D1413246

JOB SATISFACTION
AND MOTIVATION

JOB SATISFACTION AND MOTIVATION

An Annotated Bibliography

Z
7164
.C81
W25

Compiled and edited by
Ruth M. Walsh and Stanley J. Birkin

GREENWOOD PRESS
Westport, Connecticut • London, England

INDIANA
U̶ ̶ ̶ ̶TY
̶ ̶ ̶ ̶Y
OCT 2 1979

NORTHWEST

Library of Congress Cataloging in Publication Data

Walsh, Ruth M
    Job satisfaction and motivation.

    Includes indexes.
     1. Job satisfaction--Bibliography.
  2. Motivation (Psychology)--Bibliography.
 I. Birkin, Stanley J., joint author. II. Title.
Z7164.C81W25 [HF5549.5.J63] 016.15877 78-67915
ISBN 0-313-20635-X

Copyright © 1979 by Ruth M. Walsh and Stanley J. Birkin

All rights reserved. No portion of this book may be
reproduced, by any process or technique, without the
express written consent of the publisher.

Library of Congress Catalog Card Number: 78-67915
ISBN: 0-313-20635-X

First published in 1979

Greenwood Press, Inc.
51 Riverside Avenue, Westport, Connecticut 06880

Printed in the United States of America

10 9 8 7 6 5 4 3 2 1

Contents

Preface

A measure of the significance of individual behavior on organizations can be taken from the amount of research completed during the past ten years on job satisfaction and motivation. The compilation that follows is intended to facilitate the search process for the student who needs to know what work has already been done and for the organizational development professional seeking an entré to this area of applied research and its results. The size of this three-part compilation provides a concept of the enormous task of grasping the whole spectrum of studies dealing with job satisfaction and motivation.

The material is arranged alphabetically by author in Part I. A knowledgeable student would, most likely, identify material by author. On the other hand, the practitioner would probably seek subject listings. The alphabetical subject listing in Part II is actually a key-word-in-context arrangement, where the key word in the title of the articles, monographs, or books appears. Each entry in parts I and II is numerically coded. That numerical code number provides access to the annotations, which form Part III. The annotations are not strictly alphabetical since the very nature of this type of compilation is dynamic: the listing is designed for growth, updating, and expansion as new research on job satisfaction and motivation accumulates. To locate a description of the research, use the identifying number next to either the author or subject listing. For example, in the author listing is found:

> Mobley, William H.
> Construct Validation of an Instrumentality-Expectancy-Task-Goal Model of Work Motivation: Some Theoretical Boundary Conditions.   M 0082

Under "Instrumentality-Expectancy-Task" in the keyword listing, one finds the complete title, followed by "M 0082." The full title also appears under the keywords "Construct," "Validation," "Goal," "Model," "Work," "Motivation," "Theoretical," "Boundary," and "Conditions." Each time the full title appears, the code is included. "M 0082" in Part III appears as follows:

M0082   Dachler, Peter H.   Mobley, William H. Construct Validation of an Instrumentality-Expectancy-Task-Goal Model of
Work Motivation: Some Theoretical Boundary Conditions.
Journal of Applied Psychology, 58 (December 1973):
397-418.

The purpose of the present research to attempt to improve the understanding of the motivation process delineated by VIE (Valence-Instrumentality-Expectancy) Theory
through greater specificity in the conceptualization and
measurement of the key variables and the significant inter-
relations among key variables and behavior.

A detailed VIE model was explained and results of tests
of the model in two organizations were reported. In one
organization, predictions of the model were supported; in
the other organization, predictions were not supported.

The inclusion of basic bibliographical data tells the researcher that "Construct Validation . . ." is a coauthored article in a journal whose volume
number and pages are included. Students familiar with stylistic details understand that article titles should appear in quotations and that journal titles, on
typescripts, should be underscored or, in print, should appear in italics.
These details are ignored here due to computer restraints.

We wish to acknowledge the efforts of undergraduate and graduate students who shared some part of this book's total effort by contributing their
time for identifying entries, keypunching, and proofreading.

Dr. Ruth M. Walsh
Associate Professor of Management

Dr. Stanley J. Birkin
Associate Professor of Management

University of South Florida
Tampa, Florida
June 1978

I
Author Index

ABER, EDWARD

    WOMEN IN ARMY JOBS.   M0002

ABRAHAMSON, MARK.

    THE ACHIEVEMENT PROCESS: AN EXPLORATORY STUDY OF CAREER
    BEGINNINGS.   M0332

ABRAMSON, SAMUEL R.

    ACHIEVEMENT MOTIVATION AS A MODERATOR OF THE RELATIONSHIP
    BETWEEN EXPECTANCY TIMES VALENCE AND EFFORT.   M0845

ABT ASSOCIATES

    ASSESSMENT OF EXPERIMENTAL AND DEMONSTRATION INTERSTATE
    PROGRAM FOR SOUTH TEXAS MIGRANT WORKERS.   M0001

ACE, MERLE E.

    DIMENSIONS OF THRESHOLD WORK EXPERIENCE FOR HIGH SCHOOL
    GRADUATES AND DROPOUTS: A FACTOR ANALYSIS.   M0089

ACITO, FRANKLIN.

    DECISIONAL PARTICIPATION AND SOURCES OF JOB SATISFACTION: A
    STUDY OF MANUFACTURING PERSONNEL.   M0008

ACKERMAN, LEONARD.

    LET'S PUT MOTIVATION WHERE IT BELONGS -- WITHIN THE
    INDIVIDUAL.   M0003

ADAMS, E. F.

    INVESTIGATION OF THE INFLUENCE OF JOB LEVEL AND FUNCTIONAL
    SPECIALTY ON JOB ATTITUDES AND PERCEPTIONS.   M0745

ADAMS, P. G. III

    WORK GROUPS AND EMPLOYEE SATISFACTION.   M0004

AHR, C. JONATHAN.

    BEHAVIORAL TRAINING OF SUPERVISORS IN AN INDUSTRIAL SETTING
    FOR THE BLIND.   M0846

AKULA, WILLIAM G.

    FACE-TO-FACE INTERACTION IN THE PEER-NOMINATION PROCESS.   M0281

ALDAG, RAMON J.

    WORK VALUES AS MODERATORS OF PERCEIVED LEADER
    BEHAVIOR-SATISFACTION RELATIONSHIPS.   M0505

ALDAG, RAMON J.   CONTINUATION

    AGE AND REACTIONS TO TASK CHARACTERISTICS.   M0569

    CORRECTIONAL EMPLOYEES' REACTIONS TO JOB CHARACTERISTICS: A
    DATA BASED ARGUMENT FOR JOB ENLARGEMENT.   M0753

ALDERFER, CLAYTON P.

    ORGANIZATION DEVELOPMENT.   M0621

    A CRITIQUE OF SALANCIK AND PFEFFER'S EXAMINATION OF NEED
    SATISFACTION THEORIES.   M0669

ALMAN, LLOYD.

    LABOR MARKETS AND MANPOWER POLICIES IN PERSPECTIVE.   M0005

ALPER, S. WILLIAM.

    MOTIVATE THEM THROUGH THEIR JOBS.   M0006

ALTIMUS, CYRUS A.

    CHRONOLOGICAL AGE AND JOB SATISFACTION: THE YOUNG
    BLUE-COLLAR WORKER.   M0007

ALUTTO, JOSEPH A.

    DECISIONAL PARTICIPATION AND SOURCES OF JOB SATISFACTION: A
    STUDY OF MANUFACTURING PERSONNEL.   M0008

ANDREWS, FRANK M.

    TIME PRESSURE AND PERFORMANCE OF SCIENTISTS AND ENGINEERS:
    A FIVE PANEL STUDY.   M0010

ANNABLE, JAMES E.

    AN EARNINGS FUNCTION FOR HIGH LEVEL MANPOWER.   M0011

ANSARI, S. L.

    BEHAVIORAL FACTORS IN VARIANCE CONTROL: REPORT ON A
    LABORATORY EXPERIMENT.   M0634

APPEL, GARY L.

    AN ANALYSIS OF MICHIGAN'S EXPERIENCE WITH WORK INCENTIVES. M0012

ARAM, JOHN D.

    RELATION OF COLLABORATIVE INTERPERSONAL RELATIONSHIPS TO
    INDIVIDUAL SATISFACTION AND ORGANIZATIONAL PERFORMANCE.   M0013

AUNE, GEORGE A.

    A STUDY OF THE JOB SATISFACTION AND JOB PERCEPTION OF
ORGANIZED AND NON-ORGANIZED PUBLIC SCHOOL PRINCIPALS.   M0902

AUSMUS, MARLENE.

    PUT THIS UNDER F FOR FILE CLERKS.   M0019

AUSTIN, MICHAEL J.

    OCCUPATIONAL MENTAL HEALTH AND THE HUMAN SERVICES: A
REVIEW.   M0880

AWAD, E. M.

    PREDICTION OF SATISFACTION OF SYSTEMS ANALYSTS,
PROGRAMMERS.   M0807

BABCOCK, RICHARD.

    IMPACT OF MANAGEMENT BY OBJECTIVES ON MASLOW'S NEED
HIERARCHY: AN EMPIRICAL STUDY.   M0617

BACHMAN, JERALD GRAYBILL.

    THE WORKER ATTITUDES AND EARLY OCCUPATIONAL EXPERIENCES OF
YOUNG MEN -- ANALYSIS BASED ON A 4-YEAR LONGITUDINAL STUDY.   M0020

BADIN, IRWIN J.

    SOME MODERATOR INFLUENCES ON RELATIONSHIPS BETWEEN
CONSIDERATION, INITIATING STRUCTURE, AND ORGANIZATION
CRITERIA.   M0021

BAIRD, LLOYD S.

    RELATIONSHIP OF PERFORMANCE TO SATISFACTION IN STIMULATING
AND NONSTIMULATING JOBS.   M0848

BAKER, J. C.

    A COMPARATIVE STUDY OF THE SATISFACTION OF DOMESTIC U. S.
MANAGERS AND OVERSEAS U. S. MANAGERS.   M0226

BAKER, SALLY H.

    JOB DESIGN AND WORKER SATISFACTION: A CHALLENGE TO
ASSUMPTIONS.   M0571

BAKKENIST, NEIL.

    JOB ATTITUDES OF STUDENT PERSONNEL WORKERS AND THEIR JOB
SITUATIONS.   M0707

BAMUNDO, PAUL J.

    THE RELATIONSHIP BETWEEN JOB SATISFACTION AND LIFE
    SATISFACTION: AN EMPIRICAL TEST OF THREE MODELS ON A
    NATIONAL SAMPLE.   M0903

BANAS, PAUL A.

    WHY DO THEY LEAVE.   M0114

BARNHART, WILLIAM.

    JOB ATTITUDES OF STUDENT PERSONNEL WORKERS AND THEIR JOB
    SITUATIONS.   M0707

    THE DYNAMICS OF UNDERGRADUATE ACADEMIC ADVISING.   M0750

BARONE, SAM.

    THE SELF-CONCEPT, PERSONAL VALUES, AND MOTIVATIONAL
    ORIENTATIONS OF BLACK AND WHITE MANAGERS.   M0668

BARTH, RICHARD T.

    INTERGROUP CLIMATE ATTAINMENT, SATISFACTION, AND URGENCY.   M0705

BARTOL, KATHRYN M.

    SEX EFFECTS IN LEADER BEHAVIOR SELF-DESCRIPTIONS AND JOB
    SATISFACTION.   M0499

BASS, ALAN R.

    SOCIAL AND PSYCHOLOGICAL INFLUENCES ON EMPLOYMENT OF
    MARRIED NURSES.   M0755

BASS, BERNARD M.

    INFLUENCES ON THE FELT NEED FOR COLLECTIVE BARGAINING BY
    BUSINESS AND SCIENCE PROFESSIONALS.   M0572

    MANAGEMENT STYLES ASSOCIATED WITH ORGANIZATIONAL, TASK,
    PERSONAL, AND INTERPERSONAL CONTINGENCIES.   M0748

BAUMAN, ALVIN.

    EMPLOYMENT CHARACTERISTICS OF LOW-WAGE WORKERS.   M0418

BEASLEY, JAMES THOMAS JR.

    SATISFACTION WITH TRAINING AND GENERAL JOB SATISFACTION OF
    AGENCY HOMEMAKERS WORKING WITH THE ELDERLY AND DISABLED.   M0904

BEATON, ALBERT E.

    PREDICTION OF ORGANIZATIONAL BEHAVIOR.   M0139

BEATTY, JAMES U.

   LONGITUDINAL STUDY OF ABSENTEEISM AND HARD-CORE UNEMPLOYED. M0500

BEATTY, RICHARD W.

   BLACKS AS SUPERVISORS: A STUDY OF TRAINING, JOB
   PERFORMANCE, AND EMPLOYEE'S EXPECTATION.   M0023

   PERSONNEL SYSTEMS AND HUMAN PERFORMANCE.   M0024

   LONGITUDINAL STUDY OF ABSENTEEISM AND HARD-CORE UNEMPLOYED. M0500

BECKER, M. H.

   JOB SATISFACTION AND JOB PERFORMANCE: AN EMPIRICAL TEST OF
   SOME THEORETICAL PROPOSITIONS.   M0323

BEDROSIAN, HRACH.

   JOB PERFORMANCE AND THE NEW CREDENTIALISM.   M0099

BEGALLA, MARTHA E.

   ANALYZING THE HOMEMAKER JOB USING THE POSITION ANALYSIS
   QUESTIONNAIRE.   M0497

BELL, CECIL H.

   EFFECTS OF JOB ENRICHMENT AND TASK GOALS ON SATISFACTION
   AND PRODUCTIVITY: IMPLICATIONS FOR JOB DESIGN.   M0619

BEMIS, STEPHEN E.

   SEX STEREOTYPING: ITS DECLINE IN SKILLED TRADES.   M0197

BENCH, JOSEPH E.

   A STUDY OF THE RELATIONSHIP BETWEEN HERZBERG'S MOTIVATION
   HYGIENE FACTORS AND HOLLAND'S PERSONALITY PATTERNS FOR LAW
   ENFORCEMENT PERSONNEL.   M0850

BENN, MARTHA.

   COMPUTER MYSTIQUE AND FEMININE MYSTIQUE JOIN FORCES. M0058

BENNIS, WARREN.

   LEADERSHIP: BELEAGURED SPECIES?   M0586

BERGER, CHRIS J.

   ORGANIZATIONAL STRUCTURE: HOW DOES IT INFLUENCE ATTITUDES
   AND PERFORMANCE.   M0578

BERGLAND, BRUCE.

  THE VOCATIONAL EXPLORATION GROUP AND MINORITY YOUTH: AN
  EXPERIMENTAL OUTCOME STUDY.   M0749

BEROFF, JOSEPH.

  COMPONENTS OF ACHIEVEMENT MOTIVATION AS PREDICTORS OF
  POTENTIAL FOR ECONOMIC CHANGE.   M0458

BERRY, N. H.

  INDIVIDUAL AND ENVIRONMENTAL FACTORS ASSOCIATED WITH THE
  JOB SATISFACTION AND RETENTION OF NAVY HOSPITAL CORPSMEN
  SERVING WITH THE U.S. MARINE CORPS.   M0574

  BACKGROUND AND PERSONALITY CHARACTERISTICS RELATED TO
  STUDENT SATISFACTION AND PERFORMANCE IN FIELD MEDICAL
  SERVICE SCHOOL.   M0575

BETZ, ELLEN L.

  AN INVESTIGATION OF JOB SATISFACTION AS A MODERATOR
  VARIABLE IN PREDICTING JOB SUCCESS.   M0025

BEVAN, G.

  MOTIVATING YOUR JUNIORS.   M0026

BHARADWAJ, L.K.

  OCCUPATIONAL SATISFACTION OF FARM HUSBANDS AND WIVES.   M0706

BIDDLE, DEREK.

  TOWARD A TOLERANCE THEORY OF WORKER ADAPTATION.   M0573

BIGGS, DONALD A.

  JOB ATTITUDES OF STUDENT PERSONNEL WORKERS AND THEIR JOB
  SITUATIONS.   M0707

  THE DYNAMICS OF UNDERGRADUATE ACADEMIC ADVISING.   M0750

BIRCH, DAVID.

  DYNAMICS OF ACTION.   M0018

BIRCHALL, D.W.

  PERCEIVED JOB ATTITUDES, JOB ATTRIBUTES AND THE BEHAVIOR OF
  BLUE-COLLAR WORKERS: A RESEARCH NOTE.   M0751

BIRKIN, STANLEY J.

  LET'S ADMIT IT: ZERO DEFECTS IS NO PANACEA.   M0027

BLAIWES, ARTHUR S.

    LEADERSHIP DIMENSIONS OF NAVY RECRUIT MORALE & PERFORMANCE.   M0564

BLAKE, JENNY.

    EXPERIMENTS IN JOB SATISFACTION.   M0029

BLAKELY, THOMAS J.

    A PHENOMENOLOGY OF HUMAN LABOR.   M0378

BLOOD, MILTON R.

    THE VALIDITY OF IMPORTANCE.   M0030

BLUM, ALBERT A.

    THE EFFECT OF MOTIVATIONAL PROGRAMS ON COLLECTIVE BARGAINING.   M0032

BLUMENTHAL M.D.

    DEPRESSIVE SYMPTOMATOLOGY AND ROLE FUNCTION IN A GENERAL POPULATION.   M0752

BOISVERT, M. P.

    THE QUALITY OF WORKING LIFE: AN ANALYSIS.   M0502

BOOTH, R. F.

    INDIVIDUAL AND ENVIRONMENTAL FACTORS ASSOCIATED WITH THE JOB SATISFACTION AND RETENTION OF NAVY HOSPITAL CORPSMEN SERVING WITH THE U.S. MARINE CORPS.   M0574

    BACKGROUND AND PERSONALITY CHARACTERISTICS RELATED TO STUDENT SATISFACTION AND PERFORMANCE IN FIELD MEDICAL SERVICE SCHOOL.   M0575

BOUCHER, HENRY C.

    JOB SATISFACTION AND EXPECTATIONS OF DISTRIBUTIVE EDUCATION GRADUATES.   M0905

BOULIAN, PAUL V.

    ORGANIZATIONAL COMMITMENT, JOB SATISFACTION, AND TURNOVER AMONG PSYCHIATRIC TECHNICIANS.   M0353

BOWEN, DONALD.

    AN EVALUATION OF MOTIVATIONAL SIMILARITY IN WORK GROUPS.   M0033

    SATISFACTION AND PERFORMANCE: CAUSAL RELATIONSHIPS AND MODERATING EFFECTS.   M0395

BOWERS, DAVID G.

   SYSTEMS OF ORGANIZATION: MANAGEMENT OF THE HUMAN RESOURCE.   M0670

BOWIN, ROBERT B.

   MANAGERS INTEREST IN WORK.   M0034

BOWMAN, JAMES S.

   THE MEANING OF WORK AND THE MIDDLE MANAGER.   M0675

BOYATZIS, RICHARD E.

   BUILDING EFFICACY: AN EFFECTIVE USE OF MANAGERIAL POWER.   M0035

BRADSHAW, THOMAS.

   EMPLOYMENT AND UNEMPLOYMENT -- A REPORT ON 1973.   M0036

BRAGG, EMMA W.

   REVIEW OF LITERATURE ON WORK MOTIVATION: BULLETIN 12. A
   STUDY OF WORK MOTIVATION OF URBAN AND RURAL APPAREL WORKERS
   IN TENNESSEE.   M0503

BRECHER, CHARLES.

   UPGRADING BLUE-COLLAR AND SERVICE WORKERS.   M0037

BRENNAN, PETER J.

   REALIZING APPRENTICESHIP'S POTENTIAL.   M0038

BRIEF, ARTHUR P.

   WORK VALUES AS MODERATORS OF PERCEIVED LEADER
   BEHAVIOR-SATISFACTION RELATIONSHIPS.   M0505

   AGE AND REACTIONS TO TASK CHARACTERISTICS.   M0569

   CORRECTIONAL EMPLOYEES' REACTIONS TO JOB CHARACTERISTICS: A
   DATA BASED ARGUMENT FOR JOB ENLARGEMENT.   M0753

BRIGGS, NORMA.

   WOMEN APPRENTICES: REMOVING THE BARRIERS.   M0039

BRISTO, CLOIS E.

   DO YOU MOTIVATE YOUR SUBORDINATES.   M0040

BRODIE, JANE S.

   THE DYNAMICS OF UNDERGRADUATE ACADEMIC ADVISING.   M0750

BRODSKY, CARROLL M.

    THE HARASSED WORKER.   M0504

BROWN, COLIN A.

    ABSENCE FROM WORK AND JOB SATISFACTION.   M0604

BROWN, JAMES.

    UNDERSTANDING DRUG USE MOTIVATION: A NEW LOOK AT A CURRENT
    PROBLEM.   M0788

BROWN, SIDNEY E.

    JOB SATISFACTION OF GEORGIA SCHOOL SUPERINTENDENTS AND
    THEIR PERCEPTION OF THE LOCAL SCHOOL BOARD PRESIDENT'S
    LEADER BEHAVIOR.   M0906

BROWN, STEPHEN.

    WOMEN SHIPBUILDERS: JUST DOING A JOB.   M0041

BROWN, ZENIA H.

    CHANGING SCHEDULES OF WORK: PATTERNS AND IMPLICATIONS.   M0159

BRUYNS, R. A. C.

    WORK AND WORK MOTIVATION IN AN AUTOMATED INDUSTRIAL
    PRODUCTION-PROCESS.   M0042

BRYANT, CLIFTON D.

    THE SOCIAL DIMENSIONS OF WORK.   M0047

BRYANT, J. H.

    SURVEY OF VALUES AND SOURCES OF DISSATISFACTION.   M0635

BRYMAN, ALAN.

    STRUCTURE IN ORGANIZATION: A RECONSIDERATION.   M0576

BUCCHIERI, THERESA F.

    SOCIAL AND WELFARE PROGRAMS FOR THE HANDICAPPED ABROAD.   M0043

BUCHHOLTZ, ROGENE.

    MANAGERIAL BELIEFS ABOUT WORK IN SCOTLAND AND THE U.S.A.   M0756

BURKE, RONALD J.

    THE EFFECTS OF AGING ON ENGINEERS' SATISFACTION AND MENTAL
    HEALTH: SKILL OBSOLESCENCE.   M0044

BURKE, RONALD J.   CONTINUATION

EFFECTS OF DIFFERENT PATTERNS AND DEGREES OF OPENNESS IN
SUPERIOR-SUBORDINATE COMMUNICATION ON SUBORDINATE JOB
SATISFACTION.   M0045

OCCUPATIONAL STRESSES AND JOB SATISFACTION.   M0506

INFORMAL HELPING RELATIONSHIPS IN WORK ORGANIZATIONS.   M0650

BURTON, ARTHUR.

THERAPIST SATISFACTION.   M0754

BURTON, G. E.

SHIFTING TO THE HUMAN SIDE.   M0646

BUSH, JOSEPH C.

INCENTIVE PAY PATTERNS IN THE STEEL INDUSTRY.   M0046

BUXTON, BARRY MILLER.

JOB SATISFACTION OF COLLEGE PRESIDENTS.   M0907

BYHAM, WILLIAM.

INTERACTION MODELING: A NEW CONCEPT IN SUPERVISORY
TRAINING.   M0507

CAREY, MARLENE AUSMUS.

GOODS WELL BOUGHT ARE QUICKLY SOLD.   M0048

CAREY, MAX.

THE CRAFTS -- FIVE MILLION OPPORTUNITIES.   M0049

CARNALL, C.

JOB ATTITUDES AND OVERALL JOB SATISFACTION: THE EFFECT OF
BIOGRAPHICAL AND EMPLOYMENT VARIABLES: RESEARCH NOTE.   M0050

CARNEY, ROBERT T.

A STUDY OF THE RELATIONSHIP AMONG (1) JOB SATISFACTION AND
(2) TEACHER ATTITUDE.   M0908

CARROLL, A. B.

CONCEPTUAL FOUNDATIONS OF JOB ENRICHMENT.   M0051

UNMIXING CURRENT MOTIVATIONAL STRATEGIES.   M0052

CASTELLANO, J. J.

    RURAL AND URBAN DIFFERENCES: ONE MORE TIME.   M0808

CHADWICK-JONES, J.

    ABSENCE FROM WORK AND JOB SATISFACTION.   M0604

CHAKRAVARTY, T. K.

    NEED ORIENTATION AS RELATED TO EXTENSION JOB SATISFACTION:
    A PROFILE ANALYTIC EXPLORATION.   M0508

CHAMPAGE, JEAN.

    ADAPTING JOBS TO PEOPLE: EXPERIMENTS AT ALCAN.   M0053

CHAMPOUX, J. E.

    CENTRAL LIFE INTERESTS AND JOB SATISFACTION.   M0812

CHASE, RICHARD B.

    DOES JOB PERFORMANCE AFFECT EMPLOYEE SATISFACTION.   M0056

CHEN, WEN-SHYONG.

    THE JOB SATISFACTION OF SCHOOL TEACHERS IN THE REPUBLIC OF
    CHINA AS RELATED TO PERSONAL AND ORGANIZATIONAL
    CHARACTERISTICS.   M0909

CHERNS, ALBERT.

    PERSPECTIVES ON THE QUALITY OF WORKING LIFE.   M0577

CHESSER, R. J.

    RELATIONSHIP OF PERSONAL INFLUENCE DISSONANCE TO JOB
    TENSION SATISFACTION AND INVOLVEMENT.   M0817

CHRISTENSEN, L.

    COMPUTER MYSTIQUE AND FEMININE MYSTIQUE JOIN FORCES.   M0058

CHUNG, KAE H.

    A MARKOV CHAIN MODEL OF HUMAN NEEDS.   M0057

CHURCHILL, G. A.

    ORGANIZATIONAL CLIMATE AND JOB SATISFACTION IN THE SALES
    FORCE.   M0509

CLARK, MAMIE P.

    ADOLESCENT MINORITY FEMALES IN AN URBAN LABOR MARKET.   M0060

CLARY, THOMAS C.

MOTIVATION THROUGH POSITIVE STROKING. M0059

CLELAND, V.

SOCIAL AND PSYCHOLOGICAL INFLUENCES ON EMPLOYMENT OF
MARRIED NURSES. M0755

CLEMENT, ROBERT JOHN.

A STUDY OF JOB SATISFACTION OF ADMINISTRATORS AT UNITED
METHODIST RELATED CHURCHES. M0910

CLOWARD, RICHARD.

ADOLESCENT MINORITY FEMALES IN AN URBAN LABOR MARKET. M0060

COAKLEY, NORMAN.

FOREMEN: MAN IN THE MIDDLE. M0061

COBB, WILLIAM L., JR.

MOTIVATION OF THE BLACK WORKER: A REVIEW OF TRADITIONAL
APPROACHES AND CRITICAL ISSUES IN CURRENT THEORY. M0062

COCKRELL, GARY.

WHAT MAKES JOHNNY MOP ? M0559

COHEN, ARTHUR M.

COMMUNITY COLLEGE FACULTY JOB SATISFACTION. M0708

COHN, JULES.

ORGANIZATIONAL EXPERIENCES AND THEIR EFFECTS ON THE
ATTITUDES OF EMPLOYEES, INCLUDING THE DISADVANTAGED, TOWARD
WORK. M0063

ORGANIZATIONAL EXPERIENCES AND THEIR EFFECTS ON THE
ATTITUDES OF EMPLOYEES, INCLUDING THE DISADVANTAGED. M0064

COLE, DENNIS W.

AN ANALYSIS OF JOB SATISFACTION AMONG ELEMENTARY, MIDDLE
LEVEL, AND SENIOR HIGH SCHOOL TEACHERS. M0911

COLE, JOHN D. R.

SHIFTING GEARS IN PME. M0065

COLLINS, DONALD C.

A STUDY OF EMPLOYEE RESISTANCE TO JOB ENRICHMENT. M0066

COLTRIN, SALLY.

    THE EFFECT OF LEADERSHIP ROLES ON THE SATISFACTION AND
    PRODUCTIVITY OF UNIVERSITY RESEARCH PROFESSORS.   M0510

CONSTAS, PERRY A.

    ALIENATION-COUNSELING IMPLICATIONS AND MANAGEMENT THERAPY.   M0068

COOK, PHILIP.

    THE EFFECT OF LEGITIMATE OPPORTUNITIES ON THE PROBABILITY
    OF PAROLEE RECIDIVISM.   M0069

COOPER, ROBERT.

    TASK CHARACTERISTICS AND INTRINSIC MOTIVATION.   M0070

COOPER, S.

    ACCOUNTING FOR CORPORATE SOCIAL RESPONSIBILITY.   M0071

CORDTZ, DAN.

    CITY HALL DISCOVERS PRODUCTIVITY.   M0072

COSTELLO, JOHN M.

    NEEDS FULFILLMENT AND JOB SATISFACTION OF PROFESSIONALS.   M0074

COUNTS, JOHN ELDRIDGE.

    CAREER COMMITMENT: AN ANALYSIS OF SELECTED INDIVIDUAL, JOB
    AND ORGANIZATIONAL FACTORS AS RELATED TO SATISFACTION AND
    COMMITMENT OF MIDDLE LEVEL ARMY OFFICERS.   M0912

COWAN, DR. GLORIA.

    STAFF ATTITUDE AND SUCCESS OF THE WIN PROGRAM, A REPORT ON
    PHASE I RETURNS.   M0075

COX, JOHN HOWELL.

    TIME AND INCENTIVE PAY PRACTICES IN URBAN AREAS.   M0076

CRANDALL, RICK.

    CONTRIBUTION OF JOB AND LEISURE SATISFACTION TO QUALITY OF
    LIFE.   M0774

CROSS, JOHN.

    WOMEN AT WORK -- OUTDOORS.   M0077

CROWLEY, MICHAEL F.

    PROFESSIONAL MANPOWER: THE JOB MARKET TURN-AROUND.   M0078

CSOKA, LOUIS S.

    RELATIONSHIP BETWEEN ORGANIZATIONAL CLIMATE AND THE
    SITUATIONAL FAVORABLENESS DIMENSION OF FIEDLER'S
    CONTINGENCY MODEL.   M0709

CUMMINGS, L. L.

    THEORIES OF PERFORMANCE AND SATISFACTION.   M0079

    THEORIES OF PERFORMANCE AND SATISFACTION: A REVIEW.   M0080

    ORGANIZATIONAL STRUCTURE: HOW DOES IT INFLUENCE ATTITUDES
    AND PERFORMANCE.   M0578

    OPERATIONALIZING THE CONCEPTS OF GOALS AND GOAL
    INCOMPATIBILITIES IN ORGANIZATIONAL BEHAVIOR RESEARCH.   M0595

    MODERATING EFFECTS OF ENVIRONMENT AND STRUCTURE ON THE
    SATISFACTION-TENSION-INFLUENCE NETWORK.   M0828

CUMMINGS, PAUL W.

    DOES HERZBERG'S THEORY REALLY WORK.   M0081

DACHLER, PETER H.

    CONSTRUCT VALIDATION OF AN INSTRUMENTALITY-EXPECTANCY-TASK-
    GOAL MODEL OF WORK MOTIVATION: SOME THEORETICAL BOUNDARY
    CONDITIONS.   M0082

DALENA, DONALD T.

    A STEELWORKER TALKS MOTIVATION.   M0083

DALTON, GENE W.

    THE FOUR STAGES OF PROFESSIONAL CAREERS - A NEW LOOK AT
    PERFORMANCE BY PROFESSIONALS.   M0711

DAMICO, JOSEPH U.

    IN EXECUTIVE DEVELOPMENT . . . THE FUTURE IS NOW.   M0084

DANZIG, SELIG.

    CHARTING AND CHANGING THE ORGANIZATIONAL CLIMATE.   M0410

DAVIS, H. E.

    NEGOTIATED RETIREMENT PLANS -- A DECADE OF BENEFIT
    IMPROVEMENTS.   M0085

DAVIS, H. E.   CONTINUATION

   PRIVATE PENSION PLANS, 1960 TO 1969 -- AN OVERVIEW.   M0086

DAVIS, LOUIS E.

   JOB SATISFACTION RESEARCH: THE POST-INDUSTRIAL VIEW.   M0087

   RESEARCH, INTERVENTION, AND EXPERIENCE IN ENHANCING THE
   QUALITY OF WORKING LIFE.   M0088

   ENHANCING THE QUALITY OF WORKING LIFE: DEVELOPMENTS IN THE
   UNITED STATES.   M0809

DAVIS, MARGARET K.

   INTRAROLE CONFLICT AND JOB SATISFACTION ON PSYCHIATRIC
   UNITS.   M0712

DAVIS, RENE V.

   DIMENSIONS OF THRESHOLD WORK EXPERIENCE FOR HIGH SCHOOL
   GRADUATES AND DROPOUTS: A FACTOR ANALYSIS.   M0089

   THE IMPACT OF THE ORGANIZATION ON THE STRUCTURE OF JOB
   SATISFACTION: SOME FACTOR ANALYTIC FINDINGS.   M0471

DAVIS, STANLEY M.

   THE HUMAN SIDE OF THE MATRIX.   M0727

DECHARMS, RICHARD.

   PERSONAL CAUSATION: THE INTERNAL EFFECTIVE DETERMINANTS OF
   BEHAVIOR.   M0090

DECI, EDWARD L.

   EFFECTS OF EXTERNALLY MEDIATED REWARDS ON INTRINSIC
   MOTIVATION.   M0091

DEMING, D. D.

   REEVALUATING THE ASSEMBLY LINE.   M0810

DENZLER, RICHARD D.

   PEOPLE AND PRODUCTIVITY: DO THEY STILL EQUAL PAY AND
   PROFITS?   M0092

DERAKHSHANI, MANOUCHEHR.

   INTERNAL VERSUS EXTERNAL LOCUS OF CONTROL AND JOB
   SATISFACTION IN IRAN.   M0851

DILLION, DONALD.

    TOWARD MATCHING PERSONAL AND JOB CHARACTERISTICS.   M0105

DIMARCO, NICHOLAS.

    LIFE STYLE, WORK GROUP STRUCTURE, COMPATIBILITY, AND JOB
    SATISFACTION.   M0651

DODD, WILLIAM E.

    MANAGING MORALE THROUGH SURVEY FEEDBACK.   M0684

DODSON, C.

    WHY PUBLIC WORKERS STAY.   M0636

DONNELLY, J. H.

    A STUDY OF ROLE CLARITY AND NEED FOR CLARITY FOR THREE
    OCCUPATIONAL GROUPS.   M0227

    RELATION OF ORGANIZATIONAL STRUCTURE TO JOB SATISFACTION,
    ANXIETY-STRESS, AND PERFORMANCE.   M0766

    RETAIL STORE PERFORMANCE AND JOB SATISFACTION: A STUDY OF
    ANXIETY-STRESS PROPENSITY TO LEAVE AMONG RETAIL EMPLOYEES.   M0811

DONNELLY, JOHN F.

    INCREASING PRODUCTIVITY BY INVOLVING PEOPLE IN THEIR TOTAL
    JOB.   M0107

DOOLITTLE, MARY E.

    HELPING THE HAVE-NOT GIRLS.   M0108

DORE, RUSSELL

    SELF-CONCEPT AND INTERESTS RELATED TO JOB SATISFACTION OF
    MANAGERS.   M0109

DOWLING, WILLIAM F.

    CONSENSUS MANAGEMENT AT GRAPHIC CONTROLS.   M0713

DOWNEY, H. KIRK.

    CONGRUENCE BETWEEN INDIVIDUALS' NEEDS, ORGANIZATIONAL
    CLIMATE, JOB SATISFACTION AND PERFORMANCE.   M0110

    ANALYSIS OF RELATIONSHIPS AMONG LEADER BEHAVIOR,
    SUBORDINATE JOB PERFORMANCE, AND SATISFACTION: A PATH-GOAL
    APPROACH.   M0652

DUNNETTE, M. D.

    WHY DO THEY LEAVE.   M0114

DYER, LEE.

    THE DETERMINANTS OF PAY SATISFACTION.   M0582

EARLY, JOHN F.

    QUITS IN MANUFACTURING: A STUDY OF THEIR CAUSES.   M0014

EDEN, DOV.

    ORGANIZATIONAL MEMBERSHIP VS. SELF-EMPLOYMENT: ANOTHER BLOW
    TO THE AMERICAN DREAM.   M0583

EDWARDS, RICHARD A.

    SHIFT WORK: PERFORMANCE AND SATISFACTION.   M0511

EHRLE, RAYMOND A.

    BUSINESS HEALTH--MENTAL HEALTH: GROWTH ALTERNATIVE TO
    INTERVENTION.   M0117

EISON, CHARLES L.

    THE MEASUREMENT OF SATISFACTION AND DEPARTMENTAL
    ASSOCIATION AT WESTERN KENTUCKY UNIVERSITY: TESTING THE
    HOLLAND AND BIGLAN MODELS.   M0914

ELIZUR, D.

    STRUCTURES OF ATTITUDES TOWARD WORK AND TECHNOLOGICAL
    CHANGE WITHIN AN ORGANIZATION.   M0639

    VOCATIONAL NEEDS, JOB REWARDS, AND SATISFACTION: A
    CANONICAL ANALYSIS.   M0640

ENGELEN-KEFER, U.

    HUMANISATION OF WORK IN THE FEDERAL REPUBLIC OF GERMANY: A
    LABOR-ORIENTED APPROACH.   M0881

EPSTEIN, SEYMOUR.

    RELATIVE STEEPNESS OF APPROACH AND AVOIDANCE GRADIENTS AS A
    FUNCTION OF MAGNITUDE AND VALENCE OF INCENTIVE.   M0775

ERICSSON, TORE.

    RESPONSIBILITY IN MANAGEMENT -- WHAT DOES IT REALLY MEAN. M0118

ESBECK, HOWARD S.

RELATION OF COLLABORATIVE INTERPERSONAL RELATIONSHIPS TO
INDIVIDUAL SATISFACTION AND ORGANIZATIONAL PERFORMANCE.   M0013

ETZEL, M. J.

RETAIL STORE PERFORMANCE AND JOB SATISFACTION: A STUDY OF
ANXIETY-STRESS PROPENSITY TO LEAVE AMONG RETAIL EMPLOYEES.   M0811

ETZIONI, AMITAI.

MUTUAL ADAPTABILITY OF WORKERS AND ORGANIZATIONS.   M0119

EVANS, MARTIN G.

EXTENSIONS OF A PATH-GOAL THEORY OF MOTIVATION.   M0120

LEADERSHIP AND MOTIVATION: A CORE CONCEPT.   M0121

THE MODERATING EFFECTS OF INTERNAL VERSUS EXTERNAL CONTROL
ON THE RELATIONSHIP BETWEEN VARIOUS ASPECTS OF JOB
SATISFACTION.   M0122

EVANS, ROBERT, JR.

JAPAN'S LABOR ECONOMY -- PROSPECT FOR THE FUTURE.   M0123

EVERLY, GEORGE S.

PERCEIVED DIMENSIONS OF JOB SATISFACTION FOR STAFF
REGISTERED NURSES.   M0882

EWEN, ROBERT B.

THE JOB ATTITUDES OF WORKERS FROM DIFFERENT ETHNIC
BACKGROUNDS.   M0246

RACIAL DIFFERENCES IN JOB ATTITUDES AND PERFORMANCE: SOME
THEORETICAL CONSIDERATIONS AND EMPIRICAL FINDINGS.   M0717

FARGHER, K.

ACHIEVEMENT DRIVE AND CREATIVITY AS CORRELATES OF SUCCESS
IN SMALL BUSINESS.   M0730

FARR, J. L.

INCENTIVE SCHEDULES, PRODUCTIVITY, AND SATISFACTION IN WORK
GROUPS: A LABORATORY STUDY.   M0814

FARRELL, DANIEL J.

A CAUSAL MODEL OF JOB SATISFACTION.   M0915

FARRIS, GEORGE F.

TIME PRESSURE AND PERFORMANCE OF SCIENTISTS AND ENGINEERS:
A FIVE PANEL STUDY.   M0010

MOTIVATING R & D PERFORMANCE IN A STABLE ORGANIZATION.   M0124

A PREDICTIVE STUDY OF TURNOVER.   M0125

FARROW, DANA L.

MANAGEMENT STYLES ASSOCIATED WITH ORGANIZATIONAL, TASK,
PERSONAL, AND INTERPERSONAL CONTINGENCIES.   M0748

FEHD, CAROLYN S.

PRODUCTIVITY IN THE PETROLEUM PIPELINES INDUSTRY.   M0126

FELDMAN, DANIEL C.

CONTINGENCY THEORY OF SOCIALIZATION.   M0642

A PRACTICAL PROGRAM FOR EMPLOYEE SOCIALIZATION.   M0714

FELDMAN, EDWIN B.

HIGH MOTIVATION, HIGH PRODUCTIVITY.   M0127

FELDMAN, JACK M.

RACE, EMPLOYMENT, AND THE EVALUATION OF WORK.   M0128

FELDMAN, M. P.

PSYCHOLOGY IN THE INDUSTRIAL ENVIRONMENT.   M0129

FENLON, JOHN.

RECENT TRENDS IN OVERTIME HOURS AND PREMIUM PAY.   M0130

FIEDLER, FRED E.

PERSONALITY, MOTIVATIONAL SYSTEMS, AND BEHAVIOR OF HIGH AND
LOW LPC PERSONS.   M0131

CORRELATES OF PERFORMANCE IN COMMUNITY COLLEGES.   M0715

FINE, BARRY DOV.

COMPARISON OF ORGANIZATIONAL MEMBERSHIP AND
SELF-EMPLOYMENT.   M0132

FITZGERALD, THOMAS H.

WHY MOTIVATION THEORY DOESN'T WORK.   M0133

FRANCIS, H. MINTON.

   HOW EQUAL OPPORTUNITY AFFECTS DEFENSE CONTRACTS.   M0140

FRANKENHAEUSER, M.

   UNDERLOAD AND OVERLOAD IN WORKING LIFE: OUTLINE OF A
   MULTI-DISCIPLINARY APPROACH.   M0643

FRANKLIN, JACK L.

   ROLE PERFORMANCE AND COMMITMENT TO THE ORGANIZATION.   M0141

FRANKLIN, JEROME L.

   CHARACTERISTICS OF SUCCESSFUL AND UNSUCCESSFUL ORGANIZATION
   DEVELOPMENT.   M0513

FRASER, CHRISTOPHER R. P.

   THE IMPACT OF COLLECTIVE BARGAINING ON JOB SATISFACTION.   M0916

FREEMAN, EVELYN L.

   A STUDY OF BLACK MALE PROFESSIONALS IN INDUSTRY.   M0143

FRENCH, EARL B.

   WHAT A MACHINE DOESN'T KNOW.   M0144

FRIDL, JAMES J.

   RELEVANCE OF MOTIVATIONAL CONCEPTS TO INDIVIDUAL AND
   CORPORATE OBJECTIVES.   M0331

FROHMAN, ALAN L.

   THE JOINING-UP PROCESS: ISSUES IN EFFECTIVE HUMAN RESOURCE
   DEVELOPMENT.   M0758

FRONTZ, HAROLD O.

   WORK VALUES AND JOB SATISFACTION OF PSYCHIATRIC AIDES.   M0917

FROST, KEITH R.

   MOTIVATION AND CAREER PATH PLANNING.   M0146

FRUITMAN, F.

   AN EARNINGS FUNCTION FOR HIGH LEVEL MANPOWER.   M0011

FULCO, LAWRENCE J.

   CHANGES IN PRODUCTIVITY AND UNIT LABOR COSTS -- A YEARLY
   REVIEW.   M0203

FURUKAWA, HISATAKA.

    AN EXPERIMENTAL ANALYSIS OF THE RELATIONSHIP BETWEEN JOB
    SATISFACTION AND JOB IMPORTANCE.   M0514

GALLEGOS, ROBERT.

    EFFECTS ON PRODUCTIVITY AND MORALE OF A SYSTEMS-DESIGNED
    JOB-ENRICHMENT PROGRAM IN PACIFIC TELEPHONE.   M0515

GALVIN, JOHN.

    TRAINING CORRECTIONAL MANPOWER.   M0147

GANNON, MARTIN J.

    A PROFILE OF THE TEMPORARY HELP INDUSTRY AND ITS WORKERS.   M0148

GARAWSKI, ROBERT A.

    A NORMATIVE STUDY OF THE SECONDARY SCHOOL ASSISTANT
    PRINCIPALSHIP IN SELECTED PENNSYLVANIA SCHOOL DISTRICTS
    WITH AN EMPHASIS UPON JOB SATISFACTION.   M0918

GARDELL, BERTIL.

    REACTIONS AT WORK AND THEIR INFLUENCE ON NON-WORK
    ACTIVITIES: AN ANALYSIS OF A SOCIOPOLITICAL PROBLEM IN
    AFFLUENT SOCIETIES.   M0587

    UNDERLOAD AND OVERLOAD IN WORKING LIFE: OUTLINE OF A
    MULTI-DISCIPLINARY APPROACH.   M0643

GARFIELD, SOL L.

    TRAINING AND CAREER SATISFACTION AMONG CLINICAL
    PSYCHOLOGISTS.   M0759

GASTWIRTH, JOSEPH L.

    ON THE DECLINE OF MALE LABOR FORCE PARTICIPATION.   M0149

GATES, DAVID POOLE.

    JOB SATISFACTION, JOB CHARACTERISTICS, AND OCCUPATIONAL
    LEVEL.   M0919

GAVIN, JAMES F.

    SELF-ESTEEM AS A MODERATOR OF THE RELATIONSHIP BETWEEN
    EXPECTANCIES AND JOB PERFORMANCE.   M0150

    RACIAL DIFFERENCES IN JOB ATTITUDES AND PERFORMANCE: SOME
    THEORETICAL CONSIDERATIONS AND EMPIRICAL FINDINGS.   M0717

GECHMAN, ARTHUR S.

    JOB INVOLVEMENT AND SATISFACTION AS RELATED TO MENTAL
HEALTH AND PERSONAL TIME DEVOTED TO WORK.   M0718

    COMMITMENT: A BEHAVIORAL APPROACH TO JOB INVOLVEMENT.   M0899

GENTZ, SUSAN.

    CAREER OPPORTUNITIES IN THE POSTAL SERVICE.   M0152

GETZ, INGRI.

    WORK ORGANIZATION AT A BANKING BRANCH: TOWARDS A
PARTICIPATIVE RESEARCH TECHNIQUE.   M0622

GHOZEIL, SUE.

    STAFF AND DISTAFF: WHY WOMEN WORK.   M0154

GIBLIN, EDWARD J.

    MOTIVATING EMPLOYEES: A CLOSER LOOK.   M0516

GIBSON, CHARLES H.

    VOLVO INCREASES PRODUCTIVITY THROUGH JOB ENRICHMENT.   M0155

GILLO, MARTIN W.

    CORRELATES OF PERFORMANCE IN COMMUNITY COLLEGES.   M0715

GILROY, CURTIS L.

    EMPLOYMENT AND UNEMPLOYMENT -- A REPORT ON 1973.   M0036

    BLACK AND WHITE UNEMPLOYMENT: THE DYNAMICS OF THE
DIFFERENTIAL.   M0156

    JOB LOSERS, LEAVERS, AND ENTRANTS: TRAITS AND TRENDS.   M0157

GINNOLD, RICHARD E.

    URBAN-RURAL DIFFERENCES IN JOB SATISFACTION.   M0585

GITTLER, HARVEY.

    ANATOMY OF A SUCCESS.   M0158

GLASER, EDWARD M.

    STATE OF THE ART QUESTIONS ABOUT QUALITY OF WORKLIFE.   M0517

GLENN, NORVAL D.

    AGE AND JOB SATISFACTION AMONG MALES AND FEMALES: A

GLENN, NORVAL D.   CONTINUATION

    MULTI-VARIATE, MULTISURVEY STUDY.   M0518

GLICKEN, DAVID M.

    A REGIONAL STUDY OF THE JOB SATISFACTION OF SOCIAL WORKERS.   M0920

GLICKMAN, A. S.

    CHANGING SCHEDULES OF WORK: PATTERNS AND IMPLICATIONS.   M0159

GLICKMAN, S. E.

    NEUROLOGICAL BASIS OF MOTIVATION: AN ENDURING PROBLEM IN
    PSYCHOLOGY.   M0160

GLUECK, WILLIAM F.

    THE EFFECT OF LEADERSHIP ROLES ON THE SATISFACTION AND
    PRODUCTIVITY OF UNIVERSITY RESEARCH PROFESSORS.   M0510

GOBLE, JESSE W.

    RELATIONSHIPS BETWEEN JOB SATISFACTION, DEMOGRAPHIC
    FACTORS, ABSENTEEISM AND TENURE OF WORKERS IN A DELMARVA
    BROILER PROCESSING PLANT.   M0921

GOLDBERG, ALBERT I.

    THE RELEVANCE OF COSMOPOLITAN/LOCAL ORIENTATIONS TO
    PROFESSIONAL VALUES AND BEHAVIOR.   M0588

GOLDBERG, JOSEPH P.

    PUBLIC EMPLOYEE LABOR RELATIONS IN OTHER DEMOCRACIES.   M0161

GOLDEN, STANFORD.

    ATTITUDE SIMILARITY AND ATTRACTION TO A COMPANY.   M0720

GOLDFARB, R. S.

    A NEW APPROACH TO LOCAL LABOR MARKET ANALYSIS: A
    FEASIBILITY STUDY.   M0162

GOLDRING, PATRICK.

    MULTI PURPOSE MAN.   M0163

GOLDSTEIN, H.

    RESTRUCTURING PARAMEDICAL OCCUPATIONS: A CASE STUDY.   M0169

    OCCUPATIONAL MANPOWER TRAINING NEEDS.   M0170

GOLEMBIEWSKI, R. T.

TESTING SOME STEREOTYPES ABOUT THE SEXES IN ORGANIZATIONS:
DIFFERENTIAL SATISFACTION WITH WORK.   M0815

GOMEZ, LUIS R.

AN APPLICATION OF JOB ENRICHMENT IN A CIVIL SERVICE
SETTING: A DEMONSTRATION STUDY.   M0719

GONZALES, JOSEPH P.

STOCKTON UNIFIED SCHOOL DISTRICT.   M0164

GOOD, KATHERINE C.

ATTITUDE SIMILARITY AND ATTRACTION TO A COMPANY.   M0720

GOOD, LAWRENCE R.

ATTITUDE SIMILARITY AND ATTRACTION TO A COMPANY.   M0720

GOODALE, JAMES G.

BACKGROUND CHARACTERISTICS, ORIENTATION, WORK EXPERIENCE,
AND WORK VALUES OF EMPLOYEES HIRED FROM HUMAN RESOURCES
DEVELOPMENT APPLICANTS BY COMPANIES AFFILIATED WITH THE
NATIONAL ALLIANCE OF BUSINESSMAN.   M0165

GOODMAN, PAUL S.

FACTORS AFFECTING ACQUISITION OF BELIEFS ABOUT A NEW REWARD
SYSTEM.   M0589

GOODWIN, LEONARD.

DO THE POOR WANT TO WORK.   M0166

A STUDY OF THE WORK ORIENTATIONS OF WELFARE RECIPIENTS
PARTICIPATING IN THE WORK INCENTIVE PROGRAM.   M0167

WELFARE MOTHERS AND THE WORK ETHIC.   M0168

GORDON, M.E.

RELATIONSHIP BETWEEN EDUCATION AND SATISFACTION WITH JOB
CONTENT.   M0885

GOTTLIEB, DAVID.

YOUTH AND THE MEANING OF WORK.   M0171

GOUDY, WILLIS J.

THE WORK SATISFACTION, RETIREMENT-ATTITUDE TYPOLOGY:
PROFILE EXAMINATION.   M0590

GOUDY, WILLIS J.   CONTINUATION

WORK AND RETIREMENT: A TEST OF ATTITUDINAL RELATIONSHIPS.   M0721

GOULD, BRUCE R.

LONGITUDINAL INFERENCES OF JOB ATTITUDE AND TENURE
RELATIONSHIPS FROM CROSS-SECTIONAL DATA.   M0591

DIMENSIONS OF JOB SATISFACTION: INITIAL DEVELOPMENT OF THE
AIR FORCE OCCUPATIONAL ATTITUDE INVENTORY.   M0802

GRANT, JOSEPH O.

OPEN SPACE ELEMENTARY SCHOOL: EFFECTS ON TEACHERS' JOB
SATISFACTION, PARTICIPATION IN CURRICULUM DECISION-MAKING,
AND PERCEIVED SCHOOL EFFECTIVENESS.   M0922

GREABELL, LEON C.

ROLE DISSATISFACTION AND CAREER CONTINGENCIES AMONG FEMALE
ELEMENTARY TEACHERS.   M0722

GREENBERG, N. E.

DEVELOPMENT OF ASSESSMENT MEASURES FOR COUNSELING YOUTH
WORK -- TRAINING ENROLLEES.   M0142

GREENE, CHARLES N.

THE SATISFACTION-PERFORMANCE CONTROVERS   M0172

AN EVALUATION OF CAUSAL MODELS LINKING THE RECEIVED ROLE
WITH JOB SATISFACTION.   M0335

PERCEIVED PURPOSEFULNESS OF JOB BEHAVIOR: ANTECEDENTS AND
CONSEQUENCES.   M0336

GREENE, ZINA.

THE CHANGING ROLE OF WOMEN: IMPLICATIONS FOR PLANNERS.   M0173

GREENHAUS, J.

SELF-ESTEEM AS AN INFLUENCE ON OCCUPATIONAL CHOICE AND
OCCUPATIONAL SATISFACTION.   M0174

RELATIONSHIP BETWEEN LOCUS OF CONTROL AND REACTIONS OF
EMPLOYEES TO WORK CHARACTERISTICS.   M0530

PERSONNEL ATTITUDES AND MOTIVATION.   M0624

GREEVER, KATHRYN.

A STUDY OF REHABILITATION COUNSELORS: LOCUS OF CONTROL AND
ATTITUDES TOWARD THE POOR.   M0888

GREINER, LARRY E.

    WHAT MANAGERS THINK OF PARTICIPATIVE LEADERSHIP.   M0175

GRELLER, MARTIN M.

    SUBORDINATE PARTICIPATION AND REACTIONS TO THE APPRAISAL
    INTERVIEW.   M0760

GRIFFIN, LARRY J.

    CAUSAL MODELING OF PSYCHOLOGICAL SUCCESS IN WORK
    ORGANIZATIONS.   M0520

GROFF, GENE K.

    WORKER PRODUCTIVITY: AN INTEGRATED VIEW.   M0177

GROSS, RONALD H.

    SATISFACTION IN THE HOMEMAKER JOB.   M0879

GROTE, RICHARD C.

    IMPLEMENTING JOB ENRICHMENT.   M0176

GROVES, D. L., AND OTHERS.

    PLANNING -- SATISFACTION AND PRODUCTIVITY.   M0816

GUION, ROBERT M.

    THE MEANING OF WORK AND THE MOTIVATION TO WORK.   M0179

    INDIVIDUAL DIFFERENCES IN WORK SATISFACTION.   M0417

GUNDERSON, E. K.

    CONVERGENT AND DISCRIMINANT VALIDITIES OF PERFORMANCE
    EVALUATIONS IN EXTREMELY ISOLATED GROUPS.   M0180

    CORRELATES OF JOB SATISFACTION IN NAVAL ENVIRONMENTS.   M0291

GUPTA, NINA.

    THE IMPACT OF PERFORMANCE-CONTINGENT REWARDS ON JOB
    SATISFACTION: DIRECT AND INDIRECT EFFECTS.   M0686

GURIN, PATRICIA B.

    EXPECTANCY THEORY AND ITS IMPLICATIONS FOR HIGHER EDUCATION
    AMONG BLACK YOUTH.   M0210

GUTTMAN, L.

    STRUCTURES OF ATTITUDES TOWARD WORK AND TECHNOLOGICAL

GUTTMAN, L.   CONTINUATION

    CHANGE WITHIN AN ORGANIZATION.   M0639

HACKMAN, J. R.

    EMPLOYEE REACTIONS TO JOB CHARACTERISTICS.   M0181

    CONDITIONS UNDER WHICH EMPLOYEES RESPOND POSITIVELY TO
    ENRICHED WORK.   M0606

    DEVELOPMENT OF THE JOB DIAGNOSTIC SURVEY.   M0723

    MOTIVATION THROUGH THE DESIGN OF WORK: TEST OF A THEORY.   M0761

HADWIGER, DON F.

    EXPERIENCE OF BLACK FARMERS HOCE ADMINISTRATION LOCAL
    OFFICE CHIEFS.   M0182

HALL, DOUGLAS T.

    ORGANIZATIONAL AND INDIVIDUAL RESPONSE TO EXTERNAL STRESS.   M0184

    JOB CHARACTERISTICS AND PRESSURES AND THE ORGANIZATIONAL
    INTEGRATION OF PROFESSIONALS.   M0268

    ORGANIZATIONAL RESEARCH ON JOB INVOLVEMENT.   M0609

    WHAT'S NEW IN CAREER MANAGEMENT.   M0724

HALL, FRANCINE S.

    WHAT'S NEW IN CAREER MANAGEMENT.   M0724

HALPERN, MICHAEL.

    THE IMPACT OF JOB LEVEL AND SEX DIFFERENCES ON THE
    RELATIONSHIP BETWEEN LIFE AND JOB SATISFACTION. M0529

HAMERMESH, D. S.

    A NEW APPROACH TO LOCAL LABOR MARKET ANALYSIS: A
    FEASIBILITY STUDY.   M0162

    ECONOMIC CONSIDERATIONS IN JOB SATISFACTION TRENDS.   M0644

HAMILTON, BILL.

    WOMANPOWER IN DUNGAREES.   M0430

HAMILTON, G. S.

    HOW EMPLOYERS SCREEN DISADVANTAGED JOB APPLICANTS.   M0185

HAMMERTON, JAMES C.

    MANAGEMENT AND MOTIVATION.   M0186

HAMPTON, DAVID R.

    THE PLANNING-MOTIVATING DILEMMA.   M0187

HAND, HERBERT H.

    PREDICTION OF JOB SUCCESS AND EMPLOYEE SATISFACTION FOR
    EXECUTIVES AND FOREMEN.   M0402

HANSEN, RICHARD A.

    JOB DESIGN AND WORKER SATISFACTION: A CHALLENGE TO
    ASSUMPTIONS.   M0571

HANSER, LAWRENCE MORLEY.

    EMPLOYEE INFORMATION ENVIRONMENTS AND JOB SATISFACTION: A
    CLOSER LOOK.   M0854

HARDIN, D.

    DOES DIVORCE HAMPER JOB PERFORMANCE.   M0261

HARRIS, OLITA E.D.

    TASK OPPORTUNITY PROFESSIONAL GROWTH NEED FULFILLMENT AND
    INTRINSIC JOB SATISFACTION OF PUBLIC SOCIAL SERVICE WORKERS
    IN COLORADO.   M0923

HARRIS, THOMAS C.

    REPLICATION OF WHITE-COLLAR-BLUE-COLLAR DIFFERENCES IN
    SOURCES OF SATISFACTION AND DISSATISFACTION.   M0188

HARRISON, DON K.

    SIMILARITY-DISSIMILARITY IN COUNSELOR-COUNSELEE ETHNIC
    MATCH AND ITS RELEVANCE TO GOAL BEHAVIORS OF JOB TRAINEES.   M0189

HARRISON, FRANK.

    THE MANAGEMENT OF SCIENTISTS: DETERMINANTS OF PERCEIVED
    ROLE PERFORMANCE OF 95 SCIENTISTS IN THREE LARGE RESEARCH
    LABORATORIES TO THE ORGANIC SYSTEM OF MANAGEMENT CONCEIVED
    BY BURNS AND STALKER.   M0190

HARTMAN, RICHARD.

    FOUR FACTORS INFLUENCING CONVERSION TO A FOUR-DAY WORK
    WEEK.   M0687

HARVEY, DAVID W.

    CORPORATE DROPOUTS: A PRELIMINARY TYPOLOGY.   M0616

HASKETT, G. T.

    EMPLOYEE ATTITUDES REGARDING VARIOUS CHARACTERISTICS OF JOB
OPPORTUNITY AND JOB PERFORMANCE ACROSS THREE DIFFERENT WORK
SHIFTS AT AN INSTITUTION FOR THE RETARDED.   M0900

HASKEW, B.

    WHY PUBLIC WORKERS STAY.   M0636

HAYDEN, ROBERT J.

    PERFORMANCE APPRAISAL: A BETTER WAY.   M0191

HAYES, J.

    THE PERCEPTION OF OTHER WORK ROLES: IMPLICATIONS FOR JOB
CHANGE.   M0192

HAYGHE, HOWARD.

    LABOR FORCE ACTIVITY OF MARRIED WOMEN.   M0193

    MARITAL AND FAMILY CHARACTERISTICS OF THE LABOR FORCE IN
MARCH 1973.   M0194

HAYNES, JOEL B.

    UNDERSTANDING FRUSTRATION-INSTIGATED BEHAVIOR.   M0743

HAZEL, JOE T.

    DIMENSIONS OF JOB SATISFACTION: INITIAL DEVELOPMENT OF THE
AIR FORCE OCCUPATIONAL ATTITUDE INVENTORY.   M0802

HAZER, JOHN T.

    JOB SATISFACTION: A POSSIBLE INTEGRATION OF TWO THEORIES.   M0886

HEATH, BROOKS N.

    WESTERN ELECTRICS MOTIVATION AND ENRICHMENT TRIAL.   M0195

HEATH, DOUGLAS H.

    ADOLESCENT AND ADULT PREDICTORS OF VOCATIONAL ADAPTATION.   M0592

HEBDEN, JOHN.

    PITFALLS OF PARTICIPATION.   M0679

HEDGES, JANICE N.

    A LOOK AT THE 4-DAY WORKWEEK.   M0196

    SEX STEREOTYPING: ITS DECLINE IN SKILLED TRADES.   M0197

    ABSENCE FROM WORK: A LOOK AT SOME NATIONAL DATA.   M0198

    TRENDS IN LABOR AND LEISURE.   M0319

HEDLEY, R. ALAN.

    JOB SPECIALIZATION, WORK VALUES, AND WORKER
    DISSATISFACTION.   M0557

HELLRIGEL, DON.

    CONGRUENCE BETWEEN INDIVIDUALS' NEEDS, ORGANIZATIONAL
    CLIMATE, JOB SATISFACTION AND PERFORMANCE.   M0110

HENDERSON, RICHARD I.

    MONEY IS, TOO, AN INCENTIVE: ONE COMPANY'S EXPERIENCE.   M0199

    CREATING A "QUALITY" QUALITY CONTROL PROGRAM AT SPP.   M0688

HENDRIX, WILLIAM.

    PREFERRED JOB ASSIGNMENT EFFECT ON JOB SATISFACTION.   M0598

HENLE, PETER.

    WORKER DISSATISFACTION: A LOOK AT THE ECONOMIC EFFECTS.   M0200

HERBST, PHILIP G.

    WORK ORGANIZATION AT A BANKING BRANCH: TOWARDS A
    PARTICIPATIVE RESEARCH TECHNIQUE.   M0622

HERMAN, ARTHUR S.

    RAPID PRODUCTIVITY GAINS REPORTED FOR SELECTED INDUSTRIES
    FOR 1971.   M0201

HERMAN, JEANNE B.

    MANAGERIAL SATISFACTIONS AND ORGANIZATIONAL ROLES: AN
    INVESTIGATION OF PORTER'S NEED DEFICIENCY SCALES.   M0202

    PERCEIVED CONSEQUENCES OF ABSENTEEISM.   M0603

HERMAN, SHELBY W.

    CHANGES IN PRODUCTIVITY AND UNIT LABOR COSTS -- A YEARLY
    REVIEW.   M0203

HERMAN, SHELBY W.   CONTINUATION

   PRODUCTIVITY AND COST MOVEMENTS IN 1971.   M0204

HERRICK, N. Q.

   GOVERNMENT APPROACHES TO THE HUMANIZATION OF WORK.   M0205

   WORKING CONDITIONS SURVEY AS A SOURCE OF SOCIAL INDICATORS. M0206

HERZBERG, F. I.

   NEW PERSPECTIVES ON THE WILL TO WORK.   M0207

   EFFICIENCY IN THE MILITARY.   M0522

   ORTHODOX JOB ENRICHMENT: MEASURING TRUE QUALITY IN JOB
   SATISFACTION.   M0523

HICKS, THOMAS H.

   SECOND CAREER CATHOLIC PRIESTS: A STUDY OF THEIR LEVEL OF
   JOB SATISFACTION, MATURITY, AND MORALE.   M0924

HILGERT, RAYMOND L.

   POSITIVE PERSONAL MOTIVATION: THE MANAGER'S GUIDE TO
   INFLUENCING OTHERS.   M0208

HINES, GEORGE H.

   CROSS-CULTURAL DIFFERENCES IN TWO-FACTOR MOTIVATION THEORY. M0209

HOARD, A. K.

   EXPECTANCY THEORY AND ITS IMPLICATIONS FOR HIGHER EDUCATION
   AMONG BLACK YOUTH.   M0210

HODGE, CLAIRE C.

   THE NEGRO JOB SITUATION: HAS IT IMPROVED.   M0211

HOFFMAN, FRANK O.

   TEAM SPIRIT AS IT AFFECTS PRODUCTIVITY.   M0212

HOFFMAN, LOIS W.

   THE EMPLOYMENT OF WOMEN, EDUCATION, AND FERTILITY.   M0725

HOFSTEDE, GEERT

   NATIONALITY AND ESPOUSED VALUES OF MANAGERS.   M0593

HOLLENBACK, J. H.

   ROLE OF JOB SATISFACTION IN ABSENCE BEHAVIOR.   M0818

HOLLON, C. J.

   RELATIONSHIP OF PERSONAL INFLUENCE DISSONANCE TO JOB
   TENSION SATISFACTION AND INVOLVEMENT.   M0817

HOLMES, JOHN P.

   BUILD EMPLOYEES' CONFIDENCE AND SELF-ESTEEM.   M0524

HOLT, GEORGE.

   EFFECTIVE LEADERSHIP.   M0113

HOLT, K.

   WORK FRUSTRATION IN ENGINEERING DEPARTMENTS.   M0763

HOOKER, ALFRED L.

   A STUDY OF THE PERCEPTIONS OF SELECTED SCHOOL-BASED
   ADMINISTRATORS IN FLORIDA RELATIVE TO CERTAIN VARIABLES IN
   SECONDARY SCHOOL ADMINISTRATION AS THEY RELATE TO JOB
   SATISFACTION.   M0925

HOPKINS, PHYLLIS FREDERICKA.

   THE RELATIVE VALIDITIES OF TRADITIONALLY USED JOB
   SATISFACTION AND ORGANIZATIONAL COMMITMENT MEASURES VERSUS
   WOMEN-SPECIFIC MEASURES FOR THE PREDICTION OF FEMALE TENURE
   IN A MALE DOMINATED JOB.   M0856

HOROWITZ, M. A.

   RESTRUCTURING PARAMEDICAL OCCUPATIONS: A CASE STUDY.   M0169

HOSEK, J.

   JOB INVOLVEMENT: CONCEPTS AND MEASUREMENTS.   M0834

HOUGH, P.

   THE PERCEPTION OF OTHER WORK ROLES: IMPLICATIONS FOR JOB
   CHANGE.   M0192

HOUSE, JAMES.

   OCCUPATIONAL STRESS AND PHYSICAL HEALTH.   M0213

HOWELL, M. A.

   NARRATIVE AND CHECK-OFF EVALUATIONS OF EMPLOYEE
   PERFORMANCE.   M0215

HOY, STEPHEN.

LANGUAGE, TIME, AND PERSON EFFECTS ON ATTITUDE SCALE
TRANSLATIONS.   M0770

HUBBARD, ROBERT L.

FUTURE ORIENTATION AND EXPECTATIONS AS PREDICTORS OF
EMPLOYMENT SUCCESS.   M0216

FUTURE ORIENTATION AND EXPECTATIONS AS PREDICTORS OF
EMPLOYMENT SUCCESS.   M0217

COMPONENTS OF ACHIEVEMENT MOTIVATION AS PREDICTORS OF
POTENTIAL FOR ECONOMIC CHANGE.   M0458

HUBER, GEORGE P.

OPERATIONALIZING THE CONCEPTS OF GOALS AND GOAL
INCOMPATIBILITIES IN ORGANIZATIONAL BEHAVIOR RESEARCH.   M0595

RELATIONS AMONG PERCEIVED ENVIRONMENTAL UNCERTAINTY,
ORGANIZATION STRUCTURE, AND BOUNDARY-SPANNING BEHAVIOR.   M0671

HUBNER, WALTER.

INDIVIDUAL NEED SATISFACTION IN WORK AND NONWORK.   M0218

HULIN, C. L.

MANAGERIAL SATISFACTIONS AND ORGANIZATIONAL ROLES: AN
INVESTIGATION OF PORTER'S NEED DEFICIENCY SCALES.   M0202

EFFECTS OF CHANGES IN JOB SATISFACTION LEVELS ON EMPLOYEE
TURNOVER.   M0219

HUNT, J. W.

RELATIONSHIP OF AGE, TENURE AND JOB SATISFACTION IN MALES
AND FEMALES.   M0525

HUTTON, GEOFFREY.

TOWARD A TOLERANCE THEORY OF WORKER ADAPTATION.   M0573

ILGEN, DANIEL R.

SATISFACTION WITH PERFORMANCE AS A FUNCTION OF THE INITIAL
LEVEL OF EXPECTED PERFORMANCE AND THE DEVIATION FROM
EXPECTATIONS.   M0221

ROLE OF JOB SATISFACTION IN ABSENCE BEHAVIOR.   M0818

IMBERMAN, WOODRUFF.

LETTING THE EMPLOYEE SPEAK HIS MIND.   M0526

IMES, I. E.

    ORGANIZATIONAL VOIDS THAT IMPROVE PERFORMANCE.   M0222

INDIRESAN, J.

    CONVERGENT AND DISCRIMINANT VALIDITY OF A JOB SATISFACTION
    INVENTORY: A CROSS-CULTURAL REPORT.   M0764

IVANCEVICH, J. M.

    A COMPARATIVE STUDY OF THE SATISFACTION OF DOMESTIC U. S.
    MANAGERS AND OVERSEAS U. S. MANAGERS.   M0226

    A STUDY OF ROLE CLARITY AND NEED FOR CLARITY FOR THREE
    OCCUPATIONAL GROUPS.   M0227

    A COMPARATIVE ANALYSIS OF THE JOB SATISFACTION OF
    INDUSTRIAL MANAGERS AND CERTIFIED PUBLIC ACCOUNTANTS.   M0228

    AN EXPLORATORY INVESTIGATION OF ORGANIZATIONAL CLIMATE AND
    JOB SATISFACTION IN A HOSPITAL.   M0286

    EFFECTS OF GOAL SETTING ON PERFORMANCE AND JOB
    SATISFACTION.   M0594

    STUDY OF CONTROL IN MANUFACTURING ORGANIZATION: MANAGERS
    AND NONMANAGERS.   M0645

    GROUP DEVELOPMENT, TRAINER STYLE AND CARRY-OVER JOB
    SATISFACTION AND PERFORMANCE.   M0653

    PREDICTING JOB PERFORMANCE BY USE OF ABILITY TESTS AND
    STUDYING JOB SATISFACTION AS A MODERATING VARIABLE.   M0765

    RELATION OF ORGANIZATIONAL STRUCTURE TO JOB SATISFACTION,
    ANXIETY-STRESS, AND PERFORMANCE.   M0766

    SHORTENED WORKWEEK: A FIELD EXPERIMENT.   M0767

    DIFFERENT GOAL SETTING TREATMENTS AND THEIR EFFECTS ON
    PERFORMANCE AND JOB SATISFACTION.   M0819

JACKSON, ERWIN.

    OCCUPATIONAL MENTAL HEALTH AND THE HUMAN SERVICES: A
    REVIEW.   M0880

JACOBS, IRENE.

    MANPOWER TRAINING AND BENEFIT-COST ANALYSIS.   M0229

JACOBS, JEFFREY L.

    SATISFACTION WITH YOUR JOB: A LIFE-TIME CONCERN.   M0689

JACOBS, RICK.

    STRATEGIES FOR ENHANCING THE PREDICTION OF JOB PERFORMANCE
FROM JOB SATISFACTION.   M0768

JACOBSON, D.

    ORGANIZATIONAL AND OCCUPATIONAL COMMITMENT: A FACET
THEORETICAL ANALYSIS OF EMPIRICAL DATA.   M0747

JALCIONE, R. L.

    PERCEIVED DIMENSIONS OF JOB SATISFACTION FOR STAFF
REGISTERED NURSES.   M0882

JANTZ, ALFRED H.

    ENCOURAGEMENT OF EMPLOYEE CREATIVITY AND INITIATIVE.   M0527

JENKINS, DAVID.

    DEMOCRACY IN THE WORKPLACE: THE HUMAN FACTORIES.   M0230

    THE DEMOCRATIC FACTORY.   M0680

JENSEN, OLLIE.

    PREDICTION OF ORGANIZATIONAL BEHAVIOR.   M0139

JOHNSON, ALEEN M.

    THE PROFESSIONAL WOMAN IN GAO.   M0236

JOHNSON, BEVERLY B.

    THE OCCUPATIONAL INFORMATION CENTER: WHERE ATLANTA
EMPLOYERS AND EDUCATORS MEET.   M0237

JOHNSON, ROSSALL.

    PROBLEM RESOLUTION AND IMPOSITION OF CHANGE THROUGH A
PARTICIPATING GROUP EFFORT.   M0238

JOHNSON, RUTH E.

    HOW DO SECRETARIES RATE.   M0239

JOHNSON, T. W.

    TASKS, INDIVIDUAL DIFFERENCES, AND JOB SATISFACTION.   M0841

JOHNSTON, DENIS F.

    THE FUTURE OF WORK: THREE POSSIBLE ALTERNATIVES.   M0240

JOHNSTON, W.

    CHANGES IN WORK: MORE EVOLUTION THAN REVOLUTION.   M0276

    JOB REDESIGN, REFORM, ENRICHMENT -- EXPLORING THE
    LIMITATIONS.   M0277

JONES, A. P., AND OTHERS.

    BLACK-WHITE DIFFERENCES IN WORK ENVIRONMENT PERCEPTIONS AND
    JOB SATISFACTION AND ITS CORRELATES.   M0820

JONES, B. D.

    ABC OF MOTIVATION.   M0241

JONES, J. P.

    LEADERSHIP, MOTIVATION, AND COMMUNICATION.   M0242

JONES, LAURENCE C. III.

    EVALUATION AND IMPLEMENTATION OF THE NEW YORK FIRE
    DEPARTMENT EXAMINATION TRAINING PROJECT FOR CULTURALLY
    DISADVANTAGED RESIDENTS OF THE CITY OF NEW YORK.   M0243

JUROVSKY, A.

    WORK MOTIVATION, A MENTAL PROCESS.   M0528

JURY, PHILLIP A.

    THE IMPACT OF THE ORGANIZATION ON THE STRUCTURE OF JOB
    SATISFACTION: SOME FACTOR ANALYTIC FINDINGS.   M0471

KAKABADSE, ANDREW

    CORPORATE MANAGEMENT IN LOCAL GOVERNMENT: A CASE STUDY.   M0769

KALLEBERG, ARNE L.

    WORK VALUES, JOB REWARDS AND JOB SATISFACTION: A THEORY OF
    THE QUALITY OF WORK EXPERIENCE.   M0690

KANTER, ROSABETH.

    THE IMPACT OF HIERARCHICAL STRUCTURES ON THE WORK BEHAVIOR
    OF WOMEN AND MEN.   M0757

KAPLAN, H. ROY.

    HOW DO WORKERS VIEW THEIR WORK IN AMERICA.   M0244

KAPUST, JEFFRY.

    BEHAVIORAL TRAINING OF SUPERVISORS IN AN INDUSTRIAL SETTING

KAPUST, JEFFRY.   CONTINUATION

    FOR THE BLIND.   M0846

KARP, WILLIAM.

    MANAGEMENT'S FUTURE ROLE: PICKING UP WHERE THE COMPUTER
    LEAVES OFF.   M0245

KATERBERG, RALPH.

    LANGUAGE, TIME, AND PERSON EFFECTS ON ATTITUDE SCALE
    TRANSLATIONS.   M0770

KATZELL, R. A.

    THE JOB ATTITUDES OF WORKERS FROM DIFFERENT ETHNIC
    BACKGROUNDS.   M0246

KAUN, DAVID E.

    OCCUPATIONAL MIGRATION, DISCRIMINATION, AND THE CENTRAL
    CITY LABOR FORCE.   M0247

KAVANAGH, MICHAEL.

    THE IMPACT OF JOB LEVEL AND SEX DIFFERENCES ON THE
    RELATIONSHIP BETWEEN LIFE AND JOB SATISFACTION.   M0529

KEENE, DON G.

    MAN'S INHERENT REBELLION AGAINST GOD AND SATISFACTION.   M0248

KEITH, PATRICIA.

    THE WORK SATISFACTION, RETIREMENT-ATTITUDE TYPOLOGY:
    PROFILE EXAMINATION.   M0590

    WORK AND RETIREMENT: A TEST OF ATTITUDINAL RELATIONSHIPS.   M0721

KELLER, ROBERT T.

    ROLE CONFLICT AND AMBIGUITY: CORRELATES WITH JOB
    SATISFACTION AND VALUES.   M0249

    EMPLOYEE REACTIONS TO LEADER REWARD BEHAVIOR.   M0654

    ROLE DYNAMICS, LOCUS OF CONTROL, AND EMPLOYEE ATTITUDES AND
    BEHAVIOR.   M0667

KENSTANT, RAYMOND O.

    JOB VACANCIES IN 1970.   M0250

KERR, ELIZABETH A.

CAPABILITIES OF MIDDLE-AGED AND OLDER WORKERS: A SURVEY OF
THE LITERATURE.   M0778

KERR, STEVEN.

ON THE FOLLY OF REWARDING A, WHILE HOPING FOR B.   M0655

KESSELMAN, G. A.

RELATIONSHIPS BETWEEN PERFORMANCE AND SATISFACTION UNDER
CONTINGENT AND NONCONTINGENT REWARD SYSTEMS.   M0251

KETS DE VRIES, M.

THE ENTREPRENEURIAL PERSONALITY: A PERSON AT THE
CROSSROADS.   M0771

KETTERING, MERLYN H.

SEGREGATION AND JOB SATISFACTION IN THE WORK PLACE: THE
MEASUREMENT OF RACIAL DISPARITIES IN ORGANIZATIONS AND
THEIR INFLUENCE ON EMPLOYEE WORK ATTITUDES.   M0927

KILB, DAVID A.

ORGANIZATIONAL PSYCHOLOGY (A BOOK OF READINGS).   M0257

KIMMONS, GARY.

RELATIONSHIP BETWEEN LOCUS OF CONTROL AND REACTIONS OF
EMPLOYEES TO WORK CHARACTERISTICS.   M0530

KING, ALBERT S.

MANAGEMENT'S ECTASY AND DISPARITY OVER JOB ENRICHMENT:
EXPECTATIONS IN PLANNING JOB CHANGE: A CASE STUDY.   M0531

KIPNIS, DOROTHY M.

INNER DIRECTION, OTHER DIRECTION AND ACHIEVEMENT
MOTIVATION.   M0726

KLEIN, GEORGE STUART.

PERCEPTION, MOTIVES, AND PERSONALITY.   M0252

KLEIN, KENNETH L.

INTEREST CONGRUENCY AS A MODERATOR OF THE RELATIONSHIPS
BETWEEN JOB TENURE AND JOB SATISFACTION AND MENTAL HEALTH.   M0623

KLEIN, STUART M.

PARTICIPATIVE MANAGEMENT IN THE UNITED STATES: A CORPORATE

KOTTER, JOHN P.

    THE JOINING-UP PROCESS: ISSUES IN EFFECTIVE HUMAN RESOURCE
    DEVELOPMENT.   M0758

KRAFT, W. PHILIP.

    JOB REDESIGN IMPROVES PRODUCTIVITY. (BANKERS TRUST, N.Y.).   M0533

KRECK, LOTHAR A.

    SEMANTIC DISTANCE AND JOB SATISFACTION IN FORMAL
    ORGANIZATIONS.   M0599

KREISER, L.

    LOCAL FIRM AND JOB SATISFACTION.   M0821

KRIEGSMANN, J. K.

    DOES DIVORCE HAMPER JOB PERFORMANCE.   M0261

KUHN, DAVID G.

    DOES JOB PERFORMANCE AFFECT EMPLOYEE SATISFACTION.   M0056

KULECK, WALTER.

    JOB CHOICE AND POST DECISION DISSONANCE.   M0772

KURTZ, RICHARD M.

    TRAINING AND CAREER SATISFACTION AMONG CLINICAL
    PSYCHOLOGISTS.   M0759

KWIECINSKI, P. D.

    BUILD EMPLOYEES' CONFIDENCE AND SELF-ESTEEM.   M0524

LABVITZ, SANFORD.

    INDIVIDUAL REACTIONS TO ORGANIZATIONAL CONFLICT AND CHANGE.   M0311

LANDY, FRANK J.

    THE MEANING OF WORK AND THE MOTIVATION TO WORK.   M0179

    MOTIVATIONAL TYPE AND THE SATISFACTION-PERFORMANCE
    RELATIONSHIP.   M0263

LASHER, HARRY J.

    HOW THE PURCHASING MANAGER CAN IMPROVE EMPLOYEE
    PERFORMANCE.   M0264

    THERE IS NO HUMBUG TO JOB ENRICHMENT.   M0265

LATHAM, GARY P.

REVIEW OF RESEARCH ON THE APPLICATION OF GOAL SETTING IN
ORGANIZATIONS. M0657

EFFECTS OF ASSIGNED AND PARTICIPATIVE GOAL SETTING ON
PERFORMANCE AND JOB SATISFACTION. M0887

LAWLER, EDWARD E.

EMPLOYEE REACTIONS TO JOB CHARACTERISTICS. M0181

JOB DESIGN AND EMPLOYEE MOTIVATION. M0267

JOB CHARACTERISTICS AND PRESSURES AND THE ORGANIZATIONAL
INTEGRATION OF PROFESSIONALS. M0268

EFFECTIVENESS IN WORK ROLES. M0386

HIGH SCHOOL STUDENTS PERCEPTIONS OF WORK. M0535

JOB CHOICE AND POST DECISION DISSONANCE. M0772

MEASURING THE FINANCIAL IMPACT OF EMPLOYEE ATTITUDES. M0780

LAWRENCE, JAMES E.

COMPLETING THE EXTENSION TEAM. M0269

LAWRENCE, P. S.

BEHAVIORAL TRAINING OF SUPERVISORS IN AN INDUSTRIAL SETTING
FOR THE BLIND. M0846

LAWRENCE, PAUL R.

THE HUMAN SIDE OF THE MATRIX. M0727

LAZER, ROBERT IRA.

PERCEIVED LEADER BEHAVIOR AND EMPLOYEE SATISFACTION WITH
SUPERVISION AND THE JOB: THE EFFECTS OF REWARD AND
PUNISHMENT. M0859

LEAHY JOHN I.

TOTAL MOTIVATION = TOP PERFORMANCE. M0270

LEAVITT, HAROLD J.

READINGS IN MANAGERIAL PSYCHOLOGY, 2ND ED. CHICAGO. M0271

LEE, M. BLAINE.

DESIGNING A MOTIVATING AND TEAM BUILDING EMPLOYEE APPRAISAL
SYSTEM. M0534

LEE, M. SANG.

    NEEDS FULFILLMENT AND JOB SATISFACTION OF PROFESSIONALS.   M0074

    AN EMPIRICAL ANALYSIS OF ORGANIZATIONAL IDENTIFICATION.   M0272

LEHMANN, PHYLLIS.

    TEACHER TRAINING TAKES TO THE ROAD.   M0273

LEIFER, RICHARD.

    RELATIONS AMONG PERCEIVED ENVIRONMENTAL UNCERTAINTY,
    ORGANIZATION STRUCTURE, AND BOUNDARY-SPANNING BEHAVIOR.   M0671

LENTZ, WILLIAM.

    OCCUPATIONAL MIGRATION, DISCRIMINATION, AND THE CENTRAL
    CITY LABOR FORCE.   M0247

LEVINSON, HARRY.

    ASININE ATTITUDES TOWARD MOTIVATION.   M0274

    ORGANIZATIONAL DIAGNOSIS.   M0275

    SYSTEMS OF ORGANIZATION: MANAGEMENT OF THE HUMAN RESOURCE.   M0670

LEVITAN, SAR.

    CHANGES IN WORK: MORE EVOLUTION THAN REVOLUTION.   M0276

    JOB REDESIGN, REFORM, ENRICHMENT -- EXPLORING THE
    LIMITATIONS.   M0277

    HAS THE BLUE-COLLAR WORKER'S POSITION WORSENED?   M0278

LEVITIN, TERESA E.

    A SOCIAL PSYCHOLGICAL EXPLORATION OF POWER MOTIVATION AMONG
    DISADVANTAGED WORKERS.   M0279

LEVOU, ROBERT P.

    HOW TO KEEP STAFF MORALE AND MOTIVATION IN HIGH GEAR.   M0280

LEWIN, ARIE Y.

    FACE-TO-FACE INTERACTION IN THE PEER-NOMINATION PROCESS.   M0281

LIDDELL, W. W.

    THE EFFECTS OF INDIVIDUAL-ROLE COMPATIBILITY UPON GROUP
    PERFORMANCE: AN EXTENSION OF SCHUTZ'S FIRO THEORY.   M0658

LUNDQUIST, G. W.

    THE VOCATIONAL EXPLORATION GROUP AND MINORITY YOUTH: AN
    EXPERIMENTAL OUTCOME STUDY.   M0749

LUTHANS, FRED.

    MOTIVATION VS. LEARNING APPROACHES TO ORGANIZATIONAL
    BEHAVIOR.   M0285

LYNAGH, P. M.

    JOB SATISFACTION AND THE PD MANAGER: AN EMPIRICAL
    ASSESSMENT.   M0831

LYON, HERBERT L.

    AN EXPLORATORY INVESTIGATION OF ORGANIZATIONAL CLIMATE AND
    JOB SATISFACTION IN A HOSPITAL.   M0286

    SHORTENED WORKWEEK: A FIELD EXPERIMENT.   M0767

MACDONALD, A.P.

    A STUDY OF REHABILITATION COUNSELORS: LOCUS OF CONTROL AND
    ATTITUDES TOWARD THE POOR.   M0888

MACEACHRON, ANN E.

    JOB LEVEL, INDIVIDUAL DIFFERENCES, AND JOB SATISFACTION: AN
    INTERACTIVE APPROACH.   M0691

    TWO INTERACTIVE PERSPECTIVES ON THE RELATIONSHIP BETWEEN
    JOB LEVEL AND JOB SATISFACTION.   M0823

MACKENZIE, R. A.

    THE CREDIBILITY GAP IN MANAGEMENT.   M0135

MACKINNON, NEIL L.

    MOTIVATING PEOPLE WITH MEANINGFUL WORK.   M0293

MACY, B.A.

    METHODOLOGY FOR ASSESSMENT OF QUALITY OF WORK LIFE AND
    ORGANIZATIONAL EFFECTIVENESS IN BEHAVIORAL-ECONOMIC TERMS.   M0536

MAIER, NORMAN R. F.

    PSYCHOLOGY IN INDUSTRIAL ORGANIZATIONS.   M0296

MAIER, STEVEN F.

    LEARNED HELPLESSNESS: THEORY AND EVIDENCE.   M0776

MAJUMDER, RANJIT.

    A STUDY OF REHABILITATION COUNSELORS: LOCUS OF CONTROL AND
    ATTITUDES TOWARD THE POOR.   M0888

MALI, PAUL.

    A PRACTICAL SCHEME THAT MOTIVATES PEOPLE.   M0297

MALOY, RICHARD.

    THE PROFIT MOTIVE: CAN IT MOTIVATE INDUSTRY TO HIRE THE
    HARD CORE.   M0298

MALPASS, LESLIE F.

    SELECTED CHARACTERISTICS, ROLES, GOALS, AND SATISFACTIONS
    OF DEPARTMENT CHAIRMEN IN STATE AND LAND-GRANT
    INSTITUTIONS.   M0777

MANCHANDA, YASH P.

    MOTIVATION OF ENGINEERS: AN ANALYSIS OF PERCEIVED
    MOTIVATIONAL FACTORS.   M0692

MANDILOVITCH, M.

    EVALUATING WORKING CONDITIONS IN AMERICA.   M0356

MANGIONE, T. W.

    EVALUATING WORKING CONDITIONS IN AMERICA.   M0356

MANGUN, GARTH L.

    A DECADE OF MANPOWER TRAINING.   M0300

MANNARI, HIROSKI.

    ORGANIZATIONAL COMMITMENT AND TURNOVER: A PREDICTION STUDY. M0627

MANOFF, ALBERT W.

    VALUES -- NOT ATTITUDES -- ARE THE REAL KEY TO MOTIVATION. M0301

MANSFIELD, ROGER.

    ORGANIZATIONAL AND INDIVIDUAL RESPONSE TO EXTERNAL STRESS. M0184

MAPLES, MARY ANGELA F.

    RELATIONSHIPS BETWEEN WORK VALUES AND JOB SATISFACTION
    AMONG COLLEGE STUDENT PERSONNEL WORKERS.   M0928

MARA, THOMAS G.

    LEADERSHIP METHODS THAT MOTIVATE.   M0302

MARK, JEROME A.

    PROGRESS IN MEASURING PRODUCTIVITY IN GOVERNMENT.   M0303

MARLAND, SIDNEY P.

    AMERICA'S NEED FOR CAREER EDUCATION.   M0304

MARQUIS, KENT.

    INTERACTION EFFECTS OF PERSONALITY, JOB TRAINING, AND LABOR
    MARKET CONDITIONS ON PERSONAL EMPLOYMENT AND INCOME.   M0305

    COMPONENTS OF ACHIEVEMENT MOTIVATION AS PREDICTORS OF
    POTENTIAL FOR ECONOMIC CHANGE.   M0458

MARSH, JOHN.

    THE MANAGERIAL CONVOLUTION .   M0306

MARSH, ROBERT M.

    ORGANIZATIONAL COMMITMENT AND TURNOVER: A PREDICTION STUDY.   M0627

MARSHALL, PATRICIA.

    POLICEWOMEN ON PATROL.   M0307

MARTINSON, OSCAR.

    FEELINGS OF POWERLESSNESS AND SOCIAL ISOLATION AMONG LARGE
    SCALE FARM PERSONNEL.   M0596

MASON, PHILLIP.

    EMPLOYMENT, WELFARE, AND MOTHERS' MOTIVATION.   M0308

MASON, SANDRA L.

    COMPARING UNION AND NONUNION WAGES IN MANUFACTURING.   M0309

MASTERSON, T. R.

    LEADERSHIP METHODS THAT MOTIVATE.   M0302

MCARTHUR, JOHN.

    IS MOTIVATION BY MONEY STILL FASHIONABLE?   M0287

MCCALL, M.W.

    HIGH SCHOOL STUDENTS PERCEPTIONS OF WORK.   M0535

MCCLELLAND, DIANA.

OPENING JOB DOORS FOR MATURE WOMEN.   M0288

MCCONKEY, DALE.

THE POSITION AND FUNCTION OF BUDGETS IN AN MBO SYSTEM.   M0289

MCCORMICK, TOM.

SHE CAME A LONG, LONG WAY.   M0290

MCDONALD, BLAIR W.

CORRELATES OF JOB SATISFACTION IN NAVAL ENVIRONMENTS.   M0291

MCEADDY, B. J.

WHERE WOMEN WORK -- AN ANALYSIS BY INDUSTRY AND OCCUPATION. M0464

MCHUGH, NORMA.

SOCIAL AND PSYCHOLOGICAL INFLUENCES ON EMPLOYMENT OF
MARRIED NURSES.   M0755

MCINTIRE,WALTER G.

WORK VALUES AND JOB SATISFACTION OF YOUNG ADULT MALES.   M0579

MCINTYRE, JAMES M.

ORGANIZATIONAL PSYCHOLOGY (A BOOK OF READINGS).   M0257

MCKELVEY, B.,

TOWARD A CAREER-BASED THEORY OF JOB INVOLVEMENT: A STUDY OF
SCIENTISTS AND ENGINEERS.   M0824

MCKIBBIN, CARROLL R.

THE QUIT RATE AS A MEASURE OF MORALE IN THE PUBLIC SERVICE:
THE CASE OF THE UNITED STATES FOREIGN SERVICE.   M0292

MCLAUGHLIN, G.W.

SELECTED CHARACTERISTICS, ROLES, GOALS, AND SATISFACTIONS
OF DEPARTMENT CHAIRMEN IN STATE AND LAND-GRANT
INSTITUTIONS.   M0777

MCMAHON, J. T.

STUDY OF CONTROL IN MANUFACTURING ORGANIZATION: MANAGERS
AND NONMANAGERS.   M0645

GROUP DEVELOPMENT, TRAINER STYLE AND CARRY-OVER JOB
SATISFACTION AND PERFORMANCE.   M0653

MCMAHON, J. T.   CONTINUATION

PARTICIPATIVE AND POWER-EQUALIZED ORGANIZATIONAL SYSTEMS:
AN EMPIRICAL INVESTIGATION AND THEORETICAL INTEGRATION.   M0889

MCNALLY, M. S.

INDIVIDUAL AND ENVIRONMENTAL FACTORS ASSOCIATED WITH THE
JOB SATISFACTION AND RETENTION OF NAVY HOSPITAL CORPSMEN
SERVING WITH THE U.S. MARINE CORPS.   M0574

BACKGROUND AND PERSONALITY CHARACTERISTICS RELATED TO
STUDENT SATISFACTION AND PERFORMANCE IN FIELD MEDICAL
SERVICE SCHOOL.   M0575

MCNULTY, L. A.

JOB ENRICHMENT: HOW TO MAKE IT WORK.   M0294

MEACHOM, MERLE.

SELF-CONCEPT AND INTERESTS RELATED TO JOB SATISFACTION OF
MANAGERS.   M0109

MEARS, PETER.

GUIDELINES FOR THE JOB ENRICHMENT PRACTITIONER.   M0538

MEDNICK, MARTHA T.

MOTIVATIONAL AND PERSONALITY FACTORS RELATED TO CAREER
GOALS OF BLACK COLLEGE WOMEN.   M0310

MEIER, ELIZABETH.

CAPABILITIES OF MIDDLE-AGED AND OLDER WORKERS: A SURVEY OF
THE LITERATURE.   M0778

MELA, RICHARD L.

CORPORATE DROPOUTS: A PRELIMINARY TYPOLOGY.   M0616

MERRYMAN, C.

GROWTH AND SATISFACTION OF EMPLOYEES IN ORGANIZATIONS.   M0825

MEYER, HERBERT.

THE PAY-FOR-PERFORMANCE DILEMMA.   M0779

MICHIGAN UNIVERSITY. SURVEY RESEARCH CENTER.

SURVEY OF WORKING CONDITIONS. FINAL REPORT OF UNIVARIATE
AND BIVARIATE TABLES.   M0266

MILES, RAYMOND E.

A FACTOR ANALYTIC STUDY OF JOB SATISFACTION ITEMS DESIGNED
TO MEASURE MASLOW NEED CATEGORIES.   M0365

MILES, ROBERT H.

RELATIONSHIPS BETWEEN ROLE CLARITY, NEED FOR CLARITY AND
JOB TENSION AND SATISFACTION FOR SUPERVISORY AND
NONSUPERVISORY ROLES.   M0539

ORGANIZATIONAL ROLE CONFLICT: ITS ANTECEDENTS AND
CONSEQUENCES.   M0601

ROLE-SET CONFIGURATION AS A PREDICTOR OF ROLE CONFLICT AND
AMBIGUITY IN COMPLEX ORGANIZATIONS.   M0626

MILLAR, JEAN.

MOTIVATIONAL ASPECTS OF JOB ENRICHMENT.   M0540

MILLER, DONALD B.

HOW TO IMPROVE THE PERFORMANCE AND PRODUCTIVITY OF THE
KNOWLEDGE WORKER.   M0602

MILLER, GLENN W.

MULTIJOBHOLDING OF WICHITA PUBLIC SCHOOL TEACHERS.   M0729

MILLER, JON.

INDIVIDUAL REACTIONS TO ORGANIZATIONAL CONFLICT AND CHANGE.   M0311

MILLER, NEIL.

CAREER CHOICE, JOB SATISFACTION, AND THE TRUTH BEHIND THE
PETER PRINCIPLE.   M0541

MILLER, R.W.

IS WORK THE CENTRAL LIFE INTEREST? NOT FOR MOST PEOPLE --
FINDING THE COMMITED FEW.   M0826

MILLER, S.

PHYSICAL ENVIRONMENT AND JOB SATISFACTION IN A COMMUNITY
MENTAL HEALTH CENTER.   M0883

MILNER, PETER M.

NEUROLOGICAL BASIS OF MOTIVATION: AN ENDURING PROBLEM IN
PSYCHOLOGY.   M0160

MILUTINOVICH, J.S.

IMPACT OF PERCEIVED COMMUNITY PROSPERITY ON JOB
SATISFACTION OF BLACK AND WHITE WORKERS.   M0542

MINER, JOHN B.

THE MANAGEMENT CONSULTING FIRM AS A SOURCE OF HIGH-LEVEL
MANAGERIAL TALENT.   M0312

THE REAL CRUNCH IN MANAGERIAL MANPOWER.   M0313

SUCCESS IN MANAGEMENT CONSULTING AND THE CONCEPT OF
ELITENESS MOTIVATION.   M0314

MIRSBURGER, GERALD

RESPONSIBILITY IN MANAGEMENT -- WHAT DOES IT REALLY MEAN.   M0118

MIRVIS, P.H.

METHODOLOGY FOR ASSESSMENT OF QUALITY OF WORK LIFE AND
ORGANIZATIONAL EFFECTIVENESS IN BEHAVIORAL-ECONOMIC TERMS.   M0536

MEASURING THE FINANCIAL IMPACT OF EMPLOYEE ATTITUDES.   M0780

MISSHAUK, M. J.

JOB SATISFACTION AND PRODUCTIVITY.   M0315

SUPERVISORY SKILLS AND EMPLOYEE SATISFACTION.   M0316

MISUMI, JYUJI.

EFFECTS OF ACHIEVEMENT MOTIVATION ON THE EFFECTIVENESS OF
LEADERSHIP PATTERNS.   M0317

MITCHELL, C. W.

INFLUENCES ON THE FELT NEED FOR COLLECTIVE BARGAINING BY
BUSINESS AND SCIENCE PROFESSIONALS.   M0572

MITCHELL, T. R.

MOTIVATION AND PARTICIPATION: AN INTEGRATION.   M0318

EFFECTS OF JOB ENRICHMENT AND TASK GOALS ON SATISFACTION
AND PRODUCTIVITY: IMPLICATIONS FOR JOB DESIGN.   M0619

LOCUS OF CONTROL: SUPERVISION AND WORK SATISFACTION.   M0660

MOBLEY, WILLIAM H.

CONSTRUCT VALIDATION OF AN INSTRUMENTALITY-EXPECTANCY-TASK-
GOAL MODEL OF WORK MOTIVATION: SOME THEORETICAL BOUNDARY
CONDITIONS.   M0082

MOBLEY, WILLIAM H.   CONTINUATION

    INTERMEDIATE LINKAGES IN THE RELATIONSHIP BETWEEN JOB
    SATISFACTION AND EMPLOYEE TURNOVER.   M0781

MOCH, MICHAEL K.

    JAMES G. MARCH AND JOHAN P. OLSEN, AMBIGUITY AND CHOICE IN
    ORGANIZATIONS.   M0672

MOLES, ROBERT H.

    ROLE REQUIREMENTS AS SOURCES OF ORGANIZATIONAL STRESS.   M0597

MOLINARI, JANICE.

    ORGANIZATIONAL DIAGNOSIS.   M0275

MONCZKA, ROBERT M.

    MOTIVATING THE PUBLIC EMPLOYEE: FACT VS. FICTION.   M0890

MONTANO, JOCELYN.

    SOCIAL AND PSYCHOLOGICAL INFLUENCES ON EMPLOYMENT OF
    MARRIED NURSES.   M0755

MONTGOMERY, J.

    SELECTED CHARACTERISTICS, ROLES, GOALS, AND SATISFACTIONS
    OF DEPARTMENT CHAIRMEN IN STATE AND LAND-GRANT
    INSTITUTIONS.   M0777

MOORE, BRIAN E.

    FACTORS AFFECTING ACQUISITION OF BELIEFS ABOUT A NEW REWARD
    SYSTEM.   M0589

MOORE, GEOFFREY H.

    TRENDS IN LABOR AND LEISURE.   M0319

MOORE, MICHAEL L.

    THE EFFECT OF MOTIVATIONAL PROGRAMS ON COLLECTIVE
    BARGAINING.   M0032

MOORE, PERRY.

    REWARDS AND PUBLIC EMPLOYEES' ATTITUDES TOWARD CLIENT
    SERVICE.   M0693

    REWARDS AND PUBLIC EMPLOYEES' ATTITUDES TOWARD CLIENT
    SERVICE.   M0929

MORANO, RICHARD.

    CONTINUING EDUCATION IN INDUSTRY.   M0320

MORGAN, CYRIL P.

    RELATION OF COLLABORATIVE INTERPERSONAL RELATIONSHIPS TO
    INDIVIDUAL SATISFACTION AND ORGANIZATIONAL PERFORMANCE.   M0013

MORGAN, LILLIE.

    PERCEIVED CONSEQUENCES OF ABSENTEEISM.   M0603

MORGAN, MARTY.

    HE GIVES A DAMN.   M0321

MORRIS, JOHN L.

    ACHIEVEMENT DRIVE AND CREATIVITY AS CORRELATES OF SUCCESS
    IN SMALL BUSINESS.   M0730

MORSE, STEPHEN.

    MANAGEMENT BY NORMS.   M0681

MOUNT, MICHAEL KELLY.

    PERSON-ENVIRONMENT CONGRUENCE, EMPLOYEE JOB SATISFACTION,
    AND TENURE: A TEST OF HOLLAND'S THEORY.   M0863

MOWDAY, RICHARD T.

    ORGANIZATIONAL COMMITMENT, JOB SATISFACTION, AND TURNOVER
    AMONG PSYCHIATRIC TECHNICIANS.   M0353

MUCHINSKY, P. M.

    ORGANIZATIONAL COMMUNICATION: RELATIONSHIPS TO
    ORGANIZATIONAL CLIMATE AND JOB SATISFACTION.   M0827

MUNRO, JIM.

    CORRECTIONAL EMPLOYEES' REACTIONS TO JOB CHARACTERISTICS: A
    DATA BASED ARGUMENT FOR JOB ENLARGEMENT.   M0753

MUSSIO, STEPHEN J.

    AN APPLICATION OF JOB ENRICHMENT IN A CIVIL SERVICE
    SETTING: A DEMONSTRATION STUDY.   M0719

MYERS, ROBERT I.

    SCHOOL BOARD DOGMATISM AND MORALE OF PRINCIPALS.   M0731

NASSTROM, RAY R.

SCHOOL BOARD DOGMATISM AND MORALE OF PRINCIPALS.   M0731

NATHANSON, C. A.

JOB SATISFACTION AND JOB PERFORMANCE: AN EMPIRICAL TEST OF
SOME THEORETICAL PROPOSITIONS.   M0323

NELSON, MARIAN.

RAILROAD APPRENTICES STAY ON THE TRACK.   M0324

NESSLEIN, SSGT. THOMAS S.

MANAGEMENT, MOTIVATION AND JOB ENRICHMENT.   M0325

NEVAS, SUSAN R.

A DEFINITIONAL CHALLENGE: INTEREST AND WORK ITSELF
SATISFACTIONS.   M0543

NEWBOULD, G.D.

ACADEMIC SALARIES -- A PERSONAL APPLICATION OF MANAGERIAL
ECONOMICS.   M0782

NEWMAN, JOHN.

PREDICTING ABSENTEEISM AND TURNOVER: A FIELD COMPARISON OF
FISHBEIN'S MODEL AND TRADITIONAL JOB ATTITUDE MEASURES.   M0326

NEWMAN, SIDNEY H.

NARRATIVE AND CHECK-OFF EVALUATIONS OF EMPLOYEE
PERFORMANCE.   M0215

NEWSTROM, JOHN W.

MOTIVATING THE PUBLIC EMPLOYEE: FACT VS. FICTION.   M0890

NEWTON, RUSSEL MARION.

SUPERVISOR EXPECTATIONS AND BEHAVIOR: EFFECTS OF
CONSISTENT-INCONSISTENT SUPERVISORY PAIRINGS ON SUPERVISEE
SATISFACTION WITH SUPERVISION, PERCEPTIONS OF SUPERVISORY
RELATIONSHIPS AND RATED COUNSELOR COMPETENCY.   M0864

NICHOLSON, N.

ABSENCE FROM WORK AND JOB SATISFACTION.   M0604

ABSENCE BEHAVIOR AND ATTENDANCE MOTIVATION: A CONCEPTUAL
SYNTHESIS.   M0783

NICHOLSON, TOM

    THE JOB BLAHS: WHO WANTS TO WORK.   M0327

NIGHTINGALE, D. V.

    VALUES, STRUCTURE, PROCESS, AND REACTIONS/ADJUSTMENTS: A
    COMPARISON OF FRENCH AND ENGLISH-CANADIAN INDUSTRIAL
    ORGANIZATIONS.   M0628

NISBERG, JAY N.

    PERFORMANCE IMPROVEMENT WITHOUT TRAINING.   M0545

    WHEN DOES WORK RESTRUCTURING WORK? ORGANIZATIONAL
    INNOVATION AT VOLVO AND GM.   M0740

NO AUTHOR CITED

    GETTING CINDERELLA TO THE BALL.   M0153

    SPECIAL TASK FORCE WILL REVIEW ROLE OF GS AND FS
    SECRETARIES.   M0411

    TESTING, TESTING.   M0649

NOORDHOFF, LYMAN J.

    EXTENSION WOMEN OVERSEAS.   M0328

NORD, WALTER R.

    CONCEPTS AND CONTROVERSY IN ORGANIZATIONAL BEHAVIOR.   M0605

NORMAN, JAMES H.

    A QUALITIATIVE APPROACH TO PERFORMANCE PREDICTABILITY AND
    LEGAL COMPLIANCE.   M0329

NORTH, DAVID S.

    WOMEN OFFENDERS: BREAKING THE TRAINING MOLD.   M0330

NOTHNAGEL, GEORGE E.

    CONFLICT AND DISSONANCE IN A DISLOCATED WORKER POPULATION.   M0930

NOURI, CLEMENT J.

    RELEVANCE OF MOTIVATIONAL CONCEPTS TO INDIVIDUAL AND
    CORPORATE OBJECTIVES.   M0331

O'CONNEL, M. J.

    MODERATING EFFECTS OF ENVIRONMENT AND STRUCTURE ON THE
    SATISFACTION-TENSION-INFLUENCE NETWORK.   M0828

O'HAIR, JAMES P.

THE ACHIEVEMENT PROCESS: AN EXPLORATORY STUDY OF CAREER
BEGINNINGS.   M0332

O'LEARY, LOUIS K.

MOTIVATING THE NOW GENERATION.   M0333

O'REILLY, C. A.

PERSONALITY-JOB FIT: IMPLICATIONS FOR INDIVIDUAL ATTITUDES
AND PERFORMANCE.   M0829

PHYSICAL ENVIRONMENT AND JOB SATISFACTION IN A COMMUNITY
MENTAL HEALTH CENTER.   M0883

OLDHAM, GREG R.

CONDITIONS UNDER WHICH EMPLOYEES RESPOND POSITIVELY TO
ENRICHED WORK.   M0606

EFFECTS OF VARYING GOAL TYPES AND INCENTIVE SYSTEMS ON
PERFORMANCE AND SATISFACTION.   M0659

IMPACT OF SUPERVISORY CHARACTERISTICS ON GOAL ACCEPTANCE.   M0661

DEVELOPMENT OF THE JOB DIAGNOSTIC SURVEY.   M0723

MOTIVATION THROUGH THE DESIGN OF WORK: TEST OF A THEORY.   M0761

OLIVER, RICHARD.

ANTECEDENTS OF SALESMEN'S COMPENSATION PERCEPTIONS: A PATH
ANALYSIS INTERPRETATION.   M0785

OLSON, JOHN A.

ROLE DISSATISFACTION AND CAREER CONTINGENCIES AMONG FEMALE
ELEMENTARY TEACHERS.   M0722

ONDRACK, D. A.

DEFENSE MECHANISMS AND THE HERZBERG THEORY: AN ALTERNATE
TEST.   M0334

ORGAN, DENNIS W.

AN EVALUATION OF CAUSAL MODELS LINKING THE RECEIVED ROLE
WITH JOB SATISFACTION.   M0335

PERCEIVED PURPOSEFULNESS OF JOB BEHAVIOR: ANTECEDENTS AND
CONSEQUENCES.   M0336

ORGANT, G. J.

    DETERMINANTS OF PAY AND PAY SATISFACTION.   M0367

ORPEN, C.

    SOCIAL DESIRABILITY AS A MODERATOR OF THE RELATIONSHIP
    BETWEEN JOB SATISFACTION AND PERSONAL ADJUSTMENT.   M0337

    JOB ENLARGEMENT, INDIVIDUAL DIFFERENCES, AND WORKER
    RESPONSES: A TEST WITH BLACK WORKERS IN SOUTH AFRICA.   M0546

    THE LIMITATIONS OF THE MOTIVATOR-HYGIENE THEORY OF
    SATISFACTION: AN EMPIRICAL STUDY WITH BLACK FACTORY WORKERS
    IN SOUTH AFRICA.   M0607

    DISCRIMINATION AND JOB SATISFACTION: AN EMPIRICAL STUDY
    WITH A SOUTH AFRICAN MINORITY GROUP.   M0733

    THE RELATIONSHIP BETWEEN MANAGERIAL SUCCESS AND PERSONAL
    VALUES IN SOUTH AFRICA: A RESEARCH NOTE.   M0786

    THE EFFECT OF URBANIZATION ON SOURCES OF JOB SATISFACTION
    AMONG BLACK SUPERVISORS IN SOUTH AFRICA.   M0891

OSBALDESTON, M.D.

    SKANDIA INSURANCE GROUP: RESTRUCTURING THE WORK AND
    ENRICHING THE JOB.   M0547

OSBORN, RICHARD N.

    SEX STEREOTYPES: AN ARTIFACT IN LEADER BEHAVIOR AND
    SUBORDINATE SATISFACTION ANALYSIS.   M0662

OTTEMAN, ROBERT.

    MOTIVATION VS. LEARNING APPROACHES TO ORGANIZATIONAL
    BEHAVIOR.   M0285

OVERBECK, D.

    JOB SATISFACTION AND PERFORMANCE WITH RETARDED FEMALES.   M0738

PACKARD, MARY E.

    A NATIONAL STUDY OF ASSOCIATE DEGREE MENTAL HEALTH SERVICES
    WORKERS.   M0806

PAJER, ROBERT G.

    A SYSTEMS APPROACH TO RESULTS ORIENTED PERFORMANCE
    EVALUATION.   M0338

PARKE, E. LAUCK.

MYTHOLOGY OF JOB ENRICHMENT: SELF-ACTUALIZATION REVISITED.   M0548

PARKER, FAULY B.

THE EFFECT OF MOTIVATIONAL PROGRAMS ON COLLECTIVE
BARGAINING.   M0032

PARKER, WARRINGTON S.

BLACK-WHITE DIFFERENCES IN LEADER BEHAVIOR RELATED TO
SUBORDINATES' REACTIONS.   M0608

PARNES, HERBERT S.

NATIONAL LONGITUDINAL STUDIES OF THE LABOR FORCE BEHAVIOR
OF NATIONAL SAMPLES OF MEN (45-59), WOMEN (30-44), AND MALE
AND FEMALE YOUTH (14-24).   M0339

PARRELLA, VERA C.

MOONLIGHTERS: THEIR MOTIVATIONS AND CHARACTERISTICS.   M0345

PARRISH, JOHN B.

WOMEN IN PROFESSIONAL TRAINING.   M0340

PASRICHA, V.

JOB ORIENTATION AND WORK BEHAVIOR.   M0665

PATCHEN, MARTIN.

PARTICIPATION, ACHIEVEMENT, AND INVOLVEMENT ON THE JOB.   M0342

PATHAK, D. S.

SHIFTING TO THE HUMAN SIDE.   M0646

PATTENAUDE, RICHARD L.

INCREASING THE IMPORTANCE OF PERSONNEL: A STRATEGY.   M0549

PEARCE, JONE L.

CONDITIONS UNDER WHICH EMPLOYEES RESPOND POSITIVELY TO
ENRICHED WORK.   M0606

PEMBROKE, JAMES D.

MARKETING WELFARE MOTHERS' JOB SKILLS.   M0343

PERLOFF, STEPHEN H.

COMPARING MUNICIPAL, INDUSTRY, AND FEDERAL PAY.   M0344

PERREAULT, W.

   ORGANIZATIONAL ROLE CONFLICT: ITS ANTECEDENTS AND
   CONSEQUENCES.   M0601

PETERMANN, LESTER L.

   FRINGE BENEFITS OF URBAN WORKERS.   M0346

PETTY, M. M.

   RELATIONSHIPS BETWEEN ROLE CLARITY, NEED FOR CLARITY AND
   JOB TENSION AND SATISFACTION FOR SUPERVISORY AND
   NONSUPERVISORY ROLES.   M0539

   THE USE OF EXPECTANCY THEORY IN THE EXPLANATION OF TURNOVER
   IN ROTC.   M0732

PFEFFER, J.

   AN EXAMINATION OF NEED-SATISFACTION MODELS OF JOB
   ATTITUDES.   M0673

PHELAN, JOSEPH G.

   EFFECTS ON PRODUCTIVITY AND MORALE OF A SYSTEMS-DESIGNED
   JOB-ENRICHMENT PROGRAM IN PACIFIC TELEPHONE.   M0515

PHESEY, DIANA C.

   MANAGERS' OCCUPATIONAL HISTORIES, ORGANIZATIONAL
   ENVIRONMENTS, AND CLIMATES FOR MANAGEMENT DEVELOPMENT.   M0787

PHILLIPS, IRVING.

   BUSINESS MACHINES AND COMPUTER MANUFACTURING -- CAREER
   OPPORTUNITIES ARE EXCELLENT.   M0347

PINKARD, MARY.

   THE FEDERAL WOMEN'S PROGRAM: A HUD PERSPECTIVE.   M0348

PINKERTON, JAMES R.

   SOCIOECONOMIC DETERMINANTS OF URBAN POVERTY AREA WORKERS.   M0349

PINTO, PATRICK R.

   THE IMPACT OF THE ORGANIZATION ON THE STRUCTURE OF JOB
   SATISFACTION: SOME FACTOR ANALYTIC FINDINGS.   M0471

   THE DEVELOPMENT OF A MANAGERIAL JOB TAXONOMY: A SYSTEM FOR
   DESCRIBING, CLASSIFYING, AND EVALUATING EXECUTIVE
   POSITIONS.   M0618

PITTERMAN, LAWRENCE.

AN EXAMINATION OF BRAINSTORMING PROCEDURE, GROUP SIZE AND
MOTIVATIONAL ORIENTATION IN THE JOB ENRICHMENT GREENLIGHT
SESSION.   M0932

PLATER, JOHN.

SAFEGUARDING OUR WATER -- POLLUTION CONTROL WORKERS.   M0350

POIST, R. F.

JOB SATISFACTION AND THE PD MANAGER: AN EMPIRICAL
ASSESSMENT.   M0831

POLLACK, MAXWELL A.

AS YOU WERE SAYING -- THERE'S MORE TO WORK THAN WORK.   M0351

POMOZAL, RICHARD.

UNDERSTANDING DRUG USE MOTIVATION: A NEW LOOK AT A CURRENT
PROBLEM.   M0788

PONDY, LOUIS R.

READINGS IN MANAGERIAL PSYCHOLOGY, 2ND ED. CHICAGO.   M0271

JAMES G. MARCH AND JOHAN P. OLSEN, AMBIGUITY AND CHOICE IN
ORGANIZATIONS.   M0672

PORTER, LYMAN W.

ORGANIZATIONAL COMMITMENT, JOB SATISFACTION, AND TURNOVER
AMONG PSYCHIATRIC TECHNICIANS.   M0353

WHAT DO EXECUTIVES REALLY THINK ABOUT THEIR ORGANIZATIONS?   M0737

POTTS, ELMER R.

REVIEW OF LITERATURE ON WORK MOTIVATION: BULLETIN 12. A
STUDY OF WORK MOTIVATION OF URBAN AND RURAL APPAREL WORKERS
IN TENNESSEE.   M0503

POTYRT, RLDS S.

INFORMATION SHARING FOR PRODUCTIVITY IMPROVEMENT.   M0352

POWELL, MARY LOUISE.

PERCEPTIONS OF ORGANIZATIONAL CLIMATE AS MEDIATORS OF THE
RELATIONSHIPS BETWEEN INDIVIDUAL NEEDS AND JOB SATISFACTION
OF COUNSELORS IN THE NORTH CAROLINA COMMUNITY COLLEGE
SYSTEM.   M0933

POWERS, EDWARD A.

    THE WORK SATISFACTION, RETIREMENT-ATTITUDE TYPOLOGY:
    PROFILE EXAMINATION.   M0590

    WORK AND RETIREMENT: A TEST OF ATTITUDINAL RELATIONSHIPS.   M0721

PRASAD, R.

    MEASUREMENT OF SOCIOECONOMIC AND PSYCHOLOGICAL
    CHARACTERISTICS: A METHOD.   M0789

PREWITT, LENA B.

    DISCONTENT IN THE RANKS: IS THE OPERATIVE WORKER REALLY
    TRAPPED.   M0354

PRICE, RAYMOND L.

    THE FOUR STAGES OF PROFESSIONAL CAREERS - A NEW LOOK AT
    PERFORMANCE BY PROFESSIONALS.   M0711

PRICE, W.N.

    MOTIVATION AND HARD TIMES.   M0355

PRITCHARD, R.

    THE EFFECTS OF VARYING SCHEDULES OF REINFORCEMENT ON HUMAN
    TASK PERFORMANCE.   M0790

PYKE, SANDRA W.

    DESIRED JOB CHARACTERISTICS FOR MALES AND FEMALES.   M0629

QUINN, R. P.

    WORKING CONDITIONS SURVEY AS A SOURCE OF SOCIAL INDICATORS. M0206

    EVALUATING WORKING CONDITIONS IN AMERICA.   M0356

    EFFECTIVENESS IN WORK ROLES.   M0386

QUINN, ROBERT E.

    COPING WITH CUPID: THE FORMATION, IMPACT, AND MANAGEMENT OF
    ROMANTIC RELATIONSHIPS IN ORGANIZATIONS.   M0630

RABINOWITZ, S.

    ORGANIZATIONAL RESEARCH ON JOB INVOLVEMENT.   M0609

RAFALKO, EDMUND A.

    EFFICIENCY IN THE MILITARY.   M0522

RAIBORN, M.

ACCOUNTING FOR CORPORATE SOCIAL RESPONSIBILITY. M0071

RAIMO, NURMI.

PRODUCING MAN'S CASE FOR SATISFACTION. M0610

RAMOS, ALBERT A.

THE RELATIONSHIP OF SEX AND ETHNIC BACKGROUND TO
JOB-RELATED STRESS OF RESEARCH AND DEVELOPMENT
PROFESSIONALS. M0695

RANDELL, JOAN.

WORK ADJUSTMENT OF THE METHADONE-MAINTAINED CORPORATE
EMPLOYEE. M0567

RANI, KALA.

JOB MOTIVATIONS FOR WORKING WOMEN. M0791

RAUBOLT, ROBERT R.

A STUDY OF EMPLOYEE RESISTANCE TO JOB ENRICHMENT. M0066

RAUSCH, ERWIN.

THE EFFECTIVE ORGANIZATION: MORALE VS. DISCIPLINE. M0357

REDDIN, W.J.

CONFESSIONS OF AN ORGANIZATIONAL CHANGE AGENT. M0631

REIF, WILLIAM E.

A DIAGNOSTIC APPROACH TO JOB ENRICHMENT. M0358

MOTIVATING THE PUBLIC EMPLOYEE: FACT VS. FICTION. M0890

REINHARTH, L.

EXPECTANCY THEORY AS A PREDICTOR OF WORK MOTIVATION, EFFORT
EXPENDITURE, AND JOB PERFORMANCE. M0663

A TEST OF ALTERNATIVE MODELS OF EXPECTANCY THEORY. M0892

REPP, WILLIAM.

MOTIVATING THE NOW GENERATION. M0360

RHODE, JOHN.

JOB CHOICE AND POST DECISION DISSONANCE. M0772

RICHARDSON, JOHN G.

A COMPARISON OF PROFESSIONAL INSTITUTIONAL COMMUNITY
CORRECTIONS WORKERS ON JOB SATISFACTION AND SELF-CONCEPT.   M0696

RICHMOND, CHARLOTTE.

LOGGING -- A JOB FOR THE HARDY.   M0362

TOUR ESCORTING -- GLAMOUR OR HARD WORK.   M0363

RIDGELY, Q. B.

DESEGREGATION AND CAREER GOALS. CHILDREN OF AIR FORCE
FAMILIES.   M0491

ROBBINS, ANTHONY.

ROLE OF ON-THE-JOB TRAINING IN A CLINICAL LABORATORY.   M0477

ROBBINS, PAULA I.

CORPORATE DROPOUTS: A PRELIMINARY TYPOLOGY.   M0616

ROBERTS, K. H.

TWENTY QUESTIONS: UTILIZING JOB SATISFACTION MEASURES.   M0364

A FACTOR ANALYTIC STUDY OF JOB SATISFACTION ITEMS DESIGNED
TO MEASURE MASLOW NEED CATEGORIES.   M0365

PHYSICAL ENVIRONMENT AND JOB SATISFACTION IN A COMMUNITY
MENTAL HEALTH CENTER.   M0883

ROBINSON, J.

INTERACTION MODELING: A NEW CONCEPT IN SUPERVISORY
TRAINING.   M0507

ROCHE, WILLIAM J.

MOTIVATING PEOPLE WITH MEANINGFUL WORK.   M0293

RODEFIELD, R.

FEELINGS OF POWERLESSNESS AND SOCIAL ISOLATION AMONG LARGE
SCALE FARM PERSONNEL.   M0596

ROEHL, CAROL E.

THE MENTAL HEALTH ASSOCIATE: THE EFFECT OF SOCIAL
ENVIRONMENTAL FACTORS ON JOB SATISFACTION.   M0697

ROESSNER, J. D.

HOW EMPLOYERS SCREEN DISADVANTAGED JOB APPLICANTS.   M0185

ROUSTANG, G.

    WHY STUDY WORKING CONDITIONS VIA JOB SATISFACTION? A PLEA
    FOR DIRECT ANALYSIS.   M0833

RUBIN, IRWIN M.

    ORGANIZATIONAL PSYCHOLOGY (A BOOK OF READINGS).   M0257

RUDNEY, SHIRLEY.

    THE PUBLIC EMPLOYMENT SERVICE REACHES OUT TO THE URBAN
    POOR.   M0374

RUH, ROBERT A.

    EFFECTS OF PERSONAL VALUES ON THE RELATIONSHIP BETWEEN
    PARTICIPATION AND JOB ATTITUDES.   M0476

    JOB INVOLVEMENT, VALUES, PERSONAL BACKGROUND, PARTICIPATION
    IN DECISION MAKING, AND JOB ATTITUDES.   M0664

RUSH, HAROLD M. G.

    MOTIVATION THROUGH JOB DESIGN.   M0375

SALANCIK, G. R.

    AN EXAMINATION OF NEED-SATISFACTION MODELS OF JOB
    ATTITUDES.   M0673

SALEH, S. D.

    WORK VALUES OF WHITE-COLLAR EMPLOYEES AS A FUNCTION OF
    SOCIOLOGICAL BACKGROUND.   M0376

    JOB ORIENTATION AND WORK BEHAVIOR.   M0665

    JOB INVOLVEMENT: CONCEPTS AND MEASUREMENTS.   M0834

SANCHEZ VILLANUEVA, JOSE.

    PSCHOPHYSIOLOGICAL INFLUENCES ON THE WORK ENVIRONMENT: NEW
    CONCEPTS.   M0550

SANTANGELI, F.

    IMPROVING PRODUCTIVITY THROUGH JOB ENRICHMENT.   M0647

SAUER, JOHN R.

    MANAGEMENT-BY-MISSION FOR ACTIVATING PEOPLE.   M0377

SAUL, R. N.

    RELATIONSHIP OF AGE, TENURE AND JOB SATISFACTION IN MALES

SAUL, R. N.   CONTINUATION

   AND FEMALES.   M0525

SAVAGE, CHARLES M.

   A PHENOMENOLOGY OF HUMAN LABOR.   M0378

SAVAGE, FREDERICK.

   TWENTY QUESTIONS: UTILIZING JOB SATISFACTION MEASURES.   M0364

SCANLAN, BURT K.

   MOTIVATING SALESMEN THROUGH BETTER SALES MANAGEMENT.   M0379

   DETERMINATES OF JOB SATISFACTION AND PRODUCTIVITY.   M0551

SCHEIN, VIRGINIA E.

   POLITICAL STRATEGIES FOR IMPLEMENTING ORGANIZATIONAL
   CHANGE.   M0632

SCHLENKER, ROBERT

   AN ANALYSIS OF MICHIGAN'S EXPERIENCE WITH WORK INCENTIVES. M0012

SCHMIDT, STUART M.

   INTERORGANIZATIONAL RELATIONSHIPS: PATTERNS AND
   MOTIVATIONS.   M0674

SCHNEIDER, BEN.

   SOME RELATIONSHIPS BETWEEN JOB SATISFACTION AND
   ORGANIZATION CLIMATE.   M0734

SCHNEIDER, BENJAMIN.

   THREE STUDIES OF MEASURES OF NEED SATISFACTION IN
   ORGANIZATIONS.   M0380

   ORGANIZATIONAL CLIMATES: AN ESSAY.   M0893

SCHOLTES, PETER R.

   CONTRACTING FOR CHANGE.   M0792

SCHRIESHEIM, C.

   THE PATH-GOAL THEORY OF LEADERSHIP: A THEORETICAL AND
   EMPIRICAL ANALYSIS.   M0835

SCHULER, RANDALL S.

   THE EFFECTS OF ROLE PERCEPTIONS ON EMPLOYEE SATISFACTION

SCHULER, RANDALL S.   CONTINUATION

AND PERFORMANCE MODERATED BY EMPLOYEE ABILITY.   M0553

PARTICIPATION WITH SUPERVISOR AND SUBORDINATE
AUTHORITARIANISM: A PATH GOAL THEORY RECONCILIATION.   M0554

ROLE PERCEPTIONS, SATISFACTION AND PERFORMANCE MODERATED BY
ORGANIZATION LEVEL AND PARTICIPATION IN DECISION MAKING.   M0895

SCHWAB, DONALD P.

THEORIES OF PERFORMANCE AND SATISFACTION.   M0079

THEORIES OF PERFORMANCE AND SATISFACTION: A REVIEW.   M0080

CONFLICTING IMPACTS OF PAY ON EMPLOYEE MOTIVATION,
SATISFACTION.   M0381

SCHWARTZ, STANLEY J.

CURE FOR THE I DON'T CARE SYNDROME.   M0382

SCHWEITZER, S.

THE PERSISTENCE OF THE DISADVANTAGED WORKER EFFECT.   M0383

SCOBEL, D. N.

DOING AWAY WITH THE FACTORY BLUES.   M0648

SCOTT, RICHARD D.

JOB ENLARGEMENT -- THE KEY TO INCREASING JOB SATISFACTION.   M0384

JOB EXPECTANCY -- AN IMPORTANT FACTOR IN LABOR TURNOVER.   M0385

SEALS, GARY W.

CONTRIBUTION OF JOB AND LEISURE SATISFACTION TO QUALITY OF
LIFE.   M0774

SEASHORE, S. E.

EFFECTIVENESS IN WORK ROLES.   M0386

SEAY,DONNA.

MODEL PROGRAM TO INSTRUCT MANPOWER TRAINING PERSONNEL IN
SELECTION AND APPLICATION OF REMEDIAL INSTRUCTIONAL
MATERIALS TO MEET INDIVIDUAL TRAINEE NEEDS.   M0387

SEKARAN, U.

TOWARD A CAREER-BASED THEORY OF JOB INVOLVEMENT: A STUDY OF
SCIENTISTS AND ENGINEERS.   M0824

SEKI, FUMIYASU.

    EFFECTS OF ACHIEVEMENT MOTIVATION ON THE EFFECTIVENESS OF
LEADERSHIP PATTERNS.   M0317

SELIGMAN, M.

    LEARNED HELPLESSNESS: THEORY AND EVIDENCE.   M0776

SEYBOLT, JOHN W.

    WORK SATISFACTION AS A FUNCTION OF THE PERSON-ENVIRONMENT
INTERACTION.   M0836

SHANI, E.

    GROWTH AND SATISFACTION OF EMPLOYEES IN ORGANIZATIONS.   M0825

SHAPIRO, H. JACK.

    FREDRICK W. TAYLOR -- 62 YEARS LATER.   M0390

    JOB SATISFACTION: MALE AND FEMALE, PROFESSIONAL AND
NON-PROFESSIONAL.   M0552

    MODELS OF PAY SATISFACTION: A COMPARATIVE STUDY.   M0613

SHAW, GRAHAM.

    PITFALLS OF PARTICIPATION.   M0679

SHEIL, TIMOTHY J.

    THE USE OF EXPECTANCY THEORY IN THE EXPLANATION OF TURNOVER
IN ROTC.   M0732

SHEPARD, JON M.

    ON ALEX CAREY'S RADICAL CRITICISMS OF THE HAWTHORNE
STUDIES.   M0391

SHEPPARD, H. L.

    ASKING THE RIGHT QUESTIONS ON JOB SATISFACTION.   M0392

    DISCONTENTED BLUE-COLLAR WORKERS -- A CASE STUDY.   M0393

SHERIDAN, JOHN E.

    ANALYSIS OF RELATIONSHIPS AMONG LEADER BEHAVIOR,
SUBORDINATE JOB PERFORMANCE, AND SATISFACTION: A PATH-GOAL
APPROACH.   M0652

SHIMONKEVITZ, RUTH.

    OFFICE LANDSCAPING -- NEW LOOK FOR THE WORKPLACE.   M0394

SHIPP, CHRISTOPHER.

    THE IMPACT OF ORGANIZATION SIZE ON EMPLOYEE MOTIVATION.   M0735

SHREY, DONALD EUGENE.

    VOCATIONAL SATISFACTION, SUCCESS AND STABILITY: A
    COMPARATIVE STUDY OF MALE AND FEMALE NON-PROFESSIONAL
    WORKERS.   M0869

SHUBKAGEL, BETTY LOU.

    THE RELATIONSHIPS BETWEEN THE TASK-HUMAN RELATIONS
    MOTIVATIONAL STRUCTURES OF INDIVIDUALS IN SMALL WORK GROUPS
    AND THEIR SATISFACTION WITH CO-WORKERS AND IMMEDIATE
    SUPERVISION.   M0868

SHYE, S.

    ORGANIZATIONAL AND OCCUPATIONAL COMMITMENT: A FACET
    THEORETICAL ANALYSIS OF EMPIRICAL DATA.   M0747

SIEGEL, JACOB P.

    SATISFACTION AND PERFORMANCE: CAUSAL RELATIONSHIPS AND
    MODERATING EFFECTS.   M0395

SILBER, MARK B.

    MANAGERS MANAGE MOTIVATION: THEY DON'T MOTIVATE.   M0396

SIMON, YVES R.

    WORK, SOCIETY AND CULTURE.   M0397

SIMPKINS, EDWARD.

    THE WORK ETHIC IS NOT ENOUGH.   M0398

SIMS, HENRY P.

    ROLE DYNAMICS, LOCUS OF CONTROL, AND EMPLOYEE ATTITUDES AND
    BEHAVIOR.   M0667

    LEADER STRUCTURE AND SUBORDINATE SATISFACTION FOR TWO
    HOSPITAL ADMINISTRATIVE LEVELS: A PATH ANALYSIS APPROACH.   M0736

    JOB CHARACTERISTICS RELATIONSHIPS: INDIVIDUAL AND
    STRUCTURAL MODERATORS.   M0896

    THE RELATIONSHIP OF LEADERSHIP STYLE TO EMPLOYEE JOB
    SATISFACTION.   M0935

SINGER, JACK N.

    JOB STRAIN AS A FUNCTION OF JOB LIFE AND STRESSES.   M0698

SINGER, JILL M.

    FILLING THE POLICE LINEUP.   M0399

SINGH, RAMADHAR.

    INFORMATION INTEGRATION THEORY APPLIED TO EXPECTED JOB
    ATTRACTIVENESS AND SATISFACTION.   M0793

SINGH, T.

    WORK VALUES OF WHITE-COLLAR EMPLOYEES AS A FUNCTION OF
    SOCIOLOGICAL BACKGROUND.   M0376

SINGHAL, SUSHILA

    NEED-RATIFICATION, ABSENTEEISM AND ITS OTHER CORRELATES.   M0794

SIROTA, DAVID

    AN EXPERIMENTAL CASE STUDY OF THE SUCCESSES AND FAILURES OF
    JOB ENRICHMENT IN A GOVERNMENT AGENCY.   M0600

SKAGGS, C. T.

    WORK VALUES AND JOB SATISFACTION OF YOUNG ADULT MALES.   M0579

SKVORC, LORA R.

    WOMEN IN INDUSTRY: ALIENATION, SATISFACTION, AND CHANGE.   M0699

SLEZAK, LESTER.

    EFFECTS OF CHANGES IN PAYMENT SYSTEM ON PRODUCTIVITY IN
    SWEDEN.   M0400

SLOCUM, JOHN W.

    WORK GROUPS AND EMPLOYEE SATISFACTION.   M0004

    DOES JOB PERFORMANCE AFFECT EMPLOYEE SATISFACTION.   M0056

    CONGRUENCE BETWEEN INDIVIDUALS' NEEDS, ORGANIZATIONAL
    CLIMATE, JOB SATISFACTION AND PERFORMANCE.   M0110

    PERCEPTIONS OF JOB SATISFACTION IN DIFFERING OCCUPATIONS.   M0256

    JOB SATISFACTION AND PRODUCTIVITY.   M0315

    MOTIVATION IN MANAGERIAL LEVELS: RELATIONSHIP OF NEED
    SATISFACTION TO JOB PERFORMANCE.   M0401

    PREDICTION OF JOB SUCCESS AND EMPLOYEE SATISFACTION FOR
    EXECUTIVES AND FOREMEN.   M0402

    ANALYSIS OF RELATIONSHIPS AMONG LEADER BEHAVIOR,

SLOCUM, JOHN W.   CONTINUATION

   SUBORDINATE JOB PERFORMANCE, AND SATISFACTION: A PATH-GOAL
   APPROACH.   M0652

   THE EFFECTS OF INDIVIDUAL-ROLE COMPATIBILITY UPON GROUP
   PERFORMANCE: AN EXTENSION OF SCHUTZ'S FIRO THEORY.   M0658

SMALL, SYLVIA S.

   WORK TRAINING PROGRAMS AND THE UNEMPLOYMENT RATE.   M0403

SMITH, F. S. AND OTHERS.

   TEN YEAR JOB SATISFACTION TRENDS IN A STABLE ORGANIZATION.   M0837

   TRENDS IN JOB-RELATED ATTITUDES OF MANAGERIAL AND
   PROFESSIONAL EMPLOYEES.   M0838

SMITH, FRANK J.

   WHAT DO EXECUTIVES REALLY THINK ABOUT THEIR ORGANIZATIONS?   M0737

   LANGUAGE, TIME, AND PERSON EFFECTS ON ATTITUDE SCALE
   TRANSLATIONS.   M0770

   WORK ATTITUDES AS PREDICTORS OF ATTENDANCE ON A SPECIFIC
   DAY.   M0795

SMITH, FREDERICK DOWNING.

   A NETWORK ANALYSIS OF A BUREAU OF INDIAN AFFAIRS SCHOOL
   SYSTEM TO DETERMINE FACTORS INVOLVED IN JOB SATISFACTION.   M0934

SMITH, GERALD.

   OCCUPATIONAL GUIDANCE MATERIALS FOR THE DISADVANTAGED: A
   PILOT PROGRAM.   M0404

SMITH, HOWARD P.

   KEYS TO EMPLOYEE MOTIVATION.   M0405

SMITH, HOWARD R.

   THE HALF-LOAF OF JOB ENRICHMENT.   M0555

SMITH, J. H.

   CAN INTERNAL AUDITORS FIND JOB SATISFACTION?   M0840

SMITH, R.

   THE PERSISTENCE OF THE DISADVANTAGED WORKER EFFECT.   M0383

SMYSER, CHARLES M.

LOCUS OF CONTROL: SUPERVISION AND WORK SATISFACTION.   M0660

SNIDERMAN, MARK.

MULTIJOBHOLDING OF WICHITA PUBLIC SCHOOL TEACHERS.   M0729

SNOW, WILLIAM E.

PREDICTING THE PERFORMANCE OF JUNIOR ACHIEVEMENT COMPANIES
ACCORDING TO THE LEADERSHIP STYLE OF TWO LEVELS OF
MANAGEMENT: A FIELD STUDY OF THE CONTINGENCY MODEL.   M0700

PREDICTING THE PERFORMANCE OF JUNIOR ACHIEVEMENT ACCORDING
TO THE LEADERSHIP STYLE OF TWO LEVELS OF MANAGEMENT: A
FIELD STUDY OF THE CONTINGENCY MODEL.   M0872

SNYDER, ROBERT A.

SOME RELATIONSHIPS BETWEEN JOB SATISFACTION AND
ORGANIZATION CLIMATE.   M0734

SOLOMAN, ROBERT J.

THE IMPORTANCE OF MANAGER-SUBORDINATE PERCEPTUAL
DIFFERENCES TO THE STUDY OF LEADERSHIP.   M0701

MANAGEMENT STYLES ASSOCIATED WITH ORGANIZATIONAL, TASK,
PERSONAL, AND INTERPERSONAL CONTINGENCIES.   M0748

SOLOMON, TRUDY.

STRATEGIES FOR ENHANCING THE PREDICTION OF JOB PERFORMANCE
FROM JOB SATISFACTION.   M0768

SOMMERS, DIXIE.

OCCUPATIONAL RANKING FOR MEN AND WOMEN BY EARNINGS.   M0408

SONTAG, MARVIN.

MUTUAL ADAPTABILITY OF WORKERS AND ORGANIZATIONS.   M0119

SORCHER, MELVIN.

MOTIVATION, PARTICIPATION, AND MYTH.   M0409

CHARTING AND CHANGING THE ORGANIZATIONAL CLIMATE.   M0410

SORENSEN, JAMES.

JOB CHOICE AND POST DECISION DISSONANCE.   M0772

SORENSON, PETER F.

IMPACT OF MANAGEMENT BY OBJECTIVES ON MASLOW'S NEED
HIERARCHY: AN EMPIRICAL STUDY.   M0617

SPECTOR, PAUL E.

RELATIONSHIPS OF ORGANIZATIONAL FRUSTRATION WITH REPORTED
BEHAVIORAL REACTIONS OF EMPLOYEES.   M0796

SPENCER, GEORGE J.

EFFECTS OF PARTICIPATION ON SATISFACTION AND PRODUCTIVITY.   M0702

SPIKE, ROBERTA D.

CLIENT SELF-SELECTION OF TESTS AND WORK SAMPLES IN
VOCATIONAL EVALUATION.   M0897

SPINK, PETER.

SOME COMMENTS ON THE QUALITY OF WORKING LIFE.   M0614

SPOHN, ANDREW G.

ORGANIZATIONAL DIAGNOSIS.   M0275

SPRINGER, PHILIP B.

WORK ATTITUDES OF DISADVANTAGED BLACK MEN.   M0412

STAHL, O. GLENN.

WHAT THE PERSONNEL FUNCTION IS ALL ABOUT.   M0413

STANDING, T. E.

AN APPLICATION OF INFORMATION THEORY TO INDIVIDUAL WORKER
DIFFERENCES IN SATISFACTION WITH WORK ITSELF.   M0416

INDIVIDUAL DIFFERENCES IN WORK SATISFACTION.   M0417

STARKE, F. A.

A TEST OF TWO POSTULATES UNDERLYING EXPECTANCY THEORY.   M0666

STARRY, RICHARD.

WELFARE ISN'T WORKING.   M0625

STEERS, RICHARD M.

ORGANIZATIONAL COMMITMENT, JOB SATISFACTION, AND TURNOVER
AMONG PSYCHIATRIC TECHNICIANS.   M0353

FACTORS AFFECTING JOB ATTITUDE IN GOAL SETTING ENVIRONMENT. M0556

STEERS, RICHARD M.   CONTINUATION

    ANTECEDENTS AND OUTCOMES OF ORGANIZATIONAL COMMITMENT.   M0633

STERN, LOUIS W.

    JOB SATISFACTION: MALE AND FEMALE, PROFESSIONAL AND
    NON-PROFESSIONAL.   M0552

STERNLIEB, STEVEN,

    EMPLOYMENT CHARACTERISTICS OF LOW-WAGE WORKERS.   M0418

STEVENSON, GLORIA.

    CAREER PLANNING FOR HIGH SCHOOL GIRLS.   M0420

    COUNSELING BLACK TEENAGE GIRLS.   M0421

    DOES A COLLEGE EDUCATION PAY.   M0422

    PHYSICIAN'S ASSISTANT -- MEDICAL OCCUPATION IS THE MAKING. M0423

    WHAT YOUNG PEOPLE SHOULD KNOW ABOUT LABOR UNIONS.   M0424

    WORKING FOR YOURSELF -- WHAT'S IT LIKE.   M0425

    WOMEN: UNCLE SAM WANTS YOU.   M0426

STEWART, JEAN.

    JOB RESTRUCTURING. . . ONE ROAD TO INCREASED OPPORTUNITIES. M0427

STEWART, ROBERT A.

    WHERE SUCCESS LIES.   M0797

    PSYCHOLOGICAL ATTITUDES AND BELIEFS OF MINISTERS.   M0804

STINSON, J. E.

    TASKS, INDIVIDUAL DIFFERENCES, AND JOB SATISFACTION.   M0841

STONE, EUGENE.

    HIGHER ORDER NEED STRENGTHS AS MODERATORS OF THE JOB
    SCOPE-JOB SATISFACTION RELATIONSHIP.   M0798

STRASSER, A.

    PRIVATE PENSION PLANS, 1960 TO 1969 -- AN OVERVIEW.   M0086

    DIFFERENTIALS AND OVERLAPS IN EARNINGS OF BLACKS AND
    WHITES.   M0428

STRAUSS, GEORGE.

    WORKER DISSATISFACTION: A LOOK AT THE CAUSES.   M0429

    WORKER DISSATISFACTION: A LOOK AT THE CAUSE   M0615

STRAUSS, JUDI.

    IMPACT OF MANAGEMENT BY OBJECTIVES ON MASLOW'S NEED
    HIERARCHY: AN EMPIRICAL STUDY.   M0617

STRAWSER, R. H.

    A COMPARATIVE ANALYSIS OF THE JOB SATISFACTION OF
    INDUSTRIAL MANAGERS AND CERTIFIED PUBLIC ACCOUNTANTS.   M0228

    PERCEPTIONS OF JOB SATISFACTION IN DIFFERING OCCUPATIONS.   M0256

STRAY, S.J.

    ACADEMIC SALARIES -- A PERSONAL APPLICATION OF MANAGERIAL
    ECONOMICS.   M0782

STREETER, TOM.

    WOMANPOWER IN DUNGAREES.   M0430

STREIT, FRED.

    EMPLOYEES LEARN WHAT THEY LIVE NOT WHAT THEY ARE TOLD.   M0431

SUSKIN, HAROLD.

    TESTING A NEW APPROACH TO EVALUATION.   M0433

SUTERMUSTER, ROBERT A.

    EMPLOYEE PERFORMANCE AND EMPLOYEE NEED SATISFACTION --
    WHICH COMES FIRST.   M0434

SVENSON, A. L.

    MORATORIUM ON MOTIVATION.   M0435

SZILAGYI, A. D.

    EMPLOYEE REACTIONS TO LEADER REWARD BEHAVIOR.   M0654

    ROLE DYNAMICS, LOCUS OF CONTROL, AND EMPLOYEE ATTITUDES AND
    BEHAVIOR.   M0667

    LEADER STRUCTURE AND SUBORDINATE SATISFACTION FOR TWO
    HOSPITAL ADMINISTRATIVE LEVELS: A PATH ANALYSIS APPROACH.   M0736

    AN EMPIRICAL TEST OF CAUSAL INFERENCE BETWEEN ROLE
    PERCEPTIONS, SATISFACTION WITH WORK, PERFORMANCE AND

SZILAGYI, A. D.   CONTINUATION

    ORGANIZATIONAL LEVEL.   M0839

    JOB CHARACTERISTICS RELATIONSHIPS: INDIVIDUAL AND
    STRUCTURAL MODERATORS.   M0896

    THE RELATIONSHIP OF LEADERSHIP STYLE TO EMPLOYEE JOB
    SATISFACTION.   M0935

TAGGART, ROBERT.

    HAS THE BLUE-COLLAR WORKER'S POSITION WORSENED?   M0278

    MANPOWER PROGRAMS FOR CRIMINAL OFFENDERS.   M0436

TALKINGTON, L.

    JOB SATISFACTION AND PERFORMANCE WITH RETARDED FEMALES.   M0738

TANNEHILL, ROBERT E.

    MOTIVATION AND MANAGEMENT DEVELOPMENT.   M0438

TAUSKY, CURT.

    MYTHOLOGY OF JOB ENRICHMENT: SELF-ACTUALIZATION REVISITED.   M0548

TAVEGGIA, T. C.

    JOB SPECIALIZATION, WORK VALUES, AND WORKER
    DISSATISFACTION.   M0557

TAYLOR, P. A.

    AGE AND JOB SATISFACTION AMONG MALES AND FEMALES: A
    MULTI-VARIATE, MULTISURVEY STUDY.   M0518

TEMKIN, SUZANNE MARA.

    PERSONALITY TRAITS, WORK FUNCTIONS, AND VOCATIONAL
    SATISFACTION OF PHYSICIANS IN THREE MEDICAL SPECIALTIES.   M0875

TEMPLETON, JANE.

    MANPOWER MANAGEMENT: NO ONE'S SELLING YOUTH ON SELLING.   M0440

TERBORG, JAMES R.

    THE MOTIVATIONAL COMPONENTS OF GOAL SETTING.   M0799

TERRILL, ROBERT C.

    THE RELATIONSHIP OF LEADERSHIP STYLE TO EMPLOYEE JOB
    SATISFACTION.   M0935

TERSINE, RICHARD J

    CHRONOLOGICAL AGE AND JOB SATISFACTION: THE YOUNG
    BLUE-COLLAR WORKER.   M0007

THEODORE, GEORGE V.

    TAKING THE STING OUT OF PROJECT REASSIGNMENT.   M0441

THERIAULT, ROLAND.

    THE DETERMINANTS OF PAY SATISFACTION.   M0582

THOMAS, L. E.

    CORPORATE DROPOUTS: A PRELIMINARY TYPOLOGY.   M0616

THOMPSON, ANTHONY PETER.

    SUBJECTIVE EXPECTATIONS AND JOB FACET PREDICTABILITY IN JOB
    SATISFACTION.   M0876

THOMPSON, PAUL H.

    BOUNDARY CONDITIONS FOR EXPECTANCY THEORY PREDICTIONS OF
    WORK MOTIVATION AND JOB PERFORMANCE.   M0656

    THE FOUR STAGES OF PROFESSIONAL CAREERS - A NEW LOOK AT
    PERFORMANCE BY PROFESSIONALS.   M0711

TICHY, NOEL M.

    AN ANALYSIS OF CLIQUE FORMATION AND STRUCTURE IN
    ORGANIZATIONS.   M0445

    WHEN DOES WORK RESTRUCTURING WORK? ORGANIZATIONAL
    INNOVATION AT VOLVO AND GM.   M0740

TIMM, DONALD.

    IMPACT OF MANAGEMENT BY OBJECTIVES ON MASLOW'S NEED
    HIERARCHY: AN EMPIRICAL STUDY.   M0617

TINNELL, R. C.

    A DIAGNOSTIC APPROACH TO JOB ENRICHMENT.   M0358

TODD, JOHN.

    MANAGEMENT CONTROL SYSTEMS: A KEY LINK BETWEEN STRATEGY,
    STRUCTURE, AND EMPLOYEE PERFORMANCE.   M0741

TORBERT, W. R.

    BEING FOR THE MOST PART PUPPETS.   M0443

TORNOW, WALTER W.

THE DEVELOPMENT OF A MANAGERIAL JOB TAXONOMY: A SYSTEM FOR
DESCRIBING, CLASSIFYING, AND EVALUATING EXECUTIVE
POSITIONS.   M0618

TOSI, HENRI.

ORGANIZATION STRESS AS A MODERATOR OF THE RELATIONSHIP
BETWEEN INFLUENCE AND ROLE RESPONSE.   M0444

TOULOUSE, J

VALUES, STRUCTURE, PROCESS, AND REACTIONS/ADJUSTMENTS: A
COMPARISON OF FRENCH AND ENGLISH-CANADIAN INDUSTRIAL
ORGANIZATIONS.   M0628

TRIPATHI, RAMA C.

RELATIVE SALIENCY OF JOB FACTORS DURING STRIKE.   M0558

TROST, JAN.

AN INVESTIGATION OF ATTITUDES AMONG PRIVATES AT KA55
FOURTEENTH YEAR.   M0739

TRUE, JOHN E.

A NATIONAL STUDY OF ASSOCIATE DEGREE MENTAL HEALTH SERVICES
WORKERS.   M0806

TSAKLANGANOS, A.

IMPACT OF PERCEIVED COMMUNITY PROSPERITY ON JOB
SATISFACTION OF BLACK AND WHITE WORKERS.   M0542

TSENG, M. S.

JOB PERFORMANCE AND SATISFACTION OF SUCCESSFULLY
REHABILITATED VOCATIONAL REHABILITATION CLIENTS.   M0801

TUTTLE, THOMAS C.

DIMENSIONS OF JOB SATISFACTION: INITIAL DEVELOPMENT OF THE
AIR FORCE OCCUPATIONAL ATTITUDE INVENTORY.   M0802

TZINER, AHARON.

VOCATIONAL NEEDS, JOB REWARDS, AND SATISFACTION: A
CANONICAL ANALYSIS.   M0640

U. S. BUREAU OF LABOR STATISTICS.

IMPROVING PRODUCTIVITY; LABOR AND MANAGEMENT APPROACHES.   M0446

THE MEANING AND MEASUREMENT OF PRODUCTIVITY.   M0447

U. S. BUREAU OF LABOR STATISTICS.   CONTINUATION

   PRODUCTIVITY ANALYSIS IN MANUFACTURING PLANTS.   M0448

U. S. CIVIL SERVICE COMMISSION.

   EXECUTIVE MANPOWER MANAGEMENT.   M0449

   JOB ANALYSIS: KEY TO BETTER MANAGEMENT. SEPTEMBER 1971.   M0450

U. S. DEPARTMENT OF LABOR.

   DRIVING AMBITION PAYS OFF IN JOBS.   M0453

   JOB SATISFACTION: IS THERE A TREND.   M0454

   MANPOWER PROGRAMS IN FOUR CITIES.   M0455

U. S. DEPARTMENT OF THE AIR FORCE.

   ANALYSIS OF RACIAL DIFFERENCES IN TERMS OF WORK
   ASSIGNMENTS, JOB INTEREST, AND FELT UTILIZATION OF TALENTS
   AND TRAINING, BY RAYMOND E. CHRISTEL.   M0451

   REPORTED JOB INTEREST AND PERCEIVED UTILIZATION OF TALENTS
   AND TRAINING BY AIRMEN IN 97 CAREER LADDERS, BY R. BRUCE
   GOULD. PROJECT 7734, DECEMBER 1972.   M0452

U. S. NATIONAL COMMISSION ON PRODUCTIVITY.

   PRODUCTIVITY AND THE NATIONAL INTEREST.   M0456

U. S. VETERANS ADMINSTRATION.

   SURVEY OF FACTORS RELATING TO JOB SATISFACTION AMONG VA
   NURSES.   M0457

UECKER, W. C.

   CAN INTERNAL AUDITORS FIND JOB SATISFACTION?   M0840

UMSTOT, DENIS D.

   EFFECTS OF JOB ENRICHMENT AND TASK GOALS ON SATISFACTION
   AND PRODUCTIVITY: IMPLICATIONS FOR JOB DESIGN.   M0619

VALENZI, ENZO R.

   MANAGEMENT STYLES ASSOCIATED WITH ORGANIZATIONAL, TASK,
   PERSONAL, AND INTERPERSONAL CONTINGENCIES.   M0748

VARNEY, GLENN H.

   THERE IS NO HUMBUG TO JOB ENRICHMENT.   M0265

VELGHE, J. C.

WHAT MAKES JOHNNY MOP ? M0559

VERNEY, THOMAS P.

AN INVESTIGATION OF THE RELATIONSHIP BETWEEN INTRINSIC AND
EXTRINSIC JOB INSTRUMENTALITY EFFORT, JOB SATISFACTION,
INDIVIDUAL AND PERCEIVED TASK CHARACTERISTICS. M0938

VEROFF, JOSEPH.

FUTURE ORIENTATION AND EXPECTATIONS AS PREDICTORS OF
EMPLOYMENT SUCCESS. M0216

FUTURE ORIENTATION AND EXPECTATIONS AS PREDICTORS OF
EMPLOYMENT SUCCESS. M0217

A SOCIAL PSYCHOLGICAL EXPLORATION OF POWER MOTIVATION AMONG
DISADVANTAGED WORKERS. M0279

VICARS, WILLIAM M.

SEX STEREOTYPES: AN ARTIFACT IN LEADER BEHAVIOR AND
SUBORDINATE SATISFACTION ANALYSIS. M0662

VON HALLER, GILMER B.

INDUSTRIAL AND ORGANIZATIONAL PSYCHOLOGY. M0460

VONDER HAAR, R. A.

MOTIVATION THROUGH NEED FULFILLMENT. M0459

VONGLINOW, M. A.

THE PATH-GOAL THEORY OF LEADERSHIP: A THEORETICAL AND
EMPIRICAL ANALYSIS. M0835

WADSWORTH, M. D.

HOW TO EVALUATE THE JOB SATISFACTION OF CRITICAL EMPLOYEES. M0560

WAHBA, MAHMOUD A.

FREDRICK W. TAYLOR -- 62 YEARS LATER. M0390

EXPECTANCY THEORY AS A PREDICTOR OF WORK MOTIVATION, EFFORT
EXPENDITURE, AND JOB PERFORMANCE. M0663

A TEST OF ALTERNATIVE MODELS OF EXPECTANCY THEORY. M0892

WALDMAN, E.

MARITAL AND FAMILY CHARACTERISTICS OF THE LABOR FORCE. M0462

WALDMAN, E.   CONTINUATION

    VIET-NAM WAR VETERANS -- TRANSITION TO CIVILIAN LIFE.   M0463

    WHERE WOMEN WORK -- AN ANALYSIS BY INDUSTRY AND OCCUPATION.   M0464

WALKER, ORVILLE C.

    ORGANIZATIONAL CLIMATE AND JOB SATISFACTION IN THE SALES
    FORCE.   M0509

WALL, TOBY D.

    EGO-DEFENSIVENESS AS A DETERMINANT OF REPORTED DIFFERENCES
    IN SOURCES OF JOB SATISFACTION AND JOB DISSATISFACTION.   M0465

    ATTITUDES TOWARD PARTICIPATION AMONG LOCAL AUTHORITY
    EMPLOYEES.   M0773

WALLER, R. J.

    JOB SATISFACTION: THE THROWAWAY SOCIETY.   M0466

WALSH, JOHN.

    A DECADE OF MANPOWER TRAINING.   M0300

WALTER, GORDON A.

    A FACTOR ANALYTIC STUDY OF JOB SATISFACTION ITEMS DESIGNED
    TO MEASURE MASLOW NEED CATEGORIES.   M0365

WALTER, VERNE.

    SELF-MOTIVATED PERSONAL CAREER PLANNING: A BREAKTHROUGH IN
    HUMAN RESOURCE MANAGEMENT (PART I).   M0561

WALTON, RICHARD E.

    QUALITY OF WORKING LIFE: WHAT IS IT.   M0467

WANOUS, JOHN P.

    A CROSS-SECTIONAL TEST OF NEED HIERARCHY THEORY.   M0562

WARD, ERNEST H.

    ELEMENTS OF AN EMPLOYEE MOTIVATION PROGRAM.   M0469

WARD, JOE H.

    PREFERRED JOB ASSIGNMENT EFFECT ON JOB SATISFACTION.   M0598

WATKINS, DAVID.

    SELF-ESTEEM AS A MODERATOR IN VOCATIONAL CHOICE: A TEST OF

WATKINS, DAVID.   CONTINUATION

   KORMAN'S HYPOTHESIS.   M0803

WATSON, JOHN G.

   THE SELF-CONCEPT, PERSONAL VALUES, AND MOTIVATIONAL
   ORIENTATIONS OF BLACK AND WHITE MANAGERS.   M0668

WEAVER, CHARLES N.

   AGE AND JOB SATISFACTION AMONG MALES AND FEMALES: A
   MULTI-VARIATE, MULTISURVEY STUDY.   M0518

   WHAT WORKERS WANT FROM THEIR JOBS.   M0563

   RELATIONSHIPS AMONG PAY, RACE, SEX, OCCUPATIONAL PRESTIGE,
   SUPERVISION, WORK AUTONOMY, AND JOB SATISFACTION IN A
   NATIONAL SAMPLE.   M0842

WEAVER, MARK K.

   FOUR FACTORS INFLUENCING CONVERSION TO A FOUR-DAY WORK
   WEEK.   M0687

WEBSTER, ALAN C

   PSYCHOLOGICAL ATTITUDES AND BELIEFS OF MINISTERS.   M0804

WEDGEWOOD, HENSLEIGH.

   MEATBALLS AND MOTIVATION.   M0470

WEED, STAN E.

   LOCUS OF CONTROL: SUPERVISION AND WORK SATISFACTION.   M0660

WEINROTH, ELISSA D.

   MOTIVATION, JOB SATISFACTION, AND CAREER ASPIRATIONS OF
   MARRIED WOMEN TEACHERS AT DIFFERENT CAREER STAGES.   M0940

WEIR, ROBERT M.

   COMPARATIVE APPRAISALS OF JOB PERFORMANCE OF FULL-TIME
   ELEMENTARY PRINCIPALS BY THE PRINCIPALS AND THEIR
   SUPERVISORS IN CLASS I MONTANA SCHOOL DISTRICTS.   M0941

WEISENBERG, FAYE.

   DESIRED JOB CHARACTERISTICS FOR MALES AND FEMALES.   M0629

WEITZEL, W.

   THE IMPACT OF THE ORGANIZATION ON THE STRUCTURE OF JOB
   SATISFACTION: SOME FACTOR ANALYTIC FINDINGS.   M0471

WEITZEL, WILLIAM AND OTHERS.

    PREDICTING PAY SATISFACTION FROM NONPAY WORK VARIABLES.   M0843

WELCH, ROBERT J.

    THE EFFECT OF ORGANIZATIONAL CHANGE ON ADMINISTRATOR JOB
    SATISFACTION, ORGANIZATIONAL CLIMATE, AND PERCEIVED
    ORGANIZATIONAL EFFECTIVENESS.   M0942

WELLER, DENNIS R.

    LEADERSHIP DIMENSIONS OF NAVY RECRUIT MORALE & PERFORMANCE. M0564

WERTHER, WILLIAM B.

    BEYOND JOB ENRICHMENT TO EMPLOYMENT ENRICHMENT.   M0565

WESTLEY, M. W.

    THE EMERGING WORKER.   M0472

WESTLEY, W. A.

    THE EMERGING WORKER.   M0472

WHITE, HAROLD C.

    HOW THE LEADER LOOKS TO THE LED.   M0474

WHITE, J. K.

    EFFECTS OF PERSONAL VALUES ON THE RELATIONSHIP BETWEEN
    PARTICIPATION AND JOB ATTITUDES.   M0476

    JOB INVOLVEMENT, VALUES, PERSONAL BACKGROUND, PARTICIPATION
    IN DECISION MAKING, AND JOB ATTITUDES.   M0664

WHITE, JOHN M.

    SPECIAL WORK PROJECTS FOR THE UNEMPLOYED AND UPGRADING FOR
    THE WORKING POOR.   M0475

WHITE, ROBERT D.

    DEMOCRATIZING THE REWARD SYSTEM.   M0742

WHITE, SAMMY EUGENE.

    AN EXPERIMENTAL STUDY OF THE EFFECTS OF GOAL SETTING,
    EVALUATION APPREHENSION, AND SOCIAL CUES ON TASK
    PERFORMANCE AND JOB SATISFACTION.   M0878

WHITE, WARREN L.

    THE EFFECT OF FLEXIBLE WORKING HOURS ON ABSENTEEISM AND JOB

WHITE, WARREN L.   CONTINUATION

SATISFACTION AND THE RELATIONSHIP BETWEEN LOCUS OF CONTROL
AND UTILITY OF FLEXIBLE WORKING HOURS.   M0943

WHITE, WILLIAM D.

ROLE OF ON-THE-JOB TRAINING IN A CLINICAL LABORATORY.   M0477

WHITE, WILLIAM L.

INCENTIVES FOR SALESMEN DESIGNING A PLAN THAT WORKS.   M0703

WHITEHILL, ARTHUR M.

MAINTENANCE FACTORS: THE NEGLECTED SIDE OF WORKER
MOTIVATION.   M0620

WIENER, YOASH

JOB INVOLVEMENT AND SATISFACTION AS RELATED TO MENTAL
HEALTH AND PERSONAL TIME DEVOTED TO WORK.   M0718

COMMITMENT: A BEHAVIORAL APPROACH TO JOB INVOLVEMENT.   M0899

WIENER, YOASH.

INTEREST CONGRUENCY AS A MODERATOR OF THE RELATIONSHIPS
BETWEEN JOB TENURE AND JOB SATISFACTION AND MENTAL HEALTH.   M0623

WIER, TAMARA.

INFORMAL HELPING RELATIONSHIPS IN WORK ORGANIZATIONS.   M0650

WIGGINS, J. D.

THE RELATION OF JOB SATISFACTION TO VOCATIONAL PREFERENCES
AMONG TEACHERS OF THE EDUCABLE MENTALLY RETARDED.   M0805

WILCOX, DOUGLAS S.

EFFECTS OF DIFFERENT PATTERNS AND DEGREES OF OPENNESS IN
SUPERIOR-SUBORDINATE COMMUNICATION ON SUBORDINATE JOB
SATISFACTION.   M0045

WILD, RAY.

JOB ATTITUDES AND OVERALL JOB SATISFACTION: THE EFFECT OF
BIOGRAPHICAL AND EMPLOYMENT VARIABLES: RESEARCH NOTE.   M0050

PERCEIVED JOB ATTITUDES, JOB ATTRIBUTES AND THE BEHAVIOR OF
BLUE-COLLAR WORKERS: A RESEARCH NOTE.   M0751

WILKENING, E. A.

FEELINGS OF POWERLESSNESS AND SOCIAL ISOLATION AMONG LARGE

WILKENING, E. A.   CONTINUATION

   SCALE FARM PERSONNEL.   M0596

   OCCUPATIONAL SATISFACTION OF FARM HUSBANDS AND WIVES.   M0706

WILKENS, PAUL L.

   UNDERSTANDING FRUSTRATION-INSTIGATED BEHAVIOR.   M0743

WILKINSON, RODERICK.

   MOTIVATED WORKERS AND HARD WORKERS.   M0479

WILLIAMS, GEORGE A.

   OLNEY CENTRAL COLLEGE DENTAL ASSISTING PROGRAM GRADUATES
   PERCEPTIONS OF PROGRAM COMPONENTS, JOB SATISFACTION AND
   CAREER GOALS.   M0944

WILLIAMS, JOAN.

   MAKING THE JOB CORPS MORE FLEXIBLE.   M0480

WILLIAMS, K.

   JOB REDESIGN IMPROVES PRODUCTIVITY. (BANKERS TRUST, N.Y.).   M0533

WILLIAMS, LANNY.

   EMPLOYEE ATTITUDES REGARDING VARIOUS CHARACTERISTICS OF JOB
   OPPORTUNITY AND JOB PERFORMANCE ACROSS THREE DIFFERENT WORK
   SHIFTS AT AN INSTITUTION FOR THE RETARDED.   M0900

WILLIAMS, MARGARET RUTH.

   THE RELATIONSHIPS AMONG THE PERSONALITY TYPES, JOB
   SATISFACTIONS, AND JOB SPECIALTIES OF A SELECTED GROUP OF
   MEDICAL TECHNOLOGISTS.   M0945

WILLIS, E.

   LOCAL FIRM AND JOB SATISFACTION.   M0821

WILSON, K.W.

   ACADEMIC SALARIES -- A PERSONAL APPLICATION OF MANAGERIAL
   ECONOMICS.   M0782

WILSON, SIDNEY R.

   MOTIVATING MANAGERS WITH MONEY.   M0481

WINCHESTER, DAVID.

   THE BRITISH COAL MINE STRIKE OF 1972.   M0483

WINPISINGER, WILLIAM W.

JOB ENRICHMENT: A UNION VIEW. M0484

WITTMAN, JOHN.

THE COMPRESSED WORKWEEK: MORE QUESTIONS THAN ANSWERS. M0486

WNUK-LIPINSKI, E.

JOB SATISFACTION AND THE QUALITY OF WORKING LIFE: THE
POLISH EXPERIENCE. M0844

WOLFSON, ALAN D.

AN EXPERIMENTAL CASE STUDY OF THE SUCCESSES AND FAILURES OF
JOB ENRICHMENT IN A GOVERNMENT AGENCY. M0600

WOOD, MICHAEL T.

RELATIONSHIPS BETWEEN PERFORMANCE AND SATISFACTION UNDER
CONTINGENT AND NONCONTINGENT REWARD SYSTEMS. M0251

WOOD, ROBERT R.

JOB INVOLVEMENT, VALUES, PERSONAL BACKGROUND, PARTICIPATION
IN DECISION MAKING, AND JOB ATTITUDES. M0664

WOODRUFF, CHARLES KENNETH.

AN EMPIRICAL STUDY OF INDIVIDUAL CONGRUENCE AND THE
PERCEIVED ORGANIZATIONAL PRACTICES - JOB SATISFACTION - JOB
PERFORMANCE RELATIONSHIP IN SELECTED ELECTRONIC COMPUTER
DATA PROCESSING CENTERS. M0946

WOOL, HAROLD.

WHAT'S WRONG WITH WORK IN AMERICA? -- A REVIEW ESSAY. M0490

WORTMAN, MAX S.

SEX EFFECTS IN LEADER BEHAVIOR SELF-DESCRIPTIONS AND JOB
SATISFACTION. M0499

YANKELOVICH, D.

TURBULENCE IN THE WORKING WORLD: ANGRY WORKERS, HAPPY
GRADS. M0744

YANKOWITZ, R.

WORK ADJUSTMENT OF THE METHADONE-MAINTAINED CORPORATE
EMPLOYEE. M0567

YMAN, DAVID H.

    CONVERGENT AND DISCRIMINANT VALIDITIES OF PERFORMANCE
    EVALUATIONS IN EXTREMELY ISOLATED GROUPS.   M0180

YOHALEM, ALICE.

    DESEGREGATION AND CAREER GOALS. CHILDREN OF AIR FORCE
    FAMILIES.   M0491

YORKS, LYLE.

    KEY ELEMENTS IN IMPLEMENTING JOB ENRICHMENT.   M0492

YOUNG, ANN M.

    WORK EXPERIENCE OF THE POPULATION IN 1972.   M0493

YOUNG, CARL E.

    A NATIONAL STUDY OF ASSOCIATE DEGREE MENTAL HEALTH SERVICES
    WORKERS.   M0806

YUKL, GARY A.

    REVIEW OF RESEARCH ON THE APPLICATION OF GOAL SETTING IN
    ORGANIZATIONS.   M0657

    EFFECTS OF ASSIGNED AND PARTICIPATIVE GOAL SETTING ON
    PERFORMANCE AND JOB SATISFACTION.   M0887

YURAN, NEIL A.

    CORRECTIVE MOTIVATION.   M0494

ZARKIN, DAVID A.

    ONCE THEY WOULDN'T ACCEPT A WOMAN.   M0495

ZAUTRA, ALEX.

    ORTHODOX JOB ENRICHMENT: MEASURING TRUE QUALITY IN JOB
    SATISFACTION.   M0523

ZENGER, JOHN

    INCREASING PRODUCTIVITY: HOW BEHAVIORAL SCIENTISTS CAN
    HELP.   M0568

ZIEGLER, SHIRLEY MELAT.

    ANDROGYNY IN NURSING: NURSE ROLE EXPECTATION, SATISFACTION,
    ACADEMIC ACHIEVEMENT, AND SELF-ACTUALIZATION IM MALE AND
    FEMALE STUDENTS.   M0877

ZWANY, ABRAM.

    A CROSS-SECTIONAL TEST OF NEED HIERARCHY THEORY.   M0562

ZWERMAN, W. L.

    DESIGNING A MOTIVATING AND TEAM BUILDING EMPLOYEE APPRAISAL
    SYSTEM.   M0534

II
Subject Index

ABILITY

    THE EFFECTS OF ROLE PERCEPTIONS ON EMPLOYEE SATISFACTION
    AND PERFORMANCE MODERATED BY EMPLOYEE ABILITY.   M0553

    PREDICTING JOB PERFORMANCE BY USE OF ABILITY TESTS AND
    STUDYING JOB SATISFACTION AS A MODERATING VARIABLE.   M0765

ABROAD

    SOCIAL AND WELFARE PROGRAMS FOR THE HANDICAPPED ABROAD.   M0043

ABSENCE

    ABSENCE FROM WORK: A LOOK AT SOME NATIONAL DATA.   M0198

    ABSENCE FROM WORK AND JOB SATISFACTION.   M0604

    ABSENCE BEHAVIOR AND ATTENDANCE MOTIVATION: A CONCEPTUAL
    SYNTHESIS.   M0783

    ROLE OF JOB SATISFACTION IN ABSENCE BEHAVIOR.   M0818

ABSENTEEISM

    PREDICTING ABSENTEEISM AND TURNOVER: A FIELD COMPARISON OF
    FISHBEIN'S MODEL AND TRADITIONAL JOB ATTITUDE MEASURES.   M0326

    LONGITUDINAL STUDY OF ABSENTEEISM AND HARD-CORE UNEMPLOYED. M0500

    PERCEIVED CONSEQUENCES OF ABSENTEEISM.   M0603

    NEED-RATIFICATION, ABSENTEEISM AND ITS OTHER CORRELATES. M0794

    RELATIONSHIPS BETWEEN JOB SATISFACTION, DEMOGRAPHIC
    FACTORS, ABSENTEEISM AND TENURE OF WORKERS IN A DELMARVA
    BROILER PROCESSING PLANT.   M0921

    THE EFFECT OF FLEXIBLE WORKING HOURS ON ABSENTEEISM AND JOB
    SATISFACTION AND THE RELATIONSHIP BETWEEN LOCUS OF CONTROL
    AND UTILITY OF FLEXIBLE WORKING HOURS.   M0943

ACADEMIC

    THE DYNAMICS OF UNDERGRADUATE ACADEMIC ADVISING.   M0750

    ACADEMIC SALARIES -- A PERSONAL APPLICATION OF MANAGERIAL
    ECONOMICS.   M0782

    ANDROGYNY IN NURSING: NURSE ROLE EXPECTATION, SATISFACTION,
    ACADEMIC ACHIEVEMENT, AND SELF-ACTUALIZATION IM MALE AND
    FEMALE STUDENTS.   M0877

ACCEPT

    ONCE THEY WOULDN'T ACCEPT A WOMAN.   M0495

ACCEPTANCE

    IMPACT OF SUPERVISORY CHARACTERISTICS ON GOAL ACCEPTANCE.   M0661

ACCOUNTANTS

    A COMPARATIVE ANALYSIS OF THE JOB SATISFACTION OF
    INDUSTRIAL MANAGERS AND CERTIFIED PUBLIC ACCOUNTANTS.   M0228

ACCOUNTING

    ACCOUNTING FOR CORPORATE SOCIAL RESPONSIBILITY.   M0071

ACHIEVEMENT

    EFFECTS OF ACHIEVEMENT MOTIVATION ON THE EFFECTIVENESS OF
    LEADERSHIP PATTERNS.   M0317

    THE ACHIEVEMENT PROCESS: AN EXPLORATORY STUDY OF CAREER
    BEGINNINGS.   M0332

    PARTICIPATION, ACHIEVEMENT, AND INVOLVEMENT ON THE JOB.   M0342

    COMPONENTS OF ACHIEVEMENT MOTIVATION AS PREDICTORS OF
    POTENTIAL FOR ECONOMIC CHANGE.   M0458

    PREDICTING THE PERFORMANCE OF JUNIOR ACHIEVEMENT COMPANIES
    ACCORDING TO THE LEADERSHIP STYLE OF TWO LEVELS OF
    MANAGEMENT: A FIELD STUDY OF THE CONTINGENCY MODEL.   M0700

    INNER DIRECTION, OTHER DIRECTION AND ACHIEVEMENT
    MOTIVATION.   M0726

    ACHIEVEMENT DRIVE AND CREATIVITY AS CORRELATES OF SUCCESS
    IN SMALL BUSINESS.   M0730

    ACHIEVEMENT MOTIVATION AS A MODERATOR OF THE RELATIONSHIP
    BETWEEN EXPECTANCY TIMES VALENCE AND EFFORT.   M0845

    PREDICTING THE PERFORMANCE OF JUNIOR ACHIEVEMENT ACCORDING
    TO THE LEADERSHIP STYLE OF TWO LEVELS OF MANAGEMENT: A
    FIELD STUDY OF THE CONTINGENCY MODEL.   M0872

    ANDROGYNY IN NURSING: NURSE ROLE EXPECTATION, SATISFACTION,
    ACADEMIC ACHIEVEMENT, AND SELF-ACTUALIZATION IM MALE AND
    FEMALE STUDENTS.   M0877

ACQUISITION

    FACTORS AFFECTING ACQUISITION OF BELIEFS ABOUT A NEW REWARD
    SYSTEM.   M0589

ACTION

    DYNAMICS OF ACTION.   M0018

ACTIVATING

MANAGEMENT-BY-MISSION FOR ACTIVATING PEOPLE. M0377

ACTIVITIES

REACTIONS AT WORK AND THEIR INFLUENCE ON NON-WORK
ACTIVITIES: AN ANALYSIS OF A SOCIOPOLITICAL PROBLEM IN
AFFLUENT SOCIETIES. M0587

ACTIVITY

LABOR FORCE ACTIVITY OF MARRIED WOMEN. M0193

ADAPTABILITY

MUTUAL ADAPTABILITY OF WORKERS AND ORGANIZATIONS. M0119

ADAPTATION

TOWARD A TOLERANCE THEORY OF WORKER ADAPTATION. M0573

ADOLESCENT AND ADULT PREDICTORS OF VOCATIONAL ADAPTATION. M0592

ADAPTING

ADAPTING JOBS TO PEOPLE: EXPERIMENTS AT ALCAN. M0053

ADJUSTERS

INSURANCE ADJUSTERS AND EXAMINERS. M0101

ADJUSTMENT

SOCIAL DESIRABILITY AS A MODERATOR OF THE RELATIONSHIP
BETWEEN JOB SATISFACTION AND PERSONAL ADJUSTMENT. M0337

WORK ADJUSTMENT OF THE METHADONE-MAINTAINED CORPORATE
EMPLOYEE. M0567

ADJUSTMENTS

VALUES, STRUCTURE, PROCESS, AND REACTIONS/ADJUSTMENTS: A
COMPARISON OF FRENCH AND ENGLISH-CANADIAN INDUSTRIAL
ORGANIZATIONS. M0628

ADMINISTRATION

EXPERIENCE OF BLACK FARMERS HOCE ADMINISTRATION LOCAL
OFFICE CHIEFS. M0182

A STUDY OF THE PERCEPTIONS OF SELECTED SCHOOL-BASED
ADMINISTRATORS IN FLORIDA RELATIVE TO CERTAIN VARIABLES IN
SECONDARY SCHOOL ADMINISTRATION AS THEY RELATE TO JOB
SATISFACTION. M0925

ADMINISTRATIVE

HUMANIZING THE BUDGETARY SYSTEM FOR ADMINISTRATIVE
REINFORCEMENT.   M0138

LEADER STRUCTURE AND SUBORDINATE SATISFACTION FOR TWO
HOSPITAL ADMINISTRATIVE LEVELS: A PATH ANALYSIS APPROACH.   M0736

AN INVESTIGATION OF EDUCATIONAL ADMINISTRATIVE STYLE AND
JOB SATISFACTION OF ELEMENTARY SCHOOL PRINCIPALS.   M0901

ADMINISTRATOR

THE EFFECT OF ORGANIZATIONAL CHANGE ON ADMINISTRATOR JOB
SATISFACTION, ORGANIZATIONAL CLIMATE, AND PERCEIVED
ORGANIZATIONAL EFFECTIVENESS.   M0942

ADMINISTRATORS

A STUDY OF JOB SATISFACTION OF ADMINISTRATORS AT UNITED
METHODIST RELATED CHURCHES.   M0910

A STUDY OF THE PERCEPTIONS OF SELECTED SCHOOL-BASED
ADMINISTRATORS IN FLORIDA RELATIVE TO CERTAIN VARIABLES IN
SECONDARY SCHOOL ADMINISTRATION AS THEY RELATE TO JOB
SATISFACTION.   M0925

JOB SATISFACTION AND LEADER BEHAVIOR OF ADULT EDUCATION
ADMINISTRATORS.   M0936

ADOLESCENT

ADOLESCENT MINORITY FEMALES IN AN URBAN LABOR MARKET.   M0060

ADOLESCENT AND ADULT PREDICTORS OF VOCATIONAL ADAPTATION.   M0592

ADULT

WORK VALUES AND JOB SATISFACTION OF YOUNG ADULT MALES.   M0579

ADOLESCENT AND ADULT PREDICTORS OF VOCATIONAL ADAPTATION.   M0592

JOB SATISFACTION AND LEADER BEHAVIOR OF ADULT EDUCATION
ADMINISTRATORS.   .   M0936

ADVISING

THE DYNAMICS OF UNDERGRADUATE ACADEMIC ADVISING.   M0750

AFFAIRS

A NETWORK ANALYSIS OF A BUREAU OF INDIAN AFFAIRS SCHOOL
SYSTEM TO DETERMINE FACTORS INVOLVED IN JOB SATISFACTION.   M0934

AFFLUENT

REACTIONS AT WORK AND THEIR INFLUENCE ON NON-WORK
ACTIVITIES: AN ANALYSIS OF A SOCIOPOLITICAL PROBLEM IN
AFFLUENT SOCIETIES.   M0587

AFRICA

JOB ENLARGEMENT, INDIVIDUAL DIFFERENCES, AND WORKER
RESPONSES: A TEST WITH BLACK WORKERS IN SOUTH AFRICA.   M0546

THE LIMITATIONS OF THE MOTIVATOR-HYGIENE THEORY OF
SATISFACTION: AN EMPIRICAL STUDY WITH BLACK FACTORY WORKERS
IN SOUTH AFRICA.   M0607

THE RELATIONSHIP BETWEEN MANAGERIAL SUCCESS AND PERSONAL
VALUES IN SOUTH AFRICA: A RESEARCH NOTE.   M0786

THE EFFECT OF URBANIZATION ON SOURCES OF JOB SATISFACTION
AMONG BLACK SUPERVISORS IN SOUTH AFRICA.   M0891

AFRICAN

DISCRIMINATION AND JOB SATISFACTION: AN EMPIRICAL STUDY
WITH A SOUTH AFRICAN MINORITY GROUP.   M0733

AGE

CHRONOLOGICAL AGE AND JOB SATISFACTION: THE YOUNG
BLUE-COLLAR WORKER.   M0007

AGE AND JOB SATISFACTION AMONG MALES AND FEMALES: A
MULTI-VARIATE, MULTISURVEY STUDY.   M0518

RELATIONSHIP OF AGE, TENURE AND JOB SATISFACTION IN MALES
AND FEMALES.   M0525

AGE AND REACTIONS TO TASK CHARACTERISTICS.   M0569

AGENCY

AN EXPERIMENTAL CASE STUDY OF THE SUCCESSES AND FAILURES OF
JOB ENRICHMENT IN A GOVERNMENT AGENCY.   M0600

SATISFACTION WITH TRAINING AND GENERAL JOB SATISFACTION OF
AGENCY HOMEMAKERS WORKING WITH THE ELDERLY AND DISABLED.   M0904

AGENT

CONFESSIONS OF AN ORGANIZATIONAL CHANGE AGENT.   M0631

AGING

THE EFFECTS OF AGING ON ENGINEERS' SATISFACTION AND MENTAL
HEALTH: SKILL OBSOLESCENCE.   M0044

AIDES

   WORK VALUES AND JOB SATISFACTION OF PSYCHIATRIC AIDES.   M0917

AIR

   DESEGREGATION AND CAREER GOALS. CHILDREN OF AIR FORCE
   FAMILIES.   M0491

   DIMENSIONS OF JOB SATISFACTION: INITIAL DEVELOPMENT OF THE
   AIR FORCE OCCUPATIONAL ATTITUDE INVENTORY.   M0802

AIRMEN

   REPORTED JOB INTEREST AND PERCEIVED UTILIZATION OF TALENTS
   AND TRAINING BY AIRMEN IN 97 CAREER LADDERS, BY R. BRUCE
   GOULD. PROJECT 7734, DECEMBER 1972.   M0452

ALCAN

   ADAPTING JOBS TO PEOPLE: EXPERIMENTS AT ALCAN.   M0053

ALIENATION

   WORKER ALIENATION AND THE MENTALLY RETARDED.   M0532

   WOMEN IN INDUSTRY: ALIENATION, SATISFACTION, AND CHANGE.   M0699

ALIENATION-COUNSELING

   ALIENATION-COUNSELING IMPLICATIONS AND MANAGEMENT THERAPY.   M0068

ALLIANCE

   BACKGROUND CHARACTERISTICS, ORIENTATION, WORK EXPERIENCE,
   AND WORK VALUES OF EMPLOYEES HIRED FROM HUMAN RESOURCES
   DEVELOPMENT APPLICANTS BY COMPANIES AFFILIATED WITH THE
   NATIONAL ALLIANCE OF BUSINESSMAN.   M0165

ALTERNATE

   DEFENSE MECHANISMS AND THE HERZBERG THEORY: AN ALTERNATE
   TEST.   M0334

ALTERNATIVE

   BUSINESS HEALTH--MENTAL HEALTH: GROWTH ALTERNATIVE TO
   INTERVENTION.   M0117

   A TEST OF ALTERNATIVE MODELS OF EXPECTANCY THEORY.   M0892

ALTERNATIVES

   THE FUTURE OF WORK: THREE POSSIBLE ALTERNATIVES.   M0240

AMBIGUITY

AMBITION

ANALYSIS

ANALYSIS   CONTINUATION

SATISFACTION AND JOB IMPORTANCE.   M0514

REACTIONS AT WORK AND THEIR INFLUENCE ON NON-WORK
ACTIVITIES: AN ANALYSIS OF A SOCIOPOLITICAL PROBLEM IN
AFFLUENT SOCIETIES.   M0587

VOCATIONAL NEEDS, JOB REWARDS, AND SATISFACTION: A
CANONICAL ANALYSIS.   M0640

ANALYSIS OF RELATIONSHIPS AMONG LEADER BEHAVIOR,
SUBORDINATE JOB PERFORMANCE, AND SATISFACTION: A PATH-GOAL
APPROACH.   M0652

SEX STEREOTYPES: AN ARTIFACT IN LEADER BEHAVIOR AND
SUBORDINATE SATISFACTION ANALYSIS.   M0662

MOTIVATION OF ENGINEERS: AN ANALYSIS OF PERCEIVED
MOTIVATIONAL FACTORS.   M0692

LEADER STRUCTURE AND SUBORDINATE SATISFACTION FOR TWO
HOSPITAL ADMINISTRATIVE LEVELS: A PATH ANALYSIS APPROACH.   M0736

ORGANIZATIONAL AND OCCUPATIONAL COMMITMENT: A FACET
THEORETICAL ANALYSIS OF EMPIRICAL DATA.   M0747

ANTECEDENTS OF SALESMEN'S COMPENSATION PERCEPTIONS: A PATH
ANALYSIS INTERPRETATION.   M0785

WHY STUDY WORKING CONDITIONS VIA JOB SATISFACTION? A PLEA
FOR DIRECT ANALYSIS.   M0833

THE PATH-GOAL THEORY OF LEADERSHIP: A THEORETICAL AND
EMPIRICAL ANALYSIS.   M0835

AN ANALYSIS OF JOB SATISFACTION AMONG ELEMENTARY, MIDDLE
LEVEL, AND SENIOR HIGH SCHOOL TEACHERS.   M0911

CAREER COMMITMENT: AN ANALYSIS OF SELECTED INDIVIDUAL, JOB
AND ORGANIZATIONAL FACTORS AS RELATED TO SATISFACTION AND
COMMITMENT OF MIDDLE LEVEL ARMY OFFICERS.   M0912

A NETWORK ANALYSIS OF A BUREAU OF INDIAN AFFAIRS SCHOOL
SYSTEM TO DETERMINE FACTORS INVOLVED IN JOB SATISFACTION.   M0934

ANALYSTS

PREDICTION OF SATISFACTION OF SYSTEMS ANALYSTS,
PROGRAMMERS.   M0807

ANALYTIC

A FACTOR ANALYTIC STUDY OF JOB SATISFACTION ITEMS DESIGNED
TO MEASURE MASLOW NEED CATEGORIES.   M0365

ANALYTIC CONTINUATION

THE IMPACT OF THE ORGANIZATION ON THE STRUCTURE OF JOB
SATISFACTION: SOME FACTOR ANALYTIC FINDINGS. M0471

NEED ORIENTATION AS RELATED TO EXTENSION JOB SATISFACTION:
A PROFILE ANALYTIC EXPLORATION. M0508

ANALYZING

ANALYZING THE HOMEMAKER JOB USING THE POSITION ANALYSIS
QUESTIONNAIRE. M0497

ANATOMY

ANATOMY OF A SUCCESS. M0158

ANDROGYNY

ANDROGYNY IN NURSING: NURSE ROLE EXPECTATION, SATISFACTION,
ACADEMIC ACHIEVEMENT, AND SELF-ACTUALIZATION IM MALE AND
FEMALE STUDENTS. M0877

ANTECEDENTS

PERCEIVED PURPOSEFULNESS OF JOB BEHAVIOR: ANTECEDENTS AND
CONSEQUENCES. M0336

ORGANIZATIONAL ROLE CONFLICT: ITS ANTECEDENTS AND
CONSEQUENCES. M0601

ANTECEDENTS AND OUTCOMES OF ORGANIZATIONAL COMMITMENT. M0633

ANTECEDENTS OF SALESMEN'S COMPENSATION PERCEPTIONS: A PATH
ANALYSIS INTERPRETATION. M0785

ANTICIPATED

INSTRUMENTALITY THEORY PREDICTIONS OF EXPERIENCED AND
ANTICIPATED JOB SATISFACTION. M0858

ANXIETY-STRESS

RELATION OF ORGANIZATIONAL STRUCTURE TO JOB SATISFACTION,
ANXIETY-STRESS, AND PERFORMANCE. M0766

RETAIL STORE PERFORMANCE AND JOB SATISFACTION: A STUDY OF
ANXIETY-STRESS PROPENSITY TO LEAVE AMONG RETAIL EMPLOYEES. M0811

APPAREL

REVIEW OF LITERATURE ON WORK MOTIVATION: BULLETIN 12. A
STUDY OF WORK MOTIVATION OF URBAN AND RURAL APPAREL WORKERS
IN TENNESSEE. M0503

APPLICANTS

APPLICATION

APPLIED

APPRAISAL

APPRAISALS

APPREHENSION

ASSESSMENT   CONTINUATION

    ORGANIZATIONAL EFFECTIVENESS IN BEHAVIORAL-ECONOMIC TERMS.   M0536

    JOB SATISFACTION AND THE PD MANAGER: AN EMPIRICAL
    ASSESSMENT.   M0831

ASSIGNED

    EFFECTS OF ASSIGNED AND PARTICIPATIVE GOAL SETTING ON
    PERFORMANCE AND JOB SATISFACTION.   M0887

ASSIGNMENT

    PREFERRED JOB ASSIGNMENT EFFECT ON JOB SATISFACTION.   M0598

ASSIGNMENTS

    ANALYSIS OF RACIAL DIFFERENCES IN TERMS OF WORK
    ASSIGNMENTS, JOB INTEREST, AND FELT UTILIZATION OF TALENTS
    AND TRAINING, BY RAYMOND E. CHRISTEL.   M0451

ASSISTANT

    PHYSICIAN'S ASSISTANT -- MEDICAL OCCUPATION IS THE MAKING.   M0423

    A NORMATIVE STUDY OF THE SECONDARY SCHOOL ASSISTANT
    PRINCIPALSHIP IN SELECTED PENNSYLVANIA SCHOOL DISTRICTS
    WITH AN EMPHASIS UPON JOB SATISFACTION.   M0918

ASSISTING

    OLNEY CENTRAL COLLEGE DENTAL ASSISTING PROGRAM GRADUATES
    PERCEPTIONS OF PROGRAM COMPONENTS, JOB SATISFACTION AND
    CAREER GOALS.   M0944

ASSOCIATE

    THE MENTAL HEALTH ASSOCIATE: THE EFFECT OF SOCIAL
    ENVIRONMENTAL FACTORS ON JOB SATISFACTION.   M0697

    A NATIONAL STUDY OF ASSOCIATE DEGREE MENTAL HEALTH SERVICES
    WORKERS.   M0806

ASSOCIATION

    THE MEASUREMENT OF SATISFACTION AND DEPARTMENTAL
    ASSOCIATION AT WESTERN KENTUCKY UNIVERSITY: TESTING THE
    HOLLAND AND BIGLAN MODELS.   M0914

ASSUMPTIONS

    JOB DESIGN AND WORKER SATISFACTION: A CHALLENGE TO
    ASSUMPTIONS.   M0571

ATLANTA

   THE OCCUPATIONAL INFORMATION CENTER: WHERE ATLANTA
   EMPLOYERS AND EDUCATORS MEET.   M0237

ATTAINMENT

   EDUCATIONAL ATTAINMENT OF WORKERS, MARCH 1973.   M0094

   INTERGROUP CLIMATE ATTAINMENT, SATISFACTION, AND URGENCY.   M0705

ATTENDANCE

   ABSENCE BEHAVIOR AND ATTENDANCE MOTIVATION: A CONCEPTUAL
   SYNTHESIS.   M0783

   WORK ATTITUDES AS PREDICTORS OF ATTENDANCE ON A SPECIFIC
   DAY.   M0795

ATTITUDE

   STAFF ATTITUDE AND SUCCESS OF THE WIN PROGRAM, A REPORT ON
   PHASE I RETURNS.   M0075

   PREDICTING ABSENTEEISM AND TURNOVER: A FIELD COMPARISON OF
   FISHBEIN'S MODEL AND TRADITIONAL JOB ATTITUDE   MEASURES.   M0326

   FACTORS AFFECTING JOB ATTITUDE IN GOAL SETTING ENVIRONMENT.   M0556

   LONGITUDINAL INFERENCES OF JOB ATTITUDE AND TENURE
   RELATIONSHIPS FROM CROSS-SECTIONAL DATA.   M0591

   ATTITUDE SIMILARITY AND ATTRACTION TO A COMPANY.   M0720

   LANGUAGE, TIME, AND PERSON EFFECTS ON ATTITUDE SCALE
   TRANSLATIONS.   M0770

   DIMENSIONS OF JOB SATISFACTION: INITIAL DEVELOPMENT OF THE
   AIR FORCE OCCUPATIONAL ATTITUDE INVENTORY.   M0802

   A STUDY OF THE RELATIONSHIP AMONG (1) JOB SATISFACTION AND
   (2) TEACHER ATTITUDE.   M0908

ATTITUDES

   THE WORKER ATTITUDES AND EARLY OCCUPATIONAL EXPERIENCES OF
   YOUNG MEN -- ANALYSIS BASED ON A 4-YEAR LONGITUDINAL STUDY.   M0020

   JOB ATTITUDES AND OVERALL JOB SATISFACTION: THE EFFECT OF
   BIOGRAPHICAL AND EMPLOYMENT VARIABLES: RESEARCH NOTE.   M0050

   ORGANIZATIONAL EXPERIENCES AND THEIR EFFECTS ON THE
   ATTITUDES OF EMPLOYEES, INCLUDING THE DISADVANTAGED, TOWARD
   WORK.   M0063

   ORGANIZATIONAL EXPERIENCES AND THEIR EFFECTS ON THE

ATTITUDES   CONTINUATION

ATTITUDES OF EMPLOYEES, INCLUDING THE DISADVANTAGED.   M0064

ATTITUDES AND SOCIAL CHANGE -- COMMITTEE REPORT.   M0067

THE JOB ATTITUDES OF WORKERS FROM DIFFERENT ETHNIC
BACKGROUNDS.   M0246

ASININE ATTITUDES TOWARD MOTIVATION.   M0274

VALUES -- NOT ATTITUDES -- ARE THE REAL KEY TO MOTIVATION.   M0301

A COMPARATIVE STUDY OF TEACHERS' ATTITUDES TOWARD MEN AND
WOMEN DEPARTMENT HEADS IN LARGE CITY SECONDARY SCHOOLS.   M0366

WORK ATTITUDES OF DISADVANTAGED BLACK MEN.   M0412

EFFECTS OF PERSONAL VALUES ON THE RELATIONSHIP BETWEEN
PARTICIPATION AND JOB ATTITUDES.   M0476

ORGANIZATIONAL STRUCTURE: HOW DOES IT INFLUENCE ATTITUDES
AND PERFORMANCE.   M0578

PERSONNEL ATTITUDES AND MOTIVATION.   M0624

STRUCTURES OF ATTITUDES TOWARD WORK AND TECHNOLOGICAL
CHANGE WITHIN AN ORGANIZATION.   M0639

JOB INVOLVEMENT, VALUES, PERSONAL BACKGROUND, PARTICIPATION
IN DECISION MAKING, AND JOB ATTITUDES.   M0664

ROLE DYNAMICS, LOCUS OF CONTROL, AND EMPLOYEE ATTITUDES AND
BEHAVIOR.   M0667

AN EXAMINATION OF NEED-SATISFACTION MODELS OF JOB
ATTITUDES.   M0673

REWARDS AND PUBLIC EMPLOYEES' ATTITUDES TOWARD CLIENT
SERVICE.   M0693

JOB ATTITUDES OF STUDENT PERSONNEL WORKERS AND THEIR JOB
SITUATIONS.   M0707

RACIAL DIFFERENCES IN JOB ATTITUDES AND PERFORMANCE: SOME
THEORETICAL CONSIDERATIONS AND EMPIRICAL FINDINGS.   M0717

AN INVESTIGATION OF ATTITUDES AMONG PRIVATES AT KA55
FOURTEENTH YEAR.   M0739

INVESTIGATION OF THE INFLUENCE OF JOB LEVEL AND FUNCTIONAL
SPECIALTY ON JOB ATTITUDES AND PERCEPTIONS.   M0745

PERCEIVED JOB ATTITUDES, JOB ATTRIBUTES AND THE BEHAVIOR OF
BLUE-COLLAR WORKERS: A RESEARCH NOTE.   M0751

ATTITUDES   CONTINUATION

ATTITUDES TOWARD PARTICIPATION AMONG LOCAL AUTHORITY
EMPLOYEES.   M0773

MEASURING THE FINANCIAL IMPACT OF EMPLOYEE ATTITUDES.   M0780

WORK ATTITUDES AS PREDICTORS OF ATTENDANCE ON A SPECIFIC
DAY.   M0795

PSYCHOLOGICAL ATTITUDES AND BELIEFS OF MINISTERS.   M0804

PERSONALITY-JOB FIT: IMPLICATIONS FOR INDIVIDUAL ATTITUDES
AND PERFORMANCE.   M0829

TRENDS IN JOB-RELATED ATTITUDES OF MANAGERIAL AND
PROFESSIONAL EMPLOYEES.   M0838

A STUDY OF REHABILITATION COUNSELORS: LOCUS OF CONTROL AND
ATTITUDES TOWARD THE POOR.   M0888

EMPLOYEE ATTITUDES REGARDING VARIOUS CHARACTERISTICS OF JOB
OPPORTUNITY AND JOB PERFORMANCE ACROSS THREE DIFFERENT WORK
SHIFTS AT AN INSTITUTION FOR THE RETARDED.   M0900

SEGREGATION AND JOB SATISFACTION IN THE WORK PLACE: THE
MEASUREMENT OF RACIAL DISPARITIES IN ORGANIZATIONS AND
THEIR INFLUENCE ON EMPLOYEE WORK ATTITUDES.   M0927

REWARDS AND PUBLIC EMPLOYEES' ATTITUDES TOWARD CLIENT
SERVICE.   M0929

ATTITUDINAL

WORK AND RETIREMENT: A TEST OF ATTITUDINAL RELATIONSHIPS.   M0721

ATTRACTION

ATTITUDE SIMILARITY AND ATTRACTION TO A COMPANY.   M0720

ATTRACTIVENESS

INFORMATION INTEGRATION THEORY APPLIED TO EXPECTED JOB
ATTRACTIVENESS AND SATISFACTION.   M0793

ATTRIBUTES

GOAL-SETTING ATTRIBUTES, PERSONALITY VARIABLES, AND JOB
SATISFACTION.   M0570

PERCEIVED JOB ATTITUDES, JOB ATTRIBUTES AND THE BEHAVIOR OF
BLUE-COLLAR WORKERS: A RESEARCH NOTE.   M0751

AUDITORS

CAN INTERNAL AUDITORS FIND JOB SATISFACTION?   M0840

AUTHORITARIANISM

PARTICIPATION WITH SUPERVISOR AND SUBORDINATE
AUTHORITARIANISM: A PATH GOAL THEORY RECONCILIATION.   M0554

AUTHORITY

ATTITUDES TOWARD PARTICIPATION AMONG LOCAL AUTHORITY
EMPLOYEES.   M0773

AUTOMATED

WORK AND WORK MOTIVATION IN AN AUTOMATED INDUSTRIAL
PRODUCTION-PROCESS.   M0042

AUTONOMY

RELATIONSHIPS AMONG PAY, RACE, SEX, OCCUPATIONAL PRESTIGE,
SUPERVISION, WORK AUTONOMY, AND JOB SATISFACTION IN A
NATIONAL SAMPLE.   M0842

AVENUE

APPRENTICESHIP -- AVENUE TO THE SKILLED CRAFTS.   M0419

AVIATION

WAC MECHANICS JOIN ARMY AVIATION COMMUNITY.   M0461

AVOIDANCE

RELATIVE STEEPNESS OF APPROACH AND AVOIDANCE GRADIENTS AS A
FUNCTION OF MAGNITUDE AND VALENCE OF INCENTIVE.   M0775

BACKGROUND

BACKGROUND CHARACTERISTICS, ORIENTATION, WORK EXPERIENCE,
AND WORK VALUES OF EMPLOYEES HIRED FROM HUMAN RESOURCES
DEVELOPMENT APPLICANTS BY COMPANIES AFFILIATED WITH THE
NATIONAL ALLIANCE OF BUSINESSMAN.   M0165

WORK VALUES OF WHITE-COLLAR EMPLOYEES AS A FUNCTION OF
SOCIOLOGICAL BACKGROUND.   M0376

BACKGROUND AND PERSONALITY CHARACTERISTICS RELATED TO
STUDENT SATISFACTION AND PERFORMANCE IN FIELD MEDICAL
SERVICE SCHOOL.   M0575

JOB INVOLVEMENT, VALUES, PERSONAL BACKGROUND, PARTICIPATION
IN DECISION MAKING, AND JOB ATTITUDES.   M0664

THE RELATIONSHIP OF SEX AND ETHNIC BACKGROUND TO
JOB-RELATED STRESS OF RESEARCH AND DEVELOPMENT
PROFESSIONALS.   M0695

BEHAVIOR   CONTINUATION

PERCEIVED PURPOSEFULNESS OF JOB BEHAVIOR: ANTECEDENTS AND
CONSEQUENCES.   M0336

NATIONAL LONGITUDINAL STUDIES OF THE LABOR FORCE BEHAVIOR
OF NATIONAL SAMPLES OF MEN (45-59), WOMEN (30-44), AND MALE
AND FEMALE YOUTH (14-24).   M0339

SEX EFFECTS IN LEADER BEHAVIOR SELF-DESCRIPTIONS AND JOB
SATISFACTION.   M0499

THE RELEVANCE OF COSMOPOLITAN/LOCAL ORIENTATIONS TO
PROFESSIONAL VALUES AND BEHAVIOR.   M0588

OPERATIONALIZING THE CONCEPTS OF GOALS AND GOAL
INCOMPATIBILITIES IN ORGANIZATIONAL BEHAVIOR RESEARCH.   M0595

CONCEPTS AND CONTROVERSY IN ORGANIZATIONAL BEHAVIOR.   M0605

BLACK-WHITE DIFFERENCES IN LEADER BEHAVIOR RELATED TO
SUBORDINATES' REACTIONS.   M0608

ANALYSIS OF RELATIONSHIPS AMONG LEADER BEHAVIOR,
SUBORDINATE JOB PERFORMANCE, AND SATISFACTION: A PATH-GOAL
APPROACH.   M0652

EMPLOYEE REACTIONS TO LEADER REWARD BEHAVIOR.   M0654

SEX STEREOTYPES: AN ARTIFACT IN LEADER BEHAVIOR AND
SUBORDINATE SATISFACTION ANALYSIS.   M0662

JOB ORIENTATION AND WORK BEHAVIOR.   M0665

ROLE DYNAMICS, LOCUS OF CONTROL, AND EMPLOYEE ATTITUDES AND
BEHAVIOR.   M0667

RELATIONS AMONG PERCEIVED ENVIRONMENTAL UNCERTAINTY,
ORGANIZATION STRUCTURE, AND BOUNDARY-SPANNING BEHAVIOR.   M0671

UNDERSTANDING FRUSTRATION-INSTIGATED BEHAVIOR.   M0743

PERCEIVED JOB ATTITUDES, JOB ATTRIBUTES AND THE BEHAVIOR OF
BLUE-COLLAR WORKERS: A RESEARCH NOTE.   M0751

THE IMPACT OF HIERARCHICAL STRUCTURES ON THE WORK BEHAVIOR
OF WOMEN AND MEN.   M0757

ABSENCE BEHAVIOR AND ATTENDANCE MOTIVATION: A CONCEPTUAL
SYNTHESIS.   M0783

ROLE OF JOB SATISFACTION IN ABSENCE BEHAVIOR.   M0818

PERCEIVED LEADER BEHAVIOR AND EMPLOYEE SATISFACTION WITH
SUPERVISION AND THE JOB: THE EFFECTS OF REWARD AND
PUNISHMENT.   M0859

BEHAVIOR   CONTINUATION

SUPERVISOR EXPECTATIONS AND BEHAVIOR: EFFECTS OF
CONSISTENT-INCONSISTENT SUPERVISORY PAIRINGS ON SUPERVISEE
SATISFACTION WITH SUPERVISION, PERCEPTIONS OF SUPERVISORY
RELATIONSHIPS AND RATED COUNSELOR COMPETENCY.   M0864

JOB SATISFACTION OF GEORGIA SCHOOL SUPERINTENDENTS AND
THEIR PERCEPTION OF THE LOCAL SCHOOL BOARD PRESIDENT'S
LEADER BEHAVIOR.   M0906

JOB SATISFACTION AND LEADER BEHAVIOR OF ADULT EDUCATION
ADMINISTRATORS.   M0936

BEHAVIOR-SATISFACTION

WORK VALUES AS MODERATORS OF PERCEIVED LEADER
BEHAVIOR-SATISFACTION RELATIONSHIPS.   M0505

BEHAVIORAL

INCREASING PRODUCTIVITY: HOW BEHAVIORAL SCIENTISTS CAN
HELP.   M0568

BEHAVIORAL FACTORS IN VARIANCE CONTROL: REPORT ON A
LABORATORY EXPERIMENT.   M0634

RELATIONSHIPS OF ORGANIZATIONAL FRUSTRATION WITH REPORTED
BEHAVIORAL REACTIONS OF EMPLOYEES.   M0796

BEHAVIORAL TRAINING OF SUPERVISORS IN AN INDUSTRIAL SETTING
FOR THE BLIND.   M0846

COMMITMENT: A BEHAVIORAL APPROACH TO JOB INVOLVEMENT.   M0899

BEHAVIORAL-ECONOMIC

METHODOLOGY FOR ASSESSMENT OF QUALITY OF WORK LIFE AND
ORGANIZATIONAL EFFECTIVENESS IN BEHAVIORAL-ECONOMIC TERMS.   M0536

BEHAVIORS

SIMILARITY-DISSIMILARITY IN COUNSELOR-COUNSELEE ETHNIC
MATCH AND ITS RELEVANCE TO GOAL BEHAVIORS OF JOB TRAINEES.   M0189

BELEAGURED

LEADERSHIP: BELEAGURED SPECIES?   M0586

BELIEFS

FACTORS AFFECTING ACQUISITION OF BELIEFS ABOUT A NEW REWARD
SYSTEM.   M0589

MANAGERIAL BELIEFS ABOUT WORK IN SCOTLAND AND THE U.S.A.   M0756

BELIEFS   CONTINUATION

    PSYCHOLOGICAL ATTITUDES AND BELIEFS OF MINISTERS.   M0804

BELL

    MA BELL MOTIVATES.   M0295

BENEFIT

    NEGOTIATED RETIREMENT PLANS -- A DECADE OF BENEFIT
    IMPROVEMENTS.   M0085

BENEFIT-COST

    MANPOWER TRAINING AND BENEFIT-COST ANALYSIS.   M0229

BENEFITS

    FRINGE BENEFITS OF URBAN WORKERS.   M0346

    EARNINGS FUNCTION AND NONPECUNIARY BENEFITS.   M0638

BIAS

    JOB BIAS AND THE INVISIBLE MINORITY.   M0231

    SEX BIAS IN LONGSHORING.   M0389

BIGLAN

    THE MEASUREMENT OF SATISFACTION AND DEPARTMENTAL
    ASSOCIATION AT WESTERN KENTUCKY UNIVERSITY: TESTING THE
    HOLLAND AND BIGLAN MODELS.   M0914

BIOGRAPHICAL

    JOB ATTITUDES AND OVERALL JOB SATISFACTION: THE EFFECT OF
    BIOGRAPHICAL AND EMPLOYMENT VARIABLES: RESEARCH NOTE.   M0050

BIVARIATE

    SURVEY OF WORKING CONDITIONS. FINAL REPORT OF UNIVARIATE
    AND BIVARIATE TABLES.   M0266

BLACK

    BLACK PROFESSIONALS: PROGRESS AND SKEPTICISM.   M0028

    MOTIVATION OF THE BLACK WORKER: A REVIEW OF TRADITIONAL
    APPROACHES AND CRITICAL ISSUES IN CURRENT THEORY.   M0062

    A STUDY OF BLACK MALE PROFESSIONALS IN INDUSTRY.   M0143

    BLACK AND WHITE UNEMPLOYMENT: THE DYNAMICS OF THE
    DIFFERENTIAL.   M0156

BLACK   CONTINUATION

EXPERIENCE OF BLACK FARMERS HOCE ADMINISTRATION LOCAL
OFFICE CHIEFS.   M0182

EXPECTANCY THEORY AND ITS IMPLICATIONS FOR HIGHER EDUCATION
AMONG BLACK YOUTH.   M0210

MOTIVATIONAL AND PERSONALITY FACTORS RELATED TO CAREER
GOALS OF BLACK COLLEGE WOMEN.   M0310

WORK ATTITUDES OF DISADVANTAGED BLACK MEN.   M0412

COUNSELING BLACK TEENAGE GIRLS.   M0421

WANTED BLACK ENGINEERS.   M0468

IMPACT OF PERCEIVED COMMUNITY PROSPERITY ON JOB
SATISFACTION OF BLACK AND WHITE WORKERS.   M0542

JOB ENLARGEMENT, INDIVIDUAL DIFFERENCES, AND WORKER
RESPONSES: A TEST WITH BLACK WORKERS IN SOUTH AFRICA.   M0546

THE LIMITATIONS OF THE MOTIVATOR-HYGIENE THEORY OF
SATISFACTION: AN EMPIRICAL STUDY WITH BLACK FACTORY WORKERS
IN SOUTH AFRICA.   M0607

THE SELF-CONCEPT, PERSONAL VALUES, AND MOTIVATIONAL
ORIENTATIONS OF BLACK AND WHITE MANAGERS.   M0668

THE EFFECT OF URBANIZATION ON SOURCES OF JOB SATISFACTION
AMONG BLACK SUPERVISORS IN SOUTH AFRICA.   M0891

BLACK-WHITE

BLACK-WHITE DIFFERENCES IN LEADER BEHAVIOR RELATED TO
SUBORDINATES' REACTIONS.   M0608

BLACK-WHITE DIFFERENCES IN WORK ENVIRONMENT PERCEPTIONS AND
JOB SATISFACTION AND ITS CORRELATES.   M0820

BLACKS

BLACKS AS SUPERVISORS: A STUDY OF TRAINING, JOB
PERFORMANCE, AND EMPLOYEE'S EXPECTATION.   M0023

DIFFERENTIALS AND OVERLAPS IN EARNINGS OF BLACKS AND
WHITES.   M0428

BLIND

BEHAVIORAL TRAINING OF SUPERVISORS IN AN INDUSTRIAL SETTING
FOR THE BLIND.   M0846

BLUE-COLLAR

BOARD

BONUSES

BOUNDARY

BOUNDARY-SPANNING

BRAINSTORMING

BREADWINNER

    HELP FOR THE WOMAN BREADWINNER.   M0096

BRITISH

    THE BRITISH COAL MINE STRIKE OF 1972.   M0483

BUDGETARY

    HUMANIZING THE BUDGETARY SYSTEM FOR ADMINISTRATIVE
    REINFORCEMENT.   M0138

BUDGETS

    THE POSITION AND FUNCTION OF BUDGETS IN AN MBO SYSTEM.   M0289

BUSINESS

    BUSINESS HEALTH--MENTAL HEALTH: GROWTH ALTERNATIVE TO
    INTERVENTION.   M0117

    BUSINESS MACHINES AND COMPUTER MANUFACTURING -- CAREER
    OPPORTUNITIES ARE EXCELLENT.   M0347

    INFLUENCES ON THE FELT NEED FOR COLLECTIVE BARGAINING BY
    BUSINESS AND SCIENCE PROFESSIONALS.   M0572

    ACHIEVEMENT DRIVE AND CREATIVITY AS CORRELATES OF SUCCESS
    IN SMALL BUSINESS.   M0730

BUSINESSMAN

    BACKGROUND CHARACTERISTICS, ORIENTATION, WORK EXPERIENCE,
    AND WORK VALUES OF EMPLOYEES HIRED FROM HUMAN RESOURCES
    DEVELOPMENT APPLICANTS BY COMPANIES AFFILIATED WITH THE
    NATIONAL ALLIANCE OF BUSINESSMAN.   M0165

CANADIAN

    THE RELATIONSHIP OF JOB SATISFACTION MEASURES TO
    SELF-REPORT AND OBJECTIVE CRITERIA MEASURES AND THE EFFECT
    OF MODERATOR VARIABLES FOR CANADIAN MILITARY PERSONNEL.   M0853

CANONICAL

    VOCATIONAL NEEDS, JOB REWARDS, AND SATISFACTION: A
    CANONICAL ANALYSIS.   M0640

CAPABILITIES

    CAPABILITIES OF MIDDLE-AGED AND OLDER WORKERS: A SURVEY OF
    THE LITERATURE.   M0778

CAREER

MOTIVATION AND CAREER PATH PLANNING.   M0146

CAREER OPPORTUNITIES IN THE POSTAL SERVICE.   M0152

AMERICA'S NEED FOR CAREER EDUCATION.   M0304

MOTIVATIONAL AND PERSONALITY FACTORS RELATED TO CAREER
GOALS OF BLACK COLLEGE WOMEN.   M0310

THE ACHIEVEMENT PROCESS: AN EXPLORATORY STUDY OF CAREER
BEGINNINGS.   M0332

BUSINESS MACHINES AND COMPUTER MANUFACTURING -- CAREER
OPPORTUNITIES ARE EXCELLENT.   M0347

CAREER PLANNING FOR HIGH SCHOOL GIRLS.   M0420

REPORTED JOB INTEREST AND PERCEIVED UTILIZATION OF TALENTS
AND TRAINING BY AIRMEN IN 97 CAREER LADDERS, BY R. BRUCE
GOULD. PROJECT 7734, DECEMBER 1972.   M0452

DESEGREGATION AND CAREER GOALS. CHILDREN OF AIR FORCE
FAMILIES.   M0491

CAREER CHOICE, JOB SATISFACTION, AND THE TRUTH BEHIND THE
PETER PRINCIPLE.   M0541

SELF-MOTIVATED PERSONAL CAREER PLANNING: A BREAKTHROUGH IN
HUMAN RESOURCE MANAGEMENT (PART I).   M0561

ROLE DISSATISFACTION AND CAREER CONTINGENCIES AMONG FEMALE
ELEMENTARY TEACHERS.   M0722

WHAT'S NEW IN CAREER MANAGEMENT.   M0724

TRAINING AND CAREER SATISFACTION AMONG CLINICAL
PSYCHOLOGISTS.   M0759

AN INVESTIGATION OF FACTORS INVOLVED IN CAREER SATISFACTION
FOR THE PHYSICIAN.   M0847

CAREER COMMITMENT: AN ANALYSIS OF SELECTED INDIVIDUAL, JOB
AND ORGANIZATIONAL FACTORS AS RELATED TO SATISFACTION AND
COMMITMENT OF MIDDLE LEVEL ARMY OFFICERS.   M0912

SECOND CAREER CATHOLIC PRIESTS: A STUDY OF THEIR LEVEL OF
JOB SATISFACTION, MATURITY, AND MORALE.   M0924

MOTIVATION, JOB SATISFACTION, AND CAREER ASPIRATIONS OF
MARRIED WOMEN TEACHERS AT DIFFERENT CAREER STAGES.   M0940

OLNEY CENTRAL COLLEGE DENTAL ASSISTING PROGRAM GRADUATES
PERCEPTIONS OF PROGRAM COMPONENTS, JOB SATISFACTION AND
CAREER GOALS.   M0944

CAREER-BASED

TOWARD A CAREER-BASED THEORY OF JOB INVOLVEMENT: A STUDY OF
SCIENTISTS AND ENGINEERS.   M0824

CAREERS

THE FOUR STAGES OF PROFESSIONAL CAREERS - A NEW LOOK AT
PERFORMANCE BY PROFESSIONALS.   M0711

CAROLINA

PERCEPTIONS OF ORGANIZATIONAL CLIMATE AS MEDIATORS OF THE
RELATIONSHIPS BETWEEN INDIVIDUAL NEEDS AND JOB SATISFACTION
OF COUNSELORS IN THE NORTH CAROLINA COMMUNITY COLLEGE
SYSTEM.   M0933

CARRY-OVER

GROUP DEVELOPMENT, TRAINER STYLE AND CARRY-OVER JOB
SATISFACTION AND PERFORMANCE.   M0653

CATHOLIC

SECOND CAREER CATHOLIC PRIESTS: A STUDY OF THEIR LEVEL OF
JOB SATISFACTION, MATURITY, AND MORALE.   M0924

CAUSAL

AN EVALUATION OF CAUSAL MODELS LINKING THE RECEIVED ROLE
WITH JOB SATISFACTION.   M0335

SATISFACTION AND PERFORMANCE: CAUSAL RELATIONSHIPS AND
MODERATING EFFECTS.   M0395

CAUSAL MODELING OF PSYCHOLOGICAL SUCCESS IN WORK
ORGANIZATIONS.   M0520

AN EMPIRICAL TEST OF CAUSAL INFERENCE BETWEEN ROLE
PERCEPTIONS, SATISFACTION WITH WORK, PERFORMANCE AND
ORGANIZATIONAL LEVEL.   M0839

A CAUSAL MODEL OF JOB SATISFACTION.   M0915

CAUSATION

PERSONAL CAUSATION: THE INTERNAL EFFECTIVE DETERMINANTS OF
BEHAVIOR.   M0090

CAUSES

QUITS IN MANUFACTURING: A STUDY OF THEIR CAUSES.   M0014

WORKER DISSATISFACTION: A LOOK AT THE CAUSES.   M0429

WORKER DISSATISFACTION: A LOOK AT THE CAUSE   M0615

CENSUS

REMOVAL OF SEX STEREOTYPING IN CENSUS OCCUPATIONAL
CLASSIFICATION.   M0359

CENTRAL

OCCUPATIONAL MIGRATION, DISCRIMINATION, AND THE CENTRAL
CITY LABOR FORCE.   M0247

CENTRAL LIFE INTERESTS AND JOB SATISFACTION.   M0812

IS WORK THE CENTRAL LIFE INTEREST? NOT FOR MOST PEOPLE --
FINDING THE COMMITED FEW.   M0826

OLNEY CENTRAL COLLEGE DENTAL ASSISTING PROGRAM GRADUATES
PERCEPTIONS OF PROGRAM COMPONENTS, JOB SATISFACTION AND
CAREER GOALS.   M0944

CERTIFIED

A COMPARATIVE ANALYSIS OF THE JOB SATISFACTION OF
INDUSTRIAL MANAGERS AND CERTIFIED PUBLIC ACCOUNTANTS.   M0228

CHAIRMEN

SELECTED CHARACTERISTICS, ROLES, GOALS, AND SATISFACTIONS
OF DEPARTMENT CHAIRMEN IN STATE AND LAND-GRANT
INSTITUTIONS.   M0777

CHALLENGE

A DEFINITIONAL CHALLENGE: INTEREST AND WORK ITSELF
SATISFACTIONS.   M0543

JOB DESIGN AND WORKER SATISFACTION: A CHALLENGE TO
ASSUMPTIONS.   M0571

CHANGE

ATTITUDES AND SOCIAL CHANGE -- COMMITTEE REPORT.   M0067

THE PERCEPTION OF OTHER WORK ROLES: IMPLICATIONS FOR JOB
CHANGE.   M0192

PROBLEM RESOLUTION AND IMPOSITION OF CHANGE THROUGH A
PARTICIPATING GROUP EFFORT.   M0238

INDIVIDUAL REACTIONS TO ORGANIZATIONAL CONFLICT AND CHANGE. M0311

GREENER PASTURES: WHY EMPLOYEES CHANGE JOBS.   M0372

COMPONENTS OF ACHIEVEMENT MOTIVATION AS PREDICTORS OF
POTENTIAL FOR ECONOMIC CHANGE.   M0458

MANAGEMENT'S ECTASY AND DISPARITY OVER JOB ENRICHMENT:

CHARACTERISTICS   CONTINUATION

AND WORK VALUES OF EMPLOYEES HIRED FROM HUMAN RESOURCES
DEVELOPMENT APPLICANTS BY COMPANIES AFFILIATED WITH THE
NATIONAL ALLIANCE OF BUSINESSMAN.   M0165

EMPLOYEE REACTIONS TO JOB CHARACTERISTICS.   M0181

MARITAL AND FAMILY CHARACTERISTICS OF THE LABOR FORCE IN
MARCH 1973.   M0194

JOB CHARACTERISTICS AND PRESSURES AND THE ORGANIZATIONAL
INTEGRATION OF PROFESSIONALS.   M0268

MOONLIGHTERS: THEIR MOTIVATIONS AND CHARACTERISTICS.   M0345

EMPLOYMENT CHARACTERISTICS OF LOW-WAGE WORKERS.   M0418

MARITAL AND FAMILY CHARACTERISTICS OF THE LABOR FORCE.   M0462

CHARACTERISTICS OF SUCCESSFUL AND UNSUCCESSFUL ORGANIZATION
DEVELOPMENT.   M0513

RELATIONSHIP BETWEEN LOCUS OF CONTROL AND REACTIONS OF
EMPLOYEES TO WORK CHARACTERISTICS.   M0530

AGE AND REACTIONS TO TASK CHARACTERISTICS.   M0569

BACKGROUND AND PERSONALITY CHARACTERISTICS RELATED TO
STUDENT SATISFACTION AND PERFORMANCE IN FIELD MEDICAL
SERVICE SCHOOL.   M0575

THE MEASUREMENT AND DIMENSIONALITY OF JOB CHARACTERISTICS.   M0580

REACTIONS TO JOB CHARACTERISTICS: MODERATING EFFECTS OF THE
ORGANIZATION.   M0581

DESIRED JOB CHARACTERISTICS FOR MALES AND FEMALES.   M0629

IMPACT OF SUPERVISORY CHARACTERISTICS ON GOAL ACCEPTANCE.   M0661

CORRECTIONAL EMPLOYEES' REACTIONS TO JOB CHARACTERISTICS: A
DATA BASED ARGUMENT FOR JOB ENLARGEMENT.   M0753

SELECTED CHARACTERISTICS, ROLES, GOALS, AND SATISFACTIONS
OF DEPARTMENT CHAIRMEN IN STATE AND LAND-GRANT
INSTITUTIONS.   M0777

MEASUREMENT OF SOCIOECONOMIC AND PSYCHOLOGICAL
CHARACTERISTICS: A METHOD.   M0789

TECHNOLOGICAL DIFFERENCES IN JOB CHARACTERISTICS, EMPLOYEE
SATISFACTION, AND MOTIVATION: A SYNTHESIS OF JOB DESIGN
RESOURCE AND SOCIOTECHNICAL SYSTEMS THEORY.   M0832

JOB CHARACTERISTICS RELATIONSHIPS: INDIVIDUAL AND

CHARACTERISTICS   CONTINUATION

STRUCTURAL MODERATORS.   M0896

EMPLOYEE ATTITUDES REGARDING VARIOUS CHARACTERISTICS OF JOB
OPPORTUNITY AND JOB PERFORMANCE ACROSS THREE DIFFERENT WORK
SHIFTS AT AN INSTITUTION FOR THE RETARDED.   M0900

THE JOB SATISFACTION OF SCHOOL TEACHERS IN THE REPUBLIC OF
CHINA AS RELATED TO PERSONAL AND ORGANIZATIONAL
CHARACTERISTICS.   M0909

JOB SATISFACTION, JOB CHARACTERISTICS, AND OCCUPATIONAL
LEVEL.   M0919

AN INVESTIGATION OF THE RELATIONSHIP BETWEEN INTRINSIC AND
EXTRINSIC JOB INSTRUMENTALITY EFFORT, JOB SATISFACTION,
INDIVIDUAL AND PERCEIVED TASK CHARACTERISTICS.   M0938

CHARTING

CHARTING AND CHANGING THE ORGANIZATIONAL CLIMATE.   M0410

CHECK-OFF

NARRATIVE AND CHECK-OFF EVALUATIONS OF EMPLOYEE
PERFORMANCE.   M0215

CHICAGO

READINGS IN MANAGERIAL PSYCHOLOGY, 2ND ED. CHICAGO.   M0271

CHILDREN

DESEGREGATION AND CAREER GOALS. CHILDREN OF AIR FORCE
FAMILIES.   M0491

CHINA

FORM CHINA WITH SKILL -- MESBIC FOUNDER WANTS TO SHARE HER
TALENT.   M0145

THE JOB SATISFACTION OF SCHOOL TEACHERS IN THE REPUBLIC OF
CHINA AS RELATED TO PERSONAL AND ORGANIZATIONAL
CHARACTERISTICS.   M0909

CHOICE

SELF-ESTEEM AS AN INFLUENCE ON OCCUPATIONAL CHOICE AND
OCCUPATIONAL SATISFACTION.   M0174

CAREER CHOICE, JOB SATISFACTION, AND THE TRUTH BEHIND THE
PETER PRINCIPLE.   M0541

JAMES G. MARCH AND JOHAN P. OLSEN, AMBIGUITY AND CHOICE IN
ORGANIZATIONS.   M0672

CHOICE   CONTINUATION

   JOB CHOICE AND POST DECISION DISSONANCE.   M0772

   SELF-ESTEEM AS A MODERATOR IN VOCATIONAL CHOICE: A TEST OF
   KORMAN'S HYPOTHESIS.   M0803

CHRONOLOGICAL

   CHRONOLOGICAL AGE AND JOB SATISFACTION: THE YOUNG
   BLUE-COLLAR WORKER.   M0007

CHURCHES

   A STUDY OF JOB SATISFACTION OF ADMINISTRATORS AT UNITED
   METHODIST RELATED CHURCHES.   M0910

CITIES

   MANPOWER PROGRAMS IN FOUR CITIES.   M0455

CITY

   CITY HALL DISCOVERS PRODUCTIVITY.   M0072

   EVALUATION AND IMPLEMENTATION OF THE NEW YORK FIRE
   DEPARTMENT EXAMINATION TRAINING PROJECT FOR CULTURALLY
   DISADVANTAGED RESIDENTS OF THE CITY OF NEW YORK.   M0243

   OCCUPATIONAL MIGRATION, DISCRIMINATION, AND THE CENTRAL
   CITY LABOR FORCE.   M0247

   A COMPARATIVE STUDY OF TEACHERS' ATTITUDES TOWARD MEN AND
   WOMEN DEPARTMENT HEADS IN LARGE CITY SECONDARY SCHOOLS.   M0366

CIVIL

   AN APPLICATION OF JOB ENRICHMENT IN A CIVIL SERVICE
   SETTING: A DEMONSTRATION STUDY.   M0719

CIVILIAN

   VIET-NAM WAR VETERANS -- TRANSITION TO CIVILIAN LIFE.   M0463

CLARITY

   A STUDY OF ROLE CLARITY AND NEED FOR CLARITY FOR THREE
   OCCUPATIONAL GROUPS.   M0227

   RELATIONSHIPS BETWEEN ROLE CLARITY, NEED FOR CLARITY AND
   JOB TENSION AND SATISFACTION FOR SUPERVISORY AND
   NONSUPERVISORY ROLES.   M0539

CLASSIFICATION

   REMOVAL OF SEX STEREOTYPING IN CENSUS OCCUPATIONAL

CLASSIFICATION   CONTINUATION

   CLASSIFICATION.   M0359

CLASSIFYING

   THE DEVELOPMENT OF A MANAGERIAL JOB TAXONOMY: A SYSTEM FOR
   DESCRIBING, CLASSIFYING, AND EVALUATING EXECUTIVE
   POSITIONS.   M0618

CLERKS

   PUT THIS UNDER F FOR FILE CLERKS.   M0019

CLIENT

   REWARDS AND PUBLIC EMPLOYEES' ATTITUDES TOWARD CLIENT
   SERVICE.   M0693

   CLIENT SELF-SELECTION OF TESTS AND WORK SAMPLES IN
   VOCATIONAL EVALUATION.   M0897

   REWARDS AND PUBLIC EMPLOYEES' ATTITUDES TOWARD CLIENT
   SERVICE.   M0929

CLIENTS

   JOB PERFORMANCE AND SATISFACTION OF SUCCESSFULLY
   REHABILITATED VOCATIONAL REHABILITATION CLIENTS.   M0801

CLIMATE

   CONGRUENCE BETWEEN INDIVIDUALS' NEEDS, ORGANIZATIONAL
   CLIMATE, JOB SATISFACTION AND PERFORMANCE.   M0110

   AN EXPLORATORY INVESTIGATION OF ORGANIZATIONAL CLIMATE AND
   JOB SATISFACTION IN A HOSPITAL.   M0286

   CHARTING AND CHANGING THE ORGANIZATIONAL CLIMATE.   M0410

   ORGANIZATIONAL CLIMATE AND JOB SATISFACTION IN THE SALES
   FORCE.   M0509

   INTERGROUP CLIMATE ATTAINMENT, SATISFACTION, AND URGENCY.   M0705

   RELATIONSHIP BETWEEN ORGANIZATIONAL CLIMATE AND THE
   SITUATIONAL FAVORABLENESS DIMENSION OF FIEDLER'S
   CONTINGENCY MODEL.   M0709

   SOME RELATIONSHIPS BETWEEN JOB SATISFACTION AND
   ORGANIZATION CLIMATE.   M0734

   ORGANIZATIONAL COMMUNICATION: RELATIONSHIPS TO
   ORGANIZATIONAL CLIMATE AND JOB SATISFACTION.   M0827

   RIGHT CLIMATE FOR SALESMEN.   M0830

CLIMATE   CONTINUATION

PERCEPTIONS OF ORGANIZATIONAL CLIMATE AS MEDIATORS OF THE
RELATIONSHIPS BETWEEN INDIVIDUAL NEEDS AND JOB SATISFACTION
OF COUNSELORS IN THE NORTH CAROLINA COMMUNITY COLLEGE
SYSTEM.   M0933

THE EFFECT OF ORGANIZATIONAL CHANGE ON ADMINISTRATOR JOB
SATISFACTION, ORGANIZATIONAL CLIMATE, AND PERCEIVED
ORGANIZATIONAL EFFECTIVENESS.   M0942

CLIMATES

MANAGERS' OCCUPATIONAL HISTORIES, ORGANIZATIONAL
ENVIRONMENTS, AND CLIMATES FOR MANAGEMENT DEVELOPMENT.   M0787

ORGANIZATIONAL CLIMATES: AN ESSAY.   M0893

CLINICAL

ROLE OF ON-THE-JOB TRAINING IN A CLINICAL LABORATORY.   M0477

TRAINING AND CAREER SATISFACTION AMONG CLINICAL
PSYCHOLOGISTS.   M0759

CLIQUE

AN ANALYSIS OF CLIQUE FORMATION AND STRUCTURE IN
ORGANIZATIONS.   M0445

CO-WORKERS

THE RELATIONSHIPS BETWEEN THE TASK-HUMAN RELATIONS
MOTIVATIONAL STRUCTURES OF INDIVIDUALS IN SMALL WORK GROUPS
AND THEIR SATISFACTION WITH CO-WORKERS AND IMMEDIATE
SUPERVISION.   M0868

COAL

THE BRITISH COAL MINE STRIKE OF 1972.   M0483

COHESION

WORKERS UNDER STRESS (THE IMPACT OF WORK PRESSURE ON GROUP
COHESION).   M0255

COLLABORATIVE

RELATION OF COLLABORATIVE INTERPERSONAL RELATIONSHIPS TO
INDIVIDUAL SATISFACTION AND ORGANIZATIONAL PERFORMANCE.   M0013

COLLECTIVE

THE EFFECT OF MOTIVATIONAL PROGRAMS ON COLLECTIVE
BARGAINING.   M0032

COLLECTIVE   CONTINUATION

INFLUENCES ON THE FELT NEED FOR COLLECTIVE BARGAINING BY
BUSINESS AND SCIENCE PROFESSIONALS.   M0572

THE IMPACT OF COLLECTIVE BARGAINING ON JOB SATISFACTION.   M0916

COLLEGE

JOB PROSPECTS FOR COLLEGE GRADUATES IN 1974.   M0233

MOTIVATIONAL AND PERSONALITY FACTORS RELATED TO CAREER
GOALS OF BLACK COLLEGE WOMEN.   M0310

DOES A COLLEGE EDUCATION PAY.   M0422

COMMUNITY COLLEGE FACULTY JOB SATISFACTION.   M0708

JOB SATISFACTION OF COLLEGE PRESIDENTS.   M0907

RELATIONSHIPS BETWEEN WORK VALUES AND JOB SATISFACTION
AMONG COLLEGE STUDENT PERSONNEL WORKERS.   M0928

PERCEPTIONS OF ORGANIZATIONAL CLIMATE AS MEDIATORS OF THE
RELATIONSHIPS BETWEEN INDIVIDUAL NEEDS AND JOB SATISFACTION
OF COUNSELORS IN THE NORTH CAROLINA COMMUNITY COLLEGE
SYSTEM.   M0933

OLNEY CENTRAL COLLEGE DENTAL ASSISTING PROGRAM GRADUATES
PERCEPTIONS OF PROGRAM COMPONENTS, JOB SATISFACTION AND
CAREER GOALS.   M0944

COLLEGES

CORRELATES OF PERFORMANCE IN COMMUNITY COLLEGES.   M0715

COLORADO

TASK OPPORTUNITY PROFESSIONAL GROWTH NEED FULFILLMENT AND
INTRINSIC JOB SATISFACTION OF PUBLIC SOCIAL SERVICE WORKERS
IN COLORADO.   M0923

COMMITMENT

ROLE PERFORMANCE AND COMMITMENT TO THE ORGANIZATION.   M0141

ORGANIZATIONAL COMMITMENT, JOB SATISFACTION, AND TURNOVER
AMONG PSYCHIATRIC TECHNICIANS.   M0353

ORGANIZATIONAL COMMITMENT AND TURNOVER: A PREDICTION STUDY. M0627

ANTECEDENTS AND OUTCOMES OF ORGANIZATIONAL COMMITMENT.   M0633

ORGANIZATIONAL AND OCCUPATIONAL COMMITMENT: A FACET
THEORETICAL ANALYSIS OF EMPIRICAL DATA.   M0747

COMMITMENT   CONTINUATION

THE RELATIVE VALIDITIES OF TRADITIONALLY USED JOB
SATISFACTION AND ORGANIZATIONAL COMMITMENT MEASURES VERSUS
WOMEN-SPECIFIC MEASURES FOR THE PREDICTION OF FEMALE TENURE
IN A MALE DOMINATED JOB.   M0856

COMMITMENT: A BEHAVIORAL APPROACH TO JOB INVOLVEMENT.   M0899

CAREER COMMITMENT: AN ANALYSIS OF SELECTED INDIVIDUAL, JOB
AND ORGANIZATIONAL FACTORS AS RELATED TO SATISFACTION AND
COMMITMENT OF MIDDLE LEVEL ARMY OFFICERS.   M0912

COMMUNICATION

EFFECTS OF DIFFERENT PATTERNS AND DEGREES OF OPENNESS IN
SUPERIOR-SUBORDINATE COMMUNICATION ON SUBORDINATE JOB
SATISFACTION.   M0045

LEADERSHIP, MOTIVATION, AND COMMUNICATION.   M0242

ORGANIZATIONAL COMMUNICATION: RELATIONSHIPS TO
ORGANIZATIONAL CLIMATE AND JOB SATISFACTION.   M0827

COMMUNITY

WAC MECHANICS JOIN ARMY AVIATION COMMUNITY.   M0461

IMPACT OF PERCEIVED COMMUNITY PROSPERITY ON JOB
SATISFACTION OF BLACK AND WHITE WORKERS.   M0542

A COMPARISON OF PROFESSIONAL INSTITUTIONAL COMMUNITY
CORRECTIONS WORKERS ON JOB SATISFACTION AND SELF-CONCEPT.   M0696

COMMUNITY COLLEGE FACULTY JOB SATISFACTION.   M0708

CORRELATES OF PERFORMANCE IN COMMUNITY COLLEGES.   M0715

PHYSICAL ENVIRONMENT AND JOB SATISFACTION IN A COMMUNITY
MENTAL HEALTH CENTER.   M0883

PERCEPTIONS OF ORGANIZATIONAL CLIMATE AS MEDIATORS OF THE
RELATIONSHIPS BETWEEN INDIVIDUAL NEEDS AND JOB SATISFACTION
OF COUNSELORS IN THE NORTH CAROLINA COMMUNITY COLLEGE
SYSTEM.   M0933

COMPANIES

BACKGROUND CHARACTERISTICS, ORIENTATION, WORK EXPERIENCE,
AND WORK VALUES OF EMPLOYEES HIRED FROM HUMAN RESOURCES
DEVELOPMENT APPLICANTS BY COMPANIES AFFILIATED WITH THE
NATIONAL ALLIANCE OF BUSINESSMAN.   M0165

PREDICTING THE PERFORMANCE OF JUNIOR ACHIEVEMENT COMPANIES
ACCORDING TO THE LEADERSHIP STYLE OF TWO LEVELS OF
MANAGEMENT: A FIELD STUDY OF THE CONTINGENCY MODEL.   M0700

COMPANY

COMPARATIVE

COMPARISON

COMPATIBILITY

COMPENSATION

COMPETENCY

SUPERVISOR EXPECTATIONS AND BEHAVIOR: EFFECTS OF
CONSISTENT-INCONSISTENT SUPERVISORY PAIRINGS ON SUPERVISEE
SATISFACTION WITH SUPERVISION, PERCEPTIONS OF SUPERVISORY
RELATIONSHIPS AND RATED COUNSELOR COMPETENCY.   M0864

COMPLEX

ROLE-SET CONFIGURATION AS A PREDICTOR OF ROLE CONFLICT AND
AMBIGUITY IN COMPLEX ORGANIZATIONS.   M0626

COMPLIANCE

A QUALITIATIVE APPROACH TO PERFORMANCE PREDICTABILITY AND
LEGAL COMPLIANCE.   M0329

COMPONENTS

COMPONENTS OF ACHIEVEMENT MOTIVATION AS PREDICTORS OF
POTENTIAL FOR ECONOMIC CHANGE.   M0458

THE MOTIVATIONAL COMPONENTS OF GOAL SETTING.   M0799

OLNEY CENTRAL COLLEGE DENTAL ASSISTING PROGRAM GRADUATES
PERCEPTIONS OF PROGRAM COMPONENTS, JOB SATISFACTION AND
CAREER GOALS.   M0944

COMPUTER

COMPUTER MYSTIQUE AND FEMININE MYSTIQUE JOIN FORCES.   M0058

MANAGEMENT'S FUTURE ROLE: PICKING UP WHERE THE COMPUTER
LEAVES OFF.   M0245

BUSINESS MACHINES AND COMPUTER MANUFACTURING -- CAREER
OPPORTUNITIES ARE EXCELLENT.   M0347

AN EMPIRICAL STUDY OF INDIVIDUAL CONGRUENCE AND THE
PERCEIVED ORGANIZATIONAL PRACTICES - JOB SATISFACTION - JOB
PERFORMANCE RELATIONSHIP IN SELECTED ELECTRONIC COMPUTER
DATA PROCESSING CENTERS.   M0946

CONCEPT

LEADERSHIP AND MOTIVATION: A CORE CONCEPT.   M0121

SUCCESS IN MANAGEMENT CONSULTING AND THE CONCEPT OF
ELITENESS MOTIVATION.   M0314

INTERACTION MODELING: A NEW CONCEPT IN SUPERVISORY
TRAINING.   M0507

CONCEPTS

RELEVANCE OF MOTIVATIONAL CONCEPTS TO INDIVIDUAL AND

CONCEPTS CONTINUATION

CONCEPTUAL

CONDITIONS

CONFESSIONS

CONFIDENCE

CONFIGURATION

CONFLICT

CONFLICTING

CONGRUENCE

CONGRUENCY

CONSENSUS

CONSEQUENCES

CONTINGENCY   CONTINUATION

CONTINGENT

CONTRACTING

CONTRACTS

CONTRIBUTION

CONTROL

CONTROL   CONTINUATION

    MANAGEMENT CONTROL SYSTEMS: A KEY LINK BETWEEN STRATEGY,
    STRUCTURE, AND EMPLOYEE PERFORMANCE.   M0741

    INTERNAL VERSUS EXTERNAL LOCUS OF CONTROL AND JOB
    SATISFACTION IN IRAN.   M0851

    A STUDY OF REHABILITATION COUNSELORS: LOCUS OF CONTROL AND
    ATTITUDES TOWARD THE POOR.   M0888

    THE EFFECT OF FLEXIBLE WORKING HOURS ON ABSENTEEISM AND JOB
    SATISFACTION AND THE RELATIONSHIP BETWEEN LOCUS OF CONTROL
    AND UTILITY OF FLEXIBLE WORKING HOURS.   M0943

CONTROLS

    CONSENSUS MANAGEMENT AT GRAPHIC CONTROLS.   M0713

CONTROVERSY

    THE SATISFACTION-PERFORMANCE CONTROVERS   M0172

    CONCEPTS AND CONTROVERSY IN ORGANIZATIONAL BEHAVIOR.   M0605

CONVERGENT

    CONVERGENT AND DISCRIMINANT VALIDITIES OF PERFORMANCE
    EVALUATIONS IN EXTREMELY ISOLATED GROUPS.   M0180

    CONVERGENT AND DISCRIMINANT VALIDITY OF A JOB SATISFACTION
    INVENTORY: A CROSS-CULTURAL REPORT.   M0764

CONVERSION

    FOUR FACTORS INFLUENCING CONVERSION TO A FOUR-DAY WORK
    WEEK.   M0687

CONVOLUTION

    THE MANAGERIAL CONVOLUTION .   M0306

CORE

    LEADERSHIP AND MOTIVATION: A CORE CONCEPT.   M0121

    THE PROFIT MOTIVE: CAN IT MOTIVATE INDUSTRY TO HIRE THE
    HARD CORE.   M0298

    THE HARD CORE AND THE PURITIAN WORK ETHIC.   M0370

    THE WORLD OF WORK THROUGH THE EYES OF THE HARD CORE.   M0371

CORPORATE

    ACCOUNTING FOR CORPORATE SOCIAL RESPONSIBILITY.   M0071

CORPORATE   CONTINUATION

    CORPORATE DROPOUT.   M0073

    PARTICIPATIVE MANAGEMENT IN THE UNITED STATES: A CORPORATE
    EXPERIENCE.   M0253

    RELEVANCE OF MOTIVATIONAL CONCEPTS TO INDIVIDUAL AND
    CORPORATE OBJECTIVES.   M0331

    WORK ADJUSTMENT OF THE METHADONE-MAINTAINED CORPORATE
    EMPLOYEE.   M0567

    CORPORATE DROPOUTS: A PRELIMINARY TYPOLOGY.   M0616

    CORPORATE MANAGEMENT IN LOCAL GOVERNMENT: A CASE STUDY.   M0769

CORPS

    MAKING THE JOB CORPS MORE FLEXIBLE.   M0480

    INDIVIDUAL AND ENVIRONMENTAL FACTORS ASSOCIATED WITH THE
    JOB SATISFACTION AND RETENTION OF NAVY HOSPITAL CORPSMEN
    SERVING WITH THE U.S. MARINE CORPS.   M0574

CORPSMEN

    INDIVIDUAL AND ENVIRONMENTAL FACTORS ASSOCIATED WITH THE
    JOB SATISFACTION AND RETENTION OF NAVY HOSPITAL CORPSMEN
    SERVING WITH THE U.S. MARINE CORPS.   M0574

CORRECTIONAL

    TRAINING CORRECTIONAL MANPOWER.   M0147

    CORRECTIONAL EMPLOYEES' REACTIONS TO JOB CHARACTERISTICS: A
    DATA BASED ARGUMENT FOR JOB ENLARGEMENT.   M0753

CORRECTIONS

    A COMPARISON OF PROFESSIONAL INSTITUTIONAL COMMUNITY
    CORRECTIONS WORKERS ON JOB SATISFACTION AND SELF-CONCEPT.   M0696

CORRECTIVE

    CORRECTIVE MOTIVATION.   M0494

CORRELATES

    INFLUENCE STYLES OF PROJECT MANAGERS: SOME PROJECT
    PERFORMANCE CORRELATES.   M0151

    ROLE CONFLICT AND AMBIGUITY: CORRELATES WITH JOB
    SATISFACTION AND VALUES.   M0249

    CORRELATES OF JOB SATISFACTION IN NAVAL ENVIRONMENTS.   M0291

CORRELATES   CONTINUATION

    CORRELATES OF PERFORMANCE IN COMMUNITY COLLEGES.   M0715

    ACHIEVEMENT DRIVE AND CREATIVITY AS CORRELATES OF SUCCESS
    IN SMALL BUSINESS.   M0730

    NEED-RATIFICATION, ABSENTEEISM AND ITS OTHER CORRELATES.   M0794

    BLACK-WHITE DIFFERENCES IN WORK ENVIRONMENT PERCEPTIONS AND
    JOB SATISFACTION AND ITS CORRELATES.   M0820

COSMOPOLITAN

    THE RELEVANCE OF COSMOPOLITAN/LOCAL ORIENTATIONS TO
    PROFESSIONAL VALUES AND BEHAVIOR.   M0588

COST

    PRODUCTIVITY AND COST MOVEMENTS IN 1971.   M0204

COSTS

    CHANGES IN PRODUCTIVITY AND UNIT LABOR COSTS -- A YEARLY
    REVIEW.   M0203

COUNSELING

    DEVELOPMENT OF ASSESSMENT MEASURES FOR COUNSELING YOUTH
    WORK -- TRAINING ENROLLEES.   M0142

    COUNSELING BLACK TEENAGE GIRLS.   M0421

COUNSELOR

    SUPERVISOR EXPECTATIONS AND BEHAVIOR: EFFECTS OF
    CONSISTENT-INCONSISTENT SUPERVISORY PAIRINGS ON SUPERVISEE
    SATISFACTION WITH SUPERVISION, PERCEPTIONS OF SUPERVISORY
    RELATIONSHIPS AND RATED COUNSELOR COMPETENCY.   M0864

COUNSELOR-COUNSELEE

    SIMILARITY-DISSIMILARITY IN COUNSELOR-COUNSELEE ETHNIC
    MATCH AND ITS RELEVANCE TO GOAL BEHAVIORS OF JOB TRAINEES.   M0189

COUNSELORS

    A STUDY OF REHABILITATION COUNSELORS: LOCUS OF CONTROL AND
    ATTITUDES TOWARD THE POOR.   M0888

    PERCEPTIONS OF ORGANIZATIONAL CLIMATE AS MEDIATORS OF THE
    RELATIONSHIPS BETWEEN INDIVIDUAL NEEDS AND JOB SATISFACTION
    OF COUNSELORS IN THE NORTH CAROLINA COMMUNITY COLLEGE
    SYSTEM.   M0933

CRAFTS

    THE CRAFTS -- FIVE MILLION OPPORTUNITIES.   M0049

    APPRENTICESHIP -- AVENUE TO THE SKILLED CRAFTS.   M0419

CREATING

    CREATING A "QUALITY" QUALITY CONTROL PROGRAM AT SPP.   M0688

CREATIVITY

    ENCOURAGEMENT OF EMPLOYEE CREATIVITY AND INITIATIVE.   M0527

    ACHIEVEMENT DRIVE AND CREATIVITY AS CORRELATES OF SUCCESS
IN SMALL BUSINESS.   M0730

CREDENTIALISM

    JOB PERFORMANCE AND THE NEW CREDENTIALISM.   M0099

CREDIBILITY

    THE CREDIBILITY GAP IN MANAGEMENT.   M0135

CREDIT

    JOBS, SALARY, CREDIT, LEGAL STATUS ALL IN FOCUS OF WOMEN'S
YEAR.   M0235

CRIMINAL

    MANPOWER PROGRAMS FOR CRIMINAL OFFENDERS.   M0436

CRITERIA

    SOME MODERATOR INFLUENCES ON RELATIONSHIPS BETWEEN
CONSIDERATION, INITIATING STRUCTURE, AND ORGANIZATION
CRITERIA.   M0021

    THE RELATIONSHIP OF JOB SATISFACTION MEASURES TO
SELF-REPORT AND OBJECTIVE CRITERIA MEASURES AND THE EFFECT
OF MODERATOR VARIABLES FOR CANADIAN MILITARY PERSONNEL.   M0853

CRITICAL

    MOTIVATION OF THE BLACK WORKER: A REVIEW OF TRADITIONAL
APPROACHES AND CRITICAL ISSUES IN CURRENT THEORY.   M0062

    HOW TO EVALUATE THE JOB SATISFACTION OF CRITICAL EMPLOYEES.   M0560

CRITICISMS

    ON ALEX CAREY'S RADICAL CRITICISMS OF THE HAWTHORNE
STUDIES.   M0391

CRITIQUE

A CRITIQUE OF SALANCIK AND PFEFFER'S EXAMINATION OF NEED
SATISFACTION THEORIES.   M0669

CROSS-CULTURAL

CROSS-CULTURAL DIFFERENCES IN TWO-FACTOR MOTIVATION THEORY.   M0209

CONVERGENT AND DISCRIMINANT VALIDITY OF A JOB SATISFACTION
INVENTORY: A CROSS-CULTURAL REPORT.   M0764

CROSS-SECTIONAL

A CROSS-SECTIONAL TEST OF NEED HIERARCHY THEORY.   M0562

LONGITUDINAL INFERENCES OF JOB ATTITUDE AND TENURE
RELATIONSHIPS FROM CROSS-SECTIONAL DATA.   M0591

CROSSROADS

THE ENTREPRENEURIAL PERSONALITY: A PERSON AT THE
CROSSROADS.   M0771

CUES

AN EXPERIMENTAL STUDY OF THE EFFECTS OF GOAL SETTING,
EVALUATION APPREHENSION, AND SOCIAL CUES ON TASK
PERFORMANCE AND JOB SATISFACTION.   M0878

CULTURALLY

EVALUATION AND IMPLEMENTATION OF THE NEW YORK FIRE
DEPARTMENT EXAMINATION TRAINING PROJECT FOR CULTURALLY
DISADVANTAGED RESIDENTS OF THE CITY OF NEW YORK.   M0243

CULTURE

WORK, SOCIETY AND CULTURE.   M0397

CUPID

COPING WITH CUPID: THE FORMATION, IMPACT, AND MANAGEMENT OF
ROMANTIC RELATIONSHIPS IN ORGANIZATIONS.   M0630

CURE

CURE FOR THE I DON'T CARE SYNDROME.   M0382

CURRENT

UNMIXING CURRENT MOTIVATIONAL STRATEGIES.   M0052

MOTIVATION OF THE BLACK WORKER: A REVIEW OF TRADITIONAL
APPROACHES AND CRITICAL ISSUES IN CURRENT THEORY.   M0062

CURRENT   CONTINUATION

UNDERSTANDING DRUG USE MOTIVATION: A NEW LOOK AT A CURRENT
PROBLEM.   M0788

CURRICULUM

OPEN SPACE ELEMENTARY SCHOOL: EFFECTS ON TEACHERS' JOB
SATISFACTION, PARTICIPATION IN CURRICULUM DECISION-MAKING,
AND PERCEIVED SCHOOL EFFECTIVENESS.   M0922

CUTTING

CUTTING INTO THE SAWMILL SKILL SHORTAGE.   M0115

DATA

ABSENCE FROM WORK: A LOOK AT SOME NATIONAL DATA.   M0198

LONGITUDINAL INFERENCES OF JOB ATTITUDE AND TENURE
RELATIONSHIPS FROM CROSS-SECTIONAL DATA.   M0591

ORGANIZATIONAL AND OCCUPATIONAL COMMITMENT: A FACET
THEORETICAL ANALYSIS OF EMPIRICAL DATA.   M0747

CORRECTIONAL EMPLOYEES' REACTIONS TO JOB CHARACTERISTICS: A
DATA BASED ARGUMENT FOR JOB ENLARGEMENT.   M0753

AN EMPIRICAL STUDY OF INDIVIDUAL CONGRUENCE AND THE
PERCEIVED ORGANIZATIONAL PRACTICES - JOB SATISFACTION - JOB
PERFORMANCE RELATIONSHIP IN SELECTED ELECTRONIC COMPUTER
DATA PROCESSING CENTERS.   M0946

DECADE

NEGOTIATED RETIREMENT PLANS -- A DECADE OF BENEFIT
IMPROVEMENTS.   M0085

A DECADE OF MANPOWER TRAINING.   M0300

DECISION

JOB INVOLVEMENT, VALUES, PERSONAL BACKGROUND, PARTICIPATION
IN DECISION MAKING, AND JOB ATTITUDES.   M0664

JOB CHOICE AND POST DECISION DISSONANCE.   M0772

ROLE PERCEPTIONS, SATISFACTION AND PERFORMANCE MODERATED BY
ORGANIZATION LEVEL AND PARTICIPATION IN DECISION MAKING.   M0895

DECISION-MAKING

OPEN SPACE ELEMENTARY SCHOOL: EFFECTS ON TEACHERS' JOB
SATISFACTION, PARTICIPATION IN CURRICULUM DECISION-MAKING,
AND PERCEIVED SCHOOL EFFECTIVENESS.   M0922

DECISIONAL

DECISIONAL PARTICIPATION AND SOURCES OF JOB SATISFACTION: A
STUDY OF MANUFACTURING PERSONNEL.   M0008

DECLINE

ON THE DECLINE OF MALE LABOR FORCE PARTICIPATION.   M0149

SEX STEREOTYPING: ITS DECLINE IN SKILLED TRADES.   M0197

DEFECTS

LET'S ADMIT IT: ZERO DEFECTS IS NO PANACEA.   M0027

DEFENSE

HOW EQUAL OPPORTUNITY AFFECTS DEFENSE CONTRACTS.   M0140

DEFENSE MECHANISMS AND THE HERZBERG THEORY: AN ALTERNATE
TEST.   M0334

DEFICIENCY

MANAGERIAL SATISFACTIONS AND ORGANIZATIONAL ROLES: AN
INVESTIGATION OF PORTER'S NEED DEFICIENCY SCALES.   M0202

DEFINITIONAL

A DEFINITIONAL CHALLENGE: INTEREST AND WORK ITSELF
SATISFACTIONS.   M0543

DEGREE

A NATIONAL STUDY OF ASSOCIATE DEGREE MENTAL HEALTH SERVICES
WORKERS.   M0806

DEGREES

EFFECTS OF DIFFERENT PATTERNS AND DEGREES OF OPENNESS IN
SUPERIOR-SUBORDINATE COMMUNICATION ON SUBORDINATE JOB
SATISFACTION.   M0045

DEHUMANIZE

DOES THE INDUSTRIAL ENGINEER DEHUMANIZE JOBS.   M0136

DELICATELY

INSTILLING APPREHENSION DELICATELY AND OTHER MOTIVATORS.   M0017

DELMARVA

RELATIONSHIPS BETWEEN JOB SATISFACTION, DEMOGRAPHIC
FACTORS, ABSENTEEISM AND TENURE OF WORKERS IN A DELMARVA
BROILER PROCESSING PLANT.   M0921

DEMOCRACIES

PUBLIC EMPLOYEE LABOR RELATIONS IN OTHER DEMOCRACIES.   M0161

DEMOCRACY

DEMOCRACY IN THE WORKPLACE: THE HUMAN FACTORIES.   M0230

DEMOCRATIC

THE DEMOCRATIC FACTORY.   M0680

DEMOCRATIZING

DEMOCRATIZING THE REWARD SYSTEM.   M0742

DEMOGRAPHIC

RELATIONSHIPS BETWEEN JOB SATISFACTION, DEMOGRAPHIC
FACTORS, ABSENTEEISM AND TENURE OF WORKERS IN A DELMARVA
BROILER PROCESSING PLANT.   M0921

DEMONSTRATION

ASSESSMENT OF EXPERIMENTAL AND DEMONSTRATION INTERSTATE
PROGRAM FOR SOUTH TEXAS MIGRANT WORKERS.   M0001

AN APPLICATION OF JOB ENRICHMENT IN A CIVIL SERVICE
SETTING: A DEMONSTRATION STUDY.   M0719

DENTAL

OLNEY CENTRAL COLLEGE DENTAL ASSISTING PROGRAM GRADUATES
PERCEPTIONS OF PROGRAM COMPONENTS, JOB SATISFACTION AND
CAREER GOALS.   M0944

DEPARTMENTAL

THE MEASUREMENT OF SATISFACTION AND DEPARTMENTAL
ASSOCIATION AT WESTERN KENTUCKY UNIVERSITY: TESTING THE
HOLLAND AND BIGLAN MODELS.   M0914

DEPARTMENTS

WORK FRUSTRATION IN ENGINEERING DEPARTMENTS.   M0763

DEPRESSIVE

DEPRESSIVE SYMPTOMATOLOGY AND ROLE FUNCTION IN A GENERAL
POPULATION.   M0752

DESCRIBING

THE DEVELOPMENT OF A MANAGERIAL JOB TAXONOMY: A SYSTEM FOR
DESCRIBING, CLASSIFYING, AND EVALUATING EXECUTIVE
POSITIONS.   M0618

DESEGREGATION

    DESEGREGATION AND CAREER GOALS. CHILDREN OF AIR FORCE
    FAMILIES.   M0491

DESIGN

    JOB DESIGN AND EMPLOYEE MOTIVATION.   M0267

    MOTIVATION THROUGH JOB DESIGN.   M0375

    JOB DESIGN AND WORKER SATISFACTION: A CHALLENGE TO
    ASSUMPTIONS.   M0571

    EFFECTS OF JOB ENRICHMENT AND TASK GOALS ON SATISFACTION
    AND PRODUCTIVITY: IMPLICATIONS FOR JOB DESIGN.   M0619

    MOTIVATION THROUGH THE DESIGN OF WORK: TEST OF A THEORY.   M0761

    TECHNOLOGICAL DIFFERENCES IN JOB CHARACTERISTICS, EMPLOYEE
    SATISFACTION, AND MOTIVATION: A SYNTHESIS OF JOB DESIGN
    RESOURCE AND SOCIOTECHNICAL SYSTEMS THEORY.   M0832

DESIGNED

    A FACTOR ANALYTIC STUDY OF JOB SATISFACTION ITEMS DESIGNED
    TO MEASURE MASLOW NEED CATEGORIES.   M0365

DESIGNING

    DESIGNING A MOTIVATING AND TEAM BUILDING EMPLOYEE APPRAISAL
    SYSTEM.   M0534

    INCENTIVES FOR SALESMEN DESIGNING A PLAN THAT WORKS.   M0703

DESIRABILITY

    SOCIAL DESIRABILITY AS A MODERATOR OF THE RELATIONSHIP
    BETWEEN JOB SATISFACTION AND PERSONAL ADJUSTMENT.   M0337

DESIRED

    DESIRED JOB CHARACTERISTICS FOR MALES AND FEMALES.   M0629

DETERMINANT

    EGO-DEFENSIVENESS AS A DETERMINANT OF REPORTED DIFFERENCES
    IN SOURCES OF JOB SATISFACTION AND JOB DISSATISFACTION.   M0465

DETERMINANTS

    PERSONAL CAUSATION: THE INTERNAL EFFECTIVE DETERMINANTS OF
    BEHAVIOR.   M0090

    THE MANAGEMENT OF SCIENTISTS: DETERMINANTS OF PERCEIVED
    ROLE PERFORMANCE OF 95 SCIENTISTS IN THREE LARGE RESEARCH

DETERMINANTS   CONTINUATION

DETERMINANTS

LABORATORIES TO THE ORGANIC SYSTEM OF MANAGEMENT CONCEIVED
BY BURNS AND STALKER.   M0190

SOCIOECONOMIC DETERMINANTS OF URBAN POVERTY AREA WORKERS.   M0349

DETERMINANTS OF PAY AND PAY SATISFACTION.   M0367

THE DETERMINANTS OF PAY SATISFACTION.   M0582

DETERMINANTS OF PAY SATISFACTION: A DISCREPANCY MODEL
EVALUATION.   M0852

DETERMINATES

EXPECTANCIES AS DETERMINATES OF PERFORMANCE.   M0258

DETERMINATES OF JOB SATISFACTION AND PRODUCTIVITY.   M0551

DEVELOPMENT

IN EXECUTIVE DEVELOPMENT . . . THE FUTURE IS NOW.   M0084

PROBLEM OF MOTIVATION IN MANAGEMENT DEVELOPMENT.   M0098

DEVELOPMENT OF ASSESSMENT MEASURES FOR COUNSELING YOUTH
WORK -- TRAINING ENROLLEES.   M0142

BACKGROUND CHARACTERISTICS, ORIENTATION, WORK EXPERIENCE,
AND WORK VALUES OF EMPLOYEES HIRED FROM HUMAN RESOURCES
DEVELOPMENT APPLICANTS BY COMPANIES AFFILIATED WITH THE
NATIONAL ALLIANCE OF BUSINESSMAN.   ·M0165

MOTIVATION AND MANAGEMENT DEVELOPMENT.   M0438

CHARACTERISTICS OF SUCCESSFUL AND UNSUCCESSFUL ORGANIZATION
DEVELOPMENT.   M0513

THE DEVELOPMENT OF A MANAGERIAL JOB TAXONOMY: A SYSTEM FOR
DESCRIBING, CLASSIFYING, AND EVALUATING EXECUTIVE
POSITIONS.   M0618

ORGANIZATION DEVELOPMENT.   M0621

GROUP DEVELOPMENT, TRAINER STYLE AND CARRY-OVER JOB
SATISFACTION AND PERFORMANCE.   M0653

THE RELATIONSHIP OF SEX AND ETHNIC BACKGROUND TO
JOB-RELATED STRESS OF RESEARCH AND DEVELOPMENT
PROFESSIONALS.   M0695

DEVELOPMENT OF THE JOB DIAGNOSTIC SURVEY.   M0723

THE JOINING-UP PROCESS: ISSUES IN EFFECTIVE HUMAN RESOURCE
DEVELOPMENT.   M0758

DEVELOPMENT   CONTINUATION

    MANAGERS' OCCUPATIONAL HISTORIES, ORGANIZATIONAL
    ENVIRONMENTS, AND CLIMATES FOR MANAGEMENT DEVELOPMENT.   M0787

    DIMENSIONS OF JOB SATISFACTION: INITIAL DEVELOPMENT OF THE
    AIR FORCE OCCUPATIONAL ATTITUDE INVENTORY.   M0802

DEVELOPMENTS

    ENHANCING THE QUALITY OF WORKING LIFE: DEVELOPMENTS IN THE
    UNITED STATES.   M0809

DEVIATION

    SATISFACTION WITH PERFORMANCE AS A FUNCTION OF THE INITIAL
    LEVEL OF EXPECTED PERFORMANCE AND THE DEVIATION FROM
    EXPECTATIONS.   M0221

DIAGNOSIS

    ORGANIZATIONAL DIAGNOSIS.   M0275

DIAGNOSTIC

    A DIAGNOSTIC APPROACH TO JOB ENRICHMENT.   M0358

    DEVELOPMENT OF THE JOB DIAGNOSTIC SURVEY.   M0723

DIFFERENTIAL

    BLACK AND WHITE UNEMPLOYMENT: THE DYNAMICS OF THE
    DIFFERENTIAL.   M0156

    TESTING SOME STEREOTYPES ABOUT THE SEXES IN ORGANIZATIONS:
    DIFFERENTIAL SATISFACTION WITH WORK.   M0815

DIFFERENTIALS

    DIFFERENTIALS AND OVERLAPS IN EARNINGS OF BLACKS AND
    WHITES.   M0428

DIFFERING

    PERCEPTIONS OF JOB SATISFACTION IN DIFFERING OCCUPATIONS.   M0256

DILEMMA

    THE PLANNING-MOTIVATING DILEMMA.   M0187

    THE PAY-FOR-PERFORMANCE DILEMMA.   M0779

DIMENSION

    RELATIONSHIP BETWEEN ORGANIZATIONAL CLIMATE AND THE
    SITUATIONAL FAVORABLENESS DIMENSION OF FIEDLER'S

DISADVANTAGED   CONTINUATION

A SOCIAL PSYCHOLGICAL EXPLORATION OF POWER MOTIVATION AMONG
DISADVANTAGED WORKERS.   M0279

THE PERSISTENCE OF THE DISADVANTAGED WORKER EFFECT.   M0383

OCCUPATIONAL GUIDANCE MATERIALS FOR THE DISADVANTAGED: A
PILOT PROGRAM.   M0404

WORK ATTITUDES OF DISADVANTAGED BLACK MEN.   M0412

DISCIPLINE

THE EFFECTIVE ORGANIZATION: MORALE VS. DISCIPLINE.   M0357

DISCONTENT

DISCONTENT IN THE RANKS: IS THE OPERATIVE WORKER REALLY
TRAPPED.   M0354

DISCONTENTED

DISCONTENTED BLUE-COLLAR WORKERS -- A CASE STUDY.   M0393

DISCOURAGE

DISCOURAGE WORKERS AND CHANGES IN UNEMPLOYMENT.   M0134

DISCOVERS

CITY HALL DISCOVERS PRODUCTIVITY.   M0072

DISCREPANCY

DETERMINANTS OF PAY SATISFACTION: A DISCREPANCY MODEL
EVALUATION.   M0852

DISCRIMINANT

CONVERGENT AND DISCRIMINANT VALIDITIES OF PERFORMANCE
EVALUATIONS IN EXTREMELY ISOLATED GROUPS.   M0180

CONVERGENT AND DISCRIMINANT VALIDITY OF A JOB SATISFACTION
INVENTORY: A CROSS-CULTURAL REPORT.   M0764

DISCRIMINATION

OCCUPATIONAL MIGRATION, DISCRIMINATION, AND THE CENTRAL
CITY LABOR FORCE.   M0247

DISCRIMINATION AND JOB SATISFACTION: AN EMPIRICAL STUDY
WITH A SOUTH AFRICAN MINORITY GROUP.   M0733

DISINCENTIVES

    DISMAL DISINCENTIVES.   M0637

DISLOCATED

    CONFLICT AND DISSONANCE IN A DISLOCATED WORKER POPULATION.   M0930

DISMAL

    DISMAL DISINCENTIVES.   M0637

DISPARITIES

    SEGREGATION AND JOB SATISFACTION IN THE WORK PLACE: THE
    MEASUREMENT OF RACIAL DISPARITIES IN ORGANIZATIONS AND
    THEIR INFLUENCE ON EMPLOYEE WORK ATTITUDES.   M0927

DISPARITY

    MANAGEMENT'S ECTASY AND DISPARITY OVER JOB ENRICHMENT:
    EXPECTATIONS IN PLANNING JOB CHANGE: A CASE STUDY.   M0531

DISSATISFACTION

    REPLICATION OF WHITE-COLLAR-BLUE-COLLAR DIFFERENCES IN
    SOURCES OF SATISFACTION AND DISSATISFACTION.   M0188

    WORKER DISSATISFACTION: A LOOK AT THE ECONOMIC EFFECTS.   M0200

    SOURCES OF SATISFACTION AND DISSATISFACTION AMONG SOLID
    WASTE MANAGEMENT EMPLOYEES.   M0283

    WORKER DISSATISFACTION: A LOOK AT THE CAUSES.   M0429

    EGO-DEFENSIVENESS AS A DETERMINANT OF REPORTED DIFFERENCES
    IN SOURCES OF JOB SATISFACTION AND JOB DISSATISFACTION.   M0465

    JOB SPECIALIZATION, WORK VALUES, AND WORKER
    DISSATISFACTION.   M0557

    WORKER DISSATISFACTION: A LOOK AT THE CAUSE   M0615

    SURVEY OF VALUES AND SOURCES OF DISSATISFACTION.   M0635

    ROLE DISSATISFACTION AND CAREER CONTINGENCIES AMONG FEMALE
    ELEMENTARY TEACHERS.   M0722

DISSATISFIERS

    SATISFIERS AND DISSATISFIERS AMONG WHITE-COLLAR AND
    BLUE-COLLAR EMPLOYEES.   M0282

DISSONANCE

    JOB CHOICE AND POST DECISION DISSONANCE.   M0772

DISSONANCE   CONTINUATION

RELATIONSHIP OF PERSONAL INFLUENCE DISSONANCE TO JOB
TENSION SATISFACTION AND INVOLVEMENT.   M0817

CONFLICT AND DISSONANCE IN A DISLOCATED WORKER POPULATION.   M0930

DISTAFF

STAFF AND DISTAFF: WHY WOMEN WORK.   M0154

DISTANCE

SEMANTIC DISTANCE AND JOB SATISFACTION IN FORMAL
ORGANIZATIONS.   M0599

DISTRIBUTION

DISTRIBUTION OF JOB SATISFACTION IN THE WORK FORCE.   M0106

DISTRIBUTIVE

JOB SATISFACTION AND EXPECTATIONS OF DISTRIBUTIVE EDUCATION
GRADUATES.   M0905

DISTRICT

STOCKTON UNIFIED SCHOOL DISTRICT.   M0164

DISTRICTS

A NORMATIVE STUDY OF THE SECONDARY SCHOOL ASSISTANT
PRINCIPALSHIP IN SELECTED PENNSYLVANIA SCHOOL DISTRICTS
WITH AN EMPHASIS UPON JOB SATISFACTION.   M0918

COMPARATIVE APPRAISALS OF JOB PERFORMANCE OF FULL-TIME
ELEMENTARY PRINCIPALS BY THE PRINCIPALS AND THEIR
SUPERVISORS IN CLASS I MONTANA SCHOOL DISTRICTS.   M0941

DIVORCE

DOES DIVORCE HAMPER JOB PERFORMANCE.   M0261

DOGMATISM

SCHOOL BOARD DOGMATISM AND MORALE OF PRINCIPALS.   M0731

DOMESTIC

A COMPARATIVE STUDY OF THE SATISFACTION OF DOMESTIC U. S.
MANAGERS AND OVERSEAS U. S. MANAGERS.   M0226

DOMINATED

THE RELATIVE VALIDITIES OF TRADITIONALLY USED JOB
SATISFACTION AND ORGANIZATIONAL COMMITMENT MEASURES VERSUS

DOMINATED   CONTINUATION

WOMEN-SPECIFIC MEASURES FOR THE PREDICTION OF FEMALE TENURE
IN A MALE DOMINATED JOB.   M0856

DRIVE

ACHIEVEMENT DRIVE AND CREATIVITY AS CORRELATES OF SUCCESS
IN SMALL BUSINESS.   M0730

DROPOUT

CORPORATE DROPOUT.   M0073

DROPOUTS

DIMENSIONS OF THRESHOLD WORK EXPERIENCE FOR HIGH SCHOOL
GRADUATES AND DROPOUTS: A FACTOR ANALYSIS.   M0089

CORPORATE DROPOUTS: A PRELIMINARY TYPOLOGY.   M0616

DRUG

UNDERSTANDING DRUG USE MOTIVATION: A NEW LOOK AT A CURRENT
PROBLEM.   M0788

DYNAMICS

DYNAMICS OF ACTION.   M0018

BLACK AND WHITE UNEMPLOYMENT: THE DYNAMICS OF THE
DIFFERENTIAL.   M0156

ROLE DYNAMICS, LOCUS OF CONTROL, AND EMPLOYEE ATTITUDES AND
BEHAVIOR.   M0667

THE DYNAMICS OF UNDERGRADUATE ACADEMIC ADVISING.   M0750

EARNINGS

AN EARNINGS FUNCTION FOR HIGH LEVEL MANPOWER.   M0011

DIFFERENCES IN HOURLY EARNINGS BETWEEN MEN AND WOMEN.   M0104

OCCUPATIONAL RANKING FOR MEN AND WOMEN BY EARNINGS.   M0408

DIFFERENTIALS AND OVERLAPS IN EARNINGS OF BLACKS AND
WHITES.   M0428

EARNINGS FUNCTION AND NONPECUNIARY BENEFITS.   M0638

ECONOMIC

WORKER DISSATISFACTION: A LOOK AT THE ECONOMIC EFFECTS.   M0200

COMPONENTS OF ACHIEVEMENT MOTIVATION AS PREDICTORS OF

ECONOMIC   CONTINUATION

    POTENTIAL FOR ECONOMIC CHANGE.   M0458

    ECONOMIC CONSIDERATIONS IN JOB SATISFACTION TRENDS.   M0644

ECONOMICS

    ACADEMIC SALARIES -- A PERSONAL APPLICATION OF MANAGERIAL
    ECONOMICS.   M0782

ECONOMY

    JAPAN'S LABOR ECONOMY -- PROSPECT FOR THE FUTURE.   M0123

ECTASY

    MANAGEMENT'S ECTASY AND DISPARITY OVER JOB ENRICHMENT:
    EXPECTATIONS IN PLANNING JOB CHANGE: A CASE STUDY.   M0531

EDITORIAL

    EDITORIAL RESEARCH REPORTS ON THE AMERICAN WORK ETHIC. M0116

EDUCABLE

    THE RELATION OF JOB SATISFACTION TO VOCATIONAL PREFERENCES
    AMONG TEACHERS OF THE EDUCABLE MENTALLY RETARDED.   M0805

EDUCATION

    EXPECTANCY THEORY AND ITS IMPLICATIONS FOR HIGHER EDUCATION
    AMONG BLACK YOUTH.   M0210

    AMERICA'S NEED FOR CAREER EDUCATION.   M0304

    CONTINUING EDUCATION IN INDUSTRY.   M0320

    DOES A COLLEGE EDUCATION PAY.   M0422

    THE EMPLOYMENT OF WOMEN, EDUCATION, AND FERTILITY.   M0725

    RELATIONSHIP BETWEEN EDUCATION AND SATISFACTION WITH JOB
    CONTENT.   M0885

    JOB SATISFACTION AND EXPECTATIONS OF DISTRIBUTIVE EDUCATION
    GRADUATES.   M0905

    JOB SATISFACTION AND LEADER BEHAVIOR OF ADULT EDUCATION
    ADMINISTRATORS.   M0936

EDUCATIONAL

    EDUCATIONAL ATTAINMENT OF WORKERS, MARCH 1973.   M0094

    AN INVESTIGATION OF EDUCATIONAL ADMINISTRATIVE STYLE AND

EDUCATIONAL   CONTINUATION

    JOB SATISFACTION OF ELEMENTARY SCHOOL PRINCIPALS.   M0901

EDUCATORS

    THE OCCUPATIONAL INFORMATION CENTER: WHERE ATLANTA
    EMPLOYERS AND EDUCATORS MEET.   M0237

EFFECT

    THE EFFECT OF MOTIVATIONAL PROGRAMS ON COLLECTIVE
    BARGAINING.   M0032

    JOB ATTITUDES AND OVERALL JOB SATISFACTION: THE EFFECT OF
    BIOGRAPHICAL AND EMPLOYMENT VARIABLES: RESEARCH NOTE.   M0050

    THE EFFECT OF LEGITIMATE OPPORTUNITIES ON THE PROBABILITY
    OF PAROLEE RECIDIVISM.   M0069

    THE PERSISTENCE OF THE DISADVANTAGED WORKER EFFECT.   M0383

    THE EFFECT OF LEADERSHIP ROLES ON THE SATISFACTION AND
    PRODUCTIVITY OF UNIVERSITY RESEARCH PROFESSORS.   M0510

    PREFERRED JOB ASSIGNMENT EFFECT ON JOB SATISFACTION.   M0598

    THE MENTAL HEALTH ASSOCIATE: THE EFFECT OF SOCIAL
    ENVIRONMENTAL FACTORS ON JOB SATISFACTION.   M0697

    THE RELATIONSHIP OF JOB SATISFACTION MEASURES TO
    SELF-REPORT AND OBJECTIVE CRITERIA MEASURES AND THE EFFECT
    OF MODERATOR VARIABLES FOR CANADIAN MILITARY PERSONNEL.   M0853

    THE EFFECT OF URBANIZATION ON SOURCES OF JOB SATISFACTION
    AMONG BLACK SUPERVISORS IN SOUTH AFRICA.   M0891

    THE EFFECT OF ORGANIZATIONAL CHANGE ON ADMINISTRATOR JOB
    SATISFACTION, ORGANIZATIONAL CLIMATE, AND PERCEIVED
    ORGANIZATIONAL EFFECTIVENESS.   M0942

    THE EFFECT OF FLEXIBLE WORKING HOURS ON ABSENTEEISM AND JOB
    SATISFACTION AND THE RELATIONSHIP BETWEEN LOCUS OF CONTROL
    AND UTILITY OF FLEXIBLE WORKING HOURS.   M0943

EFFECTIVE

    BUILDING EFFICACY: AN EFFECTIVE USE OF MANAGERIAL POWER.   M0035

    PERSONAL CAUSATION: THE INTERNAL EFFECTIVE DETERMINANTS OF
    BEHAVIOR.   M0090

    EFFECTIVE LEADERSHIP.   M0113

    THE EFFECTIVE ORGANIZATION: MORALE VS. DISCIPLINE.   M0357

EFFECTS   CONTINUATION

EFFECTS   CONTINUATION

SUPERVISOR EXPECTATIONS AND BEHAVIOR: EFFECTS OF
CONSISTENT-INCONSISTENT SUPERVISORY PAIRINGS ON SUPERVISEE
SATISFACTION WITH SUPERVISION, PERCEPTIONS OF SUPERVISORY
RELATIONSHIPS AND RATED COUNSELOR COMPETENCY.   M0864

AN EXPERIMENTAL STUDY OF THE EFFECTS OF GOAL SETTING,
EVALUATION APPREHENSION, AND SOCIAL CUES ON TASK
PERFORMANCE AND JOB SATISFACTION.   M0878

EFFECTS OF ASSIGNED AND PARTICIPATIVE GOAL SETTING ON
PERFORMANCE AND JOB SATISFACTION.   M0887

OPEN SPACE ELEMENTARY SCHOOL: EFFECTS ON TEACHERS' JOB
SATISFACTION, PARTICIPATION IN CURRICULUM DECISION-MAKING,
AND PERCEIVED SCHOOL EFFECTIVENESS.   M0922

EFFICACY

BUILDING EFFICACY: AN EFFECTIVE USE OF MANAGERIAL POWER. M0035

EFFICIENCY

EFFICIENCY IN THE MILITARY.   M0522

EFFORT

PROBLEM RESOLUTION AND IMPOSITION OF CHANGE THROUGH A
PARTICIPATING GROUP EFFORT.   M0238

EXPECTANCY THEORY AS A PREDICTOR OF WORK MOTIVATION, EFFORT
EXPENDITURE, AND JOB PERFORMANCE.   M0663

ACHIEVEMENT MOTIVATION AS A MODERATOR OF THE RELATIONSHIP
BETWEEN EXPECTANCY TIMES VALENCE AND EFFORT.   M0845

AN INVESTIGATION OF THE RELATIONSHIP BETWEEN INTRINSIC AND
EXTRINSIC JOB INSTRUMENTALITY EFFORT, JOB SATISFACTION,
INDIVIDUAL AND PERCEIVED TASK CHARACTERISTICS.   M0938

EGO-DEFENSIVENESS

EGO-DEFENSIVENESS AS A DETERMINANT OF REPORTED DIFFERENCES
IN SOURCES OF JOB SATISFACTION AND JOB DISSATISFACTION.   M0465

ELDERLY

SATISFACTION WITH TRAINING AND GENERAL JOB SATISFACTION OF
AGENCY HOMEMAKERS WORKING WITH THE ELDERLY AND DISABLED. M0904

ELECTRONIC

AN EMPIRICAL STUDY OF INDIVIDUAL CONGRUENCE AND THE
PERCEIVED ORGANIZATIONAL PRACTICES - JOB SATISFACTION - JOB
PERFORMANCE RELATIONSHIP IN SELECTED ELECTRONIC COMPUTER

ELECTRONIC   CONTINUATION

    DATA PROCESSING CENTERS.   M0946

ELEMENTARY

    ROLE DISSATISFACTION AND CAREER CONTINGENCIES AMONG FEMALE
    ELEMENTARY TEACHERS.   M0722

    AN INVESTIGATION OF EDUCATIONAL ADMINISTRATIVE STYLE AND
    JOB SATISFACTION OF ELEMENTARY SCHOOL PRINCIPALS.   M0901

    AN ANALYSIS OF JOB SATISFACTION AMONG ELEMENTARY, MIDDLE
    LEVEL, AND SENIOR HIGH SCHOOL TEACHERS.   M0911

    OPEN SPACE ELEMENTARY SCHOOL: EFFECTS ON TEACHERS' JOB
    SATISFACTION, PARTICIPATION IN CURRICULUM DECISION-MAKING,
    AND PERCEIVED SCHOOL EFFECTIVENESS.   M0922

    COMPARATIVE APPRAISALS OF JOB PERFORMANCE OF FULL-TIME
    ELEMENTARY PRINCIPALS BY THE PRINCIPALS AND THEIR
    SUPERVISORS IN CLASS I MONTANA SCHOOL DISTRICTS.   M0941

ELEMENTS

    AS YOU WERE SAYING -- ELEMENTS OF MEANINGFUL WORK.   M0016

    ELEMENTS OF AN EMPLOYEE MOTIVATION PROGRAM.   M0469

    KEY ELEMENTS IN IMPLEMENTING JOB ENRICHMENT.   M0492

ELITENESS

    SUCCESS IN MANAGEMENT CONSULTING AND THE CONCEPT OF
    ELITENESS MOTIVATION.   M0314

EMERGING

    THE EMERGING WORKER.   M0472

EMPHASIS

    A NORMATIVE STUDY OF THE SECONDARY SCHOOL ASSISTANT
    PRINCIPALSHIP IN SELECTED PENNSYLVANIA SCHOOL DISTRICTS
    WITH AN EMPHASIS UPON JOB SATISFACTION.   M0918

EMPIRICAL

    AN EMPIRICAL ANALYSIS OF ORGANIZATIONAL IDENTIFICATION.   M0272

    JOB SATISFACTION AND JOB PERFORMANCE: AN EMPIRICAL TEST OF
    SOME THEORETICAL PROPOSITIONS.   M0323

    THE LIMITATIONS OF THE MOTIVATOR-HYGIENE THEORY OF
    SATISFACTION: AN EMPIRICAL STUDY WITH BLACK FACTORY WORKERS
    IN SOUTH AFRICA.   M0607

EMPIRICAL   CONTINUATION

EMPLOYEE

EMPLOYEE   CONTINUATION

JOB DESIGN AND EMPLOYEE MOTIVATION.   M0267

SUPERVISORY SKILLS AND EMPLOYEE SATISFACTION.   M0316

CONFLICTING IMPACTS OF PAY ON EMPLOYEE MOTIVATION,
SATISFACTION.   M0381

PREDICTION OF JOB SUCCESS AND EMPLOYEE SATISFACTION FOR
EXECUTIVES AND FOREMEN.   M0402

KEYS TO EMPLOYEE MOTIVATION.   M0405

EMPLOYEE PERFORMANCE AND EMPLOYEE NEED SATISFACTION --
WHICH COMES FIRST.   M0434

ELEMENTS OF AN EMPLOYEE MOTIVATION PROGRAM.   M0469

LETTING THE EMPLOYEE SPEAK HIS MIND.   M0526

ENCOURAGEMENT OF EMPLOYEE CREATIVITY AND INITIATIVE.   M0527

DESIGNING A MOTIVATING AND TEAM BUILDING EMPLOYEE APPRAISAL
SYSTEM.   M0534

THE EFFECTS OF ROLE PERCEPTIONS ON EMPLOYEE SATISFACTION
AND PERFORMANCE MODERATED BY EMPLOYEE ABILITY.   M0553

WORK ADJUSTMENT OF THE METHADONE-MAINTAINED CORPORATE
EMPLOYEE.   M0567

EMPLOYEE REACTIONS TO LEADER REWARD BEHAVIOR.   M0654

ROLE DYNAMICS, LOCUS OF CONTROL, AND EMPLOYEE ATTITUDES AND
BEHAVIOR.   M0667

A PRACTICAL PROGRAM FOR EMPLOYEE SOCIALIZATION.   M0714

THE IMPACT OF ORGANIZATION SIZE ON EMPLOYEE MOTIVATION.   M0735

MANAGEMENT CONTROL SYSTEMS: A KEY LINK BETWEEN STRATEGY,
STRUCTURE, AND EMPLOYEE PERFORMANCE.   M0741

MEASURING THE FINANCIAL IMPACT OF EMPLOYEE ATTITUDES.   M0780

INTERMEDIATE LINKAGES IN THE RELATIONSHIP BETWEEN JOB
SATISFACTION AND EMPLOYEE TURNOVER.   M0781

TECHNOLOGICAL DIFFERENCES IN JOB CHARACTERISTICS, EMPLOYEE
SATISFACTION, AND MOTIVATION: A SYNTHESIS OF JOB DESIGN
RESOURCE AND SOCIOTECHNICAL SYSTEMS THEORY.   M0832

EMPLOYEE INFORMATION ENVIRONMENTS AND JOB SATISFACTION: A
CLOSER LOOK.   M0854

EMPLOYEE   CONTINUATION

PERCEIVED LEADER BEHAVIOR AND EMPLOYEE SATISFACTION WITH
SUPERVISION AND THE JOB: THE EFFECTS OF REWARD AND
PUNISHMENT.   M0859

PERSON-ENVIRONMENT CONGRUENCE, EMPLOYEE JOB SATISFACTION,
AND TENURE: A TEST OF HOLLAND'S THEORY.   M0863

MOTIVATING THE PUBLIC EMPLOYEE: FACT VS. FICTION.   M0890

EMPLOYEE ATTITUDES REGARDING VARIOUS CHARACTERISTICS OF JOB
OPPORTUNITY AND JOB PERFORMANCE ACROSS THREE DIFFERENT WORK
SHIFTS AT AN INSTITUTION FOR THE RETARDED.   M0900

SEGREGATION AND JOB SATISFACTION IN THE WORK PLACE: THE
MEASUREMENT OF RACIAL DISPARITIES IN ORGANIZATIONS AND
THEIR INFLUENCE ON EMPLOYEE WORK ATTITUDES.   M0927

THE RELATIONSHIP OF LEADERSHIP STYLE TO EMPLOYEE JOB
SATISFACTION.   M0935

EMPLOYEE'S

BLACKS AS SUPERVISORS: A STUDY OF TRAINING, JOB
PERFORMANCE, AND EMPLOYEE'S EXPECTATION.   M0023

EMPLOYEES

ORGANIZATIONAL EXPERIENCES AND THEIR EFFECTS ON THE
ATTITUDES OF EMPLOYEES, INCLUDING THE DISADVANTAGED, TOWARD
WORK.   M0063

ORGANIZATIONAL EXPERIENCES AND THEIR EFFECTS ON THE
ATTITUDES OF EMPLOYEES, INCLUDING THE DISADVANTAGED.   M0064

BACKGROUND CHARACTERISTICS, ORIENTATION, WORK EXPERIENCE,
AND WORK VALUES OF EMPLOYEES HIRED FROM HUMAN RESOURCES
DEVELOPMENT APPLICANTS BY COMPANIES AFFILIATED WITH THE
NATIONAL ALLIANCE OF BUSINESSMAN.   M0165

SATISFIERS AND DISSATISFIERS AMONG WHITE-COLLAR AND
BLUE-COLLAR EMPLOYEES.   M0282

SOURCES OF SATISFACTION AND DISSATISFACTION AMONG SOLID
WASTE MANAGEMENT EMPLOYEES.   M0283

GREENER PASTURES: WHY EMPLOYEES CHANGE JOBS.   M0372

WORK VALUES OF WHITE-COLLAR EMPLOYEES AS A FUNCTION OF
SOCIOLOGICAL BACKGROUND.   M0376

EMPLOYEES LEARN WHAT THEY LIVE NOT WHAT THEY ARE TOLD.   M0431

MOTIVATING EMPLOYEES: A CLOSER LOOK.   M0516

EMPLOYEES   CONTINUATION

RELATIONSHIP BETWEEN LOCUS OF CONTROL AND REACTIONS OF
EMPLOYEES TO WORK CHARACTERISTICS.   M0530

HOW TO EVALUATE THE JOB SATISFACTION OF CRITICAL EMPLOYEES.   M0560

CONDITIONS UNDER WHICH EMPLOYEES RESPOND POSITIVELY TO
ENRICHED WORK.   M0606

ATTITUDES TOWARD PARTICIPATION AMONG LOCAL AUTHORITY
EMPLOYEES.   M0773

RELATIONSHIPS OF ORGANIZATIONAL FRUSTRATION WITH REPORTED
BEHAVIORAL REACTIONS OF EMPLOYEES.   M0796

RETAIL STORE PERFORMANCE AND JOB SATISFACTION: A STUDY OF
ANXIETY-STRESS PROPENSITY TO LEAVE AMONG RETAIL EMPLOYEES.   M0811

GROWTH AND SATISFACTION OF EMPLOYEES IN ORGANIZATIONS.   M0825

TRENDS IN JOB-RELATED ATTITUDES OF MANAGERIAL AND
PROFESSIONAL EMPLOYEES.   M0838

EMPLOYEES'

BUILD EMPLOYEES' CONFIDENCE AND SELF-ESTEEM.   M0524

REWARDS AND PUBLIC EMPLOYEES' ATTITUDES TOWARD CLIENT
SERVICE.   M0693

CORRECTIONAL EMPLOYEES' REACTIONS TO JOB CHARACTERISTICS: A
DATA BASED ARGUMENT FOR JOB ENLARGEMENT.   M0753

REWARDS AND PUBLIC EMPLOYEES' ATTITUDES TOWARD CLIENT
SERVICE.   M0929

EMPLOYERS

HOW EMPLOYERS SCREEN DISADVANTAGED JOB APPLICANTS.   M0185

THE OCCUPATIONAL INFORMATION CENTER: WHERE ATLANTA
EMPLOYERS AND EDUCATORS MEET.   M0237

EMPLOYMENT

EMPLOYMENT AND UNEMPLOYMENT -- A REPORT ON 1973.   M0036

JOB ATTITUDES AND OVERALL JOB SATISFACTION: THE EFFECT OF
BIOGRAPHICAL AND EMPLOYMENT VARIABLES: RESEARCH NOTE.   M0050

RACE, EMPLOYMENT, AND THE EVALUATION OF WORK.   M0128

FUTURE ORIENTATION AND EXPECTATIONS AS PREDICTORS OF
EMPLOYMENT SUCCESS.   M0216

EMPLOYMENT   CONTINUATION

    FUTURE ORIENTATION AND EXPECTATIONS AS PREDICTORS OF
    EMPLOYMENT SUCCESS.   M0217

    INTERACTION EFFECTS OF PERSONALITY, JOB TRAINING, AND LABOR
    MARKET CONDITIONS ON PERSONAL EMPLOYMENT AND INCOME.   M0305

    EMPLOYMENT, WELFARE, AND MOTHERS' MOTIVATION.   M0308

    THE PUBLIC EMPLOYMENT SERVICE REACHES OUT TO THE URBAN
    POOR.   M0374

    EMPLOYMENT CHARACTERISTICS OF LOW-WAGE WORKERS.   M0418

    BEYOND JOB ENRICHMENT TO EMPLOYMENT ENRICHMENT.   M0565

    THE EMPLOYMENT OF WOMEN, EDUCATION, AND FERTILITY.   M0725

    SOCIAL AND PSYCHOLOGICAL INFLUENCES ON EMPLOYMENT OF
    MARRIED NURSES.   M0755

ENCOURAGEMENT

    ENCOURAGEMENT OF EMPLOYEE CREATIVITY AND INITIATIVE.   M0527

ENFORCEMENT

    A STUDY OF THE RELATIONSHIP BETWEEN HERZBERG'S MOTIVATION
    HYGIENE FACTORS AND HOLLAND'S PERSONALITY PATTERNS FOR LAW
    ENFORCEMENT PERSONNEL.   M0850

ENGINEER

    DOES THE INDUSTRIAL ENGINEER DEHUMANIZE JOBS.   M0136

ENGINEERING

    WORK FRUSTRATION IN ENGINEERING DEPARTMENTS.   M0763

ENGINEERS

    TIME PRESSURE AND PERFORMANCE OF SCIENTISTS AND ENGINEERS:
    A FIVE PANEL STUDY.   M0010

    WANTED BLACK ENGINEERS.   M0468

    MOTIVATION OF ENGINEERS: AN ANALYSIS OF PERCEIVED
    MOTIVATIONAL FACTORS.   M0692

    TOWARD A CAREER-BASED THEORY OF JOB INVOLVEMENT: A STUDY OF
    SCIENTISTS AND ENGINEERS.   M0824

ENGINEERS'

    THE EFFECTS OF AGING ON ENGINEERS' SATISFACTION AND MENTAL

ENGINEERS'   CONTINUATION

   HEALTH: SKILL OBSOLESCENCE.   M0044

ENGLISH-CANADIAN

   VALUES, STRUCTURE, PROCESS, AND REACTIONS/ADJUSTMENTS: A
   COMPARISON OF FRENCH AND ENGLISH-CANADIAN INDUSTRIAL
   ORGANIZATIONS.   M0628

ENHANCE

   HOW MUSIC CAN ENHANCE THE OFFICE ENVIRONMENT.   M0214

ENLARGEMENT

   JOB ENLARGEMENT -- THE KEY TO INCREASING JOB SATISFACTION.   M0384

   JOB ENLARGEMENT, INDIVIDUAL DIFFERENCES, AND WORKER
   RESPONSES: A TEST WITH BLACK WORKERS IN SOUTH AFRICA.   M0546

   CORRECTIONAL EMPLOYEES' REACTIONS TO JOB CHARACTERISTICS: A
   DATA BASED ARGUMENT FOR JOB ENLARGEMENT.   M0753

ENOUGH

   THE WORK ETHIC IS NOT ENOUGH.   M0398

ENRICHED

   CONDITIONS UNDER WHICH EMPLOYEES RESPOND POSITIVELY TO
   ENRICHED WORK.   M0606

ENRICHING

   SKANDIA INSURANCE GROUP: RESTRUCTURING THE WORK AND
   ENRICHING THE JOB.   M0547

ENRICHMENT

   CONCEPTUAL FOUNDATIONS OF JOB ENRICHMENT.   M0051

   A STUDY OF EMPLOYEE RESISTANCE TO JOB ENRICHMENT.   M0066

   VOLVO INCREASES PRODUCTIVITY THROUGH JOB ENRICHMENT.   M0155

   IMPLEMENTING JOB ENRICHMENT.   M0176

   WESTERN ELECTRICS MOTIVATION AND ENRICHMENT TRIAL.   M0195

   THERE IS NO HUMBUG TO JOB ENRICHMENT.   M0265

   JOB REDESIGN, REFORM, ENRICHMENT -- EXPLORING THE
   LIMITATIONS.   M0277

   JOB ENRICHMENT: HOW TO MAKE IT WORK.   M0294

ENRICHMENT   CONTINUATION

ENROLLEES

ENTRANTS

ENTREPRENEURIAL

ENVIRONMENT

ENVIRONMENTAL

ENVIRONMENTS

EQUAL

EQUATIONS

EQUITY

ESCORTING

ESPOUSED

ESSAY

ETHIC

ETHNIC

EVALUATE

EVALUATING

EVALUATION

EVALUATIONS

EVIDENCE

EVOLUTION

EXAMINATION

EXPECTANCY   CONTINUATION

IN ROTC.   M0732

ACHIEVEMENT MOTIVATION AS A MODERATOR OF THE RELATIONSHIP
BETWEEN EXPECTANCY TIMES VALENCE AND EFFORT.   M0845

A TEST OF ALTERNATIVE MODELS OF EXPECTANCY THEORY.   M0892

EXPECTATION

BLACKS AS SUPERVISORS: A STUDY OF TRAINING, JOB
PERFORMANCE, AND EMPLOYEE'S EXPECTATION.   M0023

ANDROGYNY IN NURSING: NURSE ROLE EXPECTATION, SATISFACTION,
ACADEMIC ACHIEVEMENT, AND SELF-ACTUALIZATION IM MALE AND
FEMALE STUDENTS.   M0877

EXPECTATIONS

FUTURE ORIENTATION AND EXPECTATIONS AS PREDICTORS OF
EMPLOYMENT SUCCESS.   M0216

FUTURE ORIENTATION AND EXPECTATIONS AS PREDICTORS OF
EMPLOYMENT SUCCESS.   M0217

SATISFACTION WITH PERFORMANCE AS A FUNCTION OF THE INITIAL
LEVEL OF EXPECTED PERFORMANCE AND THE DEVIATION FROM
EXPECTATIONS.   M0221

MANAGEMENT'S ECTASY AND DISPARITY OVER JOB ENRICHMENT:
EXPECTATIONS IN PLANNING JOB CHANGE: A CASE STUDY.   M0531

SUPERVISOR EXPECTATIONS AND BEHAVIOR: EFFECTS OF
CONSISTENT-INCONSISTENT SUPERVISORY PAIRINGS ON SUPERVISEE
SATISFACTION WITH SUPERVISION, PERCEPTIONS OF SUPERVISORY
RELATIONSHIPS AND RATED COUNSELOR COMPETENCY.   M0864

SUBJECTIVE EXPECTATIONS AND JOB FACET PREDICTABILITY IN JOB
SATISFACTION.   M0876

JOB SATISFACTION AND EXPECTATIONS OF DISTRIBUTIVE EDUCATION
GRADUATES.   M0905

EXPENDITURE

EXPECTANCY THEORY AS A PREDICTOR OF WORK MOTIVATION, EFFORT
EXPENDITURE, AND JOB PERFORMANCE.   M0663

EXPERIENCE

AN ANALYSIS OF MICHIGAN'S EXPERIENCE WITH WORK INCENTIVES.   M0012

RESEARCH, INTERVENTION, AND EXPERIENCE IN ENHANCING THE
QUALITY OF WORKING LIFE.   M0088

EXPERIMENTAL   CONTINUATION

FACT

    MOTIVATING THE PUBLIC EMPLOYEE: FACT VS. FICTION.   M0890

FACTOR

    DIMENSIONS OF THRESHOLD WORK EXPERIENCE FOR HIGH SCHOOL
    GRADUATES AND DROPOUTS: A FACTOR ANALYSIS.   M0089

    A FACTOR ANALYTIC STUDY OF JOB SATISFACTION ITEMS DESIGNED
    TO MEASURE MASLOW NEED CATEGORIES.   M0365

    JOB EXPECTANCY -- AN IMPORTANT FACTOR IN LABOR TURNOVER.   M0385

    THE IMPACT OF THE ORGANIZATION ON THE STRUCTURE OF JOB
    SATISFACTION: SOME FACTOR ANALYTIC FINDINGS.   M0471

FACTORIES

    DEMOCRACY IN THE WORKPLACE: THE HUMAN FACTORIES.   M0230

FACTORY

    THE LIMITATIONS OF THE MOTIVATOR-HYGIENE THEORY OF
    SATISFACTION: AN EMPIRICAL STUDY WITH BLACK FACTORY WORKERS
    IN SOUTH AFRICA.   M0607

    DOING AWAY WITH THE FACTORY BLUES.   M0648

    THE DEMOCRATIC FACTORY.   M0680

FACULTY

    COMMUNITY COLLEGE FACULTY JOB SATISFACTION.   M0708

FAILURES

    AN EXPERIMENTAL CASE STUDY OF THE SUCCESSES AND FAILURES OF
    JOB ENRICHMENT IN A GOVERNMENT AGENCY.   M0600

FAMILIES

    DESEGREGATION AND CAREER GOALS. CHILDREN OF AIR FORCE
    FAMILIES.   M0491

FAMILY

    MARITAL AND FAMILY CHARACTERISTICS OF THE LABOR FORCE IN
    MARCH 1973.   M0194

    MARITAL AND FAMILY CHARACTERISTICS OF THE LABOR FORCE.   M0462

    PERSONAL REFLECTIONS OF A FAMILY THERAPIST.   M0716

FARM

FARMERS

FAVORABLENESS

FEEDBACK

FEELINGS

FEMALE

FEMALES

FEMALES   CONTINUATION

AGE AND JOB SATISFACTION AMONG MALES AND FEMALES: A
MULTI-VARIATE, MULTISURVEY STUDY.   M0518

RELATIONSHIP OF AGE, TENURE AND JOB SATISFACTION IN MALES
AND FEMALES.   M0525

DESIRED JOB CHARACTERISTICS FOR MALES AND FEMALES.   M0629

JOB SATISFACTION AND PERFORMANCE WITH RETARDED FEMALES.   M0738

FEMININE

COMPUTER MYSTIQUE AND FEMININE MYSTIQUE JOIN FORCES.   M0058

FERTILITY

THE EMPLOYMENT OF WOMEN, EDUCATION, AND FERTILITY.   M0725

FICTION

MOTIVATING THE PUBLIC EMPLOYEE: FACT VS. FICTION.   M0890

FIEDLER'S

RELATIONSHIP BETWEEN ORGANIZATIONAL CLIMATE AND THE
SITUATIONAL FAVORABLENESS DIMENSION OF FIEDLER'S
CONTINGENCY MODEL.   M0709

FILLING

FILLING THE POLICE LINEUP.   M0399

FINAL

SURVEY OF WORKING CONDITIONS. FINAL REPORT OF UNIVARIATE
AND BIVARIATE TABLES.   M0266

FINANCIAL

MEASURING THE FINANCIAL IMPACT OF EMPLOYEE ATTITUDES.   M0780

FINDING

IS WORK THE CENTRAL LIFE INTEREST? NOT FOR MOST PEOPLE --
FINDING THE COMMITED FEW.   M0826

FINDINGS

THE IMPACT OF THE ORGANIZATION ON THE STRUCTURE OF JOB
SATISFACTION: SOME FACTOR ANALYTIC FINDINGS.   M0471

RACIAL DIFFERENCES IN JOB ATTITUDES AND PERFORMANCE: SOME
THEORETICAL CONSIDERATIONS AND EMPIRICAL FINDINGS.   M0717

FIRE

    EVALUATION AND IMPLEMENTATION OF THE NEW YORK FIRE
    DEPARTMENT EXAMINATION TRAINING PROJECT FOR CULTURALLY
    DISADVANTAGED RESIDENTS OF THE CITY OF NEW YORK.   M0243

FIRM

    THE MANAGEMENT CONSULTING FIRM AS A SOURCE OF HIGH-LEVEL
    MANAGERIAL TALENT.   M0312

    PARTICIPATIVE MANAGEMENT, BONUSES BOOST PRODUCTIVITY FOR
    MICHIGAN FIRM.   M0341

    LOCAL FIRM AND JOB SATISFACTION.   M0821

FIRO

    THE EFFECTS OF INDIVIDUAL-ROLE COMPATIBILITY UPON GROUP
    PERFORMANCE: AN EXTENSION OF SCHUTZ'S FIRO THEORY.   M0658

FLEXIBLE

    MAKING THE JOB CORPS MORE FLEXIBLE.   M0480

    THE EFFECT OF FLEXIBLE WORKING HOURS ON ABSENTEEISM AND JOB
    SATISFACTION AND THE RELATIONSHIP BETWEEN LOCUS OF CONTROL
    AND UTILITY OF FLEXIBLE WORKING HOURS.   M0943

FLORIDA

    A STUDY OF THE PERCEPTIONS OF SELECTED SCHOOL-BASED
    ADMINISTRATORS IN FLORIDA RELATIVE TO CERTAIN VARIABLES IN
    SECONDARY SCHOOL ADMINISTRATION AS THEY RELATE TO JOB
    SATISFACTION.   M0925

FOCUS

    JOBS, SALARY, CREDIT, LEGAL STATUS ALL IN FOCUS OF WOMEN'S
    YEAR.   M0235

FOLLY

    ON THE FOLLY OF REWARDING A, WHILE HOPING FOR B.   M0655

FORCE

    CHANGES IN THE LABOR FORCE STATUS OF WOMEN.   M0054

    DISTRIBUTION OF JOB SATISFACTION IN THE WORK FORCE.   M0106

    ON THE DECLINE OF MALE LABOR FORCE PARTICIPATION.   M0149

    LABOR FORCE ACTIVITY OF MARRIED WOMEN.   M0193

    MARITAL AND FAMILY CHARACTERISTICS OF THE LABOR FORCE IN

FORCE   CONTINUATION

   MARCH 1973.   M0194

   OCCUPATIONAL MIGRATION, DISCRIMINATION, AND THE CENTRAL
   CITY LABOR FORCE.   M0247

   NATIONAL LONGITUDINAL STUDIES OF THE LABOR FORCE BEHAVIOR
   OF NATIONAL SAMPLES OF MEN (45-59), WOMEN (30-44), AND MALE
   AND FEMALE YOUTH (14-24).   M0339

   SPECIAL TASK FORCE WILL REVIEW ROLE OF GS AND FS
   SECRETARIES.   M0411

   MARITAL AND FAMILY CHARACTERISTICS OF THE LABOR FORCE.   M0462

   DESEGREGATION AND CAREER GOALS. CHILDREN OF AIR FORCE
   FAMILIES.   M0491

   ORGANIZATIONAL CLIMATE AND JOB SATISFACTION IN THE SALES
   FORCE.   M0509

   DIMENSIONS OF JOB SATISFACTION: INITIAL DEVELOPMENT OF THE
   AIR FORCE OCCUPATIONAL ATTITUDE INVENTORY.   M0802

FORCES

   COMPUTER MYSTIQUE AND FEMININE MYSTIQUE JOIN FORCES.   M0058

FOREIGN

   THE QUIT RATE AS A MEASURE OF MORALE IN THE PUBLIC SERVICE:
   THE CASE OF THE UNITED STATES FOREIGN SERVICE.   M0292

FOREMEN

   FOREMEN: MAN IN THE MIDDLE.   M0061

   PREDICTION OF JOB SUCCESS AND EMPLOYEE SATISFACTION FOR
   EXECUTIVES AND FOREMEN.   M0402

FORM

   FORM CHINA WITH SKILL -- MESBIC FOUNDER WANTS TO SHARE HER
   TALENT.   M0145

FORMAL

   SEMANTIC DISTANCE AND JOB SATISFACTION IN FORMAL
   ORGANIZATIONS.   M0599

FORMATION

   AN ANALYSIS OF CLIQUE FORMATION AND STRUCTURE IN
   ORGANIZATIONS.   M0445

FULL-TIME

COMPARATIVE APPRAISALS OF JOB PERFORMANCE OF FULL-TIME
ELEMENTARY PRINCIPALS BY THE PRINCIPALS AND THEIR
SUPERVISORS IN CLASS I MONTANA SCHOOL DISTRICTS.   M0941

FUNCTION

AN EARNINGS FUNCTION FOR HIGH LEVEL MANPOWER.   M0011

SATISFACTION WITH PERFORMANCE AS A FUNCTION OF THE INITIAL
LEVEL OF EXPECTED PERFORMANCE AND THE DEVIATION FROM
EXPECTATIONS.   M0221

THE POSITION AND FUNCTION OF BUDGETS IN AN MBO SYSTEM.   M0289

WORK VALUES OF WHITE-COLLAR EMPLOYEES AS A FUNCTION OF
SOCIOLOGICAL BACKGROUND.   M0376

WHAT THE PERSONNEL FUNCTION IS ALL ABOUT.   M0413

EARNINGS FUNCTION AND NONPECUNIARY BENEFITS.   M0638

JOB STRAIN AS A FUNCTION OF JOB LIFE AND STRESSES.   M0698

DEPRESSIVE SYMPTOMATOLOGY AND ROLE FUNCTION IN A GENERAL
POPULATION.   M0752

RELATIVE STEEPNESS OF APPROACH AND AVOIDANCE GRADIENTS AS A
FUNCTION OF MAGNITUDE AND VALENCE OF INCENTIVE.   M0775

WORK SATISFACTION AS A FUNCTION OF THE PERSON-ENVIRONMENT
INTERACTION.   M0836

FUNCTIONAL

INVESTIGATION OF THE INFLUENCE OF JOB LEVEL AND FUNCTIONAL
SPECIALTY ON JOB ATTITUDES AND PERCEPTIONS.   M0745

FUNCTIONS

PERSONALITY TRAITS, WORK FUNCTIONS, AND VOCATIONAL
SATISFACTION OF PHYSICIANS IN THREE MEDICAL SPECIALTIES.   M0875

FUTURE

IN EXECUTIVE DEVELOPMENT . . . THE FUTURE IS NOW.   M0084

JAPAN'S LABOR ECONOMY -- PROSPECT FOR THE FUTURE.   M0123

MANAGERIAL STRATEGY FOR THE FUTURE: THEORY Z MANAGEMENT.   M0137

FUTURE ORIENTATION AND EXPECTATIONS AS PREDICTORS OF
EMPLOYMENT SUCCESS.   M0216

FUTURE ORIENTATION AND EXPECTATIONS AS PREDICTORS OF

GLAMOUR

TOUR ESCORTING -- GLAMOUR OR HARD WORK.   M0363

GOAL

CONSTRUCT VALIDATION OF AN INSTRUMENTALITY-EXPECTANCY-TASK-
GOAL MODEL OF WORK MOTIVATION: SOME THEORETICAL BOUNDARY
CONDITIONS.   M0082

SIMILARITY-DISSIMILARITY IN COUNSELOR-COUNSELEE ETHNIC
MATCH AND ITS RELEVANCE TO GOAL BEHAVIORS OF JOB TRAINEES.   M0189

PARTICIPATION WITH SUPERVISOR AND SUBORDINATE
AUTHORITARIANISM: A PATH GOAL THEORY RECONCILIATION.   M0554

FACTORS AFFECTING JOB ATTITUDE IN GOAL SETTING ENVIRONMENT.   M0556

EFFECTS OF GOAL SETTING ON PERFORMANCE AND JOB
SATISFACTION.   M0594

OPERATIONALIZING THE CONCEPTS OF GOALS AND GOAL
INCOMPATIBILITIES IN ORGANIZATIONAL BEHAVIOR RESEARCH.   M0595

REVIEW OF RESEARCH ON THE APPLICATION OF GOAL SETTING IN
ORGANIZATIONS.   M0657

EFFECTS OF VARYING GOAL TYPES AND INCENTIVE SYSTEMS ON
PERFORMANCE AND SATISFACTION.   M0659

IMPACT OF SUPERVISORY CHARACTERISTICS ON GOAL ACCEPTANCE.   M0661

THE MOTIVATIONAL COMPONENTS OF GOAL SETTING.   M0799

DIFFERENT GOAL SETTING TREATMENTS AND THEIR EFFECTS ON
PERFORMANCE AND JOB SATISFACTION.   M0819

AN EXPERIMENTAL STUDY OF THE EFFECTS OF GOAL SETTING,
EVALUATION APPREHENSION, AND SOCIAL CUES ON TASK
PERFORMANCE AND JOB SATISFACTION.   M0878

EFFECTS OF ASSIGNED AND PARTICIPATIVE GOAL SETTING ON
PERFORMANCE AND JOB SATISFACTION.   M0887

GOAL-SETTING

GOAL-SETTING ATTRIBUTES, PERSONALITY VARIABLES, AND JOB
SATISFACTION.   M0570

GOALS

MOTIVATIONAL AND PERSONALITY FACTORS RELATED TO CAREER
GOALS OF BLACK COLLEGE WOMEN.   M0310

DESEGREGATION AND CAREER GOALS. CHILDREN OF AIR FORCE
FAMILIES.   M0491

GOALS   CONTINUATION

OPERATIONALIZING THE CONCEPTS OF GOALS AND GOAL
INCOMPATIBILITIES IN ORGANIZATIONAL BEHAVIOR RESEARCH.   M0595

EFFECTS OF JOB ENRICHMENT AND TASK GOALS ON SATISFACTION
AND PRODUCTIVITY: IMPLICATIONS FOR JOB DESIGN.   M0619

SELECTED CHARACTERISTICS, ROLES, GOALS, AND SATISFACTIONS
OF DEPARTMENT CHAIRMEN IN STATE AND LAND-GRANT
INSTITUTIONS.   M0777

OLNEY CENTRAL COLLEGE DENTAL ASSISTING PROGRAM GRADUATES
PERCEPTIONS OF PROGRAM COMPONENTS, JOB SATISFACTION AND
CAREER GOALS.   M0944

GOD

MAN'S INHERENT REBELLION AGAINST GOD AND SATISFACTION.   M0248

GOODS

GOODS WELL BOUGHT ARE QUICKLY SOLD.   M0048

GOULD

REPORTED JOB INTEREST AND PERCEIVED UTILIZATION OF TALENTS
AND TRAINING BY AIRMEN IN 97 CAREER LADDERS, BY R. BRUCE
GOULD. PROJECT 7734, DECEMBER 1972.   M0452

GOVERNMENT

GOVERNMENT APPROACHES TO THE HUMANIZATION OF WORK.   M0205

PROGRESS IN MEASURING PRODUCTIVITY IN GOVERNMENT.   M0303

AN EXPERIMENTAL CASE STUDY OF THE SUCCESSES AND FAILURES OF
JOB ENRICHMENT IN A GOVERNMENT AGENCY.   M0600

CORPORATE MANAGEMENT IN LOCAL GOVERNMENT: A CASE STUDY.   M0769

GRADIENTS

RELATIVE STEEPNESS OF APPROACH AND AVOIDANCE GRADIENTS AS A
FUNCTION OF MAGNITUDE AND VALENCE OF INCENTIVE.   M0775

GRADS

TURBULENCE IN THE WORKING WORLD: ANGRY WORKERS, HAPPY
GRADS.   M0744

GRADUATES

DIMENSIONS OF THRESHOLD WORK EXPERIENCE FOR HIGH SCHOOL
GRADUATES AND DROPOUTS: A FACTOR ANALYSIS.   M0089

GRADUATES   CONTINUATION

   JOB PROSPECTS FOR COLLEGE GRADUATES IN 1974.   M0233

   JOB SATISFACTION AND EXPECTATIONS OF DISTRIBUTIVE EDUCATION
   GRADUATES.   M0905

   OLNEY CENTRAL COLLEGE DENTAL ASSISTING PROGRAM GRADUATES
   PERCEPTIONS OF PROGRAM COMPONENTS, JOB SATISFACTION AND
   CAREER GOALS.   M0944

GRAPHIC

   CONSENSUS MANAGEMENT AT GRAPHIC CONTROLS.   M0713

GREENER

   GREENER PASTURES: WHY EMPLOYEES CHANGE JOBS.   M0372

GREENLIGHT

   AN EXAMINATION OF BRAINSTORMING PROCEDURE, GROUP SIZE AND
   MOTIVATIONAL ORIENTATION IN THE JOB ENRICHMENT GREENLIGHT
   SESSION.   M0932

GROUP

   PROBLEM RESOLUTION AND IMPOSITION OF CHANGE THROUGH A
   PARTICIPATING GROUP EFFORT.   M0238

   WORKERS UNDER STRESS (THE IMPACT OF WORK PRESSURE ON GROUP
   COHESION).   M0255

   SKANDIA INSURANCE GROUP: RESTRUCTURING THE WORK AND
   ENRICHING THE JOB.   M0547

   LIFE STYLE, WORK GROUP STRUCTURE, COMPATIBILITY, AND JOB
   SATISFACTION.   M0651

   GROUP DEVELOPMENT, TRAINER STYLE AND CARRY-OVER JOB
   SATISFACTION AND PERFORMANCE.   M0653

   THE EFFECTS OF INDIVIDUAL-ROLE COMPATIBILITY UPON GROUP
   PERFORMANCE: AN EXTENSION OF SCHUTZ'S FIRO THEORY.   M0658

   DISCRIMINATION AND JOB SATISFACTION: AN EMPIRICAL STUDY
   WITH A SOUTH AFRICAN MINORITY GROUP.   M0733

   THE VOCATIONAL EXPLORATION GROUP AND MINORITY YOUTH: AN
   EXPERIMENTAL OUTCOME STUDY.   M0749

   JOB SATISFACTION AND NEED IMPORTANCE: RACE, SEX, AND
   OCCUPATIONAL GROUP.   M0860

   AN EXAMINATION OF BRAINSTORMING PROCEDURE, GROUP SIZE AND
   MOTIVATIONAL ORIENTATION IN THE JOB ENRICHMENT GREENLIGHT

GROUP   CONTINUATION

    SESSION.   M0932

    THE RELATIONSHIPS AMONG THE PERSONALITY TYPES, JOB
    SATISFACTIONS, AND JOB SPECIALTIES OF A SELECTED GROUP OF
    MEDICAL TECHNOLOGISTS.   M0945

GROUPS

    WORK GROUPS AND EMPLOYEE SATISFACTION.   M0004

    AN EVALUATION OF MOTIVATIONAL SIMILARITY IN WORK GROUPS.   M0033

    CONVERGENT AND DISCRIMINANT VALIDITIES OF PERFORMANCE
    EVALUATIONS IN EXTREMELY ISOLATED GROUPS.   M0180

    A STUDY OF ROLE CLARITY AND NEED FOR CLARITY FOR THREE
    OCCUPATIONAL GROUPS.   M0227

    INCENTIVE SCHEDULES, PRODUCTIVITY, AND SATISFACTION IN WORK
    GROUPS: A LABORATORY STUDY.   M0814

    THE RELATIONSHIPS BETWEEN THE TASK-HUMAN RELATIONS
    MOTIVATIONAL STRUCTURES OF INDIVIDUALS IN SMALL WORK GROUPS
    AND THEIR SATISFACTION WITH CO-WORKERS AND IMMEDIATE
    SUPERVISION.   M0868

GROWTH

    BUSINESS HEALTH--MENTAL HEALTH: GROWTH ALTERNATIVE TO
    INTERVENTION.   M0117

    GROWTH AND SATISFACTION OF EMPLOYEES IN ORGANIZATIONS.   M0825

    TASK OPPORTUNITY PROFESSIONAL GROWTH NEED FULFILLMENT AND
    INTRINSIC JOB SATISFACTION OF PUBLIC SOCIAL SERVICE WORKERS
    IN COLORADO.   M0923

GUIDANCE

    OCCUPATIONAL GUIDANCE MATERIALS FOR THE DISADVANTAGED: A
    PILOT PROGRAM.   M0404

GUIDE

    GUIDE TO PART-TIME WORK.   M0178

    POSITIVE PERSONAL MOTIVATION: THE MANAGER'S GUIDE TO
    INFLUENCING OTHERS.   M0208

GUIDELINES

    GUIDELINES FOR THE JOB ENRICHMENT PRACTITIONER.   M0538

HALF-LOAF

    THE HALF-LOAF OF JOB ENRICHMENT.   M0555

HALL

    CITY HALL DISCOVERS PRODUCTIVITY.   M0072

HAMPER

    DOES DIVORCE HAMPER JOB PERFORMANCE.   M0261

HANDICAPPED

    SOCIAL AND WELFARE PROGRAMS FOR THE HANDICAPPED ABROAD.   M0043

HARASSED

    THE HARASSED WORKER.   M0504

HARD

    THE PROFIT MOTIVE: CAN IT MOTIVATE INDUSTRY TO HIRE THE
    HARD CORE.   M0298

    MOTIVATION AND HARD TIMES.   M0355

    TOUR ESCORTING -- GLAMOUR OR HARD WORK.   M0363

    THE HARD CORE AND THE PURITIAN WORK ETHIC.   M0370

    THE WORLD OF WORK THROUGH THE EYES OF THE HARD CORE.   M0371

    MOTIVATED WORKERS AND HARD WORKERS.   M0479

HARD-CORE

    LONGITUDINAL STUDY OF ABSENTEEISM AND HARD-CORE UNEMPLOYED.   M0500

HAWTHORNE

    ON ALEX CAREY'S RADICAL CRITICISMS OF THE HAWTHORNE
    STUDIES.   M0391

HEADS

    INCREASING PROPORTION OF WOMEN ARE HEADS OF HOUSEHOLD.   M0224

    A COMPARATIVE STUDY OF TEACHERS' ATTITUDES TOWARD MEN AND
    WOMEN DEPARTMENT HEADS IN LARGE CITY SECONDARY SCHOOLS.   M0366

HEALTH

    THE EFFECTS OF AGING ON ENGINEERS' SATISFACTION AND MENTAL
    HEALTH: SKILL OBSOLESCENCE.   M0044

HEALTH   CONTINUATION

   BUSINESS HEALTH--MENTAL HEALTH: GROWTH ALTERNATIVE TO
   INTERVENTION.   M0117

   OCCUPATIONAL STRESS AND PHYSICAL HEALTH.   M0213

   INTEREST CONGRUENCY AS A MODERATOR OF THE RELATIONSHIPS
   BETWEEN JOB TENURE AND JOB SATISFACTION AND MENTAL HEALTH.   M0623

   THE MENTAL HEALTH ASSOCIATE: THE EFFECT OF SOCIAL
   ENVIRONMENTAL FACTORS ON JOB SATISFACTION.   M0697

   JOB INVOLVEMENT AND SATISFACTION AS RELATED TO MENTAL
   HEALTH AND PERSONAL TIME DEVOTED TO WORK.   M0718

   A NATIONAL STUDY OF ASSOCIATE DEGREE MENTAL HEALTH SERVICES
   WORKERS.   M0806

   OCCUPATIONAL MENTAL HEALTH AND THE HUMAN SERVICES: A
   REVIEW.   M0880

   PHYSICAL ENVIRONMENT AND JOB SATISFACTION IN A COMMUNITY
   MENTAL HEALTH CENTER.   M0883

HEALTH--MENTAL

   BUSINESS HEALTH--MENTAL HEALTH: GROWTH ALTERNATIVE TO
   INTERVENTION.   M0117

HEDONIC

   HEDONIC WAGE EQUATIONS AND PSYCHIC WAGES IN THE RETURNS TO
   SCHOOLING.   M0822

HELP

   HELP FOR THE WOMAN BREADWINNER.   M0096

   A PROFILE OF THE TEMPORARY HELP INDUSTRY AND ITS WORKERS.   M0148

   INCREASING PRODUCTIVITY: HOW BEHAVIORAL SCIENTISTS CAN
   HELP.   M0568

HELPLESSNESS

   LEARNED HELPLESSNESS: THEORY AND EVIDENCE.   M0776

HERZBERG

   DEFENSE MECHANISMS AND THE HERZBERG THEORY: AN ALTERNATE
   TEST.   M0334

HERZBERG'S

   DOES HERZBERG'S THEORY REALLY WORK.   M0081

HOMEMAKER

ANALYZING THE HOMEMAKER JOB USING THE POSITION ANALYSIS
QUESTIONNAIRE.   M0497

SATISFACTION IN THE HOMEMAKER JOB.   M0879

HOMEMAKERS

SATISFACTION WITH TRAINING AND GENERAL JOB SATISFACTION OF
AGENCY HOMEMAKERS WORKING WITH THE ELDERLY AND DISABLED.   M0904

HOSPITAL

AN EXPLORATORY INVESTIGATION OF ORGANIZATIONAL CLIMATE AND
JOB SATISFACTION IN A HOSPITAL.   M0286

INDIVIDUAL AND ENVIRONMENTAL FACTORS ASSOCIATED WITH THE
JOB SATISFACTION AND RETENTION OF NAVY HOSPITAL CORPSMEN
SERVING WITH THE U.S. MARINE CORPS.   M0574

LEADER STRUCTURE AND SUBORDINATE SATISFACTION FOR TWO
HOSPITAL ADMINISTRATIVE LEVELS: A PATH ANALYSIS APPROACH.   M0736

HOURLY

DIFFERENCES IN HOURLY EARNINGS BETWEEN MEN AND WOMEN.   M0104

HOURS

RECENT TRENDS IN OVERTIME HOURS AND PREMIUM PAY.   M0130

THE EFFECT OF FLEXIBLE WORKING HOURS ON ABSENTEEISM AND JOB
SATISFACTION AND THE RELATIONSHIP BETWEEN LOCUS OF CONTROL
AND UTILITY OF FLEXIBLE WORKING HOURS.   M0943

HOUSEHOLD

INCREASING PROPORTION OF WOMEN ARE HEADS OF HOUSEHOLD.   M0224

HUD

THE FEDERAL WOMEN'S PROGRAM: A HUD PERSPECTIVE.   M0348

HUMAN

PERSONNEL SYSTEMS AND HUMAN PERFORMANCE.   M0024

A MARKOV CHAIN MODEL OF HUMAN NEEDS.   M0057

MOTIVATING HUMAN BEHAVIOR.   M0102

BACKGROUND CHARACTERISTICS, ORIENTATION, WORK EXPERIENCE,
AND WORK VALUES OF EMPLOYEES HIRED FROM HUMAN RESOURCES
DEVELOPMENT APPLICANTS BY COMPANIES AFFILIATED WITH THE
NATIONAL ALLIANCE OF BUSINESSMAN.   M0165

IMPROVEMENT

IMPROVEMENTS

INCENTIVE

INCENTIVES

INCOME

INCOMPATIBILITIES

INCREASED

INCREASES

VOLVO INCREASES PRODUCTIVITY THROUGH JOB ENRICHMENT.   M0155

INCREASING

INCREASING PRODUCTIVITY BY INVOLVING PEOPLE IN THEIR TOTAL
JOB.   M0107

INCREASING PROPORTION OF WOMEN ARE HEADS OF HOUSEHOLD.   M0224

JOB ENLARGEMENT -- THE KEY TO INCREASING JOB SATISFACTION.   M0384

INCREASING THE IMPORTANCE OF PERSONNEL: A STRATEGY.   M0549

INCREASING PRODUCTIVITY: HOW BEHAVIORAL SCIENTISTS CAN
HELP.   M0568

INDEX

VALIDATION OF THE INDEX OF ORGANIZATIONAL REACTIONS WITH
THE JDI, THE MSQ, AND FACES SCALES.   M0813

INDIAN

A NETWORK ANALYSIS OF A BUREAU OF INDIAN AFFAIRS SCHOOL
SYSTEM TO DETERMINE FACTORS INVOLVED IN JOB SATISFACTION.   M0934

INDICATORS

WORKING CONDITIONS SURVEY AS A SOURCE OF SOCIAL INDICATORS.   M0206

INDIRECT

THE IMPACT OF PERFORMANCE-CONTINGENT REWARDS ON JOB
SATISFACTION: DIRECT AND INDIRECT EFFECTS.   M0686

INDIVIDUAL

LET'S PUT MOTIVATION WHERE IT BELONGS -- WITHIN THE
INDIVIDUAL.   M0003

RELATION OF COLLABORATIVE INTERPERSONAL RELATIONSHIPS TO
INDIVIDUAL SATISFACTION AND ORGANIZATIONAL PERFORMANCE.   M0013

ORGANIZATIONAL AND INDIVIDUAL RESPONSE TO EXTERNAL STRESS.   M0184

INDIVIDUAL NEED SATISFACTION IN WORK AND NONWORK.   M0218

INDIVIDUAL REACTIONS TO ORGANIZATIONAL CONFLICT AND CHANGE.   M0311

RELEVANCE OF MOTIVATIONAL CONCEPTS TO INDIVIDUAL AND
CORPORATE OBJECTIVES.   M0331

MODEL PROGRAM TO INSTRUCT MANPOWER TRAINING PERSONNEL IN
SELECTION AND APPLICATION OF REMEDIAL INSTRUCTIONAL

INDIVIDUAL   CONTINUATION

    MATERIALS TO MEET INDIVIDUAL TRAINEE NEEDS.   M0387

    AN APPLICATION OF INFORMATION THEORY TO INDIVIDUAL WORKER
    DIFFERENCES IN SATISFACTION WITH WORK ITSELF.   M0416

    INDIVIDUAL DIFFERENCES IN WORK SATISFACTION.   M0417

    JOB ENLARGEMENT, INDIVIDUAL DIFFERENCES, AND WORKER
    RESPONSES: A TEST WITH BLACK WORKERS IN SOUTH AFRICA.   M0546

    INDIVIDUAL AND ENVIRONMENTAL FACTORS ASSOCIATED WITH THE
    JOB SATISFACTION AND RETENTION OF NAVY HOSPITAL CORPSMEN
    SERVING WITH THE U.S. MARINE CORPS.   M0574

    JOB LEVEL, INDIVIDUAL DIFFERENCES, AND JOB SATISFACTION: AN
    INTERACTIVE APPROACH.   M0691

    PERSONALITY-JOB FIT: IMPLICATIONS FOR INDIVIDUAL ATTITUDES
    AND PERFORMANCE.   M0829

    TASKS, INDIVIDUAL DIFFERENCES, AND JOB SATISFACTION.   M0841

    JOB CHARACTERISTICS RELATIONSHIPS: INDIVIDUAL AND
    STRUCTURAL MODERATORS.   M0896

    CAREER COMMITMENT: AN ANALYSIS OF SELECTED INDIVIDUAL, JOB
    AND ORGANIZATIONAL FACTORS AS RELATED TO SATISFACTION AND
    COMMITMENT OF MIDDLE LEVEL ARMY OFFICERS.   M0912

    PERCEPTIONS OF ORGANIZATIONAL CLIMATE AS MEDIATORS OF THE
    RELATIONSHIPS BETWEEN INDIVIDUAL NEEDS AND JOB SATISFACTION
    OF COUNSELORS IN THE NORTH CAROLINA COMMUNITY COLLEGE
    SYSTEM.   M0933

    AN INVESTIGATION OF THE RELATIONSHIP BETWEEN INTRINSIC AND
    EXTRINSIC JOB INSTRUMENTALITY EFFORT, JOB SATISFACTION,
    INDIVIDUAL AND PERCEIVED TASK CHARACTERISTICS.   M0938

    AN EMPIRICAL STUDY OF INDIVIDUAL CONGRUENCE AND THE
    PERCEIVED ORGANIZATIONAL PRACTICES - JOB SATISFACTION - JOB
    PERFORMANCE RELATIONSHIP IN SELECTED ELECTRONIC COMPUTER
    DATA PROCESSING CENTERS.   M0946

INDIVIDUAL-ROLE

    THE EFFECTS OF INDIVIDUAL-ROLE COMPATIBILITY UPON GROUP
    PERFORMANCE: AN EXTENSION OF SCHUTZ'S FIRO THEORY.   M0658

INDIVIDUALS

    THE RELATIONSHIPS BETWEEN THE TASK-HUMAN RELATIONS
    MOTIVATIONAL STRUCTURES OF INDIVIDUALS IN SMALL WORK GROUPS
    AND THEIR SATISFACTION WITH CO-WORKERS AND IMMEDIATE
    SUPERVISION.   M0868

INDIVIDUALS'

CONGRUENCE BETWEEN INDIVIDUALS' NEEDS, ORGANIZATIONAL
CLIMATE, JOB SATISFACTION AND PERFORMANCE.   M0110

INDUSTRIAL

WORK AND WORK MOTIVATION IN AN AUTOMATED INDUSTRIAL
PRODUCTION-PROCESS.   M0042

PSYCHOLOGY IN THE INDUSTRIAL ENVIRONMENT.   M0129

DOES THE INDUSTRIAL ENGINEER DEHUMANIZE JOBS.   M0136

A COMPARATIVE ANALYSIS OF THE JOB SATISFACTION OF
INDUSTRIAL MANAGERS AND CERTIFIED PUBLIC ACCOUNTANTS.   M0228

INDUSTRIAL AND ORGANIZATIONAL PSYCHOLOGY.   M0259

PSYCHOLOGY IN INDUSTRIAL ORGANIZATIONS.   M0296

INDUSTRIAL AND ORGANIZATIONAL PSYCHOLOGY.   M0460

VALUES, STRUCTURE, PROCESS, AND REACTIONS/ADJUSTMENTS: A
COMPARISON OF FRENCH   AND ENGLISH-CANADIAN INDUSTRIAL
ORGANIZATIONS.   M0628

BEHAVIORAL TRAINING OF SUPERVISORS IN AN INDUSTRIAL SETTING
FOR THE BLIND.   M0846

INDUSTRIES

RAPID PRODUCTIVITY GAINS REPORTED FOR SELECTED INDUSTRIES
FOR 1971.   M0201

INCENTIVE PAY IN MANUFACTURING INDUSTRIES.   M0223

INDUSTRY

INCENTIVE PAY PATTERNS IN THE STEEL INDUSTRY.   M0046

PRODUCTIVITY IN THE PETROLEUM PIPELINES INDUSTRY.   M0126

A STUDY OF BLACK MALE PROFESSIONALS IN INDUSTRY.   M0143

A PROFILE OF THE TEMPORARY HELP INDUSTRY AND ITS WORKERS.   M0148

THE PROFIT MOTIVE: CAN IT MOTIVATE INDUSTRY TO HIRE THE
HARD CORE.   M0298

CONTINUING EDUCATION IN INDUSTRY.   M0320

COMPARING MUNICIPAL, INDUSTRY, AND FEDERAL PAY.   M0344

WHERE WOMEN WORK -- AN ANALYSIS BY INDUSTRY AND OCCUPATION. M0464

INDUSTRY CONTINUATION

WOMEN IN INDUSTRY: ALIENATION, SATISFACTION, AND CHANGE. M0699

INFERENCE

AN EMPIRICAL TEST OF CAUSAL INFERENCE BETWEEN ROLE
PERCEPTIONS, SATISFACTION WITH WORK, PERFORMANCE AND
ORGANIZATIONAL LEVEL. M0839

INFERENCES

LONGITUDINAL INFERENCES OF JOB ATTITUDE AND TENURE
RELATIONSHIPS FROM CROSS-SECTIONAL DATA. M0591

INFLUENCE

INFLUENCE STYLES OF PROJECT MANAGERS: SOME PROJECT
PERFORMANCE CORRELATES. M0151

SELF-ESTEEM AS AN INFLUENCE ON OCCUPATIONAL CHOICE AND
OCCUPATIONAL SATISFACTION. M0174

ORGANIZATION STRESS AS A MODERATOR OF THE RELATIONSHIP
BETWEEN INFLUENCE AND ROLE RESPONSE. M0444

ORGANIZATIONAL STRUCTURE: HOW DOES IT INFLUENCE ATTITUDES
AND PERFORMANCE. M0578

REACTIONS AT WORK AND THEIR INFLUENCE ON NON-WORK
ACTIVITIES: AN ANALYSIS OF A SOCIOPOLITICAL PROBLEM IN
AFFLUENT SOCIETIES. M0587

INVESTIGATION OF THE INFLUENCE OF JOB LEVEL AND FUNCTIONAL
SPECIALTY ON JOB ATTITUDES AND PERCEPTIONS. M0745

RELATIONSHIP OF PERSONAL INFLUENCE DISSONANCE TO JOB
TENSION SATISFACTION AND INVOLVEMENT. M0817

SEGREGATION AND JOB SATISFACTION IN THE WORK PLACE: THE
MEASUREMENT OF RACIAL DISPARITIES IN ORGANIZATIONS AND
THEIR INFLUENCE ON EMPLOYEE WORK ATTITUDES. M0927

INFLUENCES

SOME MODERATOR INFLUENCES ON RELATIONSHIPS BETWEEN
CONSIDERATION, INITIATING STRUCTURE, AND ORGANIZATION
CRITERIA. M0021

PSCHOPHYSIOLOGICAL INFLUENCES ON THE WORK ENVIRONMENT: NEW
CONCEPTS. M0550

INFLUENCES ON THE FELT NEED FOR COLLECTIVE BARGAINING BY
BUSINESS AND SCIENCE PROFESSIONALS. M0572

SOCIAL AND PSYCHOLOGICAL INFLUENCES ON EMPLOYMENT OF

INFLUENCES   CONTINUATION

   MARRIED NURSES.   M0755

INFLUENCING

   POSITIVE PERSONAL MOTIVATION: THE MANAGER'S GUIDE TO
   INFLUENCING OTHERS.   M0208

   FOUR FACTORS INFLUENCING CONVERSION TO A FOUR-DAY WORK
   WEEK.   M0687

INFORMAL

   INFORMAL HELPING RELATIONSHIPS IN WORK ORGANIZATIONS.   M0650

INFORMATION

   QUESTIONNAIRE PROVIDES INFORMATION ON JOB OPPORTUNITIES FOR
   FS WIVES OVERSEAS.   M0015

   THE OCCUPATIONAL INFORMATION CENTER: WHERE ATLANTA
   EMPLOYERS AND EDUCATORS MEET.   M0237

   INFORMATION SHARING FOR PRODUCTIVITY IMPROVEMENT.   M0352

   AN APPLICATION OF INFORMATION THEORY TO INDIVIDUAL WORKER
   DIFFERENCES IN SATISFACTION WITH WORK ITSELF.   M0416

   INFORMATION INTEGRATION THEORY APPLIED TO EXPECTED JOB
   ATTRACTIVENESS AND SATISFACTION.   M0793

   EMPLOYEE INFORMATION ENVIRONMENTS AND JOB SATISFACTION: A
   CLOSER LOOK.   M0854

INGREDIENTS

   SOME INGREDIENTS FOR MAKING IT.   M0406

INHERENT

   MAN'S INHERENT REBELLION AGAINST GOD AND SATISFACTION.   M0248

INITIAL

   SATISFACTION WITH PERFORMANCE AS A FUNCTION OF THE INITIAL
   LEVEL OF EXPECTED PERFORMANCE AND THE DEVIATION FROM
   EXPECTATIONS.   M0221

   DIMENSIONS OF JOB SATISFACTION: INITIAL DEVELOPMENT OF THE
   AIR FORCE OCCUPATIONAL ATTITUDE INVENTORY.   M0802

INITIATING

   SOME MODERATOR INFLUENCES ON RELATIONSHIPS BETWEEN
   CONSIDERATION, INITIATING STRUCTURE, AND ORGANIZATION

INITIATING   CONTINUATION

   CRITERIA.   M0021

INITIATIVE

   ENCOURAGEMENT OF EMPLOYEE CREATIVITY AND INITIATIVE.   M0527

INNER

   INNER DIRECTION, OTHER DIRECTION AND ACHIEVEMENT
   MOTIVATION.   M0726

INNOVATION

   WHEN DOES WORK RESTRUCTURING WORK? ORGANIZATIONAL
   INNOVATION AT VOLVO AND GM.   M0740

INSPECTOR

   THE INSPECTOR IS A LADY.   M0225

INSTANT

   H.I.T. ON TARGET WITH INSTANT UPGRADING.   M0262

INSTILLING

   INSTILLING APPREHENSION DELICATELY AND OTHER MOTIVATORS.   M0017

INSTITUTION

   EMPLOYEE ATTITUDES REGARDING VARIOUS CHARACTERISTICS OF JOB
   OPPORTUNITY AND JOB PERFORMANCE ACROSS THREE DIFFERENT WORK
   SHIFTS AT AN INSTITUTION FOR THE RETARDED.   M0900

INSTITUTIONAL

   A COMPARISON OF PROFESSIONAL INSTITUTIONAL COMMUNITY
   CORRECTIONS WORKERS ON JOB SATISFACTION AND SELF-CONCEPT.   M0696

INSTITUTIONS

   SELECTED CHARACTERISTICS, ROLES, GOALS, AND SATISFACTIONS
   OF DEPARTMENT CHAIRMEN IN STATE AND LAND-GRANT
   INSTITUTIONS.   M0777

INSTRUCT

   MODEL PROGRAM TO INSTRUCT MANPOWER TRAINING PERSONNEL IN
   SELECTION AND APPLICATION OF REMEDIAL INSTRUCTIONAL
   MATERIALS TO MEET INDIVIDUAL TRAINEE NEEDS.   M0387

INSTRUCTIONAL

   MODEL PROGRAM TO INSTRUCT MANPOWER TRAINING PERSONNEL IN

INSTRUCTIONAL   CONTINUATION

SELECTION AND APPLICATION OF REMEDIAL INSTRUCTIONAL
MATERIALS TO MEET INDIVIDUAL TRAINEE NEEDS.   M0387

INSTRUMENTALITY

INSTRUMENTALITY THEORY PREDICTIONS OF EXPERIENCED AND
ANTICIPATED JOB SATISFACTION.   M0858

AN INVESTIGATION OF THE RELATIONSHIP BETWEEN INTRINSIC AND
EXTRINSIC JOB INSTRUMENTALITY EFFORT, JOB SATISFACTION,
INDIVIDUAL AND PERCEIVED TASK CHARACTERISTICS.   M0938

INSTRUMENTALITY-EXPECTANCY-TASK-

CONSTRUCT VALIDATION OF AN INSTRUMENTALITY-EXPECTANCY-TASK-
GOAL MODEL OF WORK MOTIVATION: SOME THEORETICAL BOUNDARY
CONDITIONS.   M0082

INSURANCE

INSURANCE ADJUSTERS AND EXAMINERS.   M0101

SKANDIA INSURANCE GROUP: RESTRUCTURING THE WORK AND
ENRICHING THE JOB.   M0547

INTEGRATED

WORKER PRODUCTIVITY: AN INTEGRATED VIEW.   M0177

INTEGRATION

JOB CHARACTERISTICS AND PRESSURES AND THE ORGANIZATIONAL
INTEGRATION OF PROFESSIONALS.   M0268

MOTIVATION AND PARTICIPATION: AN INTEGRATION.   M0318

INFORMATION INTEGRATION THEORY APPLIED TO EXPECTED JOB
ATTRACTIVENESS AND SATISFACTION.   M0793

JOB SATISFACTION: A POSSIBLE INTEGRATION OF TWO THEORIES.   M0886

PARTICIPATIVE AND POWER-EQUALIZED ORGANIZATIONAL SYSTEMS:
AN EMPIRICAL INVESTIGATION AND THEORETICAL INTEGRATION.   M0889

INTERACTION

FACE-TO-FACE INTERACTION IN THE PEER-NOMINATION PROCESS.   M0281

INTERACTION EFFECTS OF PERSONALITY, JOB TRAINING, AND LABOR
MARKET CONDITIONS ON PERSONAL EMPLOYMENT AND INCOME.   M0305

INTERACTION MODELING: A NEW CONCEPT IN SUPERVISORY
TRAINING.   M0507

INTERACTION   CONTINUATION

    WORK SATISFACTION AS A FUNCTION OF THE PERSON-ENVIRONMENT
    INTERACTION.   M0836

INTERACTIVE

    JOB LEVEL, INDIVIDUAL DIFFERENCES, AND JOB SATISFACTION: AN
    INTERACTIVE APPROACH.   M0691

    TWO INTERACTIVE PERSPECTIVES ON THE RELATIONSHIP BETWEEN
    JOB LEVEL AND JOB SATISFACTION.   M0823

INTEREST

    MANAGERS INTEREST IN WORK.   M0034

    ANALYSIS OF RACIAL DIFFERENCES IN TERMS OF WORK
    ASSIGNMENTS, JOB INTEREST, AND FELT UTILIZATION OF TALENTS
    AND TRAINING, BY RAYMOND E. CHRISTEL.   M0451

    REPORTED JOB INTEREST AND PERCEIVED UTILIZATION OF TALENTS
    AND TRAINING BY AIRMEN IN 97 CAREER LADDERS, BY R. BRUCE
    GOULD. PROJECT 7734, DECEMBER 1972.   M0452

    PRODUCTIVITY AND THE NATIONAL INTEREST.   M0456

    A DEFINITIONAL CHALLENGE: INTEREST AND WORK ITSELF
    SATISFACTIONS.   M0543

    INTEREST CONGRUENCY AS A MODERATOR OF THE RELATIONSHIPS
    BETWEEN JOB TENURE AND JOB SATISFACTION AND MENTAL HEALTH.   M0623

    IS WORK THE CENTRAL LIFE INTEREST? NOT FOR MOST PEOPLE --
    FINDING THE COMMITED FEW.   M0826

INTERESTS

    SELF-CONCEPT AND INTERESTS RELATED TO JOB SATISFACTION OF
    MANAGERS.   M0109

    CENTRAL LIFE INTERESTS AND JOB SATISFACTION.   M0812

INTERGROUP

    INTERGROUP CLIMATE ATTAINMENT, SATISFACTION, AND URGENCY.   M0705

INTERMEDIATE

    INTERMEDIATE LINKAGES IN THE RELATIONSHIP BETWEEN JOB
    SATISFACTION AND EMPLOYEE TURNOVER.   M0781

INTERNAL

    PERSONAL CAUSATION: THE INTERNAL EFFECTIVE DETERMINANTS OF
    BEHAVIOR.   M0090

INTERNAL   CONTINUATION

THE MODERATING EFFECTS OF INTERNAL VERSUS EXTERNAL CONTROL
ON THE RELATIONSHIP BETWEEN VARIOUS ASPECTS OF JOB
SATISFACTION.   M0122

CAN INTERNAL AUDITORS FIND JOB SATISFACTION?   M0840

INTERNAL VERSUS EXTERNAL LOCUS OF CONTROL AND JOB
SATISFACTION IN IRAN.   M0851

INTERORGANIZATIONAL

INTERORGANIZATIONAL RELATIONSHIPS: PATTERNS AND
MOTIVATIONS.   M0674

INTERPERSONAL

RELATION OF COLLABORATIVE INTERPERSONAL RELATIONSHIPS TO
INDIVIDUAL SATISFACTION AND ORGANIZATIONAL PERFORMANCE.   M0013

MANAGEMENT STYLES ASSOCIATED WITH ORGANIZATIONAL, TASK,
PERSONAL, AND INTERPERSONAL CONTINGENCIES.   M0748

INTERPRETATION

ANTECEDENTS OF SALESMEN'S COMPENSATION PERCEPTIONS: A PATH
ANALYSIS INTERPRETATION.   M0785

INTERRELATIONSHIP

THE INTERRELATIONSHIP OF INTRINSIC AND EXTRINSIC
MOTIVATION.   M0093

INTERSTATE

ASSESSMENT OF EXPERIMENTAL AND DEMONSTRATION INTERSTATE
PROGRAM FOR SOUTH TEXAS MIGRANT WORKERS.   M0001

INTERVENTION

RESEARCH, INTERVENTION, AND EXPERIENCE IN ENHANCING THE
QUALITY OF WORKING LIFE.   M0088

BUSINESS HEALTH--MENTAL HEALTH: GROWTH ALTERNATIVE TO
INTERVENTION.   M0117

INTERVIEW

SUBORDINATE PARTICIPATION AND REACTIONS TO THE APPRAISAL
INTERVIEW.   M0760

INTRAROLE

INTRAROLE CONFLICT AND JOB SATISFACTION ON PSYCHIATRIC
UNITS.   M0712

INVISIBLE

INVOLVED

INVOLVEMENT

INVOLVING

IRAN

ISOLATED

ISOLATION

JOB   CONTINUATION

JOB   CONTINUATION

JOB   CONTINUATION

JOB CONTINUATION

JOB   CONTINUATION

JOB CONTINUATION

JOB   CONTINUATION

EXPECTANCY THEORY AS A PREDICTOR OF WORK MOTIVATION, EFFORT
EXPENDITURE, AND JOB PERFORMANCE.   M0663

JOB INVOLVEMENT, VALUES, PERSONAL BACKGROUND, PARTICIPATION
IN DECISION MAKING, AND JOB ATTITUDES.   M0664

JOB ORIENTATION AND WORK BEHAVIOR.   M0665

AN EXAMINATION OF NEED-SATISFACTION MODELS OF JOB
ATTITUDES.   M0673

THE IMPACT OF PERFORMANCE-CONTINGENT REWARDS ON JOB
SATISFACTION: DIRECT AND INDIRECT EFFECTS.   M0686

SATISFACTION WITH YOUR JOB: A LIFE-TIME CONCERN.   M0689

WORK VALUES, JOB REWARDS AND JOB SATISFACTION: A THEORY OF
THE QUALITY OF WORK EXPERIENCE.   M0690

JOB LEVEL, INDIVIDUAL DIFFERENCES, AND JOB SATISFACTION: AN
INTERACTIVE APPROACH.   M0691

A COMPARISON OF PROFESSIONAL INSTITUTIONAL COMMUNITY
CORRECTIONS WORKERS ON JOB SATISFACTION AND SELF-CONCEPT.   M0696

THE MENTAL HEALTH ASSOCIATE: THE EFFECT OF SOCIAL
ENVIRONMENTAL FACTORS ON JOB SATISFACTION.   M0697

JOB STRAIN AS A FUNCTION OF JOB LIFE AND STRESSES.   M0698

JOB ATTITUDES OF STUDENT PERSONNEL WORKERS AND THEIR JOB
SITUATIONS.   M0707

COMMUNITY COLLEGE FACULTY JOB SATISFACTION.   M0708

INTRAROLE CONFLICT AND JOB SATISFACTION ON PSYCHIATRIC
UNITS.   M0712

RACIAL DIFFERENCES IN JOB ATTITUDES AND PERFORMANCE: SOME
THEORETICAL CONSIDERATIONS AND EMPIRICAL FINDINGS.   M0717

JOB INVOLVEMENT AND SATISFACTION AS RELATED TO MENTAL
HEALTH AND PERSONAL TIME DEVOTED TO WORK.   M0718

AN APPLICATION OF JOB ENRICHMENT IN A CIVIL SERVICE
SETTING: A DEMONSTRATION STUDY.   M0719

DEVELOPMENT OF THE JOB DIAGNOSTIC SURVEY.   M0723

DISCRIMINATION AND JOB SATISFACTION: AN EMPIRICAL STUDY
WITH A SOUTH AFRICAN MINORITY GROUP.   M0733

SOME RELATIONSHIPS BETWEEN JOB SATISFACTION AND
ORGANIZATION CLIMATE.   M0734

JOB   CONTINUATION

RELATIONSHIP OF PERSONAL INFLUENCE DISSONANCE TO JOB
TENSION SATISFACTION AND INVOLVEMENT.   M0817

ROLE OF JOB SATISFACTION IN ABSENCE BEHAVIOR.   M0818

DIFFERENT GOAL SETTING TREATMENTS AND THEIR EFFECTS ON
PERFORMANCE AND JOB SATISFACTION.   M0819

BLACK-WHITE DIFFERENCES IN WORK ENVIRONMENT PERCEPTIONS AND
JOB SATISFACTION AND ITS CORRELATES.   M0820

LOCAL FIRM AND JOB SATISFACTION.   M0821

TWO INTERACTIVE PERSPECTIVES ON THE RELATIONSHIP BETWEEN
JOB LEVEL AND JOB SATISFACTION.   M0823

TOWARD A CAREER-BASED THEORY OF JOB INVOLVEMENT: A STUDY OF
SCIENTISTS AND ENGINEERS.   M0824

ORGANIZATIONAL COMMUNICATION: RELATIONSHIPS TO
ORGANIZATIONAL CLIMATE AND JOB SATISFACTION.   M0827

JOB SATISFACTION AND THE PD MANAGER: AN EMPIRICAL
ASSESSMENT.   M0831

TECHNOLOGICAL DIFFERENCES IN JOB CHARACTERISTICS, EMPLOYEE
SATISFACTION, AND MOTIVATION: A SYNTHESIS OF JOB DESIGN
RESOURCE AND SOCIOTECHNICAL SYSTEMS THEORY.   M0832

WHY STUDY WORKING CONDITIONS VIA JOB SATISFACTION? A PLEA
FOR DIRECT ANALYSIS.   M0833

JOB INVOLVEMENT: CONCEPTS AND MEASUREMENTS.   M0834

TEN YEAR JOB SATISFACTION TRENDS IN A STABLE ORGANIZATION.   M0837

CAN INTERNAL AUDITORS FIND JOB SATISFACTION?   M0840

TASKS, INDIVIDUAL DIFFERENCES, AND JOB SATISFACTION.   M0841

RELATIONSHIPS AMONG PAY, RACE, SEX, OCCUPATIONAL PRESTIGE,
SUPERVISION, WORK AUTONOMY, AND JOB SATISFACTION IN A
NATIONAL SAMPLE.   M0842

JOB SATISFACTION AND THE QUALITY OF WORKING LIFE: THE
POLISH EXPERIENCE.   M0844

INTERNAL VERSUS EXTERNAL LOCUS OF CONTROL AND JOB
SATISFACTION IN IRAN.   M0851

THE RELATIONSHIP OF JOB SATISFACTION MEASURES TO
SELF-REPORT AND OBJECTIVE CRITERIA MEASURES AND THE EFFECT
OF MODERATOR VARIABLES FOR CANADIAN MILITARY PERSONNEL.   M0853

JOB   CONTINUATION

JOB   CONTINUATION

SHIFTS AT AN INSTITUTION FOR THE RETARDED.   M0900

AN INVESTIGATION OF EDUCATIONAL ADMINISTRATIVE STYLE AND
JOB SATISFACTION OF ELEMENTARY SCHOOL PRINCIPALS.   M0901

A STUDY OF THE JOB SATISFACTION AND JOB PERCEPTION OF
ORGANIZED AND NON-ORGANIZED PUBLIC SCHOOL PRINCIPALS.   M0902

THE RELATIONSHIP BETWEEN JOB SATISFACTION AND LIFE
SATISFACTION: AN EMPIRICAL TEST OF THREE MODELS ON A
NATIONAL SAMPLE.   M0903

SATISFACTION WITH TRAINING AND GENERAL JOB SATISFACTION OF
AGENCY HOMEMAKERS WORKING WITH THE ELDERLY AND DISABLED.   M0904

JOB SATISFACTION AND EXPECTATIONS OF DISTRIBUTIVE EDUCATION
GRADUATES.   M0905

JOB SATISFACTION OF GEORGIA SCHOOL SUPERINTENDENTS AND
THEIR PERCEPTION OF THE LOCAL SCHOOL BOARD PRESIDENT'S
LEADER BEHAVIOR.   M0906

JOB SATISFACTION OF COLLEGE PRESIDENTS.   M0907

A STUDY OF THE RELATIONSHIP AMONG (1) JOB SATISFACTION AND
(2) TEACHER ATTITUDE.   M0908

THE JOB SATISFACTION OF SCHOOL TEACHERS IN THE REPUBLIC OF
CHINA AS RELATED TO PERSONAL AND ORGANIZATIONAL
CHARACTERISTICS.   M0909

A STUDY OF JOB SATISFACTION OF ADMINISTRATORS AT UNITED
METHODIST RELATED CHURCHES.   M0910

AN ANALYSIS OF JOB SATISFACTION AMONG ELEMENTARY, MIDDLE
LEVEL, AND SENIOR HIGH SCHOOL TEACHERS.   M0911

CAREER COMMITMENT: AN ANALYSIS OF SELECTED INDIVIDUAL, JOB
AND ORGANIZATIONAL FACTORS AS RELATED TO SATISFACTION AND
COMMITMENT OF MIDDLE LEVEL ARMY OFFICERS.   M0912

A CAUSAL MODEL OF JOB SATISFACTION.   M0915

THE IMPACT OF COLLECTIVE BARGAINING ON JOB SATISFACTION.   M0916

WORK VALUES AND JOB SATISFACTION OF PSYCHIATRIC AIDES.   M0917

A NORMATIVE STUDY OF THE SECONDARY SCHOOL ASSISTANT
PRINCIPALSHIP IN SELECTED PENNSYLVANIA SCHOOL DISTRICTS
WITH AN EMPHASIS UPON JOB SATISFACTION.   M0918

JOB SATISFACTION, JOB CHARACTERISTICS, AND OCCUPATIONAL
LEVEL.   M0919

JOB   CONTINUATION

A REGIONAL STUDY OF THE JOB SATISFACTION OF SOCIAL WORKERS.   M0920

RELATIONSHIPS BETWEEN JOB SATISFACTION, DEMOGRAPHIC
FACTORS, ABSENTEEISM AND TENURE OF WORKERS IN A DELMARVA
BROILER PROCESSING PLANT.   M0921

OPEN SPACE ELEMENTARY SCHOOL: EFFECTS ON TEACHERS' JOB
SATISFACTION, PARTICIPATION IN CURRICULUM DECISION-MAKING,
AND PERCEIVED SCHOOL EFFECTIVENESS.   M0922

TASK OPPORTUNITY PROFESSIONAL GROWTH NEED FULFILLMENT AND
INTRINSIC JOB SATISFACTION OF PUBLIC SOCIAL SERVICE WORKERS
IN COLORADO.   M0923

SECOND CAREER CATHOLIC PRIESTS: A STUDY OF THEIR LEVEL OF
JOB SATISFACTION, MATURITY, AND MORALE.   M0924

A STUDY OF THE PERCEPTIONS OF SELECTED SCHOOL-BASED
ADMINISTRATORS IN FLORIDA RELATIVE TO CERTAIN VARIABLES IN
SECONDARY SCHOOL ADMINISTRATION AS THEY RELATE TO JOB
SATISFACTION.   M0925

SEGREGATION AND JOB SATISFACTION IN THE WORK PLACE: THE
MEASUREMENT OF RACIAL DISPARITIES IN ORGANIZATIONS AND
THEIR INFLUENCE ON EMPLOYEE WORK ATTITUDES.   M0927

RELATIONSHIPS BETWEEN WORK VALUES AND JOB SATISFACTION
AMONG COLLEGE STUDENT PERSONNEL WORKERS.   M0928

AN EXAMINATION OF BRAINSTORMING PROCEDURE, GROUP SIZE AND
MOTIVATIONAL ORIENTATION IN THE JOB ENRICHMENT GREENLIGHT
SESSION.   M0932

PERCEPTIONS OF ORGANIZATIONAL CLIMATE AS MEDIATORS OF THE
RELATIONSHIPS BETWEEN INDIVIDUAL NEEDS AND JOB SATISFACTION
OF COUNSELORS IN THE NORTH CAROLINA COMMUNITY COLLEGE
SYSTEM.   M0933

A NETWORK ANALYSIS OF A BUREAU OF INDIAN AFFAIRS SCHOOL
SYSTEM TO DETERMINE FACTORS INVOLVED IN JOB SATISFACTION.   M0934

THE RELATIONSHIP OF LEADERSHIP STYLE TO EMPLOYEE JOB
SATISFACTION.   M0935

JOB SATISFACTION AND LEADER BEHAVIOR OF ADULT EDUCATION
ADMINISTRATORS.   M0936

AN INVESTIGATION OF THE RELATIONSHIP BETWEEN INTRINSIC AND
EXTRINSIC JOB INSTRUMENTALITY EFFORT, JOB SATISFACTION,
INDIVIDUAL AND PERCEIVED TASK CHARACTERISTICS.   M0938

MOTIVATION, JOB SATISFACTION, AND CAREER ASPIRATIONS OF
MARRIED WOMEN TEACHERS AT DIFFERENT CAREER STAGES.   M0940

JOB   CONTINUATION

LANGUAGE

LANGUAGE, TIME, AND PERSON EFFECTS ON ATTITUDE SCALE
TRANSLATIONS.   M0770

LAW

A STUDY OF THE RELATIONSHIP BETWEEN HERZBERG'S MOTIVATION
HYGIENE FACTORS AND HOLLAND'S PERSONALITY PATTERNS FOR LAW
ENFORCEMENT PERSONNEL.   M0850

LEADER

HOW THE LEADER LOOKS TO THE LED.   M0474

SEX EFFECTS IN LEADER BEHAVIOR SELF-DESCRIPTIONS AND JOB
SATISFACTION.   M0499

WORK VALUES AS MODERATORS OF PERCEIVED LEADER
BEHAVIOR-SATISFACTION RELATIONSHIPS.   M0505

BLACK-WHITE DIFFERENCES IN LEADER BEHAVIOR RELATED TO
SUBORDINATES' REACTIONS.   M0608

ANALYSIS OF RELATIONSHIPS AMONG LEADER BEHAVIOR,
SUBORDINATE JOB PERFORMANCE, AND SATISFACTION: A PATH-GOAL
APPROACH.   M0652

EMPLOYEE REACTIONS TO LEADER REWARD BEHAVIOR.   M0654

SEX STEREOTYPES: AN ARTIFACT IN LEADER BEHAVIOR AND
SUBORDINATE SATISFACTION ANALYSIS.   M0662

LEADER STRUCTURE AND SUBORDINATE SATISFACTION FOR TWO
HOSPITAL ADMINISTRATIVE LEVELS: A PATH ANALYSIS APPROACH.   M0736

PERCEIVED LEADER BEHAVIOR AND EMPLOYEE SATISFACTION WITH
SUPERVISION AND THE JOB: THE EFFECTS OF REWARD AND
PUNISHMENT.   M0859

JOB SATISFACTION OF GEORGIA SCHOOL SUPERINTENDENTS AND
THEIR PERCEPTION OF THE LOCAL SCHOOL BOARD PRESIDENT'S
LEADER BEHAVIOR.   M0906

JOB SATISFACTION AND LEADER BEHAVIOR OF ADULT EDUCATION
ADMINISTRATORS.   M0936

LEADERS

SUCCESSFUL LEADERS ARE SUCCESSFUL MOTIVATORS.   M0095

LEADERSHIP

EFFECTIVE LEADERSHIP.   M0113

LEADERSHIP AND MOTIVATION: A CORE CONCEPT.   M0121

LEAVERS

    JOB LOSERS, LEAVERS, AND ENTRANTS: TRAITS AND TRENDS.   M0157

LEAVES

    MANAGEMENT'S FUTURE ROLE: PICKING UP WHERE THE COMPUTER
    LEAVES OFF.   M0245

LEGAL

    JOBS, SALARY, CREDIT, LEGAL STATUS ALL IN FOCUS OF WOMEN'S
    YEAR.   M0235

    A QUALITIATIVE APPROACH TO PERFORMANCE PREDICTABILITY AND
    LEGAL COMPLIANCE.   M0329

LEGITIMATE

    THE EFFECT OF LEGITIMATE OPPORTUNITIES ON THE PROBABILITY
    OF PAROLEE RECIDIVISM.   M0069

LEISURE

    TRENDS IN LABOR AND LEISURE.   M0319

    CONTRIBUTION OF JOB AND LEISURE SATISFACTION TO QUALITY OF
    LIFE.   M0774

LETTING

    LETTING THE EMPLOYEE SPEAK HIS MIND.   M0526

LEVEL

    AN EARNINGS FUNCTION FOR HIGH LEVEL MANPOWER.   M0011

    SATISFACTION WITH PERFORMANCE AS A FUNCTION OF THE INITIAL
    LEVEL OF EXPECTED PERFORMANCE AND THE DEVIATION FROM
    EXPECTATIONS.   M0221

    THE IMPACT OF JOB LEVEL AND SEX DIFFERENCES ON THE
    RELATIONSHIP BETWEEN LIFE AND JOB SATISFACTION.   M0529

    JOB LEVEL, INDIVIDUAL DIFFERENCES, AND JOB SATISFACTION: AN
    INTERACTIVE APPROACH.   M0691

    INVESTIGATION OF THE INFLUENCE OF JOB LEVEL AND FUNCTIONAL
    SPECIALTY ON JOB ATTITUDES AND PERCEPTIONS.   M0745

    TWO INTERACTIVE PERSPECTIVES ON THE RELATIONSHIP BETWEEN
    JOB LEVEL AND JOB SATISFACTION.   M0823

    AN EMPIRICAL TEST OF CAUSAL INFERENCE BETWEEN ROLE
    PERCEPTIONS, SATISFACTION WITH WORK, PERFORMANCE AND
    ORGANIZATIONAL LEVEL.   M0839

LEVEL

LEVELS

LIFE

LIFE   CONTINUATION

LINK

MANAGEMENT CONTROL SYSTEMS: A KEY LINK BETWEEN STRATEGY, STRUCTURE, AND EMPLOYEE PERFORMANCE.   M0741

LINKAGES

INTERMEDIATE LINKAGES IN THE RELATIONSHIP BETWEEN JOB SATISFACTION AND EMPLOYEE TURNOVER.   M0781

LINKING

AN EVALUATION OF CAUSAL MODELS LINKING THE RECEIVED ROLE WITH JOB SATISFACTION.   M0335

LITERATURE

REVIEW OF LITERATURE ON WORK MOTIVATION: BULLETIN 12. A STUDY OF WORK MOTIVATION OF URBAN AND RURAL APPAREL WORKERS IN TENNESSEE.   M0503

CAPABILITIES OF MIDDLE-AGED AND OLDER WORKERS: A SURVEY OF THE LITERATURE.   M0778

LIVE

EMPLOYEES LEARN WHAT THEY LIVE NOT WHAT THEY ARE TOLD.   M0431

LOCAL

A NEW APPROACH TO LOCAL LABOR MARKET ANALYSIS: A FEASIBILITY STUDY.   M0162

EXPERIENCE OF BLACK FARMERS HOCE ADMINISTRATION LOCAL OFFICE CHIEFS.   M0182

THE RELEVANCE OF COSMOPOLITAN/LOCAL ORIENTATIONS TO PROFESSIONAL VALUES AND BEHAVIOR.   M0588

CORPORATE MANAGEMENT IN LOCAL GOVERNMENT: A CASE STUDY.   M0769

ATTITUDES TOWARD PARTICIPATION AMONG LOCAL AUTHORITY EMPLOYEES.   M0773

LOCAL FIRM AND JOB SATISFACTION.   M0821

JOB SATISFACTION OF GEORGIA SCHOOL SUPERINTENDENTS AND THEIR PERCEPTION OF THE LOCAL SCHOOL BOARD PRESIDENT'S LEADER BEHAVIOR.   M0906

LOCUS

RELATIONSHIP BETWEEN LOCUS OF CONTROL AND REACTIONS OF EMPLOYEES TO WORK CHARACTERISTICS.   M0530

LOCUS OF CONTROL: SUPERVISION AND WORK SATISFACTION.   M0660

LOCUS   CONTINUATION

ROLE DYNAMICS, LOCUS OF CONTROL, AND EMPLOYEE ATTITUDES AND
BEHAVIOR.   M0667

INTERNAL VERSUS EXTERNAL LOCUS OF CONTROL AND JOB
SATISFACTION IN IRAN.   M0851

A STUDY OF REHABILITATION COUNSELORS: LOCUS OF CONTROL AND
ATTITUDES TOWARD THE POOR.   M0888

THE EFFECT OF FLEXIBLE WORKING HOURS ON ABSENTEEISM AND JOB
SATISFACTION AND THE RELATIONSHIP BETWEEN LOCUS OF CONTROL
AND UTILITY OF FLEXIBLE WORKING HOURS.   M0943

LOGGING

LOGGING -- A JOB FOR THE HARDY.   M0362

LONGITUDINAL

THE WORKER ATTITUDES AND EARLY OCCUPATIONAL EXPERIENCES OF
YOUNG MEN -- ANALYSIS BASED ON A 4-YEAR LONGITUDINAL STUDY.   M0020

NATIONAL LONGITUDINAL STUDIES OF THE LABOR FORCE BEHAVIOR
OF NATIONAL SAMPLES OF MEN (45-59), WOMEN (30-44), AND MALE
AND FEMALE YOUTH (14-24).   M0339

LONGITUDINAL STUDY OF ABSENTEEISM AND HARD-CORE UNEMPLOYED.   M0500

LONGITUDINAL INFERENCES OF JOB ATTITUDE AND TENURE
RELATIONSHIPS FROM CROSS-SECTIONAL DATA.   M0591

LONGSHORING

SEX BIAS IN LONGSHORING.   M0389

LORDSTOWN

THE SPREADING LORDSTOWN SYNDROME.   M0414

LOSERS

JOB LOSERS, LEAVERS, AND ENTRANTS: TRAITS AND TRENDS.   M0157

LOSSES

WINS AND LOSSES.   M0485

LOW

PERSONALITY, MOTIVATIONAL SYSTEMS, AND BEHAVIOR OF HIGH AND
LOW LPC PERSONS.   M0131

LOW-WAGE

    EMPLOYMENT CHARACTERISTICS OF LOW-WAGE WORKERS.   M0418

LPC

    PERSONALITY, MOTIVATIONAL SYSTEMS, AND BEHAVIOR OF HIGH AND
    LOW LPC PERSONS.   M0131

MACHINE

    WHAT A MACHINE DOESN'T KNOW.   M0144

MACHINES

    BUSINESS MACHINES AND COMPUTER MANUFACTURING -- CAREER
    OPPORTUNITIES ARE EXCELLENT.   M0347

MAGNITUDE

    RELATIVE STEEPNESS OF APPROACH AND AVOIDANCE GRADIENTS AS A
    FUNCTION OF MAGNITUDE AND VALENCE OF INCENTIVE.   M0775

MAINTENANCE

    MAINTENANCE FACTORS: THE NEGLECTED SIDE OF WORKER
    MOTIVATION.   M0620

MALES

    AGE AND JOB SATISFACTION AMONG MALES AND FEMALES: A
    MULTI-VARIATE, MULTISURVEY STUDY.   M0518

    RELATIONSHIP OF AGE, TENURE AND JOB SATISFACTION IN MALES
    AND FEMALES.   M0525

    WORK VALUES AND JOB SATISFACTION OF YOUNG ADULT MALES.   M0579

    DESIRED JOB CHARACTERISTICS FOR MALES AND FEMALES.   M0629

MAN'S

    MAN'S INHERENT REBELLION AGAINST GOD AND SATISFACTION.   M0248

    PRODUCING MAN'S CASE FOR SATISFACTION.   M0610

MANAGE

    MANAGERS MANAGE MOTIVATION: THEY DON'T MOTIVATE.   M0396

MANAGEMENT

    ALIENATION-COUNSELING IMPLICATIONS AND MANAGEMENT THERAPY.   M0068

    PROBLEM OF MOTIVATION IN MANAGEMENT DEVELOPMENT.   M0098

MANAGEMENT   CONTINUATION

RESPONSIBILITY IN MANAGEMENT -- WHAT DOES IT REALLY MEAN.   M0118

THE CREDIBILITY GAP IN MANAGEMENT.   M0135

MANAGERIAL STRATEGY FOR THE FUTURE: THEORY Z MANAGEMENT.   M0137

GIVE MORE, GET MORE, TOP MANAGEMENT TOLD.   M0183

MANAGEMENT AND MOTIVATION.   M0186

THE MANAGEMENT OF SCIENTISTS: DETERMINANTS OF PERCEIVED
ROLE PERFORMANCE OF 95 SCIENTISTS IN THREE LARGE RESEARCH
LABORATORIES TO THE ORGANIC SYSTEM OF MANAGEMENT CONCEIVED
BY BURNS AND STALKER.   M0190

PARTICIPATIVE MANAGEMENT IN THE UNITED STATES: A CORPORATE
EXPERIENCE.   M0253

SOURCES OF SATISFACTION AND DISSATISFACTION AMONG SOLID
WASTE MANAGEMENT EMPLOYEES.   M0283

THE MANAGEMENT CONSULTING FIRM AS A SOURCE OF HIGH-LEVEL
MANAGERIAL TALENT.   M0312

SUCCESS IN MANAGEMENT CONSULTING AND THE CONCEPT OF
ELITENESS MOTIVATION.   M0314

MANAGEMENT, MOTIVATION AND JOB ENRICHMENT.   M0325

PARTICIPATIVE MANAGEMENT, BONUSES BOOST PRODUCTIVITY FOR
MICHIGAN FIRM.   M0341

MOTIVATING SALESMEN THROUGH BETTER SALES MANAGEMENT.   M0379

MOTIVATION AND MANAGEMENT DEVELOPMENT.   M0438

MANPOWER MANAGEMENT: NO ONE'S SELLING YOUTH ON SELLING.   M0440

IMPROVING PRODUCTIVITY; LABOR AND MANAGEMENT APPROACHES.   M0446

EXECUTIVE MANPOWER MANAGEMENT.   M0449

JOB ANALYSIS: KEY TO BETTER MANAGEMENT. SEPTEMBER 1971.   M0450

SELF-MOTIVATED PERSONAL CAREER PLANNING: A BREAKTHROUGH IN
HUMAN RESOURCE MANAGEMENT (PART I).   M0561

IMPACT OF MANAGEMENT BY OBJECTIVES ON MASLOW'S NEED
HIERARCHY: AN EMPIRICAL STUDY.   M0617

COPING WITH CUPID: THE FORMATION, IMPACT, AND MANAGEMENT OF
ROMANTIC RELATIONSHIPS IN ORGANIZATIONS.   M0630

SYSTEMS OF ORGANIZATION: MANAGEMENT OF THE HUMAN RESOURCE.   M0670

MANAGEMENT CONTINUATION

MANAGEMENT-BY-MISSION

MANAGEMENT'S

MANAGER

MANAGER   CONTINUATION

JOB SATISFACTION AND THE PD MANAGER: AN EMPIRICAL
ASSESSMENT.   M0831

MANAGER-SUBORDINATE

THE IMPORTANCE OF MANAGER-SUBORDINATE PERCEPTUAL
DIFFERENCES TO THE STUDY OF LEADERSHIP.   M0701

MANAGER'S

POSITIVE PERSONAL MOTIVATION: THE MANAGER'S GUIDE TO
INFLUENCING OTHERS.   M0208

MANAGERIAL

BUILDING EFFICACY: AN EFFECTIVE USE OF MANAGERIAL POWER. M0035

THE PRACTICE OF MANAGERIAL PSYCHOLOGY.   M0112

MANAGERIAL STRATEGY FOR THE FUTURE: THEORY Z MANAGEMENT. M0137

MANAGERIAL SATISFACTIONS AND ORGANIZATIONAL ROLES: AN
INVESTIGATION OF PORTER'S NEED DEFICIENCY SCALES.   M0202

READINGS IN MANAGERIAL PSYCHOLOGY, 2ND ED. CHICAGO.   M0271

THE MANAGERIAL CONVOLUTION .   M0306

THE MANAGEMENT CONSULTING FIRM AS A SOURCE OF HIGH-LEVEL
MANAGERIAL TALENT.   M0312

THE REAL CRUNCH IN MANAGERIAL MANPOWER.   M0313

MOTIVATION IN MANAGERIAL LEVELS: RELATIONSHIP OF NEED
SATISFACTION TO JOB PERFORMANCE.   M0401

IDENTIFICATION, PERSONALITY NEEDS, AND MANAGERIAL
POSITIONS.   M0611

THE DEVELOPMENT OF A MANAGERIAL JOB TAXONOMY: A SYSTEM FOR
DESCRIBING, CLASSIFYING, AND EVALUATING EXECUTIVE
POSITIONS.   M0618

MANAGERIAL BELIEFS ABOUT WORK IN SCOTLAND AND THE U.S.A.   M0756

ACADEMIC SALARIES -- A PERSONAL APPLICATION OF MANAGERIAL
ECONOMICS.   M0782

THE RELATIONSHIP BETWEEN MANAGERIAL SUCCESS AND PERSONAL
VALUES IN SOUTH AFRICA: A RESEARCH NOTE.   M0786

TRENDS IN JOB-RELATED ATTITUDES OF MANAGERIAL AND
PROFESSIONAL EMPLOYEES.   M0838

MANAGERS

MANAGERS'

MANAGING

MANPOWER

MANPOWER   CONTINUATION

    THE REAL CRUNCH IN MANAGERIAL MANPOWER.   M0313

    MODEL PROGRAM TO INSTRUCT MANPOWER TRAINING PERSONNEL IN
    SELECTION AND APPLICATION OF REMEDIAL INSTRUCTIONAL
    MATERIALS TO MEET INDIVIDUAL TRAINEE NEEDS.   M0387

    MANPOWER PROGRAMS FOR CRIMINAL OFFENDERS.   M0436

    MANPOWER MANAGEMENT: NO ONE'S SELLING YOUTH ON SELLING.   M0440

    EXECUTIVE MANPOWER MANAGEMENT.   M0449

    MANPOWER PROGRAMS IN FOUR CITIES.   M0455

MANUFACTURING

    DECISIONAL PARTICIPATION AND SOURCES OF JOB SATISFACTION: A
    STUDY OF MANUFACTURING PERSONNEL.   M0008

    QUITS IN MANUFACTURING: A STUDY OF THEIR CAUSES.   M0014

    INCENTIVE PAY IN MANUFACTURING INDUSTRIES.   M0223

    COMPARING UNION AND NONUNION WAGES IN MANUFACTURING.   M0309

    BUSINESS MACHINES AND COMPUTER MANUFACTURING -- CAREER
    OPPORTUNITIES ARE EXCELLENT.   M0347

    PRODUCTIVITY ANALYSIS IN MANUFACTURING PLANTS.   M0448

    STUDY OF CONTROL IN MANUFACTURING ORGANIZATION: MANAGERS
    AND NONMANAGERS.   M0645

MARINE

    INDIVIDUAL AND ENVIRONMENTAL FACTORS ASSOCIATED WITH THE
    JOB SATISFACTION AND RETENTION OF NAVY HOSPITAL CORPSMEN
    SERVING WITH THE U.S. MARINE CORPS.   M0574

MARITAL

    MARITAL AND FAMILY CHARACTERISTICS OF THE LABOR FORCE IN
    MARCH 1973.   M0194

    MARITAL AND FAMILY CHARACTERISTICS OF THE LABOR FORCE.   M0462

MARKET

    ADOLESCENT MINORITY FEMALES IN AN URBAN LABOR MARKET.   M0060

    PROFESSIONAL MANPOWER: THE JOB MARKET TURN-AROUND.   M0078

    A NEW APPROACH TO LOCAL LABOR MARKET ANALYSIS: A
    FEASIBILITY STUDY.   M0162

MATRIX

    THE HUMAN SIDE OF THE MATRIX.   M0727

MATURE

    OPENING JOB DOORS FOR MATURE WOMEN.   M0288

MATURITY

    SECOND CAREER CATHOLIC PRIESTS: A STUDY OF THEIR LEVEL OF
    JOB SATISFACTION, MATURITY, AND MORALE.   M0924

MBO

    THE POSITION AND FUNCTION OF BUDGETS IN AN MBO SYSTEM.   M0289

MEAN

    RESPONSIBILITY IN MANAGEMENT -- WHAT DOES IT REALLY MEAN.   M0118

MEANINGFUL

    AS YOU WERE SAYING -- ELEMENTS OF MEANINGFUL WORK.   M0016

    MOTIVATING PEOPLE WITH MEANINGFUL WORK.   M0293

MEASURE

    THE QUIT RATE AS A MEASURE OF MORALE IN THE PUBLIC SERVICE:
    THE CASE OF THE UNITED STATES FOREIGN SERVICE.   M0292

    A FACTOR ANALYTIC STUDY OF JOB SATISFACTION ITEMS DESIGNED
    TO MEASURE MASLOW NEED CATEGORIES.   M0365

MEASUREMENT

    THE MEANING AND MEASUREMENT OF PRODUCTIVITY.   M0447

    THE MEASUREMENT AND DIMENSIONALITY OF JOB CHARACTERISTICS.   M0580

    MEASUREMENT OF SOCIOECONOMIC AND PSYCHOLOGICAL
    CHARACTERISTICS: A METHOD.   M0789

    THE MEASUREMENT OF SATISFACTION AND DEPARTMENTAL
    ASSOCIATION AT WESTERN KENTUCKY UNIVERSITY: TESTING THE
    HOLLAND AND BIGLAN MODELS.   M0914

    SEGREGATION AND JOB SATISFACTION IN THE WORK PLACE: THE
    MEASUREMENT OF RACIAL DISPARITIES IN ORGANIZATIONS AND
    THEIR INFLUENCE ON EMPLOYEE WORK ATTITUDES.   M0927

MEASUREMENTS

    JOB INVOLVEMENT: CONCEPTS AND MEASUREMENTS.   M0834

MEDICAL

PHYSICIAN'S ASSISTANT -- MEDICAL OCCUPATION IS THE MAKING.   M0423

BACKGROUND AND PERSONALITY CHARACTERISTICS RELATED TO
STUDENT SATISFACTION AND PERFORMANCE IN FIELD MEDICAL
SERVICE SCHOOL.   M0575

PERSONALITY TRAITS, WORK FUNCTIONS, AND VOCATIONAL
SATISFACTION OF PHYSICIANS IN THREE MEDICAL SPECIALTIES.   M0875

THE RELATIONSHIPS AMONG THE PERSONALITY TYPES, JOB
SATISFACTIONS, AND JOB SPECIALTIES OF A SELECTED GROUP OF
MEDICAL TECHNOLOGISTS.   M0945

MEMBERSHIP

COMPARISON OF ORGANIZATIONAL MEMBERSHIP AND
SELF-EMPLOYMENT.   M0132

ORGANIZATIONAL MEMBERSHIP VS. SELF-EMPLOYMENT: ANOTHER BLOW
TO THE AMERICAN DREAM.   M0583

MEN

THE WORKER ATTITUDES AND EARLY OCCUPATIONAL EXPERIENCES OF
YOUNG MEN -- ANALYSIS BASED ON A 4-YEAR LONGITUDINAL STUDY.   M0020

DIFFERENCES IN HOURLY EARNINGS BETWEEN MEN AND WOMEN.   M0104

NATIONAL LONGITUDINAL STUDIES OF THE LABOR FORCE BEHAVIOR
OF NATIONAL SAMPLES OF MEN (45-59), WOMEN (30-44), AND MALE
AND FEMALE YOUTH (14-24).   M0339

A COMPARATIVE STUDY OF TEACHERS' ATTITUDES TOWARD MEN AND
WOMEN DEPARTMENT HEADS IN LARGE CITY SECONDARY SCHOOLS.   M0366

OCCUPATIONAL RANKING FOR MEN AND WOMEN BY EARNINGS.   M0408

WORK ATTITUDES OF DISADVANTAGED BLACK MEN.   M0412

THE IMPACT OF HIERARCHICAL STRUCTURES ON THE WORK BEHAVIOR
OF WOMEN AND MEN.   M0757

MENTAL

THE EFFECTS OF AGING ON ENGINEERS' SATISFACTION AND MENTAL
HEALTH: SKILL OBSOLESCENCE.   M0044

WORK MOTIVATION, A MENTAL PROCESS.   M0528

INTEREST CONGRUENCY AS A MODERATOR OF THE RELATIONSHIPS
BETWEEN JOB TENURE AND JOB SATISFACTION AND MENTAL HEALTH.   M0623

THE MENTAL HEALTH ASSOCIATE: THE EFFECT OF SOCIAL
ENVIRONMENTAL FACTORS ON JOB SATISFACTION.   M0697

MENTAL   CONTINUATION

    JOB INVOLVEMENT AND SATISFACTION AS RELATED TO MENTAL
    HEALTH AND PERSONAL TIME DEVOTED TO WORK.   M0718

    A NATIONAL STUDY OF ASSOCIATE DEGREE MENTAL HEALTH SERVICES
    WORKERS.   M0806

    OCCUPATIONAL MENTAL HEALTH AND THE HUMAN SERVICES: A
    REVIEW.   M0880

    PHYSICAL ENVIRONMENT AND JOB SATISFACTION IN A COMMUNITY
    MENTAL HEALTH CENTER.   M0883

MENTALLY

    WORKER ALIENATION AND THE MENTALLY RETARDED.   M0532

    THE RELATION OF JOB SATISFACTION TO VOCATIONAL PREFERENCES
    AMONG TEACHERS OF THE EDUCABLE MENTALLY RETARDED.   M0805

MESBIC

    FORM CHINA WITH SKILL -- MESBIC FOUNDER WANTS TO SHARE HER
    TALENT.   M0145

METHADONE-MAINTAINED

    WORK ADJUSTMENT OF THE METHADONE-MAINTAINED CORPORATE
    EMPLOYEE.   M0567

METHOD

    MEASUREMENT OF SOCIOECONOMIC AND PSYCHOLOGICAL
    CHARACTERISTICS: A METHOD.   M0789

METHODIST

    A STUDY OF JOB SATISFACTION OF ADMINISTRATORS AT UNITED
    METHODIST RELATED CHURCHES.   M0910

METHODOLOGY

    METHODOLOGY FOR ASSESSMENT OF QUALITY OF WORK LIFE AND
    ORGANIZATIONAL EFFECTIVENESS IN BEHAVIORAL-ECONOMIC TERMS. M0536

METHODS

    LEADERSHIP METHODS THAT MOTIVATE.   M0302

MICHIGAN

    PARTICIPATIVE MANAGEMENT, BONUSES BOOST PRODUCTIVITY FOR
    MICHIGAN FIRM.   M0341

MICHIGAN'S

    AN ANALYSIS OF MICHIGAN'S EXPERIENCE WITH WORK INCENTIVES.   M0012

MIDDLE

    FOREMEN: MAN IN THE MIDDLE.   M0061

    THE MEANING OF WORK AND THE MIDDLE MANAGER.   . M0675

    AN ANALYSIS OF JOB SATISFACTION AMONG ELEMENTARY, MIDDLE
    LEVEL, AND SENIOR HIGH SCHOOL TEACHERS.   M0911

    CAREER COMMITMENT: AN ANALYSIS OF SELECTED INDIVIDUAL, JOB
    AND ORGANIZATIONAL FACTORS AS RELATED TO SATISFACTION AND
    COMMITMENT OF MIDDLE LEVEL ARMY OFFICERS.   M0912

MIDDLE-AGED

    CAPABILITIES OF MIDDLE-AGED AND OLDER WORKERS: A SURVEY OF
    THE LITERATURE.   M0778

MIGRANT

    ASSESSMENT OF EXPERIMENTAL AND DEMONSTRATION INTERSTATE
    PROGRAM FOR SOUTH TEXAS MIGRANT WORKERS.   M0001

MIGRATION

    OCCUPATIONAL MIGRATION, DISCRIMINATION, AND THE CENTRAL
    CITY LABOR FORCE.   M0247

MILITARY

    EFFICIENCY IN THE MILITARY.   M0522

    THE RELATIONSHIP OF JOB SATISFACTION MEASURES TO
    SELF-REPORT AND OBJECTIVE CRITERIA MEASURES AND THE EFFECT
    OF MODERATOR VARIABLES FOR CANADIAN MILITARY PERSONNEL.   M0853

MILLION

    THE CRAFTS -- FIVE MILLION OPPORTUNITIES.   M0049

MINE

    THE BRITISH COAL MINE STRIKE OF 1972.   M0483

MINISTERS

    PSYCHOLOGICAL ATTITUDES AND BELIEFS OF MINISTERS.   M0804

MINORITY

    ADOLESCENT MINORITY FEMALES IN AN URBAN LABOR MARKET.   M0060

MINORITY   CONTINUATION

    JOB BIAS AND THE INVISIBLE MINORITY.   M0231

    DISCRIMINATION AND JOB SATISFACTION: AN EMPIRICAL STUDY
    WITH A SOUTH AFRICAN MINORITY GROUP.   M0733

    THE VOCATIONAL EXPLORATION GROUP AND MINORITY YOUTH: AN
    EXPERIMENTAL OUTCOME STUDY.   M0749

MODEL

    A MARKOV CHAIN MODEL OF HUMAN NEEDS.   M0057

    CONSTRUCT VALIDATION OF AN INSTRUMENTALITY-EXPECTANCY-TASK-
    GOAL MODEL OF WORK MOTIVATION: SOME THEORETICAL BOUNDARY
    CONDITIONS.   M0082

    PREDICTING ABSENTEEISM AND TURNOVER: A FIELD COMPARISON OF
    FISHBEIN'S MODEL AND TRADITIONAL JOB ATTITUDE MEASURES. M0326

    MODEL PROGRAM TO INSTRUCT MANPOWER TRAINING PERSONNEL IN
    SELECTION AND APPLICATION OF REMEDIAL INSTRUCTIONAL
    MATERIALS TO MEET INDIVIDUAL TRAINEE NEEDS.   M0387

    PREDICTING THE PERFORMANCE OF JUNIOR ACHIEVEMENT COMPANIES
    ACCORDING TO THE LEADERSHIP STYLE OF TWO LEVELS OF
    MANAGEMENT: A FIELD STUDY OF THE CONTINGENCY MODEL.   M0700

    RELATIONSHIP BETWEEN ORGANIZATIONAL CLIMATE AND THE
    SITUATIONAL FAVORABLENESS DIMENSION OF FIEDLER'S
    CONTINGENCY MODEL.   M0709

    DETERMINANTS OF PAY SATISFACTION: A DISCREPANCY MODEL
    EVALUATION.   M0852

    PREDICTING THE PERFORMANCE OF JUNIOR ACHIEVEMENT ACCORDING
    TO THE LEADERSHIP STYLE OF TWO LEVELS OF MANAGEMENT: A
    FIELD STUDY OF THE CONTINGENCY MODEL.   M0872

    A CAUSAL MODEL OF JOB SATISFACTION.   M0915

MODELING

    INTERACTION MODELING: A NEW CONCEPT IN SUPERVISORY
    TRAINING.   M0507

    CAUSAL MODELING OF PSYCHOLOGICAL SUCCESS IN WORK
    ORGANIZATIONS.   M0520

MODELS

    AN EVALUATION OF CAUSAL MODELS LINKING THE RECEIVED ROLE
    WITH JOB SATISFACTION.   M0335

    MODELS OF PAY SATISFACTION: A COMPARATIVE STUDY.   M0613

MODELS   CONTINUATION

    AN EXAMINATION OF NEED-SATISFACTION MODELS OF JOB
    ATTITUDES.   M0673

    A TEST OF ALTERNATIVE MODELS OF EXPECTANCY THEORY.   M0892

    THE RELATIONSHIP BETWEEN JOB SATISFACTION AND LIFE
    SATISFACTION: AN EMPIRICAL TEST OF THREE MODELS ON A
    NATIONAL SAMPLE.   M0903

    THE MEASUREMENT OF SATISFACTION AND DEPARTMENTAL
    ASSOCIATION AT WESTERN KENTUCKY UNIVERSITY: TESTING THE
    HOLLAND AND BIGLAN MODELS.   M0914

MODERATED

    THE EFFECTS OF ROLE PERCEPTIONS ON EMPLOYEE SATISFACTION
    AND PERFORMANCE MODERATED BY EMPLOYEE ABILITY.   M0553

    ROLE PERCEPTIONS, SATISFACTION AND PERFORMANCE MODERATED BY
    ORGANIZATION LEVEL AND PARTICIPATION IN DECISION MAKING. M0895

MODERATING

    THE MODERATING EFFECTS OF INTERNAL VERSUS EXTERNAL CONTROL
    ON THE RELATIONSHIP BETWEEN VARIOUS ASPECTS OF JOB
    SATISFACTION.   M0122

    SATISFACTION AND PERFORMANCE: CAUSAL RELATIONSHIPS AND
    MODERATING EFFECTS.   M0395

    REACTIONS TO JOB CHARACTERISTICS: MODERATING EFFECTS OF THE
    ORGANIZATION.   M0581

    PREDICTING JOB PERFORMANCE BY USE OF ABILITY TESTS AND
    STUDYING JOB SATISFACTION AS A MODERATING VARIABLE.   M0765

    MODERATING EFFECTS OF ENVIRONMENT AND STRUCTURE ON THE
    SATISFACTION-TENSION-INFLUENCE NETWORK.   M0828

MODERATOR

    SOME MODERATOR INFLUENCES ON RELATIONSHIPS BETWEEN
    CONSIDERATION, INITIATING STRUCTURE, AND ORGANIZATION
    CRITERIA.   M0021

    AN INVESTIGATION OF JOB SATISFACTION AS A MODERATOR
    VARIABLE IN PREDICTING JOB SUCCESS.   M0025

    SELF-ESTEEM AS A MODERATOR OF THE RELATIONSHIP BETWEEN
    EXPECTANCIES AND JOB PERFORMANCE.   M0150

    SOCIAL DESIRABILITY AS A MODERATOR OF THE RELATIONSHIP
    BETWEEN JOB SATISFACTION AND PERSONAL ADJUSTMENT.   M0337

MODERATOR   CONTINUATION

    ORGANIZATION STRESS AS A MODERATOR OF THE RELATIONSHIP
    BETWEEN INFLUENCE AND ROLE RESPONSE.   M0444

    INTEREST CONGRUENCY AS A MODERATOR OF THE RELATIONSHIPS
    BETWEEN JOB TENURE AND JOB SATISFACTION AND MENTAL HEALTH.   M0623

    SELF-ESTEEM AS A MODERATOR IN VOCATIONAL CHOICE: A TEST OF
    KORMAN'S HYPOTHESIS.   M0803

    ACHIEVEMENT MOTIVATION AS A MODERATOR OF THE RELATIONSHIP
    BETWEEN EXPECTANCY TIMES VALENCE AND EFFORT.   M0845

    THE RELATIONSHIP OF JOB SATISFACTION MEASURES TO
    SELF-REPORT AND OBJECTIVE CRITERIA MEASURES AND THE EFFECT
    OF MODERATOR VARIABLES FOR CANADIAN MILITARY PERSONNEL.   M0853

MODERATORS

    WORK VALUES AS MODERATORS OF PERCEIVED LEADER
    BEHAVIOR-SATISFACTION RELATIONSHIPS.   M0505

    HIGHER ORDER NEED STRENGTHS AS MODERATORS OF THE JOB
    SCOPE-JOB SATISFACTION RELATIONSHIP.   M0798

    JOB CHARACTERISTICS RELATIONSHIPS: INDIVIDUAL AND
    STRUCTURAL MODERATORS.   M0896

MOLD

    WOMEN OFFENDERS: BREAKING THE TRAINING MOLD.   M0330

MONEY

    MONEY IS, TOO, AN INCENTIVE: ONE COMPANY'S EXPERIENCE.   M0199

    IS MOTIVATION BY MONEY STILL FASHIONABLE?   M0287

    MOTIVATING MANAGERS WITH MONEY.   M0481

MONTANA

    COMPARATIVE APPRAISALS OF JOB PERFORMANCE OF FULL-TIME
    ELEMENTARY PRINCIPALS BY THE PRINCIPALS AND THEIR
    SUPERVISORS IN CLASS I MONTANA SCHOOL DISTRICTS.   M0941

MOONLIGHTERS

    MOONLIGHTERS: THEIR MOTIVATIONS AND CHARACTERISTICS.   M0345

MORALE

    HOW TO KEEP STAFF MORALE AND MOTIVATION IN HIGH GEAR.   M0280

    THE QUIT RATE AS A MEASURE OF MORALE IN THE PUBLIC SERVICE:

MORALE   CONTINUATION

    THE CASE OF THE UNITED STATES FOREIGN SERVICE.   M0292

    THE EFFECTIVE ORGANIZATION: MORALE VS. DISCIPLINE.   M0357

    EFFECTS ON PRODUCTIVITY AND MORALE OF A SYSTEMS-DESIGNED
    JOB-ENRICHMENT PROGRAM IN PACIFIC TELEPHONE.   M0515

    LEADERSHIP DIMENSIONS OF NAVY RECRUIT MORALE & PERFORMANCE. M0564

    MANAGING MORALE THROUGH SURVEY FEEDBACK.   M0684

    SCHOOL BOARD DOGMATISM AND MORALE OF PRINCIPALS.   M0731

    SECOND CAREER CATHOLIC PRIESTS: A STUDY OF THEIR LEVEL OF
    JOB SATISFACTION, MATURITY, AND MORALE.   M0924

MORATORIUM

    MORATORIUM ON MOTIVATION.   M0435

MOTHERS

    WELFARE MOTHERS AND THE WORK ETHIC.   M0168

MOTHERS'

    EMPLOYMENT, WELFARE, AND MOTHERS' MOTIVATION.   M0308

    MARKETING WELFARE MOTHERS' JOB SKILLS.   M0343

MOTIVATE

    MOTIVATE THEM THROUGH THEIR JOBS.   M0006

    DO YOU MOTIVATE YOUR SUBORDINATES.   M0040

    THE PROFIT MOTIVE: CAN IT MOTIVATE INDUSTRY TO HIRE THE
    HARD CORE.   M0298

    MANAGER COMMENTS ON HOW TO MOTIVATE.   M0299

    LEADERSHIP METHODS THAT MOTIVATE.   M0302

    MANAGERS MANAGE MOTIVATION: THEY DON'T MOTIVATE.   M0396

    HOW TO MOTIVATE.   M0676

MOTIVATED

    MOTIVATED WORKERS AND HARD WORKERS.   M0479

MOTIVATES

    MA BELL MOTIVATES.   M0295

MOTIVATION   CONTINUATION

MOTIVATION.   M0093

PROBLEM OF MOTIVATION IN MANAGEMENT DEVELOPMENT.   M0098

EXTENSIONS OF A PATH-GOAL THEORY OF MOTIVATION.   M0120

LEADERSHIP AND MOTIVATION: A CORE CONCEPT.   M0121

HIGH MOTIVATION, HIGH PRODUCTIVITY.   M0127

WHY MOTIVATION THEORY DOESN'T WORK.   M0133

MOTIVATION AND CAREER PATH PLANNING.   M0146

NEUROLOGICAL BASIS OF MOTIVATION: AN ENDURING PROBLEM IN
PSYCHOLOGY.   M0160

THE MEANING OF WORK AND THE MOTIVATION TO WORK.   M0179

MANAGEMENT AND MOTIVATION.   M0186

WESTERN ELECTRICS MOTIVATION AND ENRICHMENT TRIAL.   M0195

POSITIVE PERSONAL MOTIVATION: THE MANAGER'S GUIDE TO
INFLUENCING OTHERS.   M0208

CROSS-CULTURAL DIFFERENCES IN TWO-FACTOR MOTIVATION THEORY.   M0209

ABC OF MOTIVATION.   M0241

LEADERSHIP, MOTIVATION, AND COMMUNICATION.   M0242

JOB DESIGN AND EMPLOYEE MOTIVATION.   M0267

TOTAL MOTIVATION = TOP PERFORMANCE.   M0270

ASININE ATTITUDES TOWARD MOTIVATION.   M0274

A SOCIAL PSYCHOLGICAL EXPLORATION OF POWER MOTIVATION AMONG
DISADVANTAGED WORKERS.   M0279

HOW TO KEEP STAFF MORALE AND MOTIVATION IN HIGH GEAR.   M0280

MOTIVATION VS. LEARNING APPROACHES TO ORGANIZATIONAL
BEHAVIOR.   M0285

IS MOTIVATION BY MONEY STILL FASHIONABLE?   M0287

VALUES -- NOT ATTITUDES -- ARE THE REAL KEY TO MOTIVATION.   M0301

EMPLOYMENT, WELFARE, AND MOTHERS' MOTIVATION.   M0308

SUCCESS IN MANAGEMENT CONSULTING AND THE CONCEPT OF
ELITENESS MOTIVATION.   M0314

MOTIVATION   CONTINUATION

WORK MOTIVATION AND JOB PERFORMANCE.   M0656

EXPECTANCY THEORY AS A PREDICTOR OF WORK MOTIVATION, EFFORT
EXPENDITURE, AND JOB PERFORMANCE.   M0663

MOTIVATION OF ENGINEERS: AN ANALYSIS OF PERCEIVED
MOTIVATIONAL FACTORS.   M0692

INNER DIRECTION, OTHER DIRECTION AND ACHIEVEMENT
MOTIVATION.   M0726

THE IMPACT OF ORGANIZATION SIZE ON EMPLOYEE MOTIVATION.   M0735

MOTIVATION THROUGH THE DESIGN OF WORK: TEST OF A THEORY.   M0761

ABSENCE BEHAVIOR AND ATTENDANCE MOTIVATION: A CONCEPTUAL
SYNTHESIS.   M0783

UNDERSTANDING DRUG USE MOTIVATION: A NEW LOOK AT A CURRENT
PROBLEM.   M0788

TECHNOLOGICAL DIFFERENCES IN JOB CHARACTERISTICS, EMPLOYEE
SATISFACTION, AND MOTIVATION: A SYNTHESIS OF JOB DESIGN
RESOURCE AND SOCIOTECHNICAL SYSTEMS THEORY.   M0832

ACHIEVEMENT MOTIVATION AS A MODERATOR OF THE RELATIONSHIP
BETWEEN EXPECTANCY TIMES VALENCE AND EFFORT.   M0845

A STUDY OF THE RELATIONSHIP BETWEEN HERZBERG'S MOTIVATION
HYGIENE FACTORS AND HOLLAND'S PERSONALITY PATTERNS FOR LAW
ENFORCEMENT PERSONNEL.   M0850

MOTIVATION, JOB SATISFACTION, AND CAREER ASPIRATIONS OF
MARRIED WOMEN TEACHERS AT DIFFERENT CAREER STAGES.   M0940

MOTIVATIONAL

THE EFFECT OF MOTIVATIONAL PROGRAMS ON COLLECTIVE
BARGAINING.   M0032

AN EVALUATION OF MOTIVATIONAL SIMILARITY IN WORK GROUPS.   M0033

UNMIXING CURRENT MOTIVATIONAL STRATEGIES.   M0052

PERSONALITY, MOTIVATIONAL SYSTEMS, AND BEHAVIOR OF HIGH AND
LOW LPC PERSONS.   M0131

MOTIVATIONAL TYPE AND THE SATISFACTION-PERFORMANCE
RELATIONSHIP.   M0263

MOTIVATIONAL AND PERSONALITY FACTORS RELATED TO CAREER
GOALS OF BLACK COLLEGE WOMEN.   M0310

RELEVANCE OF MOTIVATIONAL CONCEPTS TO INDIVIDUAL AND

MOVEMENTS

MSQ

MULTI-DISCIPLINARY

MULTI-VARIATE

MULTIJOBHOLDING

MULTISURVEY

MUNICIPAL

MUSIC

MUTUAL

MYSTIQUE

MYTH

MYTHOLOGY

NARRATIVE

NATIONAL

BACKGROUND CHARACTERISTICS, ORIENTATION, WORK EXPERIENCE, AND WORK VALUES OF EMPLOYEES HIRED FROM HUMAN RESOURCES DEVELOPMENT APPLICANTS BY COMPANIES AFFILIATED WITH THE NATIONAL ALLIANCE OF BUSINESSMAN. M0165

ABSENCE FROM WORK: A LOOK AT SOME NATIONAL DATA. M0198

NATIONAL LONGITUDINAL STUDIES OF THE LABOR FORCE BEHAVIOR OF NATIONAL SAMPLES OF MEN (45-59), WOMEN (30-44), AND MALE AND FEMALE YOUTH (14-24). M0339

PRODUCTIVITY AND THE NATIONAL INTEREST. M0456

A NATIONAL STUDY OF ASSOCIATE DEGREE MENTAL HEALTH SERVICES WORKERS. M0806

RELATIONSHIPS AMONG PAY, RACE, SEX, OCCUPATIONAL PRESTIGE, SUPERVISION, WORK AUTONOMY, AND JOB SATISFACTION IN A NATIONAL SAMPLE. M0842

THE RELATIONSHIP BETWEEN JOB SATISFACTION AND LIFE SATISFACTION: AN EMPIRICAL TEST OF THREE MODELS ON A NATIONAL SAMPLE. M0903

NATIONALITY

NATIONALITY AND ESPOUSED VALUES OF MANAGERS. M0593

NAVAL

CORRELATES OF JOB SATISFACTION IN NAVAL ENVIRONMENTS. M0291

NAVY

LEADERSHIP DIMENSIONS OF NAVY RECRUIT MORALE & PERFORMANCE. M0564

INDIVIDUAL AND ENVIRONMENTAL FACTORS ASSOCIATED WITH THE JOB SATISFACTION AND RETENTION OF NAVY HOSPITAL CORPSMEN SERVING WITH THE U.S. MARINE CORPS. M0574

NEED-RATIFICATION

NEED-RATIFICATION, ABSENTEEISM AND ITS OTHER CORRELATES. M0794

NEED-SATISFACTION

AN EXAMINATION OF NEED-SATISFACTION MODELS OF JOB ATTITUDES. M0673

NEGLECTED

MAINTENANCE FACTORS: THE NEGLECTED SIDE OF WORKER MOTIVATION. M0620

NEGOTIATED

NEGOTIATED RETIREMENT PLANS -- A DECADE OF BENEFIT
IMPROVEMENTS.   M0085

NEGRO

THE NEGRO JOB SITUATION: HAS IT IMPROVED.   M0211

NETWORK

MODERATING EFFECTS OF ENVIRONMENT AND STRUCTURE ON THE
SATISFACTION-TENSION-INFLUENCE NETWORK.   M0828

A NETWORK ANALYSIS OF A BUREAU OF INDIAN AFFAIRS SCHOOL
SYSTEM TO DETERMINE FACTORS INVOLVED IN JOB SATISFACTION.   M0934

NEUROLOGICAL

NEUROLOGICAL BASIS OF MOTIVATION: AN ENDURING PROBLEM IN
PSYCHOLOGY.   M0160

NEW

JOB PERFORMANCE AND THE NEW CREDENTIALISM.   M0099

A NEW APPROACH TO LOCAL LABOR MARKET ANALYSIS: A
FEASIBILITY STUDY.   M0162

NEW PERSPECTIVES ON THE WILL TO WORK.   M0207

EVALUATION AND IMPLEMENTATION OF THE NEW YORK FIRE
DEPARTMENT EXAMINATION TRAINING PROJECT FOR CULTURALLY
DISADVANTAGED RESIDENTS OF THE CITY OF NEW YORK.   M0243

OFFICE LANDSCAPING -- NEW LOOK FOR THE WORKPLACE.   M0394

TESTING A NEW APPROACH TO EVALUATION.   M0433

INTERACTION MODELING: A NEW CONCEPT IN SUPERVISORY
TRAINING.   M0507

PSCHOPHYSIOLOGICAL INFLUENCES ON THE WORK ENVIRONMENT: NEW
CONCEPTS.   M0550

FACTORS AFFECTING ACQUISITION OF BELIEFS ABOUT A NEW REWARD
SYSTEM.   M0589

THE FOUR STAGES OF PROFESSIONAL CAREERS - A NEW LOOK AT
PERFORMANCE BY PROFESSIONALS.   M0711

WHAT'S NEW IN CAREER MANAGEMENT.   M0724

UNDERSTANDING DRUG USE MOTIVATION: A NEW LOOK AT A CURRENT
PROBLEM.   M0788

NORMATIVE

A NORMATIVE STUDY OF THE SECONDARY SCHOOL ASSISTANT
PRINCIPALSHIP IN SELECTED PENNSYLVANIA SCHOOL DISTRICTS
WITH AN EMPHASIS UPON JOB SATISFACTION.   M0918

NORMS

MANAGEMENT BY NORMS.   M0681

NURSE

ANDROGYNY IN NURSING: NURSE ROLE EXPECTATION, SATISFACTION,
ACADEMIC ACHIEVEMENT, AND SELF-ACTUALIZATION IM MALE AND
FEMALE STUDENTS.   M0877

NURSES

SURVEY OF FACTORS RELATING TO JOB SATISFACTION AMONG VA
NURSES.   M0457

SOCIAL AND PSYCHOLOGICAL INFLUENCES ON EMPLOYMENT OF
MARRIED NURSES.   M0755

PERCEIVED DIMENSIONS OF JOB SATISFACTION FOR STAFF
REGISTERED NURSES.   M0882

NURSING

ANDROGYNY IN NURSING: NURSE ROLE EXPECTATION, SATISFACTION,
ACADEMIC ACHIEVEMENT, AND SELF-ACTUALIZATION IM MALE AND
FEMALE STUDENTS.   M0877

OBJECTIVE

THE RELATIONSHIP OF JOB SATISFACTION MEASURES TO
SELF-REPORT AND OBJECTIVE CRITERIA MEASURES AND THE EFFECT
OF MODERATOR VARIABLES FOR CANADIAN MILITARY PERSONNEL.   M0853

OBJECTIVES

RELEVANCE OF MOTIVATIONAL CONCEPTS TO INDIVIDUAL AND
CORPORATE OBJECTIVES.   M0331

IMPACT OF MANAGEMENT BY OBJECTIVES ON MASLOW'S NEED
HIERARCHY: AN EMPIRICAL STUDY.   M0617

OBSOLESCENCE

THE EFFECTS OF AGING ON ENGINEERS' SATISFACTION AND MENTAL
HEALTH: SKILL OBSOLESCENCE.   M0044

OCCUPATION

PHYSICIAN'S ASSISTANT -- MEDICAL OCCUPATION IS THE MAKING.   M0423

OCCUPATION   CONTINUATION

WHERE WOMEN WORK -- AN ANALYSIS BY INDUSTRY AND OCCUPATION.   M0464

OCCUPATIONAL

THE WORKER ATTITUDES AND EARLY OCCUPATIONAL EXPERIENCES OF
YOUNG MEN -- ANALYSIS BASED ON A 4-YEAR LONGITUDINAL STUDY.   M0020

CHANGES IN THE OCCUPATIONAL STRUCTURE OF U. S. JOBS.   M0100

OCCUPATIONAL MANPOWER TRAINING NEEDS.   M0170

SELF-ESTEEM AS AN INFLUENCE ON OCCUPATIONAL CHOICE AND
OCCUPATIONAL SATISFACTION.   M0174

OCCUPATIONAL STRESS AND PHYSICAL HEALTH.   M0213

A STUDY OF ROLE CLARITY AND NEED FOR CLARITY FOR THREE
OCCUPATIONAL GROUPS.   M0227

THE OCCUPATIONAL INFORMATION CENTER: WHERE ATLANTA
EMPLOYERS AND EDUCATORS MEET.   M0237

OCCUPATIONAL MIGRATION, DISCRIMINATION, AND THE CENTRAL
CITY LABOR FORCE.   M0247

REMOVAL OF SEX STEREOTYPING IN CENSUS OCCUPATIONAL
CLASSIFICATION.   M0359

OCCUPATIONAL GUIDANCE MATERIALS FOR THE DISADVANTAGED: A
PILOT PROGRAM.   M0404

OCCUPATIONAL RANKING FOR MEN AND WOMEN BY EARNINGS.   M0408

OCCUPATIONAL STRESSES AND JOB SATISFACTION.   M0506

OCCUPATIONAL SATISFACTION OF FARM HUSBANDS AND WIVES.   M0706

ORGANIZATIONAL AND OCCUPATIONAL COMMITMENT: A FACET
THEORETICAL ANALYSIS OF EMPIRICAL DATA.   M0747

MANAGERS' OCCUPATIONAL HISTORIES, ORGANIZATIONAL
ENVIRONMENTS, AND CLIMATES FOR MANAGEMENT DEVELOPMENT.   M0787

DIMENSIONS OF JOB SATISFACTION: INITIAL DEVELOPMENT OF THE
AIR FORCE OCCUPATIONAL ATTITUDE INVENTORY.   M0802

RELATIONSHIPS AMONG PAY, RACE, SEX, OCCUPATIONAL PRESTIGE,
SUPERVISION, WORK AUTONOMY, AND JOB SATISFACTION IN A
NATIONAL SAMPLE.   ˋ   M0842

JOB SATISFACTION AND NEED IMPORTANCE: RACE, SEX, AND
OCCUPATIONAL GROUP.   M0860

OCCUPATIONAL MENTAL HEALTH AND THE HUMAN SERVICES: A

OPENNESS

EFFECTS OF DIFFERENT PATTERNS AND DEGREES OF OPENNESS IN
SUPERIOR-SUBORDINATE COMMUNICATION ON SUBORDINATE JOB
SATISFACTION.   M0045

OPERATIONALIZING

OPERATIONALIZING THE CONCEPTS OF GOALS AND GOAL
INCOMPATIBILITIES IN ORGANIZATIONAL BEHAVIOR RESEARCH.   M0595

OPERATIVE

DISCONTENT IN THE RANKS: IS THE OPERATIVE WORKER REALLY
TRAPPED.   M0354

OPPORTUNITIES

QUESTIONNAIRE PROVIDES INFORMATION ON JOB OPPORTUNITIES FOR
FS WIVES OVERSEAS.   M0015

THE CRAFTS -- FIVE MILLION OPPORTUNITIES.   M0049

THE EFFECT OF LEGITIMATE OPPORTUNITIES ON THE PROBABILITY
OF PAROLEE RECIDIVISM.   M0069

CAREER OPPORTUNITIES IN THE POSTAL SERVICE.   M0152

BUSINESS MACHINES AND COMPUTER MANUFACTURING -- CAREER
OPPORTUNITIES ARE EXCELLENT.   M0347

JOB RESTRUCTURING. . . ONE ROAD TO INCREASED OPPORTUNITIES.   M0427

OPPORTUNITY

HOW EQUAL OPPORTUNITY AFFECTS DEFENSE CONTRACTS.   M0140

EMPLOYEE ATTITUDES REGARDING VARIOUS CHARACTERISTICS OF JOB
OPPORTUNITY AND JOB PERFORMANCE ACROSS THREE DIFFERENT WORK
SHIFTS AT AN INSTITUTION FOR THE RETARDED.   M0900

TASK OPPORTUNITY PROFESSIONAL GROWTH NEED FULFILLMENT AND
INTRINSIC JOB SATISFACTION OF PUBLIC SOCIAL SERVICE WORKERS
IN COLORADO.   M0923

ORDER

HIGHER ORDER NEED STRENGTHS AS MODERATORS OF THE JOB
SCOPE-JOB SATISFACTION RELATIONSHIP.   M0798

ORGANIC

THE MANAGEMENT OF SCIENTISTS: DETERMINANTS OF PERCEIVED
ROLE PERFORMANCE OF 95 SCIENTISTS IN THREE LARGE RESEARCH
LABORATORIES TO THE ORGANIC SYSTEM OF MANAGEMENT CONCEIVED
BY BURNS AND STALKER.   M0190

ORGANIZATION

ORGANIZATIONAL

ORGANIZATIONAL   CONTINUATION

METHODOLOGY FOR ASSESSMENT OF QUALITY OF WORK LIFE AND
ORGANIZATIONAL EFFECTIVENESS IN BEHAVIORAL-ECONOMIC TERMS.   M0536

ORGANIZATIONAL STRUCTURE: HOW DOES IT INFLUENCE ATTITUDES
AND PERFORMANCE.   M0578

ORGANIZATIONAL MEMBERSHIP VS. SELF-EMPLOYMENT: ANOTHER BLOW
TO THE AMERICAN DREAM.   M0583

OPERATIONALIZING THE CONCEPTS OF GOALS AND GOAL
INCOMPATIBILITIES IN ORGANIZATIONAL BEHAVIOR RESEARCH.   M0595

ROLE REQUIREMENTS AS SOURCES OF ORGANIZATIONAL STRESS.   M0597

ORGANIZATIONAL ROLE CONFLICT: ITS ANTECEDENTS AND
CONSEQUENCES.   M0601

CONCEPTS AND CONTROVERSY IN ORGANIZATIONAL BEHAVIOR.   M0605

ORGANIZATIONAL RESEARCH ON JOB INVOLVEMENT.   M0609

ORGANIZATIONAL COMMITMENT AND TURNOVER: A PREDICTION STUDY. M0627

CONFESSIONS OF AN ORGANIZATIONAL CHANGE AGENT.   M0631

POLITICAL STRATEGIES FOR IMPLEMENTING ORGANIZATIONAL
CHANGE.   M0632

ANTECEDENTS AND OUTCOMES OF ORGANIZATIONAL COMMITMENT.   M0633

RELATIONSHIP BETWEEN ORGANIZATIONAL CLIMATE AND THE
SITUATIONAL FAVORABLENESS DIMENSION OF FIEDLER'S
CONTINGENCY MODEL.   M0709

WHEN DOES WORK RESTRUCTURING WORK? ORGANIZATIONAL
INNOVATION AT VOLVO AND GM.   M0740

ORGANIZATIONAL AND OCCUPATIONAL COMMITMENT: A FACET
THEORETICAL ANALYSIS OF EMPIRICAL DATA.   M0747

MANAGEMENT STYLES ASSOCIATED WITH ORGANIZATIONAL, TASK,
PERSONAL, AND INTERPERSONAL CONTINGENCIES.   M0748

RELATION OF ORGANIZATIONAL STRUCTURE TO JOB SATISFACTION,
ANXIETY-STRESS, AND PERFORMANCE.   M0766

MANAGERS' OCCUPATIONAL HISTORIES, ORGANIZATIONAL
ENVIRONMENTS, AND CLIMATES FOR MANAGEMENT DEVELOPMENT.   M0787

RELATIONSHIPS OF ORGANIZATIONAL FRUSTRATION WITH REPORTED
BEHAVIORAL REACTIONS OF EMPLOYEES.   M0796

VALIDATION OF THE INDEX OF ORGANIZATIONAL REACTIONS WITH
THE JDI, THE MSQ, AND FACES SCALES.   M0813

ORGANIZATIONAL   CONTINUATION

ORGANIZATIONS

ORGANIZATIONS   CONTINUATION

ORGANIZED

ORIENTATION

ORIENTATION CONTINUATION

AN EXAMINATION OF BRAINSTORMING PROCEDURE, GROUP SIZE AND
MOTIVATIONAL ORIENTATION IN THE JOB ENRICHMENT GREENLIGHT
SESSION. M0932

ORIENTATIONS

A STUDY OF THE WORK ORIENTATIONS OF WELFARE RECIPIENTS
PARTICIPATING IN THE WORK INCENTIVE PROGRAM. M0167

THE RELEVANCE OF COSMOPOLITAN/LOCAL ORIENTATIONS TO
PROFESSIONAL VALUES AND BEHAVIOR. M0588

THE SELF-CONCEPT, PERSONAL VALUES, AND MOTIVATIONAL
ORIENTATIONS OF BLACK AND WHITE MANAGERS. M0668

ORTHODOX

ORTHODOX JOB ENRICHMENT: MEASURING TRUE QUALITY IN JOB
SATISFACTION. M0523

OUTCOME

THE VOCATIONAL EXPLORATION GROUP AND MINORITY YOUTH: AN
EXPERIMENTAL OUTCOME STUDY. M0749

OUTCOMES

ANTECEDENTS AND OUTCOMES OF ORGANIZATIONAL COMMITMENT. M0633

OUTDOORS

WOMEN AT WORK -- OUTDOORS. M0077

OUTLINE

UNDERLOAD AND OVERLOAD IN WORKING LIFE: OUTLINE OF A
MULTI-DISCIPLINARY APPROACH. M0643

OVERLAPS

DIFFERENTIALS AND OVERLAPS IN EARNINGS OF BLACKS AND
WHITES. M0428

OVERLOAD

UNDERLOAD AND OVERLOAD IN WORKING LIFE: OUTLINE OF A
MULTI-DISCIPLINARY APPROACH. M0643

OVERSEAS

QUESTIONNAIRE PROVIDES INFORMATION ON JOB OPPORTUNITIES FOR
FS WIVES OVERSEAS. M0015

A COMPARATIVE STUDY OF THE SATISFACTION OF DOMESTIC U. S.

OVERSEAS   CONTINUATION

    MANAGERS AND OVERSEAS U. S. MANAGERS.   M0226

    EXTENSION WOMEN OVERSEAS.   M0328

OVERTIME

    RECENT TRENDS IN OVERTIME HOURS AND PREMIUM PAY.   M0130

OVERVIEW

    PRIVATE PENSION PLANS, 1960 TO 1969 -- AN OVERVIEW.   M0086

PACIFIC

    EFFECTS ON PRODUCTIVITY AND MORALE OF A SYSTEMS-DESIGNED
    JOB-ENRICHMENT PROGRAM IN PACIFIC TELEPHONE.   M0515

PAIRINGS

    SUPERVISOR EXPECTATIONS AND BEHAVIOR: EFFECTS OF
    CONSISTENT-INCONSISTENT SUPERVISORY PAIRINGS ON SUPERVISEE
    SATISFACTION WITH SUPERVISION, PERCEPTIONS OF SUPERVISORY
    RELATIONSHIPS AND RATED COUNSELOR COMPETENCY.   M0864

PANACEA

    LET'S ADMIT IT: ZERO DEFECTS IS NO PANACEA.   M0027

PANEL

    TIME PRESSURE AND PERFORMANCE OF SCIENTISTS AND ENGINEERS:
    A FIVE PANEL STUDY.   M0010

PARADOX

    THE MOTIVATIONAL PARADOX.   M0368

PARAMEDICAL

    RESTRUCTURING PARAMEDICAL OCCUPATIONS: A CASE STUDY.   M0169

    RESTRUCTURING PARAMEDICAL JOBS.   M0361

PAROLEE

    THE EFFECT OF LEGITIMATE OPPORTUNITIES ON THE PROBABILITY
    OF PAROLEE RECIDIVISM.   M0069

PART-TIME

    GUIDE TO PART-TIME WORK.   M0178

PARTICIPATING

PARTICIPATION

PARTICIPATIVE

PARTICIPATIVE   CONTINUATION

WORK ORGANIZATION AT A BANKING BRANCH: TOWARDS A
PARTICIPATIVE RESEARCH TECHNIQUE.   M0622

PARTICIPATIVE MANAGEMENT AT WORK.   M0694

EFFECTS OF ASSIGNED AND PARTICIPATIVE GOAL SETTING ON
PERFORMANCE AND JOB SATISFACTION.   M0887

PARTICIPATIVE AND POWER-EQUALIZED ORGANIZATIONAL SYSTEMS:
AN EMPIRICAL INVESTIGATION AND THEORETICAL INTEGRATION.   M0889

PARTICIPATIVE MANAGEMENT AT WORK.   M0931

PARTNERS

PARTNERS IN PRODUCTIVITY.   M0369

PASTURES

GREENER PASTURES: WHY EMPLOYEES CHANGE JOBS.   M0372

PATH

MOTIVATION AND CAREER PATH PLANNING.   M0146

PARTICIPATION WITH SUPERVISOR AND SUBORDINATE
AUTHORITARIANISM: A PATH GOAL THEORY RECONCILIATION.   M0554

LEADER STRUCTURE AND SUBORDINATE SATISFACTION FOR TWO
HOSPITAL ADMINISTRATIVE LEVELS: A PATH ANALYSIS APPROACH.   M0736

ANTECEDENTS OF SALESMEN'S COMPENSATION PERCEPTIONS: A PATH
ANALYSIS INTERPRETATION.   M0785

PATH-GOAL

EXTENSIONS OF A PATH-GOAL THEORY OF MOTIVATION.   M0120

ANALYSIS OF RELATIONSHIPS AMONG LEADER BEHAVIOR,
SUBORDINATE JOB PERFORMANCE, AND SATISFACTION: A PATH-GOAL
APPROACH.   M0652

THE PATH-GOAL THEORY OF LEADERSHIP: A THEORETICAL AND
EMPIRICAL ANALYSIS.   M0835

PATROL

POLICEWOMEN ON PATROL.   M0307

PATTERNS

EFFECTS OF DIFFERENT PATTERNS AND DEGREES OF OPENNESS IN
SUPERIOR-SUBORDINATE COMMUNICATION ON SUBORDINATE JOB
SATISFACTION.   M0045

PATTERNS   CONTINUATION

PAY

PERCEIVED

PERCEPTION

THE PERCEPTION OF OTHER WORK ROLES: IMPLICATIONS FOR JOB
CHANGE.   M0192

PERCEPTION, MOTIVES, AND PERSONALITY.   M0252

A STUDY OF THE JOB SATISFACTION AND JOB PERCEPTION OF
ORGANIZED AND NON-ORGANIZED PUBLIC SCHOOL PRINCIPALS.   M0902

JOB SATISFACTION OF GEORGIA SCHOOL SUPERINTENDENTS AND
THEIR PERCEPTION OF THE LOCAL SCHOOL BOARD PRESIDENT'S
LEADER BEHAVIOR.   M0906

PERCEPTIONS

PERCEPTIONS OF JOB SATISFACTION IN DIFFERING OCCUPATIONS.   M0256

HIGH SCHOOL STUDENTS PERCEPTIONS OF WORK.   M0535

THE EFFECTS OF ROLE PERCEPTIONS ON EMPLOYEE SATISFACTION
AND PERFORMANCE MODERATED BY EMPLOYEE ABILITY.   M0553

INVESTIGATION OF THE INFLUENCE OF JOB LEVEL AND FUNCTIONAL
SPECIALTY ON JOB ATTITUDES AND PERCEPTIONS.   M0745

ANTECEDENTS OF SALESMEN'S COMPENSATION PERCEPTIONS: A PATH
ANALYSIS INTERPRETATION.   M0785

BLACK-WHITE DIFFERENCES IN WORK ENVIRONMENT PERCEPTIONS AND
JOB SATISFACTION AND ITS CORRELATES.   M0820

AN EMPIRICAL TEST OF CAUSAL INFERENCE BETWEEN ROLE
PERCEPTIONS, SATISFACTION WITH WORK, PERFORMANCE AND
ORGANIZATIONAL LEVEL.   M0839

SUPERVISOR EXPECTATIONS AND BEHAVIOR: EFFECTS OF
CONSISTENT-INCONSISTENT SUPERVISORY PAIRINGS ON SUPERVISEE
SATISFACTION WITH SUPERVISION, PERCEPTIONS OF SUPERVISORY
RELATIONSHIPS AND RATED COUNSELOR COMPETENCY.   M0864

ROLE PERCEPTIONS, SATISFACTION AND PERFORMANCE MODERATED BY
ORGANIZATION LEVEL AND PARTICIPATION IN DECISION MAKING.   M0895

A STUDY OF THE PERCEPTIONS OF SELECTED SCHOOL-BASED
ADMINISTRATORS IN FLORIDA RELATIVE TO CERTAIN VARIABLES IN
SECONDARY SCHOOL ADMINISTRATION AS THEY RELATE TO JOB
SATISFACTION.   M0925

PERCEPTIONS OF ORGANIZATIONAL CLIMATE AS MEDIATORS OF THE
RELATIONSHIPS BETWEEN INDIVIDUAL NEEDS AND JOB SATISFACTION
OF COUNSELORS IN THE NORTH CAROLINA COMMUNITY COLLEGE
SYSTEM.   M0933

OLNEY CENTRAL COLLEGE DENTAL ASSISTING PROGRAM GRADUATES
PERCEPTIONS OF PROGRAM COMPONENTS, JOB SATISFACTION AND

PERFORMANCE   CONTINUATION

SATISFACTION WITH PERFORMANCE AS A FUNCTION OF THE INITIAL
LEVEL OF EXPECTED PERFORMANCE AND THE DEVIATION FROM
EXPECTATIONS.   M0221

ORGANIZATIONAL VOIDS THAT IMPROVE PERFORMANCE.   M0222

RELATIONSHIPS BETWEEN PERFORMANCE AND SATISFACTION UNDER
CONTINGENT AND NONCONTINGENT REWARD SYSTEMS.   M0251

EXPECTANCIES AS DETERMINATES OF PERFORMANCE.   M0258

DOES DIVORCE HAMPER JOB PERFORMANCE.   M0261

HOW THE PURCHASING MANAGER CAN IMPROVE EMPLOYEE
PERFORMANCE.   M0264

TOTAL MOTIVATION = TOP PERFORMANCE.   M0270

JOB SATISFACTION AND JOB PERFORMANCE: AN EMPIRICAL TEST OF
SOME THEORETICAL PROPOSITIONS.   M0323

A QUALITIATIVE APPROACH TO PERFORMANCE PREDICTABILITY AND
LEGAL COMPLIANCE.   M0329

A SYSTEMS APPROACH TO RESULTS ORIENTED PERFORMANCE
EVALUATION.   M0338

SATISFACTION AND PERFORMANCE: CAUSAL RELATIONSHIPS AND
MODERATING EFFECTS.   M0395

MOTIVATION IN MANAGERIAL LEVELS: RELATIONSHIP OF NEED
SATISFACTION TO JOB PERFORMANCE.   M0401

EMPLOYEE PERFORMANCE AND EMPLOYEE NEED SATISFACTION --
WHICH COMES FIRST.   M0434

SHIFT WORK: PERFORMANCE AND SATISFACTION.   M0511

PERFORMANCE IMPROVEMENT WITHOUT TRAINING.   M0545

THE EFFECTS OF ROLE PERCEPTIONS ON EMPLOYEE SATISFACTION
AND PERFORMANCE MODERATED BY EMPLOYEE ABILITY.   M0553

LEADERSHIP DIMENSIONS OF NAVY RECRUIT MORALE & PERFORMANCE.   M0564

BACKGROUND AND PERSONALITY CHARACTERISTICS RELATED TO
STUDENT SATISFACTION AND PERFORMANCE IN FIELD MEDICAL
SERVICE SCHOOL.   M0575

ORGANIZATIONAL STRUCTURE: HOW DOES IT INFLUENCE ATTITUDES
AND PERFORMANCE.   M0578

EFFECTS OF GOAL SETTING ON PERFORMANCE AND JOB
SATISFACTION.   M0594

PERFORMANCE   CONTINUATION

RETAIL STORE PERFORMANCE AND JOB SATISFACTION: A STUDY OF
ANXIETY-STRESS PROPENSITY TO LEAVE AMONG RETAIL EMPLOYEES.   M0811

DIFFERENT GOAL SETTING TREATMENTS AND THEIR EFFECTS ON
PERFORMANCE AND JOB SATISFACTION.   M0819

PERSONALITY-JOB FIT: IMPLICATIONS FOR INDIVIDUAL ATTITUDES
AND PERFORMANCE.   M0829

AN EMPIRICAL TEST OF CAUSAL INFERENCE BETWEEN ROLE
PERCEPTIONS, SATISFACTION WITH WORK, PERFORMANCE AND
ORGANIZATIONAL LEVEL.   M0839

RELATIONSHIP OF PERFORMANCE TO SATISFACTION IN STIMULATING
AND NONSTIMULATING JOBS.   M0848

PREDICTING THE PERFORMANCE OF JUNIOR ACHIEVEMENT ACCORDING
TO THE LEADERSHIP STYLE OF TWO LEVELS OF MANAGEMENT: A
FIELD STUDY OF THE CONTINGENCY MODEL.   M0872

AN EXPERIMENTAL STUDY OF THE EFFECTS OF GOAL SETTING,
EVALUATION APPREHENSION, AND SOCIAL CUES ON TASK
PERFORMANCE AND JOB SATISFACTION.   M0878

EFFECTS OF ASSIGNED AND PARTICIPATIVE GOAL SETTING ON
PERFORMANCE AND JOB SATISFACTION.   M0887

ROLE PERCEPTIONS, SATISFACTION AND PERFORMANCE MODERATED BY
ORGANIZATION LEVEL AND PARTICIPATION IN DECISION MAKING.   M0895

EMPLOYEE ATTITUDES REGARDING VARIOUS CHARACTERISTICS OF JOB
OPPORTUNITY AND JOB PERFORMANCE ACROSS THREE DIFFERENT WORK
SHIFTS AT AN INSTITUTION FOR THE RETARDED.   M0900

COMPARATIVE APPRAISALS OF JOB PERFORMANCE OF FULL-TIME
ELEMENTARY PRINCIPALS BY THE PRINCIPALS AND THEIR
SUPERVISORS IN CLASS I MONTANA SCHOOL DISTRICTS.   M0941

AN EMPIRICAL STUDY OF INDIVIDUAL CONGRUENCE AND THE
PERCEIVED ORGANIZATIONAL PRACTICES - JOB SATISFACTION - JOB
PERFORMANCE RELATIONSHIP IN SELECTED ELECTRONIC COMPUTER
DATA PROCESSING CENTERS.   M0946

PERFORMANCE-CONTINGENT

THE IMPACT OF PERFORMANCE-CONTINGENT REWARDS ON JOB
SATISFACTION: DIRECT AND INDIRECT EFFECTS.   M0686

PERSISTENCE

THE PERSISTENCE OF THE DISADVANTAGED WORKER EFFECT.   M0383

PERSON

PERSON-ENVIRONMENT

PERSONAL

CONTINUATION

PERSONAL

    VALUES IN SOUTH AFRICA: A RESEARCH NOTE.   M0786

    RELATIONSHIP OF PERSONAL INFLUENCE DISSONANCE TO JOB
    TENSION SATISFACTION AND INVOLVEMENT.   M0817

    THE JOB SATISFACTION OF SCHOOL TEACHERS IN THE REPUBLIC OF
    CHINA AS RELATED TO PERSONAL AND ORGANIZATIONAL
    CHARACTERISTICS.   M0909

PERSONALITY

    PERSONALITY, MOTIVATIONAL SYSTEMS, AND BEHAVIOR OF HIGH AND
    LOW LPC PERSONS.   M0131

    PERCEPTION, MOTIVES, AND PERSONALITY.   M0252

    INTERACTION EFFECTS OF PERSONALITY, JOB TRAINING, AND LABOR
    MARKET CONDITIONS ON PERSONAL EMPLOYMENT AND INCOME.   M0305

    MOTIVATIONAL AND PERSONALITY FACTORS RELATED TO CAREER
    GOALS OF BLACK COLLEGE WOMEN.   M0310

    GOAL-SETTING ATTRIBUTES, PERSONALITY VARIABLES, AND JOB
    SATISFACTION.   M0570

    BACKGROUND AND PERSONALITY CHARACTERISTICS RELATED TO
    STUDENT SATISFACTION AND PERFORMANCE IN FIELD MEDICAL
    SERVICE SCHOOL.   M0575

    IDENTIFICATION, PERSONALITY NEEDS, AND MANAGERIAL
    POSITIONS.   M0611

    PERSONALITY VS. ORGANIZATION.   M0704

    THE ENTREPRENEURIAL PERSONALITY: A PERSON AT THE
    CROSSROADS.   M0771

    A STUDY OF THE RELATIONSHIP BETWEEN HERZBERG'S MOTIVATION
    HYGIENE FACTORS AND HOLLAND'S PERSONALITY PATTERNS FOR LAW
    ENFORCEMENT PERSONNEL.   M0850

    PERSONALITY TRAITS, WORK FUNCTIONS, AND VOCATIONAL
    SATISFACTION OF PHYSICIANS IN THREE MEDICAL SPECIALTIES.   M0875

    THE RELATIONSHIPS AMONG THE PERSONALITY TYPES, JOB
    SATISFACTIONS, AND JOB SPECIALTIES OF A SELECTED GROUP OF
    MEDICAL TECHNOLOGISTS.   M0945

PERSONALITY-JOB

    PERSONALITY-JOB FIT: IMPLICATIONS FOR INDIVIDUAL ATTITUDES
    AND PERFORMANCE.   M0829

PERSONNEL

DECISIONAL PARTICIPATION AND SOURCES OF JOB SATISFACTION: A STUDY OF MANUFACTURING PERSONNEL.   M0008

PERSONNEL SYSTEMS AND HUMAN PERFORMANCE.   M0024

MODEL PROGRAM TO INSTRUCT MANPOWER TRAINING PERSONNEL IN SELECTION AND APPLICATION OF REMEDIAL INSTRUCTIONAL MATERIALS TO MEET INDIVIDUAL TRAINEE NEEDS.   M0387

WHAT THE PERSONNEL FUNCTION IS ALL ABOUT.   M0413

INCREASING THE IMPORTANCE OF PERSONNEL: A STRATEGY.   M0549

FEELINGS OF POWERLESSNESS AND SOCIAL ISOLATION AMONG LARGE SCALE FARM PERSONNEL.   M0596

PERSONNEL ATTITUDES AND MOTIVATION.   M0624

JOB ATTITUDES OF STUDENT PERSONNEL WORKERS AND THEIR JOB SITUATIONS.   M0707

A STUDY OF THE RELATIONSHIP BETWEEN HERZBERG'S MOTIVATION HYGIENE FACTORS AND HOLLAND'S PERSONALITY PATTERNS FOR LAW ENFORCEMENT PERSONNEL.   M0850

THE RELATIONSHIP OF JOB SATISFACTION MEASURES TO SELF-REPORT AND OBJECTIVE CRITERIA MEASURES AND THE EFFECT OF MODERATOR VARIABLES FOR CANADIAN MILITARY PERSONNEL.   M0853

RELATIONSHIPS BETWEEN WORK VALUES AND JOB SATISFACTION AMONG COLLEGE STUDENT PERSONNEL WORKERS.   M0928

PERSONS

PERSONALITY, MOTIVATIONAL SYSTEMS, AND BEHAVIOR OF HIGH AND LOW LPC PERSONS.   M0131

PERSPECTIVE

LABOR MARKETS AND MANPOWER POLICIES IN PERSPECTIVE.   M0005

THE FEDERAL WOMEN'S PROGRAM: A HUD PERSPECTIVE.   M0348

PERSPECTIVES

NEW PERSPECTIVES ON THE WILL TO WORK.   M0207

PERSPECTIVES ON THE QUALITY OF WORKING LIFE.   M0577

TWO INTERACTIVE PERSPECTIVES ON THE RELATIONSHIP BETWEEN JOB LEVEL AND JOB SATISFACTION.   M0823

PLANNERS

    THE CHANGING ROLE OF WOMEN: IMPLICATIONS FOR PLANNERS.   M0173

PLANNING

    MOTIVATION AND CAREER PATH PLANNING.   M0146

    CAREER PLANNING FOR HIGH SCHOOL GIRLS.   M0420

    MANAGEMENT'S ECTASY AND DISPARITY OVER JOB ENRICHMENT:
    EXPECTATIONS IN PLANNING JOB CHANGE: A CASE STUDY.   M0531

    SELF-MOTIVATED PERSONAL CAREER PLANNING: A BREAKTHROUGH IN
    HUMAN RESOURCE MANAGEMENT (PART I).   M0561

    PLANNING -- SATISFACTION AND PRODUCTIVITY.   M0816

PLANNING-MOTIVATING

    THE PLANNING-MOTIVATING DILEMMA.   M0187

PLANS

    NEGOTIATED RETIREMENT PLANS -- A DECADE OF BENEFIT
    IMPROVEMENTS.   M0085

    PRIVATE PENSION PLANS, 1960 TO 1969 -- AN OVERVIEW.   M0086

PLANT

    RELATIONSHIPS BETWEEN JOB SATISFACTION, DEMOGRAPHIC
    FACTORS, ABSENTEEISM AND TENURE OF WORKERS IN A DELMARVA
    BROILER PROCESSING PLANT.   M0921

PLANTS

    PRODUCTIVITY ANALYSIS IN MANUFACTURING PLANTS.   M0448

PLEA

    WHY STUDY WORKING CONDITIONS VIA JOB SATISFACTION? A PLEA
    FOR DIRECT ANALYSIS.   M0833

PME

    SHIFTING GEARS IN PME.   M0065

POLICE

    FILLING THE POLICE LINEUP.   M0399

POLICEWOMEN

    POLICEWOMEN ON PATROL.   M0307

POSITIONS

    IDENTIFICATION, PERSONALITY NEEDS, AND MANAGERIAL
    POSITIONS.   M0611

    THE DEVELOPMENT OF A MANAGERIAL JOB TAXONOMY: A SYSTEM FOR
    DESCRIBING, CLASSIFYING, AND EVALUATING EXECUTIVE
    POSITIONS.   M0618

POSITIVELY

    CONDITIONS UNDER WHICH EMPLOYEES RESPOND POSITIVELY TO
    ENRICHED WORK.   M0606

POST-INDUSTRIAL

    JOB SATISFACTION RESEARCH: THE POST-INDUSTRIAL VIEW.   M0087

POSTAL

    CAREER OPPORTUNITIES IN THE POSTAL SERVICE.   M0152

POSTULATES

    A TEST OF TWO POSTULATES UNDERLYING EXPECTANCY THEORY.   M0666

POTENTIAL

    REALIZING APPRENTICESHIP'S POTENTIAL.   M0038

    COMPONENTS OF ACHIEVEMENT MOTIVATION AS PREDICTORS OF
    POTENTIAL FOR ECONOMIC CHANGE.   M0458

POVERTY

    SOCIOECONOMIC DETERMINANTS OF URBAN POVERTY AREA WORKERS.   M0349

POWER

    BUILDING EFFICACY: AN EFFECTIVE USE OF MANAGERIAL POWER.   M0035

    A SOCIAL PSYCHOLGICAL EXPLORATION OF POWER MOTIVATION AMONG
    DISADVANTAGED WORKERS.   M0279

POWER-EQUALIZED

    PARTICIPATIVE AND POWER-EQUALIZED ORGANIZATIONAL SYSTEMS:
    AN EMPIRICAL INVESTIGATION AND THEORETICAL INTEGRATION.   M0889

POWERLESSNESS

    FEELINGS OF POWERLESSNESS AND SOCIAL ISOLATION AMONG LARGE
    SCALE FARM PERSONNEL.   M0596

PRACTICAL

    A PRACTICAL SCHEME THAT MOTIVATES PEOPLE.   M0297

    A PRACTICAL PROGRAM FOR EMPLOYEE SOCIALIZATION.   M0714

PRACTICE

    THE PRACTICE OF MANAGERIAL PSYCHOLOGY.   M0112

PRACTICES

    TIME AND INCENTIVE PAY PRACTICES IN URBAN AREAS.   M0076

    AN EMPIRICAL STUDY OF INDIVIDUAL CONGRUENCE AND THE
    PERCEIVED ORGANIZATIONAL PRACTICES - JOB SATISFACTION - JOB
    PERFORMANCE RELATIONSHIP IN SELECTED ELECTRONIC COMPUTER
    DATA PROCESSING CENTERS.   M0946

PRACTITIONER

    GUIDELINES FOR THE JOB ENRICHMENT PRACTITIONER.   M0538

PREDICTABILITY

    A QUALITIATIVE APPROACH TO PERFORMANCE PREDICTABILITY AND
    LEGAL COMPLIANCE.   M0329

    SUBJECTIVE EXPECTATIONS AND JOB FACET PREDICTABILITY IN JOB
    SATISFACTION.   M0876

PREDICTING

    AN INVESTIGATION OF JOB SATISFACTION AS A MODERATOR
    VARIABLE IN PREDICTING JOB SUCCESS.   M0025

    PREDICTING ABSENTEEISM AND TURNOVER: A FIELD COMPARISON OF
    FISHBEIN'S MODEL AND TRADITIONAL JOB ATTITUDE MEASURES. M0326

    PREDICTING THE PERFORMANCE OF JUNIOR ACHIEVEMENT COMPANIES
    ACCORDING TO THE LEADERSHIP STYLE OF TWO LEVELS OF
    MANAGEMENT: A FIELD STUDY OF THE CONTINGENCY MODEL. M0700

    PREDICTING JOB PERFORMANCE BY USE OF ABILITY TESTS AND
    STUDYING JOB SATISFACTION AS A MODERATING VARIABLE. M0765

    PREDICTING PAY SATISFACTION FROM NONPAY WORK VARIABLES. M0843

    PREDICTING THE PERFORMANCE OF JUNIOR ACHIEVEMENT ACCORDING
    TO THE LEADERSHIP STYLE OF TWO LEVELS OF MANAGEMENT: A
    FIELD STUDY OF THE CONTINGENCY MODEL. M0872

PREDICTION

    PREDICTION OF ORGANIZATIONAL BEHAVIOR. M0139

PREFERENCES

THE RELATION OF JOB SATISFACTION TO VOCATIONAL PREFERENCES
AMONG TEACHERS OF THE EDUCABLE MENTALLY RETARDED.   M0805

PREFERRED

PREFERRED JOB ASSIGNMENT EFFECT ON JOB SATISFACTION.   M0598

PRELIMINARY

CORPORATE DROPOUTS: A PRELIMINARY TYPOLOGY.   M0616

PREMIUM

RECENT TRENDS IN OVERTIME HOURS AND PREMIUM PAY.   M0130

PRESIDENT'S

JOB SATISFACTION OF GEORGIA SCHOOL SUPERINTENDENTS AND
THEIR PERCEPTION OF THE LOCAL SCHOOL BOARD PRESIDENT'S
LEADER BEHAVIOR.   M0906

PRESIDENTS

JOB SATISFACTION OF COLLEGE PRESIDENTS.   M0907

PRESSURE

TIME PRESSURE AND PERFORMANCE OF SCIENTISTS AND ENGINEERS:
A FIVE PANEL STUDY.   M0010

WORKERS UNDER STRESS (THE IMPACT OF WORK PRESSURE ON GROUP
COHESION).   M0255

PRESSURES

JOB CHARACTERISTICS AND PRESSURES AND THE ORGANIZATIONAL
INTEGRATION OF PROFESSIONALS.   M0268

PRESTIGE

RELATIONSHIPS AMONG PAY, RACE, SEX, OCCUPATIONAL PRESTIGE,
SUPERVISION, WORK AUTONOMY, AND JOB SATISFACTION IN A
NATIONAL SAMPLE.   M0842

PRIESTS

SECOND CAREER CATHOLIC PRIESTS: A STUDY OF THEIR LEVEL OF
JOB SATISFACTION, MATURITY, AND MORALE.   M0924

PRINCIPALS

SCHOOL BOARD DOGMATISM AND MORALE OF PRINCIPALS.   M0731

AN INVESTIGATION OF EDUCATIONAL ADMINISTRATIVE STYLE AND

PRINCIPALS CONTINUATION

JOB SATISFACTION OF ELEMENTARY SCHOOL PRINCIPALS. M0901

A STUDY OF THE JOB SATISFACTION AND JOB PERCEPTION OF
ORGANIZED AND NON-ORGANIZED PUBLIC SCHOOL PRINCIPALS. M0902

COMPARATIVE APPRAISALS OF JOB PERFORMANCE OF FULL-TIME
ELEMENTARY PRINCIPALS BY THE PRINCIPALS AND THEIR
SUPERVISORS IN CLASS I MONTANA SCHOOL DISTRICTS. M0941

PRINCIPALSHIP

A NORMATIVE STUDY OF THE SECONDARY SCHOOL ASSISTANT
PRINCIPALSHIP IN SELECTED PENNSYLVANIA SCHOOL DISTRICTS
WITH AN EMPHASIS UPON JOB SATISFACTION. M0918

PRINCIPLE

CAREER CHOICE, JOB SATISFACTION, AND THE TRUTH BEHIND THE
PETER PRINCIPLE. M0541

PRIVATE

PRIVATE PENSION PLANS, 1960 TO 1969 -- AN OVERVIEW. M0086

PRIVATES

AN INVESTIGATION OF ATTITUDES AMONG PRIVATES AT KA55
FOURTEENTH YEAR. M0739

PRIZE

MOTIVATION IS EASY IF THE PRIZE IS RIGHT. M0322

PROBABILITY

THE EFFECT OF LEGITIMATE OPPORTUNITIES ON THE PROBABILITY
OF PAROLEE RECIDIVISM. M0069

PROBLEM

PROBLEM OF MOTIVATION IN MANAGEMENT DEVELOPMENT. M0096

NEUROLOGICAL BASIS OF MOTIVATION: AN ENDURING PROBLEM IN
PSYCHOLOGY. M0160

PROBLEM RESOLUTION AND IMPOSITION OF CHANGE THROUGH A
PARTICIPATING GROUP EFFORT. M0238

REACTIONS AT WORK AND THEIR INFLUENCE ON NON-WORK
ACTIVITIES: AN ANALYSIS OF A SOCIOPOLITICAL PROBLEM IN
AFFLUENT SOCIETIES. M0587

UNDERSTANDING DRUG USE MOTIVATION: A NEW LOOK AT A CURRENT
PROBLEM. M0788

PROBLEMS

    W. I. N. REPORT -- PROBLEMS, PROGRESS, PROGNOSIS.   M0482

PROCEDURE

    AN EXAMINATION OF BRAINSTORMING PROCEDURE, GROUP SIZE AND
    MOTIVATIONAL ORIENTATION IN THE JOB ENRICHMENT GREENLIGHT
    SESSION.   M0932

PROCESS

    FACE-TO-FACE INTERACTION IN THE PEER-NOMINATION PROCESS.   M0281

    THE ACHIEVEMENT PROCESS: AN EXPLORATORY STUDY OF CAREER
    BEGINNINGS.   M0332

    WORK MOTIVATION, A MENTAL PROCESS.   M0528

    VALUES, STRUCTURE, PROCESS, AND REACTIONS/ADJUSTMENTS: A
    COMPARISON OF FRENCH AND ENGLISH-CANADIAN INDUSTRIAL
    ORGANIZATIONS.   M0628

    THE JOINING-UP PROCESS: ISSUES IN EFFECTIVE HUMAN RESOURCE
    DEVELOPMENT.   M0758

PROCESSING

    RELATIONSHIPS BETWEEN JOB SATISFACTION, DEMOGRAPHIC
    FACTORS, ABSENTEEISM AND TENURE OF WORKERS IN A DELMARVA
    BROILER PROCESSING PLANT.   M0921

    AN EMPIRICAL STUDY OF INDIVIDUAL CONGRUENCE AND THE
    PERCEIVED ORGANIZATIONAL PRACTICES - JOB SATISFACTION - JOB
    PERFORMANCE RELATIONSHIP IN SELECTED ELECTRONIC COMPUTER
    DATA PROCESSING CENTERS.   M0946

PRODUCING

    PRODUCING MAN'S CASE FOR SATISFACTION.   M0610

PRODUCTION-PROCESS

    WORK AND WORK MOTIVATION IN AN AUTOMATED INDUSTRIAL
    PRODUCTION-PROCESS.   M0042

PRODUCTIVITY

    CITY HALL DISCOVERS PRODUCTIVITY.   M0072

    PEOPLE AND PRODUCTIVITY: DO THEY STILL EQUAL PAY AND
    PROFITS?   M0092

    INCREASING PRODUCTIVITY BY INVOLVING PEOPLE IN THEIR TOTAL
    JOB.   M0107

PRODUCTIVITY   CONTINUATION

    HELP.   M0568

    HOW TO IMPROVE THE PERFORMANCE AND PRODUCTIVITY OF THE
    KNOWLEDGE WORKER.   M0602

    EFFECTS OF JOB ENRICHMENT AND TASK GOALS ON SATISFACTION
    AND PRODUCTIVITY: IMPLICATIONS FOR JOB DESIGN.   M0619

    IMPROVING PRODUCTIVITY THROUGH JOB ENRICHMENT.   M0647

    EFFECTS OF PARTICIPATION ON SATISFACTION AND PRODUCTIVITY.   M0702

    INCENTIVE SCHEDULES, PRODUCTIVITY, AND SATISFACTION IN WORK
    GROUPS: A LABORATORY STUDY.   M0814

    PLANNING -- SATISFACTION AND PRODUCTIVITY.   M0816

PROFESSIONAL

    PROFESSIONAL MANPOWER: THE JOB MARKET TURN-AROUND.   M0078

    THE PROFESSIONAL WOMAN IN GAO.   M0236

    WOMEN IN PROFESSIONAL TRAINING.   M0340

    JOB SATISFACTION: MALE AND FEMALE, PROFESSIONAL AND
    NON-PROFESSIONAL.   M0552

    THE RELEVANCE OF COSMOPOLITAN/LOCAL ORIENTATIONS TO
    PROFESSIONAL VALUES AND BEHAVIOR.   M0588

    A COMPARISON OF PROFESSIONAL INSTITUTIONAL COMMUNITY
    CORRECTIONS WORKERS ON JOB SATISFACTION AND SELF-CONCEPT.   M0696

    THE FOUR STAGES OF PROFESSIONAL CAREERS - A NEW LOOK AT
    PERFORMANCE BY PROFESSIONALS.   M0711

    TRENDS IN JOB-RELATED ATTITUDES OF MANAGERIAL AND
    PROFESSIONAL EMPLOYEES.   M0838

    TASK OPPORTUNITY PROFESSIONAL GROWTH NEED FULFILLMENT AND
    INTRINSIC JOB SATISFACTION OF PUBLIC SOCIAL SERVICE WORKERS
    IN COLORADO.   M0923

PROFESSIONALS

    BLACK PROFESSIONALS: PROGRESS AND SKEPTICISM.   M0028

    NEEDS FULFILLMENT AND JOB SATISFACTION OF PROFESSIONALS.   M0074

    A STUDY OF BLACK MALE PROFESSIONALS IN INDUSTRY.   M0143

    JOB CHARACTERISTICS AND PRESSURES AND THE ORGANIZATIONAL
    INTEGRATION OF PROFESSIONALS.   M0268

PROGRAM   CONTINUATION

   MATERIALS TO MEET INDIVIDUAL TRAINEE NEEDS.   M0387

   OCCUPATIONAL GUIDANCE MATERIALS FOR THE DISADVANTAGED: A
   PILOT PROGRAM.   M0404

   ELEMENTS OF AN EMPLOYEE MOTIVATION PROGRAM.   M0469

   EFFECTS ON PRODUCTIVITY AND MORALE OF A SYSTEMS-DESIGNED
   JOB-ENRICHMENT PROGRAM IN PACIFIC TELEPHONE.   M0515

   CREATING A "QUALITY" QUALITY CONTROL PROGRAM AT SPP.   M0688

   A PRACTICAL PROGRAM FOR EMPLOYEE SOCIALIZATION.   M0714

   OLNEY CENTRAL COLLEGE DENTAL ASSISTING PROGRAM GRADUATES
   PERCEPTIONS OF PROGRAM COMPONENTS, JOB SATISFACTION AND
   CAREER GOALS.   M0944

PROGRAMMERS

   PREDICTION OF SATISFACTION OF SYSTEMS ANALYSTS,
   PROGRAMMERS.   M0807

PROGRAMS

   THE EFFECT OF MOTIVATIONAL PROGRAMS ON COLLECTIVE
   BARGAINING.   M0032

   SOCIAL AND WELFARE PROGRAMS FOR THE HANDICAPPED ABROAD.   M0043

   WORK TRAINING PROGRAMS AND THE UNEMPLOYMENT RATE.   M0403

   MANPOWER PROGRAMS FOR CRIMINAL OFFENDERS.   M0436

   MANPOWER PROGRAMS IN FOUR CITIES.   M0455

   WOMEN'S PROGRAMS SURVEYED AT LATIN AMERICAN POSTS.   M0488

PROGRESS

   BLACK PROFESSIONALS: PROGRESS AND SKEPTICISM.   M0028

   PROGRESS IN MEASURING PRODUCTIVITY IN GOVERNMENT.   M0303

   W. I. N. REPORT -- PROBLEMS, PROGRESS, PROGNOSIS.   M0482

PROJECT

   INFLUENCE STYLES OF PROJECT MANAGERS: SOME PROJECT
   PERFORMANCE CORRELATES.   M0151

   EVALUATION AND IMPLEMENTATION OF THE NEW YORK FIRE
   DEPARTMENT EXAMINATION TRAINING PROJECT FOR CULTURALLY
   DISADVANTAGED RESIDENTS OF THE CITY OF NEW YORK.   M0243

PROJECT   CONTINUATION

    TAKING THE STING OUT OF PROJECT REASSIGNMENT.   M0441

    REPORTED JOB INTEREST AND PERCEIVED UTILIZATION OF TALENTS
    AND TRAINING BY AIRMEN IN 97 CAREER LADDERS, BY R. BRUCE
    GOULD. PROJECT 7734, DECEMBER 1972.   M0452

PROJECTS

    SPECIAL WORK PROJECTS FOR THE UNEMPLOYED AND UPGRADING FOR
    THE WORKING POOR.   M0475

PROPENSITY

    RETAIL STORE PERFORMANCE AND JOB SATISFACTION: A STUDY OF
    ANXIETY-STRESS PROPENSITY TO LEAVE AMONG RETAIL EMPLOYEES.   M0811

PROPORTION

    INCREASING PROPORTION OF WOMEN ARE HEADS OF HOUSEHOLD.   M0224

PROPOSITIONS

    JOB SATISFACTION AND JOB PERFORMANCE: AN EMPIRICAL TEST OF
    SOME THEORETICAL PROPOSITIONS.   M0323

PROSPECT

    JAPAN'S LABOR ECONOMY -- PROSPECT FOR THE FUTURE.   M0123

PROSPECTS

    JOB PROSPECTS FOR COLLEGE GRADUATES IN 1974.   M0233

PROSPERITY

    IMPACT OF PERCEIVED COMMUNITY PROSPERITY ON JOB
    SATISFACTION OF BLACK AND WHITE WORKERS.   M0542

PROVIDES

    QUESTIONNAIRE PROVIDES INFORMATION ON JOB OPPORTUNITIES FOR
    FS WIVES OVERSEAS.   M0015

PSCHOPHYSIOLOGICAL

    PSCHOPHYSIOLOGICAL INFLUENCES ON THE WORK ENVIRONMENT: NEW
    CONCEPTS.   M0550

PSYCHIATRIC

    ORGANIZATIONAL COMMITMENT, JOB SATISFACTION, AND TURNOVER
    AMONG PSYCHIATRIC TECHNICIANS.   M0353

    INTRAROLE CONFLICT AND JOB SATISFACTION ON PSYCHIATRIC

PSYCHIATRIC   CONTINUATION

   UNITS.   M0712

   WORK VALUES AND JOB SATISFACTION OF PSYCHIATRIC AIDES.   M0917

PSYCHIC

   HEDONIC WAGE EQUATIONS AND PSYCHIC WAGES IN THE RETURNS TO
   SCHOOLING.   M0822

PSYCHOLGICAL

   A SOCIAL PSYCHOLGICAL EXPLORATION OF POWER MOTIVATION AMONG
   DISADVANTAGED WORKERS.   M0279

PSYCHOLOGICAL

   CAUSAL MODELING OF PSYCHOLOGICAL SUCCESS IN WORK
   ORGANIZATIONS.   M0520

   SOCIAL AND PSYCHOLOGICAL INFLUENCES ON EMPLOYMENT OF
   MARRIED NURSES.   M0755

   MEASUREMENT OF SOCIOECONOMIC AND PSYCHOLOGICAL
   CHARACTERISTICS: A METHOD.   M0789

   PSYCHOLOGICAL ATTITUDES AND BELIEFS OF MINISTERS.   M0804

PSYCHOLOGISTS

   TRAINING AND CAREER SATISFACTION AMONG CLINICAL
   PSYCHOLOGISTS.   M0759

PSYCHOLOGY

   THE PRACTICE OF MANAGERIAL PSYCHOLOGY.   M0112

   PSYCHOLOGY IN THE INDUSTRIAL ENVIRONMENT.   M0129

   NEUROLOGICAL BASIS OF MOTIVATION: AN ENDURING PROBLEM IN
   PSYCHOLOGY.   M0160

   ORGANIZATIONAL PSYCHOLOGY (A BOOK OF READINGS).   M0257

   INDUSTRIAL AND ORGANIZATIONAL PSYCHOLOGY.   M0259

   READINGS IN MANAGERIAL PSYCHOLOGY, 2ND ED. CHICAGO.   M0271

   PSYCHOLOGY IN INDUSTRIAL ORGANIZATIONS.   M0296

   INDUSTRIAL AND ORGANIZATIONAL PSYCHOLOGY.   M0460

PUBLIC

   PUBLIC EMPLOYEE LABOR RELATIONS IN OTHER DEMOCRACIES. M0161

PUBLIC   CONTINUATION

    A COMPARATIVE ANALYSIS OF THE JOB SATISFACTION OF
    INDUSTRIAL MANAGERS AND CERTIFIED PUBLIC ACCOUNTANTS.   M0228

    THE QUIT RATE AS A MEASURE OF MORALE IN THE PUBLIC SERVICE:
    THE CASE OF THE UNITED STATES FOREIGN SERVICE.   M0292

    THE PUBLIC EMPLOYMENT SERVICE REACHES OUT TO THE URBAN
    POOR.   M0374

    WHY PUBLIC WORKERS STAY.   M0636

    REWARDS AND PUBLIC EMPLOYEES' ATTITUDES TOWARD CLIENT
    SERVICE.   M0693

    MULTIJOBHOLDING OF WICHITA PUBLIC SCHOOL TEACHERS.   M0729

    MOTIVATING THE PUBLIC EMPLOYEE: FACT VS. FICTION.   M0890

    A STUDY OF THE JOB SATISFACTION AND JOB PERCEPTION OF
    ORGANIZED AND NON-ORGANIZED PUBLIC SCHOOL PRINCIPALS.   M0902

    TASK OPPORTUNITY PROFESSIONAL GROWTH NEED FULFILLMENT AND
    INTRINSIC JOB SATISFACTION OF PUBLIC SOCIAL SERVICE WORKERS
    IN COLORADO.   M0923

    REWARDS AND PUBLIC EMPLOYEES' ATTITUDES TOWARD CLIENT
    SERVICE.   M0929

PUNISHMENT

    PERCEIVED LEADER BEHAVIOR AND EMPLOYEE SATISFACTION WITH
    SUPERVISION AND THE JOB: THE EFFECTS OF REWARD AND
    PUNISHMENT.   M0859

PURCHASING

    HOW THE PURCHASING MANAGER CAN IMPROVE EMPLOYEE
    PERFORMANCE.   M0264

PURITIAN

    THE HARD CORE AND THE PURITIAN WORK ETHIC.   M0370

PURPOSE

    MULTI PURPOSE MAN.   M0163

PURPOSEFULNESS

    PERCEIVED PURPOSEFULNESS OF JOB BEHAVIOR: ANTECEDENTS AND
    CONSEQUENCES.   M0336

QUALITIATIVE

QUALITY

QUESTIONNAIRE

QUESTIONS

QUESTIONS   CONTINUATION

    STATE OF THE ART QUESTIONS ABOUT QUALITY OF WORKLIFE.   M0517

QUICKLY

    GOODS WELL BOUGHT ARE QUICKLY SOLD.   M0048

QUIT

    THE QUIT RATE AS A MEASURE OF MORALE IN THE PUBLIC SERVICE:
    THE CASE OF THE UNITED STATES FOREIGN SERVICE.   M0292

QUITS

    QUITS IN MANUFACTURING: A STUDY OF THEIR CAUSES.   M0014

RACE

    RACE, EMPLOYMENT, AND THE EVALUATION OF WORK.   M0128

    RELATIONSHIPS AMONG PAY, RACE, SEX, OCCUPATIONAL PRESTIGE,
    SUPERVISION, WORK AUTONOMY, AND JOB SATISFACTION IN A
    NATIONAL SAMPLE.   M0842

    JOB SATISFACTION AND NEED IMPORTANCE: RACE, SEX, AND
    OCCUPATIONAL GROUP.   M0860

RACIAL

    ANALYSIS OF RACIAL DIFFERENCES IN TERMS OF WORK
    ASSIGNMENTS, JOB INTEREST, AND FELT UTILIZATION OF TALENTS
    AND TRAINING, BY RAYMOND E. CHRISTEL.   M0451

    RACIAL DIFFERENCES IN JOB ATTITUDES AND PERFORMANCE: SOME
    THEORETICAL CONSIDERATIONS AND EMPIRICAL FINDINGS.   M0717

    SEGREGATION AND JOB SATISFACTION IN THE WORK PLACE: THE
    MEASUREMENT OF RACIAL DISPARITIES IN ORGANIZATIONS AND
    THEIR INFLUENCE ON EMPLOYEE WORK ATTITUDES.   M0927

RADICAL

    ON ALEX CAREY'S RADICAL CRITICISMS OF THE HAWTHORNE
    STUDIES.   M0391

RAILROAD

    RAILROAD APPRENTICES STAY ON THE TRACK.   M0324

RANKING

    OCCUPATIONAL RANKING FOR MEN AND WOMEN BY EARNINGS.   M0408

RANKS

DISCONTENT IN THE RANKS: IS THE OPERATIVE WORKER REALLY
TRAPPED.   M0354

RAPID

RAPID PRODUCTIVITY GAINS REPORTED FOR SELECTED INDUSTRIES
FOR 1971.   M0201

RATE

HOW DO SECRETARIES RATE.   M0239

THE QUIT RATE AS A MEASURE OF MORALE IN THE PUBLIC SERVICE:
THE CASE OF THE UNITED STATES FOREIGN SERVICE.   M0292

WORK TRAINING PROGRAMS AND THE UNEMPLOYMENT RATE.   M0403

RATED

SUPERVISOR EXPECTATIONS AND BEHAVIOR: EFFECTS OF
CONSISTENT-INCONSISTENT SUPERVISORY PAIRINGS ON SUPERVISEE
SATISFACTION WITH SUPERVISION, PERCEPTIONS OF SUPERVISORY
RELATIONSHIPS AND RATED COUNSELOR COMPETENCY.   M0864

REACTIONS

EMPLOYEE REACTIONS TO JOB CHARACTERISTICS.   M0181

INDIVIDUAL REACTIONS TO ORGANIZATIONAL CONFLICT AND CHANGE. M0311

RELATIONSHIP BETWEEN LOCUS OF CONTROL AND REACTIONS OF
EMPLOYEES TO WORK CHARACTERISTICS.   M0530

AGE AND REACTIONS TO TASK CHARACTERISTICS.   M0569

REACTIONS TO JOB CHARACTERISTICS: MODERATING EFFECTS OF THE
ORGANIZATION.   M0581

REACTIONS AT WORK AND THEIR INFLUENCE ON NON-WORK
ACTIVITIES: AN ANALYSIS OF A SOCIOPOLITICAL PROBLEM IN
AFFLUENT SOCIETIES.   M0587

BLACK-WHITE DIFFERENCES IN LEADER BEHAVIOR RELATED TO
SUBORDINATES' REACTIONS.   M0608

VALUES, STRUCTURE, PROCESS, AND REACTIONS/ADJUSTMENTS: A
COMPARISON OF FRENCH AND ENGLISH-CANADIAN INDUSTRIAL
ORGANIZATIONS.   M0628

EMPLOYEE REACTIONS TO LEADER REWARD BEHAVIOR.   M0654

CORRECTIONAL EMPLOYEES' REACTIONS TO JOB CHARACTERISTICS: A
DATA BASED ARGUMENT FOR JOB ENLARGEMENT.   M0753

REEVALUATING

    REEVALUATING THE ASSEMBLY LINE.   M0810

REFLECTIONS

    PERSONAL REFLECTIONS OF A FAMILY THERAPIST.   M0716

REFORM

    JOB REDESIGN, REFORM, ENRICHMENT -- EXPLORING THE   M0277
    LIMITATIONS.

REGIONAL

    A REGIONAL STUDY OF THE JOB SATISFACTION OF SOCIAL WORKERS.   M0920

REGISTERED

    PERCEIVED DIMENSIONS OF JOB SATISFACTION FOR STAFF   M0882
    REGISTERED NURSES.

REHABILITATED

    JOB PERFORMANCE AND SATISFACTION OF SUCCESSFULLY   M0801
    REHABILITATED VOCATIONAL REHABILITATION CLIENTS.

REHABILITATION

    JOB PERFORMANCE AND SATISFACTION OF SUCCESSFULLY   M0801
    REHABILITATED VOCATIONAL REHABILITATION CLIENTS.

    A STUDY OF REHABILITATION COUNSELORS: LOCUS OF CONTROL AND   M0888
    ATTITUDES TOWARD THE POOR.

REINFORCEMENT

    HUMANIZING THE BUDGETARY SYSTEM FOR ADMINISTRATIVE   M0138
    REINFORCEMENT.

    PAY FACTORS AS PREDICTORS TO SATISFACTION: A COMPARISON OF   M0254
    REINFORCEMENT, EQUITY, AND EXPECTANCY.

    THE EFFECTS OF VARYING SCHEDULES OF REINFORCEMENT ON HUMAN   M0790
    TASK PERFORMANCE.

RELATE

    A STUDY OF THE PERCEPTIONS OF SELECTED SCHOOL-BASED
    ADMINISTRATORS IN FLORIDA RELATIVE TO CERTAIN VARIABLES IN
    SECONDARY SCHOOL ADMINISTRATION AS THEY RELATE TO JOB
    SATISFACTION.   M0925

RELATION

    RELATION OF COLLABORATIVE INTERPERSONAL RELATIONSHIPS TO

RELATION   CONTINUATION

INDIVIDUAL SATISFACTION AND ORGANIZATIONAL PERFORMANCE.   M0013

RELATION OF ORGANIZATIONAL STRUCTURE TO JOB SATISFACTION,
ANXIETY-STRESS, AND PERFORMANCE.   M0766

THE RELATION OF JOB SATISFACTION TO VOCATIONAL PREFERENCES
AMONG TEACHERS OF THE EDUCABLE MENTALLY RETARDED.   M0805

RELATIONS

PUBLIC EMPLOYEE LABOR RELATIONS IN OTHER DEMOCRACIES.   M0161

RELATIONS AMONG PERCEIVED ENVIRONMENTAL UNCERTAINTY,
ORGANIZATION STRUCTURE, AND BOUNDARY-SPANNING BEHAVIOR.   M0671

THE RELATIONSHIPS BETWEEN THE TASK-HUMAN RELATIONS
MOTIVATIONAL STRUCTURES OF INDIVIDUALS IN SMALL WORK GROUPS
AND THEIR SATISFACTION WITH CO-WORKERS AND IMMEDIATE
SUPERVISION.   M0868

RELATIONSHIP

THE MODERATING EFFECTS OF INTERNAL VERSUS EXTERNAL CONTROL
ON THE RELATIONSHIP BETWEEN VARIOUS ASPECTS OF JOB
SATISFACTION.   M0122

SELF-ESTEEM AS A MODERATOR OF THE RELATIONSHIP BETWEEN
EXPECTANCIES AND JOB PERFORMANCE.   M0150

MOTIVATIONAL TYPE AND THE SATISFACTION-PERFORMANCE
RELATIONSHIP.   M0263

SOCIAL DESIRABILITY AS A MODERATOR OF THE RELATIONSHIP
BETWEEN JOB SATISFACTION AND PERSONAL ADJUSTMENT.   M0337

MOTIVATION IN MANAGERIAL LEVELS: RELATIONSHIP OF NEED
SATISFACTION TO JOB PERFORMANCE.   M0401

ORGANIZATION STRESS AS A MODERATOR OF THE RELATIONSHIP
BETWEEN INFLUENCE AND ROLE RESPONSE.   M0444

EFFECTS OF PERSONAL VALUES ON THE RELATIONSHIP BETWEEN
PARTICIPATION AND JOB ATTITUDES.   M0476

AN EXPERIMENTAL ANALYSIS OF THE RELATIONSHIP BETWEEN JOB
SATISFACTION AND JOB IMPORTANCE.   M0514

RELATIONSHIP OF AGE, TENURE AND JOB SATISFACTION IN MALES
AND FEMALES.   M0525

THE IMPACT OF JOB LEVEL AND SEX DIFFERENCES ON THE
RELATIONSHIP BETWEEN LIFE AND JOB SATISFACTION.   M0529

RELATIONSHIP BETWEEN LOCUS OF CONTROL AND REACTIONS OF

RELATIONSHIP   CONTINUATION

EMPLOYEES TO WORK CHARACTERISTICS.   M0530

THE RELATIONSHIP OF SEX AND ETHNIC BACKGROUND TO
JOB-RELATED STRESS OF RESEARCH AND DEVELOPMENT
PROFESSIONALS.   M0695

RELATIONSHIP BETWEEN ORGANIZATIONAL CLIMATE AND THE
SITUATIONAL FAVORABLENESS DIMENSION OF FIEDLER'S
CONTINGENCY MODEL.   M0709

INTERMEDIATE LINKAGES IN THE RELATIONSHIP BETWEEN JOB
SATISFACTION AND EMPLOYEE TURNOVER.   M0781

THE RELATIONSHIP BETWEEN MANAGERIAL SUCCESS AND PERSONAL
VALUES IN SOUTH AFRICA: A RESEARCH NOTE.   M0786

HIGHER ORDER NEED STRENGTHS AS MODERATORS OF THE JOB
SCOPE-JOB SATISFACTION RELATIONSHIP.   M0798

RELATIONSHIP OF PERSONAL INFLUENCE DISSONANCE TO JOB
TENSION SATISFACTION AND INVOLVEMENT.   M0817

TWO INTERACTIVE PERSPECTIVES ON THE RELATIONSHIP BETWEEN
JOB LEVEL AND JOB SATISFACTION.   M0823

ACHIEVEMENT MOTIVATION AS A MODERATOR OF THE RELATIONSHIP
BETWEEN EXPECTANCY TIMES VALENCE AND EFFORT.   M0845

RELATIONSHIP OF PERFORMANCE TO SATISFACTION IN STIMULATING
AND NONSTIMULATING JOBS.   M0848

A STUDY OF THE RELATIONSHIP BETWEEN HERZBERG'S MOTIVATION
HYGIENE FACTORS AND HOLLAND'S PERSONALITY PATTERNS FOR LAW
ENFORCEMENT PERSONNEL.   M0850

THE RELATIONSHIP OF JOB SATISFACTION MEASURES TO
SELF-REPORT AND OBJECTIVE CRITERIA MEASURES AND THE EFFECT
OF MODERATOR VARIABLES FOR CANADIAN MILITARY PERSONNEL.   M0853

RELATIONSHIP BETWEEN EDUCATION AND SATISFACTION WITH JOB
CONTENT.   M0885

THE RELATIONSHIP BETWEEN JOB SATISFACTION AND LIFE
SATISFACTION: AN EMPIRICAL TEST OF THREE MODELS ON A
NATIONAL SAMPLE.   M0903

A STUDY OF THE RELATIONSHIP AMONG (1) JOB SATISFACTION AND
(2) TEACHER ATTITUDE.   M0908

THE RELATIONSHIP OF LEADERSHIP STYLE TO EMPLOYEE JOB
SATISFACTION.   M0935

AN INVESTIGATION OF THE RELATIONSHIP BETWEEN INTRINSIC AND
EXTRINSIC JOB INSTRUMENTALITY EFFORT, JOB SATISFACTION,

RELATIONSHIP   CONTINUATION

    INDIVIDUAL AND PERCEIVED TASK CHARACTERISTICS.   M0938

    THE EFFECT OF FLEXIBLE WORKING HOURS ON ABSENTEEISM AND JOB
    SATISFACTION AND THE RELATIONSHIP BETWEEN LOCUS OF CONTROL
    AND UTILITY OF FLEXIBLE WORKING HOURS.   M0943

    AN EMPIRICAL STUDY OF INDIVIDUAL CONGRUENCE AND THE
    PERCEIVED ORGANIZATIONAL PRACTICES - JOB SATISFACTION - JOB
    PERFORMANCE RELATIONSHIP IN SELECTED ELECTRONIC COMPUTER
    DATA PROCESSING CENTERS.   M0946

RELATIONSHIPS

    RELATION OF COLLABORATIVE INTERPERSONAL RELATIONSHIPS TO
    INDIVIDUAL SATISFACTION AND ORGANIZATIONAL PERFORMANCE.   M0013

    SOME MODERATOR INFLUENCES ON RELATIONSHIPS BETWEEN
    CONSIDERATION, INITIATING STRUCTURE, AND ORGANIZATION
    CRITERIA.   M0021

    RELATIONSHIPS BETWEEN PERFORMANCE AND SATISFACTION UNDER
    CONTINGENT AND NONCONTINGENT REWARD SYSTEMS.   M0251

    SATISFACTION AND PERFORMANCE: CAUSAL RELATIONSHIPS AND
    MODERATING EFFECTS.   M0395

    WORK VALUES AS MODERATORS OF PERCEIVED LEADER
    BEHAVIOR-SATISFACTION RELATIONSHIPS.   M0505

    RELATIONSHIPS BETWEEN ROLE CLARITY, NEED FOR CLARITY AND
    JOB TENSION AND SATISFACTION FOR SUPERVISORY AND
    NONSUPERVISORY ROLES.   M0539

    LONGITUDINAL INFERENCES OF JOB ATTITUDE AND TENURE
    RELATIONSHIPS FROM CROSS-SECTIONAL DATA.   M0591

    INTEREST CONGRUENCY AS A MODERATOR OF THE RELATIONSHIPS
    BETWEEN JOB TENURE AND JOB SATISFACTION AND MENTAL HEALTH.   M0623

    COPING WITH CUPID: THE FORMATION, IMPACT, AND MANAGEMENT OF
    ROMANTIC RELATIONSHIPS IN ORGANIZATIONS.   M0630

    INFORMAL HELPING RELATIONSHIPS IN WORK ORGANIZATIONS.   M0650

    ANALYSIS OF RELATIONSHIPS AMONG LEADER BEHAVIOR,
    SUBORDINATE JOB PERFORMANCE, AND SATISFACTION: A PATH-GOAL
    APPROACH.   M0652

    INTERORGANIZATIONAL RELATIONSHIPS: PATTERNS AND
    MOTIVATIONS.   M0674

    WORK AND RETIREMENT: A TEST OF ATTITUDINAL RELATIONSHIPS.   M0721

    SOME RELATIONSHIPS BETWEEN JOB SATISFACTION AND

RELATIONSHIPS   CONTINUATION

ORGANIZATION CLIMATE.   M0734

RELATIONSHIPS OF ORGANIZATIONAL FRUSTRATION WITH REPORTED
BEHAVIORAL REACTIONS OF EMPLOYEES.   M0796

ORGANIZATIONAL COMMUNICATION: RELATIONSHIPS TO
ORGANIZATIONAL CLIMATE AND JOB SATISFACTION.   M0827

RELATIONSHIPS AMONG PAY, RACE, SEX, OCCUPATIONAL PRESTIGE,
SUPERVISION, WORK AUTONOMY, AND JOB SATISFACTION IN A
NATIONAL SAMPLE.   M0842

SUPERVISOR EXPECTATIONS AND BEHAVIOR: EFFECTS OF
CONSISTENT-INCONSISTENT SUPERVISORY PAIRINGS ON SUPERVISEE
SATISFACTION WITH SUPERVISION, PERCEPTIONS OF SUPERVISORY
RELATIONSHIPS AND RATED COUNSELOR COMPETENCY.   M0864

THE RELATIONSHIPS BETWEEN THE TASK-HUMAN RELATIONS
MOTIVATIONAL STRUCTURES OF INDIVIDUALS IN SMALL WORK GROUPS
AND THEIR SATISFACTION WITH CO-WORKERS AND IMMEDIATE
SUPERVISION.   M0868

JOB CHARACTERISTICS RELATIONSHIPS: INDIVIDUAL AND
STRUCTURAL MODERATORS.   M0896

RELATIONSHIPS BETWEEN JOB SATISFACTION, DEMOGRAPHIC
FACTORS, ABSENTEEISM AND TENURE OF WORKERS IN A DELMARVA
BROILER PROCESSING PLANT.   M0921

RELATIONSHIPS BETWEEN WORK VALUES AND JOB SATISFACTION
AMONG COLLEGE STUDENT PERSONNEL WORKERS.   M0928

PERCEPTIONS OF ORGANIZATIONAL CLIMATE AS MEDIATORS OF THE
RELATIONSHIPS BETWEEN INDIVIDUAL NEEDS AND JOB SATISFACTION
OF COUNSELORS IN THE NORTH CAROLINA COMMUNITY COLLEGE
SYSTEM.   M0933

THE RELATIONSHIPS AMONG THE PERSONALITY TYPES, JOB
SATISFACTIONS, AND JOB SPECIALTIES OF A SELECTED GROUP OF
MEDICAL TECHNOLOGISTS.   M0945

RELATIVE

RELATIVE SALIENCY OF JOB FACTORS DURING STRIKE.   M0558

RELATIVE STEEPNESS OF APPROACH AND AVOIDANCE GRADIENTS AS A
FUNCTION OF MAGNITUDE AND VALENCE OF INCENTIVE.   M0775

THE RELATIVE VALIDITIES OF TRADITIONALLY USED JOB
SATISFACTION AND ORGANIZATIONAL COMMITMENT MEASURES VERSUS
WOMEN-SPECIFIC MEASURES FOR THE PREDICTION OF FEMALE TENURE
IN A MALE DOMINATED JOB.   M0856

A STUDY OF THE PERCEPTIONS OF SELECTED SCHOOL-BASED

REPORT   CONTINUATION

RESEARCH CONTINUATION

RESIDENTS

RESISTANCE

RESOLUTION

RESOURCE

RESOURCES

RESPOND

RESPONSE

RESPONSES

RESPONSIBILITY

RESTRUCTURING

RESULTS

RETAIL

ROTC

    THE USE OF EXPECTANCY THEORY IN THE EXPLANATION OF TURNOVER
    IN ROTC.   M0732

RURAL

    REVIEW OF LITERATURE ON WORK MOTIVATION: BULLETIN 12. A
    STUDY OF WORK MOTIVATION OF URBAN AND RURAL APPAREL WORKERS
    IN TENNESSEE.   M0503

    RURAL AND URBAN DIFFERENCES: ONE MORE TIME.   M0808

SAFEGUARDING

    SAFEGUARDING OUR WATER -- POLLUTION CONTROL WORKERS.   M0350

SALANCIK

    A CRITIQUE OF SALANCIK AND PFEFFER'S EXAMINATION OF NEED
    SATISFACTION THEORIES.   M0669

SALARIES

    ACADEMIC SALARIES -- A PERSONAL APPLICATION OF MANAGERIAL
    ECONOMICS.   M0782

SALARY

    JOBS, SALARY, CREDIT, LEGAL STATUS ALL IN FOCUS OF WOMEN'S
    YEAR.   M0235

SALES

    MOTIVATING SALESMEN THROUGH BETTER SALES MANAGEMENT.   M0379

    ORGANIZATIONAL CLIMATE AND JOB SATISFACTION IN THE SALES
    FORCE.   M0509

SALESMEN

    MOTIVATING SALESMEN THROUGH BETTER SALES MANAGEMENT.   M0379

    INCENTIVES FOR SALESMEN DESIGNING A PLAN THAT WORKS.   M0703

    RIGHT CLIMATE FOR SALESMEN.   M0830

SALESMEN'S

    ANTECEDENTS OF SALESMEN'S COMPENSATION PERCEPTIONS: A PATH
    ANALYSIS INTERPRETATION.   M0785

SALIENCY

    RELATIVE SALIENCY OF JOB FACTORS DURING STRIKE.   M0558

SAMPLE

SAMPLES

SATISFACTION

SATISFACTION   CONTINUATION

SATISFACTION   CONTINUATION

SATISFACTION   CONTINUATION

JOB SATISFACTION: MALE AND FEMALE, PROFESSIONAL AND
NON-PROFESSIONAL.   M0552

THE EFFECTS OF ROLE PERCEPTIONS ON EMPLOYEE SATISFACTION
AND PERFORMANCE MODERATED BY EMPLOYEE ABILITY.   M0553

HOW TO EVALUATE THE JOB SATISFACTION OF CRITICAL EMPLOYEES.   M0560

GOAL-SETTING ATTRIBUTES, PERSONALITY VARIABLES, AND JOB
SATISFACTION.   M0570

JOB DESIGN AND WORKER SATISFACTION: A CHALLENGE TO
ASSUMPTIONS.   M0571

INDIVIDUAL AND ENVIRONMENTAL FACTORS ASSOCIATED WITH THE
JOB SATISFACTION AND RETENTION OF NAVY HOSPITAL CORPSMEN
SERVING WITH THE U.S. MARINE CORPS.   M0574

BACKGROUND AND PERSONALITY CHARACTERISTICS RELATED TO
STUDENT SATISFACTION AND PERFORMANCE IN FIELD MEDICAL
SERVICE SCHOOL.   M0575

WORK VALUES AND JOB SATISFACTION OF YOUNG ADULT MALES.   M0579

THE DETERMINANTS OF PAY SATISFACTION.   M0582

REPLY TO URBAN-RURAL DIFFERENCES IN JOB SATISFACTION.   M0584

URBAN-RURAL DIFFERENCES IN JOB SATISFACTION.   M0585

THE WORK SATISFACTION, RETIREMENT-ATTITUDE TYPOLOGY:
PROFILE EXAMINATION.   M0590

EFFECTS OF GOAL SETTING ON PERFORMANCE AND JOB
SATISFACTION.   M0594

PREFERRED JOB ASSIGNMENT EFFECT ON JOB SATISFACTION.   M0598

SEMANTIC DISTANCE AND JOB SATISFACTION IN FORMAL
ORGANIZATIONS.   M0599

ABSENCE FROM WORK AND JOB SATISFACTION.   M0604

THE LIMITATIONS OF THE MOTIVATOR-HYGIENE THEORY OF
SATISFACTION: AN EMPIRICAL STUDY WITH BLACK FACTORY WORKERS
IN SOUTH AFRICA.   M0607

PRODUCING MAN'S CASE FOR SATISFACTION.   M0610

MODELS OF PAY SATISFACTION: A COMPARATIVE STUDY.   M0613

EFFECTS OF JOB ENRICHMENT AND TASK GOALS ON SATISFACTION
AND PRODUCTIVITY: IMPLICATIONS FOR JOB DESIGN.   M0619

SATISFACTION   CONTINUATION

INTEREST CONGRUENCY AS A MODERATOR OF THE RELATIONSHIPS
BETWEEN JOB TENURE AND JOB SATISFACTION AND MENTAL HEALTH.   M0623

VOCATIONAL NEEDS, JOB REWARDS, AND SATISFACTION: A
CANONICAL ANALYSIS.   M0640

ECONOMIC CONSIDERATIONS IN JOB SATISFACTION TRENDS.   M0644

LIFE STYLE, WORK GROUP STRUCTURE, COMPATIBILITY, AND JOB
SATISFACTION.   M0651

ANALYSIS OF RELATIONSHIPS AMONG LEADER BEHAVIOR,
SUBORDINATE JOB PERFORMANCE, AND SATISFACTION: A PATH-GOAL
APPROACH.   M0652

GROUP DEVELOPMENT, TRAINER STYLE AND CARRY-OVER JOB
SATISFACTION AND PERFORMANCE.   M0653

EFFECTS OF VARYING GOAL TYPES AND INCENTIVE SYSTEMS ON
PERFORMANCE AND SATISFACTION.   M0659

LOCUS OF CONTROL: SUPERVISION AND WORK SATISFACTION.   M0660

SEX STEREOTYPES: AN ARTIFACT IN LEADER BEHAVIOR AND
SUBORDINATE SATISFACTION ANALYSIS.   M0662

A CRITIQUE OF SALANCIK AND PFEFFER'S EXAMINATION OF NEED
SATISFACTION THEORIES.   M0669

THE IMPACT OF PERFORMANCE-CONTINGENT REWARDS ON JOB
SATISFACTION: DIRECT AND INDIRECT EFFECTS.   M0686

SATISFACTION WITH YOUR JOB: A LIFE-TIME CONCERN.   M0689

WORK VALUES, JOB REWARDS AND JOB SATISFACTION: A THEORY OF
THE QUALITY OF WORK EXPERIENCE.   M0690

JOB LEVEL, INDIVIDUAL DIFFERENCES, AND JOB SATISFACTION: AN
INTERACTIVE APPROACH.   M0691

A COMPARISON OF PROFESSIONAL INSTITUTIONAL COMMUNITY
CORRECTIONS WORKERS ON JOB SATISFACTION AND SELF-CONCEPT.   M0696

THE MENTAL HEALTH ASSOCIATE: THE EFFECT OF SOCIAL
ENVIRONMENTAL FACTORS ON JOB SATISFACTION.   M0697

WOMEN IN INDUSTRY: ALIENATION, SATISFACTION, AND CHANGE.   M0699

EFFECTS OF PARTICIPATION ON SATISFACTION AND PRODUCTIVITY.   M0702

INTERGROUP CLIMATE ATTAINMENT, SATISFACTION, AND URGENCY.   M0705

OCCUPATIONAL SATISFACTION OF FARM HUSBANDS AND WIVES.   M0706

SATISFACTION   CONTINUATION

COMMUNITY COLLEGE FACULTY JOB SATISFACTION.   M0708

INTRAROLE CONFLICT AND JOB SATISFACTION ON PSYCHIATRIC
UNITS.   M0712

JOB INVOLVEMENT AND SATISFACTION AS RELATED TO MENTAL
HEALTH AND PERSONAL TIME DEVOTED TO WORK.   M0718

DISCRIMINATION AND JOB SATISFACTION: AN EMPIRICAL STUDY
WITH A SOUTH AFRICAN MINORITY GROUP.   M0733

SOME RELATIONSHIPS BETWEEN JOB SATISFACTION AND
ORGANIZATION CLIMATE.   M0734

LEADER STRUCTURE AND SUBORDINATE SATISFACTION FOR TWO
HOSPITAL ADMINISTRATIVE LEVELS: A PATH ANALYSIS APPROACH.   M0736

JOB SATISFACTION AND PERFORMANCE WITH RETARDED FEMALES.   M0738

THERAPIST SATISFACTION.   M0754

TRAINING AND CAREER SATISFACTION AMONG CLINICAL
PSYCHOLOGISTS.   M0759

CONVERGENT AND DISCRIMINANT VALIDITY OF A JOB SATISFACTION
INVENTORY: A CROSS-CULTURAL REPORT.   M0764

PREDICTING JOB PERFORMANCE BY USE OF ABILITY TESTS AND
STUDYING JOB SATISFACTION AS A MODERATING VARIABLE.   M0765

RELATION OF ORGANIZATIONAL STRUCTURE TO JOB SATISFACTION,
ANXIETY-STRESS, AND PERFORMANCE.   M0766

STRATEGIES FOR ENHANCING THE PREDICTION OF JOB PERFORMANCE
FROM JOB SATISFACTION.   M0768

CONTRIBUTION OF JOB AND LEISURE SATISFACTION TO QUALITY OF
LIFE.   M0774

INTERMEDIATE LINKAGES IN THE RELATIONSHIP BETWEEN JOB
SATISFACTION AND EMPLOYEE TURNOVER.   M0781

INFORMATION INTEGRATION THEORY APPLIED TO EXPECTED JOB
ATTRACTIVENESS AND SATISFACTION.   M0793

HIGHER ORDER NEED STRENGTHS AS MODERATORS OF THE JOB
SCOPE-JOB SATISFACTION RELATIONSHIP.   M0798

JOB PERFORMANCE AND SATISFACTION OF SUCCESSFULLY
REHABILITATED VOCATIONAL REHABILITATION CLIENTS.   M0801

DIMENSIONS OF JOB SATISFACTION: INITIAL DEVELOPMENT OF THE
AIR FORCE OCCUPATIONAL ATTITUDE INVENTORY.   M0802

SATISFACTION   CONTINUATION

SATISFACTION   CONTINUATION

AN EMPIRICAL TEST OF CAUSAL INFERENCE BETWEEN ROLE
PERCEPTIONS, SATISFACTION WITH WORK, PERFORMANCE AND
ORGANIZATIONAL LEVEL.   M0839

CAN INTERNAL AUDITORS FIND JOB SATISFACTION?   M0840

TASKS, INDIVIDUAL DIFFERENCES, AND JOB SATISFACTION.   M0841

RELATIONSHIPS AMONG PAY, RACE, SEX, OCCUPATIONAL PRESTIGE,
SUPERVISION, WORK AUTONOMY, AND JOB SATISFACTION IN A
NATIONAL SAMPLE.   M0842

PREDICTING PAY SATISFACTION FROM NONPAY WORK VARIABLES.   M0843

JOB SATISFACTION AND THE QUALITY OF WORKING LIFE: THE
POLISH EXPERIENCE.   M0844

AN INVESTIGATION OF FACTORS INVOLVED IN CAREER SATISFACTION
FOR THE PHYSICIAN.   M0847

RELATIONSHIP OF PERFORMANCE TO SATISFACTION IN STIMULATING
AND NONSTIMULATING JOBS.   M0848

INTERNAL VERSUS EXTERNAL LOCUS OF CONTROL AND JOB
SATISFACTION IN IRAN.   M0851

DETERMINANTS OF PAY SATISFACTION: A DISCREPANCY MODEL
EVALUATION.   M0852

THE RELATIONSHIP OF JOB SATISFACTION MEASURES TO
SELF-REPORT AND OBJECTIVE CRITERIA MEASURES AND THE EFFECT
OF MODERATOR VARIABLES FOR CANADIAN MILITARY PERSONNEL.   M0853

EMPLOYEE INFORMATION ENVIRONMENTS AND JOB SATISFACTION: A
CLOSER LOOK.   M0854

THE RELATIVE VALIDITIES OF TRADITIONALLY USED JOB
SATISFACTION AND ORGANIZATIONAL COMMITMENT MEASURES VERSUS
WOMEN-SPECIFIC MEASURES FOR THE PREDICTION OF FEMALE TENURE
IN A MALE DOMINATED JOB.   M0856

INSTRUMENTALITY THEORY PREDICTIONS OF EXPERIENCED AND
ANTICIPATED JOB SATISFACTION.   M0858

PERCEIVED LEADER BEHAVIOR AND EMPLOYEE SATISFACTION WITH
SUPERVISION AND THE JOB: THE EFFECTS OF REWARD AND
PUNISHMENT.   M0859

JOB SATISFACTION AND NEED IMPORTANCE: RACE, SEX, AND
OCCUPATIONAL GROUP.   M0860

PERSON-ENVIRONMENT CONGRUENCE, EMPLOYEE JOB SATISFACTION,
AND TENURE: A TEST OF HOLLAND'S THEORY.   M0863

SATISFACTION   CONTINUATION

SUPERVISOR EXPECTATIONS AND BEHAVIOR: EFFECTS OF
CONSISTENT-INCONSISTENT SUPERVISORY PAIRINGS ON SUPERVISEE
SATISFACTION WITH SUPERVISION, PERCEPTIONS OF SUPERVISORY
RELATIONSHIPS AND RATED COUNSELOR COMPETENCY.   M0864

THE RELATIONSHIPS BETWEEN THE TASK-HUMAN RELATIONS
MOTIVATIONAL STRUCTURES OF INDIVIDUALS IN SMALL WORK GROUPS
AND THEIR SATISFACTION WITH CO-WORKERS AND IMMEDIATE
SUPERVISION.   M0868

VOCATIONAL SATISFACTION, SUCCESS AND STABILITY: A
COMPARATIVE STUDY OF MALE AND FEMALE NON-PROFESSIONAL
WORKERS.   M0869

PERSONALITY TRAITS, WORK FUNCTIONS, AND VOCATIONAL
SATISFACTION OF PHYSICIANS IN THREE MEDICAL SPECIALTIES.   M0875

SUBJECTIVE EXPECTATIONS AND JOB FACET PREDICTABILITY IN JOB
SATISFACTION.   M0876

ANDROGYNY IN NURSING: NURSE ROLE EXPECTATION, SATISFACTION,
ACADEMIC ACHIEVEMENT, AND SELF-ACTUALIZATION IM MALE AND
FEMALE STUDENTS.   M0877

AN EXPERIMENTAL STUDY OF THE EFFECTS OF GOAL SETTING,
EVALUATION APPREHENSION, AND SOCIAL CUES ON TASK
PERFORMANCE AND JOB SATISFACTION.   M0878

SATISFACTION IN THE HOMEMAKER JOB.   M0879

PERCEIVED DIMENSIONS OF JOB SATISFACTION FOR STAFF
REGISTERED NURSES.   M0882

PHYSICAL ENVIRONMENT AND JOB SATISFACTION IN A COMMUNITY
MENTAL HEALTH CENTER.   M0883

RELATIONSHIP BETWEEN EDUCATION AND SATISFACTION WITH JOB
CONTENT.   M0885

JOB SATISFACTION: A POSSIBLE INTEGRATION OF TWO THEORIES. M0886

EFFECTS OF ASSIGNED AND PARTICIPATIVE GOAL SETTING ON
PERFORMANCE AND JOB SATISFACTION.   M0887

THE EFFECT OF URBANIZATION ON SOURCES OF JOB SATISFACTION
AMONG BLACK SUPERVISORS IN SOUTH AFRICA.   M0891

ROLE PERCEPTIONS, SATISFACTION AND PERFORMANCE MODERATED BY
ORGANIZATION LEVEL AND PARTICIPATION IN DECISION MAKING.   M0895

AN INVESTIGATION OF EDUCATIONAL ADMINISTRATIVE STYLE AND
JOB SATISFACTION OF ELEMENTARY SCHOOL PRINCIPALS.   M0901

A STUDY OF THE JOB SATISFACTION AND JOB PERCEPTION OF

SATISFACTION   CONTINUATION

ORGANIZED AND NON-ORGANIZED PUBLIC SCHOOL PRINCIPALS.   M0902

THE RELATIONSHIP BETWEEN JOB SATISFACTION AND LIFE
SATISFACTION: AN EMPIRICAL TEST OF THREE MODELS ON A
NATIONAL SAMPLE.   M0903

SATISFACTION WITH TRAINING AND GENERAL JOB SATISFACTION OF
AGENCY HOMEMAKERS WORKING WITH THE ELDERLY AND DISABLED.   M0904

JOB SATISFACTION AND EXPECTATIONS OF DISTRIBUTIVE EDUCATION
GRADUATES.   M0905

JOB SATISFACTION OF GEORGIA SCHOOL SUPERINTENDENTS AND
THEIR PERCEPTION OF THE LOCAL SCHOOL BOARD PRESIDENT'S
LEADER BEHAVIOR.   M0906

JOB SATISFACTION OF COLLEGE PRESIDENTS.   M0907

A STUDY OF THE RELATIONSHIP AMONG (1) JOB SATISFACTION AND
(2) TEACHER ATTITUDE.   M0908

THE JOB SATISFACTION OF SCHOOL TEACHERS IN THE REPUBLIC OF
CHINA AS RELATED TO PERSONAL AND ORGANIZATIONAL
CHARACTERISTICS.   M0909

A STUDY OF JOB SATISFACTION OF ADMINISTRATORS AT UNITED
METHODIST RELATED CHURCHES.   M0910

AN ANALYSIS OF JOB SATISFACTION AMONG ELEMENTARY, MIDDLE
LEVEL, AND SENIOR HIGH SCHOOL TEACHERS.   M0911

CAREER COMMITMENT: AN ANALYSIS OF SELECTED INDIVIDUAL, JOB
AND ORGANIZATIONAL FACTORS AS RELATED TO SATISFACTION AND
COMMITMENT OF MIDDLE LEVEL ARMY OFFICERS.   M0912

THE MEASUREMENT OF SATISFACTION AND DEPARTMENTAL
ASSOCIATION AT WESTERN KENTUCKY UNIVERSITY: TESTING THE
HOLLAND AND BIGLAN MODELS.   M0914

A CAUSAL MODEL OF JOB SATISFACTION.   M0915

THE IMPACT OF COLLECTIVE BARGAINING ON JOB SATISFACTION.   M0916

WORK VALUES AND JOB SATISFACTION OF PSYCHIATRIC AIDES.   M0917

A NORMATIVE STUDY OF THE SECONDARY SCHOOL ASSISTANT
PRINCIPALSHIP IN SELECTED PENNSYLVANIA SCHOOL DISTRICTS
WITH AN EMPHASIS UPON JOB SATISFACTION.   M0918

JOB SATISFACTION, JOB CHARACTERISTICS, AND OCCUPATIONAL
LEVEL.   M0919

A REGIONAL STUDY OF THE JOB SATISFACTION OF SOCIAL WORKERS.   M0920

SATISFACTION   CONTINUATION

RELATIONSHIPS BETWEEN JOB SATISFACTION, DEMOGRAPHIC
FACTORS, ABSENTEEISM AND TENURE OF WORKERS IN A DELMARVA
BROILER PROCESSING PLANT.   M0921

OPEN SPACE ELEMENTARY SCHOOL: EFFECTS ON TEACHERS' JOB
SATISFACTION, PARTICIPATION IN CURRICULUM DECISION-MAKING,
AND PERCEIVED SCHOOL EFFECTIVENESS.   M0922

TASK OPPORTUNITY PROFESSIONAL GROWTH NEED FULFILLMENT AND
INTRINSIC JOB SATISFACTION OF PUBLIC SOCIAL SERVICE WORKERS
IN COLORADO.   M0923

SECOND CAREER CATHOLIC PRIESTS: A STUDY OF THEIR LEVEL OF
JOB SATISFACTION, MATURITY, AND MORALE.   M0924

A STUDY OF THE PERCEPTIONS OF SELECTED SCHOOL-BASED
ADMINISTRATORS IN FLORIDA RELATIVE TO CERTAIN VARIABLES IN
SECONDARY SCHOOL ADMINISTRATION AS THEY RELATE TO JOB
SATISFACTION.   M0925

SEGREGATION AND JOB SATISFACTION IN THE WORK PLACE: THE
MEASUREMENT OF RACIAL DISPARITIES IN ORGANIZATIONS AND
THEIR INFLUENCE ON EMPLOYEE WORK ATTITUDES.   M0927

RELATIONSHIPS BETWEEN WORK VALUES AND JOB SATISFACTION
AMONG COLLEGE STUDENT PERSONNEL WORKERS.   M0928

PERCEPTIONS OF ORGANIZATIONAL CLIMATE AS MEDIATORS OF THE
RELATIONSHIPS BETWEEN INDIVIDUAL NEEDS AND JOB SATISFACTION
OF COUNSELORS IN THE NORTH CAROLINA COMMUNITY COLLEGE
SYSTEM.   M0933

A NETWORK ANALYSIS OF A BUREAU OF INDIAN AFFAIRS SCHOOL
SYSTEM TO DETERMINE FACTORS INVOLVED IN JOB SATISFACTION. M0934

THE RELATIONSHIP OF LEADERSHIP STYLE TO EMPLOYEE JOB
SATISFACTION.   M0935

JOB SATISFACTION AND LEADER BEHAVIOR OF ADULT EDUCATION
ADMINISTRATORS.   M0936

AN INVESTIGATION OF THE RELATIONSHIP BETWEEN INTRINSIC AND
EXTRINSIC JOB INSTRUMENTALITY EFFORT, JOB SATISFACTION,
INDIVIDUAL AND PERCEIVED TASK CHARACTERISTICS.   M0938

MOTIVATION, JOB SATISFACTION, AND CAREER ASPIRATIONS OF
MARRIED WOMEN TEACHERS AT DIFFERENT CAREER STAGES.   M0940

THE EFFECT OF ORGANIZATIONAL CHANGE ON ADMINISTRATOR JOB
SATISFACTION, ORGANIZATIONAL CLIMATE, AND PERCEIVED
ORGANIZATIONAL EFFECTIVENESS.   M0942

THE EFFECT OF FLEXIBLE WORKING HOURS ON ABSENTEEISM AND JOB
SATISFACTION AND THE RELATIONSHIP BETWEEN LOCUS OF CONTROL

SATISFACTION   CONTINUATION

 AND UTILITY OF FLEXIBLE WORKING HOURS.   M0943

 OLNEY CENTRAL COLLEGE DENTAL ASSISTING PROGRAM GRADUATES
 PERCEPTIONS OF PROGRAM COMPONENTS, JOB SATISFACTION AND
 CAREER GOALS.   M0944

 AN EMPIRICAL STUDY OF INDIVIDUAL CONGRUENCE AND THE
 PERCEIVED ORGANIZATIONAL PRACTICES - JOB SATISFACTION - JOB
 PERFORMANCE RELATIONSHIP IN SELECTED ELECTRONIC COMPUTER
 DATA PROCESSING CENTERS.   M0946

SATISFACTION-PERFORMANCE

 THE SATISFACTION-PERFORMANCE CONTROVERS   M0172

 MOTIVATIONAL TYPE AND THE SATISFACTION-PERFORMANCE
 RELATIONSHIP.   M0263

SATISFACTION-TENSION-INFLUENCE

 MODERATING EFFECTS OF ENVIRONMENT AND STRUCTURE ON THE
 SATISFACTION-TENSION-INFLUENCE NETWORK.   M0828

SATISFACTIONS

 MANAGERIAL SATISFACTIONS AND ORGANIZATIONAL ROLES: AN
 INVESTIGATION OF PORTER'S NEED DEFICIENCY SCALES.   M0202

 A DEFINITIONAL CHALLENGE: INTEREST AND WORK ITSELF
 SATISFACTIONS.   M0543

 SELECTED CHARACTERISTICS, ROLES, GOALS, AND SATISFACTIONS
 OF DEPARTMENT CHAIRMEN IN STATE AND LAND-GRANT
 INSTITUTIONS.   M0777

 THE RELATIONSHIPS AMONG THE PERSONALITY TYPES, JOB
 SATISFACTIONS, AND JOB SPECIALTIES OF A SELECTED GROUP OF
 MEDICAL TECHNOLOGISTS.   M0945

SATISFIERS

 SATISFIERS AND DISSATISFIERS AMONG WHITE-COLLAR AND
 BLUE-COLLAR EMPLOYEES.   M0282

SCALE

 FEELINGS OF POWERLESSNESS AND SOCIAL ISOLATION AMONG LARGE
 SCALE FARM PERSONNEL.   M0596

 LANGUAGE, TIME, AND PERSON EFFECTS ON ATTITUDE SCALE
 TRANSLATIONS.   M0770

SCALES

    MANAGERIAL SATISFACTIONS AND ORGANIZATIONAL ROLES: AN
    INVESTIGATION OF PORTER'S NEED DEFICIENCY SCALES.   M0202

    VALIDATION OF THE INDEX OF ORGANIZATIONAL REACTIONS WITH
    THE JDI, THE MSQ, AND FACES SCALES.   M0813

SCHEDULES

    CHANGING SCHEDULES OF WORK: PATTERNS AND IMPLICATIONS.   M0159

    THE EFFECTS OF VARYING SCHEDULES OF REINFORCEMENT ON HUMAN
    TASK PERFORMANCE.   M0790

    INCENTIVE SCHEDULES, PRODUCTIVITY, AND SATISFACTION IN WORK
    GROUPS: A LABORATORY STUDY.   M0814

SCHOOL-BASED

    A STUDY OF THE PERCEPTIONS OF SELECTED SCHOOL-BASED
    ADMINISTRATORS IN FLORIDA RELATIVE TO CERTAIN VARIABLES IN
    SECONDARY SCHOOL ADMINISTRATION AS THEY RELATE TO JOB
    SATISFACTION.   M0925

SCHOOLING

    HEDONIC WAGE EQUATIONS AND PSYCHIC WAGES IN THE RETURNS TO
    SCHOOLING.   M0822

SCHOOLS

    A COMPARATIVE STUDY OF TEACHERS' ATTITUDES TOWARD MEN AND
    WOMEN DEPARTMENT HEADS IN LARGE CITY SECONDARY SCHOOLS.   M0366

SCHUTZ'S

    THE EFFECTS OF INDIVIDUAL-ROLE COMPATIBILITY UPON GROUP
    PERFORMANCE: AN EXTENSION OF SCHUTZ'S FIRO THEORY.   M0658

SCIENCE

    INFLUENCES ON THE FELT NEED FOR COLLECTIVE BARGAINING BY
    BUSINESS AND SCIENCE PROFESSIONALS.   M0572

SCIENTISTS

    TIME PRESSURE AND PERFORMANCE OF SCIENTISTS AND ENGINEERS:
    A FIVE PANEL STUDY.   M0010

    THE MANAGEMENT OF SCIENTISTS: DETERMINANTS OF PERCEIVED
    ROLE PERFORMANCE OF 95 SCIENTISTS IN THREE LARGE RESEARCH
    LABORATORIES TO THE ORGANIC SYSTEM OF MANAGEMENT CONCEIVED
    BY BURNS AND STALKER.   M0190

    INCREASING PRODUCTIVITY: HOW BEHAVIORAL SCIENTISTS CAN

SCIENTISTS   CONTINUATION

   HELP.   M0568

   TOWARD A CAREER-BASED THEORY OF JOB INVOLVEMENT: A STUDY OF
   SCIENTISTS AND ENGINEERS.   M0824

SCOPE-JOB

   HIGHER ORDER NEED STRENGTHS AS MODERATORS OF THE JOB
   SCOPE-JOB SATISFACTION RELATIONSHIP.   M0798

SCOTLAND

   MANAGERIAL BELIEFS ABOUT WORK IN SCOTLAND AND THE U.S.A.   M0756

SECOND

   SECOND CAREER CATHOLIC PRIESTS: A STUDY OF THEIR LEVEL OF
   JOB SATISFACTION, MATURITY, AND MORALE.   M0924

SECONDARY

   A COMPARATIVE STUDY OF TEACHERS' ATTITUDES TOWARD MEN AND
   WOMEN DEPARTMENT HEADS IN LARGE CITY SECONDARY SCHOOLS.   M0366

   A NORMATIVE STUDY OF THE SECONDARY SCHOOL ASSISTANT
   PRINCIPALSHIP IN SELECTED PENNSYLVANIA SCHOOL DISTRICTS
   WITH AN EMPHASIS UPON JOB SATISFACTION.   M0918

   A STUDY OF THE PERCEPTIONS OF SELECTED SCHOOL-BASED
   ADMINISTRATORS IN FLORIDA RELATIVE TO CERTAIN VARIABLES IN
   SECONDARY SCHOOL ADMINISTRATION AS THEY RELATE TO JOB
   SATISFACTION.   M0925

SECRETARIES

   HOW DO SECRETARIES RATE.   M0239

   SPECIAL TASK FORCE WILL REVIEW ROLE OF GS AND FS
   SECRETARIES.   M0411

SEDUCTION

   SEDUCTION AIN'T MOTIVATION.   M0388

SEGREGATION

   SEGREGATION AND JOB SATISFACTION IN THE WORK PLACE: THE
   MEASUREMENT OF RACIAL DISPARITIES IN ORGANIZATIONS AND
   THEIR INFLUENCE ON EMPLOYEE WORK ATTITUDES.   M0927

SELECTION

   MODEL PROGRAM TO INSTRUCT MANPOWER TRAINING PERSONNEL IN
   SELECTION AND APPLICATION OF REMEDIAL INSTRUCTIONAL

SELECTION   CONTINUATION

    MATERIALS TO MEET INDIVIDUAL TRAINEE NEEDS.   M0387

SELF-ACTUALIZATION

    MYTHOLOGY OF JOB ENRICHMENT: SELF-ACTUALIZATION REVISITED.   M0548

    ANDROGYNY IN NURSING: NURSE ROLE EXPECTATION, SATISFACTION,
    ACADEMIC ACHIEVEMENT, AND SELF-ACTUALIZATION IM MALE AND
    FEMALE STUDENTS.   M0877

SELF-CONCEPT

    SELF-CONCEPT AND INTERESTS RELATED TO JOB SATISFACTION OF
    MANAGERS.   M0109

    THE SELF-CONCEPT, PERSONAL VALUES, AND MOTIVATIONAL
    ORIENTATIONS OF BLACK AND WHITE MANAGERS.   M0668

    A COMPARISON OF PROFESSIONAL INSTITUTIONAL COMMUNITY
    CORRECTIONS WORKERS ON JOB SATISFACTION AND SELF-CONCEPT.   M0696

SELF-DESCRIPTIONS

    SEX EFFECTS IN LEADER BEHAVIOR SELF-DESCRIPTIONS AND JOB
    SATISFACTION.   M0499

SELF-EMPLOYMENT

    COMPARISON OF ORGANIZATIONAL MEMBERSHIP AND
    SELF-EMPLOYMENT.   M0132

    ORGANIZATIONAL MEMBERSHIP VS. SELF-EMPLOYMENT: ANOTHER BLOW
    TO THE AMERICAN DREAM.   M0583

SELF-ESTEEM

    SELF-ESTEEM AS A MODERATOR OF THE RELATIONSHIP BETWEEN
    EXPECTANCIES AND JOB PERFORMANCE.   M0150

    SELF-ESTEEM AS AN INFLUENCE ON OCCUPATIONAL CHOICE AND
    OCCUPATIONAL SATISFACTION.   M0174

    BUILD EMPLOYEES' CONFIDENCE AND SELF-ESTEEM.   M0524

    SELF-ESTEEM AS A MODERATOR IN VOCATIONAL CHOICE: A TEST OF
    KORMAN'S HYPOTHESIS.   M0803

SELF-MOTIVATED

    SELF-MOTIVATED PERSONAL CAREER PLANNING: A BREAKTHROUGH IN
    HUMAN RESOURCE MANAGEMENT (PART I).   M0561

SELF-REPORT

THE RELATIONSHIP OF JOB SATISFACTION MEASURES TO
SELF-REPORT AND OBJECTIVE CRITERIA MEASURES AND THE EFFECT
OF MODERATOR VARIABLES FOR CANADIAN MILITARY PERSONNEL.   M0853

SELF-SELECTION

CLIENT SELF-SELECTION OF TESTS AND WORK SAMPLES IN
VOCATIONAL EVALUATION.   M0897

SELLING

MANPOWER MANAGEMENT: NO ONE'S SELLING YOUTH ON SELLING.   M0440

SEMANTIC

SEMANTIC DISTANCE AND JOB SATISFACTION IN FORMAL
ORGANIZATIONS.   M0599

SENIOR

AN ANALYSIS OF JOB SATISFACTION AMONG ELEMENTARY, MIDDLE
LEVEL, AND SENIOR HIGH SCHOOL TEACHERS.   M0911

SERVICE

UPGRADING BLUE-COLLAR AND SERVICE WORKERS.   M0037

CAREER OPPORTUNITIES IN THE POSTAL SERVICE.   M0152

THE QUIT RATE AS A MEASURE OF MORALE IN THE PUBLIC SERVICE:
THE CASE OF THE UNITED STATES FOREIGN SERVICE.   M0292

THE PUBLIC EMPLOYMENT SERVICE REACHES OUT TO THE URBAN
POOR.   M0374

A 'THIRD-LEVEL' INCENTIVE: WORK SEEN AS SERVICE.   M0512

BACKGROUND AND PERSONALITY CHARACTERISTICS RELATED TO
STUDENT SATISFACTION AND PERFORMANCE IN FIELD MEDICAL
SERVICE SCHOOL.   M0575

REWARDS AND PUBLIC EMPLOYEES' ATTITUDES TOWARD CLIENT
SERVICE.   M0693

AN APPLICATION OF JOB ENRICHMENT IN A CIVIL SERVICE
SETTING: A DEMONSTRATION STUDY.   M0719

TASK OPPORTUNITY PROFESSIONAL GROWTH NEED FULFILLMENT AND
INTRINSIC JOB SATISFACTION OF PUBLIC SOCIAL SERVICE WORKERS
IN COLORADO.   M0923

REWARDS AND PUBLIC EMPLOYEES' ATTITUDES TOWARD CLIENT
SERVICE.   M0929

SERVICES

    A NATIONAL STUDY OF ASSOCIATE DEGREE MENTAL HEALTH SERVICES
WORKERS.   M0806

    OCCUPATIONAL MENTAL HEALTH AND THE HUMAN SERVICES: A
REVIEW.   M0880

SERVING

    INDIVIDUAL AND ENVIRONMENTAL FACTORS ASSOCIATED WITH THE
JOB SATISFACTION AND RETENTION OF NAVY HOSPITAL CORPSMEN
SERVING WITH THE U.S. MARINE CORPS.   M0574

SESSION

    AN EXAMINATION OF BRAINSTORMING PROCEDURE, GROUP SIZE AND
MOTIVATIONAL ORIENTATION IN THE JOB ENRICHMENT GREENLIGHT
SESSION.   M0932

SETTING

    FACTORS AFFECTING JOB ATTITUDE IN GOAL SETTING ENVIRONMENT.   M0556

    EFFECTS OF GOAL SETTING ON PERFORMANCE AND JOB
SATISFACTION.   M0594

    REVIEW OF RESEARCH ON THE APPLICATION OF GOAL SETTING IN
ORGANIZATIONS.   M0657

    AN APPLICATION OF JOB ENRICHMENT IN A CIVIL SERVICE
SETTING: A DEMONSTRATION STUDY.   M0719

    THE MOTIVATIONAL COMPONENTS OF GOAL SETTING.   M0799

    DIFFERENT GOAL SETTING TREATMENTS AND THEIR EFFECTS ON
PERFORMANCE AND JOB SATISFACTION.   M0819

    BEHAVIORAL TRAINING OF SUPERVISORS IN AN INDUSTRIAL SETTING
FOR THE BLIND.   M0846

    AN EXPERIMENTAL STUDY OF THE EFFECTS OF GOAL SETTING,
EVALUATION APPREHENSION, AND SOCIAL CUES ON TASK
PERFORMANCE AND JOB SATISFACTION.   M0878

    EFFECTS OF ASSIGNED AND PARTICIPATIVE GOAL SETTING ON
PERFORMANCE AND JOB SATISFACTION.   M0887

SEX

    SEX STEREOTYPING: ITS DECLINE IN SKILLED TRADES.   M0197

    REMOVAL OF SEX STEREOTYPING IN CENSUS OCCUPATIONAL
CLASSIFICATION.   M0359

    SEX BIAS IN LONGSHORING.   M0389

SEX   CONTINUATION

SEXES

SHARE

SHARING

SHIFT

SHIFTING

SHIFTS

SHIPBUILDERS

SKILL   CONTINUATION

    CUTTING INTO THE SAWMILL SKILL SHORTAGE.   M0115

    FORM CHINA WITH SKILL -- MESBIC FOUNDER WANTS TO SHARE HER
    TALENT.   M0145

SKILLED

    SEX STEREOTYPING: ITS DECLINE IN SKILLED TRADES.   M0197

    APPRENTICESHIP -- AVENUE TO THE SKILLED CRAFTS.   M0419

SKILLS

    SUPERVISORY SKILLS AND EMPLOYEE SATISFACTION.   M0316

    MARKETING WELFARE MOTHERS' JOB SKILLS.   M0343

SMALL

    ACHIEVEMENT DRIVE AND CREATIVITY AS CORRELATES OF SUCCESS
    IN SMALL BUSINESS.   M0730

    THE RELATIONSHIPS BETWEEN THE TASK-HUMAN RELATIONS
    MOTIVATIONAL STRUCTURES OF INDIVIDUALS IN SMALL WORK GROUPS
    AND THEIR SATISFACTION WITH CO-WORKERS AND IMMEDIATE
    SUPERVISION.   M0868

SOCIAL

    SOCIAL AND WELFARE PROGRAMS FOR THE HANDICAPPED ABROAD.   M0043

    THE SOCIAL DIMENSIONS OF WORK.   M0047

    ATTITUDES AND SOCIAL CHANGE -- COMMITTEE REPORT.   M0067

    ACCOUNTING FOR CORPORATE SOCIAL RESPONSIBILITY.   M0071

    WORKING CONDITIONS SURVEY AS A SOURCE OF SOCIAL INDICATORS. M0206

    A SOCIAL PSYCHOLGICAL EXPLORATION OF POWER MOTIVATION AMONG
    DISADVANTAGED WORKERS.   M0279

    SOCIAL DESIRABILITY AS A MODERATOR OF THE RELATIONSHIP
    BETWEEN JOB SATISFACTION AND PERSONAL ADJUSTMENT.   M0337

    FEELINGS OF POWERLESSNESS AND SOCIAL ISOLATION AMONG LARGE
    SCALE FARM PERSONNEL.   M0596

    THE MENTAL HEALTH ASSOCIATE: THE EFFECT OF SOCIAL
    ENVIRONMENTAL FACTORS ON JOB SATISFACTION.   M0697

    SOCIAL AND PSYCHOLOGICAL INFLUENCES ON EMPLOYMENT OF
    MARRIED NURSES.   M0755

SOCIAL   CONTINUATION

SOCIALIZATION

SOCIETIES

SOCIETY

SOCIOECONOMIC

SOCIOLOGICAL

SOCIOPOLITICAL

SOCIOTECHNICAL

SOLID

SOURCES OF SATISFACTION AND DISSATISFACTION AMONG SOLID
WASTE MANAGEMENT EMPLOYEES.   M0283

SOURCE

WORKING CONDITIONS SURVEY AS A SOURCE OF SOCIAL INDICATORS.   M0206

THE MANAGEMENT CONSULTING FIRM AS A SOURCE OF HIGH-LEVEL
MANAGERIAL TALENT.   M0312

SOURCES

DECISIONAL PARTICIPATION AND SOURCES OF JOB SATISFACTION: A
STUDY OF MANUFACTURING PERSONNEL.   M0008

REPLICATION OF WHITE-COLLAR-BLUE-COLLAR DIFFERENCES IN
SOURCES OF SATISFACTION AND DISSATISFACTION.   M0188

SOURCES OF SATISFACTION AND DISSATISFACTION AMONG SOLID
WASTE MANAGEMENT EMPLOYEES.   M0283

EGO-DEFENSIVENESS AS A DETERMINANT OF REPORTED DIFFERENCES
IN SOURCES OF JOB SATISFACTION AND JOB DISSATISFACTION.   M0465

ROLE REQUIREMENTS AS SOURCES OF ORGANIZATIONAL STRESS.   M0597

SURVEY OF VALUES AND SOURCES OF DISSATISFACTION.   M0635

THE EFFECT OF URBANIZATION ON SOURCES OF JOB SATISFACTION
AMONG BLACK SUPERVISORS IN SOUTH AFRICA.   M0891

SOUTH

ASSESSMENT OF EXPERIMENTAL AND DEMONSTRATION INTERSTATE
PROGRAM FOR SOUTH TEXAS MIGRANT WORKERS.   M0001

JOB ENLARGEMENT, INDIVIDUAL DIFFERENCES, AND WORKER
RESPONSES: A TEST WITH BLACK WORKERS IN SOUTH AFRICA.   M0546

THE LIMITATIONS OF THE MOTIVATOR-HYGIENE THEORY OF
SATISFACTION: AN EMPIRICAL STUDY WITH BLACK FACTORY WORKERS
IN SOUTH AFRICA.   M0607

DISCRIMINATION AND JOB SATISFACTION: AN EMPIRICAL STUDY
WITH A SOUTH AFRICAN MINORITY GROUP.   M0733

THE RELATIONSHIP BETWEEN MANAGERIAL SUCCESS AND PERSONAL
VALUES IN SOUTH AFRICA: A RESEARCH NOTE.   M0786

THE EFFECT OF URBANIZATION ON SOURCES OF JOB SATISFACTION
AMONG BLACK SUPERVISORS IN SOUTH AFRICA.   M0891

SPACE

    OPEN SPACE ELEMENTARY SCHOOL: EFFECTS ON TEACHERS' JOB
    SATISFACTION, PARTICIPATION IN CURRICULUM DECISION-MAKING,
    AND PERCEIVED SCHOOL EFFECTIVENESS.   M0922

SPECIALIZATION

    JOB SPECIALIZATION, WORK VALUES, AND WORKER
    DISSATISFACTION.   M0557

SPECIALTIES

    PERSONALITY TRAITS, WORK FUNCTIONS, AND VOCATIONAL
    SATISFACTION OF PHYSICIANS IN THREE MEDICAL SPECIALTIES.   M0875

    THE RELATIONSHIPS AMONG THE PERSONALITY TYPES, JOB
    SATISFACTIONS, AND JOB SPECIALTIES OF A SELECTED GROUP OF
    MEDICAL TECHNOLOGISTS.   M0945

SPECIALTY

    INVESTIGATION OF THE INFLUENCE OF JOB LEVEL AND FUNCTIONAL
    SPECIALTY ON JOB ATTITUDES AND PERCEPTIONS.   M0745

SPECIES

    LEADERSHIP: BELEAGUERED SPECIES?   M0586

SPECIFIC

    WORK ATTITUDES AS PREDICTORS OF ATTENDANCE ON A SPECIFIC
    DAY.   M0795

SPIRIT

    TEAM SPIRIT AS IT AFFECTS PRODUCTIVITY.   M0212

    TEAM SPIRIT RESULTS IN HIGHER PRODUCTIVITY, JOB
    SATISFACTION.   M0439

SPP

    CREATING A "QUALITY" QUALITY CONTROL PROGRAM AT SPP.   M0688

SPREADING

    THE SPREADING LORDSTOWN SYNDROME.   M0414

STABILITY

    VOCATIONAL SATISFACTION, SUCCESS AND STABILITY: A
    COMPARATIVE STUDY OF MALE AND FEMALE NON-PROFESSIONAL
    WORKERS.   M0869

STAFF

STAFF ATTITUDE AND SUCCESS OF THE WIN PROGRAM, A REPORT ON
PHASE I RETURNS.   M0075

STAFF AND DISTAFF: WHY WOMEN WORK.   M0154

HOW TO KEEP STAFF MORALE AND MOTIVATION IN HIGH GEAR.   M0280

PERCEIVED DIMENSIONS OF JOB SATISFACTION FOR STAFF
REGISTERED NURSES.   M0882

STAGES

THE FOUR STAGES OF PROFESSIONAL CAREERS - A NEW LOOK AT
PERFORMANCE BY PROFESSIONALS.   M0711

MOTIVATION, JOB SATISFACTION, AND CAREER ASPIRATIONS OF
MARRIED WOMEN TEACHERS AT DIFFERENT CAREER STAGES.   M0940

STATE

STATE OF THE ART QUESTIONS ABOUT QUALITY OF WORKLIFE.   M0517

SELECTED CHARACTERISTICS, ROLES, GOALS, AND SATISFACTIONS
OF DEPARTMENT CHAIRMEN IN STATE AND LAND-GRANT
INSTITUTIONS.   M0777

STATES

PARTICIPATIVE MANAGEMENT IN THE UNITED STATES: A CORPORATE
EXPERIENCE.   M0253

THE QUIT RATE AS A MEASURE OF MORALE IN THE PUBLIC SERVICE:
THE CASE OF THE UNITED STATES FOREIGN SERVICE.   M0292

ENHANCING THE QUALITY OF WORKING LIFE: DEVELOPMENTS IN THE
UNITED STATES.   M0809

STATUS

CHANGES IN THE LABOR FORCE STATUS OF WOMEN.   M0054

JOBS, SALARY, CREDIT, LEGAL STATUS ALL IN FOCUS OF WOMEN'S
YEAR.   M0235

STEELWORKER

A STEELWORKER TALKS MOTIVATION.   M0083

STEEPNESS

RELATIVE STEEPNESS OF APPROACH AND AVOIDANCE GRADIENTS AS A
FUNCTION OF MAGNITUDE AND VALENCE OF INCENTIVE.   M0775

STEREOTYPES

    SEX STEREOTYPES: AN ARTIFACT IN LEADER BEHAVIOR AND
    SUBORDINATE SATISFACTION ANALYSIS.   M0662

    TESTING SOME STEREOTYPES ABOUT THE SEXES IN ORGANIZATIONS:
    DIFFERENTIAL SATISFACTION WITH WORK.   M0815

STEREOTYPING

    SEX STEREOTYPING: ITS DECLINE IN SKILLED TRADES.   M0197

    REMOVAL OF SEX STEREOTYPING IN CENSUS OCCUPATIONAL
    CLASSIFICATION.   M0359

STICK

    BEYOND STICK AND CARROT: HYSTERIA OVER THE WORK ETHIC.   M0111

STIMULATING

    RELATIONSHIP OF PERFORMANCE TO SATISFACTION IN STIMULATING
    AND NONSTIMULATING JOBS.   M0848

STOCKTON

    STOCKTON UNIFIED SCHOOL DISTRICT.   M0164

STORE

    RETAIL STORE PERFORMANCE AND JOB SATISFACTION: A STUDY OF
    ANXIETY-STRESS PROPENSITY TO LEAVE AMONG RETAIL EMPLOYEES.   M0811

STRAIN

    JOB STRAIN AS A FUNCTION OF JOB LIFE AND STRESSES.   M0698

STRATEGIES

    UNMIXING CURRENT MOTIVATIONAL STRATEGIES.   M0052

    POLITICAL STRATEGIES FOR IMPLEMENTING ORGANIZATIONAL
    CHANGE.   M0632

    STRATEGIES FOR ENHANCING THE PREDICTION OF JOB PERFORMANCE
    FROM JOB SATISFACTION.   M0768

STRATEGY

    MANAGERIAL STRATEGY FOR THE FUTURE: THEORY Z MANAGEMENT.   M0137

    INCREASING THE IMPORTANCE OF PERSONNEL: A STRATEGY.   M0549

    MANAGEMENT CONTROL SYSTEMS: A KEY LINK BETWEEN STRATEGY,
    STRUCTURE, AND EMPLOYEE PERFORMANCE.   M0741

STRENGTHENING

    STRENGTHENING APPRENTICESHIP.   M0432

STRENGTHS

    HIGHER ORDER NEED STRENGTHS AS MODERATORS OF THE JOB
    SCOPE-JOB SATISFACTION RELATIONSHIP.   M0798

STRESS

    ORGANIZATIONAL AND INDIVIDUAL RESPONSE TO EXTERNAL STRESS.   M0184

    OCCUPATIONAL STRESS AND PHYSICAL HEALTH.   M0213

    WORKERS UNDER STRESS (THE IMPACT OF WORK PRESSURE ON GROUP
    COHESION).   M0255

    ORGANIZATION STRESS AS A MODERATOR OF THE RELATIONSHIP
    BETWEEN INFLUENCE AND ROLE RESPONSE.   M0444

    ROLE REQUIREMENTS AS SOURCES OF ORGANIZATIONAL STRESS.   M0597

    THE RELATIONSHIP OF SEX AND ETHNIC BACKGROUND TO
    JOB-RELATED STRESS OF RESEARCH AND DEVELOPMENT
    PROFESSIONALS.   M0695

STRESSES

    OCCUPATIONAL STRESSES AND JOB SATISFACTION.   M0506

    JOB STRAIN AS A FUNCTION OF JOB LIFE AND STRESSES.   M0698

STRIKE

    THE BRITISH COAL MINE STRIKE OF 1972.   M0483

    RELATIVE SALIENCY OF JOB FACTORS DURING STRIKE.   M0558

STROKING

    MOTIVATION THROUGH POSITIVE STROKING.   M0059

STRUCTURAL

    JOB CHARACTERISTICS RELATIONSHIPS: INDIVIDUAL AND
    STRUCTURAL MODERATORS.   M0896

STRUCTURE

    SOME MODERATOR INFLUENCES ON RELATIONSHIPS BETWEEN
    CONSIDERATION, INITIATING STRUCTURE, AND ORGANIZATION
    CRITERIA.   M0021

    CHANGES IN THE OCCUPATIONAL STRUCTURE OF U. S. JOBS.   M0100

STRUCTURE CONTINUATION

AN ANALYSIS OF CLIQUE FORMATION AND STRUCTURE IN
ORGANIZATIONS.   M0445

THE IMPACT OF THE ORGANIZATION ON THE STRUCTURE OF JOB
SATISFACTION: SOME FACTOR ANALYTIC FINDINGS.   M0471

STRUCTURE IN ORGANIZATION: A RECONSIDERATION.   M0576

ORGANIZATIONAL STRUCTURE: HOW DOES IT INFLUENCE ATTITUDES
AND PERFORMANCE.   M0578

VALUES, STRUCTURE, PROCESS, AND REACTIONS/ADJUSTMENTS: A
COMPARISON OF FRENCH AND ENGLISH-CANADIAN INDUSTRIAL
ORGANIZATIONS.   M0628

LIFE STYLE, WORK GROUP STRUCTURE, COMPATIBILITY, AND JOB
SATISFACTION.   M0651

RELATIONS AMONG PERCEIVED ENVIRONMENTAL UNCERTAINTY,
ORGANIZATION STRUCTURE, AND BOUNDARY-SPANNING BEHAVIOR. M0671

LEADER STRUCTURE AND SUBORDINATE SATISFACTION FOR TWO
HOSPITAL ADMINISTRATIVE LEVELS: A PATH ANALYSIS APPROACH. M0736

MANAGEMENT CONTROL SYSTEMS: A KEY LINK BETWEEN STRATEGY,
STRUCTURE, AND EMPLOYEE PERFORMANCE.   M0741

RELATION OF ORGANIZATIONAL STRUCTURE TO JOB SATISFACTION,
ANXIETY-STRESS, AND PERFORMANCE.   M0766

MODERATING EFFECTS OF ENVIRONMENT AND STRUCTURE ON THE
SATISFACTION-TENSION-INFLUENCE NETWORK.   M0828

STRUCTURES

STRUCTURES OF ATTITUDES TOWARD WORK AND TECHNOLOGICAL
CHANGE WITHIN AN ORGANIZATION.   M0639

THE IMPACT OF HIERARCHICAL STRUCTURES ON THE WORK BEHAVIOR
OF WOMEN AND MEN.   M0757

THE RELATIONSHIPS BETWEEN THE TASK-HUMAN RELATIONS
MOTIVATIONAL STRUCTURES OF INDIVIDUALS IN SMALL WORK GROUPS
AND THEIR SATISFACTION WITH CO-WORKERS AND IMMEDIATE
SUPERVISION.   M0868

STUDENT

BACKGROUND AND PERSONALITY CHARACTERISTICS RELATED TO
STUDENT SATISFACTION AND PERFORMANCE IN FIELD MEDICAL
SERVICE SCHOOL.   M0575

JOB ATTITUDES OF STUDENT PERSONNEL WORKERS AND THEIR JOB
SITUATIONS.   M0707

STUDENT   CONTINUATION

RELATIONSHIPS BETWEEN WORK VALUES AND JOB SATISFACTION
AMONG COLLEGE STUDENT PERSONNEL WORKERS.   M0928

STUDENTS

HIGH SCHOOL STUDENTS PERCEPTIONS OF WORK.   M0535

ANDROGYNY IN NURSING: NURSE ROLE EXPECTATION, SATISFACTION,
ACADEMIC ACHIEVEMENT, AND SELF-ACTUALIZATION IM MALE AND
FEMALE STUDENTS.   M0877

STUDIES

NATIONAL LONGITUDINAL STUDIES OF THE LABOR FORCE BEHAVIOR
OF NATIONAL SAMPLES OF MEN (45-59), WOMEN (30-44), AND MALE
AND FEMALE YOUTH (14-24).   M0339

THREE STUDIES OF MEASURES OF NEED SATISFACTION IN
ORGANIZATIONS.   M0380

ON ALEX CAREY'S RADICAL CRITICISMS OF THE HAWTHORNE
STUDIES.   M0391

STUDY

DECISIONAL PARTICIPATION AND SOURCES OF JOB SATISFACTION: A
STUDY OF MANUFACTURING PERSONNEL.   M0008

TIME PRESSURE AND PERFORMANCE OF SCIENTISTS AND ENGINEERS:
A FIVE PANEL STUDY.   M0010

QUITS IN MANUFACTURING: A STUDY OF THEIR CAUSES.   M0014

THE WORKER ATTITUDES AND EARLY OCCUPATIONAL EXPERIENCES OF
YOUNG MEN -- ANALYSIS BASED ON A 4-YEAR LONGITUDINAL STUDY.   M0020

BLACKS AS SUPERVISORS: A STUDY OF TRAINING, JOB
PERFORMANCE, AND EMPLOYEE'S EXPECTATION.   M0023

A STUDY OF EMPLOYEE RESISTANCE TO JOB ENRICHMENT.   M0066

A PREDICTIVE STUDY OF TURNOVER.   M0125

A STUDY OF BLACK MALE PROFESSIONALS IN INDUSTRY.   M0143

A NEW APPROACH TO LOCAL LABOR MARKET ANALYSIS: A
FEASIBILITY STUDY.   M0162

A STUDY OF THE WORK ORIENTATIONS OF WELFARE RECIPIENTS
PARTICIPATING IN THE WORK INCENTIVE PROGRAM.   M0167

RESTRUCTURING PARAMEDICAL OCCUPATIONS: A CASE STUDY.   M0169

A COMPARATIVE STUDY OF THE SATISFACTION OF DOMESTIC U. S.

STUDY   CONTINUATION

STUDY   CONTINUATION

DISCRIMINATION AND JOB SATISFACTION: AN EMPIRICAL STUDY
WITH A SOUTH AFRICAN MINORITY GROUP.   M0733

THE VOCATIONAL EXPLORATION GROUP AND MINORITY YOUTH: AN
EXPERIMENTAL OUTCOME STUDY.   M0749

CORPORATE MANAGEMENT IN LOCAL GOVERNMENT: A CASE STUDY.   M0769

A NATIONAL STUDY OF ASSOCIATE DEGREE MENTAL HEALTH SERVICES
WORKERS.   M0806

RETAIL STORE PERFORMANCE AND JOB SATISFACTION: A STUDY OF
ANXIETY-STRESS PROPENSITY TO LEAVE AMONG RETAIL EMPLOYEES.   M0811

INCENTIVE SCHEDULES, PRODUCTIVITY, AND SATISFACTION IN WORK
GROUPS: A LABORATORY STUDY.   M0814

TOWARD A CAREER-BASED THEORY OF JOB INVOLVEMENT: A STUDY OF
SCIENTISTS AND ENGINEERS.   M0824

WHY STUDY WORKING CONDITIONS VIA JOB SATISFACTION?   A PLEA
FOR DIRECT ANALYSIS.   M0833

A STUDY OF THE RELATIONSHIP BETWEEN HERZBERG'S MOTIVATION
HYGIENE FACTORS AND HOLLAND'S PERSONALITY PATTERNS FOR LAW
ENFORCEMENT PERSONNEL.   M0850

VOCATIONAL SATISFACTION, SUCCESS AND STABILITY: A
COMPARATIVE STUDY OF MALE AND FEMALE NON-PROFESSIONAL
WORKERS.   M0869

PREDICTING THE PERFORMANCE OF JUNIOR ACHIEVEMENT ACCORDING
TO THE LEADERSHIP STYLE OF TWO LEVELS OF MANAGEMENT: A
FIELD STUDY OF THE CONTINGENCY MODEL.   M0872

AN EXPERIMENTAL STUDY OF THE EFFECTS OF GOAL SETTING,
EVALUATION APPREHENSION, AND SOCIAL CUES ON TASK
PERFORMANCE AND JOB SATISFACTION.   M0878

A STUDY OF REHABILITATION COUNSELORS: LOCUS OF CONTROL AND
ATTITUDES TOWARD THE POOR.   M0888

A STUDY OF THE JOB SATISFACTION AND JOB PERCEPTION OF
ORGANIZED AND NON-ORGANIZED PUBLIC SCHOOL PRINCIPALS.   M0902

A STUDY OF THE RELATIONSHIP AMONG (1) JOB SATISFACTION AND
(2) TEACHER ATTITUDE.   M0908

A STUDY OF JOB SATISFACTION OF ADMINISTRATORS AT UNITED
METHODIST RELATED CHURCHES.   M0910

A NORMATIVE STUDY OF THE SECONDARY SCHOOL ASSISTANT
PRINCIPALSHIP IN SELECTED PENNSYLVANIA SCHOOL DISTRICTS
WITH AN EMPHASIS UPON JOB SATISFACTION.   M0918

SUBORDINATE

SUBORDINATES

SUBORDINATES'

SUCCEED

SUCCESS

SUCCESS CONTINUATION

CAUSAL MODELING OF PSYCHOLOGICAL SUCCESS IN WORK
ORGANIZATIONS. M0520

ACHIEVEMENT DRIVE AND CREATIVITY AS CORRELATES OF SUCCESS
IN SMALL BUSINESS. M0730

THE RELATIONSHIP BETWEEN MANAGERIAL SUCCESS AND PERSONAL
VALUES IN SOUTH AFRICA: A RESEARCH NOTE. M0786

WHERE SUCCESS LIES. M0797

VOCATIONAL SATISFACTION, SUCCESS AND STABILITY: A
COMPARATIVE STUDY OF MALE AND FEMALE NON-PROFESSIONAL
WORKERS. M0869

SUCCESSES

AN EXPERIMENTAL CASE STUDY OF THE SUCCESSES AND FAILURES OF
JOB ENRICHMENT IN A GOVERNMENT AGENCY. M0600

SUCCESSFUL

SUCCESSFUL LEADERS ARE SUCCESSFUL MOTIVATORS. M0095

CHARACTERISTICS OF SUCCESSFUL AND UNSUCCESSFUL ORGANIZATION
DEVELOPMENT. M0513

SUCCESSFULLY

JOB PERFORMANCE AND SATISFACTION OF SUCCESSFULLY
REHABILITATED VOCATIONAL REHABILITATION CLIENTS. M0801

SUPERINTENDENTS

JOB SATISFACTION OF GEORGIA SCHOOL SUPERINTENDENTS AND
THEIR PERCEPTION OF THE LOCAL SCHOOL BOARD PRESIDENT'S
LEADER BEHAVIOR. M0906

SUPERIOR-SUBORDINATE

EFFECTS OF DIFFERENT PATTERNS AND DEGREES OF OPENNESS IN
SUPERIOR-SUBORDINATE COMMUNICATION ON SUBORDINATE JOB
SATISFACTION. M0045

SUPERVISEE

SUPERVISOR EXPECTATIONS AND BEHAVIOR: EFFECTS OF
CONSISTENT-INCONSISTENT SUPERVISORY PAIRINGS ON SUPERVISEE
SATISFACTION WITH SUPERVISION, PERCEPTIONS OF SUPERVISORY
RELATIONSHIPS AND RATED COUNSELOR COMPETENCY. M0864

SUPERVISION

LOCUS OF CONTROL: SUPERVISION AND WORK SATISFACTION. M0660

CONTINUATION
SUPERVISION

RELATIONSHIPS AMONG PAY, RACE, SEX, OCCUPATIONAL PRESTIGE,
SUPERVISION, WORK AUTONOMY, AND JOB SATISFACTION IN A
NATIONAL SAMPLE.   M0842

PERCEIVED LEADER BEHAVIOR AND EMPLOYEE SATISFACTION WITH
SUPERVISION AND THE JOB: THE EFFECTS OF REWARD AND
PUNISHMENT.   M0859

SUPERVISOR EXPECTATIONS AND BEHAVIOR: EFFECTS OF
CONSISTENT-INCONSISTENT SUPERVISORY PAIRINGS ON SUPERVISEE
SATISFACTION WITH SUPERVISION, PERCEPTIONS OF SUPERVISORY
RELATIONSHIPS AND RATED COUNSELOR COMPETENCY.   M0864

THE RELATIONSHIPS BETWEEN THE TASK-HUMAN RELATIONS
MOTIVATIONAL STRUCTURES OF INDIVIDUALS IN SMALL WORK GROUPS
AND THEIR SATISFACTION WITH CO-WORKERS AND IMMEDIATE
SUPERVISION.   M0868

SUPERVISOR

PARTICIPATION WITH SUPERVISOR AND SUBORDINATE
AUTHORITARIANISM: A PATH GOAL THEORY RECONCILIATION.   M0554

SUPERVISOR EXPECTATIONS AND BEHAVIOR: EFFECTS OF
CONSISTENT-INCONSISTENT SUPERVISORY PAIRINGS ON SUPERVISEE
SATISFACTION WITH SUPERVISION, PERCEPTIONS OF SUPERVISORY
RELATIONSHIPS AND RATED COUNSELOR COMPETENCY.   M0864

SUPERVISORS

BLACKS AS SUPERVISORS: A STUDY OF TRAINING, JOB
PERFORMANCE, AND EMPLOYEE'S EXPECTATION.   M0023

BEHAVIORAL TRAINING OF SUPERVISORS IN AN INDUSTRIAL SETTING
FOR THE BLIND.   M0846

THE EFFECT OF URBANIZATION ON SOURCES OF JOB SATISFACTION
AMONG BLACK SUPERVISORS IN SOUTH AFRICA.   M0891

COMPARATIVE APPRAISALS OF JOB PERFORMANCE OF FULL-TIME
ELEMENTARY PRINCIPALS BY THE PRINCIPALS AND THEIR
SUPERVISORS IN CLASS I MONTANA SCHOOL DISTRICTS.   M0941

SUPERVISORY

SUPERVISORY SKILLS AND EMPLOYEE SATISFACTION.   M0316

INTERACTION MODELING: A NEW CONCEPT IN SUPERVISORY
TRAINING.   M0507

RELATIONSHIPS BETWEEN ROLE CLARITY, NEED FOR CLARITY AND
JOB TENSION AND SATISFACTION FOR SUPERVISORY AND
NONSUPERVISORY ROLES.   M0539

SUPERVISORY   CONTINUATION

IMPACT OF SUPERVISORY CHARACTERISTICS ON GOAL ACCEPTANCE.   M0661

SUPERVISOR EXPECTATIONS AND BEHAVIOR: EFFECTS OF
CONSISTENT-INCONSISTENT SUPERVISORY PAIRINGS ON SUPERVISEE
SATISFACTION WITH SUPERVISION, PERCEPTIONS OF SUPERVISORY
RELATIONSHIPS AND RATED COUNSELOR COMPETENCY.   M0864

SURVEY

WORKING CONDITIONS SURVEY AS A SOURCE OF SOCIAL INDICATORS. M0206

SURVEY OF WORKING CONDITIONS. FINAL REPORT OF UNIVARIATE
AND BIVARIATE TABLES.   M0266

SURVEY OF FACTORS RELATING TO JOB SATISFACTION AMONG VA
NURSES.   M0457

SURVEY OF VALUES AND SOURCES OF DISSATISFACTION.   M0635

MANAGING MORALE THROUGH SURVEY FEEDBACK.   M0684

DEVELOPMENT OF THE JOB DIAGNOSTIC SURVEY.   M0723

CAPABILITIES OF MIDDLE-AGED AND OLDER WORKERS: A SURVEY OF
THE LITERATURE.   M0778

SURVEYED

WOMEN'S PROGRAMS SURVEYED AT LATIN AMERICAN POSTS.   M0488

SWEDEN

EFFECTS OF CHANGES IN PAYMENT SYSTEM ON PRODUCTIVITY IN
SWEDEN.   M0400

SYMPTOMATOLOGY

DEPRESSIVE SYMPTOMATOLOGY AND ROLE FUNCTION IN A GENERAL
POPULATION.   M0752

SYNDROME

CURE FOR THE I DON'T CARE SYNDROME.   M0382

THE SPREADING LORDSTOWN SYNDROME.   M0414

SYNTHESIS

ABSENCE BEHAVIOR AND ATTENDANCE MOTIVATION: A CONCEPTUAL
SYNTHESIS.   M0783

TECHNOLOGICAL DIFFERENCES IN JOB CHARACTERISTICS, EMPLOYEE
SATISFACTION, AND MOTIVATION: A SYNTHESIS OF JOB DESIGN
RESOURCE AND SOCIOTECHNICAL SYSTEMS THEORY.   M0832

SYSTEM

HUMANIZING THE BUDGETARY SYSTEM FOR ADMINISTRATIVE
REINFORCEMENT.   M0138

THE MANAGEMENT OF SCIENTISTS: DETERMINANTS OF PERCEIVED
ROLE PERFORMANCE OF 95 SCIENTISTS IN THREE LARGE RESEARCH
LABORATORIES TO THE ORGANIC SYSTEM OF MANAGEMENT CONCEIVED
BY BURNS AND STALKER.   M0190

THE POSITION AND FUNCTION OF BUDGETS IN AN MBO SYSTEM.   M0289

EFFECTS OF CHANGES IN PAYMENT SYSTEM ON PRODUCTIVITY IN
SWEDEN.   M0400

DESIGNING A MOTIVATING AND TEAM BUILDING EMPLOYEE APPRAISAL
SYSTEM.   M0534

FACTORS AFFECTING ACQUISITION OF BELIEFS ABOUT A NEW REWARD
SYSTEM.   M0589

THE DEVELOPMENT OF A MANAGERIAL JOB TAXONOMY: A SYSTEM FOR
DESCRIBING, CLASSIFYING, AND EVALUATING EXECUTIVE
POSITIONS.   M0618

DEMOCRATIZING THE REWARD SYSTEM.   M0742

PERCEPTIONS OF ORGANIZATIONAL CLIMATE AS MEDIATORS OF THE
RELATIONSHIPS BETWEEN INDIVIDUAL NEEDS AND JOB SATISFACTION
OF COUNSELORS IN THE NORTH CAROLINA COMMUNITY COLLEGE
SYSTEM.   M0933

A NETWORK ANALYSIS OF A BUREAU OF INDIAN AFFAIRS SCHOOL
SYSTEM TO DETERMINE FACTORS INVOLVED IN JOB SATISFACTION.   M0934

SYSTEMS

PERSONNEL SYSTEMS AND HUMAN PERFORMANCE.   M0024

PERSONALITY, MOTIVATIONAL SYSTEMS, AND BEHAVIOR OF HIGH AND
LOW LPC PERSONS.   M0131

RELATIONSHIPS BETWEEN PERFORMANCE AND SATISFACTION UNDER
CONTINGENT AND NONCONTINGENT REWARD SYSTEMS.   M0251

A SYSTEMS APPROACH TO RESULTS ORIENTED PERFORMANCE
EVALUATION.   M0338

EFFECTS OF VARYING GOAL TYPES AND INCENTIVE SYSTEMS ON
PERFORMANCE AND SATISFACTION.   M0659

SYSTEMS OF ORGANIZATION: MANAGEMENT OF THE HUMAN RESOURCE.   M0670

MANAGEMENT CONTROL SYSTEMS: A KEY LINK BETWEEN STRATEGY,
STRUCTURE, AND EMPLOYEE PERFORMANCE.   M0741

SYSTEMS   CONTINUATION

  PREDICTION OF SATISFACTION OF SYSTEMS ANALYSTS,
  PROGRAMMERS.   M0807

  TECHNOLOGICAL DIFFERENCES IN JOB CHARACTERISTICS, EMPLOYEE
  SATISFACTION, AND MOTIVATION: A SYNTHESIS OF JOB DESIGN
  RESOURCE AND SOCIOTECHNICAL SYSTEMS THEORY.   M0832

  PARTICIPATIVE AND POWER-EQUALIZED ORGANIZATIONAL SYSTEMS:
  AN EMPIRICAL INVESTIGATION AND THEORETICAL INTEGRATION.   M0889

SYSTEMS-DESIGNED

  EFFECTS ON PRODUCTIVITY AND MORALE OF A SYSTEMS-DESIGNED
  JOB-ENRICHMENT PROGRAM IN PACIFIC TELEPHONE.   M0515

TABLES

  SURVEY OF WORKING CONDITIONS. FINAL REPORT OF UNIVARIATE
  AND BIVARIATE TABLES.   M0266

TALENT

  FORM CHINA WITH SKILL -- MESBIC FOUNDER WANTS TO SHARE HER
  TALENT.   M0145

  THE MANAGEMENT CONSULTING FIRM AS A SOURCE OF HIGH-LEVEL
  MANAGERIAL TALENT.   M0312

TALENTS

  ANALYSIS OF RACIAL DIFFERENCES IN TERMS OF WORK
  ASSIGNMENTS, JOB INTEREST, AND FELT UTILIZATION OF TALENTS
  AND TRAINING, BY RAYMOND E. CHRISTEL.   M0451

  REPORTED JOB INTEREST AND PERCEIVED UTILIZATION OF TALENTS
  AND TRAINING BY AIRMEN IN 97 CAREER LADDERS, BY R. BRUCE
  GOULD. PROJECT 7734, DECEMBER 1972.   M0452

TALK

  TOUGH TALK WON'T BE ABOUT WAGES THIS TIME.   M0800

TALKS

  A STEELWORKER TALKS MOTIVATION.   M0083

TARGET

  H.I.T. ON TARGET WITH INSTANT UPGRADING.   M0262

TASK

  TASK CHARACTERISTICS AND INTRINSIC MOTIVATION.   M0070

TASK   CONTINUATION

SPECIAL TASK FORCE WILL REVIEW ROLE OF GS AND FS
SECRETARIES.   M0411

AGE AND REACTIONS TO TASK CHARACTERISTICS.   M0569

EFFECTS OF JOB ENRICHMENT AND TASK GOALS ON SATISFACTION
AND PRODUCTIVITY: IMPLICATIONS FOR JOB DESIGN.   M0619

MANAGEMENT STYLES ASSOCIATED WITH ORGANIZATIONAL, TASK,
PERSONAL, AND INTERPERSONAL CONTINGENCIES.   M0748

THE EFFECTS OF VARYING SCHEDULES OF REINFORCEMENT ON HUMAN
TASK PERFORMANCE.   M0790

AN EXPERIMENTAL STUDY OF THE EFFECTS OF GOAL SETTING,
EVALUATION APPREHENSION, AND SOCIAL CUES ON TASK
PERFORMANCE AND JOB SATISFACTION.   M0878

TASK OPPORTUNITY PROFESSIONAL GROWTH NEED FULFILLMENT AND
INTRINSIC JOB SATISFACTION OF PUBLIC SOCIAL SERVICE WORKERS
IN COLORADO.   M0923

AN INVESTIGATION OF THE RELATIONSHIP BETWEEN INTRINSIC AND
EXTRINSIC JOB INSTRUMENTALITY EFFORT, JOB SATISFACTION,
INDIVIDUAL AND PERCEIVED TASK CHARACTERISTICS.   M0938

TASK-HUMAN

THE RELATIONSHIPS BETWEEN THE TASK-HUMAN RELATIONS
MOTIVATIONAL STRUCTURES OF INDIVIDUALS IN SMALL WORK GROUPS
AND THEIR SATISFACTION WITH CO-WORKERS AND IMMEDIATE
SUPERVISION.   M0868

TASKS

TASKS, INDIVIDUAL DIFFERENCES, AND JOB SATISFACTION.   M0841

TAXONOMY

THE DEVELOPMENT OF A MANAGERIAL JOB TAXONOMY: A SYSTEM FOR
DESCRIBING, CLASSIFYING, AND EVALUATING EXECUTIVE
POSITIONS.   M0618

TAYLOR

FREDRICK W. TAYLOR -- 62 YEARS LATER.   M0390

TEACHER

TEACHER TRAINING TAKES TO THE ROAD.   M0273

A STUDY OF THE RELATIONSHIP AMONG (1) JOB SATISFACTION AND
(2) TEACHER ATTITUDE.   M0908

TENURE   CONTINUATION

THEORIES   CONTINUATION

TRAINING   CONTINUATION

    WOMEN OFFENDERS: BREAKING THE TRAINING MOLD.   M0330

    WOMEN IN PROFESSIONAL TRAINING.   M0340

    MODEL PROGRAM TO INSTRUCT MANPOWER TRAINING PERSONNEL IN
    SELECTION AND APPLICATION OF REMEDIAL INSTRUCTIONAL
    MATERIALS TO MEET INDIVIDUAL TRAINEE NEEDS.   M0387

    WORK TRAINING PROGRAMS AND THE UNEMPLOYMENT RATE.   M0403

    ANALYSIS OF RACIAL DIFFERENCES IN TERMS OF WORK
    ASSIGNMENTS, JOB INTEREST, AND FELT UTILIZATION OF TALENTS
    AND TRAINING, BY RAYMOND E. CHRISTEL.   M0451

    REPORTED JOB INTEREST AND PERCEIVED UTILIZATION OF TALENTS
    AND TRAINING BY AIRMEN IN 97 CAREER LADDERS, BY R. BRUCE
    GOULD. PROJECT 7734, DECEMBER 1972.   M0452

    ROLE OF ON-THE-JOB TRAINING IN A CLINICAL LABORATORY.   M0477

    INTERACTION MODELING: A NEW CONCEPT IN SUPERVISORY
    TRAINING.   M0507

    PERFORMANCE IMPROVEMENT WITHOUT TRAINING.   M0545

    TRAINING AND CAREER SATISFACTION AMONG CLINICAL
    PSYCHOLOGISTS.   M0759

    BEHAVIORAL TRAINING OF SUPERVISORS IN AN INDUSTRIAL SETTING
    FOR THE BLIND.   M0846

    SATISFACTION WITH TRAINING AND GENERAL JOB SATISFACTION OF
    AGENCY HOMEMAKERS WORKING WITH THE ELDERLY AND DISABLED.   M0904

TRAITS

    JOB LOSERS, LEAVERS, AND ENTRANTS: TRAITS AND TRENDS.   M0157

    PERSONALITY TRAITS, WORK FUNCTIONS, AND VOCATIONAL
    SATISFACTION OF PHYSICIANS IN THREE MEDICAL SPECIALTIES.   M0875

TRANSITION

    VIET-NAM WAR VETERANS -- TRANSITION TO CIVILIAN LIFE.   M0463

TRANSLATIONS

    LANGUAGE, TIME, AND PERSON EFFECTS ON ATTITUDE SCALE
    TRANSLATIONS.   M0770

TRAPPED

    DISCONTENT IN THE RANKS: IS THE OPERATIVE WORKER REALLY
    TRAPPED.   M0354

TREATMENTS

    DIFFERENT GOAL SETTING TREATMENTS AND THEIR EFFECTS ON
PERFORMANCE AND JOB SATISFACTION.   M0819

TREND

    JOB SATISFACTION: IS THERE A TREND.   M0454

TRENDS

    BLUE-COLLAR / WHITE-COLLAR PAY TRENDS.   M0031

    RECENT TRENDS IN OVERTIME HOURS AND PREMIUM PAY.   M0130

    JOB LOSERS, LEAVERS, AND ENTRANTS: TRAITS AND TRENDS. M0157

    TRENDS IN LABOR AND LEISURE.   M0319

    ECONOMIC CONSIDERATIONS IN JOB SATISFACTION TRENDS.   M0644

    TEN YEAR JOB SATISFACTION TRENDS IN A STABLE ORGANIZATION. M0837

    TRENDS IN JOB-RELATED ATTITUDES OF MANAGERIAL AND
PROFESSIONAL EMPLOYEES.   M0838

TRIAL

    WESTERN ELECTRICS MOTIVATION AND ENRICHMENT TRIAL.   M0195

TRUST

    JOB REDESIGN IMPROVES PRODUCTIVITY. (BANKERS TRUST, N.Y.). M0533

TRUTH

    CAREER CHOICE, JOB SATISFACTION, AND THE TRUTH BEHIND THE
PETER PRINCIPLE.   M0541

TURBULENCE

    TURBULENCE IN THE WORKING WORLD: ANGRY WORKERS, HAPPY
GRADS.   M0744

TURN-AROUND

    PROFESSIONAL MANPOWER: THE JOB MARKET TURN-AROUND.   M0078

TURNOVER

    A PREDICTIVE STUDY OF TURNOVER.   M0125

    EFFECTS OF CHANGES IN JOB SATISFACTION LEVELS ON EMPLOYEE
TURNOVER.   M0219

    PREDICTING ABSENTEEISM AND TURNOVER: A FIELD COMPARISON OF

TURNOVER CONTINUATION

FISHBEIN'S MODEL AND TRADITIONAL JOB ATTITUDE MEASURES. M0326

ORGANIZATIONAL COMMITMENT, JOB SATISFACTION, AND TURNOVER AMONG PSYCHIATRIC TECHNICIANS. M0353

JOB EXPECTANCY -- AN IMPORTANT FACTOR IN LABOR TURNOVER. M0385

ORGANIZATIONAL COMMITMENT AND TURNOVER: A PREDICTION STUDY. M0627

THE USE OF EXPECTANCY THEORY IN THE EXPLANATION OF TURNOVER IN ROTC. M0732

INTERMEDIATE LINKAGES IN THE RELATIONSHIP BETWEEN JOB SATISFACTION AND EMPLOYEE TURNOVER. M0781

TWO-FACTOR

CROSS-CULTURAL DIFFERENCES IN TWO-FACTOR MOTIVATION THEORY. M0209

TYPE

MOTIVATIONAL TYPE AND THE SATISFACTION-PERFORMANCE RELATIONSHIP. M0263

TYPES

EFFECTS OF VARYING GOAL TYPES AND INCENTIVE SYSTEMS ON PERFORMANCE AND SATISFACTION. M0659

THE RELATIONSHIPS AMONG THE PERSONALITY TYPES, JOB SATISFACTIONS, AND JOB SPECIALTIES OF A SELECTED GROUP OF MEDICAL TECHNOLOGISTS. M0945

TYPOLOGY

THE WORK SATISFACTION, RETIREMENT-ATTITUDE TYPOLOGY: PROFILE EXAMINATION. M0590

CORPORATE DROPOUTS: A PRELIMINARY TYPOLOGY. M0616

UNCERTAINTY

RELATIONS AMONG PERCEIVED ENVIRONMENTAL UNCERTAINTY, ORGANIZATION STRUCTURE, AND BOUNDARY-SPANNING BEHAVIOR. M0671

UNDERGRADUATE

THE DYNAMICS OF UNDERGRADUATE ACADEMIC ADVISING. M0750

UNDERLOAD

UNDERLOAD AND OVERLOAD IN WORKING LIFE: OUTLINE OF A MULTI-DISCIPLINARY APPROACH. M0643

UNDERLYING

A TEST OF TWO POSTULATES UNDERLYING EXPECTANCY THEORY.   M0666

UNDERSTANDING

UNDERSTANDING FRUSTRATION-INSTIGATED BEHAVIOR.   M0743

UNDERSTANDING DRUG USE MOTIVATION: A NEW LOOK AT A CURRENT
PROBLEM.   M0788

UNEMPLOYED

SPECIAL WORK PROJECTS FOR THE UNEMPLOYED AND UPGRADING FOR
THE WORKING POOR.   M0475

LONGITUDINAL STUDY OF ABSENTEEISM AND HARD-CORE UNEMPLOYED.   M0500

UNEMPLOYMENT

EMPLOYMENT AND UNEMPLOYMENT -- A REPORT ON 1973.   M0036

DISCOURAGE WORKERS AND CHANGES IN UNEMPLOYMENT.   M0134

BLACK AND WHITE UNEMPLOYMENT: THE DYNAMICS OF THE
DIFFERENTIAL.   M0156

WORK TRAINING PROGRAMS AND THE UNEMPLOYMENT RATE.   M0403

UNIFIED

STOCKTON UNIFIED SCHOOL DISTRICT.   M0164

UNION

COMPARING UNION AND NONUNION WAGES IN MANUFACTURING.   M0309

JOB ENRICHMENT: A UNION VIEW.   M0484

UNIONS

WHAT YOUNG PEOPLE SHOULD KNOW ABOUT LABOR UNIONS.   M0424

UNITED

PARTICIPATIVE MANAGEMENT IN THE UNITED STATES: A CORPORATE
EXPERIENCE.   M0253

THE QUIT RATE AS A MEASURE OF MORALE IN THE PUBLIC SERVICE:
THE CASE OF THE UNITED STATES FOREIGN SERVICE.   M0292

ENHANCING THE QUALITY OF WORKING LIFE: DEVELOPMENTS IN THE
UNITED STATES.   M0809

A STUDY OF JOB SATISFACTION OF ADMINISTRATORS AT UNITED
METHODIST RELATED CHURCHES.   M0910

UNIVARIATE

SURVEY OF WORKING CONDITIONS. FINAL REPORT OF UNIVARIATE
AND BIVARIATE TABLES.   M0266

UNIVERSITY

THE EFFECT OF LEADERSHIP ROLES ON THE SATISFACTION AND
PRODUCTIVITY OF UNIVERSITY RESEARCH PROFESSORS.   M0510

THE MEASUREMENT OF SATISFACTION AND DEPARTMENTAL
ASSOCIATION AT WESTERN KENTUCKY UNIVERSITY: TESTING THE
HOLLAND AND BIGLAN MODELS.   M0914

UNMIXING

UNMIXING CURRENT MOTIVATIONAL STRATEGIES.   M0052

UNSUCCESSFUL

CHARACTERISTICS OF SUCCESSFUL AND UNSUCCESSFUL ORGANIZATION
DEVELOPMENT.   M0513

UPGRADING

UPGRADING BLUE-COLLAR AND SERVICE WORKERS.   M0037

H.I.T. ON TARGET WITH INSTANT UPGRADING.   M0262

SPECIAL WORK PROJECTS FOR THE UNEMPLOYED AND UPGRADING FOR
THE WORKING POOR.   M0475

URBAN

ADOLESCENT MINORITY FEMALES IN AN URBAN LABOR MARKET.   M0060

TIME AND INCENTIVE PAY PRACTICES IN URBAN AREAS.   M0076

FRINGE BENEFITS OF URBAN WORKERS.   M0346

SOCIOECONOMIC DETERMINANTS OF URBAN POVERTY AREA WORKERS.   M0349

THE PUBLIC EMPLOYMENT SERVICE REACHES OUT TO THE URBAN
POOR.   M0374

REVIEW OF LITERATURE ON WORK MOTIVATION: BULLETIN 12. A
STUDY OF WORK MOTIVATION OF URBAN AND RURAL APPAREL WORKERS
IN TENNESSEE.   M0503

RURAL AND URBAN DIFFERENCES: ONE MORE TIME.   M0808

URBAN-RURAL

REPLY TO URBAN-RURAL DIFFERENCES IN JOB SATISFACTION.   M0584

URBAN-RURAL DIFFERENCES IN JOB SATISFACTION.   M0585

VALIDITY

THE VALIDITY OF IMPORTANCE.   M0030

CONVERGENT AND DISCRIMINANT VALIDITY OF A JOB SATISFACTION
INVENTORY: A CROSS-CULTURAL REPORT.   M0764

VALUES

BACKGROUND CHARACTERISTICS, ORIENTATION, WORK EXPERIENCE,
AND WORK VALUES OF EMPLOYEES HIRED FROM HUMAN RESOURCES
DEVELOPMENT APPLICANTS BY COMPANIES AFFILIATED WITH THE
NATIONAL ALLIANCE OF BUSINESSMAN.   M0165

ROLE CONFLICT AND AMBIGUITY: CORRELATES WITH JOB
SATISFACTION AND VALUES.   M0249

VALUES -- NOT ATTITUDES -- ARE THE REAL KEY TO MOTIVATION.   M0301

WORK VALUES OF WHITE-COLLAR EMPLOYEES AS A FUNCTION OF
SOCIOLOGICAL BACKGROUND.   M0376

EFFECTS OF PERSONAL VALUES ON THE RELATIONSHIP BETWEEN
PARTICIPATION AND JOB ATTITUDES.   M0476

WORK VALUES AS MODERATORS OF PERCEIVED LEADER
BEHAVIOR-SATISFACTION RELATIONSHIPS.   M0505

JOB SPECIALIZATION, WORK VALUES, AND WORKER
DISSATISFACTION.   M0557

WORK VALUES AND JOB SATISFACTION OF YOUNG ADULT MALES.   M0579

THE RELEVANCE OF COSMOPOLITAN/LOCAL ORIENTATIONS TO
PROFESSIONAL VALUES AND BEHAVIOR.   M0588

NATIONALITY AND ESPOUSED VALUES OF MANAGERS.   M0593

VALUES, STRUCTURE, PROCESS, AND REACTIONS/ADJUSTMENTS: A
COMPARISON OF FRENCH AND ENGLISH-CANADIAN INDUSTRIAL
ORGANIZATIONS.   M0628

SURVEY OF VALUES AND SOURCES OF DISSATISFACTION.   M0635

JOB INVOLVEMENT, VALUES, PERSONAL BACKGROUND, PARTICIPATION
IN DECISION MAKING, AND JOB ATTITUDES.   M0664

THE SELF-CONCEPT, PERSONAL VALUES, AND MOTIVATIONAL
ORIENTATIONS OF BLACK AND WHITE MANAGERS.   M0668

WORK VALUES, JOB REWARDS AND JOB SATISFACTION: A THEORY OF
THE QUALITY OF WORK EXPERIENCE.   M0690

THE RELATIONSHIP BETWEEN MANAGERIAL SUCCESS AND PERSONAL
VALUES IN SOUTH AFRICA: A RESEARCH NOTE.   M0786

VALUES   CONTINUATION

WORK VALUES AND JOB SATISFACTION OF PSYCHIATRIC AIDES.   M0917

RELATIONSHIPS BETWEEN WORK VALUES AND JOB SATISFACTION
AMONG COLLEGE STUDENT PERSONNEL WORKERS.   M0928

VARIABLE

AN INVESTIGATION OF JOB SATISFACTION AS A MODERATOR
VARIABLE IN PREDICTING JOB SUCCESS.   M0025

PREDICTING JOB PERFORMANCE BY USE OF ABILITY TESTS AND
STUDYING JOB SATISFACTION AS A MODERATING VARIABLE.   M0765

VARIABLES

JOB ATTITUDES AND OVERALL JOB SATISFACTION: THE EFFECT OF
BIOGRAPHICAL AND EMPLOYMENT VARIABLES: RESEARCH NOTE.   M0050

GOAL-SETTING ATTRIBUTES, PERSONALITY VARIABLES, AND JOB
SATISFACTION.   M0570

PREDICTING PAY SATISFACTION FROM NONPAY WORK VARIABLES.   M0843

THE RELATIONSHIP OF JOB SATISFACTION MEASURES TO
SELF-REPORT AND OBJECTIVE CRITERIA MEASURES AND THE EFFECT
OF MODERATOR VARIABLES FOR CANADIAN MILITARY PERSONNEL.   M0853

A STUDY OF THE PERCEPTIONS OF SELECTED SCHOOL-BASED
ADMINISTRATORS IN FLORIDA RELATIVE TO CERTAIN VARIABLES IN
SECONDARY SCHOOL ADMINISTRATION AS THEY RELATE TO JOB
SATISFACTION.   M0925

VARIANCE

BEHAVIORAL FACTORS IN VARIANCE CONTROL: REPORT ON A
LABORATORY EXPERIMENT.   M0634

VARIOUS

THE MODERATING EFFECTS OF INTERNAL VERSUS EXTERNAL CONTROL
ON THE RELATIONSHIP BETWEEN VARIOUS ASPECTS OF JOB
SATISFACTION.   M0122

EMPLOYEE ATTITUDES REGARDING VARIOUS CHARACTERISTICS OF JOB
OPPORTUNITY AND JOB PERFORMANCE ACROSS THREE DIFFERENT WORK
SHIFTS AT AN INSTITUTION FOR THE RETARDED.   M0900

VARYING

EFFECTS OF VARYING GOAL TYPES AND INCENTIVE SYSTEMS ON
PERFORMANCE AND SATISFACTION.   M0659

THE EFFECTS OF VARYING SCHEDULES OF REINFORCEMENT ON HUMAN
TASK PERFORMANCE.   M0790

WAR

    VIET-NAM WAR VETERANS -- TRANSITION TO CIVILIAN LIFE.   M0463

WASTE

    SOURCES OF SATISFACTION AND DISSATISFACTION AMONG SOLID
    WASTE MANAGEMENT EMPLOYEES.   M0283

WATER

    SAFEGUARDING OUR WATER -- POLLUTION CONTROL WORKERS.   M0350

WELFARE

    SOCIAL AND WELFARE PROGRAMS FOR THE HANDICAPPED ABROAD.   M0043

    A STUDY OF THE WORK ORIENTATIONS OF WELFARE RECIPIENTS
    PARTICIPATING IN THE WORK INCENTIVE PROGRAM.   M0167

    WELFARE MOTHERS AND THE WORK ETHIC.   M0168

    EMPLOYMENT, WELFARE, AND MOTHERS' MOTIVATION.   M0308

    MARKETING WELFARE MOTHERS' JOB SKILLS.   M0343

    WELFARE ISN'T WORKING.   M0625

WESTERN

    WESTERN ELECTRICS MOTIVATION AND ENRICHMENT TRIAL.   M0195

    THE MEASUREMENT OF SATISFACTION AND DEPARTMENTAL
    ASSOCIATION AT WESTERN KENTUCKY UNIVERSITY: TESTING THE
    HOLLAND AND BIGLAN MODELS.   M0914

WHITE

    BLACK AND WHITE UNEMPLOYMENT: THE DYNAMICS OF THE
    DIFFERENTIAL.   M0156

    IMPACT OF PERCEIVED COMMUNITY PROSPERITY ON JOB
    SATISFACTION OF BLACK AND WHITE WORKERS.   M0542

    THE SELF-CONCEPT, PERSONAL VALUES, AND MOTIVATIONAL
    ORIENTATIONS OF BLACK AND WHITE MANAGERS.   M0668

WHITE-COLLAR

    BLUE-COLLAR / WHITE-COLLAR PAY TRENDS.   M0031

    SATISFIERS AND DISSATISFIERS AMONG WHITE-COLLAR AND
    BLUE-COLLAR EMPLOYEES.   M0282

    WORK VALUES OF WHITE-COLLAR EMPLOYEES AS A FUNCTION OF
    SOCIOLOGICAL BACKGROUND.   M0376

WHITE-COLLAR-BLUE-COLLAR

    REPLICATION OF WHITE-COLLAR-BLUE-COLLAR DIFFERENCES IN
    SOURCES OF SATISFACTION AND DISSATISFACTION.   M0188

WHITES

    DIFFERENTIALS AND OVERLAPS IN EARNINGS OF BLACKS AND
    WHITES.   M0428

WHO'S

    WHO'S UNHAPPY AT WORK AND WHY.   M0478

WICHITA

    MULTIJOBHOLDING OF WICHITA PUBLIC SCHOOL TEACHERS.   M0729

WIN

    STAFF ATTITUDE AND SUCCESS OF THE WIN PROGRAM, A REPORT ON
    PHASE I RETURNS.   M0075

WINS

    WINS AND LOSSES.   M0485

WIVES

    QUESTIONNAIRE PROVIDES INFORMATION ON JOB OPPORTUNITIES FOR
    FS WIVES OVERSEAS.   M0015

    OCCUPATIONAL SATISFACTION OF FARM HUSBANDS AND WIVES.   M0706

WOMAN

    HELP FOR THE WOMAN BREADWINNER.   M0096

    THE PROFESSIONAL WOMAN IN GAO.   M0236

    A WOMAN IN THAT JOB.   M0487

    ONCE THEY WOULDN'T ACCEPT A WOMAN.   M0495

WOMANPOWER

    WOMANPOWER IN DUNGAREES.   M0430

WOMEN

    WOMEN IN ARMY JOBS.   M0002

    WOMEN APPRENTICES: REMOVING THE BARRIERS.   M0039

    WOMEN SHIPBUILDERS: JUST DOING A JOB.   M0041

WOMEN   CONTINUATION

    CHANGES IN THE LABOR FORCE STATUS OF WOMEN.   M0054

    WOMEN AT WORK -- OUTDOORS.   M0077

    DIFFERENCES IN HOURLY EARNINGS BETWEEN MEN AND WOMEN.   M0104

    STAFF AND DISTAFF: WHY WOMEN WORK.   M0154

    THE CHANGING ROLE OF WOMEN: IMPLICATIONS FOR PLANNERS.   M0173

    LABOR FORCE ACTIVITY OF MARRIED WOMEN.   M0193

    INCREASING PROPORTION OF WOMEN ARE HEADS OF HOUSEHOLD.   M0224

    OPENING JOB DOORS FOR MATURE WOMEN.   M0288

    MOTIVATIONAL AND PERSONALITY FACTORS RELATED TO CAREER
    GOALS OF BLACK COLLEGE WOMEN.   M0310

    EXTENSION WOMEN OVERSEAS.   M0328

    WOMEN OFFENDERS: BREAKING THE TRAINING MOLD.   M0330

    NATIONAL LONGITUDINAL STUDIES OF THE LABOR FORCE BEHAVIOR
    OF NATIONAL SAMPLES OF MEN (45-59), WOMEN (30-44), AND MALE
    AND FEMALE YOUTH (14-24).   M0339

    WOMEN IN PROFESSIONAL TRAINING.   M0340

    A COMPARATIVE STUDY OF TEACHERS' ATTITUDES TOWARD MEN AND
    WOMEN DEPARTMENT HEADS IN LARGE CITY SECONDARY SCHOOLS.   M0366

    OCCUPATIONAL RANKING FOR MEN AND WOMEN BY EARNINGS.   M0408

    WOMEN: UNCLE SAM WANTS YOU.   M0426

    WHERE WOMEN WORK -- AN ANALYSIS BY INDUSTRY AND OCCUPATION.   M0464

    WOMEN IN INDUSTRY: ALIENATION, SATISFACTION, AND CHANGE.   M0699

    THE EMPLOYMENT OF WOMEN, EDUCATION, AND FERTILITY.   M0725

    THE IMPACT OF HIERARCHICAL STRUCTURES ON THE WORK BEHAVIOR
    OF WOMEN AND MEN.   M0757

    JOB MOTIVATIONS FOR WORKING WOMEN.   M0791

    MOTIVATION, JOB SATISFACTION, AND CAREER ASPIRATIONS OF
    MARRIED WOMEN TEACHERS AT DIFFERENT CAREER STAGES.   M0940

WOMEN-SPECIFIC

    THE RELATIVE VALIDITIES OF TRADITIONALLY USED JOB
    SATISFACTION AND ORGANIZATIONAL COMMITMENT MEASURES VERSUS

                                                  Job Satisfaction and Motivation

WOMEN-SPECIFIC   CONTINUATION

WOMEN-SPECIFIC MEASURES FOR THE PREDICTION OF FEMALE TENURE IN A MALE DOMINATED JOB.   M0856

WOMEN'S

JOBS, SALARY, CREDIT, LEGAL STATUS ALL IN FOCUS OF WOMEN'S YEAR.   M0235

THE FEDERAL WOMEN'S PROGRAM: A HUD PERSPECTIVE.   M0348

WOMEN'S PROGRAMS SURVEYED AT LATIN AMERICAN POSTS.   M0488

WOMEN'S WEEK -- AUGUST 26-30.   M0489

WORK

WORK GROUPS AND EMPLOYEE SATISFACTION.   M0004

AN ANALYSIS OF MICHIGAN'S EXPERIENCE WITH WORK INCENTIVES.   M0012

AS YOU WERE SAYING -- ELEMENTS OF MEANINGFUL WORK.   M0016

AN EVALUATION OF MOTIVATIONAL SIMILARITY IN WORK GROUPS.   M0033

MANAGERS INTEREST IN WORK.   M0034

WORK AND WORK MOTIVATION IN AN AUTOMATED INDUSTRIAL PRODUCTION-PROCESS.   M0042

THE SOCIAL DIMENSIONS OF WORK.   M0047

ORGANIZATIONAL EXPERIENCES AND THEIR EFFECTS ON THE ATTITUDES OF EMPLOYEES, INCLUDING THE DISADVANTAGED, TOWARD WORK.   M0063

WOMEN AT WORK -- OUTDOORS.   M0077

DOES HERZBERG'S THEORY REALLY WORK.   M0081

CONSTRUCT VALIDATION OF AN INSTRUMENTALITY-EXPECTANCY-TASK-GOAL MODEL OF WORK MOTIVATION: SOME THEORETICAL BOUNDARY CONDITIONS.   M0082

DIMENSIONS OF THRESHOLD WORK EXPERIENCE FOR HIGH SCHOOL GRADUATES AND DROPOUTS: A FACTOR ANALYSIS.   M0089

MAN AT WORK.   M0097

DISTRIBUTION OF JOB SATISFACTION IN THE WORK FORCE.   M0106

BEYOND STICK AND CARROT: HYSTERIA OVER THE WORK ETHIC.   M0111

EDITORIAL RESEARCH REPORTS ON THE AMERICAN WORK ETHIC.   M0116

WORK   CONTINUATION

WORKING   CONTINUATION

WORSENED

    HAS THE BLUE-COLLAR WORKER'S POSITION WORSENED?   M0278

WRONG

    WHAT'S WRONG WITH WORK IN AMERICA? -- A REVIEW ESSAY.   M0490

YEAR

    JOBS, SALARY, CREDIT, LEGAL STATUS ALL IN FOCUS OF WOMEN'S
    YEAR.   M0235

    AN INVESTIGATION OF ATTITUDES AMONG PRIVATES AT KA55
    FOURTEENTH YEAR.   M0739

    TEN YEAR JOB SATISFACTION TRENDS IN A STABLE ORGANIZATION.   M0837

YEARLY

    CHANGES IN PRODUCTIVITY AND UNIT LABOR COSTS -- A YEARLY
    REVIEW.   M0203

YEARS

    FREDRICK W. TAYLOR -- 62 YEARS LATER.   M0390

YORK

    EVALUATION AND IMPLEMENTATION OF THE NEW YORK FIRE
    DEPARTMENT EXAMINATION TRAINING PROJECT FOR CULTURALLY
    DISADVANTAGED RESIDENTS OF THE CITY OF NEW YORK.   M0243

YOUNG

    CHRONOLOGICAL AGE AND JOB SATISFACTION: THE YOUNG
    BLUE-COLLAR WORKER.   M0007

    THE WORKER ATTITUDES AND EARLY OCCUPATIONAL EXPERIENCES OF
    YOUNG MEN -- ANALYSIS BASED ON A 4-YEAR LONGITUDINAL STUDY.   M0020

    WHAT YOUNG PEOPLE SHOULD KNOW ABOUT LABOR UNIONS.   M0424

    WORK VALUES AND JOB SATISFACTION OF YOUNG ADULT MALES.   M0579

YOURSELF

    WORKING FOR YOURSELF -- WHAT'S IT LIKE.   M0425

YOUTH

    DEVELOPMENT OF ASSESSMENT MEASURES FOR COUNSELING YOUTH
    WORK -- TRAINING ENROLLEES.   M0142

    YOUTH AND THE MEANING OF WORK.   M0171

III
Abstracts

M0001 ABT ASSOCIATES
ASSESSMENT OF EXPERIMENTAL AND DEMONSTRATION INTERSTATE
PROGRAM FOR SOUTH TEXAS MIGRANT WORKERS.
CAMBRIDGE, MASS.
NTIS PB 199 487, 204 550, 204 551, 204 552, 211 190 (1972).

RESULTS OF THREE YEARS OF WORK BY THE UNITED STATES
EMPLOYMENT SERVICE WITH TEXAS MIGRANT WORKERS IN AN ATTEMPT
TO UPGRADE THEIR VOCATIONAL SKILLS AND GET THEM OUT OF THE
MIGRANT STREAM. THROUGH BILINGUAL OUTREACH WORKERS, GRANTS
AND LOANS, ADULT EDUCATION PROGRAMS, VOCATIONAL SKILLS
TRAINING AND COUNSELING SOME MIGRANT FAMILIES LOCATED OTHER
JOBS. CONCLUSION: IT IS POSSIBLE TO EXPAND ON THIS SUCCESS
IF CAPABLE AND ENTHUSIASTIC EMPLOYMENT SERVICE OFFICIALS
SUPPORT THE PROGRAM IN EACH STATE OF A MULTI-STATE NETWORK
OF MANPOWER AND RELATED SERVICE ORGANIZATIONS.

M0002 ABER, EDWARD
WOMEN IN ARMY JOBS.
SOLDIERS, JULY 1974, PP. 2-25.

MILITARY LIFE OFFERS QUITE A FEW ADVANTAGES OVER OTHER LIFE-
STYLES -- AND FOR WOMEN THESE PLUSES HAVE BECOME A BONANZA
OF OPPORTUNITIES AND VOCATIONAL CHALLENGES.

M0003 ACKERMAN, LEONARD.
LET'S PUT MOTIVATION WHERE IT BELONGS -- WITHIN THE
INDIVIDUAL.
PERSONNEL JOURNAL, 49 (JULY 1970): 559-62.

THE PURPOSE OF THIS ARTICLE IS TO SHOW THAT MOTIVATION IS
WITHIN THE INDIVIDUAL, RATHER THAN GIVEN TO HIM BY ANOTHER
AND, RECOGNIZING THIS, COULD CAUSE MORE EFFECTIVE EMPLOYEE
PERFORMANCE. BEHAVIOR IS CONSIDERED TO BE DIRECTED TOWARD
FULFILLING SOME NEED. THE CHOICE OF FULFILLING A PARTICULAR
NEED IS DETERMINED BY THE STRENGTH OF THE NEED, THE VALUE OF
VARIOUS ALTERNATIVES, AND THE AMOUNT OF TIME AND EFFORT
USED. ACKERMAN STATES THAT MOTIVATION IS THEREFORE A
FUNCTION OF NEED.
     THREE APPROACHES TO MOTIVATION ARE GIVEN: THE
PROJECTIVE APPROACH--THE MANAGER REFLECTS HIS OWN NEEDS TO
THE EMPLOYEES; THE NORMATIVE APPROACH--USE OF INFORMATION
GAINED FROM OBSERVATIONS TO GENERALIZE ABOUT EMPLOYEES'
NEEDS; THE INDIVIDUALISTIC APPROACH--EACH EMPLOYEE IS
DEALT WITH AS HAVING HIGHLY DIFFERENTIATED NEEDS. THE LAST
APPROACH IS THE BEST BECAUSE IT IS THE ONLY ONE THAT IS
ORIENTED TO THE REAL WORLD OF THE EMPLOYEE, THE MANAGER, AND
THE ORGANIZATION. THE APPROACH IS BASED ON THE CONCEPT THAT
JOBS GIVE A PERSON PHYSIOLOGICAL AND PSYCHOLOGICAL INCOME
BUT HIS NEEDS CAN ONLY BE MET THROUGH INTERACTION WITH
OTHERS. THE INTERACTION MUST BE OF A GIVE AND TAKE NATURE
FOR THERE TO BE OPTIMUM FULFILLMENT OF AN INDIVIDUAL'S
NEEDS. THE ARTICLE STATES THAT THE INTERACTION CAN BE
COMPLICATED BY CHANGING NEEDS OF THE EMPLOYEE OR THE
ORGANIZATION. THE INDIVIDUALISTIC APPROACH IS DESIGNED TO
MEET THE CHANGING NEEDS BECAUSE THERE MUST BE CONSIDERABLE

M0003   DISCUSSION BETWEEN THE MANAGER AND THE EMPLOYEE IN ORDER FOR
MEANINGFUL COMMUNICATION TO EXIST.
    TWO MAJOR LIMITATIONS TO THE APPROACH ARE GIVEN: THE
MANAGER'S LACK OF AUTHORITY FOR PROMOTIONS, AWARDS, AND
DISCIPLINARY ACTION AND THE EMPLOYEE'S LEVEL OF ASPIRATION.
THESE, AND OTHER VARIABLES, MAKE IT DIFFICULT TO ACCURATELY
ASSESS THE NEEDS OF AN EMPLOYEE AND TO CREATE A CLIMATE
WHICH ALLOWS SUFFICIENT OPPORTUNITY TO MEET THE NEEDS.

M0004   ADAMS, P. G. III   SLOCUM, JOHN W.
WORK GROUPS AND EMPLOYEE SATISFACTION.
PERSONNEL ADMINISTRATION   34 (MARCH 1971): 37-43.

    THIS STUDY WAS UNDERTAKEN TO EXAMINE THE COHESIVENESS
OF WORK GROUPS AND RELATE IT TO SATISFACTION OF MEMBERS
IN AN INDUSTRIAL ENVIRONMENT.   IT ATTEMPTS TO ANSWER THE
QUESTION DO MEMBERS OF GROUPS CHARACTERIZED BY A HIGH
DEGREE OF COHESIVENESS TEND TO EXHIBIT A HIGHER LEVEL OF ALL
AROUND SATISFACTION THAN MEMBERS OF GROUPS CHARACTERIZED BY
LOW COHESIVENESS?
    THE SURVEY WAS PERFORMED AT A GLASS WORKS PLANT IN
CENTRAL PENNSYLVANIA. TWELVE DISTINCT GROUPS TOTALING 142
OPERATIVE EMPLOYEES WERE USED. EIGHT GROUPS HAD ROUTINE,
REPETITIVE TASKS; THREE GROUPS WERE MACHINE OPERATORS; ONE
GROUP WAS SKILLED. NINETY-THREE MALE AND 49 FEMALE WORKERS
MADE UP THE 142 TOTAL.
    TO MEASURE GROUP COHESIVENESS, FIVE LIKERT TYPE
QUESTIONS WERE USED ON A QUESTIONNAIRE DEVELOPED BY STANLEY
SEASHORE IN 1954. IF MEMBERS PERCEIVED THEMSELVES TO BE A
PART OF A GROUP, PREFERRED TO REMAIN IN THE GROUP THAN
LEAVE, AND THOUGHT THEIR GROUP WAS BETTER THAN OTHER GROUPS
IN RESPECT TO THE WAY THEY GOT ALONG TOGETHER, HELPED EACH
OTHER, AND STUCK TOGETHER, THEN THEY WERE RATED HIGHLY ON
COHESIVENESS.
    THE SCIENCE RESEARCH ASSOCIATES EMPLOYEE INVENTORY AND
THE MORSE INDEX OF EMPLOYEE SATISFACTION WERE USED TO
DEVELOP A TWO PART QUESTIONNAIRE TO TEST EMPLOYEE
SATISFACTION. FIVE ENVIRONMENTAL WORK FACTORS TESTING THE
SATISFACTION WITH THE JOB ITSELF, SUPERVISION, COMPANY AND
MANAGEMENT, DEGREE OF FREEDOM, AND PAY COMPRISED ONE PART,
WHILE THE OTHER PART DETERMINED THE IMPORTANCE OF THESE FIVE
FACTORS TO THE EMPLOYEE.
    IT WAS FOUND THAT HIGHLY COHESIVE GROUPS WERE MORE
SATISFIED WITH THEIR JOB, FREEDOM TO PERFORM THEIR JOB, AND
THEIR EMPLOYEE BENEFITS THAN LOW COHESIVE GROUPS. WORK
SATISFACTION OF LOW SKILLED EMPLOYEES WAS POSITIVELY
RELATED TO GROUP COHESIVENESS WHEREAS THIS IS UNRELATED TO
THE SATISFACTION OF HIGHLY SKILLED EMPLOYEES. LOW SKILLED
EMPLOYEES IN A HIGHLY COHESIVE GROUP PLACED LESS IMPORTANCE
ON THE ENVIRONMENTAL WORK FACTORS THAN DID LOW SKILLED
WORKERS IN LOW COHESIVE GROUPS, EXCEPT FOR SUPERVISION.
HIGHLY SKILLED WORKERS IN COHESIVE GROUPS WERE LESS
SATISFIED IN MOST AREAS THAN THOSE IN LOW SKILLED POSITIONS,
DUE TO THEIR INCREASED ABILITIES.
ADVANCED HIGH INTENSITY TRAINING.
FIRMS CAN ONLY ACCOMMODATE A SMALL DEGREE OF ORGANIZATIONAL
CHANGE, MODEST PAY INCREASES AND VERY SMALL
INCREMENTS IN RESPONSIBILITY FOR THE GRADUATES OF SUCH

M0004 PROGRAMS.

M0005 ALMAN, LLOYD.
LABOR MARKETS AND MANPOWER POLICIES IN PERSPECTIVE.
MONTHLY LABOR REVIEW, 95 (SEPTEMBER 1972):22-28.

HOW AN ACTIVE LABOR MARKET POLICY CAN BE USED AS AN
INSTRUMENT OF REDISTRIBUTION OR STABILIZATION.

M0006 ALPER, S. WILLIAM.
MOTIVATE THEM THROUGH THEIR JOBS.
SUPERVISORY MANAGEMENT, 19 (FEBRUARY 1974): 28-32.

THE ARTICLE OUTLINES THE CHARACTERISTICS OF A MOTIVATING
JOB. SUCH A JOB MUST MEET THE FOLLOWING REQUIREMENTS: (1)
THE JOB MUST BE A WHOLE JOB COMPOSED OF A SERIES OF TASKS
AND PROCEDURES THAT ALLOW THE WORKER TO RECOGNIZE THE START
AND FINISH OF WHAT HE'S ACCOMPLISHED, AND (2) EACH WORKER
SHOULD MANAGE HIS OWN JOB TO THE GREATEST EXTENT POSSIBLE.

M0007 ALTIMUS, CYRUS A.   TERSINE, RICHARD J.
CHRONOLOGICAL AGE AND JOB SATISFACTION: THE YOUNG
BLUE-COLLAR WORKER.
ACADEMY OF MANAGEMENT JOURNAL, 16 (MARCH 1973):   53-66.

THE STUDY INVESTIGATES THE JOB SATISFACTION LEVEL OF YOUNG
BLUE COLLAR WORKERS. THE YOUNGER WORKERS WERE FOUND TO BE
SIGNIFICANTLY LOWER IN SATISFACTION WITH WORK ITSELF,
ESTEEM, SELF-ACTUALIZATION AND TOTAL WORK SATISFACTION. THE
PERCEPTIONS AND SATISFACTION LEVEL OF YOUNG BLUE COLLAR
WORKERS WERE QUITE DEFFERENT FROM THEIR OLDER COUNTERPARTS.

M0008 ALUTTO, JOSEPH A.   ACITO, FRANKLIN.
DECISIONAL PARTICIPATION AND SOURCES OF JOB SATISFACTION:
A STUDY OF MANUFACTURING PERSONNEL.
ACADEMY OF MANAGEMENT JOURNAL, 17 (MARCH 1974): 160-67.

PARTICIPATIVE DECISION MAKING AS A MANAGERIAL STRATEGY
HAS BEEN ADVOCATED AS A MEANS OF IMPROVING BOTH THE
PERFORMANCE AND SATISFACTION OF INDIVIDUALS IN
ORGANIZATIONS. THE PRESENT STUDY REPLICATES AND EXTENDS
RECENT RESEARCH ON CORRELATES OF DECISIONAL PARTICIPATION
USING A POPULATION OF SCHOOL TEACHERS.

M0009 ANALYSIS (FOR MANAGERS OF PEOPLE AND THINGS).
ASSISTANT SECRETARY OF DEFENSE.
WASHINGTON, D. C.:   U. S. GOVERNMENT PRINTING OFFICE NO.
729-489/6, 1973.

AN ELEMENTARY TEXT FOR DEPARTMENT OF DEFENSE MANAGERS IN
THEIR ROLES AS DECISION MAKERS.

M0010 ANDREWS, FRANK M.   FARRIS, GEORGE F.
TIME PRESSURE AND PERFORMANCE OF SCIENTISTS AND ENGINEERS:
A FIVE PANEL STUDY.
ORGANIZATIONAL BEHAVIOR AND HUMAN PERFORMANCE, 8 (OCTOBER
1972):   185-200.

THE DATA COLLECTED BY THE AUTHORS IN 1965 AND 1970 ON
SCIENTISTS AND ENGINEERS IN A NASA RESEARCH DIVISION SEEM TO
CONTRADICT THE THEORY THAT SCIENTISTS PERFORM BEST IN AN
UNHURRIED ATMOSPHERE. THE FINDINGS OF THIS STUDY SUGGEST
THAT A SENSE OF TIME PRESSURE CAN ENHANCE SEVERAL QUALITIES
OF SCIENTIFIC PERFORMANCE--INCLUDING INNOVATION. IN
ADDITION TO EXPERIENCING THE MOST TIME PRESSURE, THE HIGHEST
PERFORMING SCIENTISTS ALSO TENDED TO WANT RELATIVELY
LARGE AMOUNTS OF PRESSURE. WHEN THE PRESSURE ACTUALLY
EXPERIENCED WAS MARKEDLY OUT OF LINE WITH THE PRESSURE
DESIRED--EITHER IN BEING TOO LOW OR TOO HIGH--PERFORMANCE
WAS LIKELY TO SUFFER.

M0011 ANNABLE, JAMES E.   FRUITMAN, F.
AN EARNINGS FUNCTION FOR HIGH LEVEL MANPOWER.
INDUSTRIAL AND LABOR RELATIONS REVIEW, 26 (JULY 1973):
1107-21.

THE AUTHORS DEVELOP A SIMPLE ANALYTICAL FRAMEWORK
TO INTEGRATE THOSE FACTORS WHICH HAVE FREQUENTLY BEEN USED
TO EXPLAIN INCOME DIFFERENTIALS.
EXPLICITLY KEYING ON THE OPERATION OF INDIVIDUAL ENDOWMENT
CONSTRAINTS, A SET OF SIMULTANEOUS EQUATIONS WERE DEVELOPED,
A PART OF WHICH IS AN EARNINGS FUNCTION. WHILE RESULTS ARE
ONLY GENERALIZABLE TO COLLEGE TRAINED OR OTHER HIGH STATUS
INDIVIDUALS, THE STUDY INDICATES THAT STATISFACTION IS A
POSITIVE DETERMINANT OF INCOME.

M0012 APPEL, GARY L.   SCHLENKER, ROBERT E.
AN ANALYSIS OF MICHIGAN'S EXPERIENCE WITH WORK INCENTIVES.
MONTHLY LABOR REVIEW, 94 (SEPTEMBER 1971): 15-22.

INVESTIGATION OF A NEW FEDERAL WORK INCENTIVE PROGRAM
IN MICHIGAN AND THE REASONS FOR AN INCREASE IN EMPLOYMENT
AMONG AFDC MOTHERS.

M0013 ARAM, JOHN D.   MORGAN, CYRIL P.   ESBECK, HOWARD S.
RELATION OF COLLABORATIVE INTERPERSONAL RELATIONSHIPS TO
INDIVIDUAL SATISFACTION AND ORGANIZATIONAL PERFORMANCE.
ADMINISTRATIVE SCIENCE QUARTERLY, 16 (SEPTEMBER 1971):
289-96.

THE CENTRAL IDEA EXPRESSED IN THE FOLLOWING HYPOTHESIS
IS THAT COLLABORATION AND CONSENSUS IN INTERPERSONAL
RELATIONS BENEFIT BOTH THE INDIVIDUALS AND THE ORGANIZATION.
UNDER CONDITIONS OF GREATER EXPERIENCED COLLABORATION
AND CONSENSUS IN ORGANIZATION RELATIONSHIPS:
      1. A PERSON REALIZES GREATER SELF-ACTUALIZATION.
      2. A PERSON REALIZES GREATER SATISFACTION OF OTHER
          NEEDS AND EXPERIENCES WELL BEING.
      3. A PERSON REALIZES HIGHER LEVELS OF PERSONAL
          EFFECTIVENESS.
      4. A WORK GROUP ATTAINS HIGHER LEVELS OF TASK
          EFFECTIVENESS.
AN INSTRUMENT WAS DEVELOPED IN THE FORM OF A
QUESTIONNAIRE, WHICH WAS GIVEN TO SCIENTISTS, ENGINEERS,
AND LABORATORY TECHNICIANS IN AN INDUSTRIAL ORGANIZATION.
ANOTHER INSTRUMENT USED WAS DEVELOPED BY PELZ AND ANDREWS

M0013 (1966).
THE RESULTS OF THE EXPERIMENT SUPPORTED HYPOTHESES
ONE, TWO AND THREE, MENTIONED ABOVE. AS FOR HYPOTHESIS
FOUR, IT WAS SHOWN THAT THERE WAS NO RELATIONSHIP BETWEEN
COLLABORATION AND TASK EFFECTIVENESS.
ACCORDING TO THE RESEARCHERS, THE STUDY IS
INCONCLUSIVE WITH RESPECT TO THE COLLABORATION-CONSENSUS
THEORY AS STATED, BUT SUGGESTS 1) THAT THE HYPOTHESES ARE
ACCURATE WITH RESPECT TO THE SATISFACTION OF INDIVIDUAL
NEEDS, 2) THAT THE CONCEPT OF COLLABORATION IS TOO BROAD TO
BE EMPIRICALLY VALIDATED FOR ORGANIZATIONAL PERFORMANCE AND
3) THAT RATHER THAN A SIMPLE CAUSAL SYSTEM OF COLLABORATION
BEHAVIOR LEADING TO ORGANIZATIONAL PERFORMANCE, THERE
SEEMS TO BE A MORE COMPLEX SET OF INTERACTIVE RELATIONSHIPS
WITH INDIVIDUAL AND GROUP PERFORMANCE.

M0014 ARMKNECT, PAUL A. EARLY, JOHN F.
QUITS IN MANUFACTURING: A STUDY OF THEIR CAUSES.
MONTHLY LABOR REVIEW 95 (NOVEMBER 1972): 31-37.

THE REASONS FOR QUITTING ARE CHANGEABLE AND THE
RATE OF VOLUNTARY SEPARATIONS IS A GOOD ECONOMIC INDICATOR.

M0015 QUESTIONNAIRE PROVIDES INFORMATION ON JOB OPPORTUNITIES FOR
FS WIVES OVERSEAS.
DEPARTMENT OF STATE NEWSLETTER, JANUARY 1975, PP. 26-27.

LIMITED STATISTICS GATHERED BY THIS ASSOCIATION SHOW
THE RISING NUMBER OF FOREIGN SERVICE WIVES OVERSEAS AND
THE KINDS OF WORK AVAILABLE TO THEM.

M0016 AS YOU WERE SAYING -- ELEMENTS OF MEANINGFUL WORK.
PERSONNEL JOURNAL 51 (MARCH 1972): 208-14.

ATTEMPTS TO ISOLATE ELEMENTS THAT MAKE WORK
MEANINGFUL. MARSHALL BURGESS, A SENIOR COUNSELLOR WITH THE
CANADIAN DEPARTMENT OF MANPOWER AND IMMIGRATION IN VICTORIA,
B. C., CLAIMS THAT CONTEMPORARY MANAGEMENT SHOULD KEEP
FOREMOST IN MIND THAT AN INCREASING NUMBER OF NORTH AMERICAN
WORKERS ARE FINDING THEIR DAILY WORK LESS SATISFYING AND
LACKING IN BOTH MEANING AND PURPOSE. ANY MANAGEMENT FACED
WITH HIGH TURNOVER RATES, ABSENTEEISM, ALCOHOLISM AND DRUG
ABUSE, MENTAL ILLNESS AND VACANT POSITIONS DESPITE HIGH
UNEMPLOYMENT RATES SHOULD NOT NEED TO BE REMINDED OF THIS.
IN ADDITION, THERE IS A GROWING NEED IN WORKERS FOR
SELF-REALIZATION AND FULFILLMENT BEING SATISFIED THROUGH
HOME CRAFTS AND VOLUNTEER WORK.
MR. BURGESS FEELS THAT INSTEAD OF ATTACKING THE
USUAL MANAGEMENT EFFORTS, SUCH AS HIGHER PAY, PROFIT
SHARING, SENSITIVITY TRAINING FOR SUPERVISORS, MORE RAPID
TALENT RECOGNITION AND PROMOTION, WE SHOULD ATTEMPT TO
ISOLATE THE ELEMENTS OF THE HOME CRAFTS AND VOLUNTEER WORK.
IT IS FELT THAT THE WILLINGNESS TO SEEK OUT AND ACCOMPLISH
TASKS AND RECEIVE NO PAY FOR THE EFFORT WILL YIELD THE
ELEMENTS OF WORK WHICH OFFER MEANING AND SELF-REALIZATION
TO EMPLOYEES. THESE ELEMENTS APPEAR TO BE THREE:
1. WHOLENESS OF TASK; NOT JUST A MERE PART OF A
PROCESS

M0016   2. A SENSE OF CRAFTSMANSHIP
             3. FLEXIBILITY OF HOURS
             THIS CAN BE ILLUSTRATED BY THE EMPLOYEE WHO IS
LEARNING AT HOME TO BUILD AN ELECTRONIC INSTRUMENT. HE
PROBABLY WORKS HARD AT IT AND IT IS VERY SATISFYING WORK.
HE PERFORMS THE WHOLE TASK BY HIMSELF, HE HAS THE PRIDE IN
MASTERING A NEW SKILL, AND HE DOESN'T HAVE SET HOURS WHEN HE
MUST WORK AT HIS TASK.
             MR. BURGESS FEELS THAT BY BUILDING THESE THREE
ELEMENTS, WHOLENESS OF TASK, A SENSE OF CRAFTMANSHIP AND
FLEXIBILITY OF HOURS, INTO OCCUPATIONAL POSITIONS, WORKERS
WILL BEGIN TO APPROACH THE DEGREE OF SATISFACTION AND
MEANING THEY RECEIVE FROM HOME CRAFTS AND VOLUNTEER WORK.

M0017   ATELLA, JOHN T.
         INSTILLING APPREHENSION DELICATELY AND OTHER MOTIVATORS.
         ADMINISTRATIVE MANAGEMENT   35 (APRIL 1974): 56.

             ACCORDING TO THIS ARTICLE, MANAGERS MUST CREATE THE
         KIND OF ENVIRONMENT THAT WILL FOSTER INNER MOTIVATION ON THE
         PART OF EMPLOYEES.

M0018   ATKINSON, JOHN W.   BIRCH, DAVID.
         DYNAMICS OF ACTION.
         NEW YORK: WILEY. 1970.

             HIGHLY TECHNICAL AND THEORETICAL ACCOUNT ON THE
         BEHAVIORAL TENDENCIES THAT MOTIVATE ACTIONS.

M0019   AUSMUS, MARLENE.
         PUT THIS UNDER F FOR FILE CLERKS.
         OCCUPATIONAL OUTLOOK QUARTERLY   15 (SPRING 1971): 33-34.

             A LOOK AT THE JOB OF FILE CLERK AND WHERE IT MAY LEAD.

M0020   BACHMAN, JERALD GRAYBILL.
         THE WORKER ATTITUDES AND EARLY OCCUPATIONAL EXPERIENCES OF
         YOUNG MEN -- ANALYSIS BASED ON A 4-YEAR LONGITUDINAL STUDY.
         UNPUBLISHED RESEARCH, UNIVERSITY OF MICHIGAN, 1973.

             A STUDY OF WORK ATTITUDES OF HIGH SCHOOL STUDENTS FOR A
         4-YEAR PERIOD ARE USED TO CONSTRUCT JOB PAYOFF AND CHALLENGE
         INDEXES.

M0021   BADIN, IRWIN J.
         SOME MODERATOR INFLUENCES ON RELATIONSHIPS BETWEEN
         CONSIDERATION, INITIATING STRUCTURE, AND ORGANIZATION
         CRITERIA.
         JOURNAL OF APPLIED PSYCHOLOGY   59 (JUNE 1974): 380-82.

             DESCRIBES A STUDY WHICH EXAMINES POTENTIAL MODERATORS
         OF THE RELATIONSHIPS BETWEEN CONSIDERATION (C) AND
         INITIATING STRUCTURE (IS) AND EMPLOYEE SATISFACTION AND
         GROUP EFFECTIVENESS.

M0022   BANKING ON PEOPLE.
         MANPOWER, MAY 1970, PP. 8-11.

FIRST NATIONAL CITY BANK IN NEW YORK IS ACQUIRING SOME
NEW WORKING CAPITAL, IN THE FORM OF PEOPLE, FROM NEW YORK'S
IMPOVERISHED NEIGHBORHOODS AND ITS WELFARE ROLLS.

M0023 BEATTY, RICHARD W.
BLACKS AS SUPERVISORS: A STUDY OF TRAINING, JOB
PERFORMANCE, AND EMPLOYEE'S EXPECTATION.
ACADEMY OF MANAGEMENT JOURNAL 16 (JUNE 1973): 196-206.

THIS ARTICLE INVESTIGATES THE RELATIONSHIPS OF SEVERAL
TRAINING AND NONTRAINING VARIABLES WITH EMPLOYER'S
EVALUATIONS OF BLACK SUPERVISORS' JOB PERFORMANCE.

M0024 BEATTY, RICHARD W.
PERSONNEL SYSTEMS AND HUMAN PERFORMANCE.
PERSONNEL JOURNAL 52 (APRIL 1973): 307-13.

THIS ARTICLE PROPOSES A SYSTEM WHICH ANALYZES JOBS AND THE
BEHAVIOR NECESSARY TO PERFORM THEM SUCCESSFULLY AND THEN
USES THE REQUISITE BEHAVIORS AS CRITERIA FOR SELECTING
EMPLOYEES.

M0025 BETZ, ELLEN L.
AN INVESTIGATION OF JOB SATISFACTION AS A MODERATOR
VARIABLE IN PREDICTING JOB SUCCESS.
JOURNAL OF VOCATIONAL BEHAVIOR 1 (APRIL 1971): 123-28.

THE HYPOTHESIS INVESTIGATED IN THIS STUDY WAS THAT JOB
SATISFACTION OPERATES AS A MODERATOR VARIABLE IN
PREDICTING JOB SUCCESS FROM ABILITY TEST SCORES.
THREE-HUNDRED FIFTY-TWO MEN AND WOMEN ASSEMBLERS FROM A
MANUFACTURING COMPANY PARTICIPATED IN THE STUDY. RESULTS
TENDED TO SUPPORT THE HYPOTHESIS.

M0026 BEVAN, G.
MOTIVATING YOUR JUNIORS.
PERSONNEL MANAGEMENT 3 (DECEMBER 1971): 33-34

BEVAN INVESTIGATES THE FACTORS WHICH INFLUENCE THE
ATTITUDES AND MOTIVATION OF JUNIOR PERSONNEL SPECIALISTS.

M0027 BIRKIN, STANLEY J.
LET'S ADMIT IT: ZERO DEFECTS IS NO PANACEA.
PUBLIC PERSONNEL MANAGEMENT 3 (MARCH-APRIL 1974): 125-28.

REVIEWS FOUR PHASES IN IMPLEMENTING A ZERO DEFECTS
PROGRAM AND POINTS OUT THE LIMITATIONS OF THE PROGRAM.
CONCLUDES THAT MANAGEMENT IS LIKELY TO EXPECT TOO MUCH FROM
A MOTIVATIONAL PROGRAM HAVING AS ITS PHILOSOPHY THAT AN
EMPLOYEE CAN DO HIS WORK RIGHT THE FIRST TIME, AND ASSERTS
THAT A ZERO DEFECTS PROGRAM IS NO SUBSTITUTE FOR SOUND
MANAGEMENT PRACTICES.

M0028 BLACK PROFESSIONALS: PROGRESS AND SKEPTICISM.
MANPOWER 5 (JUNE 1973): 9-13.

RESULTS OF A STUDY REVEAL THAT FEW OF THOSE QUESTIONED
ARE DISSATISFIED WITH THEIR CAREER PROGRESS OR

M0028   RESPONSIBILITIES IN THEIR RESPECTIVE FIRMS.

M0029   BLAKE, JENNY.
         EXPERIMENTS IN JOB SATISFACTION.
         PERSONNEL MANAGEMENT 6 (JANUARY 1974): 32-33.

             THE AUTHOR OF THIS ARTICLE DISCUSSES THE DIFFICULTIES
         OF DOING RESEARCH ON THE QUALITY OF WORKING LIFE AND
         IN PARTICULAR HER OWN EXPERIENCE IN A VALVE ASSEMBLY PLANT.

M0030   BLOOD, MILTON R.
         THE VALIDITY OF IMPORTANCE.
         JOURNAL OF APPLIED PSYCHOLOGY 55 (OCTOBER 1971): 487-88.

             BASED ON FINDINGS FROM RESEARCH AMONG 380 CLERICAL
         WORKERS IN A LARGE CORPORATION, QUESTIONS THE USEFULNESS OF
         WEIGHTING JOB ASPECTS BY IMPORTANCE IN JOB SATISFACTION
         STUDIES.

M0031   BLUE-COLLAR / WHITE-COLLAR PAY TRENDS.
         MONTHLY LABOR REVIEW 94 (JUNE 1971): 5-12.

             ANALYSIS OF OCCUPATIONAL WAGE DIFFERENCES, CHANGING
         ATTITUDES AND PATTERNS, EARNINGS AND FAMILY INCOME, AND
         COMPENSATION PER MAN-HOUR AND TAKE-HOME PAY.

M0032   BLUM, ALBERT A.   MOORE, MICHAEL L.   PARKER, FAULY B.
         THE EFFECT OF MOTIVATIONAL PROGRAMS ON COLLECTIVE
         BARGAINING.
         PERSONNEL JOURNAL 52 (JULY 1973: 633-41.

         THE PURPOSE OF THIS ARTICLE IS TO FIND OUT THE EFFECT OF
         USING JOB ENRICHMENT AND HUMAN RESOURCES DEVELOPMENT UPON
         THE INDIVIDUAL, THE GROUP, AND THE UNION.
         THIS ARTICLE ALSO ATTEMPTS TO DISCOVER WHY MOTIVATIONAL
         PROGRAMS HAVE NOT BEEN USED IN COLLECTIVE BARGAINING BY
         ORGANIZED LABOR.
             IN THE SURVEYS TAKEN, IT IS ASSUMED THAT MCGREGOR'S
         CONCEPT, THEORY Y (MAN LIKES WORK AND RESPONSIBILITY) AND
         MASLOW'S HIERARCHY OF NEEDS THEORY PROVIDE THE BASIS BEHIND
         MODERN HUMAN SATISFACTIONS OF WANTS AND NEEDS. IT IS
         THEREFORE CONCLUDED THAT LOOSENING OF SHARP JOB BOUNDARIES
         AND RESTRICTIVE WORK RULES TEND TO INCREASE THE WORKER'S EGO
         INVOLVEMENT IN HIS WORK.
             TO INCREASE THE WORKER'S EGO INVOLVEMENT, IT IS
         SUGGESTED THAT MANAGEMENT MAY BE WILLING TO TRADE OFF
         SOME RESTRICTIVE WORK RULES. SINCE THE UNIONS HAVE IGNORED
         THESE NEEDS IN COLLECTIVE BARGAINING, THERE IS A BIG CHANCE
         THAT MANAGEMENT CAN SECURE CONTROL OF THE WORK FORCE. UNION
         LEADERS STILL REMAIN PRIMARILY CONCERNED WITH ECONOMIC
         SATISFACTION, AS THEY ARE CONVINCED THIS IS WHAT THE WORKER
         WANTS.
             OF THE FEW MOTIVATIONAL PROGRAMS INTRODUCED, MOST ARE
         CONCEPTUALIZED ON A GROUP BASIS AND IGNORE INDIVIDUAL
         WORKER DIFFERENCES AND PREFERENCES. THEY ALSO CONCENTRATE
         ON HYGIENE OR DISSATISFIER FACTORS, SUCH AS INCREASED
         SALARIES, EMPHASIS ON VACATIONS, INCREASED RELIEF TIME, AND
         EARLY RETIREMENT PLANS. THESE ARE NEGATIVE FACTORS,

M0032 STRESSING THE BURDEN OF WORK, AND ENACTED ADMINISTRATIVELY. THE SOLUTION IS TO INCREASE THE MOTIVATOR OR SATISFIER FACTORS WHICH STRESS JOB ENRICHMENT, SUCH AS ACHIEVEMENT, RECOGNITION, RESPONSIBILITY, ADVANCEMENT, AND GROWTH. UNFORTUNATELY, IN THE PAST, THESE MOTIVATIONAL FACTORS HAVE BEEN APPLIED PRIMARILY TO SUPERVISORY EMPLOYEES.

THE ANSWER FOR UNIONS IS TO BEGIN RAPIDLY THE USE OF MOTIVATIONAL PROGRAMS IN THEIR COLLECTIVE BARGAINING SCHEMES. THE AUTHOR OF THE ARTICLE SUGGESTS THAT MAYBE UNION LEADERS HAVE INTENTIONALLY IGNORED JOB ENRICHMENT PROGRAMS, AS THEY WOULD STRENGTHEN MANAGEMENT-EMPLOYEE RELATIONS AND WEAKEN THE UNIONS. THIS MAY BE TRUE BUT, IF THE UNIONS DO NOT BEGIN TO IMPLEMENT THESE PROGRAMS SOON, THEY WILL SURELY LOSE.

IN A RANDOM SAMPLING OF COLLECTIVE BARGAINING AGREEMENTS, OUT OF 12,100 CLAUSES CHOSEN, ONLY 11 INDICATED ANY MOTIVATIONAL EFFECT. ORGANIZED LABOR HAS DONE MUCH IN SATISFYING THE WORKER'S ECONOMIC NEEDS; NOW THEY SHOULD CONCENTRATE ON SOME OF MASLOW'S HIGHER NEEDS.

M0033 BOWEN, DONALD.
AN EVALUATION OF MOTIVATIONAL SIMILARITY IN WORK GROUPS. PH. D. DISSERTATION, UNIVERSITY OF MICHIGAN, 1971.

WORK GROUP MOTIVATION IS EXPLORED IN RELATION TO SELECTION PROCESSES, INDIVIDUAL WORKER NEEDS, STYLES OF LEADERSHIP, AND EMPLOYEES' JOB ATTITUDES.

M0034 BOWIN, ROBERT B.
MANAGERS INTEREST IN WORK.
PUBLIC PERSONNEL MANAGEMENT 2(MAY-JUNE 1973): 182-85.

THE STUDY WHICH THIS ARTICLE REVIEWS REPORTS THAT IT IS HIGHLY QUESTIONABLE WHETHER AS A GROUP MIDDLE MANAGERS REALLY ARE COMMITTED TO THEIR WORK AND WORKPLACE.

M0035 BOYATZIS, RICHARD E.
BUILDING EFFICACY: AN EFFECTIVE USE OF MANAGERIAL POWER. INDUSTRIAL MANAGEMENT REVIEW 11 (FALL 1969): 65-76.

THROUGH THE USE OF CASE EXAMPLES, MR. BOYATZIS DEMONSTRATES THE EFFECTIVENESS OF A LEADERSHIP STYLE BASED UPON CONFIDENCE IN HUMAN CAPACITIES RATHER THAN ON THE PRESERVATION OF PERSONAL POWER. HE DESCRIBES HOW MANAGERIAL POWER CAN BE UTILIZED TO DERIVE THE MAXIMUM BENEFIT FROM THE HUMAN RESOURCE OF THE ORGANIZATION. THE AUTHOR ALSO SHOWS THAT THE DIRECTED USE OF POWER IN A LEADERSHIP ROLE CAN INCREASE THE JOB SATISFACTION AND MOTIVATION OF EMPLOYEES.

M0036 BRADSHAW, THOMAS. GILROY, CURTIS L.
EMPLOYMENT AND UNEMPLOYMENT -- A REPORT ON 1973. MONTHLY LABOR REVIEW, FEBRUARY 1974, PP. 3-14.

UNEMPLOYMENT RATE DECLINED AND TOTAL EMPLOYMENT POSTED GREATEST PERCENTAGE INCREASE SINCE 1955, WITH ADULT MEN AND WOMEN EACH GAINING ABOUT 1.1 MILLION JOBS.

M0037 BRECHER, CHARLES.

M0037   UPGRADING BLUE-COLLAR AND SERVICE WORKERS.
        FOREWORD BY ELI GINSBERG. BALTIMORE AND LONDON: JOHNS
        HOPKINS UNIVERSITY PRESS, 1972.

            RESEARCH ON UPGRADING IN NEW YORK CITY IN THE APPAREL,
        FOOD, HEALTH, CONSTRUCTION AND TRANSIT INDUSTRIES. FOREWARD
        DISCUSSES SOCIOLOGICAL NECESSITY FOR UPGRADING JOBS AND
        PROVIDING MORE JOBS FOR ALL.

M0038   BRENNAN, PETER J.
        REALIZING APPRENTICESHIP'S POTENTIAL.
        MANPOWER, SEPTEMBER 1974, PP. 2-7.

            MORE AND MORE PEOPLE ARE REALIZING THAT WOMEN ARE
        MAKING HEADWAY IN THE SKILLED TRADES WORKPLACE.

M0039   BRIGGS, NORMA.
        WOMEN APPRENTICES: REMOVING THE BARRIERS.
        MANPOWER, DECEMBER 1974, PP. 3-11.

            A PROJECT, WOMEN IN WISCONSIN APPRENTICESHIPS,
        CHALLENGES STEREOTYPES OF SEX ROLES IN THE SKILLED TRADES
        WORKPLACE, AND TRIES TO MINIMIZE OBSTACLES FOR WOMEN.

M0040   BRISTO, CLOIS E.
        DO YOU MOTIVATE YOUR SUBORDINATES.
        SUPERVISORY MANAGEMENT 16 (SEPTEMBER 1971): 12-14.

            TO SUCCEED TODAY, MANAGERS NEED ALL THE INSPIRED
        THINKING AND ORIGINAL CONTRIBUTIONS THEY CAN GET
        FROM SUBORDINATES. THE NEED IS FOR EMPLOYEES WHO WILL PAY
        MORE THAN PERFUNCTORY ATTENTION TO THEIR JOBS. SOME
        FUNDAMENTAL TOOLS LOOKED AT ARE HONESTY, WILLINGNESS
        TO LISTEN, AND UNDERSTANDING.

M0041   BROWN, STEPHEN.
        WOMEN SHIPBUILDERS: JUST DOING A JOB.
        MANPOWER, MARCH 1975, PP. 10-13.

            AS A RESULT OF SOCIETY'S REEXAMINATION OF THEIR
        ATTITUDES TOWARD WOMEN'S ROLE AT HOME AND ON THE JOB,
        GOVERNMENT AND PRIVATE INDUSTRY ARE HUSTLING TO OPEN MORE
        JOBS -- INCLUDING NONTRADITIONAL OCCUPATIONS -- TO WOMEN.

M0042   BRUYNS, R. A. C.
        WORK AND WORK MOTIVATION IN AN AUTOMATED INDUSTRIAL
        PRODUCTION-PROCESS.
        MANAGEMENT INTERNATIONAL REVIEW 10, NOS. 4-5 (1970): 49-60.

            LITTLE HAS BEEN PUBLISHED ON THE CHANGES WHICH
        AUTOMATION MAY BRING ABOUT IN THE NATURE OF THE WORK ITSELF.
        IT IS THESE CHANGES THAT THE ATTENDANT ALTERATIONS IN WORK
        MOTIVATION STRUCTURE WHICH FORM THE OBJECT OF THE PRESENT
        ARTICLE.

M0043   BUCCHIERI, THERESA F.
        SOCIAL AND WELFARE PROGRAMS FOR THE HANDICAPPED ABROAD.
        MONTHLY LABOR REVIEW 95 (AUGUST 1972): 50-51.

M0043   DISCUSSES THE WORKSHOPS WHICH HAVE DEVELOPED IN
EUROPEAN COUNTRIES TO DEVELOP THE SKILLS AND ABILITIES OF
HANDICAPPED PERSONS.

M0044   BURKE, RONALD J.
THE EFFECTS OF AGING ON ENGINEERS' SATISFACTION AND MENTAL
HEALTH: SKILL OBSOLESCENCE.
ACADEMY OF MANAGEMENT JOURNAL 12 (DECEMBER 1969): 479-86.

        THIS STUDY IS PART OF A SERIES WHICH EXPLORE THE
SOURCES AND RESULTS OF JOB AND OFF THE JOB SOURCES OF STRAIN
AND WAYS FOR INDIVIDUALS TO COPE WITH THESE STRAINS. IT
EXAMINES THE EFFECTS OF INCREASED AGE ON THE HEALTH AND
SATISFACTION OF ENGINEERS WHERE SKILL OBSOLESCENCE IS A
VITAL CONCERN.
        FORTY-THREE MANAGERS EMPLOYED IN AN ENGINEERING
DEPARTMENT OF A LARGE CORPORATION WITH DIVISIONS THROUGHOUT
THE U. S. COMPRISED THE SAMPLE. THEY WERE MIDDLE MANAGERS
ON THE SECOND OR THIRD LEVEL. ALL OF THEM HAD EXTENSIVE
ENGINEERING TRAINING AND EXPERIENCE. ALL WERE MARRIED AND
ALL BUT TWO HAD CHILDREN. THEIR AGES RAN FROM 31 TO OVER
60, WITH THE MEAN AGE FROM 41-50.
        DATA WERE OBTAINED AT A SERIES OF SEMINARS. BEHAVIORAL
SCIENCE CONCEPTS WERE USED AT THE GROUP MEETINGS AND
QUESTIONNAIRES WERE ALSO ADMINISTERED.
        INDEXES WERE OBTAINED FOR EACH OF THE FOLLOWING
AREAS BY SUMMING WEIGHTED RESPONSES TO VARIOUS ITEMS
ASKED IN EACH AREA. SOME OF THESE INDEXES ARE INCLUDED IN
REPORTS BY INDIK, SEASHORE, AND SLESINGER AND GURIN, VEROFF,
AND FELD. THE FIRST AREA WAS JOB STRAIN, WHERE THE
RESPONDENTS WERE ASKED THE EXTENT TO WHICH A NUMBER OF
POTENTIALLY STRESSFUL JOB PROBLEMS,SUCH AS WORK OVERLOAD
AND TOO MUCH RESPONSIBILITY, BOTHERED THEM. THE SECOND AREA
WAS LIFE STRAIN, WHERE QUESTIONS OF POTENTIALLY STRESSFUL
LIFE STRAINS, SUCH AS MAJOR EXPENSES AND HOUSING PROBLEMS,
WERE ASKED TO FIND THE EXTENT TO WHICH THE RESPONDENTS WERE
BOTHERED. JOB SATISFACTION WAS THE THIRD AREA AND TWO
MAJOR QUESTIONS WERE ASKED-- ONE SPECIFIC AND THE
OTHER GENERAL. MENTAL HEALTH WAS THE LAST AREA AND
QUESTIONS WERE ASKED ABOUT HOW SPECIFIC PROBLEMS, SUCH AS
DIZZINESS OR LACK OF SLEEP, BOTHERED THE RESPONDENT.
        IT WAS FOUND THAT THE OLDER ENGINEERS ANSWERED LESS
POSITIVELY IN ALL THE ABOVE AREAS. THIS INDICATES THE
EXISTENCE OF DETRIMENTAL EFFECTS ON THE INDIVIDUAL OF AGING
AND/OR SKILL OBSOLESCENCE. BUT THE SURVEY DOES NOT PRESENT
ENOUGH INFORMATION TO BREAK DOWN THE EFFECTS ON EACH
AREA DISCUSSED ABOVE. FINDING A WAY TO RELIEVE THESE
TENSIONS REQUIRES FURTHER STUDY.

M0045   BURKE, RONALD J.   WILCOX, DOUGLAS S.
EFFECTS OF DIFFERENT PATTERNS AND DEGREES OF OPENNESS IN
SUPERIOR-SUBORDINATE COMMUNICATION ON SUBORDINATE JOB
SATISFACTION.
ACADEMY OF MANAGEMENT 12 (SEPTEMBER 1969): 319-26.

        THE PURPOSE OF THIS ARTICLE IS TO SEE IF OPEN
TWO-WAY COMMUNICATION IS ASSOCIATED WITH A SATISFYING AND
EFFECTIVE SUPERIOR-SUBORDINATE WORK RELATIONSHIP.

M0045   DIFFERENT PATTERNS AND DEGREES OF OPENNESS WERE RELATED TO
        FIVE AREAS OF SUBORDINATE WORK SATISFACTION. THE DATA WERE
        OBTAINED FROM INFORMATION COLLECTED FROM EMPOYEES USING A
        QUESTIONNAIRE SURVEY CONDUCTED IN SIX OFFICES OF A LARGE
        PUBLIC UTILITY COMPANY. THE EMPLOYEES WERE INFORMED OF THE
        SURVEY A FEW WEEKS BEFORE IT WAS CONDUCTED. QUESTIONNAIRES
        WERE THEN MAILED TO THE EMPLOYEES AND THEY WERE REQUESTED
        TO COMPLETE THE QUESTIONNAIRES AND MAIL THEM BACK TO
        THE RESEARCH STAFF. RESPONDENT ANONYMITY WAS ASSURED TO THE
        EMPLOYEES.
            QUESTIONNAIRES WERE OBTAINED FROM 323 INDIVIDUALS,
        48.0 PER CENT OF THE RESPONDENT POPULATION. ALL MEMBERS OF
        THE RESPONDENT SAMPLE WERE FEMALE TELEPHONE OPERATORS. TWO
        QUESTIONS MEASURED OPENNESS OF COMMUNICATION; ONE FROM THE
        STANDPOINT OF THE SUBORDINATE, THE OTHER FROM THE STANDPOINT
        OF THE SUPERIOR. THREE SEPARATE QUESTIONS WERE USED TO
        MEASURE TELEPHONE OPERATOR SATISFACTION WITH THE COMPANY.
        TWELVE ITEMS WERE USED TO MEASURE SATISFACTION WITH THE JOB.
        EIGHT QUESTIONS WERE USED TO MEASURE TELEPHONE OPERATOR
        SATISFACTION WITH SUPERVISION.
            EACH RESPONDENT WAS ASKED TO INDICATE THE EXTENT TO
        WHICH A NUMBER OF BEHAVIORS TOOK PLACE DURING HER LAST
        PERFORMANCE REVIEW SESSION WITH HER SUPERIOR. THREE ITEMS
        WERE INCLUDED TO DETERMINE THE EXTENT TO WHICH EACH
        SUPERVISOR APPROACHED AN IDEAL STATE IN HER RELATIONSHIPS
        WITH THE TELEPHONE OPERATORS REPORTING TO HER. IN ALL OF
        THESE QUESTIONS THAT WERE ASKED THE RESPONSE CATEGORIES
        RANGED ON A FIVE-POINT SCALE WITH 1 THE MOST FAVORABLE
        ALTERNATIVE AND 5 THE LEAST FAVORABLE ALTERNATIVE.
            RESULTS: THERE WAS A CLEAR-CUT EFFECT ATTRIBUTABLE IN
        THE OPENNESS IN SUPERIOR-SUBORDINATE COMMUNICATION. THE
        GREATER THE OPENNESS OF EITHER SUPERIOR OR SUBORDINATE
        SATISFACTION WITH FIVE DEPENDENT VARIABLES THE GREATER THE
        SATISFACTION. THESE VARIABLES INCLUDE: SATISFACTION WITH
        THE JOB, SATISFACTION WITH PERFORMANCE APPRAISAL (CLIMATE
        FOR GROWTH), PRESENCE OF A HELPING RELATIONSHIP, AND
        SATISFACTION WITH THE SUPERVISOR. ALSO THE STUDY INDICATED
        THAT GREATER OPENNESS OF COMMUNICATION BY ONE OR BOTH
        MEMBERS OF THE RELATIONSHIP WAS ASSOCIATED WITH INCREASED
        SATISFACTION. IN ADDITION, THE OPENNESS OF ONE MEMBER OF
        THE PAIR WAS SIGNIFICANTLY RELATED TO OPENNESS OF THE OTHER
        MEMBERS.

M0046   BUSH, JOSEPH C.
        INCENTIVE PAY PATTERNS IN THE STEEL INDUSTRY.
        MONTHLY LABOR REVIEW, 97 (AUGUST 1974): 75-76.

            STUDY OF INCENTIVE PAY PATTERNS AND THEIR EFFECT ON
        WORKER PRODUCTIVITY.

M0047   BRYANT, CLIFTON D.
        THE SOCIAL DIMENSIONS OF WORK.
        ENGLEWOOD CLIFFS, N. J. : PRENTICE-HALL, INC., 1972.

            A COLLECTION OF ARTICLES ANALYZING WORK FROM A
        SOCIOLOGICAL STANDPOINT. VERY, VERY INTERESTING TOPICS ARE
        INCLUDED, E. G., "OCCUPATIONAL STRUCTURE AND CRIMINAL
        BEHAVIOR: PRESCRIPTION VIOLATION BY RETAIL PHARMACISTS."

M0047   TOWARD AN ASSESSMENT OF THE MENTAL HEALTH OF FACTORY
         WORKERS: A DETROIT STUDY," "DEMOTION," "THE SELF-IMAGE OF
         THE PROSTITUTE," "THE LIFE CYCLE OF THE SOCIAL ROLE OF THE
         HOUSEWIFE." ARTICLES ARE REFRESHINGLY DOWN TO EARTH AND
         EASY TO READ. MR. BRYANT IS A FACULTY MEMBER OF WESTERN
         KENTUCKY UNIVERSITY.

M0048   CAREY, MARLENE AUSMUS.
         GOODS WELL BOUGHT ARE QUICKLY SOLD.
         OCCUPATIONAL OUTLOOK QUARTERLY, FALL 1974, PP. 2-5.

             CAREER OPPORTUNITIES FOR BUYERS AND MERCHANDISE
         MANAGERS ARE EXPLORED.

M0049   CAREY, MAX.
         THE CRAFTS -- FIVE MILLION OPPORTUNITIES.
         OCCUPATIONAL OUTLOOK QUARTERLY 15 (SPRING 1971): 2-11.

             ECONOMIC REWARDS COUPLED WITH A HERITAGE OF
         CREATIVITY THAT MEAN SELF-FULFILLMENT FOR THE SKILLED
         WORKER.

M0050   CARNALL, C.   WILD, RAY.
         JOB ATTITUDES AND OVERALL JOB SATISFACTION: THE EFFECT
         OF BIOGRAPHICAL AND EMPLOYMENT VARIABLES: RESEARCH NOTE.
         JOURNAL OF MANAGEMENT STUDIES, 11 (FEBRUARY 1974): 62-67.

             STUDY OF THE IMPORTANCE OF ATTITUDES TO SELF
         ACTUALIZATION IN RELATION TO OVERALL JOB SATISFACTION.
         RESULTS SUGGEST SEX, MARITAL STATUS, LENGTH OF SERVICE AND
         AGE HAVE SIGNIFICANT EFFECTS. RESULTS ALSO SUGGEST
         POSSIBLE NEED FOR REGULAR REASSESSMENT OF ATTITUDES TO JOBS
         TO DETECT NEED FOR REDEPLOYMENT OF LABOR OR JOB REDESIGN.

M0051   CARROLL, A. B.
         CONCEPTUAL FOUNDATIONS OF JOB ENRICHMENT.
         PUBLIC PERSONNEL MANAGEMENT 3 (JANUARY 1974): 35-38.

             DISCUSSES ENRICHMENT CONCEPTS AND THEIR INTEGRATION
         INTO TOTAL MANAGEMENT PHILOSOPHY.

M0052   CARROLL, A. B.
         UNMIXING CURRENT MOTIVATIONAL STRATEGIES.
         PERSONNEL ADMINISTRATOR 18 (JULY 1973): 53-55.

             THIS ARTICLE DISCUSSES HOW THE SIMILAR OBJECTIVES
         OF JOB ENRICHMENT, JOB ENLARGEMENT AND JOB ROTATION CAN
         CONFUSE THE MOST EXPERIENCED PERSONNEL EXECUTIVE.

M0053   CHAMPAGE, JEAN.
         ADAPTING JOBS TO PEOPLE: EXPERIMENTS AT ALCAN.
         MONTHLY LABOR REVIEW 96 (APRIL 1973): 49-51.

             STAFF EMPLOYEES AND PRODUCTION EMPLOYEES ARE TREATED
         SOMEWHAT DIFFERENTLY IN REGARD TO ADAPTATION OF THEIR JOBS.
         ON STAFF JOBS, FOUR TYPES OF SOLUTIONS HAVE BEEN TRIED:
             FIRST, THE TASK FORCE APPROACH ALLOWS THE EMPLOYEE A
         VARIETY OF DUTIES THAT ARE DIFFERENT FROM THE ONE SUGGESTED

M0053   BY HIS OFFICIAL TITLE.
        SECOND, INSTITUTION OF A MULTIPROMOTIONAL LADDER
SYSTEM, TO PERMIT PROFESSIONAL WORKERS TO PURSUE A CAREER
WITHOUT SWITCHING TO MANAGEMENT JOBS IN ORDER TO GAIN MORE
STATUS OR MORE MONEY. PARALLEL CAREER PATHS CAN BE
ESTABLISHED.
        THIRD, FORMAL CAREER PLANNING CAN BE IMPLEMENTED TO
OBTAIN EMPLOYEE INPUTS IN PROGRAMMING STAFF MOVEMENTS.
        FINALLY, COORDINATION OF JOB PROFILES WITH PROFILES OF
INDIVIDUALS WOULD HELP ADAPTATION.
        THESE APPROACHES REQUIRE MODIFIED PERSONNEL SYSTEMS IN
PERFORMANCE EVALUATION AND THE SELECTION PROCESS. THEY ALSO
REQUIRE A GREAT DEAL OF TRUST AMONG EMPLOYEES, A HIGH DEGREE
OF INTERPERSONAL RELATIONS, AND A GREAT DEAL OF OPENNESS AS
TO THE OBJECTIVES OF THE ORGANIZATION.
        TO FACILITATE THE USE OF THESE APPROACHES, INSTALLATION
OF PEOPLE PLANNING TO IDENTIFY HUMAN NEEDS, WHICH ANALYZES
THE COMPANY NEEDS AND THE EMPLOYEE NEEDS, COULD BE
IMPLEMENTED.
        OTHER EXPERIMENTS HAVE BEEN PERFORMED ON PRODUCTION
EMPLOYEES. IN ONE PLANT, TIMECLOCKS WERE REMOVED AND
SALARIES, INSTEAD OF WAGES, WERE PAID. THIS PLAN MADE
THE WORKERS FEEL MORE RESPONSIBLE, REDUCED ABSENTEEISM, AND
RAISED THE QUALITY OF THE WORK DONE.
        THE KEY TO ADAPTATION OF JOBS TO PEOPLE IS TO ALLOW
PEOPLE TO UNDERSTAND THE GOALS AND OBJECTIVES OF MANAGEMENT
AND HAVE SUFFICIENT TIME TO ADJUST THEIR OWN LIFE STYLE
ACCORDINGLY.

M0054   CHANGES IN THE LABOR FORCE STATUS OF WOMEN.
        MONTHLY LABOR REVIEW, AUGUST 1973, P. 76.

        THIS ARTICLE DISCUSSES FACTORS WHICH HAVE CHANGED BLACK
AND WHITE WOMEN'S STATUS IN THE LABOR FORCE.

M0055   CHANGING PATTERNS.
        MANPOWER, DECEMBER 1974, PP. 12-13.

        WOMEN AIR FORCE MACHINISTS FIND THE JOB IS A LOT LIKE
SEWING AND PAYS OVER SIX DOLLARS AN HOUR.

M0056   CHASE, RICHARD B.   KUHN, DAVID G.   SLOCUM, JOHN W.
        DOES JOB PERFORMANCE AFFECT EMPLOYEE SATISFACTION.
        PERSONNEL JOURNAL 50 (JUNE 1971): 455-59.

        THIS ARTICLE EXPLAINS A STUDY THAT WAS CONDUCTED IN
ORDER TO DETERMINE A RELATIONSHIP BETWEEN JOB PERFORMANCE
AND SATISFACTION OF WORKERS. THE STUDY IS
BASED ON MASLOW'S THEORY OF MOTIVATION, WHICH STATES THAT IF
HUMAN NEEDS ARE DIVIDED INTO FIVE LEVELS (PHYSIOLOGICAL,
SAFETY, SOCIAL, ESTEEM, AND SELF-ACTUALIZATION,
RESPECTIVELY), THEN THE NEEDS AT A PARTICULAR LEVEL MUST BE
SATISFIED BEFORE THE NEEDS OF A HIGHER LEVEL CAN BE TAKEN
INTO ACCOUNT. MASLOW CONTENDS THAT HIGHER LEVELS ARE
CHARACTERIZED BY DECREASING PERCENTAGES OF SATISFACTION.
        THE MODEL OF THE STUDY IS BASED ON THE ASSUMPTION THAT
SATISFACTION DIRECTLY AFFECTS PERFORMANCE. THE MODEL
SUGGESTS THAT PERFORMANCE LEADS TO REWARDS,WHICH LEADS TO

M0056 SATISFACTION. THEREFORE, SATISFACTION, RATHER THAN CAUSING IT, IS CAUSED BY PERFORMANCE. TWO TYPES OF REWARDS ARE DIFFERENTIATED: EXTRINSIC, WHICH ARE CONTROLLED REWARDS SUCH AS PAY, PROMOTION, AND SECURITY, AND INTRINSIC, WHICH ARE REWARDS THAT SATISFY HIGHER ORDER NEEDS. EXTRINSIC REWARDS TEND TO BE ASSOCIATED WITH MEMBERSHIP IN THE ORGANIZATION, THEREFORE, INTRINSIC REWARDS ARE CLOSELY RELATED WITH PERFORMANCE SINCE THIS TYPE OF REWARD IS GIVEN TO THE EMPLOYEE BY HIMSELF. THROUGH THIS KIND OF REWARD SYSTEM, THE AUTHORS FOUND THAT AN EMPLOYEE'S SATISFACTION IS A FUNCTION OF BOTH THE MAGNITUDE AND THE FREQUENCY OF THE REWARDS, AS WELL AS HIS EXPECTATION OF THE REWARD.

FROM THE CONCLUSIONS OF THE STUDY, SECURITY AND SOCIAL NEEDS ARE POSITIVELY RELATED TO JOB PRODUCTIVITY, WHILE SELF-ACTUALIZATION NEEDS ARE LEAST RELATED. THE MAGNITUDE OF THE DIFFERENCE OF THE FINDINGS INDICATE THAT EXTRINSIC REWARDS ARE MORE CLOSELY ASSOCIATED WITH PERFORMANCE THAN INTRINSIC REWARD SATISFACTION. THE REASON FOR THIS IS THAT WORKERS DO NOT EXPECT TO FIND PERSONAL FULFILLMENT AT WORK, SO THEY CHANNEL HIGHER ORDER NEEDS INTO NON-WORK ACTIVITIES, SUCH AS HOBBIES. THE AUTHORS CONCLUDE THAT AN INCENTIVE PAY PLAN WILL STRENGTHEN THE RELATIONSHIP BETWEEN EXTRINSIC NEEDS AND PERFORMANCE.

M0057 CHUNG, KAE H.
A MARKOV CHAIN MODEL OF HUMAN NEEDS.
ACADEMY OF MANAGEMENT JOURNAL, 12 (JUNE 1969): 223-34.

IN ORDER TO CAUSE AN EMPLOYEE TO PRODUCE, THE EMPLOYER MUST BE ABLE TO APPLY THE CORRECT INCENTIVES. THIS NECESSITATES THE UNDERSTANDING OF THE EMPLOYEE'S NEED STRUCTURE. THIS PAPER DISCUSSES THE . . . HUMAN NEED STRUCTURE, EXAMINES . . . EXISTING MODELS WHICH HAVE SOUGHT TO ANALYZE THIS STRUCTURE, AND PROPOSES A MARKOV CHAIN MODEL FOR DEALING WITH . . . THE HUMAN NEEDS. (P. 223).

MASLOW'S THEORY OF NEEDS.
ALTHOUGH MASLOW IS BEST KNOWN FOR HIS HEIRARCHY OF NEEDS, HE ALSO DEVELOPED A THEORY HE CALLED HOLISM. HOLISM SHOWS THAT THE FIVE BASIC HUMAN NEEDS (PHYSIOLOGICAL, SAFETY, SOCIAL, SELF-RESPECT, AND SELF-ACTUALIZATION) ARE INTERDEPENDENT, RATHER THAN ORDERED WITH ONE NEED BEING FULFILLED BEFORE ANOTHER IS SOUGHT AS IN THE CLASSICAL HEIRARCHY. THE HOLISTIC NEED SYSTEM MAKES IT POSSIBLE FOR A PERSON TO WORK FOR HIS GOALS IN MULTIDIRECTIONAL MOVEMENTS. THEREFORE, THE INDIVIDUAL MAY NOT ONLY WORK UP THE SCALE TO SATISFY HIS HIGHER NEEDS, HE MAY ALSO MOVE BACK DOWN THE SCALE TO BETTER SATISFY LOWER LEVEL NEEDS BY UPGRADING THE MEANS OF SATISFYING THEM. (P. 226).

TECHNIQUES FOR ANALYZING THE HUMAN NEED SYSTEM.
THE VECTOR ANALYSIS IS A TECHNIQUE WHICH STATES THAT THE HYPOTHETICAL PERSON HAS DIFFERENT NEEDS, EACH OF WHICH PULL HIM IN DIFFERENT DIRECTIONS WITH VARYING STRENGTHS. THESE FACTORS ARE CALLED VECTORS.

THE UNIDIMENSIONAL ANALYSIS IS ANOTHER ANALYTIC TECHNIQUE. THIS ANALYSIS MEASURES THE FORCE OF OPPOSING NEEDS AND PLOTS THIS FORCE ON A SINGLE DIMENSIONAL SCALE. A THIRD TECHNIQUE IS THE MARGINAL UTILITY ANALYSIS.

M0057   THE CONCEPT OF MARGINAL UTILITY STATES THAT THE INDIVIDUAL
        TRIES TO OPTIMIZE HIS OVERALL SATISFACTION OF VARIOUS
        NEEDS THE BEST HE CAN WITH THE LIMITED CAPACITIES AND
        RESOURCES AVAILABLE TO HIM. (P. 228). ANOTHER TECHNIQUE,
        GOAL DISTANCE ANALYSIS, MEASURES THE STRENGTH OF A PERSON'S
        MOTIVATION TO SATISFY A GOAL. HIERACHICAL CHANCE IS A
        FIFTH TECHNIQUE. THIS TECHNIQUE IS INTERPRETED AS A CAREER
        STAGE MODEL: THAT IS, THE STRENGTH OF VARIOUS NEEDS IS MORE
        CLOSELY RELATED TO THE INTERACTION OF AGE AND ROLE THAN
        TO THE DEGREE OF LOWER NEED GRATIFICATION (P.229).
            MARKOV'S CHAIN ANALYSIS IS A METHOD OF ANALYZING A
        SYSTEM WHOSE BEHAVORIAL CHARACTERISTICS INVOLVE
        MULTIVARIATE, PROBABILISTIC, AND DYNAMIC ELEMENTS. (P. 234)
        IT MAKES IT POSSIBLE TO PREDICT FUTURE BEHAVORIAL PATTERNS
        IF PAST PATTERNS ARE KNOWN.

M0058   CHRISTENSEN, L.   BENN, MARTHA.
        COMPUTER MYSTIQUE AND FEMININE MYSTIQUE JOIN FORCES.
        EXTENSION SERVICE REVIEW, JANUARY-FEBRUARY 1975, PP. 16-17.

            FEMALE AGRICULTURAL ECONOMISTS PROGRAMMED A COMPUTER
        WITH A WOMAN'S VOICE TO AID IN NUTRITION PLANNING FOR
        PEOPLE.

M0059   CLARY, THOMAS C.
        MOTIVATION THROUGH POSITIVE STROKING.
        PUBLIC PERSONNEL MANAGEMENT 2 (MARCH-APRIL 1973):   113-17.

            THE AUTHOR MAINTAINS THAT THE BEST CLIMATE FOR
        MOTIVATION TOWARD ACHIEVING THE MOST EFFECTIVE RESULTS FOR
        AN ORGANIZATION IS SET BY POSITIVE STROKING TECHNIQUES.
        THE AUTHOR GIVES THE EXAMPLE OF THESE TECHNIQUES AND METHODS
        OF IMPLEMENTING A PLANNED STROKING PROGRAM. THE AUTHOR
        ALSO INCLUDES ANECDOTAL RECORDS OF SUCCESSFUL STROKING
        UTILIZATION.

M0060   CLOWARD, RICHARD.   CLARK, MAMIE P.
        ADOLESCENT MINORITY FEMALES IN AN URBAN LABOR MARKET.
        NEW YORK: METROPOLITAN APPLIED RESEARCH CENTER, INC.,
        DECEMBER, 1974.

            THIS PROJECT IS ATTEMPTING TO TEST AND DETERMINE THE
        IMPACT AND EFFECTIVENESS OF A MODEL YOUTH PROGRAM UPON THE
        MOTIVATION OF BLACK WOMEN SCHOOL DROPOUTS AGED 16 THROUGH
        19, IN AN URBAN GHETTO. PEER GROUPS REINFORCEMENT IS USED
        AND PEERS AIDS ARE USED AS ROLE MODELS. THE TENTATIVE
        FINDINGS INDICATE THAT THE PEER GROUP REINFORCEMENT MODEL IS
        IS A USEFUL MEANS OF IMPROVING EMPLOYMENT BEHAVIOR.

M0061   COAKLEY, NORMAN.
        FOREMEN: MAN IN THE MIDDLE.
        OCCUPATIONAL OUTLOOK QUARTERLY 13 (SUMMER 1969): 8-11.

            PLANT MANAGERS HAVE AUTHORITY . . . WORKERS HAVE
        RIGHTS . . . AND FOREMEN HAVE HEADACHES.

M0062   COBB, WILLIAM L., JR.
        MOTIVATION OF THE BLACK WORKER: A REVIEW OF TRADITIONAL

M0062 APPROACHES AND CRITICAL ISSUES IN CURRENT THEORY.
UNPUBLISHED RESEARCH, UNIVERSITY OF MICHIGAN, 1973.
THIS STUDY REVIEWED VARIOUS HYPOTHESES CONCERNING THE
ATTITUDES AND BEHAVIOR OF THE BLACK WORKER, WITH PARTICULAR
FOCUS ON ATTEMPTS TO UNDERSTAND HIS SPECIAL PROBLEMS IN
TERMS OF A MOTIVATION-SITUATION DICHOTOMY.

M0063 COHN, JULES.
ORGANIZATIONAL EXPERIENCES AND THEIR EFFECTS ON THE
ATTITUDES OF EMPLOYEES, INCLUDING THE DISADVANTAGED, TOWARD
WORK.
NEW YORK: AMERICAN JEWISH COMMITTEE. SEPTEMBER 1973

THIS PROJECT HAS TWO MAJOR OBJECTIVES: (1) TO
ORGANIZE AND ANALYZE AVAILABLE FINDINGS ON THE ATTITUDES OF
EMPLOYEES, PARTICULARLY THE DISADVANTAGED, TOWARD THEIR WORK
AND THE ORGANIZATIONAL ENVIRONMENT; AND (2) TO SEARCH THE
EXPANDING BODY OF LITERATURE GROWING OUT OF THE CURRENT
HUMANIZATION OF WORK MOVEMENT FOR SIGNIFICANT THEMES FOR
THE FUTURE STUDY OF WORKER MOTIVATION. FINDINGS WILL HELP
ILLUMINATE ISSUES THAT BEAR NOT ONLY UPON EMPLOYEE MORALE
AND JOB SATISFACTION BUT ALSO UPON PRODUCTIVITY AND TURNOVER
RATES.

M0064 COHN, JULES.
ORGANIZATIONAL EXPERIENCES AND THEIR EFFECTS ON THE
ATTITUDES OF EMPLOYEES, INCLUDING THE DISADVANTAGED.
NEW YORK: AMERICAN JEWISH COMMITTEE. DECEMBER 1974

THE PURPOSE OF THIS STUDY WAS TO PULL TOGETHER THE
AVAILABLE INFORMATION ON THE ATTITUDES OF EMPLOYEES,
INCLUDING THE DISADVANTAGED, TOWARD WORK. AFTER REVIEWING
THE AVAILABLE LITERATURE, A STATE-OF-THE-ART PAPER WAS
PRODUCED WHICH SYNTHESIZED AND ANALYZED THE KNOWLEDGE
AND FINDINGS OF R&D WORK THAT HAD FOCUSED ON THE MEANING OF
WORK, THE MOTIVATION FOR WORK, THE RELATIONSHIPS BETWEEN
LIFE STYLE AND WORK, AND BETWEEN RACIAL-ETHNIC GROUP
AND WORK.

M0065 COLE, JOHN D. R.
SHIFTING GEARS IN PME.
CIVIL SERVICE JOURNAL, 14 (OCTOBER-DECEMBER 1973): 16-20.

JOB PERFORMANCE EVALUATION WITHIN THE FEDERAL
GOVERNMENT.

M0066 COLLINS, DONALD C. RAUBOLT, ROBERT R.
A STUDY OF EMPLOYEE RESISTANCE TO JOB ENRICHMENT.
PERSONNEL JOURNAL, 54 (APRIL 1975): 232-35.

THE ASSOCIATION BETWEEN EMPLOYEE BACKGROUND AND
OCCUPATIONAL CHARACTERISTICS AND DEGREE OF RESISTANCE TO A
JOB ENRICHMENT PROGRAM WERE EXAMINED IN A LARGE SCALE
MANUFACTURING FIRM. THE IMPORTANT DETERMINANTS OF
RESISTANCE WERE FOUND TO BE EDUCATIONAL LEVEL, AGE, TASK
PERFORMANCE AND NUMBER OF YEARS TO RETIREMENT.
COMMITTEE ON ATTITUDES AND SOCIAL CHANGE.

M0067   ATTITUDES AND SOCIAL CHANGE -- COMMITTEE REPORT.
         DEPARTMENT OF STATE NEWSLETTER, MARCH 1975, PP. 38-43.
                 THIS REPORT CONCERNS SOCIAL ATTITUDES TOWARD
         SECRETARIAL FORCES AND RECOMMENDATIONS ON HOW TO PROVIDE AN
         UPWARD MOBILITY LADDER FOR THOSE WITHIN THE FORCES.

M0068   CONSTAS, PERRY A.
         ALIENATION-COUNSELING IMPLICATIONS AND MANAGEMENT THERAPY.
         PERSONNEL JOURNAL 52 (MAY 1973):   349-56.

                 IDENTIFIES SOME POSSIBLE SYMPTOMS AND CAUSES OF
         WORKER ALIENATION AND PRESENTS GUIDELINES FOR COUNSELING THE
         ALIENATED PERSON.   INCLUDES SEVERAL SUGGESTIONS FOR
         INVESTIGATING THE WORK ENVIRONMENT AND ITS IMPACT ON
         EMPLOYEES.

M0069   COOK, PHILIP.
         THE EFFECT OF LEGITIMATE OPPORTUNITIES ON THE PROBABILITY OF
         PAROLEE RECIDIVISM.
         BERKELEY: UNIVERSITY OF CALIFORNIA, OCTOBER 1973.

                 THE PURPOSE OF THIS STUDY WAS TO DETERMINE WHETHER
         IMPROVING THE QUALITY OF JOB OPPORTUNITIES AVAILABLE TO
         PAROLEES AFFECTS RECIDIVISM. THE RESULTS OF THE STUDY
         SHOWED THAT PAROLEES WHO FIND SATISFACTORY JOBS ARE LESS
         LIKELY TO RECIDIVATE.

M0070   COOPER, ROBERT.
         TASK CHARACTERISTICS AND INTRINSIC MOTIVATION.
         HUMAN RELATIONS 26 (AUGUST 1973):   387-408.

                 THE MAJOR AIM OF THIS ARTICLE IS TO ISOLATE THOSE
         CHARACTERISTICS OF INDUSTRIAL TASKS WHICH SERVE TO AROUSE
         AND/OR SATISFY THE INTRINSIC MOTIVES.

M0071   COOPER, S.   RAIBORN, M.
         ACCOUNTING FOR CORPORATE SOCIAL RESPONSIBILITY.
         MSU BUSINESS TOPICS 22 (SPRING 1974): 19-26.

                 ACCORDING TO THIS ARTICLE, TECHNIQUES FOR
         MEASURING AND REPORTING SOCIAL PERFORMANCE ARE INVESTIGATED
         SEPARATE FROM THE TRADITIONAL FINANCIAL APPROACH.

M0072   CORDTZ, DAN.
         CITY HALL DISCOVERS PRODUCTIVITY.
         FORTUNE   OCTOBER 1971 PP. 92-96.

                 CONSIDERS THE EFFECT MODERN TECHNOLOGY AND BETTER
         MANAGEMENT COULD HAVE ON THE RUN-AWAY COSTS OF URBAN
         SERVICES AND URBAN ADMINISTRATION. POLICE, FIRE, PARK
         SANITATION SERVICES ARE DISCUSSED AND THE GROWING ROLE OF
         LABOR UNIONS IN THE PUBLIC SECTOR IS COVERED.

M0073   CORPORATE DROPOUT.
         IRON AGE 205 (JANUARY 1, 1970):   81-96.

                 THE VIEWS OF SEVERAL CORPORATE DROPOUTS--MEN WHO,
         ACCORDING TO INDUSTRIAL PSYCHOLOGISTS, HAVE TURNED-OFF,

M0073   DEAD-ENDED OR OTHERWISE SUFFERED CAREER ARREST. THE CLAIMS
OF CONSULTANTS, INDUSTRIAL PSYCHOLOGISTS, AND OTHER CLOSE
OBSERVERS OF LIFE IN THE U. S. CORPORATE EXECUTIVE SUITES
ARE REPRESENTED.

M0074   COSTELLO, JOHN M.   LEE, M. SANG.
NEEDS FULFILLMENT AND JOB SATISFACTION OF PROFESSIONALS.
PUBLIC PERSONNEL MANAGEMENT, 3 (SEPTEMBER-OCTOBER 1974):
454-61.

A STUDY OF PERSONAL GOAL SATISFACTION INVOLVES THE
ANALYSIS OF THE INDIVIDUAL'S NEEDS AND THEIR PERCEIVED
IMPORTANCE. THIS STUDY FOCUSES ON THIS IMPORTANT AREA OF
EMPLOYEE STATISFACTION. IT ANALYZES THE RELATIONSHIP
BETWEEN NEEDS FULFILLMENT AND JOB SATISFACTION AMONG
PROFESSIONAL EMPLOYEES IN A PUBLICLY OWNED UTILITY FIRM.

M0075   COWAN, DR. GLORIA.
STAFF ATTITUDE AND SUCCESS OF THE WIN PROGRAM, A REPORT ON
PHASE I RETURNS.
NTIS PB 205988 (1972).

EVALUATION OF STAFF AND ENROLLEE INTERACTION AND
ITS IMPORTANCE IN THE SUCCESS OF THE WORKER. IT WAS
DETERMINED THAT IT IS THE ENROLLEE'S ATTITUDE ALONE THAT
MAKES THE DIFFERENCE. RESEARCH PERFORMED AT WAYNE STATE
UNIVERSITY UNDER A GRANT FROM THE MANPOWER ADMINISTRATION.

M0076   COX, JOHN HOWELL.
TIME AND INCENTIVE PAY PRACTICES IN URBAN AREAS.
MONTHLY LABOR REVIEW, 94 (DECEMBER 1971): 53-56.

STUDY EXAMINES TRENDS IN PAY PRACTICES OF VARIOUS
EMPLOYMENT AREAS, AND THE EFFECTS OF THESE PRACTICES
ON PRODUCTIVITY OF EMPLOYEES.

M0077   CROSS, JOHN.
WOMEN AT WORK -- OUTDOORS.
SOIL CONSERVATION, JUNE 1974, PP. 9-10.

WOMEN SOIL CONSERVATIONISTS BECOME ABSORBED IN THE
PROBLEMS OR EROSION, SEDIMENTATION, AND ENVIRONMENTAL
PROBLEMS AS ONLY THEIR MALE COLLEAGUES DID A YEAR AGO.

M0078   CROWLEY, MICHAEL F.
PROFESSIONAL MANPOWER: THE JOB MARKET TURN-AROUND.
MONTHLY LABOR REVIEW 95 (OCTOBER 1972): 9-15.

PROJECTIONS OF EMPLOYMENT PROSPECTS FOR PROFESSIONALS
SUGGESTS THAT MANY COLLEGE GRADUATES STARTING WORK IN THE
1970'S MAY HAVE TO CHANGE CAREER GOALS.

M0079   CUMMINGS, L. L.   SCHWAB, DONALD P.
THEORIES OF PERFORMANCE AND SATISFACTION.
PERSONNEL ADMINISTRATOR 18 (MARCH 1973): 39-46.

THIS ARLICLE REPRESENTS AN IN-DEPTH VIEW OF THE
RELATIONSHIP BETWEEN SATISFACTION AND PERFORMANCE WHICH

M0079 COULD OPEN UP NEW AVENUES OF THOUGHT FOR THE CONTEMPORARY
PERSONNEL EXECUTIVE.

M0080 CUMMINGS, L. L.   SCHWAB, DONALD P.
THEORIES OF PERFORMANCE AND SATISFACTION: A REVIEW.
INDUSTRIAL RELATIONS 9 (OCTOBER 1970): 413-16.

THIS PAPER REVIEWS AND EVALUATES THEORICAL PROPOSITIONS
CONCERNING THE RELATIONSHIP BETWEEN SATISFACTION AND
PERFORMANCE. IT DOES NOT PRESENT ANY ONE THEORY BUT
RATHER ANALYZED VARIOUS STUDIES AND THEORIES THAT SHOW
A CONNECTION BETWEEN JOB PERFORMANCE AND EMPLOYEE
SATISFACTION.
EARLY HUMAN RELATIONS RESEARCH HAS CONCLUDED THAT BY
SATISFYING NEEDS OF AN EMPLOYEE, PRODUCTIVITY ATTEMPTS TO
INCREASE. CURRENT THEORY RESEARCH HAS BEEN GREATLY
INFLUENCED BY HERZBERG AND HIS COLLEGUES. THEY SEPARATE JOB
VARIABLES INTO TWO GROUPS: HYGIENE FACTORS AND MOTIVATORS.
HYGIENE FACTORS ARE VARIABLES SUCH AS SUPERVISION, SALARY,
AND BENEFITS WHICH ARE POTENTIAL SOURCES OF DISSATISFACTION.
MOTIVATORS ARE ASSOCIATED WITH THE WORK ITSELF AND ITS
ACCOMPLISHMENTS. IT IS FELT THAT THESE FACTORS CONTRIBUTE
TO SATISFACTION AND ARE CLOSELY RELATED TO PERFORMANCE. THE
AUTHORS STATE THAT THIS IS AN ESSENTIALLY UNSUPPORTED
INTERPRETATION AND THEREFORE, SUBSEQUENT RESEARCHERS MIGHT
MISINTERPRET THE MEANING OF THEIR DATA. RESEARCH DONE BY
THE UNIVERSITY OF MICHIGAN IS IMPORTANT BECAUSE IT
REPRESENTS EARLY EMPIRICAL EVIDENCE OFFERING LITTLE REASON
FOR OPTIMISM ABOUT THE ASSOCIATION BETWEEN SATISFACTION AND
PERFORMANCE. A STUDY DONE BY BRAYFIELD AND CROCKETT
CONCLUDED THAT HIGH SATISFACTION AND HIGH PERFORMANCE TEND
TO OCCUR WHEN PRODUCTIVITY IS PERCEIVED AS A PATH TO CERTAIN
IMPORTANT GOALS. THE THEORY OF WORK ADJUSTMENT STATES THAT
SATISFACTION RESULTS FROM COMMUNICATION OF THE EMPLOYEE'S
NEEDS AND THE ORGANIZATION'S REINFORCEMENT SYSTEM.
PERFORMANCE REFERS TO THE ORGANIZATION'S EVALUATION OF THE
BEHAVIOR OF THE EMPLOYEES. THE THEORY OF PRESSURE FOR
PRODUCTION STATES THAT ORGANIZATIONAL PRESSURE DECREASES
SATISFACTION WHILE PERFORMANCE IS CURVILINEARLY RELATED TO
THE PRESSURE. A MODEL PROPOSED BY MARCH AND SIMON SHOWS
PERFORMANCE IS A FUNCTION OF 1) THE DEGREE OF
DISSATISFACTION, AND 2) THE PERCEIVED USAGE OF PERFORMANCE
FOR GOAL ATTAINMENT.
THE AUTHORS CONCLUDE THAT EXPERIMENTAL STUDIES PERMIT
CONTROL AND OBSERVATION OF POTENTIAL MODERATORS BUT THEY ARE
PESSIMISTIC ABOUT THE VALUE OF ADDITIONAL THEORIES AT THIS
TIME. THEY FURTHER SUGGEST WORK ON THEORIES THAT DEAL WITH
JUST SATISFACTION OR THEORIES OF PERFORMANCE.

M0081 CUMMINGS, PAUL W.
DOES HERZBERG'S THEORY REALLY WORK.
MANAGEMENT REVIEW 64 (FEBRUARY 1975): 35-37.

THE AUTHOR DRAWS SEVEN CONCLUSIONS FROM A STUDY OF HIS
OWN BASED ON HERZBERG'S THEORIES THAT THE FACTORS LEADING TO
JOB SATISFACTION ARE SEPARATE AND DISTINCT FORM FACTORS
LEADING TO JOB DISSATISFACTION.

M0082   DACHLER, PETER H.   MOBLEY, WILLIAM H.
        CONSTRUCT VALIDATION OF AN INSTRUMENTALITY-EXPECTANCY-TASK-
        GOAL MODEL OF WORK MOTIVATION: SOME THEORETICAL BOUNDARY
        CONDITIONS.
        JOURNAL OF APPLIED PSYCHOLOGY, 58 (DECEMBER 1973):   397-418.

             THE PURPOSE OF THE PRESENT RESEARCH WAS TO ATTEMPT TO
        IMPROVE THE UNDERSTANDING OF THE MOTIVATION PROCESS
        DELINEATED BY VIE (VALENCE-INSTRUMENTALITY-EXPECTANCY)
        THEORY THROUGH GREATER SPECIFICITY IN THE CONCEPTUALIZATION
        AND MEASURMENT OF THE KEY VARIABLES AND THE SIGNIFICANT
        INTERRELATIONS AMONG KEY VARIABLES AND BEHAVIOR.
             A DETAILED VIE MODEL WAS EXPLAINED AND RESULTS OF TESTS
        OF THE MODEL IN TWO ORGANIZATIONS WERE REPORTED.   IN ONE
        ORGANIZATION, PREDICTIONS OF THE MODEL WERE SUPPORTED;
        IN THE OTHER ORGANIZATION, PREDICTIONS WERE NOT SUPPORTED.

M0083   DALENA, DONALD T.
        A STEELWORKER TALKS MOTIVATION.
        MANAGEMENT REVIEW, 63 (MAY 1974):   36-42.
             CONDENSED FROM INDUSTRY WEEK, JANUARY 14, 1974.

             DALENA HOLDS THAT THERE ARE THREE KEYS TO HUMAN
        PROGRESS IN THE WORKPLACE: CARE, CONTINOUS FEEDBACK, AND
        THE FEELING OF MUTUAL NEED.

M0084   DAMICO, JOSEPH U.
        IN EXECUTIVE DEVELOPMENT . . . THE FUTURE IS NOW.
        CIVIL SERVICE JOURNAL, 14 (OCTOBER-DECEMBER 1973): 7-10.

        METHODS BY WHICH FEDERAL MANAGERS ARE BEING DEVELOPED.

M0085   DAVIS, H. E.
        NEGOTIATED RETIREMENT PLANS -- A DECADE OF BENEFIT
        IMPROVEMENTS.
        MONTHLY LABOR REVIEW 92 (MAY 1969):   11-15.

             PENSION BENEFITS CONTINUE TO RISE RAPIDLY AND BECOME
        PAYABLE SOONER.

M0086   DAVIS, H. E.   STRASSER, A.
        PRIVATE PENSION PLANS, 1960 TO 1969 -- AN OVERVIEW.
        MONTHLY LABOR REVIEW 93(JULY 1970):   45-56.

             COVERAGE REMAINED STABLE DURING THE
        1960'S WHILE BENEFITS WERE LIBERALIZED.

M0087   DAVIS, LOUIS E.
        JOB SATISFACTION RESEARCH: THE POST-INDUSTRIAL VIEW.
        INDUSTRIAL RELATIONS 10 (MAY 1971):   176-93.

             DISCUSSES RELATIONSHIP BETWEEN CULTURAL VALUES
        EXHIBITED DURING THE INDUSTRIAL ERA AND JOB SATISFACTION
        RESEARCH AS PRACTICED DURING THE LAST 40 YEARS.   THEN
        EXAMINES CHANGING JOB DESIGN IN THE POST-INDUSTRIAL ERA AND
        IMPLICATIONS FOR FUTURE JOB SATISFACTION STUDIES.

M0088   DAVIS, LOUIS E.

M0088   RESEARCH, INTERVENTION, AND EXPERIENCE IN ENHANCING THE
        QUALITY OF WORKING LIFE.
        UNPUBLISHED RESEARCH, UNIVERSITY OF CALIFORNIA, 1973.

        ANALYSIS OF PROFESSIONAL AND BUSINESS LITERATURE FOR
        IMPROVING THE QUALITY OF WORK AND WORKING LIFE.

M0089   DAVIS, RENE V.   ACE, MERLE E.
        DIMENSIONS OF THRESHOLD WORK EXPERIENCE FOR HIGH SCHOOL
        GRADUATES AND DROPOUTS: A FACTOR ANALYSIS.
        JOURNAL OF VOCATIONAL BEHAVIOR, 3 (APRIL 1973): 221-31.

        FACTOR ANALYSES WERE MADE FROM DATA ON 19 THRESHOLD
        WORK EXPERIENCE VARIABLES OBTAINED FROM 183 HIGH SCHOOL
        GRADUATES AND 90 DROPOUTS 1 1/2 YEARS AFTER LEAVING SCHOOL.
        SEVEN VARIABLES FOUND TO REPRESENT THE FACTOR DIMENSIONS
        ADEQUATELY, CORRELATED ONLY SLIGHTLY WITH JOB SATISFACTION
        VARIABLES, "SUPPORTING THE CONCEPTUALIZATION OF JOB
        SATISFACTORINESS AND JOB SATISFACTION AS RELATIVELY
        INDEPENDENT SETS OF VARIABLES."

M0090   DECHARMS, RICHARD.
        PERSONAL CAUSATION: THE INTERNAL EFFECTIVE DETERMINANTS OF
        BEHAVIOR.
        NEW YORK: ACADEMIC PRESS. 1970.

        THIS BOOK IS PRIMARILY INTENDED TO MAKE A THEORETICAL
        CONTRIBUTION TO SUGGEST A SOMEWHAT NOVEL WAY OF
        APPROACHING THE PROBLEMS OF HUMAN MOTIVATION, TO BREAK
        FROM TRADITION. THE AIM OF THIS WORK IS TO STIMULATE THE
        READER TO THINK ON A BROAD SCALE ABOUT BIG PROBLEMS OF
        EMPIRICAL INVESTIGATIONS.

M0091   DECI, EDWARD L.
        EFFECTS OF EXTERNALLY MEDIATED REWARDS ON INTRINSIC
        MOTIVATION.
        JOURNAL OF PERSONALITY AND SOCIAL PSYCHOLOGY 18
        (APRIL 1971): 105-15.

        RESEARCH TESTED THE EFFECTS OF EXTERNAL REWARDS ON
        PERSONS INTRINSICALLY MOTIVATED TO PERFORM AN ACTIVITY. IT
        WAS FOUND THAT MONEY AS A REWARD TENDED TO DECREASE
        INTRINSIC MOTIVATION WHILE VERBAL REINFORCEMENT AND
        POSITIVE FEEDBACK TENDED TO ENHANCE INTRINSIC MOTIVATION.

M0092   DENZLER, RICHARD D.
        PEOPLE AND PRODUCTIVITY: DO THEY STILL EQUAL PAY AND
        PROFITS?
        PERSONNEL JOURNAL 53 (JANUARY 1974): 59-63.

        AFTER EXAMINING RECENT RESEARCH IN JOB ENRICHMENT IN
        THE PERSPECTIVE OF CLASSICAL THEORIES OF WORKER MOTIVATION,
        THE AUTHOR CONCLUDES THAT BOTH JOB ENRICHMENT AND MONEY
        MOTIVATION APPROACHES HAVE VALIDITY AND THAT THE SUCCESSFUL
        MOTIVATIONAL PLAN MUST INCLUDE BOTH.

M0093   DERMER, JERRY.
        THE INTERRELATIONSHIP OF INTRINSIC AND EXTRINSIC

M0093 MOTIVATION.
ACADEMY OF MANAGEMENT JOURNAL 18 (MARCH 1975): 125-29.
THE STUDY'S PURPOSE IS TO AID MANAGEMENT IN RESOLVING
THE DILEMMA OF WHETHER OR NOT TO TIE REWARD TO PERFORMANCE
BY INVESTIGATING THE RELATIONSHIP OF INTRINSIC AND EXTRINSIC
MOTIVATOR IN THE CONTEXT OF A BUDGET SYSTEM. THE STUDY
SURVEYED MANAGERS OF A MULTI-STATE DEPARTMENT
STORE CHAIN. THE FINDINGS SUPPORT THE CONTENTION THAT
INTRINSIC MOTIVATION IS A NECESSARY COREQUISITE FOR
EXTRINSIC MOTIVATION SINCE THOSE HIGHER IN INTRINSIC
MOTIVATION ARE ALSO HIGHER IN THEIR MOTIVATION FOR
PERFORMANCE-CONTINGENT EXTRINSIC REWARDS.

M0094 DEUTERMANN, WILLIAM V.
EDUCATIONAL ATTAINMENT OF WORKERS, MARCH 1973.
MONTHLY LABOR REVIEW, JANUARY 1974, PP. 58-62.

A SPECIAL LABOR FORCE REPORT SHOWS CONTINUED NARROWING
OF THE EDUCATIONAL GAP BETWEEN THE SEXES, AND BETWEEN
WHITES AND MEMBERS OF RACIAL MINORITIES.

M0095 DEVILLE, JARD.
SUCCESSFUL LEADERS ARE SUCCESSFUL MOTIVATORS.
SUPERVISORY MANAGEMENT 18 (JULY 1973): 23-26+.

THE ARTICLE SETS FORTH A NUMBER OF TECHNIQUES THAT
SUPERVISORS CAN USE TO MOTIVATE WORKERS. AMONG THEM ARE THE
FOLLOWING: 1) ENCOURAGE COOPERATION; 2) ESTABLISH POSITIVE
DISCIPLINE; 3) OFFER REGULAR AND WELL SPECIFIED REWARDS;
4) MAINTAIN CONSISTENCY; 5) ACCEPT INDIVIDUALITY, AND
6) RECOGNIZE FLEXIBILITY WITH RESPECT TO COMPANY POLICY.

M0096 DEVIVO, PAUL.   DEVIVO, SANDY.
HELP FOR THE WOMAN BREADWINNER.
MANPOWER, FEBRUARY 1973, PP. 9-14.

THE FEMALE JOB PLACEMENT PROGRAM ATTEMPTS TO CHANGE
THE PERCEPTIONS OF ITS ENROLLEES ABOUT THE KINDS OF WORK
THEY CAN DO, SO THAT WOMEN WHO ARE HEADS OF HOUSEHOLDS
CAN HAVE JOB OPTIONS AND PAY INCREASED.

M0097 DEWITT, GEORGE L.
MAN AT WORK.
PERSONNEL JOURNAL 49 (OCTOBER 1970): 824-26.

OF LATE, EMPHASIS HAS BEEN PLACED ON HOW THE FACTORY
SHOULD ADJUST TO THE WORKER. A TRAINING SUPERVISOR ATTEMPTS
TO EXPLAIN HOW THE WORKER GOT INTO HIS DILEMMA AND HOW
PART OF THE ADJUSTMENT HAS TO MADE BY THE MAN ON THE JOB.

M0098 DHIR, KRISHNA S.
PROBLEM OF MOTIVATION IN MANAGEMENT DEVELOPMENT.
PERSONNEL JOURNAL 49 (OCTOBER 1970): 837-42.

WHY DO MANAGERS EXHIBIT RESISTANCE TO DEVELOPMENT
PROGRAMS? SEVERAL REASONS ARE GIVEN AND THE AUTHOR
DISCUSSES OTHER PROBLEMS ENCOUNTERED IN MOTIVATING
MANAGERS TO ACHIEVE THROUGH MANAGEMENT DEVELOPMENT

M0098   PROGRAMS THEIR GOAL OF BECOMING BETTER MANAGERS.

M0099   DIAMOND, D. E.   BEDROSIAN, HRACH.
        JOB PERFORMANCE AND THE NEW CREDENTIALISM.
        CALIFORNIA MANAGEMENT REVIEW 15 (SUMMER 1972):   21-28.

        NEW AND POWERFUL RESTRICTIONS TO OCCUPATIONAL MOBILITY
HAVE EMERGED WHICH ARE BASED ON THE TECHNOLOGICAL CHARACTER
OF THE WORK AND THE WORK PLACE. BECAUSE THEY ARE
ARBITRARILY CONCEIVED AND APPLIED TO WORK SITUATIONS,
RELIGION, ETHNIC BACKGROUND AND SEX,   AFFECT   THE JOB
MARKET FOR BLUE COLLAR WORKERS.

        IN THE LAST FEW YEARS AMERICA HAS BECOME INCREASINGLY
CREDENTIALS-MINDED. SUCH THINGS AS EDUCATION, AGE, UNION
MEMBERSHIP, PREVIOUS WORK EXPERIENCE AND APPEARANCE NORMS
HAVE BECOME REQUIREMENTS FOR JOBS IN OUR TECHNOLOGICAL
SOCIETY, BUT THEY HAVE ALSO BECOME OBSTACLES FOR MANY
WORKERS. IT IS DIFFICULT TO FORECAST A WORKER'S JOB
PERFORMANCE IN THE FUTURE, SO EMPLOYEES RELY HEAVILY ON
CREDENTIALS. EMPLOYERS ARE USING CREDENTIALS AS A METHOD OF
SCREENING AND HIRING WORKERS.
        THE MOST PREDOMINATE CREDENTIAL I   544
CREDENTIAL IS THE ONE MOST LOOKED FOR ON JOB APPLICATIONS
AND MAYBE ONE THAT NEEDS THE CLOSEST ATTENTION. WHILE OUR
MODERN TECHNOLOGY MAKES MANY JOBS EASIER AND IN REALITY
THEY REQUIRE LESS EDUCATION TO DO, DEMANDS FOR A HIGHER
EDUCATION STILL GO UP. STUDIES SHOW THAT DISSATISFACTION
AMONG WORKERS IN LOW-SKILLED JOBS INCREASED AS EDUCATION
INCREASED. THIS INCREASES WORKER TURNOVER AND ABSENTEEISM.
        THESE UNWARRANTED CREDENTIAL REQUIREMENTS IMPOSE
SEVERAL UNNECESSARY COSTS ON EMPLOYERS. WORKERS THAT ARE
OVER QUALIFIED ARE GIVEN JOBS THAT LEAD THEM TO
DISSATISFACTION, WHICH LEADS TO HIGH WORKER TURNOVER.
WORKERS THAT ARE UNDERQUALIFIED ACCORDING TO THE
CREDENTIALS REQUIRED ARE NEVER GIVEN THE JOBS EVEN IF
THEY MAY BE THE BEST QUALIFIED FOR THE JOB.   THIS
LABOR SHORTAGE COULD CUT PRODUCTION, RAISE OVERTIME
PAY, OR KEEP CUSTOMERS FROM BEING SERVICED PROPERLY.
ANOTHER IMPORTANT DRAWBACK TO HIGH CREDENTIAL STANDARDS IS
THAT THE EMPLOYER MAY BE PAYING HIGHER WAGES THAN NEED BE
FOR A PARTICULAR JOB.
                IN ORDER TO CURB THIS PROBLEM, EMPLOYERS SHOULD
REASSESS THEIR HIRING MINIMUMS AND PREFERENCES FOR THE
LOW-AND SEMI-SKILLED JOBS. EACH JOB SHOULD BE CAREFULLY
ANALYZED AND THE VERY MINIMUM REQUIREMENTS WRITTEN DOWN
IN ORDER FOR THE BEST QUALIFIED, AND NOT OVER QUALIFIED,
MAN TO GET THE JOB.

M0100   DICESARE, CONSTANCE B.
        CHANGES IN THE OCCUPATIONAL STRUCTURE OF U. S. JOBS.
        MONTHLY LABOR REVIEW, MARCH 1975, PP. 24-34.

        ANALYSIS OF CENSUS DATA SHOWS THAT WOMEN'S JOB GROWTH
BETWEEN 1960 AND 1970 WAS GREATEST IN CLERICAL AND SERVICE
JOBS, ALREADY DOMINATED BY WOMEN.

M0101   DICESARE, CONSTANCE B.

M0101   INSURANCE ADJUSTERS AND EXAMINERS.
OCCUPATIONAL OUTLOOK QUARTERLY 15 (SUMMER 1971):   25-30.
          WHEN A CLAIM IS MADE, THESE WORKERS MUST MAKE A
CAREFUL INVESTIGATION OF THE CIRCUMSTANCES. EMPLOYMENT
OUTLOOK FOR ADJUSTERS IS PARTICULARLY PROMISING.

M0102   DICHTER, ERNEST.
MOTIVATING HUMAN BEHAVIOR.
NEW YORK: MCGRAW-HILL BOOK COMPANY, 1971.

          WRITTEN BY THE PRESIDENT OF THE INSTITUTE FOR
MOTIVATIONAL RESEARCH AT CROTON-ON-HUDSON, NEW YORK.
TAKES POINT OF VIEW WE NEED MORE SCIENCE, NOT LESS TO
SOLVE HUMAN PROBLEMS. WE SHOULD TAKE UP OUR NEW FOUND
TOOLS AND MOTIVATE MAN'S BEHAVIOR. HE DOES, HOWEVER,
ADMIT TO QUESTIONS SUCH AS WHO WILL MOTIVATE? WHO? TO DO
WHAT? THE BOOK IS A COLLECTION OF TECHNIQUES
DISCOVERED IN THIRTY YEARS OF STUDY.

M0103   DICKSON, JOHN W.
WHAT'S IN A JOB.
PERSONNEL MANAGEMENT   3 (JUNE 1972):   38-40.

          THERE ARE THREE KEY FEATURES THAT ARE FOUND IN A JOB.
THEY ARE: . . . THE PREDICTABILITY, THE VARIETY, AND THE
MEANING WHICH THE INDIVIDUAL DISCOVERS IN THE WORK
SITUATION.
          TECHNOLOGICAL FACTORS ARE THE BACKGROUND FOR MOST JOB
DESIGNS TODAY. IT IS BECAUSE OF THESE FACTORS THAT
PEOPLE ARE HAVING TO MAKE ADJUSTMENTS TO THEIR JOBS. THIS
ADJUSTMENT LEADS TO THE AMOUNT OF IMPORTANCE AN EMPLOYEE
PLACES ON HIS WORK.
          THE WORK SITUATION HAS THREE CHARACTERISTICS WHICH THE
EMPLOYEE FINDS TO BE OF GREAT HELP IN DETERMINING THE
IMPORTANCE OF THE JOB HE IS PERFORMING. THEY ARE
PREDICTABILITY, VARIETY, AND MEANING OF THE WORK SITUATION.
          PREDICTABILITY MAY BE EXPRESSED AS . . .THE EXTENT TO
WHICH AN INDIVIDUAL IS NOT CONFRONTED BY UNEXPECTED EVENTS
IN WORK.   THE LESS PREDICTABLE A JOB IS, THE MORE AND
LARGER THE NUMBER OF DECISIONS AND THE MORE AND
LARGER THE AMOUNT OF VARIETY THE WORKER MUST POSSESS IN
ORDER TO PERFORM HIS WORK.
          ONE WAY THAT WAS USED TO MEASURE VARIETY IN THE WORK
SITUATION WAS TO DETERMINE THE AMOUNT OF CHANGE THAT TAKES
PLACE WITHIN A CERTAIN LENGTH OF TIME. THIS CAN BE A NUMBER
OF TASKS THAT HAVE BEEN FINISHED IN AN HOUR, DAY, WEEK, OR
EVEN A MONTH. FOR EXAMPLE,IN J. W. DICKSON'S STUDY OF A
MEAT FACTORY, THE CURERS SAID VARIETY OCCURRED ONCE A WEEK,
COINCIDING WITH A CHANGE IN KINDS OF MEAT. THE PACKERS
IN THE SAME FACTORY SAID THEY HAD VARIETY EVERYDAY.
          FRAGMENTATION, OR THE MEANING OF THE WORK SITUATION, IS
THE LACK OF COHESIVE TASKS THAT AN INDIVIDUAL MIGHT
PERFORM. PEOPLE WHO HAVE BACKGROUNDS FROM THE RURAL AREAS
ARE NOT AS SUITED TO PERFORM WORK THAT CONTAINS
FRAGMENTATION OF JOBS. THOSE WORKERS COMING FROM THE URBAN
AREAS ARE BETTER SUITED FOR THIS KIND OF WORK.
          J. W. DICKSON BELIEVES THAT ONCE PREDICTABILITY,
VARIETY, AND FRAGMENTATION OF TASKS ARE UNDERSTOOD, PEOPLE

M0103   WILL START TO DESIGN SYSTEMS THAT WILL MEET THE NEEDS OF THE
        WORKERS. ONCE THIS HAS BEEN DONE THE WORKERS' BEHAVIOR
        WILL COME TO MEET THE NEEDS OF THE EMPLOYER.

M0104   DIFFERENCES IN HOURLY EARNINGS BETWEEN MEN AND WOMEN.
        MONTHLY LABOR REVIEW 94 (MAY 1971):   9-15.

            THE DIFFERENTIAL IS LARGE: ON AVERAGE, WOMEN EARN
        ONLY 60 PERCENT AS MUCH AS MEN.

M0105   DILLION, DONALD.
        TOWARD MATCHING PERSONAL AND JOB CHARACTERISTICS.
        OCCUPATIONAL OUTLOOK QUARTERLY 15 (WINTER 1971):   11-22.

            TWENTY-FIVE PERSONAL AND OCCUPATIONAL CHARACTERISTICS
        AND REQUIREMENTS ARE CROSSMATCHED WITH 268 OCCUPATIONS
        TO HELP YOUNG PEOPLE AND THEIR COUNSELORS IN MAKING CAREER
        DECISIONS.

M0106   DISTRIBUTION OF JOB SATISFACTION IN THE WORK FORCE.
        MANPOWER RESEARCH MONOGRAPH NO. 30, 1974, PP. 22-27.

            HOW OCCUPATION, SEX, AND EDUCATION AFFECT JOB
        SATISFACTION.
        STATISTICAL DATA USED IN THIS PARTICULAR ARTICLE WERE
        DRAWN FROM THE 1972-73 QUALITY OF EMPLOYMENT SURVEY. THE
        SURVEY WAS BASED ON A 28-QUESTION MEASURE OF OVERALL JOB
        SATISFACTION.
            THE ARTICLE DEALT WITH VARYING LEVELS OF JOB
        SATISFACTION ACCORDING TO THE EMPLOYEE'S OCCUPATION, SEX,
        AND EDUCATIONAL LEVEL.
            WHEN DEALING WITH OCCUPATIONAL CATEGORIES,
        PROFESSIONAL-TECHNICAL WORKERS AND MANAGERS, OFFICIALS,
        AND PROPRIETORS REGISTER THE HIGHEST LEVELS OF JOB
        SATISFACTION. TWO MAIN REASONS WHY WORKERS IN THESE
        OCCUPATIONS ARE MORE SATISFIED THAN OTHERS IS THE FINANCIAL
        ASPECTS OF THE WORK AND THE AMOUNT OF CHALLENGE THEIR
        JOBS OFFER. THOSE WORKERS REGISTERING THE LEAST
        SATISFACTION ARE OPERATIVES AND NONFARM LABORERS.
            THERE WAS LITTLE DIFFERENCE IN THE LEVEL OF JOB
        SATISFACTION BETWEEN MEN AND WOMEN--NEVER MORE THAN A 7%
        DIFFERENCE (THAT BEING IN 1969, WITH 7% MORE MEN THAN WOMEN
        SATISFIED WITH THEIR PRESENT OCCUPATIONAL LEVEL.
            WHERE SEX DEFFERENCES IN JOB SATISFACTION DID OCCUR,
        THEY WERE ONLY SLIGHT, WITH THE EXCEPTION OF ONE CATEGORY--
        THAT BEING THE PRESENCE OF PRESCHOOL CHILDREN IN THE
        WORKER'S HOUSEHOLD. ACCORDING TO THE SURVEY, WOMEN WITH ONE
        OR MORE CHILDREN UNDER 6 YEARS OF AGE IN THE HOUSEHOLD ARE
        SIGNIFICANTLY LESS SATISFIED WITH THEIR JOBS THAN WERE WOMEN
        WITHOUT YOUNG CHILDREN. THESE WOMEN ARE ALSO LESS
        SATISFIED THAN MALE WORKERS, REGARDLESS OF WHETHER OR NOT
        THERE ARE PRESCHOOLERS IN A MAN'S HOUSEHOLD.
            WHEN THE WORKER'S EDUCATIONAL LEVEL IS CONSIDERED, THE
        DISTRIBUTION OF JOB SATISFACTION DOES NOT CORRELATE AS ONE
        MIGHT EXPECT. WHAT THE ARTICLE DID BRING OUT IS THAT FOR
        EACH INCREMENT IN EDUCATION, THERE WAS NOT A CORRESPONDING
        PAYOFF IN TERMS OF INCREMENT IN JOB SATISFACTION.
        THE SURVEY SHOWS THAT THE ASSOCIATION BETWEEN JOB

M0106   SATISFACTION AND EDUCATIONAL LEVEL IS DISTINCTLY ONOLINEAR.
        IF THE SURVEY IS LOOKED AT ON A GENERAL BASIS ONE COULD
        CONCLUDE THAT THERE IS A NEGATIVE CORRELATION BETWEEN THE
        WORKER'S EDUCATIONAL LEVEL AND JOB SATISFACTION.

M0107   DONNELLY, JOHN F.
        INCREASING PRODUCTIVITY BY INVOLVING PEOPLE IN THEIR TOTAL
        JOB.
        PERSONNEL ADMINISTRATION 34 (SEPTEMBER-OCTOBER 1971):   8-13.

            HOW DONNELLY MIRRORS, INC. INCREASED PRODUCTIVITY AND
        PROFITS THROUGH BEHAVIORAL SCIENCE APPROACHES. AN ACCOUNT
        OF HOW THE COMPANY BECAME INVOLVED, WHAT IT DID
        SPECIFICALLY, WHAT RESULTS WERE ACHIEVED, AND HOW A PERSON
        MIGHT GET HIS COMPANY TO TAKE ON SUCH A PROGRAM.

M0108   DOOLITTLE, MARY E.
        HELPING THE HAVE-NOT GIRLS.
        MANPOWER, MARCH 1973, PP. 8-13.

            A FORMER CENTER DIRECTOR TALKS ABOUT LIFE IN THE JOB
        CORPS-- ITS JOYS AND PROBLEMS, AND WHAT IT TAKES TO HELP
        DISADVANTAGED YOUNG WOMEN GAIN CONFIDENCE IN THEMSELVES
        AND THE COMPETENCE TO MAKE A LIVING.

M0109   DORE, RUSSELL   MEACHOM, MERLE.
        SELF-CONCEPT AND INTERESTS RELATED TO JOB SATISFACTION OF
        MANAGERS.
        PERSONNEL PSYCHOLOGY, 26 (SPRING 1973):   49-60.

            THIS STUDY OF 140 MANAGERS IN A MEDIUM SIZED INSURANCE
        COMPANY FOCUSED ON FOUR HYPOTHESES WHICH INVESTIGATED THE
        AGREEMENT BETWEEN DIFFERENT ASPECTS OF SELF AND THE
        RELATIONSHIP OF THIS AGREEMENT TO JOB SATISFACTION. ALL
        FOUR HYPOTHESES WERE SUPPORTED IN THAT SELF-CONCEPT WAS
        SHOWN TO BE RELATED TO JOB SATISFACTION.

M0110   DOWNEY, H. KIRK.   HELLRIGEL, DON.   SLOCUM, JOHN W.
        CONGRUENCE BETWEEN INDIVIDUALS' NEEDS, ORGANIZATIONAL
        CLIMATE, JOB SATISFACTION AND PERFORMANCE.
        ACADEMY OF MANAGEMENT JOURNAL, 18 (MARCH 1975):   149-55.

            THE ARTICLE TESTS THE PROPOSITION THAT ORGANIZATIONAL
        CLIMATE INTEREACTS WITH INDIVIDUAL PERSONALITY IN
        INFLUENCING JOB SATISFACTION AND PERFORMANCE.

M0111   DRUCKER, PETER F.
        BEYOND STICK AND CARROT: HYSTERIA OVER THE WORK ETHIC.
        PSYCHOLOGY TODAY 7(NOVEMBER 1973): 86-7, 89-92.

        IN THIS EXCERPT FORM HIS FORTHCOMING BOOK, DRUCKER ANALYZES
        WORKER RESISTANCE TO MANIPULATION. HE FINDS THAT THE
        TRADITIONAL CARROT AND STICK DO NOT WORK FOR MANUAL WORKERS
        IN DEVELOPED COUNTRIES AND THAT THEY WORK NOT AT ALL FOR
        KNOWLEDGE WORKERS. HE FEELS, HOWEVER, THAT WE DO KNOW HOW
        TO MAKE WORK PRODUCTIVE AND THAT WORKER AND WORK-GROUP NEED
        TO TAKE RESPONSIBILITY FOR JOB DESIGN AND FOR WORKGROUP
        STRUCTURE AS WELL AS FOR FRINGE BENEFITS.

M0112   DUBRIN, ANDREW.
        THE PRACTICE OF MANAGERIAL PSYCHOLOGY.
        NEW YORK: PERGAMON PRESS, 1972.

        A TEXTBOOK SHOWING METHODS USED BY MANAGERIAL
        PSYCHOLOGISTS. DISCUSSES MOTIVATION AND GROUP APPROACHES
        TO DEVELOPMENT AS WELL AS THE IMPORTANT ROLE PLAYED BY
        THE SUPERVISOR IN THE DEVELOPMENT OF MIDDLE MANAGEMENT.

M0113   DUGARD, GEORGE A.   HOLT, GEORGE.
        EFFECTIVE LEADERSHIP.
        THE NAVIGATOR, 21 (FALL 1974): 9-11.

        GOAL IDENTIFICATION AS RELATED TO LEADERSHIP IN THE AIR
        FORCE.

M0114   DUNNETTE, M. D.   ARVEY, RICHARD D.   BANAS, PAUL A.
        WHY DO THEY LEAVE.
        PERSONNEL, 30 (MAY-JUNE 1973): 25-39.

        OVER 1,000 COLLEGE GRADUATES WERE SURVEYED TO FIND OUT
        WHY OVER HALF OF THEM LEAVE THEIR JOB AFTER THE FIRST FOUR
        OR FIVE YEARS.
            LARGE LOSSES OF EMPLOYEES WITH COLLEGE DEGREES AND THE
        ABILITY TO MOVE AHEAD IN JOB POSITIONS ARE BEING FELT BY THE
        EMPLOYERS WHO HAVE TRIED HARD TO EMPLOY THEM. TO FIND OUT
        WHY THESE PEOPLE LEAVE THEIR JOBS, M. D. DUNNETTE, R. D.
        ARVEY, AND P. A. BANAS SURVEYED PRESENT AND PAST EMPLOYEES
        OF ONE COMPANY.
            UPON GRADUATION FROM COLLEGE, THE TERMINEES AND
        NONTERMINEES HELD MUCH THE SAME MOTIVATIONAL IDEAS. THE
        MOST IMPORTANT JOB FACTOR WAS SALARY, FOLLOWED BY
        OPPORTUNITIES FOR ACHIEVEMENT, ACCOMPLISHMENT, USES OF
        ABILITIES, AND INTERESTING WORK. THE LEAST IMPORTANT WAS
        HIGH STATUS. THE FIRST JOB EXPERIENCE WAS A SOURCE
        OF GREAT DISSATISFACTION IN HOPES AND PROSPECTS OF USING
        THEIR ABILITIES. THE FEELING OF ACCOMPLISHMENT WAS THE ONLY
        ONE OUT OF THE FIVE MOTIVATIONAL AREAS THAT WAS SATISFIED.
            IN THE BOOK, WORK AND MOTIVATION, VICTOR H. VROOM
        THEORIZES . . . THE FORCE IMPELLING A PERSON TO EXERT EFFORT
        IN A JOB AND/OR TOWARD STAYING IN A PARTICULAR JOB
        SITUATION DEPENDS ON THE INTERACTION BETWEEN WHAT THE PERSON
        WANTS IN A JOB AND THE DEGREE TO WHICH HE BELIEVES THAT
        A COMPANY WILL REWARD EFFORT EXERTED ON THAT JOB WITH
        THE THINGS HE WANTS.
            THE THREE CHARACTERS IN THIS THEORY ARE VALENCE
        (DESIRABILITY OF A TASK AS PERCEIVED BY AN INDIVIDUAL),
        INSTRUMENTALITY (CONNECTION BETWEEN ACCOMPLISHMENTS AND THE
        REWARDS FOR THEM), AND EXPECTANCY (THE BELIEF THAT THROUGH
        WORK COMES ACCOMPLISHMENTS).
            VALENCE IS MEASURED BY THE AMOUNT OF IMPORTANCE GIVEN
        TO JOB FEATURES. INSTRUMENTALITY IS MEASURED BY THE
        CERTAINTY OF GOOD JOB PERFORMANCE AND THE ADVANCEMENT IN
        POSITIONS. EXPECTANCY IS MEASURED BY THAT WHICH ONE
        BELIEVES THAT JOB RECOGNITION AND JOB PERFORMANCE ARE
        RELATED.
            THE ABOVE MOTIVATION INDEX POINTS OUT THAT MANY COLLEGE
        GRADUATES ARE DISSATISFIED WITH THE EXPERIENCE THEY ARE

M0114   RECEIVING AND THEIR DESIRES WHEN THEY FIRST START TO WORK.
         THIS MOTIVATIONAL INDEX IS NOT ONLY USED TO POINT OUT
         TROUBLED AREAS, BUT ALSO, ENABLES CHECKS ON WORK UNITS AS
         NEW PRACTICES ARE TRIED.

M0115   DRUKETT, NANCY.
         CUTTING INTO THE SAWMILL SKILL SHORTAGE.
         MANPOWER 3 (JUNE 1971): 29-30.

         THE HAYWOOD INSTITUTE MADE A STUDY OF THE LUMBER
         INDUSTRY AND FOUND A SEVERE SHORTAGE OF SKILLED SAWMILL
         TECHNICIANS.
         W. J. SEIBERT, HAYWOOD'S DIRECTOR OF OCCUPATIONAL
         EDUCATION, AND WALTER D. RICE, HEAD OF THE SCHOOL'S
         FORESTRY DIVISION, VISITED COLLEGES IN FOUR STATES AND FOUND
         THAT WHILE SOME WERE TRAINING SAWYERS AND SAW FILERS,
         THEY HAD NOT MADE A DENT IN THE DEMAND. AFTER FINDING OUT
         APPROXIMATELY WHAT THE COST WOULD BE, THEY REALIZED THE
         STATE DID NOT HAVE THAT KIND OF MONEY AVAILABLE. A COUPLE
         OF MONTHS LATER, HAYWOOD, WHICH IS PART OF NORTH CAROLINA'S
         STATEWIDE COMPLEX OF COMMUNITY COLLEGES AND TECHNICAL
         INSTITUTES, WAS BLESSED WITH A WINDFALL. CHAMPION PAPER
         COMPANY HAD PURCHASED A 9,000-ACRE TRACT OF WOODLAND WHICH
         INCLUDED A LARGE INDUSTRIAL CIRCULAR SAWMILL. THE COMPANY
         HAD NO USE FOR THE MILL SO THEY GAVE IT TO HAYWOOD. SHORTLY
         THEREAFTER THE GIFTS BEGAN TO ROLL IN. ACCORDING TO
         SEIBERT, THE WELL-EQUIPPED SAWMILL COMPLEX, AS IT STANDS
         TODAY, IS VALUED AT $600,000. ONLY $40,000 OF THIS AMOUNT
         CAME FROM STATE GOVERNMENT FUNDS. THE REMAINDER CAME FROM
         DONATIONS.
         ACTUAL TRAINING GOT UNDERWAY IN JUNE 1969 AFTER THE
         U. S. DEPARTMENT OF LABOR'S MANPOWER ADMINISTRATION
         APPROVED THE PROGRAM FOR FUNDING UNDER THE MANPOWER
         DEVELOPMENT AND TRAINING ACT. STUDENTS RANGE FROM 18 TO 45
         YEARS OLD. SOME ARE BLACK AND SOME ARE WHITE, AND ALL
         WERE UNEMPLOYED OR UNDEREMPLOYED WHEN THEY ENTERED THE
         PROGRAM. THEY TRAIN 40 HOURS A WEEK FOR 40 WEEKS. AT THE
         BEGINNING OF THE COURSE, MOST TRAINING IS CLASSROOM WORK.
         TOWARD THE END, NEARLY ALL THE STUDENTS' TIME IS SPENT IN
         SKILL INSTRUCTION. OVERALL, SKILL TRAINING ACCOUNTS FOR
         ABOUT TWO-THIRDS OF THE STUDENTS' TIME.
         TRAINEES WHO COMPLETE THE COURSE ARE IN CONSIDERABLE
         DEMAND. SAWMILLS THROUGHOUT THE REGION SEND RECRUITERS
         ON CAMPUS BEFORE GRADUATION MUCH THE SAME WAY AS THE
         NATION'S LARGE INDUSTRIAL CORPORATIONS USED TO GO AFTER
         ENGINEERING STUDENTS.
         THE IMPORTANCE OF KEEPING IN CLOSE TOUCH WITH WHAT IS
         HAPPENING IN INDUSTRY IS REFLECTED IN THE SELECTION OF
         INSTRUCTORS. ALL ARE EXPERIENCED CRAFTSMEN RATHER THAN
         PROFESSIONAL TEACHERS. COURSE CONTENT REFLECTS CURRENT
         INDUSTRY PRACTICES. AN INDUSTRY ADVISORY COMMITTEE REVIEWS
         THE COURSES AND SKILL TECHNIQUES TAUGHT TO MAKE CERTAIN
         THEY ARE UP TO DATE.
         ONE OF THE THINGS INDUSTRY MOST WANTS, OF COURSE, IS AN
         ADEQUATE SUPPLY OF COMPETENT MANPOWER. AND ON THAT SCORE
         THE HAYWOOD PROGRAM ALREADY HAS WON STRONG ENDORSEMENT.

M0116   EDITORIAL RESEARCH REPORTS ON THE AMERICAN WORK ETHIC.

M0116 CONGRESSIONAL QUARTERLY, INC., WASHINGTON, D. C.
       A GROUP OF ARTICLES EXPLORING THE WIDENING PROBLEM
OF MAKING PEOPLE WANT TO WORK. PERHAPS WORKERS BECOME
MORE BORED AS THEY BECOME BETTER EDUCATED? MUCH INFORMATION
IN A CLEAR AND CONCISE FORMAT. AMONG ARTICLES ARE
ARGUMENTS ABOUT A FOUR-DAY WORK WEEK AND NEW ATTITUDES OF
BLUE COLLAR WORKERS.
EDUCATIONAL COMPUTER CORPORATION.
ACCELERATED TRAINING OF UNEMPLOYED AND UNDEREMPLOYED THROUGH
SPECIALIZED PROGRAM INSTRUCTION AND THE SMART TRAINER.
PHASES I AND II.
NTIS PB 199976 AND 210864.   (1972)
       TRAINING THROUGH USE OF A WORK SIMULATION DEVICE
FOR PEOPLE WHO DO NOT READ WELL. PEOPLE WERE TRAINED IN
THREE AREAS: AUTO MECHANICS, APPLIANCE SERVICE,
HEATING MECHANICS. MAJOR FINDING: THE TRAINING PROGRAM
USING PROGRAMMED INSTRUCTION WAS SUCCESSFUL.
THE TRAINING MACHINE APPEALED TO THE STUDENTS; THERE
WAS A LOW DROP OUT RATE; WHEN WORKERS ENTERED THE JOB
MARKET THEY WERE OFFERED TEN CENTS AN HOUR OVER THE
MINIMUM; NINETY-ONE PERCENT OF THE WORKERS WERE STILL
EMPLOYED A YEAR AND A HALF LATER; CONSEQUENTLY, MOTIVATION
WAS HIGH BECAUSE OF THEIR SUCCESS. LOCATION OF EXPERIMENT
- PAOLI, PA.

M0117 EHRLE, RAYMOND A.
       BUSINESS HEALTH--MENTAL HEALTH: GROWTH ALTERNATIVE TO
INTERVENTION.
PERSONNEL JOURNAL 51 (DECEMBER 1973): 898-905.

M0118 ERICSSON, TORE.   MIRSBURGER, GERALD.
       RESPONSIBILITY IN MANAGEMENT -- WHAT DOES IT REALLY MEAN.
SAM ADVANCED MANAGEMENT JOURNAL 38 (OCTOBER 1973):   36-45.

       THIS ARTICLE VOICES THE NEED FOR GUIDELINES AND
STANDARDS AGAINST WHICH PERFORMANCE CAN BE MEASURED.

M0119 ETZIONI, AMITAI.   SONTAG, MARVIN.
       MUTUAL ADAPTABILITY OF WORKERS AND ORGANIZATIONS.
WASHINGTON, D. C.: U. S. DEPARTMENT OF LABOR, MANPOWER
ADMINISTRATION, 1971.

       THE PRINCIPAL OBJECTIVE OF THIS STUDY WAS TO
DEVELOP CONCEPTUAL AND OPERATIONAL TOOLS FOR ACHIEVING
A MORE EFFECTIVE MATCH OF PERSONS WITH JOBS, THEREBY
FACILITATING BOTH JOB RETENTION AND WORK PERFORMANCE.

M0120 EVANS, MARTIN G.
       EXTENSIONS OF A PATH-GOAL THEORY OF MOTIVATION.
JOURNAL OF APPLIED PSYCHOLOGY, 59 (APRIL 1974):   172-78.

       ARTICLE EXPLORES IMPLICATIONS OF THE GOAL-PATH THEORY
OF MOTIVATION IN THE BEHAVIOR OF SUPERIORS AND SUBORDINATES.
OF THE THREE MODERATORS USED, (SUBORDINATE'S LOCUS OF
CONTROL, THE SUBORDINATE'S POSITION IN THE WEB OF ROLE
RELATIONSHIPS, AND THE SUPERVISOR'S UPWARD INFLUENCE) ONLY
THE FIRST WAS FOUND TO AFFECT THE SUPERIOR/SUBORDINATE
RELATIONSHIP.

M0121   EVANS, MARTIN G.
         LEADERSHIP AND MOTIVATION: A CORE CONCEPT.
         ACADEMY OF MANAGEMENT JOURNAL   13 (MARCH 1970):   91-102.

         THE OBJECTIVE OF THIS ARTICLE IS TO DISCUSS HOW THE
BEHAVIOR OF THE SUPERVISOR CAN AFFECT THE EMPLOYEE. IN
ORDER TO DISCUSS THIS RELATIONSHIP, EVANS EXPLORES A WORKING
THEORY OF MOTIVATION, AND A THEORY WHICH RELATES
SUPERVISORY BEHAVIOR TO EMPLOYEE MOTIVATION.
         THERE ARE TWO STRANDS TO THIS WORKING THEORY OF
MOTIVATION. THE FIRST CONCERNS THE NATURE OF THE
NEEDS AND GOALS OF THE INDIVIDUAL AND THE INTERRELATIONSHIP
BETWEEN THESE NEEDS. (PP. 92-93). MAN'S BASIC NEEDS ARE
LISTED IN A HIERARCHY FROM PHYSIOLOGICAL NEEDS TO THE NEED
FOR SELF-ACTUALIZATION.
BECOMES THE INDIVIDUAL'S GOAL.
WORKING THEORY IS REFERRED TO AS THE PATH-GOAL APPROACH
TO MOTIVATION. (P. 93). IT CONCERNS THE INTERRELATIONSHIP
BETWEEN THE ACTION OR BEHAVIOR OF THE INDIVIDUAL AND HIS
GOAL ATTAINMENT AND NEED SATISFACTION. (P. 93). IT ASSUMES
THAT THE INDIVIDUAL IS BASICALLY GOAL ORIENTED AND THAT HE
WILL FOLLOW THE PATH THAT HE PERCEIVES AS LEADING HIM TOWARD
HIS GOAL. THE COMBINATION OF THESE TWO STRANDS REFLECTS
THAT THE INDIVIDUAL WILL CHOOSE A LEVEL OF PERFORMANCE THAT
IS PERCEIVED AS INSTRUMENTAL FOR THE ATTAINMENT OF HIS
GOALS. (P. 95).
ARTICULATION BETWEEN SUPERVISORY BEHAVIOR AND SUBORDINATE
MOTIVATION.
         TWO MAJOR COMPONENTS OF SUPERVISORY BEHAVIOR ARE GIVEN:
THEY ARE INITIATION OF STRUCTURE AND CONSIDERATION.
INITIATION OF STRUCTURE SEEMS TO EMPHASIZE OVERT ATTEMPTS
TO ACHIEVE ORGANIZATIONAL GOALS. (P. 96). THE EMPLOYEE
WANTS HIS REWARDS AND PUNISHMENTS . . . (TO COME) . . . TO
HIM AS A RESULT OF HIS SPECIFIC BEHAVIOR. (P. 97). THE
RESPONSIBILITY OF THE SUPERVISOR, THEREFORE, IS TO INDICATE A
PATH TO FOLLOW BASED ON THE SUBORDINATE'S ABILITIES AND
ASPIRATIONS, AND TO REWARD THE SUCCESSFUL FOLLOWING OF THAT
PATH. THIS RESPONSIBILITY IS ALSO THAT OF CONSIDERATION-
THE OTHER MAJOR COMPONENT OF SUPERVISORY BEHAVIOR,
CONSIDERATION EMPHASIZES A DEEPER CONCERN FOR GROUP
MEMBERS' NEEDS AND INCLUDES SUCH BEHAVIOR AS ALLOWING
SUBORDINATES MORE PARTICIPATION IN DECISION-MAKING AND
ENCOURAGING MORE TWO-WAY COMMUNICATION. (P. 96).
         SUBORDINATE MOTIVATION IS INTERTWINED WITH SUPERVISORY
LEADERSHIP. THE THEORY THAT WORKER BEHAVIOR AND
SATISFACTION DEPEND UPON SUPERVISORY INITIATION OF STRUCTURE
AND CONSIDERATION SEEMS TO HOLD STRONGLY.

M0122   EVANS, MARTIN G.
         THE MODERATING EFFECTS OF INTERNAL VERSUS EXTERNAL
         CONTROL ON THE RELATIONSHIP BETWEEN VARIOUS ASPECTS OF JOB
         SATISFACTION.
         STUDIES IN PERSONNEL PSYCHOLOGY, 5 (SPRING 1973): 37-45.

         THIS STUDY EXPLORES THE UNIVERSALITY OF THE
DISCREPANCY MODEL ('SHOULD BE' --' IS NOW') OF DETERMINING
JOB SATISFACTION (EVANS, 1969; PORTER, 1962). FOLLOWING
KORMAN (1967), A CHARACTERISTIC OF THE INDIVIDUAL (IN THIS

M0122   CASE, THE INTERNAL V. EXTERNAL) CONTROL
        DIMENSION DEVELOPED BY ROTTER (1966) WAS USED TO MODERATE
        THE RELATIONSHIP BETWEEN A MEASURE OF OVERALL
        SATISFACTION AND DISCREPANCY SCORES FOR A NUMBER OF JOB
        FACETS.

M0123   EVANS, ROBERT, JR.
        JAPAN'S LABOR ECONOMY -- PROSPECT FOR THE FUTURE.
        MONTHLY LABOR REVIEW 95 (OCTOBER 1972):   3-8.

            THE PATERNALISTIC INDUSTRIAL SYSTEM IS NOT LIKELY TO
        BE DISCARDED SOON; IT AFFORDS COST FLEXIBILITY AND
        EMPLOYMENT SECURITY.

M0124   FARRIS, GEORGE F.
        MOTIVATING R & D PERFORMANCE IN A STABLE ORGANIZATION.
        RESEARCH MANAGEMENT, 36 (SEPTEMBER 1973):   22-27..

            ARTICLE SUGGESTS TO MANAGERS SOME TECHNIQUES FOR
        INCREASING TECHNICAL PERFORMANCE OF EMPLOYEES WHO HAVE BEEN
        ACCUSTOMED TO WORKING IN A FAST GROWTH SITUATION AND ARE NOW
        IN A STABLE NO-GROWTH ONE.

M0125   FARRIS, GEORGE F.
        A PREDICTIVE STUDY OF TURNOVER.
        PERSONNEL PSYCHOLOGY 24 (1971):   311-28.

        HYPOTHESES
        1.   TURNOVER IS POSITIVELY ASSOCIATED WITH THE PERCEIVED
        EASE OF MOVEMENT AND THE PERCEPTION THAT TURNOVER WOULD HELP
        THE PERSON'S CAREER.
        2.   TURNOVER IS NEGATIVELY ASSOCIATED WITH A PERSON'S
        INVOLVEMENT WITH HIS WORK.
        3.   TURNOVER IS NEGATIVELY ASSOCIATED WITH A PERSON'S
        USEFULNESS TO HIS ORGANIZATION.
        4.   TURNOVER IS NEGATIVELY ASSOCIATED WITH INCOME,
        PROVISION IN THE JOB FOR SELF ACTUALIZATION, PROVISION FOR
        STATUS AND   SOCIAL   PROVISION.
        5.   TURNOVER IS ASSOCIATED POSITIVELY WITH AN OUTSIDE
        ORIENTATION, POSITIVELY WITH A PROFESSIONAL ORIENTATION,
        NEGATIVELY WITH AN INSTITUTIONAL ORIENTATION, POSITIVELY
        WITH INDEPENDANCE, AND POSITIVELY ASSOCIATED WITH HAVING A
        REFERENCE GROUP OUTSIDE THE ORGANIZATION.
        6.   TURNOVER IS ASSOCIATED NEGATIVELY WITH A PERSON'S AGE,
        NEGATIVELY WITH HIS CAREER LEVEL, POSITIVELY WITH HIS
        EDUCATIONAL ACHIEVEMENT, AND NEGATIVELY WITH A LONG RANGE
        TIME PERSPECTIVE.
        7.   TURNOVER IS ASSOCIATED NEGATIVELY WITH THE EXTENT TO
        WHICH THE PERSON CAN INFLUENCE DECISIONS CONCERNING HIS
        WORK GOALS, NEGATIVELY WITH THE DIVERSITY OF THE PERSON'S
        WORK ACTIVITIES, NEGATIVELY WITH THE PERSON'S CONTACTS
        INSIDE THE ORGANIZATION, POSITIVELY WITH THE PERSON'S
        CONTACTS OUTSIDE THE ORGANIZATION, AND NEGATIVELY WITH A
        PERSON'S WORKING HOURS.
        8.   TURNOVER IS ASSOCIATED NEGATIVELY WITH THE FREQUENCY
        OF GROUP MEETINGS, NEGATIVELY WITH THE AMOUNT OF
        ORGANIZATION IN THE GROUP, POSITIVELY WITH GROUP SIZE,
        NEGATIVELY WITH COMPETITION BETWEEN GROUPS, AND

M0125 POSITIVELY WITH SECRECY WITHIN THE GROUP.
9. ORGANIZATIONAL GENERALITY. SIMILAR RELATIONSHIPS
ARE EXPECTED BETWEEN THE PREDICTORS AND TURNOVER IN THE TWO
ORGANIZATIONS PARTICIPATING IN THE STUDY.
10. PERFORMANCE GENERALITY. HYPOTHESES 1-8 ARE EXPECTED TO
APPLY FOR BOTH HIGH AND LOW PERFORMERS.
CONCLUSIONS
1. IT IS POSSIBLE TO PREDICT TURNOVER ON THE BASIS OF
RESPONSES TO AN ANONYMOUS QUESTIONNAIRE COMPLETED WHILE THE
PERSON IS STILL EMPLOYED. THIS ABILITY TO PREDICT TURNOVER
IN THE ABOVE MANNER IS FAR FROM BEING PERFECTED.
2. PREDICTION WAS STRONGER FOR HIGH PERFORMERS THAN FOR LOW
PERFORMERS.

M0126 FEHD, CAROLYN S.
PRODUCTIVITY IN THE PETROLEUM PIPELINES INDUSTRY.
MONTHLY LABOR REVIEW 94 (APRIL 1971): 46-48.

EXAMINES CONDITIONS IN THE PETROLEUM INDUSTRY AND
ITS ROLE IN THE RISE OF OUTPUT PER MAN-HOUR.

M0127 FELDMAN, EDWIN B.
HIGH MOTIVATION, HIGH PRODUCTIVITY.
SUPERVISORY MANAGEMENT 16 (JANUARY 1971): 30-33.

THE UNDERLYING IDEA OF THIS ARTICLE IS THAT EMPLOYEES
WHO ARE HIGHLY MOTIVATED WILL CONSEQUENTLY BE MORE
PRODUCTIVE. SEVERAL FACTORS UPON WHICH SUCCESSFUL
PERFORMANCE DOES AND DOES NOT DEPEND ARE LISTED AND
DISCUSSED.
SUCCESSFUL PERFORMANCE DOES NOT DEPEND UPON THE DATE,
THE LABOR CLIMATE, SOCIAL CONDITIONS, PERSONAL FACTORS,
SALARY OR EXPERIENCE. AS FOR THE DATE, MANY LABOR PROBLEMS
THAT EXISTED THOUSANDS OF YEARS AGO ARE STILL EXISTING. IT
HAS ALSO BEEN SHOWN THAT EVEN THOUGH THE LABOR CLIMATE,
SOCIAL CONDITIONS, AND PERSONAL FACTORS (SUCH AS PHYSICAL
LIMITATIONS) MAY BE DISADVANTAGEOUS IN SOME CIRCUMSTANCES,
THERE IS NO REAL CONNECTION BETWEEN THESE FACTORS AND
AND EMPLOYEE MOTIVATION. ALTHOUGH SALARY WOULD SEEM
TO BE A GREAT MOTIVATOR, IT HAS BEEN SHOWN THAT PAY
INCREASES ALONE DO NOT BRING ABOUT SUSTAINED BOOSTS IN
PRODUCTIVITY. (P. 32). PREVIOUS EXPERIENCE AS WELL IS NOT
AN INDICATOR THAT AN EMPLOYEE WILL PERFORM WELL.
FOUR FACTORS ON WHICH SUCCESSFUL PERFORMANCE DOES
DEPEND ARE BALANCED WORK LOADS, CONTINUITY, ADEQUATE
EQUIPMENT AND SUPPLIES, AND DEFINED ASSIGNMENTS. PEOPLE
MORE TYPICALLY COMPLAIN ABOUT HAVING MORE TO DO THAN
SOMEONE ELSE THAN THEY DO ABOUT THE TOTAL WORKLOAD.
(P. 32). THEREFORE, AN EQUAL BALANCE OF WORKLOADS SHOULD
CONTRIBUTE TO GOOD PERFORMANCE. CONTINUITY CAN BE
ACHIEVED BY AVOIDING THE SWITCHING AROUND OF AN EMPLOYEE
FROM ONE TASK TO ANOTHER. IF THE EMPLOYEE CAN WORK TOWARD A
GOAL AND MAKE PROGRESS, HE WILL PERFORM MUCH BETTER. A THIRD
FACTOR LEADING TOWARD SUCCESSFUL PERFORMANCE IS HAVING THE
RIGHT EQUIPMENT AND SUPPLIES FOR THE JOB. NO JOB CAN BE
COMPLETED SATISFACTORILY WITHOUT THE NECESSARY TOOLS.
DEFINED ASSIGNMENTS IS THE FINAL FACTOR LISTED IN THIS
ARTICLE. AN EMPLOYEE NEEDS TO KNOW SPECIFICALLY WHAT IS

M0127   EXPECTED OF HIM. THIS KNOWLEDGE ENABLES HIM TO WORK MORE
         CONFIDENTLY BECAUSE HE CAN KNOW WHETHER OR NOT HE IS
         COMPLETING HIS JOB CORRECTLY.
              THE MANAGER WHO WISHES TO IMPROVE PRODUCTIVITY BY
         INCREASING WORKERS' MOTIVATION SHOULD BEGIN BY RECOGNIZING
         WHAT IT IS THAT MOTIVATES PEOPLE. BY IGNORING THOSE
         IRRELEVANT FACTORS AND CONCENTRATING ONLY ON THOSE THAT DO
         INFLUENCE MOTIVATION, THE MANAGER CAN EFFECTIVELY INCREASE
         HIS WORKERS' PRODUCTIVITY.

M0128   FELDMAN, JACK M.
         RACE, EMPLOYMENT, AND THE EVALUATION OF WORK.
         JOURNAL OF APPLIED PSYCHOLOGY, 58 (AUGUST 1973): 10-15.

              THIS PAPER AND THE ONE WHICH FOLLOWS IT, RACE,
         ECONOMIC CLASS, AND PERCEIVED OUTCOMES OF WORK AND
         UNEMPLOYMENT,   PP. 16-22, ARE BASED ON THE AUTHOR'S
         DOCTORAL DISSERTATION AT THE UNIVERSITY OF ILLINOIS. BOTH
         PAPERS DEAL WITH RESEARCH ON RACIAL AND ECONOMIC CLASS
         DIFFERENCES IN ATTITUDES TOWARD WORK AND UNEMPLOYMENT.

M0129   FELDMAN, M. P.
         PSYCHOLOGY IN THE INDUSTRIAL ENVIRONMENT.
         LONDON: BUTTERWORTHS, 1971.

              FITTING THE MAN TO THE JOB: A GUIDE TO MEASUREMENT
         OF FACTORS CONTRIBUTING TO PROPER SELECTION OF A JOB AS WELL
         AS ADJUSTMENT TO THE JOB SITUATION.

M0130   FENLON, JOHN.
         RECENT TRENDS IN OVERTIME HOURS AND PREMIUM PAY.
         MONTHLY LABOR REVIEW 94 (AUGUST 1971): 29-35.

              STUDY OF DOWNWARD TREND IN OVERTIME WORKERS, AND
         MOTIVATIONS BEHIND THE DECLINE.

M0131   FIEDLER, FRED E.
         PERSONALITY, MOTIVATIONAL SYSTEMS, AND BEHAVIOR OF HIGH AND
         LOW LPC PERSONS.
         HUMAN RELATIONS 25 (NOVEMBER 1972): 391-412.

              THIS ARTICLE PRESENTS A NEW INTERPRETATION OF THE LPC
         SCORE WHICH THROWS LIGHT NOT ONLY ON THE LEADERSHIP
         MEASURE BUT ALSO THE DYNAMICS UNDERLYING THE LEADER'S
         INTERPERSONAL AND TASK BEHAVIOR.

M0132   FINE, BARRY DOV.
         COMPARISON OF ORGANIZATIONAL MEMBERSHIP AND
         SELF-EMPLOYMENT.
         PH. D. DISSERTATION, UNIVERSITY OF MICHIGAN, 1971.

              COMPARES THE JOB SATISFACTION AND MENTAL STRAIN
         BETWEEN ORGANIZATIONAL WORKERS AND SELF-EMPLOYED.

M0133   FITZGERALD, THOMAS H.
         WHY MOTIVATION THEORY DOESN'T WORK.
         HARVARD BUSINESS REVIEW 49 (JULY 1971): 37-44.

WE SHOULD DISCARD THE DISMAL VOCABULARY OF MOTIVES,
MOTIVATORS, AND MOTIVATION AND THINK ABOUT BECOMING A
SOCIETY OF PERSONS. INSTEAD OF THINKING OF EMPLOYEES
AS OBJECTS, MANIPULATED BY THIS OR THAT THEORETICAL
APPROACH, MANAGEMENT MUST STRIVE TO EFFECT FUNDAMENTAL,
VALUE-ORIENTED CHANGES IN THE STRUCTURE OF RATIONALIZED WORK
SYSTEMS.

M0134   FLAIM, PAUL O.
        DISCOURAGE WORKERS AND CHANGES IN UNEMPLOYMENT.
        MONTHLY LABOR REVIEW 96 (MARCH 1973): 8-16.

        ANALYSIS OF DATA FROM THE CURRENT POPULATION SURVEY
        INDICATE THE NUMBER OF DISCOURAGED WORKERS RISES AS
        UNEMPLOYMENT INCREASES.

M0135   FLORY, CHARLES D.   MACKENZIE, R. A.
        THE CREDIBILITY GAP IN MANAGEMENT.
        NEW YORK: VAN NOSTRAND REINHOLD COMPANY, 1971.

        A PLEA FOR BETTER ETHICS ON THE PART OF MANAGEMENT
        AND A BETTER GROUP OF LEADERS FOR BUSINESS.

M0136   FOLKER, DAVID A.
        DOES THE INDUSTRIAL ENGINEER DEHUMANIZE JOBS.
        PERSONNEL 50 (JULY 1973): 62-67.

        THIS ARTICLE WAS WRITTEN IN ANSWER TO THE STATEMENT
        MADE BY A BEHAVORIAL SCIENTIST: INDUSTRIAL ENGINEERS,
        ENCOURAGED AND SUPPORTED BY MANAGEMENT, HAVE DEHUMANIZED
        JOBS AND SO, TO A CONSIDERABLE DEGREE, ARE RESPONSIBLE FOR
        ALIENATING THE WORKER AND MAKING HIM A COMBATANT AGAINST
        MANAGEMENT. THIS STATEMENT IS NOT SUPPORTED BY THE
        PRESENT WRITER, WHO HAS SPENT THE PAST 14 YEARS AS AN
        INDUSTRIAL ENGINEER.
        TO BEGIN WITH, THE WRITER ATTACKS THE TIME FRAME USED
        BY THE BEHAVORIAL SCIENTIST, FREDERICK TAYLOR. TAYLOR'S
        STUDY COMPARES WORK ORGANIZATION OF TODAY WITH THAT OF AN
        ERA WHEN NO COLLECTIVE BARGAINING EXISTED, AND THE WORKER
        HAD NO DEFENSES, NO APPEALS, AND NO REPRESENTATION. ALSO,
        TAYLOR DRAWS AN ANALOGY BETWEEN THE EFFICIENCY EXPERT OF
        THE PRODUCTION REVOLUTION, AND THE HIGHLY EDUCATED AND
        SKILLED ENGINEER WHO HAS EMERGED SINCE THE LATE 1970'S.
        LABOR DIVISION IS A NECESSARY PART OF THE MASS
        PRODUCTION INDUSTRIES OF TODAY. USING THE ECONOMIC MAN
        THEORY, WE PRODUCE AS MUCH QUANTITY AND QUALITY AS MAKE
        GOOD SENSE. FOLKER STATES THAT IN ORDER TO MAKE ALL THIS
        POSSIBLE CERTAIN WORK STANDARDS MUST BE ESTABLISHED. AFTER
        ALL, THE WORKER WOULD RATHER KNOW HIS CHALLENGE AND HAVE
        SOMETHING TO WORK FOR THAN HAVE NO CONTROL OVER THE JOB.
        IN HIS EXPERIENCE IN THE FIELD, THE AUTHOR STATES HE HAS
        NEVER SEEN A STANDARD THAT EXCLUDED ALL VALUES CONCERNED
        WITH CREATIVE COMFORT AND PERSONAL NEEDS. THESE JOB
        STANDARDS ARE AS IMPORTANT TO MANAGEMENT AS SIMILAR DATA FOR
        MATERIALS AND EQUIPMENT.
        UNIONS MAY BE A MAJOR CULPRIT TO THE PROBLEM. THESE
        INSTITUTIONS REPRESENT THE WORKERS THEMSELVES. UNIONS OFTEN
        REJECT LABOR-SAVING EQUIPMENT TO KEEP MEN ON THE JOB. THE

M0136 RESULT--JOBS ARE KEPT DULL. WAGES ARE APPARENTLY NOT THE
       ANSWER. AS THEY HAVE RISEN, PRODUCTIVITY HAS FALLEN.
              IT ALL COMES DOWN TO A TRADE-OFF OF PRIORITIES. FOLKER
       STATES, IT IS NOT LIKELY THAT INDUSTRY CAN PRODUCE THE
       TOTAL JOB FULFILLMENT DEMANDED BY PSYCHOLOGISTS AND
       BEHAVORIAL SCIENTISTS AND AT THE SAME TIME SUSTAIN THE
       GROWTH OF THE GNP. NEARLY ALL OF THESE GOODS PRODUCED ARE
       CONSUMED BY THE VAST MAJORITY OF PEOPLE, INCLUDING
       PSYCHOLOGISTS.
              THERE WILL ALWAYS BE SOME DIRTY, BORING JOBS FOR
       WORKERS TO PERFORM. HOWEVER, THERE ARE EXTENSIVE
       EDUCATIONAL AND RETRAINING PROGRAMS AVAILABLE TODAY. THESE
       MAKE THE WORKER ELIGIBLE FOR THE VAST MAJORITY OF JOBS
       AVAILABLE, MANY CREATED THROUGH THE EXPERTISE OF THE
       INDUSTRIAL ENGINEER.

M0137 FOSS, LAURENCE.
       MANAGERIAL STRATEGY FOR THE FUTURE: THEORY Z MANAGEMENT.
       CALIFORNIA MANAGEMENT REVIEW, 15 (SPRING 1973): 68-81.

              THEORY Z MANAGEMENT IS DESCRIBED AS AN APPROACH THAT
       INCORPORATES THE RECOGNITION OF MOTIVATIONAL CHANGE AMONG
       TODAY'S EMPLOYEES, PARTICULARLY AMONG YOUNGER WORKERS. IT
       IS COMPARED WITH THE CONCEPTS OF OTHER MAJOR BEHAVIORAL
       THEORISTS SUCH AS MCGREGOR, HERZBERG, ARGYRIS, LIKERT,
       MASLOW, AND BLAKE AND MOUTON.

M0138 FOX, HAROLD W.
       HUMANIZING THE BUDGETARY SYSTEM FOR ADMINISTRATIVE
       REINFORCEMENT.
       PERSONNEL JOURNAL 52 (MARCH 1973): 198-204.

              THE AUTHOR OF THIS ARTICLE ATTEMPTS TO DEFINE HOW
       ENLIGHTENED BUDGETING CAN HELP TO ACHIEVE SELF-FULFILLMENT
       AND IMPROVE BUSINESS PRODUCTIVITY.

M0139 FRADERIKSEN, N   JENSEN, OLLIE.   BEATON, ALBERT E.
       PREDICTION OF ORGANIZATIONAL BEHAVIOR.
       NEW YORK: PERGAMON PRESS, 1972.

              STUDY OF MATERIALS FURNISHED BY THE OFFICE OF NAVAL
       RESEARCH, CALIFORNIA STATE PERSONNEL BOARD AND EDUCATIONAL
       TESTING SERVICE. SITUATIONAL TESTS AND EXPERIMENTS
       DONE ON 270 STATE EMPLOYEES TO ISOLATE VARIABLES INFLUENCING
       POSSIBLE DECISIONS OF MANAGEMENT. A VERY SCHOLARLY
       TREATMENT.

M0140 FRANCIS, H. MINTON.
       HOW EQUAL OPPORTUNITY AFFECTS DEFENSE CONTRACTS.
       COMMANDERS DIGEST, OCTOBER 1974, PP. 2-8.

              THE DEFENSE CONTRACT COMPLIANCE PROGRAM'S OBJECTIVES
       ARE TO INCREASE GENERAL EMPLOYMENT OF MINORITIES AND WOMEN
       IN THE WORK FORCES OF ALL FIRMS WHICH HOLD FEDERAL CONTRACTS
       AND INSURE THESE WORKERS ARE PROVIDED OPPORTUNITY FOR UPWARD
       MOBILITY.

M0141 FRANKLIN, JACK L.

M0141   ROLE PERFORMANCE AND COMMITMENT TO THE ORGANIZATION.
        PH. D. DISSERTATION, INDIANA UNIVERSITY FOUNDATION, 1972.
              THIS STUDY EXAMINED THE RELATIONSHIPS BETWEEN POWER
        USED BY THE ORGANIZATION, COMMITMENT TO THE ORGANIZATION,
        AND TASK PERFORMANCE.

M0142   GREENBERG, N. E.   REILLY, RICHARD R.   BARNETT, SAMUEL
        DEVELOPMENT OF ASSESSMENT MEASURES FOR COUNSELING YOUTH WORK
        -- TRAINING ENROLLEES.
        EDUCATIONAL TESTING SERVICE, PRINCETON, N. J.
        NTIS PB 202807.

              STANDARDS OF ASSESSMENT FOR YOUTHS APPLYING FOR JOBS
        IN NEIGHBORHOOD YOUTH CORPS. LACK OF TROUBLE WITH
        POLICE, GOOD SUPERVISOR RATINGS AND LOW ABSENTEEISM
        RATES SEEMS TO BE THE CRITERION FOR EVALUATION.

M0143   FREEMAN, EVELYN L.
        A STUDY OF BLACK MALE PROFESSIONALS IN INDUSTRY.
        UNPUBLISHED RESEARCH, NEW YORK: RECRUITING MANAGEMENT
        CONSULTANTS, INC., 1972.

              THE OBJECTIVE OF THIS STUDY WAS TO ANALYZE PROBLEMS
        CONFRONTING BLACK PROFESSIONALS IN INDUSTRY AS A BASIS FOR
        DEVELOPING AND PROMOTING PROGRAMS IN GOVERNMENT AND INDUSTRY
        TO MAKE FULL USE OF THEIR SKILLS.

M0144   FRENCH, EARL B.
        WHAT A MACHINE DOESN'T KNOW.
        PERSONNEL ADMINISTRATOR 16 (MAY-JUNE 1971):   7-9.

              MACHINE THEORY MANAGERS TEND TO IGNORE SUCH FACTORS AS
        HUMAN VALUES AND WORK ENVIRONMENT WHICH AFFECT EMPLOYEE
        MORALE AND PRODUCTIVITY. SUGGESTS FACTORS AFFECTING
        WORKERS' ATTITUDES FOR MANAGEMENT'S CONSIDERATION.

M0145   FORM CHINA WITH SKILL -- MESBIC FOUNDER WANTS TO SHARE HER
        TALENT.
        COMMERCE TODAY, APRIL 1974, P. 7.

              MRS. ROSA LEONG, FOUNDER OF MINORITY ENTERPRISE SMALL
        BUSINESS INVESTMENT COMPANY, ELEVATES MINORITIES TO ACCEPT
        THEIR POSITION IN THE ECONOMIC STRUCTURE AND CREATES A
        FEELING THAT THEY CAN MAKE IT IF THEY TRY.

M0146   FROST, KEITH R.
        MOTIVATION AND CAREER PATH PLANNING.
        DATA MANAGEMENT 12 (SEPTEMBER 1974):   18-22.

              THE AUTHOR MAINTAINS THAT THE DEVELOPMENT AND
        MAINTENANCE OF A CLIMATE OF PRODUCTIVITY MUST BE BASED ON
        MEETING THE NEEDS OF EMPLOYEES. THE KEY TO THIS CLIMATE
        LIES IN MAKING PEOPLE FEEL THEY ARE AN IMPORTANT PART OF
        COMPANY OBJECTIVES THROUGH PARTICIPATION IN DECISION
        MAKING AND PROBLEM SOLVING. IT IS THESE FACTORS OF
        INVOLVEMENT WHICH GIVE RISE TO EMPLOYEE MOTIVATION.

M0147   GALVIN, JOHN.

M0147 TRAINING CORRECTIONAL MANPOWER.
       MANPOWER 3 (JANUARY 1971): 14-19.
            THIS ARTICLE IS ESSENTIALLY A REPORT OF THE PRESIDENT'S
       COMMISSION ON LAW ENFORCEMENT AND THE ADMINISTRATION OF
       JUSTICE AND OF STUDIES OF CORRECTIONS OPERATIONS IN 1967-69
       WHICH CONFIRMED AND UPDATED THE FINDINGS OF THE COMMISSION.
            TREATMENT OF OFFENDERS REFLECTS A LACK OF CONSENSUS AS
       TO WHAT MAN'S PROBLEMS ARE AND WHAT TO DO ABOUT THEM. IN
       1966 IT WAS FOUND THAT ON AN AVERAGE DAY CORRECTIONAL
       WORKERS WERE RESPONSIBLE FOR OVER 1.2 MILLION OFFENDERS.
       THIRTY PERCENT (345,000) WERE JUVENILES. EIGHTY PERCENT OF
       THE JUVENILES WERE ON PROBATION OR PAROLE, THE OTHERS IN
       CORRECTIONAL INSTITUTIONS. SIXTY PERCENT OF THE ADULTS WERE
       IN JAIL OR PRISON. OPERATIONAL COSTS OF CORRECTIONAL
       PROGRAMS WERE $1 BILLION A YEAR BUT ONLY 20 PERCENT WENT FOR
       SERVICES TO PAROLEES AND PROBATIONERS ALTHOUGH THEY WERE
       2/3 OF THE TOTAL. CORRECTIONAL AGENCIES EMPLOYED 121,163
       PEOPLE AND 55% OF THESE WERE PEOPLE WHO PROVIDED SUPERVISION
       AND CONTROL. TWENTY PERCENT WERE PROBATION OFFICERS
       COUNSELORS, TEACHERS, ETC. IT WAS ESTIMATED
       THAT BY 1975 CORRECTIONS WOULD EMPLOY 250,000 PEOPLE WITH A
       RECRUITMENT NEED OF 30,000.
            THE COMMISSION'S MAIN MESSAGE SEEMS TO BE THAT
       CORRECTIONS NEED THE HELP OF THE PUBLIC AND PRIVATE
       AGENCIES, INDIVIDUAL CITIZENS, ETC. AND MUST TREAT THE
       OFFENDER CLIENTS AS POTENTIAL ALLIES. CORRECTIONAL MANPOWER
       SHOULD BE GROUPED INTO THESE CATEGORIES:
            1) ADMINISTRATORS
            2) STAFF SPECIALISTS
            3) CARE CORRECTIONAL PRACTITIONERS
            4) SPECIALISTS UNDER CONTRACT
       THE COMMISSION ALSO FOUND THAT CORRECTIONS EMPLOYEES NEED
       LEGAL ADVISORS TO KEEP THEM UP TO DATE ON COURT DECISIONS
       AFFECTING OPERATIONS. THE COMMISSION
       ONLY SOUGHT TO MAKE CLEAR THE DIMENSIONS OF THE PROBLEMS
       NOT THE SOLUTIONS. REPORTS ACCROSS THE COUNTRY SHOW THAT
       THERE ARE INNOVATIONS BEING IMPLEMENTED. SOME ARE--(1)
       LEADERSHIP BY CORRECTIONAL PEOPLE IN NEW PLANNING
       ORGANIZATIONS, (2) CLASSES TO TEACH PROGRAM BUDGETING,
       OBJECTIVES AND OPERATIONS RESEARCH, (3) MUSHROOMING OF TWO
       AND FOUR YEAR AND GRADUATE LEVEL COURSES TO PREPARE PEOPLE
       FOR A CAREER IN CRIMINAL JUSTICE (4) SPREAD OF COLLABORATION
       BETWEEN CORRECTIONAL AND OTHER AGENCIES, (5) EASING OF LABOR
       PROBLEMS THROUGH COLLECTIVE BARGAINING, AND (6) INCREASED
       USE OF VOLUNTEER WORKERS.

M0148 GANNON, MARTIN J.
       A PROFILE OF THE TEMPORARY HELP INDUSTRY AND ITS WORKERS.
       MONTHLY LABOR REVIEW, MAY 1974, PP. 44-49.

            A REVIEW OF AVAILABLE DATA SHOWS MAJORITY OF EMPLOYEES
       ARE WOMEN AND MOST ARE IN CLERICAL JOBS IN THIS RAPIDLY
       GROWING INDUSTRY.

M0149 GASTWIRTH, JOSEPH L.
       ON THE DECLINE OF MALE LABOR FORCE PARTICIPATION.
       MONTHLY LABOR REVIEW 95 (OCTOBER 1972): 44-46.

EXAMINES THE CAUSE OF THE DECLINE IN PARTICIPATION OF
PRIME AGE MALES IN THE LABOR FORCE.

M0150 GAVIN, JAMES F.
SELF-ESTEEM AS A MODERATOR OF THE RELATIONSHIP BETWEEN
EXPECTANCIES AND JOB PERFORMANCE.
JOURNAL OF APPLIED PSYCHOLOGY 58 (AUGUST 1973):   83-88.

THIS STUDY EXAMINES THE IMPLICATION OF KORMAN'S
CONSISTENCY HYPOTHESIS FOR PREDICTIONS OF WORK BEHAVIOR,
DERIVED FORM PORTER AND LAWLER'S EXPECTANCY MODEL AND
EVALUATES THE FEASIBILITY OF MODERATING THE
EXPECTANCY-PERFORMANCE RELATIONSHIPS WITH RELEVANT
VARIABLES.   FINDINGS OF THE STUDY OF MANAGEMENT TRAINEES IN
AN INSURANCE COMPANY DID NOT SUPPORT THE SPECIFIC HYPOTHESIS
THAT THE RELATIONSHIP BETWEEN REWARD EXPECTANCIES AND JOB
PERFORMANCE WOULD BE SUPPORTED FOR HIGH SELF-ESTEEM
INDIVIDUALS ONLY, BUT DID GIVE SOME SUPPORT TO THE
GENERAL HYPOTHESIS OF THE UTILITY OF MODERATING THE
RELATIONSHIP WITH RELEVANT VARIABLES.

M0151 GEMMILL, G.   THAMHAIN, H.
INFLUENCE STYLES OF PROJECT MANAGERS: SOME PROJECT
PERFORMANCE CORRELATES.
ADMINISTRATIVE MANAGEMENT 216-24.

THE RELATIONSHIPS BETWEEN INFLUENCE METHODS OF
PROJECT MANAGERS AND THEIR PROJECT PERFORMANCE ARE
INVESTIGATED IN THIS ARTICLE.

M0152 GENTZ, SUSAN.
CAREER OPPORTUNITIES IN THE POSTAL SERVICE.
OCCUPATIONAL OUTLOOK QUARTERLY 16 (WINTER 1972):   3-15.

OUTLINES BOTH THE ADVANTAGES AND DISADVANTAGES OF
POSTAL WORK, WITH EMPHASIS ON JOBS AS MAIL CARRIER AND
POSTAL CLERK.

M0153 NO AUTHOR CITED
GETTING CINDERELLA TO THE BALL.
MANPOWER, JULY, 1970, PP. 11-13.

REPORT REVIEWS EXPERIENCE OF 100 COMPANIES IN HIRING
THE HARD CORE.

M0154 GHOZEIL, SUE.
STAFF AND DISTAFF: WHY WOMEN WORK.
MANPOWER, 5 (DECEMBER 1973):   11-15.

STUDIES OF MOTIVATIONS OF WORKING WOMEN AND WHAT
FACTORS AFFECT THEIR DECISIONS TO WORK.

M0155 GIBSON, CHARLES H.
VOLVO INCREASES PRODUCTIVITY THROUGH JOB ENRICHMENT.
CALIFORNIA MANAGEMENT REVIEW, 15 (SUMMER 1973):   64-66.

THE AUTHOR REPORTS ON A MAJOR EFFORT BY VOLVO TO
INCREASE PRODUCTIVITY BY WAY OF JOB ENRICHMENT.

M0156   GILROY, CURTIS L.
        BLACK AND WHITE UNEMPLOYMENT: THE DYNAMICS OF THE
        DIFFERENTIAL.
        MONTHLY LABOR REVIEW, FEBRUARY 1974, PP. 38-47.

        A NEW ANALYSIS ADDS SUPPORT TO BELIEFS THAT BLACKS
        FARE BETTER IN PROSPERITY THAN IN OTHER PHASES OF THE
        BUSINESS CYCLE.

M0157   GILROY, CURTIS L.
        JOB LOSERS, LEAVERS, AND ENTRANTS: TRAITS AND TRENDS.
        MONTHLY LABOR REVIEW 96 (AUGUST 1973): 3-15.

        STUDY SHOWS THAT CLASSIFICATION OF UNEMPLOYED
        ACCORDING TO THEIR STATUS AT THE TIME OF EMPLOYMENT CAN
        HAVE GREAT IMPACT ON MANAGEMENT POLICY.

M0158   GITTLER, HARVEY.
        ANATOMY OF A SUCCESS.
        INDUSTRIAL ENGINEERING 5 (SEPTEMBER 1973):   54-57.

        THIS ARTICLE EXPLAINS A SUPERVISORY IMPROVEMENT
        PROGRAM THAT EMPHASIZES POSTING BETTER PERFORMANCE RECORDS.

M0159   GLICKMAN, A. S.   BROWN, ZENIA H.
        CHANGING SCHEDULES OF WORK: PATTERNS AND IMPLICATIONS.
        UNPUBLISHED RESEARCH, SILVER SPRING: AMERICAN INSTITUTE FOR
        RESEARCH, 1972.

        STUDY OF PSYCHOLOGICAL AND SOCIOLOGICAL ADJUSTMENT AND
        CHANGES RESULTING FROM DIFFERENT LEISURE/WORK PATTERNS.

M0160   GLICKMAN, S. E.   MILNER, PETER M.
        NEUROLOGICAL BASIS OF MOTIVATION: AN ENDURING PROBLEM IN
        PSYCHOLOGY.
        NEW YORK: VANNOSTRAND REINHOLD.   1969.

        THIS COLLECTION OF ARTICLES IS DESIGNED TO PROVIDE
        A DIVERSE SAMPLE OF CURRENT THEORY AND RESEARCH CONCERNING
        THE PSYCHOLOGICAL BASIS OF MOTIVATION.

M0161   GOLDBERG, JOSEPH P.
        PUBLIC EMPLOYEE LABOR RELATIONS IN OTHER DEMOCRACIES.
        MONTHLY LABOR REVIEW 95 (OCTOBER 1972):   37-43.

        SERIES OF 12 MONOGRAPHS PRESENTS ALTERNATIVE APPROACHES
        TO A VARIETY OF PROBLEMS CONFRONTING GOVERNMENTS AND THEIR
        EMPLOYEES.

M0162   GOLDFARB, R. S.   HAMERMESH, D. S.
        A NEW APPROACH TO LOCAL LABOR MARKET ANALYSIS: A
        FEASIBILITY STUDY.
        PRINCETON, N. J.:   PRINCETON UNIVERSITY PRESS, 1969.

        THE STUDY SOUGHT INFORMATION ON THE POLICIES AND
        CHARACTERISTICS OF A FIRM WHICH AFFECT ITS ABILITY TO
        ATTRACT AND RETAIN WORKERS.

M0163 GOLDRING, PATRICK.
MULTI PURPOSE MAN.
NEW YORK: TAPINGER PUBLISHING CO., INC., 1974.

IN THE AUTO INDUSTRY ANALYZES REASONS FOR DISCONTENT
AND RESULTS OF THE FRUSTRATION OF WORKERS. PRESCRIPTION:
CHANGE-ACCEPTANCE OF PART-TIME WORKERS AS EQUALS IN WORK
WEEKS OF TWENTY-FOUR HOURS ON ONE JOB, TWENTY HOURS ON A
DIFFERENT JOB. VERY INTERESTING, THOUGHT-PROVOKING IDEA.

M0164 GONZALES, JOSEPH P.
STOCKTON UNIFIED SCHOOL DISTRICT.
STOCKTON: SUMMER/IN-SCHOOL NYC VOCATIONAL EXPLORATION
EXPERIMENT. GRANT 42-06-72-05.

THE PROJECT WAS ESTABLISHED TO TEST THE HYPOTHESIS THAT
DROPOUT-PRONE DISADVANTAGED 10TH GRADE STUDENTS WOULD REMAIN
IN SCHOOL AND PLAN A VOCATIONAL CAREER IF THEY WERE EXPOSED
TO A VARIETY OF STRUCTURED WORK EXPERIENCES IN PUBLIC AND
PRIVATE ORGANIZATIONS. THE PROJECT SOUGHT TO: (1) MAKE 63
EXPERIMENTAL GROUP STUDENTS, RANDOMLY SELECTED FROM A LARGE
POOL OF NEIGHBORHOOD YOUTH CORP (NYC) ENROLLEES, MORE AWARE
OF THE LABOR MARKET AND THE PREREQUISITES FOR ENTRANCE INTO
CAREER-TYPE OCCUPATIONS; (2) MOTIVATE THEM TO COMPLETE HIGH
SCHOOL BY REVEALING TO THEM THEIR EDUCATIONAL AND VOCATIONAL
NEEDS; . . . . AND (7) DEVELOP A . . . MODEL FOR OTHER NYC
PROGRAM SPONSORS TO REPLICATE THE PROJECT'S FUNCTIONS OR
UTILIZE ITS FINDINGS TO IMPROVE THE MERITS OF THEIR NYC
PROGRAMS. THE PROJECT CONCLUDED THAT DISADVANTAGED
STUDENTS IN THE EXPERIMENTAL SAMPLE WERE BETTER ABLE TO PLAN
THEIR EMPLOYMENT FUTURE AFTER COMPLETING A WORK EXPLORATION
PROGRAM, AND THAT THEIR CAREER INTERESTS WILL BE INFLUENCED
BY PROFESSIONAL VOCATIONAL GUIDANCE, BY EMPLOYERS, AND BY
EXPERIENCE.

M0165 GOODALE, JAMES G.
BACKGROUND CHARACTERISTICS, ORIENTATION, WORK EXPERIENCE,
AND WORK VALUES OF EMPLOYEES HIRED FROM HUMAN RESOURCES
DEVELOPMENT APPLICANTS BY COMPANIES AFFILIATED WITH THE
NATIONAL ALLIANCE OF BUSINESSMAN.
PH. D. DISSERTATION, BOWLING GREEN STATE UNIVERSITY, 1972.

THIS STUDY FOCUSED ON DIFFERENCES IN THE WORK VALUES OF
TRAINEES IN NAB PROGRAMS AND THOSE OF REGULARLY EMPLOYED
UNSKILLED AND SEMI-SKILLED PERSONS.

M0166 GOODWIN, LEONARD.
DO THE POOR WANT TO WORK.
WASHINGTON, D. C. : THE BROOKINGS INSTITUTE, 1972.

RESULTS OF A SURVEY OF 4000 PERSONS CONTRASTING THE
WORK ORIENTATIONS OF POOR AND MORE AFFLUENT GROUPS.
CONCLUSION: LIVING IN POVERTY AFFECTS A PERSON'S BELIEF IN
HIS ABILITY TO ACHIEVE SUCCESS BUT DOES NOT DIMINISH HIS
DESIRE FOR A GOOD LIFE OR BELIEF THAT WORKING CONTRIBUTES TO
HIS SELF-RESPECT.

M0167 GOODWIN, LEONARD.

M0167   A STUDY OF THE WORK ORIENTATIONS OF WELFARE RECIPIENTS
        PARTICIPATING IN THE WORK-INCENTIVE PROGRAM.
        WASHINGTON, D. C. THE BROOKINGS INSTITUTION CONTRACT
        51-09-39-02.

        THIS STUDY OF THE WORK ORIENTATION OF WORK INCENTIVE (WIN)
        PROGRAM TRAINEES COMPARED THE TRAINEES' ATTITUDES TOWARD
        WORK WITH THOSE OF MIDDLE-CLASS WORKERS AND EXAMINED THE
        INTERACTION OF THE TRAINEES' WORK ORIENTATIONS WITH THEIR
        POST-TRAINING WORK PERFORMANCE AND EXPERIENCES. IT ALSO
        PROBED THE PERCEPTIONS OF TRAINEES' WORK ATTITUDES HELD BY
        MIDDLE-CLASS PERSONS AND WIN STAFF MEMBERS. SINCE WIN
        TRAINEES IN FACT HAVE THE SAME POSITIVE ORIENTATION TOWARD
        WORK AS DO EMPLOYED PERSONS, THE RESEARCHER CONCLUDED THAT
        THEY DO NOT NEED SPECIAL EFFORTS TO MOTIVATE THEM TO WORK.
        WHAT THEY DO NEED IS GREATER EFFORTS TO HELP THEM EXPERIENCE
        JOB SUCCESS RATHER THAN FAILURE. RECOMMENDATIONS FOR
        ACCOMPLISHING THIS WERE MADE.

M0168   GOODWIN, LEONARD.
        WELFARE MOTHERS AND THE WORK ETHIC.
        MONTHLY LABOR REVIEW 95 (AUGUST 1972):   35-37.

        DISCUSSION OF MOTIVATION OF DIFFERENT GROUPS OF
        MOTHERS, AND THE IMPACT OF WORKING MOTHERS ON THE JOB
        MOTIVATION OF THEIR CHILDREN.

M0169   GOLDSTEIN, H.   HOROWITZ, M. A.
        RESTRUCTURING PARAMEDICAL OCCUPATIONS: A CASE STUDY.
        UNDER AUSPICES OF NORTHEASTERN UNIVERSITY THROUGH GRANT
        FROM THE MANPOWER ADMINISTRATION. NTIS PB 211113 AND
        PB 211114.

        RESEARCHERS FOUND MUCH OVERLAP OF JOB FUNCTIONS IN
        NURSING AND RELATED OCCUPATIONS. EDUCATIONAL REQUIREMENTS
        AND OTHER BARRIERS PREVENT PARAMEDICAL PERSONNEL FROM
        ADVANCING AND LITTLE MORE TRAINING WAS OFFERED.
        RECOMMENDATIONS: CREATION OF A JOB LADDER CONSISTING
        OF THREE NEW PARAMEDICAL OCCUPATIONS--NURSING ASSISTANT,
        MEDICAL ASSISTANT, AND PHYSICIAN'S ASSISTANT, AND
        ESTABLISHMENT OF TRAINING PROGRAMS TO ENABLE PERSONNEL TO
        CLIMB THE LADDER WITHIN TWO YEARS. THE MESSRS. GOLDSTEIN
        AND HOROWITZ ARE HOPING TO SEE THEIR IDEAS TAKEN
        UP BY OTHER HOSPITALS IN ADDITION TO THE CAMBRIDGE FACILITY
        IN WHICH THEY DID THEIR RESEARCH.

M0170   GOLDSTEIN, H.   ROSENTHOL, NEAL.
        OCCUPATIONAL MANPOWER TRAINING NEEDS.
        OCCUPATIONAL OUTLOOK QUARTERLY 15 (FALL 1971):   28-31.

        NEW B L S REPORT HELPS CURRICULUM AND TRAINING
        PLANNERS DETERMINE TYPES OF WORKERS IN DEMAND BY
        PROVIDING COMPLETIONS OF THESE FIELDS.

M0171   GOTTLIEB, DAVID.
        YOUTH AND THE MEANING OF WORK.
        UNPUBLISHED RESEARCH, PENNSYLVANIA STATE UNIVERSITY, 1973.

EXAMINES THE ATTITUDE OF COLLEGE SENIORS TOWARD WORK
AND A CAREER, BEFORE AND AFTER FULL-TIME EMPLOYMENT.

M0172 GREENE, CHARLES N.
THE SATISFACTION-PERFORMANCE CONTROVERSY
BUSINESS HORIZONS 15 (OCTOBER 1972): 31-41.

RESEARCHERS HAVE CONCLUDED THAT THERE IS NO PRESENT
TECHNIQUE FOR DETERMINING THE CAUSE-AND-EFFECT OF
SATISFACTION AND PERFORMANCE.
THAT SATISFACTION DETERMINES PERFORMANCE IS FREQUENTLY
ACCEPTED SINCE THE DEGREE OF JOB SATISFACTION FELT BY AN
EMPLOYEE DETERMINES HIS PERFORMANCE.
THAT PERFORMANCE CAUSES SATISFACTION HOLDS THAT REWARDS
CONSTITUTE A NECESSARY INTERVENING VARIABLE AND, THUS,
SATISFACTION IS CONSIDERED TO BE A FUNCTION OF
PERFORMANCE-RELATED REWARDS.
REWARDS AS A CAUSAL FACTOR CONSIDER BOTH SATISFACTION AND
PERFORMANCE TO BE FUNCTIONS OF REWARDS. FROM THIS POINT OF
VIEW IT IS SAID THAT REWARDS CAUSE SATISFACTION
AND THAT REWARDS BASED ON CURRENT PERFORMANCE AFFECT
SUBSEQUENT PERFORMANCE.
THESE FINDINGS ON SATISFACTION AND PERFORMANCE HAVE MANY
IMPLICATIONS FOR MANAGEMENT IN THE CONSISTENT REJECTION OF
SATISFACTION-CAUSES-PERFORMANCE: INCREASING SUBORDINATES'
SATISFACTION WILL HAVE NO EFFECT ON THEIR PERFORMANCE.
IF A MANAGER GRANTS REWARDS ON THE BASIS OF DIFFERENCE IN
HIS SUBORDINATES' PERFORMANCE THIS WILL CAUSE VARYING
DEGREES OF SATISFACTION OR DISSATISFACTION. THIS STRATEGY
IS GOOD BECAUSE THE HIGHER-REWARDED PERFORMERS ARE GOING TO
STAY IN THE ORGANIZATION AND DO THE BEST JOB POSSIBLE.
REWARD IS THE MOST FREQUENT AND DIRECT CAUSE OF EFFORT.
DIRECTION, ABILITY AND PERFORMANCE OBSTACLES MAY INDIRECTLY
AFFECT EFFORT. A PERSON WILL MOST LIKELY NOT PUT FORTH MUCH
EFFORT IN HIS PERFORMANCE UNLESS THE REWARD HE RECEIVES
IS OF SOME VALUE TO HIM.
REWARDS ARE CLASSIFIED INTO TWO CATEGORIES: EXTRINSIC AND
INTRINSIC. EXTRINSIC REWARDS ARE THOSE EXTERNAL TO THE JOB
OR IN THE CONTEXT OF THE JOB. INTRINSIC REWARDS ARE REWARDS
THAT ARE ASSOCIATED WITH THE DOING OF THE JOB SUCH AS A
SENSE OF ACCOMPLISHMENT.
IN THIS ARTICLE THE EVIDENCE PROVIDES STRONG INDICATIONS
THAT THE RELATIONSHIPS ARE MORE COMPLEX IN THAT THE REWARDS
CONSTITUTE A MORE DIRECT CAUSE OF SATISFACTION THAN
PERFORMANCE DOES AND REWARDS BASED ON CURRENT PERFORMANCE
CAUSE SUBSEQUENT PERFORMANCE. REWARDS DO CAUSE
SATISFACTION. THEREFORE, THE MANAGER OF A COMPANY MUST
PROVIDE REWARDS THAT HAVE VALUE TO HIS EMPLOYEES.

M0173 GREENE, ZINA.
THE CHANGING ROLE OF WOMEN: IMPLICATIONS FOR PLANNERS.
HUD CHALLENGE, MAY 1974, PP. 2-4.

THE CHANGING SOCIAL AND ECONOMIC ROLES OF WOMEN IMPLY A
NEED FOR NEW DIRECTIONS IN PLANNING AT EVERY LEVEL OF
GOVERNMENT.

M0174 GREENHAUS, J.

M0174   SELF-ESTEEM AS AN INFLUENCE ON OCCUPATIONAL CHOICE AND
        OCCUPATIONAL SATISFACTION.
        JOURNAL OF VOCATIONAL BEJAVIOR 1 (JANUARY 1971):   75-83.

        RESEARCH INVESTIGATED THE ROLE OF SELF-ESTEEM IN
        OCCUPATIONAL CHOICE AND OCCUPATIONAL SATISFACTION. PERSONS
        WITH LOW SELF-ESTEEM TENDED TO LOOK AT SOCIAL CUES RATHER
        THAT OCCUPATIONAL FIT IN DETERMINING THEIR OCCUPATIONAL
        SATISFACTIONS WHILE PERSONS WITH HIGHER SELF-ESTEEM LOOKED
        TOWARD THE RELEVANCE OF THEIR PERCEIVED ATTRIBUTES IN MAKING
        THEIR DETERMINATIONS.

M0175   GREINER, LARRY E.
        WHAT MANAGERS THINK OF PARTICIPATIVE LEADERSHIP.
        HARVARD BUSINESS REVIEW 51 (MARCH-APRIL 1973):   111-17.

        THIS ARTICLE DEALS WITH A STUDY ON HOW MANAGERS FEEL ABOUT
        PARTICIPATIVE MANAGEMENT. TWO OBJECTIVES OF THE STUDY WERE
        TO DISCOVER WHAT MANAGERS CONSIDER TO BE CONCRETE
        CHARACTERISTICS OF PARTICIPATIVE LEADERSHIP AND TO
        DETERMINE WHETHER THEY THINK SUCH A STYLE LEADS TO EFFECTIVE
        RESULTS. IN THE STUDY 318 MANAGERS WERE GIVEN A
        QUESTIONNAIRE CONTAINING 39 LEADERSHIP CHARACTERISTICS.
        THEY WERE THEN DIVIDED INTO TWO GROUPS.
        THE FIRST GROUP CONSISTED OF 157 MANAGERS AND THEY WERE TOLD
        TO RATE EACH CHARACTERISTIC ON A SCALE FROM 1 TO 7 WITH 1
        EQUAL TO LOW PARTICIPATION AND 7 EQUAL TO HIGH
        PARTICIPATION. THEY WERE TOLD TO BASE THEIR RATINGS ON
        THEIR PAST EXPERIENCES.
        THE SECOND GROUP WAS 161 MANAGERS AND THEY WERE TOLD TO
        CHECK THE 5 CHARACTERISTICS THAT THEY FOUND TO BE MOST
        EFFECTIVE IN HANDLING MANAGERIAL SITUATIONS, AND THE 5
        CHARACTERISTICS THAT THEY FOUND TO BE MOST EFFECTIVE IN
        HANDLING MANAGERIAL SITUATIONS, AND THE 5 CHARACTERISTICS
        THAT THEY FOUND TO BE LEAST EFFECTIVE. THEY ALSO BASED
        THEIR JUDGEMENTS ON PAST EXPERIENCES.
        FROM THE SURVEY WE GET THE MESSAGE THAT THE MANAGERS FEEL
        THERE WAS ENOUGH TALK OF PARTICIPATIVE MANAGEMENT AND THAT
        MANAGERS SHOULD NOW IMPLEMENT IT INTO ACTUAL PRACTICE.
        WHILE THERE ARE MANY LEADERSHIP STYLES TO CHOSE FROM, THE
        CONSENSUS WAS THAT IN ACTUAL PRACTICE A MANAGER MAY PULL
        DIFFERENT ASPECTS FROM DIFFERENT STYLES TO USE AS AN
        EFFECTIVE PARTICIPATIVE MANAGERIAL STYLE. THE MANAGERS NOT
        ONLY CHOSE SPECIFIC CHARACTERISTICS THAT COMPRISE A
        PARTICIPATIVE STYLE, BUT WERE ALSO IN GENERAL AGREEMENT
        THAT CERTAIN PARTICIPATIVE LEADERSHIP CHARACTERISTICS
        PRODUCE MORE EFFECTIVE RESULTS.
        THE OPINIONS OF MANAGERS REPRESENTED IN THIS SURVEY SAY THAT
        PARTICIPATIVE MANAGEMENT IS A GOOD, SOUND CONCEPT.
        THE MANAGERS FELT THIS CONCEPT MUST BE PRESENTED IN A
        GENERAL MODEL FORM, FROM WHICH MANAGERS CAN SHOW A VARIETY
        OF ACTIONS TO SATISFY DIFFERENT PERSONAL AND CAREER NEEDS.

M0176   GROTE, RICHARD C.
        IMPLEMENTING JOB ENRICHMENT.
        CALIFORNIA MANAGEMENT REVIEW 15 (FALL 1972):   16-21.

        JOB ENRICHMENT IS A STRATEGY FOR INCREASING JOB MOTIVATION.

M0176 THE STRATEGY OF JOB ENRICHMENT INVOLVES CHANGING THE JOB TO
MEET CERTAIN CONDITIONS CONCERNING THE INDIVIDUAL ON THE
JOB. THIS ARTICLE ACCORDING TO THE AUTHOR EXPLAINS THE
NECESSARY STEPS THAT NEED TO BE TAKEN TO SUCCESSFULLY
IMPLEMENT JOB ENRICHMENT.
MOST ORGANIZATIONS WHICH HAVE IMPLEMENTED SUCCESSFUL JOB
ENRICHMENT PLANS HAVE STARTED WITH AN EXPERIMENT.
THIS EXPERIMENT INVOLVES ENRICHING A FEW JOBS, ESTABLISHING
EXPERIMENTAL AND CONTROL GROUPS, AND COLLECTING DATA ON
JOB SATISFACTION AND PRODUCTIVITY BEFORE AND AFTER
IMPLEMENTING CHANGES IN THE JOB TO DETERMINE THE IMPACT OF
THOSE CHANGES. THIS GIVES THE COMPANY AN ADVANTAGE
WHEN THE EXPERIMENT IS FINISHED AND IMPLEMENTING THE JOB
THROUGHOUT THE COMPANY TAKES PLACE.
THE EXPERIMENT TO BE DONE BY THE ORGANIZATION FOLLOWS
THIRTEEN STEPS WHICH ARE CALLED THE JOB ENRICHMENT MODEL:
        ASSEMBLE REQUIRED RESOURCES
              1. SELECT THE JOB
              2. ESTABLISH JOB ENRICHMENT TEAM
              3. APPOINT JOB ENRICHMENT PROJECT MANAGER
              4. DETERMINE REQUIRED RESOURCES
              5. DETERMINE ITEMS TO BE MEASURED
              6. DESIGN INSTRUMENTS
              7. CONDUCT SURVEY AND ANALYZE DATA
        IMPLEMENT CHANGES IN CONTENT AND DISCRETION
              8. IDENTIFY POSSIBLE CHANGES IN CONTENT
AND DISCRETION
              9. SCREEN CHANGES TO DETERMINE FINAL TEST
              10. PLAN IMPLEMENTATION
              11. IMPLEMENT CHANGES
        ASSESS RESULTS
              12. MEASURE EFFECTIVENESS
              13. DETERMINE ORGANIZATIONAL IMPLICATION
THE EXPERIMENT IS THE FIRST STEP IN INCREASING MOTIVATION OF
EMPLOYEES THROUGHOUT THE ORGANIZATION. THE JOB CHANGES IN
THE EXPERIMENT MUST BE IMPLEMENTED THROUGHOUT THE
ORGANIZATION AND THE RESULTS OF THE EXPERIMENT SHOULD ALSO
BE SENT TO EVERYONE CONNECTED WITH THE EXPERIMENT.
IT MUST BE REMEMBERED THAT MOTIVATING EMPLOYEES IS AN
ON-GOING RESPONSIBILITY OF MANAGEMENT AND THAT THE
EXPERIMENTAL JOB ENRICHMENT PROJECTS WILL SET THE
GUIDELINES FOR EFFECTIVE ACTION TO MEET THAT RESPONSIBILITY.

M0177 GROFF, GENE K.
WORKER PRODUCTIVITY: AN INTEGRATED VIEW.
BUSINESS HORIZONS 14 (APRIL 1971): 78-86.

        THREE OF THE MOST IMPORTANT VARIABLES IN INFLUENCING
EMPLOYEE EFFORT ARE SUPERVISORY BEHAVIOR, INCENTIVE PAY AND
THE NATURE OF THE TASK ITSELF. REINFORCEMENT THROUGH
EXTRINSIC REWARD IS PROVIDED BY THE FIRST TWO; DIRECT
SATISFACTION IS PROVIDED BY THE THIRD. GROFF SUGGESTS THE
WAYS IN WHICH THESE AND OTHER VARIABLES AFFECT PRODUCTIVITY.

M0178 GUIDE TO PART-TIME WORK.
OCCUPATIONAL OUTLOOK QUARTERLY, FALL 1974, PP. 10-13.

        SINCE TWO-THIRDS OF ALL PART-TIME WORKERS ARE WOMEN,

M0178   SUGGESTIONS FOR PROMISING OCCUPATIONS ARE OFFERED.

M0179   GUION, ROBERT M.   LANDY, FRANK J.
        THE MEANING OF WORK AND THE MOTIVATION TO WORK.
        ORGANIZATIONAL BEHAVIOR AND HUMAN PERFORMANCE   7 (APRIL
        1972):   308-39.

            REPORTS RESEARCH WHICH SOUGHT TO MEASURE THE MEANING OF
        WORK AND THE MOTIVATION TO WORK AMONG NEWLY GRADUATED
        ENGINEERS HIRED BY EIGHT COMPANIES THROUGH COLLEGE
        RECRUITING PROGRAMS.   STRONGLY TASK ORIENTED INDIVIDUALS WHO
        WERE NOT GIVEN TO HIGH LEVELS OF ACTIVITY WERE MOTIVATED TO
        WORK TO THE DEGREE THAT THEY FOUND THE WORK TO BE
        MEANINGFUL WHILE PERSONS OF HIGH ACTIVITY LEVELS EXPENDED
        THEIR ENERGIES REGARDLESS OF THE MEANINGFULNESS OF THE WORK.
        MEANING OF WORK APPEARED ALSO TO BE CLOSELY RELATED TO JOB
        SATISFACTION.

M0180   GUNDERSON, E. K.   RYMAN, DAVID H.
        CONVERGENT AND DISCRIMINANT VALIDITIES OF PERFORMANCE
        EVALUATIONS IN EXTREMELY ISOLATED GROUPS.
        PERSONNEL PSYCHOLOGY 24 (WINTER 1971):   715-24.

            THIS PAPER DEALS WITH RESEARCH OVER A FOUR YEAR SPAN IN
        WHICH CIVILIAN SCIENTISTS AND NAVY PERSONNEL AT ANTARCTIC
        STATIONS WERE RATED INDEPENDENTLY BY THE SCIENTIFIC LEADER,
        THE OFFICER IN CHARGE AND BY PEERS IN ORDER TO EVALUATE
        THEIR SOCIAL, TASK AND EMOTIONAL PERFORMANCES AND
        ADJUSTMENT.
            TWO-HUNDRED SEVENTY NAVY PERSONNEL WERE RATED BY
        STATION LEADERS TWICE DURING THE WINTER PERIOD.   ANOTHER
        PERSONAL EVALUATION AND PERFORMANCE FORM WAS ADMINISTERED TO
        ALL STATION MEMBERS.
            THE STUDY ATTEMPTS TO DEVELOP SOME IDEAS FOR MEASURES
        FOR AN UNUSUAL AND STRESSFUL ENVIRONMENT.   SUPERVISOR
        RATINGS AND PEER EVALUATION TURNED OUT TO BE THE MOST
        EFFECTIVE PERFORMANCE EVALUATIONS HERE.
            EMOTION AND TASK AREAS OF BEHAVIOR COULD BE GENERALLY
        RECOGNIZED BY UNTRAINED OBSERVERS, AFTER SEVERAL MONTHS.
        THE EMOTION AND SOCIAL ADJUSTMENT COULD NOT BE AS CLEARLY
        SEEN TO THE OBSERVERS, HOWEVER.

M0181   HACKMAN, J. R.   LAWLER, EDWARD E.
        EMPLOYEE REACTIONS TO JOB CHARACTERISTICS.
        JOURNAL OF APPLIED PSYCHOLOGY 55 (JUNE 1971):   259-86.

            PROPOSES AND TESTS A CONCEPTUAL FRAMEWORK FOR
        MEASURING THE IMPACT OF JOB CHARACTERISTICS ON INDIVIDUAL
        WORK BEHAVIOR, ATTITUDES, MOTIVATION AND JOB SATISFACTION.
         IT WAS PREDICTED AND FOUND THAT WHEN JOBS ARE HIGH ON THE
        FOUR CORE DIMENSIONS (VARIETY, AUTONOMY, TASK IDENTITY,
        FEEDBACK), EMPLOYEES WHO ARE DESIROUS OF HIGHER-ORDER
        NEED-SATISFACTION TEND TO HAVE HIGH MOTIVATION, HAVE HIGH
        JOB SATISFACTION, ARE ABSENT FROM WORK INFREQUENTLY, AND
        ARE RATED BY SUPERVISORS AS DOING HIGH QUALITY WORK.

M0182   HADWIGER, DON F.
        EXPERIENCE OF BLACK FARMERS HOCE ADMINISTRATION LOCAL

M0182   OFFICE CHIEFS.
        PUBLIC PERSONNEL MANAGEMENT 2 (JANUARY-FEBRUARY 1973):
        49-54.

        THIS ARTICLE REPORTS THAT BLACKS IN RESPONSIBLE JOBS
        WERE ABOVE AVERAGE IN PERFORMANCE, MOTIVATION, AND
        ACHIEVEMENT.

M0183   GIVE MORE, GET MORE, TOP MANAGEMENT TOLD.
        CHEMICAL WEEK 108 (FEBRUARY 19, 1971): 12.

        REPORT OF AN AMERICAN MANAGEMENT ASSOCIATION
        CONFERENCE WHICH EMPHASIZED PRODUCTIVITY THROUGH MOTIVATION.
        HOW TO STEP UP EXECUTIVE EFFICIENCY IN LEAN TIMES.

M0184   HALL, DOUGLAS T.   MANSFIELD, ROGER.
        ORGANIZATIONAL AND INDIVIDUAL RESPONSE TO EXTERNAL STRESS.
        ADMINISTRATIVE SCIENCE QUARTERLY 16 (DECEMBER 1971):
        533-47.

        BECAUSE OF THE ECONOMIC SITUATION OF THE DAY AND
        ASSOCIATED PROBLEMS THIS RESEARCH IS FOCUSED ON STRESS IN
        THREE CHANGING ORGANIZATIONS AND THE PROBLEMS THAT
        ARISE.
        THREE CONNECTICUT RESEARCH AND DEVELOPMENT ORGANIZATIONS
        WERE USED TO CONDUCT THE SURVEY OF THE THREE COMPANIES.
        HALF HOUR INTERVIEWS WERE CONDUCTED WITH PROFESSIONAL
        MEMBERS OF THE RESEARCH STAFF. THEY WERE THEN ASKED TO
        FILL OUT QUESTIONNAIRES WHICH MEASURED NEEDS, JOB ATTITUDES,
        SELF-IMAGE, REWARD STRUCTURE, AND PERCEIVED ORGANIZATIONAL
        CLIMATE.
        INSTRUMENTS USED WERE PORTERS' (1971), THE LODAHL AND
        KEJNER (1965) SCALE, AND THE 7 POINT LIKERT SCALE.
        IT WAS FOUND, AS A RESULT OF DECREASES IN EXTERNAL
        FINANCIAL RESOURCES THAT THERE WAS A STRAIN ON THE
        ORGANIZATION WHICH CAUSED THE COMPANIES TO RESTRICT OR
        REORGANIZE SOME POLICIES. THIS IN TURN CAUSED STRESS AND
        STRAIN AT THE TOP OF A NEED-HIERARCHY SUCH AS MASLOWS'.
        THE MAIN RESULT WAS AN INTERNAL STRAIN AND INCREASED
        ALIENATION FROM THE ORGANIZATION.

M0185   HAMILTON, G. S.   ROESSNER, J. D.
        HOW EMPLOYERS SCREEN DISADVANTAGED JOB APPLICANTS.
        MONTHLY LABOR REVIEW 95 (SEPTEMBER 1972): 14-22.

        NEW EVIDENCE CALLS INTO QUESTION THE RELATIONSHIP
        BETWEEN HIRING STANDARDS AND ACTUAL TASKS A WORKER MUST
        PERFORM.

M0186   HAMMERTON, JAMES C.
        MANAGEMENT AND MOTIVATION.
        CALIFORNIA MANAGEMENT REVIEW 13 (WINTER 1970):   51-56.

        THE PROBLEM ADDRESSED HEREIN IS THAT OF MANAGING
        INTERDISCIPLINARY GROUPS OF PROFESSIONALS. EXPERIENCE
        INDICATES THAT A MORE THOROUGH-GOING APPLICATION OF THE
        GROUP PROJECT TEAM APPROACH IS THE WAY TO DEVELOP A
        PRODUCTIVE WORKING ENVIRONMENT WHICH RETAINS THE LOYALTY

M0186   AND ENTHUSIASM OF THE PROFESSIONAL EMPLOYEE.

M0187   HAMPTON, DAVID R.
        THE PLANNING-MOTIVATING DILEMMA.
        BUSINESS HORIZONS, 16 (JUNE 1973):   79-87.

            THE NEEDS AND DESIRES OF THE INDIVIDUAL INTERACT WITH
        CHARACTERISTICS OF THE WORK SITUATION AND EFFECTIVE
        MANAGEMENT MUST CONSIDER BOTH THE MOTIVES OF THE INDIVIDUAL
        AND ORGANIZATIONAL GOALS.

M0188   HARRIS, THOMAS C.   LOCKE, EDWIN A.
        REPLICATION OF WHITE-COLLAR-BLUE-COLLAR DIFFERENCES IN
        SOURCES OF SATISFACTION AND DISSATISFACTION.
        JOURNAL OF APPLIED PSYCHOLOGY, 59 (JUNE 1973):   369-70.

            SMALL SAMPLES OF WHITE-COLLAR AND BLUE-COLLAR
        EMPLOYEES WERE ASKED TO DESCRIBE SOURCES OF SATISFACTION AND
        DISSATISFACTION ON THE JOB.   THESE CRITICAL INCIDENTS WERE
        CLASSIFIED USING THE SCHNEIDER-LOCKE EVENT-AGENT
        CLASSIFICATION SYSTEM.

M0189   HARRISON, DON K.
        SIMILARITY-DISSIMILARITY IN COUNSELOR-COUNSELEE ETHNIC
        MATCH AND ITS RELEVANCE TO GOAL BEHAVIORS OF JOB TRAINEES.
        PH. D. DISSERTATION, UNIVERSITY OF MICHIGAN, 1972.

            THIS STUDY EXPLORED THE ATTITUDES OF BLACK MANPOWER
        TRAINEES TOWARD COUNSELORS WHO DIFFERED IN RACE AND EXAMINED
        THE EFFECTS OF COUNSELOR RACE ON GOAL PERSISTING BEHAVIOR
        AS PERCEIVED BY MANPOWER TRAINEES.

M0190   HARRISON, FRANK.
        THE MANAGEMENT OF SCIENTISTS: DETERMINANTS OF PERCEIVED
        ROLE PERFORMANCE OF 95 SCIENTISTS IN THREE LARGE RESEARCH
        LABORATORIES TO THE ORGANIC SYSTEM OF MANAGEMENT CONCEIVED
        BY BURNS AND STALKER.

M0191   HAYDEN, ROBERT J.
        PERFORMANCE APPRAISAL: A BETTER WAY.
        PERSONNEL JOURNAL 18 (JULY 1973):   53-55.

            SOME ORIGINAL IDEAS ARE PRESENTED IN THIS ARTICLE
        WHICH WILL BE USEFUL TO THOSE RESPONSIBLE FOR THE DESIGN
        OR MODIFICATION OF PERFORMANCE APPRAISAL SYSTEMS.

M0192   HAYES, J.   HOUGH, P.
        THE PERCEPTION OF OTHER WORK ROLES: IMPLICATIONS FOR JOB
        CHANGE.
        MANAGEMENT STUDIES 2 (MAY 1974):   143-48.

            IT IS HYPOTHESIZED IN THIS ARTICLE THAT WORK EXPERIENCE
        DOES NOT INFLUENCE THE WAY IN WHICH A PERSON THINKS ABOUT
        OCCUPATIONS OTHER THAN HIS OWN.

M0193   HAYGHE, HOWARD.
        LABOR FORCE ACTIVITY OF MARRIED WOMEN.
        MONTHLY LABOR REVIEW, APRIL 1973, PP. 31-396

M0193   A SPECIAL LABOR FORCE REPORT ON MARITAL AND FAMILY
CHARACTERISTICS SHOWS AN INCREASE IN THE NUMBER OF FAMILIES
WITH MORE THAN ONE WORKER.

M0194   HAYGHE, HOWARD.
MARITAL AND FAMILY CHARACTERISTICS OF THE LABOR FORCE IN
MARCH 1973.
MONTHLY LABOR REVIEW, APRIL 1974, PP. 21-27.

A SPECIAL LABOR FORCE REPORT SHOWS A CONTINUED
DECLINE IN LABOR FORCE PARTICIPATION RATES OF MARRIED MEN
AND AN INCREASE IN RATES OF MARRIED WOMEN WITH YOUNG
CHILDREN.

M0195   HEATH, BROOKS N.
WESTERN ELECTRICS MOTIVATION AND ENRICHMENT TRIAL.
MANAGEMENT REVIEW 64 (MARCH 1975):   40-43.

THE AUTHOR PRESENTS A BRIEF SUMMATION OF A PROJECT
CONDUCTED IN A WESTERN ELECTRIC PLANT WHICH SOUGHT TO
DEVELOP POTENTIAL OF THE INDUSTRIAL WORKER.   THE ARTICLE
OUTLINES THE PROJECTS GOALS, METHODS AND RESULTS.

M0196   HEDGES, JANICE N.
A LOOK AT THE 4-DAY WORKWEEK.
MONTHLY LABOR REVIEW 94 (OCTOBER 1971):   33-37.

A 4-DAY WORKWEEK IS EXAMINED AND CONCLUSIONS ABOUT ITS
FUTURE ARE PRESENTED.

M0197   HEDGES, JANICE N.   BEMIS, STEPHEN E.
SEX STEREOTYPING: ITS DECLINE IN SKILLED TRADES.
MONTHLY LABOR REVIEW, MAY 1974, PP. 14-22.

ABOUT ONE EMPLOYED WOMAN IN SIXTY IS IN A SKILLED
TRADE; MOVEMENT INTO SKILLED JOBS ACCELERATES AS EMPLOYMENT
BARRIERS FALL.

M0198   HEDGES, JANICE N.
ABSENCE FROM WORK: A LOOK AT SOME NATIONAL DATA.
MONTHLY LABOR REVIEW, JULY 1973, PP. 24-31.

INFORMATION USED IN THIS WAS TAKEN FROM THE CURRENT
SURVEY OF HOUSEHOLDS, CONDUCTED EACH MONTH BY THE BUREAU OF
THE CENSUS.
THIS PARTICULAR ARTICLE ATTEMPTED TO POINT OUT SOME OF
THE PROBLEM AREAS AND ACCESS THE INFLUENCE OF VARIOUS
FACTORS OFTEN CITED AS MAJOR CAUSES OF UNSCHEDULED PERSONAL
ABSENCE.   (THE ARTICLE WAS CONFINED TO WAGE AND SALARY
WORKERS, EXCLUDING FARM AND PRIVATE HOUSEHOLD WORKERS.)
IN A COMPARISON OF THIS SURVEY AND ONE TAKEN FIVE YEARS
EARLIER, IT WAS FOUND THAT, FOR WHAT EVER REASON THERE MIGHT
BE UNSCHEDULED PERSONAL ABSENCES OF LESS THAN A WEEK, WAS
SIGNIFICANTLY HIGH IN 1972.   TOTAL MAN HOURS LOST AS A
RESULT OF THESE SHORT-TERM ABSENCES AVERAGED 43.8 MILLION
HOURS PER WEEK IN 1972.
THE MAJOR FACTORS SUGGESTED AS CONTRIBUTING TO THE
INCREASE IN ABSENCES ARE: A DISPROPORTIONATE INCREASE IN

M0198 INDUSTRIES OR OCCUPATION HIGH WITH ABSENCE RATES; AN
       INCREASE IN THE AVERAGE AGE OF WORKERS; OR A DECREASE IN THE
       AVERAGE AGE OF WORKERS.
            ANOTHER REASON THAT HAS BEEN SUGGESTED WHY WORKERS ARE
       MORE LIKELY TO TAKE OFF ILL IS THAT THERE IS AN INCREASING
       PREVALENCE OF PAID SICK LEAVE.
            WHEN THE SURVEY WAS NARROWED TO INDUSTRY WORKERS, IT
       WAS FOUND THAT IN 1972, OPERATIVES, LABORERS, AND SERVICE
       WORKERS HAD THE HIHGEST RATES OF ABSENCE ON THE ASSEMBLY
       LINES, WHICH ARE SOMETIMES ATTRIBUTED TO MANDATORY OVERTIME,
       POOR WORKING CONDITIONS, OR BOREDOM WITH THE JOB, AND
       SOMETIMES TO THE INCREASING COMPLEXITY OF LIFE.
            THERE IS CERTAIN LITERATURE ON ABSENCE THAT GIVES
       VARIOUS CHARACTERISTICS THAT ARE RELATED TO ABSENCE. THESE
       INCLUDE AGE, SEX, AND MARITAL STATUS.
            YOUTH HAS BEEN A CENTRAL FACT ASSOCIATED WITH HIGH
       RATES OF ABSENCE ON ASSEMBLY LINES. PART-WEEK ABSENCE WAS
       HIGHEST AMONG TEENAGE WORKERS AND LOWEST AMONG THOSE AGE
       64-75. HOWEVER, FULL-WEEK UNSCHEDULED ABSENCE WAS LESS
       FREQUENT FOR THE YOUNGER WORKERS AND INCREASED GRADUALLY
       WITH AGE.
            WOMEN WERE MORE LIKELY THAN MEN (GENERALLY SPEAKING) TO
       MISS MORE DAYS, DUE TO THE FACT THAT THEY WERE LIKELY TO BE
       NEW EMPLOYEES IN THE LOWER SKILLED, LOWER PAID OCCUPATIONS.

M0199 HENDERSON, RICHARD I.
       MONEY IS, TOO, AN INCENTIVE: ONE COMPANY'S EXPERIENCE.
       SUPERVISORY MANAGEMENT, 5 (MAY 1974): 20-25.

            ARTICLE DESCRIBES THE FINANCIAL INCENTIVE PROGRAM. IN
       EFFECT, A BONUS SYSTEM IS INCLUDED.

M0200 HENLE, PETER.
       WORKER DISSATISFACTION: A LOOK AT THE ECONOMIC EFFECTS.
       MONTHLY LABOR REVIEW 97 (FEBRUARY 1974): 58.

            THERE IS EVIDENCE THAT SUPPORTS THE PROPOSITION THAT
       THERE IS INCREASING JOB DISSATISFACTION, INCLUDING, FOR
       EXAMPLE, THE INCREASE IN THE RATE OF ABSENCES AND THE
       INCREASING PROPORTION OF STRIKES OVER WORKING CONDITIONS.
            HOWEVER, EACH OF THESE POINTS MUST BE QUALIFIED. THE
       SIGNIFICANCE OF THE INCREASED RATE OF UNSCHEDULED ABSENCES
       IS NOT CLEAR; TO SOME EXTENT IT MAY SIMPLY REFLECT WORKERS'
       TAKING ADVANTAGES OF THE NEW PAID-LEAVE PRIVILEGES. THE
       INCREASE IN THE PROPORTION OF STRIKES OVER WORKING
       CONDITIONS CONTAINS SUCH A LARGE NUMBER OF VARIABLES THAT
       ITS IMPLICATIONS IN TERMS OF ATTITUDES TOWARD WORK ARE
       UNCERTAIN.
            HENLE BELIEVES THAT WORKERS MAY NOT BE HAPPY AT WORK,
       BUT THERE IS LITTLE EVIDENCE THAT THIS HAS AFFECTED THEIR
       ECONOMIC PERFORMANCE. THE ABSENCE OF ANY CLEAR-CUT
       ECONOMIC DATA INDICATING JOB DISSATISFACTION RAISES THE
       POSSIBILITY THAT PEOPLE MAY BE MORE SATISFIED WITH THEIR
       JOBS THAN MANY PEOPLE HAVE SUGGESTED.
            THERE HAVE BEEN DEVELOPMENTS THAT HAVE CREATED A MORE
       FAVORABLE WORKING ENVIRONMENT. THEY MAY HAVE THE EFFECT OF
       MAKING WORK MORE TOLERABLE ECONOMICALLY THAN IN THE PAST.
            THERE IS ONLY LIMITED EVIDENCE THAT JOB DISSATISFACTION

M0200 HAS INTERFERED WITH THE PERFORMANCE OF THE NATIONAL ECONOMY.
IF WORK IS TO RETAIN ITS ATTRACTION, MANAGEMENT AND LABOR
MAY HAVE TO CHANGE SOME ATTITUDES AND APPROACHES TO THE WORK
ENVIRONMENT.

M0201 HERMAN, ARTHUR S.
RAPID PRODUCTIVITY GAINS REPORTED FOR SELECTED INDUSTRIES
FOR 1971.
MONTHLY LABOR REVIEW 95 (AUGUST 1972): 41-43.

EXAMINES THE GROWTH IN PRODUCTIVITY FOR CERTAIN FIRMS.

M0202 HERMAN, JEANNE B. HULIN, C. L.
MANAGERIAL SATISFACTIONS AND ORGANIZATIONAL ROLES: AN
INVESTIGATION OF PORTER'S NEED DEFICIENCY SCALES.
JOURNAL OF APPLIED PSYCHOLOGY 2 (APRIL 1973): 118-24.

THIS RESEARCH ON THE RELATIONSHIP BETWEEN JOB
SATISFACTION OF SUPERVISORS AND FOREMEN AND LEVEL IN THE
ORGANIZATIONAL HIERARCHY UTILIZED PORTER'S NEED
SATISFACTION QUESTIONNAIRE AND THE JOB DESCRIPTION INDEX.
THE JDI SUPPORTED THE RELATIONSHIP BUT THE PORTER
QUESTIONNAIRE DID NOT. THE AUTHORS INDICATE THAT THE
POINT OF THIS DISCUSSION IS NOT TO DISCREDIT THE VALIDITY
OF THE HEIRARCHICAL LEVEL-JOB SATISFACTION HYPOTHESIS, ONLY
TO QUESTION THE SUPPORT OF THAT HYPOTHESIS IN THE NEED
SATISFACTION STUDIES.

M0203 HERMAN, SHELBY W. FULCO, LAWRENCE J.
CHANGES IN PRODUCTIVITY AND UNIT LABOR COSTS -- A YEARLY
REVIEW.
MONTHLY LABOR REVIEW 94 (MAY 1971): 3-15.

DISCUSSES EMPLOYMENT CHANGES AND INCOME DISTRIBUTION IN
RELATION TO UNIT LABOR COSTS, NONLABOR PRODUCTION COSTS, AND
PRODUCTIVITY DEVELOPMENTS.

M0204 HERMAN, SHELBY W.
PRODUCTIVITY AND COST MOVEMENTS IN 1971.
MONTHLY LABOR REVIEW 95 (MAY 1972): 12-16.

CONTRIBUTES A RAPID USE IN PRODUCTIVITY TO RETRENCHMENT
IN MAN-HOURS.

M0205 HERRICK, N. Q.
GOVERNMENT APPROACHES TO THE HUMANIZATION OF WORK.
MONTHLY LABOR REVIEW 96 (APRIL 1973): 52-54.

HERRICK SAYS THAT THERE ARE FOUR BASIC CONDITIONS OF
WORK: SECURITY, EQUITY, INDIVIDUATION, AND DEMOCRACY.
THE GOVERNMENT HAS TRIED TO ATTAIN THESE CONDITIONS IN
SEVERAL WAYS. FOR EXAMPLE, THE SOCIAL SECURITY ACT OF 1935
PRODUCED AN UNEMPLOYMENT SYSTEM, A RETIREMENT SYSTEM, AND
AID TO PEOPLE LOOKING FOR WORK. THE FAIR LABOR STANDARDS
ACT OF 1938 SETS MINIMUM STANDARDS AS TO THE EQUITY OF
COMPENSATION. THE CIVIL RIGHTS ACT OF 1964 AIMS TOWARD
EQUITY FOR MINORITIES. THE MANPOWER DEVELOPMENT AND
TRAINING ACT OF 1972 PROVIDES OPPORTUNITIES FOR LEARNING AND

M0205   GROWTH, ESPECIALLY FOR THE DISADVANTAGED.
        THESE ACCOMPLISHMENTS HAVE NOT BEEN ENOUGH. THE
        PRESENT   DAY WORK FORCE HAS NEEDS OF AUTONOMY AND DEMOCRACY.
        THE NATIONAL COMMISSION ON PRODUCTIVITY PLANS TO SPONSOR A
        QUALITY OF WORK PROGRAM, WHICH CONSISTS OF WORK HUMANIZATION
        EFFORTS IN A NUMBER OF MAJOR CORPORATIONS. IT PLANS TO
        MEASURE THE HUMAN AND ECONOMIC OUTCOMES OF EXISTING
        CONDITIONS, TO SET UP WORKER-MANAGEMENT COUNCILS THAT WILL
        CONSIDER WAYS TO IMPROVE THE QUALITY OF WORK, AND TO
        PERIODICALLY MEASURE THE HUMAN AND ECONOMIC OUTCOMES AS
        WORK BECOMES MORE HUMANIZED. OTHER GOVERNMENT TASK FORCES
        WILL PERFORM ADDITIONAL STUDIES.
             STUDIES INDICATE THAT WORKERS ARE CONCERNED WITH
        BOREDOM, LACK OF STIMULATION, AND THE WASTE OF THEIR
        ABILITIES. HAVING DEFINED THE PROBLEM, THE GOVERNMENT IS
        ENCOURAGING PROGRAMS DESIGNED TO MEET THE NEEDS OF THE
        WORKERS.

M0206   HERRICK, N. Q.   QUINN, R. P.
        WORKING CONDITIONS SURVEY AS A SOURCE OF SOCIAL
        INDICATORS.
        MONTHLY LABOR REVIEW 94 (APRIL 1971):   15-24.

        THIS SURVEY IS BASED ON PRELIMINARY FINDINGS OF A SURVEY
        CONDUCTED BY THE UNIVERSITY OF MICHIGAN SURVEY RESEARCH
        CENTER. IT ATTEMPTED TO RELATE INTRINSIC AND EXTRINSIC
        ELEMENTS OF WORK TO WORKERS SATISFACTION WITH THEIR JOBS.
        A NATIONAL PROBABILITY SAMPLE OF 1533 EMPLOYED PERSONS OF
        AGE 16 OR OLDER WHO WORKED 20 HOURS OR MORE PER WEEK WAS
        TAKEN IN NOVEMBER AND DECEMBER OF 1969. THIS FORMED THE
        BASIS FOR THE RESULTS FOUND.
        THERE WERE 23 QUESTIONS USED TO PROVIDE SIX SCORES
        REFLECTING WORKERS TOTAL SATISFACTION WITH THEIR JOBS AND
        THEIR SATISFACTION WITH FIVE MORE SPECIFIC ASPECTS OF THEIR
        JOBS.   THESE SPECIFIC ASPECTS WERE SATISFACTION WITH PAY,
        RESOURCES FOR DOING THE JOB, CO-WORKERS, CHALLENGE PROVIDED
        BY THE JOB, AND COMFORT ASPECT OF THE JOB.   THE WORKERS
        RATED THESE AREAS IN THE ORDER OF THE ASPECT CONTRIBUTING
        MOST TO SATISFACTION AS CHALLENGE, PAY, COMFORT, RESOURCE
        ADEQUACY, AND LASTLY RELATIONS WITH CO-WORKERS.
        SEVERAL MAJOR DEMOGRAPHIC AND OCCUPATIONAL SUB-GROUPS
        WERE CONTRASTED IN TERMS OF THEIR MEAN SCORES ON OVERALL JOB
        SATISFACTION.   IT WAS FOUND THAT WORKERS LEAST SATISFIED
        WERE WOMEN, BLACKS, YOUNGER WORKERS, WAGE AND SALARY
        WORKERS, BLUE-COLLAR WORKERS, THOSE IN SERVICE OCCUPATIONS,
        AND THOSE WITH LOW INCOMES.   THESE PEOPLE WERE ALSO THE
        LEAST SATISFIED WITH THE CHALLENGE OF THEIR JOBS. OTHER
        SUCH COMPARISONS WERE MADE.
        A TABLE PREPARED IN THE SURVEY LISTED THE CHARACTERISTICS OF
        WORKERS OR JOBS MOST HIGHLY RELATED TO OVERALL JOB
        SATISFACTION.   LISTED MOST IMPORTANTLY WERE ITEMS RELATING
        SUPERVISION, RESOURCES, AUTONOMY, CHALLENGE AND ENRICHMENT,
        FRINGE BENEFITS, SECURITY, AND SAFETY CONDITIONS.
        JOB SATISFACTION HAS A GREAT CORRELATION WITH JOB
        CONTENT-RESOURCE ADEQUACY, AUTONOMY, CHALLENGE, ETC.
        WORKERS HAVE CONSIDERABLE MOTIVATION TOWARD PRODUCTIVITY
        AND ACHIEVEMENT.   THEREFORE, JOBS SHOULD BE DESIGNED
        TO OFFER PEOPLE NOT ONLY ECONOMIC AND TANGIBLE RETURNS, BUT

M0206 ALSO MORE SELF-FULFILLMENT THROUGH THEIR WORK.

M0207 HERZBERG, F. I.
NEW PERSPECTIVES ON THE WILL TO WORK.
MANAGEMENT REVIEW 63 (NOVEMBER 1974): 52-54.

THE AUTHOR OUTLINES THREE MAJOR MANAGERIAL
PHILOSOPHIES. WHILE ALL THREE HAVE HAD THEIR SUCCESS, THEY
ARE FAILURES TODAY. HERZBERG MAINTAINS THAT ORTHODOX JOB
ENRICHMENT IS THE MOST PROMISING OF ALL THE ORGANIZATIONAL
IMPROVMENT STRATEGIES.

M0208 HILGERT, RAYMOND L.
POSITIVE PERSONAL MOTIVATION: THE MANAGER'S GUIDE TO
INFLUENCING OTHERS.
PERSONNEL JOURNAL 53 (NOVEMBER 1974): 832-34.

THE AUTHOR OUTLINES A PROGRAM OF POSITIVE
SELF-DEVELOPMENT FOR MANAGERS WHICH WILL ALSO HELP TO
MOTIVATE OTHERS.

M0209 HINES, GEORGE H.
CROSS-CULTURAL DIFFERENCES IN TWO-FACTOR MOTIVATION
THEORY.
JOURNAL OF APPLIED PSYCHOLOGY 3 (DECEMBER 1973): 375-77.

THE APPLICABILITY OF HERZBERG'S THEORY TO CONDITIONS IN
NEW ZEALAND WAS TESTED BY COMPARING JOB FACTOR RATINGS AND
OVERALL JOB SATISFACTION OF MIDDLE MANAGERS AND SALARIED
EMPLOYEES. CONTRARY TO FINDINGS IN OTHER COUNTRIES, THE
RESULTS INDICATED THE THEORY APPEARS TO HAVE VALIDITY
ACROSS OCCUPATIONAL LEVELS. FOR MANAGERS AND SALARIED
EMPLOYEES THERE WAS NO STATISTICALLY SIGNIFICANT DIFFERENCE
BETWEEN THE MOTIVATOR AND HYGIENE FACTORS FOR EITHER
SATISFIED OR DISSATISFIED PERSONNEL.

M0210 HOARD, A. K.   GURIN, PATRICIA B.
EXPECTANCY THEORY AND ITS IMPLICATIONS FOR HIGHER EDUCATION
AMONG BLACK YOUTH.
ANN ARBOR: THE UNIVERSITY OF MICHIGAN, DECEMBER 1973.

THIS STUDY OF BLACKS IN THEIR SENIOR YEAR OF HIGH SCHOOL
INVESTIGATES SOME OF THE SOCIO-PSYCHOLOGICAL AND
ENVIRONMENTAL DETERRENTS TO THE PURSUIT OF POST-HIGH SCHOOL
EDUCATION OR TRAINING, AND APPRAISES THE EFFECTIVENESS OF
DIFFERENT TYPES OF GUIDANCE PROGRAMS IN OVERCOMING THESE
DETERRENTS. SPECIAL ATTENTION IS BEING GIVEN TO THE ROLE OF
EXPECTANCY (I.E., AN INDIVIDUAL'S PERCEPTIONS OF
OPPORTUNITIES AND OF THE LIKELIHOOD OF SUCCESS) IN BLACK
YOUTHS' DECISIONS TO CONTINUE THEIR EDUCATION.

M0211 HODGE, CLAIRE C.
THE NEGRO JOB SITUATION: HAS IT IMPROVED.
MONTHLY LABOR REVIEW 92 (JANUARY 1969): 20-28.

BLS SURVEY SHOWS OCCUPATIONAL GAINS BY BLACK WORKERS:
MORE EMPLOYED IN BETTER JOBS.

M0212 HOFFMAN, FRANK O.
       TEAM SPIRIT AS IT AFFECTS PRODUCTIVITY.
       PERSONNEL ADMINISTRATOR 16 (MAY-JUNE 1971): 11-15.

          DESCRIBES THE DIMENSIONS OF MORALE AND THEIR IMPACTS ON
       WORKERS PRODUCTIVITY AS INDIVIDUALS AND AS TEAMS. LISTS
       OBSTACLES TO BEST PERFORMANCE AND MAXIMUM JOB SATISFACTION

M0213 HOUSE, JAMES.
       OCCUPATIONAL STRESS AND PHYSICAL HEALTH.
       MANPOWER, 5 (OCTOBER 1973): 3-9.

          DISCUSSION OF EFFECT OF STRESS ON PHYSICAL AND MENTAL
       HEALTH, AND THEREBY ON PERFORMANCE. ALSO, CAUSES OF STRESS
       IN VARIOUS JOB SITUATIONS.

M0214 HOW MUSIC CAN ENHANCE THE OFFICE ENVIRONMENT.
       THE OFFICE 73 (JUNE 1973): 70-73.

          JOHN FINN, OFFICE SERVICES MANAGER, NATIONWIDE
       INSURANCE COMPANIES, WHITE PLAINS, N. Y., HAS INSTITUTED AND
       FOUND SUCCESSFUL A MUZAK SYSTEM SPECIFICALLY DESIGNED TO
       IMPROVE EMPLOYEE EFFICIENCY. THE APPROACH IS BRIEFLY
       DESCRIBED.

M0215 HOWELL, M. A.   NEWMAN, SIDNEY H.
       NARRATIVE AND CHECK-OFF EVALUATIONS OF EMPLOYEE
       PERFORMANCE.
       PUBLIC PERSONNEL REVIEW 32 (JULY 1971): 148-50.

          REPORTS ON RESEARCH WHICH COMPARED RESULTS OF NARRATIVE
       AND CHECK-OFF TYPES OF PERFORMANCE EVALUATIONS AMONG
       PHYSICIANS IN THE COMMISSIONED CORPS OF THE U. S. PUBLIC
       HEALTH SERVICE. EVIDENCE INDICATED THAT NARRATIVE
       APPRAISALS, WHEN PROPERLY CODED AND SCORED ARE AS VALID AS
       CHECK-OFF EVALUATIONS. HOWEVER, THE LATTER ARE GENERALLY
       MORE RELIABLE, EASIER TO SCORE, AND QUICKER TO ADMINISTER.

M0216 HUBBARD, ROBERT L. VEROFF, JOSEPH.
       FUTURE ORIENTATION AND EXPECTATIONS AS PREDICTORS OF
       EMPLOYMENT SUCCESS.
       ANN ARBOR: THE UNIVERSITY OF MICHIGAN.
       SCHEDULED FOR COMPLETION FISCAL YEAR 1975.

          THIS PROJECT BUILDS ON AN ONGOING STUDY OF THE INFLUENCE OF
       ACHIEVEMENT MOTIVATION ON TRAINEES' JOB SUCCESS (GRANT
       91-24-70-15) WHOSE PRELIMINARY FINDINGS SUGGEST THAT
       MOTIVATION IS AFFECTED BY LABOR MARKET CONDITIONS AT THE
       TIME OF APPRAISAL AND THE INDIVIDUAL'S GENERAL ORIENTATION
       TO THE FUTURE. JOB HISTORIES AND MEASURES OF MOTIVATION ARE
       BEING USED IN THIS PROJECT.

M0217 HUBBARD, ROBERT L.   VEROFF, JOSEPH.
       FUTURE ORIENTATION AND EXPECTATIONS AS PREDICTORS OF
       EMPLOYMENT SUCCESS.
       ANN ARBOR: THE UNIVERSITY OF MICHIGAN.
       SCHEDULED FOR COMPLETION FISCAL YEAR 1974.

THIS PROJECT BUILDS ON AN ONGOING STUDY OF THE INFLUENCE OF
ACHIEVEMENT MOTIVATION ON TRAINEES'JOB SUCCESS WHOSE
PRELIMINARY FINDINGS SUGGEST THAT MOTIVATION IS AFFECTED BY
LABOR MARKET CONDITIONS AT THE TIME OF APPRAISAL AND THE
INDIVIDUAL'S GENERAL ORIENTATION TO THE FUTURE. IT
ADDRESSES SUCH QUESTIONS AS: WHAT FACTORS AFFECT TRAINEES'
EXPECTATIONS? HOW DO FUTURE ORIENTATION AND EXPECTATIONS
FUNCTION AS PREDICTORS OF JOB SUCCESS? WHAT CAUSED THESE
EXPECTATIONS TO CHANGE? JOB HISTORIES AND MEASURES OF
MOTIVATION AND EXPECTATIONS FOR
APPROXIMATELY 150 TRAINEES FROM THE OTHER STUDY ARE BEING
USED IN THIS PROJECT.

M0218 HUBNER, WALTER.
INDIVIDUAL NEED SATISFACTION IN WORK AND NONWORK.
PH. D. DISSERTATION, UNIVERSITY OF WISCONSIN, 1971.

STUDY EXPLORES BLUE-COLLAR WORKERS' MOTIVATIONS AND
THE SATISFACTION THEY FIND IN WORK (AS OPPOSED TO LEISURE),
AND IN SPECIFIC JOBS.*

M0219 HULIN, C. L.
EFFECTS OF CHANGES IN JOB SATISFACTION LEVELS ON EMPLOYEE
TURNOVER.
JOURNAL OF APPLIED PSYCHOLOGY 52 (1968): 122-26.

EXAMINES THE RELATIONSHIP OF JOB SATISFACTION TO EMPLOYEE
TURNOVER.
SETTING
RESEARCH TOOK PLACE WITHIN A LARGE INTERNATIONAL
MANUFACTURING COMPANY, EMPLOYING APPROXIMATELY 400 FEMALE
CLERICAL WORKERS IN THE CORPORATE OFFICE. TURNOVER RATE IN
THE THREE YEARS PRECEDING THE INITIAL STUDY WAS
APPROXIMATELY 30% IN EACH YEAR. THIS RATE SEEMED TO BE
STABLE, SHOWING NO TENDENCY IN EITHER DIRECTION FOR THE TEN
YEARS PRECEEDING THE STUDY. TURNOVER RATE WAS COMPUTED BY
OBTAINING THE RATIO OF NUMBER OF QUITS PER YEAR TO THE
AVERAGE NUMBER OF FEMALE EMPLOYEES. (AVERAGE WAS TAKEN
OF THE NUMBER EMPLOYED AT THE BEGINNING OF THE YEAR AND
THE NUMBER EMPLOYED AT THE END OF THE YEAR.)
SUBJECTS
THE ENTIRE FEMALE CLERICAL STAFF WAS ASKED TO PARTICIPATE
IN THE SURVEY CONDUCTED BY THE COMPANY. ANONYMITY WAS
ASSURED. OF 350 PRESENT DURING THE WEEK OF THE SURVEY,
298 (85.1%) PARTICIPATED.
VARIABLES
SATISFACTION WAS MEASURED BY THE JOB DESCRIPTION INDEX.
IN ADDITION TO THE FIVE SATISFACTION VARIABLES MEASURED,
WORKER'S AGE, EDUCATION LEVEL, JOB LEVEL, SOCIOECONOMIC
BACKGROUND AND MOTHER TONGUE WERE ALSO MEASURED. VARIABLES
WERE MEASURED DURING THE FIRST WEEK OF JULY
1966 AND BY THE FIRST WEEK OF APRIL 1967, 32 HAD QUIT OF
WHOM 20 COULD BE POSITIVELY IDENTIFIED. FOUR OF THE
TWENTY WERE ELIMINATED BECAUSE 3 WERE SUMMER STUDENTS AND
ONE DIDN'T SUBMIT ENOUGH BIOGRAPHICAL INFORMATION TO YIELD
MEASURES OF THE CONTROL VARIABLES SO THAT IT WAS
POSSIBLE TO OBTAIN CONTROL SS.
RESULTS

M0219 TURNOVER RATE IN 1964, BEFORE ANY CHANGES IN COMPANY
       POLICY AND PROCEDURE, WAS 30%. IN 1965, THE TURNOVER RATE
       DROPPED TO 18% AND IN 1966, THE YEAR OF THE STUDY, THE
       TURNOVER WAS COMPUTED AT 12%.
       CONCLUSION
       A STRONG INFERENCE IS MADE THAT THE COMPANY PROGRAM
       INITIATED IN 1964 BROUGHT ABOUT AN INCREASE IN THE
       SATISFACTION LEVELS OF THE FEMALE CLERICAL WORKERS AND
       CONSEQUENTLY, THE TURNOVER RATE WAS REDUCED BECAUSE OF
       THIS INCREASE IN SATISFACTION. HOWEVER, HULIN CONSIDERS
       SEVERAL ALTERNATIVE EXPLANATIONS.

M0220 IF AT FIRST THEY DON'T SUCCEED . . .
       MANPOWER, AUGUST 1970, PP. 9-12.

           YOUNGSTERS WHO FAIL AT JOBS GO BACK FOR MORE TRAINING.

M0221 ILGEN, DANIEL R.
       SATISFACTION WITH PERFORMANCE AS A FUNCTION OF THE INITIAL
       LEVEL OF EXPECTED PERFORMANCE AND THE DEVIATION FROM
       EXPECTATIONS.
       ORGANIZATIONAL BEHAVIOR AND HUMAN PERFORMANCE 6 (MAY 1971):
       345-61.

           THE RESEARCH FOUND: THE LEVELS OF PERFORMANCE HAD A
       DIRECT EFFECT ON PERFORMANCE SATISFACTION AND ALSO
       MODERATED THE EXTENT TO WHICH THE EXPECTATION-EXPERIENCE
       COMPARISON AFFECTED SATISFACTION.
           TO THE EXTENT THAT STIMULUS OBJECTS OTHER THAN
       PERFORMANCE CAN BE CONSIDERED IN TERMS OF THE AMOUNT OR
       QUANTITY PRESENT IN THE JOB, AN IMPLICATION OF THE PRESENT
       STUDY CAN BE RELATED TO THE MEASUREMENT OF JOB
       SATISFACTION.

M0222 IMES, I. E.
       ORGANIZATIONAL VOIDS THAT IMPROVE PERFORMANCE.
       MANAGEMENT REVIEW 58 (SEPTEMBER 1969): 15-17.

           THIS ARTICLE EXPLAINS HOW ORGANIZATIONAL VOIDS, WHICH
       ARE INTENTIONAL AND CONTROLLED DECISION-MAKING OR LEADERSHIP
       FUNCTIONS THAT ARE UNFILLED, CAN BE
       USED AS A MANAGERIAL TOOL TO MOTIVATE EMPLOYEES, DEVELOP
       THEIR ABILITIES, AND MAKE THEM MORE PERFORMANCE CONSCIOUS.
       AMONG OTHER BENEFITS, THE AUTHOR FOUND THAT GRIEVANCES AND
       COMPLAINTS DROP OFF AND RELATIONS BECAME MORE OPEN AND
       CORDIAL.
           VOIDS ARE INTENTIONALLY INSERTED BETWEEN TWO EXISTING
       LEVELS OF AN ORGANIZATION, MEANING THAT THE
       HIGHER LEVEL OPENS CERTAIN OF ITS FUNCTIONS TO THE LOWER.
       DELEGATION OF AUTHORITY IS DIFFERENTIATED FROM A VOID BY
       STATING THAT DELEGATION IS OFTEN DETERMINED TO BE
       FAIRLY DIRECT IN THAT THE SUPERVISOR PASSES OUT NEW
       RESPONSIBILITY AND THE SUBORDINATE RECEIVES IT. THE ACTION
       FOLLOWS THE CHAIN OF COMMAND. AN ORGANIZATIONAL VOID IS
       THE REVERSE: THE SUBORDINATE INITIATES TAKING ON NEW
       RESPONSIBILITY. THE SUPERVISOR'S MAIN PURPOSE IS TO CREATE
       A CLIMATE IN WHICH THE SUBORDINATE CAN SEE THAT HE HAS A
       CHOICE AND CAN FEEL FREE TO MAKE IT.

M0222 THE VOIDS ARE FIRST MADE AT THE SHIFT SUPERVISOR LEVEL,
THEN, THE FOREMEN PICK UP THE NEW PROCEDURE. VOIDS ARE THEN
OPENED AT THE HOURLY LEVEL BY ENCOURAGING THE FOREMEN TO DO
LESS OF THE OPERATING WORK.
  IMES CONCLUDES THAT THIS APPROACH IS BEST APPLIED TO
LINE FUNCTIONS BECAUSE PEOPLE WHO ARE INTERESTED AND
CHALLENGED BY THEIR WORK AND ASSOCIATE THEIR GOAL WITH
THOSE OF THE COMPANY WILL WORK MORE CONSCIENTIOUSLY.
MANAGEMENT'S ONLY PART IS TO STRENGTHEN COMMUNICATION ABOUT
RESULTS BECAUSE, AS IMES STATES, INFORMATION FREELY GIVEN
ABOUT IMPROVED PERFORMANCE REINFORCES POSITIVE ATTITUDES
ON THE PART OF THE EMPLOYEES. COMMUNICATION HAS TO BE
DEVELOPED TO PROTECT AGAINST COMPLETELY WRONG DECISIONS
OR THE ABSENCE OF THEM, AND TO MAKE THE EMPLOYEES FEEL
SECURE. IMES STRESSES THAT THIS APPROACH WILL GIVE THE
COMPANY BENEFITS FROM HAVING HIGHLY MOTIVATED AND
EFFICIENT EMPLOYEES, AND THAT EMPLOYEES WILL RECEIVE MORE
SATISFACTION FROM THEIR JOB.

M0223 INCENTIVE PAY IN MANUFACTURING INDUSTRIES.
MONTHLY LABOR REVIEW 92 (JULY 1969): 49-53.

  PIECE-RATE OR PRODUCTION BONUS PLANS COVER MORE
THAN HALF OF WORKERS IN IRON, STEEL, AND CLOTHING
INDUSTRIES.

M0224 INCREASING PROPORTION OF WOMEN ARE HEADS OF HOUSEHOLD.
MONTHLY LABOR REVIEW, APRIL 1973, P. 67.

  THE BUREAU OF CENSUS REPORTS THAT MORE AND MORE BLACK
AND WHITE AMERICAN WOMEN ARE ASSUMING THE ROLE OF HEAD OF
THE FAMILY.

M0225 THE INSPECTOR IS A LADY.
POSTAL LIFE, MARCH-APRIL 1974, P. 15.

  FOR WOMEN COLLEGE GRADUATES, AND ESPECIALLY WOMEN WHO
ARE ALREADY POSTAL EMPLOYEES, THERE ARE PLENTY OF
OPPORTUNITIES AS POSTAL INSPECTORS.

M0226 IVANCEVICH, J. M. BAKER, J. C.
A COMPARATIVE STUDY OF THE SATISFACTION OF DOMESTIC U. S.
MANAGERS AND OVERSEAS U. S. MANAGERS.
ACADEMY OF MANAGEMENT JOURNAL 13 (MARCH 1970): 69-77.

THIS STUDY EXTENDS AND ENLARGES UPON PREVIOUS RESEARCH
STUDIES CONCERNED WITH JOB SATISFACTIONS OF MANAGERS. IT
SPECIFICALLY FOCUSES ON AMERICAN MANAGERS IN THE UNITED
STATES AND AMERICAN MANAGERS IN EUROPE. COMPARISONS WERE
MADE ON THE BASIS OF MANAGERIAL LEVELS.
ONE HUNDRED AND FIFTY RANDOMLY SELECTED U. S. EXECUTIVES
WORKING FOR LARGE U. S. FIRMS IN EUROPE WERE CHOSEN, WITH
37 TOP LEVEL EXECUTIVES AND 49 MIDDLE LEVEL EXECUTIVES
REPLYING. DOMESTIC U. S. EXECUTIVES WERE CHOSEN FROM A TEN
PERCENT RANDOM SAMPLE OF MEMBERS OF THE AMERICAN MANAGEMENT
ASSOCIATION, MANAGERS IN LARGE INDUSTRIAL FIRMS (FORTUNE'S
  500), AND NAMES SUBMITTED BY FOUR CONSULTING FIRMS.
THE PORTER NEED SATISFACTION QUESTIONNAIRES WERE GIVEN TO

M0226 ALL OF THOSE PEOPLE SAMPLED. IT WAS MODIFIED TO CONTAIN 12
ITEMS BASED ON MASLOW'S THEORY OF MOTIVATION. AUTONOMY
NEEDS WERE SUBSTITUTED FOR THE PHYSIOLOGICAL NEEDS. FOR
EACH ITEM, TWO QUESTIONS WERE ASKED AND WERE TO BE RATED.
THE LOWER RATING WAS SUBTRACTED FROM THE HIGHER RATING TO
FIND THE AMOUNT OF NEED DEFICIENCY.
THE TOP EXECUTIVES IN EUROPE RANKED THE NEEDS, FROM LOWEST
TO HIGHEST, AS ESTEEM, SOCIAL, SECURITY, AUTONOMY, AND
SELF-ACTUALIZATION WHEREAS THE TOP EXECUTIVES IN THE U. S.
RANKED THEM AS SOCIAL, SECURITY, ESTEEM,
AUTONOMY, AND SELF-ACTUALIZATION. THE MIDDLE
EXECUTIVES IN EUROPE RANKED THE NEEDS,
FROM LOWEST TO HIGHEST, AS ESTEEM, AUTONOMY, SOCIAL,
SELF-ACTUALIZATION, AND SECURITY WHEREAS THE MIDDLE
EXECUTIVES IN THE U. S. RANKED THEM AS SECURITY, SOCIAL,
ESTEEM, AUTONOMY, AND SELF-ACTUALIZATION. THESE DIFFERED
COMPLETELY FROM EACH OTHER.
AUTONOMY AND SELF-ACTUALIZATION HAVE CONSISTENTLY BEEN MOST
DEFICIENT AREAS OF SATISFACTION, AND IT IS SHOWN AGAIN
HERE. TOP LEVEL EXECUTIVES IN EUROPE HAVE MORE SELF ESTEEM
SATISFACTION, BUT LESS AUTONOMY AND PRESTIGE THAN TOP LEVEL
DOMESTIC EXECUTIVES. SECURITY AND SOCIAL NEEDS ARE
DEFICIENT IN NEED SATISFACTION AMONG MIDDLE LEVEL EXECUTIVES
IN EUROPE--MUCH MORE SO THAN THOSE IN THE U. S. HOWEVER,
THE SELF-ACTUALIZATION NEED IS BETTER SATISFIED IN EUROPE.
THE RANKING ORDER OF NEED IN EUROPE DOES NOT COMPLY WITH
THOSE IN THE U. S. AND THOSE OF PORTER. THIS INFORMATION IS
IMPORTANT TO FIRMS WITH BRANCHES IN EUROPE TO DECIDE THE
TYPE OF PERSON WHO WOULD BE SATISFIED THERE. IT ALSO AIDS
IN DEVELOPING MOTIVATION PROGRAMS.

M0227 IVANCEVICH, J. M. DONNELLY, J. H.
A STUDY OF ROLE CLARITY AND NEED FOR CLARITY FOR THREE
OCCUPATIONAL GROUPS.
ACADEMY OF MANAGEMENT JOURNAL 17 (MARCH 1974): 28-36.

RESEARCH EXAMINED PERCEIVED ROLE CLARITY AMONG
SALESMEN, SUPERVISORS AND OPERATING EMPLOYEES IN A
MANUFACTURING ORGANIZATION AND ITS RELATION TO GENERAL JOB
INTEREST, OPPORTUNITIES FOR JOB INNOVATION,
SELF-ACTUALIZATION, AUTONOMY AND PHYSICAL STRESS.

M0228 IVANCEVICH, J. M. STRAWSER, R. H.
A COMPARATIVE ANALYSIS OF THE JOB SATISFACTION OF
INDUSTRIAL MANAGERS AND CERTIFIED PUBLIC ACCOUNTANTS.
ACADEMY OF MANAGEMENT JOURNAL 12 (JUNE 1969): 193-203.

THIS SURVEY WAS DONE TO EXTEND AND ENLARGE UPON PREVIOUS
RESEARCH STUDIES CONCERNED WITH THE JOB SATISFACTION OF
MANAGERIAL PERSONNEL--SPECIFICALLY INDUSTRIAL MANAGERS AND
CERTIFIED PUBLIC ACCOUNTANTS IN LARGE FIRMS. THREE
CONCLUSIONS REACHED BY PREVIOUS RESEARCH STUDIES FOUND THAT
MANAGERS ARE LEAST SATISFIED IN THE AREAS OF AUTONOMY AND
SELF-ACTUALIZATION, AND THAT TOP EXECUTIVES ARE MORE
SATISFIED THAN LOWER LEVEL EXECUTIVES. THE PAST RESEARCH
STUDIES COMPARED MANAGERS AT THE SAME LEVEL IN THE SAME
INDUSTRIES, WHEREAS THIS STUDY IS INTER-INDUSTRY.
THE C. P. A. 'S WERE GIVEN THE PORTER NEED SATISFACTION

M0228 QUESTIONNAIRE WITH TWELVE ITEMS BASED ON MASLOW'S THEORY OF
MOTIVATION. THESE QUESTIONNAIRES WERE GIVEN TO 200
RANDOMLY SELECTED C. P. A. 'S WORKING FOR THE LARGEST
ACCOUNTING FIRMS IN THE U. S. (PRICE WATERHOUSE, ARTHUR
ANDERSEN, ETC.). OF THE C. P. A.'S CHOSEN, 48 TOP LEVEL
AND 60 MIDDLE LEVEL ACCOUNTANTS REPLIED.
THE INDUSTRIAL MANAGER GROUP USED WAS ONE WHICH HAD
PREVIOUSLY BEEN SURVEYED BY PORTER. THE JOB SATISFACTION
QUESTIONNAIRE WAS ADMINISTERED TO SEVERAL THOUSAND MANAGERS
THROUGHOUT THE U. S. ONLY TOP LEVEL AND MIDDLE LEVEL
RESULTS WERE USED TO COMPARE WITH THE ACCOUNTANTS.
THE FINDINGS INDICATED THAT BOTH GROUPS HAVE THE HIGHEST
NEED DEFICIENCIES IN SELF-ACTUALIZATION. FOR THE TOP LEVEL
MANAGERS, THE CATEGORIES RANGE, FROM LOW TO HIGH NEEDS,
SOCIAL, SECURITY, ESTEEM, AUTONOMY, AND SELF-ACTUALIZATION,
WHEREAS THE TOP LEVEL ACCOUNTANTS CATEGORIZE THEIR NEEDS AS
SECURITY, AUTONOMY, SOCIAL, ESTEEM, AND SELF-ACTUALIZATION.
THE MANAGERS' RATINGS FOLLOW PORTER'S CONTENTIONS THE
CLOSEST.
FOR MIDDLE MANAGERS AND C. P. A. 'S, SELF-ACTUALIZATION
WAS ALSO THE MOST NEED-DEFICIENT. THE MANAGERS AND THE
C. P. A. 'S BOTH RATED THE CATEGORIES, FROM LOW TO HIGH
NEED, AS SECURITY, SOCIAL, ESTEEM, AUTONOMY, AND
SELF-ACTUALIZATION. THEY DID DIFFER ON THE PLACEMENT OF
SPECIFIC SUB-ITEMS.
THE NEED FOR SELF-ACTUALIZATION WAS AGAIN PROVEN TO
BE THE LEAST SATISFIED, AS FOUND IN PAST STUDIES. IT WAS
ALSO FOUND TO OCCUR IN DIFFERENT INDUSTRIES. SECURITY WAS
RELATIVELY SATISFIED. THEREFORE, THESE RESULTS SHOULD AID
IN IMPROVING MOTIVATION, SELECTION, AND TRAINING PROGRAMS.

M0229 JACOBS, IRENE.
MANPOWER TRAINING AND BENEFIT-COST ANALYSIS.
MANPOWER 5 (MARCH 1973): 28-30.

THIS ARTICLE IS AN ATTEMPT TO EXPLAIN THE BENEFIT COST
ANALYSIS METHOD OF DETERMINING WHETHER CERTAIN MANPOWER
TRAINING PROGRAMS ARE WORTHWHILE.
IRENE JACOBS USES DAVE, AN UNSKILLED, UNEMPLOYED,
EX-CONVICT, AS AN EXAMPLE AND SHOWS JUST HOW BENEFIT-COST
ANALYSIS WAS APPLIED TO HIS SITUATION AND SHOWED VERY
CLEARLY THAT THE USE OF $2000 OF THE TAXPAYERS' MONEY TO
TRAIN HIM WAS WISELY SPENT.
THE BENEFIT COST ANALYSIS TECHNIQUE WOULD APPEAR TO BE
A SIMPLE ADDITION-DIVISION EXERCISE BUT BECAUSE THIS
TECHNIQUE DOES NOT MEASURE INTANGIBLES SUCH AS A PERSON'S
SELF-IMAGE, IT SOMETIMES GIVES THE ECONOMIST HEADACHES.
HE IS CALLED UPON TO DEFINE THE BENEFITS AS WELL AS MEASURE
THEM IN TERMS OF DOLLARS AND CENTS.
IN DAVE'S CASE THE ECONOMIST FIGURED THAT SINCE DAVE
WAS 35 YEARS OLD WHEN HE FINISHED HIS TRAINING HE WOULD HAVE
29 YEARS TO WORK, ASSUMING THAT HE WOULD RETIRE AT AGE 65.
THEREFORE HIS PROJECTED LIFE TIME EARNINGS WOULD BE $290,000
IF HE EARNED $10,000 A YEAR. BUT SINCE HE CAN NOT IGNORE
THE POSSIBILTY THAT DAVE MIGHT BE INJURED OR DIE BEFORE AGE
65 HE USES STATISTICS ON PREVIOUS TRENDS TO DETERMINE THAT
DAVE HAS A PROBABILITY OF 27 YEARS LEFT TO WORK (PROJECTED
EARNINGS NOW $270,000). PRODUCTIVITY IS CONSIDERED NEXT--3%

M0229   MORE EACH YEAR. THEN THE DISCOUNT RATE FOR DAVE'S SALARY IS
         CONSIDERED. THIS IS SAYING THAT THE MONEY HE MAKES THIS
         YEAR IS WORTH MORE THAN WHAT HE WILL MAKE IN SUBSEQUENT
         YEARS BECAUSE HE CAN INVEST SOME OF IT TO EARN DIVIDENDS AND
         INTEREST. WHEN THIS INFORMATION IS FED INTO THE COMPUTER WE
         LEARN THAT DAVE'S TOTAL SALARY WILL BE $256,500 - 168,000 =
         $88,000. DAVE'S BENEFIT OF $88,000 DIVIDED BY $2,000 COST,
         RESULTS IN A RATIO OF 44 TO 1 IN INCREASED, TAXABLE INCOME
         AND PURCHASING POWER TO BENEFIT HIMSELF AND THE ECONOMY.
              CONCLUSION-- BECAUSE HUMAN FACTORS AND SUBJECTIVE
         JUDGEMENTS ARE INVOLVED, BENEFIT-COST ANALYSIS IS NOT A
         PRECISE TOOL BUT IS THE BEST WE HAVE AT PRESENT AND WILL BE
         USED UNTIL A BETTER METHOD IS DEVISED.

M0230   JENKINS, DAVID.
         DEMOCRACY IN THE WORKPLACE: THE HUMAN FACTORIES.
         THE NATION, 218 (JANUARY 1974): 45-48.

              A BRIEF DESCRIPTION OF LEGISLATION BEING CONSIDERED IN
         FRANCE TO IMPROVE SATISFACTION, FOLLOWED BY A DISCUSSION OF
         THE IMPACT OF FREDERICK TAYLOR AND FREDERICK HERZBERG ON
         AMERICAN INDUSTRY.

M0231   JOB BIAS AND THE INVISIBLE MINORITY.
         MANPOWER, OCTOBER, 1970, PP. 25-29.

              FRED SCHMIDT, OF THE INSTITUTE OF INDUSTRIAL RELATIONS
         AT THE UNIVERSITY OF CALIFORNIA, PROVIDES FRESH INSIGHT
         INTO THE LIVING AND WORKING CONDITIONS OF THE INVISIBLE
         MINORITY IN A NEW STUDY.

M0232   JOB BROKER FOR THE POOR.
         MANPOWER, JULY 1970, PP. 14-20.

              URBAN LEAGUE HELPS EMPLOYERS AND THE DISADVANTAGED
         FIND AND UNDERSTAND EACH OTHER.

M0233   JOB PROSPECTS FOR COLLEGE GRADUATES IN 1974.
         OCCUPATIONAL OUTLOOK QUARTERLY, SUMMER 1974, PP. 9-11.

              THE STRONGEST DEMAND IS SEEN FOR ENGINEERS AND
         ACCOUNTANTS. RECRUITING OF WOMEN IS UP SHARPLY OVER 1973.

M0234   JOB REDESIGN: SOME CASE HISTORIES.
         MANPOWER, MAY 1973, PP. 14-21.

              "WORK IN AMERICA" STUDY REPORT IN COMPANY EFFORTS TO
         DEAL WITH EMPLOYEES' DISCONTENT.
              THIS ARTICLE WAS BASED ON A REPORT "WORK IN AMERICA,"
         WHICH WAS DONE BY A COMMITTEE OF THE SECRETARY OF HEALTH,
         EDUCATION AND WELFARE. THE PURPOSE OF THE STUDY WAS TO
         EXAMINE THE HEALTH OF THE NATION'S WORKING LIFE, AND
         SUGGESTED WAYS THAT IT MIGHT BE IMPROVED. THE COMMITTEE
         STUDIED GENERAL FOODS NEW PLANT WHICH WAS BUILT AROUND A JOB
         REDESIGN CONCEPT.
              SOME OF THE FEATURES OF THE PROGRAM WERE
         SELF-MANAGEMENT WORK TEAMS, WHICH DECIDED WHAT WAS TO BE
         DONE AND WHO WAS TO DO IT. THE TEAM ACCEPTED FIRST AND

M0234 FINAL RESPONSIBILITY FOR PERFORMING QUALITY TESTS AND
ENSURING THAT THEY MAINTAINED QUALITY STANDARDS.
THE COMPANY REFRAINED FROM SPECIFYING IN ADVANCE ANY PLANT
RULES. THEY DESIGNED EVERY SET OF TASKS IN A WAY THAT WOULD
INCLUDE FUNCTIONS REQUIRING HIGHER HUMAN ABILITIES AND
RESPONSIBILITIES. THE REASON FOR THIS WAS TO ELIMINATE DULL
OR ROUTINE JOBS INSOFAR AS POSSIBLE.
      SOME RESULTS OF DIFFERENT TYPES OF JOB REDESIGN ARE
THAT THE WORKERS ARE MORE SATISFIED WITH THEIR JOBS. THEY
ALSO TAKE PRIDE IN THEIR WORK AND DO BETTER AT IT. IT HAS
BEEN FOUND THAT IT TAKES FEWER PEOPLE TO DO A JOB.
      ALTHOUGH SELF MANAGEMENT IS A BASIC FEATURE OF THE
REDESIGN PROGRAM, IT USUALLY DOESN'T WORK WITHOUT SOME TYPE
OF PROFIT SHARING PLAN. THE SELF MANAGEMENT PROGRAM WITHOUT
THE PROFIT SHARING PLAN MAY CAUSE THE WORKERS TO FEEL LIKE
THEY'VE BEEN MANIPULATED, AND PRODUCTIVITY MAY SLIP BACK TO
FORMER LEVELS. SOME REQUIREMENTS FOR PROFIT SHARING ARE
THAT PROFITS SHOULD BE CLEARLY IN ADDITION TO BASE PAY. THE
PROFIT SHOULD BE PAID IMMEDIATELY AND BASED ON PRODUCTIVITY.
THE PLAN MUST ALSO BE CONTRACTUAL. HUMAN GOALS (AUTONOMY
AND INTERDEPENDENCE) AND ECONOMIC GOALS (INCREASE IN
PRODUCTIVITY) CAN BE ACHIEVED THROUGH THE SHARING BY WORKERS
IN BOTH THE RESPONSIBILITIES OF PRODUCTION AND THE PROFIT
EARNED THROUGH PRODUCTION. MOST WORKERS WILL WILLINGLY
ASSUME RESPONSIBILITY FOR A WIDER RANGE OF DECISIONS IF THEY
ARE ALLOWED TO SHARE IN THE RESULTS.

M0235 JOBS, SALARY, CREDIT, LEGAL STATUS ALL IN FOCUS OF WOMEN'S
YEAR.
COMMERCE TODAY, MARCH 1975, PP. 9-10.

      THE UN COMMISSION ON THE STATUS OF WOMEN CALLED UPON
THE UNITED NATIONS TO DECLARE 1975 A YEAR FOR WOMEN TO
MOBILIZE ACTION ON BEHALF OF WOMEN THROUGHOUT THE WORLD. A
FOCUS IS PLACED ON THE PART WOMEN PLAY IN THE ECONOMIC AND
BUSINESS LIFE OF THE UNITED STATES.

M0236 JOHNSON, ALEEN M.
THE PROFESSIONAL WOMAN IN GAO.
THE GAO REVIEW, WINTER 1974, PP. 12-16.

      THIS ARTICLE DISCUSSES A FEMALE AUDITOR'S IMPRESSION OF
HER FIRST YEAR'S EXPERIENCE WITH THE UNITED STATES GENERAL
ACCOUNTING OFFICE.

M0237 JOHNSON, BEVERLY B.
THE OCCUPATIONAL INFORMATION CENTER: WHERE ATLANTA
EMPLOYERS AND EDUCATORS MEET.
OCCUPATIONAL OUTLOOK QUARTERLY 16 (WINTER 1972):   23-25.

      TEACHERS AND BUSINESSMEN FIND A COMMON CAUSE--HELPING
TOMORROW'S WORKER MAKE THE GRADE.

M0238 JOHNSON, ROSSALL.
PROBLEM RESOLUTION AND IMPOSITION OF CHANGE THROUGH A
PARTICIPATING GROUP EFFORT.
MANAGEMENT STUDIES 2 (MAY 1974):   129-42.

THE STUDY REVIEWED IN THIS ARTICLE UTILIZED GROUP
PARTICIPATION AS THE METHOD FOR BRINGING ABOUT CHANGE.

M0239   JOHNSON, RUTH E.
HOW DO SECRETARIES RATE.
DEPARTMENT OF STATE NEWSLETTER, JUNE 1974, P. 23.

MS. JOHNSON'S COMMENTS ABOUT PERFORMANCE OF SECRETARIES
COULD PROVE HELPFUL TO BOTH RATING OFFICERS AND SECRETARIES.

M0240   JOHNSTON, DENIS F.
THE FUTURE OF WORK: THREE POSSIBLE ALTERNATIVES.
MONTHLY LABOR REVIEW 95 (MAY 1972): 3-9.

PREDICTS FUTURE CHANGES IN THE ROLE OF WORK IN OUR
SOCIETY.

M0241   JONES, B. D.
ABC OF MOTIVATION.
ADMINISTRATIVE MANAGEMENT 31 (MAY 1970): 49-51.

PROVIDES A QUICK REVIEW OF THE MOTIVATION THEORIES
OF MASLOW AND HERZBERG, AND CONCLUDES THERE IS NO
STEREOTYPED ANSWER OR APPROACH TO MOTIVATION.

M0242   JONES, J. P.
LEADERSHIP, MOTIVATION, AND COMMUNICATION.
PERSONNEL ADMINISTRATION 33 (SEPTEMBER 1970):   4-7.

LOOKS AT MOTIVATION FROM THE VIEW THAT WE ARE ALL
BORN MOTIVATED, AND THE EMPLOYER HAS THE ABILITY TO
CONTROL MOTIVATION AS A HUMAN RESOURCE.

M0243   JONES, LAURENCE C. III.
EVALUATION AND IMPLEMENTATION OF THE
NEW YORK FIRE DEPARTMENT EXAMINATION TRAINING PROJECT
FOR CULTURALLY DISADVANTAGED RESIDENTS OF THE CITY OF
NEW YORK.
NTIS PB 221956

RESEARCH DONE BY THE NEW YORK CITY FIRE DEPARTMENT
UNDER A GRANT FROM THE MANPOWER ADMINISTRATION.
EXAMINES REASONS FOR FAILURE TO COMPLETE THE COURSE;
ALSO CONTRIBUTING FACTORS TO HIGH CIVIL SERVICE TEST
SCORES AMONG CULTURALLY DISADVANTAGED APPLICANTS.

M0244   KAPLAN, H. ROY.
HOW DO WORKERS VIEW THEIR WORK IN AMERICA.
MONTHLY LABOR REVIEW 96 (JUNE 1973): 46-48.

DISCUSSION OF VARIOUS APPROACHES TO JOB SATISFACTION
SURVEYS IN ORDER TO COLLECT THE DESIRED INFORMATION,
AND THE RESULTS OF THESE APPROACHES.

M0245   KARP, WILLIAM.
MANAGEMENT'S FUTURE ROLE: PICKING UP WHERE THE COMPUTER
LEAVES OFF.
MANAGEMENT REVIEW 60 (MARCH 1971):   14-17.

M0245   IN THIS AGE OF COMPUTERS, THE MANAGERS OF BIG
INDUSTRIES ARE BEING SUBJECTED TO CHANGE. THE MANAGERS ARE
NOW BEING ADVISED TO DIVERT THEIR ENERGIES INTO MORE
CREATIVE HUMAN RELATIONSHIPS.
     INDUSTRY, IN THE FUTURE, MAY EXCHANGE THE PRACTICAL
MANAGER FOR A NEW MANAGER WITH A CREATIVE IMAGINATION AND A
BROAD OUTLOOK.
THE PERSON WITH SPECIAL NARROW-GAUGE SKILLS WILL BE LESS IN
DEMAND BECAUSE THE COMPUTER WILL BE ABLE TO TAKE OVER
SUCH SPECIALIZED FUNCTIONS.
     COMPUTERS ARE WITHERING AWAY THE NEED FOR BUREAUS AND
DEPARTMENTS AND WIPE OUT BEHAVIOR PATTERNS THAT ARE
DERIVATIVE OF THE BUREAU MENTALITY. THE CHANNELS OF
INFORMATION ARE SHORTER, SO THEREFORE, THEY ARE MORE
EFFECTIVE. WITH THE USE OF COMPUTERS, MANAGERS CAN ADDRESS
THEMSELVES TO PROBLEMS THAT ARE NOT EASILY DEFINED.
     DURING THE 1980'S COMPUTER TECHNIQUES WILL HAVE
ADVANCED BY TAKING OVER A LARGE NUMBER OF PROGRAMMED
DECISIONS MADE BY MANAGERS ACROSS THE BOARD.
     WITH THE USE OF COMPUTERS, THE BURDEN OF MIDDLE
MANAGEMENT CENTERS ON THE SUPERVISOR AND HANDLING OF
WELL-STRUCTURED TASKS, SUCH AS ACCOUNTING OR INVENTORY
CONTROL. MIDDLE MANAGEMENT'S WORK WILL BECOME LESS
FRUSTRATING SINCE THE NEED FOR SUCH MANAGERS TO EXERCISE
AUTHORITY OVER OTHERS WILL DIMINISH.
     THERE ARE CHANGES IN EMPLOYEE RELATIONS POLICIES, SUCH
AS THE WORK FORCE, CHANGING FROM BLUE TO WHITE COLLAR. THE
WHITE COLLAR GROUP HAS A HIGHER EDUCATIONAL BACKGROUND.
     MOTIVATION, INNOVATION AND CREATIVITY DO NOT FLOURISH
IN AN AUTHORITIAN WORK ENVIRONMENT. A SOPHISTICATED
EXECUTIVE IS NEEDED WHO CAN INSPIRE PEOPLE. AS IT IS NOW,
THERE IS AN IMBALANCE BETWEEN TECHNOLOGICAL AND SOCIOLOGICAL
PROCESS.
     PERHAPS WITH THE HELP OF COMPUTER TECHNOLOGY, WE WILL
UNRAVEL THE MOST ELUSIVE PHENOMENON OF ALL--MAN HIMSELF.

M0246   KATZELL, R. A.   EWEN, ROBERT B.   KORMAN, ABRAHAM K.
THE JOB ATTITUDES OF WORKERS FROM DIFFERENT ETHNIC
BACKGROUNDS.
UNPUBLISHED RESEARCH, NEW YORK UNIVERSITY, 1973.

     DISCUSSES THE RELATIONSHIP BETWEEN JOB SATISFACTION AND
JOB PERFORMANCE RATINGS.

M0247   KAUN, DAVID E.   LENTZ, WILLIAM.
OCCUPATIONAL MIGRATION, DISCRIMINATION, AND THE CENTRAL
CITY LABOR FORCE.
MONTHLY LABOR REVIEW, 94 (DECEMBER 1971):   57-61.

     COMPARISON OF FLOW OF NEGRO AND WHITE WORKERS
OUT OF URBAN AREAS, AS WELL AS FROM ONE OCCUPATION TO
ANOTHER.

M0248   KEENE, DON G.
MAN'S INHERENT REBELLION AGAINST GOD AND SATISFACTION.
PERSONNEL ADMINISTRATOR 18 (SEPTEMBER-OCTOBER 1973):   33-36.

     THIS AUTHOR'S LOOK TO THE OLD AND NEW TESTAMENTS

M0248   CASTS A DOUBTFUL PERSPECTIVE ON THE DIRECTIONS OF CURRENT
         THEORIES OF JOB SATISFACTION.

M0249   KELLER, ROBERT T.
         ROLE CONFLICT AND AMBIGUITY: CORRELATES WITH JOB
         SATISFACTION AND VALUES.
         PERSONNEL PSYCHOLOGY 28 (SPRING 1975):   57-64.

             THE BASIC HYPOTHESES OF THIS STUDY WERE THAT ROLE
         CONFLICT AND AMBIGUITY WOULD BE NEGATIVELY RELATED TO JOB
         SATISFACTION AND THAT PERSONALITY RELATED VALUES WOULD BE
         RELATED TO ROLE CONFLICT   AMBIGUITY AS WELL AS JOB
         SATISFACTION.

M0250   KENSTANT, RAYMOND O.
         JOB VACANCIES IN 1970.
         MONTHLY LABOR REVIEW 94 (FEBRUARY 1971):   20-23.

             THE NEW SERIES ON JOB VACANCIES INTRODUCED IN
         1970 PROVIDES FOR THE FIRST TIME, SOME PARTIAL INFORMATION
         ON THE SHAPE AND SIZE OF UNFILLED DEMAND FOR LABOR.

M0251   KESSELMAN, G. A.   WOOD, MICHAEL T.
         RELATIONSHIPS BETWEEN PERFORMANCE AND SATISFACTION UNDER
         CONTINGENT AND NONCONTINGENT REWARD SYSTEMS.
         JOURNAL OF APPLIED PSYCHOLOGY   59 (JUNE 1974):   374-76.

             A CONTINGENT PAY SYSTEM (PIECE RATES AND PROMOTION TIED
         TO PERFORMANCE) AND A NONCONTINGENT SYSTEM (PAY BASED ON
         SENIORITY) WERE EXAMINED IN TWO SAMPLES OF FEMALE TELEPHONE
         WORKERS.   WHILE PERFORMANCE UNDER THE TWO SYSTEMS WAS
         SIMILAR,SATISFACTION IN THE CONTINGENT GROUP WAS RELATED TO
         THE WORK ITSELF, PAY, AND PROMOTIONS.   IN THE NONCONTINGENT
         GROUP, SATISFACTION RELATED TO INTERPERSONAL FACTORS, PAY,
         AND WORK.

M0252   KLEIN, GEORGE STUART.
         PERCEPTION, MOTIVES, AND PERSONALITY.
         NEW YORK: KNOPF. 1970.

             COLLECTION OF ESSAYS ON MOTIVATED COGNITION.   TECHNICAL
         APPROACH WRITTEN BASICALLY FOR STUDENTS OF PSYCHOANALYSIS.

M0253   KLEIN, STUART M.
         PARTICIPATIVE MANAGEMENT IN THE UNITED STATES: A CORPORATE
         EXPERIENCE.
         MANAGEMENT INTERNATIONAL REVIEW   12, NO. 1, (1972):   17-22.

             PARTICIPATIVE MANAGEMENT ENCOURAGES SUBORDINATES
         TO EXPRESS THEIR VIEWS AS TO THE BEST POSSIBLE MEANS
         OF GETTING A TASK DONE.   THIS ARTICLE IS A STUDY OF
         PARTICIPATIVE MANAGEMENT WITHIN IBM, TO SEE IF PARTICIPATIVE
         MANAGEMENT WILL LEAD TO MORE PRODUCTIVE, EFFICIENT
         ORGANIZATIONS WHICH SIMULTANEOUSLY TEND TO ENHANCE OVERALL
         JOB SATISFACTION.

M0254   KLEIN, STUART M.
         PAY FACTORS AS PREDICTORS TO SATISFACTION: A COMPARISON OF

M0254   REINFORCEMENT, EQUITY, AND EXPECTANCY.
ACADEMY OF MANAGEMENT JOURNAL 16 (DECEMBER 1973):   598-610.
A COMPARISON OF PAY VARIABLES SUGGESTED BY
REINFORCEMENT, EXPECTANCY, AND EQUITY THEORIES AS PREDICTORS
TO A MEASURE OF GLOBAL SATISFACTION IS PRESENTED.   EQUITY
AND EXPECTANCY VARIABLES PROVIDED PREDICTIVE CAPABILITIES
THOUGH EQUITY SEEMED SOMEWHAT MORE POWERFUL.   REINFORCEMENT
PROVIDED NO PREDICTIVE CAPABILITY BY ITSELF.

M0255   KLEIN, STUART M.
WORKERS UNDER STRESS (THE IMPACT OF WORK PRESSURE ON
GROUP COHESION).
LEXINGTON, KY.:   UNIVERSITY PRESS OF KENTUCKY, 1971.

RESULTS OF MANY TESTS MADE ON WORK PRESSURED WORKERS
IN AN INDUSTRIAL SITUATION TO ISOLATE FACTORS WHICH
WHEN MODIFIED MIGHT INCREASE JOB PERFORMANCE, PARTICULARLY
COHESION.

M0256   KOKKILA, L. M.   SLOCUM, JOHN W.   STRAWSER, R. H.
PERCEPTIONS OF JOB SATISFACTION IN DIFFERING OCCUPATIONS.
BUSINESS PERSPECTIVES 9 (FALL 1972):   5-9.

THE PURPOSE OF THIS ARTICLE WAS TO EVALUATE MASLOW'S
THEORY OF NEEDS BY AN ANALYSIS OF NUMEROUS MANAGERIAL
STUDIES THAT HAVE UTILIZED THE PORTER QUESTIONNAIRE.
THE PORTER NEED SATISFACTION QUESTIONNAIRE RANDOMLY
ARRANGED THE NEEDS AND ASKED TWO QUESTIONS ABOUT EACH NEED.
THE QUESTIONS ASKED WERE,   HOW MUCH IS THERE NOW?   AND,   HOW
MUCH SHOULD THERE BE?   THE RESPONDENT WAS ASKED TO RATE ON
A SCALE OF ONE SEVEN HOW HE FELT ABOUT HIS JOB.   ON THE
SCALE, ONE WAS THE MINIMUM OF HOW HE FELT AND SEVEN WAS THE
MAXIMUM.
THE FINDINGS WERE NOT COMPLETELY CONSISTENT WITH
MASLOW'S THEORY OF NEEDS.   OUT OF THE SIXTEEN TYPES OF JOBS
STUDIED ONLY SEVEN WERE IN GENERAL AGREEMENT WITH MASLOW.
THE STUDIES DID SHOW THAT MASLOW'S THEORY MIGHT NOT BE
COMPLETELY THE ANSWER TO MOTIVATING PEOPLE BUT IT DOES GIVE
MANAGERS A STARTING POINT TO DEVELOP AN
APPROACH TO MOTIVATING PEOPLE.
BUSINESS AND ORGANIZATIONS IN TODAY'S WORLD HAVE DONE A
REMARKABLE JOB OF SATISFYING THE LOWER ORDER NEEDS FOR THE
WORKER.   MOST COMPANIES HAVE WORKMAN'S INSURANCE,
WORKMAN'S COMPENSATION, RETIREMENT BENEFITS AND OTHER FRINGE
BENEFITS WHICH SATISFY THESE LOWER ORDER NEEDS.
ORGANIZATIONS ARE TRYING TO SATISFY THE SOCIAL AND
AFFILIATION NEEDS BY STRUCTURING JOBS IN SUCH A WAY THAT
PEOPLE CAN INTERACT AND ASSOCIATE WITH EACH OTHER WHILE
WORKING.   MANY MANAGERS REALIZE THAT THE HIGHER LEVEL NEEDS
ARE NOT BEING SATISFIED BUT THIS IN PART MAY BE DUE TO
AUTOMATION IN SOME JOBS.   IN THE FUTURE IT IS HOPED WORKERS
MAY BE ABLE TO USE MORE OF THEIR OWN DISCRETION
IN THE COURSE OF COMPLETING THEIR WORK.   MANY MANAGERS FEEL
THAT IN THE FUTURE, A MANAGER'S SUCCESS WILL DEPEND ON HIS
ABILITY TO SATISFY HIS EMPLOYEES' HIGHER ORDER NEEDS THROUGH
AN APPROPRIATE LEADERSHIP STYLE AND CREATION OF A GOOD
INDUSTRIAL WORK CLIMATE.

M0257   KILB, DAVID A.   RUBIN, IRWIN M.   MCINTYRE, JAMES M.
ORGANIZATIONAL PSYCHOLOGY (A BOOK OF READINGS).
ENGLEWOOD CLIFFS, N. J., PRENTICE-HALL, INC., 1971.

       TEXTBOOK EDITED BY THREE M. I. T. TEACHERS. HEAVY
EMPHASIS ON TRAINING, PROBLEM SOLVING. MUCH PITH IN 387
PAGES.

M0258   KORMAN, ABRAHAM K.
EXPECTANCIES AS DETERMINATES OF PERFORMANCE.
JOURNAL OF APPLIED PSYCHOLOGY 55 (JUNE 1971):   218-22.

       REPORTS RESULTS OF A SERIES OF LABORATORY AND FIELD
INVESTIGATIONS WHICH SUPPORT HYPOTHESIS THAT PERFORMANCE IS
FACILITATED BY THE HIGH EXPECTANCIES WHICH OTHERS HAVE OF
ONE'S COMPETENCY AND ABILITY.

M0259   KORMAN, ABRAHAM K.
INDUSTRIAL AND ORGANIZATIONAL PSYCHOLOGY.
ENGLEWOOD CLIFFS, N. J. ; PRENTICE-HALL, INC., 1971.

       TEXTBOOK WITH HEAVY EMPHASIS ON THEORETICAL
DEVELOPMENTS IN ALL OF PSYCHOLOGY AS APPLIED TO WORK
SITUATIONS. GOES INTO NEW DEVELOPEMENTS--URBAN DILEMMAS,
RACE HATRED, AUTOMATION AND OTHER CHARACTERISTICS OF OUR
TORMENTED SOCIETY.
MANY TABLES OF INFORMATION, CLEARLY LAID OUT. CONSIDERING
THE HIGHLY TECHNICAL NATURE OF THE BOOK, IT IS VERY
INTERESTING TO READ.

M0260   KORMAN, ABRAHAM K.
TOWARD AN HYPOTHESIS OF WORK BEHAVIOR.
JOURNAL OF APPLIED PSYCHOLOGY 54 (FEBRUARY 1970):   31-41.

       OFFERS A THEORETICAL HYPOTHESIS RELATING TO THE
INFLUENCE OF AN INDIVIDUAL'S SELF-CONCEPT OF THE TASK AT
HAND ON THE OUTCOME HE SEEKS AND ATTAINS. INCLUDES AN
EXTENSIVE REVIEW OF THE LITERATURE AND OF PREVIOUS RESEARCH.

M0261   KRIEGSMANN, J. K.   HARDIN, D.
DOES DIVORCE HAMPER JOB PERFORMANCE.
PERSONNEL ADMINISTRATOR 19 (MARCH-APRIL 1974):   22-29.

       RESEARCH FINDINGS INDICATE THAT DIVORCE PROCEEDINGS
DO AFFECT JOB PERFORMANCE AND THIS ARTICLE SUGGEST THAT
COMPANIES PROVIDE COUSELING FOR THEIR EMPLOYEES WITH
MARITAL PROBLEMS.

M0262   H.I.T. ON TARGET WITH INSTANT UPGRADING.
MANPOWER, MAY 1969, PP. 19-21.

       HIGH INTENSITY TRAINING -- AN INNOVATIVE AND
POTENTIALLY POWERFUL TOOL IN HELPING LOW-SKILL, LOW-PAID
WORKERS MOVE OUT OF THE POVERY RANKS.

M0263   LANDY, FRANK J.
MOTIVATIONAL TYPE AND THE SATISFACTION-PERFORMANCE
RELATIONSHIP.

M0263   JOURNAL OF APPLIED PSYCHOLOGY 55 (OCTOBER 1971):   406-13.
        LANDY STATES, THE PRESENT RESEARCH IS BASED ON THE
NOTION THAT MOTIVATIONAL TYPE OR SUBGROUP MIGHT ACT AS A
MULTIVARIATE MODERATOR OF THE RELATIONSHIP BETWEEN JOB
SATISFACTION AND PERFORMANCE. THE PRESENT STUDY IS THE
FIRST STEP IN DESCRIBING THE VARIOUS RELATIONSHIPS
BETWEEN SPECIFIC NEED PATTERNS, SATISFACTION WITH SPECIFIC
JOB BEHAVIORS. ITS PRIMARY INTENT WAS TO DEMONSTRATE THAT
THE PATTERN OF INDIVIDUAL NEEDS MODIFIES THE RELATIONSHIP
BETWEEN JOB SATISFACTION AND PERFORMANCE.
        THE FOUR CLASSES OF VARIABLES INCLUDED SATISFACTION,
PERFORMANCE, MOTIVATION, AND WORK HISTORY AND BIOGRAPHICAL
INFORMATION. MOTIVATIONAL TYPE WAS TESTED AS A MODERATOR OF
THE RELATIONSHIP BETWEEN FIVE FACTOR SATISFACTION DIMENSIONS
AND SIX PERFORMANCE DIMENSIONS.
        USING AN APPROPRIATE STATISTICAL METHOD, OUT OF SEVERAL
SUGGESTED, LANDY FINDS THAT MOTIVATIONAL TYPE ACTED AS A
MODERATOR OF THE RELATIONSHIP BETWEEN SATISFACTION AND
PERFORMANCE. THIS THEORY ASSUMES THAT PEOPLE WILL ENGAGE
IN WORK THAT IS PERSONALLY MEASURE MOTIVATION, AT LEAST WITH
PROFESSIONAL PEOPLE. LANDY SUGGESTS THAT EXPENDITURE
PATTERNS CAN GIVE VALUABLE INFORMATION AS TO THE
RELATIONSHIP BETWEEN JOB SATISFACTION AND JOB PERFORMANCE.

M0264   LASHER, HARRY J.
        HOW THE PURCHASING MANAGER CAN IMPROVE EMPLOYEE
        PERFORMANCE.
        JOURNAL OF PURCHASING 9 (MAY 1973):   25-33.

        THIS ARTICLE ATTEMPTS TO DEFINE EMPLOYEE PERFORMANCE
AND SUGGESTS A MANAGERIAL STRATEGY WHICH WILL STIMULATE
HIGHER PERFORMANCE WHILE HELPING THE EMPLOYEES TO DEVELOP.

M0265   LASHER, HARRY J.   VARNEY, GLENN H.
        THERE IS NO HUMBUG TO JOB ENRICHMENT.
        PERSONNEL ADMINISTRATOR 18 (JULY 1973):   42-43.

        REFUTING A RECENT ARTICLE PUBLISHED IN TPA, THESE
AUTHORS SET OUT TO PROVE THE VALUE OF JOB ENRICHMENT AS
RELATED TO ASSEMBLY LINE WORKERS.

M0266   MICHIGAN UNIVERSITY. SURVEY RESEARCH CENTER.
        SURVEY OF WORKING CONDITIONS. FINAL REPORT OF UNIVARIATE
        AND BIVARIATE TABLES.
        WASHINGTON, D.C.: GOVERNMENT PRINTING OFFICE, 1971. 484

        NATIONWIDE SURVEY OF EMPLOYED PERSONS, ON SUCH TOPICS
AS HEALTH AND SAFETY, HOURS AND OTHER TIME-RELATED PROBLEMS
TRANSPORTATION, UNION MANAGEMENT, DISCRIMINATION, JOB
SECURITY, INTERPERSONAL RELATIONS, AND CONTENT OF WORK.
THE BULK OF THE REPORT CONSISTS OF STATISTICAL TABLES
GROUPED UNDER MAJOR CONTENT AREAS WITH EACH SET OF TABLES
PRECEEDED BY A BRIEF COMMENTARY. ONE CONCLUSION DRAWN IS
THAT THERE NEED NOT NECESSARILY BE A HIGH CORRELATION
BETWEEN THE PRESENCE OF WORK RELATED PROBLEMS AND JOB
SATISFACTION.
        PREPARED UNDER CONTRACT WITH WORKPLACE STANDARDS
ADMINISTRATION (NOW EMPLOYMENT STANDARDS ADMINISTRATION),

M0266   U. S. DEPARTMENT OF LABOR.

M0267   LAWLER, EDWARD E.
        JOB DESIGN AND EMPLOYEE MOTIVATION.
        PERSONNEL PSYCHOLOGY, 22 (WINTER 1969):   426-35.

            THE PURPOSE OF THIS ARTICLE BY LAWLER IS TO FOCUS ON
        THE REASONS FOR EXPECTING CHANGES IN JOB DESIGN TO AFFECT
        EMPLOYEE MOTIVATION AND PERFORMANCE. THE ARGUMENT IN THIS
        ARTICLE IS THAT JOB DESIGN CHANGES CAN HAVE A POSITIVE
        EFFECT ON MOTIVATION, BECAUSE THEY CAN CHANGE AN
        INDIVIDUAL'S BELIEFS ABOUT THE PROBABILITY THAT CERTAIN
        REWARDS WILL RESULT FROM PUTTING FORTH HIGH LEVELS OF
        EFFORT. FIRST ONE MUST DISTINGUISH BETWEEN TWO KINDS OF
        REWARDS. THE FIRST TYPE ARE THOSE THAT ARE EXTRINSIC TO THE
        INDIVIDUAL. THESE REWARDS ARE INTRINSIC TO THE INDIVIDUAL
        AND STEM DIRECTLY FRO THE PERFORMANCE ITSELF.
            THESE REWARDS ARE INTERNALLY-MEDIATED SINCE THE
        INDIVIFUAL REWARDS HIMSELF. THESE REWARDS CAN BE SATISFYING
        NEEDS SUCH AS SELF-ESTEEM AND SELF-ACTUALIZATION. JOB
        CONTENT IS THE CRITICAL DETERMINANT OF WHETHER EMPLOYEES
        BELIEVE THAT GOOD PERFORMANCE ON THE JOB LEADS TO FEELINGS
        OF ACCOMPLISHMENT, GROWTH, AND SELF-ESTEEM. JOB CONTENT
        IS IMPORTANT HERE BECAUSE IT SERVES A MOTIVE AROUSAL
        FUNCTION WHERE HIGHER ORDER NEEDS ARE CONCERNED AND
        BECAUSE IT INFLUENCES WHAT REWARDS WILL BE SEEM TO STEM FROM
        GOOD PERFORMANCE. THERE APPEAR TO BE THREE CHARACTERISTICS
        WHICH JOBS MUST POSSESS IF THEY ARE TO AROUSE HIGHER ORDER
        NEEDS. THE FIRST IS THAT THE INDIVIDUAL MUST RECEIVE
        MEANINGFUL FEEDBACK ABOUT HIS PERFORMANCE. THE SECOND IS
        THAT THE JOB MUST BE PERCEIVED BY THE INDIVIDUAL AS
        REQUIRING HIM TO USE ABILITIES THAT HE VALUES IN ORDER FOR
        HIM TO PERFORM THE JOB EFFECTIVELY. FINALLY, THE
        INDIVIDUAL MUST FEEL HE HAS A HIGH DEGREE OF SELF-CONTROL
        OVER SETTING HIS OWN GOALS AND OVER DEFINING THE PATHS OF
        THESE GOALS.
            THE ABILITY OF JOB DESIGN FACTORS TO INFLUENCE
        EMPLOYEES' PERCEPTIONS OF THE PROBABILITY THAT GOOD
        PERFORMANCE WILL BE INTRINSICALLY REWARDING. JOB DESIGN
        FACTORS CAN DETERMINE HOW MOTIVATING A JOB WILL BE. IN THE
        REPORT OF TEN STUDIES WHERE A PROPORTION OF THE JOBS
        HAD BEEN ENLARGED ON BOTH, THE HORIZONTAL AND THE VERTICAL
        DIMENSIONS WERE FOUND. ONLY FOUR OUT OF TEN STUDIES REPORT
        THAT JOB ENLARGEMENT LED TO HIGHER PRODUCTIVITY.
        SUMMARY: WHEN A JOB IS STRUCTURED IN A WAY THAT
        MAKES INTRINSIC REWARDS APPEAR TO RESULT FROM GOOD
        PERFORMANCE THEN THE JOB ITSELF CAN BE A VERY EFFECTIVE
        MOTIVATOR. ALSO, JOB ENLARGEMENT IS MORE LIKELY TO LEAD TO
        INCREASED PRODUCT QUALITY THAN TO INCREASED PRODUCTIVITY.

M0268   LAWLER, EDWARD E.   HALL, DOUGLAS T.
        JOB CHARACTERISTICS AND PRESSURES AND THE ORGANIZATIONAL
        INTEGRATION OF PROFESSIONALS.
        ADMINISTRATIVE SCIENCE QUARTERLY 15 (SEPTEMBER 1970):
        271-80.

            THE PURPOSE OF THIS ARTICLE WAS TO EXAMINE JOB
        CHARACTERISTICS AND JOB PRESSURES AS POSSIBLE CORRELATES OF

M0268 ORGANIZATIONAL EFFECTIVENESS, NEED SATISFACTIONS, AND JOB
INVOLVEMENT OF RESEARCHERS IN LABORATORIES. THEORY AND
PREVIOUS RESEARCH WERE DONE ON JOB PRESSURES AND THREE BASIC
ASSUMPTIONS WERE MADE. THE FIRST IS THAT JOB PRESSURES
FELT BY THE INDIVIDUAL ARISE FROM BOTH EXTERNAL AND INTERNAL
FORCES. THE EXTERNAL PRESSURES ARE EXPECTATIONS AND DEMANDS
FROM THE ENVIRONMENT, SUCH AS, POSITIONAL REQUIREMENTS.
INTERNAL DEMANDS ARE PRESSURES THAT ARISE FROM PERSONAL
DEMANDS UPON ONESELF; THAT IS FROM ONE'S PARTICULAR
VALUES, NEEDS, ABILITIES, AND PAST EXPERIENCES. THESE
ENVIRONMENTAL AND PERSONAL PRESSURES CAN INFLUENCE A PERSON
THROUGH THEIR INDIVIDUAL EFFECTS. THE SECOND ASSUMPTION IS
THAT THE TERM PRESSURE COVERS EXPERIENCES THAT CAN BE EITHER
POSITIVE OR NEGATIVE, PLEASANT OR UNPLEASANT. SOME OF THESE
PRESSURES COME WITH MUCH ANXIETY AND TENSION WITH NO
POSITIVE OUTCOME. THE THIRD ASSUMPTION IS THAT PRESSURE
WILL NOT NECESSARILY ENTAIL CONFLICTING OR OPPOSING FORCES.
THERE HAS BEEN A TENDENCY TO USE THE TERM PRESSURE
SYNONYMOUSLY WITH TERMS SUCH AS STRESS, CONFLICT, TENSION,
ANXIETY, AND STRAIN.
        THE SUBJECTS IN THIS RESEARCH WERE DIRECTORS AND
PROFESSIONALS IN 22 RESEARCH AND DEVELOPMENT ORGANIZATIONS;
THEY WERE ENGAGED IN APPLIED AND DEVELOPMENTAL WORK RATHER
RATHER THAN IN BASIC RESEARCH. QUESTIONNAIRES WERE
ADMINISTERED TO THE DIRECTORS OF RESEARCH AND A RANDOM
SAMPLE OF RESEARCHERS. IN ALL, THE DATA WERE COLLECTED FROM
22 DIRECTORS AND 291 PROFESSIONALS. SCALE SCORES WERE
OBTAINED BY AVERAGING AN INDIVIDUAL'S RESPONSES TO ALL
SCALE ITEMS.
RESULTS: THE PRESSURES MOST GENERALLY REPORTED BY THE
PROFESSIONALS INTERVIEWED WERE TIME, QUALITY AND FINANCIAL
RESPONSIBILITY. THE MOST WIDELY FELT PRESSURE WAS TIME;
THIS PRESSURE WAS A NEED TO MEET SCHEDULES FOR REPORTS,
TESTS, PRODUCTS, OR PROPOSALS. THESE DEADLINES WERE
EXTERNALLY IMPOSED, EITHER BY A CUSTOMER, SPONSOR, OR HIGHER
MANAGEMENT. FINANCIAL RESPONSIBILITY WAS THE SECOND MOST
FELT PRESSURE. THIS PRESSURE WAS A CONCERN FOR THE
FINANCIAL GOALS OF THE ORGANIZATION AS A WHOLE, USUALLY
EXPRESSED THROUGH CONCERNS TO KEEP COSTS DOWN, OR TO DESIGN
NEW PRODUCTS THAT WOULD BE PROFITABLE. THE LEAST WAS
CONCERN FOR DOING A GOOD TECHNICAL JOB. THIS PRESSURE
SEEMED TO BE GENERATED BY THE RESEARCHERS THEMSELVES AND
BY THEIR COLLEAGUES.

M0269 LAWRENCE, JAMES E.
COMPLETING THE EXTENSION TEAM.
EXTENSION SERVICE REVIEW, JANUARY-FEBRUARY 1974, PP. 3-4.

        WOMEN JOIN THE RANKS OF AGRICULTURAL AGENTS.

M0270 LEAHY JOHN I.
TOTAL MOTIVATION = TOP PERFORMANCE.
SALES MANAGEMENT 110 (APRIL 30, 1973): 12-13.

        THE ARTICLE OUTLINES BLACK AND DECKER'S MOTIVATIONAL
APPROACH FOR PERSONNEL.

M0271 LEAVITT, HAROLD J. PONDY, LOUIS R.

M0271   READINGS IN MANAGERIAL PSYCHOLOGY, 2ND ED. CHICAGO.
        UNIVERSITY OF CHICAGO PRESS, 1973.
              A COLLECTION OF READINGS DEALING WITH PERSONNEL,
        MANAGEMENT AND MOTIVATION. MOST SOURCE MATERIAL IS
        FROM THE BEHAVIORAL SCIENCES. SENSITIVITY TRAINING,
        GROUP CONFLICT, IMPACT OF COMPUTERS ARE ANALYZED.   THERE IS
        NO ONE BEST WAY TO DEAL WITH PEOPLE IN ORGANIZATIONS.

M0272   LEE, M. SANG.
        AN EMPIRICAL ANALYSIS OF ORGANIZATIONAL IDENTIFICATION.
        ACADEMY OF MANAGEMENT JOURNAL 14 (JUNE 1971): 213-26.

              BASED ON RESEARCH DATA FROM 170 SCIENTIFIC EMPLOYEES
        AND THEIR SUPERVISORS IN THE U. S. PUBLIC HEALTH SERVICE,
        ANALYZED VARIABLES ASSOCIATED WITH SCIENTIST'S
        ORGANIZATIONAL IDENTIFICATION PATTERNS TO JOB ATTITUDES AND
        MOTIVATION. THOSE WITH HIGH ORGANIZATIONAL IDENTIFICATION
        WERE MORE PRODUCTIVE, BETTER MOTIVATED AND REWARDED,
        MORE SATISFIED AND HAD LESS PROPENSITY TO LEAVE THAN DID
        THOSE WITH LOWER ORGANIZATIONAL IDENTIFICATION.

M0273   LEHMANN, PHYLLIS.
        TEACHER TRAINING TAKES TO THE ROAD.
        MANPOWER 3 (MAY 1971): 2-6.

              THERE ARE SEVERAL OUTSTANDING OBJECTIVES BEHIND
        EQUIPPING A MOBILE VAN WITH COMPUTER-ASSISTED INSTRUCTION.
        IT OFFERS PRIVATE TUTORING FOR EVERY STUDENT AT HOURS
        CONVENIENT TO HIS PERSONAL SCHEDULE. AN IMPORTANT FACTOR IS
        THE METHOD OF TEACHING. EACH STUDENT RECEIVES INDIVIDUAL
        INSTRUCTION IN WHICH THE STUDENT MOVES AT HIS OWN PACE. THE
        TRAVELING CLASSROOM ALSO BRINGS UPDATED INSTRUCTION TO
        TEACHERS WHO CAN NOT CONVENIENTLY RETURN TO CAMPUS.
              THE PROGRAM WAS INITIATED AT THE BEGINNING OF 1972.
        BY JULY 1972, MORE THAN 2,100 TEACHERS IN TWELVE CITIES HAD
        COMPLETED THE COURSE KNOWN APPROPRIATELY AS C. A. I.
        (COMPUTER ASSISTED INSTRUCTION).
              TEACHERS FEEL THEY LEARN AS WELL AS OR BETTER THAN THEY
        DO FROM A HUMAN INSTRUCTOR IN THE TRADITIONAL CLASSROOM
        SETTING. YOU SEE IT, YOU HEAR IT, YOU READ IT, AND ITS ALL
        REVIEWED SO YOU SHOULD LEARN SOMETHING.
        ALTHOUGH THE PROGRAM IS MAINLY AIMED AT MIDDLE-AGED
        GROUP OF TEACHERS WITH THE EMPHASIS ON CONTINUING
        EDUCATION, IT IS ALSO STRIVING FOR SPECIALIZED TRAINING IN
        PREPARING TEACHERS TO RECOGNIZE, COPE AND TRAIN CHILDREN
        WHO ARE SEVERELY HANDICAPPED AND RETARDED, TO THOSE WHO ARE
        MILDLY RETARDED, EMOTIONALLY DISTURBED, HYPERACTIVE,
        CULTURALLY DISADVANTAGED, AND THOSE WITH SPEECH, HEARING,
        AND VISION PROBLEMS WHICH CAN HINDER LEARNING.
        IN CONCLUSION, THE AUTHOR CREDITS THE PROJECT WITH
        AWAKENING BOTH TEACHERS AND PARENTS TO THE NEED FOR
        UPDATING TEACHERS' SKILLS. SHE ALSO POINTS OUT THAT THE
        PROJECT WAS INSTRUMENTAL IN DISPELLING PEOPLE'S FEARS AND
        MISTRUST OF AUTOMATION, AND SHE BELIEVES THAT SUCH
        TECHNOLOGICAL TEACHING METHODS COULD PLAY A LARGE ROLE
        IN HER AREA FOR TRAINING NOT ONLY TEACHERS BUT ALSO
        SCHOOL DROPOUTS AND THE 80% OF HIGH SCHOOL
        GRADUATES WHO DO NOT GO TO COLLEGE.

M0273   ULTIMATELY, ASSISTANT PROJECT DIRECTOR HALL ENVISIONS
A FLEET OF TEN TO TWELVE VANS TOURING THE STATES OFFERING
COURSES TO WIDELY VARYING GROUPS, BOROUGH OFFICIALS, LAW
ENFORCEMENT AND CORRECTIONS PERSONNEL, PRISON INMATES,
ADULTS PREPARING FOR HIGH SCHOOL EQUIVALENCY EXAMINATIONS.

M0274 LEVINSON, HARRY.
ASININE ATTITUDES TOWARD MOTIVATION.
HARVARD BUSINESS REVIEW 51 (JANUARY-FEBRUARY 1973): 70-76.

    THE AUTHOR IN THIS ARTICLE IS DEALING WITH THE JACKASS
FALLACY OF MOTIVATION. THE JACKASS FALLACY OF MOTIVATION IS
THE UNCONSCIOUS MANAGERIAL ASSUMPTION ABOUT PEOPLE AND HOW
THEY SHOULD BE MOTIVATED.
    MANAGERS FAIL TO MOTIVATE WORKERS FOR MANY REASONS.
THEY GO TO SEMINARS, LECTURES AND LABORATORIES TO LEARN ALL
THE NEW BEHAVIOR SCIENCES AND WAYS TO MOTIVATE PEOPLE. THEN
THEY RETURN TO THE WORK SITUATION AND FAIL TO IMPLEMENT
THESE THINGS THEY LEARNED. THE PROBLEM HERE IS THAT THEY
EXPECT TO LEARN TOO MUCH IN SUCH A SHORT PERIOD OF TIME. A
MANAGER BECOMES FRUSTRATED WITH HIMSELF AND HIS EMPLOYEES
WHEN THEY DON'T RESPOND AS HE LEARNED THEY WOULD. NOW HE
SIMPLY DROPS THE NEW TECHNIQUES AND REVERTS TO HIS OLD SELF.
MANAGERS ARE ALSO AFRAID OF PARTICIPATIVE MANAGEMENT. THEY
DO NOT LIKE TO LET GO OF THE CONTROL THEY HAVE. THIS
CONTROL MAY HAVE TAKEN YEARS TO GAIN AND THEY DO NOT WANT TO
LOSE IT.
    THE JACKASS FALLACY IS ALSO REFERRED TO AS THE REWARD
AND PUNISHMENT OR CARROT-AND-STICK PHILOSOPHY. THIS SEEMS
TO BE THE MOST DOMINATE PHILOSOPHY OF MOTIVATION. THE
EMPLOYEE CAN SENSE THIS TECHNIQUE OF MOTIVATION AND WILL
REACT DEFENSIVELY. THE EMPLOYEE VIEWS THIS AS MANAGEMENT'S
WAY TO MANIPULATE HIM AND HE WILL RESIST. THE PROBLEMS OF
THE JACKASS FALLACY ARE COMPOUNDED FURTHER BY BUREAUCRATIC
ORGANIZATIONAL STRUCTURES. THIS TYPE OF STRUCTURE REQUIRES
EVERYONE TO BE DEPENDENT ON THOSE AT HIGHER LEVELS. THIS
CREATES INTERNAL COMPETITION, FIGHTING WITHIN THE
ORGANIZATION AND RIVALRY. IT ALSO CREATES FAILURES AND
FEELINGS OF FUTILITY WHICH CREATE DEFENSIVENESS ON THE PART
OF THE EMPLOYEE.
    THERE ARE WAYS IN WHICH A MANAGER CAN HELP HIMSELF
START TO SOLVE THESE PROBLEMS. HIS FIRST PRIORITY SHOULD BE
TO CHANGE HIS WAY OF THINKING, AS IN THE JACKASS FALLACY.
HIS NEXT STEP IS TO LOOK AT HIS ORGANIZATIONAL STRUCTURE.
HE SHOULD MAKE SURE THE ORGANIZATION'S STRUCTURE IS TO
ACCOMPLISH THE TASK IT MUST DO, AND NOT TO ACHIEVE A
HIERARCHIAL STRUCTURE. BY APPLYING NEW PRINCIPLES OF
MOTIVATION TO HIS OWN ORGANIZATION HE WILL BE IN A POSITION
NOT ONLY TO SUSTAIN THE VITALITY OF THAT ORGANIZATION BUT,
MORE IMPORTANT, TO KEEP EMPLOYEES ADAPTIVE TO CHANGING
CIRCUMSTANCES.

M0275 LEVINSON, HARRY.   MOLINARI, JANICE.   SPOHN, ANDREW G.
ORGANIZATIONAL DIAGNOSIS.
CAMBRIDGE, MASS.: HARVARD UNIVERSITY PRESS, 1972.

    SCHOLARLY OVERVIEW OF CAUSES AND CURES OF MENTAL
INSTABILITY IN INDUSTRY AND MANAGEMENT'S RELATION WITH

M0275   IT. INSTRUMENT USED IS A GUIDE DERIVED FROM MENNINGER'S
        MANUAL FOR PSYCHIATRIC CASE STUDY.

M0276   LEVITAN, SAR.   JOHNSTON, W.
         CHANGES IN WORK: MORE EVOLUTION THAN REVOLUTION.
        MANPOWER, SEPTEMBER 1973, PP. 2-8.

            JOB REDESIGN SEEN HAVING MINOR IMPACT COMPARED TO
        ONGOING CHANGES IN THE WORK PLACE.
            THIS ARTICLE IS BASED ON THE BOOK, WORK IS HERE TO
        STAY, ALAS. IT STARTS WITH THE ASSUMPTION THAT MAN IS ON
        THE VERGE OF A MORE OR LESS COMPLETE RELEASE FROM WORK AND
        DISPROVES IT. IT THEN GOES ON TO EXPLAIN WHY THIS IS NOT
        TRUE.
            AMERICANS HAVE MORE LEISURE TIME NOW THAN EVER BEFORE.
        ECONOMIC BONDS WHICH HAVE ALWAYS TIED MEN TO THEIR JOBS ARE
        NOW LOOSENED. WORKERS TODAY ARE BETTER EDUCATED. THERE IS
        A MISMATCH BETWEEN BETTER EDUCATED, BETTER PAID WORKERS AND
        ROUTINE JOBS. THESE CHANGES ARE SUPPOSED TO CAUSE A GREAT
        DECLINE IN THE NUMBER OF PEOPLE WHO ARE GOING TO WANT TO
        WORK.
            ACCORDING TO THE BUREAU OF LABOR STATISTICS,
        ABSENTEEISM HAS ONLY INSIGNIFICANTLY INCREASED IN RECENT
        YEARS. THEY ALSO STATE THAT MONEY IS STILL THE MOST
        IMPORTANT ASPECT OF WORK. SINCE 1964, WAGES HAVE BEEN THE
        PREDOMINANT ISSUE IN COLLECTIVE BARGAINING.
            THERE ARE SOME SOLUTIONS TO THE PROBLEM OF ABSENTEEISM.
        SOME OF THESE ARE THAT INDIVIDUALS SHOULD BE GIVEN MAXIMUM
        FREEDOM TO CONTROL WORK AND EDUCATION. JOBS SHOULD BE
        DESIGNED TO GIVE A PERSON A SERIES OF TASKS WHICH ARE
        VARIED, CHALLENGING, AND MEANINGFUL IN TERMS OF THE END
        PRODUCT. THE STATUS DIFFERENCES WHICH HAVE SEPARATED
        SUPERVISORS AND WORKERS SHOULD LARGELY BE ELIMINATED AND
        REPLACED BY A TEAM CONCEPT AND AN EMPHASIS ON SHARED GOALS.
        HOWEVER IN PRACTICE, REDESIGNING FAVORS INDUSTRIES' NEEDS
        MORE THAN THE WORKERS' NEEDS. REASONS FOR THIS ARE THAT
        THERE IS NO REAL WAY TO TELL IF IT WOULD BENEFIT THE
        INDUSTRY. RESTRUCTURING JOBS TO GIVE WORKERS VARYING TASKS
        WOULD BE AT ODDS WITH THE FUNDAMENTAL REQUIREMENT OF
        EFFICIENT PRODUCTION.
            EVEN THOUGH ALL THE WORK REDESIGN IN THE WORLD CAN NOT
        MAKE DULL JOBS EXCITING OR INJECT MEANING INTO MEANINGLESS
        JOBS, THERE ARE SOME GOOD POINTS TO IT. CHANGES IN WORKER'S
        ATTITUDES ARE BEING PARALLED BY CHANGES IN THE NATURE OF
        WORK. SKILL REQUIREMENTS ARE INCREASING. WORK WHICH WAS
        LARGELY DETERMINED BY ACCIDENT OF BIRTH IS NOW MORE LIKELY
        TO BE AN EXPRESSION OF PERSONAL CHOICE. WELFARE HAS RELAXED
        THE HISTORIC WORK OR STARVE LAW NOT ENTIRELY CLEAR.
        PRODUCTIVITY GAINS HAVE MADE IT POSSIBLE FOR SHORTER WORKING
        HOURS.
            SOME DAY ALL WORK MAY BE A MATTER OF CHOICE RATHER
        THAN NECESSITY. BUT AS YET THE HEAVENLY CITY OF THE
        PHILOSOPHERS IS STILL BEYOND OUR REACH.

M0277   LEVITAN, SAR.   JOHNSTON, W.
         JOB REDESIGN, REFORM, ENRICHMENT -- EXPLORING THE
        LIMITATIONS.
        MONTHLY LABOR REVIEW 96 (JULY 1973): 35-41.

M0277   DISCUSSION OF VARIOUS EXPERIMENTS AND METHODS
OF JOB REDESIGN TO INCREASE WORKER SATISFACTION AND
PRODUCTIVITY.

M0278 LEVITAN, SAR.   TAGGART, ROBERT.
HAS THE BLUE-COLLAR WORKER'S POSITION WORSENED?
MONTHLY LABOR REVIEW, 94 (SEPTEMBER 1971): 23-29.

        DISCUSSION OF DISSATISFACTION OF BLUE-COLLAR WORKERS,
WITH CONCLUSION BY THE AUTHORS THAT THEIR PROBLEMS ARE NO
DIFFERENT FROM THOSE SUFFERED BY SOCIETY IN GENERAL.

M0279 LEVITIN, TERESA E. VEROFF, JOSEPH.
A SOCIAL PSYCHOLGICAL EXPLORATION OF POWER MOTIVATION
AMONG DISADVANTAGED WORKERS.
ANN ARBOR: THE UNIVERISTY OF MICHIGAN, GRANT 91-26-71-21.

        THIS STUDY DEVELOPED AND TESTED SOME SYSTEMATIC IDEAS
ABOUT SOCIAL POWER. THREE CONCEPTUAL DISTINCTIONS WERE
INTRODUCED: (1) EFFECTANCE MOTIVATION WAS USED TO DESCRIBE
THE JOINT, OFTEN INEXTRICABLY LINKED, AROUSAL OF POWER AND
ACHIEVEMENT MOTIVATION. (2) POWER MOTIVATION WAS
DISTINGUISHED FROM ACHIEVEMENT MOTIVATION ON THE BASIS OF
THE RESPECTIVE SOCIAL AND NONSOCIAL GOALS. (3) POWER
MOTIVATION WAS CONCEPTUALIZED AS BASED IN EITHER FEAR OF
HAVING CHOICES USURPED BY OTHERS (NEGATIVE ORIENTATION)
OR DELIGHT IN TRYING TO DETERMINE THE CHOICES OF OTHERS
(POSITIVE ORIENTATION). PREDICTIONS BASED ON SPECULATION
ABOUT ATTITUDINAL AND BEHAVIORAL CORRELATES OF EACH MOTIVE
AND OF EACH ORIENTATION WERE TESTED WITH DATA OBTAINED
THROUGH INTERVIEWS WITH 211 BLACK, DISADVANTAGED MEN WHO
WERE IN EITHER A TRAINING PROGRAM OR AN ENTRY-LEVEL JOB
WITH A LARGE MANUFACTURING COMPANY. FINDINGS DID NOT
SUPPORT PREDICTIONS ABOUT EFFECTANCE MOTIVATION; POWER
MOTIVATION WAS SIGNIFICANTLY ASSOCIATED WITH FEELINGS OF
PREJUDICE, DISCRIMINATION, AND MILITANCY. PREDICTIONS ABOUT
POWER AND ACHIEVEMENT MOTIVATION AND THE ORIENTATIONS
TOWARD POWER WERE GENERALLY SUPPORTED, ALTHOUGH ACCEPTABLE
LEVELS OF SIGNIFICANCE WERE SELDOM REACHED.

M0280 LEVOU, ROBERT P.
HOW TO KEEP STAFF MORALE AND MOTIVATION IN HIGH GEAR.
PERSONNEL JOURNAL 51 (DECEMBER 1973): 913-18.

        THE AUTHOR OF THIS ARTICLE MAKES SOME SUGGESTIONS
FOR IMPROVEMENT OF MORALE AND MOTIVATION OTHER THAN
HIGHER WAGES OR FRINGE BENEFITS. INSTEAD HE RECOMMENDS
LISTENING TO EMPLOYEES' IDEAS AND BEING SENSITIVE TO CHANGE.

M0281 LEWIN, ARIE Y.   DUBNO, PETER.   AKULA, WILLIAM G.
FACE-TO-FACE INTERACTION IN THE PEER-NOMINATION PROCESS.
JOURNAL OF APPLIED PSYCHOLOGY 55 (OCTOBER 1971): 495-97.

        LEWINS' SURVEY ATTEMPTS TO DISCOVER ANY ADVANTAGE OF
PEER RATINGS AND THEIR VALIDITY IN PREDICTING FUTURE
MANAGERIAL PERFORMANCE OR LEADERSHIP. LEWIN GOES ON THE
ASSUMPTION THAT AS PEOPLE WORK TOGETHER THEY FORM OPINIONS
ABOUT EACH OTHER.

M0281   THE RESEARCHERS CONDUCTED THEIR EXPERIMENT AT A COLLEGE
OF BUSINESS ADMINISTRATION OF A LARGE EASTERN UNIVERSITY.
NINETY-FIVE STUDENTS USED MANAGEMENT GAME SIMULATION. THE
STUDENTS WERE BROKEN INTO GROUPS AND AFTER PRACTICING,
PLAYED THE GAME THREE TIMES. THE THIRD GAME WAS
VIDEO-TAPED. AFTER THE GAMES THE STUDENTS EVALUATED OTHERS
IN THE GROUP THROUGH A QUESTIONNAIRE ADAPTED FROM FIEDLER
(1967). THE QUESTIONS COVERED THE DIMENSIONS OF: A) WITH
WHOM CAN YOU WORK BEST?, B) WHO CONTRIBUTED MOST TO
ACHIEVING THE GOALS OF THE TEAM?, AND C) WHO CONTRIBUTED
MOST TO THE ANALYSIS AND SOLVING OF DAY-TO-DAY PROBLEMS?
A DIFFERENT GROUP OF 97 STUDENTS EVALUATED THE FIRST
GROUP WHO WERE ON VIDEO-TAPE. THE DATA WERE THEN SUBJECTED
TO RANKINGS AND CHI-SQUARE TESTING.
        IT WAS FOUND THAT INTERACTION DID NOT HAVE TO TAKE
PLACE FOR INDIVIDUALS TO FORM OPINIONS ABOUT OTHERS. THE
EXTERNAL VIEWERS FORMED MANY OF THE SAME OPINIONS AS THE
ACTUAL GROUP MEMBERS.
        LEWIN SUGGESTS, THEREFORE, THAT, APPARENTLY THE
FACE-TO-FACE ASPECT OF INTERACTION IS ONLY ONE SMALL
PHYSICAL INGREDIENT IN THE PROCESS THAT DOES NOT EVEN APPEAR
TO BE NECESSARY FOR ADEQUATE PEER RATING TO OCCUR. WHAT
SEEMS TO BE MUCH MORE PROBABLE IS THAT SOME ASPECT OF RULE
BEHAVIOR LIES AT THE CORE OF THE JUDGEMENT INTERACTION
PROCESS.

M0282   LOCKE, EDWIN A.
   SATISFIERS AND DISSATISFIERS AMONG WHITE-COLLAR AND
   BLUE-COLLAR EMPLOYEES.
   JOURNAL OF APPLIED PSYCHOLOGY 58 (AUGUST 1973): 67-76.

        SATISFACTION AMONG WHITE-COLLAR EMPLOYEES WAS STUDIED
BY HAVING EMPLOYEES DESCRIBE SATISFYING AND DISSATISFYING
JOB INCIDENTS AND CLASSIFYING THESE INCIDENTS ACCORDING TO
A NEW EVENT-AGENT SYSTEM. IT WAS FOUND THAT THE SAME
CATEGORIES OF EVENTS LED TO BOTH SATISFACTION AND
DISSATISFACTION WITHIN EACH JOB LEVEL. HOWEVER,
DIFFERENT AGENTS WERE SEEN AS RESPONSIBLE FOR THESE EVENTS--
THE SELF FOR SATISFYING EVENTS AND OTHERS FOR DISSATISFYING
EVENTS.

M0283   LOCKE, EDWIN A.   WHITING, ROMAN J.
   SOURCES OF SATISFACTION AND DISSATISFACTION AMONG SOLID
   WASTE MANAGEMENT EMPLOYEES.
   JOURNAL OF APPLIED PSYCHOLOGY 59 (APRIL 1974): 145-56.

        A NATIONAL RANDOM SAMPLE OF 911 EMPLOYEES IN THE SOLID
WASTE MANAGEMENT INDUSTRY WERE INTERVIEWED CONCERNING THEIR
JOB ATTITUDES. WHILE WHITE-COLLAR EMPLOYEES WERE MORE
SATISFIED WITH THEIR JOBS THAN WERE BLUE-COLLAR EMPLOYEES,
BOTH THE LATTER AND THE SECRETARIAL EMPLOYEES WERE MORE
SATISFIED THAN WERE THE EMPLOYEES AT THE SAME JOB LEVELS IN
OTHER TYPES OF WORK. THESE DIFFERENCES WERE ATTRIBUTED TO
PAY AND WORK DIFFERENCES BETWEEN SOLID WASTE MANAGEMENT AND
OTHER OCCUPATIONS. WHITE-COLLAR EMPLOYEES WERE MORE LIKELY
TO DERIVE SATISFACTIONS AND DISSATISFACTION FROM INTRINSIC
SOURCES AND LESS LIKELY TO DERIVE THEM FROM EXTRINSIC
SOURCES.

M0284 LUKIEC, MITCHELL.
MOTIVATING THE WORKER.
PERSONNEL JOURNAL, 52 (NOVEMBER 1973): 988-91.

THE AUTHOR POINTS OUT A CONFLICT BETWEEN UNION AND
MANAGEMENT VIEWS OF MOTIVATING THE WORKER.

M0285 LUTHANS, FRED. OTTEMAN, ROBERT.
MOTIVATION VS. LEARNING APPROACHES TO ORGANIZATIONAL
BEHAVIOR.
BUSINESS HORIZONS 16 (DECEMBER 1973): 55-62.

THE MOTIVATION THEORY HAS BEEN PLAYING THE DOMINANT
ROLE IN THE EMERGING FIELD OF ORGANIZATIONAL BEHAVIOR. THE
MASLOW THEORY INFERRED THAT ESTEEM AND SELF-ACTUALIZATION
WOULD MOTIVATE ORGANIZATIONAL PARTICIPANTS.
THE PROCESS APPROACH TO MOTIVATION SEEMS TO HOLD MUCH
MORE PROMISE FOR UNDERSTANDING ORGANIZATIONAL BEHAVIOR
THAN THE SIMPLISTIC CONTENT APPROACH.
MOTIVATION IS A BASIC PSYCHOLOGICAL PROCESS WHICH
INVOLVES NEEDS THAT SET UP DRIVES TO ACCOMPLISH GOALS. IT
IS DIFFICULT TO EXPLAIN ORGANIZATIONAL BEHAVIOR BECAUSE IF
YOU USE AN EXAMPLE OF A PERSON WORKING HARD, IT COULD BE
SAID THAT HE HAS A MOTIVE FOR WORKING THAT HARD IN ORDER TO
SATISFY HIS NEEDS.
SOME MANAGERS AND SUPERVISORS TYPICALLY DEPEND ON
VARIOUS FORMS OF THREAT OR PUNISHMENT IN ATTEMPTING TO
CHANGE THEIR EMPLOYEES' BEHAVIOR. PUNISHMENT ON A JOB HAS
TO BE DONE CAREFULLY. IF THE PUNISHMENT IS TOO MUCH, THE
EMPLOYEE IS NOT GOING TO KNOW PRECISELY HOW TO RESPOND
WHEN THE SAME OR SIMILIAR SITUATION ARISES AGAIN.
ADMINISTRATION OF THE PUNISHMENT MAY BECOME ASSOCIATED
THROUGH CONDITIONING WITH THE PUNISHMENT ITSELF AND TAKE ON
ACCOMPANYING NEGATIVE PROPERTIES.
THE CONTENT MOTIVATIONAL APPROACH TO THE MANAGEMENT OF
HUMAN RESOURCES HAS PRIMARILY RELIED UPON JOB ENRICHMENT
WHICH WILL PRESUMABLY LEAD TO INCREASED PERFORMANCE AND
GOAL ATTAINMENT. THIS APPROACH IS BASED ON THE IDEA THAT
THE FEELINGS OF RESPONSIBILITY OR ACHIEVEMENT WILL AFFECT
JOB SATISFACTION AND THIS IN TURN WILL IMPROVE A PERSON'S
JOB PERFORMANCE.
THE MONOCRATIC VARIETY OF BUREAUCRACY IS FROM A PURELY
TECHNICAL POINT OF VIEW, WHICH IS CAPABLE OF ATTAINING THE
HIGHEST DEGREE OF EFFICIENCY AND IS IN THIS SENSE FORMALLY
THE MOST RATIONAL KNOWN MEANS OF CARRYING OUT IMPERATIVE
CONTROL OVER HUMAN BEINGS.

M0286 LYON, HERBERT L. IVANCEVICH, J. M.
AN EXPLORATORY INVESTIGATION OF ORGANIZATIONAL CLIMATE AND
JOB SATISFACTION IN A HOSPITAL.
ACADEMY OF MANAGEMENT JOURNAL 17 (DECEMBER 1974): 635-48.

THE ORGANIZATIONAL CLIMATE OF A HOSPITAL IS
INVESTIGATED, AND ITS IMPACT ON JOB SATISFACTION IS ANALYZED
FOR NURSES AND ADMINISTRATORS. DIFFERENT CLIMATE DIMENSIONS
ARE SHOWN TO INFLUENCE INDIVIDUAL JOB SATISFACTION FACETS
FOR NURSES AND ADMINISTRATORS, AND THE IMPACT OF
ORGANIZATIONAL CLIMATE OF SATISFACTION VARIES WITH THE

M0286   CLIMATE DIMENSION AND THE TYPE OF SATISFACTION.

M0287   MCARTHUR, JOHN.
         IS MOTIVATION BY MONEY STILL FASHIONABLE?
         MANAGEMENT REVIEW 62 (MAY 1973): 64-65.

              THE AUTHOR STRESSES THAT THE NEW THEORIES OF MOTIVATION
         BECOME EFFECTIVE ONLY AFTER THE EMPLOYEE IS PAID ENOUGH TO
         DISPEL CONCERNS OVER DAY-TO-DAY SURVIVAL. THUS MONEY IS, IF
         NOT THE MOTIVATOR, AT LEAST THE KEY TO MOTIVATION.

M0288   MCCLELLAND, DIANA.
         OPENING JOB DOORS FOR MATURE WOMEN.
         MANPOWER, AUGUST 1973, PP. 8-12.

              THROUGH EXEMPLARY PROGRAMS TO HELP MATURE WOMEN, THE
         FEDERAL GOVERNMENT CAN DEMONSTRATE TO OTHER EMPLOYERS THAT
         IT IS GOOD MANAGEMENT TO MAKE THE BEST USE OF THE NATION'S
         HUMAN RESOURCES, REGARDLESS OF SEX OR AGE.

M0289   MCCONKEY, DALE.
         THE POSITION AND FUNCTION OF BUDGETS IN AN MBO SYSTEM.
         BUSINESS QUARTERLY 39 (SPRING 1974): 44-50.

              IN THIS ARTICLE THE AUTHOR DISCUSSES WHY HE BELIEVES
         THE ROLE OF THE BUDGETS MUST BE ONE WHICH CAPITALIZES ON
         THE MOTIVATIONAL QUALITIES WHICH ARE INHERENT IN THE SYSTEM.

M0290   MCCORMICK, TOM.
         SHE CAME A LONG, LONG WAY.
         EXTENSION SERVICE REVIEW, JANUARY-FEBRUARY 1974, PP. 18-19.

              IN 1974, A NATIONAL AWARD FOR EXCELLENCE IN TELEVISION
         WENT TO TV EDITOR KARIN KRISTIANSSON.

M0291   MCDONALD, BLAIR W. GUNDERSON, E. K.
         CORRELATES OF JOB SATISFACTION IN NAVAL ENVIRONMENTS.
         JOURNAL OF APPLIED PSYCHOLOGY 59 (JUNE 1974): 371-73

              FOUR VARIABLES (DEMOGRAPHIC, MILITARY STATUS,
         JOB-RELATED, HEALTH-RELATED) WERE USED IN A JOB SATISFACTION
         MEASURE OF 5851 NAVY ENLISTED MEN. HEALTH-RELATED VARIABLES
         WERE MOST HIGHLY CORRELATED WITH SATISFACTION, FOLLOWED BY
         TYPE OF JOB AND MILITARY STATUS.

M0292   MCKIBBIN, CARROLL R.
         THE QUIT RATE AS A MEASURE OF MORALE IN THE PUBLIC SERVICE:
         THE CASE OF THE UNITED STATES FOREIGN SERVICE.
         PUBLIC PERSONNEL REVIEW 32 (JANUARY 1971): 12-15.

         ANALYSIS INDICATES THAT THE QUIT RATE HAS A VERY
         LIMITED APPLICATION TO AN ASSESSMENT OF MORALE AMONG
         GOVERNMENT EMPLOYEES. USES THE FOREIGN SERVICE TO
         DEMONSTRATE NON-MORALE RELATED FACTORS WHICH
         INFLUENCE QUIT RATES: CAREER PREPARATION AND COMMITMENT,
         GOVERNMENT REGULATIONS, ACCESS, TRANSFERABILITY, AND HOPE.
         SUGGESTS MEASURING MORALE BY SIMPLY QUESTIONING EMPLOYEES.

M0293 MACKINNON, NEIL L. ROCHE, WILLIAM J.
       MOTIVATING PEOPLE WITH MEANINGFUL WORK.
       HARVARD BUSINESS REVIEW 48 (MAY 1970): 97-110.

       THIS ARTICLE SUGGESTS A PROGRAM WHICH COULD MOTIVATE
PERFORMANCE FROM EMPLOYEES BY GIVING THEM MEANINGFUL WORK.
THIS IS DESCRIBED AS A JOB THAT INVOLVES THE EMPLOYEE WITH
THE IDENTIFICATION AND SOLUTION OF PROBLEMS THAT AFFECT HIM.
THE WORK BECOMES MEANINGFUL IN A SENSE THAT THE EMPLOYEE IS
HIGHLY MOTIVATED TO SOLVE PROBLEMS WHICH ARE PERSONALLY
CLOSE TO HIM.
       IN ORDER FOR THE PROGRAM TO BE IMPLEMENTED, IT IS
NECESSARY TO HAVE TOTAL TOP MANAGEMENT SUPPORT. THE SECOND
PHASE OF THE PROGRAM IS TO RETRAIN SUPERVISORS SO THAT
EACH SUPERVISOR AND HIS GROUP CAN RUN A CONTINUOUS CYCLE
OF MEETINGS. AT EACH MEETING, THE GROUP IDENTIFIES PROBLEMS
ASSOCIATED WITH ITS WORK, ASSIGNS RESPONSIBILITY FOR
SOLVING PROBLEMS TO ONE MEMBER, AND HEARS PROGRESS REPORTS
ON PROBLEMS FROM EARLIER MEETINGS. INITIALLY, THE
SUPERVISOR HAS TO ACCEPT AND USE A NEW MANAGERIAL STYLE, AND
HIS WORKERS HAVE TO ACCEPT MORE RESPONSIBILITY THAN THEY
PROBABLY HAVE EVER HAD. IT IS SUGGESTED THAT THE SUPERVISOR
FOCUS THE GROUP'S ATTENTION TOWARD PROBLEMS THAT THE MEMBERS
CAN SOLVE. THE AUTHORS STRESS THREE POINTS AS THE MEETINGS
ARE GETTING UNDERWAY: 1) THE GROUP NEEDS TO DEVELOP A
CRITERION TO MEASURE IMPROVEMENT OVER TIME; 2) THE
SUPERVISOR SHOULD SELECT AN AREA OF HIS RESPONSIBILITY IN
WHICH THE PROGRAM WILL HAVE QUICK SUCCESS (AS HE BECOMES
EXPERIENCED, HE CAN WORK INTO THE MORE DIFFICULT AREAS); 3)
IN LATER MEETINGS, THE GROUP NEEDS TO SET ITS OWN GOALS.
       AS THE MEETINGS BECOMES A CONTINUOUS CYCLE, THE WORK
GROUP BOTH IDENTIFIES NEW PROBLEMS AND CHECKS UP ON HOW
WELL ANY SOLUTIONS ARE WORKING. THE MEETINGS TEND TO OCCUR
LESS FREQUENTLY BECAUSE THE GROUP HAS DEVELOPED EXPERIENCE
TO ANALYZE PROBLEMS AND ESTABLISH CRITERIA AND GOALS
QUICKLY, WHICH TENDS TO INCREASE AS TIME PASSES. THE
AUTHORS SUGGEST STRESSING THE WORKER'S ROLE BY TELLING THE
GROUP, REMEMBER THAT YOU KNOW THE PROBLEMS ASSOCIATED
WITH YOUR WORK BETTER THAN ANYONE IN MANAGEMENT BECAUSE YOU
ARE CLOSE TO THE PROBLEM. YOU IDENTIFY THEM.

M0294 MCNULTY, L. A.
        JOB ENRICHMENT: HOW TO MAKE IT WORK.
       SUPERVISORY MANAGEMENT 18 (SEPTEMBER 1973): 7-15.

       DISCUSSES FIVE BASIC KINDS OF JOB ENRICHMENT PROGRAMS.

M0295   MA BELL MOTIVATES.
       INDUSTRY WEEK 169 (MAY 17,1971): 34-37.

       PRESENTATION OF THE BELL SYSTEM'S HERZBERG-BASED
JOB ENRICHMENT PROGRAM TO RESTRUCTURE THE JOBS OF OVER
100,000 EMPLOYEES. INCLUDES SEVERAL CASE HISTORIES AND
COMPARISONS OF THE BELL SYSTEM APPROACH TO THOSE OF OTHER
INDUSTRIES.

M0296 MAIER, NORMAN R. F.
       PSYCHOLOGY IN INDUSTRIAL ORGANIZATIONS.

M0296   BOSTON: HOUGHTON MIFFLIN COMPANY, 1973.
        TEXTBOOK ON INDUSTRIAL AND ORGANIZATIONAL PSYCHOLOGY.
A SOURCE BOOK ON PRINCIPLES AND METHODS FOR PERSONNEL
MANAGERS. LABORATORY EXERCISES ARE DESIGNED TO DEVELOP
SKILLS THROUGH EXPERIENCE--INTERPERSONAL SKILL REQUIRES
PRACTICE. INTRIGUING EXERCISES AT THE END OF EACH CHAPTER
SHOULD HELP A STUDENT GET A FEEL FOR AN ACTUAL WORK
SITUATION.

M0297   MALI, PAUL.
        A PRACTICAL SCHEME THAT MOTIVATES PEOPLE.
        ADMINISTRATIVE MANAGEMENT 34 (MARCH 1973):   64-67.

        THE AUTHOR OF THIS ARTICLE PRESENTS A PLANNED
MODEL WHICH DEALS WITH MOTIVATORS AND DEMOTIVATORS AS
"BEST FIT" OF COMPANY NEEDS AND EMPLOYEE OBJECTIVES.

M0298   MALOY, RICHARD.
        THE PROFIT MOTIVE: CAN IT MOTIVATE INDUSTRY TO HIRE THE
        HARD CORE.
        MANPOWER, JANUARY, 1969, PP. 12-15.

        GIVEN THE PROPER CIRCUMSTANCES, AND BARRING AN
ECONOMIC RECESSION, THE PRIVATE SECTOR CAN SHARPLY
REDUCE THE NUMBER OF HARD-CORE UNEMPLOYED.

M0299   MANAGER COMMENTS ON HOW TO MOTIVATE.
        INDUSTY WEEK 166 (JUNE 29, 1970):   39.

        ONE APPROACH IS TO HUMANIZE THE WORK ENVIRONMENT
FOR MORALE, TO KEEP DOWN COSTLY TURNOVER, AND FOR
SAFETY. MANY CHANGES CAN AFFECT THE EMPLOYEE'S PRIDE
IN HIS JOB, AND PRIDE IS A FUNCTION OF SUCCESS.

M0300   MANGUN, GARTH L.   WALSH, JOHN.
        A DECADE OF MANPOWER TRAINING.
        MANPOWER 3 (APRIL 1973):   20-26.

        MANGUN AND WALSH, RESOURCES DEVELOPMENT RESEARCHERS,
TOOK A GOOD LOOK AT THE LAST TEN YEARS OF MANPOWER TRAINING
AND ARE ATTEMPTING TO ANSWER THESE QUESTIONS:
        1. WHAT DO THE EXPERIENCE OF THESE TEN YEARS TELL US
ABOUT REMEDIAL ADULT OCCUPATIONAL PREPARATION?
        2. WHAT HAVE BEEN THE MAJOR SUCCESSES OF THE PROGRAMS?
        3. WHERE HAS IT FAILED TO MATCH EXPECTATIONS?
        4. HOW MAY IT BE IMPROVED?
        THEY SAY THAT WHETHER THE INCOME GAINS ($1,250 FOR
INSTITUTIONAL TRAINEES; $1,092 FOR ON THE JOB TRAINEES)
MAKE THE PROGRAM WORTH ITS COSTS RESTS UPON A VALUE
JUDGEMENT--IS IT RIGHT TO SPEND PUBLIC MONEY ON THIS
PARTICULAR SEGMENT OF PEOPLE-- WILL THE EARNINGS GAINS LAST
FOR AT LEAST TWO YEARS? STUDIES SHOW THE ANSWER TO BOTH IS
YES AND THEREFORE WORTHWHILE.
        MDTA (MANPOWER DEVELOPMENT AND TRAINING ACT) MADE
CONTRIBUTIONS TO INSTITUTIONS TRAINING IN THREE NOTABLE
WAYS.
        1. ESTABLISHMENT OF GROUP TRAINING PROJECTS TO PREPARE
ENROLLEES FOR A SPECIFIC JOB.

M0300　　　　2. ESTABLISHMENT OF SKILL CENTERS THAT OFFER TRAINING
IN A VARIETY OF OCCUPATIONS.
　　　　3. INDIVIDUAL REFERRAL OF MDTA ENROLLEES TO OTHER ON
GOING TRAINING PROGRAMS.
　　　　THE AUTHORS SAY THAT THE MOST SERIOUS WEAKNESS OF MDTA
HAS BEEN THE OCCUPATION IN WHICH THE TRAINING HAS BEEN
OFFERED--THE OBJECTIVE SHOULD HAVE BEEN A SATISFYING CAREER
FOR THE REMAINDER OF THE TRAINEE'S WORKING LIFE INSTEAD OF
IMMEDIATE EMPLOYMENT. ANOTHER WEAKNESS HAS BEEN THE USE OF
SECOND CLASS TRAINING INSTITUTIONS, SUB-STANDARD
FACILITIES AND EQUIPMENT WHICH REDUCES THE BENEFITS.
STIPENDS IS ANOTHER CONSIDERATION-- THEY SHOULD NOT BE SO
HIGH AS TO ENCOURAGE PEOPLE TO ENROLL FOR THE STIPEND ALONE.
THE CHOICE BETWEEN INSTITUTIONAL TRAINING AND ON-THE -JOB
TRAINING HAS BEEN AS ISSUE SINCE MDTA BEGAN. ON-THE-JOB
TRAINING IS CHEAPER AND IS DIRECTLY CONNECTED TO A JOB BUT
IS LIMITED BY JOB AVAILABILITY, EMPLOYERS' WILLINGNESS
TO COOPERATE. INSTITUTIONAL TRAINING CAN BE UNDERTAKEN BY
ANYONE, ANYTIME FOR ANY OCCUPATION BUT IT COSTS MORE AND
HAS NO ASSURANCE OF A JOB.
　　　　IN CONCLUSION, ADULT REMEDIAL OCCUPATIONAL TRAINING
SHOULD BE APPROACHED AS A LONG-RUN STRATEGY.

M0301　MANOFF, ALBERT W.
VALUES -- NOT ATTITUDES -- ARE THE REAL KEY TO MOTIVATION.
MANAGEMENT REVIEW, 63 (DECEMBER 1974): 23-29.

　　　　THE AUTHOR MAINTAINS THAT TOO MUCH RELEVANCE HAS BEEN
PLACED ON ATTITUDES AS THE KEY TO MOTIVATION. RATHER THE
KEY MAY WELL BE VALUES SINCE A SINGLE VALUE MAY GIVE RISE TO
MANY ATTITUDES.
MANPOWER REPORT OF THE PRESIDENT, INCLUDING A REPORT ON
MANPOWER REQUIREMENTS, RESOURCES, UTILIZATION AND TRAINING.
U. S. DEPARTMENT OF LABOR. TRANSMITTED TO CONGRESS APRIL
1971.
　　　　GIVES PRODUCTIVITY TRENDS, WAGES AND EARNINGS,
INDUSTRY DEVELOPMENTS, EMPLOYMENT CHANGES, UNEMPLOYMENT
STATISTICS, NEGRO EMPLOYMENT PROBLEMS, CHANGING
LABOR FORCE PARTICIPATION OF WOMEN, VETERANS EMPLOYMENT,
MANPOWER PROGRAMS, PROBLEMS OF THE CITY JOB
MARKETS, RURAL DILEMMAS, GOVERNMENT EXPENSES AND OUTLOOK.
MANY, MANY STATISTICS.
RESEARCH PAPERS DONE UNDER GRANTS FROM THE MANPOWER
ADMINISTRATION UNITED STATES DEPARTMENT OF LABOR.

M0302　MARA, THOMAS G.　　　MASTERSON, T. R.
LEADERSHIP METHODS THAT MOTIVATE.
SUPERVISORY MANAGEMENT, 15 (JANUARY 1970): 3-9.

　　　　A LEADER/SUPERVISOR IN THE WORLD OF BUSINESS IS
COMPARED TO A DIRECTOR IN THE THEATER. THE LEADER PLANS
AND ORGANIZES WORK FOR HIS PEOPLE . . . . HE EVALUATES THE
PERFORMANCE OF EACH INDIVIDUAL AND OF THE GROUP; . . . HE
MAKES SUGGESTIONS AND COUNSELS THEM ON IMPROVING THEIR
PERFORMANCE. (PP. 7-8). IN ORDER TO LEAD AND MOTIVATE HIS
SUBORDINATES, THE LEADER MUST HAVE THEIR CONFIDENCE AND
RESPECT. THE PURPOSE OF THIS ARTICLE IS TO DISCUSS CERTAIN
PRINCIPLES OF LEADERSHIP AND HOW THEY RESULT IN MOTIVATING

M0302   EMPLOYEES.
            THE FOLLOWING PRINCIPLES ARE IMPORTANT FOR   CAPABLE
        LEADERSHIP AND EFFECTIVE MOTIVATION . . . (BY) . . . THE
        SUPERVISOR. (P. 8).
        PERSONAL EXAMPLE. PERSONAL EXAMPLE IS ONE OF THE MOST
        IMPORTANT MOTIVATING PRINCIPLES.   TO BRING OUT THE BEST IN
        OTHERS, YOU MUST SHOW BY YOUR OWN ACTIONS THE LEVEL OF
        PERFORMANCE THAT YOU EXPECT. (P. 8).
        CONSISTENCY IN BEHAVIOR. EMPLOYEES WANT TO PREDICT HOW
        THEIR BOSS WILL REACT IN CERTAIN SITUATIONS. IF HE
        BECOMES EXPLOSIVE, THEY WILL REACT BY BEING OVERCAUTIOUS,
        CONSERVATIVE ABOUT MAKING SUGGESTIONS FOR IMPROVEMENTS, AND
        RELUCTANT TO 'STICK THEIR NECKS OUT'. (P. 8).
        CONSISTENT BEHAVIOR IS THEREFORE IMPORTANT IN EARNING
        EMPLOYEE CONFIDENCE AND RESPECT.
        REGULAR REWARDS.   ONE OF THE STRONGEST INCENTIVES YOU CAN
        OFFER YOUR SUBORDINATES IS RECOGNITION FOR THEIR EFFORTS.
        (P. 9). THE EMPLOYEE IS MORE HIGHLY MOTIVATED IF HE KNOWS
        THAT HE WILL BE REWARDED IN SOME WAY FOR A JOB WELL DONE.
        EMPHASIS ON POSITIVE DISCIPLINE. AS A GENERAL RULE,
        EMPLOYEES WORK BETTER WHEN THEY ARE REWARDED FOR THEIR
        ACCOMPLISHMENTS RATHER THAN BEING PUNISHED FOR THEIR
        MISTAKES. WHEN THE EMPHASIS IS ON POSITIVE DISCIPLINE,
        THE EMPLOYEE WANTS TO LIVE UP TO THE RULES AND STANDARDS, (P
        SETTING AND MAINTAINING A CHALLENGING WORK PACE.
         PEOPLE WORK BEST AT A PACE THAT IS CHALLENGING BUT
        FEASIBLE. (P. 9). SO EVEN IF EMPLOYEES WORK TOWARD
        DIFFICULT GOALS, THEY WILL LOSE MOTIVATION IF THE GOAL
        IS SET TOO HIGH.
            THE LEADER THAT UTILIZES THESE PRINCIPLES WILL BE
        ABLE TO WIN THE CONFIDENCE AND RESPECT OF HIS EMPLOYEES.
        AS A RESULT, HE WILL EFFECTIVELY LEAD AND MOTIVATE THEM
        TOWARD THEIR COMMON GOALS.

M0303   MARK, JEROME A.
            PROGRESS IN MEASURING PRODUCTIVITY IN GOVERNMENT.
        MONTHLY LABOR REVIEW 95 (DECEMBER 1972):   3-6.

            RECENT REPORT ON PRODUCTIVITY IN THE FEDERAL SECTOR
        ADVANCES EFFORT TO DEVELOP A MEASURE OF OUTPUT PER MAN-HOUR
        FOR THE ENTIRE ECONOMY.

M0304   MARLAND, SIDNEY P.
            AMERICA'S NEED FOR CAREER EDUCATION.
        OCCUPATIONAL OUTLOOK QUARTERLY 16 (SUMMER 1972):   2-4.

            U. S. COMMISSIONER OF EDUCATION OUTLINES A MODEL
        PROGRAM THAT INTEGRATES CAREER ORIENTATION INTO BASIC
        ACADEMIC CURRICULUM FROM KINDERGARTEN THROUGH HIGH SCHOOL.

M0305   MARQUIS, KENT.
            INTERACTION EFFECTS OF PERSONALITY, JOB TRAINING, AND LABOR
        MARKET CONDITIONS ON PERSONAL EMPLOYMENT AND INCOME.
        ANN ARBOR: THE UNIVERSITY OF MICHIGAN. SCHEDULED FOR
        COMPLETION FISCAL YEAR 1975.

            THIS PROJECT BUILDS ON EARLIER RESEARCH WHICH INDICATES
        THAT STRONGLY MOTIVATED PEOPLE WITH WELL DEFINED HIGH

M0305 EXPECTATIONS FARE WORSE ECONOMICALLY AFTER TRAINING THAN
THOSE WHOSE MOTIVATIONS AND EXPECTATIONS ARE LOW. THE
RESEARCHER IS INTERVIEWING THREE GROUPS: (1) 90 ORIGINAL
STUDY MEN; (2) 100 NEW MEN; AND (3) A CONTROL GROUP OF
50 MEN.

M0306 MARSH, JOHN.
THE MANAGERIAL CONVOLUTION .
MANAGEMENT TODAY 28 (SEPTEMBER 1971): 71-73, 126.

    IN MANY COUNTRIES THROUGHOUT THE WORLD THERE IS AN
IMMENSE, FASCINATED, AND GROWING INTEREST IN THE ART AND
SCIENCE OF MANAGEMENT. ALL COUNTRIES ARE INTERESTED IN THE
SCIENTIFIC SIDE OF MANAGEMENT, IN THE THINGS THAT CAN BE
QUANTIFIED AND MEASURED.
    WHEN IT COMES TO PEOPLE AND THEIR TEMPERAMENTS,
CHARACTERISTICS AND CULTURES AND TO MOTIVATION AND REWARDS,
COUNTRIES DIFFER GREATLY.
IN THE WEST, THE PERIOD OF MASSIVE MANAGERIAL CHANGE BEGAN
ABOUT 1950 WHEN OUR TALENTS HAD BEEN UNHARNESSED FROM THE
WAR EFFORT.
    PEOPLE IN THE UNITED STATES WERE TOO ABSORBED WITH
THEIR OWN PROCESSES, WITH THEIR OWN MANAGERIAL GENIUS. THE
UNITED STATES USED TO HAVE A FIVE-YEAR LEAD ON ALMOST ANY
MANAGERIAL TECHNIQUE OR VEIN OF MANAGERIAL PHILOSOPHY. BUT
SINCE 1968 THE UNITED STATES HAS BEGUN RUNNING INTO
ECOLOGICAL, ENVIRONMENTAL, AND SEVERE SOCIAL PROBLEMS THERE
HAS BEEN A CHANGE.
    THE SECRET OF MAKING GOOD MANAGERS LIES IN ENTRUSTING
RESPONSIBILITY TO YOUNG MEN. A MANAGER MUST BE GIVEN
PERSONAL RESPONSIBILITY FOR HIS ENTERPRISE, OR FOR HIS
SECTION OF AN ENTERPRISE IF HE IS TO DEVELOP THE NECESSARY
CUTTING EDGE.
    THERE ARE THREE KINDS OF MANAGERS: THE ROUTINE MAN WHO
DOES A ROUTINE JOB; THE SECOND IS A ROUTINE MAN
WITH A CONCEPTUAL CAPACITY; THE THIRD IS THE INNOVATOR--THE
ENTREPRENEUR OF IDEAS. THERE ARE A NUMBER OF THESE
PEOPLE, BUT IT SEEMS AS IF THEY ARE WAITING FOR THE
OLDER PEOPLE TO MOVE OUT. THESE YOUNG PEOPLE SHOULD ASK
THEIR BOSSES FOR MORE RESPONSIBILITY AND IF THEY DON'T
RECEIVE IT, THEN THEY SHOULD MOVE ON TO A BETTER JOB.
    WITH THE 1970'S RUSHING TOWARD US IT IS NOT
SUFFICIENT FOR MEN IN RESPONSIBLE POSITIONS TO SATISFY
THEMSELVES WITH ADMINISTRATION. MANAGEMENT REQUIRES THE
APPLICATION OF CREATIVE ENERGY THAT MAKES A MAN FEEL
UNCOMFORTABLE. THE MANAGEMENT TASK IN THE FUTURE IS GOING
TO GET MORE DIFFICULT, MORE COMPLEX, AND INFINITELY MORE
OPEN TO PUBLIC CRITICISM.

M0307 MARSHALL, PATRICIA.
POLICEWOMEN ON PATROL.
MANPOWER, OCTOBER 1973, PP. 15-20.

    WASHINGTON D. C. DESEXES ASSIGNMENT OF ITS OFFICERS.
THIS ARTICLE GATHERS DATA ON THE ACTUAL PERFORMANCE OF
WOMEN ON PATROL.

M0308 MASON, PHILLIP.

M0308   EMPLOYMENT, WELFARE, AND MOTHERS' MOTIVATION.
MANPOWER, SEPTEMBER 1973, PP. 28-32.
         THE SUCCESS OF JOB PROGRAMS IS SEEN AS LINKED TO HOW
FAMILY WOMEN VIEW THEIR ROLES.

M0309   MASON, SANDRA L.
COMPARING UNION AND NONUNION WAGES IN MANUFACTURING.
MONTHLY LABOR REVIEW 94 (MAY 1971): 20-26.

         STRAIGHT-TIME PAY WAS TYPICALLY HIGHER FOR UNION
THAN NONUNION WORKERS IN THE SAME INDUSTRY IN THE 1960'S.

M0310   MEDNICK, MARTHA T.
MOTIVATIONAL AND PERSONALITY FACTORS RELATED TO CAREER
GOALS OF BLACK COLLEGE WOMEN.
UNPUBLISHED RESEARCH, HOWARD UNIVERSITY, 1973.

         THIS STUDY INVESTIGATED THE DEGREE TO WHICH TRADITIONAL
AND NONTRADITIONAL CAREER GOALS ARE SOUGHT BY BLACK COLLEGE
WOMEN IN RELATION TO SELECTED BACKGROUND, ATTITUDINAL, AND
MOTIVATIONAL FACTORS.

M0311   MILLER, JON.   LABVITZ, SANFORD.
INDIVIDUAL REACTIONS TO ORGANIZATIONAL CONFLICT AND
CHANGE.
SOCIOLOGICAL QUARTERLY 14 (1973): 556-75.

HYPOTHESES
1. A.   THE LOWER THE SATISFACTION WITH WORK AND WITH THE
ORGANIZATION, THE HIGHER THE PROBABILITY THAT AN INDIVIDUAL
WILL HAVE LEFT THE ORGANIZATION:
        B.   THE GREATER THE JOB TENSION, THE HIGHER THE
PROBABILITY THAT A MEMBER WILL HAVE LEFT THE ORGANIZATION
2.   THE PROBABILITY THAT AN INDIVIDUAL WILL HAVE LEFT THE
ORGANIZATION IS DIRECTLY RELATED TO THE PROPORTION OF HIS
MORE HIGHLY ESTEEMED COWORKERS WHO LEFT.
3.   THE PROBABILITY THAT AN INDIVIDUAL WILL HAVE LEFT THE
ORGANIZATION IS DIRECTLY RELATED TO THE PROPORTION OF HIS
INFORMATION CONTACTS WHO HAVE LEFT.
4.   THE PROBABILITY THAT AN INDIVIDUAL WILL HAVE LEFT THE
ORGANIZATION IS DIRECTLY RELATED TO THE PROPORTION OF HIS
FRIENDS IN THE ORGANIZATION WHO HAVE LEFT.
5.   THE PROBABILITY OF AN INDIVIDUAL'S LEAVING INCREASES
WITH THE DEGREE TO WHICH HE IS ISOLATED FROM THE FORMAL
AND INFORMAL POWER STRUCTURES OF THE ORGANIZATION.
6.   THE PROBABILITY OF AN INDIVIDUAL'S LEAVING INCREASES
WITH THE DEGREE TO WHICH HE IS ALIENATED FROM EXPRESSIVE
RELATIONS, INCLUDING RELATIONS WITH HIS FRIENDS AND THOSE HE
RESPECTS PROFESSIONALLY.
7.   INDIVIDUALS WHO OCCUPY INCONSISTENT STATUS
CONFIGURATIONS ARE MORE LIKELY TO HAVE LEFT THAN THOSE WITH
CONSISTENT STATUS CONFIGURATIONS.
8.   MARRIED INDIVIDUALS AND THOSE WITH CHILDREN ARE LESS
LIKELY TO HAVE MOVED, AND THE INDIVIDUALS WHO ARE MORE
HIGHLY TRAINED, MORE PROFESSIONALLY ORIENTED, AND MORE
ACTIVE IN COMMUNITY AFFAIRS ARE MORE LIKELY TO HAVE LEFT THE
ORGANIZATION.
CONCLUSIONS

M0311   GIVEN THE CHANCE, MEMBERS TENDED TO FOLLOW THEIR FRIENDS,
THEIR INFORMATION CONTACTS, AND THOSE THEY RESPECTED
PROFESSIONALLY. ATTEMPTING TO PRESERVE SOCIAL REWARDS HAD A
SOMEWHAT STRONGER AND MORE CONSISTENT INFLUENCE THAN THE
PRESSURE TO ESCAPE THE COSTS INCURRED IN SOCIAL INTERACTION,
AND IT WAS CLEARLY MORE UNIFORM IN ITS EFFECTS THAN THE
MEASURES OF STATUS CONSISTENCY AND THE VARIOUS
EXTRA-ORGANIZATIONAL VARIABLES.

M0312   MINER, JOHN B.
THE MANAGEMENT CONSULTING FIRM AS A SOURCE OF HIGH-LEVEL
MANAGERIAL TALENT.
ACADEMY OF MANAGEMENT JOURNAL 18 (JUNE 1973):   253-54.

      IN THIS ARTICLE MANAGEMENT CONSULTANTS AND CORPORATE
MANAGERS ARE COMPARED ON MEASURES OF MOTIVATION AND
MENTAL ABILITY WHICH HAVE BEEN EXHIBITED WITH SOME
RELATIONSHIP TO MANAGERIAL SUCCESS.

M0313   MINER, JOHN B.
THE REAL CRUNCH IN MANAGERIAL MANPOWER.
HARVARD BUSINESS REVIEW   57 (NOVEMBER-DECEMBER 1973):
146-58.

      THE AUTHOR PULLS TOGETHER MANY OF THE AVAILABLE DATA TO
DEMONSTRATE THE CONSISTENCY OF THE DECLINE IN TRADITIONAL
MANAGERIAL   VALUES AND ATTITUDES AMONG OUR YOUNGER PEOPLE.

M0314   MINER, JOHN B.
SUCCESS IN MANAGEMENT CONSULTING AND THE CONCEPT OF
ELITENESS MOTIVATION.
ACADEMY OF MANAGEMENT JOURNAL   14 (SEPTEMBER 1971):   367-78.

      THIS STUDY FOCUSES ON THE CHARACTERISTICS OF THE
EMPLOYEES WHO WERE PROMOTED WITHIN A CERTAIN PERIOD AND
THOSE WHO SEPARATED FROM THE COMPANY BEFORE PROMOTION. THE
THEORY IS THAT THE SUCCESSFUL EMPLOYEES HAVE CERTAIN TRAITS
THAT THEIR NON-SUCCESSFUL COUNTERPARTS LACK. TWO
HYPOTHESES ARE INVESTIGATED TO TEST THE THEORY.
THEY ARE: (1) A TOTAL LIFE PATTERN OF SUCCESSFUL
ENDEAVOR, AND (2) A MAXIMAL PRIOR EXPOSURE TO TOP
MANAGEMENT CULTURE. (P. 367).
THE STUDY CONSISTS OF THREE PARTS: A MAJOR OFFICE
STUDY, A MINOR OFFICE STUDY, AND A CROSS-VALIDATION STUDY.
IN EACH PART, THE TWO HYPOTHESES WERE TESTED. THE ITEMS TO
TEST THE PATTERN OF SUCCESS HYPOTHESIS WERE CLASS STANDING
IN COLLEGE AND GRADUATE WORK, HAVING AN ADVANCED DEGREE
(VS. NONE), BEING A COMMISSIONED OFFICER IN THE SERVICE (AS
OPPOSED TO A LOWER RANK OR NO SERVICE), AND HAVING
EXPERIENCE IN A MANAGERIAL CAPACITY (VS. A NON-MANAGERIAL
CAPACITY). THE ITEMS USED TO TEST THE SECOND HYPOTHESIS
WERE THE FATHER'S EDUCATIONAL LEVEL, WHETHER THE FATHER HELD
A HIGH POSITION IN A WHERE THE EMPLOYEE GRADUATED FROM HIGH
SCHOOL, COLLEGE, AND GRADUATE SCHOOL, HIS SERVICE IN THE
NAVY OR AIR FORCE (VS. THE ARMY), YEARS OF PRIOR BUSINESS
EXPERIENCE, AND REFERENCES OF AT LEAST ONE OFFICER OF A
BUSINESS CORPORATION. MOST OF THE DATA WERE FOUND IN THE
PERSONNEL FILES SINCE 76 PERSONS HAD LEFT THE FIRM WHILE

M0314   ONLY 28 HAD BEEN PROMOTED.
        THE FINDINGS RELATING TO THE FIRST HYPOTHESIS WERE THAT
        PREVIOUS MANAGERIAL EXPERIENCE AND SIMILAR EXPERIENCE IN
        THE ARMED FORCES ARE RELATED TO SUCCESS AND PROMOTION.
        STRANGELY, THE GRADES AND EDUCATIONAL LEVEL OF THE EMPLOYEES
        DID NOT HAVE ANY BEARING ON THEIR SUCCESS. THE FINDINGS
        RELATING TO THE SECOND HYPOTHESIS UNEXPECTEDLY SHOWED THAT
        FATHERS OF THE MORE SUCCESSFUL CONSULTANTS ARE LESS WELL
        EDUCATED AND IN LOWER LEVEL POSITIONS. (P. 373).
        GRADUATION FROM PRESTIGE SCHOOLS USUALLY LEADS TO SUCCESS,
        AS DOES SERVICE IN THE NAVY OR AIR FORCE. PRIOR BUSINESS
        EXPERIENCE AND OFFICER REFERENCES SHOWED NO CLEAR-CUT
        EVIDENCE OF BEING RELATED TO CONSULTING SUCCESS.
        ACCORDING TO THE ARTICLE, THE HYPOTHESES CANNOT BE
        CONSIDERED FULLY SUPPORTED. (P. 375). EVEN SO, THERE SEEMS
        TO BE A CONSISTENT PATTERN OF PRIOR IDENTIFICATION WITH
        AND MEMBERSHIP IN PRESTIGE ORGANIZATIONS AND GROUPS AMONG
        THE MORE SUCCESSFUL CONSULTANTS. (P. 37K). ONE FINDING NOT
        COVERED IN THE SURVEY QUESTIONS WAS THAT THE HIGHLY PAID AND
        HIGHLY RATED EMPLOYEES STAYED WITH THE FIRM LONGER.

M0315   MISSHAUK, M. J.   SLOCUM, JOHN W.
        JOB SATISFACTION AND PRODUCTIVITY.
        PERSONNEL ADMINISTRATION 33 (MARCH 1970): 52-58.

        THIS ARTICLE DEALS WITH THE ENVIRONMENTAL WORK FACTORS
        THAT EFFECT JOB SATISFACTION AND PRODUCTIVITY. THE AUTHORS
        CONDUCTED A STUDY TO EXAMINE THE SATISFACTION AND
        PRODUCTIVITY OF WORK GROUPS DIFFERING IN SKILLS AND
        JOB AUTONOMY. THERE ARE FACTORS THAT ARE DEEMED IMPORTANT
        TO EMPLOYEES: THE ENVIRONMENT, THEIR SATISFACTION WITH
        THE ENVIRONMENTAL WORK FACTOR, AND THE RELATIONSHIP
        BETWEEN SATISFACTION AND PRODUCTIVITY.
        THE STUDY WAS CONDUCTED IN A STEEL PLANT, TESTING TWO
        GROUPS OF EMPLOYEES WHICH DIFFERED IN SKILL LEVEL AND JOB
        AUTONOMY. THE FIRST GROUP HAD HIGH SKILL
        AND AUTONOMY WHILE THE SECOND HAD LOW SKILL AND AUTONOMY.
        NEITHER GROUP PERFORMED SUPERVISORY ACTIVITIES. THERE WERE
        FIVE ENVIRONMENTAL FACTORS STUDIED: THE JOB, THE PAY, THE
        SUPERVISION, THE EMPLOYEE'S FREEDOM, AND MANAGEMENT. A
        QUESTIONNAIRE WAS DEVELOPED TO MEASURE EACH OF THE
        ENVIRONMENTAL FACTORS. FIRST, THE EMPLOYEE'S PERCEPTION
        OF THE FACTORS WITHIN HIS OWN WORK AREA HAD TO BE MEASURED,
        THEN SECOND, THE IMPORTANCE OF EACH FACTOR TO THE EMPLOYEE
        HAD TO BE DETERMINED. SATISFACTION WAS MEASURED BY
        SUBTRACTING THE RESPONSE TO THE IMPORTANCE OF A WORK FACTOR
        FROM THE PERCEPTION OF THE FACTOR. A SMALL DIFFERENCE
        INDICATED HIGH SATISFACTION, AND A LARGE DIFFERENCE
        INDICATED LOW SATISFACTION.
        WHEN THE TWO GROUPS WERE COMPARED, IT WAS FOUND THAT IF
        THE HIGH SKILL WORKERS PLACED GREAT IMPORTANCE ON THE
        FREEDOM TO MAKE WORK DECISIONS, AND IF THEY PERCEIVE THEIR
        WORK REQUIREMENTS CORRECTLY, THEN THE GREATER THE
        OPPORTUNITY TO MAKE DECISIONS, THE HIGHER THE SATISFACTION.
        IN CONTRAST, WHEN THE LOW SKILLED WORKERS HAD THE
        OPPORTUNITY FOR DECISION-MAKING, THERE WAS LITTLE IMPACT
        ON SATISFACTION. THE AUTHORS CONCLUDED THAT JOB
        SATISFACTION WAS NEGATIVELY RELATED TO PRODUCTIVITY FOR THE

M0315 HIGHLY SKILLED WORKERS BECAUSE THE WORK THESE
EMPLOYEES PERFORMED WAS BELOW THEIR ASPIRATIONS OR DESIRES.
THEREFORE, THE OPPORTUNITY FOR AN EMPLOYEE TO SATISFY EGO,
AUTONOMY, AND SELF-ACTUALIZATION NEEDS WAS DIFFICULT. FOR
THE LOW SKILLED WORKERS, SATISFACTION WAS POSITIVELY RELATED
TO PRODUCTIVITY BECAUSE OF THE EMPLOYEE'S SATISFACTION
WITH SUPERVISORS.

M0316 MISSHAUK, M. J.
SUPERVISORY SKILLS AND EMPLOYEE SATISFACTION.
PERSONNEL ADMINISTRATION 34 (JULY-AUGUST 1971): 29-33.

EVIDENCE OF THE RELATIONSHIP BETWEEN SUPERVISORY SKILLS
AND EMPLOYEE SATISFACTION AND PRODUCTIVITY WAS GATHERED IN
THIS RESEARCH AMONG ENGINEERS, MECHANICS AND MACHINE
OPERATORS. THE RELATIVE IMPORTANCE OF SUPERVISORY TECHNICAL
AND ADMINISTRATIVE SKILL DID NOT CHANGE AS THE AUTONOMY AND
SKILL LEVEL OF THE EMPLOYEES VARIED, BUT GREATER EMPHASIS
WAS PLACED ON HUMAN RELATIONS SKILL BY THE ENGINEERS.
FINDINGS ARE JUDGED SIGNIFICANT TO THE DESIGN OF MANAGEMENT
TRAINING PROGRAMS.

M0317 MISUMI, JYUJI.   SEKI, FUMIYASU.
EFFECTS OF ACHIEVEMENT MOTIVATION ON THE EFFECTIVENESS OF
LEADERSHIP PATTERNS.
ADMINISTRATIVE SCIENCE QUARTERLY 16 (MARCH 1971): 51-59.

A LABORATORY EXPERIMENT TO FIND OUT THE EFFECTS OF
VARYING THE STRENGTHS OF NEED FOR ACHIEVEMENT OF
INIDVIDUALS IN A GROUP WITH RESPECT TO PRODUCTIVITY AND
MORALE, OR SATISFACTION.

M0318 MITCHELL, T. R.
MOTIVATION AND PARTICIPATION: AN INTEGRATION.
ACADEMY OF MANAGEMENT JOURNAL 16 (DECEMBER 1973): 670-79.

AN INTEGRATION OF THE RATIONAL MODEL OF EXPECTANCY
THEORY AND THE "CARING FOR PEOPLE" PHILOSOPHY OF THE
PARTICIPATIVE APPROACH TO EMPLOYEE MOTIVATION IS PRESENTED.
THE PAPER DESCRIBES FOUR WAYS IN WHICH THESE THEORIES ARGUE
THAT THE SAME PROCESSES INCREASE MOTIVATION.

M0319 MOORE, GEOFFREY H. HEDGES, JANICE N.
TRENDS IN LABOR AND LEISURE.
MONTHLY LABOR REVIEW 94 (FEBRUARY 1971): 3-11.

STUDY OF TRENDS IN LEISURE TIME, AND EFFECTS ON
EMPLOYEE MORALE AND PRODUCTIVITY. IN 1970, THE AVERAGE
AMERICAN WORKER HAD 50 HOURS MORE FREE TIME THAN 1960.

M0320 MORANO, RICHARD.
CONTINUING EDUCATION IN INDUSTRY.
PERSONNEL JOURNAL 52 (FEBRUARY 1973): 106-112.

THIS ARTICLE STUDIES THE BROAD CONCEPT OF MOTIVATION OF
THE INDIVIDUAL IN SETTING THE STAGE FOR LEARNING AND FURTHER
MOTIVATION TO CONTINUE HIS EDUCATION.

M0321   MORGAN, MARTY.
        HE GIVES A DAMN.
        MANPOWER, JULY, 1970, PP. 20-23.

            IN CLOVIS, NEW MEXICO, JOHN MARSHALL HELPS JUVENILE
        DELINQUENTS FIND 'THEMSELVES' AND EMPLOYMENT.

M0322   MOTIVATION IS EASY IF THE PRIZE IS RIGHT.
        SALES MANAGEMENT 105 (JULY 1, 1970): 49.

            A LOOK AT THE DIFFERENT SALES INCENTIVES THAT
        HAVE BEEN DANGLED BEFORE SALESMEN IN THE PAST. CASH
        BONUSES ARE NO LONGER AS ATTRACTIVE, SO THE INCENTIVE MUST
        COME FROM OTHER AREAS.

M0323   NATHANSON, C. A.   BECKER, M. H.
        JOB SATISFACTION AND JOB PERFORMANCE: AN EMPIRICAL TEST
        OF SOME THEORETICAL PROPOSITIONS.
        ORGANIZATIONAL BEHAVIOR AND HUMAN PERFORMANCE   9
        (APRIL 1973):   267-79.

            THE FINDINGS OF THIS STUDY OF 103 PHYSICIANS ENGAGED IN
        ROUTINE PEDIATRIC CARE IN AMBULATORY CLINICS GENERALLY
        SUPPORT THREE HYPOTHESES DERIVED FROM E. A. LOCK'S THEORY
        THAT SATISFACTION AND PERFORMANCE WILL BE ASSOCIATED WHEN
        PERFORMANCE LEADS TO THE ATTAINMENT OF AN INDIVIDUAL'S
        JOB VALUES.

M0324   NELSON, MARIAN.
        RAILROAD APPRENTICES STAY ON THE TRACK.
        MANPOWER 5 (JULY 1973):   13-16.

            REVIEW OF BENEFITS TO APPRENTICES OF BURLINGTON
        NORTHERN RAILROAD, AS WELL AS THE REWARDS TO THE COMPANY
        ITSELF.

M0325   NESSLEIN, SSGT. THOMAS S.
        MANAGEMENT, MOTIVATION AND JOB ENRICHMENT.
        AIR FORCE COMPTROLLER 8 (JANUARY 1974):   30-32.

            PROVIDES A RELATIONSHIP BETWEEN MANAGEMENT STATEGIES
        OF MOTIVATION AND JOB ENRICHMENT AND THE AIR FORCE
        COMPTROLLER'S ORGANIZATION.

M0326   NEWMAN, JOHN.
        PREDICTING ABSENTEEISM AND TURNOVER: A FIELD COMPARISON OF
        FISHBEIN'S MODEL AND TRADITIONAL JOB ATTITUDE MEASURES.
        JOURNAL OF APPLIED PSYCHOLOGY 59 (1974):   610-15.

            COMPARISON ASSERTS THAT BOTH METHODS ARE GOOD
        PREDICTORS IN SPECIAL CIRCUMSTANCES AND NEITHER IS SUPERIOR
        TO THE OTHER.
        PURPOSE
            TO TEST FISHBEINS' MODEL IN A REAL ORGANIZATIONAL
        SETTING AND TO EXAMINE THE EFFICACY OF TRADITIONAL JOB
        SATISFACTION MEASURES AS PREDICTORS OF WITHDRAWAL BEHAVIOR.
        FISHBEINS' MODEL

M0326   SETTING AND SUBJECTS
        108 EMPLOYEES OF A COUNTY NURSING HOME,
INCLUDING NURSE'S AIDES, LICENSED PRACTICAL NURSES,
REGISTERED NURSES, ADMINISTRATORS, STAFF, FOOD SERVICE AND
HOUSEKEEPING PERSONNEL. (88% FEMALE)
        VARIABLES AND QUESTIONNAIRE
        BI WITH RESPECT TO UNEXCUSED ABSENCES WAS MEASURED WITH
THE FOLLOWING QUESTION: I AM GOING TO BE ABSENT
(UNEXCUSED) FROM WORK ON ONE OR MORE DAYS WITHIN THE NEXT
TWO MONTHS.   THE SCALE ON THIS QUESTION WAS SCORED FROM 1-7
FROM EXTREMELY LIKELY TO EXTREMELY UNLIKELY.
        ATTITUDE TOWARD BEING ABSENT (AACT) WAS MEASURED BY
TAKING THE SUM OVER THE FOLLOWING DIFFERENTIAL SCALES WITH
HIGH LOADINGS ON THE EVALUATIVE FACTOR: BEING ABSENT
(UNEXCUSED) FROM WORK ON ONE OR MORE DAYS WITHIN THE NEXT
TWO MONTHS IS: FOOLISH--WISE
                  GOOD - BAD
                  HARMFUL- BENEFICIAL
                  REWARDING - PUNISHING
        RESULTS
DATA DERIVED FROM THE TRADITIONAL JOB ATTITUDE MEASURES
WERE RELATIVELY MORE EFFICACIOUS IN PREDICTING ABSENTEEISM
THAN THE FISHBEIN MODEL.
        REGARDING RESIGNATION PREDICTION, FISHBEINS' MODEL
SHOWED UP SLIGHTLY BETTER THAN THE TRADITIONAL MEASURES
USED.
        CONCLUSIONS
        INDICATIONS WERE THAN NEITHER JOB ATTITUDES NOR
BEHAVIORAL INTENTIONS WERE CONSISTENTLY SUPERIOR IN
ACCOUNTING FOR JOB WITHDRAWAL BEHAVIORS.
        COMMENTS
        TOO MANY POTENTIALLY IMPORTANT VARIABLES LEFT
UNCONTROLLED.   PERHAPS, IN A FIELD STUDY SUCH AS THIS, ONE
CAN'T POSSIBLY BRING ENOUGH RELEVANT VARIABLES UNDER CONTROL
TO MAKE THE STUDY CONSISTENTLY VALID INTERNALLY OR TO MAKE
IT SAFE TO GENERALIZE THE RESULTS INTO OTHER AREAS.

M0327   NICHOLSON, TOM
        THE JOB BLAHS: WHO WANTS TO WORK.
        NEWSWEEK, MARCH 26,1973 PP. 79-80.

        THIS REPORT STATES THAT   . . . NEARLY HALF OF
AMERICAN WORKERS ARE DISSATISFIED WITH THEIR JOBS AND
SUGGESTED THAT SOMETHING HAD BETTER BE DONE TO MAKE WORK
MORE ATTRACTIVE, INTERESTING, AND MEANINGFUL.
        BOREDOM, REBELLION, AND FRUSTRATION APPEAR TO BE
GROWING FASTER IN THE LABOR FORCE THAN THE LABOR FORCE
ITSELF. THIS IS THE BELIEF HELD BY MANY PEOPLE.
EXECUTIVES, AS WELL AS LABORERS, IN THE ESTIMATED 83 MILLION
WORK FORCE ARE BECOMING DISSATISFIED WITH THEIR JOBS.
        SINCE OUR ATTITUDE TOWARD WORK AFFECTS PRODUCTIVITY,
MANY COMPANIES HAVE INCORPORATED JOB ENRICHMENT PROGRAMS
FOR THEIR WORKERS. ONE AUTOMOBILE PLANT PERMITTED EMPLOYEES
TO WORK WITHOUT A FOREMAN AND HAVE THE CHANCE TO DO
PLEASANT CHORES. THE RESULT WAS THAT EMPLOYEE TURNOVER WAS
CUT IN HALF.
        A 32% JUMP IN PRODUCTION AND 20% DECREASE IN SPOILAGE
RATE WAS THE RESULT OF ONE INDUSTRY WHEN THEY GAVE THEIR

M0327   EMPLOYEES FULL RESPONSIBILITIES. A MONSANTO PLANT
        EXPERIENCED AN INCREASE IN PRODUCTIVITY BY 50% AND AT THE
        SAME TIME WASTE MATTER WAS DELETED ALL TOGETHER. THE
        EMPLOYEES OF THIS PLANT WERE SET UP IN TASK FORCES FOR THE
        PURPOSE OF REORGANIZING CERTAIN JOBS DUE TO AUTOMATION.
        A SMALLER, ADDED EXTRA RESULT WAS THE DELETION OF JOBS
        THAT THE EMPLOYEES DISLIKED.
            ALTHOUGH THERE IS STILL SOME CONTROVERSY AS TO
        WHETHER OR NOT THE ISSUE OF EMPLOYEE DISSATISFACTION HAS
        . . . BEEN BLOWN OUT OF ALL PROPORTION TO BEGIN WITH
        . . . , THE DEPARTMENT OF HEALTH, EDUCATION AND WELFARE
        SAID THE RESULTS OF A MEANINGLESS, UNCHALLENGING, AND BORING
        JOB TASKS ARE LEADING TO HIGH TURNOVER, ABSENTEEISM, LACK OF
        RESPECT FOR AUTHORITY AND WITHDRAWN BEHAVIOR.
            GAINES PET FOOD PLANT IN TOPEKA SOLVED THE PROBLEM OF
        HIGH ABSENTEEISM AND LOW PRODUCTIVITY BY LEAVING MANY OF THE
        DECISIONS TO TEAMS CONSISTING OF THE WORKERS THEMSELVES.
        THEY ARE ABLE TO SOLVE MANY DISCIPLINE MATTERS. EACH
        EMPLOYEE IS ALSO EXPECTED TO BE TRAINED ON JUST ABOUT EVERY
        JOB IN THE PLANT. THESE JOBS RANGE FROM THE LOWEST AND
        REPETITIVE JOBS TO THOSE REQUIRING MORE SKILL AND VARIETY,
        SUCH AS THE CONTROLS ON COMPLICATED MACHINES.

M0328   NOORDHOFF, LYMAN J.
        EXTENSION WOMEN OVERSEAS.
        EXTENSION SERVICE REVIEW, JANUARY-FEBRUARY 1974, P. 9.

            HOME ECONOMISTS GO ONE OVERSEAS ASSIGNMENTS TO ASSIST
        THOSE IN NEED.

M0329   NORMAN, JAMES H.
        A QUALITIATIVE APPROACH TO PERFORMANCE PREDICTABILITY AND
        LEGAL COMPLIANCE.
        PERSONNEL ADMINISTRATOR 18 (MARCH 1973): 28-29.

            THIS ARTICLE PRESENTS A RESEARCH STUDY WHICH IS
        AN EMPIRICAL APPROACH TO PERFORMANCE PREDICTABILITY AND
        STATISTICAL VALIDATION.

M0330   NORTH, DAVID S.
        WOMEN OFFENDERS: BREAKING THE TRAINING MOLD.
        MANPOWER, FEBRUARY 1975, PP. 13-19.

            VARIOUS WOMEN'S CORRECTIONAL INSTITUTES THROUGHOUT THE
        NATION PROVIDE VOCATIONAL TRAINING FOR NONTRADITIONAL JOBS.

M0331   NOURI, CLEMENT J.   FRIDL, JAMES J.
        RELEVANCE OF MOTIVATIONAL CONCEPTS TO INDIVIDUAL AND
        CORPORATE OBJECTIVES.
        PERSONNEL JOURNAL 49 (NOVEMBER 1970): 900-906.

            A PURVIEW OF EVOLUTION OF MOTIVATIONAL THEORY --
        EXPERTS TODAY SEEK TO ACCOMPLISH ORGANIZATIONS' GOALS
        BY SOLVING THE PROBLEMS OF SATISFYING INDIVIDUAL AS
        WELL AS CORPORATE NEEDS.

M0332   O'HAIR, JAMES P.   ABRAHAMSON, MARK.
        THE ACHIEVEMENT PROCESS: AN EXPLORATORY STUDY OF CAREER

M0332 BEGINNINGS.
UTICA: SYRACUSE UNIVERSITY. SCHEDULED FOR COMPLETION
FISCAL YEAR 1975.

ASSUMING THAT THE POSITIONS TO WHICH AN INDIVIDUAL MOVES
WITHIN AND BETWEEN OCCUPATIONAL STRUCTURES LARGELY
DETERMINE HIS SOCIAL STATUS, THIS STUDY IS ANALYZING THE WAY
IN WHICH STRUCTURAL AND SOCIAL-PSYCHOLOGICAL INFLUENCES
INTERACT TO DETERMINE EARLY CAREER MOBILITY AND THUS DEFINE
ACHIEVEMENT AS A PROCESS. THE RESEARCHER IS DEVELOPING A
MODEL WHICH CONCEPTUALIZES THE PROCESS AS ONE THROUGH WHICH
THE INDIVIDUAL ACQUIRES VARIOUS TYPES OF RESOURCES WHICH
INTERACT WITH HIS ENVIRONMENT TO PROVIDE HIM WITH THE MEANS
TO MAKE THE SEQUENCE OF MOVES NEEDED TO ATTAIN A DESIRED
GOAL OR STATUS. OPERATIONALLY, THE MODEL ASSOCIATES EACH OF
THE STEPS THROUGH WHICH INDIVIDUALS MUST PASS TO REACH THE
CAREER GOALS WITH THE VARIABLE CONDITIONS FOR SUCCESSFUL
MOBILITY INTO THE PARTICULAR STEP: THEIR ANTECEDENT
KNOWLEDGE OF THE GOALS IN THE ENVIRONMENT AND OF ALTERNATIVE
MEANS OF OTHER RESOURCES AS PERSONAL ATTRIBUTES, SKILLS,
MOTIVATIONS ASSOCIATED WITH SUCCESS AND FAILURE, CAPITAL OF
VARIOUS SORTS, AND ROLE MODELS.

M0333 O'LEARY, LOUIS K.
MOTIVATING THE NOW GENERATION.
PERFORMANCE 6 (NOVEMBER-DECEMBER 1973): 14-77, 32.

THE AUTHOR IS CONVINCED THAT THE NEW WORKERS ARE
DIFFERENT FROM PREVIOUS WORKERS. GIVEN THIS BELIEF, HE
RECOMMENDS THAT A DIFFERENT APPROACH TO JOB STRUCTURING BE
APPLIED, ESPECIALLY TO ASSEMBLY-LINE TYPE WORK. HE FEELS
THAT DIVIDING THE JOB INTO WORK MODULES, PROVIDING FEEDBACK
TO THE WORKER, AND GIVING HIM A CERTAIN AMOUNT OF CONTROL
OVER THE TASK ASSIGNED WILL MOTIVATE THE WORKER TO DO MORE,
TO SHOW UP MORE REGULARLY, ETC.

M0334 ONDRACK, D. A.
DEFENSE MECHANISMS AND THE HERZBERG THEORY: AN ALTERNATE
TEST.
ACADEMY OF MANAGEMENT JOURNAL 17 (MARCH 1974): 79-89.

A CONSTRUCT REPLICATION OF HERZBERG'S FINDINGS USING
THE SEMISTRUCTURED OCCUPATIONAL VALUES SCALE TO ELICIT
PROJECTIVE RESPONSES ABOUT SATISFYING AND DISSATISFYING JOB
SITUATIONS FAILED TO YIELD THE TWO FACTOR PATTERN. RESULTS
FROM THE USE OF THIS METHODOLOGY APPEAR TO SUPPORT VROOM'S
EGO-DEFENSE CRITICISM OF THE RECALL METHODOLOGY.
ONE-FOURTH OF JUNIOR OFFICERS IN FY '74 ARE WOMEN.
DEPARTMENT OF STATE NEWSLETTER, AUGUST 1974, PP. 24-25.
TWENTY-FOUR PERCENT OF THE 144 JUNIOR FOREIGN SERVICE
OFFICERS COMMISSIONED DURING FISCAL YEAR '74 ARE WOMEN --
THE HIGHEST PERCENTAGE IN THE 50-YEAR HISTORY OF THE CAREER
FOREIGN SERVICE.

M0335 ORGAN, DENNIS W.   GREENE, CHARLES N.
AN EVALUATION OF CAUSAL MODELS LINKING THE RECEIVED ROLE
WITH JOB SATISFACTION.
ADMINISTRATIVE SCIENCE QUARTERLY 18 (MARCH 1973): 94-100.

M0335   THIS ARTICLE EXAMINES THE RELATIONSHIP BETWEEN
THE RECEIVED ROLE AND SATISFACTION WITH ONE'S JOB
BASED ON FOUR VARIABLES: ROLE ACCURACY, COMPLIANCE,
PERFORMANCE EVALUATION, AND SATISFACTION.

M0336   ORGAN, DENNIS W.   GREENE, CHARLES N.
PERCEIVED PURPOSEFULNESS OF JOB BEHAVIOR: ANTECEDENTS AND
CONSEQUENCES.
ACADEMY OF MANAGEMENT JOURNAL, 17 (MARCH 1974):   69-78.

         PERCEIVED PURPOSEFULNESS OF JOB BEHAVIOR IS INTRODUCED
AS A POSSIBLE LINK THROUGH WHICH ROLE AMBIGUITY AFFECTS WORK
SATISFACTION. A MEASURE OF THIS CONCEPT WAS DEVELOPED AND
ITS EXPLORATORY VALUE TESTED. THE MEASURE WAS ABLE TO
ACCOUNT FOR THE MANNER IN WHICH TENURE, ROLE CLARITY, AND
LOCUS OF CONTROL CONTRIBUTE TO WORK SATISFACTION.

M0337   ORPEN, C.
SOCIAL DESIRABILITY AS A MODERATOR OF THE RELATIONSHIP
BETWEEN JOB SATISFACTION AND PERSONAL ADJUSTMENT.
PERSONNEL PSYCHOLOGY 27 (SPRING 1974):   103-108.

         THE PRESENT STUDY REPRESENTS A FIRST ATTEMPT TO
EXAMINE THE RELATION BETWEEN JOB SATISFACTION AND PERSONAL
ADJUSTMENT, WITH THE 'INFLATING' EFFECT OF SOCIAL
DESIRABILITY PARTIALLED OUT.

M0338   PAJER, ROBERT G.
A SYSTEMS APPROACH TO RESULTS ORIENTED PERFORMANCE
EVALUATION.
PERSONNEL ADMINISTRATOR AND PUBLIC PERSONNEL REVIEW 1
(NOVEMBER-DECEMBER 1973):   42-47.

         ACCORDING TO THIS AUTHOR, THE IDEAL SYSTEM OF
PERFORMANCE EVALUATION WOULD BE WHERE THERE IS A TOTAL
UNDERSTANDING OF THE JOB FOR WHICH THE EVALUATION OF
PERFORMANCE IS IN QUESTION AS IT EXISTS IN A SYSTEM OF
PURPOSE, GOALS, AND OBJECTIVES.

M0339   PARNES, HERBERT S.
NATIONAL LONGITUDINAL STUDIES OF THE LABOR FORCE BEHAVIOR OF
NATIONAL SAMPLES OF MEN (45-59), WOMEN (30-44), AND MALE AND
FEMALE YOUTH (14-24).
WASHINGTON, D. C., BUREAU OF THE CENSUS, U. S. DEPARTMENT OF
COMMERCE. JUNE 1974.

         THIS STUDY IS PROBING THE RELATIONSHIP OF FACTORS
INFLUENCING THE WORK BEHAVIOR AND EXPERIENCE OF FOUR GROUPS:
MEN, AGED 45 TO 59; WOMEN, 30 TO 44; AND MEN AND WOMEN, 14
TO 24. IT FOCUSES ON THE INTERACTION AMONG ECONOMIC,
SOCIOLOGICAL, AND PSYCHOLOGICAL VARIABLES THAT PERMIT SOME
MEMBERS OF A GIVEN AGE-EDUCATION-OCCUPATION GROUP TO HAVE
SATISFACTORY WORK EXPERIENCE WHILE OTHERS DO NOT. THE
COMPLETED STUDY WILL CONSTITUTE A COMPREHENSIVE BODY OF DATA
ON LABOR MOBILITY.

M0340   PARRISH, JOHN B.
WOMEN IN PROFESSIONAL TRAINING.

M0340 MONTHLY LABOR REVIEW, MAY 1974, PP. 41-43.
AMERICAN WOMEN ARE ENTERING PROFESSIONAL TRAINING IN INCREASED NUMBERS, FORESHADOWING THEIR GREATER SHARE IN HIGH-LEVEL OCCUPATIONS.

M0341 PARTICIPATIVE MANAGEMENT, BONUSES BOOST PRODUCTIVITY FOR MICHIGAN FIRM.
COMMERCE TODAY, NOVEMBER 11, 1974, PP. 12-13.

BASIC PRODUCT SELLS FOR LESS THAN IT DID 20 YEARS AGO, MOSTLY DUE TO DOUBLING OF PRODUCTIVITY; SOME WORKERS ACTUALLY VOLUNTEER FOR LAY-OFFS.

M0342 PATCHEN, MARTIN.
PARTICIPATION, ACHIEVEMENT, AND INVOLVEMENT ON THE JOB.
ENGLEWOOD CLIFFS, N. J.: PRENTICE-HALL. 1970.

THE IDEAS AND EVIDENCE IN THIS VOLUME ARE INTENDED TO FURTHER OUR UNDERSTANDING OF THE FACTORS WHICH LEAD TO GREATER OR LESSER EMPLOYEE INVOLVEMENT IN THEIR JOBS. IT REPORTS THE RESULTS OF A STUDY CONDUCTED BY THE SURVEY RESEARCH CENTER, UNIVERSITY OF MICHIGAN, IN PARTS OF THE TENNESSEE VALLEY AUTHORITY. A FIRST MAJOR FOCUS OF THE STUDY IS ON CHARACTERISTICS OF THE JOB SITUATION AND OF THE INDUVIDUAL WHICH MAY BE RELEVANT TO ACHIEVEMENT ON THE JOB.

M0343 PEMBROKE, JAMES D.
MARKETING WELFARE MOTHERS' JOB SKILLS.
MANPOWER, JANUARY 1974, PP. 28-29.

THE JOB FAIR, A DEVICE OFTEN USED TO GET JOBS FOR VETERANS, NOW IS BEING TRIED AS A WAY TO HELP WELFARE MOTHERS FIND WORK.

M0344 PERLOFF, STEPHEN H.
COMPARING MUNICIPAL, INDUSTRY, AND FEDERAL PAY.
MONTHLY LABOR REVIEW 94 (OCTOBER 1971): 46-50.

IN MOST OF THE 11 LARGE CITIES STUDIED, CITY GOVERNMENT WORKERS IN SELECTED JOBS HELD PAY ADVANTAGES OVER THEIR PRIVATE INDUSTRY AND FEDERAL GOVERNMENT COUNTERPARTS.

M0345 PARRELLA, VERA C.
MOONLIGHTERS: THEIR MOTIVATIONS AND CHARACTERISTICS.
MONTHLY LABOR REVIEW 93 (AUGUST 1970): 57-64.

SPECIAL LABOR FORCE REPORT, BASED ON 1969 SURVEY, SHOWS THAT HALF TAKE SECOND JOBS TO MEET CURRENT BILLS OR PAY DEBTS.

M0346 PETERMANN, LESTER L.
FRINGE BENEFITS OF URBAN WORKERS.
MONTHLY LABOR REVIEW 94 (NOVEMBER 1974): 41-44.

DISCUSSION OF INCREASED VACATIONS, INSURANCE, PENSION PLANS, ETC., FOR URBAN WORKERS. DATA FROM BUREAU OF LABOR STATISTICS' WAGE SURVEY PROGRAM.

M0347   PHILLIPS, IRVING.
         BUSINESS MACHINES AND COMPUTER MANUFACTURING -- CAREER
         OPPORTUNITIES ARE EXCELLENT.
         OCCUPATIONAL OUTLOOK QUARTERLY 2 (SUMMER 1971):   14-19.

            SPURRED BY THE DEMAND FOR COMPUTER EQUIPMENT,
         THIS INDUSTRY WILL NEED THOUSANDS OF NEW WORKERS
         YEARLY DURING THE 1970'S. OUTLOOK FAVORS ENGINEERS,
         SCIENTISTS, TECHNICIANS AND SYSTEM ANALYSTS AND PROGRAMMERS.

M0348   PINKARD, MARY.
         THE FEDERAL WOMEN'S PROGRAM: A HUD PERSPECTIVE.
         HUD CHALLENGE, APRIL 1974, PP. 18-21.

            THE FEDERAL WOMEN'S PROGRAM HELPS WOMEN MAKE PROGRESS
         IN THE GOVERNMENT, AND IS INTEGRATED INTO THE OVERALL EQUAL
         OPPORTUNITY PROGRAM.

M0349   PINKERTON, JAMES R.
         SOCIOECONOMIC DETERMINANTS OF URBAN POVERTY AREA WORKERS.
         LABOR FORCE PARTICIPATION AND INCOME.
         COLUMBIA: UNIVERSITY OF MISSOURI. SCHEDULED FOR COMPLETION
         FALL 1974.

         THIS PROJECT WILL FOCUS ON THE SOCIOECONOMIC CHARACTERISTICS
         OF URBAN MALE WORKERS, AGED 16 TO 64, WHO ARE LIVING IN
         LOW-INCOME NEIGHBORHOODS, IN ORDER TO IDENTIFY THE VARIOUS
         FACTORS IN GHETTO LIFE THAT COMBINE AND ACCUMULATE TO CAUSE
         INDIVIDUALS TO PERFORM POORLY IN THE LABOR MARKET OR NEVER
         TO ENTER THE LABOR MARKET. NEW KNOWLEDGE, BASED ON
         COMPREHENSIVE ANALYSES OF CHARACTERISTICS OF THE POOR AND
         THE TOTALITY OF FORCES THAT MADE IT POSSIBLE FOR SOME
         WORKERS TO BREAD OUT OF POVERTY WHILE OTHERS CANNOT, WILL
         HELP TO GUIDE POLICYMAKERS IN DISTINGUISHING THOSE
         CLIENTS WHO WOULD HAVE SUCCESS IN MANPOWER AND OTHER
         REMEDIAL PROGRAMS AS OPPOSED TO THOSE WHO WOULD EXHIBIT
         FAILURE CHARACTERISTICS. THIS WOULD HELP DETERMINE
         APPROPRIATE MANPOWER PROGRAM APPROACHES AND IMPROVED
         METHODS OF SERVICE DELIVERY FOR VARIOUS GROUPS. THE STUDY
         WILL EMPLOY TWO SPECIFIC COMPUTERIZED TECHNIQUES (AUTOMATIC
         INTERACTION DETECTOR AND MULTIPLE CLASSIFICATION ANALYSIS)
         TO EXAMINE DATA IN THE 1970 CENSUS EMPLOYMENT SURVEY (C)S)
         AND OBTAIN PREDICTIVE VALUES ON GHETTO RESIDENTS' LABOR
         FORCE PARTICIPATION AND INCOME. CES POVERTY AREAS IN
         CHICAGO, ST. LOUIS AND SAN ANTONIO WILL BE STUDIED. AMONG
         THE CHARACTERISTICS ANALYZED WILL BE RURAL/URBAN BACKGROUND,
         RACE/ETHNICITY, EDUCATION, AGE, EDUCATION OF WIFE, FAMILY
         INCOME, AND ADEQUACY OF HOUSING.

M0350   PLATER, JOHN.
         SAFEGUARDING OUR WATER -- POLLUTION CONTROL WORKERS.
         OCCUPATIONAL OUTLOOK QUARTERLY 14 (WINTER 1970):   30-34.

            A DISCUSSION OF CAREER OPPORTUNITIES FOR PROFESSIONAL
         AND TECHNICAL WORKERS CHALLENGED BY THE ENVIRONMENTAL
         CRISIS.

M0351   POLLACK, MAXWELL A.

M0351 AS YOU WERE SAYING -- THERE'S MORE TO WORK THAN WORK.
PERSONNEL JOURNAL 51 (FEBRUARY 1972): 138-39.
EMPLOYEE INVOLVEMENT ON THE JOB IS THE KEY TO INCREASED
PRODUCTIVITY.
INVOLVEMENT IS A BRIGHT NEW WORD IN MANAGEMENT LANGUAGE
TODAY. THIS INVOLVEMENT DEADS WITH THE RELATIONSHIP OF
EMPLOYEES AND THEIR JOBS. DR. MAXWELL A. POLLACK, PRESIDENT
OF VAN DYK RESEARCH CORPORATION, INDICATES THAT EMPLOYEE
NON-INVOLVEMENT ON THE JOB IS COSTLY IN TERMS OF
ABSENTEEISM, LOW PRODUCTIVITY, HIGH ACCIDENT RATES AND
PERSONAL TENSIONS WHICH LEAD TO STRIKES AND DISLOYALTY.
IN MOST CASES, DR. POLLACK BLAMES MANAGEMENT FOR
EMPLOYEE NON-INVOLVEMENT, BECAUSE MANAGEMENT HAS NOT COME TO
TERMS WITH AUTOMATION ON ONE HAND AND THE EFFECTS OF
EMPLOYEE AFFLUENCE ON THE OTHER. AUTOMATION IS REDUCING
MANY TASKS TO SIMPLE REPETITIOUS MOTIONS RESULTING IN
LOWERING EMOTIONAL COMMITMENT TO THE JOB. THE RESULTING
AFFLUENCE HAS COME ABOUT THROUGH AUTOMATION MAKING TASKS
EASIER AND PAY CHECKS LARGER. EMPLOYEES NOW HAVE MORE TIME
AND MONEY TO DEVOTE TO LEISURE TIME ACTIVITIES AND
INTERESTS. CONSEQUENTLY, THE JOB SUFFERS AS THE EMPLOYEE
BECOMES LESS INVOLVED WITH IT.
ACCORDING TO PSYCHOLOGIST FREDERICK HERZBERG, FIVE
BASIC MOTIVATORS MUST BE BROUGHT INTO PLAY TO ACHIEVE
INVOLVEMENT: LEARNING, ACHIEVEMENT, RECOGNITION,
RESPONSIBILITY AND ADVANCEMENT. DR. POLLACK MAINTAINS THAT
BUILDING THESE FACTORS INTO THE JOB MUST BE ACCOMPLISHED IF
EMPLOYEE-JOB INVOLVEMENT IS TO INCREASE.
THE BASIC KEY TO THE SUCCESS OF SUCH A PROGRAM IS THE
RESPONSIBILITY GIVEN TO THE EMPLOYEES. THEY ARE LEFT WITH
THE OPTIONS AND DECISIONS THAT INVOLVE THEM AS PRODUCTIVE
HUMAN BEINGS. THEY MAY BE GIVEN THE RESPONSIBILITY FOR NOT
PUNCHING A CLOCK, BUT FOR COMPLETING A TASK, AND WHEN
COMPLETED, FOR PROGRESSING TO ONE MORE DIFFICULT. WHAT IS
VITAL IS THAT AT EACH STEP, THEY ARE INVOLVED. WHEN
MANAGEMENT BUILDS INVOLVEMENT INTO THE JOB, IT WILL
REALIZE HIGHER PRODUCTIVITY THROUGH JOB SATISFACTION. IT
WILL ALSO EXPAND OUR ECONOMY ON THE BASIS OF HUMAN RESOURCES
RATHER THAN JUST MACHINES.

M0352 POTYRT, RLDS S.
INFORMATION SHARING FOR PRODUCTIVITY IMPROVEMENT.
CIVIL SERVICE JOURNAL, 15 (JULY-SEPTEMBER 1974): 13-15.

DISCUSSION OF THE CIVIL SERVICE COMMISSION'S
CLEARINGHOUSE ON PRODUCTIVITY AND ORGANIZATIONAL
EFFECTIVENESS.

M0353 PORTER, LYMAN W. STEERS, RICHARD M. MOWDAY, RICHARD T.
BOULIAN, PAUL V.
ORGANIZATIONAL COMMITMENT, JOB SATISFACTION, AND TURNOVER
AMONG PSYCHIATRIC TECHNICIANS.
JOURNAL OF APPLIED PSYCHOLOGY 59 (1974): 603-609.

WEST COAST HOSPITAL FOR THE MENTALLY RETARDED WITH A
HIGH TURNOVER RATE AMONG TECHNICIAN TRAINEES. (30 TO 50%
TURNOVER AFTER THE FIRST YEAR OF TRAINING AND 25%
THEREAFTER) SIXTY OF THESE NEW TECHNICIAN TRAINEES

M0353   CONSTITUTED THE INITIAL TWO GROUPS; HOWEVER, BEFORE THE
STUDY HAD BEEN COMPLETED, 45% HAD TERMINATED THEIR EMPLOY.
        THE ORGANIZATIONAL COMMITMENT QUESTIONNAIRE WAS USED TO
MEASURE THE DEGREE TO WHICH THE SUBJECTS FELT COMMITTED TO
THE EMPLOYING ORGANIZATION.
        THE JOB DESCRIPTIVE INDEX WAS USED TO MEASURE
SATISFACTION WITH FIVE ASPECTS OF THE SUBJECTS' JOBS:
SUPERVISION, WORK, COWORKERS, PAY AND PROMOTION.
        1. THE SAMPLE WAS DIVIDED INTO LEAVERS AND STAYERS
ACCORDING TO SUBSEQUENT TURNOVER DATA COLLECTED.
        2. THE MEAN AGE FOR STAYERS WAS SIGNIFICANTLY HIGHER
THAN THAT FOR LEAVERS.
        3. AS AN INDIVIDUAL APPROACHES THE POINT OF LEAVING
THE ORGANIZATION, HIS ATTITUDES ARE A MORE ACCURATE
PREDICTOR OF SUCH SUBSEQUENT BEHAVIOR.
        4. COMMITMENT TO THE ORGANIZATION WAS THE MOST
IMPORTANT VARIABLE IN DIFFERENTIATING BETWEEN STAYERS AND
LEAVERS. SATISFACTION WITH OPPORTUNITIES FOR PROMOTION AND
SATISFACTION WITH THE WORK WERE THE NEXT MOST IMPORTANT
VARIABLES.
        5. STAYERS CONSISTENTLY HAD MORE POSITIVE ATTITUDES
THAN LEAVERS.
        IN THIS TYPE OF ORGANIZATIONAL CONTEXT, GENERAL
ATTITUDES TOWARD THE ORGANIZATION MAY BE A MORE IMPORTANT
PREDICTOR THAN SPECIFIC ATTITUDES TOWARD ONE'S JOB.
        IN THIS TYPE OF ORGANIZATIONAL CONTEXT, GENERAL
ATTITUDES MAY BE A MORE IMPORTANT PREDICTOR BECAUSE OF THE
NATURE OF THE JOB. CONSEQUENTLY THESE SAME RESULTS MAY NOT
BE GENERALIZABLE INTO OTHER MORE PROFIT-ORIENTED SITUATIONS.

M0354   PREWITT, LENA B.
DISCONTENT IN THE RANKS: IS THE OPERATIVE WORKER REALLY
TRAPPED.
PERSONNEL JOURNAL 52 (OCTOBER 1973): 878-84.

        THIS AUTHOR EXPLAINS WHAT ALTERNATIVES THE EMPLOYER
HAS IF HE IS TO SATISFY THE PSYCHOLOGICAL AND ETHICAL
NEEDS OF THE WORKER.

M0355   PRICE, W.N.
MOTIVATION AND HARD TIMES.
DEFENSE MANAGEMENT JOURNAL 6 (FEBRUARY 1971): 50-53.

        THE DIRECTOR OF THE MANPOWER PLANNING DIVISION OF THE
DEPARTMENT OF THE NAVY DISCUSSES THEORIES OF MOTIVATION AND
THE EFFECT OF THE REDUCTION IN FORCE OF DEFENSE PERSONNEL
ON THE MOTIVATION AND MORALE OF BOTH THE SEPARATED AND THE
REMAINING EMPLOYEES. ANTI-DEMOTIVATIONAL MEASURES ARE ALSO
CONSIDERED.
        ARTICLE INSPIRED BY DISCUSSIONS OF FMIC PANEL 10 OF THE
FEDERAL MANAGEMENT IMPROVEMENT CONFERENCE HELD SEPTEMBER
21-22, IN WASHINGTON, D. C.

M0356   QUINN, R. P.   MANGIONE, T. W.   MANDILOVITCH, M.
EVALUATING WORKING CONDITIONS IN AMERICA.
MONTHLY LABOR REVIEW 96 (NOVEMBER 1973): 32-41.

        COMPARISON OF DATA FROM 1969-70 SURVEY OF WORKING

M0356   CONDITIONS AND A SIMILAR 1973 SURVEY, WHICH INDICATES FEW
SIGNIFICANT CHANGES IN WORKING CONDITIONS AND WORKERS'
ATTITUDES.

M0357   RAUSCH, ERWIN.
THE EFFECTIVE ORGANIZATION: MORALE VS. DISCIPLINE.
MANAGEMENT REVIEW 60 (JUNE 1971):   23-30.

        DISCUSSES THE INTERRELATIONSHIPS BETWEEN MORALE,
DISCIPLINE AND PRODUCTIVITY.   EFFECTIVE MOTIVATION REQUIRES
THE LEADER OF AN ORGANIZATION UNIT TO MAINTAIN A DELICATE
BALANCE OF APPROPRIATE MANAGEMENT STYLES FOR THE VARIETY
OF SITUATIONS HE MUST FACE . . .   AN ACCURATE SENSE OF
DIRECTION IS EVEN MORE IMPORTANT THAN A CLEAR VIEW OF THE
REALITIES OF THE MOMENT.

M0358   REIF, WILLIAM E.   TINNELL, R. C.
A DIAGNOSTIC APPROACH TO JOB ENRICHMENT.
MSU BUSINESS TOPICS 21 (AUTUMN 1973): 29-37.

        THIS ARTICLE INVOLVES USING A DIAGNOSTIC APPROACH TO
JOB ENRICHMENT.   THE ARTICLE'S KEY CONCERN IS WITH THE
PROCESS FOR SELECTING THE JOBS FOR ENRICHMENT.   THE AUTHORS
DISCUSS SEVERAL REASONS WHY JOB ENRICHMENT DOESN'T WORK ALL
THE TIME AND THEN THEY DISCUSS THE DIAGNOSTIC APPROACH TO
SELECTING JOBS FOR JOB ENRICHMENT.
        THE THREE MOST COMMON METHODS OF JOB SELECTION
CONTRIBUTE MORE TO FAILURE THAN TO SUCCESS.   A METHOD
FREQUENTLY USED BY ORGANIZATIONS THAT HAVE BECOME SOLD ON
JOB ENRICHMENT IS THE BLANKET APPROACH.   IN THIS APPROACH
THEY THINK ALL JOBS CAN SUCCESSFULLY BE ENRICHED SO THEY
DON'T REALLY STUDY THE JOB OR WORK SITUATION BEFORE
IMPLEMENTATION.   SOME FIRMS TRY TO ENRICH THE TROUBLE JOBS
FIRST.   THEY FEEL JOB ENRICHMENT IS THE SOLUTION FOR ALL
JOBS, WHICH IS NOT TRUE.   THE THIRD APPROACH IS TO TRY TO
ENRICH THE MOST CONVENIENT JOB.   LITTLE THOUGHT IS GIVEN TO
JOB CHARACTERISTICS, CONVERSIONS COSTS, WORKER ACCEPTANCE,
TECHNOLOGY, AND OTHER SITUATIONAL VARIABLES THAT AFFECT
RESULTS.
        THE DIAGNOSTIC APPROACH TO SELECTING JOBS FOR JOB
ENRICHMENT, FIRST IDENTIFIES THE ORGANIZATIONAL VARIABLES
THAT ARE PRIMARILY RESPONSIBLE FOR DETERMINING THE POTENTIAL
OF JOBS FOR ENRICHMENT AND, SECOND, IS CAPABLE OF RANKING
JOBS IN ORDER OF THEIR PROBABLE RETURN ON INVESTMENT.
FOUR SETS OF VARIABLES   ARE PRIMARILY RESPONSIBLE FOR
DETERMINING THE POTENTIALITY OF JOBS FOR ENRICHMENT: THE
JOB ITSELF, TECHNOLOGY, THE WORKERS, AND MANAGEMENT.   THE
VARIABLE, THE JOB ITSELF, IS FURTHER BROKEN DOWN
INTO: COST, QUALITY, FLEXIBILITY, COORDINATION,
SPECIALIZATION, WAGE PAYMENT PLAN, AND MAN-MACHINE
RELATIONSHIP.   UNDER WORKERS THERE ARE SEVEN INDICATORS OF
HOW THEY WILL ACCEPT JOB ENRICHMENT: SKILL LEVEL,
EDUCATION, PREVIOUS WORK EXPERIENCE, BACKGROUND, JOB
SECURITY, PRESENT JOB SATISFACTION, AND THE UNION.
        TO OPERATIONALIZE THIS INFORMATION INTO USABLE FORM THE
AUTHORS CAME UP WITH AN EVALUATION FORM WITH EIGHTEEN PAIRS
OF STATEMENTS WHICH ARE RATED ON A SCALE OF ONE TO FIVE.   IN
THIS APPROACH MANAGERS ARE PROVIDED WITH AN QUANTITATIVE

M0358   MEASURE OF ENRICHMENT POTENTIALITY. THE JOB ENRICHMENT
        RATINGS CAN BE USED TO RANK JOBS IN ORDER OF THEIR
        POTENTIALITY. IT IS ALSO HELPFUL IN IDENTIFYING LIMITING
        FACTORS AND POTENTIAL PROBLEM AREAS THAT SHOULD BE DEALT
        WITH BEFORE MANAGEMENT PROCEEDS WITH JOB ENRICHMENT.

M0359   REMOVAL OF SEX STEREOTYPING IN CENSUS OCCUPATIONAL
        CLASSIFICATION.
        MONTHLY LABOR REVIEW, JANUARY 1974, PP. 67-68.

            THE BUREAU OF THE CENSUS OCCUPATIONAL CLASSIFICATION
        SYSTEM WAS REVIEWED, AND OCCUPATIONAL TITLES WHICH DENOTE OR
        CONNOTE SEX STEREOTYPES WERE MODIFIED.

M0360   REPP, WILLIAM.
        MOTIVATING THE NOW GENERATION.
        PERSONNEL JOURNAL 50(JULY 1971):   540-43.

            THE COMPOSITION OF TODAY'S WORK FORCE PRESENTS
        MANAGEMENT WITH MANY NEW PROBLEMS. UNDERSTANDING THAT
        CHANGES IN ATTITUDE AND LIFE STYLES ARE NOT RESTRICTED
        TO THE YOUNG EMPLOYEES, BUT ARE ALSO BEING FOUND IN THE
        OLDER ONES, GIVES CLUES TO THE MORE EFFECTIVE MANAGEMENT
        OF OUR HUMAN RESOURCES.

M0361   RESTRUCTURING PARAMEDICAL JOBS.
        MANPOWER 5 (MARCH 1973):   3-7.

            EFFECTS OF REDESIGNING JOBS TO INCREASE PERFORMANCE,
        EFFICIENCY, AND JOB MOBILITY FOR PARAMEDICS.

M0362   RICHMOND, CHARLOTTE.
        LOGGING -- A JOB FOR THE HARDY.
        OCCUPATIONAL OUTLOOK QUARTERLY 15 (SUMMER 1971):   2-7.

            EXAMINES LOGGING AS A CAREER.

M0363   RICHMOND, CHARLOTTE.
        TOUR ESCORTING -- GLAMOUR OR HARD WORK.
        OCCUPATIONAL OUTLOOK QUARTERLY 15 (FALL 1971):   9-15.

            SOME TOUR GUIDES ADMIT THERE CAN BE TOO MUCH
        A GOOD THING, BUT MOST LIKE THE EXCITEMENT OF A JOB
        THAT OFTEN TAKES THEM TO EXOTIC PLACES.

M0364   ROBERTS, K. H.   SAVAGE, FREDERICK.
        TWENTY QUESTIONS: UTILIZING JOB SATISFACTION MEASURES.
        CALIFORNIA MANAGEMENT REVIEW 15 (SPRING 1972):   82-90.

            IN THIS ARTICLE THE AUTHORS DISCUSS THE IMPORTANCE OF
        ASKING A SERIES OF QUESTIONS PRIR TO ADVOCATING A JOB
        SATISFACTION SURVEY. THESE QUESTIONS ARE BROADLY CONCERNED
        WITH MANAGERIAL GOALS IN DIRECTING THE SURVEY ATTENTION TO
        CORPORATE PHILOSOPHY AND STRUCTURE, AND THE INFLUENCE OF
        EMPLOYEE CHARACTERISTICS AND THE EXTERNAL ENVIRONMENT ON JOB
        SATISFACTION. IF A SURVEY IS TO BE CONDUCTED ATTENTION MUST
        BE GIVEN TO THE SELECTION OF INSTRUMENTS BY CONSIDERING
        THEIR THEORETICAL BASES, RELIABILITY AND VALIDITY.

M0364   ALTHOUGH THIS STRATEGY IS SOMEWHAT STRUCTURED AND
SLIGHTLY ARTIFICIAL, IT PRESENTS ONE EFFECTIVE WAY TO
DETERMINE WHETHER A JOB SATISFACTION SURVEY SHOULD BE
USED, AND WHAT OUTCOMES CAN BE EXPECTED. THROUGH THESE
QUESTIONS THE MANAGER WHO USES THEM WILL BE ABLE TO CONSIDER
THE COSTS AND BENEFITS ASSOCIATED WITH JOB SATISFACTION
SURVEYS AND PROVIDE THE GROUND WORK FOR SELECTING
INSTRUMENTS.

M0365   ROBERTS, K. H.   MILES, RAYMOND E.   WALTER, GORDON A.
A FACTOR ANALYTIC STUDY OF JOB SATISFACTION ITEMS
DESIGNED TO MEASURE MASLOW NEED CATEGORIES.
PERSONNEL PSYCHOLOGY 24 (SUMMER 1971): 205-20.

        RESEARCH . . . REPORTS A SET OF ANALYSES OF THE
RESPONSES BY 380 MANAGERS FROM SEX ORGANIZATIONS TO ITEMS
PRESUMABLY RELATED TO THE ONE AVAILABLE MULTI-DIMENSIONAL
SCHEME FOR CATEGORIZING HUMAN NEEDS, THE MASLOW NEED
HIERARCHY. IT SEEKS TO DETERMINE THE EXTENT TO WHICH FACTORS
EMPIRICALLY DERIVED FROM THESE RESPONSES MATCH MASLOW'S
CONCEPTUALLY DERIVED NEED CATEGORIES.
RESULTS PROVIDE MIXED SUPPORT OF JOB SATISFACTION USING
MASLOW'S NEED CATEGORIES.

M0366   ROUSSELL, FRANCIS CECILE.
A COMPARATIVE STUDY OF TEACHERS' ATTITUDES TOWARD MEN
AND WOMEN DEPARTMENT HEADS IN LARGE CITY SECONDARY SCHOOLS.
PH. D. DISSERTATION, UNIVERSITY OF NORTH CAROLINA, 1972.

        THIS PROJECT INVESTIGATES THE RELATIONSHIP BETWEEN THE
ATTITUDES OF THE TEACHERS TOWARD THE SEX OF THEIR DEPARTMENT
HEAD AND THE RESULTING WORK CLIMATE AND LEADERSHIP
EFFECTIVENESS OF THESE HEADS.

M0367   ROMAN, W.W.   ORGANT, G. J.
DETERMINANTS OF PAY AND PAY SATISFACTION.
PERSONNEL PSYCHOLOGY 26 (JANUARY-FEBRUARY 1973): 503-20.

        DATA FROM A TOTAL OF 11, 156 PERSONS IN ONE OF THREE
GROUPS. THE STUDY INDICATED THAT THE VARIABLES RELATED TO
PAY SATISFACTION DIFFERED BY SEX AND JOB TYPE.

M0368   ROSE, EDWARD.
THE MOTIVATIONAL PARADOX.
MANAGEMENT 23 (MARCH 1971): 12-18.

        EXTRACTING OPTIMUM PRODUCTIVITY FROM LABOR APPEARS TO
BE LARGELY A MOTIVATIONAL PROBLEM, ONE OF CONVINCING
EMPLOYEES THAT THE GOALS OF MANAGEMENT AND LABOR ARE NOT
MUTUALLY EXCLUSIVE; THEY ARE, IN FACT, MUTUALLY INCLUSIVE.
SUGGESTS THAT PROGRAMS OF FRINGE BENEFITS, BONUS PAY, WAGE
INCREASES, PROMOTIONS,GRANTING OF STATUS SYMBOLS, COMPANY
EDUCATIONAL PROGRAMS, EMPLOYEE PARTICIPATION PLANS, AND
PROFIT-SHARING PLANS ARE SUCH MOTIVATORS.

M0369   ROSEN, BERNARD.
PARTNERS IN PRODUCTIVITY.
CIVIL SERVICE JOURNAL 15 (JANUARY-MARCH 1975): 16-17.

M0369   STATEMENT TO SENATE COMMITTEE ON IMPROVING PRODUCTIVITY
AND QUALITY OF WORKLIFE.

M0370   ROSEN, R. A. H.
THE HARD CORE AND THE PURITIAN WORK ETHIC.
MANPOWER, JANUARY 1970, PP. 29-31.

        DO THEY WANT TO WORK? WHAT ARE THEIR OCCUPATIONAL
ASPIRATIONS AND HOW MUCH HOPE DO THEY HAVE OF REALIZING
THEM.

M0371   ROSEN, R. A. H.
THE WORLD OF WORK THROUGH THE EYES OF THE HARD CORE.
PERSONNEL ADMINISTRATION 33 (MAY 1970): 8-21.

        THIS SURVEY ATTEMPTS TO DETERMINE FACTORS WHICH
INVOLVE THE STABLE EMPLOYMENT OF NUMBERS OF THE HARD CORE.
THE SAMPLE WAS NEGRO MALES, AGE 21-50, WHO WERE RESIDENTS OF
THE INNER CITY FOR AT LEAST ONE YEAR. THEY MUST NOT HAVE
WORKED FOR MORE THAN SIX MONTHS IN THE PREVOUS TWO YEARS
AND NOT HAD MORE THAN THREE MONTHS OF CONSECUTIVE STEADY
EMPLOYMENT IN THAT TIME. ONE QUARTER OF THEM HAD CRIMINAL
RECORDS AND ONE HALF HAD DROPPED OUT BY THE TENTH
GRADE. THIS ASSURED THAT THEIR ATTITUDES WOULD BE
INDICATIVE OF TRULY HARD CORE MEN.
        THE MAJOR RESEARCH WAS DONE AT A LARGE MIDWESTERN
UTILITY COMPANY BETWEEN APRIL 1968, WHEN 49 HARD CORE MEN
WERE HIRED, AND APRIL 1969.   AT THE END OF JUNE 1968,
UNSTRUCTURED INTERVIEWS WERE CONDUCTED ON 22 OF THE MEN BY
A PROFESSOR OF CLINICAL PSYCHOLOGY. GENERAL QUESTIONS WERE
ASKED ABOUT THE MEN'S WORK AND HISTORIES, BUT MOST OF THE
DATA SPONTANEOUS COMMENTS BY THE MEN THEMSELVES WHICH
REFLECT THEIR VALUES AND PERCEPTIONS RELATED TO WORK.
        THE FINDINGS OF THIS STUDY INDICATE THAT WORK WAS
CENTRAL TO THE MEN'S LIVES. THEY WERE MOST SATISFIED WITH
JOBS WHICH PROVIDED SUITABLE RELATIONS WITH FELLOW
WORKERS, TREATMENT BY MANAGEMENT, WAGES, WORKING CONDITIONS,
AND CHANCES FOR ADVANCEMENT.
THEY DIFFER FROM WORKERS IN GENERAL BY THE GREAT EMPHASIS
THEY PUT ON INTERPERSONAL RELATIONS AND WORKING CONDITIONS,
AND THE LOWER IMPORTANCE PUT ON ADVANCEMENT. THEY WERE
ALSO CONCERNED ABOUT THE FLEXIBILITY OF THE WORK SCHEDULING,
THE NATURE OF THE WORK, AND THE PRESTIGE OF THE WORK. JOB
SECURITY WAS NOT VERY IMPORTANT. THE UTILITY COMPANY WAS
FOUND TO BE A DESIRABLE PLACE OF EMPLOYMENT FOR MOST OF
THEM.
        THESE MEN HAVE GOALS SIMILAR TO EVERYONE ELSE'S, BUT
THEY MUST SCALE DOWN THESE GOALS DUE TO THE REALITIES OF
THEIR LIVES. THEY WANT JOBS WHICH MAKE THEM FEEL WORTHWHILE
AND LET THEM ADVANCE. IF SUCH JOBS WERE OFFERED TO THEM,
CHANCES ARE THEY WOULD STAY AT THOSE JOBS.

M0372   ROSENTHAL, EDMOND M.
GREENER PASTURES: WHY EMPLOYEES CHANGE JOBS.
PERSONNEL: THE MANAGEMENT OF PEOPLE AT WORK, 46 (JANUARY
1969): 22-30.

        COMPANIES KNOW THEY MAY LOSE EMPLOYEES TO COMPETITORS

M0372 BECAUSE OF HIGHER SALARY OFFERS. EVEN SO, THIS IS NOT A
GREAT THREAT BECAUSE MOST EMPLOYEES DO NOT LEAVE A COMPANY
SOLELY FOR AN INCREASE IN PAY. THE EMPLOYEE MAY BE
INFLUENCED TO LEAVE BY AGGRESSIVE RECRUITING EFFORTS BY
OTHER EMPLOYERS, SALARY COMPARISONS WITH FELLOW EMPLOYEES,
OR THE EMPLOYEE'S REALIZATION OF HIS CASH VALUE TO THE
COMPANY. OTHER REASONS MAY BE THE EMPLOYEE'S UNFULFILLED
AMBITIONS, COMPENSATION NEEDS CREATED BY THE COMPANY
ITSELF, AND NON-MONETARY CONSIDERATIONS THAT MAY BE
CONCEALED AS SALARY PROBLEMS.
AGGRESSIVE RECRUITING EFFORTS.
        TOP EMPLOYEES ARE FREQUENTLY OFFERED TOP SALARIES FROM
SMALL OR NEW COMPANIES WHICH NEED EXPERIENCED HELP IN A
HURRY. LARGER COMPANIES, IN TURN, ARE USUALLY UNABLE TO
OFFER A COUNTER-OFFER BECAUSE THEY MAINTAIN A FORMAL SALARY
STRUCTURE. THE LARGER, MORE ESTABLISHED COMPANIES,
HOWEVER, OFFER MORE SECURITY THAN THEIR NEW OR SMALL
COMPETITORS.
SALARY COMPARISONS AND REALIZATION OF CASH VALUE.
        ALTHOUGH DISCUSSION OF SALARIES WITH CO/WORKERS IS
SUPPOSEDLY PROHIBITED, IT IS OFTEN A TOPIC OF THE COMPANY
GRAPEVINES. THE EMPLOYEE WHO LEARNS THAT HIS SALARY IS
LOWER THAN THAT OF AN EQUALLY QUALIFIED PEER, HIS
PREVIOUSLY ADEQUATE PAYCHECK BECOMES A REFLECTION OF HIS
COMPANY'S LOW ESTIMATE OF HIS PERFORMANCE. (P. 27).
CONSEQUENTLY, HE MAY BEGIN LOOKING FOR A NEW JOB.
UNFULFILLED AMBITIONS.
THE EMPLOYEE WHO FINDS THAT MANY OF HIS EXPECTATIONS HAVE
FAILED TO MATERIALIZE MAY SOON SEEK DIFFERENT EMPLOYMENT.
SECURITY AND PRESTIGE ARE TWO AMBITIONS MOST OFTEN DESIRED
BY EMPLOYEES.
COMPENSATION NEEDS AND NON-MONETARY CONDIDERATIOSS.
        IN MANY JOBS WHERE THE MAN MAKES THE JOB--IN
MANAGEMENT AND IN CREATIVE WORK-- (P. 29), SALARY IS NOT
EVERYTHING. PERSONAL PRIDE ALSO PLAYS A LARGE PART IN JOB
SATISFACTION. THE EMPLOYEE WHO ASKS FOR A PAY INCREASE
IS REALLY ASKING FOR MANAGEMENT TO APPRECIATE (AND BE
WILLING TO PAY FOR) HIS ABILITIES.
        A GOOD MANY OBSERVERS OF THE SALARY SCENE AGREE THAT
MONEY AS A MOTIVATOR TO MOVE TO ANOTHER JOB IS GREATLY
OVERRATED.   (P. 30).

M0373 ROSOW, JEROME M.
TOWARD A BRIGHTER BLUE-COLLAR.
MANPOWER 3 (MARCH 1971): 28-32.

        STUDY OF DISSATISFACTION OF BLUE-COLLAR WORKERS
DUE TO THEIR BELIEF THAT THEY ARE NOT RECEIVING A
SUFFICIENT RETURN FOR THEIR LABOR.

M0374 RUDNEY, SHIRLEY.
THE PUBLIC EMPLOYMENT SERVICE REACHES OUT TO THE URBAN
POOR.
OCCUAPTIONAL OUTLOOK QUARTERLY 13 (SPRING 1969): 8-12.

        THREE NEW PROGRAMS HELP TO BREAK TOUGH CRUST
OF HARD-CORE UNEMPLOYMENT.

M0375   RUSH, HAROLD M. G.
        MOTIVATION THROUGH JOB DESIGN.
        THE CONFERENCE BOARD RECORD 8 (JANUARY 1971):   52-56.

            A PROBLEM OF MANAGEMENT IS TO PROVIDE THE
        OPPORTUNITY FOR INDIVIDUAL INVOLVEMENT IN WORK WHILE COPING
        WITH THE DEMANDS OF INCREASED AUTOMATION AND THE
        REQUIREMENTS OF MASS PRODUCTION. MANY FIRMS ARE BEGINNING
        TO CONSIDER WAYS TO DESIGN JOBS TO INCLUDE MOTIVATIONAL
        FACTORS. SOME APPROACHES DISCUSSED ARE JOB ROTATION,
        JOB ENLARGEMENT, JOB ENRICHMENT, AND WORK SIMPLIFICATION.

M0376   SALEH, S. D.   SINGH, T.
        WORK VALUES OF WHITE-COLLAR EMPLOYEES AS A FUNCTION OF
        SOCIOLOGICAL BACKGROUND.
        JOURNAL OF APPLIED PSYCHOLOGY, 58 (AUGUST 1973):   131-33.

            THIS PAPER INVESTIGATES THE RELATIONSHIP BETWEEN
        INTRINSIC JOB ORIENTATION, FATHER'S OCCUPATION, AND
        COMMUNITY SIZE IN A SAMPLE OF WHITE-COLLAR WORKERS.   FOR
        ANALYSIS OF THE DATA THE SAMPLE WAS CLASSIFIED BY SALARY
        LEVEL, EDUCATION AND SEX.

M0377   SAUER, JOHN R.
        MANAGEMENT-BY-MISSION FOR ACTIVATING PEOPLE.
        THE OFFICE 73 (MARCH 1971):   58-59.

            WHEN A MANAGER ISSUES CLEAR AND SIMPLE INSTRUCTIONS
        DIRECTED AT THE MISSION OF THE JOB RATHER THAN AT THE
        TECHNIQUES OF ACCOMPLISHING IT, WORKERS WILL BE ACTIVATED TO
        PERFORM THEIR BEST.
        FOUR BASIC TECHNIQUES ARE SUGGESTED.

M0378   SAVAGE, CHARLES M. BLAKELY, THOMAS J.
        A PHENOMENOLOGY OF HUMAN LABOR.
        CHESTNUT HILL: BOSTON COLLEGE PROJECT COMPLETED FISCAL YEAR
        1974

            USING A PHENOMENOLOGICAL APPROACH, THIS STUDY ATTEMPTS
        TO ANSWER THE FOLLOWING QUESTIONS: (1)   WHAT IS HUMAN WORK?
        AND (2)   WHAT MAKES IT A SIGNIFICANT OR INSIGNIFICANT HUMAN
        VENTURE?
            THE RESEARCH EXPLORES HOW THE ACTIVITY OF WORK BECOMES
        HUMANLY MEANINGFUL, VIEWING MEANINGFUL GROWTH AS A FUNCTION
        OF HUMAN TIME CONSCIOUSNESS AND IT EXAMINES THE NATURE OF
        WORK AS A   FORM-BESTOWING ACTIVITY, WHICH IS BOTH
        ACCUSATIVE AND REFLEXIVE.   TO IMPLEMENT THESE FINDINGS IT
        WILL BE NECESAARY TO FLATTEN EXISTING WORK HIERARCHIES,
        PHASE OUT ARTIFICIAL DISTINCTIONS BETWEEN MANAGEMENT AND
        LABOR, AND LESSEN THE INTENSE CONCENTRATION ON THE PRESENT
        (TO THE EXCLUSION OF THE PAST AND FUTURE).   THE REAL GROWTH
        SECTOR OF AN EMERGING HUMAN ECONOMY IS IN THE AREA OF HUMAN
        MEANING GROWTH.   WORK CAN BECOME HUMANLY SIGNIFICANT IF THE
        TEMPORAL DIMENSION OF HUMAN WORK IS RECOGNIZED.

M0379   SCANLAN, BURT K.
        MOTIVATING SALESMEN THROUGH BETTER SALES MANAGEMENT.
        SALES MANAGEMENT 106 (APRIL 10, 1971):   56.

M0379   THREE CHARACTERISTICS OF A SALESMAN'S JOB CAN
         AFFECT HIS SUBSEQUENT LEVEL OF MOTIVATION AND OVER-ALL JOB
         PERFORMANCE. THESE CHARACTERISTICS--FLUCTUATION
         BETWEEN SUCCESS AND FAILURE, A TENDENCY TO GET IN A
         RUT, AND INDEPENDENCE OF OPERATION--REQUIRE ADDITIONAL
         STIMULUS TO MOTIVATE THE SALESMAN.

M0380   SCHNEIDER, BENJAMIN.
         THREE STUDIES OF MEASURES OF NEED SATISFACTION IN
         ORGANIZATIONS.
         ADMINISTRATIVE SCIENCE QUARTERLY   4 (DECEMBER 1973):
         489-505.

         DATA FROM THREE STUDIES ARE USED TO COMPARE THE RESULTS
         GENERATED BY TWO MEASURES OF NEED CATEGORIES AS DEVELOPED
         IN MASLOW'S THEORY OF HUMAN MOTIVATION AND MEASURES
         OF TWO OR MORE DIFFERENT ORIENTATIONS.   IT IS SUGGESTED
         THAT THE FAILURE TO FIND SUPPORT FOR MASLOW'S NEED
         CATEGORIES IN ORGANIZATIONAL SETTINGS IS DUE TO: (1) AN
         INADEQUATE CONCEPTUALIZATION WHICH DOES NOT READILY
         FACILITATE THE DEVELOPMENT OF OPERATIONAL INDICATORS, AND
         (2) THE INITIAL ORIENTATION OF MASLOW'S THEORY WHICH WAS NOT
         SPECIFICALLY AIMED TOWARD ORGANIZATIONAL SETTINGS.

M0381   SCHWAB, DONALD P.
         CONFLICTING IMPACTS OF PAY ON EMPLOYEE MOTIVATION,
         SATISFACTION.
         PERSONNEL JOURNAL   53 (MARCH 1974):   196-200.

         ALL ORGANIZATIONS ARE CONCERNED WITH BOTH EMPLOYEE
         MOTIVATION TO PERFORM AND EMPLOYEE SATISFACTION.   THE
         ARTICLE PRESENTS A RECENT STUDY WHICH INDICATES THAT THE
         TYPE OF PAY SYSTEM MAY HAVE POSITIVE EFFECTS ON MOTIVATION
         AND AT THE TIME HAVE NEGATIVE EFFECTS ON SATISFACTION.

M0382   SCHWARTZ, STANLEY J.
         CURE FOR THE I DON'T CARE SYNDROME.
         PERSONNEL JOURNAL 50 (JULY 1971):   529-31.

         UNLESS THE EMPLOYER RECOGNIZES THE HUMAN-BEINGNESS OF
         HIS EMPLOYEES--IN A WAY NOT YET GENERALLY ACHIEVED--THE
         UNION ORGANIZER MAY STEP IN AND DO IT FOR HIM.   IT'S
         TIME FOR THE PRESIDENT OF THE COMPANY TO CLEARLY STATE HIS
         ORGANIZATION'S PHILOSOPHY OF PERSONNEL ADMINISTRATION.

M0383   SCHWEITZER, S.   SMITH, R.
         THE PERSISTENCE OF THE DISADVANTAGED WORKER EFFECT.
         INDUSTRIAL AND LABOR RELATIONS REVIEW 27 (JANUARY 1974):
         249-60.

         IT IS DEMONSTRATED HERE THAT SIGNIFICANT NEGATIVE
         RELATIONSHIPS DO EXIST BETWEEN CURRENT PARTICIPATION AND
         BOTH CURRENT AND PAST EMPLOYMENT.

M0384   SCOTT, RICHARD D.
         JOB ENLARGEMENT -- THE KEY TO INCREASING JOB SATISFACTION.
         PERSONNEL JOURNAL 52 (APRIL 1973):   313-17.

THE AUTHOR OF THIS ARTICLE OBSERVES THAT NOT ALL
WORKERS WILL RESPOND TO AN ENLARGED JOB IN THE SAME
MANNER DEPENDING UPON THE CULTURAL BACKGROUND OF THE WORK
FORCE.

M0385   SCOTT, RICHARD D.
        JOB EXPECTANCY -- AN IMPORTANT FACTOR IN LABOR TURNOVER.
        PERSONNEL JOURNAL 51 (MAY 1972): 360-63.

             SCOTT WROTE THIS ARTICLE TO EXPAND UPON THE REASONS
        WHY EMPLOYEES TERMINATE THEIR JOBS EARLY. HE ALSO OFFERS
        SOME SUGGESTIONS WHICH MAY HELP EMPLOYERS SUBSTANTIALLY TO
        ELIMINATE HIGH TURNOVER RATES AMONG PERSONNEL. THE
        CONCLUSIONS OF THIS ARTICLE ARE DRAWN FROM RESEARCH ON THE
        SUBJECT OF LABOR TURNOVER.
             IN THE PAST, MANY TECHNIQUES AND PROCEDURES HAVE BEEN
        USEFUL IN RETAINING EMPLOYEES. AMONG THESE ARE EMPLOYMENT
        TESTS, WEIGHTED APPLICATION BLANKS, AND SUPERVISORY TRAINING
        PROGRAMS. ONE ITEM THAT HAS BEEN OVERLOOKED ALMOST
        COMPLETELY IS THE JOB EXPECTANCY OF THE INDIVIDUAL
        APPLICANT.
             MANAGEMENT, OF COURSE, HAS NO WAY OF KNOWING WHAT THE
        NEW APPLICANT EXPECTS. BUT ONCE THE ORIENTATION PROGRAM
        BEGINS, THE COMPANY HAS CONSIDERABLE INFLUENCE OVER THE
        PROSPECTIVE EMPLOYEE TO THE JOB SITUATION. TOO MANY
        COMPANIES FAIL TO DISPEL ANY MISCONCEPTIONS THE NEW EMPLOYEE
        MAY HAVE. THIS PROVES THE INADEQUACY OF THE COMPANY'S
        ORIENTAION PROGRAM, WHICH RESULTS IN UNNECESSARY
        EXPENDITURES OF TRAINING TIME AND MONEY ON NEW PERSONNEL.
        THE PROBLEM MAY BE A SIMPLE ONE TO OVERCOME, SUCH AS
        ANSWERING THE APPLICANT'S QUESTIONS AS A MAJOR PORTION OF
        THE INTERVIEW PROCESS. AS IT STANDS NOW, HOWEVER, TOO MANY
        COMPANIES PUT TOO MUCH IMPORTANCE UPON THE APPLICATION
        BLANK, PSYCHOLOGICAL TESTS, REFERENCES, ETC. COMPANIES
        FAIL TO TELL IT LIKE IT IS.
             THERE IS CONSIDERABLE EVIDENCE OF A RELATIONSHIP AMONG
        JOB EXPECTANCIES AND TURNOVER. IN A STUDY BY SALEK, LEE,
        AND PRIEN, IT WAS DISCOVERED THAT A VAST MAJORITY OF NURSES
        LEFT THEIR JOBS AS A RESULT OF IGNORANCE OF THE JOB.
        THESE FACTORS INCLUDED NURSES NOT USING THEIR EXPERIENCE
        OR ABILITY, THEIR WORK NOT BEING RECOGNIZED, AND THEIR LACK
        OF ADVANCEMENT ON THE JOB. IN A STUDY CONDUCTED BY WEITZ
        AND NICKOLS, IT WAS FOUND THAT THERE WAS A SIGNIFICANTLY
        LARGER NUMBER OF TERMINATIONS AMONG LIFE INSURANCE AGENTS
        WHO HAD NOT RECEIVED ADEQUATE INFORMATION THROUGH THE
        INTERVIEW. THIS WAS CORRECTED BY THE ISSUANCE OF A
        BOOKLET DESCRIBING THE REQUIRED JOB DUTIES.

M0386   SEASHORE, S. E.   QUINN, R. P.   LAWLER, EDWARD E.
        EFFECTIVENESS IN WORK ROLES.
        ANN ARBOR: THE UNIVERSITY OF MICHIGAN. JUNE 1973.

             THIS STUDY IS DESIGNED TO ANSWER TWO QUESTIONS WHICH
        HAVE BEEN PLAGUING BOTH THE PRODUCERS AND USERS OF RESEARCH
        ON WORKER ATTITUDES AND JOB SATISFACTION--ONE SUBSTANTIVE
        AND THE OTHER METHODOLOGICAL. OF PRIMARY CONCERN IS THE
        SPECIFICATION OF THE BEHAVIORAL CONSEQUENCES OF WORK
        ATTITUDES TO THE WORKER, THE ORGANIZATION THAT EMPLOYS HIM,

M0386 AND SOCIETY GENERALLY. ON THE METHODOLOGICAL SIDE, THE STUDY AIMS TO DETERMINE: (1) THE EXTENT TO WHICH WORKERS REPORTS OF THE CHARACTER AND QUALITY OF THEIR JOBS ACCURATELY PORTRAY THE TRUE CONDITIONS OF THEIR EMPLOYMENT, AND (2) THE VALIDITY OF WORKERS' DESCRIPTIONS OF THEIR JOB BEHAVIORS (PRODUCTIVITY, TURNOVER, ABSENTEEISM).

M0387 SEAY,DONNA.
MODEL PROGRAM TO INSTRUCT MANPOWER TRAINING PERSONNEL IN SELECTION AND APPLICATION OF REMEDIAL INSTRUCTIONAL MATERIALS TO MEET INDIVIDUAL TRAINEE NEEDS.
CAMBRIDGE: TECHNICAL EDUCATION RESEARCH CENTER, INC.
PROJECT COMPLETED FISCAL YEAR 1974.

THE PURPOSE OF THE PROJECT WAS TO DEVELOP A STAFF TRAINING SYSTEM THAT WOULD ENABLE A STAFF TO INSTALL, IMPLEMENT, AND EVALUATE A SYSTEM OF DELIVERY OF BASIC AND PREVOCATIONAL EDUCATION IN AN INDIVIDUALIZED MANNER. IT WAS FOUND THAT EFFECTIVE AND EFFICIENT STAFF TRAINING MATERIALS COULD BE DEVELOPED AND PACKAGE FOR STAFF TRAINING. IT WAS ALSO FOUND THAT THE PROJECT COULD TRAIN OTHER TRAINERS (TEACHER-EDUCATORS) WHO COULD IN TURN DELIVER THE TRAINING EFFECTIVELY WITH THE STAFF TRAINING PACKAGE. THE TRAINING HAS BEEN SOUGHT AND FOUND HIGHLY USEFUL BY TRADE SCHOOLS, SKILL CENTERS, AND COMMUNITY COLLEGES. PRELIMINARY SUMMARY DATA ON STUDENTS WHO HAVE GONE THROUGH PROGRAMS UNDER STAFF TRAINED IN THIS MANNER INDICATE GREATER PROGRESS IN SHORTER TIME SPANS THAN USUAL.

M0388 SEDUCTION AIN'T MOTIVATION.
SALES MANAGEMENT 105 (SEPTEMBER 1, 1970): 28.

ASKED WHAT REALLY MAKES THEM WANT TO SELL, 169 INDUSTRIAL SALESMEN TOLD OLD DOMINION UNIVERSITY PROFESSOR H. B. KARP THAT THE JOYS OF ACHIEVING MAKES MONEY AND CONTESTS ALSO-RANS.

M0389 SEX BIAS IN LONGSHORING.
MONTHLY LABOR REVIEW, JUNE 1974, P. 62.

WOMEN ARE NOT ENTIRELY OUT OF THE PICTURE IN LONGSHORING, AND THERE THEY HAVE EQUAL RIGHTS WITH MEN, ACCORDING TO A RECENT DECISION OF THE NATIONAL LABOR RELATIONS BOARD.

M0390 SHAPIRO, H. JACK. WAHBA, MAHMOUD A.
FREDRICK W. TAYLOR -- 62 YEARS LATER.
PERSONNEL JOURNAL 53 (AUGUST 1974): 574-78.

THE ARTICLE PRESENTS A STUDY DESIGNED TO TEST THESIS THAT MONETARY REWARDS WOULD LEAD TO INCREASED PRODUCTIVITY, I.E., THAT MONEY IS A PRINCIPAL MOTIVATOR OF MAN'S EFFORTS. THE STUDY INVOLVING EMPLOYEES OF A NEW YORK STEEL PRODUCTS MANUFACTURING COMPANY INDICATED THAT IN SPITE OF THE 62 YEARS SINCE ITS PROMULGATION, TAYLOR'S THESIS IS STILL VIABLE.

M0391   SHEPARD, JON M.
ON ALEX CAREY'S RADICAL CRITICISMS OF THE HAWTHORNE
STUDIES.
ACADEMY OF MANAGEMENT JOURNAL 14 (MARCH 1971):   23-32.

        THIS PAPER ATTEMPTS TO PROVIDE AN UNDERSTANDING OF AND
A PERSPECTIVE FOR ALEX CAREY'S SELF-ADMITTED RADICAL
CRITICISM OF THE THAT THE HAWTHORNE RESEARCHERS DID NOT
MINIMIZE THE INFLUENCE OF MONETARY INCENTIVES TO SATISFY
THEIR PREDELICTION FOR A PARTICULAR STYLE OF SUPERVISION.
IT IS CONCLUDED THAT PART OF THE ENDURING SIGNIFICANCE OF
THIS BODY OF RESEARCH RESIDES IN ITS PLACEMENT OF
FINANCIAL INCENTIVES INTO A SOCIAL CONTEXT.

M0392   SHEPPARD, H. L.
ASKING THE RIGHT QUESTIONS ON JOB SATISFACTION.
MONTHLY LABOR REVIEW 96 (APRIL 1973):   51-52.

        ONE IMPORTANT QUESTION IS--WHAT ARE THE BEST QUESTIONS
TO USE IN MEASURING JOB SATISFACTION, AND HOW MANY OF THESE
SHOULD BE USED?
        SHEPPARD USES ONE TYPE OF QUESTION CALLED A   JOB
SATISFACTION FREQUENCY QUESTION AND CHECKS IT AGAINST
INDIRECT JOB SATISFACTION ITEMS (ADDITIONAL QUESTIONS
ASKING ABOUT DESIRE TO KEEP OR CHANGE CURRENT JOB; FEELINGS
ABOUT CHANGING JOB; AND FREQUENCY OF THINKING SERIOUSLY
ABOUT A DIFFERENT OCCUPATION).
        THE RESPONSE TO THE ADDITIONAL QUESTIONS ARE GIVEN
QUANTITATIVE WEIGHTINGS, THEREFORE, MAKING IT POSSIBLE TO
ADOPT A CLASSIFICATION OF HIGH, MEDIUM, AND LOW ATTACHMENT
TO THE JOB. THE   JOB SATISFACTION FREQUENCY MEASURE HAS A
STATISTICAL RELATIONSHIP TO THE ADDITIONAL QUESTIONS WHICH
IN TURN, ARE STATISTICALLY RELATED TO DEGREE OF TASK VARIETY
AND RESPONSIBILITY. THIS FINDING SHOULD CONTRADICT THE
CONTENTION THAT WORKERS WILL SAY THAT THEY ARE SATISFIED
WITH THEIR JOBS BECAUSE OF ONE'S EGO, OR RELUCTANCE TO ADMIT
A POOR OCCUPATIONAL CHOICE.
        SOME WORKERS VIEW THEIR JOBS PURELY AS A SOURCE OF
INCOME. THESE PEOPLE WILL ADAPT TO THEIR JOBS AND CARE
LITTLE ABOUT SATISFACTION.
        JOB SATISFACTION IS A FUNCTION OF RELATIONSHIP BETWEEN
THE NATURE OF THE WORKER AND THE NATURE OF THE JOB TASKS
AND WORK ENVIRONMENT. IT IS BECOMING LESS TRUE THAT
PEOPLE CAN GET USED TO ANYTHING WITH NO ILL EFFECTS.

M0393   SHEPPARD, H. L.
DISCONTENTED BLUE-COLLAR WORKERS -- A CASE STUDY.
MONTHLY LABOR REVIEW 94 (APRIL 1971):   25-32.

TODAY, THERE ARE MANY DISCONTENTED WORKERS WHO ARE REFERRED
TO AS HAVING THE BLUE COLLAR BLUES.   THIS SURVEY TAKES A
GROUP OF WORKERS WITH CERTAIN ARBITRARILY CHOSEN
CHARACTERISTICS THAT MAY REFLECT DISCONTENT, AND COMPARES
THEM WITH OTHER WORKERS WITH SUCH CHARACTERISTICS.
THE TOTAL SAMPLE OF 270 WHITE MALES HAD CERTAIN OTHER
CHARACTERISTICS IN COMMON. THEY WERE UNION MEMBERS WHO
LIVED AND WORKED IN FOUR INDUSTRIAL URBAN AREAS OF ONE
NORTHEASTERN STATE.

M0393 TWO SETS OF QUESTIONS WERE USED TO DETERMINE WHICH WORKERS
       WERE DISCONTENTED. THE FIRST SET WAS USED TO SEE THE DEGREE
       TO WHICH WORKERS' ASPIRATIONS HAVE BEEN MET. AN ASPIRATION
       ACHIEVEMENT DISCREPANCY INDEX WAS DEVELOPED TO RELATE A
       WORKER'S FEELINGS ABOUT HIS ACHIEVEMENTS COMPARED WITH HIS
       EARLIER ASPIRATIONS. THE SECOND SET MEASURED THE EXTENT TO
       WHICH A WORKER PERCEIVED HIS MOBILITY CHANCES. OUT OF THE
       270 MEN SAMPLED, 79 SCORED HIGH ON DISCREPANCY BETWEEN
       ASPIRATION AND ACHIEVEMENT AND ALSO REPLIED THAT THEY HAVE
       LITTLE OR NO REAL CHANCE OF GETTING AHEAD ON THEIR JOB.
       THESE ARE THE DISCONTENTED WORKERS.
       PERSONAL INTERVIEWS WERE CONDUCTED TO SURVEY: AGE,
       EDUCATION, HOURLY WAGES, FAMILY INCOME, NUMBER OF WAGE
       EARNERS IN THE FAMILY, NUMBER OF DEPENDENTS, ADEQUACY OF
       TAKE HOME PAY, PERCEPTION OF THE JOB, POLITICAL
       EFFECTIVENESS, ALIENATION, AND RACE ATTITUDES. THESE
       INTERVIEWS HELPED TO DIFFERENTIATE THE CHARACTERISTICS OF
       CONTENTED AND DISCONTENTED WORKERS.
       THE RESULTS SHOWED THAT IF THE WORKER WERE DISCOURAGED IN
       HIS STRIVING TO MEET HIS GOALS BY MIDDLE AGE, THE WORKER
       WITH MORE EDUCATION WAS LIKELY TO BE A DISCONTENTED WORKER.
       ALIENATION IS RELATED TO THE FACT THAT MORE THAN ONE
       FAMILY MEMBER MUST WORK TO OBTAIN A RELATIVELY HIGH FAMILY
       INCOME. THE NATURE OF THE JOB CAN'T BE SEPARATED FROM THE
       OFF-JOB ATTITUDES AND BEHAVIOR OF THE WORKER. A WORKER'S
       PERCEPTION OF HIS POLITICAL EFFECTIVENESS, VOTING CHOICES,
       RACE ATTITUDES, AND FEELING OF ALIENATION ARE SHAPED BY
       THESE FACTORS AND CONDITIONS. IN SUMMARY, THE DISCONTENTED
       WORKER FEELS HE HAS LITTLE EFFECT IN THE POLITICAL PROCESS
       OF THE COUNTRY; HAS LITTLE VARIETY, AUTONOMY, OR
       RESPONSIBILITY IN HIS JOB; AND IS ALIENATED.

M0394 SHIMONKEVITZ, RUTH.
       OFFICE LANDSCAPING -- NEW LOOK FOR THE WORKPLACE.
       MANPOWER 3 (MAY 1971): 20-24.
            DISCUSSION OF THE EFFECTS OF OFFICE DESIGN ON

       EMPLOYEE EFFICIENCY AND MORALE.

M0395 SIEGEL, JACOB P.   BOWEN, DONALD.
       SATISFACTION AND PERFORMANCE: CAUSAL RELATIONSHIPS AND
       MODERATING EFFECTS.
       JOURNAL OF VOCATIONAL BEHAVIOR 1 (JULY 1971): 263-69.

            USING 86 MBA'S AND QUESTIONNAIRES DEVELOPED BY
       A. ZANDER (1969), THE AUTHOR REPORTS THAT SELF-ESTEEM IS
       A FACTOR THAT MODERATES SATISFACTION-PERFORMANCE
       RELATIONSHIPS. DATA ALSO SUGGEST THAT GROUP, NOT
       INDIVIDUAL, REWARDS ARE AN IMPORTANT SOURCE MOTIVATION FOR
       GROUP-ORIENTED TASKS.

M0396 SILBER, MARK B.
       MANAGERS MANAGE MOTIVATION: THEY DON'T MOTIVATE.
       DEFENSE MANAGEMENT JOURNAL 11 (JANUARY 1975): 44-49

            MANAGEMENT BY MOTIVATION WHICH COME FROM WITHIN THE
       EMPLOYEE IS ENCOURAGED.

M0397   SIMON, YVES R.
WORK, SOCIETY AND CULTURE.
NEW YORK: FORDHAM UNIVERSITY PRESS, 1971.

A WRITTEN VERSION OF A COURSE GIVEN BY YVES SIMON
AT THE UNIVERSITY OF CHICAGO ENTITLED WORK AND THE
WORKMAN. TOPICS COVERED ARE IRKSOMENESS OF WORK,
ETHICS OF WORKERS, SOCIOLOGICAL CONCEPTION OF THE
WORKING MAN.

M0398   SIMPKINS, EDWARD.
THE WORK ETHIC IS NOT ENOUGH.
MONTHLY LABOR REVIEW 96 (APRIL 1973):   59-60.

AUTHOR BELIEVES THAT WORK ETHIC AND MOTIVATION
ALONE ARE NOT SUFFICIENT TO SOLVE THE POVERTY DILEMMA.

M0399   SINGER, JILL M.
FILLING THE POLICE LINEUP.
MANPOWER, SEPTEMBER 1974, PP. 2-7.

MANY WOMEN HAVE QUALIFICATIONS TO COMPLETE THE POLICE
LINEUP AND BECOME POLICEWOMEN.

M0400   SLEZAK, LESTER.
EFFECTS OF CHANGES IN PAYMENT SYSTEM ON PRODUCTIVITY IN
SWEDEN.
MONTHLY LABOR REVIEW, 96 (MARCH 1973):   51-52.

STUDY OF CHANGES IN PRODUCTIVITY DUE TO CHANGES
IN METHOD OF PAYMENT TO INDUSTRIAL WORKERS IN SWEDEN.

M0401   SLOCUM, JOHN W.
MOTIVATION IN MANAGERIAL LEVELS: RELATIONSHIP OF NEED
SATISFACTION TO JOB PERFORMANCE.
JOURNAL OF APPLIED PSYCHOLOGY 55 (AUGUST 1971):   312-16.

THE PURPOSE OF THIS SURVEY IS TO COMPARE THE NEED
SATISFACTION OF FIRST-LINE SUPERVISORS WITH TOP AND MIDDLE
MANAGERS AND RELATE NEED SATISFACTION TO JOB PERFORMANCE.
SLOCUM USES LAWLER AND PORTER (1967) AS BACKGROUND AND A
BASE FOR STARTING THE SURVEY.
ACCORDING TO SLOCUM ON LAWLER AND PORTER (1967), THE
RESEARCHERS CONCLUDE THAT SATISFACTION IS MORE CLOSELY
RELATED TO PERFORMANCE THAN SATISFACTION OF LOWER ORDER
NEEDS.   SLOCUM ALSO STATES, THE PURPOSE OF THIS ARTICLE IS
TO REEXAMINE THE EARLIER FINDINGS WHICH HAVE RELATED NEED
SATISFACTION TO MANAGERIAL LEVELS AND ALSO EXAMINE THE MODEL
POSITED BY PORTER AND LAWLER IN TERMS OF PERFORMANCE. THIS
ARTICLE CONSIDERS ONLY SPECIFIC PREDICTION: SATISFACTION OF
HIGHER ORDER NEEDS IS MORE CLOSELY RELATED TO TOP MANAGEMENT
PERFORMANCE THAN SATISFACTION FOR HIGH ORDER NEEDS FOR
LOWER MANAGEMENT.
DATA WERE COLLECTED FROM 87 FIRST-LINE SUPERVISORS AND
123 TOP AND MIDDLE LEVEL MANAGERS AT A STEEL MILL. THE
MANAGERS WERE RATED ON THE FOLLOWING TRAITS: A) TECHNICAL
KNOWLEDGE, B) FUNCTIONAL KNOWLEDGE, C) DRIVE/AGGRESSIVENESS,
D) RELIABILITY, E) COOPERATION AND F) ORGANIZING ABILITY.

M0401 THE PERFORMANCE MEASURES WERE TESTED FOR CONVERGENT AND
DISCRIMINANT VALIDITY ACCORDING TO THE CRITERIA SUGGESTED BY
CAMPBELL AND FISKE (1959).
   THE DATA IN THE SURVEY SUPPORT, STATISTICALLY, LAWLER
AND PORTER (1967) IN THAT AN INDIVIDUALS' DEGREE OF
HIGHER ORDER NEED SATISFACTION IS RELATED TO HIS
PERFORMANCE. ALSO SUPPORTED IS THE RELATIONSHIP BETWEEN
NEED SATISFACTION AND MANAGERIAL LEVEL.

M0402 SLOCUM, JOHN W.   HAND, HERBERT H.
PREDICTION OF JOB SUCCESS AND EMPLOYEE SATISFACTION FOR
EXECUTIVES AND FOREMEN.
TRAINING AND DEVELOPMENT JOURNAL 25 (OCTOBER 1971): 28-36.

   THE EDWARDS PERSONAL PREFERENCE SCHEDULE (EPPS) WAS THE
MEASURING INSTRUMENT USED ON 57 FOREMEN AND 37 EXECUTIVES IN
A STEEL PLANT. EMPLOYEE SATISFACTION AND PERFORMANCE AS
CORRELATES OF PERSONALITY CHARACTERISTICS WERE INVESTIGATED.
RESULTS INDICATE PROMISE IN USING PERSONALITY
CHARACTERISTICS AS PREDICTORS OF JOB PERFORMANCE AND
SATISFACTION.

M0403 SMALL, SYLVIA S.
WORK TRAINING PROGRAMS AND THE UNEMPLOYMENT RATE.
MONTHLY LABOR REVIEW 95 (SEPTEMBER 1972): 7-13.

   PROGRAMS HAVE MODEST DIRECT IMPACT ON THE UNEMPLOYMENT
RATE, BUT OVER HALF THE ENROLLEES PUT TO WORK HAD BEEN OUT
THE LABOR FORCE.

M0404 SMITH, GERALD.
OCCUPATIONAL GUIDANCE MATERIALS FOR THE DISADVANTAGED: A
PILOT PROGRAM.
OCCUPATIONAL OUTLOOK QUARTERLY 15 (SUMMER 1971): 31-33.

   PROGRESS REPORT ON A NEW PILOT PROGRAM
AIMED AT YOUNG PEOPLE WITH LIMITED READING COMPREHENSION.

M0405 SMITH, HOWARD P.
KEYS TO EMPLOYEE MOTIVATION.
SUPERVISORY MANAGEMENT 16 (FEBRUARY 1971): 40-41.

   THE PURPOSE OF THIS ARTICLE IS TO DISCUSS THE KEYS
WHICH ARE IMPORTANT IN EMPLOYEE MOTIVATION. THE AREAS
COVERED ARE THE ENCOURAGING OF BETTER PERFORMANCE, JOB
CONDITIONS WHICH INFLUENCE JOB BEHAVIOR, AND SUPERVISOR
LEADERSHIP.
ENCOURAGING BETTER PERFORMANCE.
   THE THOUGHT IN THIS ARTICLE IS THAT IF AN EMPLOYEE HAS
A LACK OF SELF-CONFIDENCE, THE MANAGER MUST BUILD THE
EMPLOYEE'S CONFIDENCE BY GIVING HIM RESPONSIBILITIES THAT
ARE WITHIN HIS RANGE OF ABILITY AND BY REINFORCING GENUINE
ACHIEVEMENT WHEN IT OCCURS. (P. 40). CONSEQUENTLY, THE
MANAGER IS NOT ACTUALLY MOTIVATING THE EMPLOYEE, BUT IS
PROVIDING THE CONDITIONS WHICH STIR THE EMPLOYEE'S DESIRE
TO ACHIEVE. (P. 41).
JOB CONDITIONS WHICH INFLUENCE JOB BEHAVIOR.
   TWO SETS OF FACTORS ARE POINTED OUT AS BEING

M0405   INFLUENTIAL TOWARD JOB BEHAVIOR: THEY ARE HYGIENE FACTORS
        AND MOTIVATION FACTORS.   HYGIENE FACTORS SURROUND THE DOING
        OF A JOB. (P. 41).   THEY INCLUDE MONEY, PHYSICAL WORKING
        CONDITIONS, RELATIONS WITH FELLOW WORKERS, AND COMPANY
        POLICY AND SUPERVISION. HYGIENE FACTORS CAN CAUSE
        DISSATISFACTION, RESULTING IN LOWER PRODUCTIVITY; BUT THEY
        DO NOT RESULT IN IMPROVED PRODUCTIVITY. MOTIVATION FACTORS,
        ON THE OTHER HAND, DO INCREASE PRODUCTIVITY BECAUSE THEY
        SATISFY THE NEED FOR FULFILLMENT. THEY ARE THOSE FACTORS
        WHICH   ARE INHERENT IN THE JOB ITSELF--NAMELY, JOB
        CHALLENGE AND OPPORTUNITY FOR ACHIEVEMENT. (P. 41).
        SUPERVISOR LEADERSHIP.
             LEADERSHIP IS THE THIRD FACTOR COVERED IN
        THIS ARTICLE THAT INFLUENCES MOTIVATIONAL BEHAVIOR. THE
        PRIMARY TASK OF THE LEADER IS TO   CREATE A CLIMATE IN WHICH
        EMPLOYEES SATISFY THEIR OWN MOTIVES BY WORKING TO FULFILL
        DEPARTMENT OBJECTIVES. (P. 41). THIS INCLUDES THE
        RESPONSIBILITY OF TASK SUPPORT AND OF ORGANIZATION. TASK
        SUPPORT INVOLVES THE MAINTAINING OF THE HYGIENE
        FACTORS AT A SATISFACTORY LEVEL. ORGANIZATION IS PRIMARILY
        CONCERNED WITH PROVIDING WORK THAT IS BOTH CONTRIBUTORY TO
        COMPANY OBJECTIVES AND IS CHALLENGING TO THE EMPLOYEE.
             SINCE   YOU CAN'T MOTIVATE OTHERS; YOU . . . (MUST) . .
        CREATE THE CONDITIONS THAT PERMIT AND ENCOURAGE
        SELF-MOTIVATION. (P. 40). THEREFORE, IT IS THE
        RESPONSIBILITY OF MANAGEMENT TO PROVIDE THE CONDITIONS
        NECESSARY TO MOTIVATE EMPLOYEES AND ENCOURAGE BETTER JOB
        PERFORMANCE.

M0406   SOME INGREDIENTS FOR MAKING IT.
        MANPOWER, AUGUST 1971, PP. 3-9.

             SURVEY SHOWS THAT THOSE WHO HAVE 'MADE IT' HAVE SOME
        CHARACTERISTICS IN COMMON.

M0407   SOMETHING OF VALUE.
        MANPOWER, MARCH 1972, PP. 2-7.

             CHANCES AT A FEDERAL JOB BRINGS OUT THE BEST IN
        DISADVANTAGED YOUTHS.
             PROJECT VALUE IS ONE WAY OF SOLVING SOME OF THE JOB
        DISSATISFACTION PROBLEM. THERE WERE THREE FEDERAL AGENCIES
        INVOLVED. THE CIVIL SERVICE COMMISSION, THE DEFENSE
        DEPARTMENT, AND THE DEPARTMENT OF LABOR'S MANPOWER
        ADMINISTRATION. THE MAIN PORTION OF THE ARTICLE DEALT WITH
        THE DEFENSE DEPARTMENT AT LOUISVILLE.
             THE GOALS WERE TO LOOSEN THE REQUIREMENTS TO GET
        IN THE   NYC.
             TRANSPORTATION AND EDUCATION PROBLEMS POPPED UP ALMOST
        IMMEDIATELY. THERE WAS ADEQUATE PUBLIC TRANSPORTATION TO
        GET THE TRAINEES TO WORK, THEN TO SCHOOL AND BACK HOME
        AGAIN, BUT THE THREE FARES A DAY WERE TOO MUCH FOR SOME OF
        THE PEOPLE TO HANDLE. SO THE GOVERNMENT PAID THE EXTRA
        FARES. EDUCATION PROVED TO BE MORE OF A PROBLEM. THE
        PARTICIPANTS WERE ALL DROPOUTS SO THEY WERE FED UP WITH
        SCHOOL AND CLASSROOMS. THE CLASSROOM WAS MOVED TO THE JOB
        SITE AND THE PARTICIPANTS PROGRESSED AT THEIR OWN SPEED.
             THE RESULTS WERE POSITIVE. THE IMPACT ON THE

M0407 LIFESTYLES OF THE SUCCESSFUL TRAINEES HAS BEEN IMPRESSIVE.
THE PARTICIPANTS NOW KNOW THE NECESSITY OF GETTING TO WORK
ON TIME, OF BEING COOPERATIVE INSTEAD OF CYNICAL, OF
LEARNING THE WORK AND DOING IT RIGHT, AND OF GETTING AN
EDUCATION. TWENTY-EIGHT OUT OF THE FIFTY ENROLLED IN THE
PROGRAMS ARE FEDERAL EMPLOYEES NOW.

M0408 SOMMERS, DIXIE.
OCCUPATIONAL RANKING FOR MEN AND WOMEN BY EARNINGS.
MONTHLY LABOR REVIEW, AUGUST 1974, PP. 34-51.

THE 1970 CENSUS CONFIRMS THAT SKILL, SEX, AND AGE ARE
LIKELY TO DETERMINE THE WORKER'S POSITION ON THE PAY
LADDER.

M0409 SORCHER, MELVIN.
MOTIVATION, PARTICIPATION, AND MYTH.
PERSONNEL ADMINISTRATION 34 (SEPTEMBER 1971):   20-24.

THIS ARTICLE IS DESIGNED TO POINT OUT SOME OF THE
STEPS THAT A MANAGER MUST TAKE IF HE WANTS TO MOTIVATE
EMPLOYEES THROUGH PARTICIPATIVE MANAGEMENT. IT SERVES
AS A SKELETAL OUTLINE OF HOW TO DO IT MANUAL, WITHOUT
A PRESENTATION OF THE THEORY AND RESEARCH WHICH ARE
THE BASIS OF THESE STEPS.

M0410 SORCHER, MELVIN.   DANZIG, SELIG.
CHARTING AND CHANGING THE ORGANIZATIONAL CLIMATE.
PERSONNEL 46 (MARCH 1969): 16-22.

DEFINES AREAS WHICH AFFECT EMPLOYEE MOTIVATION AS
CLIMATE VARIABLES, AND EXPLAINS HOW THESE VARIABLES ARE
RELATED TO EFFECTIVE ORGANIZATIONAL GOAL ACHIEVEMENT.

M0411 NO AUTHOR CITED
SPECIAL TASK FORCE WILL REVIEW ROLE OF GS AND FS
SECRETARIES.
DEPARTMENT OF STATE NEWSLETTER, AUGUST 1974, P. 11.

A SPECIAL TASK FORCE REVIEWS ALL ASPECTS OF THE ROLE OF
THE SECRETARY IN THE CIVIL SERVICE AND THE FOREIGN SERVICE
TO DETERMINE WHETHER THIS FUNCTION IN THE ACHIEVEMENT OF
NATIONAL GOALS IN FOREIGN POLICY HAS KEPT PACE WITH THE
RECENT TRENDS IN SOCIETY.

M0412 SPRINGER, PHILIP B.
WORK ATTITUDES OF DISADVANTAGED BLACK MEN.
MONTHLY LABOR REVIEW 94 (DECEMBER 1971): 66-68.

PRESENTS RESULTS OF A SURVEY ON WORK ATTITUDES IN
POVERTY AREAS.

M0413 STAHL, O. GLENN.
WHAT THE PERSONNEL FUNCTION IS ALL ABOUT.
CIVIL SERVICE JOURNAL 12 (JULY--SEPTEMBER 1971):   10-14.

HOW MANAGEMENT MUST BASE DECISIONS OF THE RESULTING
EFFECTS ON MOTIVATION AND PRODUCTIVITY OF EMPLOYEES.

M0414   THE SPREADING LORDSTOWN SYNDROME.
         BUSINESS WEEK, MARCH-APRIL 1972, PP. 69-70.
              ASSEMBLY-LINE DISPUTES CONTINUE IN AUTOMATED PLANTS.
              AUTOMATION WAS SUPPOSED TO RELIEVE THE DRUDGERY ON THE
         ASSEMBLY LINE WHILE INCREASING PRODUCTIVITY AND PRODUCT
         QUALITY AT GENERAL MOTORS' LORDSTOWN VEGA FACTORY. THIS
         SAME AUTOMATION ALSO DREW LABORS' CRITICAL CRY OF
         DEHUMANIZING WORK.
              UNTIL NOW, THE PROBLEMS OF ASSMEBLY-LINE WORK HAVE BEEN
         DEBATED ON THE ISSUE OF THE SPEED OF WORK. WORKERS NOW
         COMPLAIN THAT THE LATEST AUTOMATION TECHNOLOGY HAS MADE MUCH
         SPEEDIER PRODUCTION POSSIBLE. BUT THE WORK IS LESS CREATIVE
         AND JUST AS PHYSICALLY DEMANDING.
              FOR AUTOMAKERS AND OTHER EMPLOYERS IN THE U. S. AND
         ABROAD, WORKER COMPLAINTS IN AUTOMATED PLANTS, THE
         LORDSTOWN SYNDROME OF HARD WORK AND MORE MONOTONOUS WORK,
         SHAPES UP AS A MAJOR ISSUE IN FUTURE LABOR-MANAGEMENT
         RELATIONS. IF IT HAD NOT BEEN FOR THE HIGH UNEMPLOYMENT
         RATES OF THE RECENT PAST YEARS, THE AUTOMATION
         ISSUE MIGHT WELL HAVE SURFACED EARLIER AND MORE
         DRAMATICALLY.   IF THE ECONOMY WERE BOOMING, WE WOULD HAVE
         THE SEEDS FOR REVOLT.   SAYS GORDON FLEMING, A UNION
         OFFICIAL AT FORD LOCAL 600 IN DETROIT.
              THE SOLUTION TO EASING THE AGONY OF THE ASSEMBLY LINE
         STILL APPEARS TO REMAIN UNFOUND. GENERAL MOTORS APPEARS
         TO BE TAKING THE MOST SYSTEMATIC APPROACH TO STUDYING
         ASSEMBLY LINE WORKER MOTIVATION. IT DEVELOPED AN ENTIRE
         STAFF OF PERSONNEL ADMINISTRATORS TO STUDY THE PROBLEM.
         ONE IDEA WHICH THE STAFF PROPOSED WAS CONCERNED WITH
         CONDUCTING PERIODIC WORKER-MANAGEMENT RAP SESSIONS ON
         ABSENTEEISM AND HOW TO IMPROVE THE ASSEMBLY LINE PROCESS.
         ANOTHER PROPOSAL WAS TO ENLARGE JOBS TO GIVE WORKER
         MORE VARIETY ON THE JOB RATHER THAN ONE SIMPLE TASK.
              HOWEVER, MANY AUTO UNION OFFICIALS SEE NO REAL WAY THAT
         CAN BE CHANGED ENOUGH TO MAKE ASSEMBLY LINE JOBS SEEM MORE
         WORTHWHILE. THEY CLAIM THAT THE SOLUTION MAY LIE IN PAYING
         WORKERS TO ACCEPT THE UNPLEASANTNESS AND CUT THEIR WORK
         TIME SO THAT THEY WILL HAVE SHORTER HOURS AND FEWER YEARS TO
         WORK.

M0416   STANDING, T. E.
         AN APPLICATION OF INFORMATION THEORY TO INDIVIDUAL WORKER
         DIFFERENCES IN SATISFACTION WITH WORK ITSELF.
         PH. D. DISSERTATION, BOWLING GREEN STATE UNIVERSITY, 1972.

              AN INDIVIDUAL JOB MODEL IS USED TO EVALUATE EMPLOYEE'S
         WORK ENVIRONMENT AND RELATED JOB SATISFACTION.

M0417   STANDING, T. E.   GUION, ROBERT M.
         INDIVIDUAL DIFFERENCES IN WORK SATISFACTION.
         MANPOWER RESEARCH AND DEVELOPMENT PROJECTS.
         WASHINGTON, D. C.: U. S. DEPARTMENT OF LABOR, MANPOWER
         ADMINISTRATION, 1971.

              THIS STUDY IS CONCERNED WITH THE DIFFERENCES IN WORK
         SATISFACTION: A STUDY DEALING WITH THE INDIVIDUAL JOB
         SATISFACTION IN RELATION TO THE ENVIRONMENTAL COMPLEXITY OF
         HIS JOB.

M0418 STERNLIEB, STEVEN. BAUMAN, ALVIN.
EMPLOYMENT CHARACTERISTICS OF LOW-WAGE WORKERS.
MONTHLY LABOR REVIEW 95 (JULY 1972): 9-14.

   ANALYSIS OF CHARACTERISTICS OF LOWEST PAID ONE-FOURTH
OF WORKERS PROVIDES A YARDSTICK AGAINST WHICH TO MEASURE
FUTURE PROGRESS.

M0419 APPRENTICESHIP -- AVENUE TO THE SKILLED CRAFTS.
OCCUPATIONAL OUTLOOK QUARTERLY, 15 (SPRING 1971): 17-19.

   OVERVIEW OF APPRENTICESHIP OPPORTUNITIES IN THE
UNITED STATES TODAY, INCLUDING LISTINGS OF STATE
APPRENTICESHIP OUTREACH OFFICES.

M0420 STEVENSON, GLORIA.
CAREER PLANNING FOR HIGH SCHOOL GIRLS.
OCCUPATIONAL OUTLOOK QUARTERLY, SUMMER 1973, PP. 21-31.

   TEENAGERS MUST REALIZE THAT THEY ARE LIKELY TO WORK FOR MANY
MORE YEARS THAN MOST MAY THINK AND SHOULD BEGIN EARLY TO
WEIGH THEIR CAREER NEEDS.

M0421 STEVENSON, GLORIA.
COUNSELING BLACK TEENAGE GIRLS.
OCCUPATIONAL OUTLOOK QUARTERLY, SUMMER 1975, PP. 2-13.

   BLACK TEENAGE GIRLS HAVE HIGHER UNEMPLOYMENT RATES THAN
ANY OTHER GROUP IN THE WORK FORCE. THIS ARTICLE EXPLORES
SOME OF THE REASONS AND DESCRIBES STEPS SCHOOL COUNSELORS
MAY TAKE TO IMPROVE THE SITUATION.

M0422 STEVENSON, GLORIA.
DOES A COLLEGE EDUCATION PAY.
OCCUPATIONAL OUTLOOK QUARTERLY 15 (FALL 1971): 24-27.

   THE ANSWER LIES IN WEIGHING THE RAPIDLY RISING
COSTS OF HIGHER EDUCATION AND THE RECENT DECLINE IN
JOB OPPORTUNITIES FOR NEW GRADUATES AGAINST LONG-TERM
EARNINGS AND EMPLOYMENT BENEFITS ENJOYED BY
COLLEGE-EDUCATED WORKERS.

M0423 STEVENSON, GLORIA.
PHYSICIAN'S ASSISTANT -- MEDICAL OCCUPATION IS THE MAKING.
OCCUPATIONAL OUTLOOK QUARTERLY 15 (SUMMER 1971): 8-13.

   EXAMINES THE PROBLEMS OF JOB PERFORMANCE AND TRAINING
FOR PHYSICIANS' ASSISTANTS.

M0424 STEVENSON, GLORIA.
WHAT YOUNG PEOPLE SHOULD KNOW ABOUT LABOR UNIONS.
OCCUPATIONAL OUTLOOK QUARTERLY 16 (WINTER 1972): 26-31.

   ANSWERS TO IMPORTANT QUESTIONS ABOUT WHY WORKERS JOIN
UNIONS, WHAT UNIONS DO, AND THE BENEFITS AND OBLIGATIONS OF
MEMBERSHIP.

M0425 STEVENSON, GLORIA.

M0425   WORKING FOR YOURSELF -- WHAT'S IT LIKE.
        OCCUPATIONAL OUTLOOK QUARTERLY 17 (SPRING 1973):   21-30.
             A LOOK AT SELF-EMPLOYMENT, ITS DEMANDS AND ADVANTAGES.

M0426   STEVENSON, GLORIA.
        WOMEN: UNCLE SAM WANTS YOU.
        OCCUPATIONAL OUTLOOK QUARTERLY, WINTER 1973, PP. 2-9.

             BY 1973, THE ARMED FORCES HOPE NEARLY TO DOUBLE THEIR
        WOMANPOWER.   FEMALE RECRUITS MAY QUALIFY FOR A VAST ARRAY
        OF JOB SPECIALTIES FORMERLY FOR MEN ONLY.

M0427   STEWART, JEAN.
        JOB RESTRUCTURING. . . ONE ROAD TO INCREASED
        OPPORTUNITIES.
        CIVIL SERVICE JOURNAL 13 (APRIL-JUNE 1973):   1-25.

             THE CIVIL SERVICE IS TAKING STEPS TO RESTRUCTURE JOBS
        TO ALLOW FOR GREATER UPWARD MOBILITY WITHIN THE
        ORGANIZATION.

M0428   STRASSER, A.
        DIFFERENTIALS AND OVERLAPS IN EARNINGS OF BLACKS AND
        WHITES.
        MONTHLY LABOR REVIEW, DECEMBER, 1971, PP. 16-26.

             THOUGH AVERAGE ANNUAL EARNINGS OF BLACKS ARE
        CONSIDERABLY LOWER THAN THOSE OF WHITES, THE EARNINGS
        DISTRIBUTIONS HAVE LARGE OVERLAPPING AREAS.

M0429   STRAUSS, GEORGE.
        WORKER DISSATISFACTION: A LOOK AT THE CAUSES.
        MONTHLY LABOR REVIEW 97 (FEBRUARY 1974):   57-58.

             IN THE PAST, JOB SECURITY WAS TOP PRIORITY TO WORKERS.
        IN CONTRAST, A 1969 SURVEY SHOWED INTERESTING WORK, FIRST
        WITH JOB SECURITY COMING SEVENTH.
             WITH LOW LEVEL NEEDS FULFILLED, WORKERS MAY NOW BE IN A
        POSITION TO DEMAND HIGHER LEVEL NEED SATISFACTION FROM
        EMPLOYMENT.   IF SO, THESE WORKERS ARE LESS LIKELY TO SETTLE
        FOR A JOB THAT IS NOT CHALLENGING, DESPITE THE INCOME AND
        SOCIAL POSITION THAT GOES WITH IT.   REGARDLESS, MOST
        EMPLOYEES STATE THAT THEY ARE SATISFIED WITH THEIR JOBS.
        JOB DISSATISFACTION MAY HAVE INCREASED, BUT PROBABLY NOT BY
        MUCH.
             IT SEEMS THAT JOB SATISFACTION IS A FUNCTION OF
        TECHNOLOGY.   JOBS WITH THE MOST DISSATISFACTION ARE THOSE
        WITH SHORT JOB CYCLES OR LITTLE CHALLENGE.
             THERE ARE MANY ADJUSTMENTS WORKERS MAY MAKE TO
        CHALLENGELESS WORK.   SOME DEVELOP FULL SOCIAL LIVES BOTH ON
        AND OFF THE JOB OR BECOME ACTIVE IN THEIR UNION.
             DISSATISFACTION CAN ALSO BE CAUSED BY LOW INCOME, JOB
        INSECURITY, AND INADEQUATE FRINGE BENEFITS.   STRAUSS
        BELIEVES THAT THE LACK OF CHALLENGE IS MUCH LESS OPPRESSIVE
        THAN THE LACK OF INCOME.   PEOPLE WOULD RATHER BE BORED THAN
        HUNGRY.

M0430   STREETER, TOM.   HAMILTON, BILL.

M0430 WOMANPOWER IN DUNGAREES.
NAVAL AVIATION NEWS, FEBRUARY 1974, PP. 22-23.
FEMALE HIGH PERFORMANCE JET CAPTAINS ENTERED WHAT WAS
ONCE A MAN'S DOMAIN AND ESTABLISHED STATUS AS PROFESSIONALS.

M0431 STREIT, FRED.
EMPLOYEES LEARN WHAT THEY LIVE NOT WHAT THEY ARE TOLD.
PAPER TRADE JOURNAL 166 (JANUARY 258 1971):   36-37.

THE CONCEPT OF GROUP NORMS OF BEHAVIORAL PATTERNS
IS DISCUSSED TOGETHER WITH CONSIDERATION OF HOW
UNDERSTANDING OF THESE NORMS MAY BE USED AS AN EMPLOYEE
MOTIVATION TOOL.

M0432 STRENGTHENING APPRENTICESHIP.
MANPOWER   4 (FEBRUARY 1972):   21-25.

DISCUSSION OF METHODS TO IMPROVE APPRENTICESHIP
PROGRAMS, AND THUS IMPROVE EFFICIENCY AND PRODUCTIVITY.

M0433 SUSKIN, HAROLD.
TESTING A NEW APPROACH TO EVALUATION.
CIVIL SERVICE JOURNAL 15 (JULY-SEPTEMBER 1974):   24-31.

THE FACTOR/POINT RATING METHOD IS DESIGNED TO MAKE THE
JOB EVALUATION PROCESS MORE UNDERSTANDABLE.   IT IS ALSO
HOPED THAT THE NEW METHOD WILL IMPROVE THE ACCURACY AND
CONSISTENCY OF CLASSIFICATION JUDGEMENTS.   THIS NEW APPROACH
COMBINES SEVERAL ADDITIONAL JOB EVALUATION METHODS.
THE FIRST STEP IN DESIGNING THE FACTOR/POINT METHOD
WAS THE SELECTION OF THE FACTORS.   ANOTHER STEP WAS
SELECTION OF A SAMPLE OF POSITIONS TO REPRESENT THE 1.3
MILLION FEDERAL GENERAL SCHEDULE POSITIONS.   THE SAMPLE
CONSISTED OF 3,844 POSITIONS IN 26 FEDERAL AGENCIES AT 256
INSTALLATIONS LOCATED THROUGHOUT THE UNITED STATES.
THE FOLLOWING STEPS WERE TAKEN: A NEW DESK AUDIT WAS
CONDUCTED;   THE EXISTING GRADE LEVEL WAS CHECKED FOR
ACCURACY:THE NEW FACTOR-FORMAT POSITION DESCRIPTION WAS
REVIEWED FOR ACCURACY AND COMPLETENESS;   THE POSITION WAS
REEVALUATED USING THE NEW METHOD;   AND A NEW POSITION DATA
SUMMARY SHEET WAS COMPLETED DOCUMENTING THE EVALUATION
PROCESS.
THE EMPLOYEES AND SUPERVISORS PREFERRED THE NEW METHOD
TO THE OLD.   AN EXTENSIVE TRAINING PROGRAM IS NECESSARY TO
IMPLEMENT A FACTOR/POINT RATING APPROACH.   A LONG TERM
IMPLEMENTATION PERIOD WOULD BE NECESSARY IF A DECISION IS
MADE TO ADOPT THE NEW METHOD.

M0434 SUTERMUSTER, ROBERT A.
EMPLOYEE PERFORMANCE AND EMPLOYEE NEED SATISFACTION
-- WHICH COMES FIRST.
CALIFORNIA MANAGEMENT REVIEW 13 (SUMMER 1971):   43-47.

WHAT IS THE CAUSE AND EFFECT RELATIONSHIP BETWEEN EMPLOYEE
PERFORMANCE AND NEED SATISFACTION?   SATISFACTION WITH ONE'S
POSITION IN A NETWORK OF RELATIONSHIPS NEED NOT IMPLY STRONG
MOTIVATION TO OUTSTANDING PERFORMANCE WITHIN THAT SYSTEM.
OUTSTANDING PERFORMANCE CAN LEAD TO A GREATER SATISFACTION

M0434   OF NEEDS. MOST PEOPLE GET THEIR REWARDS IN KNOWING THAT
         THEY HAVE ACCOMPLISHED A JOB AND HAVE DONE IT WELL.
         IN THE PORTER AND LAWLER MODEL THEY PREDICT THAT
         SATISFACTION RESULTS FROM PERFORMANCE ITSELF. AS
         THE PERSON SEEKS HIGHER REWARDS HE WILL INCREASE
         HIS EFFORT SO THAT HE CAN OBTAIN THESE REWARDS.
         PEOPLE WHO HAVE NOT SATISFIED THEIR NEEDS IN A JOB IN
         WHICH THEY ARE EMPLOYED, CAN SEEK A JOB IN THE SAME FIRM
         THAT HAS BETTER REWARDS OR THEY CAN LOOK FOR ANOTHER JOB
         WITH A NEW FIRM. IF A PERSON FEELS THAT HIS CHANCES OF
         SATISFYING HIS NEEDS ARE WORTHLESS HE MAY GIVE UP. THIS
         BEHAVIOR IS STRONGLY INFLUENCED BY HIS LEVEL OF ASPIRATION.
         PEOPLE THAT ARE SATISFIED WITH THEIR REWARDS STILL WONDER IF
          THEIR EFFORT WILL DROP TO A LOWER LEVEL OR WILL BE
         MAINTAINED AT THE PRESENT LEVEL AND MANY OTHER QUESTIONS
         ALSO ARISE. A PERSON WHO IS SATISFIED WILL TRY TO DO HIS
         BEST AT ALL TIMES SO HE CAN STAY AT THE JOB HE IS DOING
         THE PRESENT TIME.
          THE DEGREE OF SATISFACTION WILL AFFECT A PERSON'S LEVEL OF
          ASPIRATION IN THE PERFORMANCE-SATISFACTION CYCLE. IF A
         PERSON WANTS HIGHER REWARDS, HE WILL WORK HARDER, IF A
         PERSON IS HAPPY WITH THE REWARDS HE IS NOW GETTING, HE WILL
         DO HIS BEST TO STAY THERE. IF A PERSON WHO HAS LOW REWARDS
         AND WANTS TO MOVE UP, HE WILL HAVE TO WORK HARDER SO THAT HE
         CAN DO SO.

M0435   SVENSON, A. L.
         MORATORIUM ON MOTIVATION.
         SAM ADVANCED MANAGEMENT JOURNAL 36 (APRIL 1971):   26-31.

              THE STATURE IN WHICH THE MEMBER OF AN ORGANIZATION
         HOLDS HIMSELF IS DIRECTLY A REFLECTION OF THE STATURE
         MANAGEMENT ACCORDS HIM IN THE DECISION-MAKING AREA. IF
         DECISION AUTHORITY IS DENIED AT THE LOCAL JOB LEVEL, THE
         COMPANY IS, IN EFFECT, TELLING THE INDIVIDUAL THAT
         HE HAS NO PROSPECT OF BECOMING INVOLVED. SINCE HE
         IS NOT INVOLVED, MANAGEMENT CANNOT EXPECT HIM TO BE
         MOTIVATED.

M0436   TAGGART, ROBERT.
         MANPOWER PROGRAMS FOR CRIMINAL OFFENDERS.
         MONTHLY LABOR REVIEW 95 (AUGUST 1972):   17-24.

              VOCATIONAL EDUCATION, WORK RELEASE, AND OTHER
         APPROACHES TO THE COMPLEX MANPOWER NEEDS OF RELEASED
         PRISONERS ARE BEING TESTED.

M0437   TAKING AIM ON JOBS.
         MANPOWER, NOVEMBER 1970, PP. 14-20.

              PROJECT AIM TRIES TO MAKE THE HARD CORE UNEMPLOYED,
         "EMPLOYABLE" THROUGH TRAINING AND MOTIVATION.

M0438   TANNEHILL, ROBERT E.
         MOTIVATION AND MANAGEMENT DEVELOPMENT.
         LONDON: BUTTERWORTH. 1970.

              EXPANSION ON THE ROLE OF ENLIGHTENED PROFESSIONAL

M0438 MANAGERS IN USE OF COLLABORATION AS OPPOSED TO FORCE.
DISCUSSION OF MOTIVATIONAL NEEDS AND DEVELOPMENT, THE
PROCESS OF MOTIVATION, AND CREATING A MOTIVATIONAL
CLIMATE.

M0439 TEAM SPIRIT RESULTS IN HIGHER PRODUCTIVITY, JOB
SATISFACTION.
COMMERCE TODAY, SEPTEMBER 30, 1974   PP. 5-6.

TEAMWORK AS A METHOD OF IMPROVING MORALE AND
PRODUCTIVITY AS USED BY THE R. G. BARRY CORPORATION.

M0440 TEMPLETON, JANE.
MANPOWER MANAGEMENT: NO ONE'S SELLING YOUTH ON SELLING.
SALES MANAGEMENT 106 (MARCH 15, 1971): 54.

A CRITICAL LOOK AT THE GENERATION GAP BETWEEN
COLLEGE GRADUATES AND MANAGEMENT AND WAYS TO CLOSE
THE GAP BY MAKING COLLEGE MORE MEANINGFUL FOR SURVIVAL.
GIVE THE COLLEGE STUDENTS A BETTER REAL-WORLD PICTURE
AND YOU WILL INCREASE YOUR BENEFITS RATHER THAN COSTS.

M0441 THEODORE, GEORGE V.
TAKING THE STING OUT OF PROJECT REASSIGNMENT.
MANAGEMENT REVIEW 60 (JANUARY 1971): 54-57.

THIS ARTICLE GIVES A GENERAL OVERVIEW OF SOME PROBLEMS
OF PROJECT MANAGEMENT.
THE MAIN PROBLEM DISCUSSED IS THE SHIFTING OF PERSONNEL
DURING THE TERMINATING PHASE OF A PROJECT AND THE RESULTING
ANXIETY AND TURNOVER.
THEORDORE POINTS OUT THAT BECAUSE OF THE NATURE OF A
PROJECT GROUP (I. E. GROWING FROM A SMALL TO A LARGE AND
COHESIVE GROUP) THERE CAN BE, SOMETIMES, A GOOD DEAL OF
FEAR AT A PROJECT END. A COMPANY THAT HAS NEVER FACED A
PROBLEM LIKE THIS IS LIKELY TO HAVE A HARD TIME ADJUSTING
ITS PERSONNEL.
INTRAGROUP RELATIONS MANY TIMES DETERMINE HOW A
GROUP WILL PERCEIVE A BREAKUP. IF DONE CORRECTLY AND IN
SUCH A WAY THAT THE INDIVIDUAL REALIZES WHY THE BREAKUP IS
HAPPENING, THEN TENSIONS MAY BE REDUCED.
THEODORE GOES ON TO DESCRIBE SOME OF THE RESULTS OF
UNSUCCESSFUL REASSIGNMENT, SUCH AS TURNOVER. HE SAYS
PROBLEMS COULD BE MINIMIZED IF CAPABILITIES WERE USED AS
CRITERIA FOR REASSIGNMENT.
THEODORE STRESSES THAT CONFLICT AND FRUSTRATION ARE
MAJOR PROBLEMS THAT CAN'T BE IGNORED BECAUSE OF POSSIBLE
ECONOMIC REPERCUSSIONS.

M0443 TORBERT, W. R.   ROGERS, MALCOLM R.
BEING FOR THE MOST PART PUPPETS.
CAMBRIDGE, MASS.: SCHENKMAN PUBLISHING COMPANY, 1973.

RESULTS OF AN EXPERIMENT ON 209 MEN IN NEW HAVEN,
CONN. TO ANALYZE RATINGS OF THEIR JOBS AND THEIR
LEISURE TIME. DONE IN 1964, RESULTS SEEM TO SHOW A
POSITIVE RELATION BETWEEN JOB INVOLVEMENT AND
CONSTRUCTIVE USE OF LEISURE TIME.

M0444 TOSI, HENRI.
       ORGANIZATION STRESS AS A MODERATOR OF THE RELATIONSHIP
       BETWEEN INFLUENCE AND ROLE RESPONSE.
       ACADEMY OF MANAGEMENT, 14 (MARCH 1971): 7-22.

            THIS ARTICLE DEALS WITH ROLE CONFLICT AND HOW IT IS
       SIGNIFICANTLY RELATED TO JOB SATISFACTION, JOB THREAT, AND
       ANXIETY, BUT NOT TO AN EFFECTIVENESS MEASURE. IN ROLE
       CONFLICT AND ROLE AMBIGUITY THERE ARE TYPES OF ROLE
       DISCREPANCY RELATED TO THE RESPONSE VARIABLES. THREE
       ASPECTS OF THE FOCAL PERSON'S RESPONSES WERE CORRELATED WITH
       ROLE CONFLICT AND ROLE AMBIGUITY. EFFECTIVENESS IS A
       RESPONSE MEASURE WHICH IS INDICATIVE OF THE DEGREE OF
       COMPLIANCE OF THE FOCAL PERSON WITH PRESSURES TO PRODUCE.
       JOB THREAT AND ANXIETY IS THE SECOND ROLE RESPONSE
       VARIABLE; IT IS A MORE SPECIFIC FORM OF THE MOTIVE OF
       ANXIETY. ANXIETY HERE IS MORE ORIENTED TOWARD THE JOB OF
       MANAGER. JOB SATISFACTION, THE THIRD VARIABLE, IS
       CONSIDERED TO BE AN AFFECTIVE RESPONSE TO ROLE PRESSURES.
       THIS ARTICLE HAD DATA THAT WERE COLLECTED FROM 488 MANAGERS
       OF CONSUMER LOAN OFFICES OF A LARGE, GEOGRAPHICALLY
       DISPERSED FINANCE ORGANIZATION. THE BRANCH MANAGER DEALS
       WITH TWO TO SEVEN EMPLOYEES IN HIS OFFICE. HE DEALS
       DIRECTLY WITH THE CUSTOMERS IN NEGOTIATING LOANS.
            THE BRANCH MANAGER REPORTS TO A REGIONAL SUPERVISOR WHO
       HAS BETWEEN 25 AND 30 BRANCHES IN HIS REGION. A
       QUESTIONNAIRE WAS DISTRIBUTED MAIL TO 537 BRANCH MANAGERS.
       MANY QUESTIONS ON JOB SATISFACTION AND JOB THREAT AND
       ANXIETY WERE MEASURED ON A SCALE RANGING FROM 1-5 WITH
       DEGREES FROM VERY MUCH TO VERY LITTLE. EFFECTIVENESS
       WAS CALCULATED BY SIMPLY COMPUTING THE PROFITABILITY OF
       EACH OFFICE. THIS IS A RATIO OF THE NET PROFITS FOR AN
       OFFICE TO THE TOTAL AMOUNT OF CAPITAL INVESTMENT IN THAT
       OFFICE. MEASURES OF ROLE CONFLICT AND ROLE AMBIGUITY WERE
       COMBINED TO FORM DIFFERENT ORGANIZATION STRESS LEVELS. THEY
       WERE MEASURED BY A 10-ITEM SUBSCALES FOR EACH CONCEPT.
            THREE LEVELS OF STRESS WERE CONSIDERED: HIGH-STRESS
       SITUATIONS WERE THOSE IN WHICH THE RESPONDENT REPORTED HE
       EXPERIENCED HIGH ROLE CONFLICT AND HIGH ROLE AMBIGUITY,
       MODERATE-STRESS SITUATIONS WERE DEFINED AS THOSE CASES IN
       WHICH THE RESPONDENT REPORTED WHETHER HIGH ROLE AMBIGUITY,
       AND LOW-STRESS SITUATIONS WERE DEFINED AS THOSE CASES IN
       WHICH THE RESPONDENT REPORTED LOW ROLE CONFLICT AND ROLE
       AMBIGUITY.
       SUMMARY: INFLUENCE WAS NOT CORRELATED WITH JOB ANXIETY OR
       TO EFFECTIVENESS IN HIGH-STRESS CONDITIONS; IT WAS IN THE
       LOW-STRESS SITUATIONS. IT MAY BE THAT IF INFLUENCE DOES
       AFFECT THE LEVEL OF EFFECTIVENESS AND JOB ANXIETY, IT DOES
       SO WHEN THERE IS A HIGHLY STABLE ORGANIZATION ENVIRONMENT.

M0445 TICHY, NOEL M.
       AN ANALYSIS OF CLIQUE FORMATION AND STRUCTURE IN
       ORGANIZATIONS.
       ADMINISTRATIVE SCIENCE QUARTERLY 13 (JUNE 1973): 194-208.

            IN THIS ARTICLE A NUMBER OF TESTABLE PROPOSITIONS
       ARE DEVELOPED WHICH RELATE THE VARIABLES OF COMPLIANCE,
       MOBILITY AND SIZE TO MOTIVATION FOR CLIQUE FORMATION AND TO

M0445 CONSTRAINTS WITHIN WHICH CLIQUES FORM.

M0446 U. S. BUREAU OF LABOR STATISTICS.
IMPROVING PRODUCTIVITY; LABOR AND MANAGEMENT APPROACHES.
(WASHINGTON, D. C., GOVERNMENT PRINTING OFFICE, 1971):
PP. 35

           THIS BULLETIN PRESENTS EXAMPLES OF FORMAL EFFORTS BY
LABOR AND MANAGEMENT TO IMPROVE PRODUCTIVITY. THE FOCUS IS
ON PLANT LEVEL PRACTICES THAT ARE WITHIN THE CONTROL OF
MANAGEMENT UNIONS, LEAVING BROAD ECONOMIC, TECHNOLOGICAL,
INSTITUTIONAL, AND OTHER FACTORS THAT AFFECT PRODUCTIVITY
CHANGE FOR EXAMINATION IN OTHER STUDIES.
           CONTENTS: RETRAINING PROGRAMS; WORK RULES
SETTLEMENTS; METHODS OF ADJUSTING TO TECHNOLOGICAL CHANGE;
MANPOWER PLANNING; PLANTWIDE PRODUCTIVITY INCENTIVE PLANS;
FORMAL UNION-MANAGEMENT COOPERATIVE PROGRAMS; JOB REDESIGN;
ABSENTEEISM AND HOURS OF WORK; SELECTED BIBLIOGRAPHY.

M0447 U. S. BUREAU OF LABOR STATISTICS.
THE MEANING AND MEASUREMENT OF PRODUCTIVITY.
(WAHINGTON, D. C.: GOVERNMENT PRINTING OFFICE, 1971):
PP. 15

PREPARED FOR THE NATIONAL COMMISSION ON PRODUCTIVITY.

M0448 U. S. BUREAU OF LABOR STATISTICS.
PRODUCTIVITY ANALYSIS IN MANUFACTURING PLANTS.
WASHINGTON,, D. C.: GOVERNMENT PRINTING OFFICE 1970):

BY BENJAMIN P. KLOTZ.
           REPORTS ON A RESEARCH STUDY WHICH MEASURED ALTERNATIVE
MEANS FOR ESTIMATING COMMON TYPES OF INDUSTRIAL PRODUCTION
FUNCTIONS IN 1729 PLANTS OF 23 INDUSTRIES.

M0449 U. S. CIVIL SERVICE COMMISSION.
EXECUTIVE MANPOWER MANAGEMENT.
PERSONNEL BIBLIOGRAPHY SERIES, VOL. 40. WASHINGTON, D.C.:
GOVERNMENT PRINTING OFFICE NO.   0-6000-0616, 1971.

           AN ANNOTATED BIBLIOGRAPHY OF PUBLICATIONS AVAILABLE
IN THE FIELD, ESPECIALLY AS IT RELATES TO PUBLIC EXECUTIVES.
INCLUDES RESEARCH STUDIES AS WELL AS BOOKS AND ARTICLES.

M0450 U. S. CIVIL SERVICE COMMISSION.
JOB ANALYSIS: KEY TO BETTER MANAGEMENT.
SEPTEMBER 1971.
PERSONNEL BIBLIOGRAPHY SERIES, VOL. 42.
WASHINGTON, D.C.: GOVERNMENT PRINTING OFFICE NO. 0-600-0618
1971.

           THE USE OF JOB ANALYSIS TOOLS USED BY MANAGEMENT.
THE PERSONNEL MANAGEMENT FUNCTION: ORGANIZATION, STAFFING
AND EVALUATION.
           AN ANNOTATED BIBLIOGRAPHY OF RESEARCH STUDIES,
ARTICLES AND BOOKS. TEXTBOOKS AND HANDBOOKS IN PERSONNEL
ADMINISTRATION ARE INCLUDED.
PLANNING ORGANIZATION AND EVALUATING TRAINING

M0450   PROGRAMS.

M0451   U. S. DEPARTMENT OF THE AIR FORCE.
        ANALYSIS OF RACIAL DIFFERENCES IN TERMS OF WORK ASSIGNMENTS,
        JOB INTEREST, AND FELT UTILIZATION OF TALENTS AND TRAINING,
        BY RAYMOND E. CHRISTEL.
        PROJECT 7723, SEPTEMBER 1972.
        U. S. GOVERNMENT PRINTING OFFICE NO. 0-600-0617, 1971.
        PERSONNEL BIBLIOGRAPHY SERIES, VOL. 41. WASHINGTON, D. C.:

            AN ANNOTATED BIBLIOGRAPHY OF RESULTS OF WORKSHOP
        SESSIONS, ARTICLES, BOOKS AND BIBLIOGRAPHIES IN THE
        FIELD OF TRAINING.
            THIS STUDY WAS MADE IN CONJUNCTION WITH A LARGER STUDY
        OF 11 CAREER LADDERS IN WHICH THE GOAL WAS TO DETERMINE
        WHETHER THE DIFFICULTY LEVEL OF WORK ASSIGNED FIRST-TERM
        AIRMEN WAS ASSOCIATED WITH APTITUDE LEVEL. BLACKS
        COMPRISED 19 PERCENT OF THE CASES STUDIED, SO THE DATA WERE,
        IN ADDITION, ANALYZED FOR RACIAL DIFFERENCES ON VARIABLES
        SUCH AS THE DIFFICULTY OF WORK LEVEL ASSIGNED, JOB INTEREST,
        AND FELT UTILIZATION.
        THE STUDY INCLUDED 380 CASES. INDIVIDUALS WERE
        ASKED TO COMPLETE GENERAL BACKGROUND INFORMATION IN WHICH
        THEY PROVIDED DATA CONCERNING THEIR IDENTIFICATION, JOB
        LOCATION, EDUCATION, MONTHS ON THE JOB, MONTHS IN THE
        CAREER LADDER, MONTHS IN THE SERVICE, COURSES TAKEN,
        EQUIPMENT WORKED ON, AND TOOLS UTILIZED. THE AIRMEN ALSO
        INDICATED THEIR INTEREST IN THE JOB, FELT UTILIZATION,
        AND REENLISTMENT INTENTIONS.
            APPLICATION OF A MULTIPLE LINEAR REGRESSION MODEL WAS
        USED AS AN APPROACH. THIS DETERMINED THE RELATIONSHIPS
        BETWEEN RACE AND OTHER CRITERIA, HOLDING CONSTANT SUCH
        VARIABLES AS APTITUDE, TIME IN MILITARY SERVICE, TECHNICAL
        SCHOOL GRADUATION STATUS, AND TIME ON THE JOB. TWO SEPARATE
        REGRESSION EQUATIONS WERE USED. ONE INCLUDED RACE AMONG THE
        PREDICTORS, AND ONE EXCLUDED RACE FROM THE PREDICTOR SET.
        IN OBSERVING THE DIFFERENCES, IT COULD BE DETERMINED WHETHER
        BLACKS SCORE LOWER OR HIGHER THAN NON-BLACKS ON A PARTICULAR
        ITEM, OTHER FACTORS BEING HELD CONSTANT.
        SLIGHTLY LESS DIFFICULT JOBS.
        AIR PASSENGER/AIR CARGO AND ADMINISTRATIVE. SINCE THE
        DIFFERENCES WERE SO SMALL, IT CAN BE CONCLUDED THAT THERE
        WERE NO PRACTICAL DIFFERENCES IN THE TYPES OF ASSIGNMENTS
        BEING GIVEN TO BLACKS AND NON-BLACKS IN THE 11 CAREER
        LADDERS INVESTIGATED. IN THE TWO LADDERS OF COMMUNICATIONS
        AND ADMINISTRATIVE CAREER, BLACKS FELT THEY WERE BEING
        BETTER UTILIZED. THERE WAS NO DIFFERENCE IN FELT
        UTILIZATION BETWEEN BLACKS AND NON-BLACKS IN THE REMAINING
        NINE LADDERS.

M0452   U. S. DEPARTMENT OF THE AIR FORCE.
        REPORTED JOB INTEREST AND PERCEIVED UTILIZATION OF TALENTS
        AND TRAINING BY AIRMEN IN 97 CAREER LADDERS, BY R. BRUCE
        GOULD. PROJECT 7734, DECEMBER 1972.

            THE PURPOSE OF THIS STUDY WAS TO REPORT FINDINGS AND
        DRAW CONCLUSIONS ON THE LEVELS OF JOB SATISFACTION IN 97
        CAREER LADDERS. ITS INITIAL GOAL WAS TO BEGIN THE STUDY ON

M0452 JOB SATISFACTION OR DISSATISFACTION AMONG SPECIFIC CAREER
LADDERS, AND WAS EXPECTED TO BE FOLLOWED UP WITH FURTHER
STUDIES. THIS REPORT IS INTENDED FOR THE USE OF BEHAVORIAL
SCIENCE RESEARCH AND IS NOT INTENDED FOR USE BY
OPERATIONAL OR MANAGERIAL PERSONNEL.

THIS STUDY COVERS 100,000 AIRMEN IN THE 3-, 5-, AND 7-
SKILL LEVELS. DATA WERE COLLECTED ON TWO DIMENSIONS OF JOB
SATISFACTION, AS PART OF THE USAF OCCUPATIONAL SURVEY
PROGRAM. RESPONDENTS WERE ASKED TO USE 7-POINT SCALES TO
INDICATE THEIR JOB INTEREST RANGING FROM EXTREMELY DULL TO
EXTREMELY INTERESTING AND THE EXTENT TO WHICH THEIR JOBS
UTILIZE THEIR TALENTS AND TRAINING WITH RESPONSES FROM
NOT AT ALL TO PERFECTLY.

THE SURVEY OF 3- AND 5-LEVEL AIRMEN INDICATED THAT
THEIR JOBS WERE SO-SO TO FAIRLY INTERESTING. THEIR
PERCEIVED UTILIZATION OF TALENTS AVERAGED FROM FAIRLY WELL
TO QUITE WELL. THE 7-LEVEL WAS FOUND TO RATE
THEIR JOBS AS VERY INTERESTING, AND THEIR PERCEIVED
UTILIZATION OF TALENTS AS VERY WELL . THIS SUGGESTS THAT,
AS THE SKILL LEVEL INCREASES, THE DEGREE OF JOB SATISFACTION
AND JOB UTILIZATION INCREASES, AND HENCE MOTIVATION.

CAUTION MUST BE EXERCISED IN MAKING COMPARISONS BETWEEN
SPECIFIC LADDERS, AS SURVEY DATES VARY OVER AN INTERVAL OF
FIVE YEARS. FOR EXAMPLE, SUBSTANTIAL CHANGES IN THE
PERCENTAGE OF EXPRESSED FEELINGS OF POOR UTILIZATION
OCCURRED AMONG THE ACCOUNTING DISBURSEMENT LADDER FROM 30 TO
45 PERCENT, AND AMONG THE AEROSPACE GROUND EQUIPMENT LADDER
FROM 19 TO 36 PERCENT. THE CONCLUSION DRAWN AMONG THE
SURVEYORS WAS THAT THE INCREASE COULD BE THE RESULT OF THE
GENERAL INCREASE IN DISSATISFACTION AMONG ENLISTEES DURING
THE TIME SPAN, CHANGES IN TASKS PERFORMED ON THE JOB, OR
CHANGES IN THE APTITUDE AND EDUCATIONAL CHARACTERISTICS OF
THE PERSONNEL ASSIGNED TO THESE CAREER FIELDS IN THE PAST
FEW YEARS.

SUMMARIZING, MOST AIRMEN SURVEYED FOUND THEIR JOBS
INTERESTING AND THEIR TALENTS UTILIZED. THERE WERE DEFINITE
DIFFERENCES IN SATISFACTION LEVELS BETWEEN CAREER LADDERS
AND INDIVIDUALS. LADDER-BY-LADDER STUDIES ARE CURRENTLY
BEING INITIATED TO IDENTIFY FACTORS CAUSING THESE
DIFFERENCES AND TO EVALUATE THE IMPACT WHICH WORK PERFORMED
HAS ON CAREER DECISIONS.

M0453 U. S. DEPARTMENT OF LABOR.
DRIVING AMBITION PAYS OFF IN JOBS.
MANPOWER 3 (APRIL 1971): 28-30.

THIS ARTICLE IS BASICALLY A STUDY OF THE SHORTAGE OF
DRIVING EDUCATION INSTRUCTORS AND WHAT IS BEING DONE TO
SOLVE THE PROBLEM.

THE U. S. DEPARTMENT OF LABOR IS FUNDING ADULTS WITH
TRAINING AT AGENCIES SUCH AS, EASY METHOD DRIVING SCHOOL
THROUGH THE JOB OPPORTUNITIES IN THE BUSINESS SECTOR (JOBS)
PROGRAM.

THE JOBS CONTRACT CALLS FOR NINE MONTHS OF TRAINING FOR
22 INSTRUCTORS AND THREE OFFICE CLERKS. EASY METHOD HIRED
NORTHERN SYSTEMS COMPANY, A SUBSIDIARY OF NORTHERN NATURAL
GAS COMPANY OF OMAHA, TO PROVIDE JOB RELATED EDUCATION,
ORIENTATION, AND COUNSELING FOR THE TRAINEES AND TO INSTRUCT

M0453   SUPERVISORS IN HANDLING DISADVANTAGED EMPLOYEES. ON-THE-JOB
        TRAINING IS THE METHOD USED BY EASY METHOD. THIS COST THE
        FEDERAL GOVERNMENT $67,000.
                TRAINEES BEGIN THEIR NINE MONTH COURSE WITH 40 HOURS
        OF ORIENTATION. FOR THE NEXT 16 WEEKS THEY GET TEN HOURS
        A WEEK OF BASIC EDUCATION, TWO HOURS OF COUNSELING, AND 28
        HOURS OF ON-THE-JOB TRAINING TAUGHT BY EXPERIENCED
        SUPERVISORS. THE BASIC EDUCATION INCLUDES TEACHING
        TECNIQUES, SOCIAL SKILLS, AND READING AND MATH IF REQUIRED.
        THE LAST 22 WEEKS ARE SPENT ALMOST SOLELY IN ON-THE-JOB
        TRAINING WITH TWO HOURS OF WEEKLY COUNSELING IF NEEDED.
                TRAINEES WHO ARE HIRED FIRST AND TRAINED LATER ARE
        PAID TWO DOLLARS AN HOUR FROM THE TIME THEY ARE ACCEPTED BY
        EASY METHOD FOLLOWING CERTIFICATION BY THE EMPLOYMENT
        SERVICE THAT THEY QUALIFY AS HARD-CORE UNEMPLOYED. THE PAY
        INCREASES TO $2.40 AN HOUR AFTER 16 WEEKS AND $2.90 AN HOUR
        PLUS DOUBLE TIME FOR OVERTIME AT THE END OF NINE MONTHS.
        ONCE THEY BEGIN TEACHING, EVEN ON AN ON-THE-JOB TRAINING
        BASIS, THEY ARE PERMITTED TO HAVE THEIR TRAINING CARS FOR
        THEIR OWN PERSONAL USE. THE PROGRAM STARTED IN AUGUST 1970.
        BY THE END OF JANUARY, 34 MEN AND WOMEN HAD BEEN HIRED, AND
        20 WERE STILL IN TRAINING. OF THE 14 DROPOUTS, TEN LEFT
        BECAUSE THEY WERE NOT QUALIFIED TO BECOME DRIVING
        INSTRUCTORS, ACCORDING TO RICHARD L. KLASS, A
        NORTHERN SYSTEMS TECHNICAL CONSULTANT AND TRAINER.
                IN CONCLUSION, NORTHERN SYSTEMS CLAIM THEY WERE HAPPY
        TO SIGN A CONTRACT WITH JOBS BECAUSE THEY SUPPORT THE
        OBJECTIVES OF THE PROGRAM TO HIRE AND TRAIN THE
        DISADVANTAGED FOR GOOD JOBS.

M0454   U. S. DEPARTMENT OF LABOR.
        JOB SATISFACTION: IS THERE A TREND.
        MANPOWER MONOGRAPH NO. 30, 1974.

                THIS REPORT REVIEWS SOME OF THE MAJOR RESEARCH ON JOB
        SATISFACTION THAT HAS BEEN CONDUCTED IN THE PAST 40 YEARS.

M0455   U. S. DEPARTMENT OF LABOR.
        MANPOWER PROGRAMS IN FOUR CITIES.
        MANPOWER 4 (JANUARY 1972): 8-12.

                MANPOWER PROGRAMS HAVE DONE A GOOD JOB OF PREPARING
        THE DISADVANTAGED FOR STEADY WORK AND BETTER PAY. THE
        OLYMPUS RESEARCH CORPORATION HAS MADE A STUDY AND COMPLETED
        A REPORT ENTITLED THE TOTAL IMPACT OF MANPOWER PROGRAMS: A
        FOUR-CITY CASE STUDY.
                THE CITIES STUDIED WERE SAN FRANCISCO, OAKLAND, BOSTON
        AND DENVER. A FOLLOW-UP SAMPLE FOR MEASURING THE IMPACT OF
        TRAINING, REMEDIAL EDUCATION, LANGUAGE, AND ORIENTATION
        PROGRAMS CONSISTED OF 1,709 PERSONS WHO WERE ENROLLED
        BETWEEN OCTOBER 1969 AND FEBRUARY 1970 IN MANPOWER PROGRAMS
        UNDER THE MANPOWER DEVELOPMENT AND TRAINING ACT. THERE WAS
        LITTLE DIFFERENCE AMONG THE ENROLLEES IN THE FOUR CITIES
        STUDIED IN AVERAGE AGE, EDUCATION, SIZE OF HOUSEHOLD OR
        NUMBER OF DEPENDENTS. AVERAGE AGE WAS 28, EDUCATION
        SLIGHTLY ABOVE 10 YEARS, AND SIZE OF HOUSEHOLDS BETWEEN 4
        AND 4.5 PEOPLE. LENGTH OF TIME IN THE PROGRAMS VARIED
        FROM 5.9 MONTHS IN BOSTON TO 10.2 IN OAKLAND.

M0455 SUPPORTIVE SERVICES, SUCH AS HEALTH AND DENTAL CARE, CHILD CARE, AND LEGAL ASSISTANCE WERE FOUND TO BE NECESSARY FOR A SUCCESSFUL PROGRAM.

ACROSS ALL CITIES AND PROGRAMS THE AVERAGE ENROLLEE IN A TRAINING PROGRAM WAS SUBSTANTIALLY AND SOMETIMES SPECTACULARLY BETTER OFF IN TERMS OF EMPLOYMENT STABILITY AND EARNINGS BECAUSE OF HIS PROGRAM PARTICIPATION. IN MEASURING THE SIZE OF GAINS MADE BY INDIVIDUAL PARTICIPANTS, THE STUDY FOUND THAT THOSE WHO STARTED FROM LOWER BASE TENDED TO MAKE THE GREATEST GAINS. THE PROGRAM'S GREATEST PROBLEM WAS THAT RELATIVELY FEW OF ITS WELFARE MOTHERS CHOSE TO SEEK EMPLOYMENT FOLLOWING ENROLLEMNT. ONE OF THE ODDITIES OF THE SURVEY WAS THAT IT SHOWED A SURPRISINGLY GOOD PERFORMANCE FOR TRAINING WITH POOR SCHOOLING.

ALTHOUGH GAINS IN INCOME AND EMPLOYMENT STABILITY WERE CONSIDERABLE, THE REPORT NOTES THAT THE INCOME OF PARTICIPANTS WAS STILL NOTHING TO CHEER ABOUT. THE AVERAGE ENROLLEE ACROSS THE FOUR CITIES GAINED $1,380 A YEAR IN EARNINGS AFTER TRAINING. HOWEVER, THE AVERAGE ENROLLEE WHO WORKED FOLLOWING TRAINING WAS STILL EARNING ONLY AT A RATE OF $3,000 PER YEAR. POVERTY HAS BEEN MADE SUBSTANTIALLY MORE COMFORTABLE BUT NOT ELIMINATED.

IN CONCLUSION THE PROGRAMS HAVE HAD THE RESOURCES TO ENROLL ONLY A FRACTION OF THOSE ELIGIBLE AND A VERY SMALL PROPORTION OF THE LABOR MARKET PARTICIPANTS. BUT IN GENERAL, THE MOST VITAL AND PRODUCTIVE SEVICES HAVE BEEN BASIC EDUCATION AND LANGUAGE TRAINING FOR THOSE WHO NEEDED IT AND SKILL TRAINING FOR THOSE WHO HAVE RECEIVED IT.

M0456 U. S. NATIONAL COMMISSION ON PRODUCTIVITY.
PRODUCTIVITY AND THE NATIONAL INTEREST.
WASHINGTON, D.C.: GOVERNMENT PRINTING OFFICE, 1971. 13 PP.

A POLICY STATEMENT ISSUED BY GEORGE P. SHULTZ AS CHAIRMAN OF THIS PRESIDENTIAL COMMISSION, WHICH WAS CREATED TO RECOMMEND WAYS TO FURTHER PRODUCTIVITY IMPROVEMENT. IDENTIFIES SIX TARGET OPPORTUNITIES, WHICH INCLUDE IMPROVED PRODUCTIVITY OF GOVERNMENT PERSONNEL RESOURCES.

M0457 U. S. VETERANS ADMINSTRATION.
SURVEY OF FACTORS RELATING TO JOB SATISFACTION AMONG VA NURSES.
1960-1970, VETERANS ADMINISTRATION, WASHINGTON, D.C. 20420.

THE PURPOSE OF THIS REPORT WAS TO STUDY THE FACTORS RELATED TO JOB SATISFACTION AMONG VA NURSES. THIS STUDY WAS PERFORMED IN 1970 AS A FOLLOW-UP TO A PREVIOUS STUDY DONE IN 1960. THE 1960 STUDY FOCUSED PRIMARILY ON CAUSES OF TURNOVER AMONG VA NURSES. IT ALSO PROVIDED MANY CLUES RELATED TO JOB SATISFACTION. A DM&S TASK FORCE DECIDED TO INVESTIGATE MORE FULLY THE JOB SATISFACTION CLUES THAT CAME TO LIGHT IN 1960, AND INITIATED A STUDY IN 1970. THE SURVEYORS FELT THAT THE ORGANIZATIONAL AND RELATIONSHIP PROBLEMS OF 1960 CLUES WERE RELATED TO THE SOCIETAL PROBLEMS OF 1970.

TO COMPILE THE DATA FOR THE 1970 STUDY, A THREE-PART QUESTIONNAIRE WAS USED. THE OBJECTIVE WAS TO LEARN WHAT

M0457   CAUSES A NURSE TO BE SATISFIED OR DISSATISFIED WITH THE VA
        SYSTEM. IT ALSO ATTEMPTED TO LEARN HOW TURNOVER,
        ESPECIALLY AVOIDABLE TURNOVER, COULD BE REDUCED. THE GOAL
        OF THESE TWO MAJOR OBJECTIVES WAS TO IMPROVE THE DELIVERY OF
        NURSING SERVICE TO PATIENTS.
            THE ANALYSIS OF TURNOVER CONCENTRATED ON JOB FACTORS.
        DIFFERENCES IN PERSONAL CHARACTERISTICS, BIOGRAPHICAL
        CHARACTERISTICS, AND ATTITUDES AND OPINIONS OF THE NURSES
        ALL HAD A MAJOR IMPACT ON THE DATA GATHERED. UNFORTUNATELY,
        WHEN ALL THE FINDINGS WERE COMPILED, NO PARTICULAR REASON
        COULD BE GIVEN FOR JOB SATISFACTION OR DISSATISFACTION
        AMONG VA NURSES.
            A MAJOR PROBLEM IN RECEIVING SUFFICIENT RESPONSES TO
        THE QUESTIONNAIRES WAS THAT THE NURSES REFUSED TO ANSWER
        MANY QUESTIONS ON THE GROUND THAT THEY DEALT WITH PERSONAL
        MATTERS. IN ADDITION, THE CHANGING SOCIAL, ECONOMIC, AND
        PROFESSIONAL CIRCUMSTANCES HAVE A DIRECT BEARING ON HOSPITAL
        POLICIES AND PRACTICES. THE RELEVANT FACTORS OF JOB
        SATISFACTION IN 1960 WERE NOT THE SAME AS THOSE IN 1970.
            COMPARISONS OF THE TWO STUDIES WERE COMPLICATED BY OTHER
        MATTERS. IN THE 1960 STUDY, DATA WERE GATHERED BY AN
        INTERMEDIATE PERSON WHO SEARCHED THE RECORDS. IN THE 1970
        STUDY, ALL QUESTIONNAIRE DATA WERE OBTAINED DIRECTLY FROM
        THE NURSES INVOLVED. THESE QUESTIONNAIRES WERE LENGTHY, AND
        A GOOD UNDERSTANDING OF THE INSTRUCTIONS WAS ESSENTIAL FOR
        ADEQUATE ANSWERS.
            IT IS SUGGESTED THAT FUTURE STUDIES IN THIS AREA BE
        PARTICIPATED IN BY HOSPITAL MANAGEMENT. QUESTIONNAIRES
        SHOULD BE SHORTENED, AND THE SIZE OF THE SAMPLE INCREASED .

M0458   BEROFF, JOSEPH.   HUBBARD, ROBERT L. MARQUIS, KENT.
        COMPONENTS OF ACHIEVEMENT MOTIVATION AS PREDICTORS OF
        POTENTIAL FOR ECONOMIC CHANGE.
        UNPUBLISHED RESEARCH, UNIVERSITY OF MICHIGAN, 1972.

            IDENTIFIES AND DISCUSSES PERSONAL ACHIEVEMENT
        ORIENTATIONS AND THEIR USE IN JOB TRAINING PROGRAMS.

M0459   VONDER HAAR, R. A.
        MOTIVATION THROUGH NEED FULFILLMENT.
        SUPERVISORY MANAGEMENT 16 (OCTOBER 1971):   10-14.

            CONCERN FOR MOTIVATION NECESSARILY SUGGESTS CONCERN
        FOR PERFORMANCE. WHAT MAKES PEOPLE PERFORM IN THE BEST
        INTERESTS OF THE ORGANIZATION IS THE SUBJECT OF THIS
        ARTICLE.

M0460   VON HALLER, GILMER B.
        INDUSTRIAL AND ORGANIZATIONAL PSYCHOLOGY.
        NEW YORK: MCGRAW-HILL BOOK COMPANY, 1971.

            A TEXTBOOK WITH CONTRIBUTIONS FROM THE FIELDS OF
        PSYCHOLOGY, ECONOMICS, MARKETING MANAGEMENT AND
        ENGINEERING, PLUS INDUSTRY.

M0461   WAC MECHANICS JOIN ARMY AVIATION COMMUNITY.
        U. S. ARMY AVIATION DIGEST, FEBRUARY 1974, P. 23.

MEMBERS OF THE WOMEN'S ARMY CORPS ARE COMPLETING
AVIATION MAINTENANCE TRAINING COURSES AND CREATING FIRSTS AS
MECHANICS.

M0462   WALDMAN, E.
MARITAL AND FAMILY CHARACTERISTICS OF THE LABOR FORCE.
MONTHLY LABOR REVIEW 93 (MAY 1970):   18-27.

SPECIAL LABOR FORCE REPORT POINTS TO AN INCREASING
PROPORTION OF YOUNG MARRIED WOMEN IN THE 1969 WORK FORCE.

M0463   WALDMAN, E.
VIET-NAM WAR VETERANS -- TRANSITION TO CIVILIAN LIFE.
MONTHLY LABOR REVIEW 93 (NOVEMBER 1970):   21-29.

SPECIAL LABOR FORCE REPORT SHOWS THAT UNEMPLOYMENT OF
YOUNG VETERANS ROSE IN THE FIRST HALF OF 1970,
AS THE MILITARY CUTBACK DEEPENED AND ECONOMIC GROWTH
SLOWED.

M0464   WALDMAN, E.   MCEADDY, B. J.
WHERE WOMEN WORK -- AN ANALYSIS BY INDUSTRY AND OCCUPATION.
MONTHLY LABOR REVIEW, MAY 1974, PP. 3-13.

WOMEN FIND JOBS IN THE FASTEST GROWING INDUSTRIES, BUT
REMAIN CLUSTERED IN FEWER OCCUPATION GROUPS THAN MEN.

M0465   WALL, TOBY D.
EGO-DEFENSIVENESS AS A DETERMINANT OF REPORTED DIFFERENCES
IN SOURCES OF JOB SATISFACTION AND JOB DISSATISFACTION.
JOURNAL OF APPLIED PSYCHOLOGY, 58 (AUGUST 1973):   125-28.

THE RESULTS OF THIS INVESTIGATION SUPPORT VROOM'S
HYPOTHESIS THAT HERZBERG'S FINDINGS RESULTING IN HIS
TWO-FACTOR THEORY OF JOB SATISFACTION-DISSATISFACTION
ARE IN PART A PRODUCT OF EGO-DEFENSIVE PROCESSES WITHIN
INDIVIDUALS.

M0466   WALLER, R. J.
JOB SATISFACTION: THE THROWAWAY SOCIETY.
BUSINESS HORIZONS 16 (OCTOBER 1973):   61-62.

THIS IS A COMPARISON OF THE COGNITIVE AND BEHAVIORISTIC
THEORIES OF MOTIVATION.

M0467   WALTON, RICHARD E.
QUALITY OF WORKING LIFE: WHAT IS IT.
SLOAN MANAGEMENT REVIEW 15 (FALL 1973):   11-21.

SEEKS TO DEFINE THE EIGHT MAJOR CRITERIA FOR THE
QUALITY OF WORKING LIFE AND EXAMINES THEIR SPECIFIC
INTERRELATIONSHIPS AND THEIR RELATIONSHIP TO PRODUCTIVITY.
ALSO DISCUSSES HOW DEFICIENCIES AFFECT DIFFERENT EMPLOYEE
GROUPS AND SOME CAUSES OF FUTURE CHANGE.

M0468   WANTED BLACK ENGINEERS.
MANPOWER, JUNE, 1971, PP. 8-10.

NEGRO STUDENTS SHUN TECHNICAL FIELDS DESPITE RISE IN
OPPORTUNITIES FOR THEM.

M0469   WARD, ERNEST H.
        ELEMENTS OF AN EMPLOYEE MOTIVATION PROGRAM.
        PERSONNEL JOURNAL 54 (MARCH 1974):   205-208.

            THE ELEMENTS WHICH IDEALLY SHOULD BE PRESENT IN
        AN EMPLOYEE MOTIVATION PROGRAM ARE DISCUSSED HERE IN
        THE PRACTICAL TERMS OF WHAT CAN ACTUALLY BE DONE IN AN
        INDUSTRIAL ENVIRONMENT TO BRING ABOUT A STRONGER AND
        MORE WIDESPREAD ACCEPTANCE OF ORGANIZATIONAL GOALS.

M0470   WEDGEWOOD, HENSLEIGH.
        MEATBALLS AND MOTIVATION.
        SUPERVISORY MANAGEMENT 15 (MAY 1970):   2-7.

            PEOPLE ARE MOTIVATED BY A VARIETY OF PERSONAL
        NEEDS, NOT BY SOME EXTERNAL TECHNIQUE. THE BEST RESULTS
        COME FROM KNOWING WHAT THESE NEEDS ARE AND GIVING
        SUBORDINATES ROOM TO SATISFY THEM WHILE ACHIEVING COMPANY
        GOALS.

M0471   WEITZEL, W.   PINTO, PATRICK R.   DAVIS, RENE V.
        JURY, PHILLIP A.
        THE IMPACT OF THE ORGANIZATION ON THE STRUCTURE OF JOB
        SATISFACTION: SOME FACTOR ANALYTIC FINDINGS.
        PERSONNEL PSYCHOLOGY 26 (JANUARY-FEBRUARY 1974):   545-59.

            THE PURPOSE OF THE STUDY WAS TO EXAMINE THE IMPACT OF
        THE ORGANIZATION UPON THE FACTOR STRUCTURE OF JOB
        SATISFACTION. USING FIVE VARIED ORGANIZATIONS AND MEASURING
        28 SATISFACTION VARIABLES, THE STUDY INDICATED THAT WHILE
        SOME DIFFERENCES WERE FOUND, THE DIFFERENCES DID NOT OBSCURE
        BASIC SIMILARITIES IN THE DIMENSIONS OF JOB SATISFACTION
        ACROSS ALL FIVE ORGANIZATIONS.

M0472   WESTLEY, W. A.   WESTLEY, M. W.
        THE EMERGING WORKER.
        MONTREAL AND LONDON: MCGILL-QUEEN'S UNIVERSITY PRESS, 1971.

            THE NEWLY EMERGING WORKER HAS A DIFFERENT VIEW OF
        HIMSELF AND HIS RELATIONSHIP TO WORK AND SOCIETY.
        (THIS WORKER IS PREDOMINANTLY UNDER 35, EITHER SEMI-SKILLED
        UNIONIZED OR LOWER LEVEL WHITE-COLLAR WORKER.)
        BOOK INVESTIGATES TRENDS WHICH ARE EMERGING-- HIGH
        EDUCATIONAL LEVELS, HIGH AND RISING INCOMES, HIGH
        EMPLOYMENT LEVELS AND HIGH CONSUMPTION NORMS. WORKER
        PARTICIPATION IN MANAGEMENT DECISIONS IS A SUGGESTED
        SOLUTION.

M0473   WHAT DO WORKERS THINK OF THEIR JOBS.
        OCCUPATIONAL OUTLOOK QUARTERLY, 16 (WINTER 1972):   36-39.

            RESULTS OF A STUDY BY THE UNIVERSITY OF MICHIGAN'S
        SURVEY RESEARCH CENTER REVEAL THAT A MAJORITY OF WORKERS
        ARE GENERALLY SATISFIED.

M0474 WHITE, HAROLD C.
HOW THE LEADER LOOKS TO THE LED.
ADMINISTRATIVE MANAGEMENT 35 (MARCH 1974): 58-60.

THE AUTHOR OF THIS ARTICLE CLAIMS THAT THE MORE
AUTOCRATIC THE LEADER IS, THE LESS EFFECTIVE HE WILL
BE IN MOTIVATING HIS WORKERS.

M0475 WHITE, JOHN M.
SPECIAL WORK PROJECTS FOR THE UNEMPLOYED AND UPGRADING
FOR THE WORKING POOR.
MONTPELIER: STATE OF VERMONT, DEPARTMENT OF EMPLOYMENT
SECURTIY. SCHEDULED FOR COMPLETION SUMMER 1974.

THIS PROJECT EXPLORED THE FEASIBILITY AND EFFECTIVENESS
OF TEMPORARY SUBSIDIZED JOB OPPORTUNITIES FOR WELFARE
RECIPIENTS AND OTHER MEMBERS OF LOW-INCOME FAMILIES AS A
MEANS OF HELPING THEM TO PERMANENT UNSUBSIDIZED EMPLOYMENT.
IT ALSO EXPLORED THE FEASIBILITY AND EFFECTIVENESS OF
UPGRADING TRAINING FOR THE WORKING POOR. COMPLETE
DOCUMENTATION OF THE PROJECT EXPERIENCE, INCLUDING ANALYSIS
OF PROJECT OUTCOMES, DESCRIPTION OF HOW VARIOUS OPERATIONAL
ISSUES WERE DEALT WITH, AND OPERATING GUIDES AND HANDBOOK,
IS CONTAINED IN A SERIES OF MONOGRAPHS AND SPECIAL REPORTS,
INCLUDING A SEPARATE GRANT OF THE UNIVERSITY OF PITTSBURGH
(GRANT 92-42-72-29).

M0476 WHITE, J. K.   RUH, ROBERT A.
EFFECTS OF PERSONAL VALUES ON THE RELATIONSHIP BETWEEN
PARTICIPATION AND JOB ATTITUDES.
ADMINISTRATIVE SCIENCE QUARTERLY 18 (DECEMBER 1973): 506-15

THE MODERATING EFFECTS OF INDIVIDUAL VALUES ON THE
RELATIONSHIPS BETWEEN PARTICIPATION IN DECISION MAKING
AND JOB ATTITUDES WERE INVESTIGATED FOR A SAMPLE OF 2, 755
EMPLOYEES FROM SIX MANUFACTURING ORGANIZATIONS.

M0477 WHITE, WILLIAM D.   ROBBINS, ANTHONY.
ROLE OF ON-THE-JOB TRAINING IN A CLINICAL LABORATORY.
MONTHLY LABOR REVIEW, 94 (MARCH 1971): 65-69.

CASE STUDY SHOWING EFFECTS OF EMPLOYEE TRAINING
ON THE PRODUCTIVITY OF A LAB.
UNFAVORABLE ASPECTS ARE POINTED UP BY THE AUTHORS.

M0478 WHO'S UNHAPPY AT WORK AND WHY.
MANPOWER, JANUARY PP. 2-8.

UNIVERSITY OF MICHIGAN SURVEY SEEKS TO IDENTIFY
DISSATISFIED WORKERS AND WHAT MAKES THEM THAT WAY.
THIS ARTICLE TAKEN FROM A CHAPTER OF THE BOOK,
WHERE HAVE ALL THE JOBS GONE? THE ARTICLE DESCRIBES WHAT
TYPE OF PEOPLE ARE USUALLY THE MOST DISSATISFIED WITH THEIR
JOBS.
THE ARTICLE STATES THAT THE HIGHER A WORKER'S WAGES
ARE, THE MORE SATISFIED HE WILL BE WITH HIS JOB.
THE SURVEY USED TOOK 107 SUBGROUPS OF WORKERS AND
BROKE THEM DOWN INTO SMALLER GROUPS ACCORDING TO RACE, AGE

M0478   AND INCOME. OF THESE GROUPS BLACK WORKERS UNDER AGE THIRTY
        WERE FAR AND AWAY THE MOST DISSATISFIED WITH THEIR JOBS.
        THE SECOND MOST DISSATISFIED GROUP WAS WORKERS AGED 29 AND
        UNDER WITH SOME COLLEGE EDUCATION. WOMEN 29 AND UNDER WERE
        THE THIRD MOST DISSATISFIED GROUP. OF ALL GROUPS TESTED,
        ONLY 10% OF EMPLOYED PERSONS AGE 55 AND OVER REPORTED
        DISSATISFACTION WITH THEIR LIVES.
              RANKING JOB SATISFACTION BY INDUSTRY OR OCCUPATION,
        CONSTRUCTION WORKERS AND THE SELF-EMPLOYED WERE AT
        THE TOP OF THE CONTENTMENT SCALE. ONLY 1 IN ABOUT 20 FROM
        THESE TWO GROUPS WERE DISSATISFIED.
              BLACKS WERE ABOUT TWICE AS LIKELY AS WHITES TO BE
        DISSATISFIED WITH THEIR JOBS. THIS HELD TRUE THROUGH AGE
        44; AT THAT POINT THE PERCENTAGE OF DISSATISFIED BLACKS
        DROPPED TO 7 PERCENT AS COMPARED TO 9 PERCENT FOR WHITES
        44 AND OVER.
              TWICE AS MANY BLACKS OVER 44 WERE DISSATISFIED WITH
        THEIR LIVES AS WERE DISSATISFIED WITH THEIR JOBS. OLDER
        WHITES WERE ABOUT AS DISSATISFIED WITH ONE AS WITH THE
        OTHER.
              WHEN WORKER DISSATISFACTION DATA WERE BROKEN DOWN BY
        EDUCATION, THERE WAS A SURPRISING RESULT: THE PERCENTAGE OF
        DISCONTENTED WORKERS WAS THE SAME AMONG THOSE WITH AN
        ELEMENTARY SCHOOL EDUCATION OR LESS, AND THOSE WHO
        PROGRESSED BEYOND HIGH SCHOOL.
              UNMARRIED PEOPLE ARE TWICE AS LIKELY TO BE UNSATISFIED
        WITH THEIR LIVES AS THEIR MARRIED COUNTERPARTS.
              WORKERS WERE ASKED HOW IMPORTANT THEY CONSIDERED
        SOME 25 ASPECTS OF WORK, INCLUDING PAY, WORKING CONDITIONS,
        AND RELATIONS WITH CO-WORKERS.
              OF THE FIVE FEATURES RATED NEXT IMPORTANT ONLY ONE HAD
        TO DO WITH TANGIBLE OR ECONOMIC BENEFITS. AND THAT ONE
        (GOOD PAY) WAS RANKED NUMBER FIVE. RANKED ABOVE PAY WERE
        INTERESTING WORK, ENOUGH HELP AND EQUIPMENT TO GET THE JOB
        DONE, ENOUGH INFORMATION TO GET THE JOB DONE AND ENOUGH
        AUTHORITY TO GET THE JOB DONE.

M0479   WILKINSON, RODERICK.
        MOTIVATED WORKERS AND HARD WORKERS.
        SUPERVISORY MANAGEMENT 18 (NOVEMBER 1973):   30-33.

              THE AUTHOR POINTS OUT THREE CONDITIONS HE VIEWS AS
        BEING ESSENTIAL TO THE MOTIVATION OF WORKERS.

M0480   WILLIAMS, JOAN.
        MAKING THE JOB CORPS MORE FLEXIBLE.
        MANPOWER, NOVEMBER, 1970, PP. 10-13.

              MEMBERSHIP IN THE MANPOWER FAMILY MEANS A SHARING
        OF TRAINING OPPORTUNITIES, RESULTING IN GREATER EFFICIENCY
        AND ECONOMY.

M0481   WILSON, SIDNEY R.
        MOTIVATING MANAGERS WITH MONEY.
        BUSINESS HORIZONS 16 (APRIL 1973):   37-43.

              THE AUTHOR LOOKS AT SALARY ADMINISTRATION AND INCENTIVE
        BONUSES AND CONCLUDES THERE MUST BE EQUALITY BETWEEN SALARY

M0481 EARNED AND SALARY RECEIVED AND COMPANIES MUST ESTABLISH
CRITERIA FOR EVALUATING AN EMPOYEE'S EARNED INCOME.

M0482 W. I. N. REPORT -- PROBLEMS, PROGRESS, PROGNOSIS.
MANPOWER, SEPTEMBER 1970, PP. 8-13.

ALTHOUGH MANY PROBLEMS REMAIN, PROGRESS HAS BEEN
MADE AND THE PROGNOSIS FOR THE FUTURE IS GOOD.

M0483 WINCHESTER, DAVID.
THE BRITISH COAL MINE STRIKE OF 1972.
MONTHLY LABOR REPORT 95 (OCTOBER 1972): 30-36.

THE CONFRONTATION RAISED QUESTIONS ABOUT INFLATION
POLICY AND ENFORCEMENT OF THE NEW INDUSTRIAL RELATIONS ACT.

M0484 WINPISINGER, WILLIAM W.
JOB ENRICHMENT: A UNION VIEW.
MONTHLY LABOR REVIEW 96 (APRIL 1973): 54-56.

VICE PRESIDENT OF INTERNATIONAL ASSOCIATION OF
MACHINISTS AND AEROSPACE WORKERS, AFL-CIO, DISCUSSES
JOB SATISFACTION FROM THE UNION'S POINT OF VIEW.
MANY PEOPLE ARE WORRIED ABOUT THE WORK ETHIC IN THE
UNITED STATES. THEY DO NOT KNOW WHAT THE NEW GENERATION IS
COMING TO, CITING THE INCIDENT AT LORDSTOWN IN THE EARLY
1970'S AS AN EXAMPLE. WINPISINGER BELIEVES THAT THE WORK
ETHIC IS ALIVE AND WELL.
JOB ENRICHMENT MEANS ENRICHING THE PAYCHECK. IT MEANS
DECREASING THE HOURS A WORKER MUST LABOR ORDER TO EARN
A DECENT LIVING. WINPISINGER BELIEVES THAT
THE TIME HAS COME TO TRANSLATE THE INCREASED PRODUCTIVITY
INTO THE KIND OF ENRICHMENT THAT COMES FROM SHORTER
WORKWEEKS, LONGER VACATIONS, AND EARLIER RETIREMENTS.
JOB ENRICHMENT MEANS DOING SOMETHING ABOUT THE NOISE,
THE HEAT, THE FUMES, AND OTHER WORKING CONDITIONS.
COMPANIES WILL SPEND MILLIONS ADVERTISING QUIETER APPLIANCES
AND CARS, BUT ARE RELUCTANT TO SPEND ONE PENNY TO REDUCE
NOISE IN THEIR PLANTS.
IF JOB ENRICHMENT IS TO BE ATTAINED, A BLUE-COLLAR
WORKER MUST NOT BE ASHAMED TO WERE COVERALLS AND TO HAVE
DIRTY FINGERNAILS. NO MATTER HOW BORING A JOB MAY BE, THE
WORKER MUST HAVE HOPE FOR SOMETHING BETTER TOMORROW.
THESE EXAMPLES OF JOB ENRICHMENT ARE NOT WHAT
MANAGEMENT HAS IN MIND. SOME INTRODUCE GIMMICKS, LIKE DOING
AWAY WITH TIMECLOCKS OR DEVELOPING WORK TEAMS.
STUDIES TEND TO PROVE THAT WORKER DISSATISFACTION TENDS
TO DECREASE WITH AGE. THAT IS BECAUSE OLDER WORKERS HAVE
ACCRUED MORE OF THE KINDS OF JOB ENRICHMENT THAT UNIONS
HAVE FOUGHT FOR--BETTER WAGES, SHORTER HOURS, A RIGHT TO
HAVE A SAY IN THEIR WORKING CONDITIONS, AND SO ON. THAT IS
THE KIND OF ENRICHMENT THAT UNIONS BELIEVE IN.

M0485 WINS AND LOSSES.
MANPOWER, NOVEMBER, 1971, PP. 24-28.

WORK INCENTIVE PROGRAM BATTLES NEW PROBLEMS BUT SHOWS
PROGRESS.

M0486   WITTMAN, JOHN.
        THE COMPRESSED WORKWEEK: MORE QUESTIONS THAN ANSWERS.
        MANPOWER, 3 (JULY 1971):   18-19.

            DISCUSSION OF POSSIBLE EFFECTS OF A SHORTER WORKWEEK
        ON PRODUCTIVITY, EMPLOYEE MORALE, AND JOB SATISFACTION.

M0487   A WOMAN IN THAT JOB.
        JOB SAFETY AND HEALTH, FEBRUARY 1974, PP. 16-17.

            AS THE OCCUPATIONAL SAFETY AND HEALTH ACT INCREASES THE
        NEED FOR SAFETY AND HEALTH PROFESSIONALS, MORE WOMEN ARE
        TAKING UP CAREERS IN THE FIELD.

M0488   WOMEN'S PROGRAMS SURVEYED AT LATIN AMERICAN POSTS.
        DEPARTMENT OF STATE NEWSLETTER, JANUARY 1974, 36-37.

            A FEDERAL WOMEN'S PROGRAM COORDINATOR VISITED EIGHT
        LATIN AMERICAN POSTS, ESTABLISHED IN 1973, THAT PROVIDE
        EQUAL EMPLOYMENT OPPORTUNITIES FOR WOMEN.

M0489   WOMEN'S WEEK -- AUGUST 26-30.
        DEPARTMENT OF STATE NEWSLETTER, AUGUST 1974, PP. 26-28.

            STATE AND FEDERAL AGENCIES AS WELL AS NON-GOVERNMENT
        ORGANIZATIONS WILL COMMEMORATE AUGUST AS THE MONTH IN 1920
        WHEN THE 19TH AMENDMENT WAS RATIFIED GRANTING WOMEN THE
        RIGHT TO VOTE, AND ALSO AS THE 10TH ANNIVERSARY OF THE CIVIL
        RIGHTS ACT OF 1974 WHICH PROHIBITED THE DISCRIMINATION IN
        EMPLOYMENT ON THE BASIS OF SEX.

M0490   WOOL, HAROLD.
        WHAT'S WRONG WITH WORK IN AMERICA? -- A REVIEW ESSAY.
        MONTHLY LABOR REVIEW   96 (MARCH 1973):   38-44.

            REVIEWER QUESTIONS THESIS OF RISING JOB DISCONTENT;
        EMPHASIZES HIGH EMPLOYMENT STRATEGY AS PRIMARY CONDITION FOR
        IMPROVING OR ELIMINATING UNDESIRABLE JOBS.

M0491   YOHALEM, ALICE.   RIDGELY, Q. B.
        DESEGREGATION AND CAREER GOALS. CHILDREN OF AIR FORCE
        FAMILIES.
        NEW YORK: PRAEGER, APRIL 1974.

            THIS STUDY SOUGHT TO APPRAISE THE IMPACT OF MILITARY
        DESEGREGATION ON THE EDUCATIONAL AND CAREER ASPIRATIONS
        IF BLACK YOUTH AND THOSE OF THEIR CIVILIAN YOUTH
        COUNTER-PARTS. THE CHILDREN OF BLACK AIRMEN HAD A HIGHER
        RATE OF COLLEGE ENROLLMENT THAN THEIR CIVILIAN PEERS IN
        COMPARABLE SOCIAL-ECONOMIC CIRCUMSTANCES.

M0492   YORKS, LYLE.
        KEY ELEMENTS IN IMPLEMENTING JOB ENRICHMENT.
        PERSONNEL 50 (SEPTEMBER 1973):   45-52.

            THIS ARTICLE WAS WRITTEN TO HELP FACILITATE THE
        IMPLEMENTATION OF JOB ENRICHMENT. YORKS DESCRIBES HOW JOB
        ENRICHMENT, WHEN PROPERLY IMPLEMENTED, INCREASES QUANTITY AN

M0492 QUALITY IN PRODUCTION AND REDUCES ABSENTEEISM AND TURNOVER.
       JOB ENRICHMENT IS DEFINED AS PROVIDING THE WORKER WITH
A JOB THAT HAS CERTAIN CHARACTERISTICS. FIRST, THE WORKER
GIVEN A COMPLETE PIECE OF WORK SO THAT HE CAN SEE THE
PROGRESS HE IS MAKING, AND IDENTIFY HIS FINISHED PRODUCT.
SECOND, THE WORKER IS GIVEN AS MUCH DECISION-MAKING
RESPONSIBILITY AND CONTROL AS POSSIBLE IN CARRYING OUT HIS
JOB. THIRD, IS THE FACT THAT THE WORKER IS PROVIDED WITH AS
MUCH FEEDBACK AS POSSIBLE SO THAT HE KNOWS HOW HE DOING HIS
JOB.
       IN ADDITION TO MODIFYING THE JOB HORIZONTALLY BY
EXPANDING HIS WORK BASE, JOB ENRICHMENT MODIFIES THE
WORKER VERTICALLY, AS HE TAKES ON NEW RESPONSIBILITIES AND
AUTHORITY FORMERLY HELD BY SUPERVISORS. FOR JOB ENRICHMENT
TO WORK, IT MUST BE IMPLEMENTED IN THE CORRECT WAY.
       TO BEGIN WITH, JOB ENRICHMENT SHOULD BE BASED ON A
CONSULTING RATHER THAN A TRAINING MODEL. THE JOB ENRICHMENT
SPECIALIST SHOULD FUNCTION AS A CONSULTANT TO MANAGERS,
INSTEAD OF ACTING AS A TEACHER OF JOB ENRICHMENT BASICS AND
PRINCIPLES. HE SHOULD FIND OUT THE NEEDS OF MANAGEMENT AND
NOT IMPLEMENT HIS OWN INDEPENDENT PLAN. MANAGERS ARE OFTEN
SKEPTICAL OF INTRODUCING NEW PLANS FOR FEAR OF EMPLOYEE
FAILURE. THE MANAGER MAY NOT HAVE THE BACK-UP SUPPORT
HE NEEDS TO IMPLEMENT JOB ENRICHMENT EFFECTIVELY. THE JOB
ENRICHMENT SPECIALIST'S JOB INCLUDES HELPING THE MANAGER
OVERCOME THESE PROBLEMS.
       AFTER THE JOB ENRICHMENT SPECIALIST HAS BEEN ASSIGNED
TO A DEPARTMENT, AND HIS DUTIES ARE UNDERSTOOD TO BE
CONSULTING ONLY, IT IS TIME TO CHOSE A KEY MAN.   A KEY
MAN IS A MEMBER OF THE CLIENT'S DEPARTMENT ASSIGNED TO WORK
CLOSELY WITH THE JOB ENRICHMENT SPECIALIST WHO, AFTER
TRAINING BY THE SPECIALIST AND IMPLEMENTATION OF THE PLAN,
TAKES OVER THE JOB ENRICHMENT DUTIES OF THE DEPARTMENT.
THE KEY MAN SERVES AS THE COORDINATOR OF THE JOB ENRICHMENT
PLAN. HE SHOULD BE ABLE TO GUARANTEE MAINTENANCE OF THE
PLAN AFTER THE SPECIALIST LEAVES, AND BE ABLE TO INTEGRATE
THE JOB ENRICHMENT PLAN INTO FUTURE OPERATIONS OF THE
BUSINESS.

M0493 YOUNG, ANN M.
       WORK EXPERIENCE OF THE POPULATION IN 1972.
       MONTHLY LABOR REVIEW, FEBRUARY 1974, PP. 48-56.

       THIS SPECIAL LABOR FORCE REPORT ON A 1973 SURVEY SHOWS
THE PROPORTION OF WOMEN AND MEN WORKERS EMPLOYED FULL-TIME
ALL YEAR INCREASED, MAINLY BECAUSE OF EXPANSION IN THE
SERVICE-PRODUCING INDUSTRIES.

M0494 YURAN, NEIL A.
       CORRECTIVE MOTIVATION.
       MANAGERIAL PLANNING 19 (JANUARY-FEBRUARY): 12-13.

       THIS PAPER TRIES TO EXPLAIN CERTAIN COURSES OF
MOTIVATIONAL CORRECTIVE ACTION THAT MANAGER CAN TAKE WHEN
VARIOUS UNIVERSAL SITUATIONS ARISE IN THE WORK ENVIRONMENT.
A MANAGER OF A COMPANY CAN USE MANY TOOLS OF CORRECTIONAL
MOTIVATION ON HIS EMPLOYEES. HERE ARE SOME OF THE MORE
COMMON DEVICES: ADDING AND REDUCING TASK RESPONSIBILITY.

M0494 TO ADD RESPONSIBILITY CAN BE A MOST POWERFUL MOTIVATIONAL
       TOOL. TO THE EMPLOYEE THIS KIND OF ENCOURAGEMENT CAN
       INCREASE HIS FEELINGS OF FULL PARTICIPATION AND CAN LIFT HIS
       MENTAL ATTITUDE. ON THE OTHER HAND, SOME PEOPLE MIGHT FEEL
       CHEATED IF THEY DEDUCE THAT THEY HAVE BEEN SUBJECTED TO
       TOO MUCH TASK RESPONSIBILITY.
            PROMISING REWARDS SUCH AS MONEY CAN IN SOME CASES BE
       USED TO CORRECT ANY HARMFUL SITUATION THAT MAY HAMPER
       WORK PERFORMANCE. SOME WORKERS ARE MOTIVATED BY COMPETITION
       WITH FELLOW WORKERS. CREATING A SECURE ATMOSPHERE AMONG THE
       EMPLOYEES WILL INCREASE SELF-CONFIDENCE. THE CREATION OF
       SECURITY WILL EASE THE FEAR SELF-INFLICTED BY THE
       SUBORDINATE. A CREATIVE MANAGER WILL STRIVE TO REWARD THE
       INDIVIDUAL ONCE HE PRODUCES GOOD WORK, WITH TOTAL
       ACCEPTANCE. REWARDS INSTILL PRIDE IN THE INDIVIDUAL.
       TEACHING A SUBORDINATE A JOB FUNCTION WILL TEND TO RELIEVE
       THE ANXIETY OF CONFUSION AND WILL TEND TO INSTILL PARTIAL
       CONFIDENCE IN THE EMPLOYEE.
       CONCLUSTION: THE MANAGER IS THE KEY INDIVIDUAL
       PARTICIPATING IN THE CORRECTIVE MEASURES; HE IS THE KEY TO
       SUCCESS OR FAILURE.

M0495 ZARKIN, DAVID A.
       ONCE THEY WOULDN'T ACCEPT A WOMAN.
       EXTENSION SERVICE REVIEW, JANUARY-FEBRUARY 1974, PP. 6-8.

            HORTICULTURISTS ARE IN THE HOT SEAT BECAUSE OF THE
       EVER-INCREASING NUMBER OF HOME GARDENERS.

M0497 ARVEY, RICHARD D.   BEGALLA, MARTHA E.
       ANALYZING THE HOMEMAKER JOB USING THE POSITION ANALYSIS
       QUESTIONNAIRE.
       JOURNAL OF APPLIED PSYCHOLOGY 60 (AUGUST 1975): 513-17.

            E.J. MC CORMICK'S POSITION ANALYSIS QUESTIONNAIRE WAS
       ADMINISTERED TO 48 FEMALE HOMEMAKERS TO (1) DETERMINE IF
       THE JOB WERE AMENABLE TO ANALYSIS, (2) ASSOCIATE A WAGE WITH
       THE JOB, (3) IDENTIFY CLOSELY RELATED JOBS, AND (4) EXAMINE
       CORRELATES, SUCH AS AGE (TAKEN FROM A BIOGRAPHICAL
       QUESTIONNAIRE) OF PAQ DESCRIPTIONS. FINDINGS SHOWED
       CONSISTENCIES IN DESCRIPTIONS, INDICATING THAT THE JOB WAS
       PERSONALLY DEMANDING. PARTICIPANTS VALUED THEIR ACTIVITY AT
       $740 PER MONTH AND COMPARED THEIR RESPONSIBILITIES MOST
       CLOSELY WITH THAT OF PATROLMEN.

M0499 BARTOL, KATHRYN M.   WORTMAN, MAX S.
       SEX EFFECTS IN LEADER BEHAVIOR SELF-DESCRIPTIONS AND JOB
       SATISFACTION.
       JOURNAL OF PSYCHOLOGY 94 (NOVEMBER 1976): 177-83.

            INVESTIGATED POSSIBLE SEX DIFFERENCES IN LEADERSHIP
       AMONG 72 SUPERVISORY EMPLOYEES OF A LARGE PSYCHIATRIC
       HOSPITAL BY COMPARING MALE AND FEMALE SELF-DESCRIPTIONS OF
       THEIR OWN LEADER BEHAVIORS, AS WELL AS THEIR SATISFACTION
       WITH VARIOUS ASPECTS OF THEIR JOBS. DATA FROM THE LEADER
       BEHAVIOR DESCRIPTION QUESTIONNAIRE SHOW THAT FEMALE LEADERS
       DESCRIBED THEMSELVES AS PERFORMING MORE CONSIDERATION AND
       TOLERANCE OF UNCERTAINTY LEADER BEHAVIOR AND AS BEING MORE

M0499 SATISFIED WITH CO-WORKERS THAN MALE LEADERS. THE POSSIBILITY, SUGGESTED BY SEX ROLE STEREOTYPES, THAT SELF PERCEPTIONS OF CONSIDERATION BEHAVIOR FOR FEMALES AND INITIATING STRUCTURE FOR MALES ARE RELATED TO JOB SATISFACTION WAS NOT SUPPORTED BY THE FINDINGS. RESULTS GENERALLY SUPPORT INDICATIONS FROM STUDIES BASED ON SUBORDINATE DESCRIPTIONS THAT THERE ACTUALLY MAY BE FEW JOB-RELATED DIFFERENCES BETWEEN MALE AND FEMALE LEADERS.

M0500 BEATTY, RICHARD W. BEATTY, JAMES U.
LONGITUDINAL STUDY OF ABSENTEEISM AND HARD-CORE UNEMPLOYED.
PSYCHOLOGICAL REPORTS 36 (APRIL 1975): 395-406.

STUDY OF ABSENTEEISM AMONG 20 FEMALE HARD-CORE UNEMPLOYED OVER A TWO-YEAR PERIOD. WORKING IN AN INSURANCE COMPANY, THEY HAD COMPLETED A TRAINING PROGRAM. ABSENTEEISM AFTER SIX MONTHS EMPLOYMENT COULD BE PREDICTED ON THE BASIS OF ORGANIZATION-WIDE FACTORS, WHILE AFTER TWENTY-FOUR MONTHS LONGITUDINAL ABSENTEEISM WAS ATTRIBUTABLE TO IMMEDIATE WORK ENVIRONMENT AND JOB CONTENT FACTORS.

M0502 BOISVERT, M. P.
THE QUALITY OF WORKING LIFE: AN ANALYSIS.
HUMAN RELATIONS 30 (FEBRUARY 1977): 155-60.

DIFFERENCES BETWEEN WORKERS' AND RESEARCHES' CONCEPTS OF THE QUALITY OF WORKING LIFE WERE IDENTIFIED THROUGH THE ANALYSIS OF 155 QUESTIONNAIRES COMPLETED BY WHITE-COLLAR WORKERS. FOR WORKERS THE CONCEPT SEEMS LIMITED TO INTRINSIC WORK ASPECTS WHILE FOR RESEARCHERS ITS SCOPE EXTENDS TO THE ORGANIZATIONAL AND CAREER DOMAINS OF ACTION. THIS DIFFERENCE INDICATES THAT MISUNDERSTANDINGS ARE LIKELY TO ARISE THAT WILL ENDANGER ANALYSIS AND REMEDIAL ACTIONS WITH RESPECT TO THE QUALITY OF WORKING LIFE.

M0503 BRAGG, EMMA W. POTTS, ELMER R.
REVIEW OF LITERATURE ON WORK MOTIVATION: BULLETIN 12. A STUDY OF WORK MOTIVATION OF URBAN AND RURAL APPAREL WORKERS IN TENNESSEE.
(NASHVILLE: TENNESSEE STATE UNIVERSITY PRESS, 1975) PROJECT 1-4178.35466 USDA, 1975.

PRESENTS AN INTERPRETIVE SUMMARY OF LITERATURE ON WORK MOTIVATION AS AN INITIAL STAGE OF A LARGE-SCALE STUDY OF THE WORK MOTIVATION OF URBAN AND RURAL APPAREL WORKERS IN TENNESSEE. TOPICS COVERED INCLUDE ACHIEVEMENT NEEDS, LOCUS OF CONTROL, WORK INCENTIVE, WORK VALUES, JOB AND ROLE PERCEPTIONS, JOB SATISFACTION, JOB PERFORMANCE, ORGANIZATIONAL FACTORS, PERSONALITY AND WORK MOTIVATION, SPECIAL MEMBERSHIP GROUPS, INSTRUMENTATION AND MEASUREMENT, AND SOCIOLOGY OF WORK.

M0504 BRODSKY, CARROLL M.
THE HARASSED WORKER.
LEXINGTON, MASS.: D. C. HEATH AND CO., 1976.

BASED ON A STUDY OF WORKERS WHO HAD BEEN INJURED ON THE JOB, AN ANALYSIS OF THE CHARACTERISTICS OF HARASSED

M0504   EMPLOYEES AND THEIR HARASSERS IS PRESENTED, FOCUSING ON
        METHODS OF ASSESSING AND DEALING WITH HARASSMENT IN WORK
        SITUATIONS, THE NATURE OF THE HARASSMENT PROCESS, WORK
        PRESSURE AS HARASSMENT, THE WORK CULTURE IN SOCIETY, AND
        RECOMMENDATIONS FOR PUBLIC POLICY.

M0505   BRIEF, ARTHUR P.   ALDAG, RAMON J.
        WORK VALUES AS MODERATORS OF PERCEIVED LEADER
        BEHAVIOR-SATISFACTION RELATIONSHIPS.
        SOCIOLOGY OF WORK AND OCCUPATIONS 4 (FEBRUARY 1977): 99-112.

            TESTED HYPOTHESES CONCERNING THE MODERATING EFFECTS OF
        JOB INVOLVEMENT AND PRO-PROTESTANT ETHIC ATTITUDES ON
        PERCEIVED LEADER BEHAVIOR-SATISFACTION RELATIONSHIPS FOR A
        SAMPLE OF 131 PRODUCTION WORKERS USING THE LEADER BEHAVIOR
        DESCRIPTION QUESTIONNAIRE AND PARTS OF THE YALE JOB
        INVENTORY. STATISTICALLY SIGNIFICANT MODERATING EFFECTS
        WERE NOT ISOLATED. HOWEVER, JOB INVOLVEMENT AND PRO-
        PROTESTANT ETHIC ATTITUDES DIFFERENTIALLY AFFECTED THE
        PERCEIVED LEADER BEHAVIOR-SATISFACTION RELATIONSHIPS. THE
        RELATIONSHIP BETWEEN JOB INVOLVEMENT AND PRO-PROTESTANT
        ETHIC ATTITUDES IS DISCUSSED.

M0506   BURKE, RONALD J.
        OCCUPATIONAL STRESSES AND JOB SATISFACTION.
        JOUNAL OF SOCIAL PSYCHOLOGY 100 (DECEMBER 1976): 235-44.

            THE HYPOTHESIS PROPOSED IN THIS ARTICLE WAS THAT SOME
        OCCUPATIONAL STRESSES ARE DESIRABLE AND SOME ARE NOT. THE
        OCCUPATIONAL STRESS INDEX WAS FOUND TO BE SIGNIFICANTLY
        RELATED TO THE JOB SATISFACTION INDEX. THE GREATER THE
        STRESS, THE LOWER THE SATISFACTION. A MORE COMPLICATED
        PICTURE EMERGED WHEN THE SPECIFIC ITEM INTERCORRELATIONS
        WERE EXAMINED. CERTAIN TYPES OF OCCUPATIONAL STRESSES,
        PRIMARILY ASSOCIATED WITH ENLARGED OR DEMANDING JOBS, WERE
        POSITIVELY RELATED TO EMPLOYEE JOB SATISFACTION.

M0507   BYHAM, WILLIAM.   ROBINSON, J.
        INTERACTION MODELING: A NEW CONCEPT IN SUPERVISORY TRAINING.
        TRAINING AND DEVELOPMENT JOURNAL 30 (FEBRUARY 1976): 20-33.

            DESCRIBES INTERACTION MODELING, A FAST-GROWING METHOD
        OF IMPROVING SUPERVISORY SKILLS WITH EMPHASIS ON POSITIVE
        MODELS OF BEHAVIOR AND A STEP-BY-STEP APPROACH TO HANDLING
        PRACTICAL SITUATIONS. NO THEORY IS TAUGHT SINCE SPECIFIC
        SKILLS ARE THE GOALS. WHILE RECOGNIZING THAT THERE MAY BE
        MANY WAYS OF HANDLING A SITUATION, SUCH AS ORIENTING NEW
        EMPLOYEES OR DEALING WITH A DISCRIMINATION COMPLAINT, THE
        PRACTICAL TRAINING OBJECTIVE IS TO BE SURE THE SUPERVISOR
        LEARNS ONE SET WAY THAT IS KNOWN TO WORK; HENCE THE EMPHASIS
        ON FOLLOWING THE CRITICAL STEPS IN ORDER AND THE USE OF FILM
        OR VIDEOTAPE MODELS OF CORRECT SITUATION RESOLUTION.
        EXERCISES DIFFER FROM TYPICAL ROLE-PLAYING IN THAT THEY
        CONFORM TO A MORE DETAILED BLUEPRINT AND ARE PRECEDED BY
        LEARNING WHAT TO DO AND WHEN TO DO IT. TO BUILD CONFIDENCE,
        FALSE STARTS AND FAILURES ARE MINIMIZED. COMMERCIAL
        MATERIALS ARE AVAILABLE WITH EACH MODULE STANDING BY ITSELF
        SO THAT AN ORGANIZATION CAN CHOOSE MODULES WITH PROBLEM

M0507 SITUATIONS OF PARTICULAR CONCERN TO ITS SUPERVISORS. INITIAL
VALIDITY STUDIES ARE PROMISING.

M0508 CHAKRAVARTY, T. K.
NEED ORIENTATION AS RELATED TO EXTENSION JOB SATISFACTION: A
PROFILE ANALYTIC EXPLORATION.
INDIAN JOURNAL OF PSYCHOLOGY 49, NO. 3 (1974): 201-12.

STUDIED 98 OFFICERS OF THE EXTENSION EDUCATION
ORGANIZATION IN NORTHERN INDIA TO INVESTIGATE THE RELATION-
SHIP BETWEEN THEIR LEVELS OF JOB SATISFACTION AND PROFILES
OF 8 PSYCHOLOGICAL NEEDS: ECONOMIC, DEPENDENCE, AFFILIATION,
RECOGNITION, DOMINANCE, AUTONOMY, ALTRUISM, AND ACHIEVEMENT.
GROUPING OF SIMILAR PROFILES WAS DONE BY THE METHOD
SUGGESTED BY W.L.K. SAWREY ET AL (1960). FOUR DIFFERENT
CLUSTERS OF SIMILAR PROFILES EMERGED. AN AFFILIATIVE-
ALTRUISTIC PERSONALITY WAS FOUND TO CONTRIBUTE TO POSITIVE
JOB SATISFACTION; WHILE THOSE WITH A PERSONALITY ORIENTED
TOWARD ACHIEVEMENT AND/OR RECOGNITION WERE GENERALLY FOUND
TO BE DISSATISFIED WITH EXTENSION WORK.

M0509 CHURCHILL, G. A.   FORD, NEIL M.   WALKER, ORVILLE C.
ORGANIZATIONAL CLIMATE AND JOB SATISFACTION IN THE SALES
FORCE.
JOURNAL OF MARKETING RESEARCH 13 (NOVEMBER 1976): 323-32.

SURVEYED 479 INDUSTRIAL SALESMEN FROM 10 COMPANIES TO
EXAMINE THE IMPACT OF 4 ORGANIZATIONAL CLIMATE VARIABLES
(THE AMOUNT OF AUTONOMY GIVEN THE INDIVIDUAL IN PERFORMING
HIS JOB, THE AMOUNT OF STRUCTURE IMPOSED UPON A POSITION AND
THE PERSON WHO OCCUPIES IT, REWARD ORIENTATION, AND THE
NATURE OF INTERPERSONAL RELATIONSHIPS) ON SS' JOB
SATISFACTION. THE RELATIONSHIP BETWEEN EACH OF THESE
VARIABLES AND EACH OF 7 COMPONENTS OF JOB SATISFACTION
(E.G., CLOSENESS OF SUPERVISION, INNOVATIVENESS DEMANDED OF
THE SALESMAN, AND EXPERIENCE) WERE ALSO EXAMINED. RESULTS
INDICATE THAT (A) ORGANIZATIONAL CLIMATE WAS AN IMPORTANT
DETERMINANT OF SALESFORCE MORALE, (B) THE HIGHLY AUTONOMOUS
AND NONROUTINE NATURE OF THE SALES JOB DIFFERENTIATED IT
FROM MOST OTHER NONMANAGERIAL POSITIONS IN A FIRM, AND (C)
THE NATURE OF THE RELATIONSHIPS BETWEEN A SALESMAN AND HIS
ROLE PARTNERS -- HIS ORGANIZATIONAL SUPERIORS, CUSTOMERS,
FAMILY MEMBERS, AND OTHERS -- ALSO HAD AN EFFECT ON HIS JOB
SATISFACTION.

M0510 COLTRIN, SALLY.   GLUECK, WILLIAM F.
THE EFFECT OF LEADERSHIP ROLES ON THE SATISFACTION AND
PRODUCTIVITY OF UNIVERSITY RESEARCH PROFESSORS.
ACADEMY OF MANAGEMENT JOURNAL 20 (MARCH 1977): 101-16.

THE SATISFACTION OF RESEARCH PROFESSORS DEPENDS ON THE
UNIVERSITY ADMINISTRATOR'S LEADERSHIP STYLE, ROLE MODEL, AND
PERCEIVED ABILITY TO REWARD THE PROFESSORS' EFFORTS, WITH
SIGNIFICANT DIFFERENCES IN THESE FACTORS AMONG ACADEMIC
DISCIPLINES. PROFESSORS' PRODUCTIVITY WAS NOT INFLUENCED BY
THE RESEARCH ADMINISTRATORS' STYLE, ROLE MODEL AND REWARD
EFFORTS IN THIS STUDY.

M0511   EDWARDS, RICHARD A.
        SHIFT WORK: PERFORMANCE AND SATISFACTION.
        PERSONNEL JOURNAL 54 (NOVEMBER 1975): 578-79.

            A STUDY OF THE RELATIONSHIP BETWEEN SATISFACTION AND
        WORKING TIMES VERSUS HUMAN EFFICIENCY AND THE TIME OF DAY
        ACTIVITIES OCCUR. EDWARDS FINDS THAT "SHIFT WORKERS APPEAR
        TO BE MORE SATISFIED IN SITUATIONS WHERE SWIFTLY ROTATING
        SHIFTS HAVE REPLACED FIXED-PERIOD ROTATING SHIFTS."

M0512   FOEGEN, J. H.
        A 'THIRD-LEVEL' INCENTIVE: WORK SEEN AS SERVICE.
        PERSONNEL JOURNAL 54 (OCTOBER 1975): 516-18.

            TRADITIONAL NEEDS SATISFACTION IS SOMEWHAT STERILE; THE
        AUTHOR SUGGESTS THAT WORK NEEDS TO BE REGARDED AS A
        "SPIRITUAL" FULFILLMENT TO PROVIDE REAL SATISFACTION.

M0513   FRANKLIN, JEROME L.
        CHARACTERISTICS OF SUCCESSFUL AND UNSUCCESSFUL ORGANIZATION
        DEVELOPMENT.
        JOURNAL OF APPLIED BEHAVIORAL SCIENCE 12 (OCT-NOV-DEC 1976):
        471-92.

            COMPARISON OF 25 ORGANIZATIONS WITH SUCCESSFUL AND
        UNSUCCESSFUL ORGANIZATIONAL DEVELOPMENT (OD) ON 8 CLUSTERS
        OF CHARACTERISTICS REVEALED THAT THE 2 TYPES OF STUCTURE
        COULD BE DIFFERENTIATED BY 3 GENERAL AREAS RELATED TO
        ADJUSTMENTS TO CHANGE AND QUALIFICATIONS OF INTERNAL CHANGE
        AGENTS. IMPLICATIONS FOR MANAGERS AND CONSULTANTS SEEKING TO
        INCREASE THE LIKELIHOOD OF SUCCESS IN OD PROJECTS ARE
        CONSIDERED.

M0514   FURUKAWA, HISATAKA.
        AN EXPERIMENTAL ANALYSIS OF THE RELATIONSHIP BETWEEN JOB
        SATISFACTION AND JOB IMPORTANCE.
        JAPANESE JOURNAL OF EXPERIMENTAL SOCIAL PSYCHOLOGY 15 (JULY
        1975): 25-34.

            SHOWED THAT CORRELATION IMPROVED BETWEEN JOB
        SATISFACTION AND EXTERNAL CRITERIA (LIKELIHOOD OF LEAVING
        PRESENT JOB, EVALUATION CONCERNING THE FUTURE OF THE JOB,
        MENTAL HEALTH, AND FEELING OF JOB ACCOMPLISHMENT) BY
        WEIGHTING WITH JOB IMPORTANCE RATINGS. A SIGNIFICANT
        INTERACTION WAS ALSO FOUND BETWEEN JOB SATISFACTION AND JOB
        IMPORTANCE RATINGS AMONG 297 JAPANESE RAILROAD WORKERS.
        RESULTS INDICATE THAT PREDICTION OF EXTERNAL VARIABLES ON
        THE BASIS OF JOB SATISFACTION MEASUREMENT CAN BE IMPROVED BY
        WEIGHTING WITH JOB IMPORTANCE RATINGS.

M0515   GALLEGOS, ROBERT.   PHELAN, JOSEPH G.
        EFFECTS ON PRODUCTIVITY AND MORALE OF A SYSTEMS-DESIGNED
        JOB-ENRICHMENT PROGRAM IN PACIFIC TELEPHONE.
        PSYCHOLOGICAL REPORTS 40 (FEBRUARY 1977): 283-90.

            TWO EXPERIMENTAL GROUPS WERE EXAMINED BEFORE, AFTER,
        AND DURING JOB-ENRICHMENT PROGRAMS. SIGNIFICANT IMPROVEMENT
        IN QUANTITY AND QUALITY OCCURRED AND WAS MAINTAINED AFTER

M0515 TERMINATION OF EXPERIMENTS. EXPRESSED JOB SATISFACTION WAS AVERAGE OR SLIGHTLY BELOW ON THE JOB DESCRIPTION INDEX FOR ALL WORKERS. THERE ARE NO SIGNIFICANT DIFFERENCES IN EXPRESSED JOB SATISFACTION DESPITE IMPROVEMENT IN PRODUCTIVITY.

M0516 GIBLIN, EDWARD J.
MOTIVATING EMPLOYEES: A CLOSER LOOK.
PERSONNEL JOURNAL 55 (FEBRUARY 1976): 68-71.

TOO LARGE A PROPORTION OF MIDDLE MANAGEMENT AND PROFESSIONALS ARE OVER-EDUCATED AND HAVE EXPECTATIONS THAT EXCEED THE DEMANDS OF THEIR JOBS.

M0517 GLASER, EDWARD M.
STATE OF THE ART QUESTIONS ABOUT QUALITY OF WORKLIFE.
PERSONNEL 53 (MAY-JUNE 1976): 39-47.

IN SPITE OF CONCERNS OVER ESTABLISHING BETTER WORK ENVIRONMENTS, MANAGEMENT STILL NEEDS ANSWERS TO THE WHY AND HOW-TO OF QUALITY OF WORKLIFE PROGRAMS.

M0518 GLENN, NORVAL D.   TAYLOR, P. A.   WEAVER, CHARLES N.
AGE AND JOB SATISFACTION AMONG MALES AND FEMALES: A MULTI-VARIATE, MULTISURVEY STUDY.
JOURNAL OF APPLIED PSYCHOLOGY 62 (APRIL 1977): 189-93.

A STUDY OF WHITE MALE AND FEMALE RESPONDENTS TO THREE RECENT NATIONAL SAMPLE SURVEYS REVEALS, FOR BOTH SEXES, A MODERATE BUT CONSISTENT POSITIVE CORRELATION BETWEEN AGE AND JOB SATISFACTION. THE CORRELATION MAY RESULT FROM INFLUENCES ASSOCIATED WITH AGING OR COHORT MEMBERSHIP, OR BOTH. TESTS, THROUGH PARTIAL CORRELATION ANALYSIS, OF ONE "AGING" AND ONE "COHORT" EXPLANATION YIELD LARGELY NEGATIVE EVIDENCE. HOWEVER, THE CORRELATION AMONG MALES SEEMS LIKELY TO RESULT TO SOME DEGREE FROM AN INCREASE WITH AGING IN EXTRINSIC JOB REWARDS.

M0520 GRIFFIN, LARRY J.
CAUSAL MODELING OF PSYCHOLOGICAL SUCCESS IN WORK ORGANIZATIONS.
ACADEMY OF MANAGEMENT JOURNAL 20 (MARCH 1977): 6-33.

THIS PAPER DEMONSTRATES THE APPLICABILITY OF PATH ANALYSIS TO THE STUDY OF PSYCHOLOGICAL SUCCESS IN WORK ORGANIZATIONS BY REANALYZING THREE PREVIOUSLY PUBLISHED STUDIES. TWO EXAMPLES TEST AND ESTIMATE TWO CAUSAL MODELS OF PSYCHOLOGICAL SUCCESS. THE FINAL EXAMPLE DEMONSTRATES THAT THE UTILITY OF PATH ANALYSIS IS DEPENDENT UPON ADEQUATE THEORETICAL FORMULATION.

M0521 HAPPY AT 3M.
SALES AND MARKETING MANAGEMENT, JUNE 14, 1976, P.12.

A SURVEY AT 3M TO DISCOVER HOW MUCH THE SALES FORCE LIKED THEIR JOBS.

M0522 HERZBERG, F. I.   RAFALKO, EDMUND A.

M0522 EFFICIENCY IN THE MILITARY.
PERSONNEL 52 (NOVEMBER-DECEMBER 1975): 38-48.
A CASE ANALYSIS OF HOW THE AIR FORCE EFFECTED
REMARKABLE SAVINGS USING MOTIVATIONAL TECHNIQUES. MILITARY
PERSONNEL CAN BE MANAGERS.

M0523 HERZBERG, F. I.   ZAUTRA, ALEX.
ORTHODOX JOB ENRICHMENT: MEASURING TRUE QUALITY IN JOB
SATISFACTION.
PERSONNEL 53 (SEPTEMBER-OCTOBER 1976): 54-68.

ENRICHING JOBS WITHOUT ALTERING THEIR STRUCTURES
PRODUCES ONLY MINIMAL RETURN IN JOB SATISFACTION. ARGUE
THE AUTHORS, EMPLOYEES RESPOND BEST, NOT TO HYGIENIC CHANGE
BUT TO TASKS LEADING TO MORE RESPONSIBILITY, MORE LEARNING,
AND NEW SKILLS.

M0524 HOLMES, JOHN P.   KWIECINSKI, P. D.
BUILD EMPLOYEES' CONFIDENCE AND SELF-ESTEEM.
PERSONNEL 52 (JULY-AUGUST 1975): 45-49.

A VALUES-CLARIFICATION PROGRAM IS USEFUL IN GETTING
PEOPLE TALKING AND COMMUNICATING. EMPLOYEES AND MANAGERS
PERFORM BETTER WHEN THEY KNOW MORE ABOUT THEMSELVES, AS WELL
AS EACH OTHER.

M0525 HUNT, J. W.   SAUL, R. N.
RELATIONSHIP OF AGE, TENURE AND JOB SATISFACTION IN MALES
AND FEMALES.
ACADEMY OF MANAGEMENT JOURNAL 18 (DECEMBER 1975): 690-702.

IN A SURVEY OF WHITE COLLAR WORKERS, AGE AND TENURE
HAD POSITIVE, LINEAR RELATIONSHIPS TO OVERALL JOB
SATISFACTION. AGE HAD A STRONGER RELATIONSHIP WITH
SATISFACTION IN MALES THAN TENURE; THE REVERSE HELD FOR
FEMALES. WHEN SIX FACETS OF SATISFACTION WERE EXAMINED,
THE RELATIONSHIPS WITH AGE AND TENURE BECAME MORE COMPLEX.

M0526 IMBERMAN, WOODRUFF.
LETTING THE EMPLOYEE SPEAK HIS MIND.
PERSONNEL (NOVEMBER-DECEMBER 1976): 12-22.

GUIDELINES ON HOW TO IMPROVE UPWARD COMMUNICATION FROM
THE SHOP FLOOR, AND WHY TO: PRODUCTION WORKERS FREQUENTLY
HAVE ANSWERS MANAGEMENT NEEDS -- BUT RARELY ARE HEARD.

M0527 JANTZ, ALFRED H.
ENCOURAGEMENT OF EMPLOYEE CREATIVITY AND INITIATIVE.
PERSONNEL JOURNAL 54 (SEPTEMBER 1975): 476-77, 500-1.

LOWER-LEVEL EMPLOYEES OFTEN GET THINGS DONE OUTSIDE
NORMAL CHAINS OF COMMAND AND TRADITIONAL AUTHORITY/RESPONSI-
BILITY SYSTEMS. CHANGES IN SOME ORGANIZATIONAL CONCEPTS
SHOULD PROVIDE FOR RECOGNITION OF TALENT -- CREATIVITY,
INITIATIVE, INFLUENCE AND POTENTIAL ACCOMPLISHMENT --
NOTWITHSTANDING ONE'S FORMAL POSITION WITHIN THE
ORGANIZATION.

M0528 JUROVSKY, A.
WORK MOTIVATION, A MENTAL PROCESS.
PSYCHOLOGIE V EKONOMICKE PRAXI 9,NO.1 (1974): 1-17.

DESCRIBES A METHOD FOR STUDYING WORK MOTIVATION BY
ASSESSING REASONS FOR A HYPOTHETICAL CHANGE OF EMPLOYMENT.
SS WERE 650 MALE AND FEMALE WORKERS IN 1969 AND 1,200 IN
1971-1972, WHO INDICATED ON A 4-POINT SCALE THE IMPORTANCE
TO THEM OF 14 MOTIVES FOR WORKING. FACTOR ANALYSIS GAVE 4
MAIN FACTORS: SOCIAL, SELF-REALIZATION, MATERIAL, AND
WORKING CONDITIONS. THE RELATIONSHIPS BETWEEN EACH OF THE
14 MOTIVES AND (A) WORK SATISFACTION AND (B) WORK ESTIMATION
WERE INVESTIGATED. SIGNIFICANT CORRELATIONS WERE FOUND BE-
TWEEN WORK SATISFACTION AND THE STRENGTH OF 13 MOTIVES FOR
JOB CHANGE. SIGNIFICANT CORRELATIONS WERE FOUND BETWEEN
WORK ESTIMATION AND THE STRENGTH OF ALL 14 MOTIVES. THESE
AND OTHER FINDINGS ARE DISCUSSED IN TERMS OF AFFECTIVE
MOTIVATIONAL THEORIES.

M0529 KAVANAGH, MICHAEL. HALPERN, MICHAEL.
THE IMPACT OF JOB LEVEL AND SEX DIFFERENCES ON THE
RELATIONSHIP BETWEEN LIFE AND JOB SATISFACTION.
ACADEMY OF MANAGEMENT JOURNAL 20 (MARCH 1977): 66-73.

QUESTIONNAIRE DATA WERE COLLECTED FROM 411 UNIVERSITY
EMPLOYEES AT THREE JOB LEVELS TO TEST TWO HYPOTHESES
RELATIVE TO DIFFERENCES IN THE RELATIONSHIP BETWEEN JOB AND
LIFE SATISFACTION FOR MALE AND FEMALES. COMPARISONS
INDICATED STRONG DIFFERENCES, PRIMARILY FOR FEMALES,
BETWEEN AN EARLIER STUDY AND THIS STUDY FOR THE LIFE-JOB
SATISFACTION RELATIONSHIP.

M0530 KIMMONS, GARY. GREENHAUS, J.
RELATIONSHIP BETWEEN LOCUS OF CONTROL AND REACTIONS OF
EMPLOYEES TO WORK CHARACTERISTICS.
PSYCHOLOGICAL REPORTS. 39 (DECEMBER 1976): 815-20.

THE PURPOSE OF THIS STUDY WAS TO DETERMINE WHETHER
EMPLOYEES' LOCUS OF CONTROL MODERATED THE RELATIONSHIP
BETWEEN SEVERAL WORK CHARACTERISTICS AND JOB SATISFACTION.
INTERNALS PERCEIVED MORE AUTONOMY, FEEDBACK, AND
PERFORMANCE-REWARD CONNECTIONS ON THEIR JOBS THAN EXTERNALS.
INTERNALS DEMONSTRATED MORE INVOLVEMENT AND SATISFACTION
WITH THEIR JOBS THAN EXTERNALS. HOWEVER, THE CORRELATIONS
BETWEEN THE WORK CHARACTERISTICS AND JOB SATISFACTION WERE
GENERALLY POSITIVE FOR BOTH INTERNALS AND EXTERNALS BUT
SMALL.

M0531 KING, ALBERT S.
MANAGEMENT'S ECTASY AND DISPARITY OVER JOB ENRICHMENT:
EXPECTATIONS IN PLANNING JOB CHANGE: A CASE STUDY.
TRAINING AND DEVELOPMENT JOURNAL. 30 (MARCH 1976): 3-8.

A STUDY OF THE EFFECT OF MANAGERIAL EXPECTATIONS ON THE
RESULT OF INNOVATIONS, CONDUCTED IN 4 PLANTS OF THE SAME
COMPANY, INDICATED THAT INCREASES IN PRODUCTIVITY WERE
GREATER IN THE 2 PLANTS WHERE MANAGERS HAD BEEN ADVISED IN
ADVANCE THAT CHANGES WOULD INCREASE PRODUCTION THAN IN THE

M0531   2 PLANTS WHERE MANAGERS HAD BEEN ADVISED THAT THE CHANGES
         WERE MERELY PROCEDURAL.

M0532   KOHN, MERVIN.
         WORKER ALIENATION AND THE MENTALLY RETARDED.
         EDUCATION AND TRAINING OF THE MENTALLY RETARDED. 12
         (APRIL 1977):   149-51.

              THIS ARTICLE CITES FOUR STRATEGIES MANAGERS CAN USE TO
         COMBAT THE PROBLEMS OF WORKER ALIENATION. THE APPROPRIATE
         MATCHING OF PEOPLE TO JOBS ALLOWS FOR CONSIDERATION OF
         HANDICAPPED WORKERS, PARTICULARLY EDUCABLE MENTALLY RETARDED
         PERSONS.

M0533   KRAFT, W. PHILIP.   WILLIAMS, K.
         JOB REDESIGN IMPROVES PRODUCTIVITY. (BANKERS TRUST, N.Y.).
         PERSONNEL JOURNAL. 54 (JULY 1975):   393-97.

              THE UNIQUE CHALLENGES PRESENTED IN GOOD BANKING
         BUSINESS ARE APPROACHED THROUGH THE CONCEPT OF JOB ENRICH-
         MENT. DESCRIBED IS A CONSULTING FIRM'S EXPERIENCE WITH A
         BANK IN TRANSFORMING JOB SATISFACTION, MOTIVATION, AND
         PERFORMANCE INTO USABLE TOOLS BENEFITING THE INDIVIDUAL AND
         THE ORGANIZATION.

M0534   LEE, M. BLAINE.   ZWERMAN, W. L.
         DESIGNING A MOTIVATING AND TEAM BUILDING EMPLOYEE APPRAISAL
         SYSTEM.
         PERSONNEL JOURNAL 55 (JULY 1976):   354-57.

              A FUNCTIONAL APPRAISAL SYSTEM RESTS ON DETERMINING THE
         THE DESIRED BEHAVIOR OF EACH CORPORATE TEAM MEMBER.

M0535   MCCALL, M.W.   LAWLER, EDWARD E.
         HIGH SCHOOL STUDENTS PERCEPTIONS OF WORK.
         ACADEMY OF MANAGEMENT JOURNAL. 19 (MARCH 1976):   17-24.

              THE WORK REWARD EXPECTATIONS AND GENERALIZED WORK
         ATTITUDES OF 453 HIGH SCHOOL STUDENTS WERE MEASURED. THE
         EFFECTS OF RACE, SEX, SOCIAL CLASS, AND PARENTAL REWARD
         VALUES ON STUDENTS' PERCEPTIONS OF WORK WERE EXAMINED.
         PREEMPLOYMENT ATTITUDES PARTIALLY ACCOUNT FOR FREQUENTLY
         REPORTED RELATIONSHIP AMONG JOB CHARACTERISTICS, DEMOGRAPHIC
         VARIABLES, AND EMPLOYEE ATTITUDES.

M0536   MACY, B.A.   MIRVIS, P.H.
         METHODOLOGY FOR ASSESSMENT OF QUALITY OF WORK LIFE AND
         ORGANIZATIONAL EFFECTIVENESS IN BEHAVIORAL-ECONOMIC TERMS.
         ADMINISTRATIVE SCIENCE QUARTERLY. 21 (JUNE 1976):   212-26.

              THIS PAPER DESCRIBES THE DEVELOPMENT AND IMPLEMENTATION
         OF A STANDARDIZED SET OF DEFINITIONS, MEASURES, AND COSTING
         METHODS FOR BEHAVIORAL OUTCOMES. UTILIZING INDUSTRIAL
         ENGINEERING, ACCOUNTING-WORK MEASUREMENTS, AND BEHAVIORAL
         CONCEPTS, THIS LONGITUDINAL FIELD RESEARCH IDENTIFIES AND
         QUANTIFIES THE COST COMPONENTS OF CERTAIN BEHAVIORS AND
         ARRIVES AT A DOLLAR FIGURE PER INCIDENT AND AN ESTIMATED
         TOTAL COST OVER THREE YEARS OF MEASUREMENT.

M0538   MEARS, PETER.
         GUIDELINES FOR THE JOB ENRICHMENT PRACTITIONER.
         PERSONNEL JOURNAL 55 (MAY 1976): 210,212.

         SINCE ONLY FOUR PERCENT OF FIRMS SURVEYED WERE
         IMPLEMENTING JOB ENRICHMENT PROGRAMS, LOW ACCEPTANCE
         SUGGESTS THAT PRACTITIONERS MAY BE EXPERIENCING DIFFICULTY
         IN APPLYING JOB ENRICHMENT. THE AUTHOR PROVIDES A QUESTION
         AND ANSWER CHECKLIST.

M0539   MILES, ROBERT H.   PETTY, M. M.
         RELATIONSHIPS BETWEEN ROLE CLARITY, NEED FOR CLARITY AND
         JOB TENSION AND SATISFACTION FOR SUPERVISORY AND
         NONSUPERVISORY ROLES.
         ACADEMY OF MANAGEMENT JOURNAL 18 (DECEMBER 1975): 877-83.

         THE STUDY FOCUSES ON ROLE DIFFERENCES (A) IN
         RELATIONSHIPS BETWEEN DEGREE OF ROLE CLARITY AND VARIOUS
         PERSONAL OUTCOMES AND (B) IN THE MODERATING EFFECTS OF
         NEED FOR CLARITY.

M0540   MILLAR, JEAN.
         MOTIVATIONAL ASPECTS OF JOB ENRICHMENT.
         MANAGEMENT INTERNATIONAL REVIEW 16,NO.2 (1976): 37-46.

         THE PAPER REVIEWS SOME DEVELOPMENTS IN MOTIVATIONAL
         THEORY AND PRACTICES AND PRESENTS A PLEA FOR "BURYING" THE
         MASLOW-HERZBERG MODELS ON THIS SUBJECT.

M0541   MILLER, NEIL.
         CAREER CHOICE, JOB SATISFACTION, AND THE TRUTH BEHIND THE
         PETER PRINCIPLE.
         PERSONNEL 53 (JULY-AUGUST 1976): 58-65.

         TOO MANY SELF-CONFIDENT MANAGERS WRITE OFF PEER
         INCOMPETENCE TO THE PETER PRINCIPLE WITHOUT EXAMINING THE
         CAUSES FOR INADEQUATE PERFORMANCE AND WITHOUT CONSIDERING
         POSSIBLE CORRECTIVES.

M0542   MILUTINOVICH, J.S.   TSAKLANGANOS, A.
         IMPACT OF PERCEIVED COMMUNITY PROSPERITY ON JOB
         SATISFACTION OF BLACK AND WHITE WORKERS.
         ACADEMY OF MANAGEMENT JOURNAL 19 (MARCH 1976): 49-65.

         DATA COLLECTED FROM BLACK AND WHITE WORKERS IN THREE
         ORGANIZATIONS INDICATE THAT WORKERS LIVING IN COMMUNITIES
         WITH DIFFERENT PERCEIVED LEVELS OF PROSPERITY HAVE
         DIFFERENT JOB SATISFACTION. A RELATIVELY LESS AFFLUENT
         COMMUNITY SEEMS TO BE A CASUAL VARIABLE IN LOWER JOB
         SATISFACTION OF WORKERS. THE IMPLICATIONS OF THESE
         FINDINGS ON WORKERS' BEHAVIOR ARE DISCUSSED.

M0543   NEVAS, SUSAN R.
         A DEFINITIONAL CHALLENGE: INTEREST AND WORK ITSELF
         SATISFACTIONS.
         VOCATIONAL GUIDANCE ABSTRACT QUARTERLY 25 (SEPTEMBER 1976):
         10-17.

DISCUSSES HOW RESEARCH ON INTERESTS HAS NOT YET YIELDED
SATISFACTORY DESCRIPTIONS OF INTRINSIC SATISFACTION IN JOB
TASKS. MAJOR INTEREST INVENTORY DEFINITIONS ARE TOO
GENERAL; THEY SUBMERGE COMPONENT INTERESTS WITHIN JOBS AND
FIELDS, AND THEY INCLUDE ELEMENTS BEYOND ATTRACTION TO THE
NATURE OF JOB TASKS. VALIDITY OF EXTANT EMPIRICALLY
DERIVED SCALES IS WEAKENED BY INCLUSION OF 2 SITUATIONAL
FACTORS UNRELATED TO INTRINSIC INTERESTS: CULTURAL
VARIABLES AND OPPORTUNITY. IN ADDITION, SVIB SCORES ARE
DISAPPOINTINGLY UNRELATED TO OVERALL WORK SATISFACTION.
IF SCHOOLS ARE TO CONTRIBUTE TO WORK SATISFACTION, THEY
MUST KNOW WHAT INTRINSIC WORK SATISFACTIONS ARE. NEEDED
INVESTIGATION IS LONG OVERDUE.

M0545   NISBERG, JAY N.
PERFORMANCE IMPROVEMENT WITHOUT TRAINING.
PERSONNEL JOURNAL 56 (DECEMBER 1976): 613-15.

JOB PERFORMANCE DEPENDS AS MUCH ON KNOWING PROPER
PROCEDURES AND METHODS AS IT DOES ON SKILLS. PERFORMANCE
WITHOUT TRAINING CAN BE EFFECTED WHEN THERE IS A RECOGNITION
BETWEEN DEFICIENCY IN KNOWLEDGE AND DEFICIENCY IN SKILLS.

M0546   ORPEN, C.
JOB ENLARGEMENT, INDIVIDUAL DIFFERENCES, AND WORKER
RESPONSES: A TEST WITH BLACK WORKERS IN SOUTH AFRICA.
JOURNAL OF CROSS-CULTURAL PSYCHOLOGY 7 (DECEMBER 1976):
473-80.

THIS STUDY TESTS THE HYPOTHESIS THAT JOB ENLARGEMENT
IS ONLY POSITIVELY ASSOCIATED WITH JOB SATISFACTION AMONG
WORKERS WHO ARE INVOLVED IN THEIR JOBS. THREE GROUPS OF
BLACK WORKERS IN SOUTH AFRICA PERFORMING JOBS OF DIFFERENT
SIZES OR DEGREES OF ENLARGEMENT WERE DIVIDED INTO WESTERN
AND TRIBAL SUBGROUPS. THE LEVEL OF JOB SATISFACTION OF THE
THREE WESTERN SUBGROUPS INCREASED SIGNIFICANTLY AS THEIR
JOBS BECAME LARGER OR MORE ENLARGED. THOSE OF THE TRIBAL
SUBGROUPS REMAINED THE SAME THUS SUPPORTING THE HYPOTHESIS.

M0547   OSBALDESTON, M.D.
SKANDIA INSURANCE GROUP: RESTRUCTURING THE WORK AND
ENRICHING THE JOB.
MANAGEMENT INTERNATIONAL REVIEW 16, NO.2 (1976): 9-22.

CASE STUDY FROM A SWEDISH INSURANCE COMPANY GENERATED
DURING A RESEARCH STUDY CONDUCTED IN 1974-75 WHICH WAS
CONCERNED WITH THE SYSTEMATIC CHANGES INTRODUCED BY VARIOUS
EUROPEAN COMPANIES IN THE ORGANIZATION OF WHITE-COLLAR WORK.

M0548   PARKE, E. LAUCK.   TAUSKY, CURT.
MYTHOLOGY OF JOB ENRICHMENT: SELF-ACTUALIZATION REVISITED.
PERSONNEL 52 (SEPTEMBER-OCTOBER 1975): 12-21.

ENRICHED JOBS MAY BE PSYCHOLOGICALLY SATISFYING TO
SOME EMPLOYEES, BUT THEY STILL EXPECT APPROPRIATE
COMPENSATION.

M0549   PATTENAUDE, RICHARD L.

M0549 INCREASING THE IMPORTANCE OF PERSONNEL: A STRATEGY.
PERSONNEL JOURNAL 54 (AUGUST 1975): 451-53.
EFFECTIVE PERSONNEL PRACTICES INVOLVE MANY MORE
DIFFICULTIES THAN MIGHT BE, AT FIRST, OBVIOUS.

M0550 SANCHEZ VILLANUEVA, JOSE.
PSCHOPHYSIOLOGICAL INFLUENCES ON THE WORK ENVIRONMENT: NEW
CONCEPTS.
REVISTA DE PSICOLOGIA GENERAL Y APLICADA 30 (JANUARY-
FEBRUARY 1975): 65-72.

DISCUSSES VARIOUS INFLUENCES ON THE WORK ENVIRONMENT
INCLUDING SPACE AND PSYCHOPHYSICAL FACTORS. IN EUROPE THE
TREND IS TO INDIVIDUALIZE SPACE FOR EACH WORKER, WHEREAS IN
NORTH AMERICA THE TREND IS TO GROUP WORKERS TOGETHER IN
LARGE SPACES. IT IS SUGGESTED THAT A TEAM OF PROFESSIONALS
(ARCHITECT, PSYCHOLOGIST, ECONOMIST, ETC.) SHOULD PLAN WORK
AREAS. FOUR TYPES OF PSYCHOPHYSICAL FACTORS ARE CONSIDERED:
SOUND. CLIMATE, VISUAL ELEMENTS, AND FURNITURE. THE EFFECTS
OF VARIOUS COMBINATIONS OF THESE FACTORS ARE DESCRIBED.

M0551 SCANLAN, BURT K.
DETERMINATES OF JOB SATISFACTION AND PRODUCTIVITY.
PERSONNEL JOURNAL 55 (JANUARY 1976): 12-14.

THE LEVEL OF JOB SATISFACTION IS POSITIVELY INFLUENCED
BY THE INTERACTION THAT OCCURS, ACCEPTANCE THAT EXISTS, AND
GROUP COHESIVENESS DUE TO SIMILARITY IN ATTITUDES.

M0552 SHAPIRO, H. JACK. STERN, LOUIS W.
JOB SATISFACTION: MALE AND FEMALE, PROFESSIONAL AND
NON-PROFESSIONAL.
PERSONNEL JOURNAL 54 (JULY 1975): 388-89.

A STUDY FINDS THAT SATISFACTION WITH WORK AND PROMOTION
IS HIGHER FOR MALES REGARDLESS OF WHETHER THE INDIVIDUAL IS
A PROFESSIONAL OR NON-PROFESSIONAL.

M0553 SCHULER, RANDALL S.
THE EFFECTS OF ROLE PERCEPTIONS ON EMPLOYEE SATISFACTION AND
PERFORMANCE MODERATED BY EMPLOYEE ABILITY.
ORGANIZATIONAL BEHAVIOR AND HUMAN PERFORMANCE 18 (FEBRUARY
1977): 98-107.

IN THIS STUDY IT WAS HYPOTHESIZED THAT EMPLOYEE ABILITY
WOULD REDUCE THE NEGATIVE RELATIONSHIP BETWEEN ROLE
PERCEPTIONS AND SATISFACTION AND PERFORMANCE. ALSO, IT
WAS HYPOTHESIZED THAT THE EFFECT OF ABILITY IS MODERATED BY
ORGANIZATIONAL LEVEL. THE RESULTS GENERALLY FAILED TO
SUPPORT THE HYPOTHESIZED RELATIONSHIPS. THERE WERE,
HOWEVER, TWO SIGNIFICANT INTERACTIONS THAT PARTIALLY
SUPPORTED ONE HYPOTHESIS. EMPLOYEES WITH HIGH ABILITY WERE
LESS AFFECTED BY ROLE AMBIGUITY THAN EMPLOYEES WITH LOW
ABILITY.

M0554 SCHULER, RANDALL S.
PARTICIPATION WITH SUPERVISOR AND SUBORDINATE
AUTHORITARIANISM: A PATH GOAL THEORY RECONCILIATION.

M0554 ADMINISTRATIVE SCIENCE QUARTERLY 21 (JUNE 1976):   320-25.
       THIS RESEARCH SOUGHT TO RECONCILE PREVIOUS STUDIES IN
WHICH PARTICIPATION AND JOB SATISFACTION OF SUBORDINATES
WERE SOMETIMES EFFECTIVELY MODERATED BY THEIR AUTHORITARI-
ANISM AND SOMETIMES NOT. THE DEGREE OF TASK REPETITIVENESS
WAS HYPOTHESIZED TO DETERMINE WHEN THE AUTHORITARIANISM OF
SUBORDINATES MODERATED BETWEEN THEIR PARTICIPATION WITH
THEIR SUPERVISORS AND JOB SATISFACTION.

M0555 SMITH, HOWARD R.
       THE HALF-LOAF OF JOB ENRICHMENT.
       PERSONNEL 53 (MARCH-APRIL 1976):   24-31.

       MANY WORKERS REJECT JOB ENRICHMENT BECAUSE THEIR
PRIORITIES DO NOT NECESSARILY JIBE WITH THE GOOD INTENTIONS
OF THEIR MANAGEMENT.

M0556 STEERS, RICHARD M.
       FACTORS AFFECTING JOB ATTITUDE IN GOAL SETTING ENVIRONMENT.
       ACADEMY OF MANAGEMENT JOURNAL 19 (MARCH 1976):   6-16.

       THE RELATIONSHIP BETWEEN VARIATIONS IN EMPLOYEES'
TASK-GOAL ATTRIBUTES, INDIVIDUAL NEED STRENGTHS, AND TWO
JOB ATTITUDES WAS STUDIED. JOB INVOLVEMENT AND SATISFACTION
WERE FOUND TO BE RELATED TO THE AMOUNT OF PARTICIPATION
ALLOWED IN GOAL-SETTING, GOAL DIFFICULTY, AND GOAL SPECIFI-
CITY; SATISFACTION WAS ALSO RELATED TO FEEDBACK. NEITHER
ATTITUDE WAS RELATED TO PEER COMPETITION.

M0557 TAVEGGIA, T. C.   HEDLEY, R. ALAN.
       JOB SPECIALIZATION, WORK VALUES, AND WORKER DISSATISFACTION.
       JOURNAL OF VOCATIONAL BEHAVIOR 9 (DECEMBER 1976): 293-309.

       THE RECENT WORK LITERATURE INCLUDES 3 CONTRADICTORY
PROPOSITIONS RELATING JOB SPECIALIZATION AND WORKER
DISSATISFACTION. THE 1ST PROPOSITION PREDICTS AN UN-
CONDITIONAL RELATIONSHIP BETWEEN THESE VARIABLES; THE 2ND
PREDICTS THAT THIS RELATIONSHIP WILL BE HIGHER AMONG WORKERS
COMMITTED TO MIDDLE CLASS WORK VALUES; THE 3RD PREDICTS THAT
THE RELATIONSHIP WILL BE HIGHER AMONG "ALIENATED" WORKERS.
FINDINGS OF A STUDY OF 3193 BRITISH INDUSTRIAL WORKERS
SUGGEST THAT, WHEN INDIVIDUALLY MEASURED AND ANALYZED, TASK
ATTRIBUTES RELATE IN DIFFERENT WAYS AND IN VARYING DEGREES
TO WORKER DISSATISFACTION. THE ABOVE PROPOSITIONS MAY BE
COMPLEMENTARY RATHER THAN COMPETING; THE VALIDITY OF EACH
MAY DEPEND UPON HOW JOB SPECIALIZATION IS MEASURED.

M0558 TRIPATHI, RAMA C.
       RELATIVE SALIENCY OF JOB FACTORS DURING STRIKE.
       INDIAN JOURNAL OF INDUSTRIAL RELATIONS 12 (JULY 1976): 81-85

       EXAMINED THE EFFECT OF STRIKING ON THE SALIENCE OF
VARIOUS JOB CHARACTERISTICS FOR 75 OF 601 MALE CLERICAL
WORKERS AT A LARGE UNIVERSITY IN NORTHERN INDIA WHO WENT ON
AN INDEFINITE STRIKE IN 1967. IT WAS HYPOTHESIZED THAT THE
PERCEPTION OF INEQUITY DURING A STRIKE SITUATION WOULD BE
EXAGGERATED BY WORKERS BY REDUCING THE VALENCE OF REWARDS
OFFERED TO THEM BY THE ORGANIZATION AND INCREASING THE

M0558   AMOUNT OF THEIR PERCEIVED PSYCHOLOGICAL INVESTMENT IN THE
        JOB AND IN THE ORGANIZATION. IT WAS FURTHER PREDICTED, BASED
        ON P. HERZBERG'S (1959) CLASSIFICATION OF JOB FACTORS INTO
        HYGIENE AND MOTIVATION FACTORS, THE SALIENCE OF THOSE JOB
        FACTORS PERTAINING TO PSYCHOLOGICAL INVESTMENTS IN THE JOB
        (MOTIVATORS) WOULD INCREASE. 25 SS SERVED AS RESPONDENTS
        DURING THE STRIKE, AND 50 SERVED AS RESPONDENTS 1 MO. AFTER
        THE STRIKE. DATA WERE OBTAINED BY A 20-ITEM JOB SATISFACTION
        QUESTIONNAIRE. RESULTS ARE TENTATIVE BUT APPEAR TO SUPPORT
        THE HYPOTHESIS FOR HYGIENE FACTORS BUT NOT FOR MOTIVATORS.

M0559   VELGHE, J. C.   COCKRELL, GARY.
        WHAT MAKES JOHNNY MOP ?
        PERSONNEL JOURNAL 54 (JUNE 1975): 324-25.

             THE AUTHORS FOUND, IN A STUDY AMONG THE HOUSEKEEPING
        STAFF OF A KANSAS CITY HOSPITAL, THAT ONCE WORKER EXPECTA-
        TIONS HAVE BEEN MET, ADDITIONAL INCREMENTS IN THE MAINTEN-
        ANCE FACTORS HAVE LITTLE, OR NO, EFFECT ON PERFORMANCE.

M0560   WADSWORTH, M. D.
        HOW TO EVALUATE THE JOB SATISFACTION OF CRITICAL EMPLOYEES.
        PERSONNEL JOURNAL 55 (SEPTEMBER 1976): 464-66.

             SYSTEMATIC EVALUATION OF A JOB PROVIDES THE FIRM WITH
        A REALISTIC PROFILE OF EACH EMPLOYEE'S JOB SATISFACTION.
        HELPFUL IN IDENTIFYING THE OVERLY-OPTIMISTIC AND THE BORED;
        USEFUL IN FUTURE CANDIDATE SELECTION AND IN MONITORING
        EMPLOYEE'S NEEDS.

M0561   WALTER, VERNE.
        SELF-MOTIVATED PERSONAL CAREER PLANNING: A BREAKTHROUGH IN
        HUMAN RESOURCE MANAGEMENT (PART I).
        PERSONNEL JOURNAL 55 (MARCH 1976): 112-15;
        (PART II): 55 (APRIL 1976): 162-67.

             EMPLOYEES WANT TO FEEL THAT THROUGH THEIR JOBS THEY CAN
        DEVELOP THEIR POTENTIAL TO THE FULLEST EXTENT POSSIBLE.
        PART II DESCRIBES HOW THROUGH A PROGRAM OF CAREER ASSESSMENT
        AND PERSONAL PLANNING WITH BENEFITS FOR BOTH MANAGEMENT
        FACILITATORS AND EMPLOYEE PLANNERS.

M0562   WANOUS, JOHN P.   ZWANY, ABRAM.
        A CROSS-SECTIONAL TEST OF NEED HIERARCHY THEORY.
        ORGANIZATIONAL BEHAVIOR AND HUMAN PERFORMANCE 18
        (FEBRUARY 1977): 78-97.

             THREE PROPOSITIONS WHICH STATE THE CAUSAL RELATIONSHIP
        BETWEEN NEED SATISFACTION AND IMPORTANCE WERE EXAMINED ON
        THE BASIS OF THREE NEED CATEGORIES. THESE WERE:
        (1) RELATIONSHIPS WITHIN THE SAME NEED CATEGORY,
        (2) RELATIONSHIPS BETWEEN NEED CATEGORIES IN AN UPWARD
        DIRECTION, AND (3) RELATIONSHIPS BETWEEN NEED CATEGORIES
        IN A DOWNWARD DIRECTION. THE DATA SUGGEST THAT NEED
        FULFILLMENT MAY BE THE BASIC PSYCHOLOGICAL VARIABLE WHICH
        ACCOUNTS FOR THE DIFFERENT RESULTS OBTAINED IN DISSIMILAR
        ORGANIZATIONS.

M0563   WEAVER, CHARLES N.
        WHAT WORKERS WANT FROM THEIR JOBS.
        PERSONNEL 53 (MAY-JUNE 1976): 48-54.

            FEW RESEARCHERS, CLAIMS THE AUTHOR, HAVE GONE TO
        EMPLOYEES AND ASKED THEM TO STATE THEIR WORKPLACE NEEDS.

M0564   WELLER, DENNIS R.   BLAIWES, ARTHUR S.R
        LEADERSHIP DIMENSIONS OF NAVY RECRUIT MORALE & PERFORMANCE.
        PSYCHOLOGICAL REPORTS 39 (DECEMBER 1976): 767-70.

            LEADERSHIP DIMENSIONS AND THEIR RELATION TO RECRUIT
        SATISFACTION AND PERFORMANCE WERE STUDIED IN 73 COMPANY
        COMMANDERS. RECRUITS COMPLETED QUESTIONNAIRES ASSESSING
        COMMANDERS' BEHAVIORS AND RECRUITS' ATTITUDES. FACTOR
        ANALYSIS YIELDED FOUR FACTORS, HUMAN, INFORMATIVE, WARM, AND
        EFFECTIVE COMUNICATOR. THE HUMAN AND WARM FACTORS WERE
        CONSISTENT WITH INTERPERSONAL COMPONENTS FOUND IN PRIOR
        RESEARCH, BUT THE INFORMATIVE AND EFFECTIVE COMMUNICATOR
        FACTORS WERE ONLY MARGINALLY CONSISTENT WITH TASK COMPONENTS
        FOUND PREVIOUSLY. CORRELATIONS WERE COMPUTED BETWEEN THE
        FACTORS AND THE SATISFACTION AND PERFORMANCE OF RECRUITS.
        ALL FACTORS CORRELATED SIGNIFICANTLY (NEGATIVELY) WITH
        RECRUITS' PERFORMANCE. POSSIBLE REASONS FOR THE LACK OF A
        TRADITIONAL TASK COMPONENT ARE DISCUSSED.

M0565   WERTHER, WILLIAM B.
        BEYOND JOB ENRICHMENT TO EMPLOYMENT ENRICHMENT.
        PESONNEL JOURNAL 54 (AUGUST 1975): 438-42.

            EMPLOYMENT ENRICHMENT CONSIDERS THE TOTAL WORK
        ENVIRONMENT AS A SYSTEM OF TWO OVERLAPPING AREAS: WORKER-JOB
        AND WORKER-ORGANIZATION SUBSYSTEMS. SAYS THE AUTHOR, JOB
        ENRICHMENT HAS IMPROVED THE WORKER-JOB SUBSYSTEM.
        THE FOCUS IN THIS ARTICLE IS ON METHODS OF IMPROVING THE
        WORKER-ORGANIZATION RELATIONSHIPS.

M0567   YANKOWITZ, R.   RANDELL, JOAN.
        WORK ADJUSTMENT OF THE METHADONE-MAINTAINED CORPORATE
        EMPLOYEE.
        REHABILITATION COUNSELLING BULLETIN 20 (MARCH 1977): 191-97.

            THE PRESENT STUDY EVALUATED AND COMPARED THE WORK AD-
        JUSTMENT OF 26 METHADONE-MAINTAINED CORPORATE EMPLOYEES IN
        RELATION TO SIMILAR EMPLOYEES WHO WERE NOT USING METHADONE.
        THEIR EMPLOYMENT SATISFACTION WAS COMPARED WITH NORMATIVE
        DATA FOR DISABLED AND NONDISABLED WORKERS IN CLOSELY RELATED
        OCCUPATIONS. THE RESULTS INDICATE THAT (A) RELATIVE TO THEIR
        NONMETHADONE-MAINTAINED COWORKERS, THE METHADONE-MAINTAINED
        EMPLOYEES HAD COMPARABLE JOB PERFORMANCE AND SUPERIOR
        PUNCTUALITY AND ATTENDANCE AND (B) THE METHADONE-MAINTAINED
        SKILLED LABORERS WERE SATISFIED WITH THEIR EMPLOYMENT AND
        THE OFFICE WORKERS WERE DISSATISFIED.

M0568   ZENGER, JOHN
        INCREASING PRODUCTIVITY: HOW BEHAVIORAL SCIENTISTS CAN HELP.
        PERSONNEL JOURNAL 55 (OCTOBER 1976): 513-15.

ZENGER SUGGESTS THAT THE BEHAVIORAL SCIENTISTS CAN
INFLUENCE PRODUCTIVITY WITHIN AN ORGANIZATION THROUGH AP-
PLICATIONS OF RESEARCH FINDINGS REGARDING MANAGEMENT
ATTITUDES, SYSTEMS, AND INTERPERSONAL RELATIONSHIPS.

M0569   ALDAG, RAMON J.   BRIEF, ARTHUR P.
AGE AND REACTIONS TO TASK CHARACTERISTICS.
JOURNAL OF EMPLOYMENT COUNSELING 13 (SEPTEMBER 1976): 109-15

        A SURVEY USING TWO SAMPLES EXAMINED THE DIFFERENCES
BETWEEN OLDER AND YOUNGER EMPLOYEES IN THE LEVELS OF SATIS-
FACTION DERIVED FROM AN "ENRICHED" JOB. SAMPLE A CONSISTED
OF 122 EMPLOYEES WITH AN AVERAGE AGE OF 36 YRS. WHO WORKED
FOR A MANUFACTURING COMPANY. SAMPLE B WAS COMPRISED OF 99
WORKERS WITH AN AVERAGE AGE OF 41 YRS. WHO WERE EMPLOYED BY
A PUBLIC SECTOR SERVICE AGENCY. FINDINGS FROM SAMPLE B TEND
TO REFUTE POPULAR STEREOTYPES THAT SUGGEST THAT OLDER
EMPLOYEES PLACE MORE IMPORTANCE ON EXTRINSIC REWARDS (E.G.
HIGH PAY) THAN DO YOUNGER EMPLOYEES. OLDER WORKERS RESPONDED
MUCH MORE FAVORABLY TO JOBS HIGH ON TASK IDENTITY THAN TO
THOSE LOW ON TASK IDENTITY. YOUNGER WORKERS ACTUALLY
RESPONDED SLIGHTLY MORE FAVORABLY TO JOBS LOW ON TASK
IDENTITY THAN TO THOSE HIGH ON TASK IDENTITY.

M0570   ARVEY, RICHARD D.   DEWHIRST, H. D.
GOAL-SETTING ATTRIBUTES, PERSONALITY VARIABLES, AND
JOB SATISFACTION.
JOURNAL OF VOCATIONAL BEHAVIOR 9 (OCTOBER 1976): 179-89.

        INVESTIGATED THE RELATIONSHIPS BETWEEN 4 GOAL-SETTING
ATTRIBUTES IDENTIFIED BY FACTOR ANALYTIC PROCEDURES AND JOB
SATISFACTION AMONG 271 SCIENTISTS AND ENGINEERS (MEAN AGE
46.5 YRS.) AT A NUCLEAR RESEARCH AND DEVELOPMENT CENTER.
SS' RESPONSES TO A COMPREHENSIVE QUESTIONNAIRE SHOWED
POSITIVE RELATIONSHIPS BETWEEN THE GOAL-SETTING ATTRIBUTES
AND SATISFACTION. FURTHER, IT WAS FOUND THAT NEED FOR
ACHIEVEMENT, NEED FOR AUTONOMY, AND NEED FOR AFFILIATION AS
MEASURED BY THE ADJECTIVE CHECK LIST DID NOT SIGNIFICANTLY
MODERATE THE GOAL-SETTING ATTRIBUTE/JOB SATISFACTION
RELATIONSHIPS.

M0571   BAKER, SALLY H.   HANSEN, RICHARD A.
JOB DESIGN AND WORKER SATISFACTION: A CHALLENGE TO
ASSUMPTIONS.
JOURNAL OF OCCUPATIONAL PSYCHOLOGY 48 (JUNE 1975): 79-91.

        SOME RECENT JOB REDESIGN EFFORTS IN THE U.S., INTRO-
DUCED TO COUNTER WORKER DISSATISFACTION AND LOW PRODUCTIVITY
REPRESENT A SHIFT FROM MORE TRADITIONAL BUT STILL PREVALENT
MODELS OF WORKER-EMPLOYER RELATIONS. THE PRESENT PAPER
REPORTS DATA FROM A STUDY OF 571 BLUE-COLLAR AND 842 WHITE-
COLLAR SEMI-SKILLED AMERICAN WORKERS WHICH CHALLENGE 2 BASIC
ASSUMPTIONS OF THESE NEWER EFFORTS: (A) THAT SMALL CHANGES
IN JOB DESIGN (HERE CONCEPTUALIZED AS "DESTRUCTURING" WORK
ROLES) ARE SUFFICIENT TO AFFECT WORKER SATISFACTION; AND (B)
THAT MATCHING EMPLOYEES' WORK ORIENTATIONS (HERE, THEIR
"TOLERANCE FOR STRUCTURE") WITH THE NATURE OF THEIR JOBS
(ITS DEGREE OF "STRUCTURE") WILL IMPROVE JOB SATISFACTION.

M0571   BLUE-COLLAR SS INCLUDED TEXTILE AND GARMENT OPERATORS,
         ELECTRONIC ASSEMBLERS, AND TAXI DRIVERS; WHITE-COLLAR
         SS WERE NURSES' AIDES, BANK CLERKS, OFFICE TEMPORARIES
         AND COLLEGE SECRETARIES. THE CONCEPTS "STRUCTURE" AND
         "TOLERANCE FOR STRUCTURE" ARE DISCUSSED IN OPERATIONAL
         TERMS. FINDINGS INDICATE THAT MODEST DIFFERENCES IN THE
         STRUCTURE OF JOBS ARE NOT SYSTEMATICALLY RELATED TO JOB
         SATISFACTION AND THAT THERE IS NO INTERACTION BETWEEN THESE
         WORKERS' ORIENTATIONS AND THE NATURE OF THEIR JOBS WHICH
         INFLUENCES SATISFACTION WITHIN THIS RANGE OF JOBS.

M0572   BASS, BERNARD M.   MITCHELL, C. W.
         INFLUENCES ON THE FELT NEED FOR COLLECTIVE BARGAINING BY
         BUSINESS AND SCIENCE PROFESSIONALS.
         JOURNAL OF APPLIED PSYCHOLOGY 61 (DECEMBER 1976): 770-73.

         EXAMINED THE EXTENT TO WHICH SAMPLES OF PROFESSIONALS
         WORKING IN INDUSTRY ARE INTERESTED IN UNIONIZATION AND SOME
         OF THE FACTORS THAT ARE ASSOCIATED WITH THIS INTEREST.
         26 "BUSINESS" PROFESSIONALS AND 38 "SCIENCE" PROFESSIONALS
         INDICATED IN A SURVEY QUESTIONNAIRE HOW THEY FELT ABOUT THE
         NECESSITY FOR COLLECTIVE BARGAINING. THEY ALSO COMPLETED
         SELECTIVE SECTIONS OF THE MANAGEMENT STYLES SURVEY TO REPORT
         HOW THEY FELT ABOUT THEIR JOBS, THE FAIRNESS OF PEOPLE,
         THEIR SUPERVISOR'S STYLE, AND THEIR ORGANIZATIONS. ALTHOUGH
         THE PROFESSIONALS AS A WHOLE WERE CLOSE TO THE MIDPOINT IN
         FELT NEED FOR COLLECTIVE BARGAINING, SCIENCE PROFESSIONALS
         FELT MUCH MORE NEED THAN DID BUSINESS PROFESSIONALS.
         ADDITIONAL COVARIANCE WAS ASSOCIATED WITH DISBELIEF IN THE
         FAIRNESS OF PEOPLE, AN AUTHORITARIAN RATHER THAN A
         CONSULTATIVE BOSS, JOB INSECURITY, AND PERCEIVED LACK OF
         TRUST IN THE ORGANIZATION.

M0573   BIDDLE, DEREK.   HUTTON, GEOFFREY.
         TOWARD A TOLERANCE THEORY OF WORKER ADAPTATION.
         HUMAN RELATIONS 29 (SEPTEMBER 1976): 833-62.

         EXAMINES THE WAYS IN WHICH PEOPLE CAN ACHIEVE TOLER-
         ATION OF WHAT IS TO THEM, AND MAY APPEAR TO OTHERS AS, AN
         UNSATISFYING OR IMPOVERISHED WORK SITUATION. THE EXAMINATION
         IS BASED ON AN EMPIRICAL STUDY OF 6 DEPARTMENTS OR
         WORKSHOPS IN AN ENGINEERING COMPANY IN THE SOUTH OF ENGLAND.
         THE ANALYSIS WAS MADE, NOT IN TERMS OF MOTIVES, NEEDS, AND
         ATTITUDES, BUT IN TERMS OF LIVING SPACE OR THE PSYCHOLOGICAL
         TERRITORY WHICH MEDIATES AND PROTECTS AN INDIVIDUAL'S INNER
         WORLD AND SENSE OF WORTH. JOBS THEMSELVES, AND ORGANIZATION-
         AL ACTION, DEFINE A PERMITTED LIVING SPACE WHICH MAY OR MAY
         NOT BE CONGRUENT WITH THE INDIVIDUAL'S REQUIRED LIVING
         SPACE. ADAPTIVE ACTIONS, TO ADJUST INDIVIDUAL LIVING SPACE
         OR TO CONSTRUCT GROUP LIVING SPACES, ARE EXEMPLIFIED FROM
         THE RESEARCH CASES, AND SHOWN TO AFFECT PEOPLE'S RELATIONS
         WITH THEIR JOBS, SUPERVISION, MANAGEMENT, AND UNIONS. LINKS
         ARE MADE WITH THE PSYCHOLOGY OF PLAY AND CREATIVITY AND THE
         SOCIAL PSYCHOLOGY OF NEIGHBORHOOD.

M0574   BOOTH, R. F.   MCNALLY, M. S.   BERRY, N. H.
         INDIVIDUAL AND ENVIRONMENTAL FACTORS ASSOCIATED WITH THE JOB
         SATISFACTION AND RETENTION OF NAVY HOSPITAL CORPSMEN SERVING

M0574 WITH THE U.S. MARINE CORPS.
CATALOG OF SELECTED DOCUMENTS IN PSYCHOLOGY 6
(NOVEMBER 1976): 123-24. (U.S. NAVAL HEALTH RESEARCH CENTER

REPORT NO. 76-24)
ASSESSED THE JOB SATISFACTION AND WILLINGNESS TO
VOLUNTEER FOR ADDITIONAL DUTY WITH THE U.S. MARINE CORPS OF
298 MALE NAVY HOSPITAL CORPSMEN (HMS) AFTER THEY HAD SERVED
WITH THE CORPS FOR APPROXIMATELY 11 MO. THOSE SS SATISFIED
WITH THEIR JOBS WERE MORE LIKELY TO HAVE BEEN SATISFIED
INITIALLY WITH THEIR ASSIGNMENT TO THE MARINE CORPS, TO HAVE
HAD HIGHER SCORES ON THE COMREY SOCIAL CONFORMITY, ACTIVITY,
EMOTIONAL STABILITY, AND EMPATHY SCALES, AND TO HAVE
PERFORMED BETTER DURING FIELD MEDICAL SERVICE TRAINING THAN
HMS WHO WERE NOT SATISFIED. WHEN THE INFLUENCE OF WORK
SETTINGS WAS CONSIDERED, IT WAS FOUND THAT HMS WORKING IN
PRIMARY CARE FACILITIES WERE MORE SATISFIED THAN HMS WORKING
IN FACILITIES THAT PROVIDED LITTLE OPPORTUNITY FOR PATIENT
CONTACT. ALTHOUGH BACKGROUND AND PERSONALITY CHARACTERISTICS
PLAYED A SIGNIFICANT ROLE IN THE WILLINGNESS OF A HM TO
VOLUNTEER FOR ADDITIONAL DUTY, AN HM'S DECISION OF WHETHER
OR NOT TO REMAIN WITH THE MARINE CORPS DEPENDED TO A
CONSIDERABLE EXTENT ON HIS EXPERIENCES ON THE JOB. FINDINGS
SUGGEST THAT CURRENT GUIDELINES USED IN SELECTING HMS FOR
MARINE CORPS DUTY SHOULD BE REVISED AND THAT GREATER
EMPHASIS SHOULD BE PLACED ON DEVELOPING A CADRE OF HMS WHO
HAVE FOUND THE MARINE CORPS ENVIRONMENT TO BE CONGRUENT WITH
THEIR NEEDS.

M0575 BOOTH, R. F.   MCNALLY, M. S.   BERRY, N. H.
BACKGROUND AND PERSONALITY CHARACTERISTICS RELATED TO
STUDENT SATISFACTION AND PERFORMANCE IN FIELD MEDICAL
SERVICE SCHOOL.
CATALOG OF SELECTED DOCUMENTS IN PSYCHOLOGY 6
(NOVEMBER 1976): 124. (U.S. NAVAL HEALTH RESEARCH CENTER
REPORT NO. 76-19.)

APTITUDE, BACKGROUND, AND PERSONALITY CHARACTERISTICS
OF 640 U.S. NAVY HOSPITAL CORPSMEN (HMS) WERE RELATED TO
SATISFACTION WITH ASSIGNMENT TO THE FLEET MARINE FORCE(FMF),
PERCEPTIONS OF THE FIELD MEDICAL SERVICE SCHOOL (FMSS)
ENVIRONMENT, AND ACADEMIC PERFORMANCE DURING THE 5-WEEK FMSS
TRAINING COURSE. INDIVIDUALS SATISFIED WITH AN ASSIGNMENT TO
THE FMF WERE MORE LIKELY TO HAVE VOLUNTEERED FOR FMF DUTY,
TO HAVE BEEN SATISFIED WITH HAVING BEEN DESIGNATED AN HM,
AND TO HAVE HAD HIGHER SCORES ON THE COMREY SOCIAL
CONFORMITY AND ACTIVITY SCALES THAN THOSE NOT SATISFIED WITH
ASSIGNMENT TO THE FMF. ALTHOUGH SATISFACTION WITH ASSIGNMENT
OF FMF DUTY WAS SIGNIFICANTLY RELATED TO STUDENT PERCEPTIONS
OF THE TRAINING ENVIRONMENT, SATISFACTION AND ENVIRONMENTAL
PERCEPTIONS WERE UNRELATED TO ACADEMIC PERFORMANCE. THE
EXPLAINED VARIANCE IN ACADEMIC PRFORMANCE WAS ACCOUNTED FOR
LARGELY BY A STUDENT'S APTITUDE TEST SCORES AND PREVIOUS
EXPERIENCE AS AN HM (PAY GRADE). RESULTS SUGGEST THAT
RECRUITING HMS WHO WOULD BE SATISFIED WITH FMF DUTY COULD BE
ACCOMPLISHED WITHOUT ANY REDUCTION IN THE QUALITY OF INPUT.

M0576 BRYMAN, ALAN.

M0576   STRUCTURE IN ORGANIZATION: A RECONSIDERATION.
        JOURNAL OF OCCUPATIONAL PSYCHOLOGY 49 (MARCH 1976): 1-9.
        REVIEWS THE LITERATURE AND DISCUSSES SCHOOLS OF THOUGHT
        ON STRUCTURE IN ORGANIZATIONS. THE "NEO-HUMAN RELATIONS" AND
        THE "ORGANISMIC" ORGANIZATION ADHERENTS CRITICIZE BUREAU-
        CRACY AND ADVOCATE THE CONSTUCTION OF ORGANIZATIONS IN
        WHICH STRUCTURE IS LESS PROMINENT. EVIDENCE IS CITED WHICH
        INDICATES THAT A CERTAIN DEGREE OF STRUCTURE MAY IN FACT BE
        BENEFICIAL TO ORGANIZATIONS AND THEIR MEMBERS. THIS IS
        LINKED TO A DISCUSSION OF 3 SOCIAL SCIENCE APPROACHES, EACH
        OF WHICH POINTS TO THE POSSIBILITY THAT STRUCTURE MAY NOT BE
        THE BETE NOIRE THAT IT IS FREQUENTLY TAKEN TO BE IN THE NEO-
        HUMAN RELATIONS AND ORGANISMIC ORIENTATIONS. IT MAY IN FACT
        BE TRUE THAT STRUCTURE IS A NECESSARY INGREDIENT OF ORGANIZ-
        ATIONAL LIFE AND THAT PEOPLE'S APPARENT NEED FOR STRUCTURE
        IS NOT A PATHOLOGICAL SYMPTOM OF MECHANISTIC BUREAUCRACY BUT
        A CENTRAL FEATURE OF SOCIAL EXISTENCE.

M0577   CHERNS, ALBERT.
        PERSPECTIVES ON THE QUALITY OF WORKING LIFE.
        JOURNAL OF OCCUPATIONAL PSYCHOLOGY 48 (SEPTEMBER 1975):
        155-67.

        OUTLINES BASIC ASSUMPTIONS AND VALUES IMPLICIT IN THE
        MOVE TO IMPROVE THE QUALITY OF WORKING LIFE. FOUR MAJOR
        GROUPS OF CRITICISMS OF THESE ASSUMPTIONS AND VALUES ARE
        DISCUSSED AT LENGTH, SOME BEING CONSIDERED OF STRONG WEIGHT
        AND SOME NEGATORY. SURVEY DATA ON JOB SATISFACTION ARE RE-
        VIEWED, ESPECIALLY THE FINDINGS OF M. ABRAMS (1973). THE
        SIGNIFICANCE OF THE QUALITY OF WORKING LIFE MOVEMENT IS THEN
        CONSIDERED, AND THE GROWTH AND DIFFUSION OF THIS APPROACH ON
        THE INTERNATIONAL SCENE ARE ASSESSED. FINALLY, PROBLEMS FOR
        THE FUTURE ARE REVIEWED FROM THE PERSPECTIVE OF THE VARIOUS
        RELEVANT DISCIPLINES (E.G., INDUSTRIAL PSYCHOLOGY AND SOCIAL
        PSYCHOLOGY).

M0578   CUMMINGS, L. L.   BERGER, CHRIS J.
        ORGANIZATIONAL STRUCTURE: HOW DOES IT INFLUENCE ATTITUDES
        AND PERFORMANCE.
        ORGANIZATIONAL DYNAMICS 5(AUTUMN 1976): 34-49.

        DATA FROM A LARGE NUMBER OF STUDIES OVER THE PAST 10
        YRS. WERE USED TO ANALYZE THE RELATIONSHIP BETWEEN STRUCTUR-
        AL PROPERTIES OF ORGANIZATIONS AND EMPLOYEE ATTITUDES AND
        BEHAVIORS. WHILE ALLOWING FOR GAPS IN RESEARCH AND METHODO-
        LOGICAL INCONSISTENCIES OR OCCASIONAL INAPPROPRIATENESS,
        THE FOLLOWING TENTATIVE CONCLUSIONS ARE OFFERED: (A) AN
        INDIVIDUAL'S POSITION IN THE ORGANIZATIONAL HIERARCHY IS
        RELATED TO SATISFACTION; (B) THE SOURCE OF SATISFACTION
        VARIES ACCORDING TO LEVEL IN THE ORGANIZATION; (C)
        SPECIFIC JOB BEHAVIORS AND LEVEL IN THE ORGANIZATION DO NOT
        APPEAR TO BE RELATED; (D) SATISFACTION OF INDIVIDUALS IN
        LINE AND STAFF POSITIONS DOES NOT SEEM TO DIFFER; (E)   A
        MANAGER'S JOB SATISFACTION INCREASES SLIGHTLY WITH THE
        NUMBER OF SUBORDINATES HE/SHE SUPERVISES; (F) DEPARTMENTAL
        SIZE IS NOT CONSISTENTLY RELATED TO EMPLOYEE ATTITUDE
        (G) INTERVENING PROCESSES MASK POTENTIAL INFLUENCES OF
        OVERALL ORGANIZATIONAL SIZE ON EMPLOYEE VARIABLES; AND (H)

M0578   HIGH-LEVEL EXECUTIVES IN TALL ORGANIZATIONS AND LOW-LEVEL
EXECUTIVES IN FLAT ORGANIZATIONS OBTAIN MORE SATISFACTION
THAN DO THEIR OPPOSITES.

M0579   DRUMMOND, R. J.   MCINTIRE,WALTER G. SKAGGS, C. T.
WORK VALUES AND JOB SATISFACTION OF YOUNG ADULT MALES.
JOURNAL OF EMPLOYMENT COUNSELING 14 (MARCH 1977): 23-26.

     USED A CAREER TRANSITION QUESTIONNAIRE DEVELOPED BY C.
T. SKAGGS AND R. J. DRUMMOND (1972) AND THE WORK VALUES IN-
VENTORY TO CLASSIFY 136 18-25 YR OLD MALE WORKERS ACCORDING
TO 3 DEGREES OF WORK SATISFACTION (HIGH, MEDIUM, AND LOW).
THE RESULTS LEND SUPPORT TO THE IDEA THAT JOB SATISFACTION
IS MORE CLOSELY LINKED TO THE INTRINSIC RATHER THAN THE EX-
TRINSIC FACTORS OF WORK. CONSIDERABLE AGREEMENT ON WHICH
FACTORS CONTRIBUTE TO WORK SATISFACTION WAS ALSO EVIDENT
REGARDLESS OF THE LEVEL OF SATISFACTION. IT IS SUGGESTED
THAT COUNSELORS WORKING WITH YOUTHS PAY CLOSE ATTENTION TO
INTRINSIC WORK FACTORS.

M0580   DUNHAM, RANDALL B.
THE MEASUREMENT AND DIMENSIONALITY OF JOB CHARACTERISTICS.
JOURNAL OF APPLIED PSYCHOLOGY 61 (AUGUST 1976): 404-409.

     INVESTIGATED THE DIMENSIONALITY OF MEASURES OF
PERCEIVED JOB CHARACTERISTICS AND MODELS FOR COMBINING THESE
DIMENSIONS TO ACCOUNT FOR AFFECTIVE RESPONSES. 3610 EXEMPT
PERSONNEL FROM A LARGE RETAIL MERCHANDISING ORGANIZATION
RESPONDED TO THE JOB DIAGNOSTIC SURVEY AND A MEASURE OF WORK
SATISFACTION. RESULTS SHOW THAT MEASURES OF TASK VARIETY AND
AUTONOMY ARE NOT EMPIRICALLY DIFFERENT AND THAT A SINGLE
DIMENSIONAL REPRESENTATION OF JOB CHARACTERISTICS MAY BE
PARSIMONIOUS. IT IS SUGGESTED THAT AN ADDITIVE, COMPENSATORY
MODEL FOR COMBINING ELEMENTS OF TASK CHARACTERISTCS SHOULD
BE CONSIDERED ALONG WITH COMPLEX NONCOMPENSATORY MODELS.

M0581   DUNHAM, RANDALL B.
REACTIONS TO JOB CHARACTERISTICS: MODERATING EFFECTS OF THE
ORGANIZATION.
ACADEMY OF MANAGEMENT JOURNAL 20 (MARCH 1977): 42-65.

     AN ANALYSIS ESTABLISHED A SIGNIFICANT RELATIONSHIP
BETWEEN TASK DESIGN AND AFFECTIVE RESPONSE MEASURES (JOB
DIAGNOSTIC SURVEY, INDEX OF ORGANIZATIONAL REACTIONS, AND
PERCEIVED ENVIRONMENTAL CHARACTERISTICS SCALES) FOR 784
MIDDLE-LEVEL EXECUTIVES. FUNCTIONAL SPECIALTY MODERATED THE
RELATIONSHIP. IT IS SUGGESTED THAT THE MODERATING EFFECT MAY
BE EXPLAINED IN TERMS OF ENVIRONMENTAL ELEMENTS WHICH CAUSE
THE WORKER TO FOCUS ON OR OFF TASK DESIGN.

M0582   DYER, LEE.   THERIAULT, ROLAND.
THE DETERMINANTS OF PAY SATISFACTION.
JOURNAL OF APPLIED PSYCHOLOGY 61 (OCTOBER 1976): 596-604.

     CONDUCTED A STUDY TO TEST EMPIRICALLY (A) THE UTILITY
OF A MODEL OF THE DETERMINANTS OF PAY SATISFACTION DEVELOPED
BY E.E. LAWLER (1971) AND (B) THE VALUE OF ADDING TO THIS
MODEL A CATEGORY OF VARIABLES NOT PREVIOUSLY INCLUDED:

M0582   PERCEPTIONS OF PAY-SYSTEM ADMINISTRATION. THE STUDY WAS
        CONDUCTED AMONG 180 U.S., 133 FRENCH-CANADIAN, AND 79
        ENGLISH-CANADIAN MANAGERS. RESULTS PROVIDE SOME SUPPORT FOR
        THE UTILITY OF LAWLER'S MODEL AND ADDITIONAL SUPPORT FOR THE
        VALUE OF ADDING THE ADMINISTRATIVE-TYPE VARIABLES. RESULTS
        OF THIS AND OTHER STUDIES ARE USED TO DEVELOP A MODIFIED
        MODEL OF THE DETERMINANTS OF PAY SATISFACTION.

M0583   EDEN, DOV.
        ORGANIZATIONAL MEMBERSHIP VS. SELF-EMPLOYMENT: ANOTHER BLOW
        TO THE AMERICAN DREAM.
        ORGANIZATIONAL BEHAVIOR AND HUMAN PERFORMANCE 13 (FEBRUARY
        1975): 79-94.

             THE CONTENTION THAT MEMBERSHIP IN WORK ORGANIZATIONS
        HAD ADVERSE EFFECTS ON INDIVIDUAL PSYCHOLOGICAL WELL-BEING
        WAS TESTED BY COMPARING NATIONAL SURVEY DATA FOR 1,902
        MEMBERS AND 183 SELF-EMPLOYED WORKERS. FORMERLY ESTABLISHED
        DEMOGRAPHIC DIFFERENCES BETWEEN SELF-EMPLOYED AND WAGE-AND-
        SALARY WORKERS WERE REPLICATED. WHILE MAJOR DIFFERENCES WERE
        NOT REVEALED IN WORK VALUES, MEASURES OF CHARACTERISTICS OF
        THE WORK SETTING SHOWED THAT THE SELF-EMPLOYED ENJOY MORE
        ENRICHING JOB REQUIREMENTS, OPPORTINITIES FOR SELF-
        FULFILLMENT AND SKILL UTILIZATION, AUTONOMY, PHYSICAL
        WORKING CONDITIONS, AUTHORITY OVER OTHER PERSONS, RESOURCES
        WITH WHICH TO DO THE JOB, AND OTHER GENERALLY HIGHLY PRIZED
        FEATURES OF THEIR JOB SETTINGS. MEMBERS REPORTED MORE
        FRIENDLY RELATIONS WITH CO-WORKERS, GREATER JOB SECURITY,
        AND MORE CONVENIENT HOURS. IN COMPARISON TO MEMBERS, THE
        SELF-EMPLOYED APPEARED TO HAVE MORE FAVORABLE JOB SETTINGS,
        REPORTED SLIGHTLY MORE JOB SATISFACTION AND ROLE STRAIN, AND
        SHOWED NO DIFFERENCE ON A MENTAL HEALTH INDEX. MULTIPLE
        CLASSIFICATION ANALYSIS SUPPORTED THE INTERPRETATION OF
        THESE FINDINGS AS EVIDENCE THAT ORGANIZATIONAL MEMBERSHIP
        HAS A POSITIVE NET EFFECT UPON PSYCHOLOGICAL OUTCOMES.
        FINDINGS ARE CONSISTENT WITH THE CONCLUSION THAT SELF-
        EMPLOYMENT, DESPITE ITS NUMEROUS OTHER ADVANTAGES, DOES NOT
        PROVIDE WORKERS WITH THE GREATER PSYCHOLOGICAL BENEFITS
        PROMISED BY THE AMERICAN DREAM.

M0584   FOSSUM, JOHN A.
        REPLY TO URBAN-RURAL DIFFERENCES IN JOB SATISFACTION.
        INDUSTRIAL AND LABOR RELATIONS REVIEW 29 (APRIL 1976):
        422-24.

             REPLIES TO R.E. GINNOLD'S CRITIQUE OF THE AUTHOR'S 1975
        ARTICLE RELATING JOB SATISFACTION TO URBAN-RURAL DIFFERENCES
        AND QUESTIONS SOME OF GINNOLD'S SUGGESTIONS FOR RESEARCH.
        FUTURE STUDIES SHOULD TRY TO DETERMINE DIFFERENCES IN URBAN
        AND RURAL ATTITUDES TOWARD WORK AND WHETHER THESE ATTITUDES
        ARE TRANSLATED INTO BEHAVIOR.

M0585   GINNOLD, RICHARD E.
        URBAN-RURAL DIFFERENCES IN JOB SATISFACTION.
        INDUSTRIAL AND LABOR RELATIONS REVIEW 29 (APRIL 1976):
        420-22.

             CRITICIZES J. FOSSUM'S 1974 STUDY WHICH FOUND AN URBAN-

M0585   RURAL EFFECT IN JOB SATISFACTION, ON THE BASIS OF
         EXPERIMENTAL CONTROL PROBLEMS, INADEQUATE SPECIFICATION OF
         THE INDEPENDENT VARIABLE, AND INTERPRETATION OF THE RESULTS.
         HYPOTHESES FOR FUTURE RESEARCH ARE OFFERED.

M0586   BENNIS, WARREN.
         LEADERSHIP: BELEAGURED SPECIES?
         ORGANIZATIONAL DYNAMICS 5 (SUMMER 1976): 3-16.

              POINTS OUT THAT THE MOST SERIOUS THREAT TO INSTITUTIONS
         AND THE CAUSE OF THE 'DIMINISHING SENSE OF ABLE LEADERSHIP'
         IS THE STEADY EROSION OF INSTITUTIONAL AUTONOMY. EXTERNAL
         FORCES WHICH CONTRIBUTE TO THIS EROSION ARE THE MULTIPLE
         DEPENDENCIES OR EXTERNAL PATRONAGE STRUCTURES WHICH 'BLUNT
         AND DIFFUSE' THE MAIN PURPOSES OF INSTITUTIONS. OTHER FORCES
         ERODING INSTITUTIONAL AUTONOMY STEM FROM FRAGMENTATION
         THROUGH THE FORMATION OF INTERNAL PRESSURE GROUPS AND THE
         CONFLICTS ARISING FROM MULTIPLE ADVOCACIES. COERCIVE
         POLITICAL AND LEGAL CONSTRAINTS ALSO CONTRIBUTE TO WEAKENED
         INSTITUTIONAL CONTROL. IT IS MAINTAINED THAT LEADERS HAVE
         FEW ALTERNATIVES BUT TO COPE WITH THESE PROBLEMS THROUGH (A)
         MANAGING, NOT LEADING; (B) 'COPPING-OUT'; (C) LEADING
         THROUGH LIMITS AND BY DIMINUENDO; AND (D) 'SWEEPING AND
         DUSTING'. SEVEN GUIDELINES FOR LEADERS IN DIRECTING THE
         PROCESS OF CHANGE ARE PROPOSED. EMPHASIS IS PLACED ON THE
         LEADER AS A 'SOCIAL ARCHITECT' WHOSE BROAD VISION FOR THE
         PRESENT AND FUTURE RESTS ON HIS/HER ABILITY TO CLARIFY AND
         DIRECT THE CONDUCT OF ORGANIZED HUMAN ENDEAVORS.

M0587   GARDELL, BERTIL.
         REACTIONS AT WORK AND THEIR INFLUENCE ON NON-WORK
         ACTIVITIES: AN ANALYSIS OF A SOCIOPOLITICAL PROBLEM IN
         AFFLUENT SOCIETIES.
         HUMAN RELATIONS 29 (SEPTEMBER 1976): 885-904.

              TRADITIONAL WAYS OF ORGANIZING WORK IN INDUSTRIALIZED
         SOCIETIES ARE IN CONFLICT WITH BASIC HUMAN NEEDS RELATED TO
         CREATIVITY, INFLUENCE, AND GROWTH. THIS CONFLICT SEEMS TO
         AFFECT ADVERSELY NOT ONLY WORK SATISFACTION AND JOB AND
         LABOR-MARKET BEHAVIOR, BUT ALSO PARTICIPATION IN AND REWARDS
         FROM NONWORK ACTIVITIES SUCH AS PARTICIPATION IN ORGANIZED
         CULTURAL, POLITICAL, AND EDUCATIONAL ACTIVITIES. EVIDENCE
         IS ALSO GIVEN FOR ADVERSE EFFECTS ON SELF-ESTEEM AND MENTAL
         HEALTH. THE ADVANCE OF THE WELFARE STATE IS SEEN AS THE
         MATERIAL FOUNDATION MAKING POSSIBLE THE PRESENT CHANGE IN
         WORK VALUES AND EXPECTATIONS, CALLING FOR INCREASED WORKER
         INFLUENCE ON DIFFERENT LEVELS IN THE PRODUCTION SYSTEM AND
         FOR AN INCREASED QUALITY OF WORKING LIFE. AT THE SAME TIME,
         HOWEVER, INCREASED EXPECTATIONS ARE MADE TOWARD THE QUALITY
         OF NONWORK ACTIVITIES AND TOWARD GREATER EQUALITY BETWEEN
         SEXES AND GENERATIONS, (E.G., IN RELATION TO FAMILY DUTIES,
         EDUCATION, AND LABOR-MARKET OPPORTINITIES.) THESE VALUE
         CHANGES CALL FOR A BROADER APPROACH TO SOCIAL CHANGE IN
         WORKING LIFE THAN IS GENERALLY IMPLIED IN SOCIOTECHNICAL
         APPROACHES TO JOB DESIGN AND ORGANIZATION HOURS, MORE
         FLEXIBLE CAREER PATTERNS, AND GREATER FLEXIBILITY IN THE
         RELATION BETWEEN WORK, FAMILY, AND NONWORK ACTIVITIES.

M0588   GOLDBERG, ALBERT I.
        THE RELEVANCE OF COSMOPOLITAN/LOCAL ORIENTATIONS TO
        PROFESSIONAL VALUES AND BEHAVIOR.
        SOCIOLOGY OF WORK AND OCCUPATIONS 3 (AUGUST 1976): 331-56.

            DISCUSSES 2 KEY CONCEPTS USED BY SOCIAL SCIENTISTS:
        COSMOPOLITANISM AND LOCALISM. IT IS ARGUED THAT THE FORMER
        HAS COME TO BE CONFUSED WITH PROFESSIONALISM.
        THIS CONFUSION CAN BE ELIMINATED BY RETURNING THE CONCEPTS
        TO THEIR ORIGINAL USAGE TO DESIGNATE OUTER AND INNER
        REFERENCE GROUPS. THIS MORE RESTRICTED DEFINITION OF COSMO-
        POLITANISM-LOCALISM WAS SERVICES ORGANIZATION. RESPONDENTS-
        54 BLACK COUNSELORS AND PEOPLE-HELPING WORKERS-DESCRIBED
        THEIR JOB SATISFACTION, ROLE CLARITY, AND THE BEHAVIOR OF
        THEIR LEADERS (N=19), WHILE THE LEADERS EVALUATED THE
        RESPONDENTS' JOB PERFORMANCE. USING SUBGROUP MODERATOR
        ANALYSES, THE EFFECT OF WORK UNIT SIZE WAS SIGNIFICANT, WITH
        LEADER STRUCTURE RELATED TO SATISFACTION IN LARGER UNITS
        AND CONSIDERATION RELATED TO SATISFACTION IN SMALLER UNITS.
        RESULTS CONFIRM EARLIER FINDINGS THAT IN LOW-STRESS JOBS
        CONSIDERATION ENHANCES SATISFACTION AND PERFORMANCE BUT THAT
        IN HIGH STRESS JOBS, STRUCTURE IS HELPFUL. ALSO CONFIRMED
        WERE RESULTS OF PREVIOUS STUDIES SHOWING THAT HIGH STRUCTURE
        HAD DYSFUNCTIONAL EFFECTS ONLY WHEN ACCOMPANIED BY LOW
        CONSIDERATION. FINALLY, ROLE CLARITY DID NOT MODERATE THE
        RELATIONSHIP BETWEEN LEADER BEHAVIOR AND SUBORDINATE
        SATISFACTION AND PERFORMANCE.

M0589   GOODMAN, PAUL S.   MOORE, BRIAN E.
        FACTORS AFFECTING ACQUISITION OF BELIEFS ABOUT A NEW REWARD
        SYSTEM.
        HUMAN RELATIONS 29 (JUNE 1976): 571-88.

            EXAMINED THE RELATIONSHIPS AMONG INDIVIDUAL, ORGANIZA-
        TIONAL, AND INTERPERSONAL VARIABLES ON THE ACQUISITION OF
        BELIEFS ABOUT A NEW ORGANIZATIONAL REWARD SYSTEM. THE
        SETTING FOR THE RESEARCH WAS THE INTRODUCTION OF AN
        INCENTIVE PLAN (SCANLON PLAN) INTO A MANUFACTURING PLANT.TWO
        TYPES OF BELIEFS WERE ANALYZED: (A) THAT SUGGESTION-MAKING
        BEHAVIOR LEADS TO A REWARD (SYSTEM EXPECTANCY) AND THAT (B)
        GIVEN THE EFFORT, THE INDIVIDUAL CAN MAKE PRODUCTIVITY-
        RELATED SUGGESTIONS (SELF-EXPECTANCY). SS WERE 70 BLUE-
        COLLAR WORKERS AND 25 MANAGERS. MANAGERS' BELIEFS ABOUT
        THIS NEW PLAN WERE MORE AFFECTED BY INDIVIDUAL LEVEL
        VARIABLES (E.G. EDUCATIONAL LEVEL), WHILE BELIEFS OF BLUE-
        COLLAR WORKERS SEEMED MORE AFFECTED BY ORGANIZATIONAL (E.G.
        NATURE OF TASK) OR INTERPERSONAL VARIABLES. A MEASUREMENT 6
        MONTHS AFTER THE PLAN HAD BEEN IN OPERATION INDICATED THAT
        THE BELIEFS REMAINED RELATIVELY STABLE; HOWEVER, DESPITE
        FREQUENT BONUSES FROM THE NEW PLAN, THERE WAS A TENDENCY FOR
        SOME PARTICIPANTS TO BE MORE SKEPTICAL ABOUT FUTURE PAYOFFS.

M0590   GOUDY, WILLIS J.   POWERS, EDWARD A.   KEITH, PATRICIA.
        THE WORK SATISFACTION, RETIREMENT-ATTITUDE TYPOLOGY: PROFILE
        EXAMINATION.
        EXPERIMENTAL AGING RESEARCH 1 (NOVEMBER 1975): 267-79.

            A NEW TYPOLOGY OF WORK SATISFACTION AND ATTITUDE TOWARD

M0590   RETIREMENT INCLUDING 4 CATEGORIES (TYPE A-POSITIVE ATTITUDES
         TOWARD WORK AND RETIREMENT; TYPE B-WORK POSITIVE, RETIREMENT
         NEGATIVE; TYPE C-WORK NEGATIVE, RETIREMENT POSITIVE; AND
         TYPE D-NEGATIVE ATTITUDES TOWARD WORK AND RETIREMENT) WAS
         DEVELOPED AND APPLIED TO QUESTIONNAIRE DATA COLLECTED IN
         1964 FROM 1,922 MALES OVER 50 YEARS OF AGE WHO WERE EITHER
         SELF-EMPLOYED PROFESSIONALS, SALARIED PROFESSIONALS, OWNER-
         MERCHANTS, FACTORY WORKERS, OR FARMERS. SOME FOLLOW-UP DATA
         FROM 1966 AND 1974 ARE ALSO REPORTED. OVERALL FINDINGS
         SUGGEST THAT MEMBERS OF SOME TYPES WILL BE MORE SUSCEPTIBLE
         TO NEGATIVE CONSEQUENCES OF CYCLE CHANGE (WORK TO
         RETIREMENT) THAN OTHERS. SOCIOECONOMIC STATUS, AGE, SOCIAL
         PARTICIPATION, HEALTH, COMMUNITY, HOUSING, FAMILY, WORK,
         MORALE, AND LONGEVITY DATA INDICATE PRERETIREMENT PLANNING
         APPROACHES SHOULD BE DEVELOPED FOR THOSE HAVING DIFFERENT
         WORK-RETIREMENT ATTITUDES.

M0591   GOULD, BRUCE R.
         LONGITUDINAL INFERENCES OF JOB ATTITUDE AND TENURE
         RELATIONSHIPS FROM CROSS-SECTIONAL DATA.
         U.S. AFHRL TECHNICAL REPORT NO. 76-46 (JULY 1976).

              ONE OBJECTIVE OF A U.S. AIR FORCE SATISFACTION RESEARCH
         PROGRAM IS THE IDENTIFICATION OF CAREER LADDERS WITH THE
         GREATEST POTENTIAL FOR IMPROVING RETENTION. THE PRESENT
         STUDY, USING 7 SURVEY GROUPS REPRESENTED BY 1,206 CASES,
         REVEALS THAT A REGRESSION MODEL (WHICH TAKES INTO ACCOUNT
         AIRMEN CAREER STATUS AND MONTHS OF SERVICE WHILE HOLDING
         CONSTANT APTITUDE DIFFERENCES) CAN BE USED TO DISPLAY AND
         INTERPRET CROSS-SECTIONAL ATTITUDE DATA IN A LONGITUDINAL
         FASHION. THE CROSS-SECTIONAL PROFILES PROVIDE A MEANS OF
         IDENTIFYING SPECIALTIES WITH THE GREATEST POTENTIAL FOR JOB
         REENGINEERING WHERE THE GOAL IS TO POSITIVELY INFLUENCE
         CAREER DECISIONS THROUGH PROVIDING MORE SATISFYING JOBS.

M0592   HEATH, DOUGLAS H.
         ADOLESCENT AND ADULT PREDICTORS OF VOCATIONAL ADAPTATION.
         JOURNAL OF VOCATIONAL BEHAVIOR 9 (AUGUST 1976): 1-19.

              CONDUCTED THE INITIAL PHASE OF A LONGITUDINAL STUDY OF
         THE MATURATION OF 68 MALES UPON THEIR ENTRY TO COLLEGE, AND
         WHEN THESE PROFESSIONAL AND MANAGERIAL MEN WERE IN THEIR
         EARLY 30'S. QUESTIONNAIRE (INCLUDING THE SELF-IMAGE
         QUESTIONNAIRE, STUDY OF VALUES, AND PERCEIVED SELF QUESTION-
         NAIRE), TEST (INCLUDING THE MMPI, SCHOLASTIC APTITUDE TEST,
         AND THE RORSCHACH), AND INTERVIEW DATA WERE PREDICTIVE OF
         THE SS' VOCATIONAL ADAPTATION MEASURED BY A 28-ITEM
         VOCATIONAL ADAPTATION SCALE COMPLETED BY EACH S, HIS WIFE,
         CLOSEST FRIEND, AND CO-WORKER. SELF-AND JUDGE-RATED
         VOCATIONAL ADAPTATION WAS DIRECTLY RELATED TO SATISFACTION
         WITH ONE'S VOCATION, CORDIALITY OF ONE'S WORK RELATIONSHIPS,
         COMPETENCE IN A VARIETY OF NONOCCUPATIONAL ROLES, BUT NOT TO
         SALARY. PSYCHOLOGICAL MATURITY, WHETHER MEASURED WHEN
         COLLEGE STUDENT OR AN ADULT MORE THAN A DECADE LATER,
         CONSISTENTLY PREDICTED VOCATIONAL ADAPTATION. RESULTS
         PROVIDED FURTHER SUPPORT FOR A DIMENSIONAL MODEL OF
         MATURING THAT IDENTIFIES THE PERSONALITY TRAITS ASSOCIATED
         WITH GOOD VOCATIONAL ADAPTATION OF PROFESSIONAL AND

M0592 MANAGERIAL MEN.

M0593 HOFSTEDE, GEERT
NATIONALITY AND ESPOUSED VALUES OF MANAGERS.
JOURNAL OF APPLIED PSYCHOLOGY 61 (APRIL 1976): 148-55.

A SAMPLE OF 372 24-45 YEAR OLD MIDDLE-LEVEL MANAGERS
FROM 40 NATIONALITIES WHO ATTENDED RESIDENT MANAGEMENT
DEVELOPMENT PROGRAMS IN LAUSANNE, SWITZERLAND, SCORED THEIR
ESPOUSED VALUES ON 2 PAPER-AND-PENCIL VALUES TESTS, L.V.
GORDON'S SURVEYS OF PERSONAL AND OF INTERPERSONAL VALUES.
ALL USED THE ENGLISH LANGUAGE FORM. SCORES DIFFERENTIATED
MEANINGFULLY BY THE AGE GROUP OF RESPONDENTS. FOR THE 15
NATIONALITIES REPRESENTED BY AT LEAST 7 RESPONDENTS, A Q
ANALYSIS OF THE SCORES PER NATIONALITY GROUP WAS CARRIED OUT
WHICH SORTED THE 15 NATIONALITIES INTO 5 CLUSTERS- NORDIC,
GERMANIC, ANGLO, LATIN, AND ASIAN. THE VALUE PROFILES OF
EACH COUNTRY AND CLUSTER ARE SHOWN. DIFFERENCES BETWEEN
CLUSTERS SHOW SIGNIFICANT AGREEMENT WITH DIFFERENCES BETWEEN
STUDENT SAMPLES FROM THE SAME COUNTRIES, OBTAINED WITH
TRANSLATED VERSIONS OF THE INSTRUMENTS. THE CLUSTER
COMPOSITION CAN BE EXPLAINED BY BOTH LINGUISTIC AND OTHER
CULTURAL REASONS.

M0594 IVANCEVICH, J. M.
EFFECTS OF GOAL SETTING ON PERFORMANCE AND JOB SATISFACTION.
JOURNAL OF APPLIED PSYCHOLOGY 61 (OCTOBER 1976): 605-12.

CONDCTED A FIELD EXPERIMENT TO COMPARE PARTICIPATIVE,
ASSIGNED, AND NO-TRAINING (COMPARISON) GOAL SETTING GROUPS.
37 SALES PERSONNEL WERE TRAINED IN PARTICIPATIVE GOAL
SETTING, AND 41 WERE TRAINED IN ASSIGNED GOAL SETTING. A 3RD
GROUP OF 44 SERVED AS A COMPARISON UNIT. MEAN AGE RANGE OF
SS WAS 34.3-36.4 YEARS. MEASURES OF 4 PERFORMANCE AND 2
SATISFACTION CRITERIA WERE COLLECTED AT 4 DATA POINTS:
BASELINE (BEFORE TRAINING), AND 6, 9, AND 12 MONTHS AFTER
TRAINING. ANALYSIS OF VARIANCE AND DUNCAN'S MULTIPLE-RANGE
TEST RESULTS INDICATE THAT FOR AT LEAST 9 MONTHS BOTH
PARTICIPATIVE AND ASSIGNED GOAL SETTING SS WERE MORE
EFFECTIVE IN IMPROVING PERFORMANCE AND SATISFACTION. THE
IMPROVEMENTS, HOWEVER, WERE GENERALLY NOT FOUND 12 MONTHS
AFTER TRAINING.

M0595 KOCHRAN, THOMAS A. CUMMINGS, L. L.   HUBER, GEORGE P.
OPERATIONALIZING THE CONCEPTS OF GOALS AND GOAL
INCOMPATIBILITIES IN ORGANIZATIONAL BEHAVIOR RESEARCH.
HUMAN RELATIONS 29 (JUNE 1976): 527-44.

DEMONSTRATES THE THEORETICAL REVELANCE AND VALIDITY OF
USING UTILITY MODELS AND SCALING TECHNIQUES AS AN APPROACH
TO MAKING THE CONCEPTS OF GOALS AND GOAL INCOMPATIBILITIES
OPERATIONAL. THE APPROACH WAS USED, WITH EMPIRICAL DATA FROM
MUNINCIPAL GOVERNMENT OFFICIALS IN 380 CITIES, TO TEST THE
PROPOSITIONS THAT (A) STRUCTURAL DIFFERENTIATION IN
ORGANIZATIONS IS ASSOCIATED WITH GOAL INCOMPATIBILITIES AND
(B) GOAL INCOMPATIBILITIES ARE CORRELATED WITH CONFLICT IN
ORGANIZATION. BOTH PROPOSITIONS WERE SUPPORTED. ON THE BASIS
OF A LITERAL REVIEW, IT IS CONCLUDED THAT (A) THE CONCEPTS

M0595 OF GOALS AND GOAL INCOMPATIBILITIES PLAY IMPORTANT, BUT
CONTROVERSIAL ROLES IN ORGANIZATION BEHAVIOR, AND (B) THERE
HAS BEEN VERY LITTLE EMPIRICAL RESEARCH DIRECTED TOWARD
OPERATIONALIZING THESE CONCEPTS. ON THE BASIS OF THE
EMPIRICAL RESEARCH, IT IS SUGGESTED THAT THE APPROACH IS
VALID. GOALS WHICH WERE SHARED ACROSS UNITS TENDED TO BE
OF MODERATE IMPORTANCE TO ORGANIZATIONAL DECISION-MAKERS
WITHIN THESE UNITS, WHILE DISAGREEMENTS REGARDING GOALS WERE
FOUND TO FOCUS ON UNIT POWER PRESERVATION AND PROCEDURES.

M0596 MARTINSON, OSCAR.   WILKENING, E. A.   RODEFIELD, R.
FEELINGS OF POWERLESSNESS AND SOCIAL ISOLATION AMONG LARGE
SCALE FARM PERSONNEL.
RURAL SOCIOLOGY 41 (WINTER 1976): 452-72.

     THE EFFECTS OF A DIFFERENTIATED PRODUCTION STRUCTURE
ON INDICATORS OF POWERLESSNESS AND SOCIAL ISOLATION WERE
EXAMINED IN INTERVIEWS WITH 180 LARGE-SCALE FARM PERSONNEL
(OWNERS, MANAGERS, AND WORKERS), USING ANALYSES OF VARIANCE
AND COVARIANCE. SIGNIFICANT EFFECTS OF THE INDEPENDENT
VARIABLE, OCCUPATION, ON BOTH DEPENDENT VARIABLES WERE
FOUND, AS WERE EFFECTS FROM ANOTHER ANTECEDENT AND MEDIATING
VARIABLES. THE USE OF ANALYSES OF COVARIANCE AND MULTIPLE
COMPARISONS FURTHER SPECIFIED THE EFFECTS OF THE MAJOR
INDEPENDENT VARIABLE AND OF SELECTED COVARIATES ON EACH OF
THE DEPENDENT VARIABLES. IT IS CONCLUDED THAT SPECIALIZED
EXPLANATIONS OF SPECIFIC INDICATORS OF ALIENATION ARE
NECESSARY TO UNDERSTAND THE WAY IN WHICH A DIFFERENTIATED
OCCUPATIONAL STRUCTURE HELPS TO EXPLAIN ALIENATION AMONG
LARGE-SCALE FARM PERSONNEL. IMPLICATIONS FOR THE QUALITY OF
LIFE OF LARGE-SCALE FARM PERSONNEL ARE DISCUSSED.

M0597 MOLES, ROBERT H.
ROLE REQUIREMENTS AS SOURCES OF ORGANIZATIONAL STRESS.
JOURNAL OF APPLIED PSYCHOLOGY 61 (APRIL 1976): 172-79.

     EXAMINED RELATIONSHIPS BETWEEN MAJOR ROLE REQUIREMENTS
AND EXPERIENCED ROLE STRESS, USING DATA FROM 202 RESEARCH
AND DEVELOPMENT PROFESSIONALS. MEASURES (INCLUDING THOSE OF
J.R. RIZZO ET AL,1970) OF ROLE STRESS INCLUDED VARIOUS TYPES
OF ROLE CONFLICT AND AMBIGUITY. ROLE REQUIREMENTS INCLUDED
INTEGRATION AND BOUNDARY-SPANNING ACTIVITIES, PERSONNEL
SUPERVISION, AND SCIENTIFIC RESEARCH. ROLE CONFLICT WAS MORE
SENSITIVE THAN ROLE AMBIGUITY TO DIFFERENCES IN RESEARCH AND
DEVELOPMENT ROLE REQUIREMENTS; AND INTEGRATION AND BOUNDARY
SPANNING ACTIVITIES WERE THE BEST PREDICTORS OF EXPERIENCED
ROLE CONFLICT, ESPECIALLY OF THE INTERSENDER VARIETY.

M0598 HENDRIX, WILLIAM.   WARD, JOE H.
PREFERRED JOB ASSIGNMENT EFFECT ON JOB SATISFACTION.
U.S. AFHRL TECHNICAL REPORT NO. 75-77, DECEMBER 1975.

     THE CURRENT POSTENLISTMENT ASSIGNMENT PROCESS USED BY
THE U.S. AIR FORCE PERMITS RECRUITS TO INDICATE 3 JOB
PREFERENCES. AN ATTEMPT WAS MADE TO LEARN WHETHER BEING
PERMITTED TO INDICATE A PREFERENCE CATEGORY AND BEING
ASSIGNED TO A PREFERRED JOB EFFECTED JOB SATISFACTION.
ANALYSES WERE PERFORMED WITH DATA FROM 15,000 MALE AND 4,156

M0598   FEMALE 1ST-TERM AIRMEN TO SEE IF THE PREFERENCES SELECTION
         PROCESS WAS RELATED TO 3 MEASURES OF JOB SATISFACTION-
         REENLISTMENT INTENT, JOB INTEREST, AND FELT UTILIZATION OF
         TALENTS AND TRAINING. RESULTS INDICATE THAT THE SELECTION
         PROCESS WAS RELATED (P<.01) TO 2 OF THE MEASURES. THE
         EXCEPTION WAS REENLISTMENT INTENT. THE QUESTION OF PRACTICAL
         SIGNIFICANCE IS RAISED AND THE RECOMENDATIONS OFFERED.

M0599   KRECK, LOTHAR A.
         SEMANTIC DISTANCE AND JOB SATISFACTION IN FORMAL
         ORGANIZATIONS.
         ETC. 31 (SEPTEMBER 1974): 249-56.

              CONSIDERS THE ROLE OF COMMUNICATION IN EMPLOYEE
         SATISFACTION. USING C.E. OSGOOD'S SEMANTIC DIFFERENTIAL
         SCALING TECHNIQUE (SD), PREVIOUS STUDIES HAVE NOTED SEMANTIC
         DISTANCE (DIFFERENCES IN CONNOTATIVE MEANINGS) AMONG
         HIERARCHICAL ORGANIZATIONAL LEVELS. TWO CHAIN INNS AND A
         HOTEL PARTICIPATED IN THIS FIELD STUDY AND THERE WERE 31
         MANAGERIAL AND 146 NONSUPERVISORY EMPLOYEES. TEN SD
         GRADIENTS WERE ADMINISTERED TO MEASURE THE MEANINGS OF 10
         ORGANIZATIONAL CONCEPTS, AND A MEAN ABSOLUTE SCORE FOR EACH
         OF THE CONCEPTS WAS OBTAINED FOR EACH S. THREE MEASURES OF
         JOB SATISFACTION (LABOR UNREST, LABOR TURNOVER, AND
         ABSENTEEISM) WERE APPLIED TO EACH ORGANIZATION. JOB
         SATISFACTION MEASURES AND INDICES OF SEMANTIC DISTANCE
         BETWEEN MANAGERS AND NONSUPERVISORS WERE ANALYZED USING
         CORRELATIONS. NEGATIVE RESULTS INDICATE THAT (A) THE FRAME
         OF REFERENCE OF MANAGERS AND NONSUPERVISORS WAS SIMILAR AND
         (B) SEMANTIC DISTANCE AND JOB SATISFACTION WERE UNRELATED.
         SEVERAL POSSIBLE EXPLANATIONS FOR THE DATA ARE ADVANCED.
         THE SD IS NOTED AS AN EFFICIENT DEVICE FOR LOCATING POSSIBLE
         AREAS OF CONCERN IN ORGANIZATIONS.

M0600   LOCKE, EDWIN A.   SIROTA, DAVID   WOLFSON, ALAN D.
         AN EXPERIMENTAL CASE STUDY OF THE SUCCESSES AND FAILURES OF
         JOB ENRICHMENT IN A GOVERNMENT AGENCY.
         JOURNAL OF APPLIED PSYCHOLOGY 61 (DECEMBER 1976): 701-11.

              AN EXPERIMENTAL JOB ENRICHMENT PROGRAM WAS INTRODUCED
         IN 3 CLERICAL WORK UNITS (N= 1,000 WORKERS) OF A FEDERAL
         AGENCY. MATCHED CONTROL GROUPS WERE SELECTED FOR EACH
         EXPERIMENTAL UNIT. THE PROGRAM WAS INTRODUCED AFTER CAREFUL
         DIAGNOSIS OF THE WORK SITUATION AND THOROUGH TRAINING OF THE
         PERSONNEL INVOLVED. WITHIN THE LIMITS IMPOSED BY THE FIELD
         SITUATION, BEFORE-AFTER MEASURES OF BOTH BEHAVIOR AND
         ATTITUDES SUGGESTED THAT CHANGES IN BEHAVIOR (E.G.
         PRODUCTIVITY, ABSENCES) OCCURRED IN FAVOR OF THE EXPERIMENT-
         AL GROUPS. JOB ENRICHMENT APPARENTLY HAD NO EFFECTS ON
         ATTITUDES, HOWEVER. ON THE BASIS OF INTERVIEWS AND
         OBSERVATIONS, THE PRODUCTIVITY CHANGES WERE ATTRIBUTED
         MAINLY TO MORE EFFICIENT USE OF MANPOWER, ELIMINATION OF
         UNNECESSARY OPERATIONS, AND FEEDBACK AND COMPETITION, WHILE
         THE ABSENCE CHANGES WERE ATTRIBUTED MAINLY TO INITIAL
         CHANGES IN MORALE BASED ON THE EXPECTATION OF EXTRINSIC
         REWARDS. IT IS CONCLUDED THAT ATTITUDES DID NOT IMPROVE
         BECAUSE THE EXPECTATIONS AND DESIRE FOR SUCH REWARDS HAD NOT
         BEEN MET. THE PROBLEM AND LIMITATIONS OF JOB ENRICHMENT ARE

M0600 DISCUSSED.

M0601 MILES, ROBERT H.   PERREAULT, W.
ORGANIZATIONAL ROLE CONFLICT: ITS ANTECEDENTS AND
CONSEQUENCES.
ORGANIZATIONAL BEHAVIOR AND HUMAN PERFORMANCE 17 (OCTOBER
1976): 19-44.

        TESTED THE LINKAGES AND UNDERLYING STRUCTURE OF A
COMPREHENSIVE MODEL RELATING ROLE CONFLICT TO ITS ANTECED-
ENTS AND CONSEQUENCES, USING MULTIVARIATE BEHAVIORAL
RESEARCH METHODOLOGY. DATA WERE DRAWN FROM 195 PROFESSIONAL-
LEVEL EMPLOYEES REPRESENTING 5 MAJOR ROLES IN 9 ORGAN-
IZATIONS. ROLE CONFLICT WAS TREATED AS A MULTIVARIATE
CONSTRUCT CONSISTING OF VARIOUS CONFLICT TYPES. ANTECEDENTS
OF ROLE CONFLICT INCLUDED OBJECTIVE ROLE REQUIREMENTS (I.E.
INTEGRATION AND BOUNDARY-SPANNING ACTIVITIES, PERSONNEL
SUPERVISION ACTIVITIES, AND NONSUPERVISORY SCIENTIFIC
RESEARCH ACTIVITIES) AND CHARACTERISTICS OF THE ROLE SET
(I.E. AVERAGE ORGANIZATIONAL DISTANCE AND AVERAGE AUTHORITY
OF ROLE SENDERS). CONSEQUENCES INCLUDED JOB-RELATED TENSION
AND SATISFACTION, PERCEIVED EFFECTIVENESS AND ATTITUDES
TOWARD ROLE SENDERS. USING A CLUSTER ANALYTIC APPROACH, 5
DISTINCT CONFLICT ORIENTATION GROUPS WERE ISOLATED. AN
ANALYSIS OF THE SIMULTANEOUS LINKAGES BETWEEN ANTECEDENTS
AND CONFLICT ORIENTATION REVEALED AN ADDITIVE CONTINUUM
COMPOSED OF OBJECTIVE ROLE CONDITIONS WHICH STRATIFIED THE 5
CONFLICT ORIENTATIONS, HIGHLIGHTING THE IMPACT OF
SIMULTANEOUS ROLE REQUIREMENTS. FINALLY, WORK-RELATED OUT-
COMES WERE SIGNIFICANTLY DIFFERENT FOR INDIVIDUALS IN
DIFFERENT CONFLICT ORIENTATION GROUPS.

M0602 MILLER, DONALD B.
HOW TO IMPROVE THE PERFORMANCE AND PRODUCTIVITY OF THE
KNOWLEDGE WORKER.
ORGANIZATIONAL DYNAMICS 5 (WINTER 1977): 62-80.

        PRESENTS EXAMPLES FROM THE AUTHOR'S EXPERIENCE WITH AN
ENGINEERING LABORATORY TO SHOW HOW PRODUCTIVITY CAN BE
INCREASED BY IMPROVING THE QUALITY OF WORKING LIFE. THE NEED
FOR CHANGE IN THE ORGANIZATION AND MANAGEMENT OF ENGINEERING
AND WORK IN GENERAL IS EXAMINED FROM A HISTORICAL PERSPECT-
IVE AND 4 KEY METHODS FOR IMPROVING THE QUALITY OF LIFE FOR
THE WORKING ENGINEER ARE PRESENTED: (A) RAISE THE VALUE
AND PRIORITY OF CONTINUED LEARNING, GROWTH, AND PERSONAL
VITALITY IN THE WORK ENVIRONMENT. (B) PROVIDE A BETTER
GROWTH ENVIRONMENT. (C) IMPROVE THE UNDERSTANDING OF
PRODUCTIVITY. (D) BUILD SELF-CONFIDENCE. EXCERPTS FROM A
PERSONAL GROWTH AND VITALITY INVENTORY ARE PRESENTED.

M0603 MORGAN, LILLIE.   HERMAN, JEANNE B.
PERCEIVED CONSEQUENCES OF ABSENTEEISM.
JOURNAL OF APPLIED PSYCHOLOGY 61 (DECEMBER 1976): 738-42.

        INVESTIGATED WHETHER ORGANIZATIONAL POLICIES AND
PRACTICES CAN BE EFFECTIVE DETERRENTS TO ABSENTEEISM.
HYPOTHESES ABOUT THE RELATIONSHIP BETWEEN CONSEQUENCES OF
ABSENTEEISM AND PAST AND FUTURE ABSENTEEISM WERE BASED ON AN

M0603   EXPECTANCY MODEL OF BEHAVIOR. DATA WERE COLLECTED FROM 60
        BLUE-COLLAR EMPLOYEES IN ONE DEPARTMENT OF A UNIONIZED
        AUTOMOBILE-PARTS FOUNDRY. RESULTS INDICATE THAT FOR SOME
        EMPLOYEES ABSENTEEISM PROVIDED AN OPPORTUNITY TO EXPERIENCE
        CONSEQUENCES THAT TENDED TO ENCOURAGE ABSENTEEISM AND THAT
        WERE NOT OFFSET BY ORGANIZATIONALLY CONTROLLED CONSEQUENCES
        THAT WOULD TEND TO DETER ABSENTEEISM. AN ABSENTEEISM POLICY
        THAT BOTH REWARDS ATTENDANCE WITH CONSEQUENCES THAT USUALLY
        MOTIVATE ABSENTEEISM AND ONE THAT PENALIZES ABSENTEEISM IS
        PROPOSED.

M0604   NICHOLSON, N.   BROWN, COLIN A.   CHADWICK-JONES, J.
        ABSENCE FROM WORK AND JOB SATISFACTION.
        JOURNAL OF APPLIED PSYCHOLOGY 61 (DECEMBER 1976): 728-37.

        A TAXONOMIC REVIEW OF 29 STUDIES REVEALS THAT THE
        POPULAR BELIEF THAT JOB DISSATISFACTION IS A MAJOR CAUSE
        OF ABSENCE FROM WORK HAS DOUBTFUL EMPIRICAL BASIS. IN AN
        ATTEMPT TO RESOLVE THE ANOMALIES OF METHOD, FINDINGS, AND
        INTERPRETATION USED IN PAST STUDIES, A SYSTEMATIC INVEST-
        IGATION OF THE RELATIONSHIP BETWEEN JOB DISSATISFACTION AND
        ABSENCE FROM WORK WAS CARRIED OUT USING 3 ABSENCE MEASURES
        (TIME LOST, FREQUENCY, AND ATTITUDINAL INDEXES) AND 5 JOB-
        SATISFACTION SCALES (A MODIFIED FORM OF THE JOB DESCRIPIIVE
        INDEX). DATA WERE GATHERED FROM 1,222 MALE AND FEMALE BLUE-
        COLLAR PRODUCTION WORKERS IN 16 SEPERATE ORGANIZATIONS IN 4
        CONTRASTING TECHNOLOGIES (CLOTHING MANUFACTURE, FOUNDRIES,
        CONTINUOUS PROCESS, AND BUS COMPANIES). RESULTS SHOW THAT IN
        MOST INSTANCES JOB DISSATISFACTION AND ABSENCE FROM WORK
        WERE UNRELATED AND THAT THE LACK OF RELATIONSHIP WAS NOT
        ATTRIBUTABLE TO ARTIFICIAL OR EXTRANEOUS INFLUENCES. IT IS
        CONCLUDED THAT THE JOB-DISSATISFACTION THEORY OF ABSENTEEISM
        IS EMPIRICALLY UNSUPPORTABLE, AND ALTERNATIVE CONCEPTUALI-
        ZATIONS OF ATTENDANCE MOTIVATION AND POTENTIALLY FRUITFUL
        FUTURE RESEARCH STRATEGIES ARE DISCUSSED.

M0605   NORD, WALTER R.
        CONCEPTS AND CONTROVERSY IN ORGANIZATIONAL BEHAVIOR.
        PACIFIC PALISADES, CALIFORNIA: GOODYEAR PUBLISHING, 1976.

        PRESENTS A REVISED EDITION OF A COLLECTION OR READINGS
        ON THEORIES, APPLICATIONS, AND RESEARCH IN ORGANIZATIONAL
        BEHAVIOR. OF 53 ARTICLES, 20 ARE NEW AND FOCUS ON RECENT
        WORK ON THE ROLE OF ENVIRONMENTAL PRESSURES IN MANAGERIAL
        BEHAVIOR, THE HISTORY OF ORGANIZATIONAL THEORY, THE CURRENT
        STATUS OF ORGANIZATIONS AS SOCIO-TECHNICAL SYSTEMS, AND
        THE IMPORTANCE OF ENVIRONMENTAL FACTORS IN ORGANIZATIONAL
        PERFORMANCE.

M0606   OLDHAM, GREG R.   HACKMAN, J. R.   PEARCE, JONE L.
        CONDITIONS UNDER WHICH EMPLOYEES RESPOND POSITIVELY TO
        ENRICHED WORK.
        JOURNAL OF APPLIED PSYCHOLOGY 61 (AUGUST 1976): 395-403.

        TESTED THE MODERATING EFFECTS OF (A) EMPLOYEE GROWTH
        NEED STRENGTH AND (B) LEVEL OF SATISFACTION WITH THE WORK
        CONTEXT ON EMPLOYEE RESPONSES TO ENRICHED WORK. DATA WERE
        COLLECTED FROM 201 EMPLOYEES WHO WORK ON 25 JOBS IN A BANK.

M0606 EMPLOYEES WHO HAD STRONG GROWTH NEEDS AND ALSO WERE
SATISFIED WITH THE WORK CONTEXT (I.E. WITH THEIR PAY, JOB
SECURITY, CO-WORKERS, AND SUPERVISORS) RESPONDED MORE
MORE POSITIVELY TO ENRICHED JOBS THAN EMPLOYEES WHO HAD WEAK
NEEDS FOR GROWTH AND/OR WHO WERE DISSATISFIED WITH THE WORK
CONTEXT. IMPLICATIONS FOR THE PRACTICE OF WORK REDESIGN ARE
DISCUSSED.

M0607 ORPEN, C.
THE LIMITATIONS OF THE MOTIVATOR-HYGIENE THEORY OF
SATISFACTION: AN EMPIRICAL STUDY WITH BLACK FACTORY WORKERS
IN SOUTH AFRICA.
JOURNAL OF BEHAVIORAL SCIENCE 2 (JUNE 1975): 137-49.

       HERZBERG'S MOTIVATION-HYGIENE THEORY OF JOB
SATISFACTION WAS TESTED USING 52 BLACK FACTORY SUPERVISORS
AND 50 BLACK FACTORY LABORERS WHO HELD WESTERN WORK VALUES
AND 49 BLACK FACTORY LABORERS WHO HELD TRIBAL WORK VALUES.
G.V. GRANT'S URBAN-RURAL SCALE WAS USED TO ASSES WORK VALUE
ORIENTATION. CONTENT FACTORS WERE FOUND TO CONTRIBUTE MORE
HIGHLY TO JOB SATISFACTION ONLY AMONG THE FACTORY
SUPERVISORS. THE CONTRIBUTION OF THE 2 FACTORS WAS THE SAME
AMONG THE FACTORY LABORERS WITH WESTERN VALUES, WHILE THE
CONTRIBUTION OF CONTEXT FACTORS TO JOB SATISFACTION WAS
GREATER THAN CONTENT FACTORS AMONG THE FACTORY LABORERS WITH
TRIBAL VALUES. MOREOVER, THE PROPOSED CONTENT-CONTEXT
DICHOTOMY WAS ONLY SUPPORTED AMONG THE FACTORY SUPERVISORS.
IT IS THEREFORE CONCLUDED THAT HERZBERG'S THEORY IS
OCCUPATION- AND CULTURE-BOUND. RESULTS ARE EXPLAINED MORE
ADEQUATELY BY THE REFERENCE GROUP THEORY OF JOB
SATISFACTION.

M0608 PARKER, WARRINGTON S.
BLACK-WHITE DIFFERENCES IN LEADER BEHAVIOR RELATED TO
SUBORDINATES' REACTIONS.
JOURNAL OF APPLIED PSYCHOLOGY 61 (APRIL 1976): 140-47.

       INVESTIGATED DIFFERENCES IN 4 MANAGERIAL LEADERSHIP
MEASURES (MANAGERIAL SUPPORT, GOAL EMPHASIS, WORK
FACILITATION, AND INTERACTION FACILITATION) AMONG 72 BLACK,
36 WHITE, AND 15 CHICANO SUBORDINATES OF 16 BLACK AND 17
WHITE SUPERVISORS IN 3 INDUSTRIAL PLANTS. THE 10 SUPERVISORY
LEADERSHIP QUESTIONS USED ARE PART OF A LARGER INSTRUMENT,
THE SURVEY OF ORGANIZATIONS. FINDINGS WERE ANALYZED TO
DETERMINE WHETHER OR NOT THE SUBORDINATES' REACTIONS TO
THEIR SUPERVISORS ON EACH MANAGERIAL LEADERSHIP MEASURE
VARIED WITH (A) THE RACE OF THE SUPERVISOR, (B) THE RACE OF
SUPERVISOR AND SUBORDINATES, AND (C) THE MAJORITY OR
MINORITY NUMERICAL STATUS OF SUBORDINATES IN WORK GROUPS
WITH SUPERVISOR OF THE SAME OR DIFFERENT RACE. RESULTS
INDICATE THAT THE BEHAVIOR OF SUPERVISORS TOWARD THEIR
SUBORDINATES IS A COMPLEX FUNCTION OF (A) THE SUPERVISOR'S
OWN RACE AND ROLE IN COMBINATION WITH (B) THE RACE OF
SUBORDINATES AND (C) THE MAJORITY OR MINORITY POSITIONS OF
RACIAL GROUPS WITHIN THE GROUPS SUPERVISED.

M0609 RABINOWITZ, S.   HALL, DOUGLAS T.
ORGANIZATIONAL RESEARCH ON JOB INVOLVEMENT.

M0609   PSYCHOLOGICAL BULLETIN 84 (MARCH 1977): 265-88.
        REVIEWS THE LITERATURE ON JOB INVOLVEMENT. FIRST THE
VARIOUS DEFINITIONS OF THE TERM ARE IDENTIFIED AND
INTEGRATED. NEXT, 3 THEORETICAL PERSPECTIVES ON JOB
INVOLVEMENT ARE CONSIDERED: JOB INVOLVEMENT AS AN INDIVIDUAL
CHARACTERISTIC, AS A SITUATIONALLY DETERMINED VARIABLE, AND
AS A PRODUCT OF PERSON-SITUATION INTERACTION. THE LITERATURE
IS REVIEWED IN TERMS OF EACH OF THESE PERSPECTIVES. A
SUMMARY TABLE IS PRESENTED SHOWING THE MAJOR CORRELATES OF
JOB INVOLVEMENT, AND A PROFILE OF THE JOB-INVOLVED PERSON IS
PRESENTED. CONCLUSIONS ARE DRAWN REGARDING THE NATURE OF JOB
INVOLVEMENT, AND NEW DIRECTIONS FOR NEEDED RESEARCH ARE
SUGGESTED.

M0610   RAIMO, NURMI.
        PRODUCING MAN'S CASE FOR SATISFACTION.
        OTANIEMI, FINLAND: TEKNILLINEN KORKEAKOULU, NO.20, 1975.

        AS A FOLLOW-UP TO AN INTERNATIONAL STUDY OF
MANUFACTURING SYSTEMS AND THE WORKER'S CHANGING ROLE, THIS
REPORT FOCUSES ON BEHAVIORAL AND ADMINISTRATIVE IMPLICATIONS
OF THE ORIGINAL RESULTS (BASED ON DATA COLLECTED BY 22
INDIVIDUALS FROM 8 COUNTRIES). PART 1 CONSIDERS BASES FOR
PRODUCING MAN'S SATISFACTION; PART 2 CONSIDERS WORK
SATISFACTION RELATIVE TO THEORY, ACTIVATION BEHAVIOR,
ACHIEVEMENT MOTIVE, AND OTHER TOPICS; AND PART 3 CONSIDERS
WHAT TO DO ABOUT SATISFACTION.

M0611   RONTONDI, THOMAS.
        IDENTIFICATION, PERSONALITY NEEDS, AND MANAGERIAL POSITIONS.
        HUMAN RELATIONS 29 (JUNE 1976): 507-15.

        EXAMINED (A) THE RELATIONSHIPS BETWEEN THE PERSONALITY
NEEDS AND IDENTIFICATION MODELS OF ORGANIZATIONAL PERSONNEL
AND (B) THE EFFECTS OF MANAGERIAL POSITION ON SUCH
RELATIONSHIPS. VARIABLES UNDER INVESTIGATION INCLUDED NEED
(N) AFFILIATION, N ACHIEVEMENT, ORGANIZATIONAL
IDENTIFICATION, WORK GROUP IDENTIFICATION, OCCUPATIONAL
IDENTIFICATION, AND EXTERNAL GROUP IDENTIFICATION. TO
REFLECT THE IMPACTS OF DIFFERING OCCUPATIONS AND
ORGANIZATIONAL PHILOSOPHIES, DATA WERE COLLECTED AND
ANALYZED FROM A GEOGRAPHICALLY DIVERSE SAMPLE OF 187 US
INDUSTRIAL EMPLOYEES (MEAN AGE, 32.5 YRS). SIGNIFICANT
FINDINGS SHOW THAT (A) AMONG MANAGERS (140 SS), BOTH N
AFFILIATION AND N ACHIEVEMENT WERE DIRECTLY ASSOCIATED WITH
EACH OF THE IDENTIFICATION MODELS, WHEREAS (B) AMONG
NONMANAGERS (47 SS), N AFFILIATION WAS RELATED DIRECTLY TO
OCCUPATIONAL IDENTIFICATION AND WORK GROUP IDENTIFICATION,
WITH N ACHIEVEMENT BEING DIRECTLY ASSOCIATED ONLY WITH
OCCUPATIONAL IDENTIFICATION.

M0613   SHAPIRO, H. JACK.
        MODELS OF PAY SATISFACTION: A COMPARATIVE STUDY.
        PSYCHOLOGICAL REPORTS 39(AUGUST 1976): 223-30

        USED DATA FROM 133 INDUSTRIAL EMPLOYEES TO ASSESS THE
VALIDITY OF 5 ALTERNATIVE MODELS OF PAY SATISFACTION. THE
MODELS DIFFER SYSTEMATICALLY FROM EACH OTHER IN TERMS OF

M0613 THEIR INPUT DATA AND THE MEASURING PROCESS USED TO DETERMINE EACH MODEL'S ESTIMATE OF PAY SATISFACTION. THE MODELS WERE EVALUATED AGAINST THE PAY SATISFACTION SUBSCALE OF THE JOB DESCRIPTIVE INDEX. THE SOCIAL COMPARISON COST OF LIVING MODEL YIELDED THE BEST RESULTS, FOLLOWED BY THE 3 DISCREPENCY MODELS AND FINALLY BY THE OBJECTIVE PAY DISTRIBUTION MODEL. FINDINGS SUGGEST THE 3 DISCREPENCY MODELS, ALTHOUGH DIFFERENT CONCEPTUALLY AND IN THE MEASUREMENT PROCESS, ARE VERY SIMILAR IN THEIR ABILITY TO PREDICT PAY SATISFACTION. THE OBJECTIVE PAY DISTRIBUTION MODEL, ALTHOUGH EXHIBITING THE LOWEST PREDICTIVE POWER OF ALL THE MODELS TESTED, MAY BE ABLE TO PROVIDE A USEFUL AND READILY AVAILABLE MEASURE OF PAY SATISFACTION WITHOUT RESORTING TO EMPLOYEES' SELF-REPORTING.

M0614 SPINK, PETER.
SOME COMMENTS ON THE QUALITY OF WORKING LIFE.
JOURNAL OF OCCUPATIONAL PSYCHOLOGY 48 (SEPTEMBER 1975): 179

STARTING FROM A VIEW OF THE PRESENT IN WHICH THERE IS GROWING AWARENESS OF THE SOCIOTECHNICAL NATURE OF WORK SYSTEMS, THE PRESENT PAPER STRESSES THE NEED TO EXPLORE OTHER LEVELS OF SYSTEM SO AS TO ADD TO EXISTING PICTURES OF THE WORLD OF WORK. THREE ASPECTS ARE CONSIDERED: THE INTERDEPENDENCE BETWEEN WORK AND NONWORK, THE ENTERING AND LEAVING PROCESS WITH ITS ATTENDANT TRANSITIONAL SYSTEMS, AND THE WIDER SOCIETAL AND GLOBAL REASSESSMENTS OF VALUES AND RELATIONSHIPS. IT IS SUGGESTED THAT AWARENESS OF THESE AND OTHER ASPECTS WILL LEAD TO DIFFERENT CONCEPTS OF WORK.

M0615 STRAUSS, GEORGE.
WORKER DISSATISFACTION: A LOOK AT THE CAUSES
JOURNAL OF EMPLOYMENT COUNSELING 13(SEPTEMBER 1976): 105-6.

NOTES THAT DURING THE 1940S AND 1950S, WORKERS LISTED STEADY WORK AS THE MOST DESIRABLE THING THEY WANTED FROM THEIR JOBS. IN CONTRAST, A 1969 SURVEY LISTED INTERESTING WORK FIRST AND JOB SECURITY SEVENTH. THE VIEW IS EXPRESSED, HOWEVER, THAT DISSATISFACTION CAN BE CAUSED AS MUCH BY LOW INCOMES, JOB INSECURITY, INADEQUATE FRINGE BENEFITS, OR TYRANNICAL SUPERVISION AS BY ANY INTRINSIC STERILITY ON THE JOB.

M0616 THOMAS, L. E.   MELA, RICHARD L.   ROBBINS, PAULA I.
HARVEY, DAVID W.
CORPORATE DROPOUTS: A PRELIMINARY TYPOLOGY.
VOCATIONAL GUIDANCE QUARTERLY 24 (MARCH 1976): 220-28.

EXPLORED REASONS WHY SUCCESSFUL MIDDLE-MANAGEMENT AND PROFESSIONAL MEN WOULD LEAVE CORPORATE POSITIONS TO BECOME SELF-EMPLOYED. 10SS FROM THE NORTHEASTERN US, AGED 37-51 YRS, PARTICIPATED IN SEMISTRUCTURED INDIVIDUAL INTERVIEWS. TWO FINDINGS EMERGED: (A) SINCE NONE OF THE S'S EMBODIED THE PERJORATIVE CHARACTERISTICS IMPLIED BY DROPOUT, THE TERM CORPORATE DROPOUT IS MISLEADING; THESE ARE NOT PEOPLE REJECTING POLITICAL VALUES AND INSTITUTIONS. (B) THE S'S COULD BE CLASSIFIED MEANINGFULLY INTO A TYPOLOGY HAVING 4 CATEGORIES BASED ON THE DIMENSIONS TOUGH-MINDED VS

M0616   TENDER-MINDED, AND HIGH-ACHIEVEMENT ORIENTED VS
         LOW-ACHIEVEMENT ORIENTED. THE TENTATIVE NATURE OF THESE
         FINDINGS IS STRESSED. FURTHER STUDY WITH LARGER, MORE
         REPRESENTATIVE SAMPLES IS NEEDED TO DETERMINE WHETHER THE
         TYPOLOGY IS VALID FOR MIDDLE-AGE CAREER BEHAVIOR AND WHETHER
         IT CAN ALSO BE USED TO UNDERSTAND CAREER BEHAVIOR AT OTHER
         LIFE STAGES.

M0617   TIMM, DONALD.   STRAUSS, JUDI.   SORENSON, PETER F.
         BABCOCK, RICHARD.
         IMPACT OF MANAGEMENT BY OBJECTIVES ON MASLOW'S NEED
         HIERARCHY: AN EMPIRICAL STUDY.
         PSYCHOLOGICAL REPORTS 40 (FEBRUARY 1977): 71-74.

             CONDUCTED A PILOT STUDY OF CHANGES IN NEED DEPRIVATION
         FOLLOWING THE INTRODUCTION OF A MANAGEMENT BY OBJECTIVES
         PROGRAM. CHANGES IN DEPRIVATION WERE MEASURED BY THE NEEDS
         QUESTIONNAIRE OF L.W. PORTER AND E.E. LAWLER (1968)
         DISTRIBUTED TO 44 PROFESSIONAL EMPLOYEES IN A COMMUNITY
         SERVICE ORGANIZATION. FINDINGS INDICATE SIGNIFICANT
         DECREASES IN DEPRIVATION FOR 4 OF 5 NEED LEVELS: SOCIAL,
         SELF ESTEEM, AUTONOMY, AND SELF-ACTUALIZATION, FOLLOWING
         THE INTRODUCTION OF THE PROGRAM.

M0618   TORNOW, WALTER W.   PINTO, PATRICK R.
         THE DEVELOPMENT OF A MANAGERIAL JOB TAXONOMY: A SYSTEM FOR
         DESCRIBING, CLASSIFYING, AND EVALUATING EXECUTIVE POSITIONS.
         JOURNAL OF APPLIED PSYCHOLOGY 61 (AUGUST 1976): 410-18.

             DEVELOPED A MANAGEMENT POSITION DESCRIPTION
         QUESTIONNAIRE (MPDQ) FOR OBJECTIVELY DESCRIBING THE JOB
         CONTENT OF EXECUTIVE AND MANAGEMENT POSITIONS IN TERMS OF
         THEIR RESPONSIBILITIES, CONCERNS, RESTRICTIONS, DEMANDS, AND
         AND ACTIVITIES. A FACTOR OF THE MPDQ RESPONSES FROM 433
         POSITION INCUMBENTS, COVERING A WIDE RANGE OF MANAGERIAL
         LEVELS AND FUNCTIONS, REVEALED 13 INDEPENDENT JOB FACTORS.
         ALL POSITIONS WERE THEN COMPARED AND GROUPED INTO 10
         HOMOGENEOUS CLUSTERS IN TERMS OF THE SIMILARITIES AND
         DIFFERENCES IN THEIR 13-FACTOR JOB PROFILES. A
         CROSS-VALIDATION OF RESULTS SHOWED THAT 73% OF THE CLUSTER
         ASSIGNMENTS FOR 56 HELD-OUT POSITIONS MATCHED THEIR
         BEHAVIORAL REQUIREMENTS IN TERMS OF SALARY GRADE AND
         FUNCTION. POSSIBLE APPLICATIONS OF THIS TAXONOMY TO MAJOR
         AREAS OF PERSONNEL PSYCHOLOGY ARE DISCUSSED.

M0619   UMSTOT, DENIS D.   BELL, CECIL H.   MITCHELL, T. R.
         EFFECTS OF JOB ENRICHMENT AND TASK GOALS ON SATISFACTION
         AND PRODUCTIVITY: IMPLICATIONS FOR JOB DESIGN.
         JOURNAL OF APPLIED PSYCHOLOGY 61 (AUGUST 1976) : 379-94

             A 2-PHASE RESEARCH PROJECT INVESTIGATED THE EFFECTS
         OF JOB ENRICHMENT AND GOAL SETTING ON EMPLOYEE PRODUCTIVITY
         AND SATISFACTION IN A WELL-CONTROLLED, SIMULATED JOB
         ENVIRONMENT.IN THE 1ST PHASE, 2 CONDITIONS OF GOAL SETTING
         (ASSIGNED GOALS VS NO GOALS) AND 2 CONDITIONS OF JOB
         ENRICHMENT (ENRICHED VS UNENRICHED) WERE ESTABLISHED,
         PRODUCING 4 EXPERIMENTAL CONDITIONS IN WHICH 42 PART-TIME
         WORKERS TOOK PART. JOB ENRICHMENT HAD A SUBSTANTIAL IMPACT

M0619 ON JOB SATISFACTION BUT LITTLE EFFECT ON PRODUCTIVITY.
GOAL SETTING, ON THE OTHER HAND, HAD A MAJOR IMPACT ON
PRODUCTIVITY AND A LESS SUBSTANTIAL IMPACT ON SATISFACTION.
IN THE 2ND PHASE(AFTER 2 DAYS' WORK), SS WITH UNENRICHED
JOBS WORKED UNDER THE ENRICHMENT CONDITIONS AND SS
ORIGINALLY WITHOUT GOALS WERE ASSIGNED GOALS. AGAIN, JOB
ENRICHMENT HAD A POSITIVE EFFECT ON JOB SATISFACTION, WHILE
GOAL SETTING HAD A POSITIVE EFFECT ON PERFORMANCE. RESULTS
ARE DISCUSSED IN TERMS OF THE CURRENT THEORETICAL
APPROACHES FOR UNDERSTANDING EMPLOYEE MOTIVATION ON THE JOB.

M0620 WHITEHILL, ARTHUR M.
MAINTENANCE FACTORS: THE NEGLECTED SIDE OF WORKER
MOTIVATION.
PERSONNEL JOURNAL 55(OCTOBER 1976): 516-19.

QUESTIONS THE VALIDITY OF JUDGING EMPLOYEE JOB
SATISFACTION BY MOTIVATIONAL FACTORS (VARIETY, INDEPENDENCE,
AND RESPONSIBILITY) AND REPORTS THE RESULTS OF AN INTERVIEW
SURVEY OF 173 PRODUCTION WORKERS IN SEVERAL TYPES OF JOBS IN
3 ENGINE PLANTS OF LEADING US AUTO MAKERS. ALTHOUGH 86%
EXPRESSED THEMSELVES AS SATISFIED WITH THEIR JOBS IN GENERAL
MARKED DISSATISFACTION WAS REGISTERED WITH 3 JOBS FACETS
CLASSIFIED AS MAINTENANCE FACTORS: PHYSICAL WORKING
CONDITIONS, SAFETY AND HEALTH, AND HOURS OF WORK. THIS
DISSATISFACTION WITH LOWER-LEVEL HYGIENE FACTORS WAS TRUE IN
ALL AGE, EDUCATION, SENIORITY, AND PAY GROUPS AMONG THOSE
INTERVIEWED. ALTHOUGH BOTH MOTIVATION AND MAINTENANCE
FACTORS CONTRIBUTE TO EMPLOYEE SATISFACTION AND
DISSATISFACTION, THE SURVEY RESULTS SUGGEST THAT MORE
ATTENTION SHOULD BE DEVOTED TO EMPLOYEE NEEDS THAT ARE
INHERENT IN THE PHYSICAL ENVIRONMENT OF THE WORK ITSELF. IT
IS POINTED OUT THAT THESE NEGLECTED MAINTENENCE FACTORS ARE
THE ONES THAT ARE EASIEST TO IMPROVE.

M0621 ALDERFER, CLAYTON P.
ORGANIZATION DEVELOPMENT.
ANNUAL REVIEW OF PSYCHOLOGY 28 (1977): 197-223

PRESENTS A 3-PART REVIEW OF THE LITERATURE ON
ORGANIZATION DEVELOPMENT (OD) THAT HAS BEEN PUBLISHED
SINCE F. FRIEDLANDER AND L. D. BROWN'S (1974) REVIEW.
PART 1 EXAMINES THE VALUE CONFLICTS WHICH ARE
CHARACTERISTIC OF THE FIELD; PART 2 DISCUSSES THE VARIETY
OF NEW SETTINGS AND TECHNIQUES THAT REPRESENT THE LATEST
PROFESSIONAL DEVELOPMENTS IN OD; AND THE FINAL SECTION
CRITICALLY REVIEWS THE MOST RECENT RESEARCH ON OD.

M0622 HERBST, PHILIP G.   GETZ, INGRI.
WORK ORGANIZATION AT A BANKING BRANCH: TOWARDS A
PARTICIPATIVE RESEARCH TECHNIQUE.
HUMAN RELATIONS 30 (FEBRUARY 1977): 209-42.

DESCRIBES A STUDY UNDERTAKEN BY WORK RESEARH INSTITUTES
(OSLO, NORWAY) IN DEVELOPING TECHNIQUES FOR PARTICIPATIVE
RESEARCH. DATA WERE GATHERED OVER A PERIOD OF ABOUT 3 DAYS
TALKING WITH EMPLOYEES AT A BRANCH OF A LARGE NORWEGIAN
BANK. EACH S WAS ASKED QUESTIONS WHICH WOULD ENABLE

M0622   RESEARCHERS TO MAP THE ORGANIZATION ACCORDING TO 3
        SUBSTRUCTURES: (A) COMPETENCE HIERARCHY, (B) WORK STRUCTURE,
        AND (C) SOCIAL SUBGROUPS. A SEQUENTIAL MAPPING OF TASK
        OULINES WAS MADE, AND COMMENTS WERE CODED TO GIVE A
        GENERAL INDEX OF JOB SATISFACTION. RESULTS SHOW (A)
        A SIMPLE, THOUGH NOT BUREAUCRATIC, HIERARCHICAL STRUCTURE
        ALONG WHICH PROMOTION TAKES PLACE; (B) A MATRIX TYPE WORK
        STRUCTURE; AND (C) A SENIOR-AND JUNIOR-GROUP SOCIAL
        STRUCTURE, WITH WORK SATISFACTION FOR THOSE IN THE SENIOR
        GROUP AND MARKED DISSATISFACTION FOR THE JUNIOR GROUP. IN
        IN ADDITION, A PERFECT CORRELATION EXISTED BETWEEN LEVEL IN
        THE COMPETENCE HIERARCHY AND WORK SATISFACTION BASED ON 3
        JOB CRITERIA: SATISFACTION WITH WORK VARIETY, PARTICIPATION
        IN DECISION MAKING, AND WORK LOAD.

M0623   KLEIN, KENNETH L.   WIENER, YOASH.
        INTEREST CONGRUENCY AS A MODERATOR OF THE RELATIONSHIPS
        BETWEEN JOB TENURE AND JOB SATISFACTION AND MENTAL HEALTH.
        JOURNAL OF VOCATIONAL BEHAVIOR 10 (FEBRUARY 1977): 92-98

              EXAMINED THE ROLE OF INTEREST/PRESENT JOB CONGRUENCY
        AS A MODERATOR OF THE RELATIONSHIP BETWEEN JOB TENURE AND
        JOB SATISFACTION AND MENTAL HEALTH. INSTRUMENTS USED
        INCLUDED THE STRONG VOCATIONAL INTEREST BLANK, JOB
        DESCRIPTIVE INDEX, AND MENTAL HEALTH MEASURES COMPRISED OF
        6 SELF-REPORT SCALES. IN 54 MIDDLE MANAGERS, SIGNIFICANT
        MODERATOR EFFECTS WERE FOUND FOR THE MENTAL HEALTH INDICES
        OF SELF-ESTEEM, LIFE-SATISFACTION, AND OVERALL MENTAL
        HEALTH AND FOR SATISFACTION WITH SUPERVISION. AS EXPECTED,
        THESE INDICES CORRELATED POSITIVELY WITH JOB TENURE FOR
        HIGH CONGRUENCY SS. FOR LOW CONGRUENCY SS, THE
        RELATIONSHIPS WERE EXPECTED TO BE NEGATIVE; HOWEVER, THE
        OBTAINED CORRELATIONS DID NOT DIFFER SIGNIFICANTLY FROM
        ZERO.

M0624   KORMAN, ABRAHAM K.   GREENHAUS, J.   BADIN, IRWIN J.
        PERSONNEL ATTITUDES AND MOTIVATION.
        ANNUAL REVIEW OF PSYCHOLOGY 28 (1977): 175-96.

              EXAMINES THE RESEARCH ON PERSONNEL ATTITUDES AND
        MOTIVATION IN TERMS OF THE USEFULNESS OF THE THEORETICAL
        APPROACHES THAT HAVE BEEN EMPLOYED IN THE FIELD OF WORK
        MOTIVATION; AND (B) THE BASIC METATHEORETICAL ASSUMPTIONS
        THAT HAVE BEEN USED TO STUDY WORK MOTIVATION AND
        SATISFACTION, AND (C) THE EFFECT OF CULTURAL CHANGES ON THE
        MEANING OF WORK.

M0625   LOOMIS, ROSEMARY   STARRY, RICHARD.
        WELFARE ISN'T WORKING.
        JOURNAL OF EMPLOYMENT COUNSELING 12 (JUNE 1975): 66-72.

              REPORTS THE EXPERIENCE OF 2 STAFF MEMBERS WORKING IN A
        FEDERALLY FUNDED WORK INCENTIVE PROGRAM (WIN) INVOLVED WITH

        WELFARE RECIPIENTS IN 4 RURAL COUNTIES IN THE MIDWESTERN US.

        WIN ACCEPTED REFERRALS FROM THE SOCIAL SERVICES AGENCY AND

ASSESSED THE CLIENT'S EMPLOYABILITY. THE AUTHORS MAINTAIN
THAT PAST NEGATIVE EXPERIENCES WITH THE SOCIAL SERVICES
DEPARTMENT PRODUCED DISTRUST IN CLIENTS WHICH INHIBITED
THEM FROM ASSUMING AGGRESSIVE ROLES IN INTERVIEWS AND
DEVELOPING TRUST RELATIONSHIPS WITH THE WIN STAFF. IT IS
ALSO STATED THAT SOCIAL SERVICES FUNCTIONED TO MAINTAIN THE
STATUS-QUO OF WELFARE RECIPIENTS BECAUSE OF SOCIAL WORKERS'
INSENSITIVITY AND LACK OF RESPECT FOR THESE PEOPLE AND THEIR
NEEDS. EXAMPLES OF SUCH INSENSITIVE TREATMENT ARE PRESENTED.
IT IS RECOMMENDED THAT PERSONS DEALING WITH WELFARE
RECIPIENTS (A) DEVELOP AWARENESS OF DIFFERENCES BETWEEN
CLIENTS, (B) BE SENSITIVE TO THE INDIVIDUAL'S NEEDS,(C)
STRIVE FOR A CLIENT-CENTERED APPROACH,(D) RECEIVE TRAINING
FOR JOB DEVELOPEMENT SKILLS, AND (E) WORK TOWARDS ABOLISHING
THE EXISTING STEREOTYPE OF THE WELFARE RECIPIENT.

M0626 MILES, ROBERT H.
ROLE-SET CONFIGURATION AS A PREDICTOR OF ROLE CONFLICT AND
AMBIGUITY IN COMPLEX ORGANIZATIONS.
SOCIOMETRY 40 (MARCH 1977): 21-54

EXAMINED ROLE-SET CONFIGURATION AS A PREDICTOR OF
ORGANIZATIONAL ROLE STRESS EXPERIENCED BY 202 RESEARCH AND
DEVELOPMENT PROFESSIONALS REPRESENTING 5 ORGANIZATIONAL
ROLES. DIMENSIONS OF THE ROLE SET INCLUDED THE
ORGANIZATIONAL DISTANCE AND RELATIVE AUTHORITY OF ROLE
SENDERS. THESE DIMENSIONS WERE FOUND TO BE IMPORTANT
THROUGH INDEPENDENT PREDICTORS OF SPECIFIC TYPES OF ROLE
CONFLICT AND ROLE AMBIGUITY. RESULTS ALSO REVEAL A
THRESHOLD EFFECT REGARDING THE STRESSFULNESS OF ROLE-SET
DISTANCE, A MEASURE OF BOUNDARY RELEVANCE, WHICH
UNDERSCORES THE NEED TO BE WARY OF THE ROLE-MASKING
ARTIFACT IN RESEARCH ON ROLE ANALYSIS AND ROLE STRESS.

M0627 MARSH, ROBERT M.   MANNARI, HIROSKI.
ORGANIZATIONAL COMMITMENT AND TURNOVER: A PREDICTION STUDY.
ADMINISTRATIVE SCIENCE QUATERLY 22 (MARCH 1977):57-75.

REEXAMINES EXPLANATIONS OF WHY JAPANESE ORGANIZATIONS
HAVE LOWER TURNOVER RATES THAN AMERICAN ORGANIZATIONS.
PREVIOUS RESEARCH IN JAPAN, ESPECIALLY THAT DONE IN TERMS OF
THE LIFETIME COMMITMENT MODEL OF JAPANESE ORGANIZATIONS,
SHOWED THAT SOME OF THE CAUSES OF TURNOVER IN JAPAN ARE
SIMILAR TO THOSE IN OTHER SOCIETIES- DEGREE OF STATUS
ENHANCEMENT AS A RESULT OF STAYING IN THE ORGANIZATION. THE
LIFETIME COMMITMENT MODEL ALSO POSITS AS CAUSES OF TURNOVER
CERTAIN DISTINCTIVELY JAPANESE NORMS AND VALUES OF LOYALTY
TO ONE'S ORGANIZATION, INDEPENDENT OF HOW MUCH STATUS
ENHANCEMENT OR SATISFACTION ONE DERIVES FROM MEMBERSHIP.
THIS EXPLANATION WAS TESTED WITH LONGITUDINAL DATA FROM 1033
EMPLOYEES IN ONE FACTORY OF ONE OF JAPAN'S 5 LEADING
ELECTRICAL APPLIANCE COMPANIES. AN INDEX WAS DEVELOPED TO
MEASURE LIFETIME COMMITMENT NORMS AND VALUES. FINDINGS FROM
THE PREDICTION STUDY, USING MULTIPLE REGRESSION ANALYSIS,
ARE NEGATIVE FOR THE LIFETIME COMMITMENT MODEL:(A)EMPLOYEES'
INTERORGANIZATIONAL MOBILITY PRIOR TO 1969 HAD NO EFFECT ON
THEIR LIFETIME COMMITMENT NORMS AND VALUES IN1969.(B) THE
VARIABLES THAT WERE RELATED TO 1969 LIFETIME COMMITMENT WERE

M0627   UNIVERSAL, NOT DISTINCTIVELY JAPANESE. (C) EMPLOYEES' LEVEL
        OF SUPPORT FOR LIFETIME COMMITMENT NORMS AND VALUES IN 1969
        HAD NO CAUSAL IMPACT ON WHETHER THEY HAD REMAINED IN THE
        SAME ORGANIZATION BY 1973.

M0628   NIGHTINGALE, D. V. TOULOUSE, J
        VALUES, STRUCTURE, PROCESS, AND REACTIONS/ADJUSTMENTS: A
        COMPARISON OF FRENCH AND ENGLISH-CANADIAN INDUSTRIAL
        ORGANIZATIONS.
        CANADIAN JOURNAL OF BEHAVIOURAL SCIENCE 9 (JANUARY 1977):
        37-48.

                PRESENTS THE FIRST MAJOR ATTEMPT SINCE THE 1969 REPORT
        OF THE ROYAL COMMISSION ON BILINGUALISM AND BICULTURALISM
        TO EXPLORE A BROAD RANGE OF VALUES, ATTITUDES, AND
        REACTIONS/ADJUSTMENTS OF FRENCH- AND ENGLISH-CANADIAN
        WORKING PEOPLE. RESPONSES FROM 1,000 WORKING PEOPLE IN A
        MATCHED SAMPLE OF 20 INDUSTRIAL ORGANIZATIONS IN ONTARIO
        AND QUEBEC PROVIDED COMPARISONS ON 4 DIMENSIONS: (A)
        THE THEORY X-THEORY Y VALUE SYSTEM OF ORGANIZATION MEMBERS;
        (B) ORGANIZATIONAL STRUCTURE (E.G., DEGREE OF
        FORMALIZATION, CENTRALIZATION, AND STANDARDIZATION OF
        PROCEDURES); (C) ORGANIZATIONAL PROCESSES (E.G., DECISION-
        MAKING AND CONFLICT RESOLUTION); AND (D) REACTIONS/
        ADJUSTMENTS OF ORGANIZATION MEMBERS (E.G., JOB SATISFACTION,
        ATTITUDES TOWARDS WORK, AND ALIENATION).

M0629   PYKE, SANDRA W.   WEISENBERG, FAYE.
        DESIRED JOB CHARACTERISTICS FOR MALES AND FEMALES.
        CANADIAN COUNSELLOR 10 (JULY 1976): 185-91

                F. HERZBERG ET AL (1959) CLASSIFIED JOB
        CHARACTERISTICS AS EITHER SELF-ACTUALIZING FACTORS
        (MOTIVATORS) OR PHYSICAL JOB FEATURES (HYGIENES). A SAMPLE
        OF 42 PROFESSIONAL AND 46 NONPROFESSIONAL MEN AND WOMEN
        REPORTED THEIR ORDER OF PREFERENCE FOR 10 JOB
        CHARACTERISTICS (5 MOTIVATORS AND 5 HYGIENES) AND ALSO
        INDICATED THEIR PERCEPTION OF THE IMPORTANCE OF THESE JOB
        TRAITS FOR MALE AND FEMALE CO-WORKERS. BOTH SEXES REGARDED
        MOTIVATORS AS PERSONALLY MORE IMPORTANT THAN HYGIENES BUT
        NONPROFESSIONAL RESPONDENTS WERE SIGNIFICANTLY MORE
        CONCERNED ABOUT HYGIENES THAN THE PROFESSIONAL GROUP.
        FEMALES, BOTH PROFESSIONAL AND NONPROFESSIONAL, DID NOT
        PERCEIVE ANY SIGNIFICANT DIFFERENCES BETWEEN THEMSELVES AND
        THEIR MALE AND FEMALE CO-WORKERS, WHILE MALES RATED
        THEMSELVES AS SIGNIFICANTLY MORE INFLUENCED BY MOTIVATORS
        THAN THEY BELIEVED THEIR FEMALE CO-WORKERS TO BE.MALE AND
        FEMALE NONPROFESSIONALS RATED THEIR MALE COLLEAGUES AS
        MORE INTERESTED IN THE SELF-ACTUALIZING FACTORS THAN THEIR
        FEMALE CO-WORKERS. RESULTS ARE DISCUSSED IN TERMS OF THE
        POSSIBLE NEGATIVE CONSEQUENCES OF THE IMAGE OF THE LESS
        COMMITTED FEMALE WORKER.

M0630   QUINN, ROBERT E.
        COPING WITH CUPID: THE FORMATION, IMPACT, AND MANAGEMENT
        OF ROMANTIC RELATIONSHIPS IN ORGANIZATIONS.
        ADMINISTRATIVE SCIENCE QUARTERLY 22 (MARCH 1977): 30-45.

ARGUES THAT A MODEL OF THE DYNAMICS OF ORGANIZATIONAL ROMANCE IS IMPORTANT BECAUSE ORGANIZATIONS ARE A NATURAL ENVIRONMENT FOR THE EMERGENCE OF ROMANTIC RELATIONSHIPS. THEIR EMERGENCE IS FEARED AND THESE FEARS INFLUENCE DECISIONS ABOUT THE ACCEPTABILTY OF WOMEN IN ORGANIZATIONS. THE FREQUENCY OF SUCH RELATIONSHIPS IS LIKELY TO INCREASE WITH MORE WOMEN IN THE WORK FORCE. QUALITATIVE DATA FROM INTERVIEWS WITH 3RD PARTIES AND NUMERICAL DATA FROM A QUESTIONNAIRE GIVEN TO PEOPLE IN AN AIRPORT ARE USED TO DELINEATE THE TYPES AND VARIETIES OF BEHAVIOR ASSOCIATED WITH THE FORMATION, IMPACT, AND MANAGEMENT OF ORGANIZATIONAL ROMANCE. FACTORS IN THE FORMATION OF ROMANTIC RELATIONSHIP INCLUDE PROXIMITY, MOTIVES, AND CHARACTERISTICS OF THE WORK GROUP OR SETTING. VISIBILITY OF THE RELATIONSHIP, BEHAVIOR CHANGES BY PARTICIPANTS, THE REACTIONS OF MEMBERS, AND OVERALL CHANGES IN THE SYSTEM ARE DELINEATED AS ELEMENTS IN UNDERSTANDING THE IMPACT OF ORGANIZATIONAL ROMANCE. IN CONSIDERING THE MANAGEMENT OF ROMANTIC RELATIONSHIPS 3 TYPES OF BEHAVIOR ARE IDENTIFIED: NO ACTION, PUNITIVE ACTIONS, AND POSITIVE ACTIONS. THE IMPACT OF ORGANIZATIONAL ROMANCE IS DISCUSSED IN TERMS OF WEBERIAN ASSUMPTIONS AND BELIEFS, EXCHANGE THEORY, PERSONAL COSTS, AND SOCIAL EQUITY.

M0631 REDDIN, W.J.
CONFESSIONS OF AN ORGANIZATIONAL CHANGE AGENT.
GROUP AND ORGANIZATIONAL STUDIES 2 (MARCH 1977): 33-41

PRESENTS AN ACCOUNT OF ERRORS MADE BY THE AUTHOR IN HIS ROLE AS ORGANIZATIONAL CHANGE AGENT WORKING AS A PROCESS CONSULTANT. FOR EACH ERROR THERE IS AN ILLUSTRATIVE CASE STUDY IN WHICH HE WAS DIRECTLY INVOLVED. THE ERRORS INCLUDE INITIATING CHANGE FROM THE BOTTOM UP, CREATING A CHANGE OVERLOAD, RAISING EXPECTATIONS BEYOND WHAT IS POSSIBLE, ALLOWING INAPPROPRIATE ATTACHMENT, BECOMING TRAPPED IN ONE PART OF THE ORGANIZATION, CHANGING ONLY A SUBSYSTEM, INAPPROPIATELY USING BEHAVIORAL INTERVENTIONS INSTEAD OF STRUCTURAL INTERVENTIONS, LOSING PROFESSIONAL DETACHMENT, ASSUMING THAT A CHANGE IS NEEDED, AND FAILING TO SEEK HELP.

M0632 SCHEIN, VIRGINIA E.
POLITICAL STRATEGIES FOR IMPLEMENTING ORGANIZATIONAL CHANGE.
GROUP AND ORGANIZATIONAL STUDIES 2 (MARCH 1977): 42-48.

ARGUES THAT POLITICAL STRATEGIES AND POWER TACTICS ARE NECESSARY FOR THE EFFECTIVE IMPLEMENTATION OF SYSTEMATIC CHANGE PROGRAMS IN ORGANIZATIONS. SINCE THE ORGANIZATION IS A HIGHLY POLITICAL ENVIRONMENT, THE CONSULTANT NEEDS TO DEVELOP BOTH POWER BASES AND POWER STRATEGIES IF HE IS TO OPERATE EFFICIENTLY WITHIN SUCH AN ENVIRONMENT. STRATEGIES THAT CAN BE USED BY THE CHANGE AGENT INCLUDE ALIGNING WITH A POWERFUL OTHER, TRADE-OFF, RESEARCH, USING A NEUTRAL COVER, LIMITING COMMUNICATIONS, AND WITHDRAWING. ALTHOUGH SUCH TACTICS MAY CURRENTLY CAUSE VALUE DILEMMAS FOR THE CONSULTANT, THEY MAY PROVE TO BE REALISTIC AND WORTHWHILE COURSES OF ACTION.

M0633   STEERS, RICHARD M.
        ANTECEDENTS AND OUTCOMES OF ORGANIZATIONAL COMMITMENT.
        ADMINISTRATIVE SCIENCE QUARTERLY 22 (MARCH 1977): 46-56.

            PROPOSES A PRELIMINARY MODEL CONCERNING THE
        ANTECEDENTS AND OUTCOMES OF EMPLOYEE COMMITMENT TO
        ORGANIZATIONS USING A CROSS-VALIDATIONAL FRAMEWORK. THE
        MODEL WAS TESTED AMONG 382 HOSPITAL EMPLOYEES AND 119
        SCIENTISTS AND ENGINEERS. IT WAS FOUND THAT FOR BOTH
        SAMPLES PERSONAL CHARACTERISTICS, JOB CHARACTERISTICS, AND
        WORK EXPERIENCES INFLUENCED COMMITMENT. MOREOVER,
        COMMITMENT WAS STRONGLY RELATED TO INTENT AND DESIRE TO
        REMAIN FOR BOTH SAMPLES AND MODERATELY RELATED TO
        ATTENDANCE TURNOVER FOR ONE SAMPLE. PEFORMANCE WAS
        GENERALLY UNRELATED TO COMMMITMENT.

M0634   ANSARI, S. L.
        BEHAVIORAL FACTORS IN VARIANCE CONTROL: REPORT ON A
        LABORATORY EXPERIMENT.
        JOURNAL OF ACCOUNTING RESEARCH 14 (AUTUMN 1976): 189-211

            IN THIS PAPER THE AUTHOR PRESENTS THE FINDINGS OF AN
        EXPERIMENT DESIGNED TO EXAMINE THE JOINT OR COMBINED
        INFLUENCE OF BOTH VARIANCE REPORTS AND LEADERSHIP STYLES ON
        EMPLOYEE SATISFACTION AND PRODUCTIVITY.

M0635   BRYANT, J. H.
        SURVEY OF VALUES AND SOURCES OF DISSATISFACTION.
        DATA MANAGEMENT 14 (FEBRUARY 1976):34-37.

            THE PURPOSE OF THE STUDY DESCRIBED IN THIS ARTICLE WAS
        TO SURVEY SEVERAL GROUPS OF DATA PROCESSING PERSONNEL SO AS
        TO DETERMINE THE RELATIVE VALUE OF A NUMBER OF JOB RELATED
        FACTORS, ASSESS THE LEVEL OF SATISFACTION WITH RESPECT TO
        THOSE FACTORS, AND OBTAIN INDICATIONS ABOUT WHAT JOB CHANGES
        WERE SEEN AS LEADING TO BETTER JOB PERFORMANCE.

M0636   DODSON, C.   HASKEW, B.
        WHY PUBLIC WORKERS STAY.
        PUBLIC PERSONNEL MANAGEMENT 5 (MARCH 1976):132-38.

            INVESTIGATIONS INTO THE COMBINATIONS OF REASONS WORKERS
        FIND FOR STAYING ON THE JOB HAVE BEEN DEVELOPED RECENTLY.
        THIS STUDY OF APPROXIMATELY 600 STATE EMPLOYEES PURSUES THE
        HYPOTHESIS THAT INERTIA ACCOUNTS FOR MOST WORKERS CONTINUING
        EMPLOYMENT.

M0637   DREYFACK, R.
        DISMAL DISINCENTIVES.
        MANAGEMENT REVIEW 65 (DECEMBER 1976): 48-51.

            SOME MOTIVATION CAREERISTS LIKE TO THINK THAT ALL IT
        TAKES TO MAKE PRODUCTIVITY ROCKET IS TO WHIP WORKERS INTO A
        FERVOR IN MUCH THE SAME WAY AS A COLLEGE COACH REVS UP HIS
        TEAM. THEY ARE LIVING FOR THE MOST PART IN A NEVER-NEVER
        DREAMLAND. . . . DISPENSING CRUMBS WHEN PEOPLE WANT BREAD IS
        AS TRANSPARENT AS A NEWLY CLEANED WINDOW.

M0638   DUNCAN, G. J.
        EARNINGS FUNCTION AND NONPECUNIARY BENEFITS.
        JOURNAL OF HUMAN RESOURCES 11 (FALL 1976): 481-83

        PAST EMPIRICAL STUDIES OF EARNINGS FUNCTIONS HAVE USED
ONLY PECUNIARY EARNING MEASURES. IN THIS ARTICLE, PECUNIARY,
FRINGE, AND CERTAIN NONPECUNIARY BENEFITS ARE TREATED AS
ADDITIVE COMPONENTS OF A MORE COMPREHENSIVE MEASURE OF
LABOR MARKET REWARD.

M0639   ELIZUR, D.   GUTTMAN, L.
        STRUCTURES OF ATTITUDES TOWARD WORK AND TECHNOLOGICAL CHANGE
        WITHIN AN ORGANIZATION.
        ADMINISTRATIVE SCIENCE QUARTERLY 21 (DECEMBER 1976): 611-22.

        THE ATTITUDES OF 340 ISRAELI GOVERNMENT EMPLOYEES
TOWARD THEIR WORK AND THE INTRODUCTION OF THE COMPUTER ARE
INVESTIGATED.

M0640   ELIZUR, D.   TZINER, AHARON.
        VOCATIONAL NEEDS, JOB REWARDS, AND SATISFACTION: A CANONICAL
        ANALYSIS.
        JOURNAL OF VOCATIONAL BEHAVIOR 10 (APRIL 1977): 205-11.

        EXAMINED THE EFFECTS OF VOCATIONAL NEEDS AND JOB
REWARDS CORRESPONDENCE ON JOB SATISFACTION BASED ON THE WORK
ADJUSTMENT THEORY OF R. V. DAWIS. RESULTS SUPPORT THE
HYPOTHESIS THAT THE HIGHER THE CORRESPONDENCE BETWEEN THE
VOCATIONAL NEEDS OF THE INDIVIDUAL AND THE REWARDS OF THE
JOB, THE HIGHER THE LEVEL OF JOB SATISFACTION TENDS TO BE,
THUS, SUPPORTING THE THEORY OF DAWIS.

M0642   FELDMAN, DANIEL C.
        CONTINGENCY THEORY OF SOCIALIZATION.
        ADMINISTRATIVE SCIENCE QUARTERLY 21 (SEPTEMBER 1976):433-52.

        A MODEL OF INDIVIDUAL SOCIALIZATION INTO ORGANIZATIONS
IS PRESENTED AND TESTED. THE MODEL (A) IDENTIFIES THREE
DISTINCT STAGES OF SOCIALIZATION, (B) SPECIFIES THE
ACTIVITIES ENGAGED IN BY AN INDIVIDUAL AT EACH STAGE, AND
(C) SPECIFIES THE PERSONAL AND ORGANIZATIONAL CONTINGENCIES
THAT CONTROL AN INDIVIDUAL'S MOVEMENT THROUGH THE STAGES.

M0643   FRANKENHAEUSER, M.   GARDELL, BERTIL.
        UNDERLOAD AND OVERLOAD IN WORKING LIFE: OUTLINE OF A
        MULTI-DISCIPLINARY APPROACH.
        JOURNAL OF HUMAN STRESS 2 (SEPTEMBER 1976):35-46.

        OUTLINES A MULTIDISCIPLINARY APPROACH TO PROBLEMS
RELATING THE IMPACT OF TECHNOLOGY ON WORKERS' HEALTH AND
SATISFACTION USING BACKGROUND AND PILOT STUDY DATA. ATTEMPTS
ARE MADE TO IDENTIFY AVERSIVE FACTORS IN THE WORK PROCESS BY
STUDYING ACUTE STRESS REACTION, IN THE COURSE OF WORK AND
RELATING THESE TO LONGTERM, NEGATIVE EFFECTS ON WELLBEING,
JOB SATISFACTION, AND HEALTH.

M0644   HAMERMESH, D. S.
        ECONOMIC CONSIDERATIONS IN JOB SATISFACTION TRENDS.

M0644   INDUSTRIAL RELATIONS 15 (FEBRUARY 1976):111-14.
         ECONOMISTS WHO HAVE DONE SUBSTANTIAL WORK ON TURNOVER
AND ABSENTEEISM AND HAVE EXPRESSED JOB DISSATISFACTION IS IN
MANY WAYS THE VOICE ANALOGUE TO THESE FORMS OF EXIT. THE
SATISFACTION-PRODUCTIVITY PROBLEM AND SOME IDEAS THAT HAVE
BEEN USED IN ARGUING FOR VARIOUS POLICIES ARE VIEWED.

M0645   MCMAHON, J. T.   IVANCEVICH, J. M.
         STUDY OF CONTROL IN MANUFACTURING ORGANIZATION: MANAGERS AND
NONMANAGERS.
ADMINISTRATIVE SCIENCE QUARTERLY 21 (MARCH 1976):66-83.

         THIS STUDY FOCUSES ON THE CONTROL PERCEPTIONS,
SATISFACTION, AND PERFORMANCE OF PERSONNEL STAFF. SEVERAL
HYPOTHESES ARE TESTED TO EXAMINE THE MANAGERS' PERCEPTIONS
OF TOTAL CONTROL, DISTRIBUTION OF CONTROL AND CONCORDANCE
AS WELL AS THE SATISFACTION AND PERFORMANCE OF LINE AND
STAFF NONMANAGERIAL EMPLOYEES. THE FINDINGS INDICATE THAT
HIGH MANAGERIAL CONCORDANCE IS THE MOST ACCURATE PREDICTOR
OF NONMANAGERIAL SATISFACTION AND PERFORMANCE.

M0646   PATHAK, D. S.   BURTON, G. E.
         SHIFTING TO THE HUMAN SIDE.
DATA MANAGEMENT 14 (DECEMBER 1976):20-24.

         INNOVATIVE FIRMS ARE SHIFTING FOCUS FROM DP MACHINES TO
THE HUMAN RESOURCE. SOCIAL NEEDS MUST BE SATISFIED TO SOME
DEGREE IN THE WORK ENVIRONMENT. THE MOST EFFECTIVE
INCENTIVE IS THE ACTION MOTIVATOR -- UNGRATIFIED YET
UNIMPORTANT TO THE WORKER. FINANCIAL INCENTIVES ARE NOT
CONNECTED TO SATISFACTION.

M0647   SANTANGELI, F.
         IMPROVING PRODUCTIVITY THROUGH JOB ENRICHMENT.
BEST'S REVIEW LIFE/HEALTH INSURANCE EDITION 76 (MARCH 1976):
80-83.

         VARIOUS TECHNIQUES ARE DISCUSSED ON HOW TO BUILD
MOTIVATING FACTORS INTO A JOB TO PROMOTE JOB SATISFACTION.
THESE TECHNIQUES ARE REFERRED TO AS IMPLEMENTING CONCEPTS.

M0648   SCOBEL, D. N.
         DOING AWAY WITH THE FACTORY BLUES.
HARVARD BUSINESS REVIEW 53 (NOVEMBER 1975):132-42.

         WHEN FACTORY EMPLOYEES ARE GIVEN THE SAME RESPECT AND
CONCERN USUALLY SHOWN ONLY TO OFFICE PEOPLE, THE RESULTS
BENEFIT BOTH EMPLOYEES AND MANAGEMENT.

M0649   NO AUTHOR CITED
         TESTING, TESTING.
ECONOMIST 259 (MAY 1976):87.

         CREATIVITY AND MORE FLEXIBILITY WITH WORKERS; A NEW
PHILOSOPHY IN WORK IMPROVEMENT PROGRAM THAT HAS RESULTED IN
HIGHER PRODUCTIVITY, BETTER QUALITY, AND LESS DISRUPTION ON
THE JOB.

M0650 BURKE, RONALD J.   WIER, TAMARA.   DUNCAN, G. J.
INFORMAL HELPING RELATIONSHIPS IN WORK ORGANIZATIONS.
ACADEMY OF MANAGEMENT JOURNAL 19 (SEPTEMBER 1976):370-77.

FIFTY-THREE MANAGERS DESCRIBED INFORMAL HELPING
INTERACTIONS IN THEIR WORK SETTINGS FROM BOTH HELPER AND
HELPEE PERSPECTIVES. TYPES OF PROBLEMS, WHO INITIATED THE
INTERACTION, NATURE OF THE HELPING ACT, AND CHARACTERISTICS
OF THE HELPERS WERE ALL EXAMINED. CONSIDERABLE SATISFACTION
AND PROGRESS WAS BELIEVED TO RESULT FROM THESE INTERACTIONS.

M0651 DIMARCO, NICHOLAS.
LIFE STYLE, WORK GROUP STRUCTURE, COMPATIBILITY, AND JOB
SATISFACTION.
ACADEMY OF MANAGEMENT JOURNAL 18 (JUNE 1975):313-22.

RELATIONSHIPS BETWEEN LIFE STYLE-WORK GROUP STRUCTURE
COMPATIBILITY, LIFE STYLE COMPATIBILITIES AMONG CO-WORKERS
AND BETWEEN SUPERIOR-SUBORDINATE PAIRS, AND SATISFACTION
WITH WORK, CO-WORKERS AND SUPERVISION, RESPECTIVELY, WERE
EXAMINED. LIFE STYLE, LIFE-STYLE GROUP STRUCTURE, CO-WORKER
LIFE STYLE, AND SUPERIOR-SUBORDINATE LIFE STYLE DIMENSION
COMPATIBILITY VARIABLES WERE FOUND TO PROVIDE PREDICTIVE
CAPABILITIES.

M0652 DOWNEY, H. KIRK.   SHERIDAN, JOHN E.   SLOCUM, JOHN W.
ANALYSIS OF RELATIONSHIPS AMONG LEADER BEHAVIOR, SUBORDINATE
JOB PERFORMANCE, AND SATISFACTION: A PATH-GOAL APPROACH.
ACADEMY OF MANAGEMENT JOURNAL 18 (JUNE 1975):253-62.

IT WAS HYPOTHESIZED THAT (A) THE MORE UNSTRUCTURED
THE TASK, THE MORE POSITIVE THE RELATIONSHIP BETWEEN
LEADER INITIATING STRUCTURE AND SUBORDINATE JOB SATISFACTION
AND PERFORMANCE, AND (B) THE MORE UNSTRUCTURED THE TASK, THE
LESS POSITIVE THE RELATIONSHIP BETWEEN LEADER CONSIDERATION
AND SUBORDINATE JOB SATISFACTION AND PERFORMANCE. THE
CORRELATIONS DO NOT SUPPORT THE FIRST PROPOSITION.

M0653 IVANCEVICH, J. M.   MCMAHON, J. T.
GROUP DEVELOPMENT, TRAINER STYLE AND CARRY-OVER JOB
SATISFACTION AND PERFORMANCE.
ACADEMY OF MANAGEMENT JOURNAL 19 (SEPTEMBER 1976):395-412.

THE EFFECTS OF VARIATIONS IN TRAINER STYLE ON GROUP
DEVELOPMENT AND BACK-HOME JOB SATISFACTION AND PERFORMANCE
WERE STUDIED. A DIRECTIVE AND STRUCTURED STYLE (TGS) AND A
FACILITATIVE OR LESS DIRECTIVE STYLE (TGMS) WERE USED IN A
COGNITIVE-BASED PROGRAM. THE RESULTS SUGGEST A NUMBER OF
SIGNIFICANT DIFFERENCES FOR THE PARTICIPANTS.

M0654 KELLER, ROBERT T.   SZILAGYI, A. D.
EMPLOYEE REACTIONS TO LEADER REWARD BEHAVIOR.
ACADEMY OF MANAGEMENT JOURNAL 19(DECEMBER 1976):619-27.

RELATIONSHIPS BETWEEN POSITIVE AND PUNITIVE LEADER
REWARDS AND EMPLOYEE ROLE CONFLICT AND AMBIGUITY,
EXPECTANCIES AND JOB SATISFACTION WERE INVESTIGATED. THE
DATA SHOWED POSITIVE LEADER REWARDS TO BE MORE STRONGLY

M0654   RELATED TO ROLE AND SATISFACTION VARIABLES. PUNITIVE LEADER
         REWARDS WERE MORE STRONGLY RELATED TO PEFORMANCE EXPECTANCY.
         IMPLICATIONS ARE DISCUSSED.

M0655   KERR, STEVEN.
         ON THE FOLLY OF REWARDING A, WHILE HOPING FOR B.
         ACADEMY OF MANAGEMENT JOURNAL 18 (DECEMBER 1975): 769-83.

             ILLUSTRATIONS ARE PRESENTED FROM SOCIETY IN GENERAL,
         AND FROM ORGANIZATIONS IN PARTICULAR, OF REWARD SYSTEMS
         THAT "PAY OFF" FOR ONE BEHAVIOR EVEN THOUGH THE REWARDER
         HOPES DEARLY FOR ANOTHER. PORTIONS OF THE REWARD SYSTEM OF
         A MANUFACTURING COMPANY AND AN INSURANCE FIRM ARE EXAMINED
         AND THE CONSEQUENCES DISCUSSED.

M0656   KOPELMAN, R. E.   THOMPSON, PAUL H.
         BOUNDARY CONDITIONS FOR EXPECTANCY THEORY PREDICTIONS OF
         WORK MOTIVATION AND JOB PERFORMANCE.
         ACADEMY OF MANAGEMENT JOURNAL 19 (JUNE 1976): 237-58.

             EXPECTANCY THEORY PREDICTIONS OF WORK MOTIVATION AND
         JOB PERFORMANCE ARE EXAMINED. AS HYPOTHESIZED, PREDICTIONS
         WERE MATERIALLY STRENGTHENED BY TAKING INTO ACCOUNT THE
         EFFECTS OF FIVE BOUNDARY CONDITIONS: (A) TIME, (B) INITIAL
         LEVEL OF CRITERION, (C) LEVEL OF REWARDS, (D) TASK-SPECIFIC
         ABILITY, AND (E) ORGANIZATIONAL CONTROL SYSTEM
         RESPONSIVENESS.

M0657   LATHAM, GARY P.   YUKL, GARY A.
         REVIEW OF RESEARCH ON THE APPLICATION OF GOAL SETTING IN
         ORGANIZATIONS.
         ACADEMY OF MANAGEMENT JOURNAL 18 (DECEMBER 1975): 824-45.

             RESEARCH ON GOAL-SETTING IN ORGANIZATIONS IS REVIEWED
         IN ORDER TO EVALUATE LOCKE'S THEORY OF GOAL SETTING AND TO
         DETERMINE THE PRACTICAL FEASIBILITY OF THIS TECHNIQUE FOR
         INCREASING EMPLOYEE MOTIVATION AND PERFORMANCE. AN ATTEMPT
         IS MADE TO IDENTIFY LIMITING CONDITIONS, MODERATOR
         VARIABLES, AND PROMISING DIRECTIONS FOR FUTURE RESEARCH.

M0658   LIDDELL, W. W.   SLOCUM, JOHN W.
         THE EFFECTS OF INDIVIDUAL-ROLE COMPATIBILITY UPON GROUP
         PERFORMANCE: AN EXTENSION OF SCHUTZ'S FIRO THEORY.
         ACADEMY OF MANAGEMENT JOURNAL 19 (SEPTEMBER 1976): 413-26.

             THIS STUDY INVESTIGATES THE EFFECTS OF DIFFERENTIAL
         DEGREES OF COMPATIBILITY BETWEEN GROUP MEMBERS'
         PERSONALITIES AND THE BEHAVIORAL REQUIREMENTS OF THEIR
         ROLES IN ONE GROUP'S DECISION-MAKING STRUCTURE. THE RESULTS
         ARE IN THE DIRECTION PREDICTED FROM THE FIRO THEORY AND
         EXPLAINED BY THE ROLE ADAPTATION PROBLEMS CONFRONTING GROUP
         MEMBERS.

M0659   LONDON, MANUEL.   OLDHAM, GREG R.
         EFFECTS OF VARYING GOAL TYPES AND INCENTIVE SYSTEMS ON
         PERFORMANCE AND SATISFACTION.
         ACADEMY OF MANAGEMENT JOURNAL 19(DECEMBER 1976): 522-36.

THE WORK VALUE SYSTEMS OF 1058 WORKERS WERE ASSESSED TO INVESTIGATE DIFFERENCE IN VALUES BETWEEN YOUNGER WORKERS AND OLDER WORKERS. BOTH EDUCATION AND AGE WERE FOUND TO STRONGLY INFLUENCE SUCH VALUES BUT LITTLE EVIDENCE WAS OBTAINED TO SUPPORT THE CONCEPT OF A PERVASIVE GENERATION GAP IN WORK VALUE SYSTEMS.

M0660   MITCHELL, T. R.   SMYSER, CHARLES M.   WEED, STAN E.
LOCUS OF CONTROL: SUPERVISION AND WORK SATISFACTION.
ACADEMY OF MANAGEMENT JOURNAL 18 (SEPTEMBER 1975): 623-31.

THE ROOTS OF 'BLUE COLLAR BLUES,' 'DEHUMANIZATION OF WORK', AND 'ALIENATION' ARE EXPLORED FROM THE VIEWPOINT THAT EMPLOYEES BELIEVE THEY HAVE LITTLE CONTROL OVER WHAT HAPPENS TO THEM IN THE JOB SETTING. ONE SCHOOL SUGGESTS THAT INDIVIDUALS HAVE GENERALIZED EXPECTANCIES ABOUT WHETHER ENVIRONMENTAL OUTCOMES ARE CONTROLLED INTERNALLY OR EXTERNALLY. THE 'INTERNAL' INDIVIDUAL BELIEVES HE CAN CONTROL HIS OWN FATE; THE 'EXTERNAL' INDIVIDUAL FEELS THAT MUCH OF WHAT HAPPENS TO HIM IS CONTROLLED BY EXTERNAL FORCES. RECENTLY, A NUMBER OF INVESTIGATIONS HAVE ATTEMPTED TO RELATE THIS INTERNAL-EXTERNAL (IE) CHARACTERISTIC TO VARIABLES RELATED TO THE WORK SETTING.

M0661   OLDHAM, GREG R.
IMPACT OF SUPERVISORY CHARACTERISTICS ON GOAL ACCEPTANCE.
ACADEMY OF MANAGEMENT JOURNAL 18 (SEPTEMBER 1975): 461-75.

THE STUDY FOUND THAT SUPERVISORY CHARACTERISTICS AFFECT SUBORDINATES' STATED ACCEPTANCE OF SUPERVISOR ASSIGNED GOALS, BUT NOT THE QUANTITY OR QUALITY OF SUBORDINATES' TASK PERFORMANCE; NOR DO SUBORDINATES WHO ACCEPT THE ASSIGNED GOAL PERFORM AT A HIGHER LEVEL THAN THOSE WHO REJECT IT. A MULTILEVEL MODEL OF GOAL ACCEPTANCE IS PROPOSED.

M0662   OSBORN, RICHARD N.   VICARS, WILLIAM M.
SEX STEREOTYPES: AN ARTIFACT IN LEADER BEHAVIOR AND SUBORDINATE SATISFACTION ANALYSIS.
ACADEMY OF MANAGEMENT JOURNAL 19 (SEPTEMBER 1976): 439-49.

DATA FROM TWO ORGANIZATIONS REVEALED NO CONSISTENT EFFECT OF LEADER SEX ON EITHER LEADER BEHAVIOR OR SUBORDINATE SATISFACTION. THE RESULTS FIT A PATTERN OF RESEARCH EVIDENCE THAT SHOWS SEX STEREOTYPES MAY BE IMPORTANT IN SOME LABORATORY SETTINGS BUT NOT IN LONG-TERM SITUATIONS. THUS, SOME LABORATORY FINDINGS MAY BE ARTIFACTUAL.

M0663   REINHARTH, L.   WAHBA, MAHMOUD A.
EXPECTANCY THEORY AS A PREDICTOR OF WORK MOTIVATION, EFFORT EXPENDITURE, AND JOB PERFORMANCE.
ACADEMY OF MANAGEMENT JOURNAL 18 (SEPTEMBER 1975): 520-37.

THE PREDICTIVE POWER OF EXPECTANCY THEORY WITH RESPECT TO WORK MOTIVATION, EFFORT EXPENDITURE, AND JOB PERFORMANCE IS TESTED IN FOUR HOMOGENEOUS SAMPLES. THE BASE OF BEHAVIORAL ALTERNATIVES IS EXPANDED TO INCLUDE BOTH

M0663   APPROACH AND AVOIDANCE ACTS. THE FINDINGS DO NOT SUPPORT
        THE CLASSICAL EXPECTANCY MODEL OR ITS COMPONENTS.

M0664   RUH, ROBERT A.   WHITE, J. K.   WOOD, ROBERT R.
        JOB INVOLVEMENT, VALUES, PERSONAL BACKGROUND, PARTICIPATION
        IN DECISION MAKING, AND JOB ATTITUDES.
        ACADEMY OF MANAGEMENT JOURNAL 18 (JUNE 1975) : 300-12.

        INTERRELATIONSHIPS AMONG JOB INVOLVEMENT, VALUES,
        PERSONAL BACKGROUND, PARTICIPATION IN DECISION MAKING, AND
        JOB ATTITUDES WERE INVESTIGATED IN MANUFACTURING
        ORGANIZATIONS. JOB INVOLVEMENT WAS FOUND TO BE AFFECTED BY
        BOTH INDIVIDUAL DIFFERENCES AND CHARACTERISTICS OF THE JOB
        SITUATION. JOB INVOLVEMENT MAY ALSO BE A POOR MODERATOR OF
        RELATIONSHIPS BETWEEN JOB CHARACTERISTICS AND ATTITUDES.

M0665   SALEH, S. D.   PASRICHA, V.
        JOB ORIENTATION AND WORK BEHAVIOR.
        ACADEMY OF MANAGEMENT JOURNAL 18(SEPTEMBER 1975): 638-45.

        'JOB ORIENTATION' SHOULD BE DIFFERENTIATED FROM 'JOB
        MOTIVATION' AND 'JOB SATISFACTION'. JOB MOTIVATION DESCRIBES
        A PROCESS BY WHICH WORK BEHAVIOR IS INSTIGATED, DIRECTED,
        SUSTAINED, AND STOPPED. IT DENOTES INTERACTION BETWEEN THE
        INDIVIDUAL AND HIS WORK ENVIRONMENT. JOB SATISFACTION
        INDICATES AN AFFECTIVE STATE AND USUALLY IS CONSIDERED THE
        CONDITION OF FEELING AT A PARTICULAR TIME TOWARDS ACHIEVING
        OR NOT ACHIEVING THE INDIVIDUAL'S WORK GOALS. JOB
        ORIENTATION IS NOT A PROCESS OR A STATE BUT AN INDIVIDUAL
        TENDENCY MANIFESTED IN INTRINSIC OR EXTRINSIC PREDICTIONS.
        INTRINSICALLY-ORIENTED INDIVIDUALS ARE MORE TASK OR JOB
        CONTENT ORIENTED; EXTRINSICALLY-ORIENTED INDIVIDUALS ARE
        MORE MAINTAINANCE OR JOB-CONTEXT ORIENTED. THIS
        CONCEPTUALIZATION IS DIFFERENT FROM THE CONCEPTUALIZATION OF
        LOCUS OF CONTROL.

M0666   STARKE, F. A.   BEHLING, ORLANDO.
        A TEST OF TWO POSTULATES UNDERLYING EXPECTANCY THEORY.
        ACADEMY OF MANAGEMENT JOURNAL 18 (DECEMBER 1975): 703-14.

        THE DESCRIPTIVE ACCURACY OF TWO OF THE AXIOMS
        UNDERLYING EXPECTANCY THEORY--INDEPENDENCE AND TRANSITIVITY
        --IS EXAMINED. IT WAS FOUND THAT MANY INDIVIDUALS DID NOT
        MAKE WORK EFFORT DECISIONS IN A MANNER CONSISTENT WITH
        THESE NORMATIVE POSTULATES. THE IMPLICATIONS FOR THE
        PREDICTIVE ACCURACY OF EXPECTANCY THEORY ARE DISCUSSED.

M0667   SZILAGYI, A. D.   SIMS, HENRY P.   KELLER, ROBERT T.
        ROLE DYNAMICS, LOCUS OF CONTROL, AND EMPLOYEE ATTITUDES AND
        BEHAVIOR.
        ACADEMY OF MANAGEMENT JOURNAL 19 (JUNE 1976): 259-76.

        A STUDY OF INTERRELATIONSHIPS AMONG ROLE VARIABLES,
        LOCUS OF CONTROL, AND SUBORDINATE SATISFACTION AND
        PERFORMANCE REVEALED THAT: (A) INTERNALS PERCEIVED LESS ROLE
        CONFLICT, WERE NEITHER MORE SATISFIED NOR PERFORMED BETTER
        THAN EXTERNALS;(B) ROLE CONFLICT AND AMBIGUITY EXPLAINED
        MORE VARIANCE IN SATISFACTION AND PERFORMANCE THAN LOCUS OF

M0667 CONTROL; AND (C) ROLE AMBIGUITY INCREASINGLY EXPLAINED MORE
VARIANCE IN JOB SATISFACTION AS OCCUPATIONAL LEVEL ROSE.

M0668 WATSON, JOHN G.   BARONE, SAM.
THE SELF-CONCEPT, PERSONAL VALUES, AND MOTIVATIONAL
ORIENTATIONS OF BLACK AND WHITE MANAGERS.
ACADEMY OF MANAGEMENT JOURNAL 19 (MARCH 1976): 36-48.

       THE SELF-CONCEPT, PERSONAL VALUES, AND LEVELS OF
ACHIEVEMENT, POWER, AND AFFILIATION MOTIVATION OF A GROUP OF
BLACK AND WHITE MANAGERS PRESENTLY WORKING IN ORGANIZATIONS
WERE EVALUATED. THE OVERALL RESULTS SUPPORT THE VIEW THAT,
AS GROUPS, BLACK AND WHITE MANAGERS HAVE VERY SIMILAR
SELF-CONCEPT, VALUE AND MOTIVATIONAL PROFILES.

M0669 ALDERFER, CLAYTON P.
A CRITIQUE OF SALANCIK AND PFEFFER'S EXAMINATION OF NEED
SATISFACTION THEORIES.
ADMINISTRATIVE SCIENCE QUARTERLY 22 (DECEMBER 1977): 658-69.

       IN THE SEPTEMBER 1977 ISSUE OF ASQ GERALD SALANCIK AND
JEFFERY PFEFFER PRESENTED AN EXAMINATION OF NEED
SATISFACTION MODELS OF JOB ATTITUDES. THEIR ARTICLE INCLUDED
A DESCRIPTION AND EVALUATION OF THE THEORETICAL
CHARACTERISTICS OF THE MODEL(P), AN ASSESSMENT OF THE
EMPIRICAL RESEARCH RELEVANT TO THE MODEL (P), AND AN
ANALYSIS OF THE PRACTICAL IMPLICATIONS OF THEIR POSITION.
THIS PAPER IS A RESPONSE TO THEIR VIEWS. IT SEEKS TO CLARIFY
A NUMBER OF THEORETICAL AND METATHEORETICAL ISSUES RAISED,
DISCUSSED, AND CONFUSED BY SALANCIK AND PFEFFER, TO PRESENT
A MORE COMPLETE VIEW OF THE DATA AND CONCEPTS RELEVANT TO
NEED THEORY THAN THEIR EXAMINATION DOES, AND TO EXPAND THE
RANGE OF PRAGMATIC AND VALUE QUESTIONS RAISED BY THEIR
PRESENTATION.

M0670 LEVINSON, HARRY.   BOWERS, DAVID G.
SYSTEMS OF ORGANIZATION: MANAGEMENT OF THE HUMAN RESOURCE.
ADMINISTRATIVE SCIENCE QUARTERLY 22 (JUNE 1977): 362-64.

       BOOK REVIEW: LEVINSON ASSERTS, 'DAVID BOWERS HAS
SUMMARIZED THE CONCEPTS AND CONTRIBUTIONS OF HIS MENTOR,
RENSIS LIKERT, ONE OF THE DOMINANT THINKERS IN CONTEMPORARY
INDUSTRIAL-SOCIAL PSYCHOLOGY. THIS BRIEF, EASILY READ VOLUME
IS A QUICK, LUCID, AND HELPFUL OVERVIEW OF LIKERT'S THINKING
FOR THOSE WHO EITHER DO NOT NEED OR DO NOT WANT TO DO THE
ORIGINALS. BOWERS HAS DONE WELL BY HIS MENTOR.'

M0671 LEIFER, RICHARD.   HUBER, GEORGE P.
RELATIONS AMONG PERCEIVED ENVIRONMENTAL UNCERTAINTY,
ORGANIZATION STRUCTURE, AND BOUNDARY-SPANNING BEHAVIOR.
ADMINISTRATIVE SCIENCE QUARTERLY 22 (JUNE 1977): 235-47.

       BOUNDARY-SPANNING ACTIVITY IS CONCEIVED OF AS AN
INTERVENING VARIABLE BETWEEN ORGANIZATIONAL STRUCTURE AND
PERCEIVED ENVIRONMENTAL UNCERTAINTY (PEU). THIS IS DUE
PRIMARILY BECAUSE, SINCE BOUNDARY SPANNERS OPERATE AT THE
SKIN OF THE ORGANIZATION, THEIR FUNCTIONS ARE TO INTERPRET
ENVIRONMENTAL CONDITIONS AND RELAY THAT INFORMATION TO

M0671   ORGANIZATION DECISION MAKERS. THREE HYPOTHESES EXAMINING
RELATIONS BETWEEN PEU, ORGANIZATION STRUCTURE, AND
BOUNDARY-SPANNING ACTIVITY WERE INVESTIGATED. IN A FIELD
STUDY COMPRISING 12 WORK UNITS (182 PEOPLE) WORKING IN A
HEALTH AND WELFARE ORGANIZATION POSITIVE RELATIONS WERE
FOUND BETWEEN ALL THREE VARIABLES... NOT ONLY IS THE NOTION
OF BOUNDARY SPANNING AS AN INTERVENING VARIABLE SUPPORTED,
BUT RESULTS SUGGEST THAT CAUSALITY IN THE RELATIONSHIP
BETWEEN STRUCTURE AND PEU MAY BE FROM STRUCTURE TO PEU
RATHER THAN CURRENT CONTINGENCY NOTIONS OF PEU AFFECTING
STRUCTURE.

M0672   MOCH, MICHAEL K.   PONDY, LOUIS R.
JAMES G. MARCH AND JOHAN P. OLSEN, AMBIGUITY AND CHOICE IN
ORGANIZATIONS.
ADMINISTRATIVE SCIENCE QUARTERLY 22 (JUNE 1977):351-61.

        BOOK REVIEW: SAY THE REVIEWERS, 'THIS IS AN IMPORTANT
BOOK. IT MAKES SIGNIFICANT THEORETICAL CONTRIBUTIONS TO OUR
UNDERSTANDING OF THE BEHAVIOR OF ORGANIZATIONS UNDER
UNCERTAINTY, AND IT DEMONSTRATES THE VALUE OF ETHNOGRAPHIC
METHODS FOR STUDYING SUCH BEHAVIOR.   THIS IS NOT A
TEXTBOOK REHASH OF FAMILIAR IDEAS. IT IS A MAJOR SCHOLARLY
WORK THAT WILL INFLUENCE THE CONCEPTS AND METHODS WE USE TO
MAKE SENSE OF AND MANAGE ORGANIZATIONS.'

M0673   SALANCIK, G. R.   PFEFFER, J.
AN EXAMINATION OF NEED-SATISFACTION MODELS OF JOB ATTITUDES.
ADMINISTRATIVE SCIENCE QUARTERLY 22 (SEPTEMBER 1977):
427-56.

        A NEED-SATISFACTION THEORETICAL MODEL HAS BEEN
UBIQUITOUS IN STUDIES AND WRITINGS ON JOB ATTITUDES AND, BY
EXTENSION, MOTIVATION, JOB DESIGN, AND OTHER ORGANIZATIONAL
PERFORMANCE IMPROVEMENT ISSUES. AN EXAMINATION OF SUCH
NEED MODELS INDICATES THAT THEY ARE FREQUENTLY FORMULATED
SO AS TO BE ALMOST IMPOSSIBLE TO REFUTE, AND THE RESEARCH
TESTING THEM HAS BEEN BESET WITH CONSISTENCY AND PRIMING
ARTIFACTS. FURTHERMORE, AVAILABLE EMPIRICAL DATA FAILS TO
SUPPORT MANY OF THE CRUCIAL ELEMENTS OF NEED-SATISFACTION
THEORIES. AN EXAMINATION OF THE COMPONENTS OF NEED-
SATISFACTION MODELS--NEEDS, JOB CHARACTERISTICS, AND JOB
ATTITUDES--INDICATES THAT ALL THREE HAVE BEEN INCOMPLETELY
CONSIDERED. NEED MODELS MAY HAVE PERSISTED IN PART BECAUSE
OF PERCEPTUAL BIASES, THEIR CONSISTENCY WITH OTHER THEORIES
OF RATIONAL CHOICE BEHAVIOR, AND BECAUSE OF WHAT THEY SEEM
TO IMPLY ABOUT HUMAN BEHAVIOR. THE MODELS APPEAR TO DENY,
HOWEVER, THAT PEOPLE HAVE THE CAPACITY TO PROVIDE THEIR OWN
SATISFACTIONS BY COGNITIVELY RECONSTRUCTING SITUATIONS.

M0674   SCHMIDT, STUART M.   KOCHRAN, THOMAS A.
INTERORGANIZATIONAL RELATIONSHIPS: PATTERNS AND
MOTIVATIONS.
ADMINISTRATIVE SCIENCE QUARTERLY 22 (JUNE 1977):220-34.

        TWO COMPETING APPROACHES, EXCHANGE AND POWER DEPENDENCY
HAVE BEEN USED IN PREVIOUS STUDIES TO CONCEPTUALIZE
INTERORGANIZATIONAL RELATIONSHIPS. THE BASIC PREMISE OF THIS

M0674 PAPER IS THAT AN INTEGRATED VIEW OF THESE RELATIONSHIPS IS
NEEDED THAT INCORPORATES PROPOSITIONS FROM BOTH OF THESE
APPROACHES. PROPOSITIONS ARE DEVELOPED FROM THESE TWO
APPROACHES FOR EXPLAINING VARIATIONS IN THE FREQUENCY OF
INTERACTION AND THE NATURE OF INTERACTIONS BETWEEN PAIRS OF
ORGANIZATIONS IN AN INTERORGANIZATIONAL SET. SPECIAL
EMPHASIS IS GIVEN TO THE NATURE OF INTERACTIONS IN AN
ASYMMETRICAL RELATIONSHIP. THE PROPOSITIONS ARE TESTED USING
DATA ON INTERACTIONS BETWEEN COMMUNITY ORGANIZATIONS AND
LOCAL OFFICES OF THE UNITED STATES TRAINING AND EMPLOYMENT
SERVICE. THE RESULTS SUGGEST THAT INTERORGANIZATIONAL
RELATIONSHIPS SHOULD BE CONCEPTUALIZED AS A MIXED-MOTIVE
SITUATION IN WHICH EACH ORGANIZATION BEHAVES IN ACCORDANCE
WITH ITS OWN SELF-INTERESTS.

M0675 BOWMAN, JAMES S.
THE MEANING OF WORK AND THE MIDDLE MANAGER.
CALIFORNIA MANAGEMENT REVIEW 19 (SPRING 1977): 63-70

IN THE CONTEXT OF THE CONTINUING CONTROVERSY OVER WORK
IN MODERN LIFE, THIS ARTICLE ATTEMPTS TO GAIN A CLEARER
UNDERSTANDING OF THE MEANING OF WORK FOR ONE KEY STRATUM OF
SOCIETY: MIDDLE MANAGERS. THE EVIDENCE FROM A VARIETY OF
STUDIES IS REVIEWED TO SHED LIGHT ON THE VIEWS OF THESE
PERSONS, WHO FORM THE MANAGERIAL BACKBONE OF ORGANIZATIONS.
THE NATURE OF THE PRESENT PROBLEM FOR THE YOUNG MANAGER IS
DISCUSSED AND THE DILEMMAS ENCOUNTERED IN THE SOLUTIONS TO
THAT PROBLEM ARE EXPLORED.

M0676 ARMSTRONG, JOHN.
HOW TO MOTIVATE.
MANAGEMENT TODAY (FEBRUARY 1977): 60-63.

PRODUCTIVITY ON SOME WELSH FARMS ROSE BY LEAPS AND
BOUNDS FOLLOWING MANAGEMENT DEVELOPMENT AND A CAREFUL PLAN
TO INVOLVE EVERYONE IN THE ACTION. WHAT WERE THE PRECISE
FACTORS WHICH BROUGHT SUCCESS? TO UNDERSTAND THAT, RESORT
HAS TO BE MADE TO THE BEHAVIOURISTS' THEORIES ABOUT REWARDS
AND MOTIVATION. GET THOSE RIGHT, AND JOB SATISFACTION LOOKS
AFTER ITSELF.

M0677 ARGENTI, JOHN.
WHATEVER HAPPENED TO MANAGEMENT TECHNIQUES.
MANAGEMENT TODAY (APRIL 1976): 76-79.

A DECADE AGO MOST MANAGERS THOUGHT OF THE MANAGERIAL
REVOLUTION PRIMARILY IN TERMS OF TECHNIQUES. TODAY MANY
TECHNIQUES THAT SEEMED TO HAVE A BRIGHT AND INDISPENSABLE
FUTURE BACK IN 1966 HAVE DISAPPEARED — IN SOME CASES WITHOUT
A TRACE. YET COMPANIES STILL EXIST WHICH DON'T USE THOSE
TECHNIQUES WHICH HAVE PASSED THE TEST OF TIME. WHAT
HAPPENED IS EXPLAINED.

M0678 FOSTER, GEOFFREY.
THE IMAGE OF MANAGEMENT.
MANAGEMENT TODAY (JANUARY 1977): 47-49.

NOBODY ELSE'S HEART BLEEDS FOR MANAGERS: THEIR IMAGE IS

M0678   STILL TOO BLURRED.   BUT RECENT DECISIONS TO 'MAKE
MANAGEMENT'S VOICE HEARD' COULD HERALD A CHANGE.   PERSUASION
IS THE PREFERRED METHOD -- BUT MORE MUSCULAR REPRESENTATION
IS NO LONGER IN THE REALM OF THE UNTHINKABLE.

M0679   HEBDEN, JOHN.   SHAW, GRAHAM.
PITFALLS OF PARTICIPATION.
MANAGEMENT TODAY (JANUARY 1976):   68-69.

        PARTICIPATIVE MANAGEMENT MIGHT OFFER A SOLUTION TO
MANY OF OUR INDUSTRIAL ILLS: BUT ONLY IF MANAGERS ARE TAUGHT
TO MAKE IT WORK.

M0680   JENKINS, DAVID.
THE DEMOCRATIC FACTORY.
MANAGEMENT TODAY (APRIL 1977):   70-73.

        WORK RESTRUCTURING MEANS QUESTIONING ROLES.   IT MAY CUT
DOWN SUPERVISION - E.G., WHERE A COMPUTER CONTROLS UNDER-
GROUND TRAINS - AND IT MAY BE DIFFICULT TO IMPLEMENT BECAUSE
OF THE ACTUAL RESHAPING OF WORK THAT IS DONE AND THE PROCESS
BY WHICH DECISIONS ARE REACHED ABOUT SUCH CHANGES.

M0681   MORSE, STEPHEN.
MANAGEMENT BY NORMS.
MANAGEMENT TODAY (FEBRUARY 1976):   66-69.

        THE NORMS OF GROUP BEHAVIOUR EXERT STRONG PRESSURE ON
PEOPLE, LARGELY UNRECOGNIZED BY THEM OR EVEN THEIR MANAGERS.
SUCCESSFUL CHANGE DEMANDS UNDERSTANDING, AND ALSO CAREFUL,
OPEN DISCUSSION.

M0684   DODD, WILLIAM E.
MANAGING MORALE THROUGH SURVEY FEEDBACK.
BUSINESS HORIZONS 20 (JUNE 1977):   36-45.

        SUGGESTS THAT A PROGRAM TEACHING MANAGEMENT HOW TO USE
OPINION SURVEY RESULTS EFFECTIVELY WILL RESULT IN MORE
EFFECTIVE MEETINGS WITH SUBORDINATES, BETTER ACTION PROGRAMS
AND IMPROVED MORALE.

M0686   GUPTA, NINA.
THE IMPACT OF PERFORMANCE-CONTINGENT REWARDS ON JOB
SATISFACTION: DIRECT AND INDIRECT EFFECTS.
PH.D. DISSERTATION, UNIVERSITY OF MICHIGAN, 1975.

        THE EFFECTS OF LINKING REWARDS TO PERFORMANCE ON JOB
SATISFACTION WAS THE SUBJECT OF THIS STUDY.   IT WAS
CONCLUDED THAT BOTH THE EMPLOYEES AND THE ORGANIZATION
BENEFIT FROM BASING ORGANIZATIONAL REWARDS ON JOB
SATISFACTION.

M0687   HARTMAN, RICHARD.   WEAVER, MARK K.
FOUR FACTORS INFLUENCING CONVERSION TO A FOUR-DAY WORK WEEK.
HUMAN RESOURCE MANAGEMENT 16 (SPRING 1977):   24-27.

        THE PURPOSE OF THIS INVESTIGATION WAS TO DETERMINE THE
ATTITUDES OF TOP MANAGEMENT TOWARD THE FACTORS WHICH RELATED

M0687   TO A SUCCESSFUL IMPLEMENTATION OF THE FOUR-DAY WORK WEEK.
        THE FOUR FACTORS REPORTED ON IN THIS ARTICLE ARE CHANGES IN
        PRODUCTIVITY, WORKFORCE JOB SATISFACTION, ABSENTEEISM
        TRENDS, AND TURNOVER RATE.

M0688   HENDERSON, RICHARD I.
        CREATING A "QUALITY" QUALITY CONTROL PROGRAM AT SPP.
        SUPERVISORY MANAGEMENT 22 (MARCH 1977): 25-30.

            THIS ARTICLE REPORTS THE RESULTS OF SOUTHERN PROTECTIVE
        PRODUCTS' USE OF OPERATIVE EMPLOYEES AS ROTATING QUALITY
        SUPERVISORS. THIS PROGRAM LED TO OTHER BENEFITS AS WELL AS
        IMPROVED QUALITY.

M0689   JACOBS, JEFFREY L.
        SATISFACTION WITH YOUR JOB: A LIFE-TIME CONCERN.
        SAM ADVANCED MANAGEMENT JOURNAL 42 (SPRING 1977): 44-50.

            THIS ARTICLE PRESENTS A FRAMEWORK FOR EVALUATING JOB
        SATISFACTION AND CAREER ALTERNATIVES THROUGHOUT A PERSON'S
        LIFETIME.

M0690   KALLEBERG, ARNE L.
        WORK VALUES, JOB REWARDS AND JOB SATISFACTION: A THEORY OF
        THE QUALITY OF WORK EXPERIENCE.
        PH.D. DISSERTATION, UNIVERSITY OF WISCONSIN, 1975.

            AN ATTEMPT IS MADE TO DEVELOP A THEORY OF VARIATION IN
        JOB SATISFACTION IN TERMS OF THE FACTORS THAT INFLUENCE THE
        DEGREE OF CONTROL INDIVIDUALS HAVE OVER THE ATTAINMENT OF
        JOB REWARDS IN AMERICAN SOCIETY. AN ADDITIVE MODEL WAS
        FOUND TO BE REPRESENTATIVE OF THE EFFECTS OF THESE FACTORS
        ON JOB SATISFACTON. THESE FACTORS MAY USUALLY BE UNDER-
        STOOD IN TERMS OF THE 'FIT' BETWEEN PARTICULAR VALUES AND
        REWARDS FOR THE TOTAL SAMPLE OF WORKERS. FITS ON THE
        INTRINSIC AND FINANCIAL DIMENSIONS HAD THE GREATEST EFFECTS
        ON OVERALL SATISFACTION.

M0691   MACEACHRON, ANN E.
        JOB LEVEL, INDIVIDUAL DIFFERENCES, AND JOB SATISFACTION: AN
        INTERACTIVE APPROACH.
        PH.D. DISSERTATION, CORNELL UNIVERSITY, 1975.

            THE HYPOTHESIS THAT KNOWLEDGE OF BOTH THE WORK ENVIRON-
        MENT AND THE INDIVIDUAL IS REQUIRED BEFORE JOB SATISFACTION
        MAY BE PREDICTED ADEQUATELY WAS TESTED IN A NURSING
        HIERARCHY OF AN URBAN PEDIATRIC HOSPITAL. MORE SPECIFI-
        CALLY, FIELD INDEPENDENCE AND ALIENATION FROM MIDDLE-CLASS
        NORMS WERE PREDICTED TO MEDIATE THE RELATIONSHIP BETWEEN JOB
        LEVEL AND JOB SATISFACTION. AN INTERACTIVE MODEL OF JOB
        SATISFACTION WAS SUPPORTED BY THE RESULTS. JOB SATISFACTION
        WAS PREDICTED WHEN A PERSON'S COGNITIVE STYLE AND VALUED
        WORK NORMS WERE CONGRUENT WITH THE COMPLEXITY OF THE TASK
        REQUIREMENTS AT EACH JOB LEVEL.

M0692   MANCHANDA, YASH P.
        MOTIVATION OF ENGINEERS: AN ANALYSIS OF PERCEIVED
        MOTIVATIONAL FACTORS.

M0692   PH.D. DISSERTATION, UNITED STATES INTERNATIONAL UNIVERSITY,
        1975.
            THE PURPOSE OF THIS STUDY WAS TO DETERMINE IF ENGINEERS
        AS A GROUP, PERCEIVED THEMSELVES AS BEING DIFFERENT FROM
        OTHER GROUPS OF SKILLED WORKERS. THE MAJORITY OF ENGINEERS
        FELT THEMSELVES TO BE DIFFERENT IN GENERAL AND IN SPECIFICS
        IN JOB APPROACH, SUPERVISION REQUIRED, RECOGNITION DESIRED,
        PERSONALITY TRAITS, AND GOAL SETTING.

M0693   MOORE, PERRY.
        REWARDS AND PUBLIC EMPLOYEES' ATTITUDES TOWARD CLIENT
        SERVICE.
        PUBLIC PERSONNEL MANAGEMENT 6 (MARCH-APRIL 1977): 98-105.

            THIS ARTICLE INVESTIGATED THE RELATIONSHIP BETWEEN
        PUBLIC EMPLOYEES' ATTITUDES ABOUT CLIENT SERVICE AND THEIR
        DESIRE FOR SPECIFIC REWARDS AND THE UTILITY OF CLIENT
        SERVICE IN OBTAINING THESE REWARDS. SEVERAL STEPS ARE
        SUGGESTED WHICH THE PUBLIC MANAGER COULD TAKE TO IMPROVE
        THE EMPLOYEES' CONCERN ABOUT CLIENT SERVICE.

M0694   PARTICIPATIVE MANAGEMENT AT WORK.
        HARVARD BUSINESS REVIEW 55 (JANUARY-FEBRUARY 1977): 117-27.

            IN THIS INTERVIEW JOHN F. DONNELLY, OF DONNELLY
        MIRRORS, INC., SUGGESTS TWO FUNDAMENTALS FOR SUCCESS. HE
        EXPLAINS THAT ALL EMPLOYEES SHOULD BE INVOLVED IN THE
        ISSUES AND PROBLEMS AND THAT BENEFITS AND BURDENS BE SHARED.

M0695   RAMOS, ALBERT A.
        THE RELATIONSHIP OF SEX AND ETHNIC BACKGROUND TO JOB-RELATED
        STRESS OF RESEARCH AND DEVELOPMENT PROFESSIONALS.
        PH.D. DISSERTATION, UNITED STATES INTERNATIONAL UNIVERSITY,
        1975.

            THE PURPOSE OF THIS STUDY WAS TO DETERMINE IF MINORITY
        RESEARCH AND DEVELOPMENT PROFESSIONALS EXPERIENCE MORE JOB-
        RELATED STRESS THAN NON-MINORITY PROFESSIONALS. IN ADDITION
        THE DIFFERENCES IN MEAN TENSION BETWEEN MALE CAUCASIANS,
        FEMALES, AND MALE ETHNIC MINORITY PROFESSIONALS WITH REGARD
        TO DEMOGRAPHIC AND JOB-RELATED FACTORS WAS EXAMINED. THE
        RESULTS INDICATE THAT, WITH THE EXCEPTION OF FEMALE PROFES-
        SIONALS, MINORITY PROFESSIONALS GENERALLY EXPERIENCE MORE
        JOB-RELATED STRESS THAN NON-MINORITY PROFESSIONALS.

M0696   RICHARDSON, JOHN G.
        A COMPARISON OF PROFESSIONAL INSTITUTIONAL COMMUNITY
        CORRECTIONS WORKERS ON JOB SATISFACTION AND SELF-CONCEPT.
        ED.D. DISSERTATION, UNIVERSITY OF CINNCINNATI, 1975.

            PROFESSIONAL INSTITUTIONAL CORRECTIONS WORKERS WERE
        COMPARED TO PROFESSIONAL COMMUNITY CORRECTIONS WORKERS ON
        JOB SATISFACTION AND SELF-CONCEPT. THE INSTITUTIONAL
        WORKERS WERE FOUND TO BE MORE SATISFIED THAN THE COMMUNITY
        WORKERS. NO DIFFERENCE WAS DISCOVERED IN THE SELF-CONCEPT
        VARIABLE. HOWEVER, BOTH GROUPS SCORED HIGHER THAN THE NORM.

M0697   ROEHL, CAROL E.

M0697   THE MENTAL HEALTH ASSOCIATE: THE EFFECT OF SOCIAL
        ENVIRONMENTAL FACTORS ON JOB SATISFACTION.
        PH.D. DISSERTATION, UNIVERSITY OF TEXAS, 1975.

            THE PURPOSE OF THIS STUDY WAS TO INVESTIGATE THE
        RELATIONSHIP BETWEEN SOCIAL ENVIRONMENT AND JOB SATISFACTION
        FOR A GROUP OF MENTAL HEALTH ASSOCIATES. THE BEST PREDICTOR
        OF JOB SATISFACTION WAS FOUND TO BE THE OPPORTUNITY FOR
        FURTHER PERSONAL AND PROFESSIONAL GROWTH.

M0698   SINGER, JACK N.
        JOB STRAIN AS A FUNCTION OF JOB LIFE AND STRESSES.
        PH.D. DISSERTATION, COLORADO STATE UNIVERSITY, 1975.

            IT WAS HYPOTHESIZED THAT JOB STRESSES WOULD HAVE A
        STRONGER EFFECT ON THE STRAIN EXPERIENCED BY WORKERS WHO
        WERE HIGHLY INVOLVED IN THEIR JOBS AND WORK, AND LIFE
        STRESSES WOULD HAVE A STRONGER EFFECT ON WORKERS WHO HAD
        RELATIVELY LITTLE JOB INVOLVEMENT. THE RESULTS INDICATE
        THAT JOB-RELATED STRAIN CAN BE EFFECTIVELY PREDICTED USING
        A COMBINATION OF JOB AND LIFE STRESSES. THE HYPOTHESIS WAS
        NOT SUPPORTED.

M0699   SKVORC, LORA R.
        WOMEN IN INDUSTRY: ALIENATION, SATISFACTION, AND CHANGE.
        PH.D. DISSERTATION, CASE WESTERN RESERVE UNIVERSITY, 1975.

            THIS STUDY WAS DESIGNED TO STUDY THE CONTEXT, STRUCTURE
        AND DYNAMICS OF INSTITUTIONAL AND ATTITUDINAL SEXISM AND
        THE EFFECTS ON JOB SATISFACTION AND ALIENATION IN WOMEN.
        THE POWER STRUCTURE OF THE ORGANIZATION EXAMINED WAS FOUND
        TO BE MALE ORIENTED AND MALE DOMINATED. WOMEN IN THIS
        ORGANIZATION WERE FOUND TO EXPERIENCE SIGNIFICANTLY LOWER
        JOB SATISFACTION AND HIGHER ALIENATION THAN DO THE MEN.
        DIFFERENTIAL MODES OF ADAPTING TO OR COPING WITH THESE
        ISSUES WERE EXAMINED.

M0700   SNOW, WILLIAM E.
        PREDICTING THE PERFORMANCE OF JUNIOR ACHIEVEMENT COMPANIES
        ACCORDING TO THE LEADERSHIP STYLE OF TWO LEVELS OF
        MANAGEMENT: A FIELD STUDY OF THE CONTINGENCY MODEL.
        PH.D. DISSERTATION, CASE WESTERN RESERVE UNIVERSITY, 1975.

            AN ATTEMPT WAS MADE TO PREDICT THE PERFORMANCE OF
        JUNIOR ACHIEVEMENT COMPANIES ON THE BASIS OF FIEDLER'S
        CONTINGENCY MODEL. THE RESULTING FAILURE IN PREDICTIVE
        VALIDITY WAS ATTRIBUTED TO INADEQUACIES IN THE CLASSIFIABLE
        FIELD STUDIES RATHER THAN IN FIEDLER'S ORIGINAL MODEL.

M0701   SOLOMAN, ROBERT J.
        THE IMPORTANCE OF MANAGER-SUBORDINATE PERCEPTUAL DIFFERENCES
        TO THE STUDY OF LEADERSHIP.
        PH.D. DISSERTATION, UNIVERSITY OF ROCHESTER, 1975.

            THE POSSIBLE EFFECT OF A DIFFERENCE IN MANAGER-SUBOR-
        DINATE PERCEPTION OF SITUATIONAL VARIABLES ON THE DEGREE OF
        RELATIONSHIP BETWEEN LEADER STYLE AND WORK GROUP OUTPUT WAS
        THE SUBJECT OF THIS STUDY. THE RESULTS SUGGEST THAT MANA-

M0701   GER-SUBORDINATE DIFFERENCES BECOME IMPORTANT WHEN THERE IS
         SMALL MARGIN FOR ERROR OR WHEN THE SITUATION LACKS TOLERANCE
         OR ROBUSTNESS.

M0702   SPENCER, GEORGE J.
         EFFECTS OF PARTICIPATION ON SATISFACTION AND PRODUCTIVITY.
         PH.D. DISSERTATION, UNIVERSITY OF MICHIGAN, 1975.

              A FIELD EXPERIMENT WAS USED IN THE STUDY OF THE EFFECTS
         OF PARTICIPATION ON SATISFACTION AND PRODUCTIVITY. THE
         RESULTS INDICATED THAT ABILITY, EFFORT, AND ROLE DEFINITIONS
         WERE SIGNIFICANTLY RELATED TO PERFORMANCE. IN GENERAL,
         PERFORMANCE WAS BEST PREDICTED BY ABILITY WHEN THE TASK WAS
         NORMATIVELY DIFFICULT. GOAL SETTING WAS FOUND TO BE RELATED
         TO PERFORMANCE ONLY THROUGH ITS IMPACT ON EFFORT AND ROLE
         DEFINITION.

M0703   WHITE, WILLIAM L.
         INCENTIVES FOR SALESMEN DESIGNING A PLAN THAT WORKS.
         MANAGEMENT REVIEW 66 (FEBRUARY 1977): 27-36.

              THIS ARTICLE SUGGESTS SIX AREAS TO CHECK IN THE ASSESS-
         MENT OR DEVELOPMENT OF AN INCENTIVE PROGRAM.

M0704   ARGYRIS, CHRIS.
         PERSONALITY VS. ORGANIZATION.
         ORGANIZATIONAL DYNAMICS 3 (FALL 1974): 2-17.

              REVIEWS THE EXTENT OF INCONGRUENCE BETWEEN THE NEEDS OF
         INDIVIDUALS AND THE REQUIREMENTS OF A FORMAL ORGANIZATION.
         A CASE FOR INCREASED NORMATIVE RESEARCH BY BEHAVIORAL SCIEN-
         TISTS IS MADE.

M0705   BARTH, RICHARD T.
         INTERGROUP CLIMATE ATTAINMENT, SATISFACTION, AND URGENCY.
         SMALL GROUP BEHAVIOR 5 (AUGUST 1974): 341-55.

              STUDIED THE RELATIONSHIP BETWEEN THE SATISFACTION AND
         ATTAINMENT PERCEIVED FOR 68 INTERGROUP CLIMATE FACTORS AND
         THE URGENCY THAT 256 ENGINEERS AND SCIENTISTS FROM 13
         RESEARCH AND DEVELOPMENT ORGANIZATIONS PLACED ON REDUCING
         DISCREPANCIES BETWEEN THEIR IMAGES OF ACTUAL AND IDEAL
         CLIMATES. THE INTERGROUP CLIMATE INVENTORY (ICI) WAS USED
         TO ASSESS INTERACTIONS BETWEEN S'S GROUP AND OTHER SPECIFIC
         GROUPS IN THE ORGANIZATION. RESULTS SUPPORT H.P. FROELICH
         AND L. WOLINS'S (1960) FINDING THAT ITEMS WITH LOW SATISFAC-
         TION AND HIGH IMPORTANCE ARE THE BEST PREDICTORS OF MEAN
         OVERALL SATISFACTION.

M0706   BHARADWAJ, L.K.   WILKENING, E. A.
         OCCUPATIONAL SATISFACTION OF FARM HUSBANDS AND WIVES.
         HUMAN RELATIONS 27 (OCTOBER 1974): 739-53.

              STUDIED 500 WISCONSIN FARM FAMILIES TO TEST THE HYPO-
         THESIS THAT HUSBANDS AND WIVES DERIVE THEIR PRIMARY SATIS-
         FACTION WITH OCCUPATIONAL SUCCESS FROM ASPIRATIONS AND
         ATTAINMENTS IN THEIR RESPECTIVE ROLE AREAS. THE DATA WERE
         OBTAINED IN 1962 BY THE WISCONSIN SURVEY LABORATORY FOR A

M0706 MULTI-STAGE AREA PROBABILITY SAMPLE. RESULTS OF A MULTIPLE
REGRESSION ANALYSIS EMPLOYING A STEPWISE FORWARD SELECTION
PROCEDURE SUGGEST THAT COUPLES UTILIZE DIFFERENT PERCEPTUAL
FRAMEWORKS IN EVALUATING OCCUPATIONAL SUCCESS WHICH REFLECT
THE RELATIVE SALIENCE OF FARM AND FAMILY ROLES. GOAL ORIEN-
TATIONS DO NOT SIMPLY REPRODUCE CULTURALLY DETERMINED SEX-
ROLE PATTERNS.

M0707 BIGGS, DONALD A.   BARNHART, WILLIAM. BAKKENIST, NEIL.
JOB ATTITUDES OF STUDENT PERSONNEL WORKERS AND THEIR JOB
SITUATIONS.
JOURNAL OF COLLEGE STUDENT PERSONNEL 16 (MARCH 1975):
114-18.

        ADMINISTERED A QUESTIONNAIRE ON JOB ALIENATION AND JOB
SATISFACTION AND THE SOCIAL AND AFFECTIVE CHARACTERISTICS
OF S'S OFFICE TO 174 PROFESSIONAL STAFF MEMBERS IN 15
OFFICES OF THE STUDENT AFFAIRS DEPARTMENT OF A LARGE STATE
UNIVERSITY. 148 RETURNED THE QUESTIONNAIRE. RESULTS SHOW
THAT THE SOCIAL CHARACTERISTICS OF THE OFFICES (E.G., AMOUNT
OF COMMUNICATION WITH STAFF MEMBERS IN OTHER OFFICES, PER-
CEIVED BENEFITS FROM BELONGING TO THE DEPARTMENT, AND PER-
CEIVED SOCIAL STATUS OF THE SPECIFIC OFFICE) BUT NOT OF THE
DEPARTMENT AS A WHOLE WERE SOMEWHAT RELATED TO STAFF JOB
SATISFACTION, AND THE SOCIAL CHARACTERISTICS OF THE OFFICES
AND OF THE DEPARTMENT AS A WHOLE WERE RELATED TO JOB
ALIENATION.

M0708 COHEN, ARTHUR M.
COMMUNITY COLLEGE FACULTY JOB SATISFACTION.
RESEARCH IN HIGHER EDUCATION 2, NO. 4 (1974): 369-76.

        THE 2-FACTOR THEORY OF F. HERZBERG (1959) SEPARATES JOB
SATISFACTION AND DISSATISFACTION BY POSTULATING THAT SATIS-
FACTION IS RELATED TO INTRINSIC FACTORS OR MOTIVATORS, WHILE
DISSATISFACTION RESULTS FROM EXTRINSIC FACTORS OR HYGIENES.
USING THE CRITICAL INCIDENT METHOD, 222 COMMUNITY COLLEGE
INSTRUCTORS FROM 12 COLLEGES WERE ASKED TO RELATE ASPECTS OF
THEIR WORK THAT LED THEM TO FEEL SATISFIED AND ASPECTS
THAT LED THEM TOWARD FEELINGS OF DISSATISFACTION. MORE THAN
TWO THIRDS OF THE GROUP INDICATED THAT THEY GAINED SATISFAC-
TION FROM STUDENT LEARNING OR FROM INTERACTION WITH STUDENTS
AND NEARLY TWO THIRDS RELATED ADMINISTRATIVE, COLLEGIAL,
AND/OR ORGANIZATIONAL DIFFICULTIES AS LEADING TO DISSATIS-
FACTION. THE 2-FACTOR THEORY WAS SUPPORTED. IMPLICATIONS
FOR COLLECTIVE BARGAINING, ADMINISTRATIVE ACTION, AND
FACULTY PROFESSIONALISM ARE NOTED.

M0709 CSOKA, LOUIS S.
RELATIONSHIP BETWEEN ORGANIZATIONAL CLIMATE AND THE
SITUATIONAL FAVORABLENESS DIMENSION OF FIEDLER'S CONTINGENCY
MODEL.
JOURNAL OF APPLIED PSYCHOLOGY 60 (APRIL 1975): 273-77.

        HYPOTHESIZED THAT ORGANIZATIONAL CLIMATE MODERATES
THE RELATIONSHIP OF LEADERSHIP MOTIVATION WITH PERFORMANCE
IN 52 US ARMY MESS HALLS IN A MANNER COMPARABLE TO F. E.
FIEDLER'S (1967) SITUATIONAL FAVORABLENESS DIMENSION. 52

M0709   ARMY STEWARDS IN THESE MESS HALLS COMPLETED FIEDLER'S LEAST
         PREFERRED CO-WORKER (LPC) MEASURE AND MEASURES ASSESSING
         SITUATIONAL FAVORABLENESS, WHILE 487 ARMY PERSONNEL RATED
         ORGANIZATIONAL CLIMATE. RESULTS SUBSTANTIATE THE HYPOTHESES
         THAT (A) FIEDLER'S SITUATIONAL OCTANTS I, III, AND VIII HAVE
         MECHANISTIC CLIMATE SCORES, WHILE OCTANT V HAS AN ORGANIC
         CLIMATE SCORE; AND (B) LOW-LPC LEADERS PERFORM BEST IN
         MECHANISTIC CLIMATES, COMPARABLE TO SITUATIONS OF HIGH OR
         LOW FAVORABLENESS, WHILE HIGH LPC LEADERS PERFORM BEST IN
         ORGANIC CLIMATES OR SITUATIONS OF INTERMEDIATE
         FAVORABLENESS.

M0711   DALTON, GENE W.   THOMPSON, PAUL H.   PRICE, RAYMOND L.
         THE FOUR STAGES OF PROFESSIONAL CAREERS - A NEW LOOK AT
         PERFORMANCE BY PROFESSIONALS.
         ORGANIZATIONAL DYNAMICS 6 (SUMMER 1977):   19-42.

              THE MODEL PRESENTED DESCRIBES HOW EACH ONE OF THE FOUR
         SUCCESSIVE CAREER STAGES - APPRENTICE, COLLEAGUE, MENTOR,
         SPONSOR - INVOLVES DIFFERENT TASKS, DIFFERENT PSYCHOLOGICAL
         ADJUSTMENTS. HIGH PERFORMANCE IS PERFORMING WELL WITHIN THE
         APPROPRIATE ROLE.

M0712   DAVIS, MARGARET K.
         INTRAROLE CONFLICT AND JOB SATISFACTION ON PSYCHIATRIC
         UNITS.
         NURSING RESEARCH 23 (NOVEMBER-DECEMBER 1974):   482-88.

              TO DETERMINE IF INTRAROLE CONFLICT EXISTED AMONG ROLE
         RECIPROCALS WHO WORKED ON 2 PSYCHIATRIC INPATIENT UNITS OF
         A UNIVERSITY HOSPITAL, A QUESTIONNAIRE REGARDING EXPECTA-
         TIONS ABOUT A NURSE'S INVOLVEMENT IN DECISION MAKING ON A
         PSYCHIATRIC UNIT WAS GIVEN TO 17 REGISTERED NURSES, 16 OTHER
         STAFF MEMBERS, 12 PATIENTS, AND 8 PHYSICIANS WHO WORKED ON
         THE UNITS. TO MEASURE HOW INTRAROLE CONFLICT WAS REFLECTED
         IN JOB SATISFACTION FOR REGISTERED NURSES ONLY, THE NURSES
         RESPONDED TO A.H. BRAYFIELD AND H.F. ROTHE'S 1951 MEASURE OF
         JOB SATISFACTION. INTRAROLE CONFLICT WAS FOUND BETWEEN THE
         NURSE GROUP AND THE PHYSICIAN GROUP AND THE NURSE GROUP AND
         THE PATIENT GROUP. THE NURSE GROUP HAD THE HIGHEST TOTAL
         MEAN EXPECTANCY SCORE FOR INVOLVEMENT IN DECISION MAKING
         WHILE THE PATIENT GROUP HAD THE LOWEST. SIGNIFICANT DIF-
         FERENCES EXISTED IN EXPECTATION SCORES BETWEEN GROUPS IN
         THE DECISIONS ABOUT PSYCHOTHERAPY, PHYSICAL CARE, WARD
         MILIEU, AND UNIT POLICY, BUT NOT ABOUT CONTINUITY OF CARE.
         INTRAROLE CONFLICT INDICATED BY INDIVIDUAL NURSES' EXPECTA-
         TION SCORES COMPARED WITH THE TOTAL EXPECTANCY SCORE OF THE
         COMBINED GROUPS WAS NOT REFLECTED IN JOB SATISFACTION.

M0713   DOWLING, WILLIAM F.
         CONSENSUS MANAGEMENT AT GRAPHIC CONTROLS.
         ORGANIZATIONAL DYNAMICS 5 (WINTER 1977):   23-29.

              POWER SHARING BY THE MAN AT THE TOP WITH THE NEXT THREE
         LEVELS BELOW HIM BOTH ENRICHES THEIR JOBS AND ENHANCES THE
         BOTTOM LINE.

M0714   FELDMAN, DANIEL C.

M0714 A PRACTICAL PROGRAM FOR EMPLOYEE SOCIALIZATION.
ORGANIZATIONAL DYNAMICS 5 (AUTUMN 1976): 64-80.
    WHAT DO SOCIALIZATION PROGRAMS AFFECT? GENERAL SATIS-
FACTION AND FEELINGS OF AUTONOMY AND INFLUENCE. WHAT CAN'T
THEY AFFECT? INTERNAL WORK MOTIVATION AND JOB INVOLVEMENT.
WITHIN THESE CONSTRAINTS, FELDMAN GIVES A STEP-BY-STEP
DESCRIPTION OF THE POLICIES AND PRACTICES REQUIRED TO MAKE
A SOCIALIZATION PROGRAM SUCCESSFUL.

M0715 FIEDLER, FRED E.   GILLO, MARTIN W.
CORRELATES OF PERFORMANCE IN COMMUNITY COLLEGES.
JOURNAL OF HIGHER EDUCATION 45 (DECEMBER 1974): 672-81.

    OBTAINED DATA FROM 55 TEACHING UNITS OF 18 COMMUNITY
COLLEGES IN THE STATE OF WASHINGTON. SIXTY-FIVE PERCENT
OF THE FACULTY RESPONDED TO A QUESTIONNAIRE ON TEACHING
STYLES, GOAL PERCEPTIONS, JOB SATISFACTION, AND PERCEIVED
FACULTY CONTROL IN DECISION-MAKING. TO OBTAIN A MEASURE OF
TEACHING EFFECTIVENESS, COLLEGE PRESIDENTS AND DEANS OF
INSTRUCTION WERE ASKED TO RANK INDIVIDUALLY EACH DIVISION OF
THEIR COLLEGE FROM BEST TO POOREST IN PROVIDING AN EFFECTIVE
EDUCATIONAL PROGRAM. RESULTS INDICATE DIFFERENCES BETWEEN
TEACHING PERFORMANCE, FACULTY ATTITUDES, AND ORGANIZATIONAL
STRUCTURE. THE TEACHING OF SOCIAL SCIENCE FACULTIES APPEARS
TO BE MORE AFFECTED BY THEIR GOALS AND ATTITUDES TOWARDS THE
COLLEGE THAN THE TEACHING OF OTHER FACULTIES. METHODS OF
TEACHING WHICH EMPHASIZE LECTURING AND ASSIGNED READINGS
RATHER THAN VISUAL AIDS, GUEST LECTURERS, AND LESS ORTHODOX
METHODS, APPEAR TO BE RELATED TO GOOD TEACHING PERFORMANCE.
SIZE OF FACULTY, EXPERIENCE, SALARY, AND FACULTY CONTROL
WERE NOT RELATED TO TEACHING PERFORMANCE.

M0716 FRAME, JAMES L.
PERSONAL REFLECTIONS OF A FAMILY THERAPIST.
JOURNAL OF MARRIAGE AND FAMILY COUNSELING 1 (JANUARY 1975)
15-28.

    DISCUSSES THE AUTHOR'S PERSONAL EVOLUTION AS A FAMILY
THERAPIST, THE POLITICS OF A SYSTEMS APPROACH IN STANDARD
SETTINGS, RESISTANCES TO FAMILY AND MARITAL THERAPY BY OTHER
PROFESSIONALS, WHETHER FAMILY OR MARITAL THERAPY WORKS AND
WHAT IS MEANT BY WORKING, THE SATISFACTIONS AND FRUSTRATIONS
AND STRESSES OF BEING A FAMILY THERAPIST, SOME HIDDEN AGEN-
DAS OF FAMILY THERAPY PRACTICES, HOW ONE'S OWN PERSONAL
FAMILY RELATIONSHIPS AFFECT AND ARE AFFECTED BY THIS KIND OF
WORK, THE CASUALTIES AMONG FAMILY AND MARITAL THERAPISTS,
AND, FINALLY, WHETHER FAMILY THERAPISTS SHOULD HAVE FAMILY
THERAPY FOR THEMSELVES AND THEIR OWN FAMILIES.

M0717 GAVIN, JAMES F.   EWEN, ROBERT B.
RACIAL DIFFERENCES IN JOB ATTITUDES AND PERFORMANCE: SOME
THEORETICAL CONSIDERATIONS AND EMPIRICAL FINDINGS.
PERSONNEL PSYCHOLOGY 27 (AUTUMN 1974): 455-64.

    COMPARED THE WORK ATTITUDES OF BLACK AND WHITE EM-
PLOYEES IN SIMILAR JOB SITUATIONS, AND STUDIED THE RELATION-
SHIP BETWEEN ATTITUDE AND PERFORMANCE CRITERIA FOR THE 2
GROUPS. A 53-ITEM JOB SATISFACTION QUESTIONNAIRE WAS AD-

M0717   MINISTERED TO 390 WHITE AND 81 BLACK, MALE, BLUE-COLLAR AIR-
         LINE EMPLOYEES. IT WAS NOT ANONYMOUSLY ADMINISTERED. THE
         DATA SUPPORTED THE CONCEPT OF RELATIVE DEPRIVATION,
         WITH BLACKS TENDING TO HAVE MORE POSITIVE WORK ATTITUDES.

M0718   GECHMAN, ARTHUR S. WIENER, YOASH
         JOB INVOLVEMENT AND SATISFACTION AS RELATED TO MENTAL HEALTH
         AND PERSONAL TIME DEVOTED TO WORK.
         JOURNAL OF APPLIED PSYCHOLOGY 60 (AUGUST 1975): 521-23.

             A WEEK-LONG DAILY RECORD AND SELF-REPORT MEASURES OF
         JOB INVOLVEMENT, SATISFACTION, AND MENTAL HEALTH WERE COM-
         PLETED BY 54 FEMALE ELEMENTARY SCHOOL TEACHERS. RESULTS
         SHOW THAT DEVOTING PERSONAL TIME TO WORK-RELATED ACTIVITIES
         WAS POSITIVELY ASSOCIATED WITH JOB INVOLVEMENT, BUT UNRE-
         LATED TO JOB SATISFACTION. MENTAL HEALTH WAS POSITIVELY
         RELATED TO JOB SATISFACTION, BUT DID NOT CORRELATE SIGNIFI-
         CANTLY WITH INVOLVEMENT. THESE DIFFERENTIAL RELATIONSHIPS
         SUPPORT THE VIEW THAT SATISFACTION AND INVOLVEMENT SHOULD
         BE THOUGHT OF AS SEPARATE AND DISTINCT JOB ATTITUDES.

M0719   GOMEZ, LUIS R.   MUSSIO, STEPHEN J.
         AN APPLICATION OF JOB ENRICHMENT IN A CIVIL SERVICE SETTING:
         A DEMONSTRATION STUDY.
         PUBLIC PERSONNEL MANAGEMENT 4 (JANUARY-FEBRUARY 1975):
         49-54.

             DESCRIBES A JOB ENRICHMENT EXPERIENCE INVOLVING 8 SS
         PERFORMING CLERICAL TASKS IN THE SELECTION DIVISION OF A
         MUNICIPAL PERSONNEL DEPARTMENT. THE TASKS WERE REORGANIZED
         INTO A MEANINGFUL MODULE OF WORK, INCREASING SS' RESPONSI-
         BILITIES, RECOGNITION, ACHIEVEMENT OPPORTUNITIES, AND
         ADVANCEMENT POTENTIAL. QUESTIONNAIRE RESULTS INDICATE
         INCREASED JOB SATISFACTION AND WORK PERFORMANCE. NO SIGNI-
         FICANT IMPACT ON ABSENTEEISM WAS NOTED. JOB ENRICHMENT IS
         CONSIDERED A VLAUABLE TOOL IN MANPOWER PLANNING AND EMPLOYEE
         DEVELOPMENT.

M0720   GOOD, LAWRENCE R.   GOOD, KATHERINE C. GOLDEN, STANFORD.
         ATTITUDE SIMILARITY AND ATTRACTION TO A COMPANY.
         PSYCHOLOGY 11 (AUGUST 1974): 52-55.

             TESTED THE HYPOTHESIS THAT ATTITUDE SIMILARITY BETWEEN
         A PERSON AND THE EMPLOYEES OF A COMPANY WOULD RESULT IN MORE
         ATTRACTION TO THE COMPANY AND DESIRE TO WORK THAN WOULD
         DISSIMILARITY. 48 UNDERGRADUATES COMPLETED A 14-ITEM SURVEY
         OF ATTITUDES CONCERNING A HETEROGENEOUS SET OF ISSUES SUCH
         AS DISCIPLINE OF CHILDREN AND WELFARE SPENDING. SS LATER
         COMPLETED A SURVEY OF EMPLOYEES' ATTITUDES AND A COMPANY
         JUDGEMENT SCALE. THE HYPOTHESIS WAS CONFIRMED.

M0721   GOUDY, WILLIS J.   POWERS, EDWARD A. KEITH, PATRICIA.
         WORK AND RETIREMENT: A TEST OF ATTITUDINAL RELATIONSHIPS.
         JOURNAL OF GERONTOLOGY 30 (MARCH 1975): 193-98.

             RECENT STUDIES REPORT CONTRADICTORY FINDINGS ON THE
         HYPOTHESIS OF AN INVERSE RELATIONSHIP BETWEEN WORK SATIS-
         FACTION AND RETIREMENT ATTITUDE. IN AN EFFORT TO CLARIFY THE

M0721   SITUATION, IT HAS BEEN SUGGESTED THAT ONLY IN INSTANCES
         WHERE WORK ACTS AS A KEY ORGANIZING FACTOR IN THE WORKERS'
         LIVES SHOULD THE INVERSE RELATIONSHIP BE OBSERVED. DATA
         TESTING THESE HYPOTHESES WERE ANALYZED FROM A STUDY OF
         EMPLOYED MALES 50 YEARS OLD AND OLDER (N=1,922) RESIDING IN
         A MIDWESTERN STATE. RESULTS OF THIS STUDY OFFER ONLY
         MARGINAL SUPPORT FOR THE HYPOTHESES. A WORK SATISFACTION
         RETIREMENT ATTITUDE TYPOLOGY BASED ON COMBINATIONS OF THE
         2 ATTITUDINAL AREAS IS DISCUSSED.

M0722   GREABELL, LEON C.   OLSON, JOHN A.
         ROLE DISSATISFACTION AND CAREER CONTINGENCIES AMONG FEMALE
         ELEMENTARY TEACHERS.
         JOURNAL OF STUDENT PERSONNEL ASSOCIATION FOR TEACHER
         EDUCATION 11 (JUNE 1973): 131-38.

             REPORTS RESULTS OF AN ASSESSMENT OF THE NATURE AND
         EXTENT OF ROLE DISSATISFACTION AMONG FEMALE ELEMENTARY
         SCHOOL TEACHERS. A 48-QUESTION INTERVIEW SCHEDULE CON-
         CERNING DEMOGRAPHIC, CAREER, AND ROLE PERCEPTION WAS AD-
         MINISTERED TO 187 FEMALE AND 20 MALE ELEMENTARY SCHOOL
         TEACHERS. IMPORTANCE OF OUTSIDE VALUE PRESSURES SUCH AS
         MARRIAGE ARE STRESSED.

M0723   HACKMAN, J. R.   OLDHAM, GREG R.
         DEVELOPMENT OF THE JOB DIAGNOSTIC SURVEY.
         JOURNAL OF APPLIED PSYCHOLOGY 60 (APRIL 1975): 159-70.

             DESCRIBES THE JOB DIAGNOSTIC SURVEY (JDS) WHICH IS
         INTENDED TO (A) DIAGNOSE EXISTING JOBS TO DETERMINE WHETHER
         (AND HOW) THEY MIGHT BE REDESIGNED TO IMPROVE EMPLOYEE MOTI-
         VATION AND PRODUCTIVITY AND (B) EVALUATE THE EFFECTS OF JOB
         CHANGES ON EMPLOYEES. THE INSTRUMENT IS BASED ON A SPECIFIC
         THEORY OF HOW JOB DESIGN AFFECTS WORK MOTIVATION, AND PRO-
         VIDES MEASURES OF (A) OBJECTIVE JOB DIMENSIONS, (B) INDI-
         VIDUAL PSYCHOLOGICAL STATES RESULTING FROM THESE DIMENSIONS,
         (C) AFFECTIVE REACTIONS OF EMPLOYEES TO THE JOB AND WORK
         SETTING, AND (D) INDIVIDUAL GROWTH NEED STRENGTH (INTER-
         PRETED AS THE READINESS OF INDIVIDUALS TO RESPOND TO
         "ENRICHED" JOBS). RELIABILITY AND VALIDITY DATA ARE SUMMA-
         RIZED FOR 658 EMPLOYEES ON 62 DIFFERENT JOBS IN 7 ORGANIZA-
         TIONS WHO RESPONDED TO A REVISED VERSION OF THE INSTRUMENT.

M0724   HALL, DOUGLAS T.   HALL, FRANCINE S.
         WHAT'S NEW IN CAREER MANAGEMENT.
         ORGANIZATIONAL DYNAMICS 5 (SUMMER 1976): 17-33.

             FRESH PROBLEMS BREED FRESH SOLUTIONS. FOR EXAMPLE, THE
         HALLS IDENTIFY THIS KEY PROBLEM: WHAT TO DO ABOUT PROMO-
         TIONS IN THE STABLE OR CONTRACTING ORGANIZATION? SOLUTIONS:
         CROSS-FUNCTIONAL MOVES, FALLBACK POSITIONS, DOWNWARD
         TRANSFERS, CORPORATE TENURE. A DISCUSSION REPLETE WITH PROS
         AND CONS, DRAWN FROM CONCRETE SITUATIONS.

M0725   HOFFMAN, LOIS W.
         THE EMPLOYMENT OF WOMEN, EDUCATION, AND FERTILITY.
         MERRILL-PALMER QUARTERLY 20 (APRIL 1974): 99-119.

EXAMINES THE FERTILITY CHOICE BEHAVIOR OF WORKING VS
NONWORKING WOMEN IN THE US FROM THE POST-WORLD WAR II ERA TO
THE PRESENT IN RELATION TO EDUCATION, CHANGING SOCIETAL
VALUES AND OPTIONS, AND POPULATION CONTROL (I.E., THE HYPO-
THESIS THAT BECAUSE WORKING WOMEN HAVE FEWER CHILDREN,
ENCOURAGING FEMALE EMPLOYMENT WILL DECREASE THE BIRTHRATE).
INCOMPATIBILITIES BETWEEN MOTHERHOOD AND EMPLOYMENT MAY BE
LESSENING, WHICH MAY INCREASE THE NUMBER OF CHILDREN FOR
WORKING WOMEN IN JOBS THAT DO NOT PROVIDE ALTERNATIVE
GRATIFICATIONS TO MOTHERHOOD. FOR WOMEN WHOSE JOBS DO PRO-
VIDE ALTERNATIVE GRATIFICATION, CHILDBEARING MAY DECREASE AS
CAREER BARRIERS LESSEN, EDUCATIONAL LEVEL RISES, AND NEGA-
TIVE SOCIETAL PERCEPTIONS OF VOLUNTARY CHILDLESSNESS ARE
MODIFIED. THESE 2 TRENDS MAY COMBINE TO RESULT IN ZERO
POPULATION GROWTH.

M0726   KIPNIS, DOROTHY M.
        INNER DIRECTION, OTHER DIRECTION AND ACHIEVEMENT MOTIVATION.
        HUMAN DEVELOPMENT 17, NO. 5 (1974):   321-43.

        RELATES THE CONCEPTS OF INNER- AND OTHER-DIRECTION
        DISCUSSED BY D. RIESMAN ET AL (1953) TO SEX DIFFERENCES IN
        CORRELATES AND ANTECEDENTS OF ACHIEVEMENT MOTIVATION AND
        BEHAVIOR. DATA SUPPORT THE CONCLUSION THAT AT THE PRESENT
        TIME, AMERICAN MALES ARE OTHER-DIRECTED IN ACHIEVEMENT
        FANTASY AND ACTION.   IF THE DEFINING CRITERIA OF OTHER-
        DIRECTION ARE CONSIDERED TO BE (A) AROUSAL OF ACHIEVEMENT-
        RELATED THOUGHT AND BEHAVIOR IN SETTINGS WHERE THE PARTICI-
        PANTS EXPECT EVALUATION, (B) LACK OF CONTINUITY OVER TIME IN
        ACHIEVEMENT-RELATED THOUGHT AND BEHAVIOR, AND (C) LACK OF
        INTERNALIZATION OF REGULATORY MECHANISMS ASSOCIATED WITH
        ACHIEVEMENT, THE CORRELATES OF NEED ACHIEVEMENT IN MALES ARE
        THOSE WHICH REISMAN ET AL ASCRIBED TO THE OTHER-DIRECTED.
        DATA ALSO SUPPORT THE CONCLUSION THAT THOSE AMERICAN FEMALES
        WHO PARTICIPATE IN CAREER AND PROFESSIONAL ACHIEVEMENT
        SETTINGS AS ADULTS ARE INNER-DIRECTED.   ALTHOUGH FEWER
        FEMALES THAN MALES PURSUE INTELLECTUAL AND PROFESSIONAL OB-
        JECTIVES, THOSE WHO DO APPEAR TO BE GUIDED BY INTERNALIZED
        GOALS RATHER THAN BY EVALUATION SETTINGS.

M0727   LAWRENCE, PAUL R.   KOLODNY, HARVEY F.   DAVIS, STANLEY M.
        THE HUMAN SIDE OF THE MATRIX.
        ORGANIZATIONAL DYNAMICS 6 (SUMMER 1977):   43

        THE MATURE MATRIX INVOLVES A RADICALLY DIFFERENT STRUC-
        TURE FOR THE ORGANIZATION. THESE CHANGES, IN TURN, REQUIRE
        DIFFERENT BEHAVIORS AT KEY LEVELS OF MANAGEMENT. THE
        AUTHORS EXPLORE THE CHANGES IN POWER, PRESSURES, AND PER-
        CEPTIONS THAT FOLLOW FROM THESE NEW MANAGEMENT ROLES.

M0729   MILLER, GLENN W.   SNIDERMAN, MARK.
        MULTIJOBHOLDING OF WICHITA PUBLIC SCHOOL TEACHERS.
        PUBLIC PERSONNEL MANAGEMENT 3 (SEPTEMBER-OCTOBER 1974):
        392-402.

        ADMINISTERED A QUESTIONNAIRE TO 702 TEACHERS AND CON-
        DUCTED INTERVIEWS WITH A RANDOM SAMPLE OF MULTIPLE JOB-
        HOLDING AND NONMULTIPLE JOB-HOLDING TEACHERS. THE DESIRE TO

M0729 ACHIEVE A HIGHER STANDARD OF LIVING AND TO SATISFY SOCIAL
AND PSYCHOLOGICAL NEEDS NOT FULFILLED THROUGH CLASSROOM
TEACHING ARE INDICATED AS THE MAIN REASONS FOR PUBLIC SCHOOL
TEACHERS TO MOONLIGHT.

M0730 MORRIS, JOHN L.   FARGHER, K.
ACHIEVEMENT DRIVE AND CREATIVITY AS CORRELATES OF SUCCESS
IN SMALL BUSINESS.
AUSTRALIAN JOURNAL OF PSYCHOLOGY 26 (DECEMBER 1974):
217-22.

    ADMINISTERED THE THEMATIC APPERCEPTION TEST AND
WALLACH'S GEOMETRIC PATTERNS TEST TO 60 MEN WHO CONTROLLED
SMALL BUSINESSES. IT WAS FOUND THAT THESE ACHIEVEMENT MOTI-
VATION AND CREATIVITY MEASURES WERE RELATED TO THE GROWTH
RATE OF SS' COMPANIES. HIGH SCORES ON EITHER VARIABLE WERE
ASSOCIATED WITH BUSINESS SUCCESS; LOW SCORES ON BOTH
VARIABLES WERE ASSOCIATED WITH STATIC OR DECLINING
BUSINESSES.

M0731 NASSTROM, RAY R.   KLINE, CHARLES E.   MYERS, ROBERT I.
SCHOOL BOARD DOGMATISM AND MORALE OF PRINCIPALS.
CALIFORNIA JOURNAL OF EDUCATIONAL RESEARCH 26 (MARCH 1975):
107-13.

    ADMINISTERED THE SOCIAL OPINION SURVEY (SHORT FORM
DOGMATISM SCALE) TO 201 SCHOOL BOARD MEMBERS AND THE SCHOOL
ADMINISTRATOR MORALE MEASURE: III TO 88 ELEMENTARY SCHOOL
PRINCIPALS, ALL FROM 52 RURAL SCHOOL DISTRICTS. RESULTS
SHOW THAT THE DOGMATISM OF SCHOOL BOARD MEMBERS HAD NO
RELATIONSHIP TO THE MORALE OF ELEMENTARY SCHOOL PRINCIPALS.
NO DIFFERENCES IN MORALE COULD BE ATTRIBUTED TO VARIANCE IN
PRINCIPALS' AGE, SEX, GRADE LEVEL RESPONSIBILITY, OR YEARS
IN POSITION. NEVERTHELESS, SOME DEGREE OF HIGHER MORALE
COULD BE ATTRIBUTED TO INCREASED PROFESSIONAL TRAINING, TO
ENTRY INTO THE PRINCIPALSHIP FROM OUTSIDE THE DISTRICT, AND
TO PARTICIPATION, ACTUAL AND PERCEIVED, IN THE FORMULATION
OF SCHOOL BOARD POLICY.

M0732 PETTY, M. M.   SHEIL, TIMOTHY J.
THE USE OF EXPECTANCY THEORY IN THE EXPLANATION OF TURNOVER
IN ROTC.
JOURNAL OF VOCATIONAL BEHAVIOR 6 (APRIL 1975): 197-204.

    ADMINISTERED A QUESTIONNAIRE ON THE IMPORTANCE OF 32
OUTCOMES IN SELECTING AN ARMY OR CIVILIAN JOB AND THE
EXPECTED LEVEL OF SATISFACTION FOR EACH OUTCOME IN EACH TYPE
OF JOB TO 142 MALE STUDENTS WHO WERE ENROLLED IN RESERVE
OFFICERS' TRAINING CORPS (ROTC) AND 18 MALE STUDENTS WHO HAD
DROPPED OUT OF ROTC. SEVERAL MONTHS LATER 7 OF THE ABOVE
142 SS DROPPED OUT OF ROTC. A RATIO EXPECTANCY THEORY MODEL
WAS DEVELOPED FROM THE QUESTIONNAIRE AS AN OPERATIONAL
DEFINITION OF MOTIVATION TO REMAIN IN ROTC. RESULTS INDI-
CATE THAT THE 25 DROPOUTS HAD A SIGNIFICANT LOWER (P<.001)
SCORE ON THIS MOTIVATIONAL MEASURE THAN THE 135 SS WHO WERE
STILL ENROLLED IN ROTC, AND ALSO THAT THESE LATTER SS WERE
AS STRONGLY ATTRACTED TO A CIVILIAN JOB AS THEY WERE TO AN
ARMY JOB. IMPLICATIONS OF THESE FINDINGS RELATIVE TO THE

M0732   ABILITY OF THE ARMY TO ATTRACT CAREER OFFICERS ARE
        DISCUSSED.

M0733   ORPEN, C.
        DISCRIMINATION AND JOB SATISFACTION: AN EMPIRICAL STUDY WITH
        A SOUTH AFRICAN MINORITY GROUP.
        JOURNAL OF SOCIAL PSYCHOLOGY 95 (APRIL 1975):   271-72.

           HYPOTHESIZED THAT, WITH EDUCATION AND THE NATURE OF THE
        JOB HELD CONSTANT, BLACK WORKERS IN SOUTH AFRICA SHOULD FEEL
        SIGNIFICANTLY LESS SATISFIED WITH THEIR JOBS AND MORE
        ALIENATED THAN WHITE WORKERS. DATA FROM 62 BLACK AND 73
        WHITE ACCOUNTING CLERKS SUPPORT THE HYPOTHESIS AND SUGGEST
        THAT FEELINGS OF ALIENATION ARE RELATED TO THE PERCEPTION OF
        A DISJUNCTION BETWEEN NORMS DEFINING APPROPRIATE "ENDS" AND
        "MEANS" (E.G., DISCRIMINATION) WHICH HAS NEGATIVE CONSE-
        QUENCES FOR JOB SATISFACTION.

M0734   SCHNEIDER, BEN.   SNYDER, ROBERT A.
        SOME RELATIONSHIPS BETWEEN JOB SATISFACTION AND ORGANIZATION
        CLIMATE.
        JOURNAL OF APPLIED PSYCHOLOGY 60 (JUNE 1975):   318-28.

           RELATIONSHIPS AMONG 2 MEASURES OF JOB SATISFACTION, 1
        MEASURE OF ORGANIZATIONAL CLIMATE, AND 7 PRODUCTION AND
        TURNOVER INDEXES OF ORGANIZATIONAL EFFECTIVENESS WERE
        INVESTIGATED IN 50 LIFE INSURANCE AGENCIES (N=522). IT WAS
        SHOWN THAT (A) CLIMATE AND SATISFACTION MEASURES WERE
        CORRELATED FOR PEOPLE IN SOME POSITIONS IN THE AGENCIES BUT
        NOT FOR OTHERS; (B) PEOPLE AGREED MORE ON THE CLIMATE OF
        THEIR AGENCY THAN THEY DID ON THEIR SATISFACTION; (C)
        NEITHER SATISFACTION NOR CLIMATE WERE STRONGLY CORRELATED
        WITH PRODUCTION DATA; AND (D) SATISFACTION BUT NOT CLIMATE,
        WAS CORRELATED WITH TURNOVER DATA. IMPLICATIONS OF THESE
        DATA FOR RESEARCH ON CLIMATE AND SATISFACTION AS WELL AS
        ORGANIZATIONAL CHANGE ARE DISCUSSED.

M0735   SHIPP, CHRISTOPHER.
        THE IMPACT OF ORGANIZATION SIZE ON EMPLOYEE MOTIVATION.
        IEEE TRANSACTIONS ON SYSTEMS, MAN, AND CYBERNETICS 5
        (JANUARY 1975):   43-45.

           ARGUES THAT BEHAVIORAL FACTORS IN THE ECONOMIES OF
        PROVIDING COMMUNICATIONS SERVICES ARE KNOWN TO BE VERY
        IMPORTANT, BUT THEY ARE ESSENTIALLY UNQUANTIFIED. WHAT IS
        KNOWN ABOUT SOME OF THE FACTORS AND RELATIONSHIPS AMONG THEM
        THAT DO AFFECT THE ECONOMIES OF SCALE, PARTICULARLY IN THE
        AREA OF EMPLOYEE MOTIVATION, IS REVIEWED.

M0736   SIMS, HENRY P.   SZILAGYI, A. D.
        LEADER STRUCTURE AND SUBORDINATE SATISFACTION FOR TWO
        HOSPITAL ADMINISTRATIVE LEVELS: A PATH ANALYSIS APPROACH.
        JOURNAL OF APPLIED PSYCHOLOGY 60 (APRIL 1975):   194-97.

           EXAMINED THE PATH-GOAL THEORY OF LEADERSHIP BY INVEST-
        IGATING RELATIONSHIPS BETWEEN LEADER INITIATING STRUCTURE
        AND SUBORDINATE SATISFACTION AT 2 HOSPITAL ADMINSTRATIVE
        LEVELS. IT ALSO HYPOTHESIZED THAT AT THE HIGHER OCCUPATION-

M0736 AL LEVELS, FOR 20 FEMALE ASSOCIATE DIRECTORS, INITIATING
STRUCTURE WOULD BE NEGATIVELY RELATED TO ROLE AMBIGUITY, AND
POSITIVELY RELATED TO EXPECTANCY II (I.E., THE PERCEPTION
OF THE PROBABLILITY OF OBTAINING A REWARD GIVEN A CERTAIN
PERFORMANCE) AND SUBORDINATE SATISFACTION. HOWEVER, AT THE
LOWER OCCUPATIONAL LEVEL, FOR 20 FEMALE HEAD NURSES, IT WAS
HYPOTHESIZED THAT INITIATING STRUCTURE WOULD BE NEGATIVELY
RELATED TO SUBORDINATE SATISFACTION AND UNRELATED TO
EXPECTANCY II. SS COMPLETED THE SUPERVISORY BEHAVIOR
DESCRIPTION, AN INSTRUMENT ADAPTED TO MEASURING AMBIGUITY,
AN INSTRUMENT ADAPTED TO MEASURING EXPECTANCY II, AND THE
JOB DESCRIPTIVE INDEX. THE HYPOTHESES WERE SUBSTANTIATED.
A PATH ANALYSIS MODEL WAS CONFIRMED FOR ASSOCIATE DIRECTORS,
BUT NOT FOR HEAD NURSES, INDICATING INITIATING STRUCTURE WAS
A MORE IMPORTANT SOURCE OF ROLE CLARIFICATION AND
SUBORDINATE SATISFACTION AT THE HIGHER OCCUPATIONAL LEVEL.

M0737 SMITH, FRANK J.   PORTER, LYMAN W.
WHAT DO EXECUTIVES REALLY THINK ABOUT THEIR ORGANIZATIONS?
ORGANIZATIONAL DYNAMICS 6(AUTUMN 1977): 68-80.

     HERE'S WHAT SEARS ROEBUCK FOUND OUT WHEN IT STOPPED
ASSUMING ITS EXECUTIVES WOULD BE NEITHER CRITICAL NOR
CANDID AND SURVEYED THEM. THE MOST CRITICAL AND MEANINGFUL
COMMENTS CAME FROM MIDDLE-AND UPPER-LEVEL-MANAGERS. THE
ARTICLE ALSO SPELLS OUT SOME SIGNIFICANT ACTIONS TAKEN BY
SEARS IN RESPONSE TO SURVEY FINDINGS.

M0738 TALKINGTON, L.   OVERBECK, D.
JOB SATISFACTION AND PERFORMANCE WITH RETARDED FEMALES.
MENTAL RETARDATION 13 (JUNE 1975): 18-19.

     DESCRIBES A STUDY WITH 2 GROUPS OF 45 MENTALLY RETARDED
FEMALES DESIGNED TO EXPLORE THE RELATIONSHIP BETWEEN
EXPRESSED SATISFACTION OR DISSATISFACTION IN WORK
ASSIGNMENTS AND ASSOCIATED PERFORMANCE. FINDINGS CONSISTENT
WITH SIMILAR STUDIES OF NONRETARDED PERSONS ARE REPORTED :
JOB SATISFACTION WAS HIGHLY RELATED TO THEIR ATTENDANCE,
DEPENDABILITY, AND GENERAL EFFICIENCY.

M0739 TROST, JAN.
AN INVESTIGATION OF ATTITUDES AMONG PRIVATES AT KA55
FOURTEENTH YEAR.
(SWED) MPI A-RAPPORT, NO. 20 (JANUARY 1974), PP. 27.

     REPORTS THE FOURTEENTH INVESTIGATION OF SATISFACTION
AND MORALE AMONG SWEDISH ARMY PRIVATES AND CORPORALS. A
GROUP QUESTIONNAIRE ON ATTITUDES TOWARD SUPERIORS, PEERS,
MILITARY EDUCATION, AND THEIR OWN PERFORMANCE WAS
ADMINISTERED TO ALL PRIVATES AND CORPORALS WHEN THEY LEFT
THEIR UNITS. A SLIGHT POSITIVE CHANGE FROM A 1972 SURVEY WAS
FOUND IN ATTITUDES TOWARD SUPERIORS, WHILE SMALL NEGATIVE
CHANGES WERE FOUND IN ATTITUDES TOWARD PEERS AND MILITARY
EDUCATION. THERE WAS NO CHANGE IN SS' EVALUATIONS OF THEIR
OWN PERFORMANCE. A NOTABLE FINDING WAS THAT 50% OF THE SS
DID NOT IDENTIFY THEMSELVES; A COMPARISON OF ATTITUDES AMONG
THESE ANONYMOUS SS AND THOSE WHO DID INDICATE THEIR I.D.
NUMBERS AND NAMES SHOWS THAT THE ANONYMOUS SS WERE MORE

M0739   NEGATIVE TOWARD MILITARY EDUCATION AND THEIR SUPERIORS, AS
        WELL AS THEIR PEERS.

M0740   TICHY, NOEL M.   NISBERG, JAY N.
        WHEN DOES WORK RESTRUCTURING WORK? ORGANIZATIONAL INNOVATION
        AT VOLVO AND GM.
        ORGANIZATIONAL DYNAMICS 5(SUMMER 1976): 63-80.

            USING A PRAGMATIC BUT CONCEPTUALLY SOPHISTICATED
        FRAMEWORK, TICHY ANALYZES TWO QUALITY OF WORKING LIFE
        PROJECTS AND EXPLAINS WHY ONE WAS AN OUTSTANDING SUCESS,
        THE OTHER A RESOUNDING FAILURE.

M0741   TODD, JOHN.
        MANAGEMENT CONTROL SYSTEMS: A KEY LINK BETWEEN STRATEGY,
        STRUCTURE, AND EMPLOYEE PERFORMANCE.
        ORGANIZATIONAL DYNAMICS 5(SPRING 1977): 65-78.

            IN A RESEARCH BASED ARTICLE, TODD IDENTIFIES SEVERAL
        ELEMENTS OF STRATEGY AND STRUCTURE THAT CONTRIBUTE TO AN
        EFFECTIVE MANAGEMENT CONTROL SYSTEM- ONE THAT MOTIVATES
        EMPLOYEE PERFORMANE. THEY ARE CLARITY OF CONTROL, STRENGTH
        OF PERFORMANCE- REWARDS RELATIONSHIP, AND AMOUNT OF
        INDIVIDUAL CONTROL AND INFLUENCE.

M0742   WHITE, ROBERT D.
        DEMOCRATIZING THE REWARD SYSTEM.
        PUBLIC PERSONNEL MANAGEMENT 3(SEPTEMBER-OCTOBER 1974): 409-
        14.

            SUGGEST INCREASED EMPLOYEE-PARTICIPATION REFORMS IN THE
        FEDERAL GOVERNMENT PERSONNEL SYSTEM. INCREASED USE OF
        BEHAVIORAL SCIENCE INSIGHTS IS RECOMMENDED.

M0743   WILKENS, PAUL L.   HAYNES, JOEL B.
        UNDERSTANDING FRUSTRATION-INSTIGATED BEHAVIOR.
        PERSONNEL JOURNAL 53(OCTOBER 1974): 770-74.

            PRESENTS MODELS CONTRASTING GOAL-DIRECTED WITH
        FRUSTRATION-INSTIGATED BEHAVIORS (FIB). FIB IS SEEN AS
        RESULTING FROM A BARRIER ARISING BETWEEN AN INDIVIDUAL'S
        WANTS AND HIS GOALS. SEVERAL DEFENSE MECHANISMS REPRESENTING
        FIB ARE DISCUSSED: AGGRESSION, RATIONALIZATION, FIXATION,
        REPRESSION, REGRESSION, AND AVOIDANCE. RECOMMENDATIONS ARE
        MADE TO THE MANAGER OF AN EMPLOYEE EXHIBITING FIB.

M0744   YANKELOVICH, D.
        TURBULENCE IN THE WORKING WORLD: ANGRY WORKERS, HAPPY GRADS.
        PSYCHOLOGY TODAY 8(DECEMBER 1974): 80-87.

            SUGGEST THAT THE GAP BETWEEN COLLEGE-EDUCATED YOUNG
        PEOPLE AND THOSE WITH LITTLE OR NO COLLEGE EDUCATION IS MORE
        CRITICAL THAN THE GENERATION GAP. BOTH GROUPS WANT SELF-
        FULFILLMENT IN WORK AND OTHER AREAS OF LIFE. HOWEVER, NON-
        COLLEGE YOUNG PEOPLE DO NOT HAVE ACCESS TO SELF-FULFILLING
        JOBS SINCE PEOPLE NO LONGER RISE FROM THE ASSEMBLY LINE TO
        BECOME MANAGERS. WORK ITSELF NO LONGER HAS DIGNITY IF THE
        WORKER DOES NOT DEFINE IT AS MEANINGFUL.

M0745 ADAMS, E. F.
INVESTIGATION OF THE INFLUENCE OF JOB LEVEL AND FUNCTIONAL
SPECIALTY ON JOB ATTITUDES AND PERCEPTIONS.
JOURNAL OF APPLIED PSYCHOLOGY 62(JUNE 1977): 335-43.

　　　　ONE HUNDRED AND FIFTY-TWO JOBS IN A LARGE (N=1,313)
MIDWESTERN PRINTING COMPANY WERE CLASSIFIED INTO VERTICAL
(JOB LEVEL) AND HORIZONTAL (FUNCTIONAL SPECIALTY)
DISTRIBUTIONS TO INVESTIGATE DIFFERENCES IN EMPLOYEE
ATTITUDES. DESCRIPTIONS OF LEADER BEHAVIOR (THE LEADER
BEHAVIOR DESCRIPTION QUESTIONNAIRE'S INITIATING STRUCTURE
SCALE) AND FOUR ASPECTS OF SATISFACTION (THE JOB DESCRIPTIVE
INDEX SCALES: SATISFACTION WITH WORK, PAY, SUPERVISION, AND
CO-WORKERS) WERE ASSESSED. A 3 (JOB LEVEL) X 5 (FUNCTIONAL
SPECIALTY) MULTIVARIATE ANALYSIS OF VARIANCE DEMONSTRATED
SIGNIFICANT DIFFERENCES IN JOB ATTITUDES FOR BOTH JOB LEVEL
AND FUNCTIONAL SPECIALTY. A DISCRIMINANT ANALYSIS SEPARATED
THE FUNCTIONAL SPECIALTY AND JOB LEVEL GROUPINGS ALONG TWO
DIMENSIONS IN TERMS OF SATISFACTION WITH WORK ITSELF AND PAY
AND INITIATING STRUCTURE. THE RESULTS SUGGEST THAT THESE TWO
ORGANIZATIONAL STRUCTURE CHARACTERISTICS SUMMARIZE INFLUENCE
OF MANAGERIAL STYLE, LOCAL NORMS, GOALS, AND JOB
REQUIREMENTS THAT AFFECT INDIVIDUAL ATTITUDES AND PERCEPTION
OF WORK SITUATION.

M0747 ARANYA, N.　　　　JACOBSON, D.　　　　SHYE, S.
ORGANIZATIONAL AND OCCUPATIONAL COMMITMENT: A FACET
THEORETICAL ANALYSIS OF EMPIRICAL DATA.
NEDERLANDS TIJDSCHRIFT VOOR DE PSYCHOLOGIE EN HARR
GRENSGEBIEDEN 31(JANUARY 1976): 13-22.

　　　　ACCORDING TO G. RITZER AND H. TRICE (1970), THE
RELATIVE STRENGTH OF OCCUPATIONAL COMMITMENTS CAN BE
ILLUSTRATED BY MEANS OF A NONMETRIC MULTIVARIATE ANALYSIS,
KNOWN AS L. GUTTMAN'S (SEE PA, VOL. 43:6108) SMALLEST SPACE
ANALYSIS (SSA). THE SSA CAN BE ILLUSTRATED BY A MAPPING
SENTENCE: 'THE DEGREE BY WHICH A PERSON IS INCLINED TO
REMAIN IN HIS FACET A (ORGANIZATION OR OCCUPATION) CAN BE
ILLUSTRATED IF HE WERE OFFERED FACET B (GREAT, LITTLE, OR
NO) INCREASE IN HIS FACET C (OPPORTUNITY TO DEVELOP SELF,
RESPONSIBILITY, STATUS, FREEDOM, OR PAY) LEADING TO THE
(HIGH OR LOW COMMITMENT) FRAMEWORK SPECIFIED.' THE SSA IS
USED TO DEPICT THE RELATIVE STRENGTH OF THE 3 FACETS OF THE
ILLUSTRATED MAPPING SENTENCE.

M0748 BASS, BERNARD M.　　　　VALENZI, ENZO R.　　　　FARROW, DANA L.
SOLOMAN, ROBERT J.
MANAGEMENT STYLES ASSOCIATED WITH ORGANIZATIONAL, TASK,
PERSONAL, AND INTERPERSONAL CONTINGENCIES.
JOURNAL OF APPLIED PSYCHOLOGY 60 (DECEMBER 1975): 720-29.

　　　　PRIOR STUDIES WITH SUBORDINATES AND MANAGERS FROM
PUBLIC AND PRIVATE AGENCIES RESULTED IN THE DEVELOPMENT OF A
31-SCALE PROFILE QUESTIONNAIRE CONCEPTUALIZED IN A SYSTEMS
FRAMEWORK OF INPUT, TRANSFORM, AND OUTPUT VARIABLES. IN THE
PRESENT STUDY, THE PROFILE WAS COMPLETED BY 78 MANAGERS AND
407 OF THEIR SUBORDINATES. CONVERGENT AND CONCURRENT
VALIDITY STUDIES GENERALLY SUPPORTED THE VALIDITY SCALES.

M0748   FIVE MANAGEMENT STYLES MEASURED WERE FOUND TO BE
        CONCEPTUALLY BUT NOT EMPIRICALLY INDEPENDENT. THE STYLES
        DIRECTION, NEGOTIATION, CONSULTATION, PARTICIPATION, AND
        DELEGATION-DIFFERENTIALLY CORRELATED WITH ORGANIZATIONAL,
        TASK, INTRAPERSONAL, AND INTERPERSONAL VARIABLES, AS WELL AS
        WITH MEASURES OF WORK-UNIT EFFECTIVENESS AND SATISFACTION.
        ACCORDING TO STEPWISE REGRESSIONS, DIRECTION WAS MORE LIKELY
        TO APPEAR WITH STRUCTURE AND CLARITY; NEGOTIATION WITH
        SHORT-TERM OBJECTIVES AND AUTHORITARIAN SUBORDINATES;
        CONSULTATION, WITH LONG-TERM OBJECTIVES AND INTRAGROUP
        HARMONY; PARTICIPATION, WITH CLARITY AND WARMTH; AND
        DELEGATION, WITH WARMTH AND LACK OF ROUTINE TASKS.

M0749   BERGLAND, BRUCE.   LUNDQUIST, G. W.
        THE VOCATIONAL EXPLORATION GROUP AND MINORITY YOUTH: AN
        EXPERIMENTAL OUTCOME STUDY.
        JOURNAL OF VOCATIONAL BEHAVIOR 7(DECEMBER 1975): 289-96.

            INVESTIGATED THE EFFECTIVENESS OF THE VOCATIONAL EXPLO-
        RATION GROUP (VEG) IN ASSISTING STUDENTS TO BECOME MORE
        AWARE OF THE WORLD OF WORK AND ITS RELEVANCE FOR THEM. 60
        MALE MEXICAN-AMERICAN 9TH GRADERS WERE RANDOMLY ASSIGNED TO
        1 OF 3 GROUPS: (A) VEG, (B) VEG WITHOUT INTERACTION, OR (C)
        CONTROL. UPON COMPLETION OF THE TREATMENTS SS WERE POST-
        TESTED WITH THE CAREER EXPLORATION QUESTIONNAIRE, AN
        INSTRUMENT DESIGNED TO ASSESS KNOWLEDGE OF FACTORS SUCH AS
        DIFFERING FUNCTIONS OF JOBS, INTEREST AND SKILLS NEEDED IN
        DIFFERENT JOBS, AND SATISFACTIONS AVAILABLE FROM WORK.
        ANALYSES REVEALED NO STATISTICALLY SIGNIFICANT DIFFERENCE
        AMONG GROUPS.

M0750   BIGGS, DONALD A.   BRODIE, JANE S.   BARNHART, WILLIAM.
        THE DYNAMICS OF UNDERGRADUATE ACADEMIC ADVISING.
        RESEARCH IN HIGHER EDUCATION 3, NO. 4 (1975): 345-57.

            DESCRIBES JOB ACTIVITIES, ROLE EXPECTATIONS, AND JOB
        SATISFACTIONS OF A SAMPLE OF ACADEMIC ADVISORS: 452 FACULTY
        AND STAFF ADVISORS IN 5 COLLEGES AT THE UNIVERSITY OF
        MINNESOTA (TWIN CITIES). 72% OF THE SAMPLE COMPLETED THE
        QUESTIONNAIRE. THEIR WORK CAN BE CLASSIFIED INTO 4 CLUSTERS
        OF JOB ACTIVITIES. THREE INVOLVE HELPING STUDENTS (A) WITH
        SPECIAL ACADEMIC, SOCIAL, OR FINANCIAL PROBLEMS; (B) WITH
        EMOTIONAL OR PSYCHOLOGICAL PROBLEMS; AND (C) WITH ACADEMIC
        AND CAREER GUIDANCE PROBLEMS. THE 4TH INVOLVES
        ADMINISTRATIVE ACTIVITIES. RESULTS ALSO SUGGEST THAT
        ADVISERS SPEND MOST OF THEIR TIME APPROVING REGISTRATION
        CARDS AND PROVIDING INFORMATION ABOUT ACADEMIC REQUIREMENTS.
        MOST ADVISERS VIEW THEMSELVES AS APPROPIATE SOURCES OF HELP
        IN ACADEMIC AND VOCATIONAL GUIDANCE AREAS RATHER THAN IN
        PERSONAL OR SOCIAL ONES. MOST ADVISERS ARE SATISFIED WITH
        THEIR WORK, BUT A SUBSTANTIAL PERCENTAGE ARE DISSATISFIED
        WITH THE AMOUNT OF RECOGNITION THEY RECEIVE. ADVISERS WITH
        MORE ADVANCED DEGREES AND THOSE WITH LARGER NUMBERS OF
        ADVISEES TEND TO BE MORE DISSATISFIED.

M0751   BIRCHALL, D.W.   WILD, RAY.
        PERCEIVED JOB ATTITUDES, JOB ATTRIBUTES AND THE BEHAVIOR OF
        BLUE-COLLAR WORKERS: A RESEARCH NOTE.

M0751 JOURNAL OF MANAGEMENT STUDIES 13 (MAY 1976): 191-96.
CERTAIN ASPECTS OR FEATURES OF JOBS HAVE BEEN
IDENTIFIED BY RESEARCHERS AS POTENTIALLY IMPORTANT
DETERMINANTS OF WORKER BEHAVIOUR AND JOB SATISFACTION. WILD
AND BIRCHALL, FOR EXAMPLE, HAVE PROPOSED A SERIES OF
DESIRABLE JOB ATTRIBUTES, INCLUDING OPTIMUM WORK VARIETY,
WORKER RESPONSIBILITY, AUTONOMY, SOCIAL INTERACTION,
UTILIZATION OF VALUED SKILLS AND ABLITIES AND PERCEIVED
CONTRIBUTION TO PRODUCT UTILITY, WHICH THEY ARGUE MIGHT BE
CONSIDERED AS NECESSARY ASPECTS OF 'BEHAVIOURALLY POSITIVE'
JOBS. CERTAIN LOW-SKILL JOBS MAY BE CONSIDERED TO BE
DEFICIENT IN RESPECT OF SUCH ATTRIBUTES AND WHILST SOME FORM
OF MEASUREMENT OF JOBS (E.G. TURNER AND LAWRENCE) MAY
SUGGEST AREAS FOR JOB IMPROVEMENT OR RESTRUCTURING, OF
COURSE, FOR THE WORKER IT IS HIS OWN (SUBJECTIVE) PERCEPTION
OF HIS JOB WHICH MAY INFLUENCE HIS ATTITUDES AND BEHAVIOUR.
THE STUDY EXAMINED IN DETAIL THE RELATIONSHIP BETWEEN
WORKERS' PERCEPTIONS OF THE EXTENT TO WHICH THEIR LOW-SKILL
BLUE-COLLAR JOBS POSSESSED SUCH 'BEHAVIOURALLY DESIRABLE'
JOB ATTRIBUTES AND THEIR WORK-RELATED BEHAVIOUR.

M0752 BLUMENTHAL M.D.
DEPRESSIVE SYMPTOMATOLOGY AND ROLE FUNCTION IN A GENERAL
POPULATION.
ARCHIVES OF GENERAL PSYCHIATRY 32 (AUGUST 1975): 985-91.

INVESTIGATED DEPRESSIVE SYMPTOMATOLOGY, MARITAL
SATISFACTION AND FUNCTIONING, JOB SATISFACTION, AND SOCIAL
RELATIONSHIPS IN 320 RESPONDENTS COMPRISING 160 MARITAL
COUPLES. RESPONSES TO THE ZUNG SELF-RATING DEPRESSION SCALE
INDICATED THAT 13% OF SS HAD SCORES SIMILAR TO THOSE
OBTAINED BY PATIENTS WITH DIAGNOSED DEPRESSIONS, AND AN
ADDITIONAL 27% HAD SCORES COMPARABLE TO THOSE OF PERSONS
WITH OTHER PSYCHIATRIC PROBEMS. RESPONSES TO QUESTIONS
ABOUT SS SOCIAL LIFE, SOCIAL SATISFACTION, AND MARITAL
FUNCTION INDICATED THAT INCREASED DEPRESSIVE SYMPTOMATOLOGY
IN THIS GENERAL POPULATION WAS ASSOCIATED WITH A DECLINE
IN SATISFACTION AND FUNCTIONING IN THESE AREAS. THE DATA
SUGGEST THAT THIS ASSOCIATION WAS NOT SOLELY DUE TO RESPONSE
BIAS BUT WAS ASSOCIATED WITH A REAL DECLINE IN FUNCTION,
PARTICULARLY IN THE AREA OF CHILD REARING.

M0753 BRIEF, ARTHUR P.   MUNRO, JIM.   ALDAG, RAMON J.
CORRECTIONAL EMPLOYEES' REACTIONS TO JOB CHARACTERISTICS: A
DATA BASED ARGUMENT FOR JOB ENLARGEMENT.
JOURNAL OF CRIMINAL JUSTICE 4(FALL 1976): 223-30.

DISCUSSES JOB ENLARGEMENT, AN INDUSTRIAL ORGANIZATIONAL
INNOVATION THAT ALLOWS WORKERS GREATER RESPONSIBILITY FOR
THEIR JOBS; IN RELATION TO CORRECTIONAL PERSONNEL. A
QUESTIONNAIRE WAS ADMINISTERED TO 104 CORRECTIONAL PERSONNEL
(78% MALE, AVERAGE AGE OF ALL SS 41.4 YEARS) IN A VARIETY OF
JOBS, AND IT WAS FOUND THAT INDUSTRIAL FINDINGS GENERALIZED
TO CORRECTIONS. SS RESPONDED MORE POSITIVELY TO A JOB THAT
OFFERED THEM SKILL VARIETY, AUTONOMY, TASK IDENTITY, AND
FEEDBACK THAN THEY DID TO A JOB THAT WAS PERCEIVED AS DULL
AND MONOTONOUS. JOB ENLARGEMENT IS RECOMMENDED TO IMPROVE
THE PERSONNEL AND MANAGERIAL ASPECTS OF THE CORRECTIONAL

M0753   INSTITUTION, TO BRING THE INSTITUTION INTO CONFORMITY WITH
        ENVIRONMENTAL REALITY, AND TO OVERCOME THE THERAPY-CUSTODY
        DICHOTOMY.

M0754   BURTON, ARTHUR.
        THERAPIST SATISFACTION.
        AMERICAN JOURNAL OF PSYCHOANALYSIS 35(SUMMER 1975): 115-22.

            DISCUSSES AREAS IN WHICH THE PSYCHOANALYST CAN DERIVE
        PERSONAL SATISFACTION FROM THE PRACTICE OF PSYCHOTHERAPY:
        INTAPSYCHIC, SENSUAL-INTERPERSONAL, INTELLECTUAL-RATIONAL,
        RESEARCH-CREATIVE, CULTIST-FRATERNAL, AND ECONOMIC. IT IS
        ARGUED THAT THE SATISFACTION OF THE THERAPIST IS AS
        IMPORTANT AS THAT OF THE PATIENT, AND CAN AFFECT THE OUTCOME
        OF TREATMENT THROUGH TRANSFERENTIAL INVASIONS. WHENEVER
        OUTSIDE SOURCES OF GRATIFICATION ARE LACKING TO THE
        THERAPIST, STRAIN IS PLACED ON PATIENT RELATIONSHIPS FOR
        SATISFACTIONS WHICH SHOULD PROPERLY COME FROM OUTSIDE
        THERAPY. STATES OF INNER DISSATISFACTION ALSO CAN INHIBIT
        THE THERAPIST'S MOTIVATION TO CURE.

M0755   CLELAND, V.   BASS, ALAN R.   MCHUGH, NORMA.
        MONTANO, JOCELYN.
        SOCIAL AND PSYCHOLOGICAL INFLUENCES ON EMPLOYMENT OF MARRIED
        NURSES.
        NURSING RESEARCH 25(MARCH-APRIL 1976): 90-97.

            SEVEN SUMMARY FACTORS WERE OBTAINED FROM A PRINCIPAL
        COMPONENTS FACTOR ANALYSIS AND VARIMAX ROTATION OF 21
        VARIABLES, BASED ON INFORMATION IN MAILED QUESTIONNAIRES
        RETURNED BY 1,998 NURSES (89% OF SAMPLE) IN A METROPOLITAN
        AREA. SS WERE UNDER 60 YEARS OF AGE, MARRIED, AND LIVING
        WITH SPOUSE, AND HAD AT LEAST ONE CHILD 18 YEARS OLD OR
        YOUNGER. FACTORS WERE CAREER DESIRABILITY, PROFESSIONAL
        ATTITUDE, PROFESSIONAL BEHAVIOR, ACHIEVEMENT PERSONALITY,
        CONDUCIVE HOME SITUATION, ECONOMIC VALUE OF WORK, AND
        SATISFACTION WITH NURSING. WHEN THESE FACTORS WERE COMPARED
        WITH (A) CURRENT EMPLOYMENT ACTIVITY OF ALL SS AND (B) SS
        WHOSE EMPLOYMENT STATUS WAS CONSTANT FOR 5 YEARS, HIGHEST
        SCORES WERE REGISTERED IN BOTH CATEGORIES ON CAREER
        DESIRABILITY, PROFESSIONAL BEHAVIOR, AND ECONOMIC VALUE OF
        WORK. BOTH GROUPS SCORED LOWEST ON SATISFACTION WITH
        NURSING, WITH THE 5-YEAR STATUS, WHILE CONTROLLING FINANCIAL
        NEED AND AGE OF YOUNGEST CHILD AT HOME, HIGHEST CORRELATION
        SCORES RESULTED FOR PROFESSIONAL BEHAVIOR, CAREER
        DESIRABILITY, AND, IN THE CASE OF THOSE WITH FINANCIAL NEED,
        ON THE ECONOMIC VALUE OF NURSING.

M0756   DICKSON, JOHN W.   BUCHHOLTZ, ROGENE.
        MANAGERIAL BELIEFS ABOUT WORK IN SCOTLAND AND THE U.S.A.
        JOURNAL OF MANAGEMENT STUDIES 14, NO. 1 (1977): 80-101.

            THE PRACTICE OF MANAGEMENT IS NOW AS NEVER BEFORE UNDER
        ATTACK FROM VARIOUS SEGMENTS OF SOCIETY. THIS QUESTIONING OF
        THE LEGITIMACY OF MANAGERIAL ROLES IS FACILITATED BY THE
        EXISTENCE OF A NUMBER OF DIFFERENT WIDELY HELD BELIEFS ABOUT
        WORK. THERE NO LONGER APPEARS TO BE ONE WIDELY HELD BELIEF
        ABOUT WORK, SUCH AS THE WORK ETHIC. RATHER A DIVERSITY OF

M0756 BELIEFS EXIST AMONG DIFFERENT INDIVIDUALS OR IN THE SAME
INDIVIDUAL. THIS STUDY EXAMINES BELIEFS ABOUT WORK WITHIN
A CONCEPTUAL FRAMEWORK THAT ALLOWS A MEASUREMENT OF THE
STRENGTH OF COMMITMENT TO VARIOUS BELIEF SYSTEMS ABOUT WORK.
THUS A COMPARISON CAN BE MADE FOR THE RELATIVE IMPORTANCE
THE IMPACT OF HIERARCHICAL ITEMS FOR THE GROUPS UNDER STUDY.

M0757 KANTER, ROSABETH.
THE IMPACT OF HIERARCHICAL STRUCTURES ON THE WORK BEHAVIOR
OF WOMEN AND MEN.
SOCIAL PROBLEMS 23(APRIL 1976): 415-30.

PROPOSES THAT THERE ARE NO SEX DIFFERENCES IN WORK
BEHAVIOR; INSTEAD WORK ATTITUDES AND WORK BEHAVIOR ARE A
FUNCTION OF LOCATION IN ORGANIZATIONAL STRUCTURES. THE
STRUCTURES OF OPPORTUNITY (E.G. MOBILITY PROSPECTS) AND
POWER (E.G. INFLUENCED UPWARD), ALONG WITH THE PROPORTIONAL
REPRESENTATION OF A PERSON'S SOCIAL TYPE, DEFINE AND SHAPE
THE WAYS THAT ORGANIZATIONAL MEMBERS RESPOND TO THEIR JOBS
AND TO EACH OTHER. IN HIERARCHICAL SYSTEMS LIKE LARGE
CORPORATIONS, THE RELATIVE DISADVANTAGE OF MANY WOMEN WITH
RESPECT TO OPPORTUNITY AND POWER RESULTS IN BEHAVIORS AND
ATTITUDES (SUCH AS LIMITED ADPIRATIONS, CONCERN WITH CO-
WORKER FRIENDSHIPS, OR CONTROLLING LEADERSHIP STYLES) THAT
ARE ALSO TRUE OF MEN IN SIMILARLY DISADVANTAGED POSITIONS.
THE STRUCTURE OF POWER IN ORGANIZATIONS, RATHER THAN
INHERENT SEXUAL ATTITUDES, CAN ALSO EXPLAIN WHY WOMEN SOME-
TIMES APPEAR TO BE LESS PREFERRED AS LEADERS. IT IS
CONCLUDED THAT IT IS NOT THE NATURE OF WOMEN BUT
HIERARCHICAL ARRANGEMENTS THAT MUST BE CHANGED IF WE ARE TO
PROMOTE EQUITY IN THE WORKPLACE.

M0758 FROHMAN, ALAN L.   KOTTER, JOHN P.
THE JOINING-UP PROCESS: ISSUES IN EFFECTIVE HUMAN RESOURCE
DEVELOPMENT.
TRAINING AND DEVELOPMENT JOURNAL 29(AUGUST 1975): 3-7.

DESCRIBES PROBLEMS OF THE INITIAL MANAGEMENT OF NEW 1ST
LEVEL MANAGERS AND PROFESSIONALS, AND SUMMARIZES METHODS FOR
SOLUTION. MISMATCHED EXPECTATIONS ARE PREVENTED BY EARLY
DISCUSSIONS USING A STRUCTURED FORMAT. STIFLING OF
CREATIVITY IS HANDLED BY IDENTIFYING JOB CONSTRAINTS AND
COACHING EMPLOYEES. LACK OF MANAGERIAL SENSITIVITY IS
COUNTERED BY OFFERING A SHORT COURSE ON HOW TO MANAGE THE
NEW EMPLOYEE. INAPPROPIATE SCREENING CRITERIA ARE AVOIDED BY
USING A DETAILED CHECKLIST TO SPECIFY ABILITIES AND
BEHAVIORS REQUIRED BY THE OPEN JOB. ACTION STEPS OF THIS
KIND HAVE PROVED EFFECTIVE IN SUPPORTING JOB SATISFACTION
AND IN PROMOTING PRODUCTIVITY ON THE JOB.

M0759 GARFIELD, SOL L.   KURTZ, RICHARD M.
TRAINING AND CAREER SATISFACTION AMONG CLINICAL
PSYCHOLOGISTS.
CLINICAL PSYCHOLOGIST 28(WINTER 1975): 6-9.

OF 855 CLINICAL PSYCHOLOGISTS (CP) SURVEYED, TWO-THIRDS
EXPRESSED SOME DEGREE OF SATISFACTION WITH THE AMERICAN
PSYCHOLOGY ASSOCIATION; MORE SATISFACTION TENDED TO BE

M0759   EXPRESSED BY THOSE IN UNIVERSITY POSITIONS THAN THOSE IN
         OTHER SETTINGS. AN OVERWHELMING MAJORITY EXPRESSED
         SATISFACTION WITH THE CAREER OF A CP IN GENERAL, AND 71%
         STATED THAT, GIVEN THE CHOICE AGAIN, THEY WOULD AGAIN CHOOSE
         CP AS THEIR LIFE'S CAREER. THERE WAS LITTLE RELATION BETWEEN
         CAREER SATISFACTION AND THE DATE WHEN THE PH.D. WAS GRANTED.
         OVER 77% EXPRESSED GREAT OR MODERATE SATISFACTION WITH THE
         TRAINING IN CP THAT THEY HAD RECEIVED. REPORTS ON
         SATISFACTION WITH TRAINING ARE ANALYZED ACCORDING TO THE
         RESPONDENTS' PRIMARY PROFESSIONAL VIEW OF THEMSELVES,
         THEORETICAL ORIENTATION, AND WORK SETTINGS. FINDINGS ARE
         PRESENTED IN DETAIL AND ARE COMPARED WITH THOSE OF THE
         SIMILAR SURVEY MADE IN 1959 BY E.L. KELLY AND L.R. GOLDBERG.
         COMMENTS AND SUGGESTIONS ON RESEARCH AND CLINICAL TRAINING
         ARE OFFERED.

M0760   GRELLER, MARTIN M.
         SUBORDINATE PARTICIPATION AND REACTIONS TO THE APPRAISAL
         INTERVIEW.
         JOURNAL OF APPLIED PSYCHOLOGY 60(OCTOBER 1975): 544-49.

              CONDUCTED 2 STUDIES WHICH EXAMINED RELATIONSHIPS OF
         SUBORDINATE PARTICIPATION IN AN APPRAISAL INTERVIEW TO
         REACTIONS TO THE APPRAISALS AND SUBORDINATE SATISFACTION.
         IN STUDY 1, 25 MANAGERS RATED THEIR LAST APPRAISAL ON (A)
         HELPFULNESS AND (B) THE WEXLEY ET AL MEASURE OF PSYCHOLOGI-
         CAL PARTICIPATION, AND THEN RATED THEIR OVERALL SATISFACTION
         WITH SUPERVISION. THE LACK OF SIGNIFICANT INTERCORRELATIONS
         AMONG THE PSYCHOLOGICAL PARTICIPATION ITEMS INDICATED THAT
         DIFFERENT CONCEPTS OF PARTICIPATION WERE REPRESENTED. ITEMS
         REPRESENTING PARTICIPATION IN INTERACTION CORRELATED
         SIGNIFICANTLY WITH APPRAISAL HELPFULNESS AND SATISFACTION,
         WHILE CONTROL OF GOAL SETTING DID NOT CORRELATE
         SIGNIFICANTLY. IN A FIELD STUDY, 56 HOURLY EMPLOYEES AND 1ST
         LEVEL MANAGERS IN A BANK RATED (A) THEIR APPRAISAL ON
         CERTAIN CHARACTERISTICS, (B) THEIR SATISFACTION WITH THE
         APPRAISAL, AND (C) THEIR JOB SATISFACTION. THE INVITATION TO
         TO PARTICIPATE WAS MORE PREDICTIVE OF APPRAISAL
         SATISFACTION. THE OCCURRENCE OF GOAL SETTING CORRELATED
         SIGNIFICANTLY WITH BOTH APPRAISAL AND JOB SATISFACTION.

M0761   HACKMAN, J. R.   OLDHAM, GREG R.
         MOTIVATION THROUGH THE DESIGN OF WORK: TEST OF A THEORY.
         ORGANIZATIONAL BEHAVIOR AND HUMAN PERFORMANCE 16(AUGUST
         1976): 250-79.

              PROPOSES A MODEL THAT SPECIFIES THE CONDITIONS UNDER
         WHICH INDIVIDUALS WILL BECOME INTERNALLY MOTIVATED TO
         PERFORM EFFECTIVELY ON THEIR JOBS. THE MODEL FOCUSES ON THE
         INTERACTION AMONG 3 CLASSES OF VARIABLES: (A) THE
         PSYCHOLOGICAL STATES OF EMPLOYEES THAT MUST BE PRESENT FOR
         INTERNALLY MOTIVATED WORK BEHAVIOR TO DEVELOP, (B) THE
         CHARACTERISTICS OF JOBS THAT CAN CREATE THESE PSYCHOLOGICAL
         STATES, AND (C) THE ATTRIBUTES OF INDIVIDUALS THAT DETERMINE
         HOW POSITIVELY A PERSON WILL RESPOND TO A COMPLEX AND
         CHALLENGING JOB. THE MODEL WAS TESTED FOR 658 EMPLOYEES WHO
         WORK ON 62 DIFFERENT JOBS (BLUE COLLAR, WHITE COLLAR, AND
         PROFESSIONAL) IN 7 ORGANIZATIONS, AND RESULTS SUPPORT ITS

M0761 VALIDITY. A NUMBER OF SPECIAL FEATURES OF THE MODEL ARE
DISCUSSED (INCLUDING ITS USE AS A BASIS FOR DIAGNOSIS OF
JOBS AND THE EVALUATION OF JOB REDESIGN PROJECTS), AND THE
MODEL IS COMPARED TO OTHER THEORIES OF JOB DESIGN.

M0762 HOW TO KEEP WORKERS HAPPY ON THE JOB.
U.S. NEWS AND WORLD REPORT (DECEMBER 26, 1977): 85-86.

DANA CORPORATION, IN TOLEDO, OHIO, HAS INSTALLED THE
SCANLON PLAN IN SEVERAL OF ITS PLANTS AROUND THE COUNTRY. THE
PLAN ENCOURAGES BOTH WORKERS AND MANAGEMENT TO COME UP WITH
LABOR-SAVING IDEAS AND THEN PAYS EVERYONE IN THE PLANTS A
BONUS IF THOSE IDEAS INCREASE PRODUCTION WHILE KEEPING
PAYROLL COSTS BELOW A CERTAIN BASE.

M0763 HOLT, K.
WORK FRUSTRATION IN ENGINEERING DEPARTMENTS.
R & D MANAGEMENT 5(OCTOBER 1974): 17-24.

NOTES THAT A LARGE NUMBER OF ENGINEERS WORK IN
ORGANIZATIONS WITH SPECIALIZED JOBS OF A ROUTINE NATURE, IN
MANY WAYS COMPARABLE TO WORKERS ON A PRODUCTION LINE.
PREVIOUS EMPIRICAL STUDIES DEMONSTRATED THAT THIS LEADS TO
FRUSTRATION. ALTHOUGH THERE IS NO STANDARD SOLUTION AVAILA-
BLE, A NUMBER OF APPROACHES ARE SUGGESTED IN THE PRESENT
ARTICLE THAT CAN LEAD TO GREATER SATISFACTION IF ONE IS
WILLING TO EXPERIMENT WITH THEM. A MORE ORGANIC, LESS
STRUCTURED MANAGEMENT SYSTEM AND MORE USE OF PROBLEM
ORIENTED PROJECT GROUPS MAY BRING BENEFITS. JOB ENRICHMENT,
WHERE ENGINEERS ARE GIVEN MORE RESPONSIBILITIES BY TRANSFER
OF TASKS PREVIOUSLY DONE BY MANAGEMENT AND SENIORS, AND
SPECIAL TRAINING, WHERE ENGINEERS ARE GIVEN AN OPPORTUNITY
TO SYSTEMATICALLY DEVELOP THEIR CAPABILITIES, SHOULD BE
CONSIDERED. ORGANIZATIONAL DEVELOPMENT MUST BE MENTIONED
WHERE AN EXTERNAL CHANGE AGENT TOGETHER WITH THE PEOPLE
INVOLVED DEVELOPS A SOLUTION AIMING AT THE SATISFACTION OF
THE NEEDS OF BOTH THE INDIVIDUAL AND THE ORGANIZATION.
FINALLY, FLEXIBLE WORKING HOURS HAVE AN INDIRECT EFFECT ON
THE JOB SITUATION BY ALLOWING FOR A RICHER LIFE OFF THE JOB.

M0764 INDIRESAN, J.
CONVERGENT AND DISCRIMINANT VALIDITY OF A JOB SATISFACTION
INVENTORY: A CROSS-CULTURAL REPORT.
JOURNAL OF THE INDIAN ACADEMY OF APPLIED PSYCHOLOGY 10, NO.
1 (1973): 17-21.

DEVELOPED AND ADMINISTERED A 3-PART LIKERT-TYPE JOB
SATISFACTION INVENTORY (JSI) TO 158 TEACHERS IN INDIAN
TECHNOLOGICAL INSTITUTIONS AND 50 ENGLISH UNIVERSITY
TEACHERS. THE MODELS FOR CONVERGENT AND DISCRIMINANT
VALIDITIES PROPOSED BY D.T. CAMPBELL AND D.M. FISKE (1959)
WERE USED TO VALIDATE THE INSTRUMENT. THE 30 ITEMS IN THE
JSI WERE DIVIDED INTO 5 NEED AREAS: PHYSICAL, SOCIAL, ESTEEM
AUTONOMY, AND SELF-ACTUALIZATION. PARTS 1, 2, AND 3 OF THE
INVENTORY MEASURED 'PERCEIVED NEED DEFICIENCY', 'EXPRESSED
SATISFACTION', AND 'PERCEIVED FUTURE ESTIMATE',
RESPECTIVELY. AN INTERCORRELATION MATRIX WAS OBTAINED,
CORRELATING THE 15 SCORES RESULTING FROM THE 3 PARTS.

M0764   CONVERGENT AND DISCRIMINANT VALIDITIES WERE TESTED FOR THE
         NEED AREAS AND FOR THE 3 METHODS USED. MOST OF THE CRITERIA
         REQUIRED TO ESTABLISH THE CONVERGENT AND DISCRIMINANT
         VALIDITY FOR THE NEED AREAS AS WELL AS THE METHODS USED WERE
         SATISFIED IN BOTH THE INDIAN AND ENGLISH SAMPLES.

M0765   IVANCEVICH, J. M.
         PREDICTING JOB PERFORMANCE BY USE OF ABILITY TESTS AND
         STUDYING JOB SATISFACTION AS A MODERATING VARIABLE.
         JOURNAL OF VOCATIONAL BEHAVIOR 9(AUGUST 1976): 87-97.

              INVESTIGATED THE MODERATING IMPACT OF JOB SATISFACTION
         IN THE PREDICTION OF JOB PERFORMANCE CRITERIA FROM ABILITY
         AS INDICATED BY THE PERFORMANCE OF 324 TECHNICIANS' (AGED
         21-59 YEARS) SCORES ON THE EMPLOYEE APTITUDE SURVEY.
         PERFORMANCE MEASURES WERE UNEXCUSED ABSENCES, TARDINESS,
         COST PER PROJECT, SUPERVISORY RATINGS, AND BEHAVIORALLY
         ANCHORED SCALES DEVELOPED BY TECHNICIANS WITHIN THE SAME
         ORGANIZATION. FINDINGS SUGGEST THAT THE TYPE OF JOB
         SATISFACTION FACET AND THE PERFORMANCE CRITERIA USED ARE
         IMPORTANT CONSIDERATIONS WHEN EXAMINING SATISFACTION AS A
         MODERATOR: ONLY FOR SOME FACETS AND CRITERIA DID
         SATISFACTION MODERATE THE RELATIONSHIP BETWEEN PREDICTED AND
         ACTUAL PERFORMANCE.

M0766   IVANCEVICH, J. M.   DONNELLY, J. H.
         RELATION OF ORGANIZATIONAL STRUCTURE TO JOB SATISFACTION,
         ANXIETY-STRESS, AND PERFORMANCE.
         ADMINISTRATIVE SCIENCE QUATERLY 20(JUNE 1975): 272-80.

              USED 295 TRADESALESMEN IN 3 ORGANIZATIONS TO STUDY THE
         RELATIONSHIP BETWEEN ORGANIZATIONAL SHAPE OR STRUCTURE (TALL
         MEDIUM, AND FLAT) TO JOB SATISFACTION, ANXIETY-STRESS, AND
         PERFORMANCE. DEPENDENT VARIABLES WERE MEASURED BY A 20-ITEM
         LIKERT SCALE OF JOB SATISFACTION, A 9-ITEM ANXIETY-STRESS
         SCALE BY R. KAHN ET AL, AND 3 INDICES OF JOB EFFECTIVENESS
         (ABSENTEEISM, EFFICIENCY RATING, AND ROUTE-COVERAGE INDEX).
         FINDINGS INDICATE THAT SALESMEN IN FLAT ORGANIZATIONS (A)
         PERCEIVE MORE SATISFACTION WITH RESPECT TO SELF-
         ACTUALIZATION, AND AUTONOMY, (B) PERCEIVE LOWER AMOUNTS OF
         ANXIETY-STRESS, AND (C) PERFORM MORE EFFICIENTLY THAN SALES-
         MEN IN MEDIUM AND TALL ORGANIZATIONS.

M0767   IVANCEVICH, J. M.   LYON, HERBERT L.
         SHORTENED WORKWEEK: A FIELD EXPERIMENT.
         JOURNAL OF APPLIED PSYCHOLOGY 62 (FEBUARY 1977): 34-37.

              EFFECTS OF THE 4-DAY, 40-HOUR WORKWEEK WERE EXAMINED IN
         THE PRESENT FIELD STUDY BY COMPARING TWO EXPERIMENTAL GROUPS
         (N=97, N=111) AND A COMPARISON GROUP (N=94) OF THE OPERATING
         EMPLOYEES IN A MEDIUM-SIZED MANUFACTURING COMPANY.
         COMPARISONS WERE MADE ON DIMENSIONS OF SELF-ACTUALIZATION,
         AUTONOMY, PERSONAL WORTH, SOCIAL AFFILIATION, JOB SECURITY,
         PAY AND OVERALL JOB SATISFACTION, ANXIETY-STRESS,
         ABSENTEEISM, AND PERFORMANCE OVER A A 13-MONTH
         EEISM, AND PERFORMANCE OVER A 13-MONTH AND A 25-MONTH
         PERIOD. THE ANALYSIS OF 13-MONTH DATA INDICATED THAT THE
         WORKERS IN THE 4-DAY, 40-HOUR GROUPS WERE (A) MORE SATISFIED

M0767 WITH AUTONOMY, PERSONAL WORTH, JOB SECURITY, AND PAY; (B)
EXPERIENCED LESS ANXIETY-STRESS; AND (C) PERFORMED BETTER
WITH REGARD TO PRODUCTIVITY THAN DID THE COMPARISON GROUP.
HOWEVER THESE IMPROVEMENTS WERE NOT FOUND WITH THE 25-MONTH
DATA.

M0768 JACOBS, RICK.   SOLOMON, TRUDY.
STRATEGIES FOR ENHANCING THE PREDICTION OF JOB PERFORMANCE
FROM JOB SATISFACTION.
JOURNAL OF APPLIED PSYCHOLOGY 62(AUGUST 1977): 417-21.

TWO MODERATOR VARIABLES, PERFORMANCE TO REWARD
CONTINGENCY AND SELF-ESTEEM, WERE INCORPORATED INTO MULTIPLE
REGRESSION EQUATIONS IN AN ATTEMPT TO INCREASE THE
PEDICTABILITY OF JOB PERFORMANCE RATINGS FROM JOB
SATISFACTION INFORMATION. TWO HUNDRED FIFTY-ONE EMPLOYEES,
OCCUPYING THREE ORGANIZATIONAL LEVELS OF A NATIONWIDE
CORPORATION, RESPONDED BY MAIL TO A QUESTIONNAIRE PACKAGE.
SUBJECTS RECEIVED SCORES ON FOUR SELF-REPORT INVENTORIES
COVERING THE AREAS OF JOB SATISFACTION, SELF-ESTEEM, AND
CONTINGENCY OF REWARDS ON JOB PERFORMANCE. ADDITIONALLY EACH
SUBJECT WAS RATED BY AN IMMEDIATE SUPERVISOR ON THE QUALITY
OF OVERALL JOB PERFORMANCE. RESULTS INDICATED THAT THE
MODERATOR VARIABLE APPROACH OPERATIONALIZED VIA INODERATED
REGRESSION, SUBSTANTIALLY INCREASED THE RELATIONSHIP BETWEEN
SATISFACTION AND PERFORMANCE.

M0769 KAKABADSE, ANDREW
CORPORATE MANAGEMENT IN LOCAL GOVERNMENT: A CASE STUDY.
JOURNAL OF MANAGEMENT STUDIES 14(OCTOBER 1977): 341-51.

THE PURPOSE OF THIS PAPER IS AN ATTEMPT TO EXAMINE THE
DEVELOPMENT OF A CORPORATE MANAGEMENT UNIT IN A NORTH-
WESTERN LOCAL AUTHORITY. THE RESEARCH TOOL IS SOCIAL
ANALYSIS TO ORGANIZATION DEVELOPMENT. THE RESEARCH WAS
UNDERTAKEN IN THE EARLY SUMMER OF 1974 WHEN A TOTAL OF
15 UNSTRUCTURED PERSON TO PERSON INTERVIEWS WERE COMPLETED
FROM A SUM OF 15 RESPONDENTS.

M0770 KATERBERG, RALPH.   SMITH, FRANK J.   HOY, STEPHEN.
LANGUAGE, TIME, AND PERSON EFFECTS ON ATTITUDE SCALE
TRANSLATIONS.
JOURNAL OF APPLIED PSYCHOLOGY 62(AUGUST 1977): 385-91.

DECENTERED TRANSLATIONS INTO SPANISH WERE OBTAINED FOR
TWO STANDARD JOB ATTITUDE INSTRUMENTS, THE JOB DESCRIPTIVE
INDEX AND THE INDEX OF ORGANIZATIONAL REACTIONS. BILINGUAL
EMPLOYEES WORKING IN DIFFERENT OFFICES OF ONE LARGE RETAIL
ORGANIZATION RESPONDED TO EACH INSTRUMENT AND ITS
TRANSLATION AT TWO TIME PERIODS. COMPLETE DATA WERE OBTAINED
FOR 57 EMPLOYEES OF PUERTO RICAN ORIGIN AND FOR 71 EMPLOYEES
OF CUBAN ORIGIN. ENGLISH AND SPANISH RESPONSES WERE COMPARED
USING ANALYSIS OF VARIANCE AND REGRESSION APPROACHES. PERSON
VARIANCE ACCOUNTED FOR THE LARGEST PORTION OF VARIANCE,
WHEREAS TIME AND LANGUAGE EFFECTS WERE NEGLIGIBLE. THE
REGRESSION ANALYSIS, COMPARING THE TRANSLATIONS WITHIN TIME
FOR EACH SCALE, SHOWED THAT ALTHOUGH RESPONSES TO THE
SPANISH VERSIONS ARE STONGLY RELATED TO THOSE OF THE ENGLISH

M0770   VERSIONS. THE TWO TRANSLATIONS DO NOT GIVE IDENTICAL
        RESULTS. THESE RESULTS ALL SUPPORT THE RELIABILITY OF THE
        TRANSLATIONS.

M0771   KETS DE VRIES. M.
        THE ENTREPRENEURIAL PERSONALITY: A PERSON AT THE CROSSROADS.
        JOURNAL OF MANAGEMENT STUDIES 14, NO. 1 (1977): 34-579

             THIS PAPER REVIEWS THE CONCEPT OF ENTREPRENEURSHIP AND
        EMPIRICAL STUDIES OF ENTREPRENEURIAL BEHAVIOUR PATTERNS. IN
        ADDITION, IT EXPLORES THE SOCIAL, ECONOMIC AND PSYCHODYNAMIC
        FORCES INFLUENCING ENTREPRENEURSHIP. A CONCEPTUALIZATION OF
        THE ENTREPRENEURIAL PERSONALITY IS PROPOSED. FINALLY, THE
        ORGANIZATIONAL IMPACT OF THESE ENTREPRENEURIAL BEHAVIOUR
        PATTERNS ON WORK ENVIRONMENT AND MANAGEMENT SUCCESSION
        IS DISCUSSED.

M0772   LAWLER, EDWARD E.   KULECK, WALTER.   RHODE, JOHN.
        SORENSEN, JAMES.
        JOB CHOICE AND POST DECISION DISSONANCE.
        ORGANIZATIONAL BEHAVIOR AND HUMAN PERFORMANCE 13(FEBUARY
        1975): 133-45.

             THE JOB CHOICE AND POSTDECISION ATTITUDES AND BEHAVIOR
        OF 431 ACCOUNTING STUDENTS WERE STUDIED. DATA ON THE
        ATTRACTIVENESS OF WORKING FOR DIFFERENT FIRMS WERE FOUND TO
        BE GOOD PREDICTORS OF BOTH THE JOB APPLICATION AND THE JOB
        CHOICE BEHAVIOR OF THE SS. DATA COLLECTED AFTER THE JOB
        CHOICE DECISION WAS MADE SHOWED THE CHOSEN FIRMS INCREASED
        IN ATTRACTIVENESS AFTER CHOICE AND THE REJECTED FIRMS
        DECREASED IN DESIRABILITY. AFTER ONE YEAR OF EMPLOYMENT, SS
        RATED ALL FIRMS IN LOWER ATTRACTIVENESS THAN THEY HAD BEFORE
        THEY APPLIED FOR JOBS. IT IS CONCLUDED THAT ATTITUDES
        TOWARD FIRM ATTRACTIVENESS DETERMINE JOB CHOICE BEHAVIOR,
        AND THAT JOB CHOICE BEHAVIOR INFLUENCES POST EMPLOYMENT
        ATTITUDES ABOUT FIRM ATTRACTIVENESS IN THE DIRECTION
        PREDICTED BY DISSONANCE THEORY.

M0773   LISCHERON, JOE   WALL, TOBY D.
        ATTITUDES TOWARD PARTICIPATION AMONG LOCAL AUTHORITY
        EMPLOYEES.
        HUMAN RELATIONS 28 (AUGUST 1975): 499-517.

             ADMINISTERED A QUESTIONNAIRE TO 127 BLUE-COLLAR
        EMPLOYEES TO DETERMINE THEIR ATTITUDES TOWARD PARTICIPATION
        IN MANAGERIAL DECISIONS. RESULTS SHOW THAT, WHILE THE SS
        EXPERIENCED LITTLE PARTICIPATION, THEY EXPRESSED STRONG
        DESIRES TO BE INVOLVED IN DECISION MAKING. THE FORM OF
        PARTICIPATION PREFERRED DEPENDED ON THE NATURE OF THE
        DECISION INVOLVED. IN MIDDLE-MANAGEMENT DECISIONS MAKING
        MOST SS WANTED TO PARTICIPATE THROUGH PERSONAL CONTACT WITH
        MANAGEMENT; IN TOP-MANAGEMENT DECISIONS EMPLOYEE
        REPRESENTATION WAS DESIRED; AND IN PAY-RELATED DECISIONS
        PARTICIPATION THROUGH TRADE UNION REPRESENTATION WAS
        FAVORED. ATTITUDES TOWARD PARTICIPATION WERE POSITIVELY
        RELATED TO JOB SATISFACTION. THE USEFULNESS OF SUCH
        QUESTIONNAIRE DATA AS A STARTING POINT FOR THE IMPLEMENT-
        ATION OF PARTICIPATIVE PRACTICES IS DISCUSSED.

M0774 LONDON, MANUEL.   CRANDALL, RICK.   SEALS, GARY W.
CONTRIBUTION OF JOB AND LEISURE SATISFACTION TO QUALITY OF
LIFE.
JOURNAL OF APPLIED PSYCHOLOGY 62(JUNE 1977): 328-34.

        THIS STUDY EXAMINES THE RELATIONSHIPS BETWEEN JOB AND
LEISURE SATISFACTION AND THEIR CONTRIBUTIONS TO THE
PERCEPTION OF QUALITY OF LIFE. THE DATA WERE COLLECTED FROM
A NATIONAL PROBABILITY SAMPLE OF 1,297 ADULT AMERICANS
INTERVIEWED IN MAY 1972. THE MAGNITUDE OF THE CORRELATIONS
BETWEEN JOB AND LEISURE SATISFACTION MEASURES WAS LOW; HOW-
EVER, BOTH ACCOUNTED FOR MEANINGFUL VARIATION IN PERCEIVED
QUALITY OF LIFE FOR THE TOTAL SAMPLE. SEPARATE ANALYSIS FOR
DEMOGRAPHIC SUBGROUPS WERE ALSO PERFORMED. THEY INDICATED
THAT THE JOB SATISFACTION AND LEISURE SATISFACTION
CONTRIBUTED RELATIVELY LITTLE TO THE LIFE QUALITY OF
MINORITIES AND OTHER OFTEN DISADVANTAGED SUBGROUPS COMPARED
TO ADVANTAGED WORKERS. IMPLICATIONS OF THE RESULTS FOR THE
APPLICATION OF MOTIVATIONAL STRATEGIES IN THE WORK SETTING
ARE DISCUSSED.

M0775 LOSCO, JEAN.   EPSTEIN, SEYMOUR.
RELATIVE STEEPNESS OF APPROACH AND AVOIDANCE GRADIENTS AS A
FUNCTION OF MAGNITUDE AND VALENCE OF INCENTIVE.
JOURNAL OF ABNORMAL PSYCHOLOGY 86(AUGUST 1977): 360-68.

        TWENTY SUBJECTS TAPPED RAPIDLY TO EITHER WIN (APPROACH)
OR AVOID LOSING (AVOIDANCE) SUMS OF MONEY. THE EXPERIMENTAL
DESIGN PERMITTED HEIGHT AND STEEPNESS OF AROUSAL GRADIENTS
TO BE EXAMINED (A) AS A FUNCTION OF MAGNITUDE OF INCENTIVE,
WITH VALENCE AND QUALITY OF INCENTIVE HELD CONSTANT, AND (B)
AS A FUNCTION OF VALENCE OF INCENTIVE, WITH MAGNITUDE AND
QUALITY OF INCENTIVE HELD CONSTANT. AN INCREASE IN INCENTIVE
INCREASED BOTH THE SLOPE AND HEIGHT APPROACH AND AVOIDANCE
AROUSAL GRADIENTS. THESE RESULTS SUPPORT THE CONCEPT-
UALIZATION OF MOTIVE STRENGTH AS A MULTIPLICATIVE FUNCTION
OF DRIVE-RELATED CUES AND AN INTERNAL STATE RATHER THAN AS
AN ADDITIVE FUNCTION, AS PROPOSED BY MILLER. AVOIDANCE
GRADIENTS WERE SIGNIFICANTLY STEEPER THAN APPROACH GRADIENTS
BUT THE EFFECT WAS NOT VERY ROBUST AND WAS FAR FROM UNIFORM
ACROSS SUBJECTS, SOME OF WHOM PRODUCED MUCH STEEPER APPROACH
THAN AVOIDANCE GRADIENTS. IT WAS CONCLUDED THAT ALTHOUGH
THERE MAY BE AN INTRINSIC TENDENCY FOR AVOIDANCE GRADIENTS
TO BE STEEPER THAN APPROACH GRADIENTS, THIS TENDENCY IS NOT
STRONG AND IS EASILY REVERSED, GIVING RISE TO AVOIDANCE-
APPROACH CONFLICT. SUCH CONFLICT HAS INTERESTING THEORETICAL
AND PRACTICAL IMPLICATIONS THAT HAVE NOT BEEN RECOGNIZED
BECAUSE OF UNCRITICAL ACCEPTANCE OF THE ASSUMPTION THAT
AVOIDANCE GRADIENTS ARE INVARIABLY STEEPER THAN APPROACH
GRADIENTS.

M0776 MAIER, STEVEN F.   SELIGMAN, M.
LEARNED HELPLESSNESS: THEORY AND EVIDENCE.
JOURNAL OF EXPERIMENTAL PSYCHOLOGY (GEN) 105(MARCH 1976): 3-
65, DISCUSSION 106(MARCH 1977): 41-46.

        IN 1967 OVERMIER AND SELIGMAN FOUND THAT DOGS EXPOSED
TO INESCAPABLE AND UNAVOIDABLE ELECTRIC SHOCKS IN ONE

M0776   SITUATION LATER FAILED TO LEARN TO ESCAPE SHOCK IN A
         DIFFERENT SITUATION WHERE ESCAPE WAS POSSIBLE. SHORTLY
         THEREAFTER SELIGMAN AND MAIER (1967) DEMONSTRATED THAT THE
         EFFECT WAS CAUSED BY THE UNCONTROLLABILITY OF THE ORIGINAL
         SHOCKS. IN THIS LATER ARTICLE WE REVIEW THE EFFECTS OF
         EXPOSING ORGANISMS TO AVERSIVE EVENTS WHICH THEY CANNOT
         CONTROL, AND WE REVIEW THE EXPLANATIONS WHICH THEY HAVE
         OFFERED. WE HAVE PROPOSED AN EXPLANATION FOR THESE EFFECTS,
         WHICH WE CALL THE LEARNED HELPLESSNESS HYPOTHESIS. IT ARGUES
         THAT WHEN EVENTS ARE UNCONTROLLABLE THE ORGANISM LEARNED
         THAT ITS BEHAVIOR AND OUTCOMES ARE INDEPENDENT, AND THAT
         THIS LEARNING PROCESSES THE MOTIVATIONAL, COGNITIVE, AND
         EMOTIONAL EFFECTS OF UNCONTROLLABILITY. WE PROVED THE
         LEARNED HELPLESSNESS HYPOTHESIS AND RESEARCH WHICH SUPPORTS
         IT.

M0777   MCLAUGHLIN, G.W.   MONTGOMERY, J.   MALPASS, LESLIE F.
         SELECTED CHARACTERISTICS, ROLES, GOALS, AND SATISFACTIONS OF
         DEPARTMENT CHAIRMEN IN STATE AND LAND-GRANT INSTITUTIONS.
         RESEARCH IN HIGHER EDUCATION 3, NO. 3 (1975): 243-59.

             A SURVEY OF 1,198 DEPARTMENT CHAIRMEN AT 38 STATE AND
         LAND-GRANT INSTITUTIONS FOUND THAT SS WERE INVOLVED IN 3
         MAJOR ROLES: ACADEMIC, ADMINISTRATIVE, AND LEADERSHIP. THE
         ACADEMIC ROLE CONSISTED OF DUTIES OF STUDENT INVOLVEMENT AND
         RESEARCH ACTIVITIES. CHAIRMEN REPORTED HIGH EMPHASIS ON
         CONCURRENT GOALS BUT FELT FRUSTRATED IN TERMS OF TIME TO
         PURSUE COMMENSURATE ACTIVITIES. THE ADMINISTRATIVE ROLE
         REQUIRED THE MAJORITY OF TIME AND ALSO CONTAINED SOME OF THE
         DESIRABLE DUTIES. IN ADDITION, ADMINISTRATIVE GOALS WERE
         SEEN AS OVEREMPHASIZED. THE LEADERSHIP ROLE INVOLVED TASKS
         RELATED TO ACADEMIC PERSONNEL AND PROGRAM DEVELOPMENT.
         DEVELOPING ABILITIES OF FACULTY MEMBERS AND MAINTAINING
         ACADEMIC FREEDOM WERE THE 2 MOST IMPORTANT GOALS IN THIS
         ROLE.

M0778   MEIER, ELIZABETH.   KERR, ELIZABETH A.
         CAPABILITIES OF MIDDLE-AGED AND OLDER WORKERS: A SURVEY OF
         THE LITERATURE.
         INDUSTRIAL GERONTOLOGY 3(SUMMER 1976): 147-56.

             A SURVEY OF THE LITERATURE OF MIDDLE-AGED AND OLDER
         WORKERS DISCONFIRMS POPULATION STEREOTYPES THAT LIMIT THE
         PARTICIPATION OF THESE WORKERS IN THE LABOR FORCE. FINDINGS
         INDICATE THAT THE PHYSICAL DEMANDS OF MOST JOBS ARE WELL
         BELOW THE CAPACITIES OF MOST NORMAL AGING WORKERS. PROPERLY
         PLACED, OLDER WORKERS FUNCTION EFFECTIVELY AND HAVE GREATER
         STABILITY ON THE JOB, FEWER ACCIDENTS, AND LESS TIME LOST
         FROM WORK THAN YOUNGER WORKERS. AT LEAST 20 STUDIES SHOW
         THAT VOCABULARY, GENERAL INFORMATION, AND JUDGMENT EITHER
         RISE OR NEVER FALL BEFORE AGE 60 YEARS. GENERALLY, OLDER
         WORKERS ARE MORE SATISFIED WITH THEIR JOBS THAN YOUNGER
         WORKERS.

M0779   MEYER, HERBERT.
         THE PAY-FOR-PERFORMANCE DILEMMA.
         ORGANIZATIONAL DYNAMICS 3(WINTER 1975): 39-50.

CRITICIZES MERIT PAY SYSTEMS AS DEMOTIVATING RATHER
THAN MOTIVATING EMPLOYEES, BECAUSE MOST PEOPLE EXAGGERATE
THEIR PERFORMANCE AND FEEL CHEATED WHENEVER THEY GET A
RAISE. MANAGERS ARE INCLINED TO MAKE RELATIVELY SMALL
DISCRIMINATIONS IN SALARY TREATMENT BETWEEN INDIVIDUALS IN
THE SAME JOB, REGARDLESS OF PERCEIVED DIFFERENCES IN
PERFORMANCE. INTEREST IN THE TASK ITSELF DECREASES TO THE
EXTENT THAT PAY IS ATTACHED DIRECTLY TO THE PERFORMANCE OF
THE TASK. A REVISED PAY SYSTEM IS SUGGESTED BASED ON AN
INDIVIDUAL'S SALARY RANGE WITHIN A JOB, INCREASING AT A
FAIRLY PREDICTABLE RATE AS LONG AS PERFORMANCE MEETS A
PREVIOUSLY NEGOTIATED CRITERIA.

M0780   MIRVIS, P.H.   LAWLER, EDWARD E.
MEASURING THE FINANCIAL IMPACT OF EMPLOYEE ATTITUDES.
JOURNAL OF APPLIED PSYCHOLOGY 62(FEBUARY 1977): 1-8.

A NEW APPROACH IN ATTACHING BEHAVIORAL COSTS TO
ATTITUDES PRESENTED IN DATA FROM 160 TELLERS IN A MID-
WESTERN BANK. ATTITUDES WERE CORRELATED WITH BEHAVIOR AND
THE BEHAVIORAL CHANGES ASSOCIATED WITH ATTITUDINAL SHIFTS
WERE ESTIMATED USING THESE RELATIONSHIPS. NEW BEHAVIORAL
COSTS PER EMPLOYEE WERE COMPARED. THE RESULTS SHOW EXPECTED
DIRECT-COST SAVINGS OF $17,664 IN ABSENTEEISM, TURNOVER, AND
PERFORMANCE FROM A .5 STANDARD DEVIATION INCREASE IN JOB
SATISFACTION; SAVINGS ASSOCIATED WITH ENHANCED JOB
INVOLVEMENT AND MOTIVATION ARE ALSO REPORTED. A CRITICAL
ANALYSIS OF THE APPROACH USED IS PRESENTED, AS IS A
DISCUSSION OF ITS USEFULNESS TO ORGANIZATIONS.

M0781   MOBLEY, WILLIAM H.
INTERMEDIATE LINKAGES IN THE RELATIONSHIP BETWEEN JOB
SATISFACTION AND EMPLOYEE TURNOVER.
JOURNAL OF APPLIED PSYCHOLOGY 62(APRIL 1977): 237-40.

THE RELATIONSHIP BETWEEN JOB SATISFACTION AND TURNOVER
IS SIGNIFICANT AND CONSISTENT, BUT NOT PARTICULARLY STRONG.
A MORE COMPLETE UNDERSTANDING OF THE PSYCHOLOGY OF THE
WITHDRAWAL DECISION PROCESS REQUIRES INVESTIGATION BEYOND
THE REPLICATION OF THE SATISFACTION TURNOVER RELATIONSHIP.
TOWARD THIS END, A HEURISTIC MODEL OF THE EMPLOYEE WITH-
DRAWAL DECISION PROCESS, WHICH IDENTIFIES POSSIBLE
INTERMEDIATE LINKAGES IN THE SATISFACTION-TURNOVER
RELATIONSHIP, IS PRESENTED. PREVIOUS STUDIES RELEVANT TO THE
HYPOTHESIZED LINKAGES ARE CITED, AND POSSIBLE AVENUES OF
RESEARCH ARE SUGGESTED.

M0782   NEWBOULD, G.D.   WILSON, K.W.   STRAY, S.J.
ACADEMIC SALARIES -- A PERSONAL APPLICATION OF MANAGERIAL
ECONOMICS.
JOURNAL OF MANAGEMENT STUDIES 13(MAY 1976): 175-82.

THE PROVISIONS OF HARD ECONOMIC FACTS TO REPLACE
INTUITION AS A BASIS FOR DISCUSSION IS THE LIFEBLOOD OF AN
ECONOMIST. THE FIRST PART OF WHAT FOLLOWS IS AN ATTEMPT TO
PUT HARD ECONOMIC FACTS IN THE PLACE OF THE INTUITION THAT
MOST ACADEMICS HAVE: THAT THEIR SALARIES HAVE FALLEN
SERIOUSLY OUT OF LINE. AS A FRAMEWORK FOR DISCUSSION,

M0782   THERE IS THEN ADVANCED A THEORY OF CAREER MOTIVATION UPON
         THE BASIS OF WHICH PREDICTIONS ARE MADE TO THE EFFECT THAT
         THE DETERIORATING FINANCIAL REWARDS TO THE ACADEMIC
         PROFESSION WILL RESULT IN A GENERAL LOWERING OF THE
         STANDARDS OF RECRUITMENT, PERFORMANCE AND DISCIPLINE IN THE
         PROFESSION.

M0783   NICHOLSON, N.
         ABSENCE BEHAVIOR AND ATTENDANCE MOTIVATION: A CONCEPTUAL
         SYNTHESIS.
         JOURNAL OF MANAGEMENT STUDIES 14(OCTOBER 1977): 231-52.

              THE PAPER PROPOSES A NEW MODEL AND ASSOCIATED METHOD-
         OLOGY FOR THE ANALYSIS AND PREDICTION OF EMPLOYEE ABSENCE.
         THE FIRST PART OF THE PAPER BRIEFLY REVIEWS THEORETICAL
         WRITINGS ON THE TOPIC AND CONCLUDES THAT A RADICALLY
         DIFFERENT ORIENTATION IS NEEDED FOR ANY USEFUL INTEGRATION
         TO BE ACHIEVED FROM THE FRAGMENTED INSIGHTS TO BE FOUND IN
         THESE WORKS. A FIRST STEP TOWARD THE BUILDING OF SUCH AN
         INTEGRATED THEORY IS A CONSIDERATION OF WHAT ARE THE
         REQUIREMENTS FOR AN ADEQUATE THEORY OF ABSENCE. TO DISCOVER
         THIS, THE NATURE OF ABSENCE IS EXPLORED IN A CONCEPTUAL
         ANALYSIS, LEADING INTO A CONSIDERATION OF METHODOLOGICAL AND
         MEASUREMENT PROBLEMS. THE 'A-B CONTINUUM' IS PROPOSED AS AN
         ANSWER TO THESE PROBLEMS, CHARACTERIZING ABSENCE-INDUCING
         EVENTS IN TERMS OF THEIR AVOIDABILITY. IT IS SUGGESTED THAT
         THE IMPACT OF THESE EVENTS VARIES FROM PERSON TO PERSON, AND
         THAT THIS VARIATION IS DUE TO THE MEDIATING INFLUENCE OF
         ATTENDANCE MOTIVATION. THE CONSTRUCT OF 'ATTACHMENT' IS
         INTRODUCED AS A MEANS OF MEASURING ATTENDANCE MOTIVATION,
         AND ITS MAIN CONSTITUENTS ARE SPECIFIED. THE FINAL SECTION
         OF THE PAPER ATTEMPTS TO SHOW HOW THE FULL MODEL MAY BE USED
         TO EXPLAIN AND PREDICT INDIVIDUAL DIFFERENCES IN ATTENDANCE
         BEHAVIOUR.

M0785   OLIVER, RICHARD.
         ANTECEDENTS OF SALESMEN'S COMPENSATION PERCEPTIONS: A PATH
         ANALYSIS INTERPRETATION.
         JOURNAL OF APPLIED PSYCHOLOGY 62(FEBUARY 1977): 20-28.

              SELECTED ANTECEDENTS OF THE VALENCE OF PAY AND THE
         INSTRUMENTALITY OF PERFORMANCE FOR PAY WERE COMBINED INTO AN
         INTEGRATIVE FRAMEWORK AND INVESTIGATED IN A STUDY OF 92 MALE
         LIFE INSURANCE AGENTS. DRAWING ON TWO MODELS PROPOSED BY
         LAWLER, IT WAS HYPOTHESIZED THAT VALENCE WOULD BE A FUNCTION
         OF AGE, JOB LEVEL, INCOME, PAY SATISFACTION, AND COMMISSION
         PAY PLAN WHILE INSTRUMENTALITY PERCEPTIONS WOULD BE A
         FUNCTION OF TENURE, COMMISSION PLAN, AND VALENCE. DATA WERE
         OBTAINED FROM COMPANY SOURCES AND FROM A JOB-ATTITUDES
         QUESTIONNAIRE. A PATH ANALYTIC INVESTIGATION OF THE
         HYPOTHESIZED LINKAGES SUGGESTED THAT A MORE PARSIMONIOUS
         MODEL OF PAY PERCEPTION DETERMINANTS MAY BE ADEQUATE.
         SPECIFICALLY, VALENCE WAS FOUND TO BE INDEPENDENTLY AND
         NEGATIVELY RELATED ONLY TO AGE AND PAY SATISFACTION, WHILE
         INSTRUMENTALITY WAS A POSITIVE FUNCTION OF VALENCE AND A
         NEGATIVE FUNCTION OF TENURE. IN ADDITION, PAY SATISFACTION
         WAS POSITIVELY RELATED TO AGE AND INCOME AND INVERSELY
         RELATED TO JOB LEVEL. IMPLICATIONS OF THE SUGGESTED MODEL

M0785 ARE DISCUSSED IN VIEW OF CURRENT PRACTICE.

M0786 ORPEN, C.
THE RELATIONSHIP BETWEEN MANAGERIAL SUCCESS AND PERSONAL
VALUES IN SOUTH AFRICA: A RESEARCH NOTE.
JOURNAL OF MANAGEMENT STUDIES 13(MAY 1976): 196-98.

THE RELATIONSHIP BETWEEN PERSONAL VALUES AND JOB
SUCESS WAS INVESTIGATED IN A SAMPLE OF 92 SOUTH AFRICAN
MANAGERS. THE CORRELATION BETWEEN SCORES ON A SPECIALLY
DEVELOPED KEY OF THE PERSONAL VALUES QUESTIONNAIRE AND
RELATIVE SALARY PER AGE (INDEX OF SUCCESS) WAS SIGNIFICANTLY
POSITIVE (R=.36, P<.001). MORE SUCCESSFUL MANAGERS HAD
DYNAMIC AND PRAGMATIC VALUES WHILE LESS SUCCESSFUL MANAGERS
HAD MORE PASSIVE AND STATIC VALUES. THE RESULTS OFFER
FURTHER CROSS-CULTURAL SUPPORT FOR THE CLOSE RELATIONSHIP
BETWEEN PERSONAL VALUES AND MANAGERIAL SUCCESS.

M0787 PHESEY, DIANA C.
MANAGERS' OCCUPATIONAL HISTORIES, ORGANIZATIONAL
ENVIRONMENTS, AND CLIMATES FOR MANAGEMENT DEVELOPMENT.
JOURNAL OF MANAGEMENT STUDIES 14, NO.1 (1977): 58-79.

SEVENTEEN INTACT COLLEGIATE GROUPS OF MANAGERS FROM
EIGHT COMPANIES AND TWO PUBLICLY OWNED ORGANIZATIONS
DESCRIBED THE ORGANIZATIONAL CLIMATES IN WHICH THEY WORKED.
THEIR PERCEPTIONS RANGED FROM HIGHLY FAVOURABLE TO HIGHLY
UNFAVOURABLE. DID THE OCCUPATIONAL HISTORIES OF THE 134
MANAGERS INFLUENCE THEIR PERCEPTIONS? COULD THE DIFFERENCES
IN THEIR EVALUATIONS HAVE ARISEN FROM OTHER FEATURES OF THE
ENVIRONMENT, FOR WHICH UNOBTRUSIVE MEASURES WERE AVAILABLE?
ALL OF THESE EXPLANATIONS HAVE SOME PLAUSIBILITY IN RELATION
TO THE DATA PRESENTED. IT IS PROBABLY IMPOSSIBLE TO CREATE
THE RIGHT CLIMATE FOR MANAGEMENT DEVELOPMENT BY PIECEMEAL
STRATEGIES WHICH IGNORE THE SIGNIFICANCE OF MARKET SUCCESS
AND DEAL ONLY WITH THE IMMEDIATE EXPERIENCE OF MANAGERS. ON
THE OTHER HAND, A GLOBAL STRATEGY WHICH CONCENTRATES ON
EXTERNAL FACTORS AND MINIMIZES THE IMPORTANCE OF THE
INDIVIDUAL'S CONTRIBUTION IN HIS PARTICULAR LOCATION IS
LIKELY TO BE EQUALLY DEFECTIVE. THE MAJOR MODERATING
VARIABLE IN THIS STUDY BETWEEN THE PERCEIVED DEVELOPMENTAL
CLIMATE OF THE ORGANIZATION AND THE MANAGER'S OCCUPATIONAL
HISTORY WAS THE SALARY HE WAS PAID.

M0788 POMOZAL, RICHARD.   BROWN, JAMES.
UNDERSTANDING DRUG USE MOTIVATION: A NEW LOOK AT A CURRENT
PROBLEM.
JOURNAL OF HEALTH AND SOCIAL BEHAVIOR 18(JUNE 1977): 212-22.

PERSONAL BELIEFS, ATTITUDES, AND OPINIONS REGARDING
SMOKING MARIJUANA WERE OBTAINED FROM 101 UNIVERSITY STUDENTS
TO TEST THE ABILITY OF A REVISED SOCIAL-PSYCHOLOGICAL THEORY
OF BEHAVIORAL INTENTION TO ACCOUNT FOR FACTORS RELATED TO
DRUG USE MOTIVATION (SMOKING MARIJUANA). A HIGHLY
SIGNIFICANT MULTIPLE CORRELATION (R=.78, P<.001) WAS
OBTAINED BETWEEN THE THEORY'S THREE COMPONENTS (ATTITUDE
TOWARD THE ACT, SOCIAL NORM, AND MORAL NORM) AND INTENTIONS
TO SMOKE MARIJUANA. ALSO AS PREDICTED, BELIEFS REGARDING THE

M0788   PERCEIVED POSITIVE AND NEGATIVE CONSEQUENCES OF SMOKING WERE
        SHOWN TO BE SIGNIFICANTLY CORRELATED (R=.69, P<.001) WITH AN
        INDIVIDUAL'S ATTITUDE TOWARD THE ACT OF SMOKING MARIJUANA.
        SMOKERS AND NONSMOKERS WERE SHOWN TO DIFFER SIGNIFICANTLY ON
        SPECIFIC BELIEFS AND VALUES CONCERNING THE EFFECTS OF
        MARIJUANA. IMPLICATIONS OF THE PRESENT RECONCEPTUALIZATION
        OF DRUG USE MOTIVATION FOR DRUG EDUCATION AND COUNSELLING
        APPROACHES ARE DISCUSSED.

M0789   PRASAD, R.
        MEASUREMENT OF SOCIOECONOMIC AND PSYCHOLOGICAL
        CHARACTERISTICS: A METHOD.
        INDIAN JOURNAL OF INDUSTRIAL RELATIONS 9(JANUARY 1974): 427-
        34.

            DESCRIBES THE DEVELOPMENT OF AN INDEX OF SOCIO-ECONOMIC
        VARIABLES. THE INDEX TAKES INTO CONSIDERATION ALL THE
        ASSIGNABLE DETERMINANTS OF THE LEVEL OF THE CHARACTERISTIC
        CONCERNED AND PROVIDES A MEASURE AS A FUNCTION OF THE
        DETERMINANTS AND THEIR IMPORTANCE IN DETERMINING THE LEVEL
        OBTAINED FROM THE RESPONDENT GROUP. THIS APPROACH IS
        CONSIDERED TO GIVE MORE UNIQUE RESULTS IN A LESS CIRCUITOUS
        MANNER THAN MOST COMMONLY USED APPROACHES. CHARACTERISTICS
        MEASURED BY THE INDEX INCLUDE JOB SATISFACTION, MOTIVATION,
        MOBILITY, AND COMMUNICATION.

M0790   PRITCHARD, R.
        THE EFFECTS OF VARYING SCHEDULES OF REINFORCEMENT ON HUMAN
        TASK PERFORMANCE.
        ORGANIZATIONAL BEHAVIOR AND HUMAN PERFORMANCE 16(AUGUST
        1976): 205-30.

            USED 4 SCHEDULES OF FINANCIAL REINFORCEMENT (HOURLY,
        FR, VR, AND VARIABLE RATIO/VARIABLE AMOUNT, VR-VA) IN AN
        ORGANIZATIONAL SIMULATION SETTING. 17-19 YEAR OLD MALES WERE
        HIRED FOR WHAT THEY PERCEIVED TO BE A REAL JOB OF 4 WEEKS
        DURATION, WHICH REQUIRED THEM TO LEARN SELF-PACED MATERIAL
        ABOUT ELECTRONICS. EACH S WORKED FOR 1 WEEK UNDER EACH OF
        THE 4 SCHEDULES OF REINFORCEMENT. PERFORMANCE WAS LOWEST
        UNDER THE HOURLY SCHEDULE; THE FR, VR, AND VR-VA SCHEDULES
        PRODUCED HIGHER PERFORMANCE. ATTITUDES WERE BEST UNDER FR.
        RESULTS ARE DISCUSSED IN TERMS OF THEIR PRACTICAL
        IMPLICATIONS AS WELL AS THEIR IMPLICATIONS FOR THEORY,
        PARTICULARLY EXPECTANCY-VALENCE THEORY.

M0791   RANI, KALA.
        JOB MOTIVATIONS FOR WORKING WOMEN.
        JOURNAL OF SOCIAL AND ECONOMIC STUDIES 3(MARCH 1975): 45-62.

            GATHERED DATA BY INTERVIEW AND OBSERVATION FROM 150
        MARRIED, EDUCATED, WORKING WOMEN IN PATNA, A MEDIUM-SIZED
        NONINDUSTRIAL CITY. SS WERE 20-55 YEARS OLD, AND NEARLY 70%
        WERE GRADUATES OR POSTGRADUATES. SS WERE ASKED TO CHOOSE 3
        FROM A LIST OF 10 MOTIVES FOR WORKING, IN ORDER OF
        PREFERENCE. SAMPLE RESPONSES ARE REPORTED. THE MOST
        IMPORTANT MOTIVATION WAS THE DESIRE TO MAKE USE OF HIGH OR
        PROFESSIONAL EDUCATION; THIS WAS FOLLOWED BY A DESIRE TO USE
        SPARE TIME. CONSTELLATIONS OF MOTIVES OF VARYING DEGREES OF

M0791 IMPORTANCE WERE COMMON.

M0792 SCHOLTES, PETER R.
CONTRACTING FOR CHANGE.
TRAINING AND DEVELOPMENT JOURNAL 29 (APRIL 1975): 8-12.

ARGUES THAT IF A STAFF IS 'AT WAR'-MAKING IT NECESSARY
TO REVAMP AN ORGANIZATION AND REMOVE BARRIERS AND DISTRUST
THAT IMPEDE COOPERATION -- A SERIES OF CONTRACTS FOR
BEHAVIORAL CHANGE MAY BE THE ANSWER. PROBLEMS ARE DEFINED AS
SMALL GROUP DISCUSSIONS WHERE THE INDIVIDUAL IS ENCOURAGED
TO TALK ABOUT WHAT HE FINDS IRKSOME, DISSATISFYING, OR
ENRAGING ABOUT WORKING IN THE ORGANIZATION. NEXT, ONE-TO-ONE
ENGAGEMENTS TO TALK OVER SPECIFIC PROBLEMS ARE ARRANGED.
SMALL GROUPS REPRESENTATIVE OF THE ORGANIZATION THEN CHOOSE
SPECIFIC PROBLEMS AND REMEDIES AND STATEMENTS OF INTENT TO
BE INCORPORATED IN A CONTRACT FOR ORGANIZATIONAL CHANGE. A
FORMAL CONTRACT FOR THE ENTIRE ORGANIZATION HELPS THE
MEMBERS AGREE ON THE DEFINITION OF PROBLEMS AND PROPOSED
REMEDIES, AND IT COMMITS MEMBERS TO INCLUDE THEMSELVES IN
CHANGING AND DETERMINING THE NEED FOLLOW-THROUGH.

M0793 SINGH, RAMADHAR.
INFORMATION INTEGRATION THEORY APPLIED TO EXPECTED JOB
ATTRACTIVENESS AND SATISFACTION.
JOURNAL OF APPLIED PSYCHOLOGY 60(OCTOBER 1975): 621-23.

128 ENGINEERING STUDENTS RATED 8 JOB DESCRIPTIONS
ACCORDING TO HOW MUCH THEY WOULD LIKE TO ACCEPT THE JOB AND
HOW SATISFIED THEY WOULD FEEL WITH THAT JOB. THE PREDICTION
THAT PLOTS OF THE CONTEXT (ROW) FACTOR (E.G. SALARY) DATA
ACROSS THE 2 LEVELS OF THE CONTENT (COLUMN) FACTOR (E.G.
NATURE OF THE TASK) SHOULD APPEAR AS SEPARATE PARALLEL
CURVES WAS CONFIRMED, SUPPORTING INFORMATION INTEGRATION
THEORY.

M0794 SINGHAL, SUSHILA
NEED-RATIFICATION, ABSENTEEISM AND ITS OTHER CORRELATES.
INDIAN JOURNAL OF INDUSTRIAL RELATIONS 2(JANUARY 1976): 351-
61.

EXAMINES THE PROBLEM OF ABSENTEEISM IN RELATION TO NEED
GRATIFICATION AND OTHER CORRELATES IN THE PERSONAL,
ORGANIZATIONAL, AND SITUATIONAL CONTEXT. DATA WERE OBTAINED
ON 2 GROUPS OF FACTORY WORKERS EACH STRATIFIED ON THE BASIS
OF PARTICIPATION IN THE ORGANIZATIONAL FUNCTION. METHODS
INCLUDED QUESTIONNAIRES, SELF-REPORTS, AND OFFICIAL RECORDS.
RESULTS INDICATE THAT PARTICIPATION LED TO REDUCED
ABSENTEEISM. OTHER ORGANIZATIONAL VARIABLES INFLUENCING
ABSENTEEISM WERE INTERPERSONAL PERCEPTION, INTERPERSONAL
COMMUNICATION, AND GROUP COHESIVENESS. IN THE PERSONAL
CORRELATES CATEGORY, ABSENTEEISM WAS AFFECTED BY THE
NUMBER OF DEPENDENTS, OTHER SOURCES OF INCOME, LENGTH OF
SERVICE, UNIONIZATION, AND ANXIETY.

M0795 SMITH, FRANK J.
WORK ATTITUDES AS PREDICTORS OF ATTENDANCE ON A SPECIFIC
DAY.

M0795   JOURNAL OF APPLIED PSYCHOLOGY 62(FEBUARY 1977): 16-19.
        THE RESEARCH EXAMINED THE RELATIONSHIP BETWEEN THE WORK
ATTITUDES AND WORK ATTENDANCE OF MANAGERIAL EMPLOYEES ON A
SPECIFIC DAY IN A NATURAL FIELD SETTING. THE JOB
SATISFACTION DATA WERE OBTAINED FROM THE INDEX OF
ORGANIZATIONAL REACTIONS (IOR). THE PRIMARY SAMPLE OF 3,010
SUBJECTS WAS LOCATED IN THE COMPANY'S HEADQUARTERS BUILDING
AND DIVIDED INTO 27 FUNCTIONAL GROUPINGS. SINCE OCCASIONAL
ABSENTEEISM AT THE MANAGERIAL LEVEL IS NOT SUBJECT TO
FINANCIAL PENALTY AND RELATIVELY FREE OF SOCIAL AND WORK-
GROUP PRESSURES, IT REPRESENTS BEHAVIOR THAT IS GENERALLY
UNDER THE CONTROL OF THE INDIVIDUAL EMPLOYEE. MOREOVER,
BECAUSE THE PARTICULAR DAY INVESTIGATED IN THE PRESENT STUDY
FOLLOWED A CRIPPLING SNOWSTORM, ATTENDANCE ON THAT DAY
INVOLVED CONSIDERABLE EFFORT. THE RESULTS SHOW SIGNIFICANT
RELATIONSHIPS BETWEEN WORK-RELATED ATTITUDES AND ATTENDANCE
ON THE SPECIFIC DAY STUDIED. THESE RESULTS GENERALLY SUPPORT
HERMAN'S POINT OF VIEW THAT WORK ATTITUDES DO PREDICT WORK-
RELATED BEHAVIOR WHEN SUCH BEHAVIOR IS UNDER THE CONTROL OF
THE SUBJECT.

M0796   SPECTOR, PAUL E.
        RELATIONSHIPS OF ORGANIZATIONAL FRUSTRATION WITH REPORTED
        BEHAVIORAL REACTIONS OF EMPLOYEES.
        JOURNAL OF APPLIED PSYCHOLOGY 60(OCTOBER 1975): 635-37.

        MAILED AN ORGANIZATIONAL FRUSTRATION QUESTIONNAIRE AND
A RESPONSE-TO-FRUSTRATION QUESTIONNAIRE TO 82 EMPLOYEES IN A
WIDE RANGE OF JOBS, MOSTLY IN A MENTAL HEALTH FACILITY. A
FACTOR ANALYSIS OF THE RESPONSES TO FRUSTRATION YIELDED 6
INTERPRETABLE FACTORS: (A) AGGRESSION AGAINST OTHERS, (B)
SABOTAGE, (C) WASTING OF TIME AND MATERIALS, (D)
INTERPERSONAL HOSTILITY AND COMPLANING, (E) INTERPERSONAL
AGGRESSION, AND (F) APATHY ABOUT THE JOB.

M0797   STEWART, ROBERT A. LIDDLE, JANE M.
        WHERE SUCCESS LIES.
        NEW ZEALAND NURSING JOURNAL 68(MARCH 1975): 13-14.

        STUDIED 75 STUDENT NURSES IN NEW ZEALAND, COMPARING
BOTH HIGH AND LOW ABILITY NURSES (AS JUDGED BY BOTH WARD AND
TUTORIAL STAFF) AND EACH OF THE 3 YEARS OF NURSING EDUCATION
CLASSES. MEASURES OF DOGMATISM, CONSERVATISM, VALUES,
PERSONALITY, AND SELF-ACTUALIZATION (E.G., 16 PF AND THE
ROKEACH DOGMATISM SCALE) WERE USED. AS JUDGED BY THE WARD
STAFF, THE HIGH-ABILITY NURSE WAS CONSERVATIVE, RELIGIOUS,
DOGMATIC, AND LOW ON POLITICAL VALUES. AS JUDGED BY THE
TUTORIAL STAFF, THE HIGH-ABILITY NURSE WAS RELAXED, HIGHER
ON SOCIAL VALUES, AND TENDED TO LIVE IN THE PAST OR FUTURE
RATHER THAN THE PRESENT. THE OVERALL PROFILE OF THE STUDENT
NURSE MOST LIKELY TO COMPLETE TRAINING (AS COMPARED TO
DROPPING OUT) SHOWS HER AS MORE POLITICAL, LESS RELIGIOUS,
LESS ACCEPTING OF AGGRESSION, AND HAVING A HIGHER WARD
RATING. RESULTS ARE COMPATIBLE WITH THOSE OF G.H. HINES
(1974) WHO FOUND THAT 3RD-YEAR STUDENT NURSES HAD A HIGH
NEED FOR POWER AND INFLUENCE RATHER THAN A HIGH NEED FOR
ACHIEVEMENT AND SERVICE TO OTHERS, WHICH CHARACTERIZES 1ST-
YEAR STUDENT NURSES.

M0798   STONE, EUGENE.
        HIGHER ORDER NEED STRENGTHS AS MODERATORS OF THE JOB
        SCOPE-JOB SATISFACTION RELATIONSHIP.
        JOURNAL OF APPLIED PSYCHOLOGY 62(AUGUST 1977): 466-71.

              QUESTIONNAIRE DATA ON JOB CHARACTERISTICS, PERSONALITY
        TRAITS, AND JOB SATISFACTION WERE OBTAINED FROM 340
        EMPLOYEES OF A MANUFACTURING ORGANIZATION. MODERATED
        REGRESSION AND SUBGROUP ANALYSES WERE PERFORMED TO DETERMINE
        THE EXTENT TO WHICH TWO PERSONALITY TRAITS, NEED FOR
        ACHIEVEMENT AND NEED FOR AUTONOMY, MODERATED THE
        RELATIONSHIP BETWEEN JOB SCOPE AND SATISFACTION WITH THE
        WORK ITSELF. THE SUBGROUP ANALYSIS SHOWED NO MODERATING
        EFFECT FOR NEED FOR AUTONOMY AND MODERATING EFFECTS
        INCONSISTENT WITH PREVIOUS RESEARCH AND THEORY FOR NEED FOR
        ACHIEVEMENT. MODERATED REGRESSION SHOWED NO MODERATING
        EFFECT FOR NEED FOR AUTONOMY AND A MODERATING EFFECT OF
        NEGLIGIBLE PRACTICAL IMPORTANCE FOR NEED FOR ACHIEVEMENT.

M0799   TERBORG, JAMES R.
        THE MOTIVATIONAL COMPONENTS OF GOAL SETTING.
        JOURNAL OF APPLIED PSYCHOLOGY 61(OCTOBER 1976): 613-21.

              EXAMINED THE RELATIONSHIPS AMONG GOAL SETTING, MONETARY
        INCENTIVES, 2 INDEXES OF MOTIVATION (I.E., EFFORT AND
        DIRECTION OF BEHAVIOR), AND PERFORMANCE. 60 17-19 YEAR OLDS
        WERE HIRED TO WORK ON A 1-WEEK JOB IN A SIMULATED COMPANY.
        RESULTS SUGGEST THAT GOAL SETTING AND MONETARY INCENTIVES
        WERE RELATED INDEPENDANTLY TO MEASURES OF MOTIVATION AND
        PERFORMANCE. INCENTIVES, HOWEVER, HAD NO IMPACT ON WHETHER
        OR NOT SS SET PERFORMANCE GOALS. THE IMPORTANCE OF
        IDENTIFYING THE PROCESSES SURROUNDING THE EFFECTS OF STATED
        TASK GOALS AND MONETARY INCENTIVES ON PERFORMANCE IS
        DISCUSSED.

M0800   TOUGH TALK WON'T BE ABOUT WAGES THIS TIME.
        U.S. NEWS AND WORLD REPORT, DECEMBER 1977, PP. 92-93.

              FEWER BIG STRIKES, LESS EMPHASIS ON OURSIZE PAY BOOSTS-
        BUT A PUSH FOR JOB SECURITY, BROAD LABOR-LAW CHANGES. THESE
        WILL BE KEY ELEMENTS IN UNIONS' DEMANDS IN 1978.

M0801   TSENG, M. S.
        JOB PERFORMANCE AND SATISFACTION OF SUCCESSFULLY
        REHABILITATED VOCATIONAL REHABILITATION CLIENTS.
        REHABILITATION LITERATURE 36 (MARCH 1975):66-72.

              OCCUPATIONAL FUNCTIONING OF DISABLED EMPLOYEES WHO HAD
        BEEN REHABILITATED BY A VOCATIONAL REHABILITATION PROGRAM
        PROGRAM AND WHO WERE GAINFULLY EMPLOYED, WAS INVESTIGATED
        THROUGH DATA COLLECTED FROM 65 OF 203 OF THESE CLIENTS
        CONTACTED AND 75 EMPLOYER RESPONDENTS. WHILE EMPLOYEES AS A
        GROUP WERE CONSIDERABLY SATISFIED WITH THEIR DISABLED
        EMPLOYEES IN TERMS OF WORK PERSONALITY, PROFICIENCY, AND
        OVERALL PERFORMANCE, THE EMPLOYEES THEMSELVES EXPRESSED A
        MODERATELY HIGH DEGREE OF JOB SATISFACTION, ATTITUDE TOWARD
        WORK AND SELF-ACCEPTANCE. IN COMPARISON TO THEIR RESPECTIVE
        EMPLOYERS' RATINGS,THE CLIENTS TENDED TO OVER-ESTIMATE THEIR

M0801   OWN PERSONAL QUALITY. AMONG THE SIGNIFICANT CORRELATES OF
        JOB SATISFACTION FOUND WERE PERSONALITY AND SELF-ACCEPTANCE.
        SELF-ACCEPTANCE PROVED TO BE A SIGNIFICANT CORRELATE
        OF ATTITUDE TOWARD WORK, WHICH IN TURN WAS SIGNIFICANTLY
        ASSOCIATED WITH SPOUSAL CONFORMITY OR FAMILY AFFAIRS.

M0802   TUTTLE, THOMAS C.   GOULD, BRUCE R.   HAZEL, JOE T.
        DIMENSIONS OF JOB SATISFACTION: INITIAL DEVELOPMENT OF THE
        AIR FORCE OCCUPATIONAL ATTITUDE INVENTORY.
        US AFHRL TECHNICAL REPORT, NO. 75-1 (JUNE 1975), 34 PP.

        DESCRIBES THE INITIAL DEVELOPMENT OF THE AIR FORCE
        OCCUPATIONAL ATTITUDE INVENTORY. FROM A SELECTIVE REVIEW OF
        STUDIES THAT ASCRIBED TO A MULTIFACETED APPROACH, SEVERAL
        CATEGORIES OR CONTENT AREAS WERE IDENTIFIED. AN EXTENSIVE
        ITEM POOL WAS PREPARED AND REVIEWED BY JUDGES TO PROVIDE
        DATA REGARDING ITEM-CATEGORY AGREEMENT, ITEM AMBIGUITY,
        AND ITEM REDUNDANCY. THE REVISED VERSION OF THE INVENTORY
        CONSISTED OF 348 ITEMS DISTRIBUTED ACROSS 35 FACETS. AN 8
        POINT BIPOLAR RATING SCALE WITHOUT A NEUTRAL POINT WAS
        DEVELOPED FOR RATING ITEMS. DETAILS OF THE FINAL VERSION
        OF THE INVENTORY BOOKLET, SUITABLE FOR ADMINISTRATION TO
        AIRMEN, ARE PROVIDED. THE ENTIRE LISTING OF 348 ITEMS AND
        DESCRIPTIONS OF THE 35 CATEGORIES ARE INCLUDED IN THE REPORT
        FOR POSSIBLE USE OF OTHER RESEARCHERS. SUBSEQUENT ACTIONS
        AND FUTURE USES OF THE OCCUPATIONAL ATTITUDE INVENTORY ARE
        DISCUSSED.

M0803   WATKINS, DAVID.
        SELF-ESTEEM AS A MODERATOR IN VOCATIONAL CHOICE: A TEST OF
        KORMAN'S HYPOTHESIS.
        AUSTRALIAN PSYCHOLOGIST 10 (MARCH 1975):75-80.

        ONE HUNDRED PRIMARY STUDENT TEACHERS (AGE RANGE 18-20)
        COMPLETED THE FOLLOWING MEASURES: (A) A SCALE DESIGNED TO
        MEASURE S'S PERCEPTIONS OF THEIR ABILITY AS TEACHERS, (B) A
        SCALE DESIGNED TO EXAMINE THE OCCUPATIONAL NEEDS OF SS BASED
        ON A QUESTIONNAIRE DEVELOPED BY TRUSTY AND SERGIVANNI, (C) A
        SELF-CONCEPT INSTRUMENT CONSISTING OF 17 BIPOLAR ADJECTIVES
        FROM THE ADJECTIVE CHECK LIST, AND (D) THE MARLOWE-CROWN
        SOCIAL DESIRABILITY SCALE. FINDINGS DO NOT SUPPORT KORMAN'S
        HYPOTHESIS. DATA INDICATE THAT HIGH AND LOW SELF-ESTEEM
        STUDENT TEACHERS CHOSE AN OCCUPATION THEY PERCEIVED AS
        SUITING THEIR ABILITIES AND ONE THAT WAS LIKELY TO SATISFY
        IMPORTANT OCCUPATIONAL NEEDS.

M0804   WEBSTER, ALAN C   STEWART, ROBERT A.
        PSYCHOLOGICAL ATTITUDES AND BELIEFS OF MINISTERS.
        ANVIL QUARTERLY 1 (MARCH 1969): 11-16

        AS AN EXTENSION OF A PREVIOUS WORK BY A. C. WEBSTER,
        77 CHRISTIAN MINISTERS WERE ADMINISTERED AN OPEN-CLOSED
        MINDEDNESS AND THEOLOGICAL CONSERVATISM-LIBERALISM; SCALES
        ON JOB SATISFACTION, ROLE CONFLICT, AND GENERAL
        CONSERVATISM; THE ROKEACH DOGMATISM SCALE; AND THE PERSONAL
        ORIENTATION INVENTORY. DATA SUPPORT THE HYPOTHESIS THAT
        (A) THERE IS A POSITIVE RELATIONSHIP BETWEEN DOGMATISM,
        THEOLOGICAL CONSERVATISM, GENERAL AND ETHROCENTRICISM; (B)

M0804   THERE IS A POSITIVE RELATION BETWEEN THEOLOGICAL LIBERALISM,
        ROLE CONFLICT, AND PSYCHOLOGICAL HEALTH; AND (C) MINISTERS
        PROFESSING "STEADY GROWTH" IN THE CHRISTIAN FAITH WERE MORE
        LIKELY THAN THE "CONVERTED" TO DISPLAY OPEN, LIBERAL, AND
        SELF-ACTUALIZING ATTITUDES. IT IS CONCLUDED THAT NEW
        EMPHASES ON PSYCHOLOGICAL HEALTH IN MINISTERS WOULD NOT ONLY
        SATISFY NEW CRITERIA OF MATURE HUMANITY, BUT WOULD DO MUCH
        TO RESTORE A CREATIVE AND RELAVANT QUALITY TO THE LIFE IN
        THE CHURCH.

M0805   WIGGINS, J. D.
        THE RELATION OF JOB SATISFACTION TO VOCATIONAL PREFERENCES
        AMONG TEACHERS OF THE EDUCABLE MENTALLY RETARDED.
        JOURNAL OF VOCATIONAL BEHAVIOR 8 (FEBRUARY 1976) :13-18.

            ADMINISTERED THE HOPPOCK JOB SATISFACTION BLANK AND THE
        VOCATIONAL PREFERENCE INVENTORY (VPI) TO 110 FEMALE TEACHERS
        OF THE EDUCABLE MENTALLY RETARDED. RESULTS SHOW THAT SS' JOB
        SATISFACTION WAS SIGNIFICANTLY AND USUALLY SUBSTANTIALLY
        CORRELATED WITH THE SOCIAL, ARTISTIC, AND REALISTIC SCALES
        OF THE VPI. THE DIRECTION OF THESE CORRELATES WAS CONSISTENT
        WITH THEORETICAL AND COMMONSENSE EXPECTATIONS. SATISFACTION
        WAS NOT SIGNIFICANTLY RELATED TO CERTIFICATION, DEGREE,
        OR TEACHING LEVEL. THE IMPLICATIONS OF THE RESULTS FOR THE
        SELECTION AND PLACEMENT OF TEACHERS AND FOR J. L. HOLLAND'S
        (1965) THEORY OF CAREER CHOICE ARE DISCUSSED.

M0806   YOUNG, CARL E.   TRUE, JOHN E.   PACKARD, MARY E.
        A NATIONAL STUDY OF ASSOCIATE DEGREE MENTAL HEALTH SERVICES
        WORKERS.
        JOURNAL OF COMMUNITY PSYCHOLOGY 4 (JANUARY 1976):89-95.

            INTERVIEWED 138 20-55 YEAR OLD GRADUATES OF ASSOCIATE
        DEGREE MENTAL HEALTH AND HUMAN SERVICES PROGRAMS TO
        IDENTIFY THEIR WORK ACTIVITIES,ADEQUACY OF WORK PERFORMANCE,
        AND JOB SATISFACTION. 77% WERE EMPLOYED IN RELEVANT HUMAN
        SERVICES JOBS. DATA FROM SS AND 91 OF THEIR SUPERVISORS
        REVEALED THAT THEY WERE PERFORMING VIRTUALLY THE ENTIRE
        RANGE OF TRADITIONAL MENTAL HEALTH FUNCTIONS AND PERFORMING
        THEM WELL. A MAJORITY WERE SATISFIED WITH THEIR WORK,
        ALTHOUGH LOW SALARY LEVELS AND RESTRICTED OPPORTUNITIES FOR
        FUTURE ADVANCEMENT WERE RECOGNIZED AS PROBLEM. MANY WERE
        RECEIVING LITTLE SUPERVISION, AND THE USER AGENCIES HAD, FOR
        THE MOST PART, NOT DEVELOPED APPROPRIATE IN-SREVICE TRAINING
        PROGRAMS. FINDINGS APPEAR TO SUPPORT THE NOTION THAT THE
        MENTAL HEALTH ASSOCIATE IS A VALUABLE NEW SOURCE OF MANPOWER
        FOR THE MENTAL HEALTH AND HUMAN SERVICES FIELD.

M0807   AWAD, E. M.
        PREDICTION OF SATISFACTION OF SYSTEMS ANALYSTS, PROGRAMMERS.
        DATA MANAGEMENT 15 (JANUARY 1977): 12-18.

            THIS RESEARCH INVESTIGATED THE DEGREE TO WHICH JOB
        SATISFACTION AS A PRIME REASON FOR TURNOVER CAN BE PREDICTED
        FROM CORRESPONDENCE BETWEEN ONE'S VOCATIONAL NEEDS AND THE
        JOB REINFORCER'S FOR A SAMPLE OF SYSTEMS ANALYSIS AND
        PROGRAMMERS IN A COMPUTER-BASED FACILITY OF A PETROLEUM
        COMPANY. MINIMAL SUPPORT WAS FOUND FOR JOB DIFFERENCES IN

M0807   VOCATIONAL NEEDS. MANAGEMENT SUCCEEDED IN SELECTING
         PROGRAMMERS WITH THE VOCATIONAL NEED STRUCTURE OF THE
         SYSTEMS ANALYSTS, BU VIEWED THE JOBS AS DISTINCT IN THE
         ORGANIZATION STRUCTURE. JOB SATISFACTION WAS ALSO FOUND TO
         BE A FUNCTION OF NEED-REINFORCER CORRESPONDENCE.

M0808   CASTELLANO, J. J.
         RURAL AND URBAN DIFFERENCES: ONE MORE TIME.
         ACADEMY OF MANAGEMENT JOURNAL 19 (SEPTEMBER 1976): 495-502.

             SIGNIFICANTLY, STUDIES WHICH HAVE ATTEMPTED TO MEASURE
         ATTITUDINAL DIFFERENCES USING INDIVIDUAL RURAL-URBAN   BACK-
         GROUND DIRECTLY HAVE FAILED TO SUPPORT THE EARLIER STUDIES.
         SHEPARD (1970), SCHULER (1973), AND SUSMAN (1973) ALL FAILED
         TO FIND SIGNIFICANT DIFFERENCES IN JOB ATTITUTES BETWEEN
         RURALS AND URBANS. IN THOSE STUDIES, A PRIMARY RESEARCH
         OBJECTIVE WAS TO DETERMINE IF WORKER BACKGROUND, WITH BACK-
         GROUND CLASSIFIED AS EITHER URBAN OR RURAL, MODERATED THE
         RELATIONSHIP BETWEEN JOB LEVEL OR QUALITY AND JOB ATTITUDES.
         IN THE PRESENT STUDY, HOWEVER, THE OBJECTIVE WAS TO DIRECTLY
         ASSESS THE INFLUENCE OF WORKER RURAL-URBAN BACKGROUND ON
         ATTITUDINAL AND BEHAVIORAL RESPONSE WHILE AVOIDING THE
         METHODOLOGICAL WEAKNESSES OF EARLIER STUDIES.

M0809   DAVIS, LOUIS E.
         ENHANCING THE QUALITY OF WORKING LIFE: DEVELOPMENTS IN THE
         UNITED STATES.
         INTERNATIONAL LABOUR REVIEW 116 (JULY 1977): 53-65.

             INTEREST IN THE QUALITY OF WORKING LIFE IS SPREADING
         RAPIDLY AND THE PHRASE HAS ENTERED THE POPULAR VOCABULARY.
         THAT THIS SHOULD BE SO IS PROBABLY DUE IN LARGE MEASURE TO
         CHANGES IN THE VALUES OF SOCIETY, NOWADAYS ACCELERATED AS
         NEVER BEFORE BY THE CONCERNS AND DEMANDS OF YOUNGER PEOPLE.
         BUT HOWEVER TOPICAL THE CONCEPT HAS BECOME, THERE IS -- AT
         LEAST IN THE UNITED STATES -- VERY LITTLE AGREEMENT ON ITS
         DEFINITION. RATHER, THE TERM APPEARS TO HAVE BECOME A KIND
         OF DEPOSITORY FOR A VARIETY OF SOMETIMES CONTRADICTORY
         MEANINGS ATTRIBUTED TO IT BY DIFFERENT GROUPS. A LIST OF
         THE ELEMENTS IT IS HELD TO COVER WOULD INCLUDE AVAILABILITY,
         SECURITY OF EMPLOYMENT, ADEQUATE INCOME, SAFE AND PLEASANT
         PHYSICAL WORKING CONDITIONS, REASONABLE HOURS OF WORK,
         EQUITABLE TREATMENT AND DEMOCRACY IN THE WORKPLACE, LESS RED
         TAPE AND BUREAUCRACY, THE POSSIBILITY OF SELF-DEVELOPMENT,
         CONTROL OVER ONE'S WORK, A SENSE OF PRIDE IN CRAFTSMANSHIP
         OR PRODUCT, WIDER CAREER CHOICES, AND FLEXIBILITY IN MATTERS
         SUCH AS THE TIME OF STARTING WORK, THE NUMBER OF WORKING
         DAYS IN THE WEEK, JOB-SHARING ETC. -- ALTOGETHER AN ARRAY
         THAT ENCOMPASSES A VARIETY OF TRADITIONAL ASPIRATIONS AND
         MANY NEW ONES REFLECTING THE ENTRY INTO THE POST-INDUSTRIAL
         ERA.

M0810   DEMING, D. D.
         REEVALUATING THE ASSEMBLY LINE.
         SUPERVISORY MANAGEMENT 32 (SEPTEMBER 1977): 2-7.

             ASSEMBLY LINES ARE LIKELY TO BE A SIGNIFICANT FACTOR IN
         MANUFACTURING PRODUCTION FOR THE FORESEEABLE FUTURE, BUT

M0810   THEY NEED NOT OCCUPY A POSITION OF SUCH LOW ESTEEM AS THEY
         DO NOW. ASSEMBLY-LINE SYSTEMS CAN BE DESIGNED WITH GREATER
         CONCERN FOR WORKERS AND THEIR NEEDS AND DESIRES. AND ABOVE
         ALL, BY RECOGNIZING AND BEING RESPONSIVE TO THE GREAT
         VARIETY OF HUMAN PERSONALITIES, IT IS POSSIBLE WITHOUT GREAT
         DIFFICULTY TO ASSIGN TO ASSEMBLY-LINE JOBS THOSE WORKERS
         WHOSE PERSONALITIES ARE SUITABLE FOR THAT KIND OF WORK. IF
         THIS COULD BE ACCOMPLISHED ON A COMPANY OR INDUSTRYWIDE
         BASIS, THE FINANCIAL AND HUMAN BENEFITS COULD BE ENORMOUS.

M0811   DONNELLY, J. H.   ETZEL, M. J.
         RETAIL STORE PERFORMANCE AND JOB SATISFACTION: A STUDY OF
         ANXIETY-STRESS PROPENSITY TO LEAVE AMONG RETAIL EMPLOYEES.
         JOURNAL OF RETAILING 53 (SUMMER 1977): 23-28.

              THE RETAILING LITERATURE IS REPLETE WITH INTERESTING
         AND USEFUL RESEARCH DEALING WITH EXTERNAL FACTORS. FOR
         EXAMPLE, CONSUMER BEHAVIOR AND CHANNEL RELATIONSHIPS ARE
         EXCLUSIVELY STUDIES AND REPORTED. IN THIS EFFORT TO BETTER
         UNDERSTAND THE FACTORS INFLUENCING RETAILING, CRITICAL
         INTERNAL ASPECTS MAY BE OVERLOOKED. THE HIGH TURNOVER RATE
         AMONG RETAIL EMPLOYEES, A GENERALLY NEGATIVE IMAGE OF RETAIL
         EMPLOYMENT AS A CAREER, AND A LARGE MAGNITUDE OF DISCONTENT
         REFLECTED IN SUCH THINGS AS EMPLOYEE THEFT AND MOVES TOWARD
         UNIONIZATION ALL REFLECT A NEED TO BETTER UNDERSTAND WHAT IS
         HAPPENING. ONE SPECIAL AREA THAT RESEARCHERS IN RETAILING
         HAVE VIRTUALLY IGNORED IS EMPLOYEE SATISFACTION, OR MORE
         SPECIFICALLY, THE RELATIONSHIP BETWEEN JOB SATISFACTION AND
         JOB PERFORMANCE.

M0812   DUBIN, R.   CHAMPOUX, J. E.
         CENTRAL LIFE INTERESTS AND JOB SATISFACTION.
         ORGANIZATION BEHAVIOR & HUMAN PERFORMANCE 18 (APRIL 1977):
         366-77.

              THE PERCEPTUAL SET OF THE INDIVIDUAL WORKER REGARDING
         THE CENTRALITY OF WORK AS A LIFE INTEREST IS SHOWN TO BE
         RELATED TO A MEASURE OF JOB SATISFACTION. WORKERS WITH A
         WORK-ORIENTED CENTRAL LIFE INTEREST HAD THE HIGHEST JOB
         SATISFACTION MEASURED BY THE JOB DESCRIPTIVE INDEX (JDI);
         THOSE WITH A NON-WORK-ORIENTED CLI THE LOWEST SATISFACTION;
         AND THOSE WITH A FLEXIBLE FOCUS CLI AN INTERMEDIATE
         LEVEL OF JOB SATISFACTION. FURTHERMORE, IT WAS FOUND THAT A
         FEATURE OF WORK THAT WAS RELATIVELY UNDESIRABLE WAS SO RATED
         ON THE JDI, REGARDLESS OF THE CLI ORIENTATION. IMPLICATIONS
         OF THESE FINDINGS ARE DISCUSSED. STUDY IS BASED ON 430 MALE,
         BLUE-COLLAR WORKERS AND 144 FEMALE CLERICAL WORKERS IN A
         TELEPHONE COMPANY, AND 336 FEMALE CLERICAL WORKERS IN 37
         BRANCHES OF A BANK.

M0813   DUNHAM, R. B. AND OTHERS.
         VALIDATION OF THE INDEX OF ORGANIZATIONAL REACTIONS WITH THE
         JDI, THE MSQ, AND FACES SCALES.
         ACADEMY OF MANAGEMENT JOURNAL 20 (SEPTEMBER 1977): 420-32.

              FACTOR ANALYTIC ANALYSES OF THE INDEX OF ORGANIZATIONAL
         REACTIONS STRONGLY CONFIRM THE A PRIORI SATISFACTION SCALES.
         IN ADDITION, THE SCALES ARE SHOWN TO HAVE GOOD CONVERGENT

M0813   AND DISCRIMINANT VALIDITY AND RELIABILITY WHEN COMPARED WITH
         THREE OTHER JOB SATISFACTION MEASURES. VALIDITY DIFFERENCES
         AS A FUNCTION OF SEX AND JOB ARE STUDIED FOR ALL FOUR
         METHODS.

M0814   FARR, J. L.
         INCENTIVE SCHEDULES, PRODUCTIVITY, AND SATISFACTION IN WORK
         GROUPS: A LABORATORY STUDY.
         ORGANIZATIONAL BEHAVIOR & HUMAN PERFORMANCE 17
         (OCTOBER 1976): 159-70.

         A FACTORIAL LABORATORY STUDY EXAMINED THE EFFECTS OF
         INDIVIDUAL INCENTIVES AND GROUP INCENTIVES. THE SUBJECTS
         WERE 144 COLLEGE STUDENTS WHO WORKED IN THREE-PERSON GROUPS
         ON A CARD-SORTING TASK. BOTH INDIVIDUAL AND GROUP INCENTIVES
         INCREASED TASK PERFORMANCE. THE EXPERIMENTAL CONDITION WHICH
         CONTAINED BOTH AN INDIVIDUAL AND GROUP INCENTIVE RESULTED IN
         THE HIGHEST LEVEL OF PERFORMANCE, BUT RESULTED PERCEPTIONS
         OF THE PAY SYSTEM AS BEING UNFAIR. PERSONAL PAY SATISFACTION
         FACTION WAS NOT AFFECTED BY ANY PAY CONDITION. RESULTS ALSO
         WERE NOT IN ACCORD WITH PREDICTIONS OF EQUITY THEORY
         CONCERNING PERFORMANCES AND SATISFACTION. IT WAS CONCLUDED
         THAT CURRENT CONCEPTIONS OF PAY INEQUITY MAY HAVE TO BE
         MODIFIED TO INCLUDE A DISTINCTION BETWEEN PERSON PAY
         SATISFACTION AND THE PERCEIVED FAIRNESS OF A PAY SYSTEM.

M0815   GOLEMBIEWSKI, R. T.
         TESTING SOME STEREOTYPES ABOUT THE SEXES IN ORGANIZATIONS:
         DIFFERENTIAL SATISFACTION WITH WORK.
         HUMAN RESOURCE MANAGEMENT 16 (SUMMER 1977): 30-32.

         THE PURPOSE IS TO TEST THE ADEQUACY OF SOME SEX
         STEREOTYPIC NOTIONS ABOUT SATISFACTION WITH WORK, USING
         HIERARCHICAL DIFFERENCES. THE FOCUS IS ON 7 VARIABLES
         DATA ABOUT WHICH ARE PROVIDED BY A SUBSTANTIAL POPULATION
         DRAWN FROM THE HEADQUARTERS OF A FIRM THAT PERFORMED THE
         FULL RANGE OF ACTIVITIES FROM RESEARCH THROUGH MARKETING
         REQUIRED FOR A DIVERSIFIED PRODUCT LINE.
         WHAT THE DATA SHOW DEPENDS ON THE SUBTLETY WITH WHICH
         THEY ARE ANALYZED. FOR THE MOST SIMPLE ANALYSIS -- WHEN ONLY
         SEX DIFFERENCES ARE CONSIDERED -- THE DATA MORE OFTEN THAN
         NOT SUPPORT THE COMMON STEREOTYPE THAT THE SEXES DERIVE
         DIFFERENTIAL SATISFACTION FROM WORK. THE SEX-STEREOTYPIC
         VIEW GETS LITTLE SUPPORT WHEN DIFFERENCES IN HIERARCHICAL
         RANK ARE ALSO TAKEN INTO ACCOUNT. THIS FINDING HIGHLIGHTS
         THE VALUE OF, AND THE NEED FOR, SENSITIVE STATISTICAL
         ANALYSIS.

M0816   GROVES, D. L., AND OTHERS.
         PLANNING -- SATISFACTION AND PRODUCTIVITY.
         LONG RANGE PLANNING 9 (AUGUST 1976): 52-57.

         THE AREAS OF WORKER SATISFACTION AND PRODUCTIVITY HAVE
         BEEN OF CONTINUAL IMPORTANCE TO MANAGERS OF ALL TYPES OF
         ORGANIZATIONS. UNFORTUNATELY, THE ANALYSIS OF THESE TOPICS
         HAVE USUALLY BEEN DONE IN A SEGMENTED MANNER. THIS ARTICLE
         ATTEMPTS TO DEVELOP A TOTAL CONCEPTUAL SCHEME FOR PLANNING
         TO INCREASE WORKER SATISFACTION AND EMPLOYEE PRODUCTIVITY.

M0816 BOTH INTERNAL WORK AND EXTERNAL ENVIRONMENTAL COMPONENTS ARE INCLUDED IN THE MODELS WHICH EXAMINE SOCIAL PSYCHOLOGICAL, PHYSICAL, AND ENVIRONMENTAL COMPONENTS OF THE WORKER'S LIFE IN A TOTAL SYSTEM'S APPROACH.

M0817 HOLLON, C. J.   CHESSER, R. J.
RELATIONSHIP OF PERSONAL INFLUENCE DISSONANCE TO JOB TENSION SATISFACTION AND INVOLVEMENT.
ACADEMY OF MANAGEMENT JOURNAL 19 (JUNE 1976): 308-14.

    THE THRUST OF RESEARCH ON DISSONANCE THEORY HAS BEEN TO SPECIFY UNDER WHAT CONDITIONS THE DISSONANCE PREDICTION WILL HOLD. THE RESULTS REPORTED HERE SUGGEST THAT THE PREDICTION HOLDS WHEN AN INDIVIDUAL EXPERIENCES A DIFFERENCE IN THE ACTUAL AND DESIRED LEVEL OF INFLUENCE IN THE JOB SITUATION.

M0818 ILGEN, DANIEL R.   HOLLENBACK, J. H.
ROLE OF JOB SATISFACTION IN ABSENCE BEHAVIOR.
ORGANIZATIONAL BEHAVIOR & HUMAN PERFORMANCE 19 (JUNE 1977): 148-61.

    TWO MODELS OF ABSENCE BEHAVIOR WERE COMPARED FOR A SAMPLE OF 166 CLERICAL WORKER IN A UNIVERSITY SETTING. THE FIRST CONSIDERED ABSENCE BEHAVIOR AS A FUNCTION OF JOB SATISFACTION. ADDITIONAL PRESSURES TOWARD ATTENDANCE, BOTH INTERNAL (THE INDIVIDUAL'S VALUE SYSTEM) AND EXTERNAL CO-WORKERS AND JOB STUCTURE), AS WELL AS FOUR DEMOGRAPHIC VARABLES WERE INCLUDED AS MODERATORS OF THE ABSENTEEISM JOB SATISFACTION RELATIONSHIP. THESE ADDITIONAL PRESSURES WERE TERMED ROLE PRESSURES. THE SECOND MODEL USED ABSENTEEISM AS A FUNCTION OF ROLE PRESURES AND JOB SATISFACTION IN AN ADDITIVE RATHER THAN A MODERATED FASHION. ONLY THE ADDITIVE MODEL WAS SUPPORTED. THE DATA ARE DISCUSSED IN LIGHT OF THE EFFECTS OF ROLE PRESSURES ON ABSENTEEISM.

M0819 IVANCEVICH, J. M.
DIFFERENT GOAL SETTING TREATMENTS AND THEIR EFFECTS ON PERFORMANCE AND JOB SATISFACTION.
ACADEMY OF MANAGEMENT JOURNAL 20 (SUMMER 1977): 406-19.

    A FIELD EXPERIMENT WAS CONDUCTED TO COMPARE THREE GOAL SETTING TREATMENTS. MEASURES OF FOUR HARD PERFORMANCE CRITERIA AND TWO JOB SATISFACTION INDICES WERE COLLECTED.THE PARTICIPATION AND ASSIGNED GROUPS SHOWED SIGNIFICANTLY MORE PERFORMANCE AND SATISFACTION IMPROVEMENTS THAN THE 'DO YOUR BEST' GROUP. HOWEVER, THE IMPROVEMENTS BEGUN TO DISSIPATE SIX TO NINE MONTHS AFTER TRAINING.

M0820 JONES, A. P., AND OTHERS.
BLACK-WHITE DIFFERENCES IN WORK ENVIRONMENT PERCEPTIONS AND JOB SATISFACTION AND ITS CORRELATES.
PERSONNEL PSYCHOLOGY 30 (SPRING 1977): 5.

    NUMEROUS STUDIES HAVE REPORTED RACIAL DIFFERENCES IN INTELLIGENCE, ABILITIES, MOTIVATION, JOB SATISFACTION, AND SO FORTH. RELATIVELY FEW OF THESE STUDIES, HOWEVER, LIMITED THEIR COMPARISONS TO BLACKS AND WHITES EXPERIENCING SIMILAR WORK CONDITIONS. THE PRESENT EFFORT COMPARED BLACK (N= 166)

M0820   AND WHITE (N= 1,451) SAILORS ASSIGNED TO THE SAME SHIPBOARD
         DIVISIONS IN ORDER TO INVESTIGATE POSSIBLE DIFFERENCES IN
         PERCEIVED WORK CONDITIONS, SATISFACTION, NEED STRENGTH, AND
         RELATIONSHIPS AMONG THESE VARIABLES. ALSO EXPLORED WERE TWO
         HYPOTHESIZED SOURCES OF RACE-RELATED SATISFACTION
         DIFFERENCES -- IN PERCEIVED WORK CONDITIONS AND ALSO IN
         NEED STRENGTH. THE RESULTS TENDED TO SUPPORT THE NEED
         STRENGTH HYPOTHESIS ALTHOUGH SATISFACTION DIFFERENCES
         WERE FEWER THAN EXPECTED.

M0821   KREISER, L.   WILLIS, E.
         LOCAL FIRM AND JOB SATISFACTION.
         JOURNAL OF ACCOUNTANCY 143 (MAY 1977) : 40+.

             THE OBJECTIVES OF THIS RESEARCH STUDY WERE TO IDENTIFY
         SOME OF THE MORE IMPORTANT OCCUPATIONAL NEEDS OF CPAS AND TO
         DETERMINE THE EXTENT TO WHICH EMPLOYERS FULFILL THESE NEEDS.
         QUESTIONNAIRES WERE MAILED TO A SAMPLE OF 482 CPA'S WHO WERE
         LISTED IN THE   MEMBERSHIP DIRECTORY OF THE OHIO SOCIETY OF
         CERTIFIED PUBLIC ACCOUNTANTS. INCLUDED IN THE SAMPLE WERE
         194 RANDOMLY SELECTED MALE CPA'S IN PUBLIC PRACTICE. 194
         RANDOMLY SELECTED MALE CPA'S NOT IN PUBLIC PRACTICE AND ALL
         OF THE 94 FEMALE CPAS LISTED IN THE DIRECTORY. REPLIES
         WERE RECEIVED FROM 203 CPA'S FOR AN OVERALL RESPONSE RATE OF
         42 PERCENT.

M0822   LUCAS, R. E. B.
         HEDONIC WAGE EQUATIONS AND PSYCHIC WAGES IN THE RETURNS TO
         SCHOOLING.
         AMERICAN ECONOMIC REVIEW 67 (SEPTEMBER 1977): 549-58.

             THESE DATA COLLECTED FOR THE DICTIONARY OF OCCUPATIONAL
         TITLES, DESCRIBE IN TERMS OF OCCUPATIONAL ATTRIBUTES THE
         NATURE OF THE WORK TASK INVOLVED IN SOME 14,000 JOBS. FOR
         EXAMPLE: THE PHYSICAL WORK ENVIRONMENT IS DESCRIBED BY
         SHOWING THE PRESENCE OF TOXIC CONDITIONS, SEVERE TEMPERATURE
         AND HAZARDS; WHETHER THE JOB IS HIGHLY REPETITIVE, OR IS
         SUPERVISORY ARE RECORDED; AND THE LEVELS OF SUCH ABILITIES
         AS STRENGTH AND GENERAL EDUCATIONAL DEVELOPMENT REQUIRED
         FOR TASK EXECUTION ARE ESTIMATED. THE PRINCIPAL OBJECTIVE
         HERE IS TO DISCOVER HOW INDIVIDUALS' WAGES VARY, CETERIS
         PARIBUS, WITH SUCH INDICATORS OF THE QUALITY OF WORKING
         LIFE, BY INSERTING THESE JOB CHARACTERISTIC VARIABLES INTO
         A WAGE EQUATION THAT ALSO EMBRACES PERSONAL DATA.

M0823   MACEACHRON, ANN E.
         TWO INTERACTIVE PERSPECTIVES ON THE RELATIONSHIP BETWEEN JOB
         LEVEL AND JOB SATISFACTION.
         ORGANIZATIONAL BEHAVIOR & HUMAN PERFORMANCE 19 (AUGUST
         1977): 226-46.

             THE FINDINGS OF THIS STUDY DID NOT REPLICATE THE JOB
         LEVEL / JOB SATISFACTION HYPOTHESIS FOR WOMEN WORKING ON A
         HOSPITAL NURSING STAFF, A TRADITIONAL OCCUPATION FOR WOMEN.
         TWO INTERACTION MODELS, A SYMMETRICAL AND ASYMMETRICAL MODEL
         WERE THEN APPLIED USING FIELD INDEPENDENCE AS THE INDIVIDUAL
         DIFFERENCES MODERATING VARIABLE. WHILE THE ASYMMETRICAL
         MODEL WAS THE BEST PREDICTOR OF JOB SATISFACTION PATTERNS,

M0823   BOTH MODELS WERE REQUIRED TO ACCOUNT FULLY FOR DIFFERENCES
IN SATISFACTION PATTERNS. THEORETICAL AND APPLIED
IMPLICATIONS WERE DISCUSSED.

M0824   MCKELVEY, B.,   SEKARAN, U.
TOWARD A CAREER-BASED THEORY OF JOB INVOLVEMENT: A STUDY OF
SCIENTISTS AND ENGINEERS.
ADMINISTRATIVE SCIENCE QUARTERLY 22 (JUNE 1977): 281-305.

MULTIPLE REGRESSION ANALYSES ARE USED TO DETERMINE THE
RELATIVE IMPORTANCE OF 49 FACTORS TO JOB INVOLVEMENT IN A
STUDY OF 441 SCIENTISTS AND ENGINEERS. OF SPECIAL IMPORTANCE
ARE CAREER AND PERSONALITY FACTORS. LEVELS OF VARIANCE
EXPLAINED INCREASE AS VARIOUS CONDITIONING FACTORS, SUCH AS
PERSONALITY, PROFESSIONAL TRAINING, AND ORIENTATION ARE
CONTROLLED BY HIGHER ORDER BREAKDOWNS OF THE SAMPLE.
THE RESULTS SUPPORT A CAREER-BASED THEORY OF INVOLVEMENT.
MENT. A DIFFERENTIATION OF THREE JOB CONTEXTS IS SUGGESTED
TO AID IN THE IDENTIFICATION OF ADDITIONAL FACTORS POSSIBLY
AFFECTING JOB INVOLVEMENT.

M0825   MERRYMAN, C.   SHANI, E.
GROWTH AND SATISFACTION OF EMPLOYEES IN ORGANIZATIONS.
PERSONNEL JOURNAL 55 (OCTOBER 1976): 492+.

A CASE STUDY INVOLVED RANDOM SAMPLING OF TWO COMPANIES,
ONE LARGE (6000 EMPLOYEES) AND ONE SMALL (1000 EMPLOYEES).
THERE WERE 44 RESPONSES FROM THE LARGER COMPANY AND 21 FROM
THE SMALLER ONE. A QUESTIONNAIRE TO MEASURE THE AMOUNT OF
COMMUNICATION AND SATISFACTION OF THE EMPLOYEES WAS DESIGNED
WITH A VERY HIGH DEGREE OF RELIABILITY (0.97), ACCORDING TO
GRONBACH'S ALPHA INTERNAL CONSISTENCY RELIABILITY. A LARGE
COMPANY THAT HAD GROWN IN RECENT YEARS WAS COMPARED TO A
SMALLER COMPANY THAT HAD NOT RECENTLY GROWN. THE COMPANIES'
ANNUAL REPORTS WERE OBTAINED AND THEIR GROWTH AND PROFITS
OVER THE LAST FIVE YEARS WERE COMPARED. IN ORDER TO FIND HOW
THE TWO COMPANIES DIFFERED IN THEIR COMMUNICATION PROBLEMS
AND THEIR SATISFACTION ON THE JOB, THE QUESTIONNAIRE WAS
ADMINISTERED TO EMPLOYEES OF BOTH COMPANIES.

M0826   MILLER, R.W.
IS WORK THE CENTRAL LIFE INTEREST? NOT FOR MOST PEOPLE --
FINDING THE COMMITED FEW.
BUSINESS QUARTERLY 41 (AUGUST 1976): 92.

IT IS IMPLIED IN MOST SURVEYS OF JOB SATISFACTION AND
ORGANIZATIONAL CLIMATE THAT EMPLOYEES WILL REACT POSITIVELY
TO DESIRABLE CHANGES IN THE WORK PLACE, IMPROVING THEIR
PERFORMANCE IN THE PROCESS. HOWEVER, WHILE WORK
SATISFACTION IS SOMEWHAT RELATED TO PERFORMANCE, TENURE,
ABSENTEEISM AND GRIEVANCES, THE CORRELATION BETWEEN
VARIOUS MEASURES OF JOB SATISFACTION (AND THERE ARE MANY)
AND PERFORMANCE IS TENUOUS, AND MANIPULATION OF VARIOUS
SATISFACTION VARIABLES (AS WITH HERZBERG,MASLOW AND OTHER
RENOWNED THEORETICIANS) SHOULD ONLY BE PRACTICED UNDER
EXPERT GUIDANCE. WHILE MAKING THE JOB SETTING A BETTER
PLACE TO WORK MAY BE A WORTHY GOAL BASED ON PURELY
BENEVOLENT SOCIAL AND HUMANITARIAN CONCERNS, THE PAYOFF

M0826 DOES NOT ALWAYS RESULT IN IMPROVED PRODUCTIVITY. WHY NOT?

M0827 MUCHINSKY, P. M.
       ORGANIZATIONAL COMMUNICATION: RELATIONSHIPS TO
       ORGANIZATIONAL CLIMATE AND JOB SATISFACTION.
       ACADEMY OF MANAGEMENT JOURNAL 20 (SEPTEMBER 1977): 592-606.

            THE PURPOSE OF THIS EXPLORATORY STUDY WAS TO EXAMINE
       RELATIONSHIPS AMONG MEASURES OF ORGANIZATIONAL
       COMMUNICATION, ORGANIZATIONAL CLIMATE, AND JOB SATISFACTION.
       SIX HUNDRED NINETY-FIVE EMPLOYEES OF A LARGE PUBLIC
       UTILITY CONSTITUTED THE SAMPLE. THE RESULTS INDICATED THAT
       CERTAIN DIMENSIONS OF ORGANIZATIONAL COMMUNICATION WERE
       HIGHLY RELATED TO BOTH ORGANIZATIONAL CLIMATE AND JOB
       SATISFACTION.

M0828 O'CONNEL, M. J.   CUMMINGS, L. L.
       MODERATING EFFECTS OF ENVIRONMENT AND STRUCTURE ON THE
       SATISFACTION-TENSION-INFLUENCE NETWORK.
       ORGANIZATIONAL BEHAVIOR & HUMAN PERFORMANCE 17 (DECEMBER
       1976): 351-66.

            RELATIONS AMONG A DEPENDENT VARIABLE NETWORK CONSISTING
       OF SATISFACTION-TENSION-INFLUENCE AND THE MODERATING EFFECTS
       OF INFORMATIONAL AND STRUCTURAL CHARACTERISTICS ARE
       REPORTED. ONE HUNDRED FORTY-FOUR SUBJECTS PARTICIPATED IN
       A 3 X 3 X 2 FACTORIAL DESIGN. DEPENDENT VARIABLES WERE
       PERCEPTIONS OF SATISFACTION, TENSION, AND INFLUENCE.
       MODERATOR VARIABLES WERE INFORMATION LOAD, INFORMATION
       SPECIFICITY, AND GROUP STRUCTURE. THE RESULTS CONFIRMED
       THE GENERAL FIELD-STUDY FINDINGS OF A NEGATIVE RELATION
       BETWEEN TENSION AND SATISFACTION AND A POSITIVE RELATION
       BETWEEN INFLUENCE AND SATISFACTION. THE TENSION AND
       SATISFACTION RELATION WAS MOST STRONGLY MODERATED BY
       INFORMATION: LESS SO BY STRUCTURE. THE INFLUENCE AND
       SATISFACTION AND INFLUENCE-TENSION RELATIONS WERE ONLY
       WEAKLY MODERATED. POSSIBLE INTERPRETATIONS ARE OFFERED IN
       TERMS OF (A) THE DEGREE TO WHICH DEPENDENT VARIABLES IN
       ORGANIZATIONAL BEHAVIOR ARE OBJECTIVELY AND ENVIRONMENTALLY
       ANCHORED AND (B) THE POSSIBILITY OF METHODOLOGICAL
       ARTIFACTS (COMBINING SELF AND OTHER PERCEPTIONS)
       INFLUENCING THE "MODERATORABILITY" OF DEPENDENT VARIABLES IN
       ORGANIZATIONAL BEHAVIOR. IT IS CONCLUDED THE (A)
       INFORMATIONAL AND ORGANIZATIONAL CHARACTERISTICS CAN
       INFLUENCE THE DEPENDENT VARIABLE NETWORK AND (B) THE
       RELATIONS AMONG DEPENDENT VARIABLES CANNOT BE ACCURATELY
       DESCRIBED WITH SIMPLE STATEMENTS IMPLYING UNIDIMENSIONAL
       MEASURES WHOSE RELATIONS ARE STABLE ACROSS CONDITIONS.

M0829 O'REILLY, C. A.
       PERSONALITY-JOB FIT: IMPLICATIONS FOR INDIVIDUAL ATTITUDES
       AND PERFORMANCE.
       ORGANIZATIONAL BEHAVIOR & HUMAN PERFORMANCE 18
       (FEBRUARY 1977): 36-46.

            RESULTS OF A TEST OF A PERSONALITY-JOB CONGRUENCY
       HYPOTHESIS USING 307 NAVY PERSONNEL IN 10 JOB CATEGORIES
       ARE REPORTED. PERSONALITY MEASURES WERE USED TO FORM TWO

M0829 INDICES OF WORK ORIENTATION: EXPRESSIVE, OR DESIRING
ACHIEVEMENT AND SELF-ACTUALIZATION WHILE ON THE JOB, AND
INSTRUMENTAL, OR DESIRING JOB SECURITY AND HIGH FINANCIAL
REWARD FROM THE JOB. THESE ORIENTATIONS WERE FOUND TO
INTERACT WITH THE TYPE OF JOB (CHALLENGING OR
NONCHALLENGING) AND TO AFFECT JOB ATTITUDES AND PERFORMANCE.
IMPLICATIONS FOR INVESTIGATING VARIATIONS IN JOB ATTITUDES
FROM STRUCTURAL AND INDIVIDUAL FRAMES OF REFERENCE ARE
DISCUSSED.

M0830 RIGHT CLIMATE FOR SALESMEN.
MANAGEMENT REVIEW 66 (SEPTEMBER 1977): 62.

THE SALES MANAGER WHO IS CONCERNED ABOUT THE JOB
SATISFACTION OF HIS SALESFORCE SHOULD PAY AS MUCH ATTENTION
TO THE GENERAL MANNER IN WHICH COMPANY POLICIES AND
PRACTICES ARE DEVELOPED, ADMINISTERED, AND CONTROLLED AS HE
DOES TO HIS SALESMEN'S FEELINGS ABOUT THE SPECIFIC POLICIES
AND PRACTICES THEMSELVES.

M0831 POIST, R. F.   LYNAGH, P. M.
JOB SATISFACTION AND THE PD MANAGER: AN EMPIRICAL
ASSESSMENT.
TRANSPORTATION JOURNAL 16 (FALL 1976): 42-51.

WITH PDM APPROACHING A STATE OF MATURITY, IT IS TIME
TO TAKE A LONG AND HARD LOOK AT THE BEHAVIORAL ASPECTS OF
SYSTEMS PLANNING AND DESIGN. AS A POSITIVE STEP IN THIS
DIRECTION A SURVEY WAS UNDERTAKEN TO ASSESS THE JOB
SATISFACTION OF A SAMPLE OF PD MANAGER.

M0832 ROUSSEAU, D. M.
TECHNOLOGICAL DIFFERENCES IN JOB CHARACTERISTICS, EMPLOYEE
SATISFACTION, AND MOTIVATION: A SYNTHESIS OF JOB DESIGN
RESOURCE AND SOCIOTECHNICAL SYSTEMS THEORY.
ORGANIZATIONAL BEHAVIOR & HUMAN PERFORMANCE 19 (JUNE 1977):
18-42.

A REVIEW OF JOB DESIGN RESEARCH AND SOCIOTECHNICAL
SYSTEMS THEORY SUGGESTS THAT BOTH OF THESE APPROACHES TO
ORGANIZATIONAL CHANGE CONVERGE IN THEIR EMPHASIS ON A COMMON
SET OF JOB CHARACTERISTICS AS IMPORTANT TO EMPLOYEE
SATISFACTION AND MOTIVATION. JOB CHARACTERISTICS SUGGESTED
BY SOCIOTECHNICAL SYSTEMS THEORY AND JOB DESIGN RESEARCH
WERE EXAMINED IN A SURVEY OF EMPLOYEES IN 19 PRODUCTION
UNITS. THESE ORGANIZATIONAL UNITS WERE CLASSIFIED INTO
THREE TECHNOLOGICAL CATEGORIES. SIGNIFICANT DIFFERENCES
WERE FOUND BETWEEN THE JOB CHARACTERISTICS, EMPLOYEE
SATISFACTION, AND MOTIVATION ACROSS TECHNOLOGY. IN
ADDITION, THERE WERE SUBSTANTIAL POSITIVE RELATIONS BETWEEN
THE JOB CHARACTERISTICS, SATISFACTION, AND MOTIVATION. THE
JOB CHARACTERISTICS VARIETY AND TASK SIGNIFICANCE WERE FOUND
TO BE PARTICULARLY IMPORTANT TO EMPLOYEE SATISFACTION AND
MOTIVATION.

M0833 ROUSTANG, G.
WHY STUDY WORKING CONDITIONS VIA JOB SATISFACTION? A PLEA
FOR DIRECT ANALYSIS.

M0833   INTERNATIONAL LABOR REVIEW 115 (MAY 1977):   277-319.
        IN RECENT YEARS THE GOVERNMENTS OF THE INDUSTRIALISED
WESTERN COUNTRIES HAVE GREATLY BROADENED THEIR TRADITIONAL
BUT LIMITED PREOCCUPATION WITH SAFEGUARDING THE WORKERS'
HEALTH AND HAVE BEGUN TO CONCERN THEMSELVES WITH IMPROVING
THE QUALITY OF WORKING LIFE IN GENERAL. A NUMBER OF
THEORIES HAVE BEEN ADVANCED TO EXPLAIN THIS DEVELOPMENT, BUT
THERE IS NO DOUBT THAT, TO A LARGE EXTENT, IT IS DUE TO THE
ALARM WHICH A CERTAIN DISAFFECTION TOWARDS INDUSTRIAL WORK
IS CAUSING AMONG BOTH EMPLOYERS AND GOVERNMENTS.
TO OVERCOME THIS MALAISE WOULD ENABLE INDIVIDUAL ENTERPRISES
AND INDUSTRIAL SOCIETY AS A WHOLE:
        TO AVOID SUCH MANIFESTATIONS OF ALIENATION AS
        ABSENTEEISM AND RAPID LABOUR TURNOVER (WHICH COST
        ENTERPRISES A GREAT DEAL OF MONEY) AND BUILD UP A MORE
        STABLE WORKFORCE;
        TO ACHIEVE BETTER PRODUCTIVITY AND QUALITY STANDARDS;
        TO MAKE MORE EFFICIENT USE OF HUMAN RESOURCES;
        TO FORESTALL FUNDAMENTAL CRITICISM OF INDUSTRIAL
        SOCIETY, IN PARTICULAR BY YOUNG PEOPLE WHO ARE LESS
        WILLING TO ACCEPT BAD WORKING CONDITIONS.

M0834   SALEH, S. D.   HOSEK, J.
        JOB INVOLVEMENT: CONCEPTS AND MEASUREMENTS.
        ACADEMY OF MANAGEMENT JOURNAL 19 (JUNE 1976):   213-24.

        MEASURES OF JOB INVOLVEMENT USED IN THE LITERATURE WERE
ADMINISTERED TO SAMPLES OF STUDENTS AND INSURANCE SALESMEN.
THREE FACTORS EMERGED IN BOTH SAMPLES. THE RESULTS WERE
EXPLAINED IN TERMS OF GERGEN'S STRUCTURAL THEORY OF THE
SELF AND WERE FOUND TO REPRESENT THE IDENTITY, THE
CONNATIVE, AND THE EVALUATIVE DIMENSIONS.

M0835   SCHRIESHEIM, C.   VONGLINOW, M. A.
        THE PATH-GOAL THEORY OF LEADERSHIP: A THEORETICAL AND
        EMPIRICAL ANALYSIS.
        ACADEMY OF MANAGEMENT JOURNAL 20 (SUMMER 1977):   398-405.

        THE EFFECTS OF DIFFERENT OPERATIONALIZATIONS OF THE
PATH-GOAL THEORY'S LEADER BEHAVIOR CONSTRUCTS ARE EXAMINED.
THE RESULTS INDICATE THAT SOME OF THE INCONSISTENT AND NON
SUPPORTIVE RESEARCH FINDINGS PERTAINING TO THE THEORY ARE
DUE TO INADEQUACIES AND DIFFERENCES IN OPERATIONALIZATIONS
OF THE THEORY'S LEADER BEHAVIOR VARIABLES. SUGGESTIONS FOR
FUTURE TESTS ARE DISCUSSED.

M0836   SEYBOLT, JOHN W.
        WORK SATISFACTION AS A FUNCTION OF THE PERSON-ENVIRONMENT
        INTERACTION.
        ORGANIZATIONAL & BEHAVIOR PERFORMANCE 17 (OCTOBER 1976):
        66-75.

        THE PRESENT STUDY EXPLORES THE RELATIONSHIPS BETWEEN
THREE CHARACTERISTICS OF THE WORK ENVIRONMENT (PAY, JOB
VARIETY, TASK COMPLEXITY) AND PERSONAL WORK SATISFACTION,
AND THE MODERATING EFFECT OF LEVEL OF FORMAL EDUCATION ON
THESE RELATIONSHIPS. THE CONCEPT OF THE PERSON-ENVIRONMENT
FIT IS USED TO PREDICT DIFFERENTIAL LEVELS OF WORK

M0836 SATISFACTION IN A PUBLIC SECTOR WORKFORCE. THE USEFULNESS
OF SUCH AN INTEGRATIVE APPROACH HAS BEEN RECOGNIZED
(E.G. KATZELL, 1957; JAHODA, 1961; FOREHAND & GILMER, 1964;
OPSAHL & DUNNETTE, 1966; PERVIN, 1968; DAWIS, LOFQUIST, &
WEISS, 1968; HACKMAN & LAWLER, 1971; KOHN & SCHOOLER, 1973)
AND THE PRESENT RESEARCH WORKS WITHIN THIS FRAMEWORK TO
EXAMINE THE ORGANIZATIONAL "INDUCEMENTS" REQUIRED FOR
EMPLOYEE SATISFACTION.

M0837 SMITH, F. S. AND OTHERS.
TEN YEAR JOB SATISFACTION TRENDS IN A STABLE ORGANIZATION.
ACADEMY OF MANAGEMENT JOURNAL 19 (SEPTEMBER 1976): 462-69.

MOST OF THE MORE THAN 4,000 JOB SATISFACTION STUDIES
(LAWLER, 1971) NOW PUBLISHED HAVE ASSESSED RESPONDENTS AT
ONLY ONE POINT IN TIME AND USED NONSTANDARDIZED MEASURES
AND SMALL, NONREPRESENTATIVE SAMPLES. GENERALIZATIONS FROM
SUCH STUDIES ARE TENUOUS, YET THEIR RESULTS ARE OFTEN USED
TO SUGGEST SOLUTIONS TO IMPORTANT ISSUES ABOUT THE AMERICAN
WORK FORCE.
BECAUSE OF THE EXPENSE INVOLVED IN CONDUCTING TRULY
LONGITUDINAL RESEARCH, THE RESULTS OF WHICH MIGHT HELP
DICTATE POLICIES BENEFICIAL TO WORKERS, IT PROBABLY WILL
NOT BE DONE. HOWEVER, A NUMBER OF PARTIALLY OVERLAPPING,
LONGITUDINAL INVESTIGATIONS USING STANDARDIZED
INSTRUMENTATION IN VARIOUS WORK SETTINGS CAN BE INTEGRATED
TO DEVELOP SPECIFIC CHANGE PROGRAMS IF THEY ARE WARRANTED.
THE STUDY REPORTED HERE IS ONE LARGE-SCALE, QUASI
LONGITUDINAL, CROSS-SECTIONAL INVESTIGATION WITH WHICH
OTHERS CAN BE INTEGRATED.

M0838 SMITH, F. S. AND OTHERS.
TRENDS IN JOB-RELATED ATTITUDES OF MANAGERIAL AND
PROFESSIONAL EMPLOYEES.
ACADEMY OF MANAGEMENT JOURNAL 20 (SEPTEMBER 1977): 454-60

THIS STUDY PRESENTS DATA FROM ONE LARGE ORGANIZATION
DEALING WITH FOUR-YEAR CHANGES IN JOB SATISFACTION OF
MANAGERIAL EMPLOYEES. IT EXPLORES THE POPULAR NOTION THAT
ORGAIZATION MEMBERS ARE BECOMING INCREASINGLY DISSATISFIED
WITH THEIR JOBS. IT HAS BEEN ARGUED THAT HIGHER LEVELS
OF EDUCATION, HIGHER STANDARDS OF LIVING, AND INCREASED WORK
FORCE MOBILITY RESULT IN HIGHER WORK FORCE EXPECTATIONS
WHICH ORGANIZATIONS ARE UNABLE TO MEET. SURPRISINGLY,
EMPIRICAL RESEARCH HAS BEEN DIRECTED TOWARD TEST OF THIS
THESIS, AND RESEARCH THAT HAS ADDRESSED THIS ISSUE IS NOT
CONCLUSIVE.

M0839 SZILAGYI, A. D.
AN EMPIRICAL TEST OF CAUSAL INFERENCE BETWEEN ROLE
PERCEPTIONS, SATISFACTION WITH WORK, PERFORMANCE AND
ORGANIZATIONAL LEVEL.
PERSONNEL PSYCHOLOGY 30 (AUGUST 1977): 375-88.

PREVIOUS RESEARCH HAS SUGGESTED THAT ORGANIZATIONAL
LEVEL MAY EXPLAIN TO A SIGNIFICANT EXTENT THE DIFFERENTIAL
IMPACT OF ROLE PERCEPTIONS ON EMPLOYEE SATISFACTION AND
PERFORMANCE. CAUSAL INFERENCES COULD NOT BE DRAWN FROM

M0839   THESE STUDIES BECAUSE OF THE PREDOMINANT USE OF STATIC
CORRELATIONAL METHODS. IN THIS STUDY, IN A HOSPITAL
SETTING, A SIX-MONTH TIME LAG BETWEEN DATA COLLECTION
PERIODS WAS USED TO DEVELOP CAUSAL INFERENCES. THE RESULTS
SUPPORTED THE HYPOTHESIS THAT ROLE AMBIGUITITY WAS A SOURCE
OF CAUSAL INFERENCE WITH SATISFACTION WITH WORK AT THE
HIGHER ORGANIZATIONAL LEVEL, WHILE ROLE CONFLICT WAS A
SOURCE OF CAUSAL INFERENCE WITH SATISFACTION WITH WORK AT
THE LOWER ORGANIZATION LEVEL. THE SOURCE AND DIRECTION OF
CAUSAL INFLUENCE WITH RESPECT TO ROLE PERCEPTIONS AND
PERFORMANCE WAS SUPPORTED ONLY AT THE HIGHER ORGANIZATIONAL
LEVEL.

M0840   SMITH, J. H.   UECKER, W. C.
CAN INTERNAL AUDITORS FIND JOB SATISFACTION?
THE INTERNAL AUDITOR 33 (OCTOBER 1976): 48-53.

        THE AUTHORS PRESENT THE FINDINGS OF A RECENTLY
COMPLETED STUDY OF THE JOB SATISFACTION OF INTERNAL AUDITORS
AND COMPARE THESE FINDINGS WITH THE JOB SATISFACTION OF
MANAGERS IN LARGE FIRMS AND CPA'S IN PUBLIC PRACTICE.

M0841   STINSON, J. E.   JOHNSON, T. W.
TASKS, INDIVIDUAL DIFFERENCES, AND JOB SATISFACTION.
INDUSTRIAL RELATIONS 16 (OCTOBER 1977): 314-22.

        JOB ENRICHMENT HAS BECOME A CONTROVERSIAL SUBJECT IN
RECENT YEARS. AN ASSORTMENT OF ILLS HAS BEEN ATTRIBUTED TO
THE OVERSIMPLIFICATION OF WORK, AND SOME AUTHORS HAVE
PROPOSED JOB ENRICHMENT AS A GENERAL PURPOSE TOOL FOR
REDUCING EMPLOYEE DISSATISFACTION, OUTPUT RESTRICTION,
ABSENTEEISM, AND TURNOVER. OTHERS BELIEVE THAT WORKER
RESPONSES TO JOB CHARACTERISTICS ARE HEAVILY INFLUENCED BY
INDIVIDUAL DIFFERENCES, AND THAT, THEREFORE, ONLY SOME
WORKERS WILL RESPOND POSITIVELY TO JOB ENRICHMENT. THIS
STUDY EXPLORES THE INFLUENCE OF INDIVIDUAL DIFFERENCES ON
WORKER RESPONSE TO JOB CHARACTERISTICS BY EXAMINING THE
MODERATING EFFECTS OF NEED FOR ACHIEVEMENT AND NEED FOR
AFFILIATION ON RELATIONSHIPS BETWEEN TASK CHARACTERISTICS
AND WORKER SATISFACTION.

M0842   WEAVER, CHARLES N.
RELATIONSHIPS AMONG PAY, RACE, SEX, OCCUPATIONAL PRESTIGE,
SUPERVISION, WORK AUTONOMY, AND JOB SATISFACTION IN A
NATIONAL SAMPLE.
PERSONNEL PSYCHOLOGY 30 (AUGUST 1977): 437-45.

        PUBLISHED EVIDENCE, BASED LARGELY ON BIVARIATE METHODS
OF ANALYSIS, GENERALLY SUGGESTS THAT PAY, RACE, OCCUPATIONAL
PRESTIGE, SUPERVISORY STATUS, AND WORK AUTONOMY ARE
ASSOCIATED WITH JOB SATISFACTION AND THAT SEX IS NOT.
REGRESSION ANALYSIS OF A REPRESENTATIVE SAMPLE OF U. S.
WORKERS, WHICH PARTIALLED OUT THE EFFECTS OF A NUMBER OF
OTHER VARIABLES, AFFIRMS THAT SUPERVISORY STATUS MAKES AN
INDEPENDENT CONTRIBUTION TO JOB SATISFACTION AND THAT SEX IS
UNRELATED, BUT SUGGESTS THAT THE ZERO-ORDER EFFECTS OF PAY,
RACE, OCCUPATIONAL PRESTIGE, AND WORK AUTONOMY ARE SPURIOUS.

M0843 WEITZEL, WILLIAM AND OTHERS.
PREDICTING PAY SATISFACTION FROM NONPAY WORK VARIABLES.
INDUSTRIAL RELATIONS 16 (OCTOBER 1977): 323-34.

PEOPLE DIFFER CONSIDERABLY IN THEIR SATISFACTION WITH
PAY. SOME OF THESE DIFFERENCES CAN BE EXPLAINED BY
DEMOGRAPHIC VARIABLES, SUCH AS AGE, EDUCATIONAL LEVEL, JOB
TYPE, AND ORGANIZATIONAL LEVEL. IT IS OUR CONTENTION HERE,
HOWEVER, THAT SATISFACTION WITH PAY IS ALSO HEAVILY
INFLUENCED BY ATTITUDES TOWARD THE JOB AS A WHOLE.

M0844 WNUK-LIPINSKI, E.
JOB SATISFACTION AND THE QUALITY OF WORKING LIFE: THE
POLISH EXPERIENCE.
INTERNATIONAL LABOUR REVIEW 115 (JANUARY 1977): 53-64.

THE NUMEROUS SURVEYS ON JOB SATISFACTION RECENTLY
UNDERTAKEN IN POLISH INDUSTRY HAVE BEEN BASED ON VARIOUS
METHODOLOGICAL ASSUMPTIONS, BUT MOST OF THEM HAVE SHARED
CERTAIN COMMON PREMISES ABOUT THE PLACE OF THE HUMAN BEING
IN A WORK SITUATION. TO PUT IT BRIEFLY, THEY SEE WORK AS AN
INTEGRAL PART OF THE BROADER BUSINESS OF LIVING IN SOCIETY;
PEOPLE WORK NOT ONLY TO SUPPORT THEMSELVES AND THEIR
FAMILIES BUT ALSO TO CONTRIBUTE TO THE WELFARE OF SOCIETY AS
A WHOLE. WORK, IT IS BELIEVED, SATISFIES AT LEAST SOME OF
THE IMPORTANT HUMAN NEEDS CREATED BY THE SOCIAL ENVIRONMENT,
FOR EXAMPLE THE NEED TO COMPETE, TO ATTAIN PROFICIENCY, TO
PARTICIPATE IN A WIDER COMMUNITY, TO DEVELOP ONE'S
PERSONALITY, AND SO ON. IN THIS VIEW OF THINGS JOB
SATISFACTION MAY BE CONSIDERED AN END IN ITSELF AND NOT JUST
A MEANS OF INCREASING PRODUCTIVITY OR INDEED OF SERVING
ANY OTHER PURPOSE AT ALL.

M0845 ABRAMSON, SAMUEL R.
ACHIEVEMENT MOTIVATION AS A MODERATOR OF THE RELATIONSHIP
BETWEEN EXPECTANCY TIMES VALENCE AND EFFORT.
PH.D. DISSERTATION, STEVENS INSTITUTE OF TECHNOLOGY, 1975.

THE MANNER IN WHICH ACHIEVEMENT ORIENTATION MODERATED
RELATIONSHIPS DERIVED FROM THE EXPECTANCY TIMES VALENCE
THEORY OF MOTIVATION WAS TESTED USING 182 MANAGERIAL
EMPLOYEES OF AN EASTERN FINANCIAL INSTITUTION. THE
MODERATING EFFECTS WERE FOUND TO BE EQUIVOCAL.

M0846 AHR, C. JONATHAN. KAPUST, JEFFRY. LAWRENCE, P. S.
BEHAVIORAL TRAINING OF SUPERVISORS IN AN INDUSTRIAL SETTING
FOR THE BLIND.
JOURNAL OF COMMUNITY PSYCHOLOGY 5 (APRIL 1977): 160-65.

SUGGESTS THAT TRAINING SUPERVISORS IN THE USE OF
BEHAVIORAL PRINCIPLES IS EFFECTIVE IN THE MODIFICATION OF
EMPLOYEE SATISFACTION WITH MANAGEMENT AND SUPERVISORY
PERSONNEL.

M0847 ARNDT, ANNE SCOLNICK.
AN INVESTIGATION OF FACTORS INVOLVED IN CAREER SATISFACTION
FOR THE PHYSICIAN.
PH.D. DISSERTATION, BOSTON COLLEGE, 1977.

M0847   AN INVESTIGATION OF THE FACTORS AFFECTING CAREER
SATISFACTION IN PHYSICIANS WAS THE SUBJECT OF THIS STUDY.
THE MAJORITY OF THE RESPONDENTS WERE FOUND TO BE VERY
SATISFIED WITH THE CHALLENGE AND GRATIFICATION OF THEIR
CAREERS, MODERATELY SATISFIED WITH PRESTIGE, INCOME, AND
SECURITY, AND LITTLE SATISFIED WITH LEISURE TIME.
PHYSICIANS WHO HAD MADE CAREER CHANGES, AS WELL AS THOSE
WHO HAD REPORTED THE PROBLEM OF DEPRESSION, HAD A LOWER
LEVEL OF JOB SATISFACTION. NO LINEAR RELATIONSHIP WAS FOUND
BETWEEN LEVEL OF SPECIALIZATION OR VIEWS ON FUTURE MEDICINE.

M0848   BAIRD, LLOYD S.
RELATIONSHIP OF PERFORMANCE TO SATISFACTION IN STIMULATING
AND NONSTIMULATING JOBS.
JOURNAL OF APPLIED PSYCHOLOGY 61 (DECEMBER 1976): 721-27.

        THE HYPOTHESIS THAT JOB SATISFACTION WOULD BE DIRECTLY
RELATED TO PERFORMANCE WITH STIMULATING JOBS WAS DISPROVED.
SATISFACTION WAS CORRELATED WITH PERFORMANCE ONLY IN
NONSTIMULATING JOBS. IT IS SUGGESTED THAT THE KEY VARIABLE
IN DETERMINING THESE RELATIONSHIPS IS THE NATURE AND USE OF
FEEDBACK.

M0850   BENCH, JOSEPH E.
A STUDY OF THE RELATIONSHIP BETWEEN HERZBERG'S MOTIVATION
HYGIENE FACTORS AND HOLLAND'S PERSONALITY PATTERNS FOR
LAW ENFORCEMENT PERSONNEL.
ED.D. DISSERTATION, WEST VIRGINIA UNIVERSITY, 1975.

        THE PURPOSE OF THIS STUDY WAS TO TEST HERZBERG'S
MOTIVATION-HYGIENE THEORY OF CAREERS WITH LAW ENFORCEMENT.
THE FOLLOWING QUESTIONS WERE PROPOSED: WHAT IS THE
RELATIONSHIP BETWEEN JOB CHARACTERISTICS AND JOB
SATISFACTION? DOES THE IMPORTANCE OF THE MOTIVATION
HYGIENE FACTORS VARY WITH PERSONALITY TYPES? AND, WHAT IS
THE MOST COMMON PERSONALITY TYPE OR PERSONALITY PATTERN FOR
LAW ENFORCEMENT PERSONNEL? THE HERTZBERG MOTIVATION
HYGIENE THEORY IS NOT SUPPORTED BY THE RESULTS OF THIS STUDY
AND HOLLAND'S THEORY OF CAREERS IS ONLY PARTIALLY SUPPORTED.

M0851   DERAKHSHANI, MANOUCHEHR.
INTERNAL VERSUS EXTERNAL LOCUS OF CONTROL AND JOB
SATISFACTION IN IRAN.
PH.D. DISSERTATION, UNIVERSITY OF UTAH, 1976.

        THE PURPOSE OF THIS STUDY WAS TO DETERMINE IF THE
PERSIAN ADAPATION OF ROTTER'S I-E SCALE HAS PSYCHOMETRIC
CHARACTERISTICS CAMPARABLE TO THE ORIGNAL, AND TO DETERMINE
THE RELATIONSHIP BETWEEN "INTERNALITY" AS MEASURED BY THE
PERSIAN I-E SCALE AND JOB SATISFACTION. THE HYPOTHESIS OF
SIMILARITY BETWEEN THE PERSIAN I-E SCALE AND THE ORIGNAL
SCALE WAS SUPPORTED. LOCUS OF CONTROL WAS FOUND TO BE
SIGNIFICANTLY RELATED TO JOB SATISFACTION ONLY IN THE
LARGEST SUB-SAMPLE. THUS, THE HYPOTHESIZED RELATIONSHIP WAS
ONLY PARTIALLY SUPPORTED.

M0852   DREHER, GEORGE FREDERICK.
DETERMINANTS OF PAY SATISFACTION: A DISCREPANCY MODEL

M0852 EVALUATION.
PH.D. DISSERTATION, UNIVERSITY OF HOUSTON, 1977.
LAWLER'S MODEL OF PAY SATISFACTION WAS EVALUATED
USING A MULTIPLE REGRESSION APPROACH TO STATISTICALLY
CONTROL THE EFFECTS OF THE VARIABLE MEASURED. COMPARATIVE
PAY, EQUITY, ADVANCEMENT, BENEFITS, EMPLOYEE GENDER, AND
SELFRATINGS ON PERFORMANCE WERE CONSISTENTLY CORRELATED WITH
THE MEASURES OF PAY SATISFACTION, AND THE CORRELATIONS
SUPPORTED LAWLER'S PREDICTIONS CONCERNING SELF.

M0853 FOURNIER, BRUCE ARTHUR.
THE RELATIONSHIP OF JOB SATISFACTION MEASURES TO SELF-REPORT
AND OBJECTIVE CRITERIA MEASURES AND THE EFFECT OF
MODERATOR VARIABLES FOR CANADIAN MILITARY PERSONNEL.
PH.D. DISSERTATION, YORK UNIVERSTIY, 1976.

THE RELATIONSHIP OF JOB SATISFACTION MEASURES TO SELF
REPORT AND OBJECTIVE CRITERIA MEASURES WAS THE SUBJECT OF
THIS STUDY. IN ADDITION, SEVERAL MODERATOR VARIABLES WERE
EXAMINED. A FACTOR ANALYSIS OF 17 JOB SATISFACTION ITEMS
YIELDED FOUR FACTORS: SELF IMAGE, INTERPERSONAL RELATIONS
AND INTRINSIC AND EXTRINSIC JOB SATISFACTION.

M0854 HANSER, LAWRENCE MORLEY.
EMPLOYEE INFORMATION ENVIRONMENTS AND JOB SATISFACTION: A
CLOSER LOOK.
PH.D. DISSERTATION, IOWA STATE UNIVERSITY, 1977

SEVERAL SOURCES OF INFORMATION WERE INVESTIGATED IN AN
ATTEMPT TO CONFIRM THE VALIDITY OF GRELLER'S AND HEROLD'S
VIEW ON THE INFLUENCE OF THE WORK ENVIRONMENT ON JOB
SATISFACTION AND PERFORMANCE. THE INFORMATION SOURCES
STUDIED WERE: THE FORMAL ORGANIZATION, CO-WORKERS,
SUPERVISOR, TASK, AND PERSONAL FEELINGS. THE RESULTS
INDICATED THAT SOURCES DO NOT PROVIDE EQUAL AMOUNTS OF
REFERENT AND APPRAISAL INFORMATION TO EMPLOYEES, AND THAT
THESE SOURCES PROVIDE DIFFERENT AMOUNTS OF INFORMATION TO
THE DIFFERENT OCCUPATIONAL CLASSES.

M0856 HOPKINS, PHYLLIS FREDERICKA.
THE RELATIVE VALIDITIES OF TRADITIONALLY USED JOB
SATISFACTION AND ORGANIZATIONAL COMMITMENT MEASURES VERSUS
WOMEN-SPECIFIC MEASURES FOR THE PREDICTION OF FEMALE TENURE
IN A MALE DOMINATED JOB.
PH.D. DISSERTATION, WAYNE STATE UNIVERSITY, 1976.

TWO FACTORS WERE INVESTIGATED IN THIS RESEARCH: (1)
THE RELATIVE VALIDITIES OF TRADITIONAL AND WOMEN-SPECIFIC
MEASURES FOR THE PREDICTION OF FEMALE TENURE IN A MALE
DOMINATED JOB, AND (2) THE EXISTENCE OF DIFFERENTIAL
VALIDITY IN THE PREDICTION OF TENURE FROM THE TRADITIONAL
MEASURES FOR BOTH MEN AND WOMEN. THE RESULTS OF THIS
RESEARCH INDICATE THAT THESE SAMPLES OF MEN AND WOMEN
SHOULD BE TREATED AS COMING FROM SEPARATE POPULATIONS AND
SHOULD, THEREFORE, REQUIRE DIFFERENT PREDICTORS AND
REGRESSION EQUATIONS IN ORDER TO AVOID BIAS.

M0858 KNEELAND, STEVEN JOHN.

M0858   INSTRUMENTALITY THEORY PREDICTIONS OF EXPERIENCED AND
        ANTICIPATED JOB SATISFACTION.
        PH.D. DISSERTATION, YORK UNIVERSITY, 1976

                THE CONCURRENT VALIDITY OF THE INSTRUMENTALITY THEORY
        OF JOB SATISFACTION WAS TESTED IN THIS STUDY. THE NINE
        PREVIOUS VALIDATION STUDIES IN THIS AREA WERE SHOWN TO BE
        INADEQUATE TESTS OF THE THEORETICAL MODEL BECAUSE OF
        CERTAIN METHODOLOGICAL SHORTCOMINGS. THIS STUDY CHECKS
        THESE SHORTCOMINGS AND EXAMINES THE USEFULNESS AND VALIDITY
        OF A NUMBER OF SPECIFIC ASSUMPTIONS INHERENT IN THE
        INSTRUMENTALITY MODEL'S INTERNAL STRUCTURE.

M0859   LAZER, ROBERT IRA.
        PERCEIVED LEADER BEHAVIOR AND EMPLOYEE SATISFACTION WITH
        SUPERVISION AND THE JOB: THE EFFECTS OF REWARD AND
        PUNISHMENT.
        PH.D. DISSERTAION, CASE WESTERN RESERVE UNIVERSITY, 1977.

                THIS STUDY TESTED THE HYPOTHESIS THAT THE SUBORDINATES
        WHO DESCRIBE THEIR LEADER'S BEHAVIOR AS BEING POSITIVELY
        REINFORCING WOULD REPORT GREATER SATISFACTION WITH
        SUPERVISION AND THE JOB. THE OPPOSITE RELATIONSHIP WAS
        PREDICTED FOR LEADER BEHAVIOR DESCRIBED AS BEING PUNISHING.
        THIS HYPOTHESIS WAS NOT SUPPORTED.

M0860   LOPEZ, ELSA MARGARITA.
        JOB SATISFACTION AND NEED IMPORTANCE: RACE, SEX, AND
        OCCUPATIONAL GROUP.
        PH.D. DISSERTATION, STEVENS INSTITUTE OF TECHNOLOGY, 1977.

                THE OBJECTIVES OF THIS STUDY WERE: (1) TO INVESTIGATE
        THE JOB SATISFACTION OF BLACK AND WHITE EMPLOYEES WITHIN
        THE THEORETICAL FRAMEWORK OF THE "NEED FULFILLMENT" AND
        "REFERNCE GROUP" MODELS OF JOB SATISFACTION, AND (2) TO
        STUDY THE IMPORTANT EFFECTS OF RACE, OCCUPATIONAL, AND SEX
        DIFFERENCES ON WORK OUTCOMES. THE RELATIONSHIP BETWEEN
        OVERALL JOB SATISFACTION AND NEED FULFILLMENT DISCREPANCY
        WAS SUPPORTED BY THE RESULTS OF THIS STUDY. THIS
        RELATIONSHIP WAS FOUND TO BE GREATER FOR BLACKS THAN
        WHITES, AND GREATER FOR HIGH SELF-ESTEEM THAN FOR LOW
        SELF-ESTEEM EMPLOYEES.

M0863   MOUNT, MICHAEL KELLY.
        PERSON-ENVIRONMENT CONGRUENCE, EMPLOYEE JOB SATISFACTION,
        AND TENURE: A TEST OF HOLLAND'S THEORY.
        PH.D. DISSERTATION, IOWA STATE UNIVERSITY, 1977.

                THE RELATIONSHIP OF HOLLAND'S THEORY OF
        PERSON-ENVIRONMENT CONGRUENCE TO JOB SATISFACTION AS
        MEASURED BY THE JOB DESCRIPTIVE INDEX AND TENURE WAS THE
        SUBJECT OF THIS RESEARCH. PARTIAL SUPPORT FOR HOLLAND'S
        PERSON-ENVIRONMENT CONGRUENCE HYPOTHESIS WAS PROVIDED BY
        THE RESULTS. CONGRUENT SUBJECTS WERE FOUND TO BE
        SIGNIFICANTLY MORE SATISFIED WITH MOST ASPECTS OF THEIR
        WORK THAN INCONGRUENT SUBJECTS.

M0864   NEWTON, RUSSEL MARION.

M0864 SUPERVISOR EXPECTATIONS AND BEHAVIOR: EFFECTS OF
CONSISTENT-INCONSISTENT SUPERVISORY PAIRINGS ON SUPERVISEE
SATISFACTION WITH SUPERVISION, PERCEPTIONS OF SUPERVISORY
RELATIONSHIPS AND RATED COUNSELOR COMPETENCY.
PH.D. DISSERTATION, UNIVERSITY OF MISSOURI, 1976.

THE TWO MAJOR OBJECTS OF THIS STUDY WERE: (1) THE
EXPLORATION OF BEHAVIORAL CORRELATES OF SUPERVISORS'
DIDACTIC OR EXPERIENTIAL EXPECTATIONS ABOUT THEIR
SUPERVISORY BEHAVIOR, OVER TIME AND IN A NATURALISTIC
SETTING, AND (2) AN EXAMINATION OF THE EFFECTS ON THE
SUPERVISEE PAIRINGS ON THE BASIS OF DIDACTIC OR
EXPERIENTIAL EXPECTATION ABOUT SUPERVISION. SEVERAL
RELATIONSHIPS WERE SUMMARIZED IN THE RESULTS.

M0868 SHUBKAGEL, BETTY LOU.
THE RELATIONSHIPS BETWEEN THE TASK-HUMAN RELATIONS
MOTIVATIONAL STRUCTURES OF INDIVIDUALS IN SMALL WORK GROUPS
AND THEIR SATISFACTION WITH CO-WORKERS AND IMMEDIATE
SUPERVISION.
PH.D. DISSERTATION, UNIVERSITY OF MARYLAND, 1976.

THE PURPOSE OF THIS STUDY WAS TO TEST THE HYPOTHESIS
THAT SIMILARITY OF TASK-HUMAN RELATIONS MOTIVATIONAL
STRUCTURES IN INDIVIDUALS WILL LEAD TO MORE SATISFACTION
WITH EACH OTHER IN SMALL WORK GROUPS. THE HYPOTHESIS WAS
ONLY PARTIALLY SUPPORTED.

M0869 SHREY, DONALD EUGENE.
VOCATIONAL SATISFACTION, SUCCESS AND STABILITY: A
COMPARATIVE STUDY OF MALE AND FEMALE NON-PROFESSIONAL
WORKERS.
PH.D. DISSERTATION, SYRACUSE UNIVERSITY, 1976.

THE VOCATIONAL SATISFACTION, VOCATIONAL SUCCESS, AND
VOCATIONAL STABILITY OF NON-PROFESSIONAL FEMALE AND MALE
WORKERS WAS THE SUBJECT OF THIS STUDY. THE RESULTS OF THIS
STUDY YIELDED SEVERAL RELATIONSHIPS.

M0872 SNOW, WILLIAM E.
PREDICTING THE PERFORMANCE OF JUNIOR ACHIEVEMENT ACCORDING
TO THE LEADERSHIP STYLE OF TWO LEVELS OF MANAGEMENT: A FIELD
STUDY OF THE CONTINGENCY MODEL.
PH.D. DISSERTATION, CASE WESTERN RESERVE UNIVERSITY, 1975.

AN ATTEMPT WAS MADE TO PREDICT THE PERFORMANCE OF
JUNIOR ACHIEVEMENT COMPANIES ON THE BASIS OF FIEDLER'S
CONTINGENCY MODEL. THE RESULTING FAILURE IN PREDICIVE
VALIDITY WAS ATTRIBUTED TO INADEQUACIES IN CLASSIFIABLE
FIELD STUDIES RATHER THAN IN FIEDLER'S ORIGINAL MODEL.

M0875 TEMKIN, SUZANNE MARA.
PERSONALITY TRAITS, WORK FUNCTIONS, AND VOCATIONAL
SATISFACTION OF PHYSICIANS IN THREE MEDICAL SPECIALTIES.
PH.D. DISSERTATION, COLUMBIA UNIVERSITY, 1975.

THIS RESEARCH TESTS THE HYPOTHESIS THAT DIFFERENCES IN
EIGHT PRESELECTED PSYCHOLOGICAL TRAITS WOULD BE OBSERVED

M0875   AMONG PHYSICIANS BASED ON THE SIMILARITY OF THEIR WORK
        FUNCTIONS AND MEMBERSHIP IN CERTAIN GROUPS. NO RELATIONSHIP
        SHIP WAS FOUND BETWEEN PERSONALITY TRAITS AND SPECIALTY.
        HOWEVER, A SIGNIFICANT RELATIONSHIP WAS FOUND BETWEEN
        PERSONALITY TRAITS AND CAREER SATISFACTION.

M0876   THOMPSON, ANTHONY PETER.
        SUBJECTIVE EXPECTATIONS AND JOB FACET PREDICTABILITY IN JOB
        SATISFACTION.
        PH.D. DISSERTATION, UNIVERSITY OF WESTERN ONTARIO, 1975.

            SUBJECTIVE EXPECTATION AND JOB FACET PREDICTABILITY
        WERE THE VARIABLES UNDER INVESTIGATION IN THIS STUDY.
        SUBJECTIVE EXPECTATION REFERRED TO AND INDIVIDUAL'S ESTIMATE
        OF THE PROBABILITY ASSOCIATED WITH A PARTICULAR LEVEL OF
        REWARD, AND JOB FACET PREDICTABILITY DEALT WITH THE CLARITY
        OF REWARD CONTINGENCIES. THE RESULTS OF SEVERAL
        EXPERIMENTAL INVESTIGATIONS ARE PROVIDED.

M0877   ZIEGLER, SHIRLEY MELAT.
        ANDROGYNY IN NURSING: NURSE ROLE EXPECTATION, SATISFACTION,
        ACADEMIC ACHIEVEMENT, AND SELF-ACTUALIZATION IM MALE AND
        FEMALE STUDENTS.
        PH.D. DISSERTATION, UNIVERSITY OF TEXAS, 1977.

            THE PURPOSE OF THIS INVESTIGATION WAS TO DETERMINE IF
        DIFFERENCES EXIST IN NURSE ROLE EXPECTATION, SATISFACTION
        WITH OCCUPATIONAL CHOICE, ACADEMIC ACHIEVEMENT, AND
        SELF-ACTUALIZATION WHICH ARE ASSOCIATED WITH ANDROGYNY AND
        SEX ROLE ORIENTATIONS. SEX ROLE ORIENTATION WAS FOUND TO
        BE ASSOCIATED WITH NURSE ROLE EXPECTATION ONLY.

M0878   WHITE, SAMMY EUGENE.
        AN EXPERIMENTAL STUDY OF THE EFFECTS OF GOAL SETTING,
        EVALUATION APPREHENSION, AND SOCIAL CUES ON TASK PERFORMANCE
        AND JOB SATISFACTION.
        PH.D. DISSERTATION, UNIVERSITY OF WASHINGTON, 1976.

            THE EFFECTS OF GOAL SETTING, EVALUATION APPREHENSION,
        AND SOCIAL CUES ON TASK PERFORMANCE AND JOB SATISFACTION IN
        A SIMULATED ORGANIZATIONAL SETTING WERE THE SUBJECT OF THIS
        RESEARCH. PRODUCTIVITY WAS FOUND TO BE MAXIMALLY INCREASED
        WHEN SPECIFIC GOALS ARE ASSIGNED, THE INDIVIDUAL EXPERIENCES
        HIGH EVALUATION APPREHENSION, AND THE WORK ENVIRONMENT
        CONTAINS POSITIVE SOCIAL CUES ABOUT THE JOB.

M0879   ARVEY, RICHARD D.   GROSS, RONALD H.
        SATISFACTION IN THE HOMEMAKER JOB.
        JOURNAL OF VOCATIONAL BEHAVIOR 10 (FEBRUARY 1977): 13-24.

            FIFTY-FIVE FEMALE FULLTIME HOMEMAKERS AND 63 FEMALE
        FULL OR PART-TIME OUTSIDE JOB HOLDERS COMPLETED A
        QUESTIONNAIRE WHICH ASSESSED THEIR SATISFACTION OVERALL AND
        THEIR SATISFACTION WITH SPECIFIC ASPECTS OF THE HOMEMAKER
        WORK ROLE OR JOB.

M0880   AUSTIN, MICHAEL J.   JACKSON, ERWIN.
        OCCUPATIONAL MENTAL HEALTH AND THE HUMAN SERVICES: A REVIEW.

M0880   HEALTH AND SOCIAL WORK 2 (FEBRUARY 1977):   92-118.
        ARGUES THAT THE DELIVERY OF MENTAL HEALTH SERVICES IN
INDUSTRY REQUIRES A COMPREHENSIVE VIEW OF THE WORKER AS
CLIENT AND MUST ADDRESS THE ISSUE OF OCCUPATIONAL MENTAL
HEALTH WITHIN THE LARGER CONTEXT OF JOB SATISFACTION AND
EXISTING OCCUPATIONAL AND UNION MENTAL HEALTH PROGRAMS.
IT IS CONCLUDED THAT EFFECTIVE INTERVENTION MUST TAKE INTO
ACCOUNT BOTH INDIVIDUAL AND ENVIRONMENTAL CAUSES OF
EMOTIONAL DISABILITY.

M0881   ENGELEN-KEFER, U.
        HUMANISATION OF WORK IN THE FEDERAL REPUBLIC OF GERMANY:
        A LABOR-ORIENTED APPROACH.
        INTERNATIONAL LABOR REVIEW 113 (MARCH 1976):   227-41.

        THE MAIN AIM OF THE ARTICLE WAS TO SHOW THAT IN THE
LIFE OF THE WORKER AND HIS FAMILY, WORK IS NOT ONLY A MEANS
TO SATISFYING MATERIAL NEEDS. THOUGH INCOME IS STILL A VERY
IMPORTANT FACTOR, SECURITY OF EMPLOYMENT AND MORE HUMANE
WORKING CONDITIONS ARE TAKING ON INCREASING SIGNIFICANCE.

M0882   EVERLY, GEORGE S.   JALCIONE, R. L.
        PERCEIVED DIMENSIONS OF JOB SATISFACTION FOR STAFF
        REGISTERED NURSES.
        NURSING RESEARCH 25 (SEPTEMBER-OCTOBER 1976):   346-48.

        TO MEASURE THE IMPORTANCE OF DIMENSIONS OF JOB
SATISFACTION, 144 FEMALES REGISTERED STAFF NURSES IN FOUR
CITY HOSPITALS WERE GIVEN AN 18-ITEM LIKERT-TYPE INSTRUMENT.
RESULTS INDICATE THAT THE TRADITIONAL INTRINSIC/EXTRINSIC
DICHOTOMY WHICH EXISTS IN ELEMENTS OF JOB SATISFACTION DID
NOT APPLY. THE STUDY IMPLIES THAT PREVIOUS CONSIDERATIONS
IN JOB SATISFACTION FOR THE PROFESSIONAL MAY NEED TO BE
EXAMINED IN TERMS BEYOND THE TRADITIONAL INTRINSIC/EXTRINSIC
DICHOTOMY.

M0883   FOLKINS, CARLYLE.   O'REILLY, C. A.
        ROBERTS, K. H.   MILLER, S.
        PHYSICAL ENVIRONMENT AND JOB SATISFACTION IN A COMMUNITY
        MENTAL HEALTH CENTER.
        COMMUNITY MENTAL HEALTH JOURNAL 13 (SPRING 1977):   24-30.

        RELOCATION OF PROFESSIONAL STAFF IN A COMMUNITY MENTAL
HEALTH CENTER PROVIDED A SETTING FOR EVALUATING THE EFFECTS
OF PHYSICAL ENVIRONMENT ON JOB SATISFACTION. RELOCATED
STAFF REPORTED SIGNIFICANT INCREASE IN SATISFACTION WITH
PHYSICAL SURROUNDINGS AS COMPARED TO STAFF THAT DID NOT
MOVE. FURTHERMORE, SATISFACTION WITH PHYSICAL SURROUNDINGS
HAD SOME IMPACT ON OVERALL SATISFACTION RATINGS. IT IS
CONCLUDED THAT PHYSICAL SURROUNDINGS IN A COMMUNITY MENTAL
HEALTH CENTER MAY BE A MEDIATING VARIABLE FOR STAFF MORALE
AND EFFECTIVENESS.

M0885   GORDON, M.E.   ARVEY, RICHARD D.
        RELATIONSHIP BETWEEN EDUCATION AND SATISFACTION WITH JOB
        CONTENT.
        ACADEMY OF MANAGEMENT JOURNAL 18 (DECEMBER 1975):   888-92.

THE STUDY EXAMINES THE PUBLICIZED PROPOSITION THAT
BETTER EDUCATED WORKERS WILL BE LESS SATISFIED WITH THE
CONTENT OF THEIR JOBS THAN WILL LESS EDUCATED WORKERS.

M0886   HAZER, JOHN T.
        JOB SATISFACTION: A POSSIBLE INTEGRATION OF TWO THEORIES.
        TRAINING AND DEVELOPMENT JOURNAL 30 (JULY 1976):   12-14.

            F. HERZBERG'S THEORY THAT JOB SATISFACTION AND
        DISSATISFACTION ARE VIEWED AS TWO SEPARATE AND PARALLEL
        CONTINUA, RATHER THAN AS THE ENDS OF THE SAME CONTINUUM,
        EVOLVED BECAUSE THE RESEARCH METHOD WAS TO ASK WORKERS TO
        DESCRIBE EXTREME CASES OF SATISFACTION OR DISSATISFACTION.
        TION. SUPPORTERS OF ALTERNATE THEORY HAVE USED METHODS
        GEARED TO THE MIDDLE RANGE OF SATISFACTION OR TO CURRENT JOB
        FEELINGS THAT ARE -- USUALLY EXTREME. NEITHER THEORY MAY BE
        UNIVERSAL; TOGETHER THEY MAY COVER THE ENTIRE RANGE OF JOB
        SATISFACTION AND PHENOMENA.

M0887   LATHAM, GARY P.   YUKL, GARY A.
        EFFECTS OF ASSIGNED AND PARTICIPATIVE GOAL SETTING ON
        PERFORMANCE AND JOB SATISFACTION.
        JOURNAL OF APPLIED PSYCHOLOGY 61 (APRIL 1976):   166-71.

            THE RESULTS OF AN EVALUATION DONE ON THE JOB PERFOR-
        MANCE OF 41 FEMALE TYPISTS UNDER PARTICIPATIVE OR ASSIGNED
        GOAL SETTING CONDITIONS OVER A TEN-WEEK PERIOD.

M0888   MAJUMDER, RANJIT.   MACDONALD, A.P.   GREEVER, KATHRYN.
        A STUDY OF REHABILITATION COUNSELORS: LOCUS OF CONTROL AND
        ATTITUDES TOWARD THE POOR.
        JOURNAL OF COUNSELING PSYCHOLOGY 24 (MARCH 1977):   137-41.

            STUDIED THE INTERRELATIONSHIPS AMONG LOCUS OF CONTROL,
        ATTITUDES TOWARD THE POOR, ATTITUDES TOWARD THE SUPERVISOR,
        JOB SATISFACTION, AND THE PERFORMANCE RATINGS OF 90
        PRACTICING REHABILITATION COUNSELORS. IMPLICATIONS OF THE
        FINDINGS ARE DISCUSSED IN THE CONTEXT OF CLIENT COUNSELOR
        RELATIONSHIPS AND OF THE CONSEQUENCE THAT THESE DATA MAY BE
        IN COUNSELOR PRESERVICE AND INSERVICE TRAINING.

M0889   MCMAHON, J. T.
        PARTICIPATIVE AND POWER-EQUALIZED ORGANIZATIONAL SYSTEMS:
        AN EMPIRICAL INVESTIGATION AND THEORETICAL INTEGRATION.
        HUMAN RELATIONS 29 (MARCH 1976):   203-14.

            TESTED THE PARTICIPATION AND POWER-EQUALIZATION
        HYPOTHESES, USING ATTITUDE DATA FROM 3 LEVELS OF MANAGEMENT
        IN TWELVE PLANTS OF A LARGE FIRM. RESULTS SUGGEST THE
        FRUITFULNESS OF A THEORETICAL INTEGRATION OF THE TWO MODELS.

M0890   NEWSTROM, JOHN W.   REIF, WILLIAM E.   MONCZKA, ROBERT M.
        MOTIVATING THE PUBLIC EMPLOYEE: FACT VS. FICTION.
        PUBLIC PERSONNEL MANAGEMENT 5 (JANUARY-FEBRUARY 1976):
        67-72.

            SURVEY CONDUCTED TO EXAMINE SOME COMMON STEREOTYPES
        ABOUT THE NATURE OF GOVERNMENT EMPLOYEES AS COMPARED TO

M0890 PRIVATE EMPLOYEES. SEVERAL CONCLUSIONS WERE DRAWN. THE
       NEED FOR PERSONNEL MANAGEMENT TO CONSTANTLY REEXAMINE BASIC
       ASSUMPTIONS ABOUT WHY EMPLOYEES WORK IS STRESSED.

M0891 ORPEN, C.
       THE EFFECT OF URBANIZATION ON SOURCES OF JOB SATISFACTION
       AMONG BLACK SUPERVISORS IN SOUTH AFRICA.
       JOURNAL OF SOCIAL PSYCHOLOGY 101 (APRIL 1977): 307-8.

           TO TEST THE VIEW THAT "URBAN"AND "RURAL" WORKERS IN THE
       SAME JOB DERIVE SATISFACTION FROM DIFFERENT ASPECTS OF THE
       WORK SITUATION, 42 BLACK SUPERVISORS WERE DIVIDED INTO URBAN
       AND RURAL GROUPS IN TERMS OF THE NUMBER OF YEARS SPENT IN
       A CITY OR TOWN. AMONG THE URBAN GROUP, THE CORRELATION
       BETWEEN SATISFACTION WITH JOB CONTENT FACTORS AND OVERALL
       JOB SATISFACTION, AS MEASURED BY THE BRAYFIELD-ROTHE INDEX,
       WAS SIGNIFICANTLY GREATER THAN THAT BETWEEN CONTEXT FACTORS
       AND OVERALL JOB SATISFACTION. AMONG THE RURAL GROUP, THE
       POSITION WAS REVERSED.

M0892 REINHARTH, L.   WAHBA, MAHMOUD A.
       A TEST OF ALTERNATIVE MODELS OF EXPECTANCY THEORY.
       HUMAN RELATIONS 29 (MARCH 1976): 257-72.

           THE INCONSISTENT FINDINGS OF PRIOR STUDIES IN EXPECTANCY
       THEORY ARE EXAMINED WITH REFERENCE TO VARIOUS LOGICAL
       AND METHODOLOGICAL ISSUES. A COMPREHENSIVE TEST OF THE
       THEORY IS PROPOSED IN BROADENING THE BASE OF THE BEHAVIORAL
       ALTERNATIVES AVAILABLE TO THE INDIVIDUAL IN THE WORK
       SOLUTION. A METHOD IS SUGGESTED FOR INCORPORATING NEGATIVE
       AS WELL AS POSITIVE ACTS.

M0893 SCHNEIDER, BENJAMIN.
       ORGANIZATIONAL CLIMATES: AN ESSAY.
       PERSONNEL PSYCHOLOGY 28 (WINTER 1975): 447-79.

           EXAMINES SOME LOGICAL AND CONCEPTUAL DISTINCTIONS
       BETWEEN JOB SATISFACTION AND ORGANIZATIONAL CLIMATE. ALSO
       DISCUSSED ARE ISSUES CONCERNING CONCEPTUALIZATION OF CLIMATE
       AS AN INDEPENDENT, DEPENDENT, AND INTERVENING VARIABLE. IT
       IS CONCLUDED THAT CLIMATE IS DIFFERENT FROM JOB
       SATISFACTION.

M0895 SCHULER, RANDALL S.
       ROLE PERCEPTIONS, SATISFACTION AND PERFORMANCE MODERATED BY
       ORGANIZATION LEVEL AND PARTICIPATION IN DECISION MAKING.
       ACADEMY OF MANAGEMENT JOURNAL 20 (MARCH 1977): 159-65.

           A STUDY CONDUCTED AND RESULTS OF MULTIPLE-LINEAR
       REGRESSION ANALYSIS SHOW THAT ROLE PERCEPTIONS,
       PARTICIPATION, AND ORGANIZATION LEVELS EXPLAINED A SMALLER
       AMOUNT OF THE VARIANCE IN PERFORMANCE AND THEN ONLY AT THE
       LOWER ORGANIZATION LEVELS THAN IN SATISFACTION WITH WORK
       ACROSS ALL ORGANIZATION LEVELS.

M0896 SIMS, HENRY P.   SZILAGYI, A. D.
       JOB CHARACTERISTICS RELATIONSHIPS: INDIVIDUAL AND
       STRUCTURAL MODERATORS.

M0896   ORGANIZATIONAL BEHAVIOR AND HUMAN PERFORMANCE 17
         (DECEMBER 1976):   211-30.
                INDICATED THE QUESTION OF HOW CHARACTERISTICS OF THE
         INDIVIDUAL MODERATE THE RELATIONSHIPS BETWEEN PERCEPTIONS
         OF JOB CHARACTERISTICS AND EMPLOYEE EXPECTANCIES,
         SATISFACTION, AND PERFORMANCE.

M0897   SPIKE, ROBERTA D.
         CLIENT SELF-SELECTION OF TESTS AND WORK SAMPLES IN
         VOCATIONAL EVALUATION.
         VOCATIONAL EVALUATION AND WORK ADJUSTMENT BULLETIN 9
         (DECEMBER 1976):   34-38.

                PERMITTED NINE EXPERIMENTAL REHABILITATION CLIENTS TO
         CHOOSE TESTS AND WORK SAMPLES USED IN A TEN-DAY EVALUATION
         PROGRAM, AND ASSIGN TEN CONTROL SS, ENTERING THE PROGRAM IN
         ALTERNATE WEEKS, TO TESTS. NO DIFFERENCE APPEARED IN THE
         EXTENT TO WHICH EVALUATION WAS FOUND HELPFUL, BUT THE
         EXPERIMENTAL GROUP WHO SELECTED THE TESTS THEMSELVES
         EXPRESSED HIGHER EXPECTATIONS OF JOB SATISFACTION.

M0899   WIENER, YOASH   GECHMAN, ARTHUR S.
         COMMITMENT: A BEHAVIORAL APPROACH TO JOB INVOLVEMENT.
         JOURNAL OF VOCATIONAL BEHAVIOR 10 (FEBRUARY 1977):   47-52.

                THE PRESENT STUDY VIEWED JOB INVOLVEMENT AND COMMITMENT
         AS INTERCHANGEABLE LABELS FOR THE SAME JOB BEHAVIOR. WORK
         COMMITMENT BEHAVIORS WERE DEFINED AS A SPECIAL CLASS OF
         SOCIALLY ACCEPTABLE WORK BEHAVIORS THAT EXCEED FORMAL AND/OR
         NORMATIVE EXPECTATIONS RELEVANT TO WORK. THE MAIN PURPOSE
         OF THIS STUDY WAS THE DEVELOPMENT OF A MEASURE OF WORK
         COMMITMENT BASED ON THIS DEFINITION.

M0900   WILLIAMS, LANNY.   HASKETT, G. T.
         EMPLOYEE ATTITUDES REGARDING VARIOUS CHARACTERISTICS OF JOB
         OPPORTUNITY AND JOB PERFORMANCE ACROSS THREE DIFFERENT WORK
         SHIFTS AT AN INSTITUTION FOR THE RETARDED.
         RESEARCH AND THE RETARDED 3 (APRIL 1976):   113-22.

                SURVEYED THE ATTITUDES REGARDING JOB OPPORTUNITY AND
         JOB PERFORMANCE OF 75 RANDOMLY SELECTED EMPLOYEES ACROSS
         THREE WORK-SHIFTS. RESULTS INDICATE MUCH DISAGREEMENT
         CONCERNING JOB PERFORMANCE, JOB EVALUATION, SUPERVISORY
         STAFF COMMUNICATION, AND PROMOTION ACROSS THE THREE SHIFTS,
         THE MOST SALIENT BEING THAT SATISFACTORY PERFORMANCE OF
         DUTIES MAY STILL NOT BE UNDERSTOOD NOR DEEMED TO BE
         EQUITABLEY EVALUATED ACROSS THE THREE SHIFTS.

M0901   ARNOLD, FREDERICK C.
         AN INVESTIGATION OF EDUCATIONAL ADMINISTRATIVE STYLE AND
         JOB SATISFACTION OF ELEMENTARY SCHOOL PRINCIPALS.
         ED.D. DISSERTATION, AMERICAN UNIVERSITY, 1977.

                THE PROBLEM WAS TO DETERMINE, ANALYZE AND COMPARE THE
         SELF-PERCEIVED ADMINISTRATIVE STYLES OF SELECTED ELEMENTARY
         SCHOOL OFFICIALS MEASURED BY THE EDUCATIONAL ADMINISTRATIVE
         STYLE DIAGNOSIS TEST (EASDT) AND THE JOB SATISFACTION
         (JS) OF THE SAME INDIVIDUALS AS MEASURED BY THE BRAYFIELD &

M0901 ROTHE JOB SATISFACTION INDEX (JSI). THREE SUB-PROBLEMS WERE
DERIVED FROM THE BASIC PROBLEM. SUB-PROBLEM ONE INVOLVED
WITH SIGNIFICANT DIFFERENCES IN MEASURES OF JS BETWEEN
PUBLIC ELEMENTARY SCHOOL PRINCIPALS WHOSE SELF-PERCEIVED
DOMINANT ADMINISTRATIVE STYLES (DAS), BASED ON THE 3-D MODEL
MODEL OF EDUCATIONAL ADMINISTRATIVE EFFECTIVENESS, ARE
EFFECTIVE AND THOSE WHOSE SELF-PERCEIVED DAS ARE INEFFECTIVE
SUBPROBLEM TWO CONCERNED RELATIONSHIPS OF SELF-PERCEIVED
TASK ORIENTATION(TO) AND SELF-PERCEIVED RELATIONSHIPS
ORIENTATION (RO) USED BY PUBLIC ELEMENTARY SCHOOL PRINCIPALS
WITH MEASURES OF JS OF THE PRINCIPALS. ALSO, SUB-PROBLEM
TWO WAS CONCERNED WITH DIFFERENCES IN THE RELATIONSHIP OF TO
TO JS AND THE RELATIONSHIP OF RO TO JS. SUB-PROBLEM THREE
DEALT WITH THE RELATIONSHIP BETWEEN SELF-PERCEIVED
EFFECTIVENESS (E) OF PUBLIC ELEMENTARY SCHOOL PRINCIPALS
AND MEASURES OF SELF-PERCEIVED JS.
CONCLUSIONS:
        1. JOB SATISFACTION (JS) OF SELECTED PUBLIC ELEMENTARY
SCHOOL PRINCIPALS IS SIGNIFICANTLY HIGHER WHEN EFFECTIVE
SELF-PERCEIVED DOMINANT ADMINISTRATIVE STYLES (DAS) ARE
UTILIZED THAN WHEN INEFFECTIVE DAS ARE USED REGARDLESS OF
WHETHER THE PRINCIPALS ARE USING EITHER A TO OR RO BEHAVIOR.
2. WHEN THE STYLE PROFILE OF SELECTED PUBLIC ELEMENTARY
SCHOOL PRINCIPALS IS FLAT (NO DAS) THE PRINCIPALS ARE
SIGNIFICANTLY MORE JOB-SATISFIED THAN PRINCIPALS WITH
EFFECTIVE DAS. 3. THE AMOUNT OF SELF-PERCEIVED TO OR RO
USED BY SELECTED PUBLIC ELEMENTARY SCHOOL PRINCIPALS IS NOT
A PREDICTOR OF JOB SATISFACTION (JS). 4. THE MEASURE OF
OF PERCEIVED EFFECTIVENESS (E) CAN BE USED AS A PREDICTOR OF
JOB SATISFACTION (JS) FOR SELECTED PUBLIC ELEMENTARY SCHOOL
PRINCIPALS. 5. THE 3-D THEORY OF EDUCATIONAL ADMINISTRATIVE
EFFECTIVENESS IS SUPPORTED AS IS THE VALIDITY OF THE
EASDT AS A RESEARCH INSTRUMENT.

M0902 AUNE, GEORGE A.
A STUDY OF THE JOB SATISFACTION AND JOB PERCEPTION OF
ORGANIZED AND NON-ORGANIZED PUBLIC SCHOOL PRINCIPALS.
PH.D. DISSERTATION, UNIVERSITY OF MICHIGAN, 1977.

        THE PURPOSE OF THIS STUDY WAS TO DETERMINE THE
RELATIONSHIP OF THE JOB SATISFACTION AND JOB PERCEPTION OF
PUBLIC SCHOOL PRINCIPALS WHO ARE MEMBERS OF RECOGNIZED
BARGAINING UNITS COMPARED WITH THE JOB SATISFACTION AND JOB
PERCEPTION OF PUBLIC SCHOOL PRINCIPALS WHO ARE NOT MEMBERS
OF SUCH LOCAL ADMINISTRATIVE BARGAINING UNITS. IMPETUS FOR
THE STUDY CAME FROM THE POSITION THAT SCHOOL PRINCIPALS
IN MICHIGAN FOUND THEMSELVES, AFTER SEVERAL YEARS OF
ORGANIZED COLLECTIVE BARGAINING, BETWEEN UNITS OF TEACHERS
AND THEIR EMPLOYERS, LOCAL BOARDS OF EDUCATION. OFTEN,
PRINCIPALS WERE CAUGHT IN THE MIDDLE OF THESE TWO GROUPS,
HAVING TO ADMINISTER A MASTER AGREEMENT TO WHICH THEY HAD
CONTRIBUTED LITTLE, IF ANY INPUT. SOME PRINCIPAL GROUPS
CHOSE TO ORGANIZE THEIR OWN BARGAINING UNITS, WHILE OTHERS
CHOSE NOT TO: SOME ADOPTED A FORM OF TEAM MANAGEMENT. TO
DETERMINE WHETHER THERE WAS ANY RELATIONSHIP IN THE JOB
SATISFACTION AND PERCEPTION OF ORGANIZED AND NON-ORGANIZED
PRINCIPALS, A SAMPLE OF BOTH GROUPS WAS SELECTED. THE
POPULATION OF THE GROUPS INCLUDED PUBLIC SCHOOL PRINCIPALS

M0902   IN THE METROPOLITAN DETROIT AREA. THE ORGANIZED
        GROUP'S SAMPLE WAS 155; THE NON-ORGANIZED GROUP, 160. IT
        WAS RECOMMENDED THAT PUBLIC SCHOOL PRINCIPALS NEED TO SEEK
        WAYS TO IMPROVE THEIR JOB SATISFACTION AND NEED TO LOOK
        CLOSELY AT WHAT HAS RESULTED WHEN PRINCIPALS HAVE ORGANIZED
        ADMINISTRATIVE BARGAINING UNITS OR HAVE ADOPTED A TEAM
        MANAGEMENT APPROACH TO THEIR SCHOOL ADMINISTRATIONS.

M0903   BAMUNDO, PAUL J.
        THE RELATIONSHIP BETWEEN JOB SATISFACTION AND LIFE
        SATISFACTION: AN EMPIRICAL TEST OF THREE MODELS ON A
        NATIONAL SAMPLE.
        PH.D. DISSERTATION, CITY UNIVERSITY OF NEW YORK, 1977.

            THE PURPOSE OF THIS STUDY WAS TO TEST THREE MODELS
        WHICH HAVE BEEN PROPOSED TO PREDICT THE RELATIONSHIP BETWEEN
        JOB SATISFACTION. THE PREDICTIONS MADE ARE A POSITIVE
        CORRELATION (GENERALIZED MODEL), A NEGATIVE CORRELATION
        (COMPENSATORY MODEL), AND A ZERO CORRELATION (SEGMENTATION
        MODEL). QUESTIONNAIRES WERE SENT TO A NATION-WIDE SAMPLE
        OF 2,200 POTENTIAL SUBJECTS; 911 USABLE QUESTIONNAIRES WERE
        RETURNED. OVERALL JOB SATISFACTION WAS MEASURED, AS WAS
        SATISFACTION WITH SPECIFIC ASPECTS OF THE JOB (SUPERVISION,
        PAY, CO-WORKERS, WORK ITSELF AND PROMOTIONS). THE LIFE
        DOMAIN MEASURES INCLUDED OVERALL SATISFACTION, HAPPINESS,
        MARITAL ADJUSTMENT, HEALTH AND ALCOHOL CONSUMPTION.
        THE HYPOTHESES TESTED AND PERTINENT RESULTS WERE AS FOLLOWS.
        HYPOTHESIS 1 PREDICTED A POSITIVE RELATIONSHIP BETWEEN JOB
        AND LIFE SATISFACTION. THIS HYPOTHESIS RECEIVED CONSISTENT
        SUPPORT ACROSS THE ENTIRE SAMPLE AND WITHIN SUBGROUPS OF THE
        SAMPLE. HYPOTHESIS 1A PREDICTED A STRONGER RELATIONSHIP
        BETWEEN JOB AND LIFE SATISFACTION FOR MEN: THIS WAS FOUND TO
        BE THE CASE. HYPOTHESIS 1B AND 1C PREDICTED AN INCREASE IN
        THE STRENGTH OF THE RELATIONSHIP WITH AGE AND EDUCATION
        RESPECTIVELY; HYPOTHESIS 1B RECEIVED ONLY PARTIAL SUPPORT,
        WHILE HYPOTHESIS 1C WAS STRONGLY SUPPORTED. HYPOTHESIS 1D
        SPECULATED THAT MARRIED PEOPLE WOULD EXHIBIT THE STRONGEST
        JOB AND LIFE RELATIONSHIP; THIS EFFECT WAS CONFIRMED.
        HYPOTHESIS 1E SPECULATED AN INCREASE IN STRENGTH OF THE
        RELATIONSHIPS OF JOB AND LIFE SATISFACTION AS A FUNCTION
        OF INCREASING INCOME; THIS WAS FOUND TO BE THE CASE.
        A STRONG RELATIONSHIP BETWEEN JOB AND LIFE SATISFACTION WAS
        PREDICTED FOR SELF-EMPLOYED PEOPLE (HYPOTHESIS 1F) AND UNION
        MEMBERS (HYPOTHESIS 1G); THE FORMER HYPOTHESIS WAS SUPPORTED
        THE LATTER WAS NOT. INCREASED TENURE WAS EXPECTED TO CAUSE
        AN INCREASE IN THE STRENGTH OF THE RELATIONSHIP BETWEEN JOB
        SATISFACTION AND LIFE SATISFACTION (HYPOTHESIS 1H); A CURVI-
        LINEAR RELATIONSHIP WAS FOUND. HYPOTHESIS 1I PREDICTED AN
        INCREASE IN THE STRENGTH OF THE RELATIONSHIP WITH HIGHER
        JOB LEVELS; THIS HYPOTHESIS WAS SUPPORTED. A COMPARISON
        OF BLUE AND WHITE-COLLAR WORKERS WAS EXPECTED TO SHOW A
        STRONGER RELATIONSHIP FOR THE WHITE-COLLAR GROUP (HYPOTHESIS
        1J); THIS WAS NOT FOUND. FINALLY, HYPOTHESIS 1K PREDICTED
        THAT THE STRENGTH OF THE RELATIONSHIP BETWEEN JOB AND LIFE
        SATISFACTION WOULD INCREASE AS CITY SIZE DECREASED; THIS
        HYPOTHESIS WAS NOT SUPPORTED. THE WEAKEST RELATIONSHIPS
        WERE FOUND AT THE EXTREMES, THAT IS, VERY LARGE AND VERY
        SMALL CITIES.

M0904   BEASLEY, JAMES THOMAS JR.
        SATISFACTION WITH TRAINING AND GENERAL JOB SATISFACTION OF
        AGENCY HOMEMAKERS WORKING WITH THE ELDERLY AND DISABLED.
        D.S.W. DISSERTATION, UNIVERSITY OF DENVER, 1977.

            THE PURPOSE OF THIS STUDY WAS TO EXPLORE SATISFACTION
        WITH JOB PREPARATION AND WITH THE JOB ITSELF AS PERCEIVED
        BY HOMEMAKERS IN A COUNTY DEPARTMENT OF SOCIAL SERVICES.
        JOB PREPARATION WAS CONCEPTUALIZED AS PRE-SERVICE TRAINING
        AND ON-GOING EDUCATION IN THE WORK ENVIRONMENT. SEVEN UNITS
        IN THE PRE-SERVICE TRAINING COURSE RECOMMENDED BY THE
        NATIONAL COUNCIL ON HOMEMAKER-HOME HEALTH AIDES, INC., WERE
        COVERED IN AN AGENCY SATISFACTION QUESTIONNAIRE CONSTRUCTED
        BY THE INVESTIGATOR. THE ON-GOING EDUCATION SECTION
        INCLUDED IN-SERVICE TRAINING, SUPERVISION, CASEWORKER
        CONTACTS, TEAM MEMBERSHIP AND DECISION-MAKING OPPORTUNITIES.
        THE GENERAL JOB SATISFACTION SECTION OF THE MINNESOTA JOB
        SATISFACTION QUESTIONNAIRE WAS ALSO UTILIZED. THE STUDY
        WAS CONDUCTED BY PERSONAL INTERVIEW WITH 62 HOMEMAKERS
        WORKING WITH THE ELDERLY AND DISABLED IN FEBRUARY, 1977.
        THE RESPONSE PATTERN WAS PREDOMINANTLY ONE OF SATISFACTION
        WITH THE JOB, AND, EXCEPT FOR CHORE SERVICE INSTRUCTION,
        WITH THE SELECTED COMPONENTS OF PRE-SERVICE TRAINING.
        HOMEMAKERS WERE ALSO SATISFIED WITH ON-GOING EDUCATION
        OPPORTUNITIES ALTHOUGH TO A SOMEWHAT LESSER EXTENT. SIX
        HYPOTHESES PREDICTING NO DIFFERENCE IN SATISFACTION BETWEEN
        COMPONENTS OF PRE-SERVICE TRAINING OR ON-GOING EDUCATION
        AND GENERAL JOB SATISFACTION WERE ACCEPTED. HOWEVER, A
        SEVENTH HYPOTHESIS WAS REJECTED; GENERAL JOB SATISFACTION
        WAS SIGNIFICANTLY HIGHER THAN SATISFACTION WITH IN-SERVICE
        TRAINING. HOMEMAKERS DESIRED MORE INPUT IN PLANNING FOR
        IN-SERVICE TRAINING, MORE AUTONOMY, AND MORE RESPECT FOR
        THEIR OPINIONS FROM CASEWORKERS.

M0905   BOUCHER, HENRY C.
        JOB SATISFACTION AND EXPECTATIONS OF DISTRIBUTIVE EDUCATION
        GRADUATES.
        PH.D. DISSERTATION, KANSAS STATE UNIVERSITY, 1977.

            THE PURPOSE OF THIS STUDY WAS TO ASSESS THE PERSONAL
        AND SOCIAL ADJUSTMENT NEEDS OF STUDENTS IN DISTRIBUTIVE
        EDUCATION PROGRAMS IN THE STATE OF LOUISIANA.
        METHODS AND PROCEDURES.   A TOTAL OF 150 DISTRIBUTIVE
        EDUCATION GRADUATES WERE SURVEYED IN 26 PARISHES IN THE
        STATE OF LOUISIANA. THE INSTRUMENT IN THIS STUDY WAS
        DEVELOPED ON THE BASIS OF EVALUATIVE INFORMATION NEEDED AS
        IT CONCERNS PERSONAL-SOCIAL ADJUSTMENT OF STUDENTS.
        THE STUDY OF THE PERSONAL-SOCIAL ADJUSTMENT NEEDS OF
        DISTRIBUTIVE EDUCATION GRADUATES TOOK INTO CONSIDERATION THE
        PRESENT JOB OF RESPONDENTS IN LOUISIANA, INCLUDING
        DELINEATION OF DEGREE-CONSQUENCE SATISFACTION.

M0906   BROWN, SIDNEY E.
        JOB SATISFACTION OF GEORGIA SCHOOL SUPERINTENDENTS AND THEIR
        PERCEPTION OF THE LOCAL SCHOOL BOARD PRESIDENT'S LEADER
        BEHAVIOR.
        ED.D DISSERTATION, UNIVERSITY OF GEORGIA, 1977.

THE PURPOSE OF THIS STUDY WAS TO INVESTIGATE THE
RELATIONSHIPS BETWEEN THE JOB SATISFACTION OF GEORGIA SCHOOL
BOARD PRESIDENTS.

THE RESEARCH DESCRIBED IN THIS REPORT REVEALED THERE
WAS A SIGNIFICANT RELATIONSHIP BETWEEN THE JOB SATISFACTION
OF GEORGIA SCHOOL SUPERINTENDENTS AND THE LEADER BEHAVIOR
OF GEORGIA SCHOOL BOARD PRESIDENTS. THE EXTRINSIC
SATISFACTION OF THE SUPERINTENDENT WAS POSITIVELY AND
SIGNIFICANTLY RELATED TO BOTH LEADER BEHAVIOR VARIABLES,
CONSIDERATION AND INITIATING STRUCTURE.

THE HYPOTHESIS OF NO SIGNIFICANT DIFFERENCE BETWEEN THE
BOARD PRESIDENT'S INITIATING STRUCTURE AND CONSIDERATION
LEADER BEHAVIOR AS PERCEIVED BY SUPERINTENDENTS WHEN
CLASSIFIED BY THE DEMOGRAPHIC VARIABLES WAS RETAINED. THE
HYPOTHESIS OF NO SIGNIFICANT DIFFERENCE BETWEEN THE JOB
SATISFACTION OF SUPERINTENDENTS ACCORDING TO CERTAIN TESTED
DEMOGRAPHIC VARIABLES WAS REJECTED.

LENGTH OF SERVICE WAS ONE OF THE MOST CRITICAL FACTORS
IN SUPERINTENDENTS' JOB SATISFACTION SCORES.SUPERINTENDENTS
WITH 11 TO 15 YEARS OF SERVICE HAD THE LOWEST INTRINSIC
AND GENERAL JOB SATISFACTION SCORES. HIGHEST INTRINSIC
AND GENERAL JOB SATISFACTION SCORES WERE INDICATED FOR
THOSE WITH MORE THAN 15 YEARS SERVICE.

METHOD OF SELECTION SIGNIFICANTLY INFLUENCED INTRINSIC
AND GENERAL JOB SATISFACTION OF SUPERINTENDENTS. THE
ELECTED SUPERINTENDENT'S INTRINSIC AND GENERAL SATISFACTION
WERE SIGNIFICANTLY LOWER THAN THOSE SUPERINTENDENTS
WHO WERE APPOINTED.

THE HYPOTHESIS THAT THERE IS NO SIGNIFICANT DIFFERENCE
IN THE LEADER BEHAVIOR SCORES AND DEMOGRAPHIC SCORES IN
PREDICTING SUPERINTENDENT'S JOB SATISFACTION WAS REJECTED.
EXTRINSIC AND GENERAL JOB SATISFACTION OF THE SUPERINTENDENT
WERE PREDICTED WITH THE COMBINATION OF THE BEHAVIOR
VARIABLE. CONSIDERATION AND THE DEMOGRAPHIC VARIABLE,
METHOD OF SELECTION. INTRINSIC SATISFACTION WAS PREDICTED
WITH THE DEMOGRAPHIC VARIABLE, METHOD OF SELECTION.

M0907   BUXTON, BARRY MILLER.
JOB SATISFACTION OF COLLEGE PRESIDENTS.
PH.D. DISSERTATION, UNIVERSITY OF NEBRASKA (LINCOLN), 1977.

THE JOB SATISFACTION OF COLLEGE AND UNIVERSITY
PRESIDENTS IS MEASURED AND ANALYZED BY USE OF A CLOSED-FORM
QUESTIONNAIRE. THE RESULTS INDICATE THAT PRESIDENTS ARE
MODERATELY SATISFIED WITH THEIR WORK. PRESIDENTS OF PRIVATE
INSTITUTIONS ARE SIGNIFICANTLY MORE SATISFIED THAN ARE
PRESIDENTS OF PUBLIC INSTITUTIONS. ADDITIONALLY, AN INVERSE
RELATIONSHIP WAS FOUND TO EXIST BETWEEN INSTITUTIONAL
ENROLLMENT AND PRESIDENTIAL SATISFACTION. INCUMBENTS OF
PH.D. DEGREE GRANTING INSTITUTIONS WERE LESS SATISFIED THAN
PRESIDENTS OF INSTITUTIONS GRANTING ONLY THE BACCALAUREATE
DEGREE. THOSE PRESIDENTS FUNCTIONING WITHIN A "UNIVERSITY
SYSTEM" REPORT LESS SATISFACTION THAN DO THEIR COUNTERPARTS
IN OTHER ORGANIZATIONAL SETTINGS. THE FIVE ITEMS ON THE
QUESTIONNAIRE MOST ASSOCIATED WITH HIGHER SATISFACTION
WERE: (1) PRESIDENTIAL RELATIONSHIPS WITH FELLOW
ADMINISTRATORS; (2) THE EXTENT TO WHICH THEY PARTICIPATE
IN INSTITUTIONAL POLICY FORMATION; (3) PRESIDENTIAL

M0907   RELATIONSHIPS WITH GOVERNING BODIES OR SUPERORDINATES;   (4)
        THE DEGREE TO WHICH PRESIDENTS HAVE ATTAINED PROFESSIONAL
        GOALS; AND (5) THE AMOUNT OF RECOGNITION PRESIDENTS
        RECEIVE FROM LEADERS OF BUSINESS AND INDUSTRY. THE FIVE
        ITEMS FOUND TO BE ASSOCIATED WITH LOW JOB SATISFACTION
        WERE: (1) THE AMOUNT OF TIME TO FULFILL JOB RESPONSIBILITIES;
        (2) THE OPPORTUNITY AVAILABLE FOR TEACHING AND / OR
        RESEARCH; (3) THE OVERALL AIMS AND OBJECTIVES OF HIGHER
        EDUCATION TODAY; (4) CURRENT MEANS OF EVALUATING PRESIDENTS'
        PERFORMANCE; AND (5) PROVISION FOR EMPLOYMENT UPON
        COMPLETION OF THEIR TERMS AS PRESIDENTS.

M0908   CARNEY, ROBERT T.
        A STUDY OF THE RELATIONSHIP AMONG (1) JOB SATISFACTION AND
        (2) TEACHER ATTITUDE.
        ED.D. DISSERTATION, SYRACUSE UNIVERSITY, 1976.

             THE PURPOSE OF THIS STUDY WAS TO DETERMINE IF THERE
        WAS ANY RELATIONSHIP AMONG JOB SATISFACTION, TEACHER
        ATTITUDE, AND INVOLVEMENT IN A TEACHER CENTER. IN ORDER TO
        ANSWER THIS QUESTION, IT WAS NECESSARY TO EXAMINE FIVE
        HYPOTHESES. THESE HYPOTHESES WERE TESTED PRE- AND POST-TEST
        BASIS, AS WELL AS BY USING EXPERIMENTAL AND CONTROL GROUPS.
        THE STUDY EXAMINED CHANGE IN TEACHER JOB SATISFACTION AND
        ALSO IDENTIFIED THOSE SUB-ELEMENTS RELATED TO THE TEACHER
        CENTER THAT CAUSED A CHANGE IN ATTITUDE TOWARD THE CENTER.
             RESULTS FROM THE MINNESOTA SATISFACTION QUESTIONNAIRE
        SHOW THAT TEACHERS INVOLVED IN THE TEACHER CENTER HAD
        A SIGNIFICANTLY LOWER LEVEL OF JOB SATISFACTION ON A PRE
        AND POST-TEST BASIS. WHEN THE EXPERIMENTAL GROUP WAS
        COMPARED TO THE CONTROL GROUP, IT WAS FOUND THERE WAS NOT
        A SIGNIFICANT DIFFERENCE IN THE CHANGE OF LEVEL OF
        BETWEEN THOSE TEACHERS INVOLVED AND THOSE NOT INVOLVED
        IN THE TEACHER CENTER.
             IN EXAMINING THE ATTITUDE LEVELS OF TEACHERS INVOLVED
        IN THE TEACHER CENTER, USING A SEMANTIC DIFFERENTIAL TEST,
        THERE WAS ONLY ONE STATISTICALLY SIGNIFICANT CHANGE IN
        ATTITUDE. THIS WAS THEIR LEARNINGS IN MORE PARAGMATIC
        CONTENT AREAS, SUCH AS: (1) TEXTILES AND CLOTHING, (2) FOODS
        AND NUTRITION, (3) FAMILY RELATIONS AND CHILD DEVELOPMENT
        THEY HAVE MOST DIFFICULTY IN SYNTHESIZING THEIR
        LEARNINGS IN MORE HIGHLY THEORETICAL CONTENT AREAS, SUCH AS:
        (1) HOUSING, HOME FURNISHING, AND EQUIPMENT AND (2) FAMILY
        ECONOMICS AND HOME MANAGEMENT.

M0909   CHEN, WEN-SHYONG.
        THE JOB SATISFACTION OF SCHOOL TEACHERS IN THE REPUBLIC OF
        CHINA AS RELATED TO PERSONAL AND ORGANIZATIONAL
        CHARACTERISTICS.
        PH.D. DISSERTATION, UNIVERSITY OF MINNESOTA, 1977.

             THE PURPOSE OF THIS STUDY WAS TO: (1) DETERMINE WHETHER
        SELECTED FACTORS AFFECT THE JOB SATISFACTION OF TEACHERS;
        (2) TO IDENTIFY WHAT DIFFERENCE IN NEED STRUCTURE EXISTS
        BETWEEN SATISFIED AND DISSATISFIED TEACHERS; (3) IDENTIFY
        THE CHARACTERISTICS OF SATISFIED AND DISSATISFIED TEACHERS
        IN THEIR RESPONSE PATTERNS ON DIFFERENT ASPECTS OF JOB
        SATISFACTION; (4) IDENTIFY WHAT JOB ASPECTS ARE SIGNIFICANT

M0909   AND CONTRIBUTE TO THE JOB SATISFACTION WHEN TEACHERS
         ARE GROUPED ON THE BASIS OF CERTAIN FACTORS; (5) MODIFY A
         VALID INSTRUMENT WHICH CAN BE APPLIED TO THE MEASUREMENT
         OF JOB SATISFACTION FOR SCHOOL TEACHERS IN TAIWAN;
         (6) DETERMINE WHETHER JOB FACTOR PRIMARY DIFFERENCES EXIST
         BETWEEN SUB-GROUPS OF RESPONDENTS FORMED ON THE BASIS OF
         CERTAIN ORGANIZATIONAL INDEPENDENT VARIABLES; (7) DETERMINE
         WHETHER JOB FACTOR PRIMARY DIFFERENCES EXIST BETWEEN
         SUB-GROUPS OF RESPONDENTS FORMED ON THE BASIS OF CERTAIN
         PERSONAL CHARACTERISTICS.

M0910   CLEMENT, ROBERT JOHN.
         A STUDY OF JOB SATISFACTION OF ADMINISTRATORS AT UNITED
         METHODIST RELATED CHURCHES.
         ED.D. DISSERTATION, UNIVERSITY OF KENTUCKY, 1976.

         THE PURPOSE OF THIS STUDY WAS TO DETERMINE IF THERE
         WERE DIFFERENCES BETWEEN THE JOB SATISFACTION OF
         ADMINISTRATORS IN SIX POSITIONS IN COLLEGES RELATED TO THE
         UNITED METHODIST CHURCH, THE LARGEST PROTESTANT
         DENOMINATIONAL SYSTEM IN HIGHER EDUCATION. POSITIONS
         INCLUDED THE CHIEF BUSINESS OFFICER, CHIEF ACADEMIC OFFICER,
         CHIEF STUDENT LIFE OFFICER, THE CHIEF LIBRARIAN, THE
         REGISTRAR, AND THE DIRECTOR OF ADMISSIONS. JOB SATISFACTION
         WAS MEASURED THROUGH THE USE OF THE PORTER NEED SATISFACTION
         QUESTIONNAIRE (PNSQ). IT CONSISTED OF A SERIES OF QUESTIONS
         THAT CALLED FOR RESPONSES ON A SEVEN-POINT NUMERICAL
         SCALE. MEAN SCORES WERE CALCULATED FROM THE RESPONSES
         FOR EACH OF THE FIVE HUMAN NEED CATEGORIES POSTULATED BY
         MASLOW AND ADAPTED BY PORTER. A SIXTH CATEGORY, (BEING IN
         THE KNOW), WAS ALSO MEASURED. A STATISTICAL TEST WAS
         EMPLOYED TO ASCERTAIN AT WHICH ADMINISTRATIVE POSITIONS
         SIGNIFICANT DIFFERENCES EXISTED.

M0911   COLE, DENNIS W.
         AN ANALYSIS OF JOB SATISFACTION AMONG ELEMENTARY, MIDDLE
         LEVEL, AND SENIOR HIGH SCHOOL TEACHERS.
         ED.D. DISSERTATION, UNIVERSITY OF COLORADO AT BOULDER, 1977.

         THE PROBLEM ADDRESSED BY THIS STUDY WAS TO COMPARE THE
         JOB SATISFACTION OF TEACHERS ACROSS THREE LEVELS OF TEACHING
         (ELEMENTARY, MIDDLE, AND SENIOR HIGH) AND FOUR TYPES OF
         COMMUNITIES. IN ADDITION, DIFFERENCES BETWEEN TEACHERS IN
         RELATION TO THE GRADE LEVEL ORGANIZATION UTILIZED BY THE
         SCHOOL EMPLOYING THEM WERE ANALYZED. (SIX CATEGORIES WERE
         CONSIDERED HERE, INCLUDING ELEMENTARY, MIDDLE LEVEL, SENIOR
         HIGH, K THROUGH 8, 7 THROUGH 12, AND K THROUGH 12.

M0912   COUNTS, JOHN ELDRIDGE.
         CAREER COMMITMENT: AN ANALYSIS OF SELECTED INDIVIDUAL, JOB
         AND ORGANIZATIONAL FACTORS AS RELATED TO SATISFACTION AND
         COMMITMENT OF MIDDLE LEVEL ARMY OFFICERS.
         PH.D. DISSERTATION, UNIVERSITY OF TEXAS AT AUSTIN, 1977.

         THE NOTION OF COMMITMENT TO A CAREER, AN ORGANIZATION,
         OR BOTH, HAS BECOME ESPECIALLY IMPORTANT BECAUSE OF THE
         POTENTIALLY CRITICAL CONSEQUENCES IN PERIODS OF INCREASING
         COMPETITION FOR COSTLY PERSONNEL RESOURCES. THIS

M0912 CIRCUMSTANCE IS PARTICULARLY RELEVANT IN PROFESSIONAL CAREER
SETTINGS SUCH AS THE MILITARY WHERE INDIVIDUALS REQUIRE
A LOT OF EDUCATION, TRAINING, AND EXPERIENCE. THEREFORE,
THE PURPOSE OF THIS STUDY WAS TO ANALYZE THE RELATIONSHIPS
AMONG SELECTED INDIVIDUAL, JOB, AND ORGANIZATION WIDE
FACTORS AND CAREER COMMITMENT OF MIDDLE LEVEL ARMY OFFICERS.
    ANALYSIS OF QUESTIONNAIRE RESPONSES OF A SAMPLE OF 352
ARMY CAPTAINS, MAJORS, AND LIEUTENANT COLONELS AND RESULTS
OF INTERVIEWS INDICATED THE MAJOR INFLUENCES ON COMMITMENT
TO BE WIDESPREAD, BUT HIGHLY INTERRELATED. SIGNIFICANT
RELATIONSHIPS WERE FOUND BETWEEN ORGANIZATION WIDE FACTORS
SUCH AS PROMOTION, SCHOOL SELECTION POLICIES, AND COMMITMENT.
PERCEPTIONS OF SATISFACTION ON SELECTED JOB DIMENSIONS,
PARTICULARLY INTRINSIC DIMENSIONS, WERE ALSO SIGNIFICANTLY
RELATED TO COMMITMENT. OF PARTICULAR IMPORTANCE WAS
THE EXTENT TO WHICH INDIVIDUAL BELIEFS ABOUT LOCUS OF
CONTROL WERE RELATED TO PERCEPTION SATISFACTION AND
COMMITMENT.

M0914 EISON, CHARLES L.
THE MEASUREMENT OF SATISFACTION AND DEPARTMENTAL ASSOCIATION
AT WESTERN KENTUCKY UNIVERSITY: TESTING THE HOLLAND
AND BIGLAN MODELS.
ED.D. DISSERTATION, UNIVERSITY OF KENTUCKY, 1976.

    OPERATIONAL AND BEHAVIORAL DIFFERENCES AMONG ACADEMIC
DISCIPLINES HAVE BEEN SUGGESTED BY A NUMBER OF RESEARCHERS
OF HIGHER EDUCATION ORGANIZATIONS. IF JOB SATISFACTION
FACTORS ARE VIEWED AS BEING A FUNCTION OF LEARNING
(PAST GRATIFICATIONS, EXPECTANCIES, FAILURES, INTERESTS,
ETC.) AND INDIVIDUAL APTITUDES (ABILITIES IN THE COGNITIVE
AND VOCATIONAL SPHERES), REINFORCEMENT REQUIREMENTS SPECIFIC
TO A DISCIPLINE MAY BE ONE DIMENSION ON WHICH UNIQUE FACULTY
GROUPS CAN BE DIFFERENTIATED. THE MAJOR QUESTION OF THIS
STUDY IS AS FOLLOWS: ARE THERE SPECIFIC FACULTY GROUPS,
CATEGORIZED BY THE HOLLAND AND BIGLAN MODELS, THAT HAVE
UNIQUE JOB SATISFACTION CONCERNS?
    THE BIGLAN AND HOLLAND MODELS ARRANGED FACULTY INTO
UNIQUE GROUPS THAT HAD SIGNIFICANTLY DIFFERENT FEELINGS
ABOUT JOB SATISFACTION AT WESTERN KENTUCKY UNIVERSITY.
THESE MODELS WERE BETTER IN DOING THIS THAN THE TRADITIONAL
COLLEGE ARRANGEMENT THAT HAD DEVELOPED AT THIS INSTITUTION.
THE JDI MAY BE A VERY APPROPRIATE INSTRUMENT FOR DESCRIBING
ORGANIZATIONAL CLIMATE AND IDENTIFYING PROBLEM AREAS WITHIN
AN INSTITUTION. THE AREA OF JOB SATISFACTION MEASUREMENT
WAS DISCUSSED AS BEING AN IMPORTANT ENDEAVOR IN THE NEAR
FUTURE FOR MANAGEMENT IN HIGHER EDUCATION.

M0915 FARRELL, DANIEL J.
A CAUSAL MODEL OF JOB SATISFACTION.
PH.D. DISSERTATION, UNIVERSITY OF IOWA, 1977.

    THIS THESIS STUDIES THE DETERMINANTS OF JOB SATISFACTION.
JOB SATISFACTION, THE FEELINGS A WORKER HAS ABOUT
HIS JOB, HAS BEEN OF INTEREST TO RESEARCHERS FOR OVER 30
YEARS. JOB SATISFACTION IS RELATED TO --BUT DISTINGUISHABLE
FROM--OTHER SOCIAL-PSYCHOLOGICAL CONCEPTS SUCH AS MORALE,
MOTIVATION, AND ALIENATION AS WELL AS FROM SUCH JOB

M0915   BEHAVIORS AS TURNOVER, TARDINESS, AND ABSENTEEISM.
         THE THESIS CONCLUDES WITH A DISCUSSION OF IMPLICATIONS
FOR FUTURE RESEARCH. MEASUREMENT OF THE INDEPENDENT
VARIABLES IS SUGGESTED AS AN AREA FOR IMPROVEMENT IN FUTURE
RESEARCH. SEVERAL POSSIBLE EXTENSIONS OF THE CAUSAL MODELS
ARE ALSO SUGGESTED.

M0916   FRASER, CHRISTOPHER R. P.
         THE IMPACT OF COLLECTIVE BARGAINING ON JOB SATISFACTION.
         PH.D. DISSERTATION, UNIVERSITY OF WISCONSIN, 1977.

         THIS STUDY EXAMINED THE RELATIONSHIP OF THE CONSTRUCT
JOB SATISFACTION WITH THE INDUSTRIAL RELATIONS SYSTEM OF THE
ENTERPRISE.   USING A COMBINATION OF CASE STUDIES AND BEFORE
AND AFTER SURVEYS, THE RESEARCH SOUGHT TO EXAMINE, FIRST,
THE EXTENT OF CHANGE IN JOB SATISFACTION, AS MEASURED BY THE
MINNESOTA SATISFACTION QUESTIONNAIRE, OVER THE PERIOD OF
COLLECTIVE BARGAINING.   SECONDLY, THE STUDY INCLUDED THE
DESIGN OF A METHODOLOGY TO ATTEMPT TO EXPLAIN ANY MEASURED
CHANGES IN JOB SATISFACTION. A CONSTRUCT LABELED PERCEPTIONS
OF THE SUCCESS WITH WHICH THE UNION BARGAINED ON BEHALF
OF ITS MEMBERS WAS HYPOTHESIZED TO ACCOUNT FOR PERCEIVED
DIFFERENCES IN THE PROCESS AND THE OUTCOMES OF COLLECTIVE
BARGAINING. FINALLY, THE STUDY SOUGHT TO EXAMINE
THE PATTERN OF RESPONSES TO PERCEPTION OF SUCCESS MEASURES,
AND ATTEMPTED TO EXPLAIN DIFFERENCES IN PERCEPTIONS
OF SUCCESS BASED ON INDIVIDUAL DIFFERENCES ON DEMOGRAPHIC
JOB-RELATED AND ATTITUDINAL VARIABLES.
         THE RESULTS OF THE STUDY INDICATED LIMITED OR LITTLE
SUPPORT FOR EXPLAINING CHANGES IN JOB SATISFACTION OR
VARIATION IN PERCEPTION OF SUCCESS MEASURES.BOTH THEORETICAL
AND MEASUREMENT PROBLEMS WERE SUGGESTED AS THE REASONS FOR
THE WEAK FINDINGS.
         THE RESULTS OF THE STUDY DO SUGGEST THAT THERE ARE
PSYCHOLOGICAL DYNAMICS OPERATING DURING THE PERIOD OF
COLLECTIVE BARGAINING THAT SHOULD BE EXPLORED FURTHER.

M0917   FRONTZ, HAROLD O.
         WORK VALUES AND JOB SATISFACTION OF PSYCHIATRIC AIDES.
         ED.D. DISSERTATION, VIRGINIA POLYTECHNIC INSTITUTE AND
STATE UNIVERSITY, 1977.

         THE PURPOSE OF THIS STUDY WAS TO INVESTIGATE THE WORK
VALUES AND JOB SATISFACTIONS OF PSYCHIATRIC AIDES AND TO
DETERMINE IF A RELATIONSHIP EXISTED BETWEEN THESE VARIABLES.
THIS WAS ACCOMPLISHED BY ADMINISTERING THE WORK VALUES
INVENTORY (WVI), THE MINNESOTA SATISFACTION QUESTIONNAIRE
(MSQ), AND A PERSONAL DATA FORM TO EACH OF 300 PSYCHIATRIC
AIDES EMPLOYED IN A RURAL, 800 BED MULTIPURPOSE HOSPITAL FOR
THE EMOTIONALLY DISTURBED.
         SEVERAL IMPLICATIONS CAN BE CONCLUDED FROM THIS STUDY
WHICH MAY BE OF INTEREST TO GUIDANCE COUNSELORS AND STATE
HOSPITAL ADMINISTRATORS. FIRST, A COMPARISON OF THE WORK
VALUES OF PARTICIPATING AIDES AND THE WORK VALUES OF OTHER
OCCUPATIONAL GROUPS PREVIOUSLY TESTED WITH THE WVI SUGGESTS
THAT AIDES MAY TEND TO EXHIBIT A PATTERN OF VALUES THAT
COULD POSSIBLY BE USED TO DIFFERENTIATE THEM FROM OTHER
WORKERS. SECOND, PARTICIPATING AIDES' RESPONSES TO THE MSQ

M0917 PROVIDED A BASIS FOR IMPROVING THE JOB OF PSYCHIATRIC AIDE.
FINALLY, THIS STUDY SUGGESTED THAT ALTHOUGH IT APPEARS TO
BE FEASIBLE TO ASSIST CLIENTS IN IDENTIFYING OCCUPATIONS
WHICH TEND TO BE HELD BY PEOPLE WITH SIMILAR VALUE SYSTEMS,
THIS STUDY DID NOT SUGGEST THAT IT IS APPROPRIATE
TO EQUATE SIMILARITY IN VALUES WITH FUTURE SATISFACTION.
HOWEVER, THESE RESULTS ARE NOT NECESSARILY APPLICABLE TO
A NATIONAL POPULATION OF PSYCHIATRIC AIDES AS RANDOM
SAMPLING PROCEDURES WERE NOT USED AND THE SAMPLE AS
RELATIVELY HOMOGENEOUS.

M0918 GARAWSKI, ROBERT A.
A NORMATIVE STUDY OF THE SECONDARY SCHOOL ASSISTANT
PRINCIPALSHIP IN SELECTED PENNSYLVANIA SCHOOL DISTRICTS
WITH AN EMPHASIS UPON JOB SATISFACTION.
ED.D. DISSERTATION, TEMPLE UNIVERSITY, 1977.

THE MAJOR OBJECTIVE OF THIS RESEARCH STUDY WAS TO
INVESTIGATE THE CURRENT STATUS OF THE ASSISTANT SECONDARY
SCHOOL PRINCIPALSHIP AND TO IDENTIFY THOSE ASPECTS OF THE
POSITION THAT HAVE GIVEN RISE TO JOB SATISFACTION AS WELL
AS JOB DISSATISFACTION.
AMONG THE MAJOR CONCLUSIONS GENERATED BY THIS RESEARCH
STUDY ARE THE FOLLOWING: 1. SECONDARY SCHOOL ASSISTANT
PRINCIPALS ARE INVOLVED IN VIRTUALLY EVERY ASPECT OF SCHOOL
ADMINISTRATION. 2. SECONDARY SCHOOL ASSISTANT PRINCIPALS
DESIRE GREATER INVOLVEMENT IN SUPERVISION OF TEACHERS; . . .
3. THE JOB TASKS THAT GENERATE THE HIGHEST DEGREE OF
JOB SATISFACTION FOR THE LARGEST PERCENTAGE OF
SECONDARY SCHOOL ASSISTANT PRINCIPALS INCLUDE TEACHER
EVALUATION, TEACHER SUPERVISION, AND SCHOOL MASTER SCHEDULE
PREPARATION. 4. THERE IS A STRONG POSITIVE RELATIONSHIP
BETWEEN EACH OF THE INDEPENDENT VARIABLES OF RESPONSIBILITY,
IMPORTANCE, AND DISCRETIONARY AUTHORITY AND THE DEPENDENT
VARIABLE OF JOB SATISFACTION. . . 6. THE RELATIVE
POSITION OF AN ASSISTANT PRINCIPAL'S SALARY LEVEL IN
COMPARISON TO PEERS, TEACHERS, AND COUNSELORS IS A
DETERMINANT OF SALARY SATISFACTION. 7. SECONDARY SCHOOL
ASSISTANT PRINCIPALS ARE, FOR THE MOST PART, SATISFIED WITH
THE ENVIRONMENTAL CONDITIONS UNDER WHICH THEY WORK.
8. DISSATISFACTION WITH ENVIRONMENTAL CONDITIONS ON THE
PART OF ASSISTANT PRINCIPALS ARE INFLUENCED BY A WORK DAY
OF TEN HOURS OR MORE; TRADITIONAL ORGANIZATIONAL STRUCTURES;
LACK OF SUFFICIENT SECRETARIAL ASSISTANCE; LACK OF
ASSISTANCE FROM IMMEDIATE SUPERIORS; BEING IGNORED BY A
SUPERIOR; COLLECTIVE BARGAINING CONSTRAINTS; TEACHER'S
PERCEPTION OF PUPIL DISCIPLINE; STUDENT PERCEPTION OF
DISCIPLINE ADMINISTRATION; STUDENT RIGHTS AND
RESPONSIBILITIES DOCUMENTS; RECENT COURT DECISIONS ABOUT
DUE PROCESS AND DISCIPLINE; AND USURPATION OF CREDIT FOR
WORK DONE BY THE PRINCIPAL.

M0919 GATES, DAVID POOLE.
JOB SATISFACTION, JOB CHARACTERISTICS, AND OCCUPATIONAL
LEVEL.
PH.D. DISSERTATION, UNIVERSITY OF NORTH CAROLINA AT CHAPEL
HILL, 1977.

DATA FROM THE UNIVERSITY OF MICHIGAN ISR SURVEY
RESEARCH CENTER 1972-73 QUALITY OF EMPLOYMENT SURVEY WERE
USED TO CLARIFY VARIOUS SUBSTANTIVE RELATIONSHIPS AMONG
THREE SETS OF VARIABLES: THOSE HAVING TO DO WITH JOB
SATISFACTION, OCCUPATION LEVEL, AND JOB CHARACTERISTICS AS
PERCEIVED BY WORKERS. ADDITIONALLY, SEVERAL METHODOLOGICAL
GOALS WERE PURSUED: THE EXPLORATION OF FACTOR STRUCTURES OF
JOB CHARACTERISTICS; THE SUCCESSFUL DEVELOPMENT OF AN
INTERACTIVE MODEL OF THE JOINT EFFECTS ON JOB SATISFACTION
OF THE PERCEIVED LEVEL OF EXISTENCE OF JOB CHARACTERISTICS
BY WORKERS ON THEIR CURRENT JOBS AND THE DEGREE TO WHICH
THESE ARE IMPORTANT TO THEM ON ANY JOB THEY MIGHT HOLD A
TESTING OF THE DIFFERENTIAL EFFECTS ON VARIABLE
RELATIONSHIPS WHEN DIFFERENT OPERATIONAL MEASURES ARE USED
FOR JOB SATISFACTION AND OCCUPATIOANL LEVEL; DEVELOPMENT OF
CANONICAL CORRELATION TECHNIQUES FOR FOR EXPLORING CAUSAL
RELATIONS AMONG MULTIPLE INDEPENDENT AND DEPENDENT
VARIABLES; AND DISCUSSION OF ISSUES HAVING TO DO WITH
CONCEPTUAL TERMINOLOGY. OF SPECIAL INTEREST IS THE FINDING
THAT THE DICTIONARY OF OCCUPATIONAL TITLES' "RELATIONS TO
DATA" MAY BE A SUPERIOR OCCUPATIONAL STATUS RANKING SYSTEM
FOR SOCIOLOGICAL RESEARCH IN THIS FIELD, AND THAT MEASURES
OF "TIME DRAG" AND "INVOLVEMENT" MAY BE MORE PERTINENT TO
THE COMPLEXITIES OF THE "JOB SATISFACTION" CONCEPT THAN
OTHER MEASURES MUCH MORE COMMONLY USED. IMPLICATIONS OF
FINDINGS FOR POLICY DECISIONS AFFECTING JOB RESTRUCTURING
AND PUBLIC EDUCATION PROGRAMS ARE DISCUSSED.

M0920 GLICKEN, DAVID M.
A REGIONAL STUDY OF THE JOB SATISFACTION OF SOCIAL WORKERS.
D.S.W. DISSERTATION, UNIVERSITY OF UTAH, 1977.

THE STUDY HAD THREE PURPOSES: TO IDENTIFY AND DESCRIBE
SELECTED CHARACTERISTICS OF SOCIAL WORKERS IN A FIVE STATE
WESTERN REGION OF THE COUNTRY; TO IDENTIFY AREAS OF
SATISFACTION AND DISSATISFACTION WITH WORK REPORTED BY
WORKERS IN THE STUDY; AND TO INTERPRET THE DATA OBTAINED
FROM VARIOUS STATISTICAL ANALYSES SO THAT THE DATA MIGHT
LEAD TO AN UNDERSTANDING OF RELATIONSHIPS BETWEEN WORK
SATISFACTION MEASURES AND SELECTED WORKER CHARACTERISTICS.
WORKERS IN THE SURVEY HAD A MEDIAN AGE OF 43 AND
REMAINED ON THEIR JOBS AN AVERAGE OF FIVE AND A HALF YEARS.
MEDIAN FULL TIME SALARY FOR ALL WORKERS WAS $17,650 WITH
FULL TIME FEMALE WORKERS AVERAGING APPROXIMATELY $4,000 LESS
IN SALARY THAN MALES. DIRECT PRACTITIONERS AND SUPERVISORS-
ADMINISTRATORS ACCOUNTED FOR 80 PERCENT OF THE WORKERS
RESPONDING TO THE SURVEY. MEN AND WOMEN WERE EVENLY
REPRESENTED IN THE GROUP RESPONDING. MEN WERE FIVE YEARS
YOUNGER THAN WOMEN BUT AVERAGED FOUR YEARS MORE OF
PROFESSIONAL EXPERIENCE.
RECOMMENDATIONS INCLUDED: A MORE ACTIVE ROLE BY NASW
IN PROVIDING FOR WORKER JOB SATISFACTION THROUGH MEDIATION,
EDUCATION, AND FACT FINDING; AGENCY POLICIES WHICH ARE
NON-DISCRETIONARY AND PROVIDE INCENTIVES AND REWARDS FOR
DIRECT PRACTITIONERS AND WOMEN; AND SERVICES TO STUDENTS
PROVIDED BY SOCIAL WORK EDUCATION TO HELP NEW WORKERS RELATE
MORE INTELLIGENTLY TO THE JOB MARKET.
AREAS FOR FUTHER RESEARCH WERE IDENTIFIED AS THE NEED

M0920   TO BETTER UNDERSTAND THE REASONS FOR THE LOWER JOB
         SATISFACTION OF FEMALE SOCIAL WORKERS; THE NEED FOR
         ADDITIONAL DATA ON WORK BEHAVIOR AND PRODUCTIVITY OF SOCIAL
         WORKERS; AND THE NEED FOR THE DEVELOPMENT OF NORMATIVE DATA
         WHICH MIGHT MAKE STUDIES OF SOCIAL WORKER JOB SATISFACTION
         MORE MEANINGFUL.

M0921   GOBLE, JESSE W.
         RELATIONSHIPS BETWEEN JOB SATISFACTION, DEMOGRAPHIC FACTORS,
         ABSENTEEISM AND TENURE OF WORKERS IN A DELMARVA BROILER
         PROCESSING PLANT.
         PH.D. DISSERTATION, UNIVERSITY OF MARYLAND, 1976.

              THE PURPOSE OF THIS STUDY WAS TO DETERMINE IF
         PRODUCTION WORKERS OF A BROILER PROCESSING PLANT WERE
         SATISFIED WITH THEIR JOBS AND WHETHER THEIR SATISFACTION WAS
         RELATED TO SELECTED DEMOGRAPHIC FACTORS, ABSENCE AND TENURE.
              RESULTS OF THE JOB SATISFACTION SURVEY REVEALED THAT
         A MAJORITY OF WORKERS WERE DISSATISFIED WITH THEIR WORK.
         THOSE 24 YEARS OF AGE AND UNDER APPEARED TO BE LESS
         SATISFIED WITH WORK AND SUPERVISION THAN OLDER WORKERS BUT
         THEY WERE MORE SATISFIED WITH PERCEIVED OPPORTUNITIES FOR
         PROMOTION. FEMALES EVIDENCED MORE DISSATISFACTION WITH
         WORK THAN DID THEIR MALE COUNTERPARTS BUT THEY EXPRESSED
         MORE SATISFACTION WITH PAY.
              WORKERS WHO WERE MOST DISSATISFIED WITH WORK AND PAY
         HAD MORE ABSENCES ATTRIBUTABLE TO EXCUSED REASONS, PERSONAL
         ILLNESSES AND TOTAL ABSENCES. EVIDENCE SUGGESTED AN INVERSE
         RELATIONSHIP EXISTED BETWEEN SATISFACTION WITH PROMOTIONAL
         OPPORTUNITIES AND ABSENCES RELATED TO FAMILY AND PERSONAL
         ILLNESSES. THOSE WORKERS LEAST SATISFIED WITH CO-WORKERS
         SEEMED TO HAVE MORE FAMILY ILLNESS RELATED ABSENCES THAN
         DID THOSE WHO WERE MORE ACCEPTABLE OF OTHERS.
              RESULTS SUGGESTED THAT JOB SATISFACTION WAS MORE
         RELEVANT TO ABSENTEEISM AND TENURE THAN WERE DEMOGRAPHIC
         FACTORS THAT MIGHT BE CONSIDERED IN THE PROCESS OF SELECTING
         NEW EMPLOYEES.

M0922   GRANT, JOSEPH O.
         OPEN SPACE ELEMENTARY SCHOOL: EFFECTS ON TEACHERS' JOB
         SATISFACTION, PARTICIPATION IN CURRICULUM DECISION-MAKING,
         AND PERCEIVED SCHOOL EFFECTIVENESS.
         PH.D. DISSERTATION, STATE UNIVERSITY OF NEW YORK AT BUFFALO,
         1977.

              THIS RESEARCH EXAMINES THE EFFECTS OF A MAJOR CHANGE
         IN ORGANIZATIONAL STRUCTURE OF ELEMENTARY SCHOOLS FOR
         INSTRUCTION, FROM TRADITIONAL STRUCTURED SCHOOLS TO OPEN
         SPACE SCHOOLS. MORE SPECIFICALLY, THE STUDY ASSESSES
         PARTICIPATION IN THE SCHOOLS' CURRICULUM DECISION-MAKING,
         TEACHERS' JOB SATISFACTION, AND PERCEIVED SCHOOL
         EFFECTIVENESS.
              OPINIONS OF 330 TEACHERS EMPLOYED IN THE SCARBOROUGH
         NORTH YORK REGION OF THE METROPOLITAN TORONTO CATHOLIC
         SCHOOL DISTRICT WERE SAMPLED, AND THE SAMPLING WAS
         STRATIFIED BY SCHOOL TYPE, TRADITIONAL AND OPEN SPACE. IN
         ADDITION TO MAJOR RESEARCH QUESTIONS ON DIFFERENCES BETWEEN
         OPEN SPACE AND TRADITIONAL SCHOOLS, OTHER SCHOOL AND

M0922   DEMOGRAPHIC DATA WERE CONTROLLED FOR: AGE, SEX, TEACHER
        QUALIFICATION, TEACHER EXPERIENCE, AND GRADE LEVEL.
            DATA WERE COLLECTED THROUGH TWO TYPES OF INSTRUMENTS:
        A MODIFIED DECISIONAL CONDITION INSTRUMENT DEVELOPED BY
        BELASCO AND ALUTTO (1972), TO MEASURE PARTICIPATIVE
        DECISION-MAKING, AND A QUESTIONNAIRE DEVELOPED BY THE
        RESEARCHER TO MEASURE JOB SATISFACTION AND PERCEIVED SCHOOL
        EFFECTIVENESS. ESSENTIAL DEMOGRAPHIC DATA WERE ALSO
        COLLECTED. MULTIVARIATE AND UNIVARIATE ANALYSES OF VARIANCE
        WERE USED TO ANALYZE THE DATA. THE SIGNIFICANT LEVEL USED
        WAS .05.
            MAJOR FINDINGS INDICATE THAT THERE IS NO OVERALL
        DIFFERENCE IN PARTICIPATIVE DECISION-MAKING, SATISFACTION
        LEVEL, OR PERCEIVED ACHIEVEMENT OF STUDENTS, BETWEEN
        TEACHERS EMPLOYED IN OPEN SPACE AND TRADITIONAL SCHOOLS.
        HOWEVER, TEACHERS IN THE OPEN SPACE SCHOOLS FEEL THAT THEY
        ARE ACHIEVING THEIR GOALS TO GREATER EXTENT THAN TRADITIONAL
        CLASSROOM TEACHERS, ESPECIALLY IN THEIR INSTRUCTION TO BOTH
        BRIGHT AND AVERAGE STUDENTS.

M0923   HARRIS, OLITA E.D.
        TASK OPPORTUNITY PROFESSIONAL GROWTH NEED FULFILLMENT AND
        INTRINSIC JOB SATISFACTION OF PUBLIC SOCIAL SERVICE WORKERS
        IN COLORADO.
        D.S.W. DISSERTATION, UNIVERSITY OF DENVER, 1977.

            THE STUDY FOCUSED ON THE MOST IMPORTANT MANPOWER
        CONSIDERATION FACING THE SOCIAL WORK PROFESSION IS THAT OF
        DEVELOPMENT, RETENTION, AND DEPLOYMENT OF SOCIAL WORKERS BY
        SOCIAL AGENCIES. THE PURPOSE OF THIS RESEARCH WAS TO TEST
        THE HYPOTHESIS THAT:
            TASK OPPORTUNITY WILL BE POSITIVELY ASSOCIATED WITH
            PROFESSIONAL GROWTH NEED FULFILLMENT AND INTRINSIC JOB
            SATISFACTION, AND WILL BE CONDITIONED BY A VARIETY OF
            INDIVIDUAL CHARACTERISTICS, E.G., AGE, SEX, EDUCATION,
            JOB TENURE, AMOUNT OF SOCIAL WORK EXPERIENCE, JOB
            POSITION, ETHNICITY, AND LENGTH OF TIME SINCE
            GRADUATION.
            AN EX POST FACTO, QUANTITATIVE-DESCRIPTIVE RESEARCH
        DESIGN WAS EMPLOYED TO TEST HYPOTHESIZED RELATIONSHIPS
        AMONG AND BETWEEN INDEPENDENT, INTERVENING, AND DEPENDENT
        VARIABLES. SOCIAL WORKERS EMPLOYED BY THE COLORADO STATE
        DEPARTMENT OF SOCIAL SERVICES SERVED AS THE STUDY
        POPULATION. A SAMPLE OF 400 RESPONDENTS WAS SELECTED.
            THREE OF THE FOUR SCALES INCLUDED IN THE DATA
        COLLECTION INSTRUMENT WERE DEVELOPED SPECIFICALLY FOR USE IN
        THIS STUDY (PROFESSIONAL GROWTH NEED FULFILLMENT SCALE,
        JOB COMPLEXITY SCALE, SERVICE AREAS CHECKLIST). THE FOURTH
        SCALE UTILIZED WAS THE SHORT FORM OF THE MINNESOTA
        SATISFACTION QUESTIONNAIRE.
            THE SUBSTANTIVE RESEARCH HYPOTHESIS FOR THIS STUDY WAS
        UPHELD AT THE .05 LEVEL OF SIGNIFICANCE. AS SPECIFIED, A
        DIRECT RELATIONSHIP WAS FOUND TO EXIST BETWEEN RESPONDENT
        PERCEPTIONS OF TASK OPPORTUNITY AND THE LEVEL OF
        RESPONDENT'S EXPERIENCED PROFESSIONAL GROWTH NEED
        FULFILLMENT AND INTRINSIC JOB SATISFACTION. THIS
        RELATIONSHIP WAS CONDITIONED BY SPECIFIC DIMENSIONS OF THE
        DEMOGRAPHIC CHARACTERISTICS. IN ADDITION, A RELATIONSHIP

M0923 BETWEEN PROFESSIONAL GROWTH NEED FULFILLMENT AND INTRINSIC
JOB SAISFACTION WAS FOUND TO EXIST WHICH TENTATIVELY
ESTABLISHED CONSTRUCT VALIDITY FOR THE PROFESSIONAL GROWTH
NEED FULFILLMENT SCALE.
THE COMMON ELEMENT WHICH APPEARED TO BE AN UNDERLYING
FACTOR NOT MEASURED IN ITSELF BUT WHICH EMERGED UPON
ANALYSIS OF THE DATA AS A DIMENSION OF THE INTERVENING
VARIABLES WAS THE LEVEL OF EXPERIENCE OF THE RESPONDENTS.
THE FINDINGS SERVED TO EMPHASIZE THE NEED TO RE-EXAMINE THE
CURRENT VIEWS AND ASSUMPTIONS ABOUT WORKER "BURN-OUT", AND
THE MIDDLE-AGE WORKER. FURTHER, THE FINDINGS REINFORCED THE
APPARENT NEED TO CONSIDER DIFFERENT JOB STRUCTURES WITH
REGARD TO THE DIVISION OF WORK WHICH COULD BE APPLIED
DIFFERENTIALLY. THE CONSIDERATION OF THE DIFFERENTIAL
APPROACHES COULD EMANATE FROM AND HAVE IMPLICATIONS FOR SUCH
SOURCES AS THE ORGANIZATION ITSELF, SOCIAL WORK RESEARCH,
AND SOCIAL WORK EDUCATION.

M0924 HICKS, THOMAS H.
SECOND CAREER CATHOLIC PRIESTS: A STUDY OF THEIR LEVEL OF
JOB SATISFACTION, MATURITY, AND MORALE.
PH.D. DISSERTATION, ST. JOHN'S UNIVERSITY, 1977.

OVER THE PAST DECADE THERE HAS BEEN A GOOD DEAL OF
DISCUSSION ABOUT THE WISDOM OF ORDAINING OLDER MEN TO THE
ROMAN CATHOLIC PRIESTHOOD. THEORETICALLY, IT IS USUALLY
ASSUMED THAT THERE SHOULD BE A RELATIONSHIP BEWTEEN "LATE
VOCATIONS" AND MORE MATURE, SATISFIED PRIESTS. BUT, AS OF
NOW, THERE HAVE BEEN NO REALLY SYSTEMATIC STUDIES OF SECOND-
CAREER CATHOLIC PRIESTS.
THE FINDINGS OF THIS STUDY DID NOT SUPPORT THE
THEORETICAL ASSUMPTIONS THAT MEN WHO ENTERED THE PRIESTHOOD
LATER IN LIFE, AFTER HAVING BEEN IN A PREVIOUS CAREER,
WOULD HAVE A GREATER DEGREE OF JOB SATISFACTION, MATURITY,
AND MORALE THAN FIRST-CAREER PRIESTS. BUT, ON THE OTHER
HAND, THE SECOND-CAREER ENTRANTS INTO THE PRIESTHOOD DID NOT
APPEAR AS A PSYCHOLOGICALLY TROUBLED OR CHRONICALLY
DISSATISFIED GROUP OF MEN. THEY CAME ACROSS AS A VERY
NORMAL GROUP OF MEN WHO WERE IDEOLOGICALLY SATISFIED WITH
BEING IN THE PRIESTHOOD BUT WERE DISSATISFIED WITH SOME
FUNCTIONAL REALITIES.

M0925 HOOKER, ALFRED L.
A STUDY OF THE PERCEPTIONS OF SELECTED SCHOOL-BASED
ADMINISTRATORS IN FLORIDA RELATIVE TO CERTAIN VARIABLES IN
SECONDARY SCHOOL ADMINISTRATION AS THEY RELATE TO JOB
SATISFACTION.
PH.D. DISSERTATION, FLORIDA STATE UNIVERSITY, 1976.

THE INVESTIGATION OF THIS STUDY CONCENTRATED ON THE
FOLLOWING MAJOR PURPOSES: 1. TO PROVIDE A PROFILE OF
SELECTED SECONDARY SCHOOL-BASED ADMINISTRATORS IN DUVAL
COUNTY, FLORIDA, 1975-76. 2. TO DETERMINE THE RELATIONSHIPS
AND CONTRIBUTIONS OF CERTAIN INDEPENDENT VARIABLES --
DEMOGRAPHIC, COMMUNICATION, PERFORMANCE EVALUATION, JOB
SECURITY, COMPENSATION, AUTHORITY AND DECISION-MAKING, JOB
PROGRESS AND CAREER NEEDS, AND WHY EMPLOYEES STAY -- TO JOB
SATISFACTION RELATIVE TO SELECTED SCHOOL-BASED

M0925   ADMINISTRATORS. 3. TO INVESTIGATE THE PERCEPTIONS OF
         SELECTED SECONDARY SCHOOL-BASED ADMINISTRATORS RELATIVE TO
         CERTAIN VARIABLES IN SECONDARY SCHOOL ADMINISTRATION AS THEY
         RELATE TO JOB SATISFACTION.
             CONCLUSIONS WERE AS FOLLOWS:
         1. PERSONNEL MANAGEMENT AS IT RELATES TO CAREER DEVELOPMENT,
         JOB PROGRESS, AND PERSONNEL EVALUATION NEEDS IMPROVING.
         2. THE HIGHER SCHOOL-BASED ADMINISTRATORS ARE ADVANCED UP
         THE ADMINISTRATIVE STRUCTURE, THE MORE SATISFIED THEY SEEM
         TO BECOME. 3. THE EVIDENCE THAT SHOWS COMPENSATION AS THE
         MOST DISSATISFYING FACTOR AND AUTHORITY AND DECISION-MAKING
         AS THE MOST SATISFYING FACTOR APPEARS TO SUBSTANTIATE THE
         APPLICABILITY OF HERZBERG'S MOTIVATION-HYGIENE THEORY OR
         PORTIONS OF HIS THEORY TO THIS STUDY'S POPULATION.
         4. CONSISTENT WITH PREVIOUS RESEARCH, IT APPEARS THAT WOMEN
         WITH SIMILAR QUALIFICATIONS AS MEN HAVE BEEN DISCRIMINATED
         AGAINST RELATIVE TO THEIR ADVANCEMENTS AND PROMOTIONS IN THE
         DUVAL COUNTY, FLORIDA PUBLIC SCHOOL SYSTEM. THIS SITUATION
         HAS APPARENTLY RESULTED IN WOMEN BEING RELATIVELY
         DISSATISFIED IN THEIR WORK.

M0927   KETTERING, MERLYN H.
         SEGREGATION AND JOB SATISFACTION IN THE WORK PLACE: THE
         MEASUREMENT OF RACIAL DISPARITIES IN ORGANIZATIONS AND
         THEIR INFLUENCE ON EMPLOYEE WORK ATTITUDES.
         PH.D. DISSERTATION, UNIVERSITY OF PITTSBURGH, 1977.

             THIS RESEARCH EXPLORES THE PROPOSITION THAT AS
         ORGANIZATIONS ACHIEVE PROPORTIONAL MINORITY EMPLOYMENT,
         RACIAL INEQUALITIES AND TENSIONS MAY ACTUALLY INCREASE.
         CONCLUSIONS FROM THE ANALYSIS EMPHASIZE THE IMPORTANCE OF
         MONITORING INTRA-ORGANIZATIONAL DYNAMICS FOR EFFECTIVE
         AFFIRMATIVE ACTION PROGRAMS. THE RESEARCH OBSERVES THAT IN
         ORGANIZATIONS WHERE RELATIVELY PROPORTIONAL MIXES OF
         MINORITY AND NON-MINORITY EMPLOYEES ARE ACHIEVED, SELECTIVE
         INTRA-ORGANIZATIONAL INDICES OF SEGREGATION AND DISPARITY
         REFLECT PERSISTENT AND EVEN EXACERBATED RACIAL IMBALANCES,
         AND THAT THESE ARE ASSOCIATED WITH WORK ATTITUDES.
             IN CONCLUSION, IT IS DEMONSTRATED THAT NEGATIVE
         UNINTENDED CONSEQUENCES (FOR INDIVIDUALS, WORK UNITS AND
         ORGANIZATIONS) FROM ACCELERATED MINORITY EMPLOYMENT CAN BE
         REDUCED BY INFORMED USE OF INTRA-ORGANIZATIONAL ANALYSIS.
         MEASUREMENT OF RACIAL DISPARITIES, SEGREGATION AND JOB
         SATISFACTION CAN ASSIST IN THE PREDICTION AND PREVENTION OF
         RACIAL IMBALANCES AND SPECIFIC ORGANIZATIONAL TENSIONS AND
         CONFLICTS.
             ORGANIZATIONS SHOULD FORMULATE POLICIES TO AVOID
         INTERNAL RACIAL IMBALANCES ACCOMPANYING ACCELERATED MINORITY
         EMPLOYMENT IMPOSED UPON EXISTING ORGANIZATIONAL FORMS. SUCH
         POLICIES MIGHT ENCOMPASS: (A) MEASURING MINORITY
         DISTRIBUTIONS IN CRITICAL AREAS; (B) JOB AND SYSTEM
         RE-DESIGN TO FACILITATE MINORITY ASSIMILATION AND REMOVE
         FUNCTIONAL BARRIERS TO INTRA-ORGANIZATIONAL INTEGRATION;
         (C) DIRECT MONITORING OF WORK ATTITUDES AS WELL AS
         ASSIGNMENTS AT WORK; AND (D) SECURING STRATEGIES FOR FULLER
         PARTICIPATION AND INFLUENCE OF ALL EMPLOYEES THROUGHOUT
         ORGANIZATIONS.
             THE ESTABLISHMENT OF INTERMEDIATE AND MEASURABLE

M0927 OBJECTIVES, BASED UPON INDICES DEVELOPED AND TESTED IN THIS STUDY, CAN HELP AVOID SOME CONFUSION AND DEFENSIVENESS SURROUNDING MINORITY RELATIONS IN MANY ORGANIZATIONS TODAY. THE ESTABLISHMENT OF REALISTIC GOALS IS ONE STEP TOWARD THE ULTIMATE AIM OF ORGANIZATIONAL INTEGRATION. MONITORING ORGANIZATIONAL PERFORMANCES THROUGH SUCH INDICES PROVIDES A FRAMEWORK TO EFFECTIVELY TEST AFFIRMATIVE ACTION POLICIES AND ACHIEVEMENTS.

M0928 MAPLES, MARY ANGELA F.
RELATIONSHIPS BETWEEN WORK VALUES AND JOB SATISFACTION AMONG COLLEGE STUDENT PERSONNEL WORKERS.
PH.D. DISSERTATION, OREGON STATE UNIVERSITY, 1977.

        THIS STUDY WAS UNDERTAKEN TO EXAMINE THE RELATIONSHIPS WHICH EXIST BETWEEN THE WORK VALUES AND JOB SATISFACTION CHARACTERISTICS OF COLLEGE STUDENT PERSONNEL WORKERS IN THE STATES OF OREGON, IDAHO, MONTANA AND WASHINGTON. WORK VALUES ARE VIEWED AS CHARACTERISTICS DESIRED ON AN IDEAL JOB AND JOB SATISFACTION CHARACTERISTICS ARE THOSE FACTORS BEING EXPERIENCED ON THE PRESENT JOB.
        SPECIFICALLY, THE STUDY WAS DESIGNED 1) TO SURVEY THE WORK VALUES, JOB SATISFACTION CHARACTERISTICS, AND AMOUNTS OF OVERALL JOB SATISFACTION AMONG 150 COLLEGE STUDENT PERSONNEL WORKERS IN THE NORTHWEST, 2) TO DETERMINE THE EFFECTS OF AGE (UNDER 30 YEARS, 30-40 YEARS, AND OVER 40 YEARS), SEX AND YEARS OF EXPERIENCE (UNDER 5, 5-10, AND OVER 10 YEARS ON THE PRESENT JOB) ON THE WORK VALUES AND JOB SATISFACTION CHARACTERISTICS OF THE POPULATION, AND 3) TO DETERMINE THE SIGNIFICANCE OF THE RELATIONSHIP BETWEEN THE WORK VALUES ON INDEPENDENCE, ACHIEVEMENT AND WAY OF LIFE ON COMPARABLE JOB SATISFACTION CHARACTERISTICS.

M0929 MOORE, PERRY.
REWARDS AND PUBLIC EMPLOYEES' ATTITUDES TOWARD CLIENT SERVICE.
PUBLIC PERSONNEL MANAGEMENT 6 (MARCH-APRIL 1977): 98-105.

        THIS ARTICLE INVESTIGATED THE RELATIONSHIPS BETWEEN PUBLIC EMPLOYEES' ATTITUDES ABOUT CLIENT SERVICE AND THEIR DESIRE FOR SPECIFIC REWARDS AND THE UTILITY OF CLIENT SERVICE IN OBTAINING THESE REWARDS. SEVERAL STEPS ARE SUGGESTED WHICH THE PUBLIC MANAGER COULD TAKE TO IMPROVE THE EMPLOYEES' CONCERN ABOUT CLIENT SERVICE.

M0930 NOTHNAGEL, GEORGE E.
CONFLICT AND DISSONANCE IN A DISLOCATED WORKER POPULATION.
PH.D. DISSERTATION, CASE WESTERN RESERVE UNIVERSITY, 1976.

        THIS STUDY EXAMINED ATTITUDES AND SATISFACTIONS OF A DISPLACED WORKER POPULATION. BASED UPON FESTINGER'S THEORY OF COGNITIVE DISSONANCE, DISSONANCE REDUCTION WAS PREDICTED TO OCCUR AFTER A JOB CHOICE IN HIGH CONFLICT EMPLOYEES. DISSONANCE REDUCTION WAS TO BE OBSERVED THROUGH MORE FAVORABLE ATTITUDES AND SATISFACTIONS BEING EXHIBITED IN HIGH CONFLICT EMPLOYEES THAN IN LOW CONFLICT EMPLOYEES. ALSO, DISSONANCE REDUCTION WAS HYPOTHESIZED TO BE A DURABLE EFFECT. NONE OF THE HYPOTHESES WERE SUPPORTED. THERE WAS

M0930   NO EVIDENCE OF DISSONANCE REDUCTION IN EITHER OF TWO
        HYPOTHESES PERTAINING TO DISSONANCE REDUCTION. STABILITY
        OF ATTITUDES WERE OBSERVED BUT THIS ALONE DID NOT INDICATE
        DURABILITY OF THE DISSONANCE REDUCTION EFFECT. CONTRARY TO
        THE HYPOTHESIZED RESULTS, LESS FAVORABLE ATTITUDES WERE
        OBSERVED IN HIGH CONFLICT EMPLOYEES THAN IN LOW CONFLICT
        EMPLOYEES. ALSO ALL DISPLACED WORKERS EXPRESSED LESS
        FAVORABLE ATTITUDES THAN A CONTROL GROUP. IT WAS CONCLUDED
        THAT DISSONANCE REDUCTION IS POSSIBLY TOO SHORT-TERM AN
        EFFECT TO BE MEASURED WITH THE PRESENT DESIGN. SUGGESTIONS
        FOR FURTHER RESEARCH MEASURING DISSONANCE REDUCTION IN A
        FIELD SETTING WERE OFFERED.

M0931   PARTICIPATIVE MANAGEMENT AT WORK.
        HARVARD BUSINESS REVIEW 55 (JANUARY-FEBRUARY 1977): 117-27.

            IN THIS INTERVIEW JOHN F. DONNELLY, OF DONNELLY
        MIRRORS, INC., SUGGESTS TWO FUNDAMENTALS FOR SUCCESS. HE
        EXPLAINS THAT ALL EMPLOYEES SHOULD BE INVOLVED IN THE
        ISSUES AND PROBLEMS AND THAT BENEFITS AND BURDENS BE SHARED.

M0932   PITTERMAN, LAWRENCE.
        AN EXAMINATION OF BRAINSTORMING PROCEDURE, GROUP SIZE AND
        MOTIVATIONAL ORIENTATION IN THE JOB ENRICHMENT GREENLIGHT
        SESSION.
        PH.D. DISSERTATION, CASE WESTERN RESERVE UNIVERSITY, 1976.

            THE PURPOSES OF THE PRESENT RESEARCH WERE TO COMPARE
        GROUP AND INDIVIDUAL BRAINSTORMING PROCEDURES FOR THREE
        GROUP SIZES IN ORDER TO DETERMINE WHICH WOULD ENHANCE THE
        GREENLIGHT SESSION'S CONTRIBUTION TO JOB ENRICHMENT
        TECHNOLOGY AND TO VALIDATE THE JOB PREFERENCE INVENTORY
        (JPI) AS A MEASURE OF MOTIVATIONAL ORIENTATION BY USING JOB
        DESIGN IDEAS GENERATED IN THE GREENLIGHT SESSION. IN JOB
        ENRICHMENT, THE GREENLIGHT SESSION PROVIDES THE PRIMARY
        MEANS FOR OBTAINING ACTUAL JOB CHANGES TO ENRICH THE TARGET
        JOB.
            IT WAS CONCLUDED THAT THE GREENLIGHT SESSION'S
        CONTRIBUTION OF JOB ENRICHING IDEAS DOES NOT DEPEND ON THE
        CHOICE OF BRAINSTORMING PROCEDURE OR GROUP SIZE. HOWEVER,
        THESE RESULTS DID EXTEND THE PREVIOUS RESEARCH CONTRADICTING
        OSBORN'S (1957) ASSERTION OF GROUP IDEATIONAL SUPERIORITY
        TO A SITUATION WHICH MORE FULLY APPROXIMATED THE PRESCRIBED
        CONDITIONS FOR GROUP BRAINSTORMING SUCCESS.
            BEYOND THESE CONCLUSIONS, IT WAS ARGUED THAT THE GROUP
        PROCEDURE MAY INVOLVE GREATER "ECONOMY" IN PRODUCING AND
        IDENTIFYING JOB ENRICHING IDEAS. THIS MAY BE A FUNCTION OF
        (1) THE INABILITY OF GROUP BRAINSTORMING TO COMPLETELY
        NEGATE THE DEVIATION-DETERRING EFFECTS OF THE GROUP PROCESS
        EVEN WITH CRITICISM PROSCRIBED, AND (2) THE LIMITING EFFECT
        OF THE TOTAL NUMBER OF JOB ENRICHING JOB CHANGES POSSIBLE
        FOR A GIVEN JOB.
            THE PRESENT STUDY WAS UNABLE TO VALIDATE THE JPI AS A
        MEASURE OF MOTIVATIONAL ORIENTATION. BOTH THE LACK OF
        VARIABILITY IN THE CRITERION DATA AND THE JPI ITSELF WERE
        THOUGHT TO CONTRIBUTE TO THE OBTAINED RESULTS. AS AN OPEN-
        ENDED PROJECTIVE MEASURE, GREATER ATTENTION MUST BE GIVEN
        IN THE FUTURE TO (1) CONTROLLING FOR RESPONSE BIASES WHICH

M0932 MAY STEM FROM A POPULATION SPECIFIC CHARACTERISTIC, AND
(2) DEVELOPING A RELIABLE CODING SYSTEM FOR EACH JOB CHOICE.

M0933 POWELL, MARY LOUISE.
PERCEPTIONS OF ORGANIZATIONAL CLIMATE AS MEDIATORS OF THE
RELATIONSHIPS BETWEEN INDIVIDUAL NEEDS AND JOB SATISFACTION
OF COUNSELORS IN THE NORTH CAROLINA COMMUNITY COLLEGE
SYSTEM.
PH.D. DISSERTATION, UNIVERSITY OF NORTH CAROLINA AT
CHAPEL HILL, 1976.

STEPWISE MULTIPLE REGRESSION ANALYSES WERE USED:
(1) TO INVESTIGATE THE MULTIVARIATE RELATIONSHIPS AMONG
BIOGRAPHICAL CHARACTERISTICS, ORGANIZATIONAL CLIMATE
DIMENSIONS, INDIVIDUAL NEEDS AND COUNSELOR JOB SATISFACTION,
AND (2) TO DETERMINE WHICH OF THE BIOGRAPHICAL
CHARACTERISTICS, ORGANIZATIONAL CLIMATE DIMENSIONS AND
INDIVIDUAL NEEDS MIGHT BE MOST PREDICTIVE OF COUNSELOR JOB
SATISFACTION. PARTIAL CORRELATIONS WERE USED TO STUDY
ORGANIZATIONAL CLIMATE DIMENSIONS AS MEDIATORS OF THE
RELATIONSHIPS BETWEEN INDIVIDUAL NEEDS AND COUNSELOR JOB
SATISFACTION.
COUNSELOR NEED FOR ORDER AND CLIMATE DIMENSION, TASK
ORIENTATION, WERE MOST PREDICTIVE OF COUNSELOR JOB
SATISFACTION. THE PREDICTIVE EFFICIENCY AMONG COMBINATIONS
OF COUNSELOR BIOGRAPHICAL FACTORS, DIMENSIONS OF
ORGANIZATIONAL CLIMATE AND INDIVIDUAL NEEDS OF COUNSELOR JOB
& SATISFACTION WAS NOT HIGH. IT WAS SUGGESTED THAT THIS
EFFICIENCY MIGHT BE IMPROVED BY: (1) NARROWING THE
GEOGRAPHICAL AREA STUDIED AND MAKING PERSONAL CONTACTS WITH
AS MANY OF THE SUBJECTS AS POSSIBLE IN ORDER TO SECURE
BETTER COOPERATION; (2) USING DIFFERENT INSTRUMENTS OR
PERSONAL INTERVIEWS TO IMPROVE THE ACCURACY OF MEASUREMENT
OF THE VARIABLES; (3) CONCEPTUALIZING ORGANIZATIONAL
CLIMATE AS AN ORGANIZATIONAL ATTRIBUTE; AND/OR (4) USING
OBJECTIVE INDICES RATHER THAN PERCEPTUAL MEASURES TO STUDY
ORGANIZATIONAL CLIMATE.

M0934 SMITH, FREDERICK DOWNING.
A NETWORK ANALYSIS OF A BUREAU OF INDIAN AFFAIRS SCHOOL
SYSTEM TO DETERMINE FACTORS INVOLVED IN JOB SATISFACTION.
PH.D. DISSERTATION, UNIVERSITY OF ARIZONA, 1977.

A SAMPLE OF TEACHERS WORKING IN THE BUREAU OF INDIAN
AFFAIRS SCHOOL SYSTEM ON THE NAVAJO RESERVATION WAS DERIVED
TO DETERMINE FACTORS INVOLVED IN THE SENSE OF SATISFACTION
THAT A TEACHER FEELS WITH HIS INVOLVEMENT IN THAT SYSTEM.
THERE WERE TWO DEPENDENT VARIABLES IN THIS STUDY:
1) SATISFACTION FELT WITH THE JOB, AND 2) SATISFACTION WITH
LIVING CONDITIONS. A QUANTITATIVE ANALYSIS BASED ON
CORRELATION COEFFICIENTS WAS CONDUCTED TO DETERMINE WHETHER
A RELATIONSHIP EXISTED BETWEEN EITHER OF THESE DEPENDENT
VARIABLES AND 1) THE FREQUENCY OF COMMUNICATION ONE HAS WITH
OTHERS IN THE LOCAL NETWORK OF SOCIAL RELATIONS, 2) THE
DEGREE OF SOCIAL DISTANCE WHICH AN INDIVIDUAL FEELS TOWARD
OTHER GROUPS LIVING ON THE NAVAJO RESERVATION. DESCRIPTIVE
RESEARCH WAS ALSO DONE TO PROVIDE FURTHER INSIGHT INTO THE
RELATIONSHIP BETWEEN THESE VARIABLES AND, MORE GENERALLY,

M0934   TO SEARCH FOR OTHER VARIABLES WHICH MIGHT BE RELATED TO JOB
        SATISFACTION OR TO SATISFACTION WITH LIVING CONDITIONS.
            SEVERAL VARIABLES WERE CONSTRUCTED TO MEASURE DIFFERENT
        FACETS OF COMMUNICATION. THESE VARIABLES DIFFERENTIATED
        COMMUNICATION FREQUENCY IN TERMS OF THE FOLLOWING
        DIMENSIONS: 1) COMMUNICATION WHICH OCCURRED ON THE JOB
        VERSUS THAT WHICH OCCURRED OFF OF THE JOB, 2) SELF-RATINGS
        OF COMMUNICATION FREQUENCY VERSUS THAT GIVEN BY OTHERS, AND
        3) COMMUNICATION WHICH OCCURRED IN A NETWORK THAT INCLUDED
        TEACHERS ONLY VERSUS A NETWORK WHICH INCLUDED EVERYONE WHO
        LIVED OR WORKED ON THE SCHOOL COMPOUND.
            A SIGNIFICANT RELATIONSHIP WAS DISCOVERED BETWEEN
        COMMUNICATION FREQUENCY AND BOTH DEPENDENT VARIABLES. A
        CONSIDERABLY STRONGER RELATIONSHIP WAS FOUND WITH JOB
        SATISFACTION THAN WAS THE CASE WITH SATISFACTION WITH
        LIVING CONDITIONS. TO PREDICT EITHER DEPENDENT VARIABLE,
        IT WAS FOUND THAT DATA MEASURING COMMUNICATION FREQUENCY
        NEED ONLY BE BASED ON A SELF-RATING OF COMMUNICATION WHICH
        OCCURS ON THE JOB. DATA BASED ON THE LARGER NETWORK OF THE
        HOUSING COMPOUND WAS A SIGNIFICANTLY BETTER PREDICTOR OF THE
        DEPENDENT VARIABLES THAN THAT WHICH WAS BASED ON THE
        SMALLER NETWORK OF THE SCHOOL.

M0935   SZILAGYI, A. D.   SIMS, HENRY P.   TERRILL, ROBERT C.
        THE RELATIONSHIP OF LEADERSHIP STYLE TO EMPLOYEE JOB
        SATISFACTION.
        HOSPITAL AND HEALTH SERVICES ADMINISTRATION 22 (WINTER 1977)
        8-21.

            THIS ARTICLE DISCUSSES THE RELATIONSHIP BETWEEN
        LEADERSHIP STYLE AND EMPLOYEE SATISFACTION. THE NATURE OF
        THE EMPLOYEE TASK WAS FOUND TO HAVE AN IMPORTANT BEARING ON
        THE LEADERSHIP STYLE WHICH IS MOST IMPORTANT. GENERALLY,
        THE LESS CLEARLY DEFINED THE JOB, THE MORE A DIRECTIVE
        STYLE WILL CONTRIBUTE TO JOB SATISFACTION.

M0936   ROSENTHAL, THOMAS G.
        JOB SATISFACTION AND LEADER BEHAVIOR OF ADULT EDUCATION
        ADMINISTRATORS.
        ED.D. DISSERTATION, ARIZONA STATE UNIVERSITY, 1977.

            RELATIONSHIPS WERE SOUGHT 1) BETWEEN THE MEAN SOURCES
        OF ADULT EDUCATION ADMINISTRATORS AND THEIR IMMEDIATE
        SUPERVISORS WHEN COMPARING THE CONSIDERATION AND INITIATING
        STRUCTURE DIMENSIONS OF LEADER BEHAVIOR AND 2) BETWEEN THE
        PERCEPTIONS OF LEADERSHIP BEHAVIOR AND JOB SATISFACTION HELD
        BY ADULT EDUCATION ADMINISTRATORS.
            A STUDY OF THE STATUS OF PROGRAMS FOR THE GIFTED AND
        TALENTED IN SELECTED INDEPENDENT SCHOOL DISTRICTS IN TEXAS
        REVEALED THAT 56 PERCENT OF THE DISTRICTS RESPONDING TO THE
        SURVEY HAD PROGRAMS. THESE PROGRAMS WERE FUNDED PRIMARILY
        FROM LOCAL FUNDS AND AT LOW LEVELS. STRATEGIES FREQUENTLY
        EMPLOYED IN PROGRAMS WERE ADVANCED CLASSES, ACCELERATED
        SUBJECT MATTER UNITS, AND INDEPENDENT STUDY. PAST SCHOOL
        PERFORMANCE WAS MOST OFTEN USED TO IDENTIFY THE GIFTED AND
        TALENTED. PARTICIPANTS IN PROGRAMS INCREASED WITH THE
        GRADE LEVEL BEING SERVED.

M0938 VERNEY, THOMAS P.
AN INVESTIGATION OF THE RELATIONSHIP BETWEEN INTRINSIC AND
EXTRINSIC JOB INSTRUMENTALITY EFFORT, JOB SATISFACTION,
INDIVIDUAL AND PERCEIVED TASK CHARACTERISTICS.
PH.D. DISSERTATION, BOWLING GREEN STATE UNIVERSITY, 1976.

THE PURPOSE OF THIS INVESTIGATION WAS TWOFOLD: (1) TO
ATTEMPT TO EXTEND THE PREDICTIVE EFFECTIVENESS OF THE
EXPECTANCY MODELS OF EFFORT AND SATISFACTION; AND (2) TO
EXAMINE THE RELATIONSHIP OF ATTITUDES TOWARD LEADERSHIP
PREFERENCE, WORK AUTONOMY, AND PERCEIVED TASK COMPLEXITY TO
PERCEPTIONS OF INSTRUMENTALITY AND EXPECTANCY.
DATA WERE OBTAINED FROM TWO MANAGERIAL SAMPLES.
SAMPLE A CONSISTED OF 67 LOW-LEVEL MANAGERS. SAMPLE B
CONSISTED OF 87 UPPER-LEVEL MANAGERS.
A FACTOR ANALYSIS WAS PERFORMED ON THE EXPECTANCY DATA
AND ON THE INSTRUMENTALITY TIMES VALENCE SCORES. FIVE
EXPECTANCY FACTORS EMERGED IN SAMPLE A AND 2 IN SAMPLE B.
IN BOTH SAMPLES THERE WERE 4 REWARD-INSTRUMENTALITY FACTORS-
TWO INTRINSIC AND TWO EXTRINSIC.
CORRELATIONS, ZERO-ORDER AND MULTIPLE, WERE COMPUTED
BETWEEN THE EXPECTANCY MODEL CONSTRUCTS AND THE CRITERIA
OF SELF-RATED EFFORT AND SATISFACTIONS.   INTRINSIC REWARD-
INSTUMENTALITY WAS THE ONLY SIGNIFICANT PREDICTOR OF EFFORT
AND SATISFACTION WITH WORK IN BOTH SAMPLES. THERE WAS NO
EVIDENCE OF AN INTERACTION BETWEEN INTRINSIC AND EXTRINSIC
REWARD-INSTRUMENTALITY. WEIGHTING BY EXPECTANCY DID NOT
SIGNIFICANTLY INCREASE THE PREDICTABILITY OF EFFORT.
MODERATED REGRESSION ANALYSES WERE MADE BETWEEN THE
PREDICTORS -- LEADERSHIP PREFERENCE, ATTITUDE TOWARD WORK
AUTONOMY, PERCEIVED TASK COMPLEXITY -- AND THE CRITERIA OF
INTRINSIC AND EXTRINSIC REWARD INSTRUMENTALITY AND
EXPECTANCY. NONE OF THE ZERO-ORDER NOR MULTIPLE
CORRELATIONS WERE SIGNIFICANT. NO MODERATOR EFFECTS WERE
EVIDENCED.
IMPLICATIONS FOR FUTURE RESEARCH WITHIN AN EXPECTANCY
MODEL FRAMEWORK ARE DISCUSSED. EXTENSIONS TO GOAL-SETTING
PROGRAMS ARE SUGGESTED.

M0940 WEINROTH, ELISSA D.
MOTIVATION, JOB SATISFACTION, AND CAREER ASPIRATIONS OF
MARRIED WOMEN TEACHERS AT DIFFERENT CAREER STAGES.
PH.D. DISSERTATION, AMERICAN UNIVERSITY, 1977.

SPECIFIC FACETS OF MOTIVATIONAL NEEDS, JOB
SATISFACTION, AND CAREER ASPIRATIONS OF MARRIED WOMEN
TEACHERS AT FOUR STAGES OF THEIR CAREERS WERE COMPARED.
FEMALE, MARRIED, ELEMENTARY SCHOOL TEACHERS IN AN AFFLUENT
SUBURBAN SCHOOL SYSTEM WERE PLACE IN ONE OF FOUR CAREER
STAGES ACCORDING TO SPECIFIC PARAMETERS. THE CRITERIA WERE
STAGE I: YOUNG, CHILDLESS, INEXPERIENCED TEACHERS;
STAGE II: YOUNG, INEXPERIENCED TEACHERS WITH PRE-SCHOOL
CHILDREN; STAGE III: OLDER, EXPERIENCED TEACHERS WITH SCHOOL
AGED CHILDREN; AND STAGE IV: EXPERIENCED TEACHERS OVER 55
YEARS OF AGE WITH OLDER CHILDREN.
THE FIRST TWO HYPOTHESES STATED THAT THERE WERE NO
DIFFERENCES IN MOTIVATIONAL NEEDS AND JOB SATISFACTION
AMONG THE FOUR STAGES. MISKEL'S EDUCATIONAL WORK COMPONENTS

M0940 STUDY MEASURED SIX SPECIFIC FACTORS OF MOTIVATION AND JOB
       SATISFACTION; ONE INTRINSIC FACTOR, TWO EXTRINSIC FACTORS,
       AND THREE FACTORS WHICH WERE A COMBINATION OF INTRINSIC
       REWARDS AND RISK. MOTIVATIONAL NEEDS WERE DETERMINED BY
       DIRECT QUESTIONING, AND JOB SATISFACTION WAS MEASURED BY
       SUBTRACTING PRESENT JOB INCENTIVES FROM IDEAL INCENTIVES TO
       YIELD A DISCREPANCY SCORE. ANALYSIS OF VARIANCE WAS
       WAS CONDUCTED TO TEST THE FIRST TWO HYPOTHESES. THE NULL
       HYPOTHESES WERE REJECTED AT THE .05 LEVEL, AND THE SCHEFFE
       PROCEDURE WAS EMPLOYED WHERE INDICATED.
             THE THIRD HYPOTHESIS STATED THAT THERE WERE NO
       RELATIONSHIPS BETWEEN CAREER STAGES AND TEACHERS' CAREER
       ASPIRATIONS AT FOUR FUTURE POINTS IN TIME. CAREER GOALS
       WERE DETERMINED BY RESPONSES TO AN ORIGINAL QUESTION. CHI
       SQUARE ANALYSIS DETERMINED INDEPENDENCE BETWEEN RESPONSES
       AND CAREER STAGES. AGAIN, THE NULL HYPOTHESIS WAS REJECTED
       AT THE .05 LEVEL.

M0941 WEIR, ROBERT M.
       COMPARATIVE APPRAISALS OF JOB PERFORMANCE OF FULL-TIME
       ELEMENTARY PRINCIPALS BY THE PRINCIPALS AND THEIR
       SUPERVISORS IN CLASS I MONTANA SCHOOL DISTRICTS.
       ED.D DISSERTATION, MONTANA STATE UNIVERSITY, 1977.

             THE PURPOSES OF THIS STUDY WAS TO: (A) DETERMINE
       IF ANY SIGNIFICANT DIFFERENCES EXISTED BETWEEN THE SELF
       APPRAISALS OF JOB PERFORMANCE OF FULL-TIME ELEMENTARY
       PRINCIPALS BY THE PRINCIPALS AS COMPARED WITH SUPERVISORS
       IN CLASS I MONTANA SCHOOL DISTRICTS; AND (B) DETERMINE IF
       THERE WAS A RELATIONSHIP BETWEEN THE PRINCIPALS' AND
       SUPERVISORS' DIFFERENCES ON SELECTED BIOGRAPHICAL VARIABLES
       AND THE DIFFERENCES IN APPRAISALS BETWEEN THE TWO GROUPS.
             THE PROBLEM WAS INVESTIGATED BY: (A) A THOROUGH REVIEW
       OF LITERATURE RELATED TO THE PROBLEM; (B) A SURVEY OF
       FIFTY-SIX RANDOMLY SELECTED CLASS I MONTANA FULL-TIME
       ELEMENTARY PRINCIPALS AND SEVENTEEN SUPERVISORS OF
       ELEMENTARY PRINCIPALS FROM THE CLASS I MONTANA SCHOOL
       DISTRICTS USING A SURVEY INSTRUMENT WITH AN ACCOMPANYING
       BIOGRAPHICAL DATA SHEET FOR BOTH GROUPS TO DETERMINE THE
       APPRAISALS OF EACH PRINCIPAL'S JOB PERFORMANCE; AND (C) A
       TABULATION, ANALYSIS, AND COMPARISON OF THE DATA COLLECTED.
             THE MAJOR RESULTS OF THE STUDY INDICATED THAT:
       (A) CLASS I MONTANA SUPERVISORS AND FULL-TIME ELEMENTARY
       PRINCIPALS COULD USE THE SURVEY INSTRUMENT FOR EVALUATION
       AND EXPECT TO FIND NO SIGNIFICANT DIFFERENCES IN SIXTEEN
       INDIVIDUAL CATEGORIES OF THE TWENTY-ONE CATEGORY EVALUATION
       INSTRUMENT; (B) DIFFERENCES IN THE APPRAISALS OF RANDOMLY
       SELECTED CLASS I MONTANA FULL-TIME ELEMENTARY PRINCIPALS AND
       THEIR SUPERVISORS CAN BE USED TO PREDICT DIFFERENCES IN
       APPRAISAL SCORES BETWEEN ALL CLASS I MONTANA FULL-TIME
       ELEMENTARY PRINCIPALS AND THEIR SUPERVISORS IN SPECIFIC
       SUB CORRELATIONS ON EIGHTEEN CATEGORIES OF THE EVALUATION
       INSTRUMENT WITH AGE BEING THE MOST CONSISTENT PREDICTOR
       VARIABLE; AND (C) SELF-APPRAISAL WAS FOUND TO POSSESS
       POTENTIALLY IMPORTANT IMPLICATIONS FOR EVALUATION OF THE
       ELEMENTARY PRINCIPLAL WHICH INCLUDED THE HONESTY WHICH
       CHARACTERIZES SELF-APPRAISAL, THE EASE AND BREVITY OF AN
       HONEST,EFFECTIVE SELF-APPRAISAL INSTRUMENT, AND THE FACT

M0941   THAT SELF-APPRAISAL CAN BE ON-GOING.
         THE MAJOR RECOMMENDATIONS OF THE STUDY WERE: (A) THAT
         EFFECTIVE CHANNELS OF COMMUNICATION SHOLD BE DEVELOPED
         WHICH WILL HELP CLARIFY AND INTERPRET IMPLICATIONS OF THE
         APPRAISALS OF THE PRINCIPAL'S JOB PERFORMANCE; (B) FURTHER
         STUDIES ARE NEEDED IN THIS AREA; AND (C) THAT ADMINSTRATOR
         PREPARATION INSTITUTIONS SHOULD ENDEAVOR TO BUILD COMMON
         PERCEPTIONS AMONG TEACHERS, PRINCIPALS, AND SUPERVISORS
         CONCERNING EFFECTIVE PROGRAMS OF EVALUATION.

M0942   WELCH, ROBERT J.
         THE EFFECT OF ORGANIZATIONAL CHANGE ON ADMINISTRATOR JOB
         SATISFACTION, ORGANIZATIONAL CLIMATE, AND PERCEIVED
         ORGANIZATIONAL EFFECTIVENESS.
         ED.D. DISSERTATION, UNIVERSITY OF KANSAS, 1976.

         1. STATEMENT OF THE PROBLEM. THE RELATIONSHIP OF
         ORGANIZATIONAL STRUCTURE TO ORGANIZATIONAL CLIMATE, JOB
         SATISFACTION, AND ORGANIZATIONAL EFFECTIVENESS HAS BEEN
         SUGGESTED IN MUCH OF THE LITERATURE. THE LITERATURE REVEALS
         THAT NUMEROUS RESEARCHERS HAVE CONSIDERED THESE VARIABLES
         TO INTERACT. THE OPPORTUNITY TO STUDY THE EFFECT OF AN
         ORGANIZATIONAL CHANGE ON THE AFOREMENTIONED VARIABLES
         PROMPTED THIS STUDY.
         4. CONCLUSION. THE HYPOTHESES RECEIVED VERY LITTLE
         SUPPORT. A RELATIONSHIP BETWEEN THE VARIABLES OF THIS STUDY
         HAS BEEN ESTABLISHED BY OTHER RESEARCHERS; A CHANGE OF
         RATHER DRASTIC NATURE DID TAKE PLACE; THE LOGIC OF THE
         RATIONALE AND HYPOTHESES REMAINS. IT WOULD SEEM REASONABLE
         TO SUGGEST THAT THE TIMING OF THE RESEARCH WAS AT FAULT AND
         THAT FURTHER STUDY OF THE EFFECT OF ORGANIZATIONAL CHANGE
         ON CLIMATE, JOB SATISFACTION AND ORGANIZATIONAL
         EFFECTIVENESS BE CONDUCTED.

M0943   WHITE, WARREN L.
         THE EFFECT OF FLEXIBLE WORKING HOURS ON ABSENTEEISM AND JOB
         SATISFACTION AND THE RELATIONSHIP BETWEEN LOCUS OF CONTROL
         AND UTILITY OF FLEXIBLE WORKING HOURS.
         PH.D. DISSERTATION, UNIVERSITY OF TEXAS AT AUSTIN, 1976.

         THE IMPACT OF FLEXIBLE WORKING HOURS ON JOB
         SATISFACTION AND ABSENTEEISM, AND THE RELATIONSHIP BETWEEN
         INTERNAL-EXTERNAL LOCUS OF CONTROL AND UTILITY FOR FLEXIBLE
         WORKING HOURS WAS EVALUATED. QUESTIONNAIRES, PERSONNEL
         RECORDS AND INTERVIEWS WERE USED TO COLLECT DATA BEFORE AND
         AFTER THE IMPLEMENTATION OF FLEXIBLE WORKING HOURS IN THE
         DIVISION OF A LARGE BANK. THE RESULTS OF DATA ANALYSIS
         INDICATE THAT JOB SATISFACTION AND ABSENTEEISM DID NOT
         CHANGE SIGNIFICANTLY, EITHER AMONG THE PERSONNEL OF THE
         TOTAL DIVISION OR AT DIFFERENT LEVELS WITHIN THE DIVISION.
         RESULTS WERE INCONCLUSIVE REGARDING THE INVERSE CORRELATION
         PREDICTED BETWEEN CHANGE IN ABSENTEEISM AND JOB
         SATISFACTION. MORE EXTERNAL LOCUS OF CONTROL WAS NOT
         FOUND TO RELATE WITH HIGHER UTILITY FOR FLEXIBLE WORKING
         HOURS. LOCUS OF CONTROL WAS NOT FOUND TO BE MORE EXTERNAL
         AMONG FEMALES THAN MALES AND UTILITY FOR FLEXIBLE WORKING
         HOURS WAS NOT FOUND TO BE LOWER AMONG FEMALES THAN MALES.

M0944   WILLIAMS, GEORGE A.
         OLNEY CENTRAL COLLEGE DENTAL ASSISTING PROGRAM GRADUATES
         PERCEPTIONS OF PROGRAM COMPONENTS, JOB SATISFACTION AND
         CAREER GOALS.
         PH.D. DISSERTATION, SOUTHERN ILLINOIS UNIVERSITY, 1977.

              THE PROBLEM OF THIS STUDY WAS TO EVALUATE THE OLNEY
         CENTRAL COLLEGE DENTAL ASSISTING PROGRAM. THE OLNEY CENTRAL
         COLLEGE DENTAL ASSISTING PROGRAM IS THE ONLY COMMUNITY
         COLLEGE PROGRAM TO HAVE BEGUN WITH 100% FEDERAL FUNDING.
         THE OBJECTIVE OF THE FOLLOW-UP STUDY WAS TO EVALUATE THE
         PROGRAM BY USING THE MAIL SURVEY TECHNIQUE. QUESTIONNAIRES
         WERE SENT TO 54 PROGRAM GRADUATES, 40 DENTISTS, AND 28
         EMPLOYERS.
              A RESEARCH INSTRUMENT WAS DEVELOPED AND VALIDATED FOR
         THIS STUDY. RETURN RATES ON THE THREE QUESTIONNAIRES WERE
         HIGH BECAUSE THE RESEARCHER GAVE A TWO-DOLLAR BILL TO
         PARTICIPATING PROGRAM GRADUATES. THE RESEARCH INSTRUMENT
         COULD BE USED FOR ANY DENTAL ASSISTING PROGRAM FOR FOLLOW-UP
         CONSISTENT WITH THE 1976 AMENDMENTS REGARDING VOCATIONAL
         EDUCATION.
              PROGRAM GRADUATES INDICATED MANY THINGS INCLUDING:
         (A) THE PROGRAM WAS GOOD AND SHOULD BE CONTINUED, (B) THE
         PROGRAM SHOULD BE EXPANDED TO INCLUDE DENTAL HYGIENE,
         (C) HIGH JOB SATISFACTION, (D) A STRONG DESIRE FOR
         EXPANDED DUTY FUNCTIONS, (E) LOW SALARIES, AND (F) 76% OF
         RESPONDENTS INDICATED THAT THEY WOULD STAY IN DENTAL
         ASSISTING.
              DENTISTS AND EMPLOYERS SUPPORT THIS PROGRAM AND ARE
         SATISFIED WITH GRADUATES THEY HAVE EMPLOYED. DENTISTS
         DESIRE ADDITIONAL OLNEY CENTAL COLLEGE DENTAL ASSISTING
         GRADUATES. DENTISTS DESIRE CERTIFIED DENTAL ASSISTANTS
         WITH EXPANDED FUNCTION DUTY TRAINING.

M0945   WILLIAMS, MARGARET RUTH.
         THE RELATIONSHIPS AMONG THE PERSONALITY TYPES, JOB
         SATISFACTIONS, AND JOB SPECIALTIES OF A SELECTED GROUP OF
         MEDICAL TECHNOLOGISTS.
         PH.D. DISSERTATION, FLORIDA STATE UNIVERSITY, 1976.

              THE PURPOSE OF THE STUDY WAS TO DETERMINE IF IN
         MEDICAL TECHNOLOGY THERE IS A RELATIONSHIP BETWEEN:
         1. PERSONALITY TYPE AND JOB SPECIALTY 2. PERSONALITY TYPE
         AND JOB SATISFACTION 3. JOB SPECIALTY AND JOB SATISFACTION
         4. PERSONALITY TYPE AND JOB SATISFACTION IN EACH OF FOUR JOB
         SPECIALTIES.
              THE POPULATION WAS OBTAINED FROM LABORATORIES
         AFFILIATED WITH RANDOMLY SELECTED MEDICAL SCHOOLS IN THE
         SOUTHEASTERN UNITED STATES. A TOTAL OF 306 TECHNOLOGISTS
         WAS TESTED. THE INSTRUMENTS USED WERE THE MYERS BRIGGS TYPE
         INDICATOR (PERSONALITY TYPE) AND THE JOB DESCRIPTIVE INDEX
         (JOB SATISFACTION).
              NEGATIVE RESULTS WERE OBTAINED ON QUESTION 1, AND IN
         HEMATOLOGY AND MICROBIOLOGY IN QUESTION 4.
              AFFIRMATIVE RESULTS WERE OBTAINED IN THE OTHER
         QUESTIONS. IN CHEMISTRY THOSE PERSONS WITH EXTROVERT
         PREFERENCE WERE LESS SATISFIED WITH THE PROMOTION POLICIES
         THAN THOSE WITH INTROVERT PREFERENCE. THE RESULTS IN

M0945 QUESTION 2 AND IN CHEMISTRY SHOW THAT THOSE WITH FEELING
PREFERENCE WERE MORE SATISFIED WITH THEIR COWORKERS THAN
THOSE WITH THINKING PREFERENCE.

        PERSONS IN BLOOD BANK WITH FEELING PREFERENCE WERE
MORE SATISFIED WITH PAY THAN THOSE WITH THINKING PREFERENCE.

M0946 WOODRUFF, CHARLES KENNETH.
AN EMPIRICAL STUDY OF INDIVIDUAL CONGRUENCE AND THE
PERCEIVED ORGANIZATIONAL PRACTICES - JOB SATISFACTION - JOB
PERFORMANCE RELATIONSHIP IN SELECTED ELECTRONIC COMPUTER
DATA PROCESSING CENTERS.
PH.D. DISSERTATION, GEORGIA STATE UNIVERSITY, 1977.

        THE PRIMARY OBJECTIVE OF THIS STUDY WAS TO DETERMINE
IF THERE ARE SIGNIFICANT RELATIONSHIPS BETWEEN THE
PERSONALITY DIMENSIONS THAT CHARACTERIZE DATA PROCESSING
PROFESSIONALS, THE MANNER WITH WHICH THEY PERCEIVE AND
INTERACT WITH THE PRACTICES OF THEIR ORGANIZATION, THEIR
JOB SATISFACTION, AND THEIR JOB PERFORMANCE. THIS RESEARCH
WAS AN EXPLORATORY FIELD STUDY EMPLOYING AN EX POST FACTO
RESEARCH DESIGN. SUBJECTS FOR THE STUDY WERE 202 DATA
PROCESSING PROFESSIONALS FROM TWELVE COMPUTER CENTERS IN
METROPOLITAN ATLANTA.
        THE RESULTS OF THE STUDY WERE AS FOLLOWS: 1. DATA
PROCESSING MALES AND FEMALES WERE FOUND TO POSSESS
REMARKABLY SIMILAR PERSONALITY NEEDS PROFILES. STUDY
SUBJECTS POSSESSED HIGH NEEDS FOR ACHIEVEMENT, COGNITIVE
STRUCTURE, ENDURANCE, HARM-AVOIDANCE, AND ORDER. LOW NEEDS
FOR AGGRESSION, CHANGE, EXHIBITION, IMPULSIVITY, PLAY, AND
SOCIAL RECOGNITION WERE FOUND. 2. STUDY SUBJECTS WERE
GENERALLY SATISFIED WITH THEIR JOBS WITH RESPECT TO MORAL
VALUES, CO-WORKERS, SECURITY, ACHIEVEMENT, AND WORKING
CONDITIONS. THEY WERE DISSATISFIED WITH ADVANCEMENT AND
COMPENSATION. OPERATIONS PERSONNEL TENDED TO BE LESS
SATISFIED WITH THEIR JOBS THAN OTHER FUNCTIONAL GROUPS.
3. STUDY SUBJECTS WERE RATED BY THEIR SUPERIORS AS
PERFORMING HIGHEST IN COOPERATION AND LOWEST IN
INNOVATIVENESS. 4. A FACTOR ANALYSIS WAS PERFORMED ON THE
ITEM RESPONSES TO THE ORGANIZATIONAL PRACTICES
QUESTIONNAIRE. AN ELEVEN FACTOR OBLIQUE ROTATION PRODUCED
THE BEST RESULTS, BUT ONE FACTOR WAS ELIMINATED DUE TO ITS
LOW RELIABILITY. 5. CANONICAL CORRELATION WAS UTILIZED FOR
TESTING OF THE HYPOTHESES. THE CONCEPT OF REDUNDANCY WAS
USED AS A MEANS OF INTERPRETING THE CANONICAL VARIATES.
6. JOB SATISFACTION AND JOB PERFORMANCE WERE FOUND TO BE
RELATED SIGNIFICANTLY. 7. PERSONALITY NEEDS AND JOB
SATISFACTION WERE FOUND TO BE RELATED SIGNIFICANTLY. 8. JOB
PERFORMANCE OF THE DATA PROCESSING SUBJECTS WAS NOT RELATED
SIGNIFICANTLY TO PERSONALITY NEEDS. 9. PERCEPTIONS OF
ORGANIZATIONAL PRACTICES HELD BY THE DATA PROCESSING
SUBJECTS WERE FOUND TO BE RELATED SIGNIFICANTLY TO JOB
SATISFACTION, BUT NOT TO JOB PERFORMANCE. 10. INTERACTIONS
OF THE PERSONALITY NEEDS OF THE DATA PROCESSING SUBJECTS
WITH THEIR PERCEPTIONS OF ORGANIZATIONAL PRACTICES WERE
FOUND TO RELATE SIGNIFICANTLY TO JOB SATISFACTION, BUT NOT
TO JOB PERFORMANCE.

About the Compiler-Editors

Ruth M. Walsh and Stanley J. Birkin are Associate Professors of Management in the School of Business Administration at the University of South Florida in Tampa. Professor Walsh's works include *Communications: Public and Private Sectors.* Professor Birkin is the author of *Problem Solving Using PI/C.*